Syria   Assad
Iraq   Saddam Hu
Jordan   Husayn King

THE MIDDLE EAST

IN WORLD AFFAIRS

ALSO BY GEORGE LENCZOWSKI

Iran under the Pahlavis (Editor)
Middle East Oil in a Revolutionary Age
Oil and State in the Middle East
The Political Awakening in the Middle East (Editor)
Political Elites in the Middle East (Editor)
Russia and the West in Iran
Soviet Advances in the Middle East
United States Interests in the Middle East (Editor)

GEORGE LENCZOWSKI

University of California at Berkeley

The Middle East in World Affairs

FOURTH EDITION

CORNELL UNIVERSITY PRESS

ITHACA AND LONDON

First edition 1952
Second edition 1956
Third edition 1962
Fourth edition 1980
First printing, paperback edition, 1980
Fourth printing 1985

International Standard Book Number (cloth) 0-8014-1273-0
International Standard Book Number (paper) 0-8014-9872-4
Library of Congress Catalog Card Number 79-17059
Printed in the United States of America
Librarians: Library of Congress cataloging information appears on the last page of the book.

TO B. L. AND J. L.

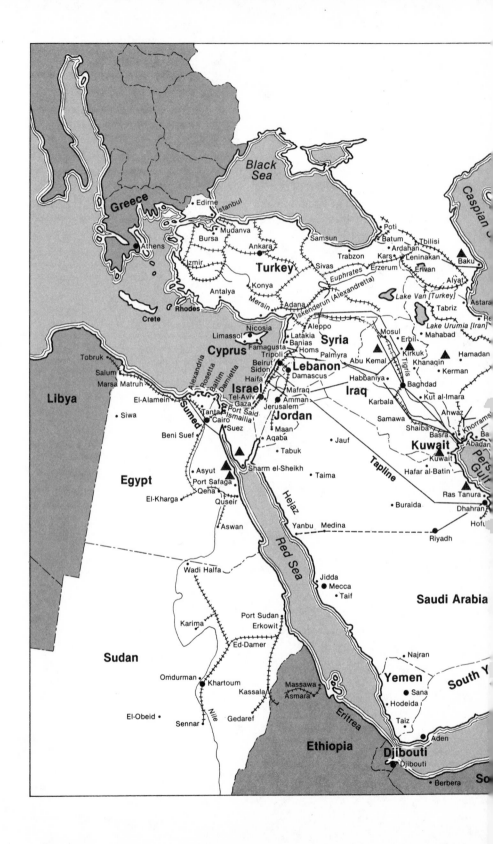

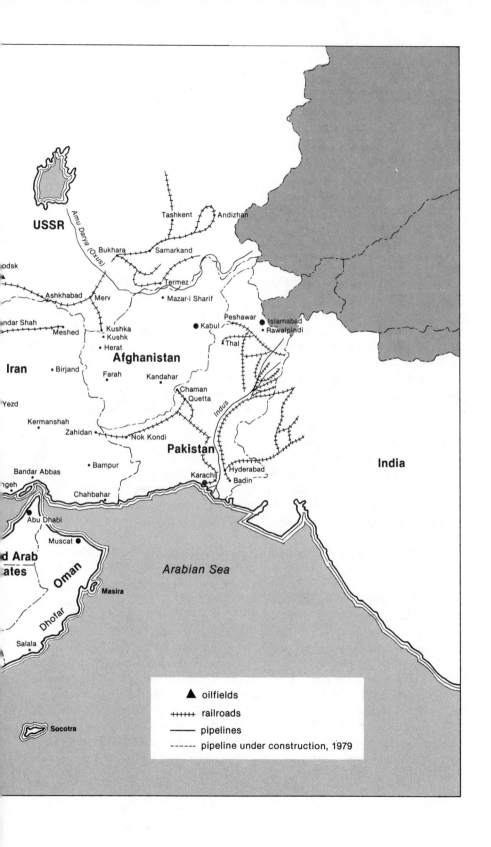

USSR

Amu Darya (Oxus)

Tashkent   Andizhan

Bukhara   Samarkand

odsk

Termez

Ashkhabad   Merv   Mazar-i Sharif

ndar Shah

Meshed   Kushka   Kabul   Peshawar   Islamabad
        • Kushk   Rawalpindi

        • Herat   Thal

Iran   • Birjand   Farah   Afghanistan

Yezd

Kermanshah   Zahidan   Nok Kondi   Kandahar   Chaman   Indus
                Quetta

                Pakistan

Bandar Abbas   • Bampur

ngeh   Karachi   Hyderabad   India
    Chahbahar   Badin

• Abu Dhabi

Muscat •

d Arab   Oman   Arabian Sea
ates

    Dhofar   Masira

Salala

Socotra

▲ oilfields
+++++ railroads
——— pipelines
------- pipeline under construction, 1979

Foreword to the
Fourth Edition

This book aims to give a comprehensive account of the political developments in the Middle East since 1914, including those in international relations, regional affairs, and domestic politics in individual countries. The Middle East is defined as an area stretching from Egypt in the west to Afghanistan in the east. The North African Arab Maghreb is not discussed, except as its member states have participated in the broader Arab unity schemes.

The Middle East deserves to be treated as a distinct geopolitical area. It shares with the rest of the Third World certain persistent issues such as decolonization, state building, and modernization, but it also possesses certain unique features: it is the cradle of Islam, the only region of the free world directly adjacent to the Soviet Union, and the principal producer of oil. It holds the world's most strategic waterways, and it is the arena of one of the most perplexing conflicts of the twentieth century, that of Arab versus Israeli nationalism.

The importance of this region in world affairs has been emphasized by the fact that the two world wars have had their Middle Eastern theaters; and events there, though not principal, weighed heavily in the final outcome of these giant international conflicts.

Similarly, two major American foreign policy doctrines—the Truman and the Eisenhower—have had the Middle East as their objective, while a third—the Nixon Doctrine—has had a definite, though indirect, impact upon the politics and diplomacy of the region.

Under the circumstances, if the Middle East could justly claim its place as a subject of study in the decade following World War II (when the first edition of this book was published), it can lay such claim with even greater justification in the 1960s and 1970s. Its persistent and complex international problems and its susceptibility to revolutionary change not only did not disappear but, if anything, became further aggravated, while the stakes of the superpowers—the Soviet Union and the United States—grew. Developments within the span of two years, 1977 and 1978 alone, provide an eloquent illustration of these complexities. During that period the Middle East was the scene of the dramatic peace initiative of President Sadat of Egypt, followed by the Camp David negotiations between Egypt and Israel; it subsequently witnessed a new polarization in the Arab world expressed by the Pan-Arab Baghdad meetings; it saw a resurgence of Palestinian nationalism; it was the arena of civil war and military intervention by Syria and Israel in Lebanon, of violent upheavals and assassinations of the heads of state in Yemen and South Yemen, and of regionwide revival of militant Islamic ideology; and it experienced revolutions in Afghanistan and Iran. At the same time, in the nearby Horn of Africa, the Somali-Ethiopian war over Ogaden and the attendant Soviet intervention added to the tension between the two superpowers.

The book presents a history and analysis of the region as a whole and of its component parts. It begins with a historical background focusing on the Ottoman and Persian empires, World War I, and the peace settlement, so as to explain the origins of the existing state system in the Middle East. Its central part consists of a review of political developments in individual countries. In this respect the fourth edition has been expanded to embrace two areas that since the appearance of the earlier editions have attained independence: the Persian Gulf and southern Arabia. The third part of the book deals with general, regional issues: it contains a brief account of World War II in the Middle East, and it has chapters on strategic waterways, Arab unity and disunity, and the policies of foreign powers in the area. Within this structure certain overlapping of material is inevitable. Some events find their ways into more than one chapter; such repetitions are justified by my desire to make each chapter self-contained so as to avoid excessive cross-references.

The sources used are both primary and secondary. Official documents such as treaties and government pronouncements are frequently cited as references.

The systems of transliterating Arabic, Persian, and Turkish words and names are geared to the needs of lay readers rather than specialists. Thus they follow the patterns adopted by newspapers and nonspecialized periodicals. As such, usage is not fully consistent, but it is familiar to the general public.

In preparing this book, I have benefited from the research assistance of my graduate students in the Political Science Department at Berkeley, especially Thomas Mattair, Rolph Wichmann, and Mine Sabuncuoglu. Additional assistance was rendered by Kamal Beyoghlow and Charles Franke. The typing of the manuscript was executed most meticulously by Florence C. Myer and Sonia Atalla.

Numerous research trips to the Middle East have helped me significantly in the preparation of this volume. I owe much, for their willingness to grant me interviews and discuss at length the politics of the area, to the Shah of Iran, the kings of Saudi Arabia and Jordan, the presidents of Egypt, Iraq, Syria, and Lebanon, the Prime Minister of Libya, and the ministers of Turkey, Iran, Israel, and various Arab states of the area. Successive secretaries-general of the Arab League, the leaders of political parties, academic colleagues in Middle Eastern universities, military officers, delegates to the United Nations, and business executives have also been most helpful in clarifying many issues discussed in this book. The rich library resources of the University of California at Berkeley and the unique collection of the Hoover Institution on War, Revolution, and Peace at Stanford have provided much precious documentary material.

Last but not least, I wish to express my warm appreciation and gratitude to my wife, who has shared my interests, assisted me in research, accompanied me on overseas trips, and gracefully accepted the pressures of publishing deadlines and the resulting disruptions of our home life.

G. L.

Berkeley, California
April 1979

Contents

Maps

Introduction

No unanimity has so far been reached on a definition of the Middle East, and even the name has not been universally accepted. Scholars, statesmen, and journalists refer to the area sometimes as the Near East, sometimes as the Middle East. The Near East is the older term. In addition to southwestern Asia it comprises those areas of southeastern Europe which have in the past been under Turkish control. The term Middle East seems to be of more recent origin and owes its widespread acceptance in modern times to its official use by the British. In this book the modern practice has been followed, with the understanding that the Middle East encompasses all those countries of Asia situated south of the Soviet Union and west of Pakistan, and Egypt on the African continent as well. The Balkans have been excluded. In the few cases in which it was necessary to include Greece and the Aegean, the older term, Near East, has been employed.

The Middle East has a unique geographical position. It is an area situated at the junction of Europe, Asia, and Africa, and as such it commands the strategic approaches to these three continents. One is tempted to call it the hub of the Eastern Hemisphere. The shortest and most convenient air and water routes from Europe to Asia go through the Middle East. Every major empire in the history of the Old World has either been included in this area, in whole or in part, or has cast covetous eyes at it. For many years the life line of the British Empire passed through the Middle East; hence whatever happened in the area was bound to have an affect on Britain.

Taken as a part of Asia (where it is chiefly located), the Middle East falls within the middle zone which extends the whole length of this gigantic continent, roughly between the 30th and 40th parallels. To the north of this middle zone lies the great land mass of Russia; to the south, those peninsular extremities of Asia which have until recently been directly controlled by the great powers of the West. The middle zone has traditionally been a contested ground between the land power of Russia and the naval power of the West. The Middle East has been and continues to be of particular importance to Russia as an area through which she might obtain access to the warm waters and major commercial routes of the globe. Moreover, Russia is particularly vulnerable to attack from the Middle East if we consider Soviet concentrations of industry in the Black Sea–Ural region.

Of all parts of the middle zone of Asia, the Middle East has been most exposed to penetration by naval powers, no doubt owing to its long and curved coast line, which is washed by the Black Sea, the Mediterranean, the Red Sea, and the Indian Ocean. It is less easily accessible by land from the north. This explains the fact that the West succeeded in obtaining a firmer foothold in the area than did Russia. Yet, there is no reason why the roles may not one day be reversed. Russia has progressed technologically; moroever, she has the advantage of being directly adjacent to the Middle East. The colonies of southern Asia, which formerly the West could freely use as bases, have been emancipated and have ceased to be a source of power to the West. In fact, Asia's middle zone, the zone of weak and independent states, has expanded southward to the detriment of Western strength. Under these conditions the balance hitherto maintained between Russia and the West on the Asiatic main-land has been seriously affected.

In addition to geographical uniqueness, the Middle East has several other distinc-tive features. Although inhabited by no more than 165 million people, it is the center of the Islamic world, a world of seven hundred million souls. It contains the holiest places of Islam as well as the highest institutions of Islamic learning. The Moslem religion and culture have permeated the whole society of the Middle East and have imbued it with philosophical attitudes such that only radical revolution is likely to effect a change in its behavior. In the Holy Land of Palestine the Middle East possesses a focus of aspirations of Jews and Christians alike. Moreover, under the arid soil of some sections of the Middle East lies the greatest single reserve of oil, the black gold of nations. For these reasons its importance transcends its geographical limits. No intelligent foreign policy today can ignore the Middle East and its impact upon the rest of the world.

Politically and culturally the Middle East may be divided into two main regions, the Northern Belt and the Arab Core. The former differs from the latter in that it is ethnically non-Arab and that it has a direct boundary with Russia. These two traits have helped to shape its destinies and its present political complexion. Turkey, Iran, and Afghanistan may differ from one another in many respects, yet the overwhelm-ing presence of the Russian giant north of their borders creates an invisible bond. Populated by about eighty-five million people, this Northern Belt separates and protects the Arab Core from Russia. As a defense line, it is uneven, the strongest link being Turkey; the weakest, Afghanistan. To a certain extent its role can be compared to the historical role of Poland in Europe: like Poland, which was a rampart of Western Christendom against the hordes from the East, so Turkey, and to a lesser extent Iran and Afghanistan, have stood guard against Muscovy's south-ward expansion. And like Poland, the countries of the Northern Belt isolated their hinterland so effectively from the great power of Muscovy that the hinterland—just as the West—tended to minimize this power and acquire a false sense of security.

Inhabited by eighty million souls, the Arab Core of the Middle East can in turn be subdivided into the Fertile Crescent and the Red Sea Region. The Fertile Crescent comprises Iraq—the once-wealthy Mesopotamia or Land of Two Rivers—and the Mediterranean coast of Asia. The latter is the home of Syria, Lebanon, Israel, and Jordan. Despite the multiplicity of races and religions in its midst, the Fertile

Crescent has certain features common to all of its component parts and, in the past, has been more than once unified under a single political power.

The Red Sea Region differs from the Fertile Crescent, but it contains tremendous contrasts within itself. On the east there is the vast and arid expanse of the Arabian peninsula, thinly populated, rich in oil, and steeped in Islamic tradition. Its way of life is still largely medieval, and wide tracts of desert separate it effectively from closer contact with the Fertile Crescent and the Mediterranean. On the west there is Egypt, a country living off the longest river in the world, with a teeming population in its lush and unhealthy delta. Egypt with her three crops a year, an abundant supply of water, and a fortunate location astride the great commercial routes has traditionally been the seat of culture and today is by far the most advanced of Arab countries.

It is practical and helpful to keep in mind this division of the Middle East. In the following pages a mass of detail may tempt one to see primarily diversity in the Middle Eastern scene. But one must never forget the basic unity of the Middle East as produced by the features of geography, culture, economy, and strategy common to the area as a whole.

PART ONE

The First World War
and the Peace

CHAPTER I

Historical Background

The history of the Middle East up to the First World War is largely a history of two empires, the Ottoman and the Persian. It is difficult to understand the politics of this area in the last quarter of a century without knowing, at least in outline, the turbulent story of these two major powers. Of the two, the Ottoman Empire should receive priority for two reasons: first, because of the empire's size, which extended to three continents, and, second, because of the involvement of practically every great European power in its foreign or domestic affairs in the course of the last three hundred years.

The Ottoman Empire

The Ottoman Turks first appeared in Asia Minor in the thirteenth century as a frontier tribe on the western confines of the Seljuk Sultanate of Rum (or Iconium). Better disciplined and organized than their immediate neighbors, they began to expand at the expense of the Seljuks and the Byzantines. The Seljuk sultanate, weakened by Mongol pressure, soon disintegrated into petty principalities which fell under the Ottomans. In the fourteenth century the Ottomans established themselves at strategic points in Greece (1399), Serbia (1389), and Bulgaria (1393). By the middle of the next century the Byzantine Empire was practically surrounded by Ottoman possessions and vulnerable to a major attack. This came with the conquest of Constantinople by the Turks in 1453. Emperor Constantine IX died defending the city. The mopping-up operations included the conquest eight years later of the tiny empire of Trebizond and the subjugation of some recalcitrant Turkoman tribes. By 1473, Asia Minor was firmly under Ottoman rule. Under Mohammed the Conqueror (1451–1481) the Turks pushed their conquests farther into Europe and Asia.

By 1468, Greece, including Morea and Euboea, was subjected to Ottoman rule, largely at the expense of the Venetian Republic. Serbia was converted into a Turkish pashalik in 1459, and Bosnia and Herzegovina were annexed by 1465.

Having established their supremacy in Anatolia and in the Balkans, the Turks then turned to the northern shores of the Black Sea. In 1475 the Genoese colonies of Azov and Crimea surrendered to the Ottomans, and the Tatars accepted the suzerainty of the Sultan. Thus the Black Sea had become a "Turkish lake."

Under Mohammed's successors the empire expanded to the East. Under Selim I (1512–1520), the Turks conquered northern Mesopotamia, Egypt, Syria, and Arabia. The conquest of Egypt was important because it ended the Abbassid caliphs. The story that the last Abbassid ruler transferred the title to the victorious sultan is not supported by historical evidence, but Ottoman rulers took the title. The caliphate implied spiritual and temporal authority over the Moslems.

The reign of Suleiman I, the Magnificent, Selim's only son, was the climax of Ottoman greatness both in foreign and in domestic affairs. Suleiman rounded out the empire's European possessions by conquering Belgrade in 1521 and by subduing Hungary at the famous battle of Mohacs in 1526. In 1547 most of Hungary and Transylvania were incorporated into the Ottoman Empire. At the same time the empire expanded toward the East. In a series of wars with Persia, Suleiman acquired large portions of Armenia and Mesopotamia, including the cities of Baghdad and Basra. Owing to his great sea power, he was able to extend his mastery to Aden and the southeastern coast of Arabia. Ambitious expansion in the Mediterranean, the Adriatic, and North Africa (Algiers acknowledged his suzerainty in 1516) completed Suleiman's impressive conquests.

At the time of Suleiman's death the Ottoman Empire stretched from the Danube to the Persian Gulf and from the Ukrainian steppes to the Tropic of Cancer in upper Egypt. It included the mastery of the great trade routes of the Mediterranean, of the Black and Red seas, and of parts of the Indian Ocean. It had an estimated population of fifty million as against some four million in England and embraced some twenty races and nationalities.

Suleiman's reign not only was the apogee of Ottoman glory, but it opened a new chapter in the empire's foreign relations. Until then the empire had been expanding at the expense of Byzantium and of relatively minor European and Asiatic nations. Suleiman's reign marked the beginning of a prolonged contest with major powers. Two of them were European, the Habsburg Empire and Venice; one was Asiatic, Persia. The contest with the Habsburgs and the Venetian Republic lasted for about a century and a half and concluded in 1699. Thereafter Austro-Ottoman relations passed to a secondary plane.

Suleiman's reign also inaugurated a new era in the empire's relations with France. This was a logical outgrowth of the contest which the Habsburgs carried on simultaneously with their eastern and western rivals. It was only natural that France and Turkey should look toward each other as friends and allies faced with the threat of the central-European power of Austria.

In 1535 a treaty was concluded between Suleiman I and Francis I of France. This was a treaty of friendship and collaboration, directed against the Habsburgs, in which the French were granted many far-reaching rights and privileges. These privileges, called thereafter capitulations (from *capitula* or chapters of the treaty), extended to the French freedom of trade and navigation in Ottoman ports, reduced the customs duty to 5 percent in their favor only, exempted French traders from Ottoman jurisdiction and placed them under French consular jurisdiction in matters both civil and criminal, guaranteed to French settlers full religious liberty as well as the custody of the Christian holy places (this, in turn, implied a quasi-protectorate of the French kings over Christians of Latin rite in Ottoman possessions), and extended to French subjects other valuable property and navigation privileges.

The treaty was the basis of a prolonged collaboration between France and Turkey, a collaboration which was to last for at least three centuries. It was confirmed several times, the most important confirmation being that of 1740 which followed a successful Ottoman campaign against the Habsburgs in Serbia. A strong Ottoman Empire was a conscious aim of France, and the maintenance of its integrity became an axiom of French foreign policy a long time before England gave thought to Turkish questions.

The contest with the Habsburgs was the main feature of Turkish history after Suleiman's death, the struggle with Venice being rather in the nature of a side show. Venice was a declining power. Only the aid of the Habsburgs and occasionally of other European powers permitted the Republic of the Doges to hold its ground against the Turks for a relatively long time.

On the other hand, Ottoman might was also declining. This decline was primarily due to internal reasons. First of all, after Suleiman's death, the empire was ruled by a succession of utterly degenerate sultans, often oblivious to the real needs of the empire and as a rule cruel and incapable. Second, corruption crept into the administration and the tax-collecting processes. And, finally, the military organization of the empire deteriorated appreciably. Here mention should be made of the special role played by the Janissaries. The Janissaries were an elite corps of the sultans, recruited among the young sons of the Christian subjects or captives of the empire. Converted to Islam, these boys were brought up under very strict discipline and taught military arts. Uprooted and isolated from other social connections, the Janissaries constituted a formidable military order, pledged to personal service to the sultan and possessing the highest military efficiency. The position of the corps underwent a revolutionary change, however, when in 1566 its members were permitted to marry. This immediately produced two results: first, the growth of a hereditary caste feeling and, second, the softening of their military valor. This circumstance as well as the fact that the sultans personally participated less and less frequently in campaigns led to a decline in the Janissaries' standards and in their loyalty to their rulers. The effects upon the military power of the empire were obviously detrimental.

In these circumstances of progressive weakening, the problem for the empire was not so much to expand and conquer as to maintain its existing possessions. This is a somewhat oversimplified statement, of course, as the Turks were still capable of initiative in expansion. The struggle with the Habsburgs centered in the mastery of the valleys of the Danube and Sava rivers, and the contest with Venice was primarily over the mastery of the seas. The latter had its dramatic development when at the Battle of Lepanto (1571), at the entrance to the Gulf of Patros, a Christian armada organized by the Venetians and commanded by Don John of Austria, utterly defeated the Turkish navy. Although the Turks retained command of the seas for a long time to come, they were no longer considered invincible.

The deteriorating position of the Ottoman Empire was best illustrated perhaps during the Thirty Years' War (1618-1648), which threw Europe into unprecedented

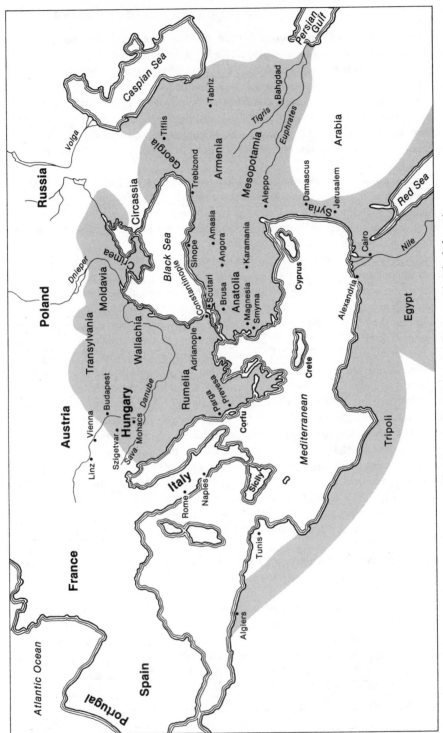

Map 1. The Ottoman Empire under Suleiman (the shaded area).

turmoil and considerably weakened the Holy Roman Empire. Instead of exploiting this weakness and pushing on toward Vienna, the Turks remained passive, a thing which would certainly not have happened in the earlier, more virile period of their history. New life was given the Ottoman Empire with the advent to power of the very able and strong-willed grand viziers of the Albanian family of Köprülü. Assuming the highest office of the empire in 1656, the Köprülüs, one after another, were able during the next half-century to arouse the weakening giant to new and bold actions.

The most remarkable of these actions was the attempt to defeat Austria and conquer Vienna in 1683. The immediate cause of this campaign was a revolt against the Habsburgs of that part of Hungary which remained under their rule. The rebels made their cause the cause of the whole of Hungary and sought the support of the sultan. This support was not denied them. A magnificent Turkish army of 200,000 which had been gathered at Adrianople under the command of Grand Vizier Kara Mustafa (a relative of the Köprülü clan), proceeded toward the Hungarian plain and approached Vienna. Emperor Leopold sent envoys to Poland asking for help. King John Sobieski of Poland, believing that the fate of Christendom was at stake, decided to come to the rescue of the Emperor and personally assumed command of a strong Polish army of 40,000 men, organized into cavalry units. The defense of the city of Vienna, itself poorly fortified, was entrusted to Count Stahremberg, who had only 10,000 men at his disposal. Other imperial forces were commanded by Charles IV, duke of Lorraine, who withdrew from the city to await the Poles' arrival. The Ottoman army appeared before the walls of Vienna, in midsummer 1683, and began the siege which was to last sixty days. In September Sobieski, after a strenuous, two-week march from Poland, arrived at Vienna and replaced the duke of Lorraine as commander of the imperial forces. At the sight of the Poles panic seized the Turks. The charge of the Polish cavalry brought confusion and disorder into the ranks of the enemy. The once invincible army was completely routed. Leaving 10,000 dead, 300 guns, and enormous quantities of equipment on the battlefield, the Turks escaped toward Hungary. Vienna and central Europe were saved. Emperor Leopold returned to his capital. Sobieski and the Christian army continued to pursue the retreating Turks. The war between the Habsburgs and the sultan continued for another fifteen years. Led by the duke of Lorraine, by the Margrave Ludwig of Baden, and by Prince Eugene of Savoy, the imperial armies inflicted many crushing defeats on the Ottomans. The Treaty of Carlowitz ended the war in 1699. Turkey was obliged to cede to the Habsburgs Transylvania, most of Hungary, and major parts of Slovenia and Croatia, and to restore parts of the Ukraine and Podolia to Poland.

From the Treaty of Carlowitz to the Treaty of Jassy

The battle of Vienna and the Treaty of Carlowitz closed a chapter in the history of the Ottoman Empire. No longer were the Turks a formidable enemy threatening western Christendom. On the contrary, their obvious weakness resulted in an exchange of roles for the Empire and for Europe. Henceforth, it was Europe that threatened the integrity of the Ottoman Empire. Among the European powers the most ambitious in this respect was Russia. Austria, while never pro-Turkish, began to play a less prominent role, though she was ever eager to enlarge her possessions in the Balkans and to prevent Russia from becoming too strong at the expense of the Turks. This new diplomatic chapter in the history of Turkey lasted for over two centuries and came to be termed "the Eastern Question." It was a story of diplomatic moves designed, in the first place, to prevent the sudden and disorderly dissolution of the Ottoman Empire and, in the second place, in case of the inevitability of such a dissolution, to secure such equal distribution of the spoils as to prevent the upsetting of the balance of power. More concretely, the Eastern Question may be narrowed down to the maneuvering of various European powers to prevent Russia from encroaching too much upon the integrity of the Ottoman Empire.

Russia appeared on the horizon of Eastern politics in the ninth century. Toward the end of the fifteenth century Ivan III, grand duke of Muscovy (1462–1505), having married Sophia, niece of the last Byzantine emperor, considered himself an heir to the Byzantine heritage. He adopted the double-headed eagle as the emblem of Russia and called Moscow the "Third Rome." But there was little political action or direct friction between Russia and Turkey beyond these vague ideological generalities. This was mainly due to the physical separation of the two states, isolated as they were by the large and sparsely populated steppes of the Ukraine. In 1575, during Ivan the Terrible's reign, an armed clash occurred between the two states for control of Astrakhan. This isolated episode did not cause any appreciable worsening of relations or any prolonged hostilities. Whatever warfare there was, was limited to the mutual raids of unruly border elements, Tatar and Cossack, upon each other. Neither the tsar nor the sultan was inclined to assume responsibility for these raids.

The situation changed appreciably with the accession of Peter the Great to the throne of Russia. Ambitious to "open the window on the Baltic" and to gain access to warm-water ports, the Tsar was determined to acquire a foothold on the Black Sea. At the time of the western offensive against the Turks, Peter in 1696, after dogged preparation, captured the fortress of Azov, which was subsequently ceded to Russia in a formal treaty concluded in 1702. In less than a decade Russia and Turkey were again at war, the result of complications in the Russo-Swedish war. Peter invaded the Ottoman Empire by way of Bessarabia in 1711 but found himself surrounded by superior Turkish forces. He was compelled to sue for peace. Actually it was a capitulation of the Russian forces, and the peace terms were damaging to Peter's foothold in and around the Black Sea. Azov and the adjoining territory were returned to the Ottomans, and the Russians had to agree to a number of restrictive measures. Because of the grand vizier's lack of foresight, the Russians managed to preserve the body of their army intact, and the great opportunity for the Turks to annihilate Russian military power was lost.

The peace concluded in 1711 was only temporary. Following the conclusion of an alliance with Austria in 1726, Russia repeatedly invaded Turkish possessions. The war of 1733–1739 resulted in the reconquest of Azov by the Russians. Catherine the Great's accession to the throne added new impetus to the policy inaugurated by Peter the Great. In fact, the Russian empress devised grandiose schemes with regard to Turkey and freely used the technique of infiltration to prepare the Slavic and Orthodox populations of the Ottoman Empire for uprising in case of a Russian invasion.

The pretext for a new war was given Catherine by differences arising out of the Polish question. The war which broke out in 1768 abounded in Russian victories, both on land—in the Rumanian principalities—and on sea. The naval operations included the dispatch of a Russian flotilla around Europe to the Mediterranean, an operation which provoked a sensation all over the world.

The war was concluded in 1774 by the Treaty of Kuchuk Kainardji. The treaty was a milestone in Russo-Turkish relations and must be considered as a major political event in the history of Turkey and of Europe. The major provisions of the treaty can be divided into four categories:

1. *Territorial.* Russia gained direct access to the Black Sea, between the mouths of the Dnieper and the Bug. In addition, she obtained Kertch and Yenikale, i.e., control of the straits between the Sea of Azov and the Black Sea, as well as Azov, Kuban, and Terek, which gave her access to the northeastern shore of the Black Sea. Thus the Tatar khanate of Crimea was surrounded by Russian possessions. Furthermore the khanate itself was declared independent of Ottoman rule.

2. *Maritime and commercial.* Russia was allowed to establish consulates in Ottoman possessions; her traders were given freedom of trade in the empire; and her merchant vessels obtained freedom of navigation in time of peace in the Black Sea and the Turkish Straits.

3. *Religious.* Russia was given the right to erect in Constantinople an Orthodox church administered by Russian ecclesiastics; her subjects were permitted to make pilgrimages to the holy places; the sultan promised to protect the Christian religion; and the Russian government was permitted to intervene in favor of the new church in the Ottoman capital.

4. *Political.* Russia obtained a protectorate over the Christian population of Moldavia and Wallachia.

The treaty obviously gave Russia enormous advantages and territorial accretions. It put an end to exclusive Turkish control of the Black Sea, and it gave some justification to the subsequent Russian claim of having the right of intervention on behalf of all Orthodox Christians throughout the Ottoman Empire. By declaring the Crimean Tatar khanate independent, it paved the way for its eventual annexation by Russia in 1783.

From that time on, Russia exercised relentless pressure on the Ottoman Empire, using the weapons of diplomacy, Pan-Slavism, Orthodoxy, and outright military aggression to achieve her ends. An additional stretch of territory on the Black Sea, between the Bug and Dniester rivers, was granted to Russia by the Treaty of Jassy after a five-year war ending in 1792. This treaty also secured Turkey's agreement to Russia's previous annexation of the Crimea.

As a result of these developments, Russia emerged as a first-rate Black Sea power. She constructed important naval bases and fortifications at Sevastopol and Odessa, and her navy achieved supremacy in Black Sea waters. Russia's progress was not without effect upon the British, who slowly became aware of the dangers inherent in these Russian successes. The younger Pitt, in particular, attempted to arouse Parliament to take action against the threat to British interests implicit in Russia's policy. Before anything could be done, however, a new complication arose, which attracted Europe's attention away from the Russian danger. The spectacular rise of Napoleon, following on the French revolution, had a disturbing effect on the pattern of European politics and on the history of the Middle East as well.

Napoleon's Middle Eastern Adventure

Initially the outbreak of the French revolution gave a somewhat pleasant relief to Turkey, since it diverted the attention of Turkey's two enemies—Russia and Austria—toward France. Yet, ultimately, even the Ottoman Empire felt the disturbing effects of the developments in France. This may be attributed to two reasons: first, Napoleon's military campaigns brought him eventually into bodily contact with the Turks; second, the ideas of popular rights and nationalism engendered by the French revolution affected various subject races of the Ottoman Empire and produced disturbing consequences.

In 1798 Napoleon organized a military expedition to Egypt for the purpose of crippling British communications with India. This naturally meant an invasion of Ottoman territory, and after centuries of friendship put France at odds with the sultan. Notwithstanding a crushing naval defeat on August 1, 1798, Napoleon persevered in his Egyptian campaign, occupying the whole of Egypt, then ruled by the Mameluke viceroys, and advancing into Palestine and Syria. Despite the valor of his armies, Bonaparte failed to take the fortress of St. Jean d'Acre (Akka), and his army did not proceed beyond Sidon in Lebanon. The French expedition, while militarily spectacular, was perhaps more significant in the cultural sense. Napoleon brought with him a number of scholars, who promptly began to study ancient Egyptian monuments, language, and history. Their work left an indelible trace in Egypt and—together with subsequent French commercial penetration—laid a firm foundation for cultural links between France and the Land of the Nile. Politically and militarily Napoleon's expedition ultimately turned out to be no more than a transitional adventure, which failed to entrench France in the East. It had, however, an important political effect in focusing British attention on the Ottoman Empire and on the latter's significance in the over-all scheme of the British imperial system. Russia's steady progress southward, both in Turkey and in Iran, was bound sooner or later to provoke British countermeasures, but Napoleon's intervention acted as a catalyst in this process. In 1799 Napoleon returned secretly to France, leaving his army behind in Egypt.

In 1801 the French in Egypt surrendered to the British. A temporary British occupation followed, but in 1802 the country was restored to the sultan. The evacuation of French forces from Ottoman territory made possible a gradual restoration of the traditionally friendly feelings between the two countries. French ascendancy in the Ottoman capital was reestablished, and by 1806 Napoleon was able to induce the Porte to take arms against Russia, with whom France was then at war. The Turks, who hoped to get rid of the Russian danger by collaborating with the seemingly invincible French Emperor, were sorely disappointed when Napoleon, after spectacular victories over the Russians, concluded the Treaty of Tilsit with Tsar Alexander I in 1807. Napoleon's betrayal of his Turkish allies stemmed from his anxiety to gain Russia's collaboration in his continental blockade of Britain. To save appearances, he offered his good offices to restore peace between Russia and Turkey. Moreover, he firmly rejected Alexander's plea for control of Constantinople. Even to the continentally minded Bonaparte it was clear that Russian control of the Turkish Straits would gravely disturb the European balance of power. In his reputed exclamation: "Constantinople? *Jamais!*" he bore witness to the importance he attached to the preservation of Ottoman independence. His mediation brought about a temporary suspension of the Russo-Turkish hostilities, but in 1809 they were resumed. Finally, the war was ended in May of 1812 by the Treaty of Bucharest. By that time Franco-Russian relations had cooled off perceptibly, and in anticipation of a French invasion Tsar Alexander was willing to grant a respite to the harassed Turks. The Treaty of Bucharest marked another step in Russia's territorial progress at the expense of Turkey. Russia annexed Bessarabia, thus extending her hold on the Black Sea shore up to the Pruth River, and secured possession of an important military road linking the Caucasian Black Sea shore with Tiflis. The latter was acquired as a result of simultaneous operations against Persia.

The Near Eastern Question, 1812–1830

In 1812 Napoleon's ill-starred expedition to Moscow closed the chapter of forceful French intervention in the affairs of the Middle East, and the traditional story of Russia's southward expansion was resumed. At this time, however, the Eastern Question presented itself in a new light, owing to aroused British interest in this part of the world. Russia henceforth had to confront not only the opposition of the Turks themselves (with the jealousy of the Habsburg Empire) but also the power of the British, who emerged in the nineteenth century as Russia's principal competitor in Asia.

It now became an axiom of British foreign policy to uphold the independence and integrity of the Ottoman Empire, in order to prevent the undue strengthening of Russia and to protect the imperial life line. The acquisition of Malta by Great Britain at the Congress of Vienna in 1815 added to the British interest in the Mediterranean and its adjacent shores.

In France, weakened after the Napoleonic wars, England found a friendly power. With minor exceptions no major conflicts separated the two nations on Middle Eastern policy. Throughout the nineteenth century the two countries presented a common front against Russia's imperialism. This concerted attitude might have arrested further Ottoman disintegration if it had not been for the seed planted involuntarily by France herself. The concept of national and popular rights which was born at the time of the revolution, spread to the four corners of Europe in the wake of Napoleonic victories. The Christian subjects of the Ottoman Empire, particularly those living in compact national groups in the Balkans, did not remain unaffected by it. The story of the struggle for national independence by the Balkan nations is outside the scope of this work. It is sufficient to state here that, beginning with the Serbian war of independence (1804–1813), one by one the Balkan nations emancipated themselves from the rule of the empire in the course of the nineteenth and twentieth centuries. Greece (1832), Rumania (1856–1878), Serbia (1834–1878), Montenegro (1878), and Bulgaria (1878–1908), all detached themselves and formed independent states.

In the liberation of the Balkan Christians, Russia played a decisive role. Her pressure on and wars with Turkey gave the Balkan peoples the encouragement and military opportunity to throw off the Ottoman yoke. The role of other European powers, in particular that of England, was difficult and often complicated. On the one hand, Europe in general and England in particular strove to preserve the life of the Ottoman Empire. On this account they were bound to oppose both Russia's aggressiveness and the disintegrating tendencies in the Balkans. On the other hand, no European power could openly place itself athwart the desire of a Christian nation to attain freedom from the rule of the infidel Moslem Empire, corrupt and decaying. Out of the dilemma thus created, the British-inspired concert of European powers attempted for the most part to adjust itself to the realities of the Eastern situation without compromising too many of the vital principles underlying European diplomacy. Autonomy under Turkish suzerainty first, and later full independence, were reluctantly conceded to the Balkan nations at a series of congresses. At the same time, care was taken to prevent Russia from gaining sole credit for and undue political advantages from such developments, and to assure that this emancipatory process would be carried out without producing a collapse of the Ottoman Empire.

Much of this basic aim was accomplished. Yet it would be erroneous to conclude that the liberation of the Balkan nations was obtained in an orderly manner. Quite the contrary, there were a number of insurrections, wars, and diplomatic crises, which might easily have led to a major European conflagration.

The Greek war of independence (1821–1829) brought Russia into conflict with Turkey in 1828. The fighting, which took place in the Balkans and in the Caucasus, ended with the Russian conquest of Adrianople, less than 150 miles from Constantinople. The Treaty of Adrianople confirmed the Russian protectorate over the Danubian principalities, provided for Turkey's agreement to any proposed solution concerning Greece, and secured for Russia new territorial acquisitions on the eastern shore of the Black Sea. These gains included the ports of Anapa and Poti, the coastal region of the Caucasus known as Abkhasia, and the fortress of Akhaltsikh in western Georgia. This newly acquired territory, in conjunction with several annexations in the general area of the Caucasus at the expense of the Persian Empire, considerably strengthened Russia's position in the Black Sea region.

The Rise of Mohammed Ali

The Treaty of Adrianople brought the Turks only a temporary respite from Russian expansionism. Scarcely three years passed before Russia scored a new success at the expense of Turkey. This time no war was necessary. Paradoxically enough, for the first and probably only time in the nineteenth century, Russia posed as a friend and ally of the Ottoman Empire. The circumstances leading to this unusual development had their roots in Egypt. Following the Napoleonic expedition, this fertile province of the Empire found itself under the rule of an Albanian adventurer,

Mohammed Ali. His rise was spectacular. He appeared in Egypt for the first time in 1801. By 1805 he was a viceroy under the sultan's suzerainty. In 1818 he subdued the Wahhabi tribes in Arabia and subjected Mecca and Medina to Ottoman control. He conquered Nubia in 1822, and in the same year he obtained the governship of Crete in return for assistance that he extended to the Ottoman government during the Greek revolt. Mohammed Ali's cooperation in quelling the Greek insurrection was to have been repaid by control not only of Crete but also of the Peloponnesus. The Greek war of liberation, however, interfered with these plans. Denied Morea, Mohammed Ali demanded Syria. When this demand was refused, he declared war on the Porte in 1831 and sent an Egyptian expeditionary force to Syria under his son Ibrahim. His troops progressed victoriously through Syria, entered Anatolia proper, and in a major battle defeated the Turkish army at Konya in 1832. The sultan, by the Treaty of Kutaya, was forced to grant to his vassal the government of Syria and Adana. At this moment Russia proferred her services to the sultan, who, bitter and revengeful, was ready to accept any assistance against further threats by the Egyptian upstart.

The Treaty of Unkiar Iskelessi, concluded in 1833, marked the climax of Russia's success in Turkey and brought the Ottoman Empire very close to complete dependence upon its powerful northern neighbor. The treaty openly provided for a defensive alliance between the two countries; its secret clauses gave Russia a uniquely privileged position concerning the Straits. Turkey promised to close the Straits to any power at war with Russia, while permitting Russia full freedom of navigation in war or peace. The result of the treaty was a veiled Russian protectorate over the Ottoman Empire and caused much concern in British government circles. Thus ended the first phase of the Mohammed Ali episode.

The second phase opened with the renewal of war between the Porte and Egypt in 1839. Ibrahim Pasha achieved another resounding victory over the Turks at the battle of Nisib on the upper Euphrates. The road to Constantinople lay virtually open to the ambitious Egyptians. At this time, however, the European powers intervened. This intervention, sponsored by the British government, was motivated by two factors: first, Europe was seriously alarmed by the extent of Russian influence in Constantinople, an influence which was bound to increase if the position of the sultan weakened as a result of Mohammed Ali's successes; second, Europe decided, under British leadership, not to permit the enfeebled Ottoman Empire to be replaced by a new empire headed by Mohammed Ali. France did not concur in this decision. Having established many commercial and cultural links with Egypt since the Napoleonic campaigns, the French viewed the rise of Mohammed Ali with favor and foresaw many advantages to them in the strengthening of his position. Eventually the intervention of the European powers took the form of an Anglo-Austrian naval blockade of the Syrian coast to cut Ibrahim's communications with his base. This was accompanied by an ultimatum demanding his withdrawal to Egypt. The Egyptians were forced to bow to this display of determination. At the Conference of London in 1840, Britain, Austria, Prussia, Russia—and also France—agreed upon a settlement by which Mohammed Ali was obliged to return Syria to the sultan. As compensation, he was made hereditary pasha of Egypt. Another part of the settlement, known as the Convention of the Straits (1841), ended the privileged position of Russia and set up an arrangement more agreeable to the other European powers. The London settlement, which quite clearly constituted intervention by outside powers into the domestic affairs of the Ottoman Empire, can be regarded as the establishment of a joint European protectorate over Turkey. As such, it replaced the exclusive Russian protectorate formulated under the Treaty of Unkiar Iskelessi.

Outwardly, it seemed that the London agreements had settled the Eastern Question for some time to come to the mutual satisfaction of most of the powers concerned. Soon, however, it developed that Britain and Russia were attaching different interpretations to these decisions. Britain was happy to see Ottoman integrity preserved and viewed with favor a reform movement in Turkey, which was bound to regenerate and strengthen the Empire. Russia, on the contrary, considered Anglo-Russian cooperation in solving Turkish domestic problems as a logical step toward further intervention and eventual partition of Ottoman territory. It was at this time that Tsar Nicholas I made his famous statement about "the Sick Man of Europe," suggesting in conversation with British statesmen and diplomats that the Sick Man's estate should be divided in an orderly manner before his impending death.

From the Crimean War to the Treaty of Berlin

This difference as to interpretation provided the setting for the Crimean War (1854–1856). When events came to a head in 1854, Russia found herself opposed by a coalition of Turkey, Britain, France, and Sardinia. The immediate cause of the war was the quarrel between France and Russia over control of the holy places in Palestine. The local dispute between the French-supported Latin monks and the Russian-protected Greek ecclesiastics led to dispatch of a Russian diplomatic mission to Constantinople. In an ultimatum Russia demanded not only the recognition of her right to protect all Orthodox Christians in the Ottoman Empire (about twelve million souls), but also an alliance with Turkey. To support this ultimatum, the Russian army entered two Rumanian principalities. Last minute attempts by a conference of European powers to effect a settlement did not produce satisfactory results, and Turkey found herself at war with her northern neighbor, In the early spring of 1854 Britain and France declared war on Russia, to be followed by a similar declaration by the small but rising kingdom of Sardinia. Military and naval operations took place predominantly in the Crimea, at a heavy cost in human lives, primarily because of poor sanitary services.

The death of Tsar Nicholas I, followed by the fall of Sevastopol, in 1855 led Russia, under Alexander II, to sue for peace. The resulting Treaty of Paris (1856) contained the following major provisions:

1. The Black Sea was to be demilitarized. This actually meant the termination of the Russian naval establishments and the destruction of shore installations and fortifications.

2. Navigation on the Danube River was to be free to all nations. This was to be a check on the Russian tendency to secure a monopolistic position there.

3. A Russian protectorate over the Rumanian principalities was to be ended. The

latter states were in turn to be granted fuller autonomy under Ottoman suzerainty with a joint guarantee by the powers.

4. Southern Bessarabia was to be ceded by Russia to the Ottoman Empire. This meant a physical separation of Russia from the banks of the Danube delta and, consequently, a check upon her control of the mouth of this important European river.

The Crimean War has often been termed utterly unnecessary. Its importance and profound consequences upon the future of the Ottoman Empire should not, however, be underrated. The defeat of Russia gave the Turks a new lease on life, and Russian expansion in the Black Sea and toward the Mediterranean suffered a serious check. The war closed a definite chapter in Ottoman history, a chapter of growing Russian influence and disquieting ascendancy in Constantinople, which started with the Treaty of Unkiar Iskelessi and was only partially checked by the London conventions of 1840–1841.

The period that followed eloquently illustrated the influence of domestic upon foreign affairs. Despite the successful outcome of the Crimean War, Turkey's troubles were by no means over. The growing nationalism of her Balkan subjects and the inefficiency and corruption of her administration were tinder for a new conflagration. Irked by the cruel exactions of the Turkish authorities, the people of Bosnia rose in revolt. The flames of insurrection soon spread to Bulgaria. Serbia and Montenegro showed solidarity with their Balkan brethren by declaring war on the Porte.

Turkish reprisals assumed cruel proportions, especially in Bulgaria, and aroused much indignation in Europe. The reaction in Russia was intense, and Moscow declared war on Turkey in 1877. As so many times before, the Russians were successful in their contest with the Turks and dictated a victor's peace in San Stefano. In this agreement, Russia annexed some territory and provided for the creation of a big Bulgarian state to extend from the Albanian mountains to the Black Sea, and from the Danube to the Aegean. Formal recognition of the independence of Serbia, Rummania, and Montenegro completed the main political provisions of the treaty. The huge state of Bulgaria, entirely dependent on Russian aid, was to constitute an outpost and an instrument of Russian influence in this region; this was to be the crowning achievement of Russian Near Eastern policy. The Treaty of San Stefano, however, was not destined to endure. Britain, Austria, and France, seriously alarmed at this new manifestation of Russian ambitions, protested. The ensuing Treaty of Berlin (1878), replacing the Treaty of San Stefano, deprived Russia of the major part of the spoils. It provided (1) for the creation of a small autonomous Bulgaria still under Turkish suzerainty, (2) for the independence of Serbia, Rumania, and Montenegro, (3) for the cession of southern Bessarabia to Russia, (4) for the cession of Kars, Ardahan, and Batum to Russia, (5) for the promise of more extended frontiers to Greece, (6) for the Austrian occupation of Bosnia and Herzegovina, and (7) for the British occupation of Cyprus.

Russia thus suffered a severe check in her Balkan diplomacy and resentfully felt that her military victory had been politically frustrated. Yet she had succeeded in enlarging her possessions at the expense of Turkey. On the other hand, with the avalanche of national liberation once set into motion, the Ottoman Empire could not avoid knowing that its domains would probably shrink again.

The Treaty of Berlin produced a new situation in Russo-Turkish relationships. Owing to the creation of an independent Rumania and of an autonomous Bulgaria, Russia lost her direct boundary with the Ottoman Empire in the west. Henceforth her territorial ambitions at the expense of Turkey had to be limited to the eastern boundary. There a pretext could be found in the Armenian people living in the Turkish vilayets. Russia was in a position to exploit this situation, and she was not hesitant about doing so. Otherwise, whatever further designs Russia might have had on the Ottoman Empire, they had perforce to be confined to political or military control of Turkey proper and of the Turkish Straits. In other words, the margin of justification of Russian imperialist actions—which in the past had been the liberation of Balkan Slavs and Christians—was now narrowed to a bare minimum. Trespass on this minimum was bound to pose the long-delayed basic problem of the existence of Turkey as an independent state. Thus the Treaty of Berlin constituted a definite landmark in Russo-Turkish relations.

On the other hand, the treaty illustrated the growing ambiguity of the attitude of the European powers. While attempting to check Russia's southward drive and while professing to desire the preservation of Ottoman integrity, they were not loath to secure advantages for themselves. The Austrian occupation of part of the Balkans and the British acquisition of Cyprus are cases in point. To this may be added the French quest for authority to occupy Tunisia and the revelation of Italian designs upon Albania and Libya. Germany was the only power that asked for nothing, a fact not without further political consequences.

It is perhaps time to turn our eyes from the main pattern of Russia vs. Turkey vs. Europe toward the oriental portions of the Ottoman Empire. The history of the empire in Asia and Africa is politically less important than its history in Europe. Nevertheless, events that developed there in the fifty years between 1864 and 1914 deserve attention because they reveal a pattern of gradual penetration or outright imperialism on the part of western European powers at the expense of the Ottoman Empire.

Western Imperialism and the Ottoman Empire

Four countries appear as contenders for various advantages or territories: France, England, Italy, and Germany.

Despite the traditional alliance between the Ottoman Empire and France, the latter was not reluctant to take advantage of the empire's weakness in those areas deemed important to French interests. And yet, although France extended her rule over Algeria (1830), Tunisia (1883), and Morocco (1906–1912), these moves could not be interpreted as anti-Turkish since the lands in question had been under only nominal and very remote control of the Porte. Egypt and Lebanon were the main areas where French interests came into direct contact or clash with those of the Turks. France's support of Mohammed Ali led to the entrenchment of her cultural and commercial influence in Egypt. This influence became obvious when the French explorer and engineer Ferdinand de Lesseps obtained in 1856, from the

Egyptian viceroy (or khedive), Ismail Pasha, a concession for the construction of a canal through the Isthmus of Suez. The canal was opened for maritime traffic in 1869 in an impressive ceremony attended by Empress Eugenie, and it seemed that it would be important as a spearhead of French influence in Egypt. Subsequent events, however, radically changed the picture. With the purchase of Khedive Ismail's interest by the Disraeli government in 1875, the British assumed a decisive role in the affairs of the canal.

Another area of traditionally strong French influence was Lebanon. Inhabited by a Christian majority, this ancient stronghold of the Crusaders had always looked toward France for inspiration and protection. The anti-Christian riots and persecutions that occurred there in the early 1860s provoked French naval and military intervention. This in turn brought about a constitutional change.

Under the pressure of the powers, the sultan in 1864 was forced to grant autonomy to the sanjak of Lebanon, which was to be governed by a Christian governor. France, to be sure, was not given any formal position of privilege as a result of these events, but she was regarded unofficially as a protecting power of the Lebanese Christians. This intervention was France's last major success in the Ottoman realm before World War I. Her defeat in the war with Prussia in 1870 weakened her and hence interfered with her ambitious designs in the Middle East. From that time on France's political influence was on the wane and she was a constant loser in the competition with Great Britain.

The British record in relation to the Ottoman Empire must at its best be described as ambiguous, and at its worst as insincere. While the preservation of the Ottoman Empire was an axiom of nineteenth-century British policy, this axiom was hedged with qualifications and practical reservations. As it was pointed out earlier, Britain, as a Christian country, was not in a position to oppose outright the struggle for national liberation of the Balkan Christians. Therefore, rather reluctantly (although it was enthusiastically at the time of Gladstone) the British supported the national aspirations of the Balkan peoples whenever their revolutionary action and corresponding Russian intervention made European intervention necessary.

Britain's interest in Ottoman integrity originated, of course, in her desire to protect her imperial line to the East. Protection of this life line sometimes demanded more than a mere negative hands-off-Turkey policy, addressed as it was to Russia. It required occasionally positive British penetration into Asiatic and African Ottoman possessions. Between 1833 and 1887 Britain was intensely interested in establishing an English-controlled land-and-river route through Mesopotamia to India. At the same time she manifested a prolonged and consistent interest in Egypt as a link in the chain leading from Gibraltar to Aden (Aden was acquired in 1839). The acquisition of Malta in 1815 and of Cyprus in 1878, the latter at the expense of the Ottoman Empire, reinforced this chain. Disraeli's decision to purchase the bankrupt khedive's interest in the Suez Canal was, therefore, a logical consequence of this policy. The 1870s witnessed a growing British commercial penetration into Egypt. When in 1882 native xenophobia caused Arabi Pasha to revolt both against the khedive and against foreign influence in Egypt, the British stake was deemed so high as to justify naval and military intervention. British bombardment of Alexandria was followed by the battle of Tel el-Kebir and resulted in the occupation of the country.

In 1883, Sir Evelyn Baring (later Lord Cromer) arrived in Cairo officially as British consul general and diplomatic agent and unofficially as virtual ruler of Egypt. This benevolent rule lasted until his retirement in 1907 and elevated Egypt from a state of bankruptcy and chaos into the richest and best-developed country in the Middle East.

Britain's involvement in Egyptian affairs brought her logically to intervention in the affairs of the Sudan, at the time of the uprising of the Mahdi in that area. British forces were sent, alongside those of the Egyptians, to quell the rebellion. The Sudanese drama can be divided into two phases. The first, between 1882 and 1855, brought defeat to the British armies and death to General Gordon at Khartoum. Thirteen years of the Mahdi's rule followed. The second phase, highlighted by Kitchener's victory at Omdurman in 1898, resulted in the final overthrow of the Mahdi and the establishment of the Anglo-Egyptian condominium over the Sudan. The grip on the Sudan strengthened the British position in Egypt and, despite early assurances in 1882, the question of British evacuation from Egypt never seriously arose thereafter. These *faits accomplis* were given their diplomatic confirmation at the time of the formation of the Entente Cordiale in 1904. In return for the recognition of French preponderance in Morocco, France recognized the British position in Egypt. Thereafter British interests in the Middle East could be challenged only by Germany, a challenge which was by no means negligible.

Germany began to show serious interest in the affairs of the Ottoman Empire around 1880. In 1881, General von der Goltz was appointed head of the German military mission to reorganize the Turkish army. In 1889 Emperor William II and the Empress paid a state visit to Constantinople, inaugurating an era of friendship and close cooperation between Germany and Turkey. The growth of German prestige coincided with the waning of British popularity, which resulted from (1) Britain's grasping attitude toward Cyprus, (2) British support of Greece in the latter's irredentism, and (3) British occupation of Egypt in 1882. Moreover, British interests in the Middle East were not well served by Gladstone's policy in the 1880s. Gladstone was outspokenly anti-Turkish. The Armenian massacres in Turkey (1897–1898) produced indignation and intervention on the part of the European powers, with the exception of the Germans, who remained cautiously aloof. As relations between Turkey and the other powers became more estranged, Germany's attitude became more cordial. During his second visit to the Ottoman Empire in 1898, the Kaiser made a simultaneous bid for the friendship of the Turks and of other Moslem peoples. "His Majesty, the Sultan Abdul Hamid and the 300 million Mohammedans, who reverence him as Caliph, may rest assured that at all times the German Emperor will be their friend," declared William II in Damascus. The effects of this diplomacy could soon be felt economically. German banking and business interests began to penetrate Turkey, and a series of concessions was awarded German firms. The most important of these, and one which caused violent international controversy, was a concession granted in 1902 to the German company of Anatolian Railways to construct the Constantinople-Baghdad railroad line. This line, if constructed, would link Berlin with Baghdad and eventually with Basra, and would serve the interests of German economic expansion. The project was deeply resented by the British, who spared no efforts to frustrate German initiative. By the turn of the century it became obvious that, in their Near Eastern policies, Berlin and Vienna worked hand in hand, the Austrians being the junior partner. Austria's role in this partnership could be described as the paving of the road to Turkey through the Balkans (where her ambitions focused). Germany would take upon herself the infiltration of Anatolia and other Asiatic domains of the Ottoman Empire. Internal developments in Turkey at this time contributed in no small measure to the success of these concerted Austro-German policies.

To complete this review of Western imperialism at the expense of the empire, a word must be said of Italy. Ever since her emancipation as a united state, Italy had been casting covetous glances toward the northern coast of Africa, an area formerly controlled by the Roman Empire. British penetration of Egypt and French annexations in Tunisia and Morocco greatly stimulated Italy's interest in the intermediate zone of North Africa, situated as it was opposite to Italy's shores and deemed strategically important by Italian statesmen. It was the Moroccan crisis of 1911 which precipitated Italy's decision to seek a solution in Africa by the force of arms. In the fall of that year Italy declared war on the Porte and sent an expeditionary army to Libya. After thirteen months peace was concluded at Lausanne in October 1912. Partly by its terms and partly by their dubious legal interpretation Italy obtained control of Libya and of the Dodecanese Islands in the Aegean. As a result, the Ottoman Empire lost its last direct stronghold on the African continent.

Attempts at Reform: The Young Turks

Thus far we have paid little attention to Turkish internal developments, which are largely outside the scope of this study. A few facts, however, deserve mention, particularly those which affected Turkey's strength or weakness. In the nineteenth century, while Turkey's international and internal situation was steadily deteriorating, a few attempts were made at reform. Mahmud II (1808–1839), the greatest of the Turkish rulers since Suleiman the Magnificent, annihilated in one bold stroke the corps of Janissaries, whose influence had become detrimental to the welfare of the empire. A series of internal reforms including military and administrative organization followed. These were interrupted, however, by constant warfare and by Mohammed Ali's rebellion and as a result never came to full fruition. The decade of the 1840s, following the settlement of the Egyptian question, brought the empire an interlude of peace. During this period, under the rule of Abdul Mejid (1839–1861), the Turkish reform party headed by Reshid Pasha undertook a number of measures destined to strengthen and modernize the empire. Following the issuance of the Charter of Liberties (or *Hatti Sherif of Gülhane*) in 1839, reforms were instituted in the fields of administration, taxation, justice, education, minorities, and military affairs. These reforms, however, were destined to be as unsuccessful as the previous ones, partly because of the domestic reactionary opposition and partly because of the new international complications which resulted in the Crimean War. Even the reaffirmation of the rights of minorities (in a decree known as *Hatti-Humayun* in

1856) did not materially change the picture. Under Abdul Aziz (1861–1876) sincere efforts for reform were exerted by an enlightened Turkish statesman of high repute, Midhat Pasha. His efforts also came largely to naught, because of the weakness of the sultan himself. Reform in the empire could be accomplished either by having a very strong-willed ruler, who would think in terms of public interest and would command public obedience, or by carrying out a radical social revolution, which would change the theocratic character of the empire and secularize it. As to the first alternative, the rulers of Turkey did not have the necessary qualifications. Neither Sultan Abdul Aziz, well-intentioned but incompetent, nor his successor Murad V—both deposed on account of mental disorders—nor Abdul Hamid II (1876–1909), corrupt and reactionary, were the leaders to carry out reform. True enough, for a brief period after Abdul Hamid's ascension, the forces of reform seemed victorious. On December 23, 1876, Midhat Pasha succeeded in inducing the new sultan to proclaim a constitution which guaranteed civil liberties and provided for parliamentary government based on general representation. But this turned out to be no more than a brief liberal interlude. Jealous of his power, Abdul Hamid soon reverted to repressive policies, dismissed and banished Midhat Pasha, and, in 1877, prorogued the newly created parliament, suspending the constitution. Thereafter for thirty years he ruled as absolute monarch.

The other alternative remained, that of a radical change by revolution. The task of shaking the empire out of its lethargy was taken up by the Young Turk movement. Composed of youthful and impatient elements, the Young Turk Party drew its inspiration from the West and wanted to remodel the empire into a liberal constitutional monarchy. Their Committee of Union and Progress was successful in creating a strong conspiratorial organization and in enlisting many army officers. In the coup d'état of 1908, the Young Turks seized power, compelled Abdul Hamid to restore the constitution, and then forced him to abdicate. In its immediate effects, the Young Turk revolution produced further shrinkage of the empire. Profiting from what they believed to be a sign of weakness, Austria annexed Bosnia and Herzegovina (under occupation since 1878), and Bulgaria proclaimed her full independence from the empire. These acts, though they came as a shock both internally and internationally, were expected to happen sooner or later. More interesting was the effect of the Young Turk revolution on German-Ottoman relations. On the surface, it appeared that the forcible elimination of Germany's friend, Sultan Abdul Hamid, might produce a radical reorientation of Turkey's foreign policy. The Young Turks professed admiration for Western democratic liberalism and could hardly be expected to feel friendly toward Prussian military autocracy. History, however, reveals surprising shifts, and ideologies are often overshadowed by personalities. Enver Pasha, a leading member of the triumvirate that ruled Turkey after 1908, turned out to be definitely pro-German and anti-British. Consequently, he facilitated German penetration and did his utmost to put Turkey into a pro-German frame of mind as the Great War approached. This frame of mind was not too difficult to create because the traditional friends of Turkey, the British and the French, effected a far-reaching rapprochement with Turkey's hereditary enemy, Russia.

As a result of the two Balkan wars (1912–1913) fought with her small Christian neighbors and largely caused by the controversial question of Macedonia, Turkey lost most of her European territory.

The outbreak of the Great War found the empire reduced territorially. Of its European possessions, only eastern Thrace remained. Egypt was under British control and virtually detached. Internally matters were far from reassuring. The empire's national minorities were resentful, and hence of doubtful loyalty. The Arabs were inclined toward nationalism. The Young Turks failed to institute the promised reforms, except in the military sphere. Here the expert advice of Prussian officers, combined with the virile characteristics of the Turkish race, made it possible to recreate the Ottoman army so that it could again be called a military factor on the international scene. German diplomatic ascendancy in Constantinople was manifest. Turkey was ready to plunge into a new war. This she did with incalculable consequences to herself and to all the rest of the Middle East.

The Persian Empire

Another country whose history is relevant to understanding of the political changes in the Middle East prior to the First World War is the ancient empire of Persia. Established in the sixth century B.C. by Cyrus, who united Media with Persia, Persia knew glory under her Achaemenid dynasty. Persia's ancient civilization, her Zoroastrian religion, and her wars with the Hellenes left an indelible mark upon the history of mankind. The dynastic history of Persia reveals periods of rule under native kings alternating with those under alien rulers. Thus, the first and truly Persian dynasty of the Achaemenids (558–331) was succeeded by Alexander the Great and the Seleucids, to be followed by more than four hundred years of the Arsacid Parthian dynasty (250 B.C.–A.D. 228). The Parthian rule gave way, in turn, to a native Persian monarchy of the Sassanids (242–642). In 642, at the battle of Nehavend, Persia was defeated and conquered by the Arabs. Conversion to the Islamic religion and rule by a series of viceroys of either Arab or Persian descent followed. Persia ceased to be a single political entity, being divided into various principalities. This era came to an end with the Mongol invasion. The capture of Baghdad in 1258 by Hulagu opened a new period of alien domination. The country rallied again under the native dynasty of the Safavids (1502–1753). Under Abbas I the Great, Persia passed through a period of regeneration and experienced a golden age in the development of her culture. The Safavi era was followed by a period of uncertainty until the establishment at the end of the eighteenth century of the Kajar dynasty, which was to rule Persia until 1925. Despotic yet weak, the Kajars proved incapable of protecting Persia against foreign encroachments.

In the course of the Kajar era, Persia entered modern world politics as a pawn in the big-power rivalry for control of the Middle East. The principal actors in this historical drama were the Russians, who, since Peter the Great, had wanted to expand toward the south. Inasmuch as Russia's approach to the Persian Gulf threatened Britain's position in India, Britain consistently opposed this expansion. Thus, the balancing of Anglo-Russian claims in Persia became a permanent feature of nineteenth-century diplomacy and was upset only when a third power threw its might on the scales. Such a situation occurred twice between 1800 and 1914. In the early 1800s and in the early 1900s, Napoleonic France and Imperial Germany, respectively, succeeded in securing paramount influence in Persia. In both cases, this interest was dictated by the basically anti-British policies of the newcomers. Influence over Persia was not treated as an end in itself but rather as a stepping stone toward the conquest of India. When such intervention occurred, Britain was, as a rule, inclined to compose her differences with Russia, such turns of British policy inevitably working to the detriment of Persia. This was so because in opposing Russian southward imperialism Great Britain acted as a virtual guarantor of Persian independence. Britain's Persian policy was dictated primarily by her concern for India, and Persia was to be an independent buffer state or neutral zone between the Indian and the Russian empires. Britain sought unimpeded commercial opportunity in Persia, and to this extent she was interested in exercising moderate influence in the area. She was unwilling, however, to assume direct imperial responsibilities similar to those in India. It was, therefore, in her interest to see Persia relatively strong and capable of withstanding Russian pressure. It was largely due to this British policy that Persia succeeded in maintaining her independence instead of falling under Russian domination.

This Russo-British rivalry could be described as almost chronic disease; it had an occasional crisis now and then, but it was essentially a disease to which the British government and public opinion were accustomed. The sudden appearance of Napoleonic France or Imperial Germany in Middle Eastern politics would throw this nicely balanced mechanism into confusion. Under such circumstances, Britain was willing temporarily to compromise with the chronic Russian danger in order to avert the more dynamic and immediate threat of the "unauthorized" adventurers. But such a compromise with Russia would obviously mean concessions at the expense of Persia. Persia's hope, in the long run, was that third-party intervention would not last too long and that the traditional pattern of Russo-British rivalry would be resumed. This fact, however, was not always recognized by the Persian rulers, who were inclined to think that the third party would give a mortal blow to both traditional protagonists and thus deliver Persia from obnoxious tutelage. Yet the uncontested historical fact is that Persia's independence in the nineteenth and twentieth centuries was gravely impaired only when, as a result of outside interference, Britain and Russia were willing to shelve their rivalry.

This picture must be kept in mind when one studies the apparently complicated policies in and over Persia from 1800 onward. Russian pressure in the direction of the Caucasus, working against Persia and Turkey, was obvious in the last decade of the eighteenth and the first decade of the nineteenth century. This threat Britain was anxious to eliminate, but her attention was temporarily diverted toward the new danger in the shape of Napoleonic imperialism. What followed was an intricate play of British and French intrigues at the shah's court in Teheran. In 1800 the British scored a diplomatic success by concluding with Persia the so-called Malcolm Treaty of Alliance. This treaty contained a French exclusion clause, and this point was of utmost importance to Britain at that time. To Shah Fath Ali, however, it was the British pledge to aid him in resisting external aggression which was of real significance. The external aggression which he most feared was that of Russia. Consequently, when it transpired that the British were lukewarm in assisting him at the time of the Russian aggression in 1802, the Shah was quite willing to abandon this alliance and turn toward France in his search for security. He first entered into negotiations with Colonel Romieu, who had arrived in Teheran to offer him an alliance and a subsidy; next he sent an envoy to Napoleon. The Franco-Persian Treaty of Finkenstein in May 1807 gave formal confirmation to the preliminary arrangements. It was followed by the dispatch to Persia of a French military mission under General Gardanne. Soon, however, Persia experienced a new disappointment. At Tilsit in July, barely two months after the Treaty of Finkenstein was signed, Napoleon and Alexander I of Russia came to terms.[1] Although no arrangements were made concerning Persia, it was clear that the latter's trust in effective French protection against Russia was to be betrayed. The French mission lost its original political usefulness and General Gardanne could do no more than offer mediation with Russia, an obviously inadequate proposal from the Persian point of view.

By 1805 it had become clear to the British that unless they recognized the primacy of the Russian danger, they would not be able to count on any stable relationship with Persia. It was futile to count on Persian collaboration against France, since France was viewed not as an enemy but as a potential ally by Teheran. In fact, some British critics maintained that any French threat to India was imaginary and that the only threat was apt to come from the north. In recognition of this new trend, Sir Hartford Jones in 1805 concluded the preliminary Treaty of Alliance with Persia, clearly directed against Russian expansion. Britain promised Persia arms, munitions, army instructors, and a subsidy. The Shah, in view of Napoleon's betrayal at Tilsit, was glad to avail himself of this assistance. With the conclusion of that treaty, the principle of the integrity of Persia became a corollary to the principle of Ottoman integrity in British foreign policy. Britain kept her word, the treaty provisions were carried out, and some British officers attached to the Shah's army came into contact with advaned Russian units on the Caucasian frontier.

Scarcely had this era of cooperation begun, when it was suspended by Napoleon's invasion of Russia in 1812. Britain, vitally interested in checkmating France, attempted reconciliation with Russia. The two-fold effects of this policy were immediately visible in Persia. On the one hand, Britain disregarded her early promises of assistance and offered instead her good offices in the Persian-Russian disputes; on the other hand, Russia, emboldened by Britain's softened attitude, increased her pressure and in October 1813 concluded with the Shah the Treaty of Gulistan, by which Persia ceded to Russia Derbend, Baku, Shirvan, Shaki, Karabagh, and part of Talish, renounced all titles to Georgia, Daghestan, Mingrelia, and Abkhasia, and agreed to domination of the Caspain by the Russian navy.

This suspension of the Anglo-Persian alliance was viewed in Great Britain as a

---

[1]Napoleon's understanding with Alexander I thus revived an earlier friendship between Napoleon and Tsar Paul. In 1800 Paul and Napoleon had planned an invasion of India by the concerted action of the Russian and French armies.

temporary expedient only. As soon as the French threat was parried, the British hastened to conclude with Persia the "definitive" Treaty of Teheran (1914), which, under somewhat emasculated terms, confirmed the Jones treaty. But the effects of the temporary relaxation of vigilance proved to be more than provisional. The Treaty of Gulistan became the opening wedge for steadily rising Russian influence. The immediate aim of the Russians was to reach the boundary which they considered to be strategic between Russia and Persia, the Aras River. The complete subjugation of Persia, by one means or another, was Russia's long-range objective. A pretext for a new war with Persia was found in 1828. Britain's assistance to Persia was limited to a few subsidies. The Treaty of Turkomanchai, concluding the war in 1828, gave Russia coveted Persian territory (Erivan and Nakhichevan) up to the Aras River[2] and supremacy over the country. Russia obtained preferential economic treatment expressed in low customs duties and in other trading privileges; secured capitulations; and in return guaranteed Persian dynastic interests, which, in itself, amounted to a veiled protectorate.

Anglo-Russian Rivalry in the Nineteenth Century

Having suffered severe territorial losses in the Caucasian region, Persia sought compensation in the east at the expense of Afghanistan. The immediate object of Persian ambitions was the strategic fortress and province of Herat. Russia encouraged this expansionist policy because it diverted Persia's attention from her northern borders and, at the same time, indirectly threatened the British position in India. Britain considered Afghanistan another link in the protective chain around India and was determined to protect it from Russian or Russian-sponsored Persian encroachments. Persia's attempts to conquer Herat in 1833 and in 1837–1838 ended in failure, despite expert advice given her by the Russians. When, however, in 1856 a Persian army succeeded in capturing the coveted fortress, Britain reluctantly declared war. British troops disembarked on the Persian Gulf coast, captured Bushire, Mohammera, and Ahwaz, and forced Persia to sue for peace. The Anglo-Persian Treaty of Paris (1957) provided for evacuation of Afghanistan and the recognition of Afghanistan's independence. The British, interested in cultivating Persian good will, displayed remarkable self-restraint and refrained from asking for territory, concessions, or indemnities.

The Anglo-Persian war over Afghanistan put an end to the adventurous policy of Persia in the east and again focused her attention on the chronic Russian danger in the north. Having acquired the naval base of Ashurada on the southern Caspian coast at the expense of Persia in 1840, the empire of the tsars now devoted its energies to the conquest of Central Asia—a process which was inevitably bound to affect Persian security. The three independent Central Asian khanates, Bukhara, Khiva, and Kokand, were conquered by Russia in 1868, 1873, and 1876, respectively. Simultaneously, Russia advanced in the Transcaspian region, conquering Krasnovodsk in 1869, capturing Geok Tepe, the Turkoman stronghold, in 1881, and subjugating Merv and Panjdeh in 1884. The latter operations affected Persia

---

[2]The boundary followed the Aras River up to the 48th meridian and then turned southeastward, putting the province of Lankoran and the town of Astara in Russia. This boundary has not changed since.

directly, inasmuch as she claimed rights over these regions. Furthermore, the subjugation of the Turkomans created a common boundary between Russia and Persia east of the Caspian. In 1881 Persia had to agree to the Atrek River boundary. Britain's worry about this advance caused a serious international crisis which brought the two protagonists close to war in 1885. Open rupture was averted by Britain's energetic stand and by the Russian decision not to cross into Afghanistan.

While Russia was thus expanding southward, the "nation of shopkeepers" attempted to secure economic advantages in Persia. In 1872 a naturalized British subject, Baron Julius de Reuter, obtained a sweeping seventy-year concession from Shah Nasser ed-Din, which gave him the right to construct a railway between the Caspian Sea and the Persian Gulf; to exploit all mines except those of gold, silver, and precious stones; to construct waterworks and regulate the rivers; and to organize streetcar transportation in Teheran.

This concession was not destined to materialize. The Shah, who in 1873 made a tour of European capitals, was frigidly received at St. Petersburg and decided, under Russian pressure, to cancel Reuter's concession. Reuter appealed to the British government for protection. In 1889, following lengthy diplomatic maneuvers, Persia, as compensation, granted two concessions to British interests: one for the "Imperial Bank of Persia" with the right to issue banknotes and one for "The Imperial Tobacco Corporation of Persia." To satisfy Russia, the Shah was compelled to allow her to establish a Russian discount and loans bank, as well as to construct a railway line in Azerbaijan. Even these concessions did not appease the northern neighbors; Russian agents skillfully instigated a popular movement against tobacco which ended in the cancellation of the British tobacco concession. This time the Persian government agreed to pay the aggrieved British investors half a million pounds sterling for damages.

At the time of Nasser ed-Din's violent death in 1896, Persia had an uncertain future and an empty treasury. The luxurious journey to Europe of his successor, Muzaffar ed-Din, did not ease the situation, and in 1900 Persia was compelled to seek a loan of twenty-two million rubles from Russia, followed by another two years later. These loans deepened Persia's dependence upon the tsar, who enjoyed his monopolistic role as creditor and who took care to ask for Persian customs revenues as a guarantee.

During this period of Russian ascendancy the first oil concession was granted to William Knox D'Arcy, an Australian financier, in 1901. This concession covered all of Persia, except the five northern provinces adjacent to Russia. Following intensive exploration in the southwest, oil was discovered in 1908, and the Anglo-Persian Oil Company, heir to D'Arcy's concession, was created. The company became a major supplier of the British navy. In 1914, shortly before the outbreak of the First World War, the British Admiralty purchased the controlling stock in this company.

Persia between 1905 and 1914

During the first decade of the twentieth century, Persia was in political ferment, partly due to the crying need for reform and partly due to the echoes of the Russian revolution of 1905. Whereas Russia supported the reactionary rulers in Teheran, Great Britain identified herself with the Democratic Party, which struggled for some semblance of political liberalism. In 1906 the crisis came to a head. Five thousand Persian merchants, representing the democratic bourgeois trend, closed their shops in the bazaar and massed together in the spacious gardens of the British legation in Teheran. Determined to resist the Shah by pressure, they encamped for several days in the legation's compound. The Democrats eventually forced the Shah to grant a constitution, which provided for a Westernized parliamentary form of government under a limited royal authority.

The success of the Democrats was intensely resented by the Russians, who felt that it was engineered by the British and considered it a threat to their own ascendancy in Persia.[3] Taking advantage of her rapprochement with Britain, which occurred in 1907, Russia encouraged Shah Mohammed Ali to repudiate the constitution in the coup d'état of 1908. The Shah's success was short-lived. In 1909 the opposition, led by the chieftains of the southern Bakhtiyari tribe, marched on Teheran and deposed the ruler. Mohammed Ali first sought refuge in the Russian legation and then, seeing that his position was untenable, fled the country. Under his minor son, Sultan Ahmed Mirza Shah, the constitutional government was restored and the Democratic Party slowly returned to power.

Ironically enough, after all this turmoil the Persian Democrats became anti-British. This change of heart on the part of the new Persian government resulted from the Anglo-Russian agreement of 1907. Russia and Britain, fearful of the rising might of Germany, finally decided to compose their differences in Asia and, for that purpose, reached a comprehensive settlement concerning Iran, Afghanistan, and Tibet. Russia promised to respect the status quo in Afghanistan (which implied the recognition of British ascendancy there), and both countries agreed to consider Tibet a no man's land, with whose affairs neither party would interfere. Persia was divided by this treaty into three zones. A Russian zone of influence was to extend over the five provinces in the north and was to embrace the central area including such cities as Qum, Kashan, Isfahan, and Yazd. Teheran was deep in the Russian zone. The British zone was to be limited to the southeastern area of Persia (Seistan and Baluchistan). The southwestern part of Persia was to constitute a neutral zone.[4]

Although the signatories declared solemnly that they were determined to respect the political independence of Persia, the publication of the agreement caused understandable anger among the Persians. The Democrats, initially pro-British but now profoundly disillusioned, turned to the Germans, who were eager to exploit this change of heart to their best advantage. Gradually Germany succeeded not only in penetrating Persia commercially but also in securing great political influence over the Democratic politicians within and without the Persian government. This new

---

[3]Readers may well ponder the similarity between Persian constitutional reform in 1906 and the adoption of a liberal constitution by the kingdom of Poland in 1791, just prior to the second partition. Both documents were designed to rescue their respective countries from anarchy and to strengthen them through much-needed governmental reform. In both cases Russia forcibly intervened to prevent such reforms from materializing.

[4]The British oil concession was situated in the neutral zone.

friendship did not, however, relieve Persia from the constant pressure of the Russians, who, following the 1907 agreement, became bolder in their actions in the northern section. Thus, when the Persian government made another attempt, in 1911, to restore order and stability within Persia's political fabric by engaging an American financial expert, Dr. Morgan Shuster, Russia promptly sabotaged the appointment. Frustrated, Dr. Shuster was compelled to leave Persia, his task unfulfilled. His book, *The Strangling of Persia,* presents an eloquent account of this situation.

While Persia was thus frantically—and unsuccessfully—trying to shake off foreign interference and to reform her internal affairs, the chasm between Germany and the Entente powers was deepening. Under these circumstances, minor agreements negotiated between 1910 and 1914 among the rival powers proved to be of little significance. The first attempt to reconcile Russian and German interests in Persia was made at Potsdam in November 1910, during the conference between Tsar Nicholas II and Emperor William II, but no formal agreement emerged at that time. Less than a year later, however, on August 19, 1911, Russia and Germany signed a treaty at St. Petersburg by which Germany implicitly recognized the Russian sphere of influence in Persia in return for the right to extend her Baghdad railway system into northern Persia under certain circumstances. The treaty gave Russia nothing of value while conceding important advantages to Germany. It could, therefore, be interpreted as a unilateral Russian appeasement move, and as such it was viewed with uneasiness in Great Britain. But this concern proved to be ill-founded. The basic incompatibility of German and Russian ambitions in Europe drove them inexorably toward war, and their agreements concerning a minor area of competition could not avert the final clash.

In 1914, when the war broke out, Persia's independence was severely curtailed as a result of Russo-British cooperation. Russian troops were stationed in several parts of Persia's northern provinces, and minor British-Indian detachments guarded the oil fields in Khuzistan. The only two efficient military formations—the Persian Cossack Brigade and the Gendarmerie Corps—were officered by the Russians and the Swedes, respectively, and were subject to foreign influences. The powerful nomad tribes in the provinces were armed, and to a marked degree remained independent of the central government. Shah Ahmed, barely sixteen years old, was too young and too weak to conduct the affairs of the state with wisdom and determination. Under these conditions, Persia's officially proclaimed neutrality meant little and could not deter the big powers from using her territory as a battlefield should their interests so dictate.

CHAPTER II

War in the Middle East

At the outbreak of the First World War on August 2, 1914, the Ottoman Empire was ruled by Sultan Mohammed V, over seventy years of age and in frail health. The Sultan, who had been held prisoner in a palace in Constantinople for thirty-two years by his predecessor, Abdul Hamid II, and who had been placed on the throne by the Young Turks, was a nominal ruler only. The real power rested in the hands of the triumvirate of Young Turkish leaders: Enver Pasha, Talaat Pasha, and Jemal Pasha. Even the grand vizier, the Egyptian Prince Said Halim, was no more than a convenient front for these three leaders. Enver, thirty-two years of age, was minister of war and chief of the General Staff, but his influence far exceeded these functions and eventually he emerged as the real master of Turkey at war.

Prior to the outbreak of the war, German influence in the Ottoman Empire had grown out of all proportion to the influence of the other powers. It was especially noticeable in the military field. In 1914 the Ottoman army was trained and instructed by a mission of forty-two German officers under the command of General Liman von Sanders.

On August 2, 1914, Germany and Turkey concluded a treaty of alliance and a military convention, both secret. Despite these agreements, Turkey continued to maintain neutrality for some time. This neutrality was outward only. On August 11, the Porte permitted two German battleships, the *Goeben* and the *Breslau,* to enter the Dardanelles and granted them refuge in Turkish territorial waters. These ships were being pursued by the British navy. The same privilege was refused to a British naval squadron under Admiral Trubridge. Upon Britain's protest the Porte accused the British of failing to supply Turkey with two battleships previously ordered in British shipyards and paid for. (The ships had been requisitioned at the last moment by British authorities.) Furthermore, the Porte officially "purchased" the two German ships and engaged their personnel to serve in the Ottoman navy. The German commanding admiral, Souchon, was given command of the Ottoman naval forces, replacing the British admiral, who was dismissed. The last link with Britain was severed, and the German hold on the Ottoman defense establishment became complete. Thus inexorably by virtue of the treaty wtth Germany and as a result of these violations of neutrality, Turkey was heading for war. The Turkish cabinet, however, was not unanimous on this issue, and some ministers manifested either pro-

52

Western or neutral attitudes. Among them were Jemal Pasha (one of the members of the triumvirate), the minister of finance, Javid, and three others. The grand vizier, Said Halim, played a double role; although sympathetic to the peace party, he hesitated to antagonize the war party headed by Enver. It was Enver's influence that eventually tipped the scales in favor of the entry into war.

Whatever hesitation the Porte had was cut short by the *Goeben* and *Breslau* incident. On orders from Enver, who acted in connivance with the Germans, these two ships, renamed *Sultan Selim* and *Medilli* but manned by their German crews, left Istanbul and on October 29 attacked the Russian fleet in the Black Sea. Russia declared war on the Ottoman Empire on November 4. This was followed by similar declarations by Britain and France one day later.

War Aims and Political Strategy of Germany

The decisive battles of the First World War were fought in Europe, and European problems had priority in the considerations of the belligerents. Although Middle Eastern operations were of secondary importance, they were vital to both sides from the point of view of general strategy. The fortunes of war in the Middle East might have profoundly influenced the outcome of the war in Europe. The decision of the Ottoman government to side with the Central powers created a new front for Russia and affected the security of the British imperial life line—and in this sense constituted a distinct advantage to Germany.

From the German point of view, Turkey had to play an auxiliary role in order to divert some Russian and British energies from the main theater of war in Europe. Furthermore, Turkish advance in the East was to pave the way for the extension of German influence and, if successful, to affect the destiny of India. The German General Staff adopted the so-called Zimmermann Plan for India. The plan foresaw support for Indian nationalists and intense propaganda both among the Moslem and Hindu peoples of the peninsula.

In order to make full use of the Turkish alliance, Germany demanded that Turkey carry out several tasks without delay. These were to close the Straits to other powers; to cut the wartime route via the Suez Canal and Aden; to invade the Caucasus in order to immobilize an appreciable number of Russian troops; and to proclaim a holy war against the Entente countries.

To ensure the fulfillment of these aims Germany was represented in Turkey by a number of able diplomats.[1] She also secured far-reaching control of the Ottoman military machine. German officers assumed the following high functions in the Turkish army: General Liman von Sanders headed a mission to organize and train the army; General von Falkenhayn commanded the Turkish army in Palestine; and Field Marshal von der Goltz commanded the army in Mesopotamia. The German General Staff was represented by General von Lossow, and Admiral Humann, the

---

[1]During World War I: Baron von Wangenheim, Count Metternich, Herr von Kuehlmann, and Count von Bernstorff, successively. In October 1917, Emperor William II himself paid a visit to Constantinople.

naval attaché at the German embassy, acted as liaison officer between Berlin and the Ottoman navy.

Diplomatic and Military Maneuvers in Iran

Germany's diplomatic and military strategy in the Middle East was not limited to Turkey. She attempted to induce Iran and Afghanistan also to enter the war on her side.

In Iran Germany was represented by Prince von Reuss. Von Reuss maintained very cordial relations with the leaders of the Iranian Democratic party. At the outbreak of the war, the latter were intensely anti-Russian and anti-British and leaned heavily toward an alliance with Germany. Their influence in the cabinet and in parliament was strong. Von Reuss's diplomacy bore fruit. In 1915 the prime minister of Iran, Mustaufi el-Mamalek, concluded a secret alliance with the Germans in return for certain political promises. These promises included a guarantee of Iran's independence and integrity, the supply of money, arms, and munitions, and the assurance of political asylum in Germany for the shah in the event that he should be compelled to flee his country. Von Reuss now proceeded to secure the cooperation of two other most important elements of strength in Iran: the Swedish-officered *gendarmerie* and the nomad tribes. The *gendarmerie* was the only independent and relatively efficient Iranian military formation. (The Iranian Cossack Brigade was Russian-officered and could not be regarded as a reliable weapon of the Iranian government.) The Swedish officers of the *gendarmerie* showed definitely pro-German proclivities and eventually decided to side openly with Germany. As to the tribes, which constituted roughly one-fifth of the Iranian population, they were armed and had an organization well suited to guerrilla warfare. In order to enlist the full cooperation of the nomad tribes and of the local governors, the German military attaché in Teheran, Count Kanitz, traveled extensively throughout the country, making lavish promises of German assitance. To aid him the German General Staff dispatched to Iran a number of military missions. The Klein mission operated in Kermanshah and the surrounding Kurd and Lur territory. The Zugmeyer mission extended its activities to Isfahan and Kerman. The Biach mission reached Yazd and Baluchistan, and former Consul Wassmus directed an uprising of the Qashqai, Bakhtiyari, and Tangistani tribes in southwestern Iran. These missions and their gendarme and tribal allies broke into many branches of the British-directed Imperial Bank of Iran, appropriated their funds, and captured a number of British citizens, including some consuls in the Iranian provincial towns.

The aim of all this German activity was to stir up anti-British and anti-Russian feelings among the people, and in this way to harmonize them with the pro-German attitude of the Teheran authorities. The Iranian government, though still persisting in outward neutrality, would thus be compelled, under the pressure of the aroused populace, to declare itself openly on the side of Germany. Such a declaration was to be accompanied—according to German plans—by a wholesale uprising of the people against the Russians and British. The resulting sabotage of the Anglo-Iranian Oil Company in Khuzistan would necessarily hinder the British war effort, inasmuch as the British navy drew heavily upon fuel supplies from that source.

By November 1915 the mood of the country was so pronouncedly anti-Entente that only a signal was needed to start the avalanche moving. The Russian and British ministers in Teheran were well informed of the state of affairs in Iran and to forestall a coup decided to act quickly. Strong warnings were issued to the Iranian government of the dire consequences of a precipitate pro-German action. Simultaneously, Russian troops, stationed in Kazvin (only thirty miles north of Teheran) moved toward the capital, threatening its occupation. Faced with such a contingency, the Iranian cabinet decided to transfer the seat of government to Isfahan in the center of the country, defying Allied pressure. Evacuation of the government offices began hastily. The German, Austrian, and Ottoman legations moved southward in a hurry, and established themselves temporarily at Qum. This evacuation, despite the necessity of abandoning the capital, actually was well suited to German plans because it meant the burning of bridges between Iran and the Entente powers. Yet the operation was not entirely successful, since at the last moment the young and weak-willed Shah Ahmed succumbed to strong Russo-British representations to remain in the capital. Faced with this turn of events, the cabinet decided to remain as well. As a result, only the outspokenly pro-German leaders of the Democratic party left Teheran.

It was not exactly what the Germans wanted. Prince von Reuss did his best and promptly proceeded to create a rival Iranian government in Qum. It was, however, dangerous to remain there, because of the proximity of Russian troops. The latter did not occupy Teheran, but they were near enough to cause uneasiness. Eventually the separatist government moved to Kermanshah, where it was close to the Turkish border and where it could count on the protection of Ottoman forces in Mesopotamia. In Kermanshah the rival government was reorganized under the presidency of Nizam es-Saltaneh, the governor of Luristan. In December 1915, Nizam concluded a treaty of alliance with Germany promising to levy 40,000 troops in the area under his control. In return he was promised weapons and munitions, German instructors, a monthly subsidy, and a guarantee of his treasury. A German legation was formally accredited to Nizam's government, and a German military mission was dispatched to train his forces.[2] Thenceforth, the political destinies of Nizam's government were linked with the fortunes of the Ottoman army in Mesopotamia. The Mesopotamian theater of war is treated in a separate section (pp. 68–69), but it may be stated here that Nizam's contribution to the Turkish-German war effort was altogether negligible.

Of all the German enterprises in Iran during the war the one conducted by Wassmuss was the most successful since he actually succeeded in provoking a rebellion of the southern tribes and in seriously threatening the British position there.[3] To Britain, German intrigue in Iran was very embarrassing. Some of the British troops in Mesopotamia had to be diverted to southern Iran to protect the oil fields, and such an extension of military commitments was most inconvenient.

[2]A detailed description of German relations with Nizam's government is contained in Wipert von Blücher, *Zeitenwende in Iran* (Biberach an der Riss, 1949), pp. 27–127.

[3]A fascinating account of his intrigues may be found in Christopher Sykes, *Wassmuss: "The German Lawrence"* (London, 1936).

Southern Iran was a traditional British preserve, and it was there that the British authorities decided to make a bold move to stop the Germans and to restore peace and order.

Following an agreement with the Iranian government, a British military mission under Brigadier General Sir Percy Sykes was sent to the Persian Gulf port of Bandar Abbas in March 1916. The object of this mission was to organize an Iranian force and with it to restore normal conditions in the country. The force, named the South Persia Rifles, was promptly recruited, and it was reinforced by some troops from India. Before long Sykes was in a position to begin a number of forced marches into the interior. Within six months he secured control of Kerman, Yazd, Isfahan (where he joined with the Russian Cossacks sent from the north), Shiraz, and a large portion of Fars. He had to wage fierce battles with the German-influenced tribes, segments of the *gendarmerie,* and other pro-German elements. The cabinet in Teheran was of no help and vacillated between recognition of the South Persia Rifles and intrigue against it. By 1917, despite all the difficulties, Sykes managed to restore order and safety for the British in southern Iran. In 1917–1918 most of the German agents operating in this area fell into his hands. Even Wassmuss, despite all his ingenuity, was eventually captured.[4]

The account of wartime Iran would be incomplete if we did not mention two further violations of neutrality by the belligerents. The northwestern province of Azerbaijan was invaded by Turkish and Russian troops early in the war. The province had to undergo all the vicissitudes of the war on the eastern Anatolian front and was also profoundly affected by Turkish operations in Transcaucasia toward the end of the war.

Eastern Iran also was not immune to the penetration of foreign troops. There Russian and British forces established what was known as the East Persian Cordon along the Afghan border. The reason for this operation lay in fear that some German or Turkish military detachments might traverse Iran and penetrate Afghanistan. This fear was not unfounded.

The German Expedition to Afghanistan

At the beginning of the war Enver Pasha persuaded the German General Staff that it would be of great advantage to the Central powers if Afghanistan entered the war on their side. According to the information available in Berlin, Afghanistan had a disciplined army of 20,000 regular troops, equipped with 350 field guns. The proximity of Afghanistan to India's most vulnerable spot—the Moslem provinces of the northwest—was a factor that Germany was eager to utilize to her own advantage. Accordingly it was decided to organize a German-Turkish mission that would proceed to Afghanistan and there induce the emir to take arms against the British Empire.

The mission in its ultimate composition was headed by Lieutenant Oskar Niedermayer and Herr von Hentig, legation secretary in the German Foreign Office. Von

[4]For the activities of the German missions, see Sir Percy M. Sykes, *A History of Persia* (London, 1930), II, 442ff.

Hentig was the bearer of a personal letter from the Kaiser to Emir Habibullah. The Turkish part of the mission included Obaydullah Effendi, a deputy to the parliament, Kazim Bey, and a number of associates. The mission was accompanied by Kumar Mahendra Pratap and Barkatullah, Indian nationalist leaders resident in Berlin. Originally it was planned to send to Afghanistan a detachment of regular Turkish troops. Rauf Bey, former commander of the special Hamidiyeh Corps, was dispatched to Baghdad to make preparations. As a result of his quarrel with the German members of the mission, this project was abandoned.

The Niedermayer-Hentig mission had to traverse the territory of Iran which was partly under Russian occupation, and to pass through several towns where local British representatives wielded considerable influence. Furthermore, it had to pierce the East Persian Cordon in order to reach the Afghan boundary. The mission's progress was slow and cautious, but it succeeded, with a somewhat reduced personnel, in evading Russian or British capture and in August 1915 reached Afghanistan. Upon their arrival in Kabul, the members of the mission were lodged as guests of Emir Habibullah. They had to wait nearly two months for an audience with the ruler. When it was accorded to them, the Germans put forward their offer of an alliance. The Emir responded with cautious reserve and delayed his answer. Afghanistan was officially neutral, but a pro-Turkish party under two influential leaders, Nasrullah Khan and Inayatullah Khan, agitated in favor of joining the Central powers. The mullahs, sensitive to the caliph's call for a holy war, also pressed the Emir to join the Turkish-German camp. The Emir's procrastination was dictated by his fear of Britain and by his desire to determine which side was likely to win the war. There is no doubt, however, that he personally favored the Central powers. In January 1916 he went so far as to sign a draft treaty of alliance with Germany. But before committing himself to an open and definite break with Britain he insisted on the fulfillment of two conditions by Germany: the dispatch of a strong force to Afghanistan and a sizable subsidy in gold. To Niedermayer and Hentig it became clear that, unless these conditions were met, there was no hope to expect more from the Emir. Consequently the mission took its leave. Niedermayer, surmounting fantastic difficulties, managed to cross Iran and reach the safety of Mesopotamia. Von Hentig went through eastern Afghanistan, reached Sin-Kiang, and through China and America returned to Germany.[5]

War Aims and Political Strategy of Turkey

The war aims of the Ottoman government could be stated as follows: (1) Turkification of the Ottoman Empire and its liberation from Western tutelage; (2) reconquest of the irredentist areas of Egypt and Cyprus (and possibly of Libya, Tunisia, and Algeria); (3) liberation and federation of the Turkish-inhabited areas of Russia (the Caucasus and Turkestan); (4) reestablishment of the caliph's authority

[5] Details about the German expedition may be found in Oskar von Niedermayer, *Unter der Glutsonne Iran's* (Dachau, 1925); Blücher, *op. cit.*, pp. 83–94; Sir Percy M. Sykes, *A History of Afghanistan* (London, 1940), pp. 246 ff.

over all Islam. This was the program of the war party headed by Enver and Talaat and one which, on their insistence, was adopted by the cabinet as a whole.[6] Enver and his friends believed that these objectives could be attained in cooperation with Germany.

To fulfill this program, Turkey needed to combine military and political strategy. Furthermore, such a strategy was bound to affect not only Turkey's foreign relations, but also the domestic situation. The Ottoman Empire at the outbreak of the war was composed of a number of nationalities. Of the total population of twenty-five million, the Turks constituted less than half, about ten million. The Arab subjects of the empire were estimated at ten million also. In addition, there were about a million and a half Kurds, about two million Armenians, and about a million and a half people of miscellaneous races. Thus the empire was far from being homogeneous, and the success of its policies depended to a great degree upon the loyalty of its subject peoples. Moreover, Turkey suffered from important limitations of sovereignty due to the existing system of capitulations and special rights accorded to foreign powers. For example, the Ottoman government was not allowed to raise the customs tariff above a level determined by international agreements; certain sources of public revenue were practically sequestered by foreign powers to assure the payment of the public debt; the Porte was forced to observe certain imposed rules with regard to the treatment of national and religious minorities; and Turkey's sovereignty over the Straits was limited.

Drifting into the war in the fall of 1914, Turkey was in a position to satisfy immediately at least the first point of her war program, that is, her liberation from foreign tutelage. On September 5, 1914, the Ottoman government formally repudiated the capitulations. The definite entry into the war in November put an end to foreign interference, at least for the duration of the hostilities.

The Problem of Loyalty: Arabs and Kurds

The loyalty problem proved to be much more complex. The Arabs were brethren in faith but had many grievances against the Ottoman administration. The Young Turks, following their revolution, had made a gesture of good will toward the Arabs. An association known as the Ottoman-Arab Fraternity (El-Ikha el-Arabi el-Uthmani) was created, and the propaganda of Ottomanism was launched with a view to assuring common loyalty to the empire on the basis of equality. But this proved to be a brief interlude only and was followed by utter disillusionment. Educated Arabs resented the Young Turks' policy of centralization and objected to the unequal representation in the Ottoman Chamber of Deputies, which had been created as a result of the 1908 revolution. Of the total of 245 representatives, 150 were Turks and only 60 were Arabs, despite the numerical parity or possible Arab majority in the empire. The Arabs did not hide their resentment, whereupon the Turkish authorities suppressed the Ottoman-Arab Fraternity. This rupture was a signal for the Arabs to organize various nationalist associations. The Literary Club

[6]For a detailed analysis of Turkish policies during World War I, see Ahmed Emin, *Turkey in the World War* (New Haven, Conn., 1930).

(El-Muntada el-Adabi), formed in 1909 in Constantinople, and the Ottoman Decentralization Party, established in 1912 in Cairo, carried on open propaganda for Arab home rule. Simultaneously the more radical Arab elements formed two secret societies. The first, El-Qahtaniya, created in 1909, was headed by Major Aziz Ali el-Masri and consisted principally of Arab officers in the Ottoman army. It operated in Constantinople and in five other centers throughout the Empire and advocated a dual Arab-Turkish monarchy. The second, El-Fatat, formed initially in Paris in 1911 among young educated Arabs, subsequently moved to Beirut and then to Damascus. It was El-Fatat which, in 1916, took Emir Faisal of Hejaz into membership and converted him to the cause of Arab liberation. The years 1912–1913 witnessed the creation of a powerful Committee of Reform in Beirut. The committee demanded Arab autonomy in the Ottoman Empire. Mention should also be made of an Arab congress in Paris in 1913, attended by twenty-four Arab nationalists, which formulated far-reaching demands for the emancipation of the Arabs.[7]

Thus when the war broke out, the politically conscious Arabs could hardly be regarded as a dependable element in the empire. Yet despite these differences, a number of purely Arab formations were in the Ottoman army. Many officers, of higher and lower ranks, were also Arabs. Under these circumstances, the Ottoman government did not fear any mass defection on their part. The revolt of the Arabs in the Hejaz in 1916 was, therefore, a severe shock to the Turkish leadership. (See pp. 67–68.) With regard to the general problem of loyalty in the Ottoman Empire, it may be pointed out that the Hejaz revolt did not produce complete unanimity in the Arab world. Certain sections remained faithful to Turkey, such as Yemen, the Arabs of Libya, and the Rashids of central Arabia.

The Arabs of Syria and Mesopotamia, while favoring the revolt, were cowed into submission by the Turkish authorities. This was especially true of Syria, where at the beginning of the war Jemal Pasha (one of the triumvirate) assumed the duties of military governor. By dealing ruthlessly with the conspiring Arab nationalists in Beirut and in Damascus, he discouraged active anti-Turkish manifestations.

The Kurds were another Moslem minority in the empire. A race of virile mountaineers, still in a seminomadic state of social organization, the Kurds were a perennial problem for the Ottoman and Iranian empires in whose borderlands they lived. They aspired toward greater freedom, and their history was marked by frequent uprisings against their overlords. If, owing to their primitve culture, they had no sense of nationality, they certainly could not be expected to have any loyalty to the vague idea of Ottomanism. Despite this the Kurds were altogether loyal to Turkey during the war. The secret of this "correct" behavior lay in the fact that the Turks skillfully channeled the Kurdish anarchistic tendencies into war against the Christians, and in particular against their close neighbors, the Armenians and the Assyrians. In this way the Kurdish minority appeased both its Islamic conscience and its predatory instincts. For the Ottoman Empire, therefore, the Kurds not only presented no problem during the war but proved relatively useful in the accom-

---

[7]The most exhaustive treatment of the Arab national movement is contained in George Antonius, *The Arab Awakening* (London, 1938).

plishment of certain disagreeable tasks in the easter provinces. Only after the end of the war were their autonomist tendencies revealed in a violent form.

The Problem of Loyalty: Armenians and Assyrians

Among the Christian minorities of the empire, three were especially affected by the war, the Armenians, the Assyrians, and the Greeks. The Greeks were not a problem between 1914 and 1918. For a long time Greece herself was on the verge of joining the Central powers, and the Greek subjects of the Empire took care not to offend the patriotic susceptibilities of the Turks. Their drama belongs properly to the aftermath of the war, when the empire lay prostrate, and it will be treated later within the general framework of the peace settlement.

The story of the Armenians was quite different. Victims of repeated massacres in the last three decades, the Armenians greeted the entry of Turkey into the war with mixed feelings of fear and hope—fear of possible Turkish reprisals, unchecked by any external pressure, and hope for the defeat of the empire and the victory of the Entente, in particular of Russia. The Russians had traditionally assumed the role of protector of the Armenians, said role being another weapon to speed up the disintegration of Turkey. The controversy over the disloyal behavior of the Armenians will probably never be resolved. The Turks maintained that the Armenians showed extreme disloyalty from the very beginning of the conflict. The Armenians claimed that their behavior was quite correct. The truth of the matter is that the wealthier and leading elements of the Armenian community, fearful of dire consequences if there were any show of disloyalty, insisted on full compliance with Turkish war regulations and discouraged any anti-Turkish manifestations. But the rank and file did not follow their leaders. Appeal to emotion was stronger than appeal to reason, and emotionally the Armenian masses were ready to greet the advancing Russian armies as liberators.

They were encouraged in this attitude by official pronouncements of the Armenian Orthodox Church, which traditionally held great sway over its communicants. In August 1914 the catholicos or head of the Armenian Church residing in Echmiadzin, Russian Armenia, proclaimed that the Russian tsar was the protector of all Armenians. This proclamation appeared in the catholicos' official organ, *Ararat*, and made it a sacred duty of all Armenians to give personal and material support to the Russian armies. This appeal was followed in November by an official Russian proclamation, exhorting the Armenians to rise against their Turkish "tyrants" and promising liberation.[8] Many Armenians responded to these appeals by deserting the Turkish army, volunterring in the Russian army, and assisting the Russian advance. There is no doubt that as a whole the Armenian minority in the villages of Turkey was hostile to the Turks and that their loyalty was highly doubtful.

The government's reaction was ruthless. In June 1915 it decided to remove the Armenian population from the eastern war zone and to deport it to the interior of Anatolia or to the northern desert areas of Syria. This mass deportation was carried

---

[8]Emin, *op. cit.*, p. 215. For the attitude of the Armenians, consult also Maurice Larcher, *La Guerre Turque dans la Guerre Mondiale* (Paris, 1926).

out in 1915 and 1916 and has become known as the Armenian massacres. This term is not inappropriate. The deportations were characterized by unspeakable cruelties and wanton destruction of life and property. They resulted in an almost total uprooting of the Armenians of the eastern vilayets, who had lived there from time immemorial, and affected not only those suspected of disloyalty, but also women, children, and other innocent persons. The cruelty of this removal was matched only by the brutality of the cattlelike transportation facilities and the horrors of internment camps and forced settlements. Two million people are estimated to have been affected, of whom 600,000 lost their lives.[9]

Attempts to soften the Turkish attitude made by Pope Pius X, by the American ambassador in Constantinople, Henry Morgenthau, and even by German authorities were of no avail. Talaat Pasha, minister of the interior, who was chiefly responsible for the deportations, was determined to pursue his course unflinchingly, and he was fully supported by the cabinet. This policy "solved" the Armenian question in Turkey proper. It generated among all remaining Armenians an undying hatred for Turkey that even the transformation of the Turkish state in the early 1920s was unable to assuage. It accounts for many reprisals against the Turks (Russian or Ottoman) on occasions when the Armenians were in a position to get vengeance. Such occasions occurred with the arrival of Russian armies into eastern Turkish territory during the war and in 1918 in Baku. It also accounts for the willingness of the Armenians living in the Middle East to respond, often favorably, to Moscow's appeal to return to Soviet Armenia at the close of World War II.[10]

Equally affected by wartime developments in the Middle East was the Assyrian minority. This group, united around its ancient Chaldean-Nestorian Church, was centered in two areas—the Lake Van region in Turkey and the Lake Urumia region in Iran. It was never so badly treated by the Turks as were the Armenians, but it was exposed to hostility and suspicion on the part of the Ottoman authorities. Encouraged by the Russian advance into eastern Anatolia in 1915, the Turkish Assyrians

[9]Simon Vratzian, *Armenia and the Armenian Question* (Boston, 1943), p. 27.

[10]The Armenian massacres undoubtedly constitute one of the blackest pages of Turkish history. Even granting the disloyalty of the Armenian people as a whole, which made it difficult to distinguish in practice between the actively disloyal and the outwardly correct in closely knit Armenian villages, no excuse can be found for the brutality with which the deportations were made. Nor can the matter be lightly dismissed, as Prof. Ernest Jackh does in *The Rising Crescent* (New York, 1944, p. 42), by stating that massacres are a time-honored device to settle political accounts in the East. It is in order, however, to keep the whole matter in proper perspective by pointing out that the Turks were not the only ones to commit mass atrocities during the First World War. First of all, the Armenians, when taking revenge, did not distinguish between guilty and innocent Moslems. Second, while the attention of the world was focused upon the tragic events in Turkey, Russia was similarly exterminating her Moslem subjects in Turkestan. Here is what Professor Toynbee says about it in *The Western Question in Greece and Turkey* (London, 1922):

"During the European war while people in England were raking up the Ottoman Turks' nomadic ancestry in order to account for their murder of 600,000 Armenians, 500,000 Turkish-speaking Central Asian nomads of the Kirghiz-Kazak Confederacy were being exterminated—also under superior orders—by that 'justest of mankind,' the Russian muzhik; men, women, children were shot down, or were put to death in a more horrible way by being robbed of their animals and equipment and then being driven forth in wintertime to perish in mountain and desert. A lucky few escaped across the Chinese frontier. These atrocities were courageously exposed and denounced by Mr. Kerensky in the Duma before the first Revolution, but who listened or cared?" (p. 342).

rose against the Turks and co-operated with the Russians. The Russian withdrawal in 1917–1918 left the Assyrians in a very exposed position; in order to avoid Turkish reprisals, about 20,000 of them fought their way to the British lines in northern Mesopotamia. The fate of those in Iran was even more dramatic. In 1918 when the Turks advanced into Iranian Azerbaijan, the Assyrians of Urumia were faced with a grave threat to their existence. Exposed to direct Turkish attacks, Kurdish depredations, and the general hostility of Iranians, the Assyrians kept their enemies at bay for a few months while feverishly seeking British protection. In the summer of 1918 the whole Assyrian population of the Urumian region was suddenly seized with panic and, led by Aga Petros, fled to the Kermanshah-Kazvin region, which was then under temporary British occupation. Only about half of the original population of 100,000 survived the hardships of the exodus. The British authorities gave them protection and subsequently moved them to Mesopotamia. There most of the Assyrians remained in refugee camps, though some were given auxiliary employment in the British army. Neither the Turkish nor the Iranian Assyrian people were allowed to return to their homes, even after the end of the war.[11]

Pan-Islamism and Pan-Turanism in Wartime

Ottoman political strategy in wartime could be summed up in two terms: Pan-Islamism and Pan-Turanism. It will be remembered that upon Turkey's entry into the war, the sultan in his capacity as caliph issued a call to a holy war or jihad addressed to all Mohammedans the world over. This proclamation, made on November 23, 1914, was signed by the highest religious dignitaries of the empire, including the Sheikh el-Islam in Constantinople. The proclamation of a jihad was the culminating point of the policy of Pan-Islamism inaugurated earlier by Sultan Abdul Hamid II. The fact that Germany as a Christian power was on the side of Turkey did not deter the sultan from issuing the call. The German emperor, pursuing his traditional policy of courting Islam, had already (September 9, 1914) issued a proclamation that Moslems fighting in the Entente armies were not to be considered as belligerents, and when taken prisoner by the Germans, would be sent to Turkey, where they would be at the disposal of the caliph.

In Constantinople it was hoped that the proclamation of a jihad would evoke vigorous response both at home and abroad. At home, i.e., within the empire, the jihad was to produce Arab loyalty. Abroad, the Turks expected an uprising of the Moslems in the colonial possessions of the Entente. These expectations proved largely futile. The Arabs did not gather in defense of "the faith and the throne," and a large segment among them, led by Sherif Hussein of Mecca, decided to pursue an independent course and chose the side of Turkey's enemies.[12] The significance of this step was tremendous and greatly outweighed the loyalty to Turkey shown by Imam Yehya of Yemen and by some nomad tribes of central Arabia.

Outside the empire also, the call to a jihad failed to produce the expected results. In the African possessions of the Entente, the Senussis in Libya and the Mahdists in

---

[11] As to the further fate of the Assyrians, see Chapter VII.
[12] For an account of the military operations of the Arab Revolt, see p. 67.

the Sudan responded. In August 1915 the Senussis rose against Italian rule. Aided by German subsidies and Turkish military instructors, they forced the Italians to vacate most of the Libyan hinterland and to limit their control to the coastal belt only. The Senussis also invaded the western extremities of Egypt and delivered a few attacks on some French posts on the Tunisian border. As to the Mahdists, there was considerable unrest among them, aggravated by the anti-British attitude of Ali Dinar, sultan of the Darfur province in western Sudan. In both cases the anti-Entente conduct of the Moslems was an isolated phenomenon and occasioned only minor military operations which could not influence the general course of the war in the Middle East.

In the Asiatic possessions of the Entente, the largest single group of people impressed by the proclamation was the Moslems of India, inhabiting the area now known as Pakistan, and numbering about seventy million souls. Yet, despite their reverence for the caliph, they did not undertake any overt military action against Great Britain. Some extremists did enter into a conspiracy and attempted to establish liaison with the Central powers, but these activities were not limited to the Moslems. A number of Hindu nationalists were included. Despite the failure of their efforts, the British bureaucracy in India was deeply concerned about the jihad and did its utmost to avoid any unnecessary provocation of the Moslem elements of the population.

This explains the political attitude of the British expeditionary force in Mesopotamia, of whose military exploits we shall speak later. The Indian-trained and Indian-oriented military and political leadership of the force was unwilling to seek Arab guerrilla support in this campaign because such support, it feared, might provoke dangerous complications in India. Indian Moslems greatly resented Britain's cooperation with Sherif Hussein of Mecca, whom they considered a traitor to the cause of Mohammedan solidarity. But at least the government of India was not responsible for these dealings with Hussein. (He was in contact with the Foreign Office through the Arab Bureau in Cairo.) If, however, the government of India were to employ Arab "traitors" in their war against the caliph in Mesopotamia, profound and violent repercussions in India might follow. This the government of India skillfully avoided, with the result that Moslem agitation never got out of hand.

The effects of the jihad, from the Turkish point of view, were deeply disappointing. In fact, Sherif Hussein's defection meant the failure of the Pan-Islamic strategy as such. In a crisis nationalism was a stronger force than was religion.

The use of Pan-Islamism as a weapon was not unanimously approved by the Turks themselves. Democratically minded leaders in the high echelons of the Union and Progress Party, such as Professor Zia Gök Alp, resented the reactionary and retarding influence of the Moslem religion upon the Ottoman Empire and wished to see a sweeping secularization of the country. They viewed with distaste any perpetuation of the hold of ecclesiastics upon Turkey as expressed by appeals to religious fanaticism. Zia Gök Alp and his friends were Turkish nationalists above everything. This meant that they rejected the vague (and in their eyes inadequate) concept of Ottomanism, which had been initially preached by the Young Turks, as well as the concept of Pan-Islamism. Ottomanism, argued Zia Gök Alp, did not prevent the Russians from disrupting the loyalty of the Balkan subjects of the Ottoman Empire by appeals to Pan-Slavism. This, according to Turkish nationalists, was one more proof that the only valid link on which a state could rely was the feeling of common blood, of belonging to a common nationality. Turkey's salvation thus lay in assuring the national consciousness of her Turkish subjects and in promoting the union of all peoples of Turkish race wherever they lived. This was the ideology of Pan-Turanism, an ideology born among the Turkic groups in Russia and now wholeheartedly adopted by Zia Gök Alp and his followers.

As to the policy of the government itself, it was eclectic. On the one hand, it did not wish to relinquish its Pan-Islamic course, still fondly hoping that it might prove useful in the prosecution of the war. On the other hand, it leaned more and more as time went on (especially after 1917) toward Pan-Turanism. That the two policies were mutually incompatible was conveniently ignored by Enver and his associates. The incompatibility was clear; it was illogical, for example, to appeal to the Iranians as Moslem coreligionists to fight on the side of Turkey (Pan-Islamism) and at the same time to threaten the disintegration of their state by appeals to Pan-Turkish unity (which would mean separation of Turkish-speaking Azerbaijan and its absorption by the Turkish Empire.) It was illogical to expect loyalty on a religious basis on the part of the Arabs and at the same time to preach a nationalist doctrine which in its logical conclusion must have provided for the independence of the Arabs as a nation.[13]

Apart from the confusion within Turkish ruling circles, there were also differences between Turkey and Germany on this account. These differences related to the content of the Central powers' propaganda in the Middle East and to the methods of carrying out their policy. With regard to the content, the German government initially approved the Pan-Islamic propaganda and even actively contributed to it. Emperor William II was represented by German agents as a friend of Islam, and rumors were circulated about his conversion to Islam. German missions in Iran and Afghanistan and the propaganda literature prepared for use in India employed Pan-Islamic slogans. The failure of Pan-Islamic propaganda caused the German Foreign Office to believe that more stress should be laid on the nationalist struggle against British or French domination as such. On this basis, it was hoped, more response could be evoked among Iranians, Egyptians, or Indians. The Germans viewed with concern the Pan-Turanian propaganda emanating from Turkey. While such a policy might prove useful with regard to the Turkish groups inside Russia, at the same time it was bound to produce complications in sectors that were of immediate concern to Germany, namely, Iran and the Arab countries. In these sectors actual military operations were conducted; and their success depended upon the attitude of the populations toward the armies in the field.

The other point of difference was the method itself. The Turkish government insisted that problems of policy and propaganda in the Mohammedan East must be left largely to the discretion of Turkey and that the Turks must assume responsibility

---

[13]On Pan-Turanism, see Emin, *op. cit.*, ch. xvi; T. Lothrop Stoddard, "Pan-Turanism" *American Political Science Review* (Feb. 1917), pp. 12–23; also Larcher, *op. cit.*, pp. 142 ff.

for them. For this reason German missions to Iran suffered all sorts of administrative chicanery in traveling through the Ottoman Empire and their entry into Iran on certain occasions was fatally delayed. The same reason accounted also for the inclusion of a Turkish staff under Obaydullah Effendi in the mission to Afghanistan headed by Niedermayer and Von Hentig. The German Foreign Office and the General Staff viewed these Turkish claims with apprehension, because the use of Turkish agents was not considered the best way to arouse confidence and friendship among the Arabs or the Iranians. Thus the failure to evoke popular enthusiasm for the Iranian separatist government of Nizam es-Saltaneh in Kermanshah was to a large extent due to the presence of Turkish battalions on Iranian soil. Iranians, because of their anti-Russian and anti-British attitudes, might become very friendly toward Germany, but hardly toward the traditional rival, Turkey.[14]

The growing inclination of the Turkish government toward Pan-Turanism, which became obvious after the Russian revolution in 1917, accentuated these differences between the allies. The Russian revolution opened before the Turks the prospect of fulfilling at least one of their major war aims, namely, the liberation and federation of the Turkish groups of Russia. Therefore, whatever strength Turkey could muster in the fourth year of the war was focused on the Caucasus. This attitude produced two consequences, both irritating to the German high command. First, it meant neglect of other theaters of war in the Middle East where Germany desired to hold up British advances. Second, active Turkish penetration in the Caucasus might deprive Germany of a rich prize in Caucasian food-stuffs and in raw materials such as manganese and oil. Hence, uncoordinated and precipitate Turkish action in this sector was greatly resented in Germany. In fact, it looked to Berlin in 1918 as if the Turks had abandoned the common war to fight their own private war for the sole benefit of Turkey.

The Military Operations in the Middle East

In the first phase of the war Turkey took the initiative by invading the Caucasus. To attain their military ends the Turks did not hesitate to violate Iranian neutrality, and their troops entered Iranian Azerbaijan. Their first offensive brought them to the gates of Batum in Russia and of Tabriz in Iran. Simultaneously, the Turks began to recruit Moslem elements in the areas occupied by them, particularly the Ajars (Moslem Georgians) and the Azeris (Turkish-speaking inhabitants of Azerbaijan). Neither Batum nor Tabriz was, however, captured. In midwinter of 1914-1915, the Russians regained the initiative and succeeded in pushing the Turks back to the Russo-Turkish frontier. Throughout the war this front was mobile in a limited sense. The Russians actually gained the upper hand by penetrating into Turkish territory as far as Trebizond, Erzerum, Erzinjan, Mush, and Van. This military line continued roughly through Lake Urumia to Kermanshah and Hamadan in Iran. Enver's dreams about a quick success in the Caucasus and the liberation of its Mohammedan populations were not realized. From the German point of view, however, this operation

[14]A vivid description of these complications may be found in Blücher, *op. cit.*, pp. 72-73, 92-94.

fulfilled its purpose of containing a number of valuable Russian divisions. Events on this front took a very dramatic turn at the end of the war as a result of the Russian revolution. They will be reviewed in the section dealing with Transcaucasia.

The Dardanelles Expedition

In March 1915 the British navy tried to force the Dardanelles, but the attempt failed. It was followed by the landing on Gallipoli, on April 25, of an Allied expeditionary force composed of British, Australian, New Zealand, and French troops. This force commanded by Sir Ian Hamilton was ordered to strike a blow at the heart of the empire, Constantinople. The idea was Winston Churchill's, who was then first lord of the Admiralty in the British cabinet. This expedition, if successful, might have resulted in the elimination of Turkey from the war. But the attempt failed. The Turks, commanded by General Liman von Sanders, offered stubborn resistance and inflicted upon the Allies heavy casualties, estimated at 25,000 men. In January 1916 the Allies were forced to evacuate Gallipoli.

The Sinai Front

In February 1915 the Turkish high command made an attempt to cross the Suez Canal. The offensive, launched under the command of Jemal Pasha, failed because of superior British forces. The British, who had occupied Egypt since 1882, had organized a powerful army in the delta of the Nile. From this army later came the bulk of the troops for the Gallipoli expedition. Now its task was to defend Egypt and the Suez Canal and to put pressure on the Turkish concentrations in Palestine and Syria.

Throughout 1915 the front shifted back and forth in the coastal region of the Sinai peninsula. By 1916 a powerful British army known as the Egyptian expeditionary force, first under General Sir Archibald Murray and later under General Sir Edmund Allenby, launched an offensive against Palestine with the ultimate objective of conquering Syria.

The slow but steady advance of the British, accompanied by British victories in Mesopotamia, produced a temporary crisis in Constantinople. In January 1917, Grand Vizier Prince Said Halim resigned and was replaced by Talaat Pasha, who was determined to give a more energetic direction to affairs. With their German allies, the Turks decided to launch a decisive, quick offensive in one of the theaters of war in the Middle East, in order to destroy at least one British expeditionary force. This project known as *Yilderim* ("Lightning") was first planned for Mesopotamia, but because of pressing need along the Mediterranean coast it was applied to the Syro-Palestinian campaign. In May 1917, General von Falkenhayn arrived from Germany at the head of a mission of sixty-five officers and assumed command of the Turkish army in Palestine. A German brigade was sent as reinforcement. One of Von Falkenhayn's staff officers was Major Franz von Papen, later to become German ambassador to Turkey,[15] while one of his corps command-

---

[15] Von Papen had been German military attaché in Washington for some time during the First World War. He was asked to leave the United States as a *persona non grata*, on account of his espionage activities.

ers was General Mustafa Kemal Pasha, who had already distinguished himself in the defense of Gallipoli. Despite heavy fighting, *Yilderim* failed. On December 9, 1917, General Allenby entered Jerusalem. The Turks were now definitely on the defensive, and nothing could stop their retreat. Even the relinquishment of high staff and command positions to the Germans did not save the situation. The final decisive battle on the Palestinian front took place at Mejiddo on September 18, 1918. It was followed by the occupation of Syria by British troops. Their progress was stopped by the conclusion of hostilities in October 1918.

The Arabian Front

At the outbreak of the war most of the Arabian peninsula, except Aden and the Persian Gulf states, was under Ottoman suzerainty. Turkish control was, however, only nominal over large portions of central Arabia. The Nejd and the Hasa in particular were virtually free, and their rulers conducted their domestic and foreign affairs independently of the will of the Ottoman government. The political status of the western part of Arabia—the Hejaz—was less clear. Turkish garrisons were stationed at some of the more important places in the Hejaz and also along the railway linking Syria with Medina. Politically the Hejaz was of doubtful loyalty because of the independent course followed by Sherif Hussein. Farther to the south there were Turkish troops in Yemen, whose ruler, Imam Yehya, was loyal to the Ottoman government.

The proclamation of the holy war, as we already know, did not produce the expected cooperation of the Arabs. Eventually two Arab princes of the peninsula allied themselves with the British: Ibn Saud of the Nejd and Sherif Hussein of the Hejaz. While Ibn Saud did not take an active part in the war against Turkey (India did not desire it), Hussein pledged the British army active military support. Hussein's decision was the result of an agreement with the British government to which we shall refer in a later section.[16]

On June 5, 1916, Hussein declared war against Turkey, a declaration which inaugurated what has since become known as the Arab Revolt. Warlike tribes were organized into a desert army whose main objective was to drive the Turks out of Arabia and to cooperate on the right flank with General Allenby's expeditionary force. The Arab army was commanded by Emir Faisal, third son of Sherif Hussein. Expert advice and leadership were provided by a number of British officers, chief among whom was Colonel T. E. Lawrence.[17]

The outbreak of the revolt threw German-Turkish plans into confusion. It occurred at a time when a German military mission, under Baron von Stotzingen, was proceeding through the Hejaz to Yemen in order to establish there a center of information and communications for the region around the southern Red Sea. Stot-

[16]See below, pp. 80–81.

[17]Among the British officers were Lt. Col. C. C. Wilson, who acted as British agent accredited to Sherif Hussein; Sir Reginald Wingate, who initially was commander-in-chief of operations in the Hejaz; Lt. Col. Alan Dawnay; Col. S. F. Newcombe, and Major P. C. Joyce. In addition, Col. E. Brémond headed a French military mission in Jidda. This mission lent to Arab forces a number of instructors, many of whom were Moroccan and Algerian officers.

zingen and his men were surprised and cut off from contact with their headquarters. After the official proclamation of revolt in the suburb of Medina by Emirs Faisal and Ali on June 5, Arab forces attacked Turkish troops in Mecca and after three days of fierce battle compelled them to surrender. Next to be liberated was the Red Sea port and town of Jidda. By September 1916 the principal towns of the Hejaz, except Medina, were under Arab control. Arab forces were then divided into two parts: the first, under the command of Ali, Abdullah, and Zaid, remained in Hejazi territory and laid siege to Medina; the second, under Faisal, proceeded northward as an auxiliary force to General Allenby's main expedition. The exploits of the Arab force were spectacular and of great value to the success of the main operation.[18] Operating east of the Jordan River, the Arabs successively captured Wajh, Aqaba, Maan, and Dara and proceeded toward their ultimate goal—Damascus. The advance of the Sherifian forces brought in their wake uprisings of Syrian and Transjordanian tribes against the Turks and caused many desertions from the Arab personnel of the Ottoman army. On October 1, 1918, British and Arab forces entered Damascus at the same time. Faisal entered at full gallop, heading a body of mounted Arab warriors. The ancient city of the Omayyads gave itself to a frenzy of enthusiasm in what was believed to be an hour of deliverance from centuries-long Turkish rule. The remainder of Syria was liberated in two operations: a British column fought its way along the coastal region through Tyre, Sidon, Beirut, and Tripoli, and a combined British-Arab force moving in a parallel direction successively captured Homs, Hama, and Aleppo in Syria's hinterland. In the last days of the war, stiff resistance was encountered at Aleppo, where the remnant of the Seventh Turkish Army under General Mustafa Kemal Pasha attempted to bar the Allies' entry into Turkey proper. A few days later the armistice put an end to the hostilities. According to British estimates, the Arab Revolt was responsible for the containment of about 65,000 Turkish troops.[19]

The Front in Mesopotamia

Allied operations against the Ottoman Empire would have been incomplete without an offensive in Mesopotamia. As early as November 6, 1914, British troops landed at Fao, the point where Shatt el-Arab flows into the Persian Gulf. This was followed by the arrival of a large expeditionary force from India. The specific objectives of this operation were to protect the British-controlled oil wells and refineries in southwestern Iran, to carry out a political countermove against the call to a jihad, and to provide a manifestation of strength to the Arab chieftains of the Persian Gulf coast (particularly those of Mohammera and Kuwait). Thus, apart from its pure military significance in the eastern theater of war, the expedition had to perform a definitely political task with regard to the Arab and Moslem world. The weight attached to these considerations was pointed up by the appointment of Sir Percy Cox, long-time British resident for the Persian Gulf, as chief political officer

---

[18]For an account of the Arab military operations, see T. E. Lawrence, *Revolt in the Desert* (New York, 1927) and *Seven Pillars of Wisdom* (London, 1935).

[19]According to Arnold J. Toynbee, *The Islamic World since the Peace Settlement (Survey of International Affairs, 1925,* vol. I; London, 1927), p. 283.

to the expeditionary force. The force, commanded in succession by Generals Dela-main, Barrett, and Maude, occupied Basra in November 1914 and undertook an offensive operation against Baghdad.[20] The ultimate aim was to effect a junction with the Russian forces operating from the Caucasus, and thus to close an iron ring around the eastern confines of the Ottoman Empire. The opposing Turkish army was under the command of an experienced German soldier, General von der Goltz Pasha, who aroused much spirit and effected great efficiency among his troops.

In contrast to Allenby's campaign in Palestine, the Mesopotamian expeditionary force had to rely entirely upon its own strength, since Arab irregulars were not accepted as allies. It was faced with an arduous task in a very unfavorable climate, and its lines of communication were extended, considering the distance from its Indian base. The force's operations were complicated by the fact that it also had to keep an eye on the developments in the nearby territory of Iran. As we know from the preceding section, the possibility that Iran might take the side of the Central powers was never completely excluded. The German-sponsored rebellion of the tribes in oil-rich Khuzistan constituted a diversion which was apt to weaken the expeditionary force in Mesopotamia and which at one time had almost catastrophic consequences.

Because of these conditions the progress of the force was slow. On April 25, 1916, the British suffered a severe defeat when over 13,000 soldiers, under General Townshend, surrendered to the Turks after a protracted siege of five months at Kut el-Amara. The almost simultaneous death of Von der Goltz, however, deprived the Ottoman army of an able leader. He was replaced by the less-competent Halil Pasha, Enver's uncle. Baghdad fell to General Maude's forces on March 11, 1917, and a further British offensive was launched toward the north. During the following months a junction was effected with the Russian army advancing toward the Mesopotamian border from Iran. As a result of the Russian revolution, this army rapidly began to disintegrate, and little could be expected from it in the way of effective cooperation. Despite this disappointment, British forces proceeded stead-ily northward and by October 1918 reached the outskirts of Mosul. At the time of the armistice, Mosul was still in Turkish hands. Following the withdrawal of the Turkish troops, however, it was promptly occupied by the British, an action which was later to lead to a bitter international controversy.

Operations in Southwestern Arabia

Isolated from the major theaters of war was a Turkish garrison in Yemen. In 1915 the Turks and their Yemenite vassals invaded the territory of the Aden Protectorate. Occupying Sheikh Said, these forces advanced toward the outskirts of Aden, which they besieged but failed to capture. This Turkish operation presented a real threat to British control of this important coaling station and military base. There was also a possibility of losing to the Turks the small but strategically situated island of Perim

[20]For an account of this campaign, see Edmund Dane, *British Campaigns in the Nearer East, 1914–1918* (London, 1917–1919); Sir Arnold T. Wilson, *Loyalties, Mesopotamia, 1914–17: A Personal and Historical Record* (London, 1930); Edmund Chandler, *The Long Road to Baghdad* (London, 1919); C. V. Townshend, *My Campaign in Mesopotamia* (London, 1920).

at the southern entrance to the Red Sea. Perim was a cable station vital to the British network of communications. The Turkish-Yemenite operation was never coordinated with other major actions of the Central powers and was therefore unlikely to affect the general course of the war.

Operations in Transcaucasia

The Russian revolution and Soviet willingness to conclude a separate peace with the Central powers had many important consequences to Turko-German relations. The Turkish government sent Ibrahim Hakki Pasha and Zeki Pasha, ambassador and military attaché, respectively, in Berlin, to Brest-Litovsk as official delegates. The grand vizier, Talaat Pasha, eventually appeared in person to support Turkish claims. These claims included (1) the return of Kars, Ardahan, and Batum; (2) freedom of action in the Caucasus and in Iran; and(3) access to raw materials. Thus formulated, these claims represented a Pan-Turanian program. Germany supported these demands, but somewhat reluctantly since they were bound to complicate the future course of Soviet-German relations and since, as pointed out previously, they diverted Turkish attention from the prosecution of the war on other fronts in the Middle East. At any rate, Turkey's value to Germany as an ally had become questionable. It was felt in Berlin that the Turks had become more of a burden than an asset. The fact that Turkey kept the Straits closed to the Entente navies—originally a most important service from the German point of view—had lost much of its earlier significance. Now, because of Rumania's defeat and Russia's defection, the Entente no longer had any military interest in the Black Sea.

The outcome of German-Soviet negotiations was the Treaty of Brest-Litovsk of March 3, 1918, by which Russia ceded to Turkey the districts of Kars, Ardahan, and Batum. This cession had a nominal and historical value only. In reality, the Soviet government had lost control of the Caucasus as a result of the nationalist movement there. Three important ethnic groups in Transcaucasia—Armenians, Georgians, and Azerbaijanis—in December 1917 had created a Transcaucasian Seym (parliament), which proclaimed the independence of the region. This coincided with the dissolution of Russian rule in Transcaucasia and the melting away of the Russian troops from the Turkish front. Not all the troops, however, deserted their positions; the Armenian and Georgian formations of the former tsarist army, for instance, remained on the front and did their utmost to stem the advance of the Turks. With its proclamation of independence, the Transcaucasian Seym assumed responsibility and command over these troops and added to them some freshly organized national formations composed of Armenians and Georgians. On December 5, 1917, the Seym managed to conclude an armistice, which was soon to be broken by a fresh Turkish advance. In this offensive the Turks not only enjoyed a superiority in numbers but also profited from inner dissensions within the enemy camp. These dissensions were due to the reluctance of the Azeris (Azerbaijanis) to cooperate with the Georgians and the Armenians. In fact, the Azeris, although members of the Transcaucasian Federation, welcomed the Turkish advance. Susceptible to Pan-Turanian ideology, they expected Turkey to protect their newly won independence from their traditional oppressor, Russia. Hence they refused outright to send troops to stop the Turkish invasion and to cooperate with other members of the Federation.

These weaknesses in the Federation led its leaders to sue for peace. Between March 1 and April 1, 1918, negotiations were conducted with the Turks in Trebizond, but they yielded nothing positive. After obtaining a legal title to Kars, Batum, and Ardahan (Georgian and Armenian areas) on March 3 at Brest-Litovsk, the Turks demanded formal recognition of this cession by theTranscaucasian Federation as a prerequisite to further negotiations. Failing to receive it, they resumed hostilities and, in a swift advance, occupied Batum on April 1 and Kars on April 12. Thereupon, the Seym renewed its plea for peace, this time on the basis of the Brest-Litovsk Treaty.[21]

The new conference, which opened in Batum on May 11, was accompanied by unceasing hostilities, especially between the Turkish and the Armenian formations. The Turks presented peace terms that were much harsher than those offered at Trebizond. They demanded important coastal regions of Georgia and impressive areas of Armenia. The latter, under these terms, was to be reduced to an area of 11,000 square miles around Erivan, the rest going either to Turkey or to what was expected to be the independent state of Azerbaijan. Apart from these territorial concessions the Turkish terms provided for virtual Turkish control of Transcaucasia politically, strategically, and economically. The harshness of Turkish terms so far as Georgian and Armenian territory was concerned and the friendly overtures to the Azeris deepened the dissensions within the Transcaucasian Federation and brought on the inevitable crisis. In order to salvage as much as they could from the disaster, the Georgians appealed to Germany for help. General von Lossow, German plenipotentiary at the Batum conference, was sympathetic toward the Georgian plea, as was the German government. On May 26, 1918, unable to continue collaboration, the Seym, at its meeting in Tiflis, proclaimed the dissolution of the Transcaucasian Federation. On the same day Georgia proclaimed her independence and placed herself under German protection, which concretely meant the guarantee of her borders against Turkish encroachments. Not displeased with this action, Azerbaijan promptly followed suit and proclaimed independence on May 26. Left alone Armenia did the same on May 28, 1918, although she would have preferred a continuation of Transcaucasian collaboration.

Faced with these developments the Turkish delegation now presented its peace terms to the three newly formed republics in the form of an ultimatum. This ultimatum affected Armenia chiefly, since Georgia enjoyed German protection, and Azerbaijan was being courted by the Turks. On June 4, 1918, the Treaty of Batum was concluded between Turkey, on the one hand, and the Georgians, Armenians and Azerbaijanis, on the other. Georgia kept Batum, but Armenia had to agree to considerable shrinkage in her territory. In addition, Armenia undertook to evacuate her troops which, as a result of wartime developments, were in Baku.

Thus Turkish plans regarding Transcaucasia were nearly fulfilled. The Turks, to

---

[21]For a more detailed account of Transcaucasian negotiations, see Larcher, *op. cit.*, pp. 140 ff., and Vratzian, *op. cit.*, pp. 32 ff.

be sure, had to renounce their designs on Georgia. The Georgians were soon encouraged by the arrival of a German division, under Colonel Kress von Kressenstein, which promptly occupied Batum and stood guard at other strategic points in the territory. A political and economic treaty with Germany, giving the latter virtual control over her resources, completed Georgia's dependence on Berlin. As to Armenia, the Turks had the satisfaction of seeing her territorially reduced and politically humiliated. A direct connection with Azerbaijan was established and the road seemed open for the fulfillment of the boldest Pan-Turanian dreams. These appeared to be close to realization because of the steps toward liberation being taken simultaneously by various Turkic groups in Russia. As a result of the March and November 1917 revolutions in Russia, the following Moslem groups attempted emancipation from Russian rule: the Tatars of Crimea (proclaimed a republic, December 26, 1917); the mountaineers of North Caucasus (formed the North-Caucasian Union, Sept. 20, 1917); the Tatars of Kazan (proclaimed a republic in October 1917); the Kirghiz of Orenburg (proclaimed independence on Dec. 20, 1917); and the Moslems of Turkestan (proclaimed independence in Kokand, December 1917). To these should be added strong nationalist and emancipatory movements among the Bashkirs of Ufa, the Turkoman tribes of Transcaspia, and the khanates of Khiva and Bukhara.

To reach the heart of the Caucasus and to cross the Caspian Sea into Central Asia constituted the ultimate aim of the Pan-Turanians. The first step on this road was the conclusion of an alliance with the government of Azerbaijan in Ganja. This was done in the summer of 1918, and it resulted immediately in the recruitment of an auxiliary, all-Islam army, composed of Azeris, Ajars, and other Caucasian Moslems, to assist the main body of the Turkish army. This new force was put under the command of Enver's brother, Nuri Pasha, who had just arrived from Turkey and who was known for his Pan-Turanian ideas. The liberation of Baku, the most important center of the Azerbaijan Republic, was his first task as the new commander. Baku was the only city in Transcaucasia which remained under Russian control after the revolution. Its history had been stormy. Following the creation of the Transcaucasian Seym, Baku had become an integral part of the Transcaucasian Federation, a state of affairs which did not last long. In March 1918, the local Communist party staged a successful coup and established a soviet under the leadership of one Stepan Shaumian, an Armenian friend of Lenin. The coup was not a mere palace revolution, and it deeply affected the Moslem masses of the city, on whom the Bolsheviks—many of them Armenians—committed shocking atrocities. It has been estimated that 10,000 Moslems perished during these few days of bloodshed. The fact that Baku was thus separated from the new republic of Azerbaijan meant that a mere political agreement between the republic and Turkey was not sufficient to assure possession of the city. It had to be conquered, and to that end the efforts of the Turkish and the All-Islam armies were directed.

Had it been only a question of capturing the city from the Bolsheviks, the problem would have been simple enough for the Turks. The Turkish forces were superior in numbers and organization, enjoyed the friendship of the population in the Azerbaijan countryside, and in case of fierce resistance could have besieged the city and starved it into submission. But, as it happened, it was not a matter of a military operation alone. There arose two complications, which were bound to make the Turkish task more difficult. The first was the German attitude. Germany viewed with definite disfavor unilateral Turkish action in this region and was ready to take her own action to frustrate Turkish plans. This had been proved earlier in Germany's sudden assumption of a protectorate over Georgia and in the occupation of Batum by the Kress division. Having succeeded in ousting the Turks from Batum, the Germans now attempted to gain control of Baku before the Turks could establish themselves there. With this purpose, the German government, in constant contact with Soviet leaders since Brest-Litovsk, concluded an agreement with Moscow, by which Soviet Russia authorized Germany to draw upon the oil resources of Baku and to organize its defense against the attack of any third party. In fulfillment of this agreement, which was later formulated as an addition to the Brest-Litovsk Treaty, a German military mission was dispatched to Baku via Astrakhan at the end of July 1918. The Soviet-German agreement provided that, in case of a Turkish approach to Baku, Germany would have to engage in hostilities against her own ally. This agreement bears witness to the extent of the deterioration in German-Turkish relations in the summer of 1918. Actually, an open clash between the two allies never came, because the German mission to Baku was not permitted to begin its real work. This was due to the fact that the Bolshevik soviet in Baku was overthrown by a rival group of Social Revolutionaries while the German mission was en route to the city (July 26). The so-called Centro-Caspian Dictatorship was subsequently established there. The new masters of the city were anti-German, and, when the German mission arrived by boat from Astrakhan on August 4, it was promptly arrested.

The sudden change of government in Baku presented the Turkish command with a new complication. The Social-Revolutionary dictators asked the British for aid, which was promptly extended to them. The British had viewed with great concern the Turko-German advance in the Caucasus as the result of the dissolution of the Russian army and were anxious to fill the gap created in the eastern front. The original British plan was to establish liaison with the three Transcaucasian republics and, exploiting their desire for independence, to assist them in the formation and training of their national armies. British representatives were sent to Tiflis to treat with the Transcaucasian nationalists, but their overtures found ready response only among the Armenians. The Georgians preferred, as we have seen, to seek German protection, which was readily available. The Azerbaijanis were pro-Turkish, and the city of Baku had been dominated since March 1918 by the Bolsheviks, who even in the face of the Turkish advance were not prepared to ask the British "imperialists" for help. After the overthrow of Bolshevik rule in the city, however, the British could gain access to it and thus take the first step toward the defense of Transcaucasia. Major General L. C. Dunsterville was dispatched with a brigade of troops through Iran and across the Caspian Sea and arrived in Baku in the middle of August. Despite his best efforts, his attempts to organize an efficient defense of the city failed, mainly because of the failure of the dictators to live up to their promises. Convinced that to remain in Baku under such circumstances would be suicidal,

Dunsterville, after a few preliminary engagements with the Turks, evacuated his troops and went back to Iran.[22] The city was left to its own devices, and soon, on September 14, fell to the Turks and the All-Islam army. Bitter over the spring massacre of their coreligionists, the Moslems now vented their anger on the Armenian population of Baku. The loss of life ran into the thousands.

The conquest of Baku opened before the Turks very alluring Pan-Turanian vistas. One had only to cross the Caspian at its narrowest point to reach Qizil Su (Krasnovodsk) and to emerge in force onto the Turkoman Steppe, from which could be reached the vast expanse of Turkestan.

This possibility roused British fears, since such an advance of the Central powers, if successful, might bring them to Afghanistan and hence to the gates of India. There might then be an uprising in the Moslem provinces of the Indian Empire. It will be remembered that to forestall such a move the British maintained during the war the so-called East Persia Cordon, a line of troops along the Afghan border, which at a certain point touched the line of tsarist Russian troops. The melting away of the Russian troops in 1918 led the British to extend this cordon up to the border of Russia, and even into Transcaspia when called to assist the Russian counterrevolutionary center that had formed in Ashkhabad. This British action was later developed into full-fledged military operations directed against the Bolsheviks in Transcaspia.

As it happened, the Turks never crossed the Caspian. Within two months after the conquest of Baku, the Ottoman government sued for peace. The armistice of Mudros, October 30, 1918, put an end to the hostilities between Turkey and the Entente powers. The armistice with Germany followed on November 11.

War Aims and Political Strategy of the Entente

From a purely military standpoint, the Turkish belligerency was an unpleasant fact for all the countries of the Entente, and all would have preferred to see Turkey remain neutral. But there the unanimity ended. To Russia, war against Turkey meant an opportunity to attain her traditional desire of controlling the Straits and, perhaps, of dismembering the Ottoman Empire. As a long-range proposition, there was no incompatibility between the basic ambitions of Russia and her struggle with Turkey. This was not the case with England. To the British, war with the Ottoman Empire was a paradox and a diplomatic tragedy. It meant the end of their longstanding policy of supporting Turkey and of the well-fixed axiom that Ottoman integrity and sovereignty must be preserved as a bulwark of the British imperial life line. Now Great Britain was to lead the Allies in defeating her traditional friend. To aggravate matters, this defeat, as planned by the Entente, was to be not only military but also political. It was to lead to the extinction of the Ottoman Empire.

Russia was determined to obtain control of Constantinople and of the Straits and to secure territorial gains in eastern Anatolia. Italy had to be bribed into joining the war by specific promises of political and territorial concessions, some of them at the

---

[22]L. C. Dunsterville, *The Adventures of Dunsterforce* (London, 1920).

expense of Turkey. Greece had to be cajoled onto the side of the Entente by a variety of dubious maneuvers and promises, which included territorial gains on the Turkish Aegean coast. And finally, it was necessary for Britain and France to reach a harmonious settlement of their respective claims. Realizing that the Ottoman Empire was doomed, Britain was not averse to claiming major portions of it for herself and was willing similarly to accommodate France. Furthermore, wartime expediency compelled Britain to reach an understanding with two other groups—the Arabs and the Zionists. This resulted in a network of agreements, some of them contradicting others but all designed to dismember the Ottoman Empire.[23]

Secret Partition Agreements

The Constantinople agreement. On March 18, 1915, a secret agreement was concluded by Russia, on the one hand, and Great Britain and France, on the other, through an exchange of notes between St. Petersburg, Paris, and London. Russia was to annex "Constantinople, the western coast of the Bosphorus, the Sea of Marmara, and the Dardanelles; Southern Thrace as far as the Enos-Midia line; the coast of Asia Minor between the Bosphorus and the river Sakaria and a point on the Gulf of Ismid to be defined later; the islands in the Sea of Marmara and the Islands of Imbros and Tenedos."

In return, Russia recognized a number of claims made by Britain and France:
1. *Concerning Turkey*
   a. Constantinople was to become a free port for the Allies, and freedom of commercial navigation was assured in the Straits.
   b. Russia agreed to recognize the special rights of Britain and France in Asiatic Turkey through a separate agreement.
   c. The Moslem holy places were to be detached from Turkey and, together with Arabia, placed under independent Moslem rule.
2. *Concerning Iran*
   a. Russia agreed to the inclusion of the neutral zone, as provided by the Anglo-Russian agreement of 1907, in the British sphere of influence.
   b. However, to this agreement there were three reservations: first, that the districts adjoining the cities of Isfahan and Yazd should be included in the Russian sphere; second, that a portion of the eastern extremity of the neutral zone, which adjoins the Afghan territory, should be included in the Russian zone; and third, that Russia gain full freedom of action in her own zone of influence. (This last reservation meant virtual annexation of the zone in the long run.)

In addition to these territorial arrangements, Russia pledged assistance to the Allies in case they attacked the Dardanelles. Italy, upon her declaration of war, gave her consent to this Russo-Anglo-French agreement.

The Constantinople agreement formally marked the end of a century-old British policy. The capital of the once mighty Empire was to pass into the control of the

[23]For relevant texts, see H. W. V. Temperley, ed., *A History of the Peace Conference of Paris* (London, 1924), VI, 1–22; also F. Seymour Cocks, ed., *The Secret Treaties and Understandings* (London, n.d.).

Russians, who were to enjoy free access to warm waters, provided, of course, the war against Turkey was victorious.

The Treaty of London. On April 26, 1915, a secret treaty was signed in London by Britain, France, Russia, and Italy. This treaty was the price paid by the Allies for Italy's joining the Allied camp. Of the many territorial concessions promised the Italians, the following pertained to the Middle East:

1. Italy was given full sovereignty over the strategic Dodecanese Islands off the Turkish coast, under Italian occupation since 1912 (Art. 8).
2. All rights and privileges in Libya belonging to the sultan by virtue of the Treaty of Lausanne (1912) were transferred to Italy (Art. 10).
3. Article 9, the most important, stated:

> Generally speaking, France, Great Britain, and Russia recognize that Italy is interested in the Mediterranean, and that in the event of a total or partial partition of Turkey-in-Asia, she [Italy] ought to obtain a just share of the Mediterranean region adjacent to the province of Adalia, where Italy has already acquired rights and interests which formed the subject of an Italo-British convention. The zone which shall eventually be allotted to Italy shall be delimited, at the proper time, due account being taken of the existing interests of France and Great Britain.
>
> The interests of Italy shall also be taken into consideration in the event of the territorial integrity of the Turkish Empire being maintained and of alterations being made in the zones of interest of the Powers.
>
> If France, Great Britain and Russia occupy any territories in Turkey-in-Asia during the course of the War, the Mediterranean region bordering on the province of Adalia within the limits indicated above shall be reserved to Italy, who shall be entitled to occupy it.[24]

As may be seen from this text, Italy's territorial claim in Anatolia was very vaguely described and could lend itself to varying interpretations. On the other hand, Italy took the precaution, as the second paragraph indicates, to safeguard her interests in the case of unforeseen changes. This passage was to serve later as legal justification for Italy's discontent with the peace settlement, insofar as it affected the Middle East.

Armed with these assurances, Italy declared war on Turkey on August 20, 1915.

The Sykes-Picot agreement. Having satisfied the main demands of Russia and Italy, the French and British governments proceeded in 1915 to adjust their own claims to the Asiatic portions of the Ottoman Empire. Sir Mark Sykes and Georges Picot were appointed to conduct negotiations. It must be pointed out that Britain had, in the meantime, entered into negotiations with Sherif Hussein of the Hejaz, with the object of securing his assistance in the war against Turkey; this assistance was to be made conditional upon British recognition of Arab national aspirations. The French government, aware of the possibility of an exclusive Arab-British deal and eager to secure for itself a portion of the Ottoman Empire, pressed for definite recognition of its claims. Such an understanding had been foreseen in the Constantinople agreement. Proceeding thus to define their rights, France and Britain desired

[24]Temperley, *op. cit.*, pp. 19, 20.

to secure Russian approval, and for this purpose Sykes and Picot were sent to St. Petersburg in the early spring of 1916. There they presented their draft agreement and secured Russia's approval, at the price, however, of recognizing further Russian claims. This bargain was subsequently formalized on April 26, 1916, under the name of the Sazonov-Paléologue agreement.[25] It formed an integral part of the general settlement reached between Russia, France, and Great Britain usually referred to as the Sykes-Picot agreement. Officially the Sykes-Picot agreement was concluded on May 16, 1916, and contained the following provisions:

1. Russia was to obtain the provinces of Erzerum, Trebizond, Van, and Bitlis (known as Turkish Armenia), as well as territory in the northern part of Kurdistan, along the line from Mush, Sairt, Ibn Omar, and Amadiya, to the Iranian border. This represented an impressive area of 60,000 square miles between the Black Sea and the Mosul-Urumia region, containing rich deposits of copper, silver, and salt.

2. France was to obtain the coastal strip of Syria, the vilayet of Adana, and the territory bounded in the south by a line from Aintab and Mardin to the future Russian frontier, and in the north by a line from Ala Dagh through Kaisariya, Ak-Dagh, Jildiz-Dagh, and Zara to Egin-Kharput (the area commonly known as Cilicia).

3. Great Britain was to obtain southern Mesopotamia with Baghdad, as well as the ports of Haifa and Acre in Palestine.

4. The zone between the French and British territories was to form a confederation of Arab states or one independent Arab state. This zone was to be further divided into a French and a British sphere of influence. The French sphere was to include the Syrian hinterland and the Mosul province of Mesopotamia. The British sphere was to extend over the territory between Palestine and the Iranian border.

5. Alexandretta was proclaimed a free port.

6. Palestine was to be internationalized.

Since secrecy was deemed as essential part of this agreement, its terms were not communicated either to Italy or to Sherif Hussein.

The St. Jean de Maurienne agreement. Despite the original secrecy of the Sykes-Picot agreement, the Italian government knew about its terms by early 1917. Consequently, Italy pressed the other three powers for a precise definition of those Italian claims in Asia Minor that had been vaguely referred to as a "region adjacent to the province of Adalia" in the London Treaty of 1915. On April 17, 1917, the prime ministers of Great Britain, France, and Italy met at St. Jean de Maurienne and there drew up an agreement that gave Italy the right to annex a large tract of purely Turkish land in southwestern Anatolia (the vilayet and city of Smyrna, the sanjaks of Menteshe, Adalia, and Itchili, and the greater part of the vilayet of Konia). In addition to this, Italy obtained a sphere of influence north of Smyrna.

The St. Jean de Maurienne agreement was the last major inter-Allied understanding concerning the partitioning of Ottoman territory. It was subject to the approval

---

[25] Sazonov was Russian foreign minister and Paléologue French ambassador in Russia.

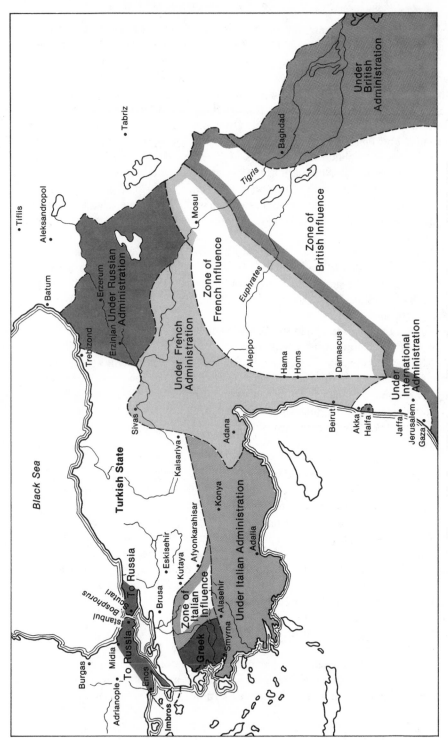

Map 2. The partitioning of Turkey according to the secret agreements of 1915–1917.

of the Russians, who were absent from the conference. This approval was never given as a result of the revolutionary change of government in Russia.

The Clemenceau-Lloyd George agreement. Following the victorious campaign in Mesopotamia, the British found themselves in occupation of the Mosul area. Inasmuch as most of the fighting in the Middle East had been done by the British, the latter believed that some revision of the Sykes-Picot treaty was needed in order to compensate them. In December 1918, during Clemenceau's visit to London, the French and the British prime ministers reached an agreement by which France consented to the inclusion of the Mosul area (formerly in the French zone) in Britain's sphere of influence. In return, France was promised a share in the north-Mesopotamian oil deposits.

British-Arab Negotiations and Agreements

The existence of a strong nationalist movement among the Arabs of the Ottoman Empire has already been mentioned. This spirit of independence manifested itself through (1) nationalist agitation and conspiratorial activities among the educated Arabs in Syria, (2) assertions of independence by the chieftains of central and eastern Arabia, and (3) the independent course pursued by the Sherif of Mecca.

Aware of these manifestations, the British decided early in the war to use Arab nationalism to their own advantage. The immediate aim was to secure Arab military support in the war against Turkey. The long-range objective was to create an independent Arab state or confederation of states, which was to serve as a substitute for the Ottoman Empire. Such a confederation was envisaged as taking over the traditional role of a friendly Moslem power serving as a bulwark of defense for the British life line to India. This scheme had the virtue of solving a serious dilemma which had beset British foreign policy ever since England found herself compelled to cross swords with Turkey. The British had to decide which group of Arabs in the Ottoman Empire was representative enough to warrant the opening of negotiations. The Syrian intellectual nationalists were the most outspoken, and the most politically conscious, in a modern sense. They were, however, physically inaccessible, since Damascus and Beirut were deep within Turkish lines and under the firm control of the Turkish authorities. The only area relatively free from Turkish control was Arabia. Here the British concentrated their efforts, which were twofold. There were agreements with Ibn Saud, ruler of the Nejd and its dependencies, and negotiations and agreement with Emir Hussein of Mecca.

Two things are worthy of note with regard to British action toward Ibn Saud. First, these negotiations were the responsibility of the government of India; consequently, they bore the imprint of the Indian school of diplomacy. Second, they were conducted for the short-range objective of securing the friendship or at least the neutrality of the ruler of the Nejd during the military operations in Mesopotamia. It will be remembered that the government of India was opposed to provoking a large-scale Arab uprising against the caliph, did not want active Arab participation in the campaign against Turkey, and gave little thought to the ultimate creation of an Arab kingdom to replace the Ottoman Empire. Indian policy was motivated by local considerations and in particular by the fear of complications with Indian Moslems if the policy of Britain was too hostile to the caliph.[26] The government of India sent the consul at Kuwait, Captain J. R. Shakespear, on a mission to Ibn Saud. The mission was successful. The visit of Sir Percy Cox, British resident in the Persian Gulf, followed, and the conclusion of a treaty of friendship came on December 26, 1915. This treaty was patterned after the treaties concluded earlier with the various chiefs of the Gulf states. The government of India recognized Ibn Saud as ruler of the Nejd and its dependencies, promised to defend him against aggression, and granted him an annual subsidy. In return, Ibn Saud pledged not to alienate any portion of his domain to foreign powers, to refrain from attacking the British-protected sheikhs along the Gulf coast, and to maintain friendly relations with Great Britain.

This treaty did not result in Ibn Saud's taking up arms against the Turks, but it did contribute to favorable developments in Arabia. Ibn Saud fought against the powerful pro-Turkish clan of the Rashids, did not respond to the Sultan's appeal for a jihad, and prevented the Turks from being supplied by sea via the Persian Gulf coast. He also refrained from attacking Sherif Hussein, with whom he might easily have picked a quarrel over some borderlands in central Arabia. His contribution to the British war effort was thus passive, but not negligible. A British mission under H. St. John Philby and Lord Belhaven added to the mutual good will.[27]

British negotiations with Emir Hussein of Mecca followed a separate course and resulted in very radical changes in the Arab situation in the Ottoman Empire. Hussein had spent many years in forced exile in Constantinople, had been appointed emir of Mecca in 1908, and by 1914 had established himself as a powerful influence in the Arab world. Having long hoped for the creation of an independent Arab kingdom and certainly not devoid of personal ambition, Hussein felt that World War I provided an excellent opportunity to realize his dreams. His unquestioned adherence to the holy war would have been of invaluable assistance to Turkey, but Hussein chose to temporize and gave the Porte various excuses of a practical nature for his delay. As early as February 1914, during a visit in Cairo, Hussein's second son, Emir Abdullah, sounded out the British on whether or not they were prepared to enter into an agreement with the Arabs. On this occasion Abdullah saw Lord Kitchener, then British high commissioner in Egypt, and intimated that the Arabs were ready for revolt if the British could give assurances of support. These suggestions first met with skepticism, but when the war began London and Cairo gave them more serious thought. Upon Kitchener's advice (he had become secretary of war in the meantime), Sir Reginald Wingate, governor general of the Sudan, and Sir Henry McMahon, high commissioner in Egypt, kept in touch with Sherif Hussein, and before long this evolved into full-scale negotiations.[28]

While these negotiations were underway, Hussein in the spring of 1915 sent his third son, Emir Faisal, to Damascus on a mission to reassure the Turkish authorities of his loyalty and also to sound out Arab public opinion in this important center of

---

[26] See below, pp. 96, 574.

[27] On British-Nejd negotiations, see H. St. John B. Philby, *Arabia* (London, 1930).

[28] A vivid account of these negotiations may be found in Antonius, *op. cit.*, chs. vii, viii, and ix, and in Ronald Storrs, *Orientations* (London, 1937), ch. viii.

nationalist propaganda. It is noteworthy that Faisal was originally pro-Turkish and did not share his father's enthusiasm for a British alliance. His visit to Damascus completely changed his attitude. There he learned of the iron rule of Jemal Pasha and of the profound discontent of the Arab population. Moreover, he was initiated into Arab secret societies. Representatives of these societies were advocating Arab revolt and a British alliance, to be based on acceptance by the latter of a set of definite conditions. These conditions, known as the Damascus Protocol, were handed over to Faisal for transmission to his father. Subsequently they constituted the basis of Hussein's territorial demands in the course of his negotiations with Great Britain.

The agreement which emerged had the form of a series of letters, exchanged between the British high commissioner in Cairo, Sir Henry McMahon, and Sherif Hussein. Hussein promised to declare war on Turkey and to raise an Arab army which would assist the British in their military operations. Sir Henry McMahon, acting on the instructions of the British government, pledged England to support "the independence of the Arabs" in the large area bounded, in the north by the 37th parallel, in the east by the Iranian border down to the Persian Gulf, and in the south by the Arab Gulf states. As to the western boundary, Hussein demanded the Red Sea and the Mediterranean coast; McMahon while readily admitting the Red Sea boundary, excluded from his pledge the whole coastal belt of Syria "lying to the west of the districts of Damascus, Homs, Hama and Aleppo." This meant the exclusion of Lebanon and the Alawi country to the north but left considerable uncertainty about Palestine.

In addition to this basic recognition of Arab nationalist claims, Great Britain guaranteed the holy places against external aggression and promised advice and assitance in the establishment of new Arab governments. In return, she secured the exclusive right of such advice and reserved for herself special administrative privileges in the vilayets of Baghdad and Basra. A corollary to this agreement granted Sherif Hussein substantial British subsidies in gold (amounting to £200,000 a month).[29]

On the strength of this agreement the Sherif gave the signal for the Arab Revolt on June 5, 1916. On November 2, 1916, Hussein proclaimed himself "King of the Arab Countries." This act proved to be too hasty and caused the British much embarrassment, especially in their relations with France. Eventually, a compromise formula was devised, according to which the Allies addressed Hussein as king of the Hejaz.

McMahon's pledge to Hussein preceded by six months the Sykes-Picot agreement. The latter was obviously incompatible with the former and, to put it bluntly, constituted a breach of the pledge to the Arabs. Its existence, therefore, was not disclosed to Sherif Hussein, except for some vague references to the need of harmonizing action with France, made during the visit which Sir Mark Sykes and Georges Picot paid to the Sherif in Jidda in May 1917.

Not until December 1917 did Hussein learn the truth about the Sykes-Picot

[29]Toynbee, *op. cit.*, p. 283.

agreement. Upon seizing power in Russia, the Soviet government promptly published the secret wartime agreements found in the archives of the tsarist Foreign Ministry. These included the Sykes-Picot treaty. Turkish authorities communicated it through secret emissaries to Sherif Hussein and, pointing out British treachery, exhorted him to break with Britain and return "to the fold of the Calph and of Islam."[30]

Profoundly disturbed, Hussein requested clarification from his British allies but obtained only vague replies, which could have been considered half-admissions and half-denials. Hoping for the best, the Arab ruler still decided to remain faithful to his ally.

Britain's Pledge to the Zionists

From the British point of view, the secret wartime agreements were dictated by the imperative necessity of gaining allies for the sake of winning the war. Russia, Italy, France, and the Arabs were such allies. It was also believed in Great Britain that an understanding with the Zionists would produce a new ally in the form of world Jewry.[31]

The Zionists, under the leadership of Dr. Chaim Weizmann, a lecturer in chemistry at Manchester University, were active in England during the war. Dr. Weizmann, who materially contributed to the British war effort by discovering a new method of producing acetone, attracted the attention of British officials to Zionist aspirations as early as 1914. Initially the outbreak of the war complicated the task of the Zionists. Zionism was an international movement, and the splitting of the world into two hostile camps was not conducive to the smoothness of organizational activity. Before the war, Zionist endeavors had been directed toward an understanding with the Ottoman Empire, as a controlling power in Palestine. The world headquarters of the Zionist Organization was situated in Berlin under the protective wing, so to speak, of the German government. Zionism had taken firm root in Russia, and the most ardent Zionists were Russian Jews. Russia's record of persecution, exclusion, and pogroms made these Zionist leaders intensely anti-Russian. Presented with an emotional and political choice between the cause of the Central powers and the cause of the Allies (including Russia), leading Zionists ardently hoped for Russia's defeat. Such a defeat at the hands of Germany would have meant a grave embarrassment if not actual disaster for the Allies. It followed, therefore, that Zionist political sympathies and the vital interests of the Allies were hardly compatible.

Inasmuch, however, as it was too risky for the future of the movement openly to join Germany, the Inner Actions Committee (the policy-making organ of the Zionist Organization) established a bureau in Copenhagan to stress their outward neutrality. Furthermore, aware of Dr. Weizmann's activity in Great Britain, the Actions Committee discouraged his intercourse with British statesmen.

---

[30]A detailed story of the British-Arab diplomacy is contained in Antonius, *op. cit.*
[31]For a history of Zionism, see pp. 388–391.

These steps did not deflect Weizmann from his purpose. In order to secure freedom of action, he cut off his contacts with the Copenhagen bureau.[32] In his pro-Ally policy he was supported by two eminent European Zionists, Sokolow and Tschlenow, who arrived in London in November 1914. He was also in touch with American Zionists. The latter, upon the outbreak of war in Europe, held an extraordinary conference and reached a decision to conduct Zionist policy autonomously in view of the practical dissolution of the Berlin headquarters. A Provisional Executive Committee for General Zionist affairs, which was then established, included Justice of the United States Supreme Court Louis Dembitz Brandeis as chairman, Rabbi Stephen S. Wise as vice-chairman, and Jacob de Haas as secretary. Among its members were Nathan Strauss, Professor Felix Frankfurter, Judge Julian W. Mack, Eugene Meyer, and a number of other prominent American Jews.

The aim of Zionists in Great Britain and in the United States was to obtain a guarantee from the Allies that, in the event of Turkey's defeat, Palestine would be recognized as a Jewish commonwealth, unrestrictedly open to immigration. To this end, Weizmann secured the sympathy and actual collaboration of a number of public figures in Great Britain. Among them were C. P. Scott and Herbert Sidebotham of the *Manchester Guardian*, who helped in organizing the British Palestine Committee; such prominent British Jews as Sir Herbert Samuel and the Rothschilds; and, finally, Lord A. J. Balfour, Britain's foreign secretary. Weizmann's talks on the government level were well advanced by 1916. Early in 1917, Sir Mark Sykes was instructed to open formal negotiations on behalf of the Allies with Nahum Sokolow, acting for the International Zionist Organization. The spring of 1917 brought two dramatic developments which proved to be decisive for the success of the Zionist cause. The first was the revolution in Russia; the second, America's entry into the war. The western Allies were intensely interested in keeping Russia in the war and in preventing a separate peace treaty with Germany. Prime Minister Lloyd George as well as Lord Balfour believed that, in view of the prominence of the Jews in the Russian revolutionary movement, it was essential to acquire their good will by responding favorably to Zionist aspirations.[33] It was also important to obtain full cooperation and maximum effort from Britain's new ally, the United States. Here, too, it was believed, the Jews could render inestimable service. Moreover, an Allied pronouncement in favor of Zionism might win over German Jewry to the Allied cause and, indirectly, help in producing internal disaffection in the Central powers. While, according to available evidence, these were the real reasons for Britain's decision to satisfy the Zionists, emotional motives guiding some statesmen and certain segments of the Allied public opinion should not be underestimated. Christian charity toward a persecuted race, the Old Testament heritage so important in shaping the historical consciousness of some Protestant groups, and democratic liberalism added the glow of virtue to purely practical calculations, or appealed to those for whom *Realpolitik* was not a sufficient in-

---

[32]Chaim Weizmann, *Trial and Error* (Philadelphia, 1949).
[33]For Lloyd George's postwar testimony on this subject, see below, pp. 85–86.

ducement. In the United States where the Jewish population was fairly large, considerations of internal politics constituted an additional incentive to support Zionism.

In their negotiations with Great Britain, the Zionists insisted upon a British protectorate over Palestine as the best guarantee for the success of their program. This involved the repudiation of that part of the Sykes-Picot agreement which provided for the internationalization of the Holy Land. This amounted to another contradictory pledge. The British government was not averse to accepting this Zionist proposal.[34]

In May 1917 Britain's foreign secretary, Lord Balfour, paid a visit to the United States. There he talked to Justice Brandeis, both a leading Zionist and a close adviser of President Wilson. The British cabinet before committing itself desired to arrange for a formal endorsement by President Wilson of a pro-Zionist pronouncement. In the meantime American Zionists displayed energetic activity in a number of appeals. These appeals did not fall on deaf ears; they could finally count on the support of eminent men in American official circles. William J. Bryan, Secretary of State; Robert Lansing; Newton D. Baker, Secretary of War; Josephus Daniels, Secretary of the Navy; Col. Edward House, and Norman Hapgood, all favored the Zionist aspirations. President Wilson not only supported Zionism but referred to himself as a Zionist in the course of his discussions with Brandeis, Frankfurter, and Wise.[35]

The Zionist's aim was to obtain from the President a public statement in support of Zionism. This Wilson was unwilling to make at that time, since the United States was not at war with Turkey. But following an official British inquiry addressed to Colonel House, Wilson instructed him, on October 16, 1917, to approve the pro-Zionist draft declaration proposed by the British cabinet. Commenting on this memorable act, Dr. Weizmann stated in his memoirs: "This was one of the most important individual factors in breaking the deadlock created by the British Jewish anti-Zionists, and in deciding the British Government to issue its declaration."[36]

Weizmann and his colleagues in Great Britain encountered more difficulties than did their counterparts in the United States. Two influential groups of English Jews voiced explicit opposition to Zionism. (See Chapter X.) In the British government Edwin Montagu, member of a prominent Jewish family and secretary of state for India, very actively opposed the issuance of any pro-Zionist declaration. His, however, was the voice of the minority. Lloyd George, Balfour, Milner, General Smuts, and Cecil all tended to favor the Zionist cause and believed in the justice and expediency of such a policy.

Dr. Weizmann's political activity was seconded in the military sector by Vladimir Zhabotinsky and Pincus Ruthenberg, who advocated the establishment of a Jewish Legion during World War I under Allied command. Their efforts bore fruit. A Zion Mule Corps was created as an auxiliary unit in Allenby's army. Composed of

[34]J. M. N. Jeffries, *Palestine: The Reality* (London, 1939), pp. 141, 144.
[35]Reuben Fink, *America and Palestine* (New York, 1945), p. 30.
[36]Weizmann, *op. cit.,* I, 208.

Jewish expellees from Syria and Palestine and including many European and American Zionists, it participated, under Colonel Patterson's command, in the Gallipoli and later Middle Eastern campaigns.

On November 2, 1917, following acceptance by the British cabinet of the major points of the draft submitted by the Zionists, Lord Balfour addressed the following letter to Lord Rothschild:

DEAR LORD ROTHSCHILD,

I have much pleasure in conveying to you, on behalf of His Majesty's Government, the following declaration of sympathy with Jewish Zionist aspirations which has been submitted to, and approved by, the Cabinet.

His Majesty's Government view with favour the establishment in Palestine of a national home for the Jewish people, and will use their best endeavours to facilitate the achievement of this object, it being clearly understood that nothing shall be done which may prejudice the civil and religious rights of existing non-Jewish communities in Palestine, or the rights and political status enjoyed by Jews in any other country.

I should be grateful if you would bring this declaration to the knowledge of the Zionist Federation.

Yours sincerely,
ARTHUR JAMES BALFOUR

The declaration was well timed because shortly afterward (in December 1917 and July 1918) Turkey and Germany tried to win Jewish favor by offering the German Zionists a chartered company in Palestine.[37] It was, however, too late to change general pro-Ally Zionist orientation.

Their task in Britain finished, the Zionists turned now to the other Allied governments to secure their approval of the Declaration. They were successful; France approved the Declaration on February 11, 1918, and Italy followed suit on February 23, 1918. Two days before the Mudros armistice President Wilson gave his open support of the Declaration in a letter addressed to Rabbi Stephen S. Wise on October 29, 1918.

Thus the destinies of Zionism became closely linked with the Allied cause. The Zionists obtained a status of unofficial allies. The Foreign Office went so far as to grant them the privilege of British diplomatic pouch. In return the Zionists were expected to render valuable assistance in the prosecution of the war. The extent to which they contributed to the Allied victory is, obviously, hard to determine, but it may be helpful to quote Britain's wartime prime minister, David Lloyd George, who made the following statement before the Palestine Royal Commission in 1936: "The Zionist leaders gave us a definite promise that, if the Allies committed themselves to giving facilities for the establishment of a national home for the Jews in Palestine, they would do their best to rally Jewish sentiment and support throughout the world to the Allied cause. They kept their word."[38] Amplifying this statement in the House of Commons in 1937, Lloyd George declared that the Zionists

[37]Royal Institute of International Affairs, *Great Britain and Palestine, 1915–1945* (London, 1946), p. 10.

[38]Quoted by Joseph Dunner, *The Republic of Israel* (New York, 1950), p. 32.

"were helpful in America and in Russia, which at that moment was just walking out and leaving us alone."[39]

When the news of the Declaration reached King Hussein, he requested elucidation from the British authorities. In response, the British sent to Arabia Commander D. G. Hogarth of the Arab Bureau in Cairo. On January 4, 1918, Hogarth delivered to Hussein a message in which he assured him that Britain's determination to assist the return of Jews to Palestine went only "so far as is compatible with the freedom of the existing population," and made no mention of a Jewish state. Hussein accepted the message but "spoke with a smile of accounts which he would settle after the war."[40]

As soon as the major part of Palestine was occupied by General Allenby, that is, just before the end of the war, Dr. Weizmann decided to visit the Holy Land. In March 1918, accompanied by several Zionist leaders and by Major Ormsby-Gore, acting as a British liaison officer, Weizmann journeyed to Jerusalem, where in an impressive ceremony he laid the cornerstone of the Hebrew University on Mount Scopus. The presence of this Zionist commission provoked adverse comments both among the Palestinian Arabs and the British officers of Allenby's staff. This was a foreshadowing of the difficulties to come.

In summing up the First World War in the Middle East, it should be stressed that political and ideological factors were as important as were military ones and that, in their complexity, the former often overshadowed the latter. On the one hand were the ambitious war aims of the Young Turkish group ruling the Ottoman Empire and the resulting interplay of Pan-Turanism, Pan-Islamism, and German imperialist ambitions. On the other was the Entente, with its often conflicting war aims, contradictory pledges, and simultaneous support of the hardly compatible claims of Zionism and Arab nationalism. Politically the war was a milestone in British foreign policy, reversing as it did traditional axioms and creating new problems for Great Britain in the Middle East.

Militarily the war could be conceived as an attempt by Turkey and Germany to expand southward and eastward by bold but ill-prepared moves, which soon brought their offensives to a halt. The Entente's strategy consisted in one attempt to strike a decisive blow at the heart of Turkey—the Gallipoli campaign—which ended in failure and was never repeated. Instead, the Allies undertook a slow movement directed from the extremities of the Ottoman Empire toward its center. Such were the Palestinian and Mesopotamian campaigns and the Russian campaign in East Anatolia. Russia's campaign, successful in the beginning, ended in failure as a result of the revolution and permitted the Turks, at the very end of the war, to obtain spectacular success in the Caucasus. This success came too late to change the general military situation and lasted too short a time to affect political developments very much. Yet it was indicative of certain long-range potentialities of Turkish foreign policy if it ever turned to Pan-Turanism. It was the victory of British arms in

[39]Jeffries, *op. cit.*, p. 190. See also R.I.I.A., *Great Britain and Palestine*, p. 9.
[40]R.I.I.A., *Great Britain and Palestine*, p. 148.

the general background of the Allied victory in Europe which ultimately proved decisive in the Middle East.

On October 31, 1918, Turkish and British plenipotentiaries, the latter acting for the Entente, signed the armistice of Mudros, which formally ended hostilities in the Middle East. The armistice authorized Allied troops to enter the hitherto unoccupied parts of Turkey. An Allied Control Commission appeared in Constantinople, and British, French, and Italian troops occupied large portions of southern Anatolia. For Turkey, the armistice was concluded by the new government of Izzet Pasha, a nonparty man, which had replaced the Union and Progress Party cabinet earlier in October. On the day of the armistice Enver, Talaat, and certain other Young Turkish politicians fled from Turkey to Germany. The Ottoman Empire lay in ruins. The victorious Allies faced a stupendous task of political and economic reconstruction in the area.

CHAPTER III

The Peace Settlement

When the statesmen of the entente met in Paris in January 1919 to discuss the peace treaties, they faced two categories of problems in the Middle East. One pertained to the actual military occupation of the area. The other, no less important, referred to secret wartime agreements.

With regard to the military occupation, the whole region could be roughly divided into three parts: the Arab countries, Turkey proper, and Iran. At the end of the war Iran was, to all practical purposes, under British military control, but she presented no major problem at the Paris Peace Conference, since Iran, as a nonbelligerent, did not participate in the conference. Of the Arab countries, Mesopotamia, Syria, and Palestine were under British occupation. The British shared their responsibility with their Arab allies under Emir Faisal. The latter established himself in Damascus and exercised authority delegated to him by General Allenby. The area under Faisal's command was known officially as Occupied Enemy Territory Administration (O.E.T.A.) East. Beirut and the Syrian coastal area were under direct British supervision. As to Turkey proper, certain parts were occupied, as we know, by Allied forces. The British first moved into Cilicia and Adana but later relinquished control of these provinces to France. Italy landed troops in Adalia. Constantinople was under a combined Allied occupation. The British occupied the major portions of the Ottoman Empire because they had carried on the major part of the military operations there. This placed them in a strong bargaining position at the Peace Conference.

The second problem concerned the wartime agreements. As we have seen in the preceding chapter, these conflicted. The major difficulty grew out of the incompatibility of these imperialist arrangements with the national aspirations of the native populations. When the conferees met in Paris, it soon became obvious that at least six different and mutually contradictory claims or attitudes had to be faced. These may be summed up as follows:

1. *Britain vs. France.* Britain was interested in a revision of the Sykes-Picot treaty, in order that her promises to the Arabs and her own interests in the area might be satisfied. France reacted negatively to all such suggestions, insisting on her "pound of flesh" and vigorously invoking the Sykes-Picot provisions and her traditional interests in Syria. The French government was opposed to any conces-

sions other than the one which gave Mosul to the British, which as we know had been made before the calling of the Peace Conference.[1]

2. *Arab claims*. Emir Faisal appeared at the conference as a delegate of the kingdom of the Hejaz and chief spokesman of the Arab cause. At a hearing before the Council of Ten, he insisted on the Arab right to self-determination and on the fulfillment of Allied promises to the Arabs.[2] His formal appearance at the conference was preceded by a state visit to France and England. In France he learned of French intransigence concerning Syria, and in England he was strongly advised to come to terms with the French and with the Zionists. Subjected to various pressures and not experienced in the ways of diplomacy, Faisal stood adamant on the principle of Arab independence, but was induced to sign an agreement with Dr. Weizmann. In this agreement, dated January 3, 1919, he welcomed Jewish immigration to Palestine, but in the postscript made his benevolent attitude to Zionism dependent upon the fulfillment of wartime promises of independence by Great Britain.

3. *Zionist claims*. Although the Zionists did not represent an established state, they sent a delegation which was accorded a rather friendly reception in Paris. The Zionist delegation included, in addition to Dr. Weizmann, Professor Frankfurter and Jacob de Haas from the United States and Messrs. Sokolow, Ussischkin, Spiré, and a number of other representatives of European Zionism.

The major political problem for the Zionists was to obtain international confirmation of the Balfour Declaration and to secure its inclusion in the text of the peace treaties. The Zionists were opposed to the incorporation of Palestine into an Arab state. They were against the principle of national self-determination, which if applied to Palestine would make it an Arab state, and they also opposed the internationalization of Palestine. Inasmuch as they favored British control of the area, their interests coincided with those of Great Britain. The Zionist delegation presented a memorandum to the Peace Conference, which was followed by a hearing. Both were given sympathetic attention, and their work was crowned with success. International instruments, such as the Treaty of Sèvres and the mandate (which will be dealt with later in this book), included explicit recognition of Zionist aspirations.

4. *Greek claims*. Greece had belatedly entered the war on the side of the Allies, succumbing to Allied pressure and inducements. The man most instrumental in aligning Greece with the Entente was Eleutherios Venizelos, who enjoyed prestige and influence in Paris quite incommensurate with the strength and role of his small country. Allied inducements had included hints of compensation at the expense of Turkey, but they were never put into formal or explicit form comparable to the other secret agreements. Despite this fact, Venizelos claimed for his country the right to occupy Smyrna and the adjacent region in western Turkey. His arguments were ethnical and historical. He pointed to the large Greek population in Smyrna, which,

---

[1] See above, p. 79.

[2] On November 7, 1918, Great Britain and France had issued a common declaration to the Arabs, in which they proclaimed their objective to be "the complete and definite emancipation of the peoples so long oppressed by the Turks and the establishment of national Governments and Administrations deriving their authority from the initiative and free choice of the indigenous population." The full text is in Royal Institute of International Affairs, *Great Britain and Palestine, 1915–1945* (London, 1946), pp. 149–150.

he alleged, constituted a majority, and to the historical link between the western and eastern shores of the Aegean—a Hellenic sea—and their economic unity. In his pleas he was backed by Britain's prime minister, Lloyd George, and the British delegation. Britain's motives in supporting Venizelos were a mixture of pro-Christian, pro-Hellenic, and anti-Turkish emotions[3] added to the political calculation (1) that Greece was a strategic bastion in the eastern Mediterranean and hence it was proper to keep her happy and friendly; (2) that inasmuch as the Straits might pass under Russian control, it would be wise to hold a reserve line from Piraeus to Smyrna across the Aegean to bar, if necessary, further Russian expansion.[4] Britain's support resulted in authorization to Greece from the Supreme Allied Council to occupy Smyrna and the vicinity. Venizelos' diplomatic triumph was complete, and he could now indulge in ambitious dreams of reconstructing some kind of Hellenic empire—an heir to Byzantium—in Asia Minor. Greek troops landed in Smyrna on May 15, 1919, and gradually advanced into the interior.

5. *Armenian claims.* The newly created republic of Armenia, having passed through the vicissitudes of war and Turkish invasion, was anxious to obtain international recognition and an increase in territory.The Armenian delegation in Paris, led by Boghos Nubar Pasha, demanded the so-called Turkish Armenia, i.e., the six-eastern vilayets of Turkey. This claim had some historical justification but little more than that. At the time the demand was made, most of the Armenians in those provinces had been uprooted; but even had they been living there, they would have been a minority of the population, the majority being decidedly Turkish.[5] The Armenian claims met with a mixed reception. Despite the friendliness generally shown the Armenians, there was an uneasy feeling at the Peace Conference that their claims were exaggerated.

6. *American attitudes.* The United States had not been a partner to the inter-Allied agreements; therefore, officially it was not bound by them. Moreover, American war aims as defined in the President's "Fourteen Points" of January 8, 1918, profoundly differed from the tenor of the secret treaties. Point One proclaimed the principle of "open covenants openly arrived at," which quite contradicted the secrecy of wartime deals. Point Twelve specifically dealt with Turkey:

> The Turkish portions of the present Ottoman Empire should be assured a secure sovereignty, but the other nationalities which are now under Turkish rule should be assured an undoubted security of life and an absolutely unmolested opportunity of development, and the Dardanelles should be permanently opened as a free passage to the ships and commerce of all nations under international guarantees.[6]

---

[3]These anti-Turkish sentiments were characteristic of only one group of British statesmen and diplomats and were by no means universal. But this group was influential at the time of Lloyd George's premiership. See Harold Nicolson, *Curzon, The Last Phase, 1919–1925: A Study in Post-War Diplomacy* (London, 1934), p. 94.

[4]*Ibid.,* p. 97.

[5]According to H. W. V. Temperley, ed., *A History of the Peace Conference of Paris* (London, 1924), VI, 82.

[6]For the full text of the Fourteen Points, see *ibid.,* I, 433.

The incompatibility of this American program with the policies of the other Allies was obvious. In Paris President Wilson refused even to consider the wartime agreements. The Allies, according to the President, had given their express approval of the Fourteen Points and hence had automatically annulled their secret agreements. They were bound to abide by the new principles of nonimperialism and national self-determination.

Had it been pushed to its logical conclusion, the President's program would have conflicted with practically every one of the secret agreements, with the exception, perhaps, of the British-Arab accord. It was incompatible with French, Italian, Greek, and Zionist plans. A device to compromise these conflicting interests and principles was found in the mandate system. The great powers were to be entrusted with mandates over some areas in the name of the League of Nations, whose covenant was being adopted in Paris. Even with the adoption of the mandate system, the question remained as to who should exercise the mandatory functions in specific areas. There were moments of tension during the conference, especially between the French delegation and the American president. In order to break the deadlock, Wilson proposed to send to the Middle East a joint Allied Commission whose task it would be to ascertain the desire of the populations "directly concerned." France refused to participate in this commission, and Britain, after brief hesitation, also decided to remain aloof from it. Notwithstanding this boycott and despite intense Zionist objections voiced by Professor Frankfurter, Wilson appointed a purely American commission composed of Dr. Henry C. King, President of Oberlin College, and Charles Crane, a prominent businessman and student of international affairs. Between May and July 1919 King and Crane made a six weeks' tour of Syria and Palestine, held hearings, and on August 28 presented their report.

In their tour of Arab centers King and Crane found an almost unanimous desire for full independence. The inhabitants of Syria, including the Palestinian Arabs, insisted on an independent and united Syrian state that would embrace not only the Syrian hinterland but also Lebanon and Palestine. Failing to achieve complete independence, the Syrians were prepared to accept the United States or Great Britain, their first and second choices, respectively, as their mandatory power. There was overwhelming opposition to France, except for a number of pro-French petitions from Lebanon. An equally overwhelming opposition to Zionism was expressed by Moslem and Christian Arabs alike.

During their visit in Aleppo, King and Crane interviewed a representative Arab delegation from Mesopotamia. The Mesopotamians also asked for independence and, in contrast to the Syrians, did not mention officially any preferences for a mandatory power. In fact, the delegation protested against Article 22 of the Covenant of the League of Nations, which had proclaimed the principle of mandates. The delegation insisted on a rather large Mesopotamia, which would include the frontier areas of Diarbekir, Deir ez-Zor, and Mosul on the northwest and Mohammera (an Iranian sheikhdom) on the southeast. It expressed preference for Abdullah or Zeid, sons of Hussein of the Hejaz, as their king, demanded complete independence for

Syria, and objected to Hindu and Jewish immigration. It also stated that, upon the achievement of independence, it would welcome technical and economic assistance from America.[7]

On the basis of the foregoing investigation, King and Crane recommended an American mandate for Syria, or as a second alternative a British mandate, and a British mandate for Mesopotamia. The two commissioners favored constitutional Arab monarchies under the mandatory system and fully endorsed Faisal for the kingship of Syria. Furthermore, they voiced serious opposition to the establishment of a Jewish state in Palestine. They recommended "that only a greatly reduced Zionist programme be attempted by the Peace Conference, and even that only very gradually initiated," that Palestine become part of a united Syrian state, and that the holy places be internationalized.[8]

Peace Settlement in the Arab Areas

The King-Crane report was not discussed by the Paris Peace Conference. The report was not rejected, but simply buried in the archives of the American delegation, and ignored by the conferees. It was not published until 1922, long after the peace settlement. This neglect of the report may be attributed to two facts: first, Wilson had left Paris for the United States in the midsummer of 1919 and in the pressure of more important business at home did not have the time or the desire to attend to what was, after all, only a secondary matter. In fact, beginning in July, the President had to fight strong domestic opposition to the League of Nations Covenant and to the whole Treaty of Versailles. This was, indeed, the basic issue; it affected the general problem of America's involvement in world affairs. And America's wishes and interests with regard to the Middle Eastern settlement depended upon solution of this fundamental question.

Second, the report was too blunt and too frank to please either France or Great

[7]Henry A. Foster, *The Making of Modern Iraq* (Norman, Okla., 1935), p. 90.

[8]The King-Crane report later elicited both favorable and unfavorable comments. Ray Stannard Baker in *Woodrow Wilson and World Settlement* (New York, 1922) says: "It was in many ways the most characteristic and interesting adventure in international politics ever undertaken by Americans, and it was the only commission appointed by the Paris Peace Conference which really carried out both the principle and the method of President Wilson, of inquiry into the real wishes of populations whose destinies were being decided. From the point of view of the old diplomacy it was truly a naïve enterprise; as unlike traditional European methods as shirt-sleeved Americans could make it" (II, 207).

Prof. Henry A. Foster in *The Making of Modern Iraq* makes the statement that "the King-Crane commission's first hand study would be a great satisfaction to the Americans, especially to Wilson, as well as to liberals everywhere. It was a procedure called for by the accepted principle of self-determination, and opposition to it by the British and the French indicated that they entertained fears as to the results" (p. 90).

Frank E. Manuel in *The Realities of American-Palestine Relations* (Washington, 1949) seems to sum up well the Zionist view when he accuses the King-Crane commission of bending to the influence of American Protestant missionaries in the Middle East (p. 239), all pro-Arab and anti-Zionist. "The final King-Crane Report," writes Dr. Manuel, "presented on August 28, 1919, was in the same spirit as the rather puerile telegrams" sent by King and Crane to President Wilson from Palestine, attesting to the bitter anti-Zionist feeling of the Arabs (p. 249). Dr. Manuel's view of the "puerility" of such objections finds another expression in his statement that "Wilson's Zionism had hit up against the wall of self-determination of peoples which meant the counting of heads" (p. 223).

Britain. In Wilson's absence the crusading spirit for self-determination ceased to be very conspicuous in the American delegation. The delegation had no desire to pick a quarrel with the British or the French over what seemed to be a minor issue. Wilson's absence, his domestic difficulties, and the resulting indifference in the American delegation left the field open for France, Great Britain, and the Zionists, all of whom were eager in greater or lesser degree to see the wartime agreements fulfilled. Britain, of course, had to choose between her pledges to the Arabs on the one hand and her promises to France and the Zionists on the other. Despite animosity toward and various differences with the French, the British were anxious to preserve French friendship and were unwilling to sacrifice the major interest of Anglo-French harmony to the minor interest of keeping Arab good will. Once this choice was made, there was no basic obstacle to satisfying the Zionists, who did not relax their efforts to secure a favorable solution.

Faisal's second appearance before the Allied Supreme Council in the fall of 1919 did not make a great impression on anybody. But, because of uncertainty as to the ultimate degree of America's participation in world affairs, the European powers did not press for an immediate assignment of mandates. The matter was delayed until the spring of 1920. By that time the Covenant of the League of Nations had become a ratified instrument and could serve as a formal basis. By that time also the American Senate had definitely repudiated all Wilsonian arrangements and had caused the United States to withdraw from an active role in the peace settlement.

The San Remo Conference

On April 24, 1920, the Peace Conference met at San Remo. There the European statesmen signed an agreement on the mandates. France was given Syria, Great Britain was assigned a mandate for Iraq and Palestine. These were all class "A" mandates, which, as outlined in the Covenant, meant that the tutelage of the mandatory powers was only temporary and was to lead to ultimate independence of the areas in question. The mandate for Palestine (made formal by an agreement between Great Britain and the League of Nations only on September 23, 1922) incorporated the Balfour Declaration. The Wilsonian principle of self-determination was thus rejected. No American delegates were present. To be sure, the American ambassador in Rome, Robert Underwood Johnson (in private life a poet and author of the ballad "Oh to Be in Paris, Now That Pershing's There") did come to San Remo. He appeared, however, to be uninformed on the issues at stake and was severely handicapped by the failure of instructions from Washington to arrive in time. "For two days the representative of the United States sat in a hotel garden reading the newspapers while the British and French settled the most important matters affecting the Middle East."[9]

The San Remo conference solved another important problem as well, the division of oil resources in Mesopotamia. In December 1918, before the Peace Conference, Clemenceau and Lloyd George had agreed to the transfer of Mosul from the French to the British sphere of influence. In return, Britain had promised France a share in

[9]Edgar A. Mowrer, *The Nightmare of American Foreign Policy* (New York, 1948), p. 51.

the Mosul oil deposits. Before the war a concession covering these deposits had been granted by the Ottoman government to the Turkish Petroleum Company. The company was 75 percent British and 25 percent German. On April 18, 1919, M. Berenger, on behalf of France, and Mr. Walter (later Lord) Long, on behalf of Great Britain, signed an agreement by which France was to receive the former German share and to permit the construction of a pipeline across the French mandated area from Mosul to the Mediterranean. This agreement could not, however, be regarded as final as long as the mandates were not officially assigned. The Berenger-Long agreement also contained clauses concerning the division of oil resources in other parts of the world, but those are beyond the scope of this discussion. At San Remo, on April 25, France and Great Britain confirmed that part of the Berenger-Long agreement which pertained to the Middle East. France was to receive a 25 percent share in the Turkish Petroleum Company and to permit transport of oil by rail or pipeline from Mesopotamia and Iran through Syria.

The San Remo agreements concluded that phase of the Peace Conference which pertained to the postwar settlement of the Arab portions of the Ottoman Empire. The Treaty of Sèvres, concluded soon afterward with Turkey, was the first public document to state officially that Syria and Mesopotamia were provisionally recognized "as independent states subject to the rendering of administrative advice and assistance by a Mandatory until such time as they are able to stand alone."

This was the formal settlement. It had to be carried out in practice, and it was here that complications arose. The Arabs of Syria, Mesopotamia, and Palestine objected to the imposition of foreign control and believed the whole arrangement to be a betrayal of the Wilsonian principles. Their resentment was manifested violently in all three areas. In each, however, this resentment followed a different course.

Settlement in Syria

In Syria, it will be remembered, Emir Faisal acted as a military governor at Damascus during the interim period following the end of the war. His leadership of the Arab national movement was universally recognized in Syria. The Syrians viewed him as their future ruler and made this clear to the King-Crane commission. At the time that the commission was touring Syria, a national Syrian conference was in session in Damascus. It voiced demands for complete independence. The Syrians expected from Faisal a strong stand in Paris and put considerable pressure on him to be uncompromising. Faisal found himself in the very delicate position of being pressed in Europe for an understanding with the French and the Zionists and of being pulled in exactly the opposite direction back in Damascus. He might have realized that Syrian intransigence was unrealistic, yet he knew that to concede to Western pressure would be tantamount to losing his popularity and leadership among the Arabs. Therefore, upon returning from his second visit to the Peace Conference (in the fall of 1919) Faisal decided to identify himself with the nationalist party, irrespective of the more or less formal understandings reached in Paris with the French and the Zionists. Having taken this stand, he grew in popularity, and in March 1920 the Syrian National Congress which met in Damascus proclaimed him king of Syria. The Congress, it may be added, claimed to represent the whole of Greater Syria, i.e., it included Palestine and Transjordan.[10]

This bold course contrasted sharply with the reality of the military situation in Syria, which was definitely becoming disadvantageous to the Arabs. Back in November 1919, the British, in fulfillment of their wartime promises to the French, had begun to evacuate the coastal area of Syria. French forces, under General Gouraud, replaced them. For a few months a tense situation prevailed between Faisal's Arab forces in Damascus and Gouraud's administration in Beirut. A provisional *modus vivendi* was finally reached, by which the French tacitly recognized Faisal's rule in the hinterland and refrained from advancing beyond Baalbek. It is a matter of speculation whether or not greater restraint on Faisal's part would have permitted him to retain direct control of the Syrian hinterland under French suzerainty. But no restraint was shown. Faisal's acceptance of the Syrian crown in the spring of 1920 appeared to the French as a direct threat to their rights in Syria. A few armed clashes between the Arab and the French outposts in the border areas added to the deterioration of relations, and in July General Gouraud decided to undertake military action against Faisal. In a swift operation the French defeated the Arabs, who attempted to barricade the road to Damascus. On August 7, 1920, General Gouraud entered the Syrian capital and deposed the king. Faisal took refuge in British-controlled Palestine. France had become supreme in Syria.

Settlement in Mesopotamia

The situation in Mesopotamia also proved explosive. Mesopotamia, like Syria, had experienced a revival of nationalism, and a number of prominent Iraqi families, such as the Gailanis, the Omaris, and the Suweidis, played an important part in the Arab national movement before and during the First World War.[11]

When the war came, many Iraqis actively supported the British in the hope of obtaining independence for their country. There were uprisings against the Turks at Nejef, Kerbela, Hilla, Kufa, and Tuweirij in 1915 and 1916. Some Iraqi officers in the Turkish army, such as Nuri es-Said, offered their services to the British and many of them eventually entered the Hejazi army to serve either on Faisal's staff or as field commanders. In fact, the number of Iraqis in the Sherifian service was considerable. The service was a school of active Arab nationalism, and it played an important role in Arab political awakening. The year 1919 was characterized by ferment and growth of anti-British feelings in Faisal's army. The revelation of secret wartime deals among the Allies, the promises to the Zionists, and above all, the possibility of losing Syria to the French combined to produce restiveness and political extremism among the Arab officers in Damascus. In Baghdad, this opposition was directed by a nationalist society of Iraqi Covenanters (El-Ahd el-Iraqiya) in which the Iraqi officers of Faisal's army often played a leading role. When, on

[10]On this stage of Syria's history, consult Philippe David, *Un Gouvernement Arabe à Damas: Le Congrès Syrien* (Paris, 1923), p. 63.

[11]In particular, Abdur Rahman el-Gailani, naqib of Baghdad, and his son, Sayid Mahmud el-Gailani; Rashid el-Omari of Mosul; Sayid Talib Pasha, son of the naqib of Basra; and Tewfik es-Suweidi.

March 8, 1920, the Syrian National Congress met in Damascus to offer the crown to Emir Faisal, the Iraqi Covenanters were instrumental in producing a resolution by which the rule of Iraq was offered to Faisal's elder brother, Emir Abdullah.

The high-pitched nationalism of Faisal's Iraqi officers coincided with the growth of discontent in Mesopotamia against British rule. Here British policy was not consistent. On the one hand, it was imperialistic. Political officers attached to the Mesopotamian expeditionary force, as members of the Indian Political Service, wanted Mesopotamia to be an extension of the British Empire in India and distrusted any manifestation of Arab nationalism. They viewed British Cairo policy in support of Hussein's ambitions as a dangerous playing with fire. They delayed the publication of Wilson's Fourteen Points for more than ten months. They regarded with dismay the influence of Faisal's Iraqi officers on popular attitudes in Mesopotamia. On the other hand, much against their will, they had to follow certain instructions from London, which reflected the liberal American trend. Thus, for example, Arnold Wilson (acting civil commissioner during Cox's mission to Teheran) was instructed in 1918–1919 to organize a "plebiscite" in order to ascertain whether the people desired a single Iraqi state under British tutelage, and, if so, which among the leading Arabs could qualify to serve as ruler. Obviously, such questioning implied deference to popular will, whetted the nationalist appetites, and contrasted with the otherwise imperialist line followed by the British civil administration in Baghdad. The latter, in contrast to the British mission with Faisal, did not act in an advisory but in an outright administrative capacity. Its members brought their families to Mesopotamia and believed that they were to remain for good. Meanwhile the nationalist movement was gaining in strength. Encouraged by the example of an independent Arab government at Damascus, Faisal's Iraqi officers demanded the immediate establishment of a similar government at Baghdad. Even the traditional religious differences between the Shiis and the Sunnis were temporarily forgotten, and a mixed front of both sects came into being in 1919–1920.

The assignment of mandates at San Remo was the spark that started the conflagration. On May 3, 1920, two British officers were killed in one of Mesopotamia's provincial towns, and by the first of July the whole country was in the throes of rebellion. The British had over 130,000 troops in Mesopotamia, but even this number did not suffice to restore order. Reinforcements had to be sent, and not until October 1920 was the insurrection quelled. Britain's losses amounted to nearly 2,500 casualties and caused a further drain on her war-strained treasury. But Britain's will prevailed and, as in Syria, the people of Mesopotamia were compelled to accept a peace settlement imposed by outside forces. The return of Sir Percy Cox in October 1920 and the inauguration of a more cautious policy, by which former British executives became advisers to the hand-picked Iraqi government, did not change the realities of the situation.

Settlement in Palestine

Finally, a word must be added about the enforcement of the decision of the big powers on Palestine. Palestine was subjected to a fervent nationalist propaganda emanating from Damascus. The people responded to it eagerly. The Palestinians desired Arab unity and, in particular, unity with Syria. The handing over of Syria to French military control meant that their desires were to be disregarded and that Arab lands were to be carved up and assigned to different rulers. Moreover, Palestine had to face Zionism. Under these circumstances, opposition to the Allied schemes became rampant, and in April 1920 anti-Jewish disturbances broke out in Jerusalem and Jaffa. A total of about fifty Jewish victims suffered its consequences. The outbreak gave a foretaste of a long series of riots that were to mark the stromy history of Palestine for the next thirty years. These disturbances did not, however, deflect Britain's determination to pursue her own policy. On April 24, the mandate for Palestine and Transjordan was assigned to Great Britain, and on July, 1, 1920, the military government gave way to a civil administration. Sir Herbert Samuel became the first British commissioner there. He set himself promptly to the task of implementing the Balfour Declaration, and in September set the first quota for Jewish immigration at 16,500.

Thus, by superior force Great Britain and France succeeded in overcoming opposition and in enforcing the decisions of the Peace Conference upon the Arab countries. Of the two, Britain's task was more difficult. Apart from Egypt, she controlled three different areas—Iraq, Palestine, and Transjordan. She felt the need of formulating some long-range policy toward these areas, a policy which would be less costly and more subtle than military occupation and which, in the long run, would correspond to the vital requirements of British political strategy in the East.

Final Arrangements: Deals with the Hashemites

To devise a unified policy for the whole region, London created a Middle East Department in December 1920. It was placed under the Colonial Office, at that time headed by Winston Churchill. The colonial secretary convoked a general British conference on Middle Eastern affairs, which met in Cairo, March 12–24, 1921. It was presided over by Churchill himself, and attended by Sir Percy Cox and Sir Herbert Samuel, high commissioners for Iraq and Palestine, respectively, and by a galaxy of prominent British Arabists, such as Lawrence, Clayton, Cornwallis, Gertrude Bell, and others.

This Cairo conference made the following decisions: The kingship of Iraq was to be offered to the deposed king of Syria, Faisal. Abdullah, Faisal's elder brother, was to be offered the emirate of Transjordan. In order to appease Iraqi nationalism the mandate was to be replaced by a treaty of alliance, which would be concluded with Faisal upon his advent to the throne.

Simple as these decisions may appear, they required the consent of both Faisal and Abdullah. Faisal had been approached by the British government as early as December 1920, during his visit to London. To the initial offer of the Iraqi throne he reacted negatively because of Abdullah's right to Iraq. Consequently Colonel Lawrence was entrusted with the task of persuading Abdullah to renounce his rights in favor of Faisal. Abdullah was at that time in Maan, east of Jordan, where he had arrived at the head of a body of Hejazi troops following Faisal's expulsion from Damascus. He was making plans for an armed incursion into Syria in order to avenge his brother and, if possible, to restore him to power. Despite his belligerent attitude, he raised no major objections to Faisal's candidacy for Iraq. Subsequently, Faisal was approached once again, and this time he accepted the offer. After the Cairo conference, Churchill went to Jerusalem, where he reached an agreement with Abdullah by which Britain would endeavor to obtain from France a liberalization of her policy in Syria in order that an Arab government under Emir Abdullah might be established in Damascus. Pending these negotiations, Abdullah was to administer, with British assistance and a subsidy, the area east of Jordan. As it happened, however, France was in no mood to change her policy in Syria and what was initially conceived as a temporary arrangement acquired all the features of permanency in the form of the emirate of Transjordan.

With the path thus cleared, all that remained was to bring Faisal to Mesopotamia and to have him accepted there as ruler. This was done and on July 11, 1921, the Council of State (an Arab body in Baghdad) declared him king of Iraq.

Thus, by 1921 the foundations for the new order in the Arab Middle East were laid. Despite the Wilsonian ideology of self-determination and despite American intervention in Paris, the new peace was imperialistic in character and corresponded in the main to the major wartime agreements. Yet for the Arabs it was not exactly a change from old to new masters. True enough, the new settlement did not fulfill the Arab political program as conceived in 1915. Nevertheless, it marked an important advance toward eventual emancipation. With the acceptance of the principle of mandates, the big powers had to pay at least lip service to self-determination and to international responsibility. Furthermore, active and violent opposition to the new system, manifested in Syria, Iraq, and Palestine, revealed new, deeply stirred forces of nationalism which the West, in the long run, would no longer be able to disregard and with which, as in the case of Iraq, it would be obliged to compromise.

Peace Settlement in Turkey

It was the intention of the victorious Allies to impose a new settlement upon Turkey without consulting her. Turkey was a defeated enemy. Her territory had been subject to wartime partition agreements. And, in contrast to the Arabs, there was no direct moral or political commitment to respect her territorial integrity. True enough, Point Twelve of Wilson's Fourteen Points had proclaimed that "the Turkish portions of the present Ottoman Empire should be assured a secure sovereignty," and in his speech on January 5, 1918, Lloyd George had stated, on behalf of Great Britain, that she was not fighting "to deprive Turkey of its capital or of the rich and renowned lands of Thrace, which are predominatly Turkish in race."[12] Both statesmen insisted upon freedom of navigation in the Straits under international control. But these pronouncements lacked precision and could hardly be construed as a guarantee that Anatolia, i.e., Turkey proper, would be left untouched. Early in the Peace Conference it became clear that the Armenians, then in favor of the Allies, would insist upon the inclusion of eastern portions of Anatolia in their newly proclaimed republic.

[12]Temperley, *op. cit.*, I, 190.

To study the problem of Armenia, President Wilson appointed a commission under Major-General James G. Harbord. The commission visited Asia Minor and in October 1919 recommended that there be a single mandatory power over Turkey and Transcaucasia, because of certain economic and ethnic considerations involved. Suggestions that the United States become a mandatory power over the Straits, Constantinople, Anatolia, and Armenia were repeatedly made by the British and other statesmen during the conference, but to no avail. President Wilson hesitated to assume any military responsibilities over the Turks with whom the United States had not been at war. The mandate idea was rejected.

Russia's absence from the conference tables (as well as her renunciation of secret agreements)[13] complicated the task of the Entente. Turkey, despite her defeat in the south at the hands of the British, was not encircled by an iron ring of victorious enemies. The Allies could assert their will in Constantinople, in the Straits, and in the Arab and south Anatolian portions of the Empire. But the center of Anatolia and its northeastern marches remained free from foreign pressure, and instead of hostile, land-grabbing tsarist Russia, Turkey faced there the revolutionary Soviets, which were hostile to the West and separated from Turkey proper by three weak Transcaucasian republics.

Under such circumstances, the Western powers might make more or less fantastic and elaborate plans as to how to implement the partition treaties, but they had to face the reality that their control of defeated Turkey was not complete. This discrepancy led to dramatic developments. On the one hand, the Allies arrived at various decisions concerning the disposal of Anatolia. These decisions, made partly in Paris and partly at San Remo in the course of 1919-1920, resulted in the Treaty of Sèvres, August 10, 1920, between the Allies and the Ottoman government.[14] But a number of political and military events occurred in Turkey, which threw Allied plans into confusion. These events rendered the Treaty of Sèvres a dead letter and resulted in a total revision of the peace settlement.

The Treaty of Sèvres

The Treaty of Sèvres was an embodiment of imperialism. Its main provisions were:

1. *Territorial clauses*
    a. *Arab lands.* Turkey was deprived of all the Arab portions of her Empire. The kingdom of Hejaz obtained recognition as an independent state. Turkey also renounced control of Syria, Palestine, and Mesopotamia, whose destinies were to be decided by the principal Allied powers.
    b. *Turkey in Europe.* Eastern Thrace was ceded to Greece up to the Chatalja line. Greece simultaneously received from the Allies Western Thrace (previously ceded to them by Bulgaria). She thus advanced her boundary to within twenty miles of the Turkish capital.
    c. *Smyrna and the Aegean islands.* The town and district of Smyrna were

---

[13]Made by the Provisional government in April 1917 and repeated—with more gusto and publicity—by the Bolshevik government upon its advent to power.

[14]The text is in *The Treaties of Peace, 1919-1923* (New York, 1924), II, 789 ff.

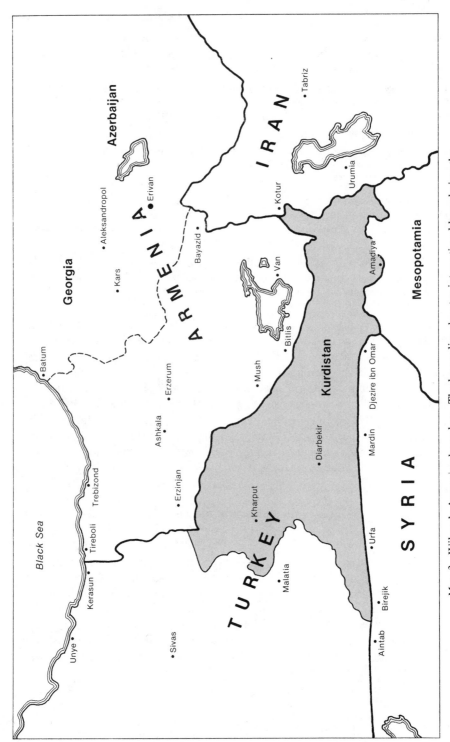

Map 3. Wilson's Armenian boundary. The heavy line denotes international boundaries; the broken line, the annulled boundary; and the shaded area, the plebiscite area.

placed under Greek administration for a period of five years, after which the population was allowed to request, by plebiscite, permanent incorporation into the kingdom of Greece. The islands of Imbros and Tenedos were ceded to Greece, and Greek sovereignty was recognized over a number of other Aegean islands. The Dodecanese Islands including the strategic Rhodes were ceded to Italy.

  d. Armenia. Turkey recognized Armenia as an independent state, and consented to accept President Wilson's arbitration with regard to the boundary between the two states.

  e. Kurdistan. Turkey agreed to grant the Kurdish area east of Euphrates local autonomy and to accept any scheme to this effect submitted by an international commission composed of the British, French, and Italian representatives. Turkey agreed also to accept modifications of her frontier with Iran in the Kurdish region. Moreover, Article 64 of the treaty stated:

If within one year from the coming into force of the present Treaty the Kurdish peoples shall address themselves to the Council of the League of Nations in such a manner as to show that a majority of the population of these areas desires independence from Turkey, and if the Council then considers that these peoples are capable of such independence and recommends that it should be granted to them, Turkey hereby agrees to execute such a recommendation and to renounce all rights and title over these areas.

The detailed provisions for such renunciation will form the subject of a separate agreement between the Principal Allied Powers and Turkey.

If and when such renunciation takes place, no objection will be raised by the Principal Allied Powers to the voluntary adhesion to such an independent Kurdish State of the Kurds inhabiting that part of Kurdistan which has hitherto been included in the Mosul vilayet.

  f. The Straits and Constantinople. Turkey agreed to international control of the Straits, and to demilitarization of adjacent zones.[15] Constantinople was to remain under Turkish sovereignty.

2. *Limitations of Turkish sovereignty*

  a. Limitation of armed forces. The Turkish army was to be limited to 50,000 men. Compulsory military service was to be abolished, and a limit was put on the armaments. The army was to be subject to the advice of Allied or neutral states. The navy was not to exceed a certain fixed maximum. Allied commissions of control were authorized to supervise the execution of these clauses.

  b. Financial clauses. Turkey agreed to accept far-reaching control by a financial commission representing Britain, France, and Italy. This commission was to have wide powers of control and supervision over the Ottoman public debt, the Turkish state budget, currency, public loans and concessions, customs, and indirect taxes. With regard to the last item, the commission's powers were to be executive in character.

  c. The capitulations. The capitulations were maintained in force, and from the Turkish standpoint, new, humiliating provisions were added.

[15]For more details, see below, Chapter XVIII.

    d. *The minorities.* Turkey accepted various clauses which compelled her to respect the rights and privileges of national and religious minorities, in particular of the Armenians, Greeks, Assyro-Chaldeans, Kurds, and Christians in general.

Simultaneously with the Treaty of Sèvres a tripartite treaty was concluded between Great Britain, France, and Italy. It provided for the division of Turkish territory into French and Italian spheres of influence. The French sphere corresponded exactly to the zone assigned to France by the Sykes-Picot agreement. The Italian zone covered the areas assigned to Italy in southwestern Anatolia according to two wartime agreements (London and St. Jean de Maurienne) minus the region of Smyrna. It also extended somewhat beyond these wartime limits in the northwestern sector. Turkey was not a party to this agreement, hence was not legally bound by it. Politically, however, the agreement affected her directly, since it represented an attempt to fulfill the wartime partition schemes. It could, therefore, not be divorced from the Sèvres Treaty and thus must be considered as part of a larger whole.

The Treaty of Sèvres thoroughly humiliated Turkey and reduced her to the status of a minor state whose territory was small and whose sovereignty was subject to limitations amounting to a virtual protectorate. It is no wonder that resentment resulted. Some observers[16] believe that, despite these humiliations, the war-weary Turks would have accepted any dictated settlement had it not been for the last drop in the cup of bitterness, the Greek invasion.

The Greek Invasion and the War of Independence

The arrangement whereby Greece was authorized by the Supreme Allied Council to occupy Smyrna and the adjacent region has already been mentioned. This operation, as was pointed out, was a part of the bargain between Greece and the Allies and was considered both as compensation for the wartime services rendered by Greece and as an additional safeguard of the maritime routes of Great Britain. It might be added here that, in addition to these considerations, it was believed in Paris that Greek contingents in Turkey would partially fill the gap created by the defection of Russia.

The Greek landing in Smyrna (May 15, 1919) acted as a powerful stimulant for Turkish action. The Turks might have surrendered to and endured Western dictation, but the thought of being invaded and occupied by the Greeks was revolting. The Turks traditionally considered the Greeks a subject race and simply could not stomach the reversal of roles. Strong resentment against Greece was manifested soon after the landing of Greek troops, i.e., long before the Treaty of Sèvres. The treaty, which formally recognized Greek territorial claims, added to the general disillusionment and intensified the revisionist action.

In this moment of crisis the Turkish nation was fortunate in finding a leader of exceptional ability and strength of will in the person of General Mustafa Kemal Pasha. Following the last stages of the Syrian campaign, Kemal found himself in

---

[16]Such as Temperley, *op. cit.,* VI, 45–46.

Constantinople, bitter and critical both of the Allies and of the impotent Ottoman government. By an almost miraculous set of circumstances, he was appointed, in May 1919, inspector general of the Third Army in eastern Anatolia. He took a boat and on May 19 landed in Samsun, a date which is now a Turkish national holiday. Soon after he left the capital, the government, yielding to Allied suspicions, issued orders recalling him. It was, however, too late. Kemal appeared in eastern Anatolia determined to save the nation from foreign bondage. He refused to obey the recall orders and proceeded to assert his undisputable authority over what was left of the Turkish army in the region under his control. He then launched an intensive propaganda campaign appealing to the national pride of the Turks. Energetic and resourceful, Kemal succeeded in arousing the nation. Two national congresses were held under his leadership, in Erzerum and Sivas in July and September of 1919, respectively. The Erzerum congress resulted in the establishment of "the League for the Defense of Rights in East Anatolia," later to become a full-fledged political party. These congresses were followed by the convocation, on April 23, 1920, of the first Grand National Assembly in Ankara, at that time a small town in the arid part of Anatolia. Attended by many deputies to the Ottoman parliament and a number of other delegates, the Assembly challenged the authority of the sultan's government in Constantinople, declaring that the government was a virtual prisoner of the Allies and could not make binding decisions for Turkey. Earlier, on January 28, 1920, a group of nationalist deputies to the Ottoman parliament had drawn up in Constantinople a six-point program which was subsequently adopted as the National Pact by the Assembly at Ankara. Its six articles included:
1. Recognition of self-determination for the Arabs with a corresponding demand of freedom and unity for those parts of the Empire "which are inhabited by an Ottoman Moslem majority" (i.e., a Turkish or Kurdish majority).
2. Acceptance of a plebiscite for the three sanjaks of Batum, Kars, and Ardahan.
3. Acceptance of a plebiscite for Western Thrace.
4. A demand for the security of Constantinople as the seat of the caliphate and of the sultanate and, if this demand was recognized, consent to an international regime for the Straits.
5. Acceptance of international protection of minorities on condition that reciprocal protection be given to "Moslem minorities in neighboring countries."
6. Demand for complete political and economic independence, with an implicit rejection of the capitulations.[17]

These articles represented a formal political program. To implement it, Kemal had recourse to military action and to diplomacy. Militarily he was in a weak but not a desperate position. He had control over the forces of eastern Anatolia, which included the famous Ninth Army of the Caucasus. The latter had never been defeated; in fact, the armistice found it in the flush of victory after it had successfully reached the Caspian Sea. Its morale was high. These forces were reinforced by over 130,000 Turkish prisoners of war, released by the Allies after the Treaty of Sèvres. By the force of his personality and his organizing genius, Kemal succeeded in

[17]The full text is in Temperley, *op. cit.*, VI, 605.

welding these elements together into a new army, imbued with patriotic spirit and eager, despite nine years of wars, to fight for independence. He had to face five enemies: the Armenians in the east, the French in Cilicia, the Italians in Adalia, the Greeks in Smyrna, and the British in Constantinople. His first offensive operation took place in Cilicia. Early in 1920 his armies attacked the French and by spring had succeeded in ejecting them from the ethnic Turkish areas toward Aleppo. The French, faced with new responsibilities in Syria and desirous of putting an end to Faisal's influence, were content to conclude an armistice with Kemal on May 30, 1920, in Ankara. This permitted him to concentrate his forces on the Armenian front.

The situation in Armenia requires a brief explanation. It will be remembered that by the Treaty of Sèvres the Armenian Republic (originally founded in the former Russian province of Erivan) had enlarged its territory at the expense of Turkey. President Wilson, authorized by the treaty to fix the boundary, awarded Armenia in 1920 a large portion of Turkish territory, which included Trebizond, Erzerum, Mush, and Van. This new territory virtually covered the area which early in the war had been assigned to tsarist Russia in the secret treaties. Its population was predominantly Turkish, and Kemal was determined to wrest it from the rather nominal control of Armenia. Free from French pressure in Cilicia, the Turks under the command of General Kiazim Kara Bekir advanced against the Armenians, and in October 1920 captured Kars. Armenia was simultaneously attacked by the Bolsheviks,[18] who conquered Erivan and installed there a Communist government. By the Treaty of Alexandropol,[19] December 3, 1920, this government ceded to the Turks major portions of its western territory, which included the fortresses of Kars and Ardahan.

Thus, by the end of 1920 Kemal's nationalists had disposed of the French and Armenian danger in the east and could concentrate on the major task in western Anatolia—the expulsion of the Greeks. Before engaging in these decisive operations, Kemal settled three important problems of foreign policy. First, on March 13, 1921, he concluded an agreement with Italy whereby the latter agreed to evacuate Anatolia in return for extensive economic concessions. By June there were no more Italian troops on Turkish soil.

Second, on March 16 Kemal signed a treaty of friendship and collaboration with Soviet Russia. The treaty settled the vexatious boundary problem; Turkey agreed to cede Batum to Russia, in return for which Russia recognized Turkish possession of Kars and Ardahan, thus confirming the Treaty of Alexandropol.[20] Even more important was a pledge of political collaboration directed against the imperialist West. The treaty gave formal endorsement to the already existing military cooperation between the two countries. Following her victory over the White forces of General Denikin in April 1920, Soviet Russia had steadily supplied the Kemalists with weapons and munitions. The operations against Armenia, as we have seen, had been conducted

---

[18]For further details, see below, p. 109.

[19]In Turkish "Gümrü," at present "Leninakan."

[20]This was later confirmed once again by the Treaty of Kars, October 13, 1921, concluded between Turkey and the Soviet Transcaucasian Federation.

simultaneously by the Turks and the Soviets. Moreover, the wiping out of the independent Armenian Republic permitted both parties to establish a land junction and greatly facilitated a further flow of supplies from Russia.

Third, on October 20, 1921, Kemal made a deal with France. Known as the Franklin-Bouillon agreement after the French plenipotentiary who negotiated it in Ankara, this instrument provided for the final evacuation of Cilicia by the French in return for favorable economic concessions. This seemingly benevolent French behavior was not difficult to explain. Since French troops had already suffered defeat at the hands of the Turks, the agreement did not bring about a material change in the military situation. Moreover France, at that time, was not hesitant in embarrassing Great Britain. The two former allies were gradually falling apart, especially in their Middle Eastern policies, and France was profoundly irritated by what seemed to her the adventurous British support of the Greeks. Greek victory in western Anatolia would mean British ascendancy in the Aegean Sea and consequent British domination of the Turkish Straits. This went counter to French views. Under these circumstances, France was only too glad to reduce her inconvenient military commitments in Cilicia and thus render it easier for Kemal to continue his war against the Greek invaders.

Having thus secured Soviet assistance and neutralized French and Italian hostility, Kemal concentrated all his strength on the Greek war. His task was not easy. Thirteen months after their landing in Smyrna, the Greeks in June 1920 undertook an offensive into the interior of Anatolia. Before long they were in control of the Ismid region, and from there they pushed eastward. Taking advantage of Kemal's preoccupation with the Armenian front, the Greeks scored several victories, including the capture of Bursa. The winter provided a temporary lull in the operations, only to be followed by a renewed Greek offensive in March 1921. Taking Afyonkarahisar and Eskisehir, the Greeks captured Kutaia and drew dangerously close to Ankara. The bloody battle of the Sakaria River, August 24 to September 16, turned the tide in favor of the Turks. Still there was a long road ahead, and it was not until August 1922 that a decisive Turkish offensive was undertaken. Once started, the offensive was a dazzling success. Within two weeks the Turks drove the Greek army back to the Mediterranean Sea. On September 11 they took Smyrna, vented their vengeance on the Greek population, and compelled the Greek army to escape on the ships available in the harbor. Master of the major part of Anatolia, Kemal turned now toward Constantinople to achieve complete liberation of Turkish territory.

The Treaty of Lausanne

Alarmed by the Greek defeat and the Kemalist threat, Lloyd George on September 15 sent out an appeal to the Allies to defend the Straits. The response from France and Italy was negative. The next day a British contingent under General Harington landed at Chanak, on the Asiatic side of the Dardanelles. Kemalist forces approached, and for a brief tense period it looked as if Britain and Turkey were to be again at war. Both parties, however, manifested remarkable restraint. The Convention of Mudania, concluded on October 11 between Kemal and the Allies, put an end to this undeclared state of war. The convention provided for the return of Eastern Thrace and Adrianople to the Turks, while Kemal accepted a proposal for international control of the Straits. The road was paved for a comprehensive discussion of all peace problems. On November 20, 1922, a peace conference was opened at Lausanne. The two main protagonists, Lord Curzon and General Ismet Pasha, had many heated disputes over controversial issues. Ismet stubbornly insisted on the inclusion of Mosul in Turkey and on the abolition of capitulations, two points unacceptable to Curzon. For two months the conference was suspended, but in April it was resumed, and on July 24, 1923, the parties signed the Treaty of Lausanne.[21] The name covered the treaty itself as well as additional instruments such as the convention of the Straits, the Turco-Greek agreement about an exchange of populations, and various annexes and minor agreements. Its provisions included:

1. *Territorial clauses.* The integrity of ethnic Turkey was recognized, and the separation of Arab lands was confirmed. Turkey regained Eastern Thrace up to the Maritza River and the town of Karagach on its western bank. The islands of Imbros and Tenedos were restored to her, but other Aegean islands went to Greece. Italian possession of the Dodecanese and British possession of Cyprus were confirmed. No mention was made of Armenia, which meant an implicit recognition of the Turkish-Soviet treaties concerning the Transcaucasian border. Smyrna was restored to Turkey as an integral part of Anatolia. The boundary with Syria was to follow the line fixed by the Franklin-Bouillon agreement of October 20, 1921, which meant exclusion from Turkish territory of the sanjak of Alexandretta. The boundary with Iraq was left to future agreement between Great Britain as the mandatory power and Turkey. If such an agreement failed to materialize within a year, the parties promised to accept arbitration by the League of Nations. In the meantime, the status quo was to prevail; i.e., the Mosul area was to be under British-Iraqi jurisdiction. The problem of independence or autonomy for Kurdistan was not mentioned.

2. *Limitations of sovereignty.* In comparison with this aspect of the humiliating Treaty of Sèvres, the Treaty of Lausanne was a victory for Turkey. Capitulations were abolished, and in return Turkey agreed to accept neutral observers of her judicial system, with purely nominal powers. She was freed from foreign economic and financial control and from any Allied claim to reparations. No limit was placed on the size of her military and naval establishment, but she was to demilitarize a zone thirty kilometers wide along the Thracian border. Turkey accepted the standard treaties to protect minorities, such as were devised for certain European nations at the Paris Peace Conference. No specific mention was made either of Greeks or of the Armenians in this respect, and the antiquated millet system was implicitly abandoned.

3. *The Straits.* The one major limitation of Turkish sovereignty was on control of the Straits, which were to be internationalized. But even here Turkey notably improved her position. The new Straits convention provided for an international commission presided over by a Turkish citizen under the auspices of the League of Nations. A limited freedom of navigation through the Straits was proclaimed,[22] and

---

[21]The text is in *The Treaties of Peace, 1919–1923,* II, 959 ff.
[22]For more details, see Chapter XVIII.

four demilitarized zones on the European and Asiatic shores of the Bosphorous and the Dardanelles were established. Islands in the Sea of Marmara were also demilitarized. Turkey was allowed, however, a garrison of 12,000 troops in Constantinople as well as freedom of transit for her troops across the specified neutral zones.

4. *Exchange of populations.* A separate Greco-Turkish agreement provided for compulsory exchange of the Greek minority living in Turkey and the Turkish minority living in Greece. Greeks in Constantinople and Turks in Western Thrace were excluded from this transfer.[23]

The Treaty of Lausanne was a signal victory for the Turkish nationalists. By signing it, Kemal's government obtained formal international recognition and buried forever the remnants of Ottoman tradition. It fulfilled, in the main, the program outlined in the National Pact of Ankara. Turkey regained her independence and secured the unity of her ethnic territory. She threw off the shackles of foreign control in judicial, military, and economic matters. She emerged from this ordeal with her national pride restored, enjoying a new and progressive leadership, impoverished but confident in the future, and homogeneous in population. The Treaty of Lausanne was a difficult one to draft, but inasmuch as it was a freely negotiated and not an imposed treaty, it provided a sounder foundation for peace in the Middle East than had its ill-fated predecessor.

This feature of free-negotiation was purchased at a heavy price of bloodshed and human suffering. But the peace settlement as it emerged in relation to Turkey was quite different from the settlement in the Arab portions of the defunct Ottoman Empire. In both cases the original intention of the European powers was to impose upon these areas an imperialistic peace which would subject them to semicolonial rule and which would conform to the wartime partition agreements. In both cases, however, there was a native revolt against these schemes. But whereas the Arabs, divided and ill-prepared, did not succeed, the Turks succeeded beyond all expectations. The West imposed its will, under the form of the mandatory system, upon the Arabs but saw its designs frustrated by the tough resolution of the Turks. In the long run, such a turn of events was to serve the real interests of the West. A healthy and strong Turkey in two decades was to become a bulwark protecting world peace against the destructive inroads of modern totalitarian states.

[23]This agreement was greatly criticized during and after the conference for its inhumanitarian surgery, but it should be borne in mind that the bitterness engendered as a result of the Greek invasion of Anatolia made any other solution impracticable. Moreover, the exodus of thousands of Greek civilians in the wake of the Greek military evacuation of Smyrna was already an accomplished fact, which was followed and not created by the agreement. The exchange affected approximately 1,500,000 Greeks and 500,000 Turks. To Turkey it proved to be something of a blessing, since it eliminated from her territory a minority of questionable loyalty and vacated many professions and trades for younger Turkish intellectuals. There was, no doubt, an immediate economic loss resulting from the disappearance of a commercially skilled element of the population, but it was not a loss which, in the long run, could not be compensated by native forces. Furthermore, Turkey could fill certain depopulated areas with the Turkish deportees from Greece—an operation not without definite advantages. To Greece the forcible exchange was a tragic episode. The newly arrived refugees and deportees constituted about one-fifth of the total Greek population and proved to be both an economic burden and a chronic source of unrest in turbulent Greek politics during the interwar period. In human terms the suffering was incalculable, and the ruination of the once prosperous Greek colony of Asia Minor was complete. Such was the sad harvest reaped from Venizelos' adventure in 1919.

The Aftermath of War in Caucasia and Central Asia

Although hostilities between the Entente and the Central powers ended in October-November 1918, turmoil on Russia's southern periphery continued for some time. There were two main causes for the unrest and the resulting prolongation of military operations: (1) the emancipatory movement of non-Russian nationalities of the Russian Empire; (2) Allied intervention against Bolshevism in Russia. Both causes were to complicate the peaceful conclusion of war.

The Russian revolution produced a pronounced weakness in the strength of the empire, a weakness verging on complete disintegration. The subject nations of Russia, long aspiring to freedom, seized this opportunity to achieve independence. Georgia, Armenia, and Azerbaijan emerged as independent states in May 1918, and a similar movement toward emancipation developed at the same time in Central Asia. In Kokand a free government of Turkestan was proclaimed in December 1917, the emirs of Khiva and Bukhara asserted their independence, and the Kirghiz population also manifested emancipatory tendencies. As pointed out earlier, several other Turkish-speaking groups in Russia also made attempts at emancipation, but we shall limit our observations to those groups which belong to the wider geographical area of the Middle East. Other movements, while important and indicative of the resentment of the Turkish-Tatar peoples against the Russian rule, were either geographically isolated or too remote from the Middle Eastern area of operations to be counted as factors in the dramatic developments which followed the armistice.

The exigencies of war with the Central powers had brought British troops to the soil of the Russian Empire. These troops came either to oppose directly Turko-German penetration eastward (such was the case in Baku) or to oppose it indirectly (by fighting the Bolsheviks). This indirect opposition requires some elucidation. In 1918 a general intervention by the Western powers into the affairs of Russia began. Its aim was to aid the anti-Communist elements in Russia to reestablish themselves in order to keep Russia in the war on the side of the Allies. Therefore any British expedition into Central Asia or the Caucasus could be interpreted in this light. But the Central Asiatic regions of the Russian Empire presented additional reasons for intervention. Upon its seizure of power, the Communist Soviet at Tashkent began to launch vigorous anti-British propaganda directed toward India and Britain's colonial empire. Having released from captivity about 200,000 German and Austro-Hungarian prisoners of war interned in Turkestan, the Tashkent Bolsheviks organized them into military formations to serve the new Communist government. The economic cooperation inaugurated between Soviet Russia and Germany after the Brest-Litovsk Treaty meant that the Tashkent Soviet, if allowed to act freely, would be in a position to supply Germany with millions of bales of cotton—a raw material needed badly by Berlin for the production of nitrate. Soviet cooperation with Germany, the presence of Communist-guided German and Austrian troops in Turkestan, the Communist propaganda emanating from Tashkent toward India, and the possibility of a junction between the German-Turkish elements in Transcaucasia and other anti-British forces in Turkestan produced considerable alarm in British quarters and were the main factors leading them to undertake an expedition to

Turkestan.[24] Actually two different British actions occurred. The first involved the sending of a small military mission, led by Colonel Sir George Macartney, by a roundabout route to Tashkent, in order to learn on the spot what the ultimate intentions of the Bolsheviks were. This mission was compelled to leave Tashkent after a brief stay in order to avoid being arrested by the local Soviet. Only one member, Lieutenant Colonel F. M. Bailey, remained in disguise in Turkestan, attempting to establish contact with anti-Soviet Moslem nationalists.[25] The second was the sending of a British force to Ashkhabad in Transcaspia in response to an appeal addressed to the British by a counterrevolutionary Russian government there. This force, under the command of General Sir Wilfrid Malleson, fought Bolshevik troops and their German and Austro-Hungarian mercenaries along the Transcaspain railway line between Ashkhabad and Tashkent. The furthest point reached by the British was the oasis of Merv.

When in October and November 1918, armistices had been concluded with the Central powers, the original anti-German objective behind the British expeditions into the Caucasus and Central Asia lost its significance. Thenceforward their continued presence in those regions was motivated by the anti-Soviet feeling of the British government and by protective measures in defense of India. The support of either Russian counterrevolutionary forces like those in Ashkhabad or of centers of anti-Soviet nationalist movements like those in the Caucasus or in Turkestan fitted well into this general policy. For this reason the Malleson force in Transcaspia was not withdrawn immediately following the armistice with the Central powers but remained there and fought with the Tashkent Communists until 1920. Similarly, following the armistice British troops reappeared in Baku and spread over other parts of Transcaucasia. They were accompanied by some French and Italian contingents. Their presence there, apart from assuring the evacuation of Turkish and German troops, was a guarantee against a possible Soviet thrust toward the area. The troops were instrumental in preserving the independence of Georgia, Armenia, and Azerbaijan. By the end of 1919 the British cabinet, and with it the governments of othe other leading Entente powers, decided to put an end to their intervention in Russia. Orders were issued to the troops to evacuate the areas under their control. By the spring of 1920 British troops had withdrawn from the Caucasus and Transcaspia. The military vacuum thus created permitted the Soviet government to penetrate these areas. One by one centers of native resistance to communism fell. In Central Asia, Khiva was captured in June 1919, Ashkhabad in October of the same year, and Bukhara in September 1920. The rulers of Khiva and Bukhara fled to Afghanistan. In Transcaucasia, Azerbaijan experienced a Communist coup and Soviet invasion in April 1920. Armenia followed suit in November 1920, and Georgia in March 1921. All three countries were proclaimed Soviet Socialist republics. The attempt to free these non-Russian areas from Russian rule had failed, and the Soviet government succeeded in reestablishing its authority over the whole

[24]For a general summary of British Central Asian expeditions, see George Lenczowski, *Russia and the West in Iran, 1918–1948* (Ithaca, N.Y., 1949), pp. 31–41.

[25]A vivid account of his extraordinary adventures is contained in F. M. Bailey, *Mission to Tashkent* (London, 1946).

former area of the tsarist empire in Asia. This whole episode left a bitter legacy. On the part of the adjacent Moslem nations it resulted in a feeling of suspicion and hostility toward the new masters of Russia; with regard to England it created a constant worry over Soviet designs upon India and the British position in the Middle East; and on the part of Soviet Russia it produced a determination to wipe out the traces of independent nationalist thought among its subject Mohammedan races. Therefore, to some extent, the basic prewar pattern was reinstated—Russia vs. Britain and vs. native nationalism in the Middle East. This time, however, Russia was armed with the powerful weapon of Communist ideology, which in case of a Russian victory would mean not only imperialist bondage but also a radical change in the pattern of life of Middle Eastern peoples.

PART TWO

The Northern Belt

CHAPTER IV

Turkey

Even before the replacement of the humiliating Treaty of Sèvres with the more honorable Treaty of Lausanne, profound changes took place in Turkey's internal politics. On November 1, 1922, barely three weeks after the armistice of Mudania, the Grand National Assembly proclaimed the abolition of the sultanate. A Kemalist leader, Refet Pasha, who later was to assume command in Thrace, appeared with Allied permission in Constantinople and promptly engineered a coup d'état to depose the sultan and his cabinet and to extend nationalist control over the capital. The sultan escaped aboard a British naval vessel. On November 18 the Assembly proclaimed the ex-sultan's cousin, Abdul Mejid, caliph with the clear understanding that his functions were to be limited to spiritual matters only. The Allies accepted these changes with good grace (in fact with a sigh of relief, since it ended the abnormal situation of having to treat with two Turkish governments at the same time). The negotiations that began soon afterward at Lausanne were conducted with the Ankara government, which represented Turkey de facto as well as de jure. At the time of the conference Kemal's fame was firmly established. He had been given by the Assembly the title of *Ghazi* ("Victorious"), as well as the rank of field marshal, after his victory at the decisive battle of the Sakaria River. His trusted friend and chief of staff, General Ismet Pasha, victor of the great battle of Inönü, ably headed the Turkish delegation.

Establishment of the Republic

From the constitutional point of view, the conference coincided with a period of transition. By the fall of 1923 basic decisions had been made. On October 29, the Grand National Assembly proclaimed Turkey a republic, and elected Mustafa Kemal its first president. It soon transpired that, despite the clear limitation of the caliph's functions to the religious sphere, the very existence of this institution did not suit the reformist spirit of the new republic. On March 3, 1924, the last link with the past was severed. The Assembly formally abolished the caliphate. The caliph went quietly into retirement abroad, and a law was passed forever banning all members of the Osmanli dynasty from Turkish soil.

Soon afterward, on April 20, the assembly adopted a constitution which, though

1 1 3

it had a few peculiarities of its own, generally followed Western European patterns. It declared that the Grand National Assembly possessed "legislative authority and executive powers," the latter being exercised by the president of the republic and a council of ministers. The principle of responsibility to the parliament by the cabinet was established. Judicial authority was vested in the tribunals, which were proclaimed independent. The franchise was established on the basis of literacy. A four-year term was set for members of the assembly, and the president was to be elected by the assembly. Chapter V of the constitution was entitled "General Rights of Turkish Citizens" and laid stress on those civic freedoms and privileges which are characteristic of the heritage of the West. In particular it provided for individual liberty; the abolition of individual and group privileges; freedom of conscience, of thought, of speech, and of the press; the right to work; the right of private property and of association; freedom from arbitrary arrest; the prohibition of torture and forced labor; the sanctity of private residence; the inviolability of mail; compulsory and free primary education; and freedom from discrimination on account of religion and race.[1]

The letter of the constitution thus provided a legal framework for the new Turkish state. It was characteristic of new Turkish trends that the constitution followed a Western, democratic pattern, and not the Soviet model, in spite of the political alliance with new Russia. Yet it was not the letter but the spirit that actually counted. It is characteristic of the nations of the twentieth century to display fine-sounding constitutions, providing beautifully constructed democratic machinery and containing impressive bills of rights, which in effect find no reflection in the real life of those nations. For this reason, the Turkish constitution, like any other similar instrument, could not accomplish a change in Turkey merely by being officially adopted. Nor could any rational person expect an immediate introduction of true Western democracy into a country which for centuries had known nothing but absolute rule.

Yet it is undeniable that Turkey, under Kemal, experienced a radical transformation, indeed a revolutionary change from the old order to the new. The most remarkable thing about the Turkish revolution is that it largely, though gradually, conformed to its professed ideals. It avoided the pitfalls of the Nazi and Soviet revolutions, which replaced the old order by a new absolutism. Despite all the temptations that the Fascist and Communist examples provided, and despite the temptation which possession of power in itself afforded, Kemal and his new Turkey represented a basically different trend than did the contemporary totalitarian machines. Instead of scorning and rejecting the Western heritage (which the totalitarians did with particular gusto), the new Turkish republic considered it an ideal worth struggling for.

In her search for a new, more prosperous, and more humane future, the new Turkey in the period between two world wars passed through a transitional stage which, in China, Sun Yat-sen termed "tutelage." This was a stage of reeducation,

[1]The full text of the constitution is contained in Helen M. Davis, ed., *Constitutions, Electoral Laws, Treaties of States in the Near and Middle East* (Durham, N.C., 1947), p. 341.

sometimes employing forcible methods, under the guidance of a strong national leader. Once this reeducation was accomplished, Turkey could hope to realize her democratic ideals.

It would be difficult to deny that, following the abolition of the sultanate and the caliphate, Kemal was a virtual dictator. This dictatorship was, however, tempered by at least three factors: (1) Kemal's basic Western liberal inclinations; (2) his benevolence and unselfishness; and (3) the sharing of power with the People's party, the real source of his political strength, whose attitude he could not disregard.

The People's party (Halk Firkasi; later renamed Republican People's party, Cümhüriyet Halk Partisi) had grown out of the original Association for the Defense of Anatolia and Rumelia (created at the Erzerum and Sivas congresses) and was officially founded on September 9, 1923. It was dedicated to the wholesome regeneration of Turkey. It manifested a truly missionary zeal in the pursuance of its objective and took care not to repeat the errors previously committed by the Committee of Union and Progress. The People's party professed a philosophy of nationalism and was willing to abide by the consequences of this profession. Thus, it demanded the right of self-determination for Turkey proper and in return recognized the same right for the Arabs. It rejected the idea of imperialism and argued that the expansion of the Ottoman Empire had brought more misfortunes than advantages to the Turkish nation. It condemned Pan-Islamism as a nefarious movement which not only retarded the modern secular development of Turkey but also entangled her in adventures and responsibilities that were of no concern to the people of Turkey. Pan-Islamism, it maintained, was also a chronic source of friction with foreign powers. Despite its emphasis on national ties, the party was also willing to abandon the concept of Pan-Turanism, which in practical terms meant denying support to irredentist tendencies among twenty million Turkish-speaking Mohammedans in the Soviet Union. Such a policy would facilitate good neighborly relations with the new Russia. In fact, of all the nationalist movements in the twentieth-century world, that of Turkey had the distinction of being sober-minded, restrained, and nonadventurous.

At the third congress in Ankara, the People's party adopted "Six Principles of Kemalism," which expressed the fundamental political philosophy of the new Turkish republic. These principles were later (in 1937) formally incorporated into the constitution. They included (1) *Republicanism,* (2) *Nationalism,* based not on religion or race but on common citizenship and devotion to the national ideal; (3) *Populism,* meaning equality in law and repudiation of class privileges and of class war as well as of the abuses of capitalism; (4) *Etatisme,* meaning constructive intervention of the state in national economy; (5) *Secularism,* definite separation of church and state; and (6) *Revolutionism,* meaning the determination to depart radically from tradition and precedent if they did not serve national interests.

Kemalist Reforms

The National Pact of Ankara, the constitution, and the Six Principles provided the legal and ideological basis for the new life of the nation. Action was needed, and this action—vigorous and determined—came in a series of far-reaching reforms that radically transformed Turkey. Chronologically, the reforms in the new Turkish Republic may be divided into (1) those that occurred during the middle twenties and (2) those carried out in the middle thirties. It seems more practical, however, for the purposes of this discussion, to group them according to their subject matter.

The major objective of Turkish reform was, in a general sense, to separate Turkey from the ancient Asiatic-Arabic sphere of culture and tradition and to transform her into a modern, Westernized nation.[2] The main attack was, therefore, directed against those institutions which were likely to perpetuate the old order. The abolition of the caliphate proved to be a good point of departure. It cleared the way not only to the establishment of a new kind of government, while freeing Turkey from an embarrassing complication in foreign relations, but also opened the way for a radical secularization of the Turkish body politic. One month after the abolition of the caliphate, in April 1924, the national assembly abolished the authority of religious (Sharia) courts in civil matters and did away with the Ministry of Pious Foundations (Evkaf) and the priests' schools. The dervish orders were disbanded and their monasteries closed. Secret sects were banned. (The top religious position of Sheikh el-Islam had been abolished with the sultanate in 1922.) To deal with religious matters, two civilian bodies—the Board of Religious Affairs and the Board of Pious Foundations—were established.

Linked with religious reform and symbolical of the new spirit was the abolition of the fez and of the veil. Instructions concerning the dress to be worn by the clergy and public officials followed. In 1926 the European calendar replaced the old Islamic computation of the year.

The transfer of the national capital from Constantinople, the old seat of the caliphs, to the new city of Ankara provided another major move toward secularization. The new capital assumed a definitely modern exterior, and no mosques were constructed in its newer section. In 1935 Friday was replaced by Sunday as a weekly holiday. Finally, an amendment to the constitution, passed in 1928, deleted the article which stated that Islam was a state religion, and another amendment of 1937 proclaimed full freedom of conscience.

The record of laicization is impressive. It should be pointed out, however, that at no time did the Turkish republic fight religion as such. The Kemalist platform did not contain any doctrinaire materialistic principles. And although Kemal himself was indifferent to religion, some of his best friends, like Ismet and Fevzi Çakmak, were deeply religious.

Many other reforms, although not directly concerning religion, stemmed from the basic policy of secularization. Such were, for example, the judicial reforms, which were introduced in 1926. The Turkish republic in a sweeping move discarded old Ottoman laws, both religious and civil, abolished the millet system, and adopted the Swiss civil code, the Italian penal code, and the German-type commercial code as

---

[2] A comprehensive account of Kemalist reforms may be found in August von Kral, *Kamâl Atatürk's Land: The Evolution of Modern Turkey* (London, 1938), and Donald E. Webster, *The Turkey of Atatürk: Social Progress in the Turkish Reformation* (Philadelphia, 1939). See also Arnold J. Toynbee, ed., *Survey of International Affairs, 1928,* and Henry E. Allen, *The Turkish Transformation: A Study in Social and Religious Development* (Chicago, 1935).

laws of the land. The new code of civil procedure also followed the Swiss model. These laws established full equality of citizens before the law, a very important aspect of which was the emancipation of women. Polygamy was abolished, and women were made eligible for public offices, professions, and positions of trust in the economic and intellectual life of the country. In 1934 an amendment to the constitution gave women the right of suffrage, and soon afterward a number of women deputies appeared in the Grand National Assembly.

Another reform linked to the general policy of secularization was that of the alphabet. At the invitation of the Soviet government Turkey sent a delegation to a Turkological Congress which met in Baku between February 26 and March 6, 1926. The Congress recommended abandonment of the Arabic script as unscientific and detrimental to the Turkic languages. Turkey adopted its recommendations in 1928. The Latin alphabet was introduced, and the government sponsored intensive studies looking toward the revival of the Turkish language and its purification of foreign ingredients.

Following this reform, foreign-sounding geographical names in Turkey gave way in 1930 to purely Turkish names. The Byzantine *Constantinople* was replaced by the Turkish *Istanbul, Adrianople* by *Edirne, Smyrna* by *Izmir,* and so on.

The development of a modern system of education was another result of the policy of secularization. Public education was divorced from church influences, and a constitutional provision concerning free and compulsory tuition on the primary level was put into effect. This was accompanied by a corresponding growth of secondary schools and institutions of higher learning. Trade, agriculture, forestry, and commerce schools were built, and the government did not hesitate to hire foreign teachers in order to assure high educational standards. At the invitation of the government a Swiss professor, Dr. Malche, presented a plan for the reform of university studies. A Medical Faculty, employing twenty foreign professors, was established in Istanbul and a School of Political and Social Sciences, which produced a number of able civil servants, diplomats, and statesmen, in Ankara. Athletics were encouraged, sports clubs flourished throughout the country, and Boy Scout organizations enjoyed popularity among teenagers. In 1935 Russian specialists were invited to instruct Turkish athletes in the arts of gliding and parachuting.

The secret of Kemal's success may largely be attributed to the strict enforcement of educational reform. The new generation of village and high-school teachers constituted—with the People's party members—a zealous cadre which spread Kemalist ideals and trained the minds of Turkish youth. Teachers became Kemal's most devoted propagandists, and—in contrast to many Western countries—were exceptionally well compensated for their services.

The old Ottoman state machinery also underwent a thorough overhauling. Badly needed reforms in the administrative system gave the new republic new efficiency. The country was divided into 62 *vilayets* (provinces), the latter subdivided into 430 *kazas* (districts), and these in turn parceled into a number of *nahiyes* (boroughs). General inspectorates, uniting some vilayets into larger districts, were created for certain special regions such as Kurdistan.

The Kemalist government successfully balanced the state budget, carried out a tax reform, and brought order into what had traditionally been a weak spot in Turkey, public finances. Throughout the 1920s a French financial expert was employed to advise on the financial recovery, and in 1933 Turkey successfully concluded a new agreement concering the debts of the old Empire. The debt was reduced from 107 million to 8 million Turkish pounds.

Closely linked to the financial reform was the inauguration of general economic progress. Following its principle of *étatisme,* the government assumed direct control of several enterprises and engaged in a great deal of general overall planning. Kemal acted on the basic premise that war-ravaged and foreign-exploited Turkey was poor in native capital, and that it was the state's responsibility to step in where private enterprise would not or could not operate. The government established state monopolies in such industries as tobacco, salt, liquors, matches, playing cards, arms, and munitions. It also acquired and established a number of factories in other fields. Without going to the extreme of compulsory nationalization, it gradually bought up most of the foreign-owned railways, coordinated their services, and embarked upon an ambitious program for their development. This program proved to be of tremendous importance in raising Turkey's economic and cultural life and served the purposes of national integration, industrialization, and defense.

The general economic policy of the new Turkey was that of autarchy and industrialization. This policy—a logical outcome of the principle of *étatisme*—required certain temporary sacrifices of the Turkish people, but in the long run assured them economic independence. The Soviet example played an important part in the formulation of this policy. While rejecting the extremist and doctrinaire aspects of the Soviet experiment, Kemalist Turkey willingly adopted the principle of economic planning. In the interwar period, a four-year plan for agriculture, a five-year plan for industry,[3] a three-year plan for mining, and a ten-year plan for the development of roads were formulated and carried out. To the extent that it served the national interest and did not endanger national independence or security, Turkey had recourse to the services of various foreign experts and construction firms. Soviet, German, Austrian, Hungarian, American, British, and other European experts were employed in the development of various economic enterprises.

The elimination of commercially skilled Armenian and Greek elements from many fields of economic endeavor caused some difficulties, especially as their services were often replaced by the bureaucratic machinery of new state-controlled enterprises. On the other hand, Turkey gained training in economic pursuits, and employed her own ethnic population. The former picture of Turkey split into a caste of "smart" aliens or minorities and another caste of "uncouth" Turks, either soldiers or peasants, was now replaced with a new one of the republic, unified by a homogeneous and soundly balanced Turkish society.

Of great importance in the economic development of the country were a number of government-controlled banks. The Central Bank issued notes and supervised overall financial policies. The Sümer Bank financed new state-owned industries, the

[3]Initiated in 1934 and repeated in 1938 and 1946.

Eti Bank promoted mining, the Iş Bank dealt with business transactions, and the older Agricultural Bank assisted farm production. The confidence generated abroad in the soundness of the new system was exemplified by a series of foreign loans granted Turkey during the interwar period.

The state spared no effort to promote foreign trade by concluding barter agreements, organizing fairs and exhibitions,[4] and establishing chambers of commerce. Care was taken to balance foreign trade properly, and this was successfully achieved throughout the interwar period. Because of the prevailing *étatisme* in Turkey and of general autarchic trends in Europe, by 1939 80 to 90 percent of Turkey's foreign trade was transacted on the basis of clearing agreements.

A further reform of family names broke still another link with the past. Family names are by no means a universal feature in Moslem countries, and their absence frequently contributed to confusion. In 1934 all Turks were ordered by law to choose legal surnames. At the same time old Ottoman titles and decorations were abolished. The Grand National Assembly gave the name *Atatürk* ("Father of the Turks") to Kemal, Ismet Pasha transformed himself into Ismet Inönü in commemoration of his victory over the Greeks, and other Turkish leaders were obliged to follow suit.

Turkey conducted a consistent demographic policy. Kemalist leaders were aware of the fact that their new state was deficient in manpower. Wars for twelve years had exacted a heavy toll of men. The Mesopotamian and Syrian campaigns during World War I were particularly costly, and if all the ambitious plans of the German High Command regarding the *Yilderim* had been put into effect, the loss of life to the Turks might have been even greater. In fact, if it had not been for large numbers of desertions[5] from the Turkish army in the last phases of the war, the biological survival of the nation might have been questioned. Both for economic and for military purposes it was essential to fill the gaps, and in 1934 the Grand Assembly passed an immigration law that encouraged Turks resident abroad to return and settle in Turkey. The new arrivals, who came mostly from the Balkans (Rumania and Bulgaria) but partly from Russia, were directed toward the western and central provinces of Anatolia. Some were settled in Eastern Thrace.

Finally, mention should be made of the social legislation. The latter kept pace with the growing industrialization of the country. A Central Labor Office in Ankara, with branches in provincial towns, administered the Labor Law, which was passed in 1936. Public health and social security matters were cared for by the Ministry of Hygiene and Social Welfare. Despite the cultivation of poppies there was never any widespread addiction to opium among the Turks (as was the case in Iran), and the state opium monopoly reduced the danger of an indiscriminate use of narcotics by the population.

---

[4]Of which the Izmir fairs have gained international reputation.

[5]This, by the way, is no reflection on the military valor of the Turkish soldier, which is of the highest order. The testimony of T. E. Lawrence, General Wavell, and other authorities supports this statement. Mass desertions at the end of the war resulted primarily from the complete breakdown of many essential supplies and services, which in many cases made desertion the only practical way of survival.

Political Opposition and Kurdish Revolts

These reforms were severely criticized and bitterly resented by some groups in Turkey. *Etatisme* and its economic policies were opposed by business circles in Istanbul (preponderantly non-Turkish), who disliked high taxes and tariffs and the general autarchic tendency. It was, however, the secularization of public life that met with the strongest opposition, particularly among the backward Kurdish tribes in the east.

The first major Kurdish revolt occurred in February 1925. Led by Sheikh Said of Genj (west of Lake Van), the Kurds seized control in a number of southeastern vilayets, demanding the restoration of Islam to its old status as well as local autonomy. The government accused Said of intrigue with the Ottoman pretender, Prince Selim, and procaliphate circles, mobilized its army, and sternly suppressed the rebellion. Moreover, the government set up the so-called "independence courts," which dealt with cases of treason and sedition in a summary way. Kurdish revolts were repeated in 1929 and 1930, but never reached equally alarming proportions. The government succeeded in restoring order in both cases. A number of Kurds were deported to the interior or to Thrace. A general inspectorate for the area was established, and the eastern vilayets have become virtually inaccessible to foreign visitors.

Opposition to Kemal's rule was not limited to business and religious circles. The dynamic way in which Kemal forced Turkey to Westernize herself necessitated strong and uncompromising measures which did not harmonize with the professed democracy of the regime. Critics accused Kemal of being intoxicated with power, denounced the group of servile "desperadoes" with whom he surrounded himself, deplored drinking bouts in his residence in the Chankaya suburb of Ankara, and demanded curtailment of his authority. In 1926, Kemal decided to curb this opposition. In the summer his cabinet announced the discovery of a plot to assassinate him and proceeded to arrest considerable numbers of Young Turkish politicans, supporters of the deposed sultan, and also some dissidents from Kemal's own party. In the trial that ensued, eighteen of those arrested were sentenced to death. The dissidents from Kemal's party were treated more leniently, being generally banished for a period of ten years.[6]

Having thus smashed the opposition, Kemal and his party remained undisputed masters of the country. It was essentially a one-party system of government. The party's secretary-general traditionally combined his duties with those of the minister of interior. The democratic processes of free discussion and majority vote were visible more within the People's party itself than in the official façade which was the Grand National Assembly. Most of the basic political decisions, including important legislation, were first debated in closed party sessions. Once a decision was made, the matter was sent to the Grand Assembly, where the same party members—now in their official capacity as deputies—made it law by formal vote.

[6]The penalty of banishment was imposed on General Kazim Kara Bekir and Refet and Ali Fuat Pasha; on Hussein Reuf and Dr. Adnan Bey and his wife, Halide Edib, a well-known writer; and on a number of others.

There were a few temporary exceptions to this one-party system. In the early twenties there was an opposition group known as the Republican, later the Republican Progressive, party. It was suppressed in 1925 on the order of an "independence court" in Ankara because of its alleged complicity with the Kurdish rebels. In 1930, with Kemal's permission and encouragement, another small opposition party was established. It was the Independent Republican party, and its leadership was entrusted to Kemal's old friend, Fethi Okyar. Kemal wanted constructive criticism and hoped that a moderate opposition party would provide it. The experiment, however, proved disappointing, and the party was soon disbanded. In 1935, Kemal decided to allow the election of sixteen independent deputies from a number of vilayets. These included, among others, two Greeks, one Jew, and one Armenian. This small independent group thereafter became a permanent feature in the Grand National Assembly.

The government's policies were supported by a number of dailies and periodicals. These were under the general supervision of the press department in the ministry of interior and were serviced by the government-owned Anatolian News Agency. The semiofficial *Ulus* of Ankara usually reflected the official opinions of the government. Among other major newspapers were *Cümhüriyet, Tan,* and *Akşam.* The People's House in the capital published a weekly, *Ankara,* in French, seconded by a monthly, *La Turquie Kemaliste,* a Press Department publication. Both served to interpret Turkey to foreign observers. Official influence on the press, especially in matters of foreign policy, was considerable. It was possible for the government to inspire the publication of certain articles in outwardly independent journals in order to test the reaction of foreign powers. This device was frequently used during the periods of international crisis.

Turkish Foreign Policy

The transformation from the Ottoman Empire into a republic reduced Turkey from a major power to a small nation. This, however, was only an outward manifestation, since in reality the old empire had been weak and disintegrating while the reborn Turkey of Kemal proved to be a relatively strong, closely knit, and homogeneous political organism. The new Turkey, however, was only a medium-sized country with a population of sixteen million bordering on giant Russia with her two hundred million people and exposed to the influence of the naval powers which dominated the Mediterranean. Thus, no matter how perfect Turkey's political and military machine was, her strength had obvious limitations. Perhaps the greatest merit of Kemal and his followers was their sober realization of these limitations and their moderate, realistic foreign policy, which corresponded to the strength of their country. There was nothing romantic or adventurous in Kemal's foreign policy—except, of course, during the initial period between his landing at Samsun and the Lausanne Treaty. During that brief period he and his patriotic friends achieved exactly the objectives that a sober mind would have deemed impossible of accomplishment. They—the nationalists—then challenged the authority of the victorious Entente and fought a successful war against several powerful enemies at once. But even if one considers this behavior romantic, one must realize that Kemal and his friends had little to lose except their lives. The Treaty of Sèvres had practically reduced Turkey to the status of a Western colony, and it would have been hard to conceive of any appreciably worse treatment for a defeated nation.

Victory over their enemies gave Kemal and his followers tremendous confidence in their own strength and ability and raised the morale throughout the entire nation. It would have been easy to adopt a dangerous and ambitious course of aggrandizement and unrealistic imperialism. Yet this was not done. Since the signing of the Treaty of Lausanne, Turkey has been essentially a status quo power. The Turks have had as great a stake in the preservation of peace as has had any other status quo country. There have, however, been some differences between the Versailles powers, such as France or Great Britain, and Turkey. These have been due largely to two chief factors: First, Turkey could not shake off overnight the emotional load of resentment, especially against the British, which her revisionist war had generated. Second, the Treaty of Lausanne left three matters unsettled, at least from Turkey's point of view—the problem of Mosul (i.e., of the boundary with Iraq); the problem of Alexandretta (i.e., of the boundary with Syria and the autonomy of the sanjak); and the problem of the Straits. (Here, true enough, a definite convention was signed, but it imposed irritating limitations on Turkish sovereignty.) In these three matters only did Turkey favor any revision of the peace settlement. These three problems, added to the above-mentioned emotional bias against the "imperialist" Entente, led Turkey in the early twenties to seek the friendship of the new proletarian state. Soviet Russia, because of her revolutionary program and her basic opposition to the Paris Peace Settlement and the League of Nations, also favored revisionism. When in 1921, Bekir Sami Bey, Kemal's foreign minister, went to Moscow to negotiate a treaty of friendship, both parties considered themselves revisionist and anti-Entente. After Lausanne, however, this was no longer true, since Turkey became quite satisfied with her own peace settlement. Nevertheless, since Russia continued in her policy of opposition to the status quo and since Turkey was still at odds on a few minor points with Great Britain and France, countries whose relations with Soviet Russia were strained, Turkey found it advantageous to continue her collaboration with Russia despite differences in their respective political ideologies. Russia had an equally good reason to reciprocate, because Turkey was anti-imperialist and anti-Entente. It was one of the cardinal points of Soviet foreign policy of that period to cultivate Turkey's good will and friendship, in order to show the exploited nations of Asia that Moscow was their only and true friend. Furthermore, Turkish friendship carried with it the promise of an advantageous accommodation in the Straits, in case of war with the capitalist West—a consideration which no Russian government could disregard.

At the Lausanne conference the Soviet delegation (permitted to participate on a limited basis) staunchly supported Turkey on the question of the Straits, but the Entente's will prevailed to the chagrin of both delegations.

The Mosul Controversy

The case of Mosul indirectly contributed to the cementing of Turko-Soviet friendship. According to the Treaty of Lausanne, Mosul was to remain under the temporary occupation of Great Britain, pending the conclusion of a definitive agreement. If no agreement was reached within a year, the matter was then to be referred to the Council of the League of Nations. Great Britain brought the Mosul controversy to the League in 1924. An international commission, headed by the Estonian General Laidoner, was appointed to investigate the matter. Following the receipt of its report, the Council, on December 16, 1925, awarded Mosul to Iraq on the condition that the British mandate over that state should continue for twenty-five years.[7] Disappointed, Turkey questioned the legality of the award, contending that the Council's function was that of conciliation and not of arbitration. The following day, December 17, the Turkish foreign minister rushed to Paris and there concluded a new treaty of friendship and nonaggression with the Soviet plenipotentiaries. The treaty, amounting to a virtual political alliance, was to last for ten years, at which time it could be renewed. It marked the apogee of cordiality in Soviet-Turkish relations. Although the friendship was maintained and as late as 1934 Russia granted Turkey an industrial credit and expert assistance for the execution of the Turkish five-year plan of industrialization, a gradual cooling off in the relations could be observed. Soviet Russia could not wholeheartedly approve the stern measures taken by Kemal against Communist propaganda in Turkey, nor could she be too enthusiastic about the gradual reconciliation between Turkey and the West, as evidenced by a series of treaties.

The most important act of reconciliation occurred with Great Britain. As pointed out earlier, resentment had accumulated against the British. British support of the Greeks in 1919, the championing of national minorities, British occupation of Constantinople after the war and the resulting arbitrary arrests and deportations, the British pro-Arab attitude and support of the Kurds, together with the Mosul problem, accounted for this resentment. The Kurdistan problem seemed particularly irritating. A number of British intelligence officers in the Iraqi mandatory administration entertained the idea that an independent Kurdish state under British influence might be carved out of the territories of Iraq, Turkey, and possibly Iran. This idea originated long before the Lausanne Treaty, and the support of Kurdish aspirations was used as a weapon against the recalcitrant Turkish nationalists. The provision about Kurdish autonomy in the Treaty of Sèvres, the Kurdish rebellion of 1925 (which coincided with the Mosul controversy), and finally British insistence on retention of the Kurdish-inhabited province of Mosul appeared to the Turks as evidences of a sinister plot to undermine Turkish political and territorial integrity.[8]

Much wisdom and moderation were required to put aside these suspicions and to make a friendly advance toward their former enemies. On June 5, 1926, Turkey concluded a treaty with Great Britain definitely settling the Mosul question. Turkey agreed to relinquish her claims to Mosul in return for the promise that 10 percent of Mosul's oil production should be available for her use. To Turkey's satisfaction, no

---

[7]For a detailed account of the conflict, see Leon Crutiansky, *La Question de Mossoul* (Paris, 1927). For a general background, consult Harry C. Luke, *Mosul and Its Minorities* (London, 1925).

[8]These fears seemed exaggerated. It is true that field agents of the British intelligence (Major Soane and his group) often supported the scheme of Kurdish independence, but other and prominent specialists on the Middle East, including Sir Percy Cox, opposed it, and the latter's views ultimately prevailed. See Philip P. Graves, *Briton and Turk* (London, 1941), pp. 221–222.

mention was made of Kurdish autonomy or independence. Moreover, the British accepted the Turkish decision not to allow the Assyrian expellees of World War I to return to their homes in Turkey. The treaty resulted in definite improvement in Anglo-Turkish relations. In 1929 part of the British Mediterranean fleet paid a courtesy visit to Istanbul, and former enmity gave place to a steadily growing friendship.

Turkey and the Balkans

Political settlement with Britain was followed by a reconciliation with Britain's traditional protégé, Greece. Here again in a truly statesmanlike fashion, emotion was overcome by sober wisdom. Following the Greek adventure in Asia Minor and the drastic exchange of populations, no real political ground for continued enmity remained. The two countries shared an equal interest in preserving the peace and in preventing Bulgaria from embarking upon a revisionist drive in Thrace. Reconciliation took the form of a Greek-Turkish treaty concluded on October 30, 1930, in Ankara. It settled the property claims of the exchanged populations and many other controversial questions. The two parties reaffirmed their attachment to the territorial status quo and accepted the principle of naval equality in the eastern Mediterranean.

Turkey's entry into the League of Nations on July 18, 1932, confirmed her peaceful intentions and her rapprochement to the status quo camp in Europe.

The treaty with Greece marked the beginning of an active Turkish policy in the Balkans, an area of traditional interest. Turkey dreaded Italy's revisionism. Mussolini's indiscreet remarks concerning the Mediterranean as "mare nostrum" and his undisguised ambitions in the Near East, together with the Italian possession of the strategic Dodecanese Islands just off the Turkish coast, filled Turkish leaders with grave anxiety. The Turks, to whom the Balkans were the first line of defense in case of Italian expansionism, were vitally interested in the stability of the peninsula and in the political solidarity of those southeastern European nations. They greeted with enthusiasm and actively encouraged the trend toward unity manifested by the Balkan states. On February 9, 1934, Turkey became a party to the Balkan Entente Pact which united Greece, Yugoslavia, Rumania, and herself in a mutual guarantee of peace, independence, and territorial integrity and which established consultative machinery among its signatories. An ideal settlement would have been to create a Balkan federation which would include Bulgaria as well. Despite various overtures to join the Entente, Bulgaria remained sulkily apart, ardently revisionist, and a hotbed of Macedonian terroristic intrigue. The Bulgars insisted on access to the Mediterranean and on the return of southern Dobruja, and refused to commit themselves to accept existing boundaries. The openly expressed determination of the Entente to preserve the status quo put a practical check on Bulgarian revisionism. It also served as a timely reminder to the major European revisionists that they could not count on dissension among the Entente members.

Turkey's fears of Italy were not unfounded. In a major speech on March 18, 1934, Mussolini announced his African and Asian ambitions. In the fall of 1935 Italy invaded Abyssinia. Turkey faithfully supported League action against the aggressors. Undeterred by sanctions, Italy completed this conquest by spring, and thus made a serious alteration in the Middle Eastern-African structure. This trend was accentuated by Hitler's unilateral violations of the peace treaty, such as the rearmament of Germany announced in March 1935, and the remilitarization of the Rhineland a year later. The European totalitarians were obviously on the move, and diplomatic revisionism had given place to military action.

Attached to peaceful reform and reconstruction, Turkey could not but view with apprehension these imperialistic manifestations. She was, therefore, irresistibly drawn toward closer cooperation with France and Great Britain, two pillars of the European status quo. The trend toward rapproachement was reciprocal, since these two countries also needed Turkey's cooperation. Aware of this, Turkey was in a position to bargain and thus to settle the two remaining questions that prevented complete harmony between her and the West—the problems of the Straits and of Alexandretta.

The Straits question was settled to Turkey's satisfaction by the Agreement of Montreux on July 20, 1936.[9] Turkey's main request—the remilitarization of the Straits—was accepted by the Lausanne Treaty signatories, with the exception of Italy, who boycotted the conference. By this act Turkey regained military control of this strategic waterway and strengthened her position in the Mediterranean-Black Sea region.

Sanjak of Alexandretta

The problem of Alexandretta proved more complicated because of the involvement of a third party, Syria, in this Franco-Turkish dispute. The Franklin-Bouillon agreement of 1921[10] provided for a special administrative regime of the sanjak of Alexandretta, which had an estimated 40 percent Turkish population. For a number of years the matter remained unchanged, the Turks hoping that one day a revision might be reached with France. The conclusion of the Franco-Syrian Treaty of September, 1936, by which Syria was promised independence[11] including Alexandretta, made the question more acute and provoked Turkish protests. Turkey brought the matter to the League of Nations Council. The Council, having first secured French and Turkish acceptance, drew up in May 1937 a special statute calling for demilitarization, autonomy, and special guarantees for the Turkish population of the sanjak. Despite these arrangements, unrest and disorders prevailed in the district. They led, in December of that year, to the denouncement by Turkey of the Turko-Syrian treaty of friendship of 1926 and to a campaign of recrimination with France. On July 3, 1938, following the dispatch of a military mission to Ankara, France and Turkey reached an agreement whereby the sanjak was proclaimed a Franco-Turkish condominium. It was to be policed by French and Turkish troops pending a general election which would determine the sanjak's future status. On July 5, Turkish troops entered the disputed area, and in September the popula-

[9] See Chapter XVIII.
[10] See above, p. 105.
[11] See below, p. 318.

tion went to the polls in the midst of feverish pro-Turkish and pro-Arab agitation. The election gave the Turks a majority of twenty-two out of forty seats in the Assembly, which promptly, on September 2, proclaimed autonomy under the name of the Republic of Hatay. The republic hoisted Turkish flags and sent a delegation to Ankara asking for union with the mother country. French troops were still in the territory, in a rather awkward position, and their unwarlike appearance contrasted sharply with the spick-and-span Turkish regiments sent into the sanjak with the obvious aim of impressing the populace. For all practical purposes, Turkey was supreme in the sanjak, and this fact only awaited official bilateral confirmation.

Alliance with France and Britain, 1939

Such a confirmation came on June 23, 1939, when France and Turkey concluded a nonaggression pact, preliminary to a full-fledged alliance, toward which they were driven by the onward march of the Axis powers. France consented to the annexation by Turkey of the Republic of Hatay and granted her credits for the purchase of armaments. By this act the last remaining grievance against the West was eliminated, and the road was paved for closer cooperation.

Reconciliation with France found a parallel development in the strengthening of Anglo-Turkish bonds. Ever since Mussolini's Ethiopian adventure, the two countries had been drawing closer together. During his short-lived reign, Edward VIII visited Istanbul while cruising in the Mediterranean on his yacht. The Turkish fleet paid a courtesy visit to the British naval base of Valetta at Malta, and Ismet Inönü, Kemal's closest associate and foremost statesman, attended the coronation of George VI. On May 27, 1938, Britain and Turkey concluded three credit agreements, and a year later (May 12, 1939) both countries issued a "declaration of mutual guarantee" which was soon followed by the above-mentioned Franco-Turkish pact.

In the summer months of 1939, Great Britain and France sought to establish a common front with Russia, in view of the German threats to world peace. Turkey followed these developments with close attention, interested as she was in the strengthening of the peace front. The conclusion of the Nazi-Soviet pact of August 23, 1939, gave Turkish leaders a severe shock. Since Ataturk's death and Ismet Inönü's election to the presidency (November 10, 1938), they had been determined to cultivate the great Kemalist heritage, to preserve peace, and to avoid dangerous entanglements. Their disappointment was keen when they learned that their formidable Soviet neighbor, hitherto friendly and since 1934 openly espousing the status quo and collective security, had joined hands with the Nazi proponents of armed revision. It meant, moreover, that their friendship with France and Great Britain, instead of being approved, would now be criticized in Moscow. After the Nazi-Soviet pact, Turkish-Soviet relations became strained. The German attack on Poland on September 1 and the Soviet invasion of Poland's eastern provinces on September 17 added considerably to the tension. War had become a reality, and a false step by Turkish diplomacy might easily prove disastrous to the cause of national survival.

Moscow Negotiations, 1939

In late September the Turkish foriegn minister, Şükrü Saracoglu, left for Moscow for the purpose of concluding a new pact with Russia.[12] Conversations toward such a pact had been going on for some time between the Soviet ambassador at Ankara, Terentieff, and the Turkish government. Both parties, however, sought different objectives. Turkey desired a pact that would reaffirm Soviet support of the status quo in the Black Sea region, and by the same token confirm Soviet respect of Turkish independence and territorial integrity, and that would clear the way for a proposed Turkish alliance with Great Britain and France. Russia's objectives were quite different. Having moved closer to Germany, she now resented the prospect of a British-French-Turkish alliance. Germany at that time was primarily interested in keeping Britain and France from building a chain of encircling alliances in the Balkans and the Near East. She viewed with concern the guarantee that London and Paris in April 1939 had given to Greece and Rumania to defend their integrity and she sought to neutralize the Balkan states and Turkey. Turkey held a key position, since Franco-British aid to Rumania would have to pass through the Straits. To keep Turkey from cooperating with the West thus became one of the major objectives of German foreign policy at the beginning of the war.

German persuasion alone, however, would not be sufficient to sway Turkey's decision. Germany needed the aid of Russia, who as a close and powerful neighbor was in a much stronger position to press for a change in Turkish policy. Captured wartime documents show that the German ambassador in Moscow, Count von der Schulenburg, one of the main architects of the Soviet-Nazi Pact, was in constant contact with the Kremlin during Saracoglu's visit to Moscow and pressed Foreign Commissar Molotov to heed German desiderata. Soviet leaders were willing to follow his advice. Having chosen neutrality in the German-Western war, Russia was ready to aid Germany in nuetralzing the Black Sea region, and thus to bar the opening of a second front in the Balkans. Such a front would bring hostilities close to the Soviet border, a situation Russia wanted to avoid. Moreover, the presence of a Franco-British fleet in the Black Sea—a possible result of an alliance with Turkey—might create serious security problems for "collaborationist" Russia. Thus, both to appease Germany and to keep the conflict away from her borders, Russia desired Turkish neutrality.

Considering the basic divergence in objectives, it is no wonder that Saracoglu's mission to Moscow failed. It was an extraordinary visit in the annals of diplomacy, because the foreign minister remained away from home for almost a month at a time of great international crisis. His trip coincided with the visit that the German foreign minister, Joachim von Ribbentrop, paid to the Soviet Union. The Nazi minister, who had come to discuss the division of eastern Europe into the German and Soviet

[12]David J. Dallin, *Soviet Russia's Foreign Policy, 1939–1942* (New Haven, Conn., 1942), p. 111. An exhaustive documentary treatment of the Soviet-Turkish negotiations is contained in Harry N. Howard, *Germany, the Soviet Union, and Turkey during World War II* (Department of State Bull.; Washington, D.C., 1948), pp. 63 ff.

spheres, was given priority in Moscow, and Saracoglu was kept waiting for weeks between conferences.

Stalin and Molotov submitted to him two proposals: (1) to close the Straits to British and French warships, and (2) to conclude a mutual assistance pact with the Soviet Union, which would draw Turkey away from her contemplated alliance with Britain and France.

Saracoglu flatly refused the first demand inasmuch as it would mean a unilateral violation of the Montreux Straits Convention and would cause hostilities with the West. As to the second proposal, lengthy negotiations ensued, during which the Turkish minister constantly consulted London and Paris. By that time Turkish-British-French conversations for a definitive alliance were far advanced, and most of the major points of the agreement settled. In order to reconcile her Western friendships with Soviet objections, Turkey was willing to formulate her proposed alliance with Britain and France in such a way that it would explicitly exclude any common anti-Soviet action. This concession was made with the approval of the British and the French, who fully understood Turkey's difficult position. Such an arrangement might prove satisfactory to Russia, and at one time during the Moscow negotiations the Soviet leaders seemed to be ready to conclude a pact on that basis. But German pressure prevailed, and Moscow insisted that, in her treaty of alliance with the West, Turkey must promise to refrain from engaging in war with Germany. This, of course, was unacceptable to Saracoglu, as it would render the Turko-British-French alliance meaningless. Germany preferred to see no Russo-Turkish pact at all than a pact which would result in safeguards to Russia only, and not to herself. Anxious to oblige the Nazis, the Soviet leaders finally informed the Turkish foreign minister that they were not interested in the pact.

The net result of Saracoglu's visit to Moscow was that he learned, much to his uneasiness, of a rather pronounced degree of Nazi-Soviet cooperation and of consequent Soviet opposition to Turkish links with the West. The trip impressed upon Turkish leaders the need for great caution in their international relations but did not deflect them from the basic course of cooperation with the West.

Saracoglu left Moscow on October 17, and before he reached Ankara Prime Minister Refik Saydam on October 19 signed the Treaty of Alliance with Great Britain and France. The treaty was not quite an equal arrangement. On the one hand, Great Britain and France promised Turkey aid and assistance in case of aggression by a European power. On the other, Turkey pledged help to her partners only if the war extended to the Mediterranean area. Turkey's aid and cooperation with the other two signatories was explicit in case the latter had to fulfill their guarantees to Greece and Rumania. No signatory was allowed to sign a separate armistice or peace treaty with enemy powers. Protocol no. 2, added to and forming an integral part of the treaty, stated: "The obligations undertaken by Turkey in virtue of the above-mentioned Treaty cannot compel that country to take action having as its effect, or involving as its consequence, entry into armed conflict with the U.S.S.R."

The treaty was to be valid for fifteen years and was accompanied by a financial agreement, according to which Britain and France granted Turkey a credit of £25 million for the purchase of war materials, a loan of £15 million in gold, and an additional credit of £3 million to liquidate British and French "frozen" commercial assets.

Moscow was highly critical of the treaty when it was officially announced, and Molotov in his speech of October 31 made vocal his disapproval of Turkey's action.[13]

Turkey and World War II, 1939–1941

During the Second World War Turkey's foreign policy was motivated by desire to avoid attack or occupation by the totalitarian powers. The Turks were anxious to avoid German bombing and they believed that Germany would prefer to conciliate rather than crush them. Distrust and fear of Russia were always present in Turkish minds, and they were dominant in Turkey's foreign policy.

Until spring of 1940 her only major move was to close the Straits (in 1939) to foreign warships, in line with Articles 20 and 21 of the Montreux Convention. The defeat of France and the last-minute intervention of Italy posed a problem for the Turkish government. War had, indeed, extended into the Mediterranean, and, if the Tripartite Treaty of Alliance was to be literally observed, Turkey was bound to take action against Italy. With the surrender of France on June 26, 1940, however, it became clear that conditions had changed so radically that it would be unrealistic to expect Turkey to rush headlong into the conflict. This was precisely the stand taken by Prime Minister Saydam when in June he told the Grand Assembly that Turkey would remain nonbelligerent.

Throughout 1940 Turkey feared a German move eastward, and she was active, as Britain's partner, in promoting greater unity among the Balkan states. The main obstacle was, as usual, Bulgarian revisionism, and to overcome this Turkey advised Rumania to reach some compromise over the controversial territorial issues. Her advice fell on deaf ears, and both Rumania and Bulgaria gradually slipped into the German orbit.

Mussolini's invasion of Greece in October 1940 brought Fascist aggression close to Turkey's door. The Greek crisis prompted Britain's foreign secretary, Anthony Eden, to pay a hurried visit to Ankara in February 1941 in order to review the war situation with Turkish leaders and to obtain their approval for the use of British troops in defense of Greece. Such a step meant a diversion of some forces that might be needed later to aid Turkey. Hence the British felt it necessary to consult Ankara. This visit was preceded by Anglo-Turkish staff talks, which took place in the autumn of 1940.

The first half of 1941 witnessed smashing German victories in Yugoslavia and Greece, the conquest of Crete, and the dispatch of a German force to Libya. The situation was further aggravated by an anti-British rebellion in Iraq and Axis infiltration into Vichy-held Syria. The German army was also in occupation of Rumania and Bulgaria. All Greek islands in the Aegean, even those close to the Turkish coast, were in German hands. By June 1941 Turkey was almost surrounded by

[13]Dallin, *op. cit.*, p. 111.

countries dominated by German military might or political influence. The sole exception was her frontier with Russia, but the latter's enigmatic policy was far from reassuring.

Turkish-German Relations

The physical approach of German power to Turkey's frontiers brought Turkish-German relations to a showdown. In the course of their relations with each other there had been friendship and there were still some romantic memories of a common struggle in the days of World War I. While many Turks resented Germany's intention to make Turkey another "Egypt," i.e., a virtual protectorate, many others, especially among the military, hard a warm feeling for the martial and efficient Teutonic nation. Despite political controversies during World War I, there had been surprisingly little mutual recrimination after defeat in 1918. Whatever emotional hostility remained in both nations was directed against the victorious Versailles powers who, as viewed from Berlin and Ankara, imposed humiliating peace terms upon the vanquished. Under these circumstances it was not difficult for the Weimar republic to regain the friendship and confidence of the Turks. The employment of numerous German professors, experts, and construction firms by the Kemalist administration eloquently testified to the speedy revival of the old bonds of friendship.

Hitler's advent to power did not per se alienate Turkey from Germany. After all, the Turks were not prone to shed tears over the ill treatment of a national minority by another country. Moreover, some dynamic features of the new regime in Berlin filled them with a certain amount of admiration. As for the lack of parliamentary democracy under Hitler's rule, few worried about that in Turkey. Economically, cooperation with Germany was promising, and the barter agreements which Dr. Hjalmar Schacht skillfully negotiated in Ankara in the 1930s increased the volume of Turkish foreign trade, relieved the pressure of depression, and permitted Turkey to sell some goods to Germany at prices 20 to 40 percent higher than those of the world market. By 1939 up to 90 percent of Turkey's foreign trade was transacted through clearing agreements, and Germany received about one-half of all Turkish exports.

The basically revisionist character of Nazi foreign policy did not quite comport with the Turkish devotion to the status quo, but, so long as Germany kept her hands off southeastern Europe, Turkey had no particular cause for alarm. The cooling of Turko-German relations came gradually as a result of the formation of the Rome-Berlin Axis. Turkish fears of Italian expansionism have already been discussed.[14] Implicit German support of Italian claims underlined the difference between German and Turkish objectives. By her participation in the Nyon conference of 1937, on the policing of the Mediterranean during the Spanish Civil War, Turkey stressed her interest in preserving the status quo and the principle of collective security, both features unpleasant to Germany. The Munich agreement of 1938 gave Turkey new concern since it illustrated the close collaboration between the European dictators.

[14]See above, p. 124.

Mussolini's attack on Albania on April 7, 1939, precipitated Turkish negotations with Britain and France and definitely marked a point of separation from the Axis camp. Eager to prevent Turkey from joining the Western powers, in late April 1939, Hitler sent as ambassador to Ankara, the exchancellor of the Reich, Franz von Papen. It was hoped in Berlin that Von Papen, a former staff officer in Falkenhayn's army in Syria and a man possessing much diplomatic skill and good Turkish contacts, would be able to influence Turkey's policies. This was not the case, however, as the conclusion of the Turkish—French-British alliance subsequently proved. But Von Papen did not relent in his efforts to improve Turkish-German relations. Generally speaking, his diplomacy in Ankara passed through three distinct stages. During the first (1939-1940), he attempted to keep Turkey neutral and to dissuade her from an Anglo-French alliance. During the second (1941-1943), he exerted pressure to bring about closer economic, political, and military ties between Berlin and Ankara. During the third (1944), he again reverted to an effort to keep the Turks neutral.

While the Turks needed no urging to stay neutral, it was more difficult to get them to cooperate with the Axis. In the spring of 1941 Germany's position was so strong after her Balkan victories that Turkey reluctantly agreed to begin negotiations on a bilateral treaty. Von Papen sought to secure Ankara's permission to unlimited transit of German war materials and passage of a disguised contingent of troops through Turkish territory toward Iraq, Syria, and Iran. In return he was authorized to promise rectification of the Turkish border in Thrace, a few Greek islands in the Aegean, and a guarantee of Turkish security and the safety of the Straits.[15]

On June 18, 1941, Von Papen succeeded in concluding a ten-year treaty of nonaggression with Turkey. The Turks accepted it as a safeguard against German aggression but took care to insert a clause which stated that previous commitments of the signatories would not be affected by the treaty. German motivation was clear; they desired to neutralize Turkey and isolate Russia prior to their invasion of that country scheduled for June 22.

The rapid advance of the Reichswehr in Russia emboldened Germany in her relations with Turkey. Berlin began to exert pressure on Ankara for closer collaboration. Germany was interested in Turkish raw materials, especially in chrome, which was essential for the production of high-grade steel. Turkey, however, had a chrome agreement with Great Britain, which she refused to violate.

What ensued could be called a "chrome war" between Germany and the Western Allies, with Turkey as a reluctant battleground. Economically, the efforts of the two protagonists to outbid each other netted Turkey tremendous gains, since the prices paid to her were far above the world market price. Politically, however, the whole process was most embarrassing and dangerous.

On October 9, 1941, partly succumbing to German pressure, Turkey concluded with the Reich a trade pact to last until March 31, 1943. It provided for the sale of 90,000 tons of chrome ore to Germany in 1943-1944 (i.e., after the expiration of

---

[15] *La Politique Allemande, 1941-1943; Documents Secrets du Ministère des Affaires Etrangères d'Allemagne* (Paris, 1946).

the Anglo-Turkish chrome agreement). In return, Germany promised to deliver war equipment worth 100 million Turkish pounds, of which 18 million pounds' worth would be shipped before the end of 1942.

Throughout 1941 and 1942 Von Papen pressed Turkey to become "more and more friendly" toward Germany and to grant the Reichswehr transit facilities to the Arab countries and the Suez Canal. In addition to the inducements mentioned in connection with the Turkish-German pact of June 18, 1941, Germany used two other devices to win Turkey's support. The first was the revelation of the far-reaching Soviet ambitions to secure military control of the Straits, which Molotov had repeatedly stressed to the German government during the period of Nazi-Soviet collaboration. Considering these Soviet claims, Turkey had, according to Berlin, nothing to gain and much to lose from an Allied victory. The second device was an attempt to revive and encourage Pan-Turanian tendencies in Turkey. The advance of the German army into the southern, Moslem-inhabited regions of the Soviet Empire (the Crimea and the Caucasus) gave Germany a trump card of major importance in her relations with Turkey. The German Foreign Office wanted to give these Turkish-speaking areas autonomy and invited some Turks to aid in the administration as expert advisers. Germany showed a disposition to negotiate with Turkey about the future status of the areas in question. By conceding to Turkey the right to organize the liberated Turko-Tatar areas of the Soviet Union into a federation, Von Papen and an influential group in the German Foreign Office hoped to secure Turkish collaboration during the war.

Although these inducements profoundly impressed Turkish Pan-Turanians and attracted the attention of some military leaders including Marshal Çakmak, the official Turkish attitude was noncommittal. In an important conversation with Von Papen on August 27, 1942, Prime Minister Saracoglu stated that as a Turk he "passionately [desired] the annihilation of Russia," and that such an exploit, about to be accomplished by the Führer, did not occur more than once in a century. He believed that Germany had a major mission to carry out in liberating the Turkish peoples of Russia. As prime minister of Turkey, however, he must take care not to give the Russians the slightest pretext to annihilate, by way of reprisals, the Turko-Mongol minorities. For this reason it was necessary for him to maintain absolute neutrality.[16]

Turkey was unwilling to compromise her neutral position by embracing Pan-Turanism. Moreover, it was doubtful whether any tangible arrangement could result from these talks because of the opposition of Alfred Rosenberg's German Ministry for the East to any schemes of Turko-Tatar autonomy. Rosenberg and his clique of power-grasping Nazis did not share the view of the foreign ministry on this situation. Selfishly looking for governorships of the occupied areas and anticipating a speedy conquest of the Caucasus, they went so far as to dispatch to Turkey a man who loudly advertised himself as the "Gauleiter of Tiflis," much to the mortification of the German ambassador.[17] In September 1942 Ribbentrop abruptly in-

[16] *Ibid*, pp. 89 ff.
[17] L. C. Moyzisch, *Operation Cicero* (New York, 1950), p. 5.

structed Von Papen to discontinue the Pan-Turanian conversations in view of the stubborn Turkish neutrality.

This attitude could not be shaken by Von Papen's personal skill, or by his lavish use of money to foster German propaganda,[18] or even by the great advantage of having access, during the critical period, to the secret documents of the British embassy.[19] The maximum advantage Germany could obtain was to conclude two new trade agreements with Turkey: the first on June 2, 1942, followed by a Turkish promise in September to ship her 45,000 tons of chrome, representing half of Turkey's annual production, and the second on April 21, 1943, for the exchange of $30 million worth of goods in the next year.

From the time of the Battle of Stalingrad and the Anglo-American landing in North Africa in the fall of 1942, Germany's military position steadily deteriorated, and so did her diplomatic position. On April 20, 1944, Turkey stopped further shipments of chrome to Germany. On June 15 she put an end to the secret passage of minor German naval craft through the Straits, and on August 2, 1944, she broke diplomatic relations with the Reich.

Turkey and the Western Allies

Turkish attitudes were obviously influenced by the changing fortunes of the war and also by skillful Allied diplomacy. The entry of the United States into the war profoundly affected Turkish political thought. Even before this happened, Turkey had been granted, on December 3, 1941, American lend-lease assistance. This proved to be valuable because of the wartime collapse of foreign trade and the fact that, throughout the war, Turkey was obliged to maintain an army of two million men, thus diverted from their productive occupations.

During the war Turkey maintained close contact with the British, who played a major part in supplying her with military equipment. In December 1942 the British cabinet decided "in principle" to try to bring Turkey into the war on the Allied side. In early February 1943, Prime Minister Churchill and President Inönü, accompanied by high military advisers, met in Adana to look into the problem of Turkish belligerency. Both parties agreed that before Turkey made any move she must be properly equipped militarily. The Adana meeting was consequently followed by visits to Ankara of top British commanders in the Middle East.[20] These men counted on Turkey's entry into the war by the fall of 1943. The result of these talks was an infiltration of Turkey by Royal Air Force personnel, incognito.[21] But, faced with the threat of German reprisal bombing of Istanbul, the Turkish government refused to

[18]In December 1942, Ribbentrop reportedly sent Von Papen five million Reichsmarks in gold to support pro-German elements in Turkey (*La Politique Allemande*, p. 115).

[19]Between October 1943 and April 1944 the valet of the British ambassador, Sir Hughe Knatchbull-Hugessen, regularly opened the ambassador's safe, photographed the documents, and supplied them to the German secret service agent, L. C. Moyzisch. He was paid £5,000 for a roll of films. Details of this fascinating story are contained in Moyzisch, *op. cit.*, and in the article by Robert W. Kempner, "The Highest Paid Spy in History," *Saturday Evening Post*, Jan. 28, 1950.

[20]Sir Sholto Douglas, Sir Henry Maitland Wilson, and Sir John Cunningham, representing the R.A.F., the Army, and the Navy, respectively.

[21]Moyzisch, *op. cit.*, p. 56.

abandon its position of non-belligerency. Yet Turkey was not absolutely neutral. In September 1943 she gave evidence of this by aiding, first to supply and then to evacuate, those British troops who. following Italy's collapse, had taken over some of the Dodecanese Islands and who were later forced to give them up to the Germans. The evacuation could be attributed to German air superiority, and it served as a reminder to the Turks to proceed with caution.

Although the Turkish position found sympathetic understanding in London and in Washington, at the Moscow and Teheran conferences in October and November 1943, the United States, Russia, and Great Britain agreed that Turkish belligerency should be secured by the end of 1943. What followed constituted another chapter in the "diplomacy of pressure." On his way from the Moscow conference, British Foreign Secretary Anthony Eden met Turkish Foreign Minister Numan Menemen-cioglu in Cairo and pressed him for a declaration of war. In December, again in Cairo, President Roosevelt and Prime Minister Churchill, fresh from their meeting in Teheran, reiterated this demand to President Inönü, requesting as a first step Allied use of Turkish air bases. The Turks agreed "in principle" but made their agreement conditional upon further supply of arms from the West. A British military and air delegation that arrived in Ankara in late January 1944 left empty-handed. The Allies did not conceal their disappointment.

Beginning with the spring of 1944, however, Turkey, as has been pointed out, made several moves to sever economic and political relations with Germany, and this trend was culminated by the declaration of war on the Reich on February 23, 1945. This last act did not evoke much enthusiasm in Ankara, inasmuch as the Turks did not like to imitate Mussolini by entering the war at the eleventh hour.[22] The decision was made largely in order to gain admittance to the United Nations Conference at San Francisco.

Turkish-Soviet Relations

Turkey's relations with Russia were strained. On the one hand, Turkey feared Soviet revisionism in the Straits, and these fears, as we have seen, were skillfully fanned by Von Papen. On the other, Russia resented, first, Turkey's alliance with the Western powers, and then after the Nazi invasion, Turkey's neutrality. After France's collapse in 1940 the German government published a White Book, which revealed that at the time of the Russo-Finnish war in 1939–1940, France had planned, with Turkish approval, to use Turkish bases to bombard Baku in the event of war with Russia.[23] Although vigorous denials were subsequently made by Ankara, this revelation was not conducive to the lessing of tension.

After the German invasion Russia desired Turkey's entry into the war on the Allied side. On September 2, 1943, a Soviet propaganda mouthpiece, *The War and*

[22]Sir Hughe Knatchbull-Hugessen, *Diplomat in Peace and War* (London, 1949), p. 196. The book contains four chapters on Turkey between 1939 and 1944.

[23]This was the so-called "Gamelin Plan," to attack Russia through the Caucasus. It was presented at the request of French Premier Edouard Daladier, and based on recommendations of General Maxime Weygand, commander-in-chief in Syria. Réné Massigli, French ambassador in Ankara, allegedly informed his government that Turkey would cooperate in the execution of these plans. For details, see Dallin, *op. cit.*, pp. 166 ff.

the Working Class, accused Turkey of prolonging the war by protecting Germany's flank in the Balkans. It was clear that the old friendship was rapidly giving way to open hostility. The increase of Pan-Turanian sentiment in Turkey added another element of friction. In fact, the Turkish government became so alarmed lest the Soviets might be provoked to action that in mid-May 1944 it publicly dissociated itself from Pan-Turanism. This took the form of arresting a number of Pan-Turanian leaders and of issuing dramatic official declarations about the alleged discovery of a plot against the government, hatched by the "Gray Wolf Society." On May 18 martial law was imposed, and Radio Ankara, in feigned indignation, called the group of plotters a "pro-German one, based on racialism and Fascist principles." On May 13, at a public celebration of National Youth Day, President Inönü intimated that the plot might have been abetted by "foreigners," and paid tribute to the Soviets who "were our [only] friends" during the War of Independence. In June the Pan-Turanian leaders, mostly school teachers but with a sprinkling of bigger names, were court-martialed.

Following this episode, anti-German articles critical of fascism and racialism appeared more frequently in the Turkish press. The Grand Assembly revoked the recently imposed Varlik-Vergisi law which, by instituting a capital levy, proved to be a particular nuisance to the Jews and other national minorities. It was obvious that Turkey was taking pains to ensure her place in the camp of the Allies.

On January 12, 1945, Turkey agreed to open the Straits for the flow of supplies to Russia and on January 29 severed relations with Japan. These steps did not assuage Russian hostility. On March 21 the Soviet government denounced the Soviet-Turkish pact of friendship and nonaggression, which had originally been concluded in 1925 and which had repeatedly been renewed. Turkish-Soviet relations entered in a new and dangerous phase.

From June 1945 on, it was public knowledge that Russia insisted upon four conditions as terms for the renewal of the nonaggression treaty. They included (1) the return to Russia of Kars and Ardahan, (2) the granting of military bases in the Bosphorous and the Dardanelles, (3) a revision of the Montreux Straits Convention, and (4) a revision of the Thracian boundary in favor of Communist-dominated Bulgaria.[24] The nature of these demands became clear when, on December 20, three important Soviet newspapers published an article written by two Georgian scholars who demanded that Turkey restore to the Georgian SSR a Black Sea coastal region situated southwest of Batum, 180 miles long and 75 miles wide. The region included the districts of Artvin, Ardahan, Oltü, Tortum, Ispir, Bayburt, Gümüsane, Giresun, and the important port of Trebizond.

Throughout 1946 Soviet pressure for the revision of the Montreux Convention continued. Russia demanded that the Straits should come under the control of Turkey as well as other Black Sea powers and that defense of the Straits should be jointly organized by Turkey and Russia.[25] These demands were steadily rejected by Ankara to the growing impatience of Moscow.

[24]Howard, *op. cit.*
[25]For details of the Straits problem, see Chapter XVIII.

Uneasiness in Turkey at this time was reflected by the extension of martial law, despite the end of the war. From Moscow came a mounting barrage of anti-Turkish propaganda, intensified by the publication in the summer of 1946 of German Foreign Office documents concerning Nazi relations with Turkey. In December the Turkish government announced the arrest of over seventy members of the Turkish Socialist Workers' and Peasants' Party and the Turkish Socialist Party for Communist subversive activities. The two groups were banned and their six press organs suppressed.

By the spring of 1947 Turkish-Soviet relations had reached an all-time low, and Turkey seriously feared armed intervention. On March 12, 1947, President Truman delivered his famous message to Congress in which he proposed assistance to Turkey and Greece, in view of the grave Soviet threats to their security. While this American action introduced a new factor of stability into the Near East which could not be ignored by the Soviets, it did not improve the strained relations between Moscow and Ankara. Later in the year the Russians lodged an official protest against the activities of the Turkish repatriation mission in Germany, Greece, and Italy. The mission had offered Turkish citizenship and other inducements to Moslem displaced persons (mostly fugitives from Russia) if they emigrated to Turkey. In December 5,000 university students in Ankara demonstrated against five reputedly pro-Communist professors, demanding their dismissal. The attitude in the country became increasingly anti-Soviet. It was highlighted on April 27, 1950, when an official communiqué declared that Turkey had "finally and conclusively" rejected Soviet demands for joint control of the Turkish Straits.

Turkish-American Friendship

Much of this growing defiance of Soviet pressure must be ascribed to the rapprochement between Turkey and the United States. American diplomacy initially endeavored to accommodate Russia when the latter brought up the question of the Montreux Convention. At the Big Three Conference of Potsdam, July 5, 1945, the American delegation, with the British, endorsed what they believed to be legitimate Soviet demands concerning maritime traffic to and from the Black Sea. On November 2, 1945, the United States went so far as to set forth its own formal proposals, very favorable to Russia and, in fact, somewhat reminiscent of the privileged status that tsarist Russia had enjoyed under the Treaty of Unkiar Iskelessi (See Chapter XVIII). But the United States, with Britain, steadfastly refused to accept Soviet contentions concerning the administration and the defense of the Straits by the Black Sea powers. In a note of August 19, 1946, addressed to Moscow, the American government made it clear that it would oppose any virtual monopoly of power by Russia in the strategic waterway.

The "Truman Doctrine" of opposition to Soviet imperialism, previously referred to, was proclaimed when Soviet pressure on Turkey and Greece was at its highest. In Greece Soviet-sponsored guerrillas endeavored to overthrow the legitimate Athens government; their success would have gravely impaired Turkish security. The British, who had hitherto been mainly responsible for the bolstering of Greek defense and for the supply of war equipment to Turkey, declared that they were no longer in a position to continue these responsibilities. In a bold decision the American government assumed the burden, declaring that the preservation of Greek and Turkish independence was vital to the security of the United States. This was the first major commitment of the United States in the Middle East of a semimilitary nature, and Congress, not quite ready to face the realities, spent a number of weeks debating the necessary appropriations. By mid-May 1947 Congress approved the expenditure of $400 million, to be spent on economic and military aid, of which $100 million was assigned to Turkey. Turkey greeted this action with relief and gratitude. President Truman's message marked the beginning of an era of growing American interest in the welfare and security of Turkey and set in motion a number of measures to aid and reassure that country. On May 2, 1947, elements of the United States Mediterranean fleet visited Istanbul, giving rise to enthusiastic pro-American demonstrations. In June an American military mission arrived in Ankara to become a permanent addition to the diplomatic representation. In the same month Turkey signed a contract with two American firms for construction and modernization of airfields.[26] The Turkish chief of staff paid an official visit to the United States in the fall of the same year. American experts were hired to advise on railway, sea transport, telegraph, and telephone organization. In the spring of 1948 Turkey received from the United States a number of naval vessels, including long-range submarines, and a contingent of attack bombers, granted under the Turkish assistance act. Simultaneously, arrangements were made for the training of Turkish naval crews in America.

The adoption by Congress of the European Recovery Program contributed to the strengthening of the ties between the two countries, Turkey being included among the sixteen recipients of American aid. A permanent mission of the Economic Cooperation Administration (ECA) was added to the growing number of private and official American institutions in Ankara.

The year 1949 brought, in the midst of the mounting East-West crisis, further manifestations of cooperation between Washington and Ankara. Aware of the increased American interest in the defense of Europe, Turkey made skillful diplomatic efforts to lay stress on her European character from the strategic and the political points of view. In February the Turkish government suggested the conclusion of a Mediterranean defense pact, and in August, much to her gratification, Turkey was admitted to the Council of Europe, a deliberative body recently created at Strasbourg.

The negotiation and conclusion by the United States of the North Atlantic Treaty on April 4, 1949, aroused in Turkey keen interest and a desire to be included in the alliance, alongside Greece. The North Atlantic partners were not yet ready to extend their formal commitments so far. However, largely to assuage Turkish fears, Dean Acheson, the American secretary of state, declared on March 23, 1949, that the United States' continuous interest in the security of the nations of the Middle East,

---

[26]Westinghouse Electric and J. G. White. Previously, in October 1946, a contract had been signed with the Radio Corporation of America for the installation of modern radio equipment aboard 31 ships of the Turkish merchant marine.

particularly Greece, Turkey, and Iran, had in no way been lessened by the negotiations on the North Atlantic Treaty.

On December 27, 1949, the United States and Turkey concluded a cultural pact providing for the use of $5 million worth of lend-lease surplus property for student exchange. In May 1950 the Department of State informed the public that in three years under the Truman Doctrine and the Marshall Plan Greece and Turkey together had received a total of $700 million in military and of $764 million in economic assistance. Scarcely a month later it was announced that the Economic Cooperation Administration had allocated to Turkey $275,000 to carry out a major maritime rehabilitation project and that a nine-man group of American shipping experts was to advise Ankara on the execution of this plan.

The outbreak of the Korean war in June 1950 found Turkey eager to show her devotion to the principles of world peace. On July 25 she offered the United Nations a brigade of 4,500 fully equipped troops, which without much delay were shipped to Korea. There they participated in some of the fiercest battles of the war, displaying great military valor and gaining universal praise from the military experts. These troops suffered heavy casualties in the dramatic retreat of midwinter 1950-1951 caused by the sudden Chinese Communist intervention, but their morale remained unimpaired. The American press paid glowing tributes to the gallantry of the Mehmetciks.

Following the official Turkish application on August 1, 1950, for membership in the North Atlantic Treaty Organization, much sympathetic thought was given on both sides of the Atlantic to this request.[27]

Turkey's New Democracy

The steadily growing friendship with America was strengthened by notable domestic developments in Turkey. Since the termination of the war, progressive liberalization in Turkish political life could be noticed. The one-party system virtually ended when, in January 1947, a newly created Democratic party held its first national congress in Ankara. Six months later press dispatches announced the inauguration of another organization, the Turkish Conservative party (Türk Muhafazakar Partisi), headed by Rifat Atilhan, which proclaimed its support of religious instruction. The ending of martial law early in 1948 marked a gradual relaxation of strict government controls and made life easier for the opposition.

This new trend found its dramatic (and to many observers unexpected) expression in May 1950 when freely conducted national elections resulted in complete victory for the new Democratic party.[28] This was followed by the election of Celal Bayar, founder of the Democratic party, to the presidency of the republic. The new presi-

---

[27]On September 20, 1951, the North Atlantic Council at its meeting at Ottawa formally extended to Turkey (and Greece) an invitation to join the alliance. Soon afterward Ambassador W. A. Harriman and Gen. Omar N. Bradley, chairman of the U.S. Joint Chiefs of Staff, visited Ankara to explore with Turkish leaders the practical aspects of Turkey's inclusion in NATO.

[28]The Democratic party secured 387 seats out of a total of 487 in the Assembly. The People's Party gained 63 seats.

dent entrusted the formation of a new cabinet to fifty-one-year-old Adnan Menderes. Fuat Köprülü became foreign minister. The Democratic party program laid greater emphasis on free enterprise in the nation's economic life but otherwise differed little from the People's party platform. The Democrats owed their resounding victory primarily to the popular desire for a change of administration. The People's party government had been in office ever since 1922 and, like any human institution, had developed burdensome bureaucratic characteristics. The immediate cause could be found in the high cost of living, resulting partly from the economic inefficiency of state-owned enterprises and partly from the impact of the uncertain international situation upon the domestic life of the nation. The important fact was that the Turkish people wanted a change and they obtained it in an orderly and peaceful manner. With regard to Turkey's international position, no division of opinion was registered. Bayar, the president-elect, declared on the day of electoral victory: "It is important for this country's security and even for the cause of world peace that friend and foe alike should know that any change whatsoever in the Government is not going to change our foreign policy."

The new government's action upheld the statement. The new regime relaxed the stress on secularism, emphasized so greatly during the preceding period.[29] On July 7, 1950, the twenty-seven-year-old ban on religious radio programs was lifted. Radio Ankara began brief broadcasts of readings from the Koran.

Although the Turks, and their foreign friends, had good reasons to rejoice at Turkey's smooth transition from tutelage to democracy, they soon found that democracy could not be speedily implanted without much work and tribulation. Such questions as the choice between a two-party or a multiparty system, the immutability or flexibility of Kemalist principles, and the role of religion in the state had to be considered in terms of their relevance to an orderly development of democratic processes. With regard to the number of parties, there was a definite trend toward a two-party system, although attempts were made to introduce other parties. While such parties as the Socialist, Peasant, Democratic Islamic, or National Uplift could be considered as minor and ephemeral, this was not true of the Nation (Millet) party, which rallied to its standard important conservative and proreligious elements. But precisely because the Millet party stood for principles opposed to the basic tenets of the Republic, in particular to secularism, it incurred accusations of sedition, and its very existence posed the problem of limits to free speech and assembly in the new democracy.

The party's fourth Congress held in Ankara in June 1953 could be regarded as a major anti-Kemalist manifestation. Alarmed at the reactionary course the party was following, the government took energetic steps to put an end to its activities. After search and closure of the party's headquarters, the government suspended the party's press organ *Millet* and indicted fifteen of its members for advocating return to the turban and veil, polygamy, teaching in the Arabic alphabet, and restoration of

---

[29]The first sign of change came as early as 1947, when the People's party government decided to permit religious instruction in schools. It was, however, largely a political move, designed to offset the successes which the opposition Democratic party scored with the peasantry by appealing to their religious emotions.

the monarchy, i.e., in general terms, propaganda in favor of a theocratic state. On January 27, 1954, a court in Ankara ordered dissolution of the party, but the verdict was subsequently voided by Turkey's highest tribunal, the Court of Cassation. Moreover, the party promptly reconstituted itself as a Republican Nation party, thus, at least through its title, indicating abandonment of royalist schemes. In the May 1954 elections the party, campaigning under its new name, won five seats to the Grand National Assembly on the basis of 480,249 votes cast in its favor.[30]

Although this figure was far from impressive, it could not be taken as fully indicative of the party's position in the country. This was due to two factors. In the first place, the Republican People's party (R.P.P.), one of the two major parties in the country, managed to secure only 31 seats out of a total of 541, and yet its strength—as represented by 3,193,471 votes—was much greater than the negligible number of seats acquired would indicate. If this was true of the R.P.P., there was no reason to apply a different yardstick to the Republican Nation party. In the second place, the 1950s witnessed a widespread revival of religious fraternities such as Ticani, Badi al-Zaman, Bektaşi, Nakşibendi, and Kadiriya and of pro-Islamic political organizations such as the Democratic Islamic Party, the National Uplift party, and a militant association known as Büyük Doğu. All these groups professed an extreme pro-Islamic philosophy and, at times, practiced terrorism and vandalism, the latter directed at statues of Kemal Ataturk. Their aggressiveness received considerable publicity when in the fall of 1952 some members of Büyük Doğu and the Islamic Democratic party assaulted and seriously wounded Ahmet Emin Yalman, editor of the respected *Vatan* and one of the foremost figures of Turkish journalism, for his allegedly "anti-Islamic" attitudes. Thus, it was certain that the poor showing of the Millet at the elections did not truly portray the strength of traditionalist and proreligious feelings in the country.

But how strong was the religious reaction, and why did it reveal itself under the Democratic administration? As for the first question, any answer must be tentative inasmuch as Turkey has not yet developed all the modern methods of gauging public opinion used in the more advanced West. It seems fairly certain that, qualitatively, the religious reaction represented a hard core of irreconcilables who were thoroughly dedicated and determined to wage an intense struggle to achieve their objectives. Quantitatively, however, they were definitely in a minority inasmuch as both major parties, the Democratic and the People's Republican, favored secularism. Moreover, most of the younger and of the educated elements opposed return to Islam as a guiding principle of the state.

With reference to the second question, the revival of religious reaction was due partly to the relaxation of government controls in conformity with the new spirit of democracy and partly to the policy and tactics of the Democratic party itself. This party, in order to win the contest with the old party of Ataturk, tried to woo to itself all those elements in Turkish society which for one reason or another had grievances against the dictatorial controls of the Kemal-İnönü era. Thus the Democrats appealed to businessmen, intellectuals, and urban consumers who had grown restive

---

[30] *Cahiers de l'Orient Contemporain,* 1954, 1. (Henceforth referred to as *Cahiers.*)

under the regime of *étatisme*, lack of civil liberties, and inflation, respectively. But the Democrats' greatest untapped source was the conservative countryside, to which the People's party, urban-minded and reformist, had never paid adequate attention. To gain popularity in the rural and provincial communities, Democrats did not hesitate to entice voters by moderate (and never too explicit) promises of greater tolerance toward religion, especially in the school and in radio programs. Furthermore, the party allowed the gradual formation among its members of a pro-Islamic wing.[31] These tactics were responsible for the confusion created in the minds of many concerning the party's true intentions. In reality, the Democratic leaders were as dedicated to the Kemalist principles as were the People's Republicans. But because of tactical concessions made in the heat of the campaign, they later had to face a strong Islamic movement, which, if unchecked, was likely to shake the foundations of the Republic.

To cope with these dangerous trends the Democrats resorted partly to legislation and partly to police action and judicial proceedings within the framework of such laws as existed. On July 25, 1951, the Grand National Assembly adopted a law protecting the memory of Ataturk. The Democrats also banned, through appropriate judicial channels, certain anticonstitutional groups and, as mentioned above, took steps against the Millet party, which appeared as the most serious challenger of the existing system.

In the initial stages this policy met with full approval from the People's Republicans. Their leader, former President Inönü, declared on January 21, 1953: "We cannot but give our support to the government for the measures it has taken with a view to protecting the structure of the country against all reactionary movements." In another speech delivered shortly afterward, he added: "It is good that the government . . . has decided to defend the reforms of the Republic. The duty of the government is to prevent the religion from being used for political purposes and the duty of the opposition is to help the government in this task."[32]

But repression (however clothed in judicial vestments) immediately posed the problem of where the line between licit and illicit political activity should be drawn. It also created the danger that, once used, it might be applied to other political foes as well. In fact, this was precisely what happened. The Democrats did not withstand the temptation of curbing the opposition as a whole. The sharp edge of this policy pointed against their most formidable rivals, the People's Republicans. The method used was the passage of a series of legislative acts by the Democrat-dominated Grand National Assembly. These acts included a law depriving the Republican People's party of its "People's Houses" (August 8, 1951); an amendment to the penal code making offensive criticism of cabinet members a punishable crime (June 1, 1953); a law placing a ban on the political activities of professors (July 21, 1953);

---

[31] A typical manifestation of the pro-Islamic tendency within the Democratic party was a petition presented at a local party conference held in Konya in March 1951. The petition asked for the substitution of the fez for the European hat, the reintroduction of veils, the abandonment of Latin script in favor of Arabic, the suppression of statues, the banning of the civil code, and the reestablishment of religious law and polygamy.

[32] *Cahiers*, 1953, 1.

a law confiscating certain properties of the Republican People's party (December 12, 1953); a press law instituting penalties for articles offending official persons (March 7, 1954); and two laws directed against the privilege of tenure of officials, professors, and judges (fall 1954). The People's Republicans naturally opposed this legislation, and, when on July 23, 1953, the Democrats introduced a bill forbidding the use of religion for political purposes, they voted against it, despite their earlier approval of the Democrats' secularist policy. The bill in question, together with the ban on political activities of professors just mentioned, had been presented by the Democrats as "laws of national safety," an ominous-sounding title.

Bolstered by this kind of legislation and the mental climate it engendered, the Democrats scored a resounding citory at the polls on May 2, 1954, gaining 503 seats out of a total of 541. Increasingly intolerant of criticism, they did not hesitate to put on trial the dean of Turkish journalism, Husein Cahit Yalçin, and a number of other newspapermen, who, in due course, received jail sentences. By August 1955 the rift between the Democrats and their Republican opponents became so intense that the latter refused to run in the municipal and provincial elections.

While thus trying to silence the opposition, the Democrats suffered dissension within their own ranks. Both the rightist wing in the party and the liberal elements began to oppose the leading group headed by Premier Adnan Menderes. The latter did not hesitate to deal harshly with those whose extreme pro-Islamic stand brought them close to the outlawed traditionalists.[33] In one case expulsion from the party was followed by indictment and punishment. The liberal critics were aggrieved by the premier's economic policies and his repressive political measures. In mid-October 1955 nine deputies, including two former ministers, were expelled from the party for revolting against Menderes' leadership. Shortly afterward ten more deputies, in a gesture of solidarity, severed their party links to act henceforth as independents. A few days later their example was followed by sixty delegates, who walked out of the party's annual conference. These defections led, in December, to the creation of a new party named Hürriyet (Freedom). Headed by Fevzi Lütfi Karaosmanoglu, a deputy from Manisa, and Ibrahim Oktem, a deputy from Bursa, the party rallied around itself twenty-nine deputies, thus becoming the third most important force in the Assembly.

In the conduct of national affairs the Democratic cabinet focused its attention on economic development, which, largely due to American assistance, took a bold swing upward. It will be recalled that the Democrats, in contrast to their predecessors, tried to deemphasize *étatisme*. In conformity with this objective they passed two laws designed to promote free enterprise. The first, of January 18, 1954, encouraged investments by foreign capital. The second, of March 7, 1954, reversed a long tradition by virtually inviting foreign oil enterprises to start prospecting and

---

[33]Early in 1953 the party expelled a few deputies for belonging to an illegal "Nationalist Association," a proreligious group. At the party congress held in February 1953, Premier Menderes strongly attacked religious trends within the party, stating that the "Democratic Party is not a boarding-house or a hotel" which will harbor people disagreeing with the party's ideas and convictions. "The Democratic Party," he said, "favors manifestations of all sorts of respect toward Islam in Turkey, but opposes the Sharia because" its reintroduction would produce "confusion of religion with politics and with mundane affairs" (*Oriente Moderno*, Feb. 1953).

production under attractive terms. Speaking at the opening of the tenth session of the Grand National Assembly in November 1954, President Celal Bayar proudly pointed out that in the last few years agricultural production had increased by 200 percent; that Turkey then had six to seven times as many tractors as she had in 1950; that industrial production had registered a 100 percent increase, and that the power output had been raised from 800 million K.W.H. to 3 billion in four years. Similarly impressive advances had been made in the road network, which increased from 2,630 kilometers in 1950 to 22,000 in 1954; in bridge construction (an increase from 289 to 1,189 units); and in the merchant marine, which by reaching a level of 700,000 tons had doubled its previous tonnage.[34]

Yet this spectacular development was not without its drawbacks, the principal of which was undoubtedly the inflationary spiral, which gravely affected Turkey's economic stability while exposing millions of people to suffering and shortages. In their zeal to develop and modernize, the Democrats seemed to disregard certain persistent laws of economics as well as the capacity of their underdeveloped country to assimilate the new wealth and technology. Consequently, by the end of 1954 they found themselves in need of a new "injection" of funds to meet their foreign and domestic commitments. Rather naturally, they turned toward the United States for help, asking for a $300 million loan, in addition to all the regular grants currently received from Washington under the heading of Mutual Security or Technical Assistance. But for the first time since the proclamation of the Truman Doctrine, they met with a refusal. Official Washington was critical of the overextension of their economy and resented their disregard of the recommendations made by American experts assisting in Turkish development plans. Linked to the criticism and the resentment was undoubtedly a feeling of uneasiness in American circles over the turn the internal politics of Turkey were taking. This uneasiness had, to be sure, never become a matter of public record, but the West had given too much publicity to the happy growth of Turkish democracy to accept with complete equanimity developments not consonant with the professed ideal.

Turkey's International Position in the 1950s

Turkey's Democratic government continued the foreign policy of its predecessors in its entirety. Based on recognition of Soviet imperialism as danger Number One, this policy aimed at consolidation of political links with the West and improvement of Turkey's military and strategic position. In conformity with these objectives the Turks sought not only to cultivate their friendship with the United States and Britain but also to improve relations with their immediate neighbors in the Balkans and the Middle East. Marshal Tito's defection from the Soviet camp and his veering toward the West enabled the Turks to work for an entente of free Balkan states as an additional barrier to Soviet expansionism. Negotiations aiming at this objective resulted, first, in the signing on February 28, 1953, of a pact of collaboration between Turkey, Yugoslavia, and Greece. This was not a mean achievement,

[34]*Cahiers*, 1954, 2.

considering the ideological divergencies and the distrust existing among the states in question. With mutual confidence thus restored, the three countries took a further step by concluding a formal treaty of alliance on August 9, 1954.

Unfortunately, this new spirit of friendship was not destined to last long. Barely had the new treaty been signed when Greece raised the question of Cyprus. This strategic island in the eastern Mediterranean was a crown colony of the British Empire, but its inhabitants are predominantly Greek with a sizable Turkish minority. During 1954 the Cypriot Greeks began to urge union with Greece, but their demands met with strong opposition on the part of both the island Turks and the Ankara government. The latter objected, on strategic grounds, to any change in the status of Cyprus. Following the evacuation of British troops from the Suez Canal Zone (see p. 527), Cyprus was to become the principal British (and therefore Western) base in the Middle East. A surrender of this valuable stronghold to the vagaries of Greek politics and administration would entail considerable weakening of the West's strategic position. The Turks were most anxious to have in their hinterland a strong Allied base, from which, in case of emergency, aid and supplies could be rushed. Needless to say, the British, as masters of the island, fully shared their views. Though fully aware of the Turkish and British stand on the matter, the Athens government not only lent its support to the Cypriots' demands but went so far as to submit the question to the United Nations. Real political solutions, however, are rarely reached through the United Nations. As with Iran, Indonesia, Palestine, and Korea, so now with Cyprus, local events tended to determine the decision.

Although rebuffed twice in the United Nations, which refused to place the dispute on its agenda,[35] the Greeks did not relent in their campaign for union. Before long Cyprus became the scene of widespread terrorism, directed mainly against the British but involving Turkish victims as well. A British-Greek-Turkish conference convoked in London early in September 1955 emphasized, instead of reducing, the existing divergencies. It was immediately followed, on September 6, by bloody rioting in Istanbul, in the course of which angry mobs attacked and burned most of the Greek (and some Armenian) establishments in the city, killing and wounding a good many of their owners and employees.

With Yugoslavia turning back toward neutralism[36] and the Cyprus issue dividing Greece and Turkey, the usefulness of the Balkan Pact became highly questionable. By the end of 1955 relations between Athens and Ankara had reached their lowest point in the thirty-five years following the Peace Settlement.

Greater success was Turkey's in her relations with the states in the Middle East. Anxious to secure her right flank by closer ties with Asian countries threatened by Soviet expansion, Turkey spearheaded the action to bring about an alliance of the Northern Tier states. As a first step a mutual assistance pact was concluded with

[35]On December 17, 1954, and September 23, 1955.

[36]In 1954–1955 President Tito of Yugoslavia made conciliatory gestures toward Moscow, and in May 1955 Premier Bulganin and Communist Party Secretary Khrushchev visited Belgrade. In December 1955, Tito visited Egypt in an attempt to establish closer relations with the neutralist bloc in the Middle East.

Pakistan on April 2, 1954. Subsequently a treaty was signed with Iraq (February 24, 1955). This became the basis for a regional alliance, to be known as the Baghdad Pact. In the course of the year Britain, Pakistan, and Iran formally adhered to the pact, thereby establishing the Middle East Treaty Organization (METO), with a permanent secretariat in Baghdad.[37] Premier Menderes, with Iraq's Nuri es-Said, could be regarded as the principal architect of this new alliance. By inducing Iraq and, especially, long-hesitant Iran to join the alliance, Menderes successfully forged a chain stretching from the Bosphorus to the highlands of Kashmir and uniting four Moslem states along the Soviet periphery in a common policy of defense.

Although Turkey's accession to the Baghdad Pact ostensibly strengthened her security, it also presented her with certain complications and dangers. The effect of the pact on the Arab world was to produce a split in the Arab ranks, to isolate Iraq, and to deepen the neutralist or anti-Western orientation of some governments and political movements. Such conditions were conducive to the rapprochement between the Soviet Union and the two main centers of Arab nationalism, Cairo and Damascus. What began in 1955 as a purely commercial transaction between Egypt and Russia—namely, the famous arms deal[38]—had assumed by 1957 the proportions of massive economic, political, and cultural Soviet penetration of Syria. Communist advances in Syria were, furthermore, intensified by a crisis in Jordan in April 1957 in which a Communist-Socialist-nationalist coalition almost succeeded in overthrowing the monarchy and radically reorienting Jordan's foreign policy toward close cooperation with the Soviet bloc.[39] Thus, owing to the leap that Moscow had made over the Northern Tier into the heartland of Arabism, Turkey found herself suddenly facing the Communist danger on both her northern and southern borders. The fear of encirclement led her to take certain diplomatic and military actions with an eye to averting the danger to her security. In the diplomatic sector Turkish spokesmen made a point of impressing upon Western public opinion the danger to the Free World that the possible communization and satellization of Syria (and of Jordan) presented. In the summer of 1957 the Turks massed major land forces along the Syrian border in a gesture that was not free from ambiguity. These troop concentrations were loudly denounced by Syria and Egypt as evidence of aggressive intentions. Furthermore, the Soviet government, trying to make political gains out of the situation of tension, publicly warned Ankara that it would not stand idly by should Turkey take aggressive action against Syria. Actually it was doubtful whether, even in case of a Communist take-over in Syria, Turkey would want to resort to force and thus expose herself to the double charge of aggression and intervention in Syria's internal affairs. More likely the Turks' intention was to dramatize the issue before the world and indicate, especially to the United States, that Turkey would fully support some kind of intervention or preventive action in Syria—if the United States decided upon such a move. Turkey's anxiety about the trends in Syria was not ill-founded. The United States shared it to a considerable

[37]For further details, see the section "The Baghdad Pact," pp. 283–286.
[38]See p. 528 below.
[39]See p. 485 below.

extent, and the mission undertaken in the summer of 1957 by Deputy Undersecretary of State Loy Henderson to Ankara and several Middle Eastern capitals
further emphasized the gravity of the situation.

The Turko-Syrian crisis was eventually overshadowed and displaced by the
movement for the unification of Syria with Egypt, which gained momentum in the
fall of 1957.

Effects of Arab Upheavals

The year 1958 opened in the Middle East with the proclamation of the Syrian-
Egyptian union, which was followed by a series of events substantially changing the
political climate in the area. These included the Iraq-Jordan federation, the civil war
in Lebanon, and the revolution in Iraq, the latter followed by American landings in
Lebanon and the dispatch of British troops to crisis-ridden Jordan. The Turks
watched these developments with considerable concern inasmuch as any weakening
of Western influence in the area was bound to affect their own security adversely.
Iraq's defection from the Baghdad Pact posed the immediate problem of the
viability and continuity of this regional alliance. At this point the Moslem member
states of the pact felt more acutely than ever before the gap in the area's defense
structure caused by America's nonparticipation in the pact in a formal capacity.
Consequently, at a London conference of the pact powers and the United States
called in midsummer following the Iraqi revolution, they asked for, and obtained, a
pledge from Washington of a formal guarantee of their security in the form of
bilateral treaties to be concluded at an early date between each of them and the
United States. A few months later, on March 5, 1959, a bilateral treaty of mutual
defense was concluded between the United States and Turkey, thus giving the latter
the much-sought-for specific American commitment, which hitherto, despite Turkey's membership in NATO and the Baghdad Pact, had been lacking. As a result of
this treaty Turkey opened her territory to the establishment of intermediate range
ballistic missile bases. This development, as might be expected, was strongly resented by Moscow, which in the course of 1959 did not fail to issue threats and
warnings, alternating with offers of economic and technical aid "with no strings
attached." Despite this, Turkey did not falter in her policy, and, in fact, her links
with the West were strengthened by a major loan granted her in August 1958 and the
ratification in February 1959 of an investment guarantee agreement concluded with
the United States. The loan, which was for $350 million, was granted jointly by the
United States ($234 million), the Organization for European Economic Cooperation
($100 million), and the International Monetary Fund ($25 million) for the purpose
of strengthening the Turkish economy, which, as will be seen in a subsequent
section, suffered from a serious crisis in 1958. The investment agreement envisaged
special guarantees and procedures to protect and ensure American investors against
possible nationalization. It followed the pattern of similar agreements concluded by
the United States with thirty-four countries prior to that date.

The Cyprus Settlement

Simultaneously with the upheavals in the Arab hinterland, another major issue
claimed Turkey's attention between 1958 and 1960, namely, the problem of the

future status of Cyprus. A Greek guerrilla movement, led by Colonel George Grivas and endorsed by Archbishop Makarios, carried on a prolonged struggle for independence or union with Greece. Initially the British were reluctant to grant either demand, partly because of their solicitude for one of their last remaining strongholds in the Middle Eastern Mediterranean area and partly out of consideration for Turkish susceptibilities. The Turkish government was definitely opposed to the emancipation of Cyprus under purely Greek rule, insisting instead on the partition of the island. between its Greek and Turkish components if the British rule were to come to an end. Eventually, after protracted negotiations involving Britain, Greece, Turkey, and Greek and Turkish representatives from Cyprus, a conference called in London produced an agreement on February 19, 1959 whereby: (1) Cyprus was to become independent as of February 19, 1960; (2) the government of Cyprus was to be shared by the Greeks and Turks in the proportion of seven to three;[40] (3) Britain was to retain her military and naval base in a defined area; and (4) both Greece and Turkey were to station contingents of their forces in Cyprus in recognition of their special interest in the island. The London agreement was signed by the premiers of Greece and Turkey, Konstantin Karamanlis and Adnan Menderes, who thus succeeded in putting an end to a dispute which had plagued their relations ever since 1955 and had threatened seriously to weaken NATO defenses in this part of the world. On August 16, 1960, in fulfillment of the agreement a Turkish army unit of 650 men landed at Famagusta to be garrisoned in the new republic.

Economic Crisis under the Democrats

In contrast to some of her Middle Eastern neighbors whose subsoil is rich in oil, Turkey has thus far not succeeded in discovering any substantial mineral resources. Despite her *étatisme* and serious endeavors toward industrialization, her economy is still predominantly based on agriculture. In order to survive and prosper, Turkey must continuously expand her agricultural production, both to keep pace with her steadily growing population[41] and to assure exportable surpluses with which to earn enough foreign exchange for the payment of much-needed industrial imports. For a number of decades the stark fact is that the Turkish economy has been chronically afflicted by the basic imbalance between her productive capacity and her need for foreign imports. The maintenance of a large army, an obligation dictated both by her security requirements and by her international obligations, constituted a continuous burden on her economy, which was only partly relieved by American military aid programs. In addition, the Menderes government forced upon the country an intensive program of development representing 32 percent of the budget for 1958. The fruits of this program would be manifest only in the decades to come; its immediate effect was to widen the gap between Turkey's import needs and her export capacities. The semiarid Anatolian Plateau is periodically subject to droughts, and Turkey's wheat production, instead of increasing, showed actual

[40]Dr. Fazil Kuchuk became vice-president on behalf of the Turkish minority, while Archbishop Makarios assumed the presidency as representative of the Greek majority.

[41]According to the census of October 23, 1960, the Turkish population was 27,600,000. By 1978 it grew to about 42,000,000.

signs of decline in the 1950s. Her chrome, which had commanded high prices in wartime, ceased to represent a significant proportion in her economic assets, and oil, though discovered in a few places in the 1950s and in 1960, could be produced only in modest quantities designed to fill a part of the country's requirements. As one observer aptly phrased it, "How does a nation maintain modern armor, jets and rockets by peddling pistachios?"[42]

Under the circumstances it was inevitable that the trade deficit, which by 1958 was more than $200 million should bring about the devaluation of the Turkish lira, whose market price fell to between one-fifth to one-fourth of the artificial official rate. Restrictions in imports followed, first limited to luxury goods but eventually affecting even such items of daily consumption as coffee, which began to be rationed. The resulting inflation hurt first of all the urban population. The latter's plight was further aggravated by the peculiar Turkish tax structure, which virtually exempted the peasants from payment of taxes, thus transferring the burden to the 15 or 20 percent of the Turks in the cities. By the summer of 1958 the Turkish economy was in a critical state. Turkey's economic crisis rather dangerously coincided in time with the earlier-mentioned political crisis in the Arab countries of the neighboring Fertile Crescent. The danger was further heightened by repeated attempts of Russia to extend her aid-and-trade policy to Turkey, attempts that met with partial success inasmuch as the hard-pressed Menderes government did accept, prior to 1958, Soviet offers of investment and technical advice in a few industrial plants.

It should be pointed out that all through the 1950s Turkey benefited from American aid. This aid, however, was primarily geared to help Turkey maintain her large military establishment. Repeated attempts of the Menderes government to secure continuous high-level economic assistance met with less success, partly because the United States government entertained serious doubts as to the soundness of ambitious Turkish development programs. By midsummer of 1958 these considerations had to give place to the urgency of the Turkish economic crisis viewed against the background of turmoil in the Arab East and the possibility of substantial Soviet penetration in the area as a whole. The rescue operation took the form of the loan mentioned earlier totaling $359 million. An American mission headed by Under Secretary of State C. Douglas Dillon soon afterward visited Turkey to study her economic stabilization program. Dillon questioned the Turks about their investment deals with the Soviets and reportedly obtained reassurances that no major involvement with Russia was either existent or contemplated. About twenty months later, in March 1960, the Turkish government made public the first results of the stabilization program. While imports had been maintained at an annual rate of $450 million, exports rose from $247 million in 1958 to $385 million in 1959. Their eventual rise to $400 million was hopefully expected by the Turks.

Even with this narrowing of the trade balance gap, Turkey was still facing continuous deficits which, unless there were drastic reductions in imports, could be removed only if she substantially increased her agricultural productive capacity. This was made clear in a report prepared for the Food and Agriculture Organization

---

[42]C. L. Sulzberger, "Bearing a Burden through a Marsh," *New York Times,* Sept. 25, 1957.

(FAO) by Dr. Fritz Baade of Kiel University in September 1959.[43] Turkish agriculture, according to the report, was in a state of "spiraling destruction" because of erosion, droughts, and a variety of other factors. To save her economy and provide livelihood for the anticipated forty-million population by 1975, Turkey should aim at doubling her agricultural production in fifteen years from its 1959 level of $4.5 billion a year to $9 billion a year. To accomplish this, 5,583,000 acres of irrigated land would have to be added to the then cultivated area at a cost of $2.5 billion.

Internal Political Tensions

The economic crisis had its counterpart in the worsening political situation. Once in power the Democrats showed little generosity toward their political opponents. In fact, many signs pointed to their determination to stay in power in disregard of constitutional legality and thus to discard, for all practical purposes, the mechanism of peaceful change. While maintaining the parliamentary façade and electoral processes, the Democrats resorted to a variety of measures designed to frustrate the opposition's attempts to regain power legally. These measures included the adoption of a new stringent press law in 1956, which made criticism of official policies and officeholders well-nigh impossible. By virtue of this law and its subsequent additions a number of newspapers suffered suspensions, and their editors received fines and jail sentences. The imprisonment of the veteran Turkish journalist Ahmet Emin Yalman, a man in his seventies enjoying prestige far beyond the confines of Turkey, is illustrative of these repressive policies. The International Press Institute in Geneva noted with concern these excesses, but its public criticisms did not deter the Menderes government from pursuing its dictatorial methods. Another significant measure was the enactment of an antielectionerring law in 1956. This placed a virtual ban on any political activity, including public speeches and assemblies. Rigidly applied, it resulted in such extreme steps as, for example, the jailing of Kasim Gülek, secretary-general of the Republican People's party, for shaking hands with the well-wishers who met him at a provincial railway station. The lifting of the parliamentary immunity of several opposition deputies, interference with academic freedom (resulting in the much-discussed resignations of Professors Fevzioglu and Yalçin from the University of Ankara), and the imprisonment of the leader of the National Republican party, Osman Bolukbasi were further expressions of this policy, which was gradually reestablishing in Turkey the old one-party system.

Availing himself of the constitutional provision which permits the government in power to accelerate the date of elections, Premier Menderes, obviously confident of the victory of his party, called for elections in the fall of 1957 instead of in 1958 after the regular four-year interval. To hamstring the opposition, the Democrat-dominated parliament passed a law which forbade the forming of election fronts and common electoral lists by coalitions of political parties. The law was designed to prevent the three opposition parties then in existence, the Republican People's party, the Republican Nation party, and the Freedom party, from cooperating during the electoral campaign.

[43]See *FAO Mediterranean Development Project, Turkey, Country Report, 1959.*

Despite these restrictions the elections of October 1957 brought substantial gains to the opposition. The People's Republicans, who had secured only 31 seats in 1954, emerged now with an impressive 178 seats, strengthened by 4 seats for the Freedom party and 4 seats for the Republican Nation party. The Democrats, who thus suffered a moral defeat, reacted by enacting further restrictions, the most notable of which was the limiting of the question period in the parliament and the ban on full reporting of parliamentary debates by the press. The opposition did not succumb to intimidation, but rather closed its ranks and displayed greater activity than usual in asserting its influence among the people. In November 1958 the Freedom party voted to merge with the People's Republicans, and throughout 1959 and early 1960 the latter's chief leader and former president of the Republic, Ismet Inönü, made several speaking tours of the provinces, braving police interference and the general hostility of the government administrative apparatus.

The Military Coup of 1960 and Its Aftermath

The government's repressive policies reached their peak when on April 18, 1960, the Grand National Assembly set up a fifteen-man committee of inquiry, composed entirely of Democrats, to look into "the destructive and illegal activities" of the Republican People's party. Simultaneously the Assembly suspended all party activity for three months and banned publication of all news about the inquiry to be conducted. These decisions initiated a series of events which were to lead to a major political upheaval. As often happens in the history of revolutions, the protest movement began with the intellectuals: shortly after these enactments by the Assembly three professors of Istanbul University issued a declaration criticizing the Assembly's actions as unconstitutional. On April 28 students of the same university joined in protest, and their demonstration, quelled by police with the use of firearms, led to the proclamation of martial law and the gradual suspension of a good many newspapers. These events were embarrassing to the government, which was to be host early in May to a meeting of the NATO foreign ministers in Istanbul. Despite continuing student demonstrations—by May 14 they extended to Ankara as well—there was hope that Turkey would not follow in the footsteps of Korea, where, only a few weeks earlier, the conservative government of Syngman Rhee had been overthrown as a result of student riots sparked by the rigging of national elections. Much depended on the attitude of the army. The latter, in contrast to most of the Arab military establishments, enjoyed the reputation of strict professionalism untainted by interference in domestic politics. Precisely because of this, the question arose whether the army would allow itself to be used as a tool of one political party—a role which Premier Menderes tried to assign to it in the growing number of clashes with the student demonstrators. An indication that not everything was smooth in government-army relations was given on May 5, when General Cemal Gürsel, commander of the ground forces, tendered his resignation. This was further confirmed on May 21, when about a thousand military cadets staged a silent protest march in Ankara in support of the students' demonstrations. Seriously alarmed, the government the next day closed all universities and colleges until the fall semester.

At the same time it prepared hasty plans to disperse the protesting cadets so as to prevent any further show of antigovernment solidarity.

All these measures proved of no avail. On May 27 the army under the command of General Cemal Gürsel seized power and in a swift move imprisoned President Bayar, Permier Menderes, and other cabinet members. Soon afterward they arrested virtually all Democratic deputies in the Grand National Assembly. General Gürsel assumed the functions of head of the state, prime minister, defense minister, and commander in chief. He was assisted by a junta of middle-bracket and junior officers (originally thirty-eight in number) calling itself the Committee of National Unity.

In his initial declaration Gürsel said that the coup aimed at the restoration of democracy, which had been gravely violated by the preceding tyrannical regime. To give weight to these utterances he promptly set up a committee of jurists to draft a new constitution that would safeguard democratic liberties and prevent the recurrence of previous anticonstitutional abuses.[44] At the same time a predominantly civilian cabinet was appointed. Its only member linked with the defunct regime was Selim Sarper, the foreign minister, who had previously served as Turkish delegate to the United Nations and undersecretary of Foreign Affairs. His appointment symbolized the new regime's intention to stress the continuity of Turkish foreign policy.

Assurances that Turkey would honor her international obligations and cultivate close relations with the West were given both by Gürsel and by Sarper in public statements. Furthermore, General Gürsel politely but firmly rejected a Soviet suggestion that the new Turkish government should follow a neutralist policy as the best means of reducing the burden of armaments. This suggestion, contained in a letter sent by Premier Nikita Khrushchev on June 28, was countered by General Gürsel's assertion that Turkey's armament burdens were likely to be lessened by her defensive association with the NATO powers.[45]

If we assume that this foreign policy orientation represented the genuine and unfaltering conviction of General Gürsel and his military associates, the main problem concerning Turkey's new regime revolved around its true intentions concerning the restoration of democratic political processes in the country. The issue was whether the ruling military group viewed its role as merely transitional, to be concluded as soon as a civilian authority emerged from the fresh procedures to be established by the new constitution, or whether it contemplated exercising political tutelage over an extended period of time. Even if the first alternative proved to be true, the process of transition would not be easy. This would be due to the following three factors: (1) no matter how much devoted to the principles of democracy and the multiparty system it was, the junta had taken a definite stand on the political responsibility of the Democrats and, in fact, did take punitive measures against their leadership; (2) soon after assuming power the new government's spokesmen began

---

[44]The committee was originally composed of seven professors of law of Istanbul University under the chairmanship of Dr. Sidik Omar, rector of the university. It included the three professors who had signed the initial protest in April. Later three more members, professors at Ankara University, were added.

[45]For the texts of the correspondence, as revealed by *Pravda* on September 1, 1960, *see Oriente Moderno*, 40 (Sept. 1960), 561–564.

stressing the need for certain long-overdue reforms which, said they, should be carried out even before the restoration of the parliamentary regime; and (3) there is always a temptation to prolong one's term of office once the advantages of wielding power are tasted.

Officially, the government more than once stressed that it aimed at a speedy restoration of the democratic process. In fact, it took several measures which were either questionable as regards their conformity with democratic procedures or puzzling with reference to their ultimate objectives. Among these measures were the official dissolution of the Democratic party, the institution of revolutionary tribunals, and a series of purges carried out in the army, the cabinet, and the officers' junta, as well as in the universities. Early in August 235 senior officers, including many generals and admirals, were retired in an obvious attempt to rejuvenate and change the leadership of the military establishment. This was followed by the removal of ten out of nineteen cabinet ministers three weeks later, on orders of the Committee of National Unity. Furthermore, the committee itself suffered a similar fate when fourteen of its members were dismissed in mid-November and after a period of house detention were offered positions in various Turkish missions abroad. The group in question, led by Colonel Alparslan Turkes, was charged by General Gürsel with the intention of removing him from power and was generally credited with more extreme, i.e., dictatorial, tendencies than the rest of the committee. While these personnel changes were not undemocratic per se, their suddenness and the mystery in which they were enveloped testified to some serious inner strains within the ruling revolutionary group. More dubious from the point of view of democratic procedures was the dismissal in October of 147 university professors, including those who had originally protested against the anticonstitutional actions of the Democrat regime and who, after the revolution, were invited to serve on the constitution-drafting committee. This action provoked so much criticism (two Turkish university heads resigned in protest) that General Gürsel shortly promised to review the dismissals because of possible mistakes.

These dramatic personnel shifts were soon followed by steps likely to restore a measure of cautious confidence in the democratic objectives of the new regime. On December 13, 1960, the government issued a decree calling for the establishment of a bicameral Constituent Assembly. Its lower chamber (House of Representatives) was to consist of 262 members chosen partly on a territorial and partly on a corporate basis, and the Committee of National Unity, with its postpurge strength of 23, was to serve as the upper chamber. The objective of the assembly was to adopt a new constitution and an electoral law, following which elections were to be held not later than in October 1961. On January 6, 1961, the Constituent Assembly convened. A week later the ban on political parties was removed.

On May 27, 1961, exactly a year after the revolution, the assembly adopted a new constitution, which was subsequently approved in a referendum on July 9, 1961. The referendum was free of any pressure and thus genuinely reflected Turkish attitudes toward the new regime. Of those eligible to vote, 82 percent cast their ballots. Sixty-two percent of those voting favored the constitution, thus assuring its adoption. If, however, abstentions are added to the negative votes, it would appear that 49.16 percent of Turkish voters were either opposed or indifferent to the new fundamental law. Their stand could be interpreted as a symbolic protest against the coup of the preceding year rather than as an objection to the provisions of the constitution.

The new constitution forcefully emphasized the democractic principles and the Kemalist concept of Turkey as a secular and modern republic. It was strongly explicit in all those articles which dealt with the safeguarding of individual freedoms, the protection of citizens and their political groupings against abuses of power by the state, and due process of law. Its main innovations were the establishment of a bicameral Grand National Assembly, to be composed of the National Assembly and the Republican Senate, and the creation of the Constitutional Court, whose task was to pronounce on the conformity of laws with the constitution. The National Assembly was to have 450 members, elected for four-year terms. The Senate was to be composed of 150 elected senators, 15 senators appointed by the President of the Republic (both of these groups serving for six years), and the 23 members of the Committee of National Unity, the latter to serve for life so long as they did not join any political party. The division of powers between legislative and executive authorities followed the west-European parliamentary pattern rather than the American presidential system.[46]

During the campaign preceding the referendum as well as in the period between it and the first postrevolution elections, Turkey experienced a revival of regular political life on a party basis. Altogether fourteen political parties made their appearance. Of these, four stood out as the most important: the Republican People's party (R.P.P.), which campaigned actively for the new constitution; the Justice party and the New Turkey party, both new creations drawing to themselves many former Democrats; and the Republican Peasants Nation party, a fusion of the older rightist Republican Nation party with the newer Peasant party. In the electoral campaign conducted in the early fall of 1961 the R.P.P. clearly identified itself with the objectives of the revolutionary military regime. Although not openly refuting these objectives, the other three parties vigorously opposed R.P.P.'s bid to return to power and therefore tended to rally to themselves all those who were critical of the new government. "We are," said Ekrem Alican, leader of the New Turkey party, "the reincarnation of the Democratic party but with the difference that we carry a new soul."[47]

In mid-September, while the electoral campaign was in progress, the special court sitting in judgment on the Democratic leaders on the island of Yassi Ada issued its verdict, sentencing to death fifteen of the principal figures of the old regime. A majority of these sentences were commuted to life terms by the Committee of National Unity. Three death sentences, however, were confirmed, namely, those against former Premier Adnan Menderes and two ministers of his cabinet, Fatin Rustu Zorlu and Hassan Polatkan. They were executed on September 16 and

[46]For a detailed analysis, see Ismet Giritli, "Some Aspects of the New Turkish Constitution," *Middle East Journal*, 16, 1 (Winter, 1962).

[47]From a statement made at the party congress held at Karaman on August 25, 1961 (*Daily News*, Istanbul, Aug. 26, 1961).

17. By applying such harsh (though legally justified) measures to its Democrat enemies, the Committee of National Unity gave notice of its uncompromising opposition to any return to political conditions such as existed before the military coup d'état. Although this might have served as a warning to all those who, through the instrumentality of the "reincarnated" parties, hoped for the relatively easy restoration of the status quo ante, it also deepened the cleavage dividing the Turkish nation. It was to the credit of the military rulers, however, that in accordance with the new constitution they scrupulously abstained from any interference in the elections. The members elected to the National Assembly and the Senate on October 17, 1961, were divided among the parties as follows:

Party	National Assembly	Senate
Republican People's Party	173	36
Justice Party	158	70
New Turkey Party	65	28
Republican Peasants Nation Party	54	16
Total	450	150

Returns showed the strong position of the R.P.P. in many urban centers. The three other parties tended to score heavily in the rural areas, where the defunct Democratic party had consistenly wooed the peasants. The elections were inconclusive in that they did not give a clear-cut majority to any single party. Although the R.P.P. secured a plurality in the Assembly, it was significantly outdistanced by the Justice party in the Senate. If the votes cast for the three parties opposed to the R.P.P. are totaled, it is clear that a majority of the electorate voiced its reservations if not its actual opposition to the new dispensation. It was also clear that no single party could claim the right to form a government and that a coalition cabinet would have to be created. There was the obvious possibility of a coalition of the three parties other than the R.P.P.; this would have commanded a sufficient majority in the Grand National Assembly. But such a solution would have meant virtual repudiation of the May revolution and its objectives. At this juncture the Committee of National Unity—about to be dissolved according to its own professed aims— intervened again, presenting to the party leaders the following main demands: (1) that a coalition government include all four principal parties; (2) that General Gürsel, head of the junta, be elected President of the Republic; (3) that there be no amnesty to more than four hundred sentenced leaders of the outlawed Democratic party; (4) that there be no change in the status of thousands of military officers retired from active duty after May 27, 1960. The party leaders assented, and on October 26 the Grand National Assembly elected General Gürsel to the presidency for a seven-year term.

Gürsel in turn appointed a coalition cabinet headed by the former president of the Republic, Ismet Inönü, and composed of representatives of the two major parties, the R.P.P. and the Justice party. With this act the transitional period of military rule officially came to an end and Turkey was launched anew on the path of democracy. It remained to be proved in practice how sound and workable this democracy would be. No realistic appraisal of Turkish politics could disregard the continued existence, despite its formal dissolution, of the military group that had seized power in 1960. In the long run much was bound to hinge on the kind of relationship which developed between the civilian and military leaders and on the willingness of both to abide by the new constitution of the Republic.

The Internal Political Process after 1960

The era after the 1960 military coup d'etat was characterized by fluctuations in the voting patterns, and the lack of a strong parliamentary majority. Political opinion became increasingly polarized. Political parties proliferated, and splinter parties and groups made their appearance, along with militant and revolutionary organizations.[48] There were recurrent military interventions. The internal political process presented a paradoxical dualism: on the one hand, the country appeared to benefit from greater freedoms in the political sector; on the other, the military were playing an increasingly active role. Two successive presidents of Turkey were generals; first, Cemal Gürsel (1960–1966), and second, Cevdet Sunay (1966–1973). This succession of military presidents was broken only in April 1973, when, after many

---

[48]The following political parties were in existence in Turkey in the 1960s and 1970s: *Republican People's party* (Cumhuriyet Halk Partisi, CHP) (left-of-center); chairman (since May 14, 1971), Bülent Ecevit. *Justice party* (Adalet Partisi, AP) (conservative laissez faire); founded in 1961 as immediate successor to outlawed Democrat party; leader (since 1961), Süleyman Demirel. *Democratic party* (Demokratik Partisi, DP) (conservative laissez faire; more Islamic traditional in orientation); established December 18, 1970, by right-wing AP members who had resigned or been expelled; President, Ferruh Bozbeyli; vice-presidents (shared), Sadettin Bilgiç and Yüksel Menderes, son of the late prime minister. *Republican Reliance party* (Cumhuriyetçi Güven Partisi, CGP) (right-of-center, but leaning to moderate positions; conservative Kemalists); leader, Turhan Feyzioglu; formed on February 28, 1973, out of three groups: (1) National Reliance party (Milli Güven Partisi, MGP); a conservative split from the R.P.P. in 1967; leader, Turhan Feyzioglu. (2) Republican party (Cumhuriyetçi Partisi, CP); formed on September 4, 1972, from another conservative faction in ever leftward-drifting R.P.P.; leader Kemal Satir. (3) Various Independent Republicans that had left R.P.P. during 1972. *National Salvation party* (Milli Silamet Partisi, MSP) (traditional/conservative/Islamic); formed in 1973 to replace the National Order party (Milli Nizam Partisi, MNP), which was founded by Necmettin Erbakan in January 1970 and outlawed on May 21, 1971, by Constitutional Court; leader, Necmettin Erbakan. *Turkish Workers party* (also Turkish Labor party) (Türkiye Işçi Partisi, TIP) (Marxist); outlawed since July 1971; founded February 1961; first Chairman, Mehmet Ali Aybar (1962) forced out by orthodox wing of party after his criticism of Soviet invasion of Czechoslovakia, succeeded by Behice Boran. *National Action party* (Milli Hareket Partisi, MHP) (neofascist); essentially new name of Republican Peasant National party adopted in early 1969; leader, Alparslan Turkes. *Republican Peasant National party* (Cumhuriyetçi Köylü Millet Partisi, CKMP) (conservative/traditional/landowning class); founded in 1948; name of party official as of 1957. First chairman, Osman Bolukbasi (left in 1961 to establish conservative Nation party [Millet Partisi, MP]); second chairman, Ahmet Oguz (1961–1965); third chairman (as National Action party), Alparslan Turkes (1965). *Nation or National party* (Millet Partisi, MP) (conservative/Islamic traditional within constitutional limits); established by Osman Bolukbasi in 1961 from faction within CKMP; leader Osman Bolukbasi. *Union or Unity party* (Birlik Partisi, BP) (centrist); founded October 1966; first chairman, Hasan Tahsin Berkman, replaced later by Hüseyin Balan, who left Nation Party to join this one; secretary-general, Cemal Özbey. *New Turkey party* (Yeni Türkiye Partisi, YTP) (liberal conservative); established in February 1961, dissolved in 1973, members joined Justice Party; leader, Ekrem Alican.

Political spectrum and leaders of principal Turkish parties in the mid-1970s: left, Turkish Workers; left-center, Republican People's (B. Ecevit), Unity (H. Balan); right-center, Justice (S. Demirel), Republican Reliance (T. Feyzioglu); right, National Action (A. Turkes), National Salvation (N. Erbakan), Democratic (F. Bozbeyli).

ballots, the Grand National Assembly elected a civilian, senator Fahri Korutürk, as president of the republic.

Because no single party emerged as a dominant force, the prevailing pattern was one of a succession of coalition governments. In this respect the post-1960 period could be divided into three subperiods. First, between 1960 and 1965, Turkey witnessed a series of coalition governments in which the two largest components were the Republican People's party and the Justice party. Between 1965 and 1971 the Justice party won a relatively clear but not overwhelming majority. During those six years the Justice party was responsible for the formation of a number of cabinets with Suleiman Demirel serving most of the time as prime minister. Meanwhile, its principal opponent, the Republican People's party, experienced an internal split which by 1971 led to the resignation and withdrawal of its long-standing leader, former president Ismet Inönü, and his replacement by Bülent Ecevit, who was broadly identified with the left-wing trend in the party. Military intervention in March 1971 ushered in an era of coalition governments, and the pattern established after the first military coup of 1960 was resumed.

Military Intervention of 1971

Beginning with the late 1960s, but particularly in 1970-1971, Turkish politics began to show disquieting signs of polarization. The most characteristic feature of this process was the appearance of various protest groups which freely resorted to violence to express their dissatisfaction with the prevailing conditions. These groups were recruited in two principal sectors—universities and urban workers. Protest demonstrations by the students included seizures of university buildings, occupation of administration offices, barricading of streets, and other acts of violence and vandalism. In the working class sector there was a proliferation of strikes (which were allowed by recent legislation), and a new radical labor union organization, DISK, emerged.[49] A new Turkish workers' party with Marxist tendencies was formed. Gradually these open manifestations of defiance led to the appearance of urban guerrillas, well-organized, clandestine groups of Marxist and Maoist persuasion. These groups engaged in kidnapings, held hostages for ransom, hijacked airplanes, bombed public buildings, and killed selected public figures. At one time their hostage was a fourteen-year-old girl. In the case of two airplane hijackings, considerable numbers of civilian passengers, including women and children, were involved. The guerrillas captured and killed the Israeli consul general, taking him from Ankara to Istanbul and executing him there. Similarly, the guerrillas kidnaped and subsequently killed three NATO radar technicians of British and Canadian nationality.

Against this background the four principal military commanders—the chief of staff and the commanders of the army, air force, and navy—submitted a memoran-

---

[49]DISK is an abbreviation of Devrimci işçi sendikalari konfederasyonu (Federation of Revolutionary Workers' Trade Unions). For further details, see J. M. Landau, *Radical Politics in Modern Turkey*, Social, Economic and Political Studies of the Middle East, 14 (Leiden, 1974).

dum to the president of the republic demanding swift and radical action on the part of the government to put an end to the deterioration of security and the growing anarchy in the country. This virtual ultimatum resulted in the resignation of the Justice party leader, Premier Suleiman Demirel. His place was taken by Professor Nihad Erim who, in forming his new government, pledged to direct his efforts toward the restoration of law and order. Although Erim was a leader of the Republican People's party, he had to rely on a coalition government. Erim resigned about a year later, to be replaced by a succession of coalition cabinet premiers. Much of the effort of the successive governments was directed toward the restoration of internal tranquillity. They were partly but not entirely successful in these endeavors. While violence abated, the guerrilla groups were not completely eradicated. Moderate and conservative leaders in Turkey as well as many ordinary citizens regarded the guerrilla groups as elements bent on sedition and banditry and strongly suspected them of being encouraged and financed by foreign powers. Some commentators, however, claimed that the guerrilla phenomenon was merely a symptom of a deeper malaise of a society in the process of transition which left many vital problems unattended.[50] Critics of the regime, especially among the more liberal academic groups, claimed that under the aegis of the defunct Democratic party but also under its successors Turkey was engaged in developing an economic system reminiscent of the nineteenth-century capitalism which, with its laissez-faire philosophy, tended to produce glaring inequalities in income among individuals and social classes, extremely high profits for certain groups, inflation and growing unemployment, particularly for the young graduates. They tended under the circumstances to justify the guerilla activity and protest movements as an understandable reaction of new generations against the established order. These varying interpretations of the Turkish reality by the conservatives and the liberals were in themselves expressive of the growing polarization in the Turkish political process. On the one hand the conservatives were unwilling to take too seriously the social and economic background of the protest activities. On the other, liberals with their exaggerated idealism tended to forget both the basic ideological Marxist commitment of leading elements among the protestors and the likelihood of their links with Communist powers.[51]

The successive cabinets after 1971 aimed both at curbing the political excesses of the dissenters and at certain reforms. Amendments were proposed and adopted for the constitution with the objective of limiting certain freedoms and making them subject to higher interests of law, order, and preservation of state integrity.[52] Several hundred revolutionary activists were captured and placed on trial. In the early 1970s three major trials of these individuals took place, and many were given prison

[50]See Feroz Ahmad, "The Turkish Guerillas: Symptom of a Deeper Malaise," *New Middle East* (London), no. 55 (April 1973).

[51]For varying interpretations of radical politics, see also C. Wakebridge, "The Problem Turkey Has Yet to Solve," *New Middle East,* no. 52/53 (Jan.-Feb. 1973), and A. Hottinger, "The Persecution of the Left in Turkey," *Swiss Review of World Affairs,* 22, no. 12 (March 1973).

[52]For a useful review of Turkish constitutional development, see "The Constitutional System," *Area Handbook for the Republic of Turkey* (Washington, D.C., 1973), pp. 192-198.

sentences. The governments generally adopted a firm attitude toward the guerrillas, refusing to negotiate with them even at the risk of jeopardizing the lives of the hostages. Turkey resembled in her attitude Israel, preferring to set a pattern of firmness rather than allowing the government to be blackmailed. Furthermore, because of evidence of seditious involvement of some military elements in these revolutionary activities, fifty-seven junior officers were dismissed from service.

Commenting on the causes of instability and dissent, neutral observers have pointed to the substantial changes that had taken place in Turkey in the postwar period, a period corresponding to the end of the tutelary system established by Ataturk. The end of the tutelary period resulted in the ushering in of greater freedom and relaxation of government controls. Workers were permitted to unionize freely and to resort to strike. Abolition of a single-party system meant opening of the doors to more political groups. In the universities students often took their cue from developments on campuses in the United States in the 1960s as well as from the "Student Revolution" in France in 1968.[53] Similarly the appearance in various parts of the world of the so-called liberation movements or guerrilla groups acted as an encouraging example, particularly the Palestinian *fedayeen* and the struggle in Vietnam and other parts of Southeast Asia. Broadly speaking, Turkey was experiencing a crisis of authority. Respected authority in any political entity may be established on either of two bases: the charismatic leadership of an individual, which was clearly the case of Kemal Ataturk with his tutelary system; or a clear majority for a political party that would enjoy the confidence of the electorate in a democratic system. But democracy cannot be easily established in a society that was subjected to nondemocratic methods for a long time and that lacked many social and economic ingredients important or essential for the establishment of democracy. In Turkish circumstances after 1960 there was a clear lack of popular leadership by a widely accepted and perhaps heroic personality. Following Ataturk's death, Turkey was led either by men personally associated with the great leader, such as Ismet Inönü, or during the democratic period between 1950 and 1960 by a man endowed with both a degree of charisma and an authoritarian personality, namely Adnan Menderes. Following the first military intervention in 1960, no such strong personalities were evident in Turkish political life. In all likelihood a society in the state of transition and rapid development such as Turkey in the postwar period requires either the presence of a strong leadership or at least a clearcut political ideology or philosophy. A purely rational democratic process is apparently not quite sufficient.

Economic Ingredients of the Political Situation

An underdeveloped and for the most part arid country of thirty-five million people, Turkey in the 1960s and 1970s experienced demographic pressure in the form of about one million births a year. At the same time, villagers attracted by the benefits of urban life tended to migrate in large numbers to the cities. Changes in consumption patterns consequently put great pressure on the Turkish economy of

[53]See J. S. Szyliowicz, "Students and Politics in Turkey," *Middle Eastern Studies* (London), no. 2 (May 1970).

scarcity. As any other underdeveloped country, Turkey was therefore exposed to the evils of unemployment and underemployment. Unemployment was partly alleviated by the opportunities for Turkish laborers in the booming economy of Europe, particularly during the 1960s. By 1970–1971 as many as 600,000 Turkish workers were employed in European industries, services, and agriculture.[54] The remittances they were sending back home reached half a billion dollars in 1971–72. Unfortunately, European and world inflation and recession compelled the repatriation of many of these workers while the general trend was to reduce their numbers. The returned workers did not necessarily find similar opportunities in Turkey and might have added to the problem of discontent in certain quarters.

At the same time, under Premier Menderes in the 1950s, Turkey developed a momentum not only in its economy but also in its consumption, with a corresponding demand for Western industrial goods. Keeping an eye on the political benefits of development, Menderes tended to disregard the rational principles of balancing revenue with expenditure, while deficits mounted and the indebtedness of the Turkish state grew. His successors found it difficult to break away from this pattern. Moreover, Turkey was committed not only to the development of its economy under free enterprise but also to the concept of a mixed economy. Consequently in 1960 the State Planning Commission was created and in 1962 the first postwar five-year plan was launched. It was followed by the second five-year plan in 1968 and the third in 1973.[55] Turkish exports were chronically insufficient to provide enough foreign exchange to cover Turkish import needs, but in some sectors the country could reduce or abandon its dependence on imports. Oil production in the 1970s has reached three million barrels of crude a year, an amount sufficient to meet Turkish domestic needs. Considering the rise in international oil prices in 1974 and the following years, the development of Turkish oil production saved her from a new financial embarrassment. The construction of the Keban Dam on the Euphrates River, which was begun in 1966 and completed in 1972, added considerably to Turkish agricultural potential in the southern provinces and provided a new source of hydro-electric power.

The production and export of opium has been an important source of foreign exchange. As part of the worldwide struggle against the illicit traffic in narcotics, Turkey was persuaded by the United States to impose a ban on the production of opium in June 1971. To compensate Turkey for losses in this connection the United States offered the Turkish government a grant of $35 million. The crusade against worldwide narcotic trafficking was only partly successful. Displeased with the lax controls existing in certain countries, Iran rescinded its ban on opium production. Before long the Turkish authorities began reassessing their own policies in this respect and in July 1974 they also annulled their ban. While this decision aided the Turkish struggle to close the gap between foreign exchange expenditures and revenues, on the whole Turkey had to rely on foreign loans and grants to maintain her economy. The United States was a major provider of financial assistance. Between

---

[54] *OECD Economic Surveys, 1973–74, Turkey* (Paris, 1974), p. 21.
[55] Useful data on planning may be found in *Area Handbook for the Republic of Turkey*, pp. 267–274.

1946 and 1971 American aid to Turkey totalled $5.7 billion. Of this, $3 billion were earmarked for military assistance and $2.7 billion for economic aid. Similarly Turkey was a recipient of various loans and credits from a number of European countries. Difficulties in repaying these debts and improving the balance of payments situation led in 1962 to the creation of a Western consortium within the Organization for Economic Cooperation and Development (OECD) to help Turkey.[56]

Foreign Policy after 1960

The most general characterization that could be given to the trends in Turkish foreign policy was that the government emphasized independence and freedom of action. This meant a change in attitudes toward the Soviet Union as well as a weakening of ties with the United States. Beginning in 1964 when cabinet-level visits were exchanged between Ankara and Moscow, an era of "normalization" of relations was inaugurated between the two countries. Preoccupied with other problems—in the Far East, in Eastern Europe, and in the Americas—the Soviet leadership modified, at least outwardly, its earlier attitude of hostility toward Turkey. Instead it began stressing peaceful coexistence and economic cooperation. These political overtures were accompanied by concrete offers of economic and technical assistance, some of which Turkey accepted. As a result a number of Soviet technicians appeared in Turkey, an innovation contrasting strongly with the mood of mutual hostility characteristic of the 1950s. It is a moot question how seriously the Turkish leadership was treating the change in Soviet attitude. Imbued with deep historical distrust of Soviet and Russian motivations, the Turkish leadership, of any political party, was not prepared to take Soviet protestations of friendship at face value, hence in all probability it did not treat the Soviet change of policy as more than a change in tactics. As long as it suited Turkey's needs, however, there was no reason for the Turkish leaders to reject any peaceful Soviet manifestation and thus they responded positively to such overtures as did not affect other basic ties and commitments to the West or to their neighbors in the Middle East.

For this reason they concluded in 1964 at a conference in Istanbul an agreement with the Asian members of CENTO, Iran and Pakistan, establishing an organization called Regional Cooperation for Development (RCD).[57] To some extent RCD could be regarded as duplicating the nonmilitary functions of the already existing organization, CENTO. But the political and psychological purpose of RCD was to stress the independent regional planning of Turkey, Iran, and Pakistan and to show Moscow that these three countries were interested in mutual cooperation not neces-

[56]Members of the Consortium for Aid to Turkey were Austria, Belgium, Canada, Denmark, France, West Germany, Italy, Luxemburg, Netherlands, Norway, Sweden, Switzerland, United Kingdom, United States; and the International Monetary Fund, the World Bank (IBRD), and the European Investment Bank as observers. (Source: International Monetary Fund, *Directory of Regional Economic Organizations and Intergovernmental Commodity Organizations* [Washington, D.C.], April 1974).

[57]Text in R. H. Magnus, ed., *Documents on the Middle East* (Washington, D.C., 1969), p. 137.

sarily for military purposes. Accordingly a secretariat of RCD was established with headquarters in Ankara and with a rotating position of secretary-general.

The launching of RCD was accompanied in Turkey, Iran, and Pakistan by many official and semiofficial criticisms of CENTO as an organization that either did not quite fit the new political conditions in the world or had disappointed its Asian members by failing to give them adequate assurances and guarantees.

In 1962 the Cuban missile crisis, which involved the United States and the Soviet Union in a major diplomatic quarrel with possible implications of global war, indirectly contributed to the weakening of American-Turkish ties. In return for his decision to withdraw Soviet missiles from Cuba, Premier Khrushchev insisted on the withdrawal of American missiles from sites in northern Turkey. Although President John F. Kennedy refused formally to accept this demand, nevertheless, to give the Soviets proof of American good will he ordered the withdrawal of missiles located on the north Turkish coast.[58] American-Turkish relations did not experience serious deterioration, however, until the Cyprus crisis, which occurred in two installments, in 1964 and 1974.[59] Because of its bearing on the totality of Turkey's relations with the United States and its effects on NATO, a brief review will be useful.

The Cyprus Crisis

The dramatic chain of events in Cyprus began on December 2, 1963, when the president of Cyprus, Archbishop Makarios, announced his intention to make thirteen revisions in the constitution of Cyprus which would reduce the rights of the Turkish minority. It will be recalled that Cyprus was established as an independent state in 1960 on the basis of three formal documents—its constitution, a four-power treaty of guarantee concluded among Greece, Turkey, Great Britain, and Cyprus, and a three-power treaty of alliance concluded among Cyprus, Turkey, and Greece. The constitution gave the Turkish minority, which represented about 20 percent of the population, 30 percent representation in the Cyprus legislature and bureaucracy. It provided for a Turkish vice president of the republic who obtained the right of veto over certain important acts of the state, and it provided certain safeguards for the Turkish minority. Makarios' announcement met with strong protests on the part of the Turkish minority, and there were violent clashes between Turks and Greeks in Cyprus. These clashes were probably not occasioned merely by the announcement of intended constitutional changes, for relations between the Greek majority and Turkish minority had worsened generally. The Greeks not only enjoyed preponderance of numbers; they also were dominant in the economic and political arenas, so that the Turkish minority considered itself definitely underprivileged. There was among the Turks a sense of being continuously wronged and ill-treated by the Greek-Cypriot authorities. As violence increased in the early months of 1964,

---

[58]For further details, see G. Lenczowski, *Soviet Advances in the Middle East* (Washington, D.C., 1971), p. 48.

[59]For a detailed analysis, see G. S. Harris, *Troubled Alliance: Turkish-American Problems in Historical Perspective, 1945–1971* (Washington, D.C., and Stanford, Calif., 1972).

various international endeavors were launched to mediate in the conflict and to restore tranquillity in Cyprus. Greece and Turkey, closely connected with Cyprus by ethnic bonds and through international treaties, automatically became involved in the conflict. International action to restore peace in Cyprus was undertaken by the United Nations, by NATO, and by the United States. Moreover, the Soviet Union also gave evidence of being actively interested in the situation.

On March 2, 1964, the United Nations Security Council decided to establish a peace-keeping force of 7,000 soldiers to be called the United Nations Force in Cyprus (UNFICYP), although the actual numbers never exceeded 4,500. This international force was initially commanded by an Indian general while the United Nations was represented also by a mediator of Finnish nationality. In spite of the presence of this force and the mediation efforts of the United Nations, the attitude of Archbishop Makarios toward the Turkish minority became steadily more aggressive. On April 3 he unilaterally denounced the treaty of alliance of July 6, 1960, among Turkey, Greece, and Cyprus while giving signs of making good his intention to abolish the four-power guarantee treaty. Following this announcement he excluded from participation in the government the Turkish-Cypriot vice president, Fazil Kuchuk. To back up his words, government forces took military action against Turkish settlements and villages while a paramilitary Greek-Cypriot militia 25,000 strong was formed. This militia abducted a number of Turkish-Cypriots and kept them hostage. At the same time official Greek-Cypriot forces made an attack on the Turkish stronghold in Kyrenia in northern Cyprus. In due course the Greek forces established a blockade of many Turkish villages, depriving them of food, water, and other necessities. The situation became further complicated on July 3 when the old fighter for Cypriot independence, General Grivas, arrived in Cyprus from Greece and announced his intention to work for *enosis,* the union of Greece and Cyprus. Confident of their ability to overcome Turkish resistance, the Greek-Cypriot authorities looked with considerable hostility upon various international mediation efforts and particularly opposed the UN-sponsored conference to be held in the summer in Geneva to resolve the conflict. The Turks in both Cyprus and Turkey responded to these Greek attitudes and initiatives with understandable hostility. Terming the unilateral abrogation of the guarantee treaty by Makarios an illegal action, the Turkish government declared that the aim of the Greek-Cypriots was "total annihilation of the Turkish-Cypriot community." There was a strong sentiment in Turkey to intervene militarily in Cyprus in order to rescue the beleaguered Turkish minority. In this connection Turkish air force planes twice made low passes over Greek positions in Cyprus. Under the leadership of Rauf Denktash the Turkish-Cypriots tried to defend themselves in their enclaves and to retaliate with violence against the Greeks. According to the original treaty of guarantee, Greece and Turkey were permitted to keep small contingents of troops in Cyprus (950 men for Greece and 650 men for Turkey). When the Turkish force in Cyprus attempted to safeguard the lives and property of some Turkish settlements, President Makarios strongly protested, saying that the presence of Greek and Turkish forces in Cyprus was for the defense of Cyprus and not for intervention in internal struggles.

The United States became seriously concerned with the deteriorating situation on the island and the effect it might have on the integrity of the eastern flank of NATO. With this in view, President Lyndon Johnson dispatched several emissaries to Cyprus and to Greece and Turkey in an attempt to provide mediation and a peaceful resolution of the conflict. These emissaries included Senator J. W. Fulbright (May 1964), General Lyman Lemnitzer, NATO commander (in June), former secretary of state Dean Acheson (to the conference in Geneva in August), and the president's special envoy, Cyrus R. Vance (in November). It was felt in Washington that the situation was deteriorating beyond the limits of safety, that President Makarios was drifting dangerously toward closer relations with the Soviet Union while at the same time courting Nasser of Egypt, and that the Soviet attitude itself was far from reassuring. At one point during the crisis Khrushchev accused the United States and Britain of an "imperialist plot" to use Cyprus as a base of aggression in the area. Similarly, Khrushchev issued stern warnings to Turkey to abstain from any military action in Cyprus, implying Soviet counteraction.

Despite the seriousness of American mediation endeavors, United States initiatives were treated with resentment in virtually every quarter, that is, in Turkey, in Greece, and in Cyprus itself. The Greek government under the leadership of George Papandreou not only sided with Archbishop Makarios but also supported him on his contention that the basic pact of 1959, which provided the foundation for the subsequent Cyprus constitution and the treaties of guarantee and alliance, was no longer valid. On the other hand, the Turkish government was unhappy about the specific formulation of American attitude provided by President Johnson. First of all, on June 4, Johnson issued a warning to Premier Inönü not to invade Cyprus. Later that month Inönü visited the president in Washington but no definite settlement was reached. In mid-August, however, Johnson informed Inönü that should Turkey invade Cyprus and thus provoke outside aggression against itself (meaning Soviet aggression), the United States would not feel itself obligated to defend Turkey. Strongly deploring what he believed to be a partial repudiation of its NATO obligations by the United States, Inönü addressed a lengthy letter to Johnson deploring the American attitude and pointing out that such an attitude was undermining solemn American obligations toward Turkey taken as a member of NATO.[60] Initially conceived as a confidential exchange of communications, this Johnson-Inönü correspondence was soon published, providing a public cause for serious deterioration in American-Turkish relations. Ultimately, largely as a result of Vance's mediation, Greece, Turkey, and Cyprus accepted a pact by virtue of which the conflict was to be resolved on the basis of the removal of all foreign troops in Cyprus, disarming of local militias (the Greek-Cypriot national guard), and the numerical expansion of the UN peace-keeping force.

Following this agreement the situation in Cyprus did not quite return to normal, but it permitted the resumption of orderly activities by the Greek and Turkish communities, while the UN force was keeping a watchful eye over the possible outbreaks of new hostilities. Occasionally an incident occurred but during the next ten years relative quiet prevailed on Cyprus. The advent to power of a junta of

[60]Relevant texts in G. Lenczowski, *Soviet Advances,* pp. 50–51.

Greek colonels in Athens in 1967 had the repercussion in Cyprus of strengthening the desire of certain Cypriot elements for union with Greece. On July 25, 1974, a dissident Greek-Cypriot group headed by Nikos Sampson carried out a coup d'etat overthrowing President Makarios and compelling him to flee into exile. There were strong indications that the colonels' government in Greece had connived in this coup d'etat and that the Greek officers present in the Greek force on Cyprus were instrumental. Because the new government in Cyprus declared its intention of effecting union with Greece, reaction in Turkey was serious and immediate. On July 20, Turkish forces invaded Cyprus and proceeded to occupy its northeastern part.[61] This time, interestingly enough, the Soviet Union took the side of Turkey in contrast to its behavior ten years earlier. Looking upon the Greek colonels' government as an instrument of American policy, Moscow was strongly critical of its performance and of that of its Greek-Cypriot allies; hence it justified Turkish actions and adopted a protective tone toward Turkey. The ill-advised adventure in Cyprus cost the Greek colonels' junta its existence. On July 23, three days after the Turkish invasion, the colonels' government fell and was replaced by a new democratic government in Greece, soon to be headed by Constantine Caramanlis, a man who initially negotiated on behalf of Greece the Cyprus agreements in 1959–1960. This new Greek government, however, was disappointed that the United States did not take stronger action against Turkey as a result of its occupation of northern Cyprus. In fact the United States disapproved of the Turkish action but hesitated to go beyond verbal protests. As a result, the Greek government withdrew officially from the military structure of NATO on August 14. This action left the fate of the United States naval base in Greece in doubt. Simultaneously an even greater complication arose in American-Turkish relations. Strong lobbying by pro-Greek elements in Washington brought about legislation in both houses of Congress in September 1974 to ban further sales of arms to Turkey so long as Turkey persisted in the occupation of northern Cyprus. This attitude of the Senate and the House of Representatives was based on the view that according to the laws governing American assistance to Turkey, American armaments delivered to Ankara were to be used only for purposes of fulfilling the NATO objectives and other obligations undertaken under a special alliance relationship between the United States and Turkey. Any diversion of these arms for other purposes was considered unlawful and contrary to the original spirit of the alliance. Considering these bills unjustified and dangerous to the alliance with Turkey, President Gerald Ford vetoed them. In the ensuing struggle between the president and Congress, congressional pressures appeared to be stronger. As a result, on February 5, 1975, United States military aid to Turkey was officially suspended until Turkey agreed to negotiate her withdrawal from Cyprus. In July, Turkey retaliated by halting most of the operations at twenty-six American military installations. Following further pleading with Congress by President Ford, the arms ban was somewhat modified in favor of Turkey in October.[62] In spite of this modification, the United States was compelled to suspend

[61]The story of Cyprus up to 1974 is to be found in C. Foley and W. I. Scobie, *The Struggle for Cyprus* (Stanford, Calif., 1975).

[62]For details, see "Turkey Arms Bill Voted by Senate and Sent to Ford," *New York Times*, Oct. 4, 1975; and "Eased Turkish Embargo Signed into Law by Ford," *New York Times*, Oct. 8, 1975.

the operations of its radar stations monitoring Soviet military moves from the Turkish territory. As a result, the half-million strong Turkish armed forces became seriously weakened and the estimated effectiveness of their airforce declined by 50 percent. Although, under the Carter administration, Congress finally agreed to rescind the ban on August 1, 1978, the whole episode left a somewhat bitter legacy. Some observers feared that the relations between the two countries based on close political and military cooperation would never resume their previous level of cordiality.

Conclusion

As the 1970s progressed, Turkey found herself facing fundamental dilemmas in her internal politics and foreign policies. In internal politics Turkey's main challenge was to reestablish political stability based on a workable majority which would reaffirm the government's authority over a variety of centrifugal forces without jeopardizing the momentum of economic development begun under the combined free enterprise and state-supported system. In the foreign sector Turkey's main challenge was to rethink and reassess her international position both on the regional scale and in regard to the two main superpowers. On the regional scale three sectors could be distinguished: the Northern Tier allies of Iran and Pakistan, the Arab world, and her western neighbor, Greece. Of the three sectors the first two appeared to pose no major problems. Relations with Iran and Pakistan followed a normal course based on cooperation within the framework of RCD and to some extent on CENTO. With regard to the Arab world, Turkey maintained a generally friendly and cooperative relationship while not repudiating her diplomatic relations with Israel. But relations with Greece suffered a great deterioration on account of Cyprus. They became further aggravated by the dispute that erupted in the 1970s over the competing Greek and Turkish claims to the Aegean Sea bed with its discovered and potential oil resources. Because the Aegean Sea is studded with islands belonging to Greece, the Greek government claimed a virtual monopoly of exploration and exploitation of oil on most of the Aegean Sea bed. This claim was contested by Turkey, whose concepts of continental shelf rights did not square with those of Greece. Of the two powers, Turkey appeared to be more conciliatory in that she insisted on a negotiated settlement. Ultimately on May 31, 1975, the two parties agreed to submit their dispute to the International Court of Justice in The Hague.

As for Cyprus, the initial objective of Turkey was to prevent its union with Greece. This objective, however, appeared to give place to a new objective in the course of 1975. Invading Turkish forces proceeded to occupy as much as 40 percent of the territory of Cyprus, north of the line from Lefka to Famagusta. The military occupation led to massive exodus of the Greek population from the northern occupied parts to the south and to a less pronounced migration of Turkish Cypriots from the south to the north. Under these circumstances, Turkey began to insist on the creation of a federal Cypriot state to be composed of autonomous Greek and Turkish parts. The other alternative kept more or less in reserve was a complete division of Cyprus between two separate governments with a possibility that each of them would affiliate itself to Greece and Turkey respectively. With the massive Turkish military presence in Cyprus, Turkey's position appeared appreciably stronger than that of either Greece or the Greek-Cypriot government, and the possibility of reunifying Cyprus as a single state appeared to be more and more remote. Moreover, the Turkish Cypriots headed by Denktash made various moves to establish their own autonomous authorities.

The advantages of the Turkish position had to be considered in the light of repercussions that it produced in Turkish-Greek relations as well as in Turkey's position within the Western alliance. Higher strategic and defense priorities might have dictated to the Turks a more restrained course of action and at least a partial withdrawal from the northern territory in Cyprus, which was a larger share of the island than could be justified by the proportional strength of the Turkish population in Cyprus. But here it was where the internal and foreign policies were mutually entangled. In the absence of a clear majority and of a strong government, Turkey could not make decisions that might appear as concessions to the other party. This was true of both the government of Premier Bülent Ecevit, on whose initiative the invasion of Cyprus was undertaken in 1974, and the successor government of Suleiman Demirel. Neither government was strong enough to make any concessions on the Cyprus issue, thus vitiating any rational process that might have been established for formulating the overall foreign policy of Turkey.

CHAPTER V

Iran

At the end of World War I Iran found herself in an unusual position. Russia, convulsed from a revolution and civil war, relaxed her traditional pressure. The new Soviet government had to fight for its life against foreign intervention. In contrast, Britain's strength appeared increased. British troops were in occupation of most of the Middle East. They were stationed throughout Iranian territory, using it freely as a transit ground for their expeditions to the Caucasus and Transcaspia. Britain was to be Iran's neighbor not only in India but also in Iraq. There was a strong temptation in British official circles to round out their possessions by including Iran in the British-influenced protective zone adjacent to India and the Persian Gulf. Consequently, considering Iran as her own preserve, Great Britain influenced the Allies to refuse to seat the Iranian delegation when it appeared at the Peace Conference in Paris.[1] Instead, Britain's foreign secretary, Lord Curzon, instructed Sir Percy Cox in Teheran to negotiate a treaty that would assure Britain political ascendancy in Iran. The treaty was signed on August 9, 1919, in London. Its provisions included British assistance to Iran through military and financial missions, which would have extensive powers in the reorganization of the Iranian army and treasury, and a loan of £2 million to Iran.

The treaty amounted to a virtual protectorate and produced widespread resentment among Iran's democrats and nationalists. Curzon, an old imperialist of the nineteenth-century Indian school, greatly underestimated the strength of postwar Asiatic nationalism and hoped that it would be possible to extend Britain's influence without committing his country to direct colonial administration and responsibility. Events proved him wrong. The Iranian Majlis (parliament) refused to ratify the treaty, and the two British missions—the military under General W. E. R. Dickson and the financial under Armitage Smith—were eventually compelled to leave Teheran after a period of inactivity. Nothing could be done about the treaty unless force

[1]The official reason for the refusal was that Iran, being neutral in the war, was not entitled to participation in the conference. This was, however, a flimsy excuse, considering that Zionists and other nongovernmental delegations were accorded full hearings. The Iranian delegation, true enough, had little to contribute to a realistic solution of Middle Eastern problems, having come to present extravagant territorial claims which included Transcaspia, Merv, and Khiva up to the Oxus River, several districts in the Caucasus, including Nakhichevan, and the Kurdish area of Mesopotamia as far as the Euphrates.

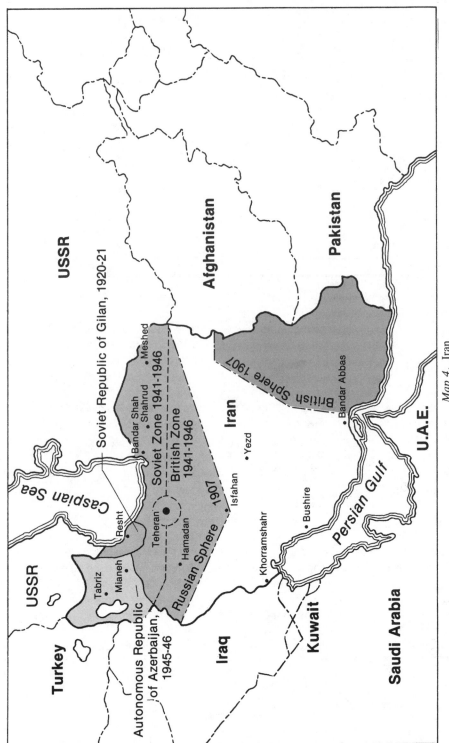

Map 4. Iran

was used. Britain was not prepared to go that far. In fact, according to the traditional British doctrine, Iran was never treated as an area of direct colonial expansion but simply as a buffer state between India and Russia. Moreover, Britain was demobilizing, and the taxpayers were loath to assume more commitments in the Middle East. At the end of 1919 British troops commenced to evacuate the Asiatic borderlands of Russia, leaving the counterrevolutionary forces to their own devices. The British military establishment in Iran was reduced in 1920, and between January and April of 1921 it was withdrawn entirely. Under such circumstances, Britain could hardly expect Iran to ratify the abortive treaty.

In contrast to Anglo-Iranian relations, Iran's postwar dealings with Soviet Russia augured well. In 1918 the revolutionary government in Moscow voluntarily renounced all the privileges and concessions that tsarist Russia had secured in Iran. In its proclamation "To the toiling Moslems of Russia and the East," the Soviet government declared itself a staunch friend and ally of the exploited peoples of Asia and at the Conference of the Peoples of the East, held in Baku in September 1920, it launched a great anti-imperialist propaganda offensive. In 1920 negotiations for the conclusion of a treaty of friendship began in Moscow between Iranian and Soviet representatives. The new Russian regime was eager to secure collaboration with her southern neighbors—Turkey, Iran, and Afghanistan. Treaty arrangements with these countries would put an end to Soviet diplomatic isolation and would constitute a victory over the Western imperialists in Asia and the Middle East.

Unfortunately, these initial friendly moves were marred by an episode which caused many people to question the sincerity of Soviet protestations. Pursuing the remnants of Denikin's White Russian forces, the Soviet fleet and expeditionary force under Commissar Raskolnikov landed in the Iranian Caspain port of Enzeli (Pahlavi) on May 18, 1920, compelling a small British garrison to withdraw. The Red army troops soon occupied most of the area between the Caspian coast and the Elburz Mountains, joined hands with the local rebel, Kuchik Khan, and helped him proclaim in Resht the Soviet Republic of Gilan. Iran vigorously protested. Moscow explained that Raskolnikov's expedition was the work of the newly established Soviet republic of Azerbaijan, over whose actions it had no control, and later insisted on retaining the Red army there so long as the British kept their troops in Iran. These two explanations failed to convince the Iranians. Despite these difficulties negotiations proceeded, and on February 26, 1921, Iran and Soviet Russia concluded a treaty of friendship. The treaty was a pleasant contrast to the abortive British treaty inasmuch as it reiterated previous Soviet renunciation of old Russian concessions and properties and, in many ways, gave expression to Soviet friendship toward the people of Iran. An annex to the treaty provided for common exploitation of the Caspian fisheries. This was about the only remnant of the old subservient attitude toward Russia. Article 6 of the treaty reserved for Soviet Russia the right to send troops into Iranian territory should the latter become a base for anti-Soviet aggression.[2]

---

[2]From the Iranian point of view, this was an unfortunate clause in the treaty. The Soviets insisted on its inclusion on the ground that Iran, even against her will, might be occupied by Western imperialists and hence one day serve as a base for counterrevolutionary White forces. No documented evidence has so far

The conclusion of the Soviet-Iranian treaty marked the end of what may be called a period of postwar settlement in Iran. Soviet troops were withdrawn from Gilan nine months later (October 1921), and Kuchik Khan's regime collapsed following an Iranian military expedition into that area. The British treaty was officially rejected by the Iranian government. After seven years of war, tribal rebellion, insurrection, and general chaos, Iran had at last regained her independence. One is tempted to describe it as "independence by default," since it was largely due to domestic developments in Russia and to Britain's reluctance to commit herself to further imperial action. Basically, Iran was still a very weak country, whose continued existence as a sovereign nation depended upon two factors: (1) the attitude of her neighbors, and (2) the strength of her own political leadership.

Reza Khan and His Reforms

Five days before the signing of the Soviet-Iranian Treaty, Iran experienced a coup staged by Reza Khan and Sayid Zia ed-Din Taba-Tabai. Reza commanded the Iranian Cossack Division, and Zia, a man in his early thirties, was a radical writer and reformer. Reza's force, the Cossack Division, was at that time the only efficient unit of the Iranian army. It had been created in 1878 as a brigade and followed the Russian pattern of organization. Russian officers traditionally held key positions in this unit, and during the period of Russian political ascendancy the brigade served as an additional safeguard to Russian interests in Iran. After the Soviet revolution this formation continued to be officered by Russian Whites under Colonel Starosselsky, who rendered meritorious service to Iran, taking Resht from the Red army in 1920. Reza Khan had been first a trooper and then an officer under Starosselsky's command.[3] Ambitious, he was determined to exploit Russia's temporary weakness after the revolution in order to get rid of the Russian officers in the division. His views coincided with those of the British, who, following their treaty with Iran in 1919, hoped for control of the Iranian army. Aided by the British commander in northwestern Iran, Reza took advantage of the momentary setback suffered by the division at Enzeli in August 1920 and engineered the dismissal of all Russian officers.[4] Their positions were filled by British officers commanded by Colonel Smyth, who remained with the division until 1921. Reza himself assumed command of the

---

been revealed to explain why Iran agreed to this clause, but it is probable that Iran was eager to effect the evacuation of Soviet troops in Gilan and at the same time to oppose any extension of British influence by speedily concluding the treaty. In the official communication appended to the treaty, the Soviet envoy in Teheran made it clear, however, that Article 6 was intended "to apply only to cases in which preparations have been made for a considerable armed attack upon Russia," and that it was "in no sense intended to apply to verbal or written attacks directed against the Soviet Government." (The relevant texts are included in George Lenczowski, *Russia and the West in Iran, 1918–1948* [Ithaca, N.Y., 1949], p. 318.)

[3]As a noncommissioned officer, he had at one time been in charge of a small detachment guarding the German legation in Teheran, and in this capacity he maintained friendly relations with the more important native servants such as the chief butler. After the war when he once visited the legation as the Shah, he was served food by some of his former friends who were still in the legation's employment. *Tempora mutantur!* (See Wipert von Blücher, *Zeitenwende in Iran* [Biberach an der Riss, 1949], p. 165.)

[4]This action was formally confirmed by the Iranian government under Premier Sepahdar.

division. British officers gave him technical advice during his march on Teheran, and hence he has often been considered by his adversaries as a British creation. The accusation was not quite just, because Reza, while ready to avail himself of British aid at a certain moment of his career, was essentially a nationalist opposed to any foreign interference in the affairs of Iran.

His rise to power was rapid. As a result of the coup of February 1921, he became the Iranian commander-in-chief and minister of war. Zia ed-Din assumed the premiership and in his zeal for radical reforms adopted harsh measures against many wealthy conservatives. Three months later Reza forced Zia to resign and flee the country; thereafter he exercised paramount influence in government. He became prime minister in 1923 and soon afterward forced the weak-willed shah, Ahmed, to depart for an "extended trip to Europe." For some time he toyed with the idea of republicanism and encouraged agitation to this end. Widespread clerical opposition to these schemes, however, made him change his mind to the extent that any mention of a republic was formally prohibited by law. On October 31, 1925, the Majlis deposed the absentee shah and on December 13 proclaimed Reza Shah-an-Shah of Iran. Thus, the century-and-a-quarter-old Kajar dynasty came to an end, and the new Pahlavi dynasty came into power.

Reza Khan's chief ambition was to emulate his Turkish counterpart, Mustafa Kemal. He wanted to emancipate Iran from foreign influence and to strengthen her by adopting Western reforms and technology. To achieve these ends he needed first to strengthen his own position and the power of the central government.

The army became the object of his particular attention. Only a well-organized, well-paid, and disciplined military force could assure him success. His first job was to restore order in the country. In a series of successful expeditions—and he often had recourse to ruthless means—Reza defeated the pro-Communist rebel Kuchik Khan, put an end to provincial rebellions in Khorasan and Azerbaijan, and subdued unruly nomad tribes including the powerful Kurdish tribes of the north. He also ended the semiautonomous status of Sheikh Khazal of Mohammera, who had wielded control over the oil-rich area of the southwest. By the time of his coronation in the spring of 1926, Reza's one man rule was undisputed and the Majlis was just an appendage filled with the Shah's nominees.

Reza turned next toward internal reforms.[5] These played a double role by marking at once the steps of internal progress and of external emancipation. Aware that the political dependence of the Kajar rulers often resulted directly from an empty treasury, Reza Shah decided to tackle this problem first. As early as 1922 he invited an American expert, Dr. Arthur Chester Millspaugh, to reorganize Iran's public finances. Millspaugh stayed in Iran until 1927, and through his skillful administration provided the government with a steady income. This success permitted the Shah to proceed with a technical project of major significance—the construction of the great Trans-Iranian Railway, which would link Teheran with both the Caspian

[5]For a review of Iranian reforms, consult L. P. Elwell-Sutton, *Modern Iran* (London, 1941), chs. v-vii; William S. Haas, *Iran* (New York, 1946), pp. 137 ff.; and A. Banani, *The Modernization of Iran, 1921-1941* (Stanford, Calif., 1961).

Sea and the Persian Gulf. The Shah believed, and rightly, that much would depend upon the development of communications in the country. The maintenance of effective government control over outlying regions, the security of the country, and its economic prosperity would all be enhanced if roads and transportation were in good condition. The Trans-Iranian Railway was begun in 1927, to be completed in 1939. The remarkable feature about it was that the whole scheme was financed entirely by the government of Iran itself from special taxes placed on tea and sugar. The technical side of the construction was entrusted to a number of foreign engineering firms, with no preponderance given to any one nation.

In addition to this, the Shah ordered the construction of many important highways and promoted the establishment of air communications. Between 1927 and 1932 the German Junkers airline provided a passenger and mail service between the capital and a number of provincial towns, and in 1928 the Shah granted a concession to the Imperial Airways, a British firm, to fly over the Iranian coast between Iraq and India. In 1931, Iran took over from the British management the Iranian network of the Indo-European Telegraph Company.

Reza's plans for reform were not restricted to technological advances only. He wanted to modernize the country in the social and educational fields as well. In 1927 he introduced the French judicial system, thus challenging the competence of the religious courts in civil matters. A year later he formally abolished the capitulations. Another law in 1931 forbade foreigners to own agricultural land. The trend toward secularization was clearly discernible, but never did it assume proportions similar to those in Turkey. Reza Shah wanted no sharing of authority with any independent group in Iran, and he considered the influence of backward Shia clergy as detrimental to the Westernization of the country. But he proceeded cautiously. The failure of prorepublican agitation in 1924 and the defeat of his reforming neighbor, King Amanullah of Afghanistan, at the hands of the mullahs in 1929 taught him that what was possible in half-Europeanized Turkey was not yet possible in Iran. Furthermore, the Iranian constitution[6] expressly stated that "the official religion of Iran is Islam, and the true sect is the Jafariya. The Shah of Iran must profess and propagate this faith." It also forbade the Majlis to pass legislation contrary to the principles of Islam and provided for consultation of the theologians in the legislative process; furthermore, such consultation was to be binding. The Shah did not feel that he could openly challenge these provisions. As a result, instead of launching a frontal attack, he used various devious ways, evading and ignoring the Shia hierarchy rather than curbing them directly.

In fact, everything that pertained to the establishment of a modern educational system or the emancipation of women was bound to reduce the influence of the clergy. And in these fields a good deal was done in the interwar period. Officially, compulsory primary education was decreed; and though it never worked perfectly in practice, because of the shortage of teachers and funds, impressive advances were made in spreading the network of schools. Since the beginning of the century Iran had possessed some institutions of higher learning, but in 1934 a university of six

[6]Supplementary Constitutional Law of October 8, 1907.

faculties was established in Teheran and provided with spacious modern buildings. It had also a theological faculty, but since 1930 compulsory religious education has been eliminated from the primary and secondary schools. The school curricula stressed patriotism and civic-mindedness. As a reaction to external influence, a law of 1932 forbade foreign primary schools in the country. It eventually affected all schools sponsored by foreign missionaries, and Teheran College, an American Presbyterian secondary school, had to close its doors. Sports were encouraged, and a number of modern stadia were erected in the principal towns. The government made participation in Boy Scout and Girl Guide organizations compulsory for teenagers mainly to imbue the young generation with the spirit of nationalism. These activities obviously kept the youth of the country from religious pursuits and contemplation. Quite a blow, though indirectly, was delivered to religious influence by the prohibition of oriental dress in 1928. The fez and the turban were replaced first by the so-called Pahlavi hat (a kind of French kepi, which was compulsory for all males) and later by a regular European hat.

The Shah also promoted various measures to emancipate women. Under his influence the Majlis passed legislation curbing the exaggerated divorce privileges hitherto possessed by husbands and made women eligible for public offices, though not to representative political functions. Through instructions given to army officers and government officials, the Shah encouraged the adoption of Western dress for women, and in 1935 his wife and daughters made a public appearance in European costumes. From that time veils were forbidden. This reform caused some riots, but enforcement was strict and all had to comply with the law.

The Shah also ordered the revision of the language, with a view to purifying it from Arabic influences. This became one of the specific tasks of the Iranian Academy of Literature, founded in 1935. In contrast to Turkey, however, no reform of the alphabet was attempted despite the fact that the Arabic script does not meet the requirements of the Persian language. In March 1935 the state was officially named Iran to replace the Hellenistic name of Persia.

Hygiene also became a subject of official solicitude, and in the twenties and thirties an impressive number of modern hospitals were built. To cope with labor questions in the nascent Iranian industry, a factory act was passed in 1938. The daily and periodical press was expected to propagandize these reforms and it fulfilled its task. The press was discouraged from criticizing the government, and the number of dailies in Teheran was restricted to four. In 1940 the first government-owned broadcasting station was inaugurated in the capital. Its programs were primarily educational.

Economic Developments

With social reform went economic development under governmental control and inspiration. Iran did not officially adopt the principle of *étatisme* as did Turkey, but government intervention in economic life was practiced on a large scale. After the resignation of Dr. A. C. Millspaugh, the Shah entrusted Dr. Lindenblatt, a German economist, with the organization of the National Bank of Iran in 1928. The bank was given the privilege of issuing banknotes, a privilege that had been withdrawn from the British-controlled Imperial Bank of Iran. The government made an impressive effort to establish many new industries in Iran (usually with German assistance) and to promote foreign trade. In 1931, largely as a protective measure against Soviet trade tactics, the government established the so-called foreign trade monopoly, which left transactions to free enterprise but subjected them to strict governmental controls. The Shah himself took an active part in the process of industrialization by investing his personal funds in a number of enterprises and constructions. Using either public or private capital, he spurred the construction of modern buildings; he himself owned some impressive hotels in some of Iran's showier places.

Reza Shah's reforms certainly stirred Iran from lethargy, and, if the Shah had been permitted to continue them for another decade, much benefit might have accrued to Iran. But his work was interrupted by the Second World War. Of his two aims—emancipation from foreign influence and Westernization—Reza Shah succeeded in the first but did not quite accomplish the second. His task was more difficult than was Kemal Ataturk's because his was a more backward country and because his education and personality were different from Kemal's. Reza Shah had never been in Europe, and his concepts of modernization were sometimes naïve. Moreover, he was a despotic and greedy individual, inclined to arbitrary acts in order to satisfy his personal ambitions, possessing no real concept of the rule of law, and lacking the unselfishness that rendered Kemal a true statesman and father of his nation.

Iran's Foreign Policy

As a small nation that had almost miraculously retained her threatened sovereignty in 1919, Iran was essentially a status quo power, unwilling and unable to pursue active expansionist policies. But at times Iranian political leadership manifested a disturbing lack of political realism. Such was the case when, at the Paris Peace Conference, Iran attempted to present far-reaching claims to the Kurdish areas of northern Iraq and to formerly Iranian, but for many decades Russian, territories in the Caucasus and Central Asia. This was true also of Iran's claims to the British-protected Bahrain Islands, situated in the Persian Gulf and inhabited by the Arabs. While the claims to Iraqi and Russian territory were quickly forgotten, the claim to the islands was often revived for demagogic purposes by groups seeking popularity in Iran.

Iran's foreign policies can be classified under two major headings: (1) those relating to the other countries of the Middle East, and (2) those relating to the great powers.

With regard to the Middle East, Irán sought peace and friendship with her neighbors. This is noteworthy because there had long been enmity between Iran and Turkey, on the one hand, and between Iran and Afghanistan, on the other. On April 22, 1926, with the encouragement of the Soviet Union, Iran, Turkey, and Afghanistan concluded a treaty of friendship. Despite this, the vexatious Kurdish problem stood in the way of a complete reconciliation between Ankara and Teheran. The Kurdish uprising that occurred during June and July 1930 accentuated these difficulties. The basic desire for good neighborly relations brought a settlement of outstanding frontier problems in 1932. In the same year King Faisal of Iraq paid a state visit to Iran, and in 1934 Turkish-Iranian friendship was confirmed by Reza Shah's visit to Ankara. In 1937, Iran, Turkey, Iraq, and Afghanistan concluded the Saadabad pact, which established an Eastern Entente. The pact provided for nonaggression, consultation, and mutual cooperation in stamping out subversive activities among the signatory states. It was viewed with thinly disguised hostility by Russia, who believed it to be another type of *cordon sanitaire*.

Little can be said about Iran's relations with Arab countries other than Iraq. Countries like Syria, Lebanon, or Palestine were still under mandates and did not have policies of their own. Egypt and the states of the Arabian peninsula were geographically removed, without points of contact except for occasional pilgrim traffic to Saudi Arabia. Generally, Iran stood aloof from the problems of the Arab countries and did not share their agitation over Palestine. As with most of the Middle Eastern states, Iran's main problems centered in her relationships with the big powers and not with her oriental neighbors.

Irano-Soviet Relations

Traditionally these powers were Russia and Great Britain. After the conclusion of the 1921 treaty, Iran's relations with the Soviet Union could be described as correct but not cordial. Cordiality was precluded because of several factors. The unfortunate episode in Gilan, previously referred to, imbued the Iranians with considerable distrust, despite friendly protestations from the Soviet Union. Furthermore, rebellions that broke out later in Iranian Azerbaijan and in Khorasan occurred dangerously close to the Soviet border, and Reza Shah had good grounds on which to suspect the sponsorship or connivance of Soviet authorities. On the other hand, his ruthless determination to stamp out communism drove the Iranian Communist party underground. This fact irked Moscow, despite the official doctrinal stand that classified Reza's regime as an antifeudal semi-bourgeois revolution, and, hence, a positive step forward, according to Marxist dialectics. In addition, economic problems considerably marred the felicity of Irano-Soviet relations.

The question of northern oil concessions was one of these problems. Freed by the treaty of 1921 from subjection to tsarist Russia, Iran repeatedly attempted to grant concessions to British and American corporations. A special clause in the Irano-Soviet treaty forbade Iran to grant to foreigners those concessions which had been renounced by Soviet Russia. Moscow therefore protested vigorously against any new deals between Iran and the Western capitalists. It was open to question whether or not Russia was right from a legal standpoint, since, as the interested British party claimed, the disputed concessions did not belong to Russian but to Georgian subjects at the time of the treaty. It was not, however, the legal argument that prevailed in the last analysis, but rather political considerations. Fearful lest it completely alienate Russia, the Iranian government canceled all arrangements with British and American corporations in 1924. The question was not reopened until 1937, when Iran granted to the Amiranian Oil Company, a subsidiary of the Seaboard Oil Company of Delaware, a concession extending to the northern provinces. No Soviet protests were recorded this time, but the concession never became operative because the company renounced its rights in 1938, owing to general world conditions.

Irano-Soviet trade constituted another bone of contention. Petrovsky, Soviet ambassador in Teheran, once gave the following fitting description of Russo-Iranian relations: "What counts in Persia is North Persia only and the latter is fully dependent on Russia. All North Persian products that must be exported can find their only market in Russia. If we Russians stop buying them, Persia is bankrupt in one month. This is Russia's strength which has no equivalent on the British side."[7] Petrovsky's statement was not inaccurate, and Russia more than once made use of this economic weapon in her dealings with Iran. In 1926 a dispute over fishery rights in the Caspian moved Russia to place an embargo on imports from Iran (with the exception of cotton), and Iran's northern provinces suffered severely as a result. Sporadically Soviet commercial representatives in Iran would grant import permits to Iranian traders as a means of influencing people and decisions or as compensation for services rendered. In 1927 the boycott was lifted at the price of a new fishery agreement, which favored Soviet interests. Motivated by political considerations, Russia did not hesitate to dump her products, such as sugar and oil, on the Iranian market to the detriment of Iran's trade with other countries. During the 1920s, Iran was constantly harassed by these spasmodic crises in her trade with Russia. Iran was also in a weak position because her system of free enteprise could not withstand the pressures applied by the Soviet monopolistic trade organization. Largely to circumvent these inconveniences, Reza Shah in 1931 decided to establish a foreign trade monopoly and, with the advent of Hitler to power, gradually began to reorient Iranian trade toward Germany.

Although the Iranian Communist party was weak, decimated, and intimidated, Soviet Russia never ceased to keep a vigilant eye on the affairs of Iran. Soviet trade officials, spies, GPU, and Comintern agents roamed freely throughout the country, which in many ways was ideally suited to such undercover activities. As long, however, as Reza Shah was in power, there was no likelihood of a revolution, despite growing discontent with his autocratic methods. If Iran were to fall prey to communism, it would be only as a result of external aggression, and this, in the interwar period, Russia was unwilling to undertake.

Irano-British Relations

Iran's relations with Britain during this time passed through various phases ranging from outward correctness to open quarreling. Even when their relations were not too friendly, Iran was closer to Britain than to any other power. This was due partly to Britain's presence in India and in Iraq and to her supremacy in the Persian Gulf. Primarily, however, it was the result of the operations of the Anglo-Iranian Oil Company in the province of Khuzistan. The presence of this large company with one of the world's biggest refineries on the island of Abadan necessitated the development of a network of services directly or indirectly connected with the basic oil interest. The British Residency for the Persian Gulf in Bushire, a number of consulates staffed by Indian Political Service officers, branches of the Imperial

[7]Blücher, *op. cit.*, p. 187.

Bank of Iran, official and unofficial agents working among the tribes—all contributed to the fact that for Britishers, civil or military, Iran was familiar ground. In Iran the British had a twofold diplomatic system: on the one hand, through their embassy in Teheran, they dealt with the Iranian government and, on the other, through local consuls and agents, with the provincial potentates and powerful nomad tribes of Qashqais, Bakhtiyaris, Lurs, and Kurds. Even the power of Reza Shah did not affect to any great degree this traditional pattern.

In 1927 a quarrel broke out between the two countries over the oil-rich Bahrain Islands. Iran claimed sovereignty over Bahrain on historical grounds, but Britain refused to consider the problem. By 1928 Britain and Iran were at odds over a number of issues. Britain resented Iran's unilateral denunciation of capitulations and asked for some *quid pro quo* to protect her subjects. Iran refused to grant Britain the right to fly over her coast to India, in the meantime concluding air agreements with Germany and the Soviet Union. Reza Shah was determined to curb the power of Sheikh Khazal of Mohammera, an old-time British protegé whose domains extended over the oil-rich Khuzistan. Britain claimed payment of debts by Iran in connection with the wartime formation of the South-Persia Rifles. Iran for some time refused to recognize the British-controlled government of Iraq. And, finally, there was a controversy over the customs tariff.

All these problems were successfully solved by the conclusion on May 16, 1928, of an Anglo-Iranian treaty which restored normal relations. The treaty gave certain safeguards to British nationals resisdent in Iran in lieu of the old capitulations. It also cleared the path to an agreement between Iran and the Imperial Airways (concluded in December 1928), which gave the latter the right to fly over the Iranian coastal area on the Persian Gulf. In 1932 a new crisis broke out, this time of major proportions. Desirous of obtaining a higher share in the profits of the Anglo-Iranian Oil Company and accusing the British of dishonest accounting practices, Reza Shah unilaterally canceled the company's concession. Britain protested, sent warships to the Persian Gulf, and brought the matter to the Council of the League of Nations. The latter's consideration of the case was, however, dropped when it was learned in 1933 that the government of Iran and the company had concluded a mutually satisfactory agreement. The new concession was to be valid for sixty years and provided for a considerable increase in royalties to Iran, as well as for the gradual "Iranization" of the company's personnel. It was greeted in Iran as a major diplomatic victory, which, indeed, it was. From that time on relations between Iran and Britain were on the whole friendly, but there was a visible waning of British influence.

To sum up Irano-Soviet-British relations, it may safely be asserted that, under Reza's energetic rule, Iran succeeded in emancipating herself from the domination of her two powerful neighbors. This emancipation was political and to a large extent economic as well.

Irano-German Relations

The process of emancipation was accompanied by growing friendship between Iran and Germany. Reviving her pet theory of the "Third Power," Iran turned toward the Reich when it became obvious that the latter had recuperated from wartime defeat. From 1928 on, Iran availed herself more and more of the economic and technical services of Germany. This trend took on a definite upward swing when Hitler came to power. To Iran's desire for a powerful friend, the Third Reich reciprocated by displaying special interest in the affairs of the Middle East in general and of Iran in particular. Germany began to supply Iran with ever-growing numbers of experts and goods. Iranian communications, industry, building, hospitals, and agriculture owed a great deal to German assistance. Trade between the two countries grew by leaps and bounds. A clearing agreement negotiated by Dr. Hjalmar Schacht during his visit in Teheran in 1935 laid solid foundations for trade between the two states. Iranian dignitaries paid state visits to Berlin, and the Reich was not slow in sending men like Baldur von Schirach, a Nazi youth leader, to Iran on good-will tours. By 1939, Germany accounted for 41 percent of the total foreign trade in Iran, and the number of Germans resident in Iran as technicians, traders, or "tourists" had risen to 2,000. Nazi propaganda scored notable successes by emphasizing the common Aryan background of the two peoples, as well as their struggle for equality and independence under the leadership of "enlightened" rulers. Reza Shah did not hesitate to praise the authoritarian regime in Germany as the best safeguard against communism.[8]

The general outcome of these policies was, on the one hand, the enhancement of Germany's position in Iran to the detriment of Soviet and British influence and, on the other hand, the strengthening of Iranian nationalism. The latter began to manifest overconfidence rather than sober political thinking.

Iran and World War II

Upon the outbreak of the war in 1939, Iran proclaimed her neutrality. Iranian ruling circles were mostly pro-German, and trade with Germany, carried on via Russia, increased. The German invasion of Russia in June 1941 presented the West with the problem of supplying the Russian allies. There were four possible routes: through Murmansk, through Vladivostok, through the Turkish Straits, and over the Iranian highlands. Neither the Murmansk nor the Vladivostok routes could handle really large supplies. Turkey closed the Straits. To force their opening would have necessitated war with her, an alternative the Allies refused consider in view of the fact that Turkey was a nonbelligerent ally of the West. Thus Iran remained the only practical transit route to Russia, through which, given proper organization, bulky supplies could be shipped. But there were many German technicians in Iran who, on orders from Berlin, could sabotage Allied transportation arrangements should Iran open her territory. Consequently, Soviet Russia and Great Britain twice (June and August 1941) asked Iran to expel the Germans. Iran refused, whereupon on August 25 British and Soviet forces entered the country and soon occupied it. Iranian military resistance was negligible. Russia and Britain divided the country into two zones of occupation: Russia obtained control of the five northern provinces of Azerbaijan, Gilan, Mazanderan, Gorgan, and Khorasan, and Great Britain got the rest of the country. Teheran became a neutral enclave. Under Soviet and British

[8]*Ibid.*, p. 331.

pressure Reza Shah abdicated in favor of his twenty-two-year-old son, Mohammed Reza, and left the country aboard a British vessel for South Africa. There he died in 1944. A new pro-Ally cabinet came into power. On January 29, 1942, it concluded a Tripartite Treaty of Alliance with Great Britain and the Soviet Union. The treaty stated that the presence of foreign troops on Iranian territory did not constitute a military occupation, gave the Allies transit and communications facilities in Iran, reaffirmed Iranian independence, and provided for the withdrawal of the Allied troops within six months after the end of the war with the Axis. Toward the end of 1942, 30,000 noncombatant American troops moved in and took charge of lend-lease supplies to Russia.

To Iran, these swift events were a severe shock, revealing as they did the country's weaknesses and the error of counting on Germany for protection. Iranian foreign policy had to be completely reoriented. Everything receded into the background before the major task of regaining full independence. This was not an easy task to accomplish. Iran had to change overnight from neutrality to alliance, revamp the enemy occupation into friendly cooperation, gain the recognition and gratitude of the Allies, obtain a seat at the future peace conference, and secure the evacuation of the Allied armies. The last of these objectives seemed especially difficult inasmuch as the Soviet Union showed signs of considering her occupation as more than a temporary expedient.

As to internal affairs, foreign occupation and Reza's abdication brought in their wake an interruption of the reforms, an upsetting of normal economic life, and pronounced inflation and unrest. The loudly advertised democracy, which was supposed to follow Reza's dictatorship, had little chance to flourish. Because of the presence of foreign troops, most of the old internal problems were now linked to Iran's foreign relations. There was a visible recrudescence of extremist movements. On the one hand, the hitherto restrained Shia clergy reasserted their influence. This was accompanied by a return of the nomad tribes to militant autonomy. On the other hand, the radical leftist elements emerged in the shape of the Communist-dominated Tudeh ("Masses") party, thus complicating the nation's turbulent politics.

The policy of the occupying powers was of the utmost importance. Russia's interest in Iran was traditional, and published Nazi-Soviet documents reveal that in the fall of 1940 the Soviet Union seriously contemplated including Iran and Iraq in her sphere of influence.[9] Less than a year later Soviet troops were in actual occupation of Iran's richest provinces, Iran's anti-Soviet ruler had been deposed, and the country was open to intrigue and infiltration. Russia did not waste a good opportunity. Soviet wartime policy in Iran was both revolutionary and imperialistic— revolutionary in the sense that Soviet organs did everything possible to upset Iran's stability and to create conditions for a violent change, and imperialistic because Russia gave plentiful evidence of desiring permanent extension of her power over Iran. Russia carried on her revolutionary tactics through a variety of means. She supported the Communist Tudeh party, whose leaders owed liberation from Reza's

---

[9]"Nazi-Soviet Relations 1939-1941," *Documents from the Archives of the German Foreign Office* (Department of State, Pub. 3023; Washington, D.C., 1948), p. 257.

jails to the Red army, stirred up labor trouble, supported a number of pro-Soviet newspapers, bribed politicians and intellectuals, and operated a huge propaganda machine. Soviet imperialism was evidenced by intrigue among and support of national minorities, such as the Armenians and the Kurds, propaganda favoring separation for Turkish-speaking Iranian Azerbaijan, arbitrary censorship on all the in- and out-going news in Iran, economic pressure and exploitation, and intimidation of Iranian officials, police, and army. In the fall of 1944, Soviet Assistant Commissar for Foreign Affairs Kavtaradze arrived in Teheran and demanded an oil concession to cover the northern provinces. When Prime Minister Mohammed Saed refused it, a veritable storm broke out. Soviet-supported newspapers vociferously asked for the granting of the concession, accusing the government of pro-Fascist tendencies; big rallies of the Tudeh party, protected by Soviet tanks, were held in Teheran and other cities and passed pro-Soviet resolutions; and, at a press conference in Teheran, Kavtaradze publicly censured Saed for his stubbornness. The situation became so tense that Saed was forced to resign and was replaced by a more conciliatory successor. At the same time, on the motion of a deputy, Dr. Mohammed Mossadegh, the Majlis passed a law forbidding the government, under severe penalties, to grant or even negotiate oil concessions without parliamentary approval. Having failed in his mission, Kavtaradze left for Moscow. This was a setback for the Soviets, but only a temporary one as later events were to prove.

To Iran, all these pressures were highly embarrassing, but little could be done to counteract them. In the British zone, the government had relative freedom of action and could, at least, keep the native Communist activities under control. The Soviet zone, however, was completely at the mercy of Soviet authorities. The only effective resistance to Soviet schemes had to come from the big powers, i.e., Great Britain or the United States.

The main burden of resistance fell to Great Britain. British authorities in Iran were fully aware of the uneasy Irano-Soviet situation and did their best to offset Soviet propaganda and pressure. The British, realistically enough, tried to oppose Soviet encroachment by using, with moderation, somewhat similar weapons. Thus to counteract Tudeh activity, they supported a nationalist party Eradeye Melli ("National Will") formed by former Premier Zia ed-Din, who had returned from prolonged exile in Palestine. To the activities of official Soviet propaganda, they opposed their own propaganda emanating from the embassy's public relations bureau and the British Council. They handled skillfully an impressive number of anti-Soviet dailies and periodicals and cooperated, instead of obstructing, in the solution of Iran's economic problems.

In this cold war of propaganda and political intrigue Britain was handicapped by the moderation if not the actual timidity of her tactics. Eager to maintain unity with her Soviet ally, Great Britain acted under inhibitions alien to the Soviet mind. For this reason she was usually on the defensive. She hesitated to use the same offensive language, a normal feature of Soviet propaganda, and in the overall balance sheet of psychological warfare she appeared to be losing ground. This was not so much the result of lack of attempts at persuasion but rather of Iranian respect for and fear of strength. And strength was manifested primarily by the Soviet Union.

What was, under such circumstances, the attitude of the United States? The most important fact about American policy was that it was not at all coordinated with that of the British. Coordination existed only in the economic sphere and in the purely technical sphere of speeding up the supplies to Russia. Both Britain and the United States assisted Iran through their wartime regional agency, the Middle East Supply Center. Otherwise, their ways parted, not because there was any basic discrepancy in principles but because the United States appeared to be quite indifferent to and aloof from the political problems of Iran.

The United States extended both technical and economic assistance. Early in 1943, at the request of the Iranian government, Dr. A. C. Millspaugh arrived for the second time to administer Iran's public finances. He was granted wide executive powers by the Majlis and was authorized to hire sixty American aides. An American military mission was invited to advise on the administration of the army, and another mission, headed by Colonel Norman Schwarzkopf of Lindbergh kidnaping fame, was entrusted with the reorganization of the rural police. American experts were active also in the departments of agriculture, municipal police, health, and others. Unfortunately a quarrel developed between Dr. Millspaugh and some powerful members of the government, and early in 1945 Dr. Millspaugh resigned in the midst of a recriminatory campaign in the press.[10] Iran benefited also from American economic assistance. In 1942 lend lease was extended to her, and Americans assumed their share of responsibility in the previously mentioned Middle East Supply Center.

Politically, Americans showed good will and friendliness toward the Iranians. This good will was symbolized by the release on December 1, 1943, during the Teheran Conference of President Roosevelt, Prime Minister Churchill, and Premier Stalin, of a communiqué complimentary to Iran. This communiqué was Roosevelt's idea. It acknowledged Iran's services in "the transportation of supplies from overseas to the Soviet Union," promised her economic assistance both during and after the war, and, invoking the Atlantic Charter, reiterated the Big Three's "desire for the maintenance of the independence, sovereignty and territorial integrity of Iran." The communiqué was greeted with joy by the Iranians who were eager to hear good tidings concerning their eventual return to full independence, but it was not a legal commitment on the part of the United States. In that period of blooming friendship with Russia, the United States was neither ready nor willing to give any far-reaching political guarantees to Russia's small neighbors. Washington apparently believed that an optimistic joint statement from the Big Three would be sufficient. In pursuing such a policy, the American government indicated that (1) it valued wartime unity with the Soviet Union above other considerations and (2) that it was either unaware of or indifferent to Soviet pressure on Iran. The official American attitude was correct, but not much more. At the time of Kavtaradze's visit, it became known, for example, that some British and American corporations were seeking oil concessions in southeastern Iran. Premier Saed's refusal to grant concessions ex-

---

[10]His own account of his mission may be found in A. C. Millspaugh, *Americans in Persia* (Washington, D.C., 1946).

tended to those powers as well. This elicited a statement from the American ambassador, Leland B. Morris, that the United States respected Iran's sovereign right to refuse concessions. When Dr. Millspaugh was dismissed by the Iranian government, the American embassy officially washed its hands of what was described as a controversy between Iran and a private American citizen. This was no doubt an honorable, but a purely negative, policy. The United States did nothing to oppose deliberately Soviet schemes in Iran and it left the burden of counteraction to the British. The Iranians, who after Germany's ouster, had looked toward America as a friendly Third Power (and who for this reason had invited many American experts), were disappointed. By the same token the Soviet authorities, encountering no common Anglo-American front, were greatly emboldened.

The Azerbaijan Crisis

As soon as the Japanese surrender was signed on September 2, 1945, serious antigovernment disturbances broke out in the Soviet-controlled province of Azerbaijan. Attempts by the Iranian government to quell them proved unavailing, nor did the Western powers show any firmness toward Russia when the case of Iran was discussed at the September meeting of foreign ministers in London. Encouraged by these manifestations of indecision, the Soviet Union made a daring bid for the control of Iran. On December 12, 1945, former Tudeh members, acting under the new name of Democrats and aided by thousands of Soviet agents who crossed the border, deposed the Iranian governor at Tabriz and proclaimed the Autonomous Republic of Azerbaijan. The Red army gave them full protection, intimidated local Iranian officials, and prevented the central government troops, sent by Teheran, from reaching the province. The autonomous Azerbaijan government under the veteran Comintern agent Jaafar Pishevari openly thanked the Red army for assistance and proceeded to carry out revolutionary changes in the economic and social structure of the province. Soon afterward an independent Kurdish republic was set up under Soviet auspices in Mahabad. Its leaders, supplied with Soviet uniforms and weapons, concluded an alliance with the Tabriz rebels.[11]

Unable to do anything at home, Iran appealed to the newly formed United Nations, accusing Russia of aggressive interference. The Soviet delegate in the Security Council denied the accusation but averred that the Red army had, indeed, stopped the Iranian army from marching to Azerbaijan in order, as he put it, "to avoid bloodshed." Iran's case was strengthened when on March 2, 1946, the Soviet Union failed to live up to its pledge in the Tripartite Treaty of 1942 to remove her troops six months after the end of the war. This was a second count in Iran's complaint. The Security Council did not manifest any particular energy in the handling of the dispute and limited its debates to procedural questions. In the meantime (February and March 1946) Iranian Premier Qavam es-Saltaneh went to Moscow in an attempt to negotiate a solution. Communist agitation in Teheran reached disturbing proportions and prevented the Majlis from assembling. Unable to

[11] See A. Roosevelt, Jr., "The Kurdish Republic of Mahabad," *Middle East Journal*, 1 (July 1947), and W. Eagleton, Jr., *The Kurdish Republic of 1946* (London, 1963).

prolong its sessions, the parliament disbanded leaving the prime minister to face Soviet pressure alone. Acting under duress, Qavam made three important concessions to Russia. First, on April 4 he concluded an agreement establishing a joint Soviet-Iranian company for the exploitation of oil in the north. The agreement was to be valid for twenty-five years and was to be renewable. Russia and Iran were to have 51 and 49 percent of the stock, respectively. The agreement, moreover, acknowledged Soviet interest in the welfare of Azerbaijan. Second, Qavam instructed the Iranian delegate in the United Nations, Hussein Ala, to withdraw Iran's complaint from the Council's agenda. Despite formal Soviet concurrence and Secretary General Trygve Lie's support of these requests, the Security Council decided, nevertheless, to continue consideration of the matter. Third, on August 2, Qavam offered three portfolios in his cabinet to the Communists. This was Russia's price to evacuate her troops from Iran. The Red army left Iran's territory on May 9, 1946, more than two months after the stipulated deadline.[12]

Iran's position was difficult. She had to buy her freedom by alienating her northern oil resources to Russia, by permitting Communist infiltration into her government, and by leaving unsolved the Azerbaijan issue, in which Russia expressly reserved continuous interest.

Despite this high ransom, it was a matter of surprise to many that Russia agreed to withdraw her troops. While the truth can only be guessed at, so long as Soviet archives remain closed to the outside world, a few hypothetical explanations may be attempted. One is that Russia desired the ratification of the oil agreement by the Majlis, and the Majlis could not be elected so long as the Red army remained in northern Iran. Another is that Russia feared the effects of adverse publicity upon the still influential pro-Soviet "liberals" in the Western world. A third explanation is that, just as she did twenty-five years earlier during the Gilan episode, Moscow decided to turn from a direct to an indirect method of conquering Asia, once the direct method proved too embarrassing. Finally, rather stiff resistance by Secretary of States James Byrnes at Lake Success and the encouragement given Iran by the American ambassador, George V. Allen, may have been influential. In fact, this last factor may have been decisive.

The withdrawal of Soviet troops removed a major intimidating factor in Soviet-Iranian relations. The problem arose as to how long, if at all, Iran would have to honor the servitudes imposed upon her under duress. The premier seemed hesitant and willing to fulfill his part of the bargain, but he met with stiff opposition in the southern part of the country, a traditionally British preserve. There, in the summer of 1946, a confederation of tribes was formed, which demanded immediate dismissal of the Tudeh ministers from the cabinet and a suppression of Communist agitation. The latter was particularly intense in the Anglo-Iranian oil fields. The riots provoked by the Tudeh in Abadan induced Great Britain to send troops into the neighboring port of Basra in Iraq in order to safeguard her interests there. Threats of forming a separate southern state were heard, also demands from certain Arab

---

[12]American troops left Iran by December 31, 1945, and the British evacuated their forces by March 2, 1946, the latter thus honoring the Tripartite Treaty.

chieftains that parts of Arab-inhabited Khuzistan should be joined to Iraq. Under these pressures, Premier Qavam reoriented his policy. First he dismissed the Tudeh ministers. Then, after a few months of inconclusive negotiations with the Azerbaijan separatists, he ordered government troops into Azerbaijan, encountering only weak and spasmodic resistance. After a full year of separate existence, the rebel regime collapsed as soon as the army reached Tabriz, December 15, 1946.

On October 22, 1947, the newly elected Majlis refused by almost unanimous vote[13] to ratify the Irano-Soviet oil agreement. What followed can be described as a state of continuous tension between Russia and Iran. Russia protested against the Majlis' decision and, in a series of diplomatic notes, accused Iran of all sorts of misbehavior. Soviet broadcasts intensified their hostile propaganda, the recurrent theme of which was that by favoring Western "imperialists" Iran was permitting her territory to be used as a base of aggression against the Soviet Union.

Postwar Problems and Anxieties

The rejection of the oil concession closed a definite chapter in Iran's history. The last tangible consequence of the war period was eliminated, and the country was again free to seek its own salvation. Internally, however, the situation was far from reassuring. The expulsion of Reza Shah did not automatically solve any major problems, and the new democracy had a difficult task to prove its superiority over the old paternalistic rule. In fact, the new system resembled more an oligarchy of a thousand wealthy families than a democracy in the Western sense. The Majlis was representative, with a few exceptions, of the rich landowning and merchant class, and as such it reflected conservative and essentially status quo trends. What the country needed was sweeping reform, but parliament could hardly be expected to serve as an instrument of any radical changes. Under such circumstances, there was a marked revival of disturbing political extremism both on the left and on the right. Step by step the Tudeh rose to the surface after the initial shock of Communist defeat in Azerbaijan. On the other hand, utterly obscurantist clerical circles whipped up religious fanaticism among the ignorant masses. This movement was reinforced by the extreme nationalism of a bloc of Majlis deputies under the leadership of Dr. Mohammed Mossadegh.

One ray of hope in this rather gloomy picture came from the youthful Shah, Mohammed Reza Pahlavi, who seemed fully aware of both the internal and external dangers menacing Iran and seriously desired the improvement of economic and social conditions. His was not an easy task, however. If he pursued the truly democratic policy of following the parliament's wishes, his dreams of reform would be reduced to naught. If he attempted to act on his own, he could easily be accused of dictatorial ambitions. As it was, the Shah chose the middle road, conforming to the duties of a constitutional monarch, but at the same time, trying to strengthen his own position. Pursuing this line, he brought about an important constitutional change. In 1948, the Constituent Assembly, called specifically for this purpose,

---

[13]With the exception of two Communist deputies.

established a senate which had initially been authorized by the constitution of 1906 but which had never been set up. The advantage of this measure was that, out of sixty senators, the Shah was entitled to appoint thirty and thus to gain more voice in parliamentary decisions. The Shah favored also a literacy test for elections. This outwardly undemocratic move was really quite progressive, since such a test would assure greater influence to the more independent urban electorate and would reduce the power of great landowners, whose elections to the Majlis were assured by the masses of illiterate and economically dependent peasantry. The project, however, was defeated in the parliament.

The economic system loudly cried for radical reforms. The withdrawal of foreign troops produced unemployment and a general deflationary trend. Business suffered severely, and by 1949 Iran experienced an alarming number of bankruptcies. The hard winters of 1948 and 1949 caused catastrophic crop failures, especially in the rich provinces of Azerbaijan and Mazanderan. The cereal and fruit crops were especially affected. The results were a sudden reduction in fruit exports, the slaughtering of cattle by the peasants, and actual famine. Government income from taxes fell to an alarming low. This was made worse by the fact that many unscrupulous land magnates were considerably in arrears. In 1951 the treasury found itself in such a state that the payment of the salaries of public officials had to be delayed for a two-month period.

Such circumstances naturally caused unrest, and extremists found it relatively easy to gain adherents. In April 1948 Iranian authorities had to resort to mass arrests of Tudeh members in the northern provinces. Political assassinations multiplied,[14] and the government was more than once obliged to proclaim martial law in large areas of the country. A Kurdish rebellion in September 1950 added to the general sense of insecurity.

These conditions provided ideal grounds for Soviet intrigue. Ever since the rejection of the oil agreement an uneasy tenseness had prevailed in Russo-Iranian relations. Soviet diplomacy alternated between intimidation and blandishments, and Russia used both direct and indirect methods to bring pressure upon Iran. The nonratification of the oil agreement brought forth energetic Soviet notes, accusing Iran of breaking her word and of general hostility toward Russia. In the spring of 1948, in another series of notes, the Soviet Union severely blamed Iran for the activities of American military and *gendarmerie* missions, who were charged with trying to convert Iran into a Western bloc state for anti-Soviet operations. The growing rapprochement between Iran and the United States (which will be discussed later) was greatly resented by Russia. Soviet-Iranian relations deteriorated steadily. A clandestine radio of "free Azerbaijan," situated just across the border in Soviet territory, broadcast vituperative propaganda against Iran, promising freedom and justice to the Azerbaijanis and Kurds if they rose against the oppressive rule of the government. The Soviet press published a number of intimidating articles with frequent references to Article 6 of the unfortunate 1921 treaty, which, it will be

---

[14]On November 4, 1949, Court Minister and former Premier Hazhir was assassinated by a member of a religious sect.

remembered, permitted Russia under specific circumstances to enter Iranian territory. At the same time Soviet authorities obstructed the appointment of an Iranian director to the jointly operated Caspain fisheries and applied a virtual economic boycott of Iranian export products.

By the spring of 1949 Soviet-Iranian relations reached a crisis. On February 4, 1949, a Tudeh follower[15] made an attempt on the life of the Shah, wounding him slightly. The following day the Tudeh party was officially outlawed. Soon afterward arrests were made among its members, to be followed, on March 2, by the trial of fourteen prominent Communist leaders, including Dr. Morteza Yazdi, ex-minister of health; Hussein Jowdat, a Tudeh youth leader; and Nur ed-Din Kianuri, leader of a Tudeh workers' union. On February 27 martial law was proclaimed following the discovery of an alleged countrywide plot to overthrow the government. In March and April official Iranian sources announced three clashes on the Soviet-Iranian border in which Soviet armored divisions made deep forays into Iran. This resulted in the kidnaping of a number of Iranian soldiers. In April Soviet Ambassador Sadchikov left Iran for Moscow, and his departure was followed by the closing of Soviet consulates in Tabriz, Rezayeh, Maku, and Ardebil. Simultaneously, Russia ordered Iran to close her consulate in Baku. Russia also deported some 150 Iranian nationals resident in the USSR—a time-honored Soviet device for introducing her agents into Iran.

Iran reacted to this campaign in two ways. First, she attempted to retaliate in kind by reviving an old claim for gold and currency, which the Soviet Union had owed Iran since 1942.[16] She also demanded prompt payment of $10 million in customs charges and more than $1 million in railway charges, which Russia had failed to pay Iran. Furthermore, the government made an effort to put an end to foreign infiltration by expelling some satellite nationals[17] and threatening the expulsion of two Armenian archbishops reputed to be Soviet agents. A decree of July 27, 1949, amplified these measures by declaring that all leaders of non-Moslem religious groups must be subjects of Iran and "concerned with religious matters only."

Second, the Iranian government questioned the validity of the Soviet-Iranian Treaty of 1921. According to some press preports, Iran denounced the treaty in a note to the Soviet Union, but this was not officially confirmed. Anyway, Iranian official circles argued that the United Nations Charter invalidated the controversial Article 6 of the Treaty,[18] and it was rumored that Iran might bring the question of Soviet pressure before the Security Council. This did not materialize. Instead, Iran's ambassador in Washington, Hussein Ala, handed over to Secretary of State Dean Acheson a detailed memorandum which contained pertinent documentation and appealed for United States support. On March 23, 1949, Secretary Acheson made a public statement in which he declared that Soviet charges that Iran was being transformed into an American military base were "altogether false and demon-

---

[15] According to the official version, he also had some links with a fanatical Islamic group.

[16] In 1941, 11.5 tons of gold, $9 million in American currency, and $11 million in Iranian currency, were deposited by Iran in the Soviet Union. These deposits were not returned by Russia until 1955.

[17] Czechoslovak engineers.

[18] See above, p. 169.

strably untrue.'' He added that American interest in the security of the Middle East, ''particularly in Greece, Turkey and Iran,'' had in no way been reduced by the negotiation of the North Atlantic Treaty.

Growth of Friendship with the United States

This significant declaration climaxed a lengthy period of growing friendship between Iran and the United States. In resisting Soviet pressure Iran frequently looked toward the United States, whose military and economic power filled the Iranian leaders with hopeful expectancy. The Truman Doctrine speech of March 12, 1947, proclaiming the policy of containment of communism and the pledge of assistance to Greece and Turkey, was greeted in Iran as evidence of American interest in the security of the Middle East. On October 6, 1947, the two countries concluded an agreement extending the life of the American advisory military mission to the Iranian army. It included a clause preventing military experts from other states from advising the Iranian army without the consent of the United States. This was followed, on July 29, 1948, by a grant of $10 million in American credits for the purchase of surplus military equipment and of $16 million for repair and shipping costs. The first shipment of these arms arrived in Iran in March 1949 a few days after Secretary Acheson's declaration.

American aid was not limited to the military realm and did not exhaust itself in mere official activity. In 1947 the engineering firm of Morrison-Knudsen from Boise, Idaho, made thorough surveys of Iranian economic conditions. These served as the basis for a subsequent seven-year plan of development. The plan was approved by the Majlis on February 15, 1949. It provided for an expenditure of $650 million and was one of the boldest and most comprehensive ventures ever attempted to improve social, educational, economic, and technical conditions in Asia. Iran invited an American consortium, Overseas Consultants, Inc. (O.C.I.), to prepare detailed blueprints and to act in an advisory capacity. The first O.C.I. team arrived in Iran in January 1949 and was soon enlarged by a number of experts and technicians. Paying $600,000 to the O.C.I. per year, Iran hopefully counted on American loans, although basically the plan was to be financed from the royalties paid by the Anglo-Iranian Oil Company.

It seemed, therefore, a good omen when, on October 6, 1949, the United States Congress adopted the Mutual Defense Assistance Act, which in the framework of a general billion-dollar appropriation contained a special fund of $27,640,000 for military aid to Iran, the Philippines, and Korea. It was estimated that from this sum Iran would receive about $10 million.[19] This, however, was too small an amount to cope with Iranian military and economic needs. Iran hoped for a $250 million loan from the International Bank of Reconstruction and Development and for a grant or loan of the same size directly from the United States.

In the meantime, as previously mentioned, Soviet-Iranian relations were deteriorating, and Iran felt an urgent need of some reassuring decisions. In order to seek

[19] A formal agreement to this effect was signed with Iran on May 23, 1950. Iran was the thirteenth—and last—of the series of states with which such agreements were concluded.

such increased military and economic aid, Shah Mohammed Reza made a trip to the United States. Arriving on November 16, 1949, he paid a state visit to official Washington, addressed the United Nations at Lake Success, and made a six-week good-will tour through the country. Outwardly it was a success. The press gave him excellent coverage, and the youthful Shah favorably impressed the American public with his charm and modesty. Columbia University inaugurated an Iranian Study Center, and arrangements were made for the rebroadcasting of the Voice of America programs through the Teheran radio. Prior to his departure on December 30, the Shah and the President issued a joint statement in which Truman, recalling the Three Power Declaration of Teheran on December 1, 1943, confirmed American interest in and "desire for the maintenance of the independence and territorial integrity of Iran," promised support for International Bank loans for Iran, expressed readiness "to facilitate Iranian economic development through the provisions under Point 4," and offered on the basis of the existing congressional authorization "certain military assistance essential to enable Iran . . . to develop effective measures for its self-defense."[20] This statement, however, did not contain any definite military commitment, nor did it mention any concrete loan. From the military and economic point of view, the visit was a failure, and the Iranians did not conceal their disappointment. The Shah, who had arrived in the United States in the President's plane "Independence," refused to accept the offer of an official plane for his return trip and went, instead, on board a Dutch air liner.

The reasons for American reticence are not hard to discover. The year 1949 was the year of Chiang Kai-shek's collapse in China, and the fall of the graft-ridden Kuomintang despite extensive American aid shocked American public opinion. A firm conviction was forming in Washington that while aid to Western Europe was put to good use, financial aid to the corrupt governments of Asia was just "money poured down the rat-hole."[21] This meant that unless Iran adopted measures of reform and purged her government of undesirable elements, she could not expect much from the United States. This was, in fact, what the American ambassador, John Wiley (1948–1949), conveyed to Iranian leaders.

Attempt at Reform

Obviously impressed by the Chinese debacle and by American admonishments, the Shah returned to Iran firmly determined to purge his administration and to institute the much-needed reforms. The year 1950 was to be the year of administrative, social, and economic reform to prove to the West that Iran was worthy of its aid. In February the Shah transferred his royal estates to the Imperial Organization for Social Welfare, to be parceled out on convenient terms to the poor peasants. Soon afterward the government shook up the administration of the vulnerable province of Azerbaijan. Five governors, nine prefects, six chiefs of police, and seven

---

[20]The text is in the *New York Times,* Dec. 31, 1949.

[21]In the fall of 1949 and the spring of 1950, conferences of American envoys to the Middle East countries were held in Istanbul and Cairo, respectively. The reports of the participants on the internal situations in their respective countries were far from reassuring, and the reports of Iran were said to be particularly gloomy.

high grain-office officials were suspended. These measures, taken in conjunction with the previously mentioned steps to strengthen the Shah's constitutional authority, testified to the young ruler's earnest desire to pull his country out of the morass and imbue it with a new spirit.

Meanwhile Soviet pressure was renewed.[22] Determined to form a cabinet that would fully support him in his reformist plans, the Shah in June 1950 appointed General Ali Razmara prime minister, and this appointment of an honest and energetic man met with warm approval in the West. Razmara's task was to clamp down on corruption, carry out the reforms under the seven-year plan, and prove by his actions that Iran was following a new path. His appointment coincided with that of Henry F. Grady as United States ambassador to Iran. Mr. Grady had gained renown as the official "watchdog" of American aid to Greece and was viewed by many as an "operating" ambassador, who would supervise the hoped-for economic aid to Iran. In fact, he brought with him three State Department economists, whose presence was an encouraging sign of active American interest.

To deserve further American aid, the Shah and his new prime minister vigorously pushed the work of reform. A plan for regional councils, prepared by Razmara, provided for increased provincial self-government and for a curb on centralistic bureaucracy. In the early fall a new purge in the administration resulted in the dismissal of 400 officials, and soon afterward, in the midst of an uproar in the Majlis, the Imperial Anticorruption Commission presented a list of 500 names of high officials unfit to hold public office. These measures were popular with the masses, but they met with strong criticism in influential political circles and threatened to bring on a cabinet crisis. Yet both the Shah and General Razmara pursued their course with determination.

Under these circumstances, the announcement in September (officially confirmed on October 10) of a mere $25 million loan from the Export-Import Bank of Washington came as a severe shock to the Iranians. The quest for more substantial loans was refused both by the World Bank and by the American government. The United States was apparently not prepared to go beyond this sum and beyond the token appropriation of a half-million dollars made additionally under the Point Four Program.[23]

Iranians were disappointed and angered. In several interviews with American correspondents, the Shah made public his deep disappointment and wondered why the United States had given generous help to former Axis countries, while refusing more extensive aid to an ally, Iran. There was an angry anti-American outburst on October 4 in the Majlis when one of the deputies asked why Iran "bothered" with the United States. The deputy questioned the expensive activities of Overseas Con-

---

[22]In May 1950 a widespread Soviet spy network in Iran was revealed by an escaped Soviet employee, and soon afterward the Soviet Union formally complained that the oil surveys made for the government by American experts close to the Soviet border resulted in the taking of aerial photographs of Soviet territory and thereby created an "abnormal situation" in Soviet-Iranian relations.

[23]On October 19, 1950, the United States and Iran announced that a fund of $500,000 was made available to the Joint Iranian-American Commission for Rural Improvement. The commission set up its headquarters in Isfahan.

sultants, Inc., and asked whether or not the United States had paid Iran for the use of her railway during wartime. Growth of a pronouncedly anti-American feeling was strongly felt throughout the country. In mid-November the generally pro-Western Razmara canceled the relaying facilities of the Voice of America and the BBC and allowed the publication of Soviet Tass dispatches in the Iranian press. Ambassador Grady's position became embarrassing inasmuch as, despite his reputation as a "watchdog," he had nothing to watch over, and in November he went back to Washington for consultation. The seven-year plan suffered a severe setback due to the lack of expected funds, a setback intensified by a quarrel between Overseas Consultants and the Iranian directorate under M. Nakhai. The American experts prepared to depart and their contract was not extended.[24]

Russia was not slow to take advantage of this situation, and instead of intimidation, she adopted a policy of part blandishments. On November 4 she concluded with Iran a $20 million trade agreement, implementing the treaty of 1940, and thus considerably eased Iran's economic position. She also offered to negotiate such outstanding questions as the afore-mentioned boundary dispute, the return of Iranian gold, and the release of Soviet-held Iranian border guards. All these inducements alternated, as usual, with threats. On December 20, General Rzamara told the press of alerting Iranian border garrisons, because of danger to the territorial integrity of the state. Soviet-Iranian negotiations were, nevertheless, proceeding, and in mid-December it was revealed that ten important Tudeh leaders, previously sentenced, had been released from prison by some Iranian officers in what was described as a "kidnaping" operation.

The Oil Crisis

The failure to obtain financial aid from the United States spurred the Majlis to press for a radical revision of the Anglo-Iranian oil concession, to increase the revenues to the state. Negotiations had already dragged on for some time. Iran argued that she was victimized by the high corporation taxes paid by the company to the British government and by the low rate of revenues. Iran pointed also to more favorable deals that Saudi Arabia and some Latin-American countries had obtained with American oil corporations. The Anglo-Iranian Company was prepared to make certain concessions, but they were regarded as insufficient by the government. In the winter of 1950–1951 Dr. Mossadegh's National Front in the Majlis began clamoring for the nationalization of the oil industry. Razmara opposed this as impractical and in doing so flirted with danger. His was not a popular attitude, but so long as he remained in power and was openly supported by the Shah, his wise counsel prevailed. The prime minister became a special target of the fanatical Islamic brotherhood Fedayan Islam ("Crusaders of Islam"), which preached liberation of Iran from foreign influences and advocated immediate nationalization of the oil industry. On March 7, 1951, a member of this brotherhood shot and killed Razmara while the general was attending a religious service in one of the mosques.

[24]The last of them left in January 1951.

The consequences were momentous. On March 15 the Majlis unanimously passed a law nationalizing Iran's oil industry. The Senate confirmed it on March 20, the day henceforth regarded as the official date of nationalization. To British protests, Iran replied firmly that the matter was entirely within her domestic jurisdiction. Early in April Communist-led riots broke out in the Anglo-Iranian fields in Khuzistan. The workers went on strike, and a number of employees, including two Britons, were killed. Speaking to Parliament, Foreign Secretary Herbert Morrison stated that his government would take action to protect British lives and property, and the press reported movements of the British navy in the Persian Gulf.

In the meantime, important cabinet changes took place in Iran. After Razmara's death, the Shah called Hussein Ala, a moderate pro-Western statesman and former ambassador to Washington, to assume the premiership. Ala endeavored to soften the effects of nationalization by making it clear that Iran did not want to deprive the West of oil supplies. At the same time it was thought that some compromise might be worked out whereby the company would become Iranian property but the technical side of production and distribution would be left to competent foreign technicians. But this was not what the extreme nationalists wanted. Their mounting pressure led to Ala's resignation on April 27. On April 28 the Shah reluctantly entrusted Mossadegh with the formation of a new cabinet. On the same day the Majlis, and on April 30 the Senate, voted immediate nationalization of the oil industry retroactive to March 20. The Shah, who did not have the right of veto, was obliged to sign these laws on May 2. The prime minister was known to oppose all foreign aid including assistance by the United States military mission to the Iranian army. But despite their outward victory, the nationalist extremists were in a predicament, because the Communists took advantage of the inflamed situation resulting from the nationalists' use of demagoguery and mob action. The Khuzistan disturbances continued, and the Anglo-Iranian Oil Company was compelled to shut down its industrial plant. Production stopped, and so did company payments to the government. Martial law was proclaimed in Khuzistan, and armored army units were dispatched to restore order. On May Day, the day following Mossadegh's appointment to the premiership, the Tudeh, still officially outlawed, organized a mass rally in the parliament square in Teheran. A crowd estimated at 30,000 carried anti-Western and pro-Soviet placards displaying anti-imperialist slogans. Even Mossadegh, father of the nationalization law, was not spared some posters depicting him as a puppet riding in the turret of an American tank.

Informed opinion held that Iran was not able to assume management of a complex industrial enterprise like the Anglo-Iranian, without gravely impairing the output. Moreover, the Anglo-Iranian's activities included marketing operations, and these were served by a fleet of company tankers, which could easily be withdrawn to prevent seizure. It was certain that any sudden transfer, such as contemplated by the law of May 2, would cause serious disruption in the company's activities and would further endanger the already precarious situation of the Iranian treasury. Little could be elicited on this subject from the new prime minister who, when queried by foreign observers, limited himself to impassioned but vague outbursts against foreign imperialism and exploitation. Mossadegh definitely rejected, however, the British government's pleas for negotiations and the company's request for arbitration, which had been provided for by the concession agreement.

Events in Iran caused well-understood concern in the United States. With Razmara's death a blow was dealt to the hopes of substantial reform, and the political curve in Iranian affairs assumed a disquietingly downward trend. Iranian oil was essential to the success of the European Recovery Program. Furthermore, the ability of the Communists so rapidly to assume quasi-leadership of the nationalist landslide constituted an additional cause for concern. The situation was not eased by the fact that the Soviet press openly accused the United States of engineering Razmara's death, allegedly to aid American oil corporations to dislodge the Anglo-Iranian. The American State Department officially proclaimed its neutrality in the conflict between Iran and Great Britain, but it took lively interest in the developments. In April, Assistant Secretary of State George McGhee and the British ambassador in Washington, Sir Oliver Franks, held a series of conferences to review the Iranian crisis. The American government considered the nationalization step as irrevocable but hoped for amicable settlement between the two parties.

Contrary, however, to the early expectations, the Anglo-Iranian oil crisis developed into a long-drawn affair which passed through the following main phases during the summer and the fall of 1951:

1. After considerable prodding from the British embassy the Iranian government agreed to receive in mid-June a mission composed of a few directors of the Anglo-Iranian Oil Company. In the course of negotiations Iran demanded that the A.I.O.C. turn over at once to the government all revenue derived from the sale of Iranian oil as of March 20, after deducting expenses and 25 percent to guarantee the company's probable claims. This proved unacceptable to the company. The latter's counter-proposals were rejected by Iran and the talks broke down.

2. On May 26 the British government brought the matter to the International Court of Justice at The Hague. On July 5 the Court, without pronoucing itself on the basic issue of its competence, issued a temporary decision enjoining both parties to preserve the status quo pending a final solution, so as to assure an uninterrupted flow of oil. Challenging the Court's competence in what she claimed to be a domestic affair, Iran gave notice of withdrawal as one of the signatories of the Court convention.

3. Four days later President Turman in a personal message appealed to Premier Mossadegh to reopen negotiations with the British and, with Mossadegh's consent, dispatched W. Averell Harriman as his personal representative to Teheran to bring about the renewal of talks.

4. After a visit in Teheran (mid-July), followed by a visit in London, Harriman succeeded in persuading both parties to reopen negotiations. This time, however, it was a British government (and not a company) mission which arrived in Teheran to negotiate. It was headed by Sir Richard R. Stokes, lord privy seal, and had two other cabinet ministers as members.

5. In their talks with the Iranians (August 6–22), the British declared themselves ready to accept the principle of nationalization provided adequate compensation was

devised and provided Iran chartered a British company to take charge of the technical aspects of production. The Iranians insisted on freedom to hire British technicians individually and not as an organized unit. This proposal was accepted by the British mission on the condition that a British general manager be appointed in a supervisory executive capacity. The Iranian government rejected this suggestion, as a result of which the negotiations broke down and the British withdrew their offer.

6. On September 27, Iranian soldiers took over the Abadan refinery and locked out British technicians. Two days earlier the Iranian government canceled the residence permits of all the British employees of the company effective October 4. On October 3 the British government duly evacuated the remaining 300 members of the company's personnel. The National Iranian Oil Company took full charge of the oil fields and the Abadan refinery.

7. Simultaneously (September 29), Britain brought the matter to the attention of the UN Security Council, urging that body to condemn Iran for a breach of international obligations. After considerable diplomatic activity and unofficial exchanges of views, Britain agreed to soften the proposed resolution to a request by the Council that both parties renew their negotiations. Premier Mossadegh, who arrived in New York to plead Iran's case, argued that the Council was not competent to deal with this matter and threatened withdrawal from further UN deliberations. Iran's plea of noncompetence was supported by the Soviet delegation, while the American delegation argued in favor of the Council's competence. Failing to reach any decision on the merits of the case, on October 19 the Council ultimately decided to ask the World Court for an advisory opinion as to the Council's competence.

8. Following this inconclusive debate, Dr. Mossadegh paid a visit to President Truman, who was reported to have urged Iran's premier to reopen his talks with the British and to follow a more realistic course of action. The ensuing four-week negotiations with Assistant Secretary of State George McGhee (conducted by Mossadegh from a sickbed in Washington's Walter Reed Hospital) ended in a deadlock, and on November 19 the Iranian premier left for Iran. Passing through Cairo he was given a rousing welcome by the Egyptians. A few weeks later it became known that the World Bank had presented certain suggestions toward the solution of the controversy. Despite the obvious loss to Iran resulting from the stoppage of oil production, the crisis did not show any signs of abatement in December 1951.

Throughout the crisis Russia seemed to play a waiting game. Her press voiced support of Iran's struggle against foreign imperialism and her representatives in the UN Security Council backed Iran on certain procedural issues, but the official attitude was that of nonintervention. By contrast, Iranian Communists eagerly seized the opportunity to advance their cause in the face of the deteriorating relations between Iran and the West. On May 8, 1951, the emboldened Tudeh party addressed an open letter to the prime minister in which it formulated seven demands. These were:

1. Expulsion of the United States military mission to Iran.
2. Legalization of the Tudeh party.
3. Recognition of Communist China.

4. Rejection of foreign arms aid.
5. Release of political prisoners.
6. An end to martial law in the southern oil fields.
7. Nationalization of the Bahrain oil fields where the American-owned Bahrain Petroleum Company was producing 10,000,000 barrels of oil a year.

In the following months the Tudeh organized a number of monster rallies and demonstrations which frequently ended in armed clashes with police or with the nationalist supporters of Mossadegh. Internal security showed disquieting signs of deterioration, and cases of prominent editors or politicians seeking refuge in the sanctuary of the Majlis multiplied. By the fall of 1951, Iran was in turmoil. Alternately threatened and cajoled by Russia, in open quarrel with Britain, and at odds with the United States, the government was far from secure, increasingly resorting to demagoguery in order to maintain its popularity. The *New York Times* gave a sober appraisal of the situation in two editorials entitled, "Recklessness in Iran" and "Emotion versus Common Sense." It required, indeed, a great deal of common sense among Iran's leaders to turn their country away from self-destruction toward sound progress and self-development. Unfortunately, Dr. Mossadegh's method of appeal to mob hysteria precluded a rational approach to the vital issues facing his people.

In the months following the expulsion of British personnel from the oil fields and the refinery, several attempts were made to solve the Anglo-Iranian oil dispute. Between December 1951 and March 1952, representatives of the World Bank visited Iran in order to advance their suggestions, but no agreement resulted. Further endeavors of the British and American governments, made either singly or jointly in the fall of 1952, in January 1953, and in the summer of 1953, also proved to be of no avail. Premier Mossadegh refused to discuss the oil problem in terms other than those provided by the nationalization law, the latter enjoining operation of the industry by Iran herself. Nor were proceedings under the auspices of international agencies any more fruitful. The Security Council's debate having proved inconclusive, attention shifted to the International Court of Justice, whose competence in the case was challenged by Iran. Ultimately, on July 22, 1953, the Court pronounced itself incompetent to deal with the dispute.

Iran's view was thus vindicated, but her victory lacked positive elements. Her oil still had to be extracted, refined, and marketed, and this could not be done so long as the dispute remained unsettled. Marketing and transportation presented two of the main difficulties. The Anglo-Iranian Oil Company announced that it would sue any buyers of Iranian oil for unlawful acquisition of its property. For this reason, as well as out of a feeling of solidarity with an expropriated concessionaire, no major world oil corporation would agree to purchase oil from Iran. By the same token, tanker tonnage, most of which was controlled by these companies, was denied to Iran. Mossadegh tried to break this virtual blockade by resorting to transactions with certain independent corporations in Italy and Japan. But these minor deals in the two years following nationalization accounted for less than one day's sales of the A.I.O.C. when the latter was in operation. From the economic point of view the results were extremely disappointing. Moreover, A.I.O.C. promptly contested these deals in the courts of Aden, Italy, and Japan, demanding the impounding of the oil cargoes in question. Although these legal actions were successful only in Aden, the Italian and Japanese courts recognizing the validity of the contracts, the judicial proceedings added new complications and delays which harmed Iranian interests.

Stoppage of the flow of oil from Iran caused considerable incovenience to its regular consumers, particularly to Britain, who was obliged to draw upon her none too abundant reserves of hard currency to purchase "dollar oil" from other areas. Similarly, certain markets east and south of Suez suffered temporary shortages. But contrary to Iranian expectations, the world at large quickly readjusted itself to the new situation, Iran being promptly replaced as producer by Saudi Arabia, Iraq, and particularly Kuwait, all of whom considerably increased their output to fill the gap. On its part, the A.I.O.C. began the construction of a new giant refinery in politically safe Aden, and other major corporations stepped up their development programs, substantially increasing the refining capacity of Europe and the British Isles. Consequently, the only real loser was Iran.

The oil dispute affected the totality of Irano-British relations. Taking the side of the company, the British government canceled the convertibility facilities hitherto granted to the Iranian sterling balances in London and placed a ban on the exportation of certain goods to Iran. Iran retaliated by closing foreign cultural institutions in the provinces, expelling certain British missionaries, curtailing the privileges enjoyed by the British Bank of Iran,[25] and in January 1952 ordering the closure of all British consulates outside Teheran. Finally, after a rather extravagant ultimatum demanding settlement of the oil question on his terms, Premier Mossadegh in October 1952 broke off diplomatic relations with Great Britain.

The worsening of British-Iranian relations had a deleterious effect on Teheran's ties with the United States. The Iranians acted in the belief that because of their strategic importance the United States would save them from economic collapse and subsequent slipping into the Soviet orbit. They therefore expected America either to buy their oil or to grant them financial assistance. Official Washington was unwilling to do either, partly out of consideration of its British ally and partly out of fear that countenancing Iranian nationalization would jeopardize the network of concessions and investments in other parts of the world. Yet, not prepared to write off the strategic importance of Iran, the American government continued to lend Iran limited aid under the technical assistance program. Such a policy, though not devoid of risks, had the advantage of preserving ties with Iran while not encouraging Dr. Mossadegh in his intransigent attitudes. Iranian extremists were, of course, very intolerant of anybody who did not side with them; hence American-Iranian relations suffered considerable strain, which in some instances was expressed by insults and attacks on Americans living in the country.

Meanwhile an internal crisis was gradually ripening within Iran. In the early stages of the oil dispute Dr. Mossadegh found support among extreme nationalists

---

[25]Previously the Imperial Bank of Iran, later renamed the British Bank of Iran and the Middle East, and finally emerging as the British Bank of the Middle East.

(mostly members of the Iran Party), religious fanatics grouped around Ayatollah Abol Ghassem Kashani, students, some bazaar merchants, Socialists, and Communists. Though ill-assorted, this coalition worked effectively so long as it aimed at relatively simple and negative objectives, such as the expulsion of the British and the silencing of opposition. Members of the latter, by the way, were so intimidated by mob action or threat of assassination that free and sober discussion of vital national issues became virtually impossible.

As for Dr. Mossadegh, who was hailed by his friends as a heroic fighter for democracy, he exulted in the atmosphere of popular hysteria and mob terror and, with the passage of time, adopted markedly antidemocratic methods of political action. Thus, in the spring of 1952, seeing that elections to the Majlis were not likely to result in a solid progovernment majority, he interrupted the electoral proceedings and convoked a truncated Majlis composed of eighty-odd deputies instead of the full strength of 136. By the same token he insisted, soon afterward, on personal control of the ministry of defense, hitherto a preserve of the crown. Failing to convince the Shah, who was anxious to maintain his prerogatives in regard to the army, Mossadegh resigned on July 16, 1952, whereupon the Shah asked Qavam es-Saltaneh to form a cabinet. Qavam immediately declared that he was determined to solve the oil controversy, restore the economic balance, and put an end to the demagoguery and religious fanaticism which were harmful to the vital interests of the nation. His declarations were met by an outburst of criticism from all the elements of the pro-Mossadegh coalition, which rallied around Mullah Kashani and resorted to rioting to defy the new premier. Abandoned by the Shah and the Majlis (both thoroughly intimidated by mob action), Qavam tendered his resignation and, fearing for his life, went into hiding.

His place was taken by Mossadegh, whose return to power on July 22 coincided with the pronouncement by the World Court of its incompetence in the oil dispute. Thus reinforced, Mossadegh asked and obtained from the Majlis the right to rule by decree during the ensuing six months. At the same time the Shah conceded to him control of the army. Soon afterward, the Majlis declared the Senate session terminated, thus to all practical purposes legislating the upper chamber out of existence. Needless to say, the Senate, composed of more conservative elements, lacked enthusiasm for Mossadegh's policies.

Armed with full powers, the premier effected a purge in the army and in certain government departments to assure loyalty to his policies on the part of officers, civil servants, and diplomats. He also issued, on August 13, 1952, a land-reform decree which enjoined landowners to turn over to their tenants 20 percent of their land revenue, half of which was to go to individual peasants and another half to village councils for communal improvements. The decree was motivated in part by the premier's desire to effect reforms, but it was largely due to his determination to steal the headlines from the Shah's program to distribute the imperial estates to needy peasants. Ultimately, under Mossadegh's prodding, the Shah agreed to transfer the administration of the imperial estates to the government, thus conceding another point to the ambitious premier.

But the stark reality of an oilless (and cashless) economy had to be faced. Fed for a year and a half on patriotic slogans, the populace could not live forever in a frenzy of enthusiasm while basic goods became scarce and the gap between prices and incomes increased. The heterogeneous coalition behind Mossadegh was bound to fall apart when confronted with positive tasks in a hopeless economic situation. Starting in January 1953, the coalition began to disintegrate. The immediate cause of dissension was Mossadegh's request for a year's extension of his powers. Both Mullah Kashani and Hussein Makki, a leading member of the National Front and the "hero of Abadan," opposed this request. Although the premier obtained his powers, the rift began to widen until, by early summer of 1953, Dr. Mossadegh found himself isolated from the majority of his former political friends. In fact, the original National Front of eight deputies lost most of its initial members. The latter were replaced by a larger but much less cohesive group in the Majlis. The premier remained surrounded by a hard core of Iran Party diehards, who now had a vested interest in preventing any settlement with Britain. By summer the Majlis had shaken off its former docility, and its debates were becoming so acrimonious as to embarrass the government. In mid-July twenty-seven National Front members resigned their seats in protest against the mounting criticism of the opposition. This step deprived the Majlis of a quorum, thus removing it as a decision-making body capable of curbing Mossadegh's excesses.

Meanwhile the Shah, thwarted in his attempts to restrain the premier, left the capital on what was officially termed a long vacation in a Caspian Sea resort. This made Mossadegh the virtual ruler of the country. The premier's next step was to call for a formal dissolution of the Majlis, to be approved by a popular referendum. Although the proposed measure was clearly unconstitutional, plans for a referendum went ahead. Between August 3 and 10 the balloting took place, resulting in 99.93 percent approval of Mossadegh's policy. Approval had been ensured by the setting up of separate voting booths for those who approved and those who opposed the contemplated decree.

This was the apogee of Mossadegh's power. From then on the decline was swift. On August 12 the premier announced the dissolution of parliament. Three days later a colonel of the Imperial Guard delivered to him a letter of dismissal from the Shah. General Fazlollah Zahedi was appointed in his place. Mossadegh defied the order, ordered the messenger arrested, and had the detachment accompanying him disarmed. Appraised of the news, the Shah and the Queen fled Iran in the Shah's airplane, first to Baghdad and later to Rome. The sovereign's flight touched off major riots in Teheran, during which Communists and extreme nationalists vied with each other in denouncing the monarchy and destroying the statues of the Shah and his father. Prominent in these antiroyalist demonstrations was Hussein Fatemi, foreign minister and Mossadegh's most trusted associate. But after two days the tide of opinion took a sharp turn in the opposite direction. Moderate elements of the population, obviously perturbed at the revolutionary chaos, spontaneously turned against the antiroyalists, while at the same time certain ani-Mossadegh units in the army defied the premier. This disaffection within the army resulted from secret preparatory activity of certain officers under the overall direction of General Zahedi, who had been in hiding to avoid arrest by Mossadegh. How well organized this group was and how much planning it had done before it acted on August 18 and 19 have not yet been fully revealed. When the group struck, General Zahedi was still in hiding, and the actual leadership, if there was any, of the military operations was not his. A tank battle raged in Teheran for many hours, ending in victory for the royalist forces. On August 19 General Zahedi emerged from concealment and took over the reins of government. The following day Mossadegh surrendered to him, while the security forces began to arrest and pursue the former premier's associates.[26] A few days later the Shah returned in triumph to Teheran. The Mossadegh era had come to an end.

Return to Normalcy

One of the first acts of General Zahedi was to appeal to the United States for financial aid. The American response came forthwith: President Eisenhower, who only two months earlier had refused a similar request from Mossadegh,[27] now promptly decided to give Iran a $45 million emergency grant-in-aid in addition to $23.4 million earmarked under the United States technical assistance program. Such aid, however, could only be a palliative, pending the basic improvement of Iran's finances, which hinged on settlement of the oil dispute. By mid-October, Herbert Hoover, Jr., a newly appointed oil adviser to the United States Department of State, arrived in Teheran to pave the way for the reopening of oil negotiations. The resumption by General Zahedi of diplomatic relations with Britain added another factor conducive to an early settlement of the dispute.

The new Iranian regime sincerely wished to reach a satisfactory solution, but it could not disregard public opinion, which was unalterably opposed to the return of the British. Even the staunchest diehards in the A.I.O.C. realized that a return to the status quo ante was impossible. Consequently, as a result of exploratory talks that took place in midwinter of 1953–1954 in Washington and London, an international consortium of eight companies[28] was formed in April 1954 to resume Iranian oil operations. On August 5, 1954, the consortium's delegation, headed by H. W. Page

---

[26]Following a trial before a military court, Dr. Mossadegh was sentenced to a three-year prison term. His foreign minister, Hussein Fatemi, received a death sentence, which was promptly carried out. Other Mossadegh collaborators were sentenced to varying prison terms.

[27]On the ground that it would be unfair to American taxpayers to extend loans or grants to Iran, the latter being in a position to utilize her oil resources.

[28]These companies and their respective shares in the consortium's stock were as follows:

British-Dutch group	Anglo-Iranian Oil Co. (British Petroleum Co.)	40%	54%
	Royal Dutch-Shell	14%	
French group	Compagnie Française des Petroles	6%	6%
American group	Standard Oil Co. of New Jersey	8%	
	Standard Oil Co. of California	8%	
	Socony-Vacuum Oil Co. (Socony Mobil Oil Co.)	8%	40%
	Texas Oil Co.	8%	
	Gulf Oil Co.	8%	

In 1955 each of the American companies agreed to cede one-eighth of its holdings (together 5 percent of the total) to American independent companies, of whom nine subsequently acquired shares in the consortium. The latter's official name became Iranian Oil Participants, Ltd.

of Standard Oil of New Jersey, signed an agreement with Iran which provided for the extraction, refining, and marketing of Iranian oil by the consortium, the profits from these operations to be divided on a 50-50 basis in accordance with the pattern prevailing in the Middle East and other oil-bearing areas. The consortium was to act on behalf of the National Iranian Oil Company through two operating companies incorporated in Holland. Over a ten-year period Iran was to pay damages to the A.I.O.C. for the nationalization of its properties, but the A.I.O.C. also recognized certain indebtednesses to Iran, as a result of which the amount of compensation was to be moderate. Moreover, the operating companies were to have international management, with Iranian representation on their boards. Soon representatives of these companies arrived in Iran and proceeded to reactivate the oil industry. On its part, the United States, acting in response to Iranian requests, made available to Iran two additional sums above the $45 million initially granted in order to save the new government from financial troubles pending the resumption of regular oil revenues.

While thus normalizing his relations with Britain and the United States, Premier Zahedi did not neglect the Soviet sector either. For reasons not yet fully clear but perhaps as a part of her peace campaign, the Soviet Union offered to settle with Iran the outstanding financial and boundary questions. Free of illusions as to the nature of Soviet objectives, Zahedi nevertheless followed up the Soviet proffer and in the ensuing negotiations reached an agreement whereby Russia was to return to Iran the eleven tons of gold she had owed since the war and the frontier was delimited in certain disputed districts. Considerable time elapsed between the agreement and the implementation of its financial clauses. In fact, the delay was so long as to make many observers skeptical concerning Russia's will to abide by her promise. On June 1, 1955, however, Moscow finally did return the gold, and its gesture was interpreted as a move designed to counter any possible military alignment of Iran with the Western powers.

In internal affairs General Zahedi concentrated on the restoration of order and security, which had reached a disquietingly low point under his predecessor. Zahedi's major achievement in this respect was discovery in the fall of 1954 of a major Communist espionage network in the Iranian army, a network which involved some six hundred officers, including a good number of colonels. This sensational discovery prevented the Communist plotters from overthrowing the government and assassinating the Shah, as they had planned to do within a few days, and allowed the Iranian police rather effectively to destroy the Tudeh organization in the country. Among the more constructive accomplishments were General Zahedi's revival of the dormant Seven-Year Plan Organization and the appointment of an outstanding Iranian financier, Abol Hassan Ebtehaj, to its directorship.

Having performed these vital services in the foreign and domestic field, Zahedi resigned in the spring of 1955, leaving the way open for a more reform-minded minister. He was replaced by Hussein Ala, a venerable statesman who, as court minister, had advised the Shah for many years. Ala's appointment was indicative of the Shah's desire to assume more direct influence in the government and gradually to transform himself from a monarch who reigns to a monarch who rules. The new premier promised a concerted drive on corruption, but within a few days of his appointment he had to leave Iran for medical treatment in Europe. During his absence Iran's basic instability once again became evident when, for reasons not yet fully explained, the government, prodded by the Shia hierarchy, applied repressive measures to the Bahai sect. These measures included the dismantling of the fine Bahai temple in the center of Teheran and resulted in instances of mob violence against peaceful Bahai communities in the provinces.

Iran's Pro-Western Course

Upon his return from abroad Premier Ala found a major international problem awaiting solution. It was the question of whether or not Iran should join the Baghdad Pact, recently concluded by Turkey, Iraq, Pakistan, and Britain and designed to serve as a regional alliance of a defensive nature. The decision was not easy to make inasmuch as Russia, in the course of the year, had twice warned Iran not to contemplate such a step, invoking the treaty of 1927 as the basis of her objections.[29] Reinforcing Russia's protests was the legacy of "Mossadeghism," i.e., suspicion and dislike of the West. However, the Shah and certain other political men realized the importance of being formally included in the Western defense system and thus benefiting from such military guarantees and economic aid as this participation was likely to provide. More specifically, adherence to this pact might mean an opportunity to modernize and strengthen Iran's army largely at Western expense. These hesitations were definitely removed after the visit of President Celal Bayar of Turkey to the Shah in September 1955. On October 11, Premier Ala announced his government's resolve to sign the Baghdad Pact, and within a week this decision was ratified by both houses of parliament. Shortly afterward Ala attended the first meeting of the Middle East Treaty Organization, which was held in Baghdad. By joining the alliance, the Shah and his government have made a bold move toward definition of Iran's position in the East-West conflict, thus creating for the first time since the war a basis for far-reaching Western commitments in favor of her defense and the strengthening of her army.

This policy was, of course, viewed with misgivings in Moscow. Yet despite its disapproval of Iran's links with the West, the Soviet government did not immediately take any overt inimical action toward Iran. Instead, for about three years it pursued a soft policy designed to woo Iran away from too close an identification with the West rather than to intimidate her. Major Soviet moves in this direction were made in 1956, when Moscow extended to Iran an offer of substantial technical aid without "political and military strings" attached and when, in midsummer, it played host to the Shah and Queen of Iran on their first state visit to Russia. Despite a great deal of persuasion by the Soviet leaders to draw the Shah away from the Baghdad Pact, they made no headway, the Shah refusing to make any commitments likely to jeopardize his newly forged links with the Western countries. As usual, the

[29]This was the "Treaty of Guarantee and Neutrality" concluded on October 1, 1927. It provided for the maintenance in force of the earlier treaty of February 26, 1921, stipulated nonaggression, and, in Art. 3, contained a mutual pledge not to participate in alliances or political agreements which might be directed against the security of either signatory. Text in J. C. Hurewitz, ed., *Diplomacy in the Near and Middle East: A Documentary Record* (Princeton, N.J., 1956), II, 154 ff.

Soviet policy operated on two levels: diplomatic relations with Iran showed all outward signs of correctness but a number of Soviet military attachés and diplomats had to be expelled from Iran for spying, and an arms-smuggling ring was apprehended in Azerbaijan. On arrest, some of the members of the outlawed Tudeh party were found to have long records of indoctrination in the Soviet Union.

Exposed as she was to Soviet pressures, Iran had two important grievances against the United States. One was that the volume and occasionally the quality of American economic and military assistance was not adequate considering her strategic role on the periphery of Russia and the risks she was undertaking as a member of the Baghdad Pact. The other was that, despite its continuous show of good will toward the pact, the United States did not join, thus withholding a formal commitment to defend Iran in the case of aggression. The Suez crisis of 1956, which severed Iran's line of oil exports to the West, and the subsequent Russian political gains in the Arab East further deepened Iran's uneasiness about the lack of firm American guarantees. This explains why the Iranians welcomed the announcement of the Eisenhower Doctrine of 1957[30] as likely to increase their security and as an evidence of intensified American interest in the defense of the Middle East.

Iran's ruling class experienced a real shock upon learning of the revolution in neighboring Iraq in July 1958. It meant not only that another monarchy was being abruptly abolished in the swift-changing Middle East but also that one of the central pillars of the Baghdad alliance was being removed in the midst of the steady advances of communism in the area as a whole. The civil war in Lebanon and the U.A.R.'s intervention in it provided another evidence of trends adverse to Western influence. For a while it seemed that the whole structure of Western-sponsored defense of the Middle East was collapsing and that in a movement of revolutionary proportions the Fertile Crescent was sliding toward decisive repudiation of its remaining ties with the West. Faced with these developments, Iran had the choice of conforming to the seemingly victorious neutralist trend or of seeking to strengthen its links with the West. Iran's policy, as enunciated by the Shah both before and after the Iraqi revolution, was that of "positive nationalism." This phrase was coined in reply to two concepts which the Shah's government was trying to combat: one was the "negative" nationalism of the Mossadegh era, which brought Iran to the verge of ruin, the other was Nasser's "positive neutralism," which, the Iranians thought, tended to facilitate Soviet infiltration in the area. "Positive nationalism" meant promotion of Iran's national interests through positive forging of links of mutual interest with those countries that were interested in the preservation of her independence and capable of assisting in her economic development and her defense against external aggression.[31] It was in pursuance of this policy that Iran joined with the other Asian members of the Baghdad Pact in urging the United States, after the revolution in Iraq, to extend direct defense guarantees to each of them. In response,

[30]See p. 797 below.

[31]For an authoritative definition of "positive nationalism" see His Imperial Majesty Mohammed Reza Shah Pahlavi, Shahanshah of Iran, *Mission for My Country* (New York, Toronto, London, 1960), pp. 125 and 297.

Secretary Dulles promised at the London conference in July 1958 to conclude bilateral defense agreements with the countries in question. In the fall and winter while negotiations were being conducted to that end, Iran was subjected to renewed Soviet pressure aimed at detaching her from the Western camp. This pressure, which first took the form of notes warning Iran against the conclusion of the bilateral agreement with the United States and of renewed offers of "unlimited aid" if the contemplated agreement were abandoned, culminated in February 1959 in the dispatch of a special Soviet mission to Teheran, headed by a vice minister of foreign affairs. Its aim was to conclude with Iran a pact of nonaggression and economic aid, involving explicit renunciation by Russia of her right to send troops to Iran by virtue of Article 6 of the Soviet-Iranian treaty of February 26, 1921. In return, Iran would be expected (1) to withdraw from the Baghdad Pact, (2) not to conclude the bilateral treaty with the United States, and (3) to deny all foreign powers the right to establish military bases on her territory. This appeared to be the Soviet maximum objective. As a minimum, the Soviet delegation was to keep Iran from signing the pact with the United States.

It is still not quite clear why the Shah—considering his policy of "positive nationalism"—agreed to receive the Soviet mission, thereby opening the door to hope on the Soviet side that, despite his earlier resistance, some agreement could be reached. Several theses have been advanced in explanation of this seemingly contradictory policy. One is that a group of high-ranking Iranian leaders and diplomats succeeded in convincing the Shah that it would be advantageous to Iran to obtain from Russia formal renunciation of her unilateral right of military intervention in return for Iran's reassurance that Russia's security would not be threatened by any intimate ties with the United States. Another thesis points to the alleged influence of Britain, who, according to certain Iranians fond of seeing Britain's hand behind every major move in their country, was bent on a policy of appeasing Russia at that time. Still another theory claims that the Shah's negotiations with the Soviets were nothing but a time-tested device to play one major power against another and thus to derive the maximum advantage to himself, in this case to prod the United States into a promise of greater financial assistance than was initially contemplated.

Whichever of these theories is correct, the fact remains that the Soviet-Iranian negotiations seriously alarmed the West. In early February 1959 it was reliably reported that the United States, Britain, Turkey, Pakistan, and West Germany sent urgent appeals to the Shah to resist Soviet pressures. The effect of this collective *démarche* was felt immediately: on February 11 the Soviet mission returned to Moscow and the following day the Soviet government publicly accused Iran of bad faith and reaffirmed the validity of the treaty of 1921. Furthermore, giving vent to their annoyance over Iran's attitude, the Russians openly boasted of their efficient intelligence apparatus in Iran: on February 24, Premier Khrushchev stated that his government had a copy of the proposed military agreement between the United States and Iran. "The secrets," he added, "are not well kept. We know everything and can tell the Shah a great deal if he wants information."[32]

[32]Quoted in *Middle East Journal*, 13 (Spring 1959), 180.

On March 4, 1959, the Irano-American agreement was signed, thus directly committing the United States to come to the aid of Iran in case of aggression. Russian reaction was undisguised resentment and hostility. Various means of pressure were applied. These included numerous violations of Iranian air space by Soviet aircraft (Iran protested against eighty-one such cases between December and mid-March), distribution of propaganda leaflets and other unlawful actions by Soviet Embassy employees, and a vigorous campaign against Iran by Soviet radio stations and the clandestine "National Voice of Iran." A special feature of this campaign was a series entitled "Behind the Walls of the Saadabad Palace," which exposed various details of the Shah's public and private life. In spite of its distortions, the series, together with other broadcasts, tended to injure the monarch's prestige by harping on the extravagance and social irresponsibility of the ruling groups in contrast to the frustrations of the poorer and middle classes.

This state of tension was further accentuated by what appeared to be Soviet advances on both flanks of Iran. The Iranians noted with misgivings the increase in the volume of Soviet aid to Afghanistan, which included economic and technical assistance as well as reported arms deliveries. On the western side of Iran, Iraq seemed to be sliding rapidly into the Soviet orbit both through its numerous pacts and exchanges with the Soviet bloc and through the substantial gains achieved by its Communist party. Directed by a largely Communist-oriented personnel, Radio Baghdad carried vicious anti-Iranian propaganda in seeming synchronization with the simultaneous outbursts of Soviet hostility. To this could be added a dispute over navigation on the Shatt el-Arab, which further envenomed relations between the two countries in the late fall of 1959.

With the advent of the year 1960, however, relations between Iran and Iraq began to improve gradually. This no doubt was a reflection of the changing internal situation in Iraq, where effective curbs began to be applied to the Communists. As a result, broadcasts hostile to Iran were stopped and by midyear Irano-Iraqi relations returned to such a state of mutual respect that the two heads of states exchanged complimentary messages on the occasion of certain national festivities in Iraq.

The normalization of their relations could also be ascribed to shared concern about the uncompromising and dynamic policies of the United Arab Republic. In contrast to the Iraqis, whose revolution, however violent, tended to be localized, Nasser's nationalists displayed a proselytizing zeal that combined the elements of social revolution, Pan-Arabism, and Afro-Asian neutralism. While General Kassem's Iraq seemed willing to seek accommodation with its neighbors such as Jordan and Iran despite the differences in political outlook, Nasser's Egypt and its affiliated Syrian province followed a path of ideological (if not territorial) expansion in the name of the policy of "liberation." As a consequence, Iran's "old order," exemplified by its monarchy and its adherence to Western alliances, tended to be contrasted by Cairo with its "new order" of revolution and nationalism. At the slightest excuse, Cairo's propaganda machinery was poised to launch an all-out campaign against Iran. Such an excuse was provided by an incident concerning Irano-Israeli relations.

On July 23, 1960, the Shah declared at a press conference in Teheran that Iran might send a diplomatic representative to Israel. The Shah's statement was received with consternation in the Arab world, Cairo's reaction being most violent and resulting, on July 27, in the rupture of diplomatic relations with Iran. A propaganda war between the two countries ensued, Radio Cairo predicting an early downfall of the "corrupt" Iranian monarchy, with Radio Teheran calling President Nasser "this light-headed Pharaoh who is ruling by bloodshed." There is no doubt that the U.A.R.'s reaction was out of proportion to Iran's "transgression." Iran had, indeed, given de facto recognition to Israel soon after her establishment as a state and for some time was represented in Tel-Aviv by a chargé d'affaires. The latter was recalled by Premier Mossadegh in the early 1950s, the post remaining vacant without any change in the formal status of Irano-Israeli relations. Thus the sending of an envoy to Israel by Iran would not have constituted a new act of recognition but merely a reactivation of the basically existing relationship. Actually the Shah did not state positively that Iran intended to send a diplomatic representative, and no official proof of such an intention was available. Yet even an intimation that such a move might be contemplated was sufficient to arouse President Nasser's ire. It may be surmised that this ire was not a matter of uncontrolled emotions but the result of a deliberate policy designed to injure and isolate any Moslem country in the Middle East that wished to disregard Arab sensibilities regarding Israel. There was some speculation among diplomatic observers in the Middle East whether the Shah's statement was intentional or accidental. Undoubtedly this incident helped to clarify, in somewhat confused Western public opinion, the fact that Iran, though Moslem, is not an Arab country. Because of the negative attitude of certain segments of Western society toward the Arabs, such a clarification represented a potential advantage from the Iranian point of view.

Whatever the truth of the matter—and the Iranian court and government were not prone to reveal their innermost thoughts on the subject—the intensity of Arab reaction seemed to take Teheran by surprise. Consequently, even if the Iranian government originally planned to send an envoy, it now hastened to proclaim that it had no intention whatsoever of effecting any changes in the existing state of its relations with Israel. From Cairo's point of view this appeared like a victory and a vindication of its uncompromising stand. But the victory was not complete: despite the U.A.R.'s strong advocacy in the Arab League that its members should sever diplomatic relations with Iran, no other Arab country followed Cairo's example.

Economic Development Problems

Ever since the return to normalcy following the Zahedi coup in 1953, much attention had been paid in Iran to problems of economic development. The conclusion of the agreement between Iran and the international oil consortium paved the way to a revival of substantial oil production, which began to bring increasing revenues to the state. These revenues rose from $90 million in 1955 to $275 million in 1960. According to laws passed by the Majlis, 62 percent (and after three years 80 percent) of these amounts were initially earmarked to finance development. As a result of the continuous budget deficits, the Majlis gradually lowered this percentage until, by 1960, it barely exceeded 50 percent. In spite of this proportional reduction, the actual amounts paid to the plan organization (a body responsible for the development program) were considerable. In the spring of 1956 the second seven-year development plan was adopted with anticipated expenditures of about one billion dollars. At the same time the plan organization signed a five-year agreement with the Development and Resources Corporation, an American firm headed by David Lilienthal and Gordon Clapp, to develop the southwestern province of Khuzistan. Under the leadership of Abol Hassan Ebtehaj, the plan organization freely availed itself of foreign expert advice and services. Instead of prematurely rushing into construction projects, it insisted on careful preliminary studies, which as a rule were entrusted on a contract basis to foreign firms of engineering consultants. Although this procedure had a delaying effect on the launching of some much-needed projects, it appeared to be based on a rational foundation. In this connection it may be observed that Iran, like many another underdeveloped country, was confronted with the competing demands of long-range schemes versus immediate-impact projects. While sound economics and basic needs of development demanded the former, internal political considerations often favored the latter. Plan Director Ebtehaj tended to emphasize the long-range needs of the country, thereby incurring considerable criticism and opposition. As long as the Shah supported him, he was able to persevere in his policies. In 1959, however, the Shah conceded to various pressures and withdrew his support, which prompted Ebtehaj's resignation and his replacement by his former deputy, engineer Khosrow Hedayatt. By that time the work of the plan organization had progressed beyond the study stage. The inauguration in 1957–1958 of two new branches of the Trans-Iranian Railroad, those linking Teheran with Meshed and Tabriz, marked an important and tangible achievement, likely to bring substantial benefits to Azerbaijan and Khorasan as well as to the rest of the country. Simultaneously work was progressing on various water-harnessing projects, such as the Karaj, the Sefid Rud, and the Dez dams, while other engineering teams were busy modernizing Iran's ports, building power plants, and enlarging the network of roads. By the late 1950s the immediate-impact projects had also gained some recognition.

Rather ambitiously conceived, the development plan necessitated financing in excess of the available portion of oil revenues. This led the Iranian government to seek additional funds from two sources. On the one hand, Iran applied for and obtained financial assistance from the United States and the World Bank, such as the latter's loan of $43 million for the Dez River project. On the other, the government aimed at increasing the oil revenues by entering into agreements with foreign firms other than the consortium. To pave the way for such agreements, the existing restrictive legislation (the Mossadegh law of 1944) had to be amended. In July 1957 the Majlis passed a new oil bill encouraging foreign exploration and allowing for a joint operation of the oil industry by foreign firms and the National Iranian Oil Company (N.I.O.C.). Shortly afterward N.I.O.C. concluded a contract with a semiofficial Italian organization, Agip Mineraria, by virtue of which a jointly owned operating enterprise to be known as Iran-Italian Petroleum Co. (S.I.R.I.P.)

was to be set up for the purpose of exploration and exploitation in the offshore areas in the Persian Gulf.

In 1958, Iran concluded similar contracts with two independent companies, American and Canadian. A common feature of these agreements was that, because of the joint ownership of the operating companies, the N.I.O.C. was to receive 50 percent of the profits remaining after the total profits had been subjected to a 50 percent tax by the Iranian government. This explains why the new agreements were generally regarded as introducing the new, 75-25 percent formula in favor of Iran and thus breaking the 50-50 profit-sharing principle established by the older concessionaire companies in the Middle East. It should be pointed out, however, that the new and seemingly more advantageous formula provided for equal sharing of expenses from the time of the discovery of oil in commercial quantities, a feature absent in the old agreements, in which such expenses were undertaken entirely by the concessionaires. By and large, however, the signing of new agreements represented a potential rather than an actual advantage in financial terms. Before the new enterprises yielded any revenues to the Iranian treasury, oil would have to be discovered and the whole intricate organization of production, transportation, and marketing established. In the immediate future, therefore, the consortium was distined to play the role of the major provider of funds for the Iranian state.

While gradual progress was registered in the sector of development, with a resulting increase of total national income, the problem of a just distribution of that income among various social classes was still awaiting solution. Although reliable statistical information on the spread of the national income among various classes was lacking, there was no doubt that a marked imbalance existed in Iran. An overwhelming majority of the population, mostly rural, lived on a mere subsistence level, while a substantial proportion of the land was owned by a few hundred wealthy families whose interest in agriculture was often tempered by a concentration on politics or pleasure seeking in the capital city. This, in turn, adversely affected the prospects for industrialization in view of the limited purchasing power of the country as a whole. In many respects agrarian reform seemed to provide the key to the sound development of the country both socially and economically. This fact has been recognized by the foreign experts who at one time or another have made surveys of Iranian society and economy[33] as well as by some of the more forward-looking Iranians. Modest beginnings had been made during the regime of Dr. Mossadegh, who, by decree legislation, increased the share the peasant tenants were to receive from the proceeds of their work. No reliable data were available as to the execution of this law by landowners or by the authorities. Skepticism on this point was justified, especially in view of the subsequent advent to power of a regime which tended to discredit everything done in the Mossadegh era.

Foremost among those favoring agrarian reform in Iran had been the Shah him-

---

[33]For a most thorough survey of Iran's needs, see Overseas Consultants, Inc., *Report on Seven Year Development Plan for the Plan Organization of the Imperial Government of Iran,* 5 vols. (New York, 1949).

self, who was reputed to appreciate the need for such a reform on both economic and political grounds. The revolution which toppled the monarchy in nearby Iraq in 1958 may have served as an ominous reminder that some action in the agrarian sector was definitely in order. In December 1959 the government submitted to the Majlis a draft agrarian reform bill aiming primarily at a reduction in the size of the great landed properties. The government-proposed maximum was 600 hectares of nonirrigated land and 300 hectares of irrigated land. This maximum was increased by the Malis to 800 and 400 hectares, respectively, when it adopted the law on March 15, 1960, after a heated debate and the Shah's personal intervention to speed up the proceedings. Furthermore, the Majlis adopted several amendments to the original government draft to ease the situation of the landowners, especially by permitting them to sell or dispose of their surplus land in the long transitional period before compulsory enforcement would begin. Critics viewed the end product with skepticism, asserting that the law had too many loopholes to be effective and that neither the efficiency nor the financial resources of the government sufficed for its effective implementation. Some went so far as to claim that in reality the only purpose of the new law was to win a psychological victory among the reform-minded urban strata of the intelligentsia and thus to reduce its hostility toward the regime. We shall return to the land reform problem in a subsequent section of this chapter.

Internal Political Stresses

Ever since the removal of Mossadegh from power the Shah had been anxious to overhaul Iran's political system with the dual objective of strengthening royal authority and assuring a more orderly and responsible parliamentary process. The first objective was achieved, at least on a temporary basis, when the nineteenth Majlis was inaugurated in May 1956, inasmuch as the overwhelming majority of its members owed their election to governmental intervention. Thus a new era of a weak and pliable parliament and a strong royal power was inaugurated, in an obvious contrast to the conditions prevailing between 1941 and 1953. As for the second objective, the Shah believed that stability in the country would be enhanced by the establishment of a two-party system, which would replace the old atomization of political life and which would tend to stress issues rather than personalities. The two parties should emulate the pattern in existence in the English-speaking democracies and alternate in office depending on the results of elections. Both parties, according to the Shah's thinking, would be dedicated to the preservation of the basic political structure of Iran, i.e., the constitutional monarchy. Then there would never again be any question as to the loyalty of the opposition. Furthermore, to assure greater stability and less political effervescence, the sessions of the Majlis should be lengthened to four years.

Partly with an eye to implementing this program and partly out of desire to create a climate of mutual trust between his new regime and the younger educated classes, the Shah chose for premier the former president of Teheran University, Dr. Manuchehr Eghbal, hitherto Court minister, who assumed his functions in April 1957. The following month the two chambers of the Majlis assembled jointly to adopt constitutional amendments that increased the number of deputies from 136 to 200 and extended their term from two to four years.

Having laid the legal foundation for greater stability, the Shah turned toward the political structure. With his encouragement, in May 1957 the opposition People's party (Mardom) was founded under the leadership of his personal friend, Asadollah Alam, at one time minister of the interior. A few months later, again acting on the Shah's suggestions, Premier Eghbal founded his progovernment National party (Mellioun). The programs of the parties did not reveal major differences, although it appeared that Mardom tended to place a somewhat stronger emphasis on the need for agrarian reform.

Politically conscious Iranians did not display much interest in the two new parties. They were inclined to treat both as artificial creations that did not represent the genuine political feelings of the country. If the court had hoped to introduce procedures of peaceful change via the parties, its hopes were largely vain. It was very unlikely that the genuine opposition would use either of the two official parties to achieve its objectives. This became evident sooner than anybody expected when in October 1957 the security police arrested seventy followers of Mossadegh on charges of subversion. Even more impressive was the incarceration in February 1958 of the former chief of army intelligence, General Vali Gharani, together with thirty-three associates and their indictment for a plot aiming at the overthrow of the regime. At the same time the Communists did not remain inactive, as occasional communiqués of arrests and executions of their adherents and leaders indicated.

A major test of the new two-party system came in late summer of 1960, when elections were held to the twentieth Majlis. Candidates for parliament could be divided into the following four categories: the progovernment Mellioun party, the "loyal opposition" Mardom party, the unaffiliated independents, and the real opposition to the regime. The latter embraced a broad array of forces calling themselves the National Front and including elements formerly associated with Mossadegh. Chief among its leaders were Allahyar Saleh, Professor Abdullah Moazzami, Dr. Karim Sanjabi, and Bagher Kazemi, all of whom had held cabinet posts under Mossadegh, and Dr. Mozaffer Baghai and Khalil Maleki, both of whom headed separate groups and were identified with socialist trends. Officially the government maintained that elections would be free. In reality the authorities exercised a great deal of interference, thus making it unlikely that any representatives of the real opposition would be elected. This led to protest meetings' and demonstrations, during which the opposition, often backed by student groups, denounced the government for muzzling democratic freedoms. When in late August the elections were completed in a majority of the constituencies, no single representative of the genuine opposition was elected. As might have been expected, the pro-government Mellioun party obtained a majority of the seats, with the Mardom and the independent (but basically progovernment) deputies following.

Thus the government's wishes seemed fulfilled to its entire satisfaction. Nevertheless, this was a Pyrrhic victory. It might be asked: What was the use of staging elections if they were not meant to be free? True enough, sham elections of this kind have been a regular feature of the totalitarian countries, and it may be argued that they accomplish a certain psychological and propagandistic task useful to the government in power. But despite all her anti-democratic features, Iran is not a totalitarian country and her intelligentsia is too sophisticated to accept such dubious procedures with equanimity. Consequently, rampant discontent was evident, especially in urban centers. It was probably this circumstance, together with the warning provided by recent student-engendered upheavals in Korea and Turkey, that led the Shah to a sudden reversal of attitude. Early in September, only a few days after the elections, he publicly declared his dissatisfaction with the electoral procedures and expressed his wish that the newly elected deputies should resign their mandates so that new elections, free from undue interference, should take place at an early date. Although reluctantly (on account of considerable sums spent on elections), the deputies, virtually all of them "King's men," complied, and the country found itself without the Majlis throughout the fall and winter. Simultaneously, engineer Sharif Emami replaced Dr. Eghbal as prime minister. The new elections held in January and February 1961 appeared like a compromise between tight government control and freedom. Police and local officialdom showed restraint, and although government influence was not totally absent it seemed to assume less obvious forms than it had in the preceding elections. This moderate liberalization of procedures made it possible for Allahyar Saleh, a leading member of the opposition, to be elected. Another consequence of this liberalization was the emergence of a larger number of independent deputies than before. Although the loyalty of the latter to the existing regime was not in doubt, their unwillingness to identify themselves rigidly with one of the two official parties was indicative of their desire to preserve a certain freedom of movement on the political arena. Basically, however, the new elections did not represent a major change in the existing political situation. Despite the election of Allahyar Saleh and a few like-minded members, loud criticisms of renewed government interference were voiced, especially at the University of Teheran, which was twice closed for long periods during the spring term of 1961 because of repeated student riots.

On the threshold of the decade of the 1960s Iran's internal situation was not free of strains and stresses which, if not removed, might jeopardize the country's chances at orderly development. In any analysis or evaluation of the causes of this malaise care should be taken not to oversimplify the issues lest one fall into serious errors. Thus, for example, it was not monarchy per se which posed the most difficult dilemma. In fact, it was highly debatable whether any attempt at removal of the monarchy would meet with popular approval. Such an attempt in 1953 resulted in a spontaneous outburst of feeling in favor of the Shah. Monarchy was an old and widely accepted institution in Iran. The Shah's marriage to an Iranian commoner, Miss Farah Diba, in 1959 and the subsequent birth of the first male heir contributed to a deeper entrenchment of this institution in the public mind. Furthermore, it should be pointed out that on a number of issues the Shah was more progressive and forward-looking than the traditional ruling classes of Iran. The question of agrarian reform may serve as an example here, and one should not forget the fact that the Shah himself pioneered in ordering the distribution of his estates to needy peasants.

Consolidation of Royalist Power

The decade between 1953 and 1963 could be regarded as a period of the Shah's struggle to assert and consolidate his power against various sources of opposition and dissent. The Shah overcame challenges to his authority from the Communist left, from the National Front, and from unreconstructed right-wing elements as well as religious circles. The Tudeh organization was almost entirely destroyed, and the party's leaders found themselves in exile, mostly in East Germany. The National Front, which frequently used students at the universities to dramatize its demands, was virtually suppressed by 1962. The right-wing groups, mostly representing big landowners who looked with hostility upon the Shah's land reform and other progressive ideas, were by and large successfully out-maneuvered by 1963, and after some violent demonstrations against the Shah's reform program which included proposals to give women the right of political participation the religious opposition was also effectively overcome. Its main spokesman, Ayatollah Khomeini, was deported from Iran. The latter part of the decade of 1953–1963 was particularly tense and fraught with dangers for the Shah. He was greatly helped by Prime Minister Ali Amini, who held office in 1961–1962, and subsequently by Asadollah Alam, who headed three successive cabinets between July 1962 and March 1964. The difference between these two prime ministers was that while Ali Amini not only used but publicly displayed his power and thus appeared to be an independent source of authority, Premier Alam was an old and trusted friend who dedicated himself entirely to the service of the Shah and the dynasty. The idea of consolidating his rule and passing on an inheritance to his heir, Crown Prince Reza, born October 31, 1960, was foremost in the Shah's mind. This concern found expression in a constitutional amendment adopted on the Shah's initiative by the Majlis on September 7, 1967, which provided for a council of regency headed by Queen Farah to rule the country after the Shah's death until the Crown Prince came of age at twenty.[34]

During these final stages of consolidation of power the Shah largely disregarded the institution of the Majlis, even although by virtue of elections held in August 1960 and then in February 1961 the Majlis was composed of deputies broadly loyal to the Shah. Yet while politically many deputies believed in the institution of the monarchy and were prepared to support the Shah's authority, where their interests, particularly as landowners were affected by reforms, they could be expected to obstruct reforming legislation. With this in view, the Shah issued an imperial decree dissolving the Majlis in May 1961. For two and a half years the government of Iran continued without a parliament. The Shah took full advantage of this situation to press for a bold reform program.

An Era of Reforms—The White Revolution

In early January 1963 the Shah announced a reform program composed of six points: (1) land reform, (2) nationalization of forests and pastures, (3) public sale of state-owned factories to finance land reform, (4) profit-sharing in industry between

[34]Text in *Kayhan*, International Edition (Teheran), Sept. 9, 1967, p. 5.

owners and workers, (5) reform of electoral law to enfranchise women, and (6) formation of a Literacy Corps.

This program was submitted to a popular referendum on January 26 (corresponding to 6 Bahman) which resulted in virtually unanimous approval by the people. Called henceforth the White Revolution, this program was subsequently enlarged by the addition of three points in 1964–1965, three other points in 1967, and five further points in 1975. These supplementary points were as follows: (7) the formation of the Health Corps, (8) the formation of the Reconstruction and Development Corps, (9) establishment of the rural courts of justice, (10) nationalization of water resources, (11) urban and rural reconstruction, (12) educational and administrative revolution, (13) transfer of 49 percent of ownership in private enterprises to employees and the public, (14) war on profiteering through price regulation, (15) free education and a daily free meal for all children from kindergarten to eighth grade, (16) nation-wide social security (to be extended to rural population).

The principal point in these reforms was undoubtedly the land reform inasmuch as its successful enactment would have serious impact upon the economic, social, and political structure of the country. It should be pointed out that the six-point program merely confirmed a land-reform law issued a year earlier by a decree dated January 9, 1962. In a purely technical sense the 1962 decree was no more than an amendment of the laws previously adopted by the Majlis. But the amendment opened a new era in land relationships in Iran. Acting on advice of his minister for agrarian reform, Hassan Arsanjani, the Shah felt that to be effective and politically useful the new land-reform law should make it possible to implement its provisions swiftly. Any law that specified the maximum number of acres to be owned by an individual would require a thorough cadastral survey in the country. Considering the enormity of the task and the slow workings of Iranian bureaucracy, such a survey might well have taken forty years to complete. Consequently the Shah decided to do away with the cadastral survey and to decree that every landowner was to transfer his land properties to his tenant peasants retaining the right to keep a maximum of one village for himself. Because villages varied greatly in size, no uniform maximum holding was established. Despite this inequality the law had the merit of swiftly transferring title and possession of land to the peasants. The law did not provide for confiscation; it called for payment by the new peasant owners for the value of the land received in installments. The value of the land thus distributed was to be determined on the basis of the taxes previously paid by the landowners, a provision which—because of the traditional undervaluing of their properties by the landowners—was clearly favorable to the new peasant proprietors. Having according to the law retained a single village, the landowners were given three further choices with regard to it: they could negotiate a sale of such a vaillage to the tenant peasants; second, they could enter with those peasants into leasehold agreements; or they could divide the village into a part directly owned by themselves and another to be distribued for the legally stipulated compensation among the peasants.[35]

[35]For details of land reform, see D. R. Denman, "Land Reforms of Shah and People," in G. Lenczowski, ed., *Iran under the Pahlavis* (Stanford, Calif., 1978), pp. 253–301, and Ann K. S. Lambton, *The Persian Land Reform, 1962–1966* (Oxford, 1969).

Subsequent legislation in the 1960s with regard to land was focused on increasing its productivity. The Shah felt that small peasant landholders, despite the new incentive of ownership, were not in a position to assure the greatest productivity because it could be achieved only by large-scale organization. Subsequent legislation provided for two forms of organized agriculture in Iran: first, it encouraged rural cooperatives among the peasants with the aid of professional cadres delegated by the ministry of agriculture, and second, it organized agricultural corporations in which the peasant landholders would transform themselves into laborers and employees of a larger corporation while reaping the benefits of greater capital investment and of modern agricultural techniques. To publicize land reform, a congress of new peasant proprietors was held in Teheran in 1963. Furthermore, the Shah made a point of traveling to many outlying villages to distribute property deeds to the new proprietors. To stress that cultivators of land ceased to be peasants in the old sense of the word, the very designation "peasant" was officially abolished by law, to be replaced by a new title, "farmer." On September 23, 1971, the Shah announced the completion of the distribution phase in Iran's land reform. From now on the reform was to enter into a new phase of emphasizing organization and productivity.

Of the other points of the reform, one that attracted considerable attention at home and abroad was that establishing a literacy corps. The Shah became known internationally as a leader promoting the struggle against illiteracy all over the world. He sponsored international congresses dedicated to the study of this problem and held in Teheran. Young men liable to do their military service were allowed to choose service in the army or work in the literacy corps, which meant teaching the villagers reading and writing in often remote provincial localities. Thus the Literacy Corps enabled young men to get acquainted with various parts of the country and to obtain the satisfaction of performing a socially useful function. The health corps and the reconstruction and development corps were subsequently created on the same principle of voluntarism combined with obligation.

Of the other points of the initial six-point program, the granting of the right of vote to women elicited protests from the fundamentalist religious circles, as mentioned earlier. But it was a single short-lived outburst of criticism, of considerable intensity and involving violence to be sure, which was soon overcome by the government. In fact, the government claimed that the religious groups were being used cynically by other elements of the opposition to intimidate the government. Enactment in March of 1975 of a law decreeing the distribution of 49 percent of ownership stock in any enterprise to its employees, workers, and the public caused considerable consternation and discontent among the business circles. There is no doubt that a radical measure of this sort needed an elaborate mechanism for implementation to avoid arbitrariness and inequities in the treatment of both the owners of the enterprises and the groups that were to benefit from it. Another law of 1975, one to curb speculation and inflationary rise in prices, met a similarly mixed reaction. The government declared that prices for all sorts of goods should be investigated by appropriate government bodies which would determine the real cost of specific goods and, by adding an appropriate amount for legitimate profit, would decide on the right price. This law posed two problems: on the one hand, it challenged the basic principle of free enterprise, namely the law of supply and demand; on the other, its implementation would be difficult. The government encouraged squads of students and other young people to make on-the-spot inspections of prices charged in the stores, restaurants, and places of public entertainment and to report to the authorities anything that appeared excessive to them. This measure introduced an opportunity for abuse and arbitrariness on the part of the young inspectors, who may have been guided by personal dislike or revenge rather than by well-considered feelings of public interest. Questionable as this method was, however, it did result in the denunciation and subsequent arrest of a good number of price-gouging businessmen ranging from small shopkeepers to multimillionaires handling wholesale businesses. The courts applied swift justice in these cases, which resulted in a number of imprisonments and public confessions by those who were sentenced. Within a few months of the enactment of this decree, the government was claiming considerable success in arresting the rise of prices.

Development Plans, Money, and Oil

Throughout the postwar period Iran based its economy on private enterprise and planning. The first plan of seven years' duration was launched as early as 1949. It called for expenditures of $646 million. It was, however, never fully implemented because of the disruption caused by the oil crisis of 1951 to 1953. Resumption of the regular flow of oil revenues in 1954 permitted the government to launch the second seven-year development plan (1955–1962). Expenditures forecast for this plan were nearly double those initially earmarked for the first plan and amounted to $1.12 billion. It was during the operation of the second plan that the initial allocation of 80 percent of oil revenues to development was reduced to 60 percent in 1959 and 55 percent in 1960. The third development plan, of five years' duration (1963–1968), had a budget of $3.07 billion. Its launching marked the beginning of the so-called take-off period in the Iranian economy which from then on grew at an impressive pace of 10 to 12 percent a year. The fourth five-year plan (1968–1973) called for total expenditures of about $11 billion. Oil revenues were expected to provide funds for a substantial part of this budget but not for the whole of it. The remaining revenue was to be secured from internal and foreign borrowing. The fifth five-year plan, launched in March 1973 to be completed by 1978, initially called for expenditures of nearly $36 billion. Within a year, however, world prices for crude oil quadrupled, thus permitting Iran to engage in even bolder planning. By the spring of 1974 the development budget was increased to nearly $70 billion.[36]

These spectacular increases in the expenditures of the successive plans reflected Iran's growing prosperity based on rising oil revenues. The ascending trend of oil revenues was due partly to the steadily rising volume of production and partly to better terms for Iran as a producer secured in numerous negotiations and agreements concluded with the oil consortium through the 1960s and 1970s. Worldwide shor-

[36] For details on the Fifth Five-Year Plan, see Plan and Budget Organization, *Iran's Fifth Development Plan 1973-1978. Revised: A Summary* (Teheran, May 1975). Also Jane P. C. Carey and Andrew G. Carey, "Industrial Growth and Development Planning in Iran," *Middle East Journal,* 29 (Winter 1975).

tages of oil caused by the collective Arab action following the outbreak of the war with Israel in 1973 gave an opportunity to the oil-producing countries, including Iran, to demand and obtain a 300-percent rise in the prices of the exported crude. The producers' decision on prices was reached through the instrumentality of the Organization of Petroleum Exporting Countries (OPEC) which had been formed in 1960 to protect their collective interests. Iran in the Middle East and Venezuela in the western hemisphere led the fight for the increase in prices. It was largely the Shah's personal leadership aided by the negotiating skills of his finance minister, Jamshid Amuzegar, that resulted in the adoption by OPEC at its conference in Teheran on December 22, 1973, of a new quadrupled price formula. Following this decision, Iran's revenue from oil reached the amount of $23.3 billion in 1974 and $19.8 billion in 1975.

Needless to say, this OPEC policy and Iran's prominent role elicited many protests abroad, mostly in the industrial countries. While adversely affected by the high price of their principal source of energy, the industrial states at least had a remedy in that they could increase their own exports and thus to some extent compensate for the loss of revenue occasioned by the high oil prices. This remedy, however, was not easily available to the underdeveloped countries of the so-called Third World who had little if anything to produce and sell that was needed by the oil-producing states. Moreover, the boost in oil prices increased tremendously the cost of the fertilizer that is vital to agriculture in the developing countries. Yet, interestingly enough, they rarely protested against the new oil prices and in a variety of public pronouncements often defended OPEC's action. Their attitude could be explained on the one hand by the somewhat unrealistic expectation that as producers of raw materials they would also be able to create cartels which would emulate OPEC policies (for such materials as copper, bauxite, manganese, aluminum, coffee, etc.), and on the other by their emotional attitude of envy and resentment against the industrial West and the corresponding feeling of affinity with the OPEC countries with which they shared an anticolonial attitude. In an effort to compensate both the developing countries and certain industrial countries for the difficulties experienced as a result of the new oil price level, Iran under the Shah's leadership committed a total of $7.5 billion in 1974–1975 to various schemes of aid and trade with the countries thus affected. India, Pakistan, and Egypt figured among the recipients and were granted about $1 billion each.

Some critics found Iran's insistence on high oil prices and the resulting embarrassment to certain key Western countries (such as Great Britain or Italy) incompatible with the essentially pro-Western Iranian orientation and the basic desire of Iran to join the free world in containing the menace of international communism. In a number of interviews given to foreign visitors and correspondents, the Shah defended his policy by pointing out that oil was too precious a resource to be used for such purposes as heating where other substitutes could be found. Oil, a quickly depleted resource, he claimed, should be used primarily for the production of petrochemicals and should be preserved as long as possible for mankind to prevent its exhaustion. The ruler also proposed that the price of oil should be determined by the price of its nearest substitute. Iran's insistence on the higher price level, argued the Shah, should spur the West to concentrate on developing new sources of energy, an endavor that would have been unprofitable with the steady supply of cheap Middle East oil.[37]

Apart from the oil price question, the Shah was among the first to change the basic relationship of the producer country to the foreign oil companies. On March 21, 1973, he announced his plan for a complete takeover of the oil industry in Iran by 1979, the date by which the consortium agreement was to expire, twenty five years after its inception. The Shah offered two alternatives to the consortium: either to continue in its present form until the end of the agreement and then change its role into that of a mere buyer along with other buyers, without any preferential treatment; or to agree to an immediate takeover of the industry by Iran while securing an agreement for twenty years giving it preferential treatment in terms of prices and guaranteed supplies. The consortium accepted the latter alternative. The new agreement, signed in July 1973, changed its status to that of a "service company" performing the tasks of exploration, production, transportation, and so forth on behalf of the Iranian government. Ultimate control of the industry, however, and policy decisions were reserved strictly for the Iranian authorities. Side by side with these developments, another interesting change took place: while as late as 1973 Iran was in the forefront of those producers who insisted on increase of the volume of production for themselves by the foreign companies, beginning in 1974 Iran began preaching the need for conservation of resources, expecting to boost its revenues not through increase in production but through increase in prices. The Iranian policy clashed to some extent with the attitude of another major producer in the Middle East, Saudi Arabia, which for economic as well as political reasons favored moderation on the price issue. In one sector, Iran practiced restraint in asking for higher prices. The price of gas exported to the Soviet Union was kept at a fraction of the prevailing world price for natural gas. But this attitude was not dictated merely by economic considerations and had to be taken within the broader context of relations between the Soviet Union and Iran.

Foreign Policy during the White Revolution

The accelerated pace of domestic developments under the White Revolution was accompanied by a corresponding intensification in Iran's foreign relations. In the most important sector of Iran's foreign policy, that of relations with the major powers, a subtle but significant change has taken place. Like Turkey, Iran responded positively to Khrushchev's pleas for coexistence and greater economic cooperation. Even before the formal proclamation of the White Revolution, in September 1962, Iran gave the Soviet Union a pledge that no foreign missile bases would be established on Iranian territory. This good-will gesture was followed by a number of other manifestations of normalization in Iranian-Soviet relations. Periodic trade agreements were concluded between the two countries, and on December 20, 1962, an agreement resolving a number of border differences was

[37]Iran's oil policy is analyzed in R. B. Stobaugh, "The Evolution of Iranian Oil Policy, 1925-1975," in G. Lenczowski, ed., *Iran under the Pahlavis,* and G. Lenczowski, "The Oil-Producing Countries," in Raymond Vernon, ed., *The Oil Crisis* (New York, 1976), pp. 68-69.

signed. In November 1963, Leonid Brezhnev, then president of the USSR but not yet in full control of the country, paid a state visit to Teheran, initiating a series of high-level visits between the heads of state or ministers of the two governments. In August 1964 a direct Teheran-Moscow air connection was inaugurated. The most spectacular event, however, was the conclusion on October 6, 1965, of a Soviet-Iranian agreement whereby the Soviet Union undertook to provide financial and technical assistance in the development of a major metallurgical complex in Isfahan which would include a steel plant of considerable capacity. Iran agreed to pay for these services by supplying gas from the southern Iranian oil fields. This gas was to be sold at a preferential price to Russia and was to be conveyed by a special pipeline to be constructed jointly by Iran and the Soviet Union.[38] The pipeline was completed in 1970. Parallel to these Soviet-Iranian transactions, Iran concluded a number of barter deals with the Soviet satellite countries of Eastern Europe. Poland, Czechoslovakia, Hungary, and East Germany figured prominently in this list. The conclusion in February 1966 of an agreement between Iran and the Soviet Union whereby Moscow undertook to supply Teheran with $100 million worth of arms attracted considerable international attention. It was the first time that a country associated with the West through collective and bilateral links of alliance turned to the Soviet Union for arms supplies. The importance of this deal should not be exaggerated, however, because Iran was purchasing only rather simple firearms such as rifles and machineguns as well as automotive equipment, particularly trucks. It appears that the deal was dictated not so much by political considerations as by the lower prices offered by the Soviet Union. In addition, the two countries concluded other agreements pertaining to the regulation of the border rivers Aras and Atrek as well as Soviet assistance in projects such as the construction of a number of grain elevators in Iran. Soviet assistance in the establishment of the Isfahan metallurgical complex meant that hundreds of Soviet technicians would work in Iran. For many years Iran resisted the introduction into its territory of Soviet technical help. Now, with the abatement of mutual political tension, Iran was more receptive to hosting a certain number of Russian technicians. On their part, the Russians seemed to abandon their earlier insistence that Iran withdraw from CENTO and generally sever its links with the United States. They appeared content with Iran's positive response to their overtures of economic and technical cooperation. With the passage of time this cooperation took a new turn. On February 25, 1975, Iran concluded an agreement with the Soviet Union whereby she undertook to finance a paper mill in the USSR.

Normalization of Iran's relations with Russia was not without effect on its relations with the United States and with the regional neighbors. While the basic multilateral and bilateral instruments linking Iran to the United States (CENTO and the bilateral agreement of 1959) preserved their official validity, the earlier close identification of Iran with the United States began to be eroded. First the Shah voiced his criticism of the United States for the inadequate level of its economic and military assistance to Iran. Subsequently, in the mid and later 1960s and early

---

[38]Text of agreement, *Kayhan,* International Edition, Oct. 6, 1965.

1970s, the Shah and his spokesmen began voicing doubts as to the significance and usefulness of CENTO. Massive involvement of the United States in the war in Vietnam was watched in Iran with mixed feelings. On the one hand, the Iranian government was encouraged by the American demonstration of will and firmness in resisting Communist aggression. On the other, the Iranians were worried lest excessive American commitment in Vietnam divert too much of America's attention from such a strategic region as the Soviet-Turkish-Iranian border. By the early 1970s Iran clearly wished the United States to disentangle itself from the Vietnam imbroglio. Yet when the American forces withdrew, leaving the South Vietnam government to its own devices and limiting its arms supplies, many Iranians began losing confidence in America's promises of support for its allies.

Moreover, the Shah and his ministers watched carefully Washington's move toward detente with the Soviet Union. First, they took it as further evidence of America's reluctance to engage in intervention and confrontations abroad to protect its friends and allies, and second, they viewed it as an indication that their own relations with Moscow must not be allowed to deteriorate below the level of the Soviet-American detente. Similarly, America's effort under President Nixon to reopen relations with Communist China was carefully noted in Teheran, and in August 1971 the Iranian government extended recognition to Peking, which was followed by a visit of Queen Farah to the Communist Chinese capital in the fall of 1972. On October 12 of that same year Iran and the Soviet Union concluded a fifteen-year treaty of cooperation. It was an agreement devoid of any military clauses, and it did not invalidate the earlier agreements between Iran, the United States, and Great Britain, but it was symbolic of a new spirit in Iranian-Soviet relations.[39]

Iran's relationship to the United States changed also in this respect, that beginning in 1967, U.S. economic and financial aid to Iran came to an end due to American conviction that further aid of this sort to a country with growing oil revenues was not warranted. From then on Iran concluded various transactions with the United States, particularly for the purchase of military equipment, on a purely commercial basis. Despite the modification in American-Iranian relations, the Shah continued to visit Washington every year or every second year and from time to time hosted the highest officials of the American government in Teheran. This was notably the case in May 1972 when President Nixon paid a state visit to the Shah's capital.

Above all, the Shah never ceased to look upon the United States as his major supplier of sophisticated arms. Iran's armament policy, geared to the enlargement and modernization of its army, experienced an expansion similar to that occurring in the economic sector. During his visit in the United States in June 1968, the Shah sought to purchase arms worth $600 million. There was some reluctance in Washington to meet the Shah's request on convenient credit terms, accompanied by doubts whether Iran needed at the time of its intensive economic development to

[39]For an analysis of this new trend, see Sepehr Zabih, "Iran's International Posture: De Facto Nonalignment within a Pro-Western Alliance," *Middle East Journal,* 24 (Summer 1970).

divert such a high proportion of its revenue to military weapons. This reluctance brought about a degree of irritation in American-Iranian relations resulting in hints from Teheran that if credits for purchase of combat arms were not forthcoming from the United States, Iran might turn to Russia. During his next visit to the United States in October 1969, the Shah expressed interest in purchasing $100 million worth of new model fighter jets in exchange for Washington's agreement to increase the quota of Iranian oil sales to the United States. The Shah argued that the antici- pated withdrawal of Great Britain from the Persian Gulf would create a military vaccum that Iran would have to fill.

Benefiting from the advice of the American military mission in Iran, the Iranian government adopted in 1971 a five-year modernization program for its armed forces. This decision paved the way for the conclusion on February 21, 1973, of a $2 billion arms deal with the United States.[40] By that time Britain's withdrawal from the Gulf was an accomplished fact, and Iran was pursuing an intensive policy of establishing political and military hegemony in the Gulf area. Iran's high oil reve- nues in the mid-1970's largely removed any lingering doubts that Washington might have had as to the wisdom of further arms supplies to Teheran. Looking upon Iran as a vital element of stability in the Middle East, Washington decided that further strengthening of Iran's military posture was justified. Furthermore, increased American arms sales were bringing back to the United States the dollars that Ameri- cans had to spend for more expensive imported oil. Thus both the American gov- ernment and American business developed a growing interest in commercial trans- actions with Iran. In line with this policy a $15 billion trade agreement was con- cluded between Washington and Iran on March 4, 1975. It provided, among other items, for the supply and construction in Iran of eight nuclear reactors.[41]

With its increased oil revenues Iran was in a position to enter into more intensive economic relationships with a number of advanced industrial countries. In June 1974, Iran concluded a ten-year development agreement with France which also provided for the construction in Iran of five nuclear reactors. Moreover, having some surplus funds to invest, the Iranian government bought in July of that same year a 25-percent share in the stock of the Krupp steel company in Germany. Iran made offers to invest in and thus rescue from financial embarrassment two major American corporations, Boeing and Pan American Airlines.

On the regional scale it is proper to differentiate between Iran's policy toward its Northern Tier neighbors and its attitude toward the Arab states of the Middle East. With regard to the Northern Tier, Iran, in agreement with Turkey and Pakistan, pursued a policy of deemphasing the importance of CENTO. Iran particularly tried to play down CENTO's military capacity as either insufficient or obsolete. This trend was temporarily interrupted in 1968 when in August the Soviet Union and its Warsaw Pact satellites invaded and occupied Czechoslovakia. There was at that time a genuine concern in Teheran whether this act represented a reversal of the

[40]For further discussion of arms supplies, see D. R. Tahtinen, *Arms in the Persian Gulf* (Washington, D.C., 1974) and A. Cottrell, "Iran's Armed Forces under the Pahlavi Dynasty," in G. Lenczowski, *Iran under the Pahlavis.*
[41]Text in *Middle East Journal,* 29, (Summer 1975), 345.

Soviet policy of detente and a return to an active and aggressive policy of territorial aggrandizement. Like Turkey, Iran as a member of Regional Cooperation for Development (RCD) was emphasizing economic and technical cooperation among the Northern Tier states. The domestic and international position of its ally, Pakistan, continued to be of interest and concern to Iran. Pakistan's hostile relations with India over Kashmir and other territorial issues, and threats to its integrity from Afghanistan, provided a subject of worry to Teheran. Furthermore, Iran and Pakistan faced a common problem, movement for national autonomy in Baluchistan, a province shared by these two countries. There Soviet and even Iraqi intrigue was suspected. Iran was also concerned, if not actually alarmed, by the aggressive role of India, with considerable Soviet involvement, in the breakaway of Pakistan's eastern province and the subsequent creation of the independent state of Bangladesh. When in 1973 the royalist government of Afghanistan was overthrown by the rebellious officers, and a republic was proclaimed in Kabul, Iran took it as another sign of disquieting instability in the region. The Iranians were looking with apprehension for possible signs of collusion between the new government of Afghanistan and the Soviet Union. To their relief, Afghanistan maintained its independent and neutral posture, which in due course permitted Iran to enter into closer relations with the Afghan rulers and even to extend economic assistance.

Iran's relations with the Arab world in the 1960s and 1970s were altogether correct and friendly but not devoid of moments of tension and suspicion. In view of the fact that the Arab world was divided by its own cold war into two camps—conservative and radical—Iran tended to side with the conservatives, and as long as Nasser lived Iranian-Egyptian relations were characterized by mutual dislike bordering on hostility. The Arab-Israeli war of 1967, however, provided a turning point in Iranian-Arab relations. Iran gradually veered from its neutral attitude to one of supporting the Arab demand for an early evacuation of the occupied Arab territories by the Israeli troops according to the resolutions of the United Nations. The gradual abatement of the Arab cold war and the death of Nasser in 1970 further opened the doors to an Iranian-Arab reconciliation. With the advent of Sadat to power in Egypt, Iranian-Egyptian relations markedly improved, and not only were full diplomatic relations restored but also Iranian economic assistance was extended to Egypt ($1 billion in 1974).

Iran traditionally maintained good relations with the neighboring Arab monarchy of Saudi Arabia. The two countries shared interest in preserving stability in the Persian Gulf area and in preventing radical and subversive movements from gaining a foothold there. Another link between the two countries was their antagonism toward Nasser's regime in Egypt. Saudi Arabia resisted the inroads of Egyptian ideology which equated Arab nationalism with revolution. This dovetailed with Iran's dislike of Nasser's objectives and methods; hence the two monarchies tended to draw closer together. As an antidote to the Egyptian brand of revolutionary nationalism, Iran and Saudi Arabia preferred to propagate the idea of the community of Islamic nations. This appeal to Islam was in turn strongly criticized in revolutionary Arab circles, which viewed it as a cynical device used by reactionary powers.

The seizure of power by the Baath Socialists in neighboring Iraq filled Iran with considerable uneasiness. The nationalist-revolutionary militancy of the Baghdad regime, particularly since 1969, led to the aggravation of five outstanding problems between Iraq and Iran. These were the Kurdish disaffection in northern Iraq, the dispute over the Shatt el-Arab River boundary between the two countries, the position of Iranian pilgrims and nationals residing in the Shii holy places of Najaf and Kerbela in southern Iraq, the sheltering by Iraqi authorities of militant and leftist Iranian dissidents engaging in conspiracies against the Iranian regime, and the rivalry for influence in the Persian Gulf. While some improvement in the relations between Iran and Iraq was registered during the rule of the two successive Aref presidents in Iraq in the 1960s, all five issues suffered further aggravation with the advent of the Baath in 1969. The Kurdish problem was perhaps the most vexing because it involved a prolonged armed rebellion of the Kurds, who were first secretly and later openly supported by Iran in their struggle against the government in Baghdad. Relations between Iran and Iraq suffered further deterioration when on April 9, 1972, Iraq concluded a fifteen-year treaty of friendship and cooperation with the Soviet Union by virtue of which it was to enjoy Soviet assistance in the military sphere and to coordinate its policies with Moscow. Coming as it did at a time when the Soviet Union was involved in the anti-Pakistan activities in the Indian subcontinent and followed soon after by the overthrow of the royalist regime in Afghanistan, the Iraqi-Soviet treaty appeared to the Shah as a sinister manifestation of a possible Soviet policy of encircling Iran while pretending to practice coexistence and detente. Under the circumstances, Iranian aid to the Kurdish rebels in northern Iraq intensified but this in turn caused the Iraqi leaders to seek further arms and assistance from the Soviet Union, thus deepening Baghdad's dependence on Moscow. Vindictive expulsion by Iraq of about 60,000 Iranian residents from its territory, followed by a series of border clashes and artillery duels, marked further deterioration of relations between Iran and Iraq.

Matters took an entirely new turn, however, when at a conference of developing nations in Algiers on March 5, 1975 the Shah of Iran and Iraq's "strongman," Saddam Hussein, concluded an agreement to resolve all Iranian-Iraqi differences. This agreement provided for noninterference in the internal affairs of either country (meaning Iranian abandonment of its support for the Kurds), the designation of the *thalweg* (the deepest channel of the river bottom) as the final boundary between the two countries on the Shatt el-Arab, and the amicable solution of all other outstanding issues including that of the expelled Iranian residents.[42] There is no doubt that agreement was a sort of Yalta for the Kurdish nationalists and that, guided by its own national interests, Iran decided to abandon their cause. On the other hand, the Kurdish military position was becoming more and more desperate owing to the progressive onslaughts by the Soviet-equipped Iraqi army. From the Iranian point of view, further aid to the Kurds meant a prolonged and embarrassing involvement in a local war beyond Iran's boundaries which could be likened on a small scale to the

---

[42]Text of the Iranian-Iraqi agreement of March 5, 1975, in *Kayhan,* International Edition, March 8, 1975.

American involvement in Vietnam. The Shah felt the time had come to extricate himself from this situation, while striking a profitable territorial bargain on the issue of the Shatt el-Arab boundary. In all fairness to Iran, however, it must be said that those Kurds who wanted to cross the border to the safety of Iranian territory were provided with food and shelter as well as the opportunity to resettle. By the same token, the Kurdish nationalist leader Mullah Mustafa Barzani made his way to Iran and as a refugee in Teheran declared that the Kurdish rebellion in Iraq had come to an end. The Iranian-Iraqi agreement had moreover this merit in the eyes of the Shah: it ipso facto lessened Iraq's dependence on the Soviet Union.

It is within the framework of these global and regional foreign policy concerns of Iran that we should look at the Iranian interest and involvement in the Persian Gulf. There is no doubt that in the 1970s the Gulf constituted the principal focus of Iranian foreign policy in the regional environment.[43] From the Iranian point of view, British withdrawal from the Gulf, announced by the Labor government in 1968 and carried out by the end of 1971, was likely to open a Pandora's box of troubles. In place of the stabilizing British military and political presence there would arise a number of small and weak independent Arab states subject to foreign pressures, domestic instability, and infiltration by subversive movements originating from such radical centers in the Middle East as Baghdad, Damascus, or the capital of the newly created People's Republic in South Yemen. The easy and swift way in which the traditionalist principalities and sultanates of the former Aden protectorate were overthrown by Marxist-oriented elements once the British withdrew from that territory served as a warning to Iran, which feared that a similar fate might befall the weak Arab sheikhdoms in the Gulf area. Should Oman and the Trucial Coast states be taken over by the Marxist-oriented revolutionaries, the security of the Persian Gulf might, from the Iranian point of view, be adversely affected. At stake were the freedom of passage and safety of the Strait of Hormuz, which links the Gulf with the Indian Ocean and provides a waterway for the export of up to twenty million barrels of crude oil a day. Furthermore, Iran, as we know, had a standing historical claim to the island of Bahrain. The withdrawal of Britain from a sovereign position there reopened the question of the political status of the island.

In spite of the early assertive moves toward Bahrain in the 1950s, the Shah decided to show restraint in this case. He declared that Bahrain should have the choice of three alternatives: to opt for incorporation by Iran, to affiliate with Iran as an autonomous entity, or to choose complete independence. The Shah expressed his readiness to accept the recommendations of the United Nations in this respect. Accordingly, a mission was dispatched to Bahrain by the United Nations Secretary General, and in May 1970, on the basis of its extensive interviews with various segments of the Bahrain population, it made a recommendation that Bahrain should become an independent state. Iran accepted this decision, and accordingly on August 14, 1971 Bahrain proclaimed its independence.

[43]For a discussion of this subject, see Amir Taheri, "Policies of Iran in the Persian Gulf Region," in Abbas Amirie, ed., *The Persian Gulf and Indian Ocean in International Politics* (Teheran, 1975), and R. K. Ramazani, "Iran's Search for Regional Cooperation," *Middle East Journal*, 30, (Spring 1976).

Iran, however, took a different attitude on the issue of the security of the Strait of Hormuz. Advancing a historical claim and strategic necessity, Iran proceeded to occupy three sparsely inhabited islands located close to its coast in the Strait of Hormuz on November 30, 1971. A similar consideration for the security of the Gulf area and its approaches led Iran to send an expeditionary force to Oman at the request of Sultan Qabus to help him fight the Aden-supported Marxist-oriented guerrillas in the province of Dhofar.

Iran's position on various Arab federation schemes in the Persian Gulf could best be described as "middle of the road." Iran opposed inclusion of Bahrain into any federative scheme in the Gulf and was pleased to see that Bahrain opted for full independence. On the other hand, Iran accepted and even welcomed the creation of the United Arab Emirates, composed of the small states of the Trucial Coast, as a device likely to strengthen these weak structures against possible internal or externally stimulated subversion. In strategic terms, Iran clearly regarded itself as an heir to Britain in the Gulf. While the Shah might have privately welcomed a stronger American presence in the area, publicly he opposed the presence of any major powers in the Gulf and even in the Indian Ocean. However, there was no doubt that he aimed at the establishment of an Iranian hegemony in the Gulf area, basing it on a realistic assumption that no other state in the Gulf region was capable of performing this function. With the impressive increase of its armaments level, Iran possessed the largest hovercraft fleet in the world and one of the largest helicopter forces. There was also a sizable increase in numbers and quality of the Iranian navy which from time to time participated in joint CENTO maneuvers in the Gulf-Indian Ocean area. Military visibility in the region was accompanied by intensive and skillful diplomacy aiming at the establishment of close and friendly relations with the United Arab Emirates and its component sheikhdoms, and also with Kuwait, Qatar, Bahrain, and Oman. Rulers of these small states were frequently invited as honored state guests to Teheran and were invariably asked to attend major Iranian military parades and shows. By the mid-1970s Iran was unmistakably in a position of hegemony in the Persian Gulf area.[44]

The Achaemenian Concept of Kingship

From the time of the assertion of the Shah's power over opposition in 1962, Iran's economic development, its oil policy, and its foreign policy could be called a story of amazing success. Much of it was due to the strong and intelligent leadership the country possessed. While this progress in the economic, social, and foreign policy fields was taking place, the political structure tended to veer toward greater authoritarianism. Neither the Shah nor his ministers tried to be hypocritical about it. As Prime Minister Amir Abbas Hoveyda put it, "The last thing Iran needs today is the Western type of democracy."[45] In saying this the prime minister was merely reflecting the basic philosophy of his ruler, who believed that at this period of rapid

---

[44]For a comprehensive review, see D. R. Tahtinen with the assistance of John Lenczowski, *Arms in the Indian Ocean: Interests and Challenges* (Washington, D.C., 1977).

[45]Personal interview with the author, August 1973.

and intensive development within the context of a changing and dangerous international situation Iran needed a strong leadership to exercise a tutelage over a people not yet ready for democratic institutions and processes and to aim at progress in every conceivable sphere of human activity. The Shah's tutelage idea—which could be compared to the political philosophy of Sun Yat-sen in China or Kemal Ataturk in Turkey—was reflected in the development of party politics in Iran. The Mellioun and Mardom parties representing the pro-government and loyal opposition trends were conceived as vehicles for the political education of the Iranians within the framework of full loyalty to the king and the existing monarchical institutions.

When a leader of a progressive circle of technocrats, Hassan Ali Mansour, was apppointed prime minister in 1964, the pro-government Mellioun party was replaced by a new party called Iran Novin, which was expected to reflect the opinion of better-educated, socially more progressive elements. Following the assassination of Mansour in January 1965, a career diplomat, Amir Abbas Hoveyda, was appointed prime minister, to hold this position for over a decade. Almost automatically Hoveyda became head of the Iran Novin party. In the meantime, the position of the loyal opposition party, Mardom, was becoming more and more difficult. It was supposed to engage in constructive criticism of the government policies but the definition of constructive criticism was gradually narrowing. A number of leaders in the Mardom party felt victimized by being placed in a somewhat artificial position to serve as a voice of dissent while in reality approving of the developments in Iran. As members of the opposition they tended to be automatically excluded from high government posts. This they believed to be a somewhat unwarranted punishment.

Finally, in a New Year's speech in March 1975, the Shah himself recognized the artificiality of this situation. He declared that the position of the Mardom party had become "impossible." Instead of dividing themselves into two groups all Iranians should join together to suport the Revolution of the Shah and the People, as the program of reforms inaugurated in 1963 was officially called. Consequently, he announced the abolition of the two parties and the launching of a new, single political organization to be called Rastakhiz (Resurgence) which would open its doors for active participation by members of both previous parties and by any Iranian willing to play a more active role in the political process in Iran.[46] The new party was expected to stress unity rather than the divisions among the Iranian people. Above all, however, there was the principle of leadership symbolized in the person of the monarch, which was to be the most vital ingredient of the political process in Iran.

The Iranian government sponsored three major events designed to propagate the idea of monarchical continuity and strength of the ruling institution in Iran.[47] These were the coronation of the Shah and Queen Farah on October 26, 1967, the ceremonies to commemorate the 2500th anniversary of the Iranian empire, held in

[46]Text in *Kayhan*, International Edition, March 8, 1975.

[47]For a discussion of the royal institution, see E. A. Bayne, *Persian Kingship in Transition* (New York, 1968); J. A. Bill, *The Politics of Iran; Groups, Classes, and Modernization* (Columbus, Ohio, 1972); and G. Lenczowski, "Political Process and Institutions in Iran: The Second Pahlavi Kingship," in Lenczowski, ed., *Iran under the Pahlavis*.

Persepolis in October 1971, and the celebration of fifty years of the Pahlavi dynasty in the jubilee year of 1975–1976. The Shah and the political elite of Iran were consciously reviving the ancient concept of Achaemenian kingship as a traditional institution capable of providing leadership for a program for modernization, and they expected to lead Iran to a position of strength and prominence in world affairs.

Revolution and Fall of the Monarchy

Yet with all these successes in domestic and foreign policies, the Iranian political system was subjected to serious strains that could briefly be called "the King's dilemma," namely, how to reconcile modernization in the social and economic sectors with a lack of corresponding progress in the political sector. Through the twenty-five years of the Shah's supremacy (since the fall of Premier Mossadegh in 1953), opposition to the system, though cowed, was never completely eliminated. Its three main components: religious leaders, the National Front, and the Communists, varied in strength and ultimate objectives but agreed on the immediate common goal of radically changing the political system. In terms of appeal to the masses, the Shii leaders—through regular contact with the praying multitudes in the mosques—had the highest mobilizing capacity. In terms of skillful clandestine operations, the Communists were the most experienced. The National Front leaders, on their part, offered the best articulation of demands for democratic freedoms and political participation.

Toward the close of 1977 these latent trends were intensified by three factors: abundance of oil-generated money, corruption, and the human rights slogans. While Iran as a whole greatly benefited from the $20 billion annual revenue which it was receiving on the average from oil in the later 1970s, the spending spree in which the government engaged produced an annual inflation of some 30 to 50 percent which victimized those strata of the population that could not quickly adjust their personal income to the rising level of prices. The stimulated economic activity, most of it government-sponsored, produced a class of "nouveau riche" contractors, often men of elastic standards, whose multimillion-dollar deals involved corruption in the highest echelons of the government. In addition, President Carter's emphasis on human rights, instead of chastizing the main violators, namely, the Communist states, in practice focused on those friends and allies of the United States that happened to have authoritarian regimes. In Iran, the tendency was to interpret this "crusade" as encouragement to dissenters.

As for Iran's government, it claimed to have started a policy of liberalization in 1976, before Carter's election. The Shah and his ministers conceded that, to ensure a peaceful transfer of power to Crown Prince Reza in the future, an orderly return to constitutionalism was desirable. Iran, the official argument ran, must be spared the tensions and dangers that Spain experienced after the death of General Franco. But, in practice, the evidence for liberalization was hard to come by.

While this discussion has thus far focused on the domestic aspects of the political situation, the foreign aspect also deserves attention. The year 1978 witnessed substantial Soviet advances in areas deemed vital to Iran's security. Thus in April 1978 a Marxist-oriented coup installed a new revolutionary regime in Afghanistan. That same spring massive Soviet and Cuban assistance to the radical government in Ethiopia against the Somali-supported Ogaden rebellion and the Eritrean liberation movement established a disturbing Soviet presence in the Horn of Africa. A militant pro-Soviet group, resorting to violence, took power in Southern Yemen. In Iran these events were viewed with increasing concern as an encircling movement. Consequently when latent dissent erupted into open defiance of the government at the beginning of 1978, strong suspicions were voiced about the synchronization of internal protest with implicit external pressures, the common objective of both being to bring down the monarchy, produce chaos, and prepare Iran for a Communist takeover.

Open defiance of the regime began on January 9, 1978, when religious dissenters influenced by Ayatollah Ghassem Shariatmadari clashed with police and troops in the holy city of Qum. In February, serious disorders took place in Tabriz, while numerous Iranian embassies abroad were repeatedly attacked by Iranian students often acting in collaboration with local Communist youth groups. Open encouragement to these violent outbreaks was provided by the exiled Ayatollah Rouhollah Khomeini from his sanctuary in Najaf in neighboring Iraq (and later from Paris.)

These violent protest demonstrations were substantially intensified in August. The burning—by arson—of a movie theater in Abadan, in which 430 people died, seriously aggravated the situation. The cabinet of Jamshid Amuzegar, an able technocrat, resigned, and the Shah asked Jafar Sharif-Emami, who was speaker of the Majlis and known for his close connections with the religious circles, to form a new government. Sharif-Emami announced a program designed, through various liberalization measures and increased attention to Islamic sensitivities, to meet the demands of the opposition.

These conciliatory moves, however, did not bring about the expected results. Instead of being appeased, the opposition became emboldened. Massive demonstrations abounding in slogans for the overthrow of the monarchy increased in size and intensity. Encouraged by their leaders, mobs usually attacked objects associated with secular modernization: banks, cabarets, liquor stores, luxury hotels, airline offices, and so on. To contain the rapidly spreading disorders, martial law was proclaimed on September 8. After an initial clash between the army and the demonstrators which cost many lives, the law was relaxed, but to no avail. Disorders were spreading; moreover, several massive strikes seriously undermined the functioning of the economy and public administration: 35,000 oil workers went on strike while voicing political demands in addition to asking for a raise in wages; many bazaar shops were closed; and some thirty government agencies (including Iranair) also engaged in work stoppage.

The Shah's attempt to explore the possibility of forming a coalition government with the participation of some National Front leaders such as Karim Sanjabi bore no fruit. Meanwhile, Ayatollah Khomeini, having left Iraq for Paris, was openly calling for the removal of the Shah and the formation of an Islamic republic.

To prevent complete chaos, the Shah appointed a military cabinet on November 6. Headed by the chief of the imperial staff, General Gholam Reza Azhari, the new government comprised the commanders of the army, air force, and navy as well as other leading generals, and a number of civilians. Its announced program consisted of three main points: the restoration of law and order, a curb on corruption, and free elections (previously promised) in the spring of 1979. Massive displays of force by the military in the main urban centers brought back a measure of tranquillity and caused some of the striking laborers and employees to resume their work. Simultaneously several dozen high officials—including former Prime Minister Hoveyda and former chief of SAVAK (the secret police), General Nematollah Nassiri—were arrested and charged with corruption.

Return to tranquillity was only partial: impressive numbers of workers and employees followed the oil workers by going on strike. They included among others thousands of teachers, editorial and technical personnel of newspapers (the latter in protest against censorship), and bank employees. With the beginning of the Shii holy month of Muharram (December 2) noted for its religious processions, a new wave of demonstrations swept the country. The army, subject to contradictory orders to avoid bloodshed and to stop riots, behaved inconsistently, alternating between toleration of certain demonstrations and violent suppression of others.

As the protest movement was gaining momentum, the Shah explored the possibility of forming a civilian cabinet that would be headed by some moderate opposition leader, with the hope that the political system would evolve into a constitutional monarchy. His attempt to enlist the cooperation of the National Front leader, Karim Sanjabi, failed. Sanjabi, who had made a brief trip to Paris to consult with Ayatollah Khomeini, refused upon his return to cooperate. Khomeini proved intransigent: he insisted on the abdication of the Shah, an end to the Pahlavi dynasty, and a proclamation of an Islamic republic. He also called for a general strike and urged soldiers to desert their military units.

December 10—the eve of the martyrdom of the Shii saint, Imam Hussein—saw a large anti-Shah demonstration in Teheran. Because the demonstration was peaceful and linked with the great religious holday, the army did not interfere. But the huge procession added significantly to the momentum of the protest movement.

While thus the situation in the country was slipping from government control, there were two important external developments. First, on November 19, Soviet President Brezhnev warned the United States against interfering in internal affairs of Iran. That same day, Secretary of State Cyrus Vance denied any intention of interfering and expressed the hope that the Soviet Union would also abstain from interference. The Soviet move was interpreted by Iranian and foreign observers as encouragement of the opposition and as a threat of possible counteraction should the Iranian army (assisted by numerous American weapons experts and advisers) attempt a coup.

The second development was the invitation addressed in early December by President Carter to former Undersecretary George Ball to offer advice regarding the situation in Iran. Ball's report, according to the press, recommended an early return to a constitutional government in Iran. But in Teheran (especially in the royal court) it was seen as a search for an alternative to the Shah's authority (and possibly to his incumbency), with attendant discouraging effect on the Shah's morale.

The Shah's efforts to find an opposition figure willing to cooperate finally bore fruit when the deputy leader of the National Front, Shahpour Bakhtiar, agreed to form a cabinet. Installed as prime minister on January 6, 1979, he pledged the launching of "a genuine social democracy" and an end to the corruption and abuses of the past. He also declared that, in foreign policy, Iran would no more be "a policeman of the Persian Gulf" and that it would leave the military "wing" of CENTO. From his sanctuary in Paris Khomeini promptly denounced him for having accepted the appointment from the Shah and called upon the people to disobey him. Similarly, the National Front expelled him from its ranks. Protest demonstrations calling for his (and the Shah's) death multiplied, and security in the country deteriorated. A high-ranking American oil executive, Paul Grimm, was killed by terrorists in the south, while—on Washington's recommendation—the forty thousand Americans serving in various technical capacities in Iran began a massive exodus, in fear for their safety.

On January 16, the Shah and the Empress with their children left for an ostensible vacation abroad, with dim prospects of a return. That same day a regency council headed by Seyyed Jalaleddin Tehrani was formed. It was reported that army commanders urged the Shah to remain; it was also reported that the United States Department of State encouraged the Shah to leave in the hope that a peaceful compromise might be found in his absence. Soon afterward, NATO's American deputy commander, General Robert E. Huyser, arrived in Teheran with a twofold mission of "extricating" from Iran certain sensitive American-made weapons so as to prevent their capture by enemy agents and of dissuading the Iranian military from attempting a pro-Shah coup. This second objective—together with the advice to the Shah to leave—was perhaps decisive in the subsequent unfolding of events. The army, until then loyal to the monarch, found less incentive to defend the empty rooms of the imperial palace than they would have had to defend the Shah himself had he stayed in his post. On the other hand, abstaining from a coup would spare Iran bloodshed and a possible civil war, but was bound to lead to a capitulation to the revolutionary forces.

The situation became aggravated when, on February 1, Khomeini (with the Bakhtiar cabinet's approval) returned in triumph to Teheran. A week later approximately one million demonstrators marched in the city demanding Bakhtiar's resignation. On February 11 a revolutionary militia launched an attack on the Shah's Imperial Guard ("The Immortals"), overcame it, seized key government buildings and the radio station, and proclaimed a victory of revolutionary forces. In this decisive moment General Abbas Qarabaghi, the last army chief of staff, proclaimed the neutrality of the armed forces. Massive desertions followed, and huge quantities of arms were seized by the rebels.

The next day, February 12, Khomeini appointed Mehdi Bazargan, a civilian noted for his religious feelings and democratic proclivities, as prime minister. Khomeini's three civilian aides, Abbas Amir Entezam, Dr. Ibrahim Yazdi, and Hashem Sabaghian, became deputy premiers. Two days later, armed bands, reportedly of leftist persuasion, attacked and temporarily occupied the American Embassy, wounding an American Marine guard and killing one of its Iranian employees.

People in Teheran and most of the country found themselves in the midst of revolutionary effervescence, with armed militias roaming the streets, looting and terrorizing the people. Supreme authority was exercised in an erratic way by Ayatollah Khomeini, first from a schoolhouse in Teheran and later from the mosque sanctuary in Qum. He was assisted by a supreme but largely anonymous committee of mullahs and civilians (the "Komiteh") and by similar local revolutionary committees. On their orders, some fifteen hundred persons associated with the Shah's regime (generals, officers, ministers, officials, and policemen) were arrested and subjected to consecutive summary trials. In the first few weeks some twenty generals of the imperial army were executed. So were also former Premier Hoveyda and former SAVAK chief Nassiri. This revolutionary justice brought not only repeated condemnations from abroad but also a serious tension between Khomeini and the liberal-leaning Premier Bazargan. Khomeini, furthermore, declared that he would seek extradition of the Shah from any country that sheltered him (Egypt, Morocco, and the Bahamas). By the same token, the Palestine Liberation Organization (PLO), whose leader, Yassir Arafat, visited Khomeini within a few days of the revolution, declared its intention to kidnap the Shah with a special squad created for this purpose.

On March 30, 1979, a referendum, carried out without safeguards to ensure secrecy of voting, resulted in a formal proclamation of an Islamic republic.

Bazargan's cabinet faced major challenges in trying to govern the country. On the domestic scene it had to cope with massive unemployment caused by the partial collapse of economic activity, with the anarchy engendered by the workers' control of a number of factories, with vindictive and erratic process of justice, with the presence of numerous armed bands and militias, and with the absence of uniformed police. The ad hoc coalition that brought down the Shah's government began to disintegrate into its religious, Communist, and liberal components. Marxist groups—the Tudeh and the Fedayan-e Khalq—repeatedly challenged the authority of both Khomeini and Bazargan.

There was, moreover, considerable uncertainty about the meaning of an Islamic republic, in particular about the effect such a system would have on the economy (with its prohibition of interest-taking, defined as usury), on corporal punishment according to the Sharia law, on the position of women, and on religious freedom. Bahais and Jews were the avowed targets of Khomeini's hostility, with the fate of Christians and Sunni Moslems also in question. Various ethnic minorities began rising in rebellion against the new government within a few weeks of the revolution. This was notably the case of the Kurds in Sanandaj and Naqadeh and Turkomans in Gonbad-e Qabous. There were also reports of unrest among the Arabs of Khuzistan and the Baluchis near Pakistan's border.

The new government revealed its foreign policy preferences soon after the seizure of power. These were: nonalignment (as contrasted with the Shah's pro-American stance), support for the PLO, hostility toward Israel (a ban proclaimed on oil exports to it), withdrawal from an active role in the Persian Gulf, and close relationships with Islamic states (especially with Libya because of its early support to Khomeini).

In the first weeks of the revolution, Iran's state machinery was in a state of advanced disintegration. The religious group around Khomeini had no skills suitable for governing a modern state; yet it imposed its will on, and partly paralyzed, the official government of Premier Bazargan. The army was demoralized after some sixty percent of its conscripts deserted and its top command underwent a bloody purge. Iran's borders were virtually defenseless. A major question was which political group among the contending religious, radical-leftist, and democratic forces was likely to emerge victorious in the chaos that followed the downfall of the monarchy.

CHAPTER VI

Afghanistan

Afghanistan was established as a separate and independent state in 1747 by Ahmed Shah, an Afghan general of the Iranian king, Nadir Shah. Ahmed Shah, a member of the Sadozai branch of the Durrani tribe, united under his rule not only Afghanistan as we know it today, but also Baluchistan, Kashmir, and Punjab. His capital was at Kandahar. Under his successors the capital was moved to Kabul and the frontiers of the state shrank. Indian provinces were lost and eventually became absorbed by the expanding British Empire. In 1809 the latter entered into the first agreements with Afghanistan in order to enlist her support against possible French or Iranian invasions of India.

Britain's interest in Afghanistan was based on strategic considerations. The main physical feature of Afghanistan is the Hindu Kush range, which passes from the northeast to the southwest through the whole length of the country. Hindu Kush is the watershed of two river systems, the Indus and the Oxus (Amu Daria), and the only natural frontier of India in the northwest. Britain had a vital interest in preventing any hostile power from dominating this great barrier. Ever since Napoleon planned a joint invasion of India with the Russians, British eyes have been on the Hindu Kush. The British had to choose between occupying the Hindu Kush and annexing Afghanistan to India or attempting to dominate the area indirectly by treating it as a satellite and a buffer state. For seventy years (1809–1879) British policy vacillated between these two alternatives. In contrast to the situation in neighboring Iran, in Afghanistan it was Britain who was on the offensive, while Russia either stood apart or, at most, tried to use the Iranians as her spearhead. Britain's overbearing policy led to two Afghan wars, the first in 1839–1842 and the second in 1878–1879. Both were caused by the pro-Russian policies of the Afghan rulers who were unwilling to subject themselves to British direction. During the first war the British conquered Kabul and captured Dost Mohammed, the great Emir and founder of the Barakzai dynasty (another branch of the dominant Durrani tribe). Then, having restored him to power, they secured his neutrality in the conflict between British and Russian interests.

In the second war the British occupied a larger part of the country, ousted the pro-Russian Emir Shir Ali, and in 1879 concluded the Treaty of Gandamak with his successor, Yakub. Yakub agreed to cede Khyber Pass to Britain and to accept

British control of his foreign relations in return for an annual subsidy of £60,000. An anti-British outbreak, however, complicated these arrangements and resulted in Yakub's abdication a few months later. On July 20, 1880, a final settlement was reached with Yakub's successor, Abdur Rahman (1880-1901): Britain transferred to him the control of the country and evacuated her troops, but retained the direction of Afghan foreign relations and pledged assistance against external aggression. This agreement was confirmed on March 21, 1905, with Emir Habibullah (1901-1919), to whom Britain extended, in addition, a yearly subsidy of £160,000. Thus, for four decades (1880-1920) Britain chose to exercise indirect control only. Afghanistan was free from British troops and enjoyed full internal independence, but her "friendly" ruler, subsidized by the government of India, was forbidden to have dealings with other powers than Britain.

Boundary Disputes

Inasmuch as Britain pledged to assist Afghanistan against external aggression, it was important to know where Afghan aboundaries lay. There was considerable doubt on this point, a doubt rendered more acute by the Russian advance in Central Asia in the 1870s and 1880s. By annexing Merv in 1884 Russia came dangerously close to Afghanistan, and by conquering the Panjdeh oasis she actually invaded Afghan territory. Britain's reaction to these moves was so strong that for a while there was talk of war, but in 1885 the two powers compromised and settled the major portion of the northern Afghan boundary. This agreement was supplemented in 1895 by exact delimitation of the Pamir boundary in the easternmost tip of Afghanistan. Two years earlier, in 1893, Britain and Afghanistan settled the Afghan-Indian boundary by the so-called Durand agreement.

The settlement of the boundaries was a positive achievement inasmuch as it removed an immediate cause of friction between the states directly concerned. But the boundaries thus established were bad and impractical. The major part of the northern boundary ran along the unprotected Oxus River or through a flat steppe, and therefore could not possibly be considered as a strategic frontier. Moreover, it split a single ethnic area in two, leaving on both sides the non-Afghan tribes of Turkomans, Uzbeks, and Tajiks, on whom Afghanistan's hold had always been tenuous. As to the southern boundary, it was better in the strategic sense, running as it did through the crests of mountains, but, unfortunately, it also divided a single ethnic area, leaving on the Indian side a few million Afghan-related tribes. The mountainous character of this borderland made effective control over them so much the more difficult.

Britain's control of Afghan foreign relations was resented by Russia. She accepted it, however, in the Anglo-Russian agreement of 1907, declaring that Afghanistan was outside her sphere of influence. During the First World War Afghanistan remained neutral, but, as we know, Emir Habibullah violated the nonintercourse pledge by receiving and parleying with the German mission under Niedermayer and Von Hentig. Mindful, however, of the proximity and power of British India, he did not dare to conclude an alliance with the Central powers.

Emancipation from British Tutelage

On February 20, 1919, Habibullah was killed by an assassin. Next day his brother, Nasrullah Khan, leader of the anti-British conservative party, was proclaimed emir by the mullahs and the tribes. This choice was challenged by Habibullah's younger son, Amanullah, then governor of Kabul, who with the aid of the army, overthrew Nasrullah and ascended the throne on February 27. One of his first steps was to sentence Nasrullah to death for alleged complicity in the murder of his father. This action aroused considerable anger in religious circles. Partly to silence domestic opposition and partly to profit from Britain's postwar weariness, Amanullah, in early May, proclaimed a Jihad against the British and ordered his army to invade India.

The Third Afghan War, as it was called, caused Britain considerable embarrassment. It came at the time of grave internal disturbances in the Punjab. An Indian nationalist, Obaydullah, known for his contacts with Berlin and Moscow, proclaimed himself head of the Provisional Government of India. In Peshawar, there was actually an attempted uprising. Native militiamen in the British service deserted their ranks and in some cases joined the enemy, while all along the Afghan border, the warlike Pathan tribes rallied around Amanullah. The British were ill-prepared to cope with this aggression in view of their postwar demobilization, but eventually they managed to gather 140,000 troops on the northwest frontier. This army, aided by air action over Kabul and Jalalabad, succeeded by the end of May in forcing the Afghans to retreat to their territory. Amanullah sued for an armistice, and it was granted to him. The British, who by that time were in a position to enter and occupy Afghanistan, refrained from doing so. It was not their intention to cause a complete disintegration of the Afghan state, which they desired to preserve as a buffer between Indian and Russia. Besides, this brief war had already cost the Indian treasury £16 million, and a military occupation would add heavy new burdens.

For these reasons, the British were glad to conclude with the Emir, on August 8, 1919, the Treaty of Rawalpindi. Despite her victory, Britain retreated from her hitherto privileged position by recognizing the complete independence of Afghanistan in internal and external affairs. This step was in keeping with the spirit of the times, but its political wisdom was debatable inasmuch as it rewarded the aggressor. Thereafter, Amanullah was able to claim victory over the British in obvious disregard of the military realities. This release from British control promptly set in motion a chain of events which Britain traditionally had tried to avoid. In the course of 1919, an Afghan mission went to Moscow and a Soviet mission was received in Kabul. Obaydullah, Mahendra Pratap, Barkatullah, and other Indian revolutionaries, who were in touch with the Soviet-sponsored Pan Hindu Revolutionary Committee at Tashkent, established a forward base on Afghan territory, and Amanullah rejected a British request for their expulsion. He further invited the Turkish general, Jemal Pasha, known for his hatred of Britain, to reorganize the Afghan army. Jemal's presence in Kabul encouraged anti-British attitudes and activities. The Afghans felt so self-confident as to demand that Britain modify the Treaty of Sèvres in favor of Turkey.

On February 28, 1921, Afghanistan and Soviet Russia concluded a treaty of friendship which provided for the exchange of diplomatic representatives and the opening of Soviet consulates in Herat, Maimena, Mazar-i-Sharif, Kandahar, and Ghazni; an annual subsidy of one million gold rubles and a supply of munitions to Afghanistan; the transfer of Panjdeh to Afghanistan; and the construction of the Kushk-Herat-Kandahar-Kabul telegraph line. This treaty was one of a series negotiated simultaneously by Russia with her southern neighbors, whose confidence and friendship she was seeking. It was a rebuff to the British, who at that time did not even possess a legation in Kabul, and it reaffirmed Afghan independence. While this treaty was being negotiated, an Afghan diplomatic mission made a tour of European capitals seeking recognition, inviting foreign technicians, and trying to establish commercial relations. This emancipation from traditional tutelage greatly irked Britain and when, during their visit in London, Afghan delegates insisted on conducting negotiations with the Foreign Office instead of the India Office, they were brusquely dismissed by the irate Lord Curzon, Britain's foreign secretary.

Amanullah's exuberance in his newly won ability to play Russia against Britain somewhat subsided when he learned of the Soviet conquest of Bukhara and of the rough treatment that the peoples of Central Asia had received from the Bolsheviks. More amenable to negotiations, he received a British mission in Kabul and on November 22, 1921, concluded a new treaty, which reaffirmed Afghan independence and the existing boundaries, provided for the exchange of diplomatic representatives and the establishment of British consulates, gave Afghanistan transit and customs facilities in India, and pledged mutual cooperation in maintaining tribal peace in frontier areas. On Britain's insistence, Amanullah agreed not to allow the establishment of Soviet consulates in Ghazni and Kandahar, two towns situated in dangerous proximity to the Indian border. On the other hand, in deference to Amanullah's wish, the treaty was concluded in the name of the British government and not on behalf of India,[1] and Britain agreed to address him as "His Majesty."

Afghan-Soviet Relations

On the whole, Amanullah leaned more heavily toward Russia than toward Britain. On March 1 and June 22, 1921, he concluded treaties of friendship with Turkey and Iran, respectively, and subsequently opened wide the gates to an influx of Turkish officers, teachers, and other experts. It will be recalled that at that time Turkey was actively cooperating with the Soviets and her relations with Britain were not good.

Amanullah displayed his pro-Soviet leanings in other instances as well. Thus he permitted the establishment of a branch of the Soviet state trading company (Vneshtorg), seriously considered a concession for a Soviet state bank, accepted the services of Russian experts in road surveys and construction, employed thirty Soviet instructors in the Afghan air force, and consented to the training of Afghan pilots in Tashkent. In 1926 he concluded with Russia a pact of neutrality and nonaggression, which was followed in 1927 by an agreement to establish an air line between Tashkent and Kabul. He also opened negotiations for a trade agreement.

Amanullah did not blindly give his body and soul to the Russians. On a few

[1]However, an Indian civil servant, Sir Henry Dobbs, negotiated it.

occasions his and their policies diverged. His ambition to pose as a defender of Islam and a champion of national self-determination fitted ill with the pattern of Soviet conquest of the neighboring khanates of Bukhara and Khiva. The emir of Bukhara, fleeing certain death at the hands of the Bolsheviks, took refuge in Afghan territory. Amanullah not only did not object to this but actually took an active interest in the Basmachi rebellion, which in 1922 seriously undermined Soviet power in Central Asia. Indeed, Amanullah went so far as to contemplate the creation of a Central Asian Confederacy under his own leadership. To this end he concentrated substantial forces along the northern border and established liaison with the Pan-Turanian leader, Enver Pasha. The Soviets demanded a declaration of neutrality and withdrawal of troops from the border regions. Amanullah complied, and Enver's death soon put an end to whatever plans these leaders had had regarding Central Asia. The Basmachi movement continued down to 1931.

In 1925 a quarrel broke out between the Afghan and Soviet governments over an island in the Oxus River. Finding that the matter was of minor importance, the Soviet government conceded the right of Afghanistan and withdrew its troops. With characteristic conceit, Amanullah's government claimed a major diplomatic victory. The fact of the matter was that, by making this truly negligible concession, Russia secured a diplomatic success which soon afterward paved the way for the above-mentioned neutrality pact and air agreement.

There is no doubt that, while maintaining the appearance of utmost correctness, Russia was consistently pursuing a slow but certain policy of penetration. She was, in the first place, taking full advantage of Amanullah's anti-British frame of mind to proffer various forms of collaboration, which the unstable ruler, believing himself very shrewd, accepted as a counterbalance to British influence. In the second place, Russia very skillfully exploited the fact that the northern part of Afghanistan was inhabited by Turkish-speaking minorities divided from their Soviet-governed brethren by an ill-protected and rather artificial boundary. And while the Soviets, in their own crude way, were paying a great deal of attention to their Central Asian possessions, the Kabul government, separated as it was from the Oxus by the powerful barrier of Hindu Kush, took slender interest in the development of Afghan Turkestan.

The Soviets, therefore, had a fertile field for propaganda. In the early twenties this propaganda had to overcome some difficulties that arose as a result of the rough handling of Afghan and Indian merchants in Bukhara and Tashkent by the Bolsheviks. The news of this treatment spread and did not help Soviet prestige, but later Russia agreed to compensate Afghan traders for their losses. While propaganda about Communist principles probably made little headway with the primitive Turkomans, Tajiks, and Uzbeks on the Afghan side of the border (and the Soviets did not stress Marxism too heavily), the road and railroad building, the telegraph connections, and the increased trade opportunities offered by the Soviets did not fail to cause favorable comment. The extension of Soviet railways to Kushk and Termez on the Afghan border helped stimulate mutual trade while serving Soviet strategic purposes. The essence of Soviet propaganda consisted in encouraging the growth of local autonomous or separatist movements, which could be used as a lever of pressure on the Afghan government in case of need. At the same time, Soviet economic penetration was bound to make Afghanistan's northern provinces more and more dependent on Russia both as a market and as a source of merchandise. This situation resembled that prevailing in northern Iran, and in both cases the mountain ranges separating the capital of the country from its northern provinces inexorably drove the latter into the arms of the Russians.

Afghan-British Relations

While Amanullah was no doubt aware of this situation, he did not consider it alarming enough to adopt countermeasures or to ally himself with Britain. On the contrary, his eyes were directed toward the turbulent borderland in the south, inhabited by native Pathan tribes. We have already mentioned that this tribal area was rather artificially divided by the Durand Line, which constituted the Afghan-Indian border. Another peculiarity was that the Pathan tribal area was not included within the administrative boundary of the government of India. British control over the area was exercised by a few scattered military outposts and political officers, and as such it was very slender. British policy with regard to the North-West Frontier Province oscillated between strictly limited commitments of the so-called "close border" policy and the more ambitious "forward movement."[2] In any case, there was always a considerable belt of mountainous territory between the last British outposts and the Afghan border, which was a virtual no man's land. Britain's reluctance to occupy this region and to subject it to the regular administration was based on the same premises that caused her to refrain from annexing Afghanistan proper. The effort and expense involved in the direct policing of these unhospitable and rugged lands would be disproportionate to the results obtained. This being the case, the rulers of Kabul claimed the right to oppose any manifestation of British control in the region. Yet some measure of control was needed, at least to protect the neighboring settled communities to the south from nomad raiding. In addition, the Afghan emirs wanted to extend their own influence over these tribes. This policy had both aggressive and defensive motivations. By favoring and subsidizing the tribes, the Afghan rulers could use them as a weapon against the British if necessary. Also as these tribes from across the border could be a major nuisance to Afghanistan herself and as their attitude could weigh heavily in domestic developments and dynastic rivalries in Kabul, it was of vital importance to Afghan rulers to cultivate their friendship.

Amanullah's conceit, coupled with his anti-British complex, led him to pursue a "pinprick" policy toward Britain through the instrumentality of these tribes, and, as a result, much of his own and British energy was devoted to this troublesome area.

Reforms and Rebellions

While trying to balance Soviet and British influences, Amanullah was also striving to Westernize his backward country. In principle, this was a commendable

[2]For a thorough discussion of the tribal problem, see Sir Kerr Fraser-Tytler, *Afghanistan: A Study of Political Developments in Central Asia* (London, 1950).

ambition, and, if successful, it could act as a deterrent to subversive doctrines or movements. But Amanullah had little understanding of Western civilization and attached undue importance to outward appearances. In an attempt to emulate Mustafa Kemal of Turkey, he promulgated, on April 9, 1923, a Fundamental Law, following which he issued a number of reform edicts aiming at the modernization of the country in every conceivable field.

To implement these reforms, Amanullah turned to foreign technicians and advisers of a number of nationalities. He gave preference to the Germans because, like Reza Shah in Iran, he sought the friendship of a "disinterested third power." This reliance on German technical aid proved to be an enduring factor in the interwar period. Even after his fall, the Germans continued to grow in numbers, providing teachers, military instructors, technicians, artisans, bank employees, nurses, doctors, and scientists. In 1924 a German school for teachers was established in Kabul. The Germans constructed paper and textile factories, built electrical plants, and flooded the Afghan market with electrical appliances and other goods. Colonel Christenn assumed the command of the Afghan Military Academy. In the thirties, with the advent of Hitler, this German penetration became more intensive, just as it did all over the Middle East. In 1935 a German scientific expedition explored the Hindu Kush, and in 1936 the Lufthansa established an air service between Berlin and Kabul.

Amanullah's reforms, especially those in the educational field, encountered considerable opposition among conservative circles. He had a forewarning of trouble when in March 1924 the Lame Mullah raised a rebellion in Khost in protest against the allegedly antireligious provisions of the new civil code. For ten months the mullah defied the authorities, and it cost the government much effort and money to restore order.

Instead of slowing down his reforms, Amanullah went ahead and in December 1927 embarked, with a large retinue, on a seven-month tour of Europe. Studiously avoiding New Delhi—another manifestation of his anti-Indian complex—he went straight to Bombay and from there proceeded to Italy, Germany, France, and England. He was received everywhere with the honors due a member of royalty, and negotiated, wherever he could, new pacts and agreements with an eye to enhancing Afghanistan's prestige and economic prosperity. On his return route, he paid a fortnight's visit to Moscow, during which the Russians undertook to supply him with thirteen airplanes and a quantity of munitions. He concluded his tour by a visit to Turkey and Iran, where his reformatory zeal experienced another upward surge. Upon his return, the king renewed his efforts to modernize the country. In a series of public speeches he outlined his program of reform, making frequent references to secular education and a new status for women. He thereby deepened the chasm between himself and the clergy, whose disapproval was becoming more and more pronounced.

Internal Crisis

On November 14, 1928, a tribal rebellion broke out. Encouraged by the mullahs and led by their conservative chieftains, the tribes rose one after another and within two months reduced the government to impotence. In the ensuing chaos, a Tajik highway robber nicknamed Bacha-i-Sakao ("'water-carrier's son'") gathered a body of tribal warriors and outlaws and on January 17, 1929, took the capital by storm. Three days earlier Amanullah had abdicated in favor of his elder brother, Inayatullah, and had fled to Kandahar. There he tried to organize resistance, but, failing to evoke popular response, he crossed the Indian border and went into exile in Europe.

In the critical days of the rebellion, the Soviet and Turkish ambassadors advised him strongly to fight to the bitter end and, should he be successful, to press his reforms. The Soviets proffered more than advice. Shortly before Amanullah's overthrow, his ambassador to Moscow, Ghulam Nabi, organized a military force on Soviet territory and, equipped and supplied by the Russians, led it into Afghanistan to rescue the king. He arrived too late, however, to change the course of events. The people of the north, who were very hostile to Amanullah, failed to rally to his banners, and after a few weeks Ghulam Nabi crossed back into Soviet territory. For several months the fate of Afghanistan hung in the balance. The destruction of the regime, however inadequate it had been, left a dangerous vacuum very tempting to foreign penetration. But neither Russia nor Britain was prepared at this juncture to divert its energies toward the conquest of Afghanistan.

Ascending the throne, Bacha-i-Sakao, or Habibullah Ghazi as he called himself, began a reign of terror. Foreign legations and many foreign residents were evacuated. Bacha-i-Sakao issued a proclamation canceling all Amanullah's reforms, thereby hoping to secure the approval of the clergy. But the mullahs were equally opposed to the usurper. Within a few months, the country was seething with restlessness, and the conditions were ripe for a counterrevolt. The opposition found a leader in the person of Mohammed Nadir Khan, a member of the Barakzai branch of the Durranis and Afghan ambassador to France. Nadir and his three brothers returned to Afghanistan in March 1929 and began recruiting a force of their own in the south. They did not limit their activities to Afghan territory but extended them to the no man's land south of the border. In fact, their army, in its final shape, was mainly composed of the Waziri and Mahsud tribes of India. With this tribal army Nadir and his brothers defeated Bacha's forces and entered Kabul. On October 16, 1929, Nadir Khan was proclaimed king of Afghanistan.

Nadir's accession provoked an angry outburst in the Soviet press, which accused Britain of using him as her instrument. The Red Shirt rebellion which broke out in the next year in Waziristan was interpreted by the British as partly resulting from Soviet machinations among the border tribes. The rebellion, coinciding with the anti-British crusade preached by the Fakir of Ipi, caused Britain considerable embarrassment at a time when she was anxious to restore normal relations with Afghanistan. Although the British disclaimed any responsibility for or connivance in Nadir's coup d'état, they greeted it with a feeling of great relief. In the hands of his irresponsible bandit predecessor, the strategic barrier of Hindu Kush was exposed to all sorts of dangers which could only result in great impairment to the security of India. Nadir Shah was a soldier[3] and a statesman of experience and maturity, acquainted with the West and thoroughly realistic.

[3]In 1919, during the Third Afghan War, Nadir Khan was a general in command of an army.

Nadir Shah

Despite the fact that he had gathered his army in British territory, Nadir Shah was not and never intended to be a British puppet. In fact, in the early twenties he had been a strong supporter of an aggressive tribal policy on the northwest frontier of India. With the assumption of royal power, however, he abandoned this adventurous course, partly because he genuinely desired good neighborly relations and partly because he believed in the pacification of tribes on both sides of the border as a prerequisite to an orderly government in Afghanistan.

His internal task was stupendous. The bandit's rule left complete anarchy in Afghanistan. The country was politically divided, and Nadir Shah's own tribal supporters looted the royal palace and the city upon entering the capital. Within four years Nadir did an impressive job of consolidation and reconstruction. In February 1932 he promulgated a new constitution which established a two-chamber assembly, the upper chamber of which was to consist of appointed notables. The constitution resembled the earlier Amanullah constitution but was devoid of the provisions irksome to the conservatives. Although the issuance of these new Fundamental Rules caused little change in the essentially autocratic and patriarchal political system, it symbolized Nadir's domestic policy as a whole. This policy was patterned where feasible on Western standards, but it was cautious, with no radical departures from the deeply ingrained habits of this Mohammedan country. There was nothing spectacular in Nadir's rule, except perhaps for two brusque executions, one of the captured Bacha-i-Sakao and another of Ghulam Nabi, who, upon his return from Russia, began to organize intrigues against the new king. As usual, the real authority in the country was divided between the ruler and the tribal chiefs. The latter were occasionally called for consultation in a Great Assembly (Loe Jirga), which was actually much more important than the bicameral legislature.

Nadir's four brothers filled the key positions in the government: Mohammed Hashim Khan was prime minister, a post he held for seventeen years from 1929 to 1946; Shah Wali Khan was minister in Paris and his special function was to keep an eye on the exiled Amanullah and his intrigues abroad; Mahmud Shah Khan was commander-in-chief of the Afghan army; and Aziz Khan was minister in Berlin, where he died of an assassin's bullet in the early 1930s. The posts of court minister, foreign minister, and minister of education were also held by the king's relatives.

Nadir's foreign policy was a traditional one, aiming at the preservation of balance between Britain and Russia, but it was more impartial than that of Amanullah. No more use was made of the services of Russian experts, but British experts were not invited either. The Germans and the nationals of other countires, France, Switzerland, Poland, and Czechoslovakia, were favored, and an impressive number of Turks were employed as military, medical, and educational advisers. These foreigners were engaged only as operating experts and not as key executives.

In 1930 a serious border incident threatened to disturb Afghan-Soviet relations. It was barely half a year after Nadir's assumption of power, and the northern provinces were not yet fully subjected to his control. A Basmachi leader from Ferghana and one of Enver's associates, Ibrahim Beg, took advantage of this state of affairs to establish a base in Afghan Turkestan from which he conducted guerrilla warfare against the Soviet authorities. The latter retaliated in June by sending a sizable force across the Oxus, forty miles deep into Afghan territory. This violation of Afghan territorial integrity spurred the Kabul government to action. In the fall of the same year a regular Afghan force crossed the Hindu Kush and after a brief fight drove Ibrahim Beg into Soviet territory. To avoid further possible misunderstandings with Moscow, Nadir Shah removed to the south the Bukharan and other Soviet refugees who had hitherto lived in Afghan Turkestan.

Nadir Shah's able rule was cut short by his assassination, in November 1933, by one of his personal enemies, yet the foundations he had laid were so solid that his twenty-year-old son, Mohammed Zahir Shah, succeeded to the throne without incident. Under the guidance of his paternal uncles, the new ruler continued his father's cautious and realistic policies. In 1937 Afghanistan joined with Iran, Iraq, and Turkey in the Saadabad pact. In the course of the next year Afghan-British relations were exposed to temporary tension as a result of the Shami Pir rebellion. Shami Pir, in an attempt to restore Amanullah, rallied a tribal force on the Indian side of the border and invaded Afghanistan. He was defeated by the government troops, and the British did their best to curb the rebellion on their side of the border. No ill feelings between Britain and Afghanistan resulted from this episode.

The Second World War and After

During the Second World War Afghanistan remained neutral. This neutrality was exposed to a severe strain when, in 1941, following their occupation of Iran, Britain and Russia asked Afghanistan to surrender all the Axis nationals resident in her territory. A Loe Jirga of tribal chieftains was called and, after a heated debate, it endorsed the government's willingness to comply with the Allied request. This realistic decision spared Afghanistan the treatment which Iran had incurred by rejecting similar Allied demands.

The war brought a serious dislocation to Afghan economy because Russia, hitherto the principal supplier of manufactured goods, was unable to export. This made Afghanistan largely dependent upon imports from India, which, in turn, resulted in increased political dependence on Britain. But the British very tactfully refrained from exploiting their superiority. By 1944 Afghan fears of British supremacy had receded to such a degree than an agreement was reached between the two governments for the training of Afghan army officers in India. Two hundred officers were sent to British training centers, and negotiations were opened for the delivery of British surplus arms after the war.[4] This change of attitude was also reflected in the increased willingness of Afghans to engage British experts in such fields as education, radio, and textiles. The British Council[5] began to function in Kabul, and British schoolmasters were invited to organize the fourth foreign secondary school

[4]For accounts of this period, see Sir Giles Squire, "Recent Progress in Afghanistan," *Royal Central Asian Journal* (Jan. 1950); Prince Peter of Greece, "Post-War Developments in Afghanistan," *R.C.A.J.*, (July–Oct. 1947); and M. Philips Price, "A Visit to Afghanistan," *R.C.A.J.* (April 1949).

[5]An organization dedicated to the spread of British culture abroad.

in the capital, the other three being French, German, and American. This growing confidence found expression in the mutual raising of their diplomatic missions to the rank of embassies in 1948.

Although Afghanistan suffered some economic inconveniences during the war, she was at the same time able to build up a considerable dollar balance as a result of the export of Persian lambskins (karakul) to the United States. In fact, for a number of years, but especially in wartime, Afghanistan enjoyed a monopoly in this field, her only competitor, Russia, having seriously dislocated production as a result of forced collectivization and an ensuing slaughtering of sheep by reluctant peasants. Thus, right after the war Afghanistan was able to plan certain public works urgently needed to raise the standard of living of her population. This was fortunate because there was a growing demand for reform, stimulated by increased contact with Westerners and by knowledge of Soviet achievements in Central Asia. The British had not been the only ones to disseminate their culture during the war; Soviet authorities had organized visits of Afghan intellectuals to Tashkent and did not miss an opportunity to impress them with the ''superiority'' of their system.

Under these circumstances, the resignation of the conservative prime minister, Hashim Khan, and his replacement in 1946 by a younger brother, Mahmud Shah Khan, was welcomed as a sign of a more liberal trend. One of the first acts of the new prime minister was to grant amnesty to political prisoners. This was followed by such acts as the inauguration of the first university in Kabul (1946) and the enlargement of the network of schools. Even some girls' schools were started, despite the grumbling of the mullahs. To cope with this dangerous clerical opposition, the government rather shrewdly opened a state college for future mullahs, hoping thereby to imbue the new generation of clergy with more liberal ideas. All these moves were, however, gradual and cautious, and despite reform Afghanistan remained one of the most backward Moslem countries, with no unveiled women to be seen in the streets and with the majority of people wearing oriental garb.[6]

Economic Needs

Economic problems towered above everything else. Despite the dollar balance accumulated in wartime, the country remained essentially poor, two-thirds of its population leading a pastoral life in rather barren hilly areas. It was clear that if Afghanistan wished to achieve greater material progress she needed to develop other exports than karakul and fruit. Karakul exports had suffered a serious setback after the war as a result of competition from South-West Africa and the Soviet Union.[7]

Under these circumstances, Afghanistan hopefully turned toward the United States. The latter had three characteristics which attracted the Afghans: it had technical know-how, it was wealthy, and it was politically disinterested. In 1946 Afghanistan engaged the Morrison-Knudsen Corporation of Boise, Idaho, to carry

[6]For a description of postwar social conditions in Afghanistan, see Arthur V. Huffman, ''The Administrative and Social Structure of Afghan Life,'' R.C.A.J. (Jan. 1951).

[7]In this connection, see Peter G. Franck, ''Problems of Economic Development in Afghanistan,'' Middle East Journal, 3 (July and Oct. 1949).

out various technical projects such as the construction of roads, bridges, dams, electrical plants, and irrigation canals. Of these, a road linking Kabul with Kandahar and regulation of the Helmand River were the most noteworthy projects. The latter, incidentally, gave rise to a quarrel with Iran, in whose territory the Helmand empties; Iran feared that the damming of the river would divert much-needed waters from the Iranian Seistan oasis. An American oil firm, Inland Exploration Company, prospected in the country, but so far the results have been modest. Negotiations were inaugurated with Trans World Airways to establish regular air communications and connections between Kabul and the outer world. In 1948 Afghan and American legations were elevated to embassies (diplomatic relations between the two countries had been established in 1943). Also in 1948 the Afghan minister of economics, Abdul Mejid Khan, visited the United States seeking a loan and technical assistance. His visit was successful. In 1949 the Export-Import Bank of the United States granted Afghanistan a $21 million loan for development purposes. The Afghan government also requested the World Bank to lend financial aid, and there was some likelihood that this American-influenced institution would favor its application. Although Afghanistan did not declare war on the Axis, she was admitted to the United Nations in 1946. Thereafter the United Nations took active interest in Afghanistan's development, and in 1950 a mission of economic experts was sent from Lake Success to Kabul to investigate Afghan needs under the technical assistance program.

Afghan-Soviet relations during and after the war were generally correct. A few outstanding boundary problems, such as the ownership of certain islands on the Oxus and the water rights in the Kushk oasis, were settled amicably by an Afghan-Soviet boundary commission on September 29, 1948. The Oxus boundary was fixed as the *thalweg* of the river. Trade between both countries was gradually revived, Russia exporting sugar, cotton goods, and petroleum and purchasing Afghan wool. But no Soviet trade agencies were permitted to operate in Afghanistan and no Afghan traders were allowed to enter Soviet territory. The exchange of goods was made at fixed points of the frontier, with not much opportunity for political penetration. In 1950 both countries concluded a trade agreement, one of a series which Russia was then negotiating with her southern neighbors. The Afghan government, fully aware of the technical and agricultural progress made in Soviet Central Asia, began to pay more attention than before to the development of Afghan Turkestan. Fears that improved conditions in Russia would contrast with the poverty and backwardness of Afghanistan were well founded, but the danger was somewhat lessened by the fact that Afghan Turkestan—the area most exposed to Soviet infiltration—was underpopulated and the land question there was never acute. In fact, the government was interested in transferring some of the nomadic Afghans from the south to farm the uncultivated lands in the north. Moreover, in contrast to many other Moslem countries, Afghanistan did not suffer from great differences in wealth. The country was generally poor, but very few beggars were in evidence. True enough, Russia did not renounce her revolutionary schemes and continued to send her agents across the border partly to operate in Afghanistan and partly to reach

Pakistan and India. The effects of Communist propaganda on the Afghans could not be easily measured,[8] but one should bear in mind the fact that Uzbeks, Tajiks, and Turkomans lived on both sides of the border and that those under Soviet rule were being drawn into a major social and economic experiment while their southern brethren continued a rather lethargic existence under the primitive conditions of slow-moving eastern society. The movement of refugees continued to be mostly in a southward direction, and their tales of oppression, secret police surveillance, and ruthlessness undid much of the Soviet propaganda. With all this, it was clear that should Russia choose to invade Afghanistan, she could do it with relative ease. The Afghan army was obviously not in a position to oppose a great power, and its role was limited to internal policing. Likewise, the Hindu Kush was no longer a formidable obstacle to a modern army as it had been in the past, and it would take only a matter of days for the Soviet troops to emerge on the frontier of Pakistan and Kashmir.

The end of British rule in India in August 1947 posed new and perplexing problems to the "Guardians of the Indu Kush." The long-feared might of Britain was replaced by two native and relatively weak countries. To Afghanistan, this meant a lessening of her external security, and she automatically became more exposed to Soviet pressure. To make matters worse, Afghan-Pakistan relations suffered serious aggravation from the very beginning. When Pakistan was about to be created, the Kabul government demanded a plebiscite in the North-West Frontier Province to determine the future allegiance of several million Pathans residing in the area. This was refused by Pakistani leaders. As a result, the no man's land south of the Durand Line was inherited by Pakistan. Afghanistan then began to advocate the creation of an independent state of Pakhtunistan (or Pushtunistan). A number of frontier incidents occurred and feeling ran high on both sides of the border between 1947 and 1949.

By 1950, however, this conflict showed signs of temporary abatement, owing to some extent to restraining British influence on both governments. Despite Pakistan's emancipation, British intelligence officers continued to be employed in the North-West Frontier Province, and Pakistan's political agent in Quetta was a Britisher. The creation of an independent Moslem state south of Afghanistan deprived Afghan extremists and such borderland troublemakers as the Fakir of Ipi of the time-tested anti-infidel slogans. On the otherhand, Pakistan, as a dominion, continued her association with the British Commonwealth. Britain, therefore, had a continuing interest in the political destinies of the Hindu Kush.

With reference to the East-West conflict, it should be pointed out that Russia was never greatly interested in Afghanistan per se. She always treated this remote country as an alternate invasion route to the subcontinent of India. In 1950–1951 she seemed to be bent on enveloping India from the east, through China and Burma. This perhaps explains why there was a lull on the Afghan front.

---

[8]According to the Afghan foreign minister, one of the captured Soviet agents, when interrogated by Afghan police, bitterly complained: "The Afghans are so stupid, they do not even understand what I am driving at." (See *R.C.A.J.*, Jan. 1950, p. 15.)

Afghanistan between East and West

In early September 1953, Mahmud Shah Khan resigned as prime minister after seven years in office. His replacement by General Mohammed Daoud Khan, hitherto minister of defense and interior, brought no appreciable change in the character of the Afghan government, which remained essentially paternalistic. It appeared, however, that the new premier was inclined to press with greater vigor than his predecessor the Pakhtunistan issue between his country and Pakistan. On December 28, 1953, he asked Britain to agree to a revision of the Treaty of Kabul of 1921, in which the Durand Line had been confirmed as the boundary between Afghanistan and British India. Legally, it was an unusual procedure, inasmuch as on August 15, 1947, Britain had been succeeded by Pakistan as a sovereign power south of Afghanistan. Politically, however, it meant a reassertion by the Kabul government of its interest in the disputed border area. Although somewhat pushed into the background during the last years of Mahmud Khan's ministry, the Pakhtunistan issue continued to impede normalization of the Afghan-Pakistani relationship. The Afghans held to their basic view that the Pathans, seven million strong (in reality they probably did not exceed two and a half million), had a right to sovereign existence as a state of Pakhtunistan, which would embrace the territory between the southern Afghan boundary and the Indus River.

How far south this territory should extend was a moot question. If literally interpreted, the expression "between Afghanistan and Indus" would mean the major part of Pakistan and would include Pakistan's capital, Karachi, as well as Baluchistan, a province bordering on Iran and the Indian Ocean. Such a claim would have some slight historical justification inasmuch as the short-lived empire of Afghanistan's founder, Ahmed Shah Durrani, did indeed extend that far south. The Afghans, to be sure, never defined the extent of their territorial claims (acting as agent for the would-be Pakhtunistan), but their official pronouncements and pamphlets contained wistful references to the historical past as well as to the necessity of obtaining access to the sea for their landlocked country. In promoting the Pakhtunistan scheme, the Afghans stressed two points: that they themselves did not covet the area in question but wanted to see it an independent state and that there should be a plebiscite to determine the wishes of the Pathans. It is noteworthy, however, that, although a substantial number of the latter inhabited Afghan territory, the Kabul government did not envisage a plebiscite on their side of the border. The issue was further confounded by the tendency of Afghan propaganda to identify two-thirds of Afghanistan's population as Pathans (or Pakhtuns), thus removing any distinction, historical or social, between them and the population of the contested area. On its part, Pakistan rejected any idea of a plebiscite in its territory.

The simmering Pakhtunistan issue came to a head late in March 1955, when the government of Pakistan announced its plan to abolish the traditional political divisions within the country and to unite all of Western Pakistan into a single province by May 31. Afghan reaction to this measure was prompt and negative. Broadcasting from Radio Kabul on March 29, Prime Minister Mohammed Daoud Khan denounced Pakistan's decision as a hostile move, warning Karachi of the "grave consequences" likely to ensue if Pakistan persisted in its plan. The next day a mob estimated at 15,000 persons attacked and plundered the Pakistani embassy in Kabul, destroying public and private property and defiling Pakistan's flag. Similar attacks occurred shortly afterward against Pakistani consulates in Jalalabad and Kandahar. Afghan police did not try to prevent these demonstrations; rather, according to some reports, they actually helped the assailants. The news of these outrages provoked widespread indignation in Pakistan, which, in turn, expressed itself in an assault on the Afghan conulate in Peshawar on April 1. Pakistan demanded official apology and "honorable amends," recalled its diplomatic and consular representatives from Afghanistan, and closed the border to commercial traffic between the two countries. Tempers rose on both sides, and a month later report of a "general mobilization" in Afghanistan was circulated in Karachi.

In the meantime Egypt and Saudi Arabia had offered to mediate the dispute, and by mid-May their offer was accepted by both sides. Subsequently a Saudi prince, Emir Musaid ibn Abdur Rahman, and an Egyptian envoy arrived in Kabul to end the conflict between the two Moslem powers. Soon Turkey and Iraq, both recent signatories of the Baghdad Pact, lent their good offices also, as a result of which Kabul in the early summer of 1955 witnessed intense diplomatic activity in which the political backgrounds of the mediators (neutralist and pro-Western, respectively) added new complications to the already difficult controversy. It should be pointed out, however, that the mediator's task was technically limited to the dispute over the insult to the flag and damage to property, inasmuch as Pakistan had accepted mediation only on condition that the issue of Pakhtunistan be kept out of the discussions.

Although these attempts at mediation virtually broke down in June (despite the vaguely optimistic communique of the Saudi mediator), the dispute was concluded by early autumn. In a ceremony in Kabul on September 13 Afghanistan's foreign minister, Sardar Naim Khan, hoisted Pakistan's flag on the embassy's building, thus satisfying Pakistani honor. In return, Pakistan lifted the ban on the movement of goods across the border. This ban, incidentally, had caused landlocked Afghanistan considerable inconvenience, exposing it to major shortages of gasoline, cement, and textiles. It proved once again how vulnerable Afghanistan was in this respect and how effectively Pakistan could use its control of access routes to Afghanistan as an instrument of pressure.

It is not surprising, therefore, that, with the basic issue of Pakhtunistan still unsolved, Afghanistan did not cease its agitation for independence for and a plebiscite in the border area. On November 19, Pakistan's prime minister, Chaudry Mohammed Ali, publicly denounced the Afghan campaign of infiltration, sabotage, and propaganda in the land of the Pathans. His declaration coincided with the five-day-long session of the Loe Jirga, which met in Kabul on November 15 to consider vital national issues. According to established tradition, this grand assembly of Afghan chieftains meets very seldom and only on occasions when issues of exceptional importance, such as war, peace, or some basic reorientation in foreign policy, are involved. Its last previous meeting had been in 1941, when it was called to decide the question of Afghanistan's position in the war.

The present session of the Loe Jirga was obviously connected with the dispute with Pakistan. Opening the session, Premier Daoud Khan declared that the "balance of power between Pakistan and Afghanistan has been destroyed by Pakistan's military alliance with the United States."[9] He then placed two questions before the assembly: (1) Should Afghanistan continue to demand a plebiscite in the disputed Pathan area? (2) Should Afghanistan take steps to restore the balance of power between itself and Pakistan? On November 20 the five hundred members of the Loe Jirga passed three resolutions, the first fully supporting Daoud's demand for a plebiscite, the second authorizing the government to "find ways and means of returning to the balance of power that was upset by Pakistan's decision to accept arms aid from the United States,"[10] and the third refusing to recognize Pakhtunistan as part of Pakistan. The intent of these deliberations was clear: inasmuch as the Afghans had not renounced their ambitions in the borderland and yet had found that Pakistan, due to its ties with America, would have the means to frustrate their plans, they were to turn to Russia for support and assistance.

From the time of this momentous decision events began to move swiftly on the Afghan scene. Exactly a month after the Loe Jirga's session, on December 15, two principal leaders of the Soviet Union, Premier Nikolai A. Bulganin and Communist Party Secretary Nikita S. Khrushchev, arrived in Kabul on a state visit, thus concluding their extended tour of Asian countries. Unprecedented in the annals of Russian-Afghan relations, this visit was in tune with the new Soviet policy of exploiting such psychological and political differences as existed between the West and Asian nations and of wooing the latter by promises of aid in their development. During their stay in the Afghan capital the Soviet leaders publicly expressed their support of Afghan views regarding Pakhtunistan and pledged economic and technical assistance to the Kabul government. No official mention was made of arms supplies, but it would not be surprising if these were on the agenda of the Soviet-Afghan conversations. In fact, there had been earlier indications that Afghanistan might import arms either from Russia or from her satellites: a year before an Afghan military mission had visited Czechoslovakia, presumably in search of weapons, and on November 1, 1955, the Afghan ambassador in Cairo had declared that if Afghanistan did not receive arms from the West it would be obliged to seek them in the Soviet Union. The Soviet visit ended with the signing of three documents. The first contained a Soviet pledge to extend a credit of $100 million to Afghanistan, to be implemented by a separate agreement. The second contained a joint Soviet-Afghan statement expressing support for the principles of peaceful coexistence and self-determination, with specific reference to the decisions of the Bandung conference, and for world peace and the admission of Communist China to the United Nations. The third was a protocol extending the 1931 Soviet-Afghan treaty of neutrality and nonaggression for the next ten years, with automatic renewal every year afterward and the possibility of termination by either party on six months' notice.

The basic pattern established in 1955 in Soviet-Afghan relations continued

[9]*New York Times*, Nov. 16, 1955.
[10]*Ibid.*, Nov. 22, 1955.

through the early 1960s. It consisted of economic and technical aid agreements, which multiplied as time went on, of increased cultural exchanges, and of occasional mutual visits of chiefs of state and government.

By 1960 the total amount of Soviet aid to Afghanistan exceeded $250 million. Granted at a low interest rate, these Soviet loans were, as a rule, extended in kind rather than in cash and included all sorts of machinery, vehicles, materials, spare parts, and services. The Soviet Union helped Afghanistan in launching a variety of projects, such as the grain silos in Pul-i-Khumri and Kabul; mills; a hospital in Jalalabad; oil storage tanks in Kabul, Herat, Mazar-i-Sharif, and Kilif; oil prospecting in the northern provinces (resulting in a discovery in May 1960); an oil pipeline between Mazar-i-Sharif and Termez (the latter in Soviet territory); roads, municipal utilities in Kabul; and the Jalalabad project on the Kabul River to provide hydroelectric power and irrigation for about 120 miles of valley land. The pipeline bringing Soviet oil to Afghan territory was especially significant because, while catering to a major need of Afghan economy, it made Afghanistan dependent on the Soviet Union. In addition, Russia also provided experts, and by the early 1960s several hundred Soviet and satellite technicians were employed in Afghanistan. Economic aid was accompanied by Soviet and Czechoslovak arms deliveries, which began in 1956 and increased in quantity as time went on.[11]

Soviet-Afghan cultural exchanges were carried on through many media. Visits of professors and writers, scholarships to Afghan students in the Soviet Union, exhibits of art, Soviet circus shows and concerts, and sports contests marked the steady progress of the Soviet cultural offensive. These Soviet "cultural" demonstrations tended to be on the showy side, catering to popular rather than refined tastes. Moreover, a standard Soviet procedure (time tested in other underdeveloped countries) was to organize visits to Russia of fairly large delegations of Afghan officials and other professional groups. These guided tours were designed to impress the visitors with the material and social achievements of the Soviet Union. They abounded in visits to model factories, agricultural experimental stations, museums, and other carefully selected institutions. Sometimes the itinerary included a visit to some Islamic center in Soviet Asia, where properly coached local Moslem functionaries (probably on the payroll of MVD[12]) invariably asserted to their visitors that their religion enjoyed not only complete freedom in the Soviet fatherland but also special support of the state. How convincing all of this was to the Afghan visitors is hard to judge. In all likelihood the Afghans had some suspicion and distrust of Soviet motives. On the other hand, one should not underestimate the impact that the hand-picked Soviet technical achievements could, and probably did, make on the half-tutored minds of many younger Afghans, for whom such a visit to

---

[11]For more detailed data on Soviet-Afghan economic relations, see R. K. Ramazani, "Afghanistan and the U.S.S.R.," *Middle East Journal* (Spring 1958); Joseph S. Berliner, *Soviet Economic Aid: The New Aid and Trade Policy in Underdeveloped Countries* (New York, 1958); and Peter G. Franck, *Afghanistan between East and West*, a pamphlet in the series "The Economics of Competitive Coexistence," National Planning Association (Washington, D.C., 1960).

[12]An abbreviation commonly used in the 1940s and 1950s for the Soviet secret police. The latter's official name has changed several times since the revolution. In chronological sequence the abbreviations were Cheka, GPU, OGPU, NKVD, NKGB, MVD, MGB, and KGB.

the powerful Russian neighbor gave perhaps the only opportunity of foreign travel they had experienced. If we add the fact that such Soviet tours provided the visitors with luxurious living (by Afghan standards) in hotels and guesthouses for periods up to a few weeks and that as such they were a not-unattractive vacation, one must conclude that they constituted a valuable weapon in the Soviet propaganda arsenal.

The intensification of the economic aid and cultural exchanges between the two countries was accompanied by a greater frequency of visits of Soviet dignitaries in Afghanistan and Afghan officials in Russia. Premier Mohammed Daoud Khan visited Moscow in October 1956, following the conclusion of military arms agreements with Russia and Czechoslovakia in August of that year, and again in May 1959. In July 1957, King Mohammed Zahir Shah paid a state visit to the Soviet Union, and in the same year Premier Daoud was a guest in two other Communist capitals, Prague and Peking. Soviet and satellite leaders reciprocated: in October 1958, Chairman of the Presidium of the USSR Klimenti Y. Voroshilov was received in Kabul, where he signed with Afghan leaders an agreement providing for a new substantial loan of 120 million rubles ($30 million) for development projects. In March 1960, Premier Khrushchev arrived in Afghanistan for his second state visit, announcing a Soviet gift of 50,000 tons of wheat. Interspersed between these major meetings were the visits of such Soviet bloc dignitaries as Premier Viliam Siroky of Czechoslovakia, Premier Joseph Cyrankiewicz of Poland, and Chinese Deputy Premier and Foreign Minister Chen Yi.

In the public statements made by Soviet leaders on these occasions, four major themes were invariably stressed: support of Afghan claims to Pakhtunistan, attack on Western-Asian alliances, reassertion of the principle of coexistence, and the contrast between "unselfish" Soviet aid and "exploitative" capitalist aid.

Despite the multiplicity of contacts between Afghanistan and the Soviet bloc, Afghan rulers persisted in their assertions that no harm, moral or political, was being done to their country as a result of these close relations and that their policy was that of strict neutralism. To prove these assertions they pointed to the continuous maintenance of economic and cultural relations with the Western world, which was, indeed, a fact, albeit these relations have been on a lesser scale than their contacts with the Soviet bloc. More specifically, Afghanistan has been willing to receive American technical and economic aid. The latter, more modest than Soviet assistance in terms of the total amounts granted, tended to be channeled primarily toward the development of the valley of the Helmand River. The river was to be dammed, the valley irrigated, and nomads settled in the newly reclaimed lands. Rather unfortunately the execution of this project (begun soon after the end of World War II) encountered numerous obstacles due to certain technical and psychological miscalculations. It appears that American experts were inclined to take too much for granted with regard to both the cooperation of the Afghan authorities and the response of the about-to-be-settled nomads. The nomads' interest in embracing a new, agricultural way of life was lukewarm. New settlers had frequently to be recruited among farmers from other, more crowded, areas, but these farmers were not always properly instructed in how to deal with the soil and water of the newly acquired properties. Salination of the land, partly due to the farmers' ignorance and neglect and partly to the failure of the Afghan government to provide adequate drainage facilities, threatened to render useless sizable tracts of the reclaimed territory. Despite the investment of more than $100 million in this project (about half of which had come from American funds), the results did not meet initial expectations, and by 1960 only 13,000 persons had been resettled, representing a small fraction of the number originally anticipated.

American assistance was not limited to the Helmand project. It included other endeavors, such as road and airport building and the training of Afghan technicians. By midsummer of 1961 its total reached $180 million. In all probability the American-sponsored projects were sound as regards the basic economic needs of the country. They tended to contrast with the Soviet works and achievements in Afghanistan in that they were often less showy and had a lesser immediate impact on the life of the population. To a minority of properly educated and unbiased Afghans this American approach might have appeared sincere, honest, and, therefore, commendable. To the majority of the populace, Soviet projects were more visible and tangible, thus assuring Russia the propaganda advantage. As in so many underdeveloped and politically sensitive areas, the United States faced the dilemma of whether or not to compete with the Russians on the latter's own terms. In Afghanistan the United States apparently leaned toward a policy of not imitating the Russians. Although fraught with certain risks, such a policy could validly be based on the argument that in the long run fleeting popular applause did not matter too much. Moreover, one could also advance the thesis that in a virtually absolutist monarchy of a patriarchal type—such as Afghanistan—public opinion was not mature and could easily be manipulated by the government. Consequently, it would be erroneous to base one's economic policy toward such a country on the mercurial manifestations of popular approval or disapproval.

The brief (six-hour) visit that President Eisenhower paid to King Mohammed Zahir in Kabul on December 9, 1959, could be considered as a case in point. The visit was part of the tour of Asian countries the President had made in that month to show American interest and good will toward a number of freshly emancipated nations. The reception accorded Mr. Eisenhower in Kabul was most cordial, both on the official as well as on the popular level. Foreign observers estimated that the crowds cheering the President were about as large as those cheering Mr. Khrushchev on his visit to Kabul three months later. In both cases the people seemed to be transported by joy at seeing the distinguished guests visit their capital. Was this enthusiasm genuine or government-generated? Was the attitude of the Afghans impartially friendly both toward their frightfully powerful northern neighbor and distant America? Was it perhaps a natural expression of Afghan courtesy mixed with understandable curiosity? Or was it a clever dissimulation of one's real feelings to prove one's ostensibly neutral conduct? While no easy answer can be found for these questions, the very uncertainty which popular manifestations of welcome and enthusiasm pose seem to confirm the thesis that to base one's policy merely on expectations of popular response is basing it on a slender reed indeed.

The general harmony in American-Afghan relations underwent a slight strain when it was learned that the American U2 reconnaissance plane which crashed in

the Soviet Union in May 1960 had flown without authorization over Afghan territory. The Afghan government lodged protests both with the United States and
Pakistan against the violation of its air space. However, no basic change in Afghan
attitudes toward Washington could be noted. In fact, the Afghan government
seemed rather solicitous to obtain further American aid in connection with its
second Five-Year Plan scheduled to begin in September 1961.

Afghanistan occupied a somewhat paradoxical position among the states adjacent
to the Soviet Union. These states, following World War II, have either been converted into Soviet satellites or, fearing such a fate, have aligned themselves with the
West to preserve their independence and territorial integrity. As a rule, neutralism
has been a luxury the states of this borderland believed they could not afford,
leaving it to countries more distant from Russia to practice. Afghanistan was an
exception to this general trend, and its "different" policies seemed to originate
largely in its continuous friction with its southern neighbor, Pakistan. The existence
of this friction greatly facilitated Moscow's good relations with Afghanistan.

Premier Daoud's First Decade: A Balance Sheet

Mohammed Daoud Khan remained in power for a decade between 1953 and
1963. A dominant figure, forceful and ambitious, he overshadowed King Zahir and
other members of the royal family. Because of his military background he enjoyed
the support of the army, to which he paid much attention. His premiership was
characterized by an energetic drive toward modernization and development of the
country, and indeed much was accomplished. During Daoud's era Afghanistan laid
foundations for its economic infrastructure by developing dams, roads, communications, and a number of basic industries. In addition, and as a vital ingredient of the
process, the school system was developed impressively. As a result,
Afghanistan—which for a long time chronically suffered a lack of educated
people—was embarrassed by having too many school and university graduates for
the restricted employment market. In the mid and later 1960s it was calculated that
Afghan schools on both secondary and higher levels were producing some 18,000
graduates a year. The student population of the capital city of Kabul reached
40,000.[13]

These impressive strides toward development would have been impossible without substantial foreign aid, which the prime minister succeeded in attracting to
Afghanistan through his shrewd diplomacy. The success in bringing foreign assistance was in no small measure due to the Cold War then prevailing between the
Soviet Union and the United States. In fact, both superpowers were engaged in a
competitive assistance race in Afghanistan.[14] While the Soviet Union channeled
much of its aid toward the provinces north of the Hindu Kush, that is, the bulk of the
Afghan territory, American aid was often directed toward the areas lying south of

[13]For the record of the first Daoud government, see Louis Dupree, *Afghanistan* (Princeton, 1973), esp.
ch. 23, "The Decade of Daoud: 1953–1963," pp. 499–558.
[14]For a more detailed treatment, see Richard S. Newell, "Afghanistan: The Dangers of Cold War
Generosity," *Middle East Journal,* 23 (Spring 1969), and Peter G. Franck, *op. cit.*

that mountain range. Of the two types of assistance, the Soviet was more substantial and probably left a greater mark on the development of the Afghan economy. Moreover, it was the Soviets who supplied and trained much of the Afghan army. Although Daoud insisted more than once that Afghan foreign policy was one of neutrality and nonalignment, to many observers it appeared that the tilt was definitely toward the Soviet side, and there was a degree of Afghan dependence upon the Soviet Union. Nevertheless, Afghanistan did not become a Soviet satellite and jealously guarded its ultimate freedom of sovereign action.

Under Daoud's regime Afghanistan, like many other developing countries, faced a classic dilemma: how to modernize and develop in the economic and technical sector while keeping the lid of political controls over the fast-growing ranks of the younger educated classes. The very process of education was bound to create expectations of political participation by its beneficiaries. Premier Daoud, however, was essentially an authoritarian personality. Without articulating his position, he clearly believed that turning over of power to a nation that was not yet fully integrated and educated, and that was inexperienced in the process of governing would be premature and detrimental to the fast development process. In some respects he was probably right, because there were many actual and potential centrifugal forces at work in the Afghan society. Despite the dominant role of the Pathans, (or Pushtuns) there existed many linguistic ethnic and national groups or minorities such as the Hazaras, Uzbeks, Turkomans, Tajiks, Baluch, Kirghiz, Nuristani, Qizilbash, Aimaq, and Brahui, which together constituted one-half of the population. Clearly some formula or device had to be adopted to keep all these groups together and to give them a sense of forming a united Afghan nation, which some of them possessed to only a small degree. But true to the long-standing tradition, Daoud preferred to embrace a strictly centralistic principle. In fact, the prime minister was reputed to be impressed by the model supplied by Nasser in Egypt. He was said to be contemplating a new constitution which would establish a strong central authority and a one-party state.

Despite his skill in governing and in the conduct of foreign relations, Premier Daoud did face some problems. The denial of meaningful political participation to the growing ranks of the intelligentsia caused the latter to become increasingly alienated from him. To this one should add the fact of growing unemployment or underemployment as well as the inevitable penetration of leftist, Marxist, or Maoist ideas into the growing ranks of the educated or semieducated groups. All of this, moreover, should be taken against the background of the general poverty of the state which in contrast to neighboring Iran, for example, did not have oil or any significant natural resources being exploited. (Afghanistan does possess major deposits of coal in certain less accessible areas and reputedly has considerable potential in certain minerals and ores, but these are not yet discovered or exploited in an economically satisfactory sense.)

Another problem which reduced Daoud's popularity and effectiveness was his handling of the Pushtunistan issue with Pakistan.[15] Daoud deliberately followed a

[15]For a background introduction, see James W. Spain, "The Pathan Borderlands," *Middle East Journal,* 15 (Spring 1961). For a more detailed coverage of the 1961 dispute, see L. Dupree, "Pushtunistan:

policy of assertiveness. It is a matter for debate whether this policy represented his genuine conviction or was merely a tactic to divert the attention of the Afghans from less pleasant realities at home and thus to unite them behind a slogan and a policy. Daoud's aggressive stance on Pushtunistan brought about retaliatory measures from Pakistan toward the Afghan transit trade through its territory, including a complete closing of the Pakistan-Afghan border between 1961 and 1963. This action in turn resulted in considerable economic embarrassment for Afghanistan; that the government had to enter into special agreements with the Soviet Union and to some extent with Iran to reroute much of its foreign trade. The business community and eventually the population as a whole suffered as a result of these measures. This mishandling of the Pushtunistan issue was the immediate cause of Daoud's downfall as prime minister.

The Decade of Constitutional Government, 1963–1973

Toward the end of the Daoud regime, a "constitutional coalition" gradually formed. It included virtually all major segments of the politically conscious Afghan society: the king, the educated elite, the business groups, the religious conservatives critical of certain secularization measures adopted by Daoud, and a variety of provincial tribal elements which felt that they had been excluded from meaningful influence upon the process of government. All in all, this constitutional coalition was in reality organized opposition to Daoud. King Zahir had a long history of being advised and dominated by various members of the royal family ever since he came to the throne as a young man of nineteen. First he was under the tutelage of his uncles and later under that of Daoud, his cousin and brother-in-law. Clearly he felt the need to emancipate himself and to become his own man. With the coalition thus formed, Zahir dismissed Daoud in 1963 ostensibly to relieve the impossible economic situation created by the severance of relations with Pakistan. And indeed, soon after Daoud's dismissal the border with Pakistan was reopened, and normal trade and transit resumed.

The same year a seven-man committee was appointed to prepare a new constitution. Its leaders were prominent members of the Afghan educated elite, some of whom had served in high diplomatic positions abroad and most of whom had been exposed through their education to Western ideas and political processes. Moreover, a French constitutional expert, Professor Louis Fauger, served as an advisor. The drafters of the new constitution had to attend to three major issues: the position of Islam, social and economic rights, and the role of the royal family. The pattern they finally adopted was influenced by the philosophy of Montesquieu, namely, a separation of powers. In 1964 the grand tribal assembly, the Loe Jirga, approved the new constitution. According to its provisions, a bicameral parliament was to be set up, to be composed of the Chamber of Deputies (Wolesi Jirga) and the Senate (Meshrano Jirga), the latter to be composed of three parts: one elected in direct

The Problem and Its Larger Implications," *American Universities Field Staff, Reports Service*, V, Nos. 2 and 3 (1961). Useful comments on this question are also contained in Leon Poullada, "The Search for National Unity," in L. Dupree and L. Albert, eds., *Afghanistan in the 1970s* (New York, 1974).

elections, one selected by the provincial councils for which the constitution provided, and one appointed by the king. Each of these groups was to number twenty-
eight members. The constitution recognized the special position of Islam by providing that no laws could be repugnant to the principles of Islam and that the Sharia law
would prevail in the absence of pertinent legislation. A substantial section of the
constitution was devoted to the social and economic rights of the people. Finally,
the royal family was to be excluded from holding government and cabinet offices.[16]

Thus under the new constitutional dispensation the first parliament was elected in
October 1965. Many of the provincial notables who held real power and influence in
their tribes or territories did not yet volunteer to serve in the parliament, suspecting
that the essence of the government, i.e., centralization of power in the ruling group
in Kabul, would remain unchanged. Consequently they allowed the second echelon
people to be elected. There were also some left-leaning deputies who were elected
from Kabul and the urban centers. In 1969 the second election took place. This
time, having discovered that the parliament had indeed a potential for influencing
the country's policies, the first rank leaders from the provinces decided to stand for
election and found their way to the parliament. As a result, the second parliament
was more definitely conservative and traditionalist in its outlook than the first.[17]

Unfortunately, the parliamentary system was new to Afghanistan and the elected
deputies had no experience in either parliamentary procedures or a constructive
debating that would end in compromise solutions and adoption of the necessary
laws. In fact, the parliament tended more to investigate than to legislate and spent
much time in acrimonious questioning and criticism of the government policies and
ministers. Old feuds and personal animosities frequently dominated the debates in
both chambers. Moreover, the Senate (Meshrano Jirga) was never constituted in its
full strength. Of the three elements previously mentioned only the directly elected
and the appointed members made their appearance. The third element—that to be
selected by the provincial councils—never took its seats because the provincial
councils were never formed, owing to the king's failure to promulgate the provincial
councils law. The king also hesitated to promulgate a political parties law and never
actually did it. Zahir's reluctance to approve these two rather important measures
was due to his fear (largely fanned by other members of the royal family including
his cousin, General Abdul Wali Khan) that the institution of political parties would
open the way for organizational efforts of the leftist, Marxist-leaning groups in the
country and that these would outdistance other groups and thus pose considerable
danger both internally and externally to Afghanistan.

All in all, the constitutional decade was one of considerable instability; government activity slowed as a result of the constant quarreling between the executive and

[16]Text of the constitution in *Middle East Journal*, 19 (Spring 1965), 217–229; also text with
glossary in L. Dupree, "Constitutional Development and Cultural Change," *American Universities
Field Staff, Reports Service*, IX, nos. 3 and 4 (1965). For a comprehensive review of the constitutional
period, see Ralph H. Magnus, "The Constitution of 1964: A Decade of Political Experimentation," in
Dupree and Albert, eds., *op. cit.*

[17]A detailed account of the parliamentary experience in Afghanistan may be found in L. Dupree,
"Comparative Profiles of Recent Parliaments in Afghanistan" and "Parliament versus the Executive in
Afghanistan, 1969-1971," *American Universities Field Staff, Reports Service*, XV, nos. 4 and 5 (1971).

legislative branches of the government, policies were inconsistent, and social, ideological, and national divisions were accentuated. Centrifugal tendencies so characteristic of the Afghans reasserted themselves with considerable strength. Two leftist groups, Parcham and Khalq, made their appearance. Students were increasingly restless. Urban workers protested against poor wages and working conditions. Young intelligentsia felt underpaid or underemployed, and various ethnic, tribal, and religious groups were each pulling in their own direction. Thus the initial constitutional coalition fell apart and in the course of the decade the country had five prime ministers.

All of this was accompanied by an economic slowdown after the completion of basic infrastructure projects in the 1950s and the early 1960s. This slowdown was partly due to the gradual fading away of the Cold War between the Soviet Union and the United States; while previously the two superpowers competed strenuously with assistance programs to Afghanistan, in the later 1960s both considerably reduced the scale of their aid. Although the Afghan government launched and tried to implement the successive five-year plans, its achievements were not commensurate with the expectations of the population.[18] By the early 1970's the country was clearly in the throes of a political and economic crisis.

Overthrow of the Monarchy and Return of Mohammed Daoud

In the early hours of July 17, 1973, former Premier Mohammed Daoud, aided by elements of the Afghan army loyal to him, executed a coup and deposed King Zahir, who was then vacationing in Italy. In his first speech broadcast over Kabul radio, Daoud proclaimed the establishment of the Afghan Republic which would "conform to the true spirit of Islam." In justifying his action, Daoud declared that the country suffered "complete decline and bankruptcy" in the economic, administrative, social, and political sectors. "In short," stated Daoud, "democracy or the government of the people was changed into anarchy and the constitutional monarchy into a despotic regime." The preceding ten years, said Daoud, were "impregnated with misery, poverty, and misfortune." The time had come "to provide a positive and real environment for the moral and material development of the people of Afghanistan, especially of the deprived classes and the youth of the nation, so that all the people of Afghanistan, without privilege or discrimination, might take a responsible part in the progress and building of the country." The true patriots, according to Daoud, and especially the Afghan armed forces, were determined to put an end to the sorry state of affairs and to eliminate a system and a regime that had become "so corrupt that no hope or expectation for its reform existed."

In the second part of his proclamation Daoud focused on foreign affairs. "Afghanistan's foreign policy will be based on neutrality, nonalignment in military blocs, and free judgment of the people of Afghanistan themselves." In conformance

---

[18]For a discussion of Afghan five-year plans, see Marvin Brant, "Recent Economic Development," in Dupree and Albert, eds., *op. cit.*, and Maxwell J. Fry, *The Afghan Economy*, esp. ch. iv, "Resource Mobilization under the Development Plans" (Leiden, 1974).

with these principles, the policy of Afghanistan would be to seek peace and friendship with all the nations and peoples of the world. Pakistan was singled out as the only nation "with whom we have a political difference over the Pushtunistan issue." Daoud pledged "permanent efforts" to find a solution to this problem.[19]

Thus began a new era of government by decree, during which the parliament and the existing constitution were abolished and freedom of the press suspended. On the eve of the coup nineteen independent newspapers had existed in Afghanistan. Following the coup they were replaced by two official organs, *Jamhuriat* and *Anis*.

Although Daoud's coup was executed smoothly and without bloodshed, it had to cope almost immediately with two counterplots. One was the attempt of the king's cousin and commander of the central forces in Kabul, Major General Abdul Wali Khan, to regain power with the aid of officers and soldiers loyal to him personally. The other was a political-military plot in which former Premier Mohammed Hashim Maiwandwal was involved. Helped by the army and his security apparatus, Daoud succeeded in thwarting both attempts. Abdul Wali was apprehended and arrested, while the abortive coup of Maiwandwal ended in his death, about which one version was that it was a suicide.

In launching his republican regime, Daoud established what appeared to be a rather typical Third World reformist-military dictatorship. At the head of the state was created the Central Committee which in turn proclaimed Daoud to be the Founder, President, and Prime Minister of the Republic. In addition he reserved for himself the portfolios of defense and foreign affairs. Pending the adoption of a new constitution, government was executed by decree. The first year of Daoud's rule was replete with many decrees pertaining to administrative reorganization and to such matters as collection of taxes, foreign and domestic investment, organization of courts and retirement and dismissal of judges, criminal procedures, traffic regulations, information and censorship, labor law, and minimum wages for workers in government enterprises. President Daoud delivered many speeches in which he proclaimed the principle of a mixed guided economy, reiterated his attachment to Islam, repudiated imported ideological slogans, and promised a wide range of political, economic, and social reforms. In the political sphere, Daoud declared that the ultimate objective would be the creation of a two-party parliamentary system. However, "since party activities and political campaigning have no precedent in our country, therefore, in order to prevent such activities from leading to strife and disunity and creating undesirable intellectual and political confusion, only one party will be allowed to operate for four years, probably equal to one term of an elected parliament."[20] Daoud reminded the people that his one-party idea had been proposed much earlier in a memorandum to King Zahir and thus represented his consistent thinking.

Daoud advocated establishment of a mixed economic system composed of a public and a private sector. The government was expected to own or control such

[19]Quotations from the text of Daoud's speech in the appendix to L. Dupree's article "A New Decade of Daoud?" *American Universities Field Staff, Reports Service,* XVII, no. 4 (1973).

[20]Quoted by L. Dupree, "A Note on Afghanistan, 1974," *American Universities Field Staff, Reports Service,* XVIII, no. 8 (1974), 6–7. Much material in this section is drawn from Dupree's account.

enterprises as mining, electricity, and heavy industry but at the same time it would encourage free enterprise in less basic fields of economic endeavor. These medium and light industries and handicrafts would be duly protected from foreign competition, presumably by appropriate licensing and tariff regulations. To put an end to social inequalities in the agrarian sector, land reforms were promised. Much emphasis was placed on social reforms which were to include improvement of conditions for the workers, a struggle against illiteracy, social security regulations, equal opportunities for women, free education for the country's youth, better health services, protection and expansion of cultural activities. Similarly, Daoud promised to end the nomadic type of existence of a substantial part of the Afghan population through appropriate resettlement schemes. Perhaps aware of criticisms leveled at him during his first period in power, 1953–1963, Daoud this time took care to emphasize his attachment to Islam. He branded as "sin" adherence to any foreign ideology or any group which repudiated the principles of Islam.

As is often the case with a regime issued from a reformist revolution, the government of Daoud Khan proceeded toward the implementation of many of these plans and pledges with considerable energy and enthusiasm. The first matter on the agenda was to collect a reliable and dedicated body of government officials who would share with the leader of the revolution his values and goals. Daoud attended to it by appointing to various administrative posts, especially in the provinces, younger people—some of a left-of-center orientation—who on basic philosophical grounds believed in the need for strong government intervention in the social and economic processes of an underdeveloped country and who thus could follow Daoud's instructions and ideas with full conviction. And, as usual in such cases, some of these appointments proved disappointing because the zeal and enthusiasm of the new officials was not always matched by practical experience and tact necessary to make the new measures acceptable to the more conservative or apathetic constituencies in the provinces.

In a major speech delivered on the first anniversary of the proclamation of the republic, July 17, 1974, President Daoud reviewed the accomplishments of his regime. He began by stressing the orderly innovations in public administration, which included the founding of a central statistical office and the 40-percent increase, as compared with the previous year, in the amount of back taxes recovered from those who owed them to the government. He pointed to the land distribution among 5,000 landless peasants and gave facts and figures pertaining to improvement in agricultural production, credit facilities to the farmers, and relief to the debt-ridden agricultural population which had suffered from recent droughts. His review included achievements in mining and industry, the opening of a copper mine in the Logar Valley, intensified exploration for minerals, increased exports of natural gas to the Soviet Union, augmented capacity of various power plants, and expansion of banks for industrial development. In the cultural and educational field, Daoud pointed to the creation of a national office for combating illiteracy and stressed the increase in the overall number of students from 147,000 in 1972 to 160,000 by 1974. He also provided information about progress in reforming the judiciary and the prison system which had long been neglected. Expansion was also noted in the field of public health, especially in rural areas. He pointed to the construction of sixty-two kilometers of new roads, of which thirty-seven were asphalted. Similarly, airport facilities were improved and extended in various locations.

It is not easy for a nonspecialist reading official government reports such as Daoud's to derive a clear picture of progress and particularly its pace as compared with the real needs of the country claimed by the regime. Reformist strongman regimes in the Third World are public-relations oriented and likely to publicize facts and figures purporting to prove advance in a variety of social, economic, and technical sectors.

It is difficult to deny that indeed the administration and economy of Afghanistan had reached a point of stagnation under the constitutional regime due to continuous friction between the executive and legislative branches of the government that paralyzed the state apparatus.

In the field of foreign policy, the performance of the Daoud regime broadly conformed to the principles enunciated by him in his inaugural declaration in July 1973. Afghanistan under his leadership followed a policy of nonalignment, neutrality, and peace. In this sense his policy was characteristic of Afghanistian's international behavior, regardless of the regime in power, for at least a half century. As for the basic Afghan neutralism (proclaimed and practiced already during World War I, in the interwar period, during World War II, and after), the only question was whether it tended to be slightly tilted toward one or another of major powers with broad interests in the Middle East. The first Daoud era, 1953–1963, was characterized by a drift toward the Soviets. The subsequent constitutional decade, by contrast, is viewed as restoring a greater evenhandedness or perhaps even a slight tilt toward the United States. With the return of Daoud to power, fears were expressed in the West and in such neighboring countries as Pakistan and Iran lest Afghanistan return again to the pro-Soviet tendency in its neutralism. This fear was particularly strong in Iran, which was apprehensive lest the Soviet-trained officers who supported Daoud's revolution display a pro-Soviet orientation in their policy and even perhaps become tools of the Soviet penetration inside Afghanistan. Similarly there was concern in Pakistan, particularly after its division and the creation of Bangladesh, that in concert with the Soviets and India, Afghanistan might become more active in sponsoring and assisting the centrifugal political tendencies of various national and ethnic groups in Pakistan, thus leading to the ultimate disintegration of Western Pakistan as a state. To the Pakistanis the name of Daoud was strictly connected with the emphasis on the Pushtunistan issue and Daoud himself made it clear in his inaugural speech that this matter would receive his special attention. Furthermore, any expression of Afghan hostility toward Pakistan was apt to produce a measure of friction with the United States. Should such friction be revived it would accentuate Soviet opportunities for maneuver and influence in Afghanistan.

Certain actions of Daoud's regime deepened these concerns and suspicions. For example, at a meeting of the Islamic heads of state in Lahore in February 1974, the Afghan delegation was almost the only one to strike a dissenting chord when it brought up the question of Pushtunistan. It was promptly criticized by Presidents

Boumedienne of Algeria and Sadat of Egypt for raising a controversial issue at an Islamic meeting dedicated to the achievement of solidarity on the Arab-Israeli issue. Furthermore, President Daoud paid a state visit to the Soviet Union in early June 1974, in the course of which he concluded an agreement providing for $150 million Soviet assistance in the development of twenty-one industrial projects in Afghanistan. The Soviet Union for some time had received 50 percent of Afghanistan's foreign trade.

However, with the passage of time it appeared that many of these apprehensions were not justified. Despite his references to the Pushtunistan problem, which to some extent were helpful to Daoud in maintaining Afghan national unity, his policy on that issue was not as forceful and aggressive as it had been during his first decade in power. True enough, irritations in Afghan-Pakistani relations did occur and once the government of Pakistan claimed that an Afghan plot to murder President Bhutto had been hatched during the Lahore Islamic conference. Despite this, relations between the two countries were not allowed to deteriorate to the point of commercial boycott and closing of borders as it had happened in the early 1960s. By the same token, after some study of the Afghan situation, Iran appeared reassured that the new regime was not about to become a Soviet satellite and thus contribute to the Communist encirclement of Iran. There was some apprehension in Iran whether an agreement concluded with the Afghan constitutional government in March 1973, which settled the Helmand waters dispute, would be honored by the government of President Daoud. To Iran's relief, Daoud's government fully confirmed the Helmand water agreement in July 1974. Furthermore, Iran entered into negotiations with Kabul to conclude various aid and trade agreements. Because Iran, since the spectacular rise in oil prices in 1974, was in a position to extend financial and economic assistance to a number of countries, it availed itself of this ability to pledge major amounts of aid to Afghanistan. This led eventually to the conclusion on February 11, 1975, of an Iranian-Afghan agreement providing for major extension of Iranian assistance up to $2 billion for a variety of Afghan development projects.

Similarly, whatever concern might have been privately nourished by the United States government regarding the nature and the policy of the Daoud regime tended to fade away when Daoud's international behavior proved in a broad outline evenhanded and responsible. Despite the remoteness and isolation of Afghanistan and its nonparticipation in any regional defense or economic schemes supported by the United States, the country continued to be of interest to the American policymakers who, not unlike the British in the nineteenth century, tended to look upon it as a welcome neutral buffer between the Soviet and the American spheres. This interest was attested by a number of official American visits to Afghanistan over a period of time. Thus Secretary of State William Rogers paid a visit to Kabul in May 1969, followed by President Richard Nixon in June 1970. This tradition was continued during the new Daoud era when in November 1974 Secretary of State Kissinger visited Kabul.

In conclusion, Afghanistan's economic and technical development faced challenges unknown in the earlier periods. The increased education and exposure to

Western patterns of government and life have created among a growing number of Afghans a desire for a speedy development coupled with interest in greater political participation. The two did not always prove compatible, as the traumatic transition from the first Daoud decade to the constitutional regime and then again to the new Daoud dispensation proved. The receding of the Cold War between the Soviet Union and the United States caused a reduction in economic assistance of both superpowers to Afghanistan precisely at a time when the country badly needed it, on both economic and psychological grounds. It is clear that the experiment in democracy in Afghanistan practiced between 1963 and 1973 did not succeed. Afghanistan historically veeered between the extremes of anarchy and despotism. In launching what some writers called a "second decade" of power, President Daoud faced the tremendous task of reconciling these various contradictory tendencies while assuring the independence and orderly development of his country.

The Marxist-oriented Coup of 1978

In February 1977, Daoud promulgated a new constitution—with emphasis on presidential powers—which was intended to entrench and legitimize his power. But there were undercurrents of violence as attested by the assassination of Ahmad Ali Khurram, minister of planning, in the fall that year and by the subsequent discovery—in February 1978—of a plot, incriminating twenty-five dissenters, to assassinate the president.

Furthermore, despite Daoud's visit to Moscow in April 1977 and the conclusion of an economic cooperation agreement, his relationship with two Afghan Marxist groups, the Parcham (Flag) and Khalq (People's) parties, was one of mistrust if not outright hostility.

Daoud's policy of neutrality began to show a tilt toward the more conservative regional powers, such as Iran and Saudi Arabia, as well as toward greater reliance in the field of technology on the United States and Western Europe. Characteristic of this trend was acceptance of a $2 billion aid program from Iran and a visit Daoud paid to Saudi Arabia. Simultaneously, relations between Daoud and Colonel Abdul Qader, who was chief of the air force and had been instrumental in bringing Daoud to power in 1973, appreciably cooled.

The assassination by unknown assailants of Akbar Khabir, one of the founders of the Communist Parcham party, late in April 1978 seems to have triggered the revolt. Two days later, on April 27, the military, led by Qader, executed a coup in the course of which Daoud, his brother Mohammed Naim, defense minister Rasuli, and a number of high government members were killed. Within three days a new revolutionary government was formed. Headed by Mohammad Taraki, leader of the Marxist Khalq party, as president and prime minister, it included Babrak Karmal, leader of the Parcham party, and Hafizullah Amin as vice premiers, and Qader as defense minister.

The new government proclaimed Afghanistan to be a "Democratic Republic" and affirmed its neutrality and nonalignment. Internally, it speedily laid the foundations of a socialist state leaning toward totalitarian patterns. Its rhetoric was definitely Marxist: Taraki called his new dispensation "a workers' revolution." Its domestic policies were severely repressive toward the figures of the old regime—"lackeys of imperialism"—and any actual or suspected opponents. Executions, arrests, and jailings followed on a large scale, accompanied by purges of "deviationists" inside the new regime itself. Thus the Parcham Party, which had helped win power, was summarily eliminated from the new political structure. Babrak Karmal was removed from office, and Qader was placed under arrest in the late summer of 1978. By the fall, Hafizullah Amin, a civilian (and a graduate of Columbia University Teachers' College) emerged as the most powerful personality of the government, next to President Taraki.

Kabul and other urban centers were subjected to a curfew, with heavily armed troops at the ready in the streets and public buildings. In spite of the repeated claims of massive public support, the new regime vividly betrayed its insecurity by posting sixty tanks in the presidential palace (renamed "People's House") and providing armed bodyguards to the ministers and high government officials. With streets emptied after dark, Kabul was illuminated by ubiquitous searchlights, eerily reminiscent of Orwell's *1984,* as if to remind the populace that "Big Brother" was watching. To add a symbolic emphasis to the left-oriented change, the regime adopted a new national flag, red in color, with one star. Such banners were draped over the buildings, and red shirts were prescribed for schoolchildren. At the same time huge pictures—Soviet style—of President Taraki were prominently displayed, suggesting the deliberate design for a "personality cult."

On the socioeconomic front, the government focused on the preparation of a new five-year plan to remold the country's development along the socialist lines. Among the first radical measures were the decrees to redistribute land and cancel all private debts.

The new course, as could be expected, generated resistance among the traditionalist religious and tribal groups, especially in the southeastern parts of Afghanistan. Army units, dispatched to quell such opposition, had to engage repeatedly in armed clashes. Groups of refugees fled toward the neighboring Pakistan.

In its foreign relations the Taraki regime definitely veered toward a close relationship with the Soviet Union. Taraki, extolled as a "great leader" by the government-controlled press, called the USSR "our very dear, close friend" and affirmed that "our fraternal ties with the Socialist camp are developing and expanding in a remarkable manner."[21] These protestations of mutual esteem soon found their practical expression in the massive influx of Soviet advisers and experts. Within the first few months after the coup their number in civilian posts was estimated at 2,000 and in military positions (some reputedly holding command assignments) at 1,000.

By the end of 1978, the Soviet Union had visibly expanded its presence and influence in Afghanistan. Yet, in view of the legacy of Afghan nationalism and

[21]Quoted in the San Francisco *Chronicle,* Nov. 22, 1978.

xenophbia, it would have been risky to assert that Afghanistan, despite its new Marxist orientation, had become a Soviet satellite according to the East European patterns. A more correct hypothesis would probably be to regard this close cooperation as a patron-client relationship. Such a relationship was subject to internal obstacles in Afghanistan itself and was potentially vulnerable to complications in the international sector.

PART THREE

The Fertile Crescent

CHAPTER VII

Iraq

On August 23, 1921, Faisal ascended the throne of Iraq. The decision to offer him the crown had been made earlier in the year, as you will recall, at a British Middle East conference. A 96 percent endorsement from the people of Iraq was obtained by means of a referendum. This referendum was described by Gertrude Bell, secretary of Sir Percy Cox, as "politics running on wheels greased with extremely well-melted grease."[1]

King Faisal's coronation marked the opening of a new period in Iraq's history. Internally, the new kingdom was confronted with the task of welding the heterogeneous peoples of Mesopotamia into a single nation, raising them from the backward condition inherited from the Ottoman Empire to a higher level, and establishing order and security. Externally, Iraq's problems revolved around her relationships with Britain. Both external and internal problems were closely intertwined.

The Iraqi Government

Purely administrative problems are outside the scope of this study; hence little will be said about them here.[2] What really mattered from the political point of view was the general trend toward emancipation from British control. Under Colonel Wilson's rule, the administration of Iraq was exercised mainly by the British, but even before Faisal's ascent it was partly transferred to the Iraqis themselves. In the transitional period of 1920 the *naqib* (chief of nobility) of Baghdad headed the administration of the state. With Faisal's arrival, a regular cabinet was formed, but the British continued to retain key functions via advisers to the various ministries, the advisers holding more permanent and better-paying positions than their nominal Iraqi superiors. Moreover, such important positions as inspector general of police and directors of health, customs and excise, agriculture, public works, irrigation, and telegraphs were all British subjects. As for the provincial administration, the

---

[1] Lady Florence Bell, ed., *The Letters of Gertrude Bell* (New York, 1927), II, 533 ff. Yet not everything was perfectly smooth: to prevent opposition, British authorities arrested and deported to Ceylon Sayid Talib Pasha, who aspired to the crown of Iraq.

[2] A thorough treatment of administrative and constitutional evolution in Iraq may be found in P. W. Ireland, *Iraq: A Study in Political Development* (London, 1937).

former British political officers were transformed into advisers (later administrative inspectors) to the Iraqi officials, but their real power remained largely undiminished. These British district advisers played a very important role in perpetuating British control over the country, irrespective of formal Anglo-Iraqi arrangements, especially in the tribal areas. The tribes constituted about one-sixth of the Iraqi population and traditionally presented a dilemma to any settled government. In the early days of their occupation the British introduced into the tribal areas the so-called Sandeman system, developed and tested in India. According to this system, control over the tribes was exercised through their hereditary chieftains. In other words, the government, instead of establishing direct control over the people, would use the local chief as its agent by recognizing his authority, by sometimes subsidizing him, and by protecting his "dynastic" interests. This system had the virtue of not destroying the age-old tribal society and of assuring a large measure of order and peace without much direct interference. The drawback of the system was that it tended to perpetuate "feudal" relationships among a large segment of the people and that it made difficult any constructive policy aiming at progress and modernization of the nation as a whole. Politically, the system meant that the tribal sheikhs were often friendlier to the British than the town dwellers and that in case of crisis the British could always, to some extent, manipulate this tribal reserve force. With the gradual transfer of administrative functions to the Iraqis, this problem was inherited by the Iraqi government itself. Like every new nationalist government, it tried to establish its uncontested supremacy over the whole area of Iraq and inevitably ran up against tribal opposition. In some cases the tribes resorted to violence. Thus, after Iraq obtained her full independence, the Middle Euphrates tribes rose, in 1935, in a large-scale rebellion, which had to be curbed by the army after severe fighting. Even in 1950, two decades after Iraq's formal emancipation, the tribal problem was far from solved.

Minority Problems

The question of tribal relationships was closely related to the question of minorities. These groups constituted slightly over 20 percent of the Iraqi population. The largest single minority was the Kurds living in the northern parts of the country, around Mosul, Kirkuk, Suleimaniya, and Rowanduz.[3] These warlike mountaineers, partly settled and partly nomadic, were a chronic source of difficulties for Iraq. Scattered throughout Iraq, Turkey, Syria, Iran, and the Soviet Union, the Kurds, whose total numbers were estimated at about four and one-half million, were too backward and immature to create their own sovereign state and yet too independent to agree to unrestricted foreign domination. At the time of the "referendum" in 1921, the Kurds for the most part abstained from voting as a token of their disapproval of being ruled by an Arab government. Throughout the interwar period the

[3]For background information on Kurdistan, see Col. W. G. Elphinston, "The Kurdish Question," *International Affairs* (Jan. 1946), and by the same author, "Kurds and the Kurdish Question," *R.C.A.J.* (Jan. 1948); also W. L. Westerman, "Kurdish Independence and Russian Expansion," *Foreign Affairs* (July 1946). For a pro-Soviet view of the Kurdish problem, consult Lucien Rambout, *Les Kurdes et le Droit* (Paris, 1947).

Kurds remained a turbulent minority, occasionally resorting to uprisings when their patience with government tyranny or corruption was exhausted. Rebellions on a larger scale occurred in 1922–1924, 1930–1931, and 1932, under the leadership of Sheikh Mahmud of Suleimaniya, and it cost the government much effort to suppress them. Although a basically internal matter affecting Iraq's security, these uprisings, like so many other domestic problems of Iraq, had their international facets as well. Because the Kurds were distributed over five countries, whatever happened in one of them was bound to affect the Kurds situated in the others. The fact that the Kurds lived in more or less compact groups in the frontier districts made it easier for them to escape across the borders to neighboring states whenever it appeared necessary for them to do so. This, in turn, was bound to provoke international quarrels between the nations involved, and between Iraq and Iran in particular, the governments accusing one another of harboring the troublemakers, even of assisting their rebellions.

The Kurdish problem was also linked with the policies of the big powers, in particular with those of Great Britain and the Soviet Union. After the First World War, the British toyed with the idea of a British-protected Kurdish state,[4] which would enable them to push their influence northward into the strategic area bordering on the Caucasus. Moreover, the support of Kurdish aspirations could be used as a lever of pressure on recalcitrant Kemalist Turkey, on Iran, and especially on Iraq, in which the percentage of Kurds was higher than in any other country. The scheme of a Kurdish puppet state was, however, abandoned, because Britain realized that the matter was too explosive, that it was likely to upset the balance and stability of the Middle East, and that its promotion would eventually benefit the Soviets more than anyone else. This view coincided with the definite British policy of influencing Iraq by winning over Arab public opinion through various political concessions. Choosing to follow a definitely pro-Arab policy, Britain found it difficult to promote at the same time schemes that would reduce the Arab-ruled area, and for this reason she changed her stand on the Kurdish question. This, however, did not mean that friendship with the Kurds was thrown overboard. On the contrary, it continued to be cultivated, especially on the local level, by various British political agents, both in Iraq and in Iran. This served two purposes at once: first, to keep the Kurdish question as a tactical reserve in case of difficulties with Baghdad or Teheran and, second, to ward off foreign penetration, whether Soviet or German. Yet, in pursuance of their basically pro-Arab policy, the British air force helped the Iraqi army suppress the Kurdish revolt of 1932.

Apart from the Kurdish, there were Turkish, Iranian, Turkoman, and Assyrian national minorities—usually settled in definite geographical areas—and a number of other minorities, such as the Jews and various religious sects, scattered all over the country or centered in towns. Of all these groups, the Assyrians posed one of the most difficult problems.[5] In contrast to other minorities, they were mostly newcom-

---

[4]See above, p. 131, and the relevant footnote; also the statement by Dr. G. M. Lees in *R.C.A.J.* (Jan. 1948), p. 50.

[5]For background information on the Assyrians, see W. A. Wigram, *The Assyrians and Their Neighbours* (London, 1929); R. S. Stafford, *The Tragedy of the Assyrians* (London, 1935).

ers, having fled to Iraq from Turkey or Iran under very trying circumstances during the First World War. Living first on British charity and later settling temporarily in a few score villages in northern Iraq, the Assyrians were protected by the British mandatory authorities, who recruited among them men for guard duty on Royal Air Force air fields and installations. As Nestorian Christians, the Assyrians enjoyed the support of the Anglican Church and had the confidence of official British circles. This dependence upon foreign protection, coupled with their state of destitution and their martial qualities, produced intergroup difficulties with the Arabs of Iraq, who always considered them as unwelcome intruders. Tension increased when the Assyrian patriarch and secular leader, Mar Shimun, asked for restoration of the millet system, which would give greater autonomy to his coreligionists. Matters came to a head when, in 1933, a desperate group of Assyrians crossed from Iraq into Syria in search of some more promising haven, only to find that the French mandatory authorities were determined to prevent their infiltration, by force, if necessary. Discouraged, the Assyrians tried to return to Iraq, but met with opposition at the Iraqi frontier posts. In the ensuing skirmish the Assyrians killed a few Iraqi soldiers and then crossed the border. The uproar which this incident created led the Iraqi government to organize a punitive expedition, which burned some twenty Assyrian villages, massacring their inhabitants. No Arab voice was raised in protest against this ruthlessness, and the commander of the expedition, Colonel Bekr Sidki, earned a reputation as a national "hero," young King Ghazi (Faisal's successor) promptly promoting him to a higher rank. The "Assyrian Massacres" caused the League of Nations to investigate the position of this unfortunate minority, and at one time it was proposed to settle all the Assyrians in Brazil, but this never materialized.

Religious Tensions

Another internal problem was the animosity between the two main Moslem sects of Iraq, the Shiis and the Sunnis. The former were slightly larger in numbers, but more backward owing to their reluctance to accept secular education. As a result, they had fewer properly trained individuals who could fill responsible government positions. The successive Iraqi cabinets contained, as a rule, a Sunni majority, sometimes including only one Shia minister to keep up the appearance of proportional representation. The Shiis were rather cool to King Faisal as an "imported" Sunni prince. Their geographical concentration in the south of Iraq added to the existing difficulties. The Shiis, through their clergy, had many links with Iran, a predominantly Shia country. Indeed, many leading mujtahids or ulema were of Iranian nationality—a fact partly due to Reza Shah's anticlerical course, which resulted in a number of migrations to Iraq. These Iranian clerical dignitaries, preoccupied with religious matters and often fanatical, owed no loyalty whatsoever to the concept of Iraqi statehood and often obstructed the normal functioning of the Iraqi administration. The Shia hierarchy was not only anti-Sunni, but also anti-British, and frequently used passive resistance to counter many common Anglo-Iraqi projects. In 1922, King Faisal was so annoyed by their preelectoral activity that he ordered forty Iranian ulema to be deported back to Iran. All in all, the Shiis, who were centered around their holy places of Nejef and Kerbela, constituted a powerful force that no Iraqi government could afford to ignore.

Iraq's Internal Politics

Iraq had been one of the most remote and least-developed corners of the Ottoman Empire and was much less advanced than the Arab nations bordering on the Mediterranean. A simple transfer from the Ottoman to the British Empire and then to native control could not quickly change these basic factors. Illiteracy was wide- spread. Iraq's educational facilities, though growing, were poor and inadequate. Baghdad did not have a single real institution of higher learning. Foreign schools, even if they carried the imposing title of "colleges" (as was the case with the American Presbyterian institutions in the Near East) were on the level of secondary schools at the very best. The Iraqi upper class was educated either in Turkey or in the West or not educated at all. The so-called intelligentsia group was infinitesimally small. Regular political parties could hardly be expected to exist, yet in the interwar period Iraq witnessed the appearance and disappearance of a number of political parties. For example, there were three nationalist parties: Hizb el-Watani (National party), Hizb el-Nahdha (Renaissance party), and Hizb el-Hurr (Independence party) in the twenties; the Ikha el-Watani (Brethren), the Ahali (People's Group), and the Society for National Reform in the thirties. But none of these groups could be compared to traditional political parties in the West. Personalities played a much more important role in Iraqi politics than programs. It was the attitude of leading families or tribal chieftains, of prominent army officers and religious leaders, that really counted. The family of the *naqib* of Baghdad, Sayid Abdur Rahman el-Gailani, wielded great influence in the capital; the same was true of the powerful Umari family of Mosul. In the south it was Sayid Talib Pasha, son of the *naqib* of Basra, who was not only one of the leading nationalists but also an aspirant to the crown. Prominent leaders among the Shia laity—Sayid Mohammed es-Sadr from Baghdad and Jafar abu Timman from Khadimain—also carried great weight in internal politics. Among the officers from the Sherifian service, Nuri es-Said, Jafar el-Askari, Yasin el-Hashimi, and a number of others emerged as influential leaders upon Faisal's ascent. Faisal tended to surround himself with his former brothers-in-arms from the Hejaz campaign, but he was careful not to antagonize others by too open favoritism. There was, for that matter, definite animosity between the Sherifian veterans and former officers from the Turkish service.

The king's popularity and strength was rather hard to gauge. A native of the Bedouin kingdom of the Hejaz, a descendant of the Prophet, commander of the Sherifian army in the desert campaign, and a short-lived ruler of Syria, Faisal had some appeal as an all-Arab leader but no deep personal links with Iraq. On the contrary, he had strong bonds with the British, to whom he owed his crown. This identification with Britain was a serious hindrance to his popularity with some Iraqi nationalists, yet no one could classify this brave soldier as a bribed collaborator. On July 10, 1924, Iraq's Constituent Assembly adopted an Organic Law (constitution) which gave the country all the external trappings of parliamentary democracy, but this act had little influence upon the actual course of Iraqi politics. In fact, Faisal emerged as a benevolent despot who did not feel too embarrassed by formal constitutional limitations. By contrast, he had to and did accommodate himself to those real centers of power in Iraq—the Shia divines, the leading families, the army officers, and the tribes. His was not an easy role because he had to act as a middleman between the British mandatory authorities and the more vocal Iraqi nationalists. There is no doubt that he himself aspired toward greater emancipation for Iraq, but at the same time he was realistic enough to know his country's limitations and Britain's strength.

Iraq's Gradual Emancipation

This brief account of King Faisal's position leads us to the external relations of Iraq in the interwar period. The pattern of these relations was relatively simple: Iraq aspired to more freedom and independence, while Britain, having invested blood and money in this area and aware of its strategic and economic value, was anxious to preserve her supremacy. Conscious of the eruptive potentialities of Iraqi nationalism, as evidenced in the 1920 uprising, Britain acted cautiously, compromising wherever possible. The transfer of Iraq affairs from the India to the Colonial Office in 1921 permitted the British government to plan and execute a more consistent policy, better coordinated with its policies toward other Arab countries in the Middle East.

Treaties with Britain

Faced with strong nationalist agitation, the British government did not ask the League of Nations for the formal assignment of a mandate but, instead, decided to exercise its control by means of a treaty with Iraq. Such a treaty was concluded on October 10, 1922. Together with four important subsidiary agreements, it confirmed British control of Iraq by giving Britain the right: (1) to appoint advisers to the Iraqi government, (2) to assist the Iraqi army, (3) to protect foreigners, (4) to advise Iraq on fiscal matters, and (5) to advise Iraq on matters of foreign relations. The treaty also provided for an open door policy to be implemented by Great Britain, foresaw British financial assistance to Iraq, and guaranteed the non-alienation of Iraqi territory by Britain. It was to operate for twenty years, but by a protocol signed in 1923, its period was reduced to four years. In its really vital provisions, the treaty did not much differ from the draft mandate that had come up for consideration before the Council of the League of Nations in September 1921, but had never been formally adopted. As for Britain's responsibility to the League of Nations, it was based on the decision of the Allied Supreme Council in San Remo on April 25, 1920, assigning Iraq to Britain as a mandate and on Article 22 of the Covenant of the League, which dealt with the mandatory system.

To the British, the treaty of 1922 was just another form of control, but properly sugar-coated for the Iraqi taste. In fact, H. A. L. Fisher, the British delegate at Geneva, had made it clear during the session of the Council in November 1921 that his government considered it advantageous to exercise the mandate by means of a treaty. This, however, was not the Iraqi view. Iraqis viewed the treaty as a definite rejection of the mandatory status and as the first step toward full independence. Much as the treaty was preferred to a mandate, many nationalists agitated against its terms. The Constituent Assembly which met in 1924 was in considerable doubt as to whether or not to ratify it. Fortunately for the British, the assembly contained forty representatives from the tribes, who favored ratification. This fact, together with strong British pressure on other members, led the assembly to ratify the treaty on March 27, 1924.

From 1924 to 1930, Iraq's demands for a greater measure of freedom grew more vocal.[6] The Anglo-Iraqi treaties of January 13, 1926, and December 14, 1927, marked further steps in the modest relaxation of British control, especially in financial and military sectors. The latter treaty, moreover, contained a British promise to support Iraq's candidacy to the League of Nations in 1932.

The treaty of 1927 did not satisfy Iraqi nationalists. There was, indeed, little change in the political realities, and the British high commissioners of the Indian school, men such as Sir Henry Dobbs, acted with virtually undiminished authority. With the arrival in 1927 of Sir Gilbert Clayton, an Arabic expert formerly associated with the Hejazi Force and a personal friend of Faisal, the atmosphere changed. Negotiations looking to a more satisfactory settlement were opened and, after Clayton's sudden death, were concluded by his successor, Sir Francis Humphrys.

On June 30, 1930, the high commissioner and Nuri es-Said Pasha, foreign minister, signed a new Anglo-Iraqi treaty, the final one of the series.[7] This treaty provided for a twenty-five-year alliance between Great Britain and Iraq; confirmed Britain's intention to support Iraq's admission to the League of Nations in 1932; and proclaimed Iraq's full independence and the termination of British mandatory responsibilities on the date of Iraq's entry into the League. In it or in the annexes were the following major provisions:

1. *Foreign policy*. Both parties agreed to "full and frank consultation in all matters of foreign policy which might affect their common interests," and each undertook not to adopt a policy "which is inconsistent with the alliance or might create difficulties for the other party."

2. *Defense*. In case of war, Britain undertook to defend Iraq. Iraq's role would "consist in furnishing to His Britannic Majesty on Iraq territory all facilities and assistance . . . including the use of railways, rivers, ports, aerodromes and means of communication."

3. *Bases and right of transit*. Iraq was to lease to Britain sites for air bases in the vicinity of Basra and west of the Euphrates; and Britain was empowered to maintain forces in these localities. She was also authorized to maintain forces in other areas of Iraq (Hinaidi and Mosul) during the transitional period, which was not to exceed

[6]In contrast with Iraqi aspirations for independence were the doubts of the Council of the League of Nations as to Iraq's fitness for self-government. These were manifested in 1925 when Mosul was assigned to Iraq on condition that the British mandate be continued for another twenty-five years. (For details of the Mosul controversy, see p. 122.)

[7]The full text may be found in Helen M. Davis, ed., *Constitutions, Electoral Laws, Treaties of States in the Near and Middle East* (Durham, N.C., 1947), p. 143.

five years. Moreover, she was granted the right of transit for her troops across Iraqi territory.

4. *Immunities*. British forces in Iraq were to enjoy immunity from local jurisdiction and taxation.

5. *Training of Iraqi army*. In case Iraq decided to invite in foreign military instructors, to train her own officers abroad, or to buy arms and equipment in foreign countries, Britain would have an exclusive right to provide such services, and armaments and equipment were "not to differ in type from those of the forces of His Britannic Majesty."

6. *Diplomatic representation*. The British high commissioner was to be replaced by an ambassador, who would enjoy a permanent position of seniority among foreign diplomatic representatives.

This treaty was of great importance because it set the pattern for other treaties with Arab countries. Britain's treaty with Egypt in 1936 and France's treaties with Syria and Lebanon in the same year followed the Iraqi treaty in their major provisions.

Release from Foreign Control

On October 3, 1932, Iraq was admitted to the League of Nations following favorable but somewhat hesitant reports from the Permanent Mandates Commission. Prior to admitting Iraq, the League asked her to give guarantees for the protection of minorities, including the Kurds; the rights of foreigners; respect for human rights, and the recognition of debts and treaties concluded by the mandatory power. In compliance with these conditions, Iraq on May 30, 1932, issued a declaration containing the required guarantees.

During the ensuing period of independence, Anglo-Iraqi relations deteriorated steadily, but Britain continued to maintain her predominant position. The deterioration was due not only to the greater freedom acquired by Iraq but also to the premature death in 1933 of King Faisal, Britain's trusted friend. His successor, the twenty-one-year-old King Ghazi, was an inexperienced and somewhat irresponsible youth whose interests lay more in automobile and motorcycle racing than in affairs of state. The country relapsed into a state of political instability characterized by constant shifts in the cabinet and a recurrence of tribal and minority unrest. Soon after Faisal's death, the government dealt severely with the Assyrian minority, and this tragedy, previously referred to, bore eloquent testimony to the dubious maturity of a new state whose national ambitions could seek an easy outlet in minority persecution.

The Organic Law of 1924, which established a pseudo-democracy for the upper stratum of elderly politicians, was obviously not likely to solve Iraq's social and economic problems. Iraq, like many other agricultural countries, suffered from the effects of worldwide depression in the early 1930s. The production of oil by the Iraq Petroleum Company began only in 1930, and some time was needed before Iraq could count on a steady and substantial income from that source.

The Coup of 1936

Iraq's ruling oligarchy was divided during this period into two main groups: those who favored the British alliance, and those who opposed it. The first group was headed by former officers of the Hejazi Force, such as General Nuri es-Said, General Jafar el-Askari, and Jamil el-Madfai. The second, more numerous, included such notables as Yasin el-Hashimi (whose brother, General Taha el-Hashimi, was a nonpolitical chief of staff of the army), Hikmat Suleiman (very pro-Turkish, brother of the prewar Young Turk General Mahmud Shevket Pasha), Rashid Ali el-Gailani, and Kamil Chadirchi. This anti-British group had formed in 1930 the Ikha el-Watani (Brotherhood) party and had opposed the signing of the Anglo-Iraqi treaty. This group dominated Iraqi politics between King Faisal's death and 1936, although it had to co-operate with some pro-British politicians.[8]

Ikha's inefficient and conservative rule provoked widespread discontent among the populace, which was especially noticeable among younger groups of Iraqi intelligentsia. Iraq's lack of progress and governmental instability were contrasted with the spectacular achievements of the new Turkish regime and the solidity of the Kemalist government. In 1931 some educated young men in Baghdad formed the Ahali (People's) Group, which began to preach "populism," a mixture of socialism and democracy, advocating radical reform in the country. As long as the group was limited to young intellectuals, its influence upon Iraqi politics was negligible, despite the fact that it published a rather popular newspaper. Ahali acquired much greater significance when, as a result of a split in the ranks of the leading Ikha group, it secured the cooperation of Hikmat Suleiman and of a few other experienced leaders. It then became possible for Ahali to aspire to political power. Simultaneously, considerable ferment could be noticed in the army. A number of officers believed that the Western-imposed division of the Arab world into separate states was highly artificial and that no radical solution for Arab ills could be found unless these states were united into some Pan-Arab federation. They blamed the politicians in power for perpetuating this division for the sake of their selfish ambitions. These officers believed that the army was the only organized group capable of accomplishing the desired change and initiating the necessary reforms. The leader of this military group was General Bekr Sidki, a divisional commander and the "hero" of the before-mentioned Assyrian punitive expedition. Hikmat Suleiman, Bekr's personal friend, helped to establish liaison between the Ahali group and the army. On Bekr's initiative, it was decided to organize a conspiracy and to overthrow the existing cabinet of Yasin el-Hashimi. On October 29, 1936, Bekr Sidki executed the coup d'état; helped by another divisional commnader, General Abdul Latif Nuri, and by the chief of the Iraqi air force, Mohammed Ali Jawad, he and his "National Reform Force" marched on Baghdad, demanding the immediate resignation of the Yasin cabinet and the appointment of Hikmat Suleiman as head of the government. Terrified by an air raid on the capital executed by Jawad's air force (actually only

[8]See Majid Khadduri, "The Coup d'Etat of 1936: A Study in Iraqi Politics," *Middle East Journal*, 2 (July 1948).

four light bombs were dropped), Yasin and his cabinet resigned, and King Ghazi, adopting a policy of nonresistance, asked Hikmat Suleiman to form the government. Jafar el-Askari, popular minister of defense in Yasin's cabinet, was the only casualty of the coup, having been treacherously murdered on Bekr's orders while attempting personal negotiation. It was characteristic of the Iraqi situation that when Yasin's cabinet gathered for its last emergency meeting in the royal palace, British Ambassador Sir Archibald Clark-Kerr (later Lord Inverchapel) attended it.

The new regime was to be based on cooperation between the progressive Ahali group and the army, but it soon became clear that the aims of these two groups were hardly compatible. The newly created progovernment party, called the Society for National Reform, was a facade behind which serious conflicts were in the making. Bekr Sidki, who reserved for himself the position of chief of staff, established a virtual military dictatorship, while Hikmat was forced to abandon his Ahali friends and to follow Bekr's line. Both men were under the spell of the Kemalist experiment, and both tried to imitate it in Iraq, with doubtful success. The only positive result of Bekr's rule was the rapprochement with Turkey which was expressed by the conclusion, on July 9, 1937, of the Saadabad pact. This pact, signed by Iraq, Turkey, Iran, and Afghanistan, provided for some cooperation among its signatories. Bekr's lack of political acumen, combined with the arrogant behavior of his close associates, caused him to lose popularity rapidly. His Kurdish background, the exiling of some influential leaders,[9] and the murder of Jafar el-Askari, who had been the real founder of the Iraqi army, were against him. On August 11, 1937, while on their way to watch Turkish military maneuvers, Bekr and Jawad were assassinated in Mosul by their rivals in the army.

As for the British attitude during these events, it was largely noncommittal. Violent changes in Iraq's government made without Britain's previous knowledge and approval were not likely to cause enthusiasm in London, but inasmuch as Bekr Sidki had not been primarily motivated by anti-British feelings, Britain made no overt attempt to get rid of him. His pro-Turkish policy even elicited some faint praise in the British press, the year 1937 being one of gradual Turko-British rapprochement as a result of the dangerous European situation. Britain's readiness to come to terms with this new power in Iraq was expressed by a loan of one million pounds granted to Bekr's government in July 1937, barely one month before his assassination. No regrets, however, were heard in London when the dictator disappeared from the scene, and British diplomacy made a quick readjustment to the new situation. A moderate statesman, Jamil el-Madfai, assumed the premiership. The old pattern of personal rivalries and intrigue was restored, with this difference, that the army, having once tasted power, constantly interfered with political developments. It was an army clique which in 1938 removed Jamil el-Madfai and replaced him with another friend of Britain, Nuri es-Said. And it was still another clique which in March 1939 attempted to oust Nuri as too pro-British.

On April 4, 1939, King Ghazi met his death in an automobile accident near

---

[9]Namely, Yasin el-Hashimi, Rashid Ali el-Gailani, and Nuri es-Said. They sought refuge in Syria and Egypt.

Baghdad. The resulting disorders and the assassination of Mr. Monckton, British consul in Mosul, by an angry mob bore testimony to the anti-British temper of the populace, which was inclined to ascribe any Iraqi misfortune to British machinations. German and Italian propaganda made their substantial contributions to this state of mind, the German minister in Baghdad, Dr. Gritz Grobba, doing much to promote pro-Axis feelings in the country. Ghazi, whose death brought a feeling of relief to London, was succeeded by his infant son Faisal II. A regency was established under the King's maternal uncle, Prince Abdul Ilah, a man acceptable to the British. At this time of growing world crisis, Britain could reasonably expect Iraq to remain faithful to her treaty pledges.

Iraq during World War II

In September 1939, in compliance with the treaty of alliance, the Iraqi government, headed by Nuri es-Said, severed diplomatic relations with Germany. The first two years of the war were rather uneventful. In March 1940, Nuri was replaced by Rashid Ali el-Gailani, a man hostile to the British. This, with Britain's initial reverses at the hands of Germany, gave rise to neutral trends in Iraqi political circles. As a leading British periodical described it, Arab neutrality was based on the following argument: "If Britain wins we shall be safe anyway. If the Nazis are going to win, our only hope is to do nothing to offend them now." Thus, as the paper pointed out, "So long as the issue is undecided, the Axis has the benefit of the doubt."[10] Iraq's cautious course was well illustrated by the government's policy of ignoring the declaration of war on Britain and France by Italy. Italian Minister Gabrielli was allowed to stay in Baghdad and to spread Axis propaganda for nearly a year after Italy's entry into the war, and no amount of British pleading caused the Iraqis to change their minds.

Iraq's position toward Britain was thus governed by Britain's strength vis-à-vis the Axis. The serious defeats suffered by the British in the spring of 1941 in the Balkans, with the Italo-German offensive in Libya, were immediately reflected in the growth of anti-British sentiment in Iraq. This sentiment was heightened by the fact that Baghdad had become a center of pro-Axis intrigue. The exiled mufti of Jerusalem, Haj Amin el-Husseini, and a number of extremist Syrian politicians established themselves there, adding considerably to the nationalist fervor.

As a result of the interplay of Iraqi politics, Rashid Ali lost his office to General Taha el-Hashimi in January 1941. Determined to return to power, Rashid, in conspiracy with a group of four colonels known as the "Golden Square,"[11] executed a coup d'état on April 3, ousting Taha and assuming the premiership. Regent Abdul Ilah, Nuri es-Said, and a majority of the cabinet members excaped to Transjordan. Despite Rashid Ali's assurances that he would honor the Anglo-Iraqi treaty, Britain was determined to restore the legitimate government to power. Sir Kinahan

[10]*The Economist*, Jan. 11, 1941.
[11]These were Colonels Saleh ed-Din es-Sabbagh, Kamil Shabib, Fahmi Said, and Mahmud Salman. For a comprehensive treatment of this period, see Majid Khadduri, *Independent Iraq, A Study in Iraqi Politics from 1932 to 1958* (London, 1960), pp. 212-243.

Cornwallis, an expert on Arab affairs of long experience, arrived in Baghdad as the new ambassador to bolster up British diplomatic action, and toward the end of April a British-Indian military contingent landed in Basra in accordance with the treaty provisions. The arrival of the second contingent, however, provoked Iraqi opposition, and fighting began on May 1. Iraqi artillery surrounded the British air base at Habbaniya, while other forces kept watch on the compound of the British embassy in Baghdad where the British colony found refuge.

Rashid Ali and his associates hoped to secure Axis military assistance. Consequently Defense Minister Sayid Naji Shawkat was dispatched to Ankara to establish liaison with German Ambassador von Papen. The results were disappointing. Germany, busy in Greece and getting ready for the invasion of Russia, was not prepared to divert any substantial amount of aid to Iraq. Moreover, she could not secure transit of arms and troops through Turkey despite pressure on Ankara. The only open channel was Vichy-controlled Syria. Syria's high commissioner, General Dentz, did grant the Germans the use of the Aleppo-Mosul railway for transport of munitions and of the airfields for transit and refueling purposes, but the Nazis were unable to organize a large-scale air operation on such short notice. Eventually, a number of German planes, reportedly not more than twenty-three, landed in Iraq, and for some time Mosul was under German control.

Meanwhile Britain rushed additional troops from Palestine, reinforced by the motorized regiment of Emir Abdullah's Arab Legion from Transjordan. These forces relieved the hard-pressed British garrison at Habbaniya, fought a successful battle at Falluja, and in co-operation with the Basra-based troops entered Baghdad at the end of May. The rebellion was crushed. Rashid Ali, whose short-lived rule was highlighted by the establishment, on May 16, of diplomatic relations with Russia, escaped to Iran. His associates and the mufti also fled abroad, by way of Teheran or Aleppo, and eventually a number of them found their way to Berlin, where they resided until the end of the war.

Under a Pro-Ally Government

The collapse of Rashid Ali's regime enabled the regent and the exiled ministers to return to Iraq. Jamil el-Madfai was installed as premier, to be followed, in October 1941, by Nuri es-Said, who remained in this post until 1944. The country was now governed by the pro-Ally group, and no major political difficulties were experienced during the next four years.[12] Large numbers of British troops poured into Iraq, to be known first as the British Tenth Army, later as the "Paiforce" (Persia and Iraq Force).[13] A Polish army, which had been formed in Russia and transferred to the Middle East, was assigned to guard the northern approaches of Iraq in 1942–1943 against a possible German breakthrough in the Caucasus. In 1942 Iraq

---

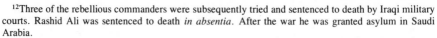

[12]Three of the rebellious commanders were subsequently tried and sentenced to death by Iraqi military courts. Rashid Ali was sentenced to death *in absentia.* After the war he was granted asylum in Saudi Arabia.

[13]For an account of its activities, see *Paiforce: The Official Story of the Persia and Iraq Command, 1941–1946* (London, 1948).

became a recipient of lend-lease aid from the United States, and an American military mission arrived in Basra to aid in forwarding war supplies to the Soviet Union. On January 16, 1943, Iraq declared war on Germany, Italy, and Japan, and on the 22nd she signed the United Nations Declaration, the first Arab country to become eligible to attend the future San Francisco conference.

In this latter part of the war, Iraq's energies, so far as foreign relations were concerned, were focused on collaboration with other Arab states in the creation of the Arab League. Nuri es-Said was very active in promoting the new league and in advocating, simultaneously, the "Greater Syria" plan, which would result in the unification of Syria, Iraq, and Transjordan under a common Hashemite crown.[14] The Iraqis manifested also a growing interest in the United States as expressed by the regent's visit to Washington in May 1945 at President Truman's invitation. Afterward Iraqi and American legations were elevated to the rank of embassies. A by-product of the wartime Soviet-British alliance was the reopening in 1942 of the Soviet legation in Baghdad.

Internally, most of the country except the Kurdish area was quiet. A Kurdish political organization, Komala, organized in Iran in 1943, spread its activities to the Kurdish centers of Iraq, keeping the nationalist spirit alive. Encouraged by Soviet sponsorship of Iranian-Kurdish independence, the Barzani tribe of Iraq, led by Mullah Mustafa, rose in rebellion in 1943 and succeeded in defying the government until the fall of 1945, when it was forced to flee to Iran. There the Barzanis joined hands with the leaders of the short-lived Kurdish republic at Mahabad. Following its collapse, they escaped northward, seeking refuge in the territory of the Soviet Union.

This Kurdish episode once again illustrated how closely internal and external developments in the Middle East were interwoven. The presence of a sizable group of Iraqi Kurds (including several well-trained Iraqi army officers) in Russia added another potential complication to the already tangled Kurdish problem.

After World War II

Upon Prime Minister Nuri's resignation in 1944, the reins of government were taken over by Hamdi el-Pachachi (1944–1946), whose policies did not basically differ from those of his predecessor. Both prime ministers stayed in power longer than any preceding or subsequent Iraqi government. Following Pachachi's term of office, Iraq fell back into the familiar merry-go-round of quickly changing cabinets whose life did not exceed an average of nine months. In 1946, in a move paralleling similar Egyptian action, Prime Minister Tewfik es-Suweidi asked Great Britain for a revision of the treaty of 1930. Iraq's aim, as could be expected, was to remove from the treaty those remnants of British control which were irksome to her national pride. Although Iraq, like the rest of the Middle East, experienced a postwar wave of resurgent nationalism, she did not have in 1946–1947 such violent anti-British

[14]For more details, see Chapters VIII and XIX.

manifestations as those in Egypt.[15] This calm could be attributed partly to the less sophisticated character of Iraqi political circles, as contrasted to the Egyptian, and partly to the nearness of the Soviet Union, whose action in Azerbaijan in 1945–1946 made the more sedate Iraqi politicians think twice before they embarked upon adventurous policies. To this we may add that, in contrast to Egyptian King Farouk, long resentful at the personal humiliations inflicted by the British, Iraq's regent, Abdul Ilah, owed much to Britain and as a Hashemite favored British-Arab understanding.

The revelation of widespread Communist activities (largely stemming from the Soviet legation in Baghdad) and the subsequent arrest and trial in January 1947 of a number of leading Communists stressed once again the reality of the Soviet danger. This undoubtedly strengthened the hand of the regent when in August 1947 he visited London in pursuance of his policy of friendship with Britain. In deference to Iraqi sensibilities, British troops were evacuated from Iraq soon afterward, in October 1947. Only Royal Air Force units remained on the treaty-provided air bases of Habbaniya and Shaiba. Subsequent negotiations for treaty revision were conducted by Foreign Minister Saleh Jabr, who brought them to a successful conclusion on January 16, 1948, by signing a new treaty with Mr. Bevin at Portsmouth. The new treaty, which in many ways resembled the old one, gave Britain the right to send troops to Iraq in the event of war or imminence of war. In return, Britain surrendered her right to occupy two air bases in Iraq but could continue to land aircraft there. The treaty also provided for the training and equipping of the Iraqi army by Great Britain.

There was every likelihood that the new instrument, though with some grumbling, would be accepted by the parliament. Events, however, took a totally unexpected course owing to the sudden emergence of the Palestinian problem. It was Saleh Jabr's misfortune that he had to negotiate with Britain just after the United Nations General Assembly had passed a resolution recommending the partition of Palestine. Public opinion in Iraq, as in other Arab countries, became highly inflamed, and, when the news of the treaty reached Baghdad, anti-British and anti-American riots occurred. Obviously frightened by these outbursts, Regent Abdul Ilah announced, on January 21, that the new treaty did not "realize the national aims of Iraq" and therefore could not be ratified. Upon Saleh Jabr's return from London, he and his cabinet resigned, and on the next day, January 28, the unfortunate prime minister fled by plane to Transjordan to escape the danger of assassination. Mohammed es-Sadr, former president of the Senate, formed a new cabinet.

The Palestinian war, in which Iraqi troops participated alongside Emir Abdullah's Arab Legion, had an upsetting effect on Iraq. The initial sober realism of 1946–1947 gave way to ill-tempered nationalist manifestations, both official and unofficial. On Iraq's demand, the advisory British mission to the Iraqi army was with-

---

[15]This led Col. V. H. Dowson, a British agent long resident in Iraq, to assert with confidence in 1946: "Official classes are now very *friendly with the British,*" and to add, no doubt with an eye to Egyptian developments: "Schoolboy government, such as they have in another country, where the students of the schools and colleges dictate the cabinet's policy, is only in its infancy; and ministers have shown admirable firmness in suppressing its manifestations" (*R.C.A.J.,* July–Oct. 1946, pp. 254 ff.).

drawn on May 16, 1948. The United States Information Office was stoned by an angry mob. Hurried legislation was passed making active Zionism a crime punishable by death. The centuries-old Jewish community in Iraq was exposed to hostility and abuse, and even anti-Zionist protestations of loyalty by Chief Rabbi Sassoon Khadduri proved of little avail. An Iraqi court sentenced to death one of the most prominent Jewish merchants, Ades, for supplying arms to Israel, and the sentence was publicly carried out before an excited multitude. Simultaneously the Jewish minority was subjected to vigorous Zionist propaganda, urging it to emigrate to Israel, a new state badly in need of manpower for both defense and economic reasons. This propaganda probably did more to induce the Jews of Iraq to abandon their homes and business establishments than any actual chicanery at the hands of Iraqis. The Iraqi government was reluctant to allow mass emigration inasmuch as it did not desire any strengthening of Israel. Some Iraqi leaders, moreover, were inclined to hold the Jews as virtual hostages to be used as a lever of pressure should Israel mistreat her own Arab minority. Militating against these considerations was the attractive prospect of "cleansing" the country of an unpopular minority group which would not only leave to aspiring Iraqi competitors its solid position in the world of trade but would also, in the process of hurried leaving, liquidate its properties at a nominal value. Ultimately the latter considerations apparently prevailed, and on March 3, 1950, the Chamber of Deputies passed an emergency bill permitting the Jews to renounce their nationality and emigrate, and soon afterward the government gave permission to an American company, Near East Transport, Inc., to fly more than 50,000 Jews to Israel. Iraq's vindictive spirit went so far as to refuse clearance for the planes if they were to fly directly to Palestine. As a result, flights had to be made first to Cyprus. It was only in 1951 that Iraq agreed to relax these cumbersome regulations. By June 1951, 160,000 Jews had emigrated from Iraq to Israel.

The Palestinian war had an upsetting effect on Iraq's finances also. By cutting the flow of oil through the pipeline linking Kirkuk with Israeli-held Haifa, Iraq deprived herself of about £1,000,000 a year in revenue. (She was, incidentally, the only Arab state to make such a substantial economic sacrifice in the "cold war" with Israel, and this in spite of the accusations of submission to imperialism made by Egypt and other critics in the Arab world.)

Internal Iraqi politics gradually resumed their normal course after the treaty crisis of 1948 with perhaps this difference, that the successive governments have become more sensitive to public opinion as expressed by student demonstrations and mob violence.[16]

Domestic Politics in the 1950s

In the early years of the 1950s Iraq's political forces were divided into two major groups: the ruling conservative group deriving its strength primarily from landown-

---

[16]That not everything was perfect in Iraq's public life was evidenced by an abortive coup staged in February 1950 by Ali Khalid, chief of police. The coup miscarried, and Khalid was promptly put under arrest by the government.

ing elements, more particularly the sheikhs of the Middle Euphrates, and the nationalist and socialist opposition relying, by and large, on support in the cities. The conservative group tended to rally around the person of Nuri es-Said, who emerged, as time went on, not only as an undisputed leader of the status quo forces, but also as the "strong man of Iraq," chief supporter and servant of the Hashemite dynasty, bold spokesman for closer ties with Britain and the West, and an all-Arab statesman of high repute. Endowed with energy and personal charm, Nuri succeeded in organizing not only a devoted following among the traditionalist rank and file but also in subordinating to his leadership an impressive number of conservative elder statesmen. Such former premiers as Jamil el-Madfai, Arshad el-Umari, Ali Jowdat, or Tewfik es-Suweidi, though they might have worked at cross-purposes under less skillful guidance, tended to cooperate with each other and with Nuri as a fairly harmonious team.

The only major defection from this "club" was that of the prominent Shia leader Saleh Jabr, who in June of 1951 formed his Socialist Party of the Nation (Umma). But while not at all negligible, Saleh Jabr's opposition could be termed "loyal" in contrast to that of some other groups, and his party really did not differ radically from Nuri's party. It agreed with the latter on foreign policy while professing a more progressive attitude in domestic matters. In social composition Saleh Jabr's party was not dissimilar to Nuri's. Its principal strength lay in Shia districts, but it should be pointed out that the Umma was not an exclusively Shia party, nor was Nuri's following recruited among the Sunnis only. In fact, Nuri's Union Constitutional party—as his organization was known—enjoyed strong support among the Shias to the extent of dominating such Shia districts as Diwaniya, Hillah, and Amara. The adjective "socialist" in the name of the Umma party should not be interpreted too literally. There was a tendency in the Middle East to equate progress with socialism, and the latter term was definitely in vogue. Actually, in its attitude to private property and free enterprise the Umma party was almost as conservative as Nuri's group.

As for the Union Constitutional party, it would be incorrect to regard it as a mere alliance of old reactionaries. To Nuri's credit it should be pointed out that he surrounded himself with a rather impressive team of competent specialists and administrators in the prime of life. Such men as Dr. Mohammed Fadhil Jamali, Iraq's foremost diplomat and foreign affairs minister; Dr. Dhia Jafar, frequent minister of finance; Dr. Nadim Pachachi, interchangeably in charge of national economy and development; and Khalil Kenna, secretary general of the Union Constitutional party and for a period minister of education, were individuals of high caliber whose talents were essential to the orderly conduct of Nuri's government. Because of this trusted team of associates it was Nuri's government which by and large ruled the country in the 1950s irrespective of whether or not Nuri headed the cabinet himself.

Apart from Saleh Jabr's Umma party, opposition forces rallied to the standards of either the Independence (Istiqlal) party or the National-Democratic party. The Independence party, led by Mohammed Mehdi Kubbah, Faiq Samarrai, and Siddiq Shanshal, stood for complete emancipation from and severance of links with Britain. It was an outspokenly nationalist group, advocating abrogation of the Anglo-Iraqi Treaty of 1930 and a policy of neutralism in the East-West conflict. In full agreement with this foreign program was the National-Democratic party, which in addition advocated socialism as a solution for domestic problems. Led by Kamil Chadirchi and Mohammed Hadid, the party had a strong appeal for students and intelligentsia while also scoring successes among the urban proletariat. Its organ, *Sawt al-Ahali,* time and again suspended by the government, steadily campaigned for the restoration of democratic processes in Iraq, for social justice, and for emancipation from Britain in both the political and the economic fields. A virtual successor to the Ahali group of the 1930s, the National-Democratic party was viewed with particular dislike and suspicion by the Nuri group. The latter, in fact, did not hesitate to accuse it of tolerance toward and infiltration by Communists.

In 1951 the ranks of the opposition were swelled by the formation of a group known as the United Popular Front. In contrast to the Istiqlal and the Socialists, the new group never assumed the proportions of a mass organization. Yet it is noteworthy that its central committee included such prominent figures as General Taha el-Hashimi and Muzahim el-Pachachi, both former premiers of moderate political views. Soon after its formation the Popular Front (El-Jabha esh-Shaabiya) decided to cooperate with Chadirchi's Socialists and went on record as favoring neutrality in world politics, revision of the Anglo-Iraqi treaty, and nationalization of oil.

For some time the oil problem provided a focusing point of political activity. The nationalization of the oil industry in neighboring Iran produced understandable repercussions in Iraq, whereon March 24, 1951, eighteen deputies in the parliament demanded that a similar measure be applied to the Iraq Petroleum Company and its affiliated groups in the country. Although the opposition was not unanimous as to whether or not the oil industry should be nationalized, it strongly campaigned for the obtainment of more favorable terms for Iraq in the negotiations conducted by the government with the company in the course of 1951. The signing of a revised concession agreement on February 3, 1952, and its subsequent ratification by the Nuri-dominated parliament on February 14 and 17 served as a new excuse for the opposition to brand the government as unpatriotic and subservient to "imperialist" interests. Attempts to sabotage the new agreement by a general strike and street demonstrations failed owing to the skill and determination of Nuri Pasha to save his country from the political and economic dangers which had beset Iran under Mossadegh's regime.

Having weathered the oil storm, Nuri resigned as premier, to be replaced by an "independent," Mustafa el-Umari, on July 11, 1952. The period of Nuri's temporary absence from the cabinet was marked by intensified activity on the part of the opposition. Influenced and encouraged by the successful revolution in Egypt (which occurred within two weeks after Nuri's resignation), on October 28 the Istiqlal, the National-Democrats, and the United Popular Front presented notes to Regent Abdul Ilah demanding universal direct suffrage, a purge of the administration, a limitation on land ownership, disarmament of the tribes, lowering of prices on consumers' goods, revision of the constitution in order to limit royal prerogatives, abrogation of the 1930 treaty with Britain, and rejection of Western-sponsored regional defense plans. A similar note was presented to the regent by Saleh Jabr in the name of his Umma party.

The regent's reply was considered unsatisfactory, and the opposition redoubled its efforts to obtain reforms and threatened to boycott the forthcoming elections unless the electoral law were amended to provide for one-degree instead of two-degree voting. A student strike at the Pharmacy School in Baghdad on November 22 became a townwide riot which severely shook the government. Anarchy threatened as security forces failed to prevent mob attacks on the headquarters of Nuri's party and of the Development Board, as well as on the United States Information office and the premises of the *Iraq Times*. The riot was symptomatic of the political situation in Iraq where urban intelligentsia and the poor were in a rebellious mood toward both the government and foreign influences. The extreme turn the demonstrations took could be attributed partly to skillful infiltration by Communists and partly to inability of the police and the opposition parties to control the mob once it was in motion.

Faced with an untenable situation, Umari and his cabinet resigned on the first day of the demonstrations. On November 23 the regent asked General Nur el-Din Mahmud, army chief of staff, to form the cabinet. Mahmud's first acts were to proclaim martial law and close the schools. Arrests of leaders of the Istiqlal and the National-Democrats followed. After having applied these repressive measures, General Mahmud the next day broadcast his cabinet's decision to implement a number of the reforms demanded by the public. Among the latter were the reduction of certain taxes, free higher education, reorganization of the army and purging of the administration, preparation of a law on social security, and, most important perhaps, adoption of universal direct suffrage. The policy was obviously designed to "steal the thunder" from the opposition without upsetting the bases of Iraqi society. Thus, while on the one hand the premier banned publication of twenty-eight newspapers including the organs of all political parties, on the other he made good his promise of direct suffrage by promulgating a new electoral law on December 16.

Legislative elections held under the new law on January 17, 1953, resulted in a victory for the progovernment forces,[17] but despite interference and intimidation charged against the government by the opposition the latter did succeed in electing twenty-one deputies, to whom could be added certain independents dissatisfied with the existing regime.

Having restored public order and normalcy to the country, General Mahmud resigned (apparently his talents were limited to matters of basic security), and a new cabinet, headed by Jamil el-Madfai, with Nuri as minister of defense, came into being. Despite the presence of another man in the driver's seat, it was still Nuri's regime. No wonder then that it was Nuri and not Madfai who was later singled out by Saleh Jabr as the man responsible for the "dictatorship" prevailing in Iraq. Thus, while the authority of the ruling group was reasserted, the basic problem of reform awaited solution. Nuri's opinion, shared by his more conservative as-

---

[17]Nuri Said's Constitutional Union party obtained 67 seats, Popular Front 11, Umma Socialists 8, Istiqlal 1, independents (many of them favoring Nuri) 48, of a total of 135 seats.

sociates, was that the country needed development—technical and economic—rather than reform. With reference to the land, Nuri opposed either limitation of property holdings or division of large estates, favoring instead reclamation and irrigation schemes which would more or less automatically tend to solve certain pressing economic problems. To use a metaphor, the veteran statesman did not believe so much in a different cutting of the cake as in an increase in the size of the cake. Consequently he attached special importance to the newly created Development Board, and as time went on tended to appoint his younger and more capable associates to direct it.

Yet even within the ruling group voices were heard indicating that the way the "cake" was cut was not a matter of indifference. These voices emanated partly from a liberal wing of Nuri's party and partly from circles close to the Court, whose dynastic interests were not always identical with those of the wealthy sheikhs. The coming of age and subsequent ascension to the throne of eighteen-year-old King Faisal II on May 2, 1953, provided an opportunity for these moderate partisans of change to suggest a change in the prevailing pattern. Although it would be hard to assess the degree of popularity of the Hashemite dynasty in Iraq—no poll being conceivable and individual opinions varying from deep attachment to profound dislike—the ascension of the young ruler undoubtedly did evoke a friendly response from great numbers of people. His youth, his position as the orphan son of a popular and nationalistic father, and his personal charm gained him many well-wishers, who looked, not without sentiment, to this young heir of the once-glorious Abbassid capital.

If there had been any doubt as to the restlessness of the discontented elements in Iraq, it was quickly dispelled by the June riots of political prisoners in Baghdad. Another outbreak of prisoners early in September, this time in Kut, seems to have broken the Madfai cabinet. A rather prolonged cabinet crisis during the first two weeks of September was terminated by the appointment, on September 17, of one of Iraq's most outstanding statesmen, Mohammed Fadhil Jamali as premier. Jamali was a good friend of Nuri and belonged to the ruling group, but, in addition, he enjoyed a special position of trust with the Court (to the extent of being dubbed the regent's righthand man) as well as a reputation as a moderate and enlightened liberal. He seemed an almost ideal leader for a peaceful transition from a somewhat petrified traditionalism to a new, more socially conscious era. Most of his associates in the new cabinet were rather young and well educated. They included, significantly enough, two members of the United Popular Front, one of whom was placed in charge of economy and social affairs. His finance minister, Abdul Karim el-Uzri, had fairly advanced ideas about progressive taxation, which he tried to embody in proposed new legislation.

Although Jamali's cabinet, a cabinet of "loyal liberals," started under good auspices, it soon faced mounting difficulties in a number of sectors. In December a major strike broke out among oil workers in Basra. The resulting violence—again attributed to Communist infiltration—led to a proclamation of martial law and to stern reprisals by the government. The Istiqlal and Socialist papers launched new attacks on the government, while the cabinet suffered its first internal dissension, the resignation of the two Popular Front ministers in protest against martial law. Even the abolition of the latter in January 1954 did not restore harmony between the premier and the Popular Front. As time went on, Jamali became a target not only for leftist and nationalist opposition but also for old-time pro-Nuri deputies in the parliament. Too conservative for the opposition, he was deemed too progressive for the old guard, who took strong exception to some agrarian and taxation projects of his cabinet. Under these circumstances, Jamali, a veteran expert in foreign affairs, had little time to concentrate on inter-Arab relations, which as the result of dramatic shifts in Egypt and Syria were entering a new and decisive phase. On January 11, 1954, Jamali presented to the Arab League's Political Committee a plan for Arab federation to be achieved by successive stages, thus reviving the Fertile Crescent plan. It was tabled by the League Committee, and subsequent events at home prevented him from pursuing the matter any further.

Toward the end of March, the Tigris overflowed in one of the worst floods in the history of Iraq, threatening Baghdad with death and destruction. All the energies of the Jamali cabinet centered on protecting the capital, which was indeed saved by the efforts and devotion of both the government and the people. After emerging from this hour of trial and tribulation, the Jamali cabinet encountered renewed hostility from the pro-Nuri majority in parliament. The problem went to the King (and his still influential uncle, Abdul Ilah, now a crown prince): Should the premier be supported and the parliament dissolved in order to produce a new legislature more in step with Jamali's program? Or should the premier be dismissed owing to the mounting opposition in parliament? Ultimately a middle-of-the-road decision was made: parliament would be dissolved, and the premier would resign.

On April 29, Arshad el-Umari formed a new "nonpartisan" cabinet, the task of which was to conduct elections to the new legislature. The elections, which took place on June 9, gave the following results: Constitutional Union party 56; Umma Socialist 14; National Front 12; United Popular Front 0; Independents 51; unidentified 2 out of a total of 135 seats in the Chamber of Deputies. The two most noteworthy features of the election were the diminution of Nuri's strength (a loss of eleven seats) and the appearance of twelve National Front deputies, all representing radical socialist or nationalist tendencies. With the fourteen Umma deputies they constituted an outspoken bloc of twenty-six members opposed to Nuri's leadership. The latter was in London at the time, but one of his associates, Dr. Dhia Jafar, accused the National Front of Communist proclivities. This statement can be taken as representing the view of Nuri and his conservative group. Following the inauguration of the new parliament, Premier Umari resigned, and Nuri, back from London, was offered the premiership. Dissatisfied as he was with the election results, Nuri accepted on the condition that the new parliament promptly be dissolved and that his own line of policy (as expressed in a memorandum to the king) be adopted. Complying with his wishes, the king decreed the dissolution of the parliament on August 3 and the following day appointed Nuri prime minister. New elections, this time supervised by Nuri and his associates, were promptly scheduled for September 12. The intervening two weeks witnessed the suppression of eighteen political newspapers, the passing of stringent decrees designed to curb communism and

Communist-infiltrated trade unions, search and closure by police of the National-Democratic party headquarters, and a decision by the Union Constitutional party to dissolve itself, thus paving the way for a nonparty system.

As could be expected, the September elections resulted in an overwhelming victory for the Nuri forces. The Popular Front (a complete loser in June) now secured two seats, and the Istiqlal two also, but these seats were secured more as a result of a "gentleman's agreement" between the ruling group and the individual deputies elected than as the result of a genuine electoral struggle. In fact, the Istiqlal soon disavowed the two members claiming to represent it. Between September 16 and 19 new stringent press and assembly decrees were passed, to be followed, a few days later, by the dissolution of all political parties.

Thus, by the fall of 1954 Iraq had returned in her internal affairs to where she stood before the "liberal" experiment of the Jamali period: the conservatives were back in power and Nuri's sway over national affairs was not only reconfirmed but further entrenched. Opposition was dispersed and driven underground, and renewed emphasis was placed on development rather than on reform. Outwardly, the country returned to normalcy, and this imposed stability distinguished it from a number of other Arab states, seething as they were with unrest and excitement.

The Baghdad Pact

Having removed the internal obstacles, Nuri es-Said was in a position to concentrate on the major foreign policy issues awaiting solution. A few years had already been spent in a search for a formula which would strengthen the Free World's defenses against Russian imperialism and yet be palatable to the peoples of the Middle East. In 1953, however, the original Western plan to form a Middle East Defense Organization had had to be abandoned reluctantly, mainly owing to Egypt's opposition. Other ways were explored, and the new formula, as devised by Washington and London, was to concentrate on the so-called Northern Tier, i.e., the chain of countries between Turkey and Pakistan, which, more conscious of the Soviet danger, were expected to enter into bilateral or multilateral military assistance agreements. With the major lines of strategy thus outlined, the initiative was promptly seized by Turkey, who first of all concluded a military assistance pact with security-minded Pakistan (April 2, 1954) and then with dynamic diplomacy followed it up with similar agreements between herself, Iraq, and Iran. Other Arab countries were further possibilities. Although not a direct participant in negotiations, the United States gave evidence of backing up these defense plans by continuing its aid to Turkey, concluding a mutual assistance treaty with Pakistan (May 19, 1954), and simultaneously offering military aid (but not a pact) to Iraq.

Iraq had to make two basic decisions: (1) whether or not to become a party in the Northern Tier defense pacts and (2) how to shape her relationship with Britain, to whom she was linked by the treaty of 1930. A decision to join in Western-sponsored military pacts would strengthen Iraq against the only real danger that might possibly threaten her—the danger of Soviet aggression and Communist subversion. This strengthening would come about through political guarantees, military assistance, and arms supplies. The latter especially would bolster up a regime which had to place much reliance on its army and police. The disadvantages of this course would be in estranging the Egyptian-led majority of the Arab League and in antagonizing sizable segments of domestic public opinion, already restive over internal issues. With regard to the second basic decision—concerning the Anglo-Iraqi treaty—public opinion in Iraq strongly favored abrogation or at least radical revision. It might be unsafe for any, even the strongest, government to flout the feelings of the majority on this question. The treaty was due to expire in 1957, and pressure not to renew it would undoubtedly mount as the termination date approached. The government could, of course, do nothing and allow the treaty to lapse in due time. But the disadvantage of such a course was that relations with Britain would deteriorate and the government in its purely passive role would get no credit from the populace.

Nuri Said had little if any hesitation regarding the course to follow. An old political realist, he was determined to join the Western-sponsored security system and at the same time he wanted to take the opportunity to rid Iraq of the unequal treaty with Britain. The reasoning behind this resolve was as follows: Iraq does not want to sever links with Britain, but she does not wish to continue them on an unequal basis (i.e., with Britain possessing air bases and special privileges in Iraq). To terminate the Anglo-Iraqi treaty and thus force the British to evacuate Iraq before the date of expiry would be a major national achievement. At the same time Iraq should not reject the security which the British alliance offered, but she should transfer it from the narrow field of bilateral relations with Britain to the broader field of a regional pact in which Britain would participate not as a sole partner but as one of a number of powers.

Considerable opposition to these plans, especially on the part of the Cairo-Riyadh axis, could be anticipated. As soon as Nuri was installed in office, he was visited by Major Saleh Salem, a member of the Egyptian military junta in charge of inter-Arab affairs,[18] who did his best, at a conference in Sarsank in mid-August, to dissuade Nuri from pursuing this policy. According to some reports, Salem went so far as to promise that Egypt would not object to a Syro-Iraqi union provided Iraq stayed out of the "foreign pacts." Nuri, however, remained unshaken and made neither promises nor commitments. Following this attempt at direct intervention, Egypt concentrated her efforts on the Arab League, trying to influence Iraq through League resolutions.

In the meantime Iraq and Turkey made further moves toward closer collaboration. Between January 6 and 14, 1955, Turkish Premier Adnan Menderes visited Baghdad, and on January 13 he and Nuri Said announced that a mutual assistance pact would soon be signed. The announcement provoked an outburst of criticism in Egypt, where Premier Colonel Gamal Abdul Nasser promptly called for a conference of Arab premiers in Cairo to discuss the League's relations with the West. Boycotted by Nuri, the conference convened on January 22. In the course of discussions the Egyptian premier insisted on a resolution which would not only declare any military pacts concluded by League members outside the League as inconsistent with the League's charter and the inter-Arab security pact but would

---

[18] His official position was that of minister of national guidance and Sudan affairs.

also condemn Iraq for her expressed desire to sign a pact with Turkey. The assembled premiers were not ready, however, to go that far and proposed instead that a commission of four (composed of the premiers of Syria, Lebanon, and Jordan and Major Salem of Egypt) be sent to Baghdad to mediate. The brief visit of this commission to the Iraqi capital (January 31–February 2) proved fruitless, and the conference ended without producing a resolution or even a final communiqué.

On February 24, 1955, the Turkish-Iraqi Pact was signed in Baghdad by the President of Turkey and the King of Iraq, who were with their premiers and foreign ministers. Strictly speaking, the pact did not provide for an alliance. But it stipulated cooperation to assure the contracting parties' security and defense, noninterference in internal affairs, the possibility of the future adhesion of other states interested in the security of the Middle East provided they are recognized by both parties, and the creation of a permanent ministerial council to implement the pact if and when at least four parties became signatories to it. The signing of the pact was followed by an exchange of interpretive letters between the Turkish and the Iraqi premiers, in which it was stated that both countries would work together toward the implementation of the United Nations resolutions concerning Palestine.[19] In a political sense this represented the price Turkey had to pay for wooing away one of the Arab states from the rest—the recognition that henceforth she would stand closer to the Arabs than to Israel on vital issues affecting the latter's security and territorial integrity. On February 26 the Turkish and the Iraqi parliaments ratified the pact by overwhelming majorities.

During subsequent months Egypt and Saudi Arabia displayed feverish activity to isolate Iraq from other members of the League, to prevent others from joining the Turkish-Iraqi Pact, and to promote a new, tripartite security pact, which would link Cairo with Riyadh and Damascus and thus constitute a counterweight to the Northern Tier alliances. Their efforts were partly successful (see Chapter XII below), but they failed to intimidate Iraq. On the contrary, their aggressiveness (which went so far as to support a "Free Iraq" radio station located in Egypt and broadcasting propaganda injurious to Nuri and his government) strengthened Iraq's resolve to follow an independent policy.

In Baghdad on March 30, 1955, Britain and Iraq initialed an agreement whereby (1) Britain adhered to the Turkish-Iraqi Pact of February 24; (2) both parties agreed to abrogate the Anglo-Iraqi Treaty of Alliance of June 30, 1930; and (3) Britain undertook to supply military aid and in case of aggression recognized by both parties as endangering Iraq's security promised, at Iraq's request, to come to the latter's assistance. On April 4 this new agreement was signed in Baghdad by both parties. It did not require ratification by the Iraqi parliament, being treated as an annex to the Turkish-Iraqi Pact, which, in Article 5, foresaw such future adhesions.[20]

Britain's adherence was of momentous significance inasmuch as it introduced the first major power into a pact hitherto linking medium or small states only. While

[19]The text is in the *Middle East Journal,* 9 (Spring 1955), 177.
[20]The text is in *Cahiers,* 1955, 1.

strengthening the pact in a military sense, this step implied also a possibility of further extension of British influence in this region. The failure of the United States (a tacitly sponsoring power) to join the pact was due partly to America's reluctance to burn the bridges in her relations with Egypt and partly to the protests of Israel, who attacked the pact as hostile to herself. From the Iraqi point of view this American hesitation had unfortunate effects inasmuch as it exposed the pact to further criticism that in reality it was nothing but a British instrument and that, instead of linking Iraq's security with the West in general (thus avoiding domination by any single power), it allowed Britain to "leave by the door but come back by the window." These objections were likely to be especially well founded in the case of Iran, should she be invited to join the pact. They were not likely, however, to deter Pakistan, already a signatory of a collaboration treaty with Turkey (see p. 145 above). Indeed, Pakistan did declare her adherence to the pact on June 30, thus completing the foursome required for the establishment of a permanent pact organization.

Adherence by Iran became the next problem on the agenda. For various reasons including those mentioned above Iran was reluctant to commit herself to the Western bloc, and as the fall of 1955 approached it looked as if the Baghdad Pact (as it has come to be known) would have to do without that geographical link between Pakistan and the rest of the signatories. But following the visit of Premier Menderes of Turkey to Teheran in early fall, Iran reversed herself and in October joined the pact.

Thus the Northern Tier defense scheme became a reality, and the pact powers could proceed, without further impediments, to set up a permanent organization. The latter came into being at the first meeting of the pact powers, which was held in Baghdad November 20–22, 1955. Presided over by Nuri Said, the meeting was attended by the premiers of the pact's Middle Eastern signatories and the foreign secretary of Britain. It resulted in the establishment of a permanent secretariat with headquarters in Baghdad and in the selection of an Iraqi, Awni Khalidi, as its first secretary general. To Nuri Said the event was a crowning of his long-range efforts and a vindication of his foreign policy. Though estranged from Egypt and Saudi Arabia, Iraq had found her place among those Islamic nations for whom the menace of Soviet imperialism and atheism overshadowed such potential dangers or inconveniences as might result from closer ties to the West.

The Last Phase of Iraqi Monarchy, 1956–1958

Following Iraq's adherence to the Baghdad Pact in 1955, its policies could be described as a forging of links with the West, isolation from the Arab world, and concentration on its own economic development. In anticipation of steady oil royalties at a rate of $220 million or more a year, the government of Iraq in 1956 launched a new phase of its development plan, which called for expenditures of $1.4 billion during the next five years. In April of the same year a Development Week was celebrated throughout the country, attended by inauguration ceremonies of several new projects, including two major water-control schemes, the Wadi Tharthar Dam near Samarra on the Tigris and the Habbaniya flood-control project with a dam at Ramadi on the Euphrates. Designed to attract public attention to the country's steady economic progress, the Development Week became an annual event, repeated in 1957 and 1958.

Had Iraq been permitted to avoid inter-Arab entanglements, it is possible that, with its concentration on domestic development, it would have reached a substantially higher economic level and that the inevitable percolating of the material benefits to various strata would have reduced social and political tensions to a minimum compatible with the safety of the country. Alas, this was not to be. As a result of various dramatic developments in the Middle East between 1956 and 1958, Iraq was continuously exposed to agitation stemming from outside sources. The Suez crisis of October-November 1956 was the first major event during that period to have a markedly unsettling effect on Iraq's inner peace. In early November Iraq's troops were sent to Jordan at the latter's request as a precautionary move in case the Egyptian-Israeli hostilities expanded beyond Sinai. On November 9 the Baghdad government broke diplomatic relations with France and simultaneously it decided to boycott any meetings of the Baghdad Pact organization attended by Britain. Iraq's delegate at the United Nations, Dr. Fadhil Jamali, proclaimed his country's full solidarity with Egypt in the face of Israeli aggression. Inside Iraq the Suez crisis gave rise to public indignation against Western imperialism to the acute embarrassment of the Western-oriented government of Premier Nuri Said. This was seized upon by the leaders of the opposition, who, in a petition addressed to the king in November, demanded a radical change in Iraq's internal and foreign policies. Soon afterward protest demonstrations and riots occurred in Mosul, Najaf, Kut, and other centers. The government met these manifestations with stern measures: late in November it ordered the arrest of five principal opposition leaders,[21] and on December 1 it proclaimed martial law for all of Iraq. Even the latter did not, however, prevent a peasant revolt from erupting with considerable violence in Al-Hai (Kut district) on December 21. A number of lives were lost before the government forces succeeded in restoring order in that locality as well as in the country as a whole.

The major challenge to Iraq's government stemmed from the fact that the Suez crisis added greatly to the stature and prestige of President Nasser of Egypt as an all-Arab leader and symbol of anti-imperialist struggle. Passive isolation was no longer possible for Iraq because Nasserism was making inroads everywhere in the Arab world, using the radio, the press, Egyptian school teachers, and a variety of other agents as a means of communication. Unless it decided to surrender to this popular wave of Cairo-sponsored Arabism, Iraq's government had no choice but to combat it and to seek allies in the struggle. Such allies could be found in the remaining monarchical regimes in the Arab world. In February 1957 Iraq's crown prince and former regent, Abdul Ilah, undertook a trip to Washington at a time when King Saud of Saudi Arabia was paying a state visit to President Eisenhower. Accompanied by four former premiers of Iraq (Tewfik es-Suweidi, Saleh Jabr,

---

[21]These were Kamil Chadirchi, leader of the National-Democratic Party; Faiq Samarrai, leader of the National Congress; Hussein Jamil, president of the Lawyers Association; Abdur Rahman Bazzaz, dean of the Law School; and Senator Mohammed Shabibi of the United Popular Front. They were subsequently given jail sentences on Dec. 19, 1956.

Fadhil Jamali, and Jamil el-Madfai), Abdul Ilah met King Saud and discussed with him thoroughly the situation in the Middle East. The gist of these discussions was that no useful purpose would be served by a continuation of the mistrust between the House of Saud and the House of Hashem; that the real threat to Saudi security was to be sought, not in the Hashemite policy of revenge which belonged to the past, but in the current revolutionary ideology of Nasser; and that the two monarchies should work together to protect themselves against this danger.

Thus the foundation stone for the "Kings' Alliance" was laid on the banks of the Potomac. In due course this alliance was enlarged by the virtual inclusion of Hashemite Jordan. It was cemented by a series of meetings mong the three kings concerned: in May 1957 King Saud paid a state visit to Baghdad which ended in a joint communiqueé in which Saud and Iraq's Faisal condemned communism, imperialism, and Zionism; in June, Faisal of Iraq and Hussein of Jordan met to discuss common policies; and in December, Faisal visited Saud in Riyadh. On his way back from the United States, Prince Abdul Ilah spent a few days in Rabat in an attempt to line up King Mohammed V of Morocco as another potential ally in the camp of conservatism.

If the formation of the Kings' Alliance could be viewed as the first reaction of the spread of Nasserism, the subsequent federation of Iraq and Jordan should be considered as the second. The act of union took place on February 14, 1958, largely in response to the merger of Syria with Egypt, which preceded it by two weeks. According to this act, a federative state called "The Arab Federation" was established by Iraq and Jordan; it was to be open to adherence by other Arab states. The two founding states were to preserve their political structures and to honor such treaty obligations as had been contracted prior to the act of union. The king of Iraq was designated as the head of the federation, with its capital alternating between Baghdad and Amman every six months. A federation cabinet and a common parliament were to be established in addition to the existing Iraqi and Jordanian cabinets and parliaments. Defense, foreign policy, customs laws, and educational curricula were to be completely unified forthwith. Unification of currency and of financial and economic policies was to be achieved "as quickly as possible."

Throughout this time, Nuri es-Said continued in power in Iraq, either directly as premier or indirectly, as was the case between June 17, 1957, and March 2, 1958, when the official duties of premiership were assumed by his trusted associates, Ali Jowdat el-Ayyubi and Abdul Wahhab Marjan, successively. On March 3, 1958, Nuri returned to the office himself, to be promoted to the premiership of the federation on May 18, while the premiership of Iraq was entrusted to Ahmed Mukhtar Baban. In the federal cabinet Iraqis and Jordanians were represented in approximately equal numbers.

The Revolution of 1958 and Its Aftermath

Outwardly it would appear that Nuri's regime had taken the necessary measures to entrench itself in power and to stave off revolutionary threats to its existence, whether of internal or external origin. In the realm of Arab politics it had obtained close cooperation with like-minded conservative regimes; in the domestic sphere it controlled the country by a combination of skillful political maneuvering and close police supervision while carrying out a well-conceived development plan; and in foreign policy it reaped the benefits of its alliance with the West by receiving arms, technical assistance, and aid in the common struggle against Communist subversion. Yet all these methods and safeguards provided no real deterrence against the bold advances of the revolutionary Pan-Arab ideology emanating from Cairo. A majority of Iraq's intelligentsia was estranged from the regime, with which it associated the evils of corruption, subservience to Western imperialism, and isolation from the mainstream of Arab thought and policies.[22]

Thus was the stage set for the coup that occurred on July 14, 1958. In the early hours of the day units of the Twentieth Brigade under the command of Brigadier-General Abdul Karim Kassem, on their way to Jordan, seized control of Baghdad. Within a few hours all members of the royal family then in Baghdad, including King Faisal II and Crown Prince Abdul Ilah, met their death. Federal and Iraqi cabinet ministers were placed under arrest, except for Nuri, who went into hiding but was discovered a few days later disguised as a woman and killed.

The new revolutionary authorities were then set up, comprising the Council of Sovereignty of three members,[23] and the cabinet, the latter headed by General Kassem, who also retained supreme command of the armed forces. Colonel Abdul Salam Mohammed Aref became deputy premier and deputy commander in chief. Outstanding leaders of the former opposition parties were invited to join the government: Mohammed Hadid of the National-Democratic party as minister of finance, Siddiq Shanshal of the Istiqlal party as minister of guidance, Fuad Rikabi of the Arab Socialist Renaissance party (Baath) as minister of development, and Ibrahim Kubbah, a man of Marxist leanings, as minister of national economy. A few other civilians and military men completed the cabinet. On July 14, the day of the coup, General Kassem as leader of the revolution issued his first public statement in which he (1) proclaimed the deliverance "of our beloved country from the corrupt clique installed by imperialism," (2) announced "the formation of a popular republic adhering to complete Iraqi unity," and (3) called for "brotherly ties with the Arab and Moslem states" and a foreign policy conforming to "the principles of the Bandung Conference," i.e., a policy of neutralism and nonalignment.[24]

On July 26 the government announced a provisional constitution which proclaimed Iraq as "part of the Arab nation," described the Kurds as associated with the Arabs "in the bosom of Iraqi unity," named Islam as the religion of the state, and designated the Council of Ministers (the cabinet) as a supreme legislative and executive authority.[25]

---

[22]For an illuminating discussion of political moods in Iraq, see Caractacus (pseud.), *Revolution in Iraq: An Essay in Comparative Public Opinion* (London, 1959).

[23]General Najib Rubai was chairman; the other two members were Mohammed Mehdi Kubbah, leader of the Istiqlal party, and Khalid el-Naqshabandi, a Kurd.

[24]Quotations are from *The Iraqi Revolution: One Year of Progress and Achievement* (Baghdad, 1959), p. 7.

[25]Text in *Oriente Moderno* (Aug.-Sept. 1958), pp. 665–667.

Within a few days after the coup Deputy Premier Colonel Aref traveled to Damascus, where on July 19, after a cordial meeting with President Nasser of the United Arab Republic, he signed on behalf of Iraq an agreement pledging close cooperation between the two countries in the military, political, economic, and cultural spheres. The rapprochement with Nasser was accompanied by the establishment of diplomatic relations with Russia and other countries of the Soviet bloc, none of which had been represented in Baghdad during the *ancien régime*. Before long various political exiles began returning to Baghdad. Foremost among them were Rashid Ali el-Gailani, leader of the anti-British coup of 1941, and Mullah Mustafa Barzani, a Kurdish rebel chieftain who had lived in the Soviet Union since the downfall of the Kurdish Republic of Mahabad in 1946. Similarly, certain Communist leaders who had fled Nuri's police in the prerevolutionary era made their way back to Iraq in the hope of reviving their political movement.

In the domestic sector the new regime left no doubt as to its profoundly revolutionary character. It promptly established a special tribunal called the People's Court, encouraged the formation of a citizens' militia known as the Popular Resistance Forces, and on September 30, 1958, enacted an agrarian reform law setting a limit of 620 acres to irrigated private lands and 1,240 acres to unirrigated ones. The People's Court soon gained wide notoriety due to the emotional outbursts of its president, Colonel Fadhil Abbas Mahdawi, a cousin of General Kassem, against the numerous old-regime politicians and army officers who stood trial on a variety of charges, including their attempts to overthrow the pro-Nasser government in Syria in 1957.

During the first months following the coup of July 14, Iraq experienced a feverish existence typical of a country in the throes of the revolution. Western embassies were surrounded by armored troops and prevented from communicating with the public; many Western technicians were compelled to leave the country, while contracts with their firms were canceled by the government; and occasionally foreigners were placed under arrest or subjected to mob violence (in one such case three Americans lost their lives). At the same time both the police and the armed militia hunted for people associated with the former regime in a general atmosphere of terror and with prisons overflowing with political detainees. Regular administrative functions of the government suffered a serious collapse, while political groups, students, and city mobs eagerly responded to any encouragement to parade and demonstrate in the streets of Baghdad and other centers. City walls were plastered with a variety of posters and pictures, those of President Nasser vying with those of General Kassem for the most prominent place.

Crisis over Relations with the U.A.R.

From the outset the Iraqi revolution had had two alternatives, either of achieving some form of union with the United Arab Republic or of staying as a separate political entity. Manifestations of joy over the successful overthrow of the old regime and protestations of Arab solidarity could only postpone but not eliminate the hour of decision. Two observations may be in order at this point. The first is that according to available evidence the Cairo government was not responsible either for the planning or the execution of the Iraqi coup, which was of General Kassem and his associates' own making. The second is that the revolutionary Pan-Arab propaganda emanating from Cairo was largely responsible for the creation of the mental and emotional climate in which the Iraqi army conspiracy could develop and thrive. In all likelihood those Iraqi army officers who helped General Kassem were as strongly motivated by their hostility to Nuri's regime on internal grounds as by their espousal of the philosophy of Arabism which condemned Iraq's isolation from the rest of the Arab community. But did it follow from the latter that they would be prepared to accept merger with Egypt and Syria, to submit to Nasser's rule, and to share the oil wealth of their country? Not necessarily. All that can be said with a degree of certainty is that opinions on this subject were divided. It appears that Premier Kassem's deputy, Colonel Abdul Salam Aref, represented a strong unionist tendency, which found its expression in his hasty trip to Damascus right after the coup and his repeated protestations of brotherhood with the Cairo regime. He may have been supported in this orientation by the returned exile, Rashid Ali el-Gailani, but we lack firm evidence on this point. Not much is known about the degree of support Aref had among army officers. As a general political law one might venture the suggestion that any organized hierarchical grouping develops a vested interest in self-preservation and is unlikely to opt for a merger with another stronger organization unless there are very alluring, if not spectacular, incentives. One doubts whether, despite their basic Pan-Arab emotional inclination, most Iraqi army officers would really have cherished the idea of becoming submerged in a larger entity dominated by the Egyptians.

This probably explains why in the contest for power and policy orientation which developed between Aref and Kassem as early as September 1958 the latter, clearly opting for Iraq's independence, emerged victorious. This contest was played in a few dramatic moves and countermoves, in the following sequence: Anxious to put an early end to the attempts to unify Iraq and Egypt, Premier Kassem in September decided to remove Aref from the Baghdad scene and persuaded him to leave for Bonn as ambassador to the West German Republic. In violation of orders Aref returned to Baghdad in October. He was immediately placed under arrest and indicted for plotting against the security of the country. On December 8, 1958, Premier Kassem announced the discovery of a conspiracy aiming at the overthrow of his regime. "The plot," said the premier, "was the work of some corrupt elements with the help of foreigners outside Iraq." Although the "foreigners" were not identified, belief that the plot was organized by Colonel Aref's followers with the assistance of Cairo has gained wide credence in Iraq and abroad. There were, moreover, rumors that the British embassy had obtained advance information of the conspiracy and had tipped off Premier Kassem.

Colonel Aref's arrest and the December crisis contributed directly to a marked deterioration in Iraqi-U.A.R. relations. Early in 1959 an exacerbated propaganda war was waged between the two countries. Inside Iraq the lines between those favoring union with Cairo and those opposing it became more clearly drawn. Among the former the Iraqi branch of the Baath party was most prominent. It soon became apparent that there were only two groups whose ideology, organization, and discipline were capable of mobilizing the Iraqi populace for the purposes of mass action: the Nasserists and the Communists. Inasmuch as the main danger to Premier Kassem's regime stemmed momentarily from the pro-Nasser elements, he seems to have allowed, if not actually encouraged, the Communists to take strong countermeasures. As a result, the winter of 1958–1959 went into history as a period of tremendous upsurge in Communist activity. Communists successfully infiltrated and often gained control of such organizations as the Popular Resistance Forces, trade unions, student federations, professional associations, and any group with a mass following, while at the same time gaining preponderant influence in a number of ministries, schools, official propaganda agencies, and the press. Their advances were greatly aided by the televised treason trials in the People's Court, whose spectacular proceedings contributed to the general atmosphere of revolutionary effervescence. The death sentences pronounced on Aref and Gailani in January 1959 were important advances in the struggle that the Kassem regime was waging against the pro-Nasser forces. In the same month the government announced a posthumous rehabilitation of certain Communist leaders who had been hanged by the pre-revolutionary government. Simultaneously, the Communist Party stepped up its demands for early execution of the old-regime politicians who had been sentenced to death in the fall of 1958 but whose sentences had not been carried out. In deference to this pressure Premier Kassem ordered the execution of three among them: former Interior Minister Said Qazzaz and two others responsible for internal security during the old era.

Soon, however, the upsurge of Communist activity was to encounter resistance. The opposition was not limited to pro-Nasser elements but embraced a wide array of forces which could most conveniently be termed nationalist and which frequently stood for an independent non-Communist Iraq neither united nor federated with Cairo. On a high government level this resistance found its expression in the resignation of six cabinet members on February 7, 1959. Foremost among them was Siddiq Shanshal, minister of national guidance. The man who replaced him, Hussein Jamil, a National-Democrat, stayed in the office for only five days, resigning for similar reasons. Simultaneously, the Baath representative in the cabinet, Fuad Rikabi, was deprived of the portfolio of development and given a rather nominal function as minister of state.

The Mosul Revolt and the Kirkuk Massacres

What the civilian leaders tried to do by peaceful methods, a dissident faction in the army decided to achieve by force. On March 8, 1959, Colonel Abdul Wahab el-Shawaf, commander of the local garrison, seized power in Mosul, proclaiming a revolt against Kassem's government. The immediate cause of this uprising was the convergence upon Mosul of thousands of Peace Partisans (a thinly disguised Communist-Front organization) who came there in government-provided trains to hold a major rally. Their aggressive behavior sparked the revolt, which had been growing for some time. Unfortunately for the rebels, their action was poorly planned and they had no air cover. Furthermore, the commander of the Mosul division, General Nadhim Tabaqchali, on whose support the rebels counted, preferred to adopt a neutral attitude pending future developments. After the initial shock the government moved against the rebels, using its loyal troops, who were supported both by the air force and by the armed Kurdish tribesmen from the vicinity of Mosul. In the course of the operations Colonel Shawaf lost his life following an air raid, and by March 13 his rebellion had collapsed.

What followed in Mosul could be likened to Dantean horror scenes. Communist liquidation squads went on a rampage, attacking homes of the Mosul bourgeoisie and perpetrating all sorts of atrocities. At the same time a self-appointed proletarian "people's court," sitting in a public square, was meting out summary justice to the "enemies of the people" on the slightest suspicion or denunciation. Sentences of death were carried out on the spot, in the view of the excited multitudes. To Mosul's leading families these were days of doom and despair. But to the people of Iraq as a whole the Mosul experience served as a shocking reminder of what might lay in store should the Communists effectively seize power in the country. From then on resistance by nationalist elements to Communist inroads steadily increased.

On the other hand, obviously intoxicated by their Mosul successes, the Communists became increasingly bolder in their advances. In April their cause was strengthened by the return from the Soviet Union of over eight hundred Kurds of the Barzani tribe. A Peace Partisans' congress on April 14 in Baghdad provided another major manifestation of their strength. And on May 1 the mass parades under their auspices were so spectacular and well attended as to cause widespread apprehension that the party's sweep to power was only a matter of time.

Washington viewed the Iraqi scene with considerable alarm. Testifying before the Senate Foreign Relations Committee on April 28, Allen W. Dulles, director of the Central Intelligence Agency, declared that the situation in Iraq was "the most dangerous in the world today." A week later, John D. Jernegan, American ambassador in Baghdad, flew to Washington for consultations on what appeared to be a steadily deteriorating situation. Although there is no doubt that the British government concurred with Washington regarding the gravity of the Iraqi developments, it is interesting to note that it had somewhat more confidence in Premier Kassem's ability to resist Communist pressures. This was expressed by the announcement on May 11, 1959, that Britain had agreed to sell a substantial quantity of arms to Iraq.

During the first half of the summer of 1959 the Communists in Iraq exerted major efforts either to share in power or to seize it. Their tactics consisted of three actions: (1) They endeavored to create a so-called United National Front with the National-Democrats and the Kurdish Democratic party. If successful, this attempt might have given them a major, and possibly a directing, role in the civilian coalition supporting Kassem's government. (2) They voiced a demand for direct participation in the cabinet. Here they scored a success when on the first anniversary of the revolution Premier Kassem reshuffled his cabinet, appointing four new ministers, of whom two were generally identified as members of the Communist party and one as pronouncedly leftist.[26] (3) By resorting to violence and terror, they

---

[26]The three Communist-leftist ministers were Madame Dr. Naziha Dulaimi (Municipalities), Awni Yusuf (Works and Housing), and Faisal el-Samir (National Guidance).

attempted to seize power in certain provincial centers of Iraq. The most notable of their terroristic excesses were the bloody disturbances in Kirkuk between July 14 and 19. There the Communists, aided by local Kurds and some detachments of the army, attacked numerous private homes and business establishments to drag their inhabitants, many of Turkoman nationality, into the streets and to inflict upon them torture and death. Eventually army units loyal to the government had to be called in to restore order and apprehend some of the culprits.

Of the three actions just mentioned, the party failed in two, while succeeding in one—namely, in gaining cabinet seats. But even in this one the success was of dubious value inasmuch as Premier Kassem was now alerted to the dangers of cooperating with the party and even of tolerating it. The Kirkuk incidents dramatized a number of questions regarding communism in Iraq, both for the people as a whole and for the Communists themselves. There was, in the first place, much speculation as to the real directing force of the Communist movement in Iraq. Was it Russian or Chinese, with implications of rivalry between the two, or was it the coordinated action of both? Various theories were advanced. One of them was that the Chinese were aiming at a quick seizure of power by the Iraqi Communist party through violent means if necessary, while the Russians were favoring gradualism and an increase in influence through friendly but correct dealings with Kassem's government on the official level. No convincing documentation is available as yet to permit a conclusive judgment. There is evidence, however, that the party itself took a second look at its own strategy and tactics.

In mid-July the Central Committee of the Iraqi Communist party held an enlarged session, at which it drew up a lengthy report, subsequently published in the party's chief press organ. Indulging freely in self-criticism, the Committee acknowledged that it had made "a wrong assessment, which exaggerated our own forces and minimized the role of the patriotic government and the other national forces in safeguarding the Republic." It admitted that "raising the slogan for participation in the government was an erroneous sectarian act" and that "the mass method which was taken as a means to express this demand . . . was another factor which deepened the negative results in the situation." In a rather amazing upsurge of frankness, the Committee furthermore confessed to have taken "a wrong stand on the excesses of the masses." "This does not mean," it added, "that we never opposed such excesses. . . . In general, however, we did not make sufficient effort in this respect." And to make its stand clear on this issue, the Committee asserted: "The use by some politically backward people of methods of dragging bodies, torturing detainees, looting and trespassing on the rights and liberties of some citizens is something which has no link with guided revolutionary struggle directed against the enemies of the Republic. . . . Our Party, which has never participated in the responsibility of government, has less chance of preventing the acts of torture which were inflicted upon detainees, in circumstances of mutiny and plotting against the Republic. Under no circumstances does it approve such methods of treating accused persons."[27]

---

[27]Central Committee of the Iraqi Communist Party, "For the Consolidation of the Unity of the Patriotic Forces, for the Defense of the Republic and the Gains of the Revolution" (report of the enlarged session held in July 1959), *Ittihad el-Shaab*, Aug. 23, 1959.

Kassem's Curbs on Communism

The two demonstrations of Communist strength and tactics, the May 1 parades and the Kirkuk massacres of mid-July, apparently made a deep impression on Premier Kassem, causing him to revise and reorient his policy toward the party. Instead of relying on it as a force capable of counteracting the pro-Nasser elements, the premier began to restrict its activities and curb its influence. The new policy was gradual and the premier avoided attacking the party openly. His preferred mode of expression in many public speeches was to condemn "the forces of anarchy" as well as "certain trends," while appealing to the unity of the "eternal Republic." More concretely, his government used its influence to eliminate the Communists from control of trade unions and professional and mass associations, restricted the freedom hitherto enjoyed by the Communist-dominated Popular Resistance Forces, and applied various repressive measures toward the Communist press, such as suspensions and arrests of the editors. Furthermore, it encouraged dissension within the Communist ranks. When, on January 6, 1960, Premier Kassem announced the restoration of political party life in the country, two Communist parties applied for a license, but only one—a small dissident group led by Daoud Sayegh and willing to follow the government's lead—was recognized. The application of the larger one, led by Khairi Said and styling itself Ittihad el-Shaab ("Union of the People"), was rejected.

Throughout 1960 the policy of curbing Communist influence was expressed by a number of new measures. These included increased toleration of articles attacking communism in the growing number of nationalist papers; the abrupt dismissal in February of the pro-Communist minister of development, Ibrahim Kubbah, followed by that of Dr. Naziha Dulaimi; virtual silencing of the flamboyant president of the People's Court, Colonel Fadhil Abbas Mahdawi, and the suspension of the court's activities; commutation of the death sentences of certain prominent figures of the old regime; the trial, for killings and atrocities, of the "people's judges" of Mosul and of some perpetrators of the Kirkuk crimes; the curbing of the Communist-inspired strikes and riots of the tobacco workers and taxi drivers; and encouragement of an anti-Communist group of socialists to form a new National Progressive party aiming at cooperation with the government.

Premier Kassem also endeavored to follow the policy of "positive neutralism" between the East and the West much more scrupulously than did Cairo. In his public utterances he carefully avoided attacking the West or singling out any particular Western countries, and though his speeches did not lack scathing references to the evil of "imperialism," such references were about matched by his equally strong condemnation of the "anarchists," a conventional name for the Communists in his revolutionary vocabulary. His policy of neutrality led him also to attempt to redress some of the imbalances that occurred in the early revolutionary period when a number of trade and cultural agreements were hastily concluded with the Soviet bloc states by some of his outspokenly pro-Communist ministers. Thus in 1960 his government signed cultural agreements with the United States and Britain, which among other things provided for the exchange of students and scholars.

Although this new policy toward communism evoked positive response from

Iraq's moderate and nationalist strata, Premier Kassem's position was by no means easy. On the one hand, the pressure from the Pan-Arab and pro-Nasser elements had still to be reckoned with as an important factor tending to undermine his position. This was vividly demonstrated in October 1959, when a group of over-zealous Baath party members shot and wounded the premier in an attempt on his life. On the other hand, Iraq's moderate nationalists (i.e., those favoring an independent state free of both Communist and Nasser domination), who represented broad strata of the country's bourgeoisie, were shocked and aggrieved to learn in September 1959 of the sentence and execution of the popularly respected General Nadhim Tabaqchali and several other officers implicated in the Mosul revolt of the preceding March.

If the history of the first year of the revolution could be summed up (with considerable oversimplification) as a series of moves by Kassem to play the Nasserists and the Communists against each other, the second year marked his definite alienation from both. Not unlike his predecessor, Nuri Said, he logically looked for support among the strata situated between the two extremes. Another similarity to Nuri Said was his reliance on the army as an ultimate source of power. The main difference between the two lay in their attitude toward social change: whereas Nuri was thoroughly conservative, Kassem favored progress. Theoretically the better-educated strata of Iraq's bourgeoisie would be expected to approve of Kassem's reformist ideas. But many of them were alienated by his initial co-operation with and tolerance of communism. If in addition they had suffered as a result of Communist excesses against themselves or their relatives, their basic hostility to the new regime and their probable desire for revenge might not be easily dismissed, even though they were outwardly loyal and favored existing policies.

Kassem's Decline and Fall

The last phase of Kassem's regime showed characteristics of deterioration in virtually every sector of public life, internal political processes, the economy, and foreign and Arab policies. Kassem's political base, never too strong, began rapidly to erode. He had no political party of his own to sustain him; he gradually alienated the pro-Nasser elements, the conservatives, the Communists, and the Baathists. He found himself increasingly isolated, having to rely on the army, police, and, to some extent, on the Popular Resistance Force, the latter of questionable loyalty because of its gradual infiltration by the Communists. The repressive measures applied to dissidents and exemplified by Colonel Mahdawi's People's Court brought Kassem hatred and resentment at home and ridicule in the Arab world. An occasional gesture of good will and clemency such as the release of his erstwhile collaborator, Colonel Abdul Salam Aref, in November 1961 after three years of detention was not sufficient to restore confidence in him and his rule. His manner was always puzzling and secretive. Continuously armed (he wore a revolver in his holster even when receiving foreign visitors), Kassem projected an image of a leader haunted by insecurity and distrusting even his closest entourage. In fact, he slept and ate in his room in the ministry of defense, which was his headquarters. Moreover, his acts and pronouncements tended to emphasize the political climate of instability, of continuous alarms, conspiracies, and defensive counteractions. The "sole leader" spoke often of plots and threats against his regime and was prone to identify the evil as imperialism, the United States, Britain, or the oil companies.

On September 16, 1961, the Kurds led by Mullah Mustafa Barzani rose in revolt against Kassem's government. Unwilling to admit that there were any genuine grievances on the part of the underprivileged Kurdish minority, Kassem promptly accused the Americans, the British, and the oil companies of having instigated this revolt. In fact, the Kurdish rebellion developed into a major cause of the ultimate demise of Kassem's regime.

Nor was the economic sector faring any better. While free enterprise was discouraged and much capital fled Iraq in search of safer havens and opportunities, the government's approach to economic development was characterized by confusion, indecision, poor planning, and general chaos. The result was felt in the general stagnation of the once developing Iraqi economy. True to the tactics followed by many revolutionary leaders, Kassem fastened his attention upon one target in particular, namely the Iraq Petroleum Company (IPC), which he presented with a number of demands. These included the cession to Iraq of 20 percent of the company's stock which Kassem claimed was promised at the time of the original signing of the concession in 1928, and a change in favor of the government of the 50-50 profit-sharing formula. Through 1961 lengthy negotiations were carried on with the IPC delegation, headed successively by Geoffrey Herridge, an Englishman, and H. W. Fisher, an American. Usually, such negotiations are conducted by the minister of petroleum or the appropriately appointed delegates of a given government. But in this case Kassem decided to head the Iraqi delegation himself, thereby putting his prestige as Head of the State and the Revolution on the line. The atmosphere of the sessions was tense and punctuated by Kassem's threats of unilateral action. Finally, when the bargaining seemed to have reached an impasse, on December 11, 1961, Kassem abruptly announced that over 99 percent of the territory of IPC's concession was being nationalized by the government. Known since as Law No. 80 of 1961, this decree deprived the company of virtually all of its concession territory except for the producing wells and the areas occupied by installations and pipelines. Outwardly, it looked like a grand and bold gesture of defiance toward an imperialist "octopus." In reality, it did not prevent the company from continuing production activities but made any further exploration effort impossible for IPC. Moreover, such a unilateral action was bound to make IPC's parent companies rethink and reorient their policies toward Iraq. It should be remembered that these parent companies possessed extensive concessions in the neighboring countries of Saudi Arabia and Iran as well as in lesser states of the Persian Gulf, not to speak of oil fields and facilities in other areas of the world. Under the circumstances, Iraq's decision to act unilaterally without being assured of coordination and support from the other producing countries in the Middle East risked countermeasures on the part of the companies, which ultimately might prove detrimental to its economic goals. And indeed, quietly and without fanfare, the companies began to direct more of their effort in exploration and production toward other areas of the Middle East in which they enjoyed a more encouraging environment. Within a few years Iraq found itself lagging behind other producing countries in the Middle East with a corresponding slowdown in its oil revenue.

In the field of foreign and Arab policies, Kassem's behavior was also somewhat erratic and unpredictable. Officially Iraq was neutral but on account of the state of irritation in its relations with the West it tended to lean more toward the Soviet Union and the Communist bloc. However, relations between Baghdad and Moscow were subject to fluctuations partly connected with Kassem's treatment of native Communists in Iraq, which as we know was following a tortuous path of occasional cooperation alternating with hostility. Moreover, when the Kurds took the warpath in September 1961, the Soviet media expressed friendly interest in the Kurdish cause. Despite Kassem's changing moods toward the Communist party in Iraq, however, the Soviet Union perceived in the situation created by Kassem's regime a considerable potential for itself in the long run. It was therefore willing to maintain friendly relations with Kassem, lend him some economic assistance, and enter into various cooperative agreements. Such was, for example, the cultural agreement signed between the two countries on February 28, 1962, which provided for 470 scholarships for Iraqi students at Soviet universities. In exchange, Iraq was to receive five Soviet students specializing in the study of the Arabic language.

In the Arab sector, Kassem's relations with a number of states in the area continued strained. This was notably the case with Nasser's Egypt because of Kassem's hostile attitude to the Iraqi Nasserites as well as his stubborn insistence on the separateness of Iraq as a state.

But the single strongest factor that put Kassem at odds with the broad community of Arab nations was the question of Kuwait. By an agreement with Britain on June 19, 1961, Kuwait was proclaimed an independent state. Barely six days later Kassem laid claim to Kuwait's territory on behalf of Iraq. His argument was that Kuwait had constituted in the past, under the Ottoman administration, an integral part of the province of Basrah. He promptly backed his demand by despatching troops toward the border of Kuwait. The newly constituted Kuwaiti authorities immediately appealed to Great Britain as a guarantor power in virtue of the independence treaty. Within a few days, on July 1, a contingent of 600 British Marines with supporting artillery and naval protection landed in Kuwait. These were promptly followed by a small expeditionary force from Saudi Arabia sent also at Kuwait's request. When on July 20, Kuwait was formally admitted to the Arab League, it secured a pledge from the Council that an Arab force would be sent to protect Kuwait and thus to replace the British troops. Such a force was not despatched until September 10—a considerable delay in view of the immediate threat to Kuwait's independence. It numbered 3300 troops from Saudi Arabia, the U.A.R., Sudan, Jordan, and Tunisia. The U.A.R. contingent was composed of Egyptian and Syrian units. At that very time Syria broke away from Egypt, and thus the United Arab Republic as a union of two countries ceased to exist. This unforeseen difficulty caused Egypt to withdraw its troops by mid-October, at about the same time that the British troops were removed upon the arrival of the Arab force.

The fact that a joint Arab expedition acting on behalf of the Arab League appeared in Kuwait to thwart Iraq's expansionist designs led to a virtual break between

Kassem and the League. By October 1962 the Iraqi government instituted a formal boycott of the Arab League, declared that Iraq would cease contributing to its budget, and stopped sending delegations to its meetings.

By alienating himself from the community of Arab nations Kassem found himself in virtually complete isolation. Almost every organized political group in Iraq, whether on the left or the right, was hostile to him, the Kurds were in a state of rebellion, and the Arab League considered him an aggressor against whom a collective Arab force had to be deployed. Moreover, Kassem's behavior and pronouncements appeared to many observers to be increasingly erratic and irrational. He oscillated between enigmatic statements and brutal denunciations of his enemies. Despite these features he was not devoid of a charismatic quality which, however, seemed to affect primarily the destitute sarifa (slum) dwellers of the poorest districts in Baghdad. By the beginning of 1963 most of the politically conscious and articulate elements in Iraq were definitely hostile toward the dictator.

The First Baath Revolution

On February 8, 1963, the Baath party, long suppressed by Kassem, executed a coup d'etat. The dictator was killed alongside some of his aides and followers including Colonel Mahdawi. As usual in such cases, the party did not act alone but in conjunction with the disaffected elements in the army. More specifically, the army was represented by Colonel Abdul Salam Aref, an erstwhile associate of Kassem. Upon his assumption of power as Head of State and Chairman of the Revolutionary Command Council (RCC) Aref proclaimed that the new regime would strive to achieve unity, freedom, and socialism, i.e., the standard Baath objectives, and would be under collective leadership. A cabinet was formed, headed by General Ahmed Hassan el-Bakr as prime minister, and Ali Saleh el-Saadi as deputy prime minister and minister of the interior. Bakr, although an officer, was a member of the Baath, while Saadi represented the militant Marxist-oriented tendency in the party. Other members of the cabinet were divided between party and nonparty members. Among the latter one was one of the "fathers of the Revolution," General Rashed Musleh, who became Military Governor General.

The seizure of power by the Baath-military coalition encountered initial resistance from the Communist party. Although the party in the latter phases of Kassem's rule experienced hostility and harassment, nevertheless it feared the rival Baath party even more. Consequently, various detachments of the Popular Resistance Force, largely dominated by the Communists, fought to defend Kassem but were overpowered by the military units and the Baath detachments. Although the world had become accustomed, by then, to the highly unorthodox procedures of the Iraqi political system—including the Mosul and Kirkuk massacres and the outrageous performance of the Mahdawi court—there was still an eerie feeling of surrealism about the new coup. Upon his assumption of power, General Aref (soon promoted to Marshal) refused to disclose to visiting journalists the names of the members of the RCC, which was the true ruling body of the new regime. These names became known only gradually without a single formal release by the government.

The Tripartite Unity Negotiations

Exactly one month after the Iraqi coup, the Syrian Baath party seized power in Damascus on March 8. As a result, three major Arab countries—Syria, Iraq, and Egypt—found themselves under socialist leaderships dedicated to Arab unity. It was therefore logical and in conformance with their ideological proclamations that the leaders of the three countries should now seek the implementation of the unity slogan. Before the end of March delegations from Iraq and Syria arrived in Cairo to conduct negotiations with President Nasser with the aim of achieving some form of unity among the three countries. These negotiations lasted approximately three weeks and abounded in lively debates between Nasser and his Baathist guests from Baghdad and Damascus. Three major issues emerged: collective versus single leadership, a federal versus unitary state, and the nature of political representation in Iraq and Syria. Iraqi and Syrian leaders insisted that the Baath party was the proper instrument for exercising power and assuring liaison between the masses and the government. Nasser countered by proposing that a broader coalition of Baathists and non-Baathists should be created. Such a coalition would presumably include pro-Nasserite and other independent socialist elements. On April 17, the three delegations signed a unity charter pledging the establishment of a federal union by stages.[28] In contrast to the previous Syrian-Egyptian union, the new political entity was to constitute a federal state. This basic decision implied also that the leadership would be collective although informally it was agreed that Nasser would become president of the federation. As for political representation, the matter was not truly settled and the text was couched in such terms as to lend itself to varying interpretations. Throughout the negotiations it was evident that considerable distrust prevailed between Nasser and his Baathist guests. The Baathists clearly suspected Nasser of dictatorial tendencies and a desire to extend the Egyptian system, and perhaps the Egyptian rule as well, to other countries. On his part, Nasser could not forget what he believed to be the disloyal behavior of the Baath party in Syria during the period of union between 1958 and 1961.[29] In fact, while these negotiations were going on, Nasser's agents and followers in both Iraq and Syria were engaged in clandestine activities aimed at overthrowing both governments. In Iraq this took the form of an abortive pro-Nasser plot by some military elements on May 25. Under the circumstances, the unity charter became a dead letter, and on July 22 it was officially repudiated. Distrust and hostility were characteristic primarily of the Syrian-Egyptian relations. The Iraqi Baathists considered themselves somewhat more neutral and attempted to revive the unity negotiations by sending a delegation under President Aref to Cairo on August 21. This new attempt to bring about agreement and reconciliation also failed and on September 2 the Iraqi delegation returned to Baghdad without achieving a new agreement.

Although an attempt to achieve unity on a more comprehensive scale had failed, the Baath leaderships in Baghdad and Damascus proceeded to explore the possibil-

[28]Text in Walid Khalidi and Yusuf Ibish, eds., *Arab Political Documents 1963* (Beirut, n.d.), pp. 227–228.

[29]Minutes of unity discussions may be found in *Arab Political Documents*, pp. 75–226.

ity of a union between Iraq and Syria. Following a number of visits between Damascus and Baghdad the two regimes were prepared by the end of October to effect unification or at least considerable coordination in the military and economic spheres. This time the goal of unity appeared more feasible owing to the fact that the Baath party exercising power in both countries possessed its own Pan-Arab organization called the National Command, to which the so-called Regional Commands (Syrian, Iraqi, Jordanian, etc.) were subordinated. Thus even without formal unity on the state level, it was conceivable that virtual unity between the two countries would be established through the operation of their ruling parties.

Internal Policies: The Communists and the Kurds

Remembering persecutions of its members by the Communists during the Kassem era, the ruling Baathists proceeded vigorously to suppress their Communist adversaries. In March and June a number of Communists were rounded up, tried, and given harsh sentences, including twenty-eight death sentences for those responsible for the Kirkuk massacres in 1959. Two prominent Communists, Aziz Sharif and Abdul Qader Ismail el-Bustani, were imprisoned. The government, on July 3, thwarted an attempt by the Communist party acting through its sympathizers in the army to carry out a coup d'etat in the Rashid military camp near Baghdad. As a result, three members of the Communist party's central committee were hanged. The militancy of the Baath against the Communists exceeded probably in its intensity even the harsh measures applied to them by the prerevolutionary regime. As could be expected, Moscow reacted to these developments very negatively, and the Soviet media carried a number of adverse comments and criticisms on the illtreatment of "democratic elements" by the Baath party.

While this settling of accounts with the Communists was taking place in Baghdad and other urban centers, the regime pursued the war with the Kurds in the north, a war it inherited from Kassem. In fact, it mounted a new anti-Kurdish offensive, in which even some Syrian battalions were taking part. This offensive, which began on June 10, promptly elicited new Soviet accusations. The Tass Agency spoke of "Nazi methods of mass extermination in Kurdistan," while the *Red Star* in Moscow accused Iraq of conducting a "genocide operation" against the Kurds.[30] This, in turn, led to further stresses in Soviet-Iraqi relations. On July 27 the Iraqi government announced the discovery of a Bulgarian spy ring in the country, and soon afterwards a group of Iraqi students returned from the Soviet Union accusing the Soviet authorities of having conducted a "provocative campaign" against them.

While the campaign against the Communists and the Kurds exposed the regime to considerable strains, it was the internecine fighting among the various factions of the Baath party that proved most harmful to the government in power. This factionalism could be traced to a midsummer pan-Arab meeting held in Damascus. That meeting, known as the Sixth National Congress of the Baath, was dominated by the Iraqi left-wing group headed by Ali Saleh el-Saadi. He was responsible for

---

[30]For further analysis of Soviet attitudes on the Kurdish question, see Aryeh Yodfat, *Arab Politics in the Soviet Mirror* (Jerusalem and New York, 1973), pp. 181–191.

the pro-Marxist tenor of many resolutions adopted by the Congress. Back in Iraq, Saadi tried to translate this ideological platform into action. His main instrument was the Baath paramilitary militia called the National Guard. This bid for power within the party organization provoked resistance from other groups. By uniting their forces, these groups succeeded at a regional Baath conference in Baghdad on November 11 in removing Saadi from any position of authority in the party. Two days later Saadi was put on a military airplane and deported to Spain. This was soon followed by the expulsion and deportation to Beirut of seven of his followers. The in-fighting in the Iraqi Baath brought about intervention by the National Command of the party based in Damascus. The party's secretary general and cofounder, Michel Aflaq, flew to Baghdad in the company of certain Syrian comrades from the national headquarters to restore peace among the warring Iraqi factions. Momentarily, this intervention appeared to be the triumph of pan-Arab unity schemes, inasmuch as it looked as if regional differences between Iraq and Syria expressed in the formal sovereignty of the two states were obliterated and effective action on a pan-Arab scale could be undertaken, at least within the framework of the unity-seeking Baath party. This, however, soon proved to be mere illusion.

The Eclipse of the Baath: The Aref Era

Actually, what the events of mid-November 1963 demonstrated was not only that the Baath possessed effective transnational organization, but also that it was weak and torn by factionalism inside Iraq itself. This inner disarray of the party gave President Aref an opportunity. On November 18, he executed a coup d'etat by which he deposed the existing Baath leadership and appointed a government of his own choosing, largely composed of his military associates. Three army generals emerged as his principal allies: these were General Taher Yahya, the new prime minister, General Rashed Musleh, minister of interior, and General Hardan Takriti, minister of defense. Only a tenuous link was maintained with the Baath through the appointment of General Hassan el-Bakr, an avowed member of the party, to the honorary position of Vice-President of the Republic. But the fiction of this collaboration soon became evident when by January 1964, Bakr resigned from his position.

Upon his advent to power, Aref immediately turned toward the crystallization of his Arab policy. Proclaiming his dedication to the principle of Arab unity, he stressed his friendship toward Cairo rather than toward Damascus. His public pronouncements were full of praise for Gamal Abdul Nasser as a pan-Arab leader and replete with assurances of an early union with Egypt as a stepping stone to a more comprehensive Arab unity. Aref found an opportunity to put his words into deeds when in late May he visited Cairo on the occasion of the inauguration of the first stage of the Aswan Dam. On May 26, Aref and Nasser signed an agreement to establish union between Egypt and Iraq by stages. These stages included first, the creation in September of an Iraq-U.A.R. Presidency Council and, in December of that year, of the unified political command. Furthermore, Nasser and Aref agreed that Egypt and Iraq should have an identical kind of political organization, in the form of the Arab Socialist Union, already in existence in Egypt as a single licensed political body and about to be established in Iraq. These unity moves were formally preceded by the adoption on May 3, 1964, of a new constitution in Iraq which described that country as an "Arab, Islamic, independent, and sovereign" state, whose aim was to establish "Arab unity, beginning with constitutional union" with the U.A.R. This constitutional formula, however, indicated that despite Aref's basic dedication to union with Egypt, he was careful not to rush it unduly. The description of Iraq as "independent and sovereign state" indicated that he had to reckon with a sizable segment of Iraqi opinion in and out of the military that was not quite prepared to follow the example of Syria back in 1958 in effecting an unconditional swift union with Egypt. Similarly, the agreement to proceed by stages indicated caution in the matter, perhaps on the part of both Aref and Nasser. These pro-Egyptian moves, however, brought about an understandable tension with the Baath-dominated Syria. Aided by Syrian elements, the Iraqi Baath attempted to seize power in early September, but the plot was discovered and thwarted by the authorities. With the passage of time, it appears that Aref's initial pro-union ardor cooled off appreciably. While always paying lip service to the principle of union and close collaboration with Egypt, Aref gave no signs of relinquishing his power, of allowing any genuine and practical joint decision-making with Egypt to take place, or of promoting Nasser's agents and followers to high positions in his government. On the contrary, the longer he stayed in power the more he appeared to cherish his position as President of the Republic and the real wielder of authority.

Nationalization, Nasserite Subversion, and the Emergence of Bazzaz

Aref's Arab policy was inextricably linked to his domestic political program. In the first place, he disbanded the National Guard as a dangerous formation filled with Baathists and other elements hostile to him. Instead, he launched the Arab Socialist Union, which, however, soon proved to be dominated by people with distinct pro-Nasserite tendencies. Pledged to close cooperation with Egypt and, in particular, to the proposition that the two systems should gradually become more alike before final union was consummated, Aref issued on July 14, 1964, the anniversary of the initial revolution, a number of nationalization decrees which put under government control banks, insurance companies, and thirty-two major industrial firms. To administer these enterprises, a State Economic Organization was formed to be headed by Socialist-leaning Dr. Khaireddin el-Hassib. Soon afterwards, a number of state monopolies for imports of staple consumption goods was established, ostensibly to protect the interests of the consumers against excessive prices. Furthermore, in line with this socialization of the economy, in January 1965, Aref announced a five-year plan for development calling for expenditures of 820 million Iraqi dinars including 500 million to be spent in the public sector. At the same time, the government drew up plans for the construction of a dam near Mosul on the Tigris River and another one on the Euphrates River.

Throughout the year 1965 the pro-Nasserite elements in Iraq expanded their influence. They were unhappy over the slow pace of union with Egypt and they were also displeased with Aref's tendency to be conciliatory toward the Kurds and the Iraq Petroleum Company. In midsummer six pro-Nasserite ministers resigned from his cabinet, and two months later in mid-September his hew prime minister, General Aref Abdur Razzaq (also a Nasserite), attempted a coup to depose Aref while he was attending a summit meeting in Casablanca in the company of Nasser and other Arab leaders. Razzaq was effectively thwarted by the acting chief of staff of the Iraqi army, General Abdur Rahman Aref, President Aref's brother. The paradox of the situation was that while the President was exchanging courtesies and words of friendship with Nasser in Casablanca, Nasser's agents—for such they really were—tried to overthrow him in Baghdad. This experience appears to have been a turning point in Aref's attitude toward Nasser and Egypt.

Immediately after his return, he formed a new cabinet, appointing a former dean of the Baghdad Law School, Professor Abdur Rahman el-Bazzaz as Prime Minister. The move was significant inasmuch as Bazzaz was the first civilian prime minister in Iraq since the Revolution of 1958. Bazzaz was an Arab nationalist with impeccable credentials both as a liberal in Iraq and as a man with a pan-Arab record, having served as Professor of Arab Studies in the Arab League-sponsored Institute of Higher Learning in Cairo. Moreover, he had suffered persecution at the hands of the Nuri government before 1958 and could be trusted by the new revolutionary generation in Iraq.

Having assumed the premier's office, Bazzaz launched a number of determined policies to correct the existing evils in Iraq, to do away with military and party intrigue, to revive respect for law, to restore, if possible, democratic procedures, and to reinstitute a climate of normalcy and security in the country. He proclaimed a policy of "prudent socialism" and abolished the inefficient State Economic Organization. He also stressed the need for freedom of the press and expression and declared on several occasions that advancement in Iraq should be on the basis of merit and not by reason of a military career or party membership. At the same time, he applied curbs to the Communist party, being careful, however, to limit only the party's illegal activities. In December of that year, a number of Communists were placed on trial. Bazzaz also disbanded a number of friendship societies between Iraq on the one hand and the Soviet Union, Czechoslovakia, Bulgaria, and other satellite states on the other, apparently considering them harmful channels for improper Communist influence in the country.

Bazzaz' major achievement was to effect a reconciliation with the Kurdish rebels. To this end he conducted negotiations with the Kurdish leader Mullah Mustafa Barzani in an attempt to find an equitable formula. These endeavors were temporarily interrupted by the sudden death of President Aref.

The Aref II Era

On April 13, 1966, President Abdul Salam Aref met his death in a helicopter accident when on an inspection tour in southern Iraq. Three days later his brother, General Abdur Rahman Aref, then acting chief of staff, was elected president in a joint session of the cabinet and the national defense council. The only other candidate was General Abdul Aziz el-Uqaili, who was known for his strong anti-Kurdish sentiments. Bazzaz was reappointed prime minister, thus assuring the continuity of policies inaugurated under the previous president.

The Kurdish dissidence continued to have high priority and on June 29, 1966, Premier Bazzaz announced a twelve-point peace plan to settle the Kurdish question.[31] Formally, this was a unilateral program announced by the Iraqi government but it gained full approval of the Kurdish leader Barzani. The plan incorporated many long-standing demands of the Kurds for the recognition of their language and for local administrative autonomy as well as for more meaningful participation in the central government. Thus for the time being at least, hostilities with the Kurds came to an end and a new era of cooperation was inaugurated.

In essence, the policies of Premier Bazzaz constituted a repudiation of the socialist and revolutionary slogans emanating from Cairo. It was not surprising, therefore, that the pro-Nasserite elements in Iraq viewed Bazzaz with considerable hostility. This opposition was expressed in a second abortive coup attempted on June 30 by General Aref Abdur Razzaq, the day after the announcement of the peace plan for Kurdistan. Bazzaz, however, persevered in his policies unflinchingly. Moreover, his anticommunist course was pursued with vigor: in mid-July the party's leader, Abdul Qader Ismail el-Bustani, was sentenced to six years in prison for his attempt to resuscitate the banned Communist party.

In the foreign and Arab sector, the Aref II–Bazzaz period was notable for moderation and steady striving to establish friendly, normal relations with the neighbor states as well as the big powers. Despite the repeated proofs of Nasser's disloyalty toward the Aref brothers, Bazzaz was anxious to establish an ostensibly friendly relationship with Cairo, and on his visit, toward the end of July, in the Egyptian capital, he stressed the bonds of amity linking both countries. He and President Abdur Rahman Aref worked in concert in this respect and both undertook at one time or another visits to Turkey and Iran. As for the major powers, the hostility characteristic of official Iraqi attitudes toward the United States in the period immediately following the 1958 Revolution gave place gradually to normal relations for which American Ambassador Robert Strong worked patiently and assiduously.   At the same time, Bazzaz—like Nasser—wanted to impress Moscow that a strict line should be drawn between the government-to-government friendship, or at least correctness in Soviet-Iraqi relations on the one hand, and the position of the Iraqi Communists inside Iraq on the other. For this reason he undertook a journey to Moscow toward the end of July, 1966, and returned, having seemingly restored the Soviet-Iraqi relationship to a level of friendly correctness devoid of mutual accusations.

The policies of Bazzaz appealed to a great many Iraqis among both the intelligentsia and the masses. It was a quiet period of unspectacular achievement but with considerable emphasis on the rule of law, the need to reduce undue military interference in the political process, the growing role of competent civilians in the

---

[31]Text in Majid Khadduri, *Republican Iraq* (London, New York, 1969) pp. 274–276; for a newspaper summary, see *New York Times*, June 30, 1966.

government, and the gradual phasing out of unprofitable and stultifying socialist controls over the economy. Iraq, moreover, emerged successfully from the isolation which the Kassem and the Baath policies had placed it in. But it was precisely those qualities of normalcy, rationality, and moderation that set various radical elements against Bazzaz. Moreover, the military, having tasted power under the preceding regimes and still considering that final authority in the state should rest with them, were growing increasingly restless at Bazzaz' vindication of civilian rights and were frequently irritated by his strong and none-too-diplomatic pronouncements about the need to draw a line between the military and the civilian responsibilities in the governing process. The military, represented by a group of high ranking generals, eventually persuaded President Aref to remove Bazzaz from the premiership. On August 6, 1966, he was dismissed and replaced as Prime Minister by General Naji Taleb. It is not clear whether the new cabinet, studded with military names, wanted to change radically the economic or foreign policies of Bazzaz. General Taleb appeared himself to be a man of reason and moderation. His acumen as a political leader was soon tested in a crisis with Syria over transit of oil. In December, in her intermittent dispute with IPC, Syria impounded the company's assets and stopped the transit of Iraqi oil to the Mediterranean coast. Although Iraq was none too friendly toward the company, nevertheless it had a vital interest in seeing that oil reached the terminals of the pipelines for transshipment. Consequently, Iraq found itself in an unusual role of mediating between IPC and the Syrian government with an eye to achieving a speedy solution so that transit would be resumed. This was eventually achieved but after much effort and irritation of the Iraqi leadership over the Syrian rigidity.

The new government was not destined to give full proof of its ability to rule the country because by June 1967 it was drawn into a brief war with Israel. Although Iraq's participation in this war was limited, certain Iraqi forces being present on the Jordanian front but not having an opportunity to engage in a full-scale battle with the Israelis, Iraq's air force was virtually annihilated by a swift Israeli surprise attack, as were the air forces of Egypt and Syria. It was again demonstrated that once the generals begin to interfere with the political process their military performance suffers. Iraq's defeat was part of the general humiliation of Arab arms in this short war.

The impact of the June war in Iraq was similar to that observed in other Arab countries. It intensified and accelerated two simultaneous trends, one of rapprochement with the Soviet Union, and the other of gradual internal radicalization. Soviet advances in Iraq were punctuated by such highly symbolic acts as the visit of President Nicolai Podgorny to Baghdad in early July, 1967, followed by a visit of Soviet Defense Minister Marshal Grechko, in March 1968. The Soviets offered and Iraq accepted many forms of Soviet aid in the military and economic sphere.[32] The Soviets in fact resupplied the shattered Iraqi air force and delivered more sophisti-

---

[32]For details, see G. Lenczowski, *Soviet Advances in the Middle East* (Washington, D.C., 1971), pp. 125-143.

cated arms to its army. A number of development projects were launched with Soviet cooperation; and last but not least the Soviets undertook to develop oil resources in certain southern areas of Iraq on the territory previously seized from Iraq Petroleum Company. In due course a Soviet team began developing production in the north Rumaila oil field in the vicinity of Basrah, a field that had been discovered by IPC before 1961.

As for internal radicalization, the sixteen private newspapers that appeared on the scene during the Aref-Bazzaz regime were abolished, and only five government-owned newspapers were licensed for the entire country. Later, the government permitted an independent organ of the Kurdish Democratic party, *el-Taakhi,* to be published in Kurdish and Arabic. This paper, however, incurred a number of temporary suspensions. In retrospect the era of two Aref brothers appeared certainly as one of normalcy and moderation, without radical slogans and ideologies. From the point of view of orderly political development in Iraq it was unfortunate that the country had to undergo the shock of war with Israel. The war seriously interfered with the process of de-revolutionizing Iraq's political system and paved the way for another turn to the left.

The Second Baath Revolution

On July 17, 1968, the Baath party, again in conjunction with the military, executed its second coup. General Hassan el-Bakr was proclaimed president and another general, Abdur Razzaq el-Nayif, became prime minister, with Dr. Nasser Hani, a professional diplomat and former ambassador to the United States, as foreign minister. Although the Baath was the prime mover in the coup, interestingly enough certain personalities in the new government, including the prime minister and the foreign minister, had moderate inclinations and soon revealed a conciliatory attitude toward the West. While Washington and London were gratified to detect friendly and moderate accents in the early pronouncements of these two leaders, the much more radically inclined Baath leadership was clearly disappointed. Within thirteen days, on July 30, a "palace coup" resulted in the ouster of Premier Nayif and Dr. Hani. President Bakr assumed the premiership and was proclaimed commander-in-chief. On September 21, a new provisional constitution was enacted which vested the Revolutionary Command Council (RCC) with full executive and legislative powers until the election of a national assembly, a representative institution which the future permanent constitution was supposed to provide for. Actually, instead of liberalizing its system, the new government subjected the country to a tighter control and by mid-July 1970, in a new constitutional enactment, it proclaimed not only that the RCC was to constitute the supreme authority, but also that it was to be composed exclusively of the Baath party members.[33] Thus within a year Iraq was transformed into a single-party regime. In a broader sense, the ruling

[33]See M. Khadduri, *Socialist Iraq: A Study in Iraqi Politics since 1968* (Washington, D.C., 1978), Appendix A.

military-party elite displayed a marked leftward trend, radicalism, and militancy in both internal and foreign sectors. As such it reflected the general trend toward the radicalization of the Arab political scene following the June 1967 war.[34]

The Domestic Scene: Repression and Radical Militancy

Once in a position of power, the Baath leaders proceeded rapidly to entrench their position by suppressing any actual or potential opposition and extending ever tighter controls over the society and economy so as to make their dictatorship impregnable. The first target of their repression was the group previously in power. Although President Abdur Rahman Aref was allowed to escape the country and settle in London, he was vilified by government propaganda and called a CIA and Israeli spy by Baghdad Radio in a broadcast on June 12, 1969.[35] Similarly, former Premier Bazzaz and General Uqaili were accused of having engaged in plots against Iraq with the help of the United States. In a much publicized trial, Bazzaz was sentenced to fifteen years in prison. The harshest treatment, however, was reserved for General Rashed Musleh, previously a minister and military governor general under the Aref brothers, who confessed to having been a CIA spy and was sentenced to death and executed. Numerous jail sentences and executions of other public figures, businessmen, and higher officials followed. The first two years of the Baath regime were clearly a period of severe repression, aggravated by a number of mysterious assassinations of prominent political figures known for differences with the regime in power. Of these, two murders received particular publicity: that of former Foreign Minister Dr. Nasser Hani in Baghdad and that of former Defense Minister General Hardan Takriti, who was killed while on a visit to Kuwait in 1970.

Repression, of course, was bound to generate clandestine opposition and conspiracies. It was not surprising, therefore, when on July 1, 1973, another coup attempt took place in Baghdad, this time carried out by the military security chief, Colonel Nazim Kazzar. Kazzar succeeded in capturing and killing the chief of staff, General Shehabi, and wounding another officer of general rank. He did not manage, however, to seize the necessary strategic points in the city, and fled toward the territory of Iran. He was apprehended, summarily tried, and put to death.

In a drive to establish maximum control over the economy, the Baath government adopted numerous measures of socialization, thus reversing the trend begun under Premier Bazzaz. There were grounds to believe that the extension of government control over the economy served not merely economic purposes but was also a means to strengthen political control over the country. Relations between the successive revolutionary governments and the Iraq Petroleum Company were never cordial. In fact, IPC served as a perfect "whipping boy" for the Iraqi nationalists and radicals. Under the circumstances, the nationalization of IPC on June 1, 1972, came as no major surprise. Because of the friendly attitude that de Gaulle's France exhibited toward the Arabs since the June 1967 war, the French component of IPC

---

[34]For further analysis, see G. Lenczowski, "Arab Radicalism: Problems and Prospects," *Current History* (January 1971).

[35]See "Iraq Accuses Ex-President Posthumously of Espionage," *New York Times,* June 13, 1969.

(accounting for a little above 23 percent of the stock) was offered exemption from nationalization and the possibility of concluding a separate agreement on more favorable terms. The nationalization decree extended to IPC itself, the principal operator in the Kirkuk oil fields, as well as to its affiliated group, the Mosul Petroleum Company. It did not extend, however, to the Basrah Petroleum Company, another affiliate of the IPC group, because the Basrah PC was in the initial stages of exploration and production, and premature nationalization might have arrested further development.[36]

In one sector of domestic policies an interesting reversal of Baath attitudes took place. This time, instead of suppressing the Communists as it did during 1963, the Baath party began to explore the ways of cooperating with them. In a first major gesture in this direction, a prominent Communist leader, Aziz Sharif, was appointed minister of justice at the end of 1969. Intermittent negotiations between the two parties eventually led, in July 1970, to the establishment of a National Front to be composed of the Baath party (with acknowledged supremacy), the Communist party, and the Kurdish Democratic party (KDP). Although the Communists were thus permitted to participate in the joint effort to "build socialism" in Iraq, they were definitely forbidden to penetrate the army, the ideological orientation of which was reserved exclusively for the Baath. When in the later 1970s the Iraqi government discovered Communist endeavors to form cells in the military establishment, its reaction was swift and severe: in the spring of 1978 twenty-one Communists were executed, while dozens were jailed in the midst of a strong press campaign against the Communist party.

A major issue to be settled in internal affairs was that of Kurdistan. Ever since the dismissal of Bazzaz as premier in the last phase of the Aref era, the Kurds felt cheated and complained about the nonfulfillment of the twelve-point program adopted in 1966. Although the Baath party had hoped to line up the left-wing element of KDP on its side, the more conservative leadership of the Kurdish resistance under Barzani viewed the Baath government with continued suspicion and resentment. Following intermittent negotiations, the government concluded on March 11, 1970, a new agreement with Barzani.[37] The agreement declared that Iraq was a country composed of two nationalities, the Arab and the Kurdish, and pledged local autonomy for the Kurds in the districts inhabited predominantly by the Kurdish population. The matter whether the oil city of Kirkuk could qualify as predominantly Kurdish was left in abeyance. The Kurds were also to be granted participation in the central government and one of the vice presidents was to be a Kurd. Considering the party's intolerance of other elements of opposition in the country, the agreement with the Kurds looked indeed like a remarkable achievement. There was some speculation that the Soviets who had previously supported the Kurdish cause decided now to throw their weight in favor of reconciliation, largely because of their growing stake in the strength and stability of Iraq. Alas, the new agreement,

---

[36]However, about three years later, on December 8, 1975, the Basrah Petroleum Company was also nationalized by a presidential announcement.

[37]Text in Khadduri, *Socialist Iraq,* Appendix C.

like those that preceded it, brought no permanent peace in the relations between Baghdad and the Kurds. By summer 1973, the accumulated mutual irritations brought about the resumption of the war. This time, however, the Iraqi army initiated the operations. Strengthened by better Soviet weapons, the army made significant progress in the northern territories, ousting the Kurds from a number of strongholds. Bombings by the Iraqi air force were significant in these operations, reducing scores of Kurdish villages and townships to rubble.

Arab and Foreign Policies

The Kurdish question was not merely an internal affair for Iraq. Kurdish rebels were known to be supported and supplied by the government of Iran, whose relations with Baghdad under the Baath regime were tense and hostile. Iran was concerned about the growth of Soviet influence in Iraq and the improvement of the latter's army with Soviet arms. Iraq, moreover, gave asylum to a dissident former chief of secret police in Iran, General Teymour Bakhtiar, as well as to Ayatollah Rouhollah Khomeini, both of whom tried to rally militant opponents to the Shah's government. A number of border clashes occurred between the two countries in the early 1970s. In January 1972, Iraq carried out a massive expulsion of over 60,000 Iranians resident in Iraq, particularly in the holy cities of Najaf and Kerbela. The seizure by Iran in late 1971 of three Arab islands in the Strait of Hormuz provided another irritation. So did the discovery by the Pakistani authorities, allied to Iran, of caches of Iraqi Soviet-made arms in the western borderland inhabited by the Baluchi tribes. There was also a longstanding dispute over the boundary line along the Shatt el-Arab River. According to an Iraqi-Iranian agreement of 1937, when Iraq was still under British influence, the boundary was to follow the eastern shore of the river, leaving the river itself under control of Iraq.[38]

Against the background of these unsettled disputes, Iran was extending help to the Kurdish insurgents. By early 1975 the deterioration of relations between Iraq and Iran had reached a point of repeated artillery exchanges along the borders, and had a potential for significant escalation. The growing crisis found its rather unexpected solution when at a summit meeting in Algiers in March 1975 under the sponsorship of the Organization of Petroleum Exporting Countries (OPEC), the Shah and Iraq's vice premier and chief civilian leader of the regime, Siddam Hussein, concluded an agreement to settle all outstanding differences.[39] The two main points of the agreement were a pledge of noninterference in each other's internal affairs and a decision to settle amicably the Shatt el-Arab boundary issue. The first point clearly meant cessation of further Iranian support for the Kurds. The second provided for the establishment of the boundary in the Shatt along the *thalweg,* the deepest channel of the river running approximately in the middle of its bottom. The agreement was signed on March 6 and its impact was immediate: on March 7 the Iraqi army undertook an offensive against the rebel Kurds which

---

[38]For details, see M. Khadduri and Herbert Dixon, "Passage through International Waterways," in M. Khadduri, ed., *Major Middle Eastern Problems in International Law* (Washington, D.C., 1972), pp. 88–94.

[39]Text in Khadduri, *Socialist Iraq,* Appendix E.

resulted in major advances of the government forces and a proclamation of a Kurdish-Iraqi cease-fire on March 13. Consequently, thousands of Kurdish fighters crossed into the Iranian territory where the authorities gave them asylum in the specially prepared camps. The Kurdish rebel leader Barzani also went into exile into Iran and there proclaimed an end to the resistance struggle.

The Baath rule in Iraq bore a certain resemblance to the rule of the late General Kassem in that it caused Iraq to be isolated in the Arab world. In the first place, although both Iraq and Syria were ruled by the Baath parties, these two branches of the erstwhile single organization developed a hostility toward each other marked by denunciations and accusations of betrayal of the original ideals. In addition, the construction in Syria, with Soviet aid, of a major dam at Tabka on the Euphrates River depleted the water resources in Iraq, provoking Baghdad to lodge complaints before the Arab League over Syria's behavior. Moreover, although both Iraq and Syria had nationalized most of their oil facilities, production and transportation, the elimination of the "imperialist" oil company, instead of bringing the two countries together, caused only further aggravation in their mutual relations over the transit fees and related questions. Iraq concluded in spring 1975 an agreement with Turkey to build a pipeline linking the Kirkuk oil fields with the Turkish Mediterranean terminal in Dörtyol in the Iskenderun province (Alexandretta). Syria, naturally, was highly displeased by this decision.

Although the Baath government in Baghdad did not renew the old claim first formulated by General Kassem to the entire territory of Kuwait, it did nevertheless present demands in the spring of 1973 toward the control of two Kuwaiti border islands, Warba and Bubiyan. Iraq claimed that control of these islands was necessary for the safeguarding of the passage to Iraq's naval port at Umm Qasr. This harbor was repeatedly visited in the late 1960s and early 1970s by a Soviet naval squadron.

Iraq avoided complete isolation, however, because it shared with certain other radical governments a negative attitude toward a compromise solution of the Arab-Israeli conflict. Iraq belonged to the so-called Rejectionist Front which on December 2 thourgh 5, 1977, met in Tripoli, Libya, to protest President Sadat's peace initiative toward Israel. (Other states attending were Libya, Syria, Algeria, and South Yemen, as well as the PLO.) Although Iraq walked out of this meeting because it found the collective stand lacking in firmness, it continued to keep in touch with other rejectionist governments. And while Iraq did not formally join the other rejectionist states which, as the newly renamed Arab Steadfastness and Confrontation Front, met in Damascus on September 20, 1978, to reject the Camp David agreements, it hosted, subsequently, the ninth Arab summit conference in Baghdad. That conference, attended by twenty Arab states, which convened on Iraq's initiative on November 2 through 5, 1978, condemned Egypt for its alleged attempt to conclude a separate peace treaty with Israel.

Against this general background of radical militancy, hostility toward the United States following the June 1967 war, and partial isolation in the Arab world, one must view the growing rapprochement between the Soviet Union and Iraq under the Baath rule. The Iraqi-Soviet relations were being strengthened not only through arms and aid-and-trade, but also through ideological cooperation carried out in the course of repeated visits of the Baath delegations in Moscow for the purpose of holding dialogues with the leaders of the Soviet Communist party. This growing cooperation between the two countries was sealed by the conclusion on April 9, 1972, of a Soviet-Iraqi treaty of friendship and cooperation during Premier Kosygin's visit in Baghdad. The Soviet premier came to Iraq on the occasion of the opening of a North Rumaila oil field which was developed with Soviet aid. The treaty was to be valid for fifteen years.[40] Soon afterward, two Communists were appointed to ministerial positions in the Iraqi cabinet.

Despite the convergence of Iraqi and Soviet policies on many points, serious differences arose between the two countries by 1978. There were seven sources of mutual irritation: (1) Iraq, by advocating complete liberation of Palestine (hence an abolition of the Israeli state), diverged from the Soviet policy that, first, recognized the legitimacy of Israel and, second, favored an Arab-Israeli peace settlement provided it was reached under certain conditions and involved Soviet sponsorship. (2) Iraq was critical of Soviet involvement in the Horn of Africa and of Soviet support of the Ethiopian junta against Arabic-speaking Somalia and Eritrea. (3) Moscow viewed with distaste the Bath government's drastic measures against the Iraqi Communists in the later 1970s. (4) Despite Soviet urgings, Iraq refused to become drawn into the Soviet involvements with China, the Vietnamese-Cambodian conflict, and Eastern Europe; it found no justification in siding with one or another party in these controversies. (5) Likewise, Iraq abstained from joining in Soviet denunciations of Eurocommunism; it viewed independent West European Communists as natural allies in its struggle against "imperialism." (6) Iraq was growing suspicious of Communist (and possibly Soviet) support for the Kurds who, after the demise of Barzani's right-wing leadership, began veering toward Communist-tinged radicalism. (5) The substantial accretion of oil wealth in the later 1970s made it possible for Iraq to expand economic relations with the West, and Iraq showed a preference for Western rather than Soviet technology.

In spite of these differences, Iraq insisted that the Soviet-Iraqi treaty of 1972 was not in jeopardy. Naim Haddad, member of the RCC and secretary-general of Iraq's National Front stated Iraqi policy: "As far as we are concerned, our strategic alliance with the USSR will not change. Our decision to conclude a treaty was not a tactical choice. The Soviet Union is a friend with whom we can cooperate as long as there is no interference in our internal affairs."[41]

In spite of controversial foreign and domestic policies, the Baath party of Iraq maintained itself in power over a period longer than any of the preceding revolutionary regimes. This success is particularly striking if we compare its record since 1968 with its dismal failure in 1963 when the party held power for merely eight months before being ousted by Abdul Salam Aref. There is no doubt that that initial failure gave the party a valuable experience from which the leaders of the

---

[40]Text in Khadduri, *Socialist Iraq,* Appendix D, and in *The Current Digest of the Soviet Press,* May 3, 1972.

[41]*The Middle East* (July 1978), p. 30.

1968 coup benefited. The party's greater durability during its second term could be ascribed to a number of factors. One was the considerable emphasis put on ideology and propaganda by which the party linked its own socialist and radical principles to the general nationalist slogans which could be freely employed in the period of continuous aggravation in Israeli-Arab relations and Arab grievances against the behavior of the United States. The second major factor was the skillful use by the party of coercive and repressive measures. These measures included highly pub- licized spy trials, jailings and executions, while dissent was freely equated with treason. Linked to this coercive behavior was the general militarization of the system, with the party infiltrating and controlling a sizable segment of the military forces. The party likewise knew how to exploit such international crises as had occurred in the 1960s and 1970s. These included, first and foremost, the two wars between the Arabs and Israel in 1967 and 1973, but also the aggravation—only later resolved—between Iran and certain Arab states. Nor should one underestimate the importance of the higher revenues which the rise in oil prices following the OPEC Teheran conference in 1973 had brought about. In contrast to the previous gov- ernments of the post-1958 period, the Baath regime was the first to possess major financial resources which it could employ both for the development of the country and for the strengthening of its military and coercive apparatus. By the late 1970s the Baath regime seemed to be well entrenched and confident of overcoming all obstacles both in the internal and external sectors.

CHAPTER VIII

Syria

General Gouraud's seizure of Damascus on July 24, 1920, put an end to Faisal's rule over the Syrian hinterland, and France extended her authority over the whole area assigned to her at the San Remo Conference. The Act of Mandate was signed in London on July 24, 1922, thus formalizing the relationship between France and the Levant under the auspices of the League of Nations.

France and the Levant

The mandate of Syria-Lebanon corresponded roughly to the war-time Sykes-Picot agreement. In this way the peace settlement confirmed the wartime arrangements. The reason why France and not some other country was awarded the countries of Levant must be sought in the long historical association between France and these countries. This association began as early as the crusades. It will be remembered that in 1535 Francis I obtained from the sultan the first capitulations, which resulted in the establishment of French trading outposts and consulates in Syria. Henry IV, Richelieu, and Louis XIV continued this relationship. Colbert actively promoted trade with the Levant in the epoch of mercantilism. By the Treaty of 1740 France obtained the renewal of the capitulations. As we know from a preceding chapter, the treaty contained special references to the Levant and to the holy places in Palestine, favoring French interests there and virtually designating France as a protector of Latin Christianity in the area. By an agreement with the sultan in 1802, Napoleon confirmed the capitulatory privileges. France's interest in the Levant has been considerable ever since. She was sympathetic toward Mohammed Ali, who, as has been mentioned earlier, extended his rule to Syria in the 1830s. Definite ties of friendship developed between France and the Maronite Christians of Lebanon. In 1842-1845 and again in 1860, France intervened in favor of Lebanon, forcing the Sublime Porte to recognize Lebanon's autonomy. French educational and religious institutions, such as the Jesuit University of Beirut, were established in the Levant, and this in turn contributed to a considerable extension of French cultural influence. It is significant that when nationalistically minded Arab intellectuals decided to hold their congress in 1913, they chose Paris as a meeting place, and the majority of its members came from Syria and Lebanon. Thus, when the partitioning of the Ottoman Empire became a reality, France considered herself as the rightful trustee of the Levant.

Her disappointment was great when she perceived that postwar Arab nationalism was not compatible with her concept of her cultural mission in the Levant. The Syrians made it clear to the King-Crane commission that they did not want any foreign tutelage, but if it was going to be imposed upon them anyway, they would favor an American or British mandate to a French one. France saw Emir Faisal ruling in Damascus at the head of a fiercely nationalistic desert army, and Faisal was susceptible to British rather than to French influences. If France was to assert her rule over Syria, the continuance of Faisal's rule in the hinterland was unthinkable. General Gouraud's action in expelling him from Damascus was, therefore, the logical sequel to the partitioning decisions and the subsequent peace settlement.

Having established her undisputed military mastery over Syria, France then faced the problem of finding the best way to perpetuate her rule. The answer seemed clear: it was the old maxim, *divide et impera*. Barely six weeks after Faisal's removal, on September 1, 1920, General Gouraud decreed the division of the mandated territory into four distinct units: Great Lebanon, the state of Damascus (including the Jebel Druze district), the state of Aleppo (including Alexandretta), and the territory of Lattakia (or Alawi territory).[1]

France was represented in the Levant by a high commissioner under whom the French governors of the component units functioned. The basic tendency to maintain the division of the Levant persisted throughout the French mandatory regime despite some territorial and administrative reshufflings. In 1922, Jebel Druze was accorded the status of a separate state, and in 1924 the French created an autonomous sanjak of Alexandretta (partly to satisfy Turkish susceptibilities and partly to conform to their basic policy of division). On January 1, 1925, however, the states of Aleppo and Damascus became unified under the title of the state of Syria. French policy in the Levant tended to follow the pattern of administration in the French colonies. It was centralized rule par excellence, with little or no regard for local autonomy. French administrators in Syria-Lebanon were not exactly of the highest caliber. (In contrast to the British, a colonial career did not attract many brilliant young Frenchmen.)

Lebanon after World War I

Of the four main divisions in the mandated territory, French policy appeared relatively successful in two, namely, in Lebanon and Lattakia. Lebanon, inhabited by a mixed population and containing a slight Christian majority, enjoyed her separate status and looked toward France for protection. In 1925, the Lebanese Representative Council drafted a constitution which, promulgated by the high commissioner, became law in May 1926. It gave Lebanon Western-patterned parliamentary institutions with a president, a cabinet, and two-chamber (later one-

---

[1] A detailed study of territorial divisions and changes may be found in A. H. Hourani, *Syria and Lebanon: A Political Essay* (London, 1946). Consult also Raymond O'Zoux, *Les Etats du Levant sous Mandat Français* (Paris, 1931), and J. Achkar, *Evolution Politique de la Syrie et du Liban, de la Palestine et de l'Iraq* (Paris, 1935).

chamber) parliament. Article 30 mentioned specifically the republic's dependent relationship to France, in conformity with the League of Nations mandate. The constitution was amended in 1927 and in 1929.

The year 1931 and the first months of 1932 were difficult for Lebanon. The country suffered an acute economic crisis, which was reflected in unemployment, strikes, and general unrest. Public finances were subjected to particular strain, and the native Lebanese authorities did little to alleviate the situation. On May 9, 1932, French High Commissioner Ponsot suspended the constitution, appointed a caretaker government, and took energetic steps to restore order in the Lebanese treasury. This crisis led the French to change their minds about the propriety of Western-modeled democratic institutions for a retarded country like Lebanon. The result was the decision to transform Lebanon from a parliamentary republic into a semiauthoritarian corporative state. On January 2, 1934, a new high commissioner, Count de Martel, promulgated a new Lebanese constitution which assured representation to the professions, limited the authority of the parliament, reinforced the executive power, and provided proper safeguards for public finances against irresponsible spending.

Gradually a tradition was established whereby the president of the republic was to be a Maronite Christian and the prime minister a Sunni Moslem, thus assuring a balance between the two prominent sections of the population. The constitution did not provide for any state religion, so freedom of worship became a reality. Some traces of the former Turkish millet system could be found in the arrangement which gave the corporate religious communities the right to regulate some matters relating to the personal status of their members. Lebanon's political forces were divided between the religious leaders, of whom the Maronite patriarch was the most influential, and the political parties. Of these, the most important were the Unionist group, headed by Emile Eddé, which was known for its insistence upon full Lebanese independence, and the Constitutionalist group, under Bishara el-Khuri, which favored closer relationships with other Arab countries. Otherwise the differences between these groups were not very profound.

Like Lebanon, the territory of Lattakia had a relatively peaceful existence. The Alawis constituted a separate Islamic sect which was anxious to preserve its identity and which feared domination by the Sunnis of Syria. The French made full use of these fears, encouraging particularism and considerably aiding the territory in its material progress.

Syria after World War I

Conditions in Syria and in the Jebel Druze[2] were far from satisfactory. French rule in these states was resented because of its centralization and because of its separation from Syria of districts which were regarded as Syrian by Sunni Arab nationalists.[3] Within five years considerable tension developed. This gave rise, by the end of 1925, to an insurrection which broke out in the Druze mountains and

[2] For conditions in the Druze district, see Narcisse Bouron, *Les Druzes* (Paris, 1930).
[3] The nationalist case is ably presented in Edmond Rabbath, *Unité Syrienne et Devenir Arabe* (Paris, 1937). See also Elizabeth P. MacCallum, *The Nationalist Crusade in Syria* (New York, 1928).

which soon spread to Damascus and other parts of Syria.[4] In order to quell the rebellion, the French sent reinforcements to Lebanon, armed Circassian and Armenian auxiliaries to fight the insurgent Arabs; under the orders of General Sarrail, the high commissioner, they bombarded Damascus in the spring of 1926. Soon afterward Suweida, the capital of Jebel Druze, was captured by French troops. By the end of 1926 the insurrection had been crushed. A new high commissioner, Henri de Jouvenel, entrusted to Ahmed Nami Bey the formation of a government in Damascus, which, it was hoped, would follow French guidance.

At the same time French policy tended to follow the constitutional pattern developed in Lebanon. In 1928 the French high commissioner directed the convocation of a Syrian Constituent Assembly. Elections to the assembly resulted in the emergence of a powerful National Bloc (Kutla) founded by Ibrahim Hananu. Among its leaders were men such as Hashim el-Atassi, Jamil Mardam Bey, Saadullah el-Jabri, and Faris el-Khuri. Within the bloc operated another group known as Istiqlal, which advocated complete independence of Syria. Headed by Shukri el-Quwatli, this group included Emir Adil Arslan and a Lebanese Nationalist, Riyadh es-Sulh. The bloc did not secure a majority of seats, but being more determined and disciplined than other groups it played a role out of proportion to its numbers and soon began to dominate Syrian politics. Its members were elected to the most important positions in the assembly.

The assembly drew up a consitution which, in some important respects, was unacceptable to the French authorities. The points objected to in particular were a provision for a united Syria (which would mean the obliteration of the separate status of Lebanon and of other areas under French mandate as well as of Palestine and Transjordan) and provisions concerning Syrian armed forces and foreign relations, which made no mention of the mandatory relationship to France. For this reason, a new high commissioner, M. Ponsot, first suspended the Assembly and then after several unsuccessful attempts at negotiation dissolved it altogether. In May 1930, he issued a constitution for Syria by his own decree. This new document embodied virtually all the articles of the old one except those to which France objected. Article 116 specifically confirmed France's responsibilities under the mandate of the League of Nations. Jebel Druze and Lattakia remained outside Syria. Special articles provided for the establishment of the so-called Common Interests (to Syria, Lebanon, and other areas) to be administered largely by French officials.

The new constitution was accepted by the people of Syria without violent opposition, and in 1932 elections to the single chamber took place. They resulted in a victory for the "moderates," i.e., those who were willing to cooperate with the French. Nevertheless, the extreme nationalists succeeded in obtaining around 25 percent of the seats. The chamber elected Mohammed Ali el-Abid president of the republic, and he in turn appointed a moderate, Haqqi el-Azem prime minister. The

[4]This insurrection was supported by a variety of political groups such as the People's Party of Syria, the Future of Islam of Konya, the Inter-Islamic Committee of Berlin, and the Third International of Moscow. Professor Faris Bey el-Khuri was an intellectual leader of the insurrection. In the Jebel Druze, the insurgents were led by the leading family of Sultan el-Atrash. In Damascus the leadership was assumed by Dr. Shahbandar.

new cabinet included, however, a number of nationalists. The latter soon emerged as the most influential group in the Chamber of Deputies, demanding a Franco-Syrian treaty to replace the mandatory regime. Their stand was strengthened by developments in British-controlled Iraq where a treaty had just been substituted for the mandate.

Treaties with France

The negotiations which ensued lasted for nearly four years. They were first conducted in Syria by High Commissioner Ponsot but, owing to the intransigence of the Kutla group, ended in failure. Eventually they were transferred to France. A Syrian delegation composed of six members with representatives of both moderates and nationalists went to Paris and there, on September 9, 1936, concluded a treaty. This document, which was signed by Vienot, French under-secretary of foreign affairs, and Hashim Bey el-Atassi, chief Syrian delegate, was composed of a main treaty, a military convention, and annexes and was to be valid for twenty-five years. The main provisions were as follows: Syria was to become independent within three years and was to be sponsored by France for membership in the League of Nations; France and Syria entered into a military alliance; France obtained the right to maintain two air bases; French land forces were permitted to stay in the Alawi and Druze districts for five years; these districts, however, were to be incorporated into Syria; French military instructors were to advise the Syrian army, and France was to supply it with armaments and military equipment; in case of war Syria's duty was to cooperate with France on her own soil by protecting and maintaining aerodromes and by furnishing communications and transit assistance as well as water.

In the annexed letters, Syria agreed to recruit technical advisers and experts in France, to establish a special judicial system for the protection of foreigners, and to accord the French ambassador the right of precedence over other diplomatic representatives. All these provisions followed the pattern of the Anglo-Iraqi treaty of 1930, but there were some differences. These consisted in the following provisions: (1) despite Syria's sovereignty over Lattakia and Jebel Druze, the administrative autonomy of these areas was expressly provided for; (2) a special regime was established for foreign schools, charitable institutions, and archeological missions; (3) a promise was made to negotiate a university convention; (4) Syria promised to respect the acquired physical and legal rights of Frenchmen; (5) a monetary agreement was concluded; (6) a financial agreement was attached to the treaty.

It was relatively easy for the French to conclude a similar treaty with Lebanon. The treaty was signed by Count de Martel and Emile Eddé on November 13, 1936, following negotiations conducted in Beirut. The Lebanese treaty was a virtual duplicate of the Syrian one except for provisions which referred to territorial and minority questions peculiar to Lebanon and for the fact that no limit was put upon the time, type, or number of French forces to be stationed in Lebanese territory.

In the late fall, elections took place in Syria. They resulted in an overwhelming victory for the National Bloc, which secured a majority in the eighty-six-members chamber.[5] The chamber elected Faris el-Khuri as its president, and, upon accepting Mohammed Ali el-Abid's resignation from the presidency of the republic, elected Hashim el-Atassi to this post. Jamil Mardam Bey became prime minister. The first important act of the new parliament was to ratify the Franco-Syrian treaty. The next was to incorporate Jebel Druze and Lattakia into the Syrian republic. Gradually the French high commissioner began transferring his functions to the Syrian government.[6] The Syrians were full of hopes, and this optimism was highlighted by the return of some prominent exiled leaders to whom amnesty had been granted.

In Lebanon political developments took a parallel course, although the Sunni Arabs did not share the Maronites' joy over the conclusion of the treaty. To them the treaty meant abandonment of hope for a reunion with Syria. In January 1937 the constitution of 1926 was restored. The new electoral law adopted in 1937 provided for a chamber whose members were to be elected in the ratio of two-thirds on a sectarian basis to one-third by nominations. The elections in the fall of 1937 were organized in accordance with this provision. No radical change could be observed in Lebanese politics, which continued to be marked by personal rivalries and sectarian issues.

The early optimism of the Syrian and Lebanese nationalists was soon dissipated. First, France delayed and eventually refused to ratify the treaties. This was due partly to political changes in France (the Blum Popular Front administration gave place to a right-of-center coalition) and partly to a feeling of national insecurity. Faced with the resurgence of German and Italian militarism, France was reluctant to liquidate her Syro-Lebanese base in the eastern Mediterranean. Second, Syria ran into difficulty almost immediately in her quest for unity. The opposition came from Turkey, and the quarrel centered on the sanjak of Alexandretta.

The Sanjak of Alexandretta

Ever since the peace settlement, Turkey had watched anxiously over the sanjak, which was inhabited by a mixed Turkish-Arab-Kurdish population. In fact, Alexandretta remained the only Turkish *terra irredenta,* Turkey being otherwise quite satisfied with her existing boundaries. When Turkey concluded the Franklin-Bouillon agreement in 1921 she made sure that the special status of Alexandretta would be recognized by France and that the sanjak would be granted adequate autonomy. With the conclusion of the Franco-Syrian treaty, which provided for a unified Syria, Turkey felt that the future of Alexandretta was jeopardized, and she immediately raised objections. The Turkish argument ran as follows: when concluding the Franklin-Bouillon agreement, Turkey had not considered France as a mandatory power over Syria; Turkey had never regarded the sanjak as a part of Syria; Turkey had entrusted the care of the Turks in Alexandretta to France alone, and for this reason she was bound to object to the transfer of responsibilities to Syria; the

---

[5]Out of this number sixteen represented religious minorities and seven the Bedouin tribes.
[6]See John Morgan Jones, *La Fin du Mandat Français en Syrie et au Liban* (Paris, 1938).

only legitimate solution was for France to conclude with the sanjak a separate treaty similar to those concluded with Syria and Lebanon.

France did not accept this Turkish thesis in its entirety but was willing to compromise. Consequently, in December 1936, the matter was brought to the Council of the League of Nations. On January 27, 1937, the Council recommended that the sanjak be granted full autonomy in its internal affairs. Its foreign relations were to be entrusted to Syria, and it was to be linked to Syria by a fiscal and monetary union. Turkish was proclaimed an official language. The Council reserved for itself the right to approve those foreign policy acts of Syria which would affect the status of the sanjak. A Council delegate of French nationality was to reside in the sanjak with the right of temporary veto. France and Turkey were to enforce, if necessary, the Council's decisions; and a statute and fundamental law for the sanjak were to be drafted and submitted for the Council's approval. On May 29, 1937, the Council adopted the statute on the basis of which the new regime was to begin on November 29. Simultaneously, France and Turkey concluded a treaty guaranteeing the integrity of the sanjak. Thus the first dent in the unity of Syria was made: the sanjak was virtually separated from the new republic and its predominantly Turkish character was recognized.[7]

In Syria, both the public and the government protested vigorously against these decisions, and the Syrian parliament refused to accept the new statute for Alexandretta. France was severely criticized for abandoning her new Syrian ally and for appeasing Turkey. The National Bloc suffered a decline in popularity for not having struggled for the sanjak with greater determination.

The Syrians viewed the 1937 arrangements as temporary and as leading inevitably, should France persist in her pro-Turkish policy, to the final incorporation of the sanjak in the Turkish state. In this they were right. Menaced by Germany and Italy, France was determined to seek allies in the Mediterranean. She believed the Turks to be more valuable and reliable than the Syrians. The same reasons which led France to suspend the ratification of her treaties with Syria and Lebanon caused her to choose the Turkish side in the sanjak controversy. By 1938 it became obvious that Turkey would regard a satisfactory solution in the sanjak as the price for linking her fate with that of France. On July 3, 1938, France and Turkey concluded an agreement in Antioch for the joint garrisoning of the sanjak by French and Turkish troops. The next day a Franco-Turkish treaty of friendship was signed at Ankara. And on July 5 impressive formations of crack Turkish troops entered the sanjak. Electoral lists, drawn up under joint Franco-Turkish supervision, showed a Turkish majority of 63 percent, which meant that the Turks would be entitled to a majority of seats in the sanjak's assembly.

The elections held in September 1938 resulted, as could be foreseen, in the establishment of a Turkish-dominated assembly. Its president, as well as the president and prime minister of the sanjak, which had become the Republic of Hatay,

---

[7]For a discussion of this problem from a French point of view, see Paul du Véou, *Le Désastre d'Alexandrette, 1934-1938* (Paris, 1938).

were all Turks. Intensive agitation followed for the joining of Hatay with Turkey. The Republic of Hatay, which was a virtual French-Turkish condominium, lasted less than a year. On June 23, 1939, in Paris, France and Turkey concluded a treaty of mutual assistance, and on the same day, by an agreement signed at Ankara, France ceded to Turkey the sanjak of Alexandretta.

Syria and Lebanon during World War II

France's refusal to ratify the treaty of 1936 had a bad effect upon Syrian political life. Splits occurred in the dominant National Bloc, and a vocal opposition, known as the Constitutionalist Party, was formed around Dr. Abdur Rahman Shahbandar, who had returned from exile. Cabinet crises followed each other in rapid succession, leading to a virtual stalemate in government activities. On July 7, 1939, the president of the republic resigned, and on July 10 the new French high commissioner, Gabriel Pueaux, suspended the constitution, dissolved the Chamber, and appointed a nonpolitical Council of Directors to govern the country under his authority. This was followed by decrees restoring separate regimes for the Druze and Lattakia districts and introducing a special administration for the northeast province of Jezira. Thus, on the eve of the Second World War France reestablished direct rule over Syria in the hope of strengthening her eastern Mediterranean bulwark. The French administration also curbed various pro-Nazi and extremist organizations, including the Communist party.

Similar measures were undertaken in Lebanon soon after the outbreak of the war. There the high commissioner also suspended the constitution and dissolved the Chamber. The president of Lebanon, however, remained in office, but the normal cabinet was replaced by a single secretary of state who governed through civil servants under French supervision.

Toward the French, who were facing a threat to their survival, Syrian and Lebanese political circles expressed, at least outwardly, their loyalty, stressing also their attachment to the camp of democracy. In reality, however, Arab public opinion was hostile to France and to the Allies in general. Resentment at what was believed to be a betrayal of the Arabs after World War I, appeasement of Turkey in the Alexandretta issue, the nonratification of the Syrian and Lebanese treaties, and the excitement over the Zionist question in Palestine—all contributed to a definitely anti-Ally trend in the Levant. As one observer has aptly phrased it, "From the point of view of the exploited nations of the East, there was nothing to choose between the oppression exercised in the name of democracy and that exercised in the name of Fascism."[8]

During the first months of the war France assembled in Syria a large force, known as the Army of the Levant, under the command of General Weygand. It was expected that, if war were to extend to the eastern Mediterranean, this army would have a major role to play. France's defeat in June 1940 put an end to these plans.

[8]Hourani, *op. cit.*, p. 230.

Syria and Lebanon found themselves under Vichy control and most members of the French civil and military administration refused to adhere to General de Gaulle's Free French Committee.

The attitude of French officialdom could be explained in part by the traditional anti-British feeling of the French in Syria. Britain had been blamed for setting a dangerous precedent by her treaty with Iraq in 1930, which greatly emboldened Syrian nationalists. Some Frenchmen had never succeeded in shaking the suspicion that, back in the 1920s, Britain would have been only too glad to see Faisal prevail and to substitute her control of Syria for French control. Moreover, the French knew of Britain's annoyance at the fact that Syria and Lebanon had become centers of intrigue for Arab refugees from Palestine, who conducted anti-British guerrilla operations from this safe shelter.

The Vichy authorities hoped to prevent the British from seizing the French Levant, but at the same time they were compelled to open their gates to Axis influence. In August 1940, the Italian and German Armistice Commissions arrived in Beirut, and before long signs of Axis infiltration began to multiply. Herr von Hentig, chief of the Near East Department of the German Foreign Office, arrived in Syria, and German propaganda, usually successful with the Arabs, was stepped up considerably. The real crisis occurred in May 1941 when General Dentz, Vichy high commissioner, permitted German aircraft to land and refuel on Syrian airfields when in transit to Iraq to aid Rashid Ali's rebellion. The pretense of Vichy neutrality could no longer be maintained, and Great Britain decided to act.

British Intervention in the Levant

On June 8, 1941, British troops, commanded by General Sir Henry Maitland Wilson, invaded Syria from Palestine, Transjordan, and Iraq. Free French elements accompanied them. Vichy forces offered resistance, but after a month of fighting General Dentz sued for peace. On July 14, an armistice was signed. Syria and Lebanon were included in the area under the British Middle East Command and subjected to occupation by the British Ninth Army. To unify Levant's economy with the rest of the Middle East, the British included it in the sterling bloc in September.

The question of Franco-Syrian-Lebanese relationships remained to be solved. On the day of the invasion, the French commander, General Catroux, issued a proclamation in which he stated that Free France intended to put an end to the mandatory regime, to proclaim Syria and Lebanon free and independent, and to negotiate a treaty which would define their mutual relations. Catroux's declaration was endorsed in a separate statement issued in Cairo on the same day by Ambassador Sir Miles Lampson in the name of Great Britain. On June 24 General de Gaulle appointed General Catroux "Delegate General and Plenipotentiary of Free France in the Levant"—a title replacing the former title of high commissioner—and instructed him to negotiate treaties with Syria and Lebanon at the earliest possible date.

In making these promises, the Free French no doubt pursued a policy advocated by the British. The dramatic changes in Syria gave the British an opportunity to restore to some degree their good standing with the Arabs, a standing which had undergone severe strain as a result of the Palestinian controversy. It soon became clear that British and French interpretations of the June 8, 1941, pledges varied. General de Gaulle conducted a policy of procrastination, trying to postpone the moment of Syrian and Lebanese liberation and insisting upon the privileged position of France even after the treaties were concluded. In contrast, Great Britain interpreted these pledges literally, and while not denying France a privileged position in the Levant, she pressed for a speedy transfer of essential controls and services to the Syrians and Lebanese. Attempts were made to reconcile these attitudes: on August 15, 1941, Oliver Lyttelton, British minister of state for the Middle East, and General de Gaulle exchanged letters in which they reaffirmed that "Great Britain has no interest in Syria or Lebanon, except to win the war" and that once independence of the Levant states has been achieved, "France should have the predominant position in Syria and Lebanon over any other European Power.'"[9] On September 9, 1941, similar declarations were made by Prime Minister Churchill in the House of Commons. But they could not dispel the basic divergence in French and British policies. Nor was the tension alleviated by the appointment of Major-General Sir Edward Spears, a staunch representative of imperial traditions, as head of the British mission to the Levant. The French resented his interference in Syrian politics and suspected him of sinister plots with the Arabs against France's position in the Levant.

Emancipation of Syria and Lebanon

In the meantime General Catroux undertook the rather ungrateful task—from the French point of view—of reaching an agreement with Syria and Lebanon that would lead toward their emancipation. On September 28, 1941, he proclaimed the independence of Syria, stating in particular that (1) she would "enjoy from now onwards the rights and prerogatives of an independent and sovereign state"; (2) she would have the power to appoint diplomatic representatives abroad; (3) she would have the right to organize her national forces; (4) she would be obliged to accord France and her Allies necessary aid and facilities during the war; and (5) the foregoing stipulations should be replaced as soon as possible by a final settlement "in the form of a Franco-Syrian Treaty which will definitely guarantee the independence of the country.'"[10]

This act was followed by the proclamation of Lebanese independence on November 26, 1941. Its terms were similar to those of the Syrian proclamation. To implement these documents, General Catroux asked Sheikh Taj ed-Din to assume the presidency of Syria and requested Alfred Naccache, president of Lebanon, to remain in that post.

Soon afterward Great Britain extended de jure recognition to both republics, and in February 1942, General Spears was appointed first British minister to Syria and

[9]Quoted by Hourani, *op. cit.*, p. 245.
[10]*Ibid.*, pp. 249–250.

Lebanon. Other recognitions followed, but the Arab states were guarded and slow in acknowledging Syrian and Lebanese independence. As for the United States, it reserved its judgment until the formal termination of the mandate, which it believed should come about by the conclusion and ratification of bilateral treaties between the two states and France. In 1942, George Wadsworth was appointed American consul general and diplomatic agent to both Levantine governments.

Despite this formal emancipation France was neither willing nor ready to transfer major functions of government to the new republics. The question of the constitutionality of both regimes remained in abeyance, both Presidents Taj ed-Din and Naccache owing their offices to General Catroux's appointment and not to the freely expressed will of their peoples. Moreover, General de Gaulle objected in the name of Free France to the holding of elections in both countries.

In consequence, the mood of expectation gradually gave way to one of hostility. Public opinion did not spare Britain either, believing that she countenanced France's behavior. In Syria the National Bloc experienced a revival, this time under the leadership of Shukri el-Quwatli, and there was a marked tendency toward left-wing extremism as expressed by the growth of Socialist and Communist movements.

Under the pressure of public opinion, the Free French authorities in March 1943 decided to reestablish the suspended constitutions in both Syria and Lebanon. Elections held in the summer of that year resulted in the establishment of nationalistically minded parliaments in Damascus and Beirut. In Syria the National Bloc regained its dominant position and its new leader, Shukri el-Quwatli, was elected to the presidency of the republic. Faris el-Khuri, Saadullah el-Jabri, Jamil Mardam Bey, old leaders of the bloc, once again took the reins of power by assuming key legislative and executive positions.

In Lebanon events followed a parallel course. The pro-French leaders were dismissed from their posts and replaced by nationalists, some of whom, as for example the new prime minister, Riyadh es-Sulh, had long-standing ties with Syrian nationalist leaders. The Lebanese Chamber, composed of thirty Christians and twenty-five Moslems, elected Bishara el-Khuri president of the republic.

The advent to power of the nationalists in both countries foreshadowed a more determined struggle for complete emancipation from French tutelage. This tutelage was expressed in a number of legislative and administrative restrictions placed upon both republics by France. In particular, the French delegate general still retained the right to issue decrees which restricted both parliaments in the free exercise of legislative power, and he could still invoke those provisions of the Syrian and Lebanese constitutions which, with reference to the League of Nations mandate, made France responsible for the maintenance of order and security and for the defense and conduct of foreign relations of both countries. Moreover, the delegate general administered directly the Common Interests, in particular the customs, maintained control over local levies known as the *Troupes Spéciales* and over the state security police, and exercised authority over nomad tribes and press censorship. He also was in a position to exert influence, through French technical advisers, in the Syrian and Lebanese administrations. Moreover, French intelligence officers, known as agents of the *Services Spéciaux*, were still much in evidence in both states.

The nationalist governments of Syria and Lebanon objected to all these preroga- tives and demanded their abolition. De Gaulle's Free French Committee retorted that France's responsibilities could not be terminated without the approval of the League of Nations or of its successor. It also argued that the special prerogatives enjoyed by France could be relinquished only as a result of treaties which would safeguard French interests in the Levant.

Nationalist reaction to this refusal was stronger than the Free French had ex- pected. On November 8, 1943, the Lebanese parliament adopted a resolution to drop from the constitution all those articles that referred to France as a mandatory power. Two days later the new French delegate general, Helleu, placed the president of the republic and the majority of his cabinet under arrest, suspended the constitu- tion, and appointed Emile Eddé as head of the state and of the government. The Lebanese replied with a general strike and anti-French riots. The British did not hide their disapproval of the precipitate French action, feeling that such action was likely to endanger order and security in the area under British military command. Faced with nationalist outbreaks and with simultaneous British pressure, General de Gaulle promptly recalled Helleu, sending General Catroux to smooth out the dif- ferences. Lebanese leaders were released and reinstated in their functions.

On January 24, 1944, a similar crisis occurred in Syria, though in less violent form. On that day the president of the republic and the members of parliament took an oath of allegiance to the constitution, expressly leaving out Article 116, which referred to French mandatory responsibilities. This action did not, however, have the same revolutionary character as the earlier Lebanese defiance, because, instead of preceding, it followed an agreement, reached on December 22, 1943, with the French Committee of National Liberation. The agreement, which extended to both Syria and Lebanon, provided for the definitive transfer of powers from the delegate general to the governments concerned. The nationalists had triumphed.

In the course of 1944, all the functions of the delegate general were transferred to the Syrian and Lebanese governments with the exception of the *Troupes Spéciales*. French delay in placing them under Syro-Lebanese command caused resentment. Mutual irritation was increased by French insistence upon the conclusion of treaties which would bind Syria and Lebanon to France and which, according to the French view, were necessary to relieve France of her mandatory responsibilities. France insisted in particular: (1) on safeguards for French cultural establishments in the Levant; (2) on the recognition of her economic rights; and (3) on the recognition of her strategic interests in the area (she asked for air and naval bases and the right to organize and command Syrian and Lebanese armies).

The Twilight of French Influence

Negotiations concerning these treaty arrangements were scheduled to begin on May 19, 1945. Four days earlier, however, fresh French reinforcements disem- barked in Beirut. The Lebanese protested vigorously against their arrival. The ensuing strikes and riots which broke out in Beirut soon spread all over Lebanon and Syria. French citizens were assaulted, and both governments broke off their negotiations with the French delegate general, General Beynet. For a few days the political situation in the Levant remained in suspense. Nothing less than the sovereignty of both states was at stake. So long as the French could maintain military control over the whole region, the independence of Syria and Lebanon would remain illusory— and both parties realized this fact perfectly well.

In this moment of tension direct British intervention again tipped the scales in favor of the two republics. At the end of May Prime Minister Winston Churchill asked General de Gaulle, in a form resembling an ultimatum, to order his troops to cease fire and withdraw to their barracks. Threatened with imminent British action, de Gaulle complied with this demand. Peace was restored, but treaty negotiations with France were not renewed. Encouraged by British support, Syria and Lebanon on June 21, 1945, issued a joint declaration dismissing all French citizens from their services and announcing the transfer of the *Troupes Spéciales* to their national control. On July 7 France gave her formal consent to this transfer. It had been accomplished in forty-five days.

In the meantime the independent international status of both republics was given explicit recognition by a number of diplomatic acts. In July 1944 the Soviet Union, and in September of the same year the United States, granted the Levant states full and unconditional recognition in which no mention was made of the special position of France. Both republics participated as independent states in the negotiations leading toward the creation of the Arab League, and both signed the League pact on March 22, 1945, as founding members. In conformity with the Yalta decisions, Syria and Lebanon declared war on Germany and Japan on March 1, 1945, signed the United Nations declaration in April, and by these acts gained admission to the United Nations conference at San Francisco. From that time on, sovereign status was accorded both republics without question by the outside world or even by France. The only question that remained to be settled was the withdrawal of foreign troops from the republics' territories. On December 13, 1945, the British and French governments issued a joint statement promising gradual evacuation of their forces from the Levant. This statement elicited protests in Beirut and Damascus, where the nationalist governments were anxious to see a speedy departure of foreign troops. On February 4, 1946, Syria and Lebanon brought the matter to the attention of the United Nations Security Council. After a brief debate the American delegation moved that the Council express its confidence that foreign troops would be evacuated as soon as practicable and that negotiations to that end would be undertaken without delay. Despite seven affirmative votes, this proposal was not adopted because of a Soviet veto. Russia voted against it on the ground that it was too vague. Thereupon France and Great Britain declared that despite the veto they would abide by the resolution. At the end of April they informed the Council that they had agreed to withdraw their troops from Syria without delay and from Lebanon by gradual stages. Withdrawal from Syria was carried out in the same month, and by December 31, 1946, the last foreign soldiers had departed from Lebanon. Thus both republics achieved complete political emancipation.

The Republic of Syria

Syria's politics after the war were full of violence and abrupt changes. More than three years after Syria's emancipation the power of government rested in the hands of the National Bloc leaders, Shukri el-Quwatli, Jamil Mardam Bey, Saadullah el-Jabri, and others, who had spent the greater part of their lives struggling for independence. Having won freedom for their country, this rather elderly generation proved to be ill-fitted for the postwar task of construction and reform. Critics maintained that the National Bloc leaders were interested only in reaping personal rewards for their victory and in perpetuating their rule. The first elections in independent Syria, in July 1947, were carried out with less corruption than in Lebanon. Yet they, too, elicited vigorous protests against government interference. In 1947 the progovernment majority passed a constitutional amendment allowing the reelection of the president for a second term. In April 1948 the Chamber availed itself of this right, reelecting Shukri el-Quwatli to the presidency of the republic.

Devoted to the principles of republicanism, the National Bloc leaders (whose political philosophy has been likened to that of late-eighteenth-century liberals) realized that their own position of power could not be divorced from Syria's sovereignty and separateness as a nation. They therefore opposed plans for the unification of the Arab world that would result in the submergence of Syria in a larger—and presumably monarchical—entity. In particular they opposed the Greater Syria scheme advocated by the Hashemite Kingdoms of Transjordan and Iraq and favored by King Abdullah of Transjordan, who made no secret of his ambition to rule the vast area comprising Syria proper, Lebanon, Iraq, Transjordan, and Palestine. King Abdullah, however, was not the only one who strongly favored this scheme. The Greater Syria plan was also advocated by Antoun Saadeh's Syrian National party, which drew its membership from the young radical elements of both republics. It was also backed by the Constitutionalist group of Aleppo men, which in 1948 assumed the name of People's party, attracting considerable numbers of moderate politicians and extending its activities to all parts of Syria. These groups, however, did not favor Abdullah for their prospective king.

It is possible that the Quwatli regime might have continued in power for an indefinite period if it had not been for the problem of Palestine. The bungling of the Palestine war in 1948 by the Quwatli-Mardam Bey government resulted in discontent and general disaffection. It vividly exposed the regime's weaknesses, causing chaos and disorder, which, in December 1948, assumed the form of antigovernment riots verging on a spontaneous mob revolution. Prime Minister Jamil Mardam Bey was forced to resign. Law and order were eventually restored by the chief of staff of the army, Colonel Husni Zaim, who toured the country and, combining force with persuasion, succeeded in saving Syria from disintegration. The failure of the Syrian government in the Palestinian war strengthened the case of the pro-unionists, who claimed that greater unity among the Arabs and closer collaboration with Iraq and Transjordan might have averted military disaster. Faced with widespread criticism, the Quwatli group tried to shift the blame for the Palestinian failure to the army. This was the spark which set off a great explosion.

The Husni Zaim Coup

On March 30, 1949, Colonel Husni Zaim executed a bloodless coup d'état.[11] Placing President Quwatli and Prime Minister Khalid el-Azem under arrest, Zaim dissolved the parliament and assumed dictatorial powers. His coup expressed the reaction of the Syrian people against the ineptitude of the Quwatli regime. There was a wide-spread desire for change, and Zaim's action met with general approval, eliciting manifestations of joy and hopeful expectation. Zaim drew his main support from two discontented yet different groups. One was the army and the other the younger reformist circles desiring a radical change. The latter were drawn from such diverse camps as the Hama branch of Saadeh's Syrian National Social party (advocating the Greater Syria scheme) and the People's party (friendly to Iraq, conservative but believing in democratic principles).

Supported by these groups, Zaim inaugurated a "New Order" based upon Turkish patterns. (He himself was reputed to be a great admirer of Kemal Ataturk.) His reforms included the extension of suffrage to literate women, the virtual separation of church and state, curbs on the clergy, the introduction of a civil code largely based upon European models, and the inauguration of extensive public works. Ideological and practical considerations pushed him toward the cooperation with Iraq and Jordan advocated by prounionists. There was also a compelling need to accept their military aid at the time of the armistice negotiations with Israel. Such aid was likely to strengthen Syria's position and guarantee her protection against the threat of an Israeli invasion. Furthermore, if Zaim's pledges of reform were not to remain an empty word, they had to be backed up by some quick steps toward economic recovery—and this was possible only with friendly foreign cooperation. Iraq and Jordan were Syria's two principal customers, accounting for over 60 percent of her exports, principally grain. Therefore, expansion of trade with them would be a basic factor in Syria's economic recovery. Soon after he assumed power, Zaim entered into negotiations with the Hashemite states. A desire for rapid economic progress led him to resume talks with the Trans-Arabian Pipe Line Company, which, if allowed transit to its Mediterranean terminal in Sidon, would supply ready cash for the war-depleted Syrian treasury. It should be pointed out that negotiations with Tapline had been interrupted by the Quwatli government as a reprisal against United States support of Israel. Zaim was no more pro-Israeli than his predecessor, but in order to obtain both private and public aid from the United States he was willing to abandon Quwatli's stubborn and impractical resistance.

Zaim was anxious to secure formal diplomatic recognition of his regime. This quest for recognition, coupled with the desire for immediate economic help from abroad, led him to change his policy rather suddenly and turn toward Egypt and Saudi Arabia as partners and friends. Barely three weeks after the coup Zaim accepted an invitation from King Farouk to visit Cairo. Received with great cordiality in the capital of the wealthiest of the Arab states, Zaim quickly secured Egyptian

[11] For an analysis of violent political changes in Syria, see Alford Carleton, "The Syrian Coups d'Etat of 1949," *Middle East Journal* (Jan. 1950).

recognition and far-reaching promises of financial and military aid. Saudi Arabia promptly followed suit, Ibn Saud readily pledging substantial loans from his gold-filled treasury. In view of these facts, Lebanon did not delay recognition.

Zaim's diplomatic victory was bought at a price. The price was his renunciation of the Greater Syria schemes and his rejection of any closer political union with Iraq. Having to choose between the promise of slow economic recovery through political cooperation with the Hashemite kingdoms and quick political and financial benefits through Egyptian and Saudi Arabian aid, Zaim decided to choose the latter. Moreover, such a solution appealed to him on purely personal grounds. A Greater Syria scheme, if implemented, would put an end to Zaim's career as head of an independent state and would make him no more than a caretaker during the transitional phase. In Cairo his ambition was fanned, and he was encouraged to make his position permanent. In addition to Egyptian and Saudi Arabian blessing, he could be reasonably sure of American and French support. Although the American legation in Damascus maintained strict neutrality toward domestic Syrian developments, it was no secret that American policy gave high priority to cordial relations between the United States and Saudi Arabia on account of the American oil investments in the latter country. Ibn Saud stubbornly resisted the Greater Syria scheme which would increase the strength of his rivals, the Hashemites, and favored the status quo with Syria as an independent state. American policy, therefore, also favored the preservation of an independent Syria. Thus Zaim's newly revealed ambition to establish himself permanently did not run counter to American aims; in fact, the United States may have welcomed the beginning of a really reformist, antifeudal movement in Damascus. Zaim's energetic anti-Communist pronouncements added to his popularity with the State Department. As for France, she had traditionally resented the Greater Syria scheme, believing it to be British-inspired. Blaming Britain for her wartime political defeat in the Levant, France was ready to back any anti-British solution in Damascus. Although unable to offer military and political support, France was still in a position to offer financial aid to Zaim, a consideration he could not disregard.

This about-face in Zaim's foreign policy had immediate domestic repercussions. Abandoning closer union with Iraq and Jordan, Zaim had to part with the pro-unionist elements who had initially supported him and to rely more heavily upon the army. This policy alienated from him large numbers of the aspiring younger generation of Syrian politicians. Zaim's ban on all political parties in the summer of 1949 and his failure to form a party of his own produced a dangerous political vacuum, testifying to his lack of skill in handling domestic politics.

Gradually the initial enthusiasm over his advent to power wore off, and the people began to become aware of his mistakes. These included some moves interpreted as pro-French and, as such, subject to severe criticism; certain measures toward self-aggrandizement, such as the assumption of the title of marshal amid pompous ceremonies; his move into luxurious quarters; his assumption of the title of head of the state following a dubious referendum; the extradition to Lebanon of fugitive leader Antoun Saadeh after the latter had been granted the right of asylum

(Saadeh was subsequently sentenced to death in Lebanon); and delay in economic reforms. It was, however, his loss of the army's support which ultimately tipped the scales against him. Zaim relied chiefly on Kurdish and Circassian units, employing them in the interior while leaving the purely Arab formations on the Palestinian border. This produced resentment and resulted in an anti-Zaim conspiracy.

The Hinnawi and the Shishakli Coups

On August 14, 1949, Zaim and his prime minister, Muhsin el-Barazi, were captured and summarily executed in a coup engineered by Colonel Sami Hinnawi. In a statement released shortly afterward, Hinnawi declared that this action had been taken by the army in fulfillment of the aims of the first coup, which had been betrayed by Zaim and his government. Hinnawi then asked former President of the Republic Hashim Bey el-Atassi to form a civilian caretaker government pending the formation of a Constituent Assembly. The task of the assembly was to adopt a new constitution in place of the one which had been suspended by Zaim. Although the Hinnawi coup was the work of the army alone, it gave a new chance to the People's party. Frustrated by Zaim, it now came into prominence. In the November 1949 elections to the Constituent Assembly (in which women were permitted to vote for the first time), the People's party secured 42 of the total of 114 seats, becoming the largest single party in the Assembly. Its leader, Rushdi el-Kikhya, was elected president of the Assembly. Quwatli's National Bloc party boycotted the elections. Hashim el-Atassi was made temporary president of the republic.

Reversing Zaim's policy of friendship with Egypt and Saudi Arabia, Colonel Hannawi reopened negotiations with Iraq and Jordan for closer political bonds. In this he was supported by the People's party, which consistently favored friendship with Baghdad. When the Assembly met for the first time on December 12, it gave the problem of union with Iraq high priority as a basic constitutional question. The leading clique in the army did not, however, favor this solution. To forestall a move for the union of Syria and Iraq, the army, led by Lieutenant-Colonel Adib Shishakli, deposed Hinnawi in the third coup of the year. In the name of the army, Shishakli proclaimed his belief in Syria's separate sovereignty but disavowed any intention of ruling the country himself. Despite these assurances the army watched political developments very carefully, however, and it intervened actively each time the government appeared about to take an action of which it did not approve. Thus, shortly after Shishakli's coup, in late December 1949, the army vetoed the appointment of Nazem el-Qudsi, deputy leader of the People's party, to the office of prime minister. Instead, President Hashim el-Atassi was obliged to ask Khalid el-Azem, an independent, to form a cabinet. In Azem's cabinet, the People's party lost all three of the key portfolios of foreign affairs, defense, and interior, which were given to men whom the army trusted.

The army's chief civilian spokesman in the succeeding cabinets was Akram Hourani, head of the Department of Defense. Hourani attempted to counter the influence of the People's party by founding a new group named the Arab Socialist party and by organizing a forty-five-man Republican bloc in the assembly.

The new regime's policy toward the big powers tended to be neutral and almost isolationist. It was certainly not pro-French.[12] Nor was it pro-British, if we realize Britain's interest in the achievement of the Greater Syria scheme. Indirectly, it suited the United States, inasmuch as the Shishakli-Azem government renewed friendly ties with Egypt and Saudi Arabia. (Ibn Saud went so far as to grant Syria a substantial loan in January 1950 in an apparent effort to bolster up its anti-Hashemite regime.) But the cordial relations with the United States which characterized the Zaim regime were definitely abandoned. Instead, Syria followed a tortuous path, vacillating between negotiation concerning limited technical assistance and loud denunciations of Washington because of its pro-Israeli policy. In Syria, as in other Arab countries, there was a feeling of frustration and disenchantment regarding America. This caused some prominent members of Azem's government to declare themselves publicly in favor of pro-Soviet policy. The recurrent theme of these statements was that the Arabs would rather become "Sovietized" than "Judaized" and that it was proper to collaborate with the Soviet Union as "an enemy of our enemy," i.e., of the United States, in the same way that the Arabs had collaborated with Nazi Germany as the enemy of Britain.[13]

As early as February 1950, Khalid el-Azem made it clear that Syria would not seek an American loan and that she proposed to "go it alone" in her development schemes. To the best of their ability, Syrian authorities obstructed American-sponsored United Nations aid to Palestine Arab refugees and adopted a hostile attitude toward the Clapp mission. The United States legation's protests against the anti-American tenor of Syrian editorials in 1950 provoked an even stronger press campaign against what was termed American interference with the freedom of the press. Repeated pronouncements of American public figures about Israel as the "principal stronghold of democracy and American ideology" in the Middle East had the effect of keeping Syrian anger alive. Incidents such as the tearing down of the American flag and the exploding of a bomb in the garden of the United States legation, as well as official plans for a discriminatory tax rate upon American goods, testified to the depth of Syrian hostility. Syrian newspapers vigorously attacked President Truman's message of May 24, 1951, promising aid to the Middle East on the ground that it placed Israel on the same level with the Arab states. Syrian journalists boycotted a press reception organized soon afterward by the United States Information Services. On June 7, 1951, Prime Minister Khalid el-Azem publicly rejected American technical aid under the Point Four program.

So far, however, Syria's bitterness toward the United States had not resulted in an understanding with Russia. Syria's reply to the United Nations' appeal for aid to the republic of Korea was to declare her support of all resolutions aimed against aggres-

---

[12]Syria definitely broke her economic ties with France. On January 31, 1948, she left the "franc bloc," thus differing from Lebanon, which reached an agreement with France on this issue. In February 1949 France and Syria signed a monetary agreement providing for the latter's final separation from the franc bloc and repayment by France of the Syrian currency cover.

[13]Statements to this effect were made in the spring of 1950 by three members of Khalid el-Azem's cabinet: Maaruf Dawalibi, minister of national economy (in April); Mustafa Sibai, Moslem Brotherhood leader and minister of education (April 29); and Akram Hourani, minister of defense (May 22). Dawalibi opened negotiations for an extensive trade agreement with Russia but subsequently was dropped from the cabinet.

sion, thus both approving the action taken in Korea and implicitly registering regret that different standards were applied in Palestine.[14]

Shishakli's Dictatorship

Adib Shishakli's rule lasted a little over four years. Between December 1949 and December 1951 the colonel allowed a civilian government to function, contenting himself with the role of power behind the scenes; between December 1951 and February 1954 he exercised direct rule.

The first phase was characterized by an uneasy cooperation between the People's party—the dominant group in Syria's politics after President Quwatli's overthrow in 1949—and the army. Cabinets created during those two years usually represented coalitions of Populists, Independents, and certain other elements, with the premiership being rotated between Independents and Populists. Work on the constitution, suddenly interrupted by the coup of December 1949, was resumed, and the constitution was adopted in September 1950.[15] It contained strong Pan-Arab accents, but made no explicit references to union with Iraq. The cooperation between Shishakli and the Populists was severely tested early in November 1951 by the differences that arose with regard to Syria's attitude toward Middle East defense plans and certain internal jurisdictional questions. Behind these divergencies was the basic question of Syria's possible union with Iraq, a matter which was far from buried. The only element capable of keeping peace between Shishakli and his civilian opponents was Syria's president, venerable Hashim el-Atassi. A civilian and a strong believer in constitutional government, he leaned toward the Populists, thus frustrating Shishakli's designs and putting a brake on his influence.

Unable to cooperate with Shishakli, Premier Hassan Hakim (an Independent of pro-Western tendencies) resigned on November 10, 1951. The prolonged cabinet crisis that ensued was resolved only eighteen days later, when a Populist known for his strong nationalist attitudes, Dr. Maaruf Dawalibi, formed a cabinet basically unchanged; i.e., it was composed of Populists and Independents. Obviously discontented with the prolonged Populist hold on cabinet offices, Shishakli decided to end the pretense of noninterference and on the night of November 28–29 executed a new coup in the course of which he placed under arrest the prime minister, his cabinet members, and certain other leaders. In the declarations that followed, Shishakli delivered a scathing attack on the Populists, accusing them of "destructive work" and of trying to achieve a federation which would restore "the throne" and destroy Syrian independence. He also declared that the immediate cause of the coup was the Populist determination to appoint a civilian to the ministry of defense and detach the gendarmerie from the army. On December 2, Shishakli dissolved the Chamber. On the same day President Atassi resigned, leaving the door open for Shishakli to assume the highest office himself. The latter decided, however, to remain in his

---

[14]This declaration was made on July 8, 1950. For details concerning the attitudes of Arab states during the Korean crisis, see *Middle Eastern Affairs* (Aug.-Sept. 1950), pp. 247 ff.

[15]See Majid Khadduri, "Constitutional Development in Syria," *Middle East Journal* (Spring 1951).

position as chief of staff, while entrusting his associate, Colonel Fawzi Salu (later promoted to general) with the functions of "chief of state," prime minister, and minister of defense.

The coup ushered in the second phase of Shishakli's rule, a phase of undisguised dictatorship. During this period a number of typically dictatorial measures were applied, such as the banning of political parties and of the Moslem Brotherhood; the launching of the "Arab Liberation Movement," designed to substitute for the old parties "patriotic" work for the state and the "Arab nation" (August 1952); "consolidation" of the press, i.e., forcible reduction in the number of papers; glorification of the army; a ban on the political activities of civil servants; the removal of tenure and the dismissal of a number of university professors;[16] and a ban on student strikes and unauthorized demonstrations. Decree 151 of March 3, 1952, made it mandatory for any foreign company operating in Syria to be represented in the country by a Syrian citizen or a Syrian company. Another decree forbade direct communications between Syrians (including the Syrian University, the Arab Academy, and the Directorate of Antiquities) and foreign cultural institutions. Decree 189 forbade the acquisition of real estate by foreigners, while still another regulation imposed a number of restrictions on the admission of foreigners to Syria. Not all of these measures, however, were of a repressive type. Among the more positive ones could be mentioned a decree of October 23, 1952, on agrarian reform, which provided for the distribution of domanial estates, and a decree abolishing honorary titles and titles of nobility.

Following the rather well-worn patterns of military dictatorships Shishakli emphasized order, security, and patriotism. The first anniversary of his second coup was celebrated with military parades and oratory. In a speech Shishakli called Damascus the "capital of present Arabism and the heart of the Arab nation, where rests Saladin, hero-liberator of Palestine." His servile press spoke of Syria as a "giant in an armor of steel and iron"[17] and recalled Omayyad conquests. But references to the "Arab nation" were no more than lip service to the popular cause of Pan-Arabism, for in reality the dictator and his clique clung tenaciously to the separateness of Syria as the only solution apt to guarantee the preservation of their high positions and honors. Repeated emphasis on discipline and "Arabism" could not conceal the growing political isolation of Shishakli and his army friends. Barely a year after the second coup the government announced the discovery of a plot among some "subaltern officers," who, it claimed, as former members of certain political parties, had succumbed to subversive ideas. Actually, higher ranks were involved as well, and on December 30, 1952, a number of colonels and majors were cashiered.[18] These army dismissals were soon followed by the escape abroad of

---

[16]This measure was applied to such prominent professors and former members of parliament as Munir Ajlani, Abdul Wahab Haumad, and Rizkallah Antaki, as well as to Mustafa Sibai, professor of sacred law and leader of the Moslem Brotherhood.

[17]*Al-Yawm*, Dec. 5, 1952.

[18]The list included the names of Col. Mustafa Safa (reputedly of Populist tendencies) and Lt. Col. Adnan Malki (with Socialist connections).

several of the principal Socialist leaders: Akram Hourani, Michel Aflaq, and Saleh el-Bitar, all three accused of conspiracy against the regime. Hourani's escape was noteworthy because earlier he had not been opposed to collaboration with Shishakli.

Despite this growing political estrangement Shishakli made several moves toward the formal legalization of his regime. Late in June 1953 he published a constitutional draft and followed it promptly on July 10 by a plebiscite, which resulted in overwhelming approval of the constitution and the election of himself (the only candidate) to the presidency of the Republic. The new constitution established a presidential system (in contrast to the parliamentary one existing until then) which markedly increased the power of the chief executive.

In the meantime, however, the opposition was gaining ground. A "national congress" of former political parties which met in Homs on July 4 called the regime "tyrannical." The Moslem Brotherhood and the ulema of Damascus, Aleppo, and Hama also raised their voices in protest against the new constitution. Despite these warnings Shishakli went ahead with his plans. On July 30 a newly passed electoral law decreased the number of seats from 108 to 82 (a device often used by power-seeking rulers to obtain greater influence upon fewer deputies), and on September 12 a presidential decree allowed the formation of political parties—with strings attached. In the subsequent electoral campaign only two parties presented candidates: Shishakli's own Liberation Movement and the Syrian National Social party.[19] As could be expected, the elections resulted in a victory for Shishakli's Movement, with one deputy being elected on behalf of the P.P.S. and a number of deputies remaining independent.

On October 24 the newly elected parliament met and chose Maamun Kuzbari as speaker. Simultaneously Shishakli made gestures of reconciliation toward the opposition: between July and October he released some politicians (such as Dawalibi) from prison and guaranteed safe return to the exiled Socialist leaders. This was accompanied by another measure designed to win popular applause and whip up nationalist feelings: on October 8, 1953, a new press decree forbade newspapers to accept advertisements from foreign companies and institutions without prior official authorization. Yet even this popularity seeking was not of much avail. In December a wave of student demonstrations and lawyer strikes profoundly rocked the country as it spread from Aleppo to other centers. In January 1954, Shishakli had to resort to repression once again: he placed under arrest eleven leaders of the old regime, including former President Hashim el-Atassi, and followed this with a proclamation of martial law in several provinces. To add to his difficulties, two hundred Druze chiefs, meeting in the security of Lebanese territory, passed resolutions against the regime. A few days later a leading Druze, Sultan Pasha el-Atrash, fled from Suwaida to Jordan.

Ultimately it was the army that decided Shishakli's fate. On February 25 troops under Colonel Mustafa Hamdun mutinied in Aleppo, and the rebellion soon spread

---

[19]Hizb es-Suri el-Qaumi el-Ijtimai, known also, especially in Lebanon, as P.P.S. (Parti Populaire Syrien, the French rendering of the original name, by which the party was known to many bilingual inhabitants of the Levant). Because of the prevalence of this abbreviation, it will be used in this book. The party should not be confused with the People's Party (Hizb esh-Shaab).

to other cities. Seeing the futility of resistance, Shishakli resigned and immediately left Syria, first for Lebanon and later for Saudi Arabia and France. After a brief interim period during which Speaker Maamun Kuzbari assumed the duties of the presidency, the old president, Hashim el-Atassi, was reinstated. On March 1 a new cabinet came into being. Although headed by a Nationalist prime minister (Sabri el-Assali), it was dominated by the Populists, who reserved for themselves the key ministries of defense (Maaruf Dawalibi), foreign affairs (Faidi el-Atassi), and interior (Ali Buzu, secretary general of the party). Simultaneously the last legally elected speaker, Nazem el-Qudsi, convoked the pro-Shishakli parliament, which had been dissolved in December 1951. Not invited to attend were those deputies who had served in Shishakli's parliament. The new regime promptly re-established the constitution of September 1950 and reinstated the army officers who had been dismissed by the dictator between 1951 and 1954.

Return to Constitutional Life

With the passing of the dictator Syria resumed her constitutional life, and the assumption of power by the Populist-led coalition reflected rather accurately the actual political configuration in the country. A complete return to the conditions antedating the period of dictatorship was unthinkable. The National party, which had dominated Syrian politics before Zaim's coup, lost too much of its popularity as a result of the "bungling" of the Palestinian War to gain full reinstatement. The Nationalists' loss was the Populists' gain, and, had it not been for army intervention between 1949 and 1954, the Populists would have assumed control of Syria and, perhaps, brought about a union with Iraq.

It would be unwise, however, to write off army intervention as a mere accident stemming from the ambitions of restless officers. The undeniable fact is that the dictators enjoyed initial success and that this was due to a favorable response by the people. The traditional parties, whether the National or the Populist, did not suffice as channels of expression for those elements in Syrian society which chafed under existing economic and social inequalities. They sought to find a satisfactory solution either by supporting the dictators or by joining the more radical groups, whether leftist or rightist. This explains why, even under the repressive conditions of Shishakli's regime, such groups as the Moslem Brotherhood, the Arab Socialist Renaissance party,[20] the Syrian National Social party (P.P.S.), and the Communists gained considerable ground. The restitution of the constitution lifted the lid on the activities of these groups, and their true strength was revealed.

This strength was tested in September 1954 at the time of the first postdictatorship elections. The elections were preceded by the formation in June of a "neutral" cabinet under Said Ghazzi, an Independent, chosen to assure impartiality. Prior to disbanding parliament adopted a new electoral law raising the number of seats to 142. This measure helped to register more accurately the moods prevailing in the

[20]This party was a result of the fusion of Akram Hourani's Socialist party and Michel Aflaq's Arab Renaissance party. The new organization inherited from the latter its Pan-Arabism, spreading from Syria into Jordan, Iraq (where it met with reprisals), and Lebanon (where it was purely nominal and generally unknown to the public, due to the rallying of Socialist elements around the person of Kamal Jumblat).

country. The results of the balloting were as follows: Independents 64; Populists 34: Nationalists 12: Socialists 16; P.P.S. 2; National Liberation Movement 2; Socialist Cooperative party 2; Tribes 9; Communists 1. Of the organized parties, the Populists scored the greatest success, but they did not gain a stable majority in the new legislature. The Socialists' sixteen members was a spectacular achievement in view of their newness and their negligible representation in the past. Damascus proved to be quite a mixed city politically, with no single group able to claim ascendancy. Socialists were strong in Hama, Akram Hourani's native town; and Populists asserted themselves in their traditional strongholds of Aleppo, Homs, and the Jezira province. A Populist, Nazem el-Qudsi, was reelected speaker, and, inasmuch as the elections had confirmed the Populists' lead, a cabinet largely staffed by Populists was formed in October, with Independent Faris el-Khuri as prime minister.

Intermingling of Foreign and Domestic Problems

The Populists' hold on the government was soon exposed to a severe strain by the Baghdad Pact. Though originally designed to group the Northern Tier states (see pp. 283-286), this pact was never intended to be exclusive, and both Iraq and Turkey attempted to draw into it other Arab states. The presence of the Populists at the helm in Syria seemed to favor their hopes. With a few exceptions the Populists were not averse to collaboration with the West. They had, moreover, a traditionally friendly attitude toward both Iraq and Turkey. The removal of Shishakli—whom Iraq had refused to recognize until late in 1952—seemed to have eliminated a major block barring a closer entente between Syria and her pro-Western neighbors. Nevertheless, the Populists proceeded cautiously, mindful of the hazards that lay ahead. The experience of being overthrown twice within four years for desiring union with Iraq could not be ignored. Neither could the general mood of the populace, hostile as it was to any dealings with the West. The masses, as is often the case, were motivated more by emotion than by reason. Hence no matter how beneficial a link with the West might be, popular opinion was decidedly against it. It would be easy for any demagogue—and these were not lacking—to whip up a cry against "imperialism" threatening Syria by extension of the Hashemite rule of Iraq, against the Turks (had not they snatched Alexandretta from the Syrians?), or against the West in general on account of its responsibility in setting up the state of Israel. By contrast, Egypt's support of the Arab League evoked sympathetic response, and the League, despite its failure in the Palestinian War, was still regarded as the best hope for Arab unity and strength. To advocate action ignoring these feelings was, to say the least, a risky undertaking. This explains why the Populist ministers behaved noncommittally at the December 1954 conference of the Arab League, when collaboration with the West was made subject to rather exacting conditions. This also explains why Prime Minister Faris el-Khuri and Foreign Minister Faidi el-Atassi refused, at the subsequent conference of Arab premiers, to take a clear stand for or against Iraq.

A few days earlier Turkish Premier Adnan Menderes had stopped for a few hours in Damascus on his return trip from Baghdad. But even this brief visit embarrassed the Populists and prompted self-defensive explanations. In a public statement Faidi el-Atassi argued that there was nothing wrong in trying to improve relations with Turkey. "If one has an enemy such as Israel, one prefers to have one enemy only," he declared. On his part, discussing the projected Baghdad Pact, Faris el-Khuri defended its political legitimacy by saying: "Besides, the intended pact is directed against the state of Israel."[21]

These cautious remarks were not sufficient to avert popular wrath. The Populists' refusal to take a clear stand against Iraq brought about a government crisis which resulted in their elimination from power. The crisis was precipitated by the resignation from the cabinet of two Nationalist ministers. On February 12, Sabri el-Assali formed a new cabinet composed of Nationalists, Democratic bloc members,[22] one Socialist, and one member of the Liberation Movement. Khalid el-Azem, leader of the Democratic bloc, took charge of foreign affairs. The change thus accomplished was equivalent to a radical reorientation of Syria's policy, particularly in foreign affairs. In order to secure a workable majority in the Chamber the Nationalists, a minority group of barely twelve deputies, had to ally themselves with their erstwhile enemies, the Socialists, and with certain other elements with whom they had relatively little in common. Opposition to the Baghdad Pact provided the only real unifying link among these heterogeneous elements. It was claimed that Saudi Arabian and Egyptian influence was largely responsible for the formation of this coalition.

Shortly after the formation of his cabinet Sabri el-Assali made a policy statement in which he declared:

Our government follows in its foreign policy the recommendation adopted at the conference of Arab ministers of foreign affairs which was held in Cairo last December, namely, that the policy of Arab states is based on the [Arab] pact of defense and economic co-operation.[23] It views, however, with reserve, the recommendation enjoining collaboration with Western powers subject to specific conditions.... Our government agrees with the recommendation of the conference of chiefs of Arab governments which was recently held in Cairo, the recommendation which enjoins us not to accept alliances and not to adhere to the Turkish-Iraqi Pact.[24]

Syria's opposition to the Baghdad Pact was thus clear. In the dramatic contest between the pro-Iraqi and pro-Egyptian forces, the latter have carried the field for the third time in the last five years.[25] But how far would the new government go in espousing the Egyptian policy? Pressures and inducements from the Cairo-Riyadh axis began to mount steadily. Syria was urged to sign a tripartite treaty which would link herself, Egypt, and Saudi Arabia in defense and economic cooperation. She was also wooed by Saudi Arabia with the promise of a loan.

Although personal convictions—and tangible interests—led some members of the

[21]*Cahiers*, 1955, 1.
[22]The Democratic bloc accounted for some nineteen deputies originally elected as Independents.
[23]For details of the pact, see p. 744.
[24]*Cahiers*, 1955, 1.
[25]Zaim's about-face after his visit to Cairo was the first Egyptian victory, and Shishakli's coup of 1949, the second.

Assali cabinet to advocate a complete alignment with Cairo and Riyadh, the cabinet as a whole hesitated to commit itself to a policy fraught with many dangers. These dangers were both internal and external. Internally, the position of the Populists, still strong, especially in the north, could not be disregarded. As soon as they were pushed into opposition, the Populists began to claim that Assali's cabinet managed to survive only at the price of major concessions to the leftist elements. Rather than see Syria go Communist the Populists might separate the north from the rest of the country. The suggestion was also advanced that a "Free Syrian Government" might be created somewhere on the territory of Iraq and, to save Syria from communism, might invite the Iraqi army to intervene. Such a procedure would involve a possible external danger to the sovereignty and territorial integrity of Syria. It might be noted here that Turkey did not hide her disappointment over the turn of events in Damascus. A series of notes and speeches accusing Syria of anti-Turkish policy were delivered by the Turks, while border incidents began to multiply. Some relief was felt in Damascus when Molotov, in late March, reassured the Syrian envoy that Russia "would not stand with crossed arms" if Turkey resorted to force in her dealings with Syria. But this was not adequate compensation for the feeling of growing isolation from immediate neighbors: Turkey, Iraq, Jordan, Israel, and Lebanon.

All these fears explain why Syria, despite overt protestations of loyalty to the Egyptian-led Arab League and a verbal promise to conclude a pact with Cairo and Riyadh, was delaying her signature in obvious procrastination.

In the spring of 1955 the depth of Syria's political division became obvious in connection with dramatic developments in the army. On April 22 Lieutenant-Colonel Adnan Malki, chief of the Third Bureau of the Syrian army staff, was assassinated by a sergeant who happened to be a member of the Syrian National Social party. What followed could be called a mass persecution of the P.P.S. Army officers with links to the party were purged, the immunity of its deputy to parliament was lifted, and a trial involving charges of treason and conspiracy was instituted. The proceedings were definitely political despite the outward forms of legality observed by the authorities. One of the official statements called Malki's assassination "the first act of a plot to suppress the Chief-of-Staff and the officers hostile to certain foreign projects." By "foreign projects" were meant both the Baghdad Pact and the Syro-Iraqi federation.

The purge and trial of the P.P.S. revealed a number of interesting—and disquieting—aspects of the Syrian situation. These could be listed as follows: (1) Despite Shishakli's eclipse, the army had regained its influence on Syria's government and had again become an important factor in the country's politics. (2) Aware of this, various political parties were trying to infiltrate the military establishment. (3) The two groups which were competing most vigorously for the officers' loyalties were the Arab Socialist Renaissance (Baath) party and the P.P.S. (4) The ideological struggle between these two parties could be summed up as a contest between, on the one hand, leftist, pro-Egyptian, and partly pro-Soviet orientation and, on the other, rightist, pro-Western, and profederation tendencies. (5) Colonel Malki was a foremost leader of the Socialist wing in the army. (6) The legal proceedings notwithstanding, it was not certain that Malki's assassination was an act of premeditated conspiracy. Certain evidence pointed to personal motives, and the connection of the assassin with P.P.S. might have been purely coincidental. Yet the removal of Malki from the scene was undoubtedly a major blow to Socialist influence in the army. (7) Because Assali's Nationalist government had made common cause (at least tactically) with the Socialists, it tried to exploit to the maximum the indignation caused by the murder of a popular and youthful officer and to capitalize upon the frenzy of nationalism which this act evoked. (8) The purge and prosecution of P.P.S. thus served two purposes: to stop a dangerous political rival from influencing the army and to gain acclaim by making the pro-Western P.P.S. a scapegoat of popular wrath. (9) Indirectly, the prosecution was an attempt on the part of the Nationalists and Socialists to discredit anybody who dared to advocate closer links with the West or with Turkey and Iraq. This implied a warning to their most formidable rivals, the Populists. (10) The proceedings against P.P.S. revealed another recurring aspect of Syrian politics, namely, the readiness of the ostensibly democratic government to subordinate law to its political interests. Premier Assali wanted to introduce martial law in the country, which would have permitted him to set up special tribunals designed to apply swift procedures. This proposal was vetoed by President Atassi and it met with significant opposition within the cabinet. Consequently, when the matter was put up to the parliament, the premier managed only to secure some modification of penal procedures.

To sum up, by the early summer of 1955 it seemed that the Nationalist-Socialist coalition could maintain itself in power only by constantly whipping up popular resentments against real or imaginary foreign dangers. It was a fairly dangerous situation in which the Nationalists believed that they could hold power without conceding on essential points to the Socialists, while the latter treated the Nationalists as a convenient front and a vehicle to be used to spread their influence and secure a firmer foothold in the army. Sooner or later both partners would have to face a showdown because of the incompatibility of their objectives. The summer months brought the expected crisis and the occasion for it was supplied by the presidential elections.

President Atassi's five-year term was due to expire on September 5, 1955, and it soon became known that former President Shukri el-Quwatli (an old-time Nationalist, then resident in Egypt), Foreign Minister Khalid el-Azem, and one of the Populist leaders would contest for the vacancy. The Nationalists were ready, naturally enough, to campaign for Quwatli (the "campaigning" meaning political persuasion of the deputies in parliament, who elect the president). But at the outset the Socialists announced their opposition to Quwatli, a man too symbolical of the *ancien régime* to be palatable to the radically minded youths flocking to Socialist standards. It was, therefore, on the issue of the presidency that the Nationalist and the Socialist roads parted. The Socialists decided to throw their support to Khalid el-Azem, who also enjoyed the friendship of Egypt and Saudi Arabia—not altogether a negligible factor. Under the circumstances there was no hope of reconstituting the coalition, and no single candidate could be sure of a majority in the chamber. The only solution was a possible withdrawal of one of the candidates, and this was, indeed, what happened. In a rather bold maneuver the Populists decided at the last minute not to present a candidate of their own; instead they threw their support to Quwatli. As a result, on August 18 the latter was elected to the presidency by ninety-one votes. Forty-one deputies voted for Khalid el-Azem, who, upon learning of his defeat, promptly resigned his cabinet position.

Despite minor demonstrations by some young army officers against the president-elect, Quwatli was installed without obstruction. As he owed his election to the solid bloc of the Populists and their Independent allies, Quwatli was politically indebted to both, a debt exceeding his obligation to the rather small number of Nationalists. On September 13 he asked Said Ghazzi, a former premier, to form a cabinet. In the new government the Populists regained their former pre-eminence, with their party secretary, Ali Buzu, again becoming minister of the interior. Some posts were given to Independents. The Nationalists remained outside the cabinet and soon declared themselves in opposition.

Thus the presidential elections resulted in a political configuration similar to that prevailing after Shishakli's demise. This time, however, the Populists were wiser: they had learned the inflammable nature of the issue of "foreign pacts." In order to continue in office, they would have to tread very cautiously on the slippery ground of inter-Arab relations and, in all probability, disguise some of their true feelings by catering to the masses. On the other hand, Quwatli's moderate friendship with the Egyptians could not be overlooked either. No surprise was registered, therefore, when, on October 20, 1955, the new government acceded to the Egyptian demand to sign a mutual defense pact,[26] but the pact did not include Saudi Arabia as a third partner. The official Syrian formula was to promote "bilaterality" and to shun exclusive multilateral agreements such as that initially suggested by Egypt. This formula left the door open for economic negotiations with Saudi Arabia or, if need be, a military pact with Iraq. Thus the Syrian government responded to the popular demand for a closer military link with Egypt without burning the bridges of understanding with Iraq. The Populists sincerely hoped that this formula would work and consequently did not hesitate to conclude, on November 9, 1955, an economic pact with Saudi Arabia, whereby the latter granted Syria the long-expected $10 million loan.[27]

When it came to the next step which would have balanced the Syrian position—the conclusion of a pact with Iraq—difficulties arose. A combination of latent factors and the immediate cause contributed to the problem. The immediate cause was an Israeli attack, on December 11, 1955, on the Syrian outposts east of Lake Tiberias. Fifty-six Syrian lives were lost. Syria's complaint to the UN Security Council and her demand that Israel be expelled from the United Nations, important as it was, was overshadowed by the emotional wave which flooded the country. The pent-up resentments against Zionism and imperialism found new expression in the mass demonstrations that accompanied the burials of victims of Israeli aggression. Under those circumstances, to suggest rapprochement with pro-Western Iraq was too dangerous for anyone with political aspirations in Syria.

[26]The text is in the *Middle East Journal,* 10 (Winter 1956).
[27]The text is in the *Bulletin de la Presse Syrienne,* no. 770 (1955).

Victory of Pan-Arabism, 1956–1958

The two years 1956 and 1957 constituted a period of profound transition in Syria's postwar history. In these years Syria underwent two major changes: a radical change in political leadership and a complete turn in her national policy from separate independence to union with Egypt. The two were naturally interconnected. The drama of this transition was played in three acts. Act One (the first half of 1956), the opening period, saw the hitherto dominant People's Party (Hizb esh-Shaab) demoted from its position of prominence and compelled to share power with other groups; Act Two (the second half of 1956) was a period of intensive Communist and Pan-Arab offensives and of defeat for the conservatives; and Act Three (the whole of 1957) was a headlong rush toward a revolutionary climax, in the course of which Syria barely missed becoming a Soviet satellite, ending instead as a province of the United Arab Republic. These three acts of the Syrian drama will be briefly reviewed in the lines that follow.

Act One (the first half of 1956). Although the Populists (Ash-Shaab) and their conservative allies held a dominant position in Said Ghazzi's cabinet, they gradually lost the initiative and were forced instead to fight a defensive struggle against the surging waves of Pan-Arabism, socialism, and communism. Among the factors which contributed to the dynamic expansion of these three movements was opposition to the Baghdad Pact, which served as a rallying point for all forces hostile to the West and the status quo in the Arab states. Another factor was anger over Colonel Malki's assassination. The Baath party and its allies in the army exploited this tragic event to the fullest extent by creating a popular myth of a brave and noble hero who gave his life for the cause of Arabism.[28] Although the primary target of hostility was the P.P.S. as a group to which the assassin belonged, the opprobrium was meant to apply to all groups standing for cooperation with the West and opposing Pan-Arab ideology. Pan-Arabists were further strengthened by continuous Egyptian propaganda as well as by Egyptian and Saudi subsidies. A major Pan-Arab event was the convocation in Damascus in March 1956 of the first conference of the newly constitued Federation of Arab Labor Unions. The Communists, who at that time threw their tactical support to the Pan-Arabists, enjoyed the material and spiritual support of the Soviet Union. Symbolic of this was the award in March of 1956 of the Stalin Peace Prize (30,000 rubles) to a fellow-traveling mullah, Sheikh Mohammed Ashmar, for his role in promoting the Peace Partisans' movement in Syria. The event was attended by a host of dignitaries and celebrities. By the middle of 1956 it became increasingly clear that the gap between the Populist-dominated government and the leftist Pan-Arab forces had widened to dangerous proportions. In order to reduce the tension, President Quwatli proposed to form a government of "national unity." In conformity with his wish Ghazzi's cabinet resigned and on June 14, 1956, a coalition cabinet under the National Party leader Sabri el-Assali came into power. All major political parties were represented in it, including, for the first time, the Baath in the persons of Saleh el-Bitar as foreign minister and Khalil Kallas

[28]For a similar evaluation, see Nicola A. Ziadeh, *Syria and Lebanon* (London, 1957), p. 163, and George E. Kirk, *Contemporary Arab Politics: A Concise History* (New York, 1961), p. 92.

as minister of national economy. The Populists entered the cabinet, still retaining the vital ministry of the interior (Ahmad Qanbar), but they had to accept a position of equality with three other major parties and their dominant role in Syrian politics had come to an end.

Act Two (the second half of 1956). Placed in the strategic portfolios of Foreign Affairs and National Economy, the Baathists took full advantage of this to press for further gains. With their Communist allies and a variety of pro-Egyptian elements they launched a rapid offensive to demolish the remnants of Western influence, to equate the pro-Iraq tendency with treason, and to establish close links with both Egypt and the Soviet bloc in the name of "positive neutralism." A week after the formation of the Assali cabinet Soviet Foreign Minister Shepilov paid a visit to Damascus on his way back from Cairo. On July 1, Syria extended recognition to Communist China. Wild enthusiasm was displayed in Damascus when Egypt nationalized the Suez Canal later in the same month. On August 20 the Assali government signed a cultural agreement with Russia, which opened the door to a stream of Syrian students going to Soviet and satellite universities and to numerous visits of scholars, artists, and cultural missions from and to Communist areas. In the summer Czechoslovakia and certain private Western firms bid for the construction of the first Syrian oil refinery at Homs. Powerful pressures were exerted on the cabinet to accept the Czechoslovak offer. At the International Fair in Damascus the Soviet bloc obtained the largest and choicest grounds for their industrial displays, dwarfing the United States and other countries. In September it was reported that Syria and Russia had concluded an arms deal similar to the Soviet-Egyptian one of the preceding year. At first denied by Foreign Minister Bitar, the deal was confirmed in December by the chief of Syrian army intelligence, Lieutenant Colonel Abdul Hamid Sarraj, who was rapidly emerging as a dominant military personality behind the Syrian government. Israeli aggression against Egypt and the subsequent Franco-British intervention added fuel to the already inflamed state of minds in Syria. The Suez War coincided with President Quwatli's visit to Moscow on November 3. A few days later, in a gesture of solidarity with Egypt, the Syrian army blew up the pipeline of the Iraq Petroleum Company traversing Syria, thereby depriving Western Europe of oil, which had flowed at the rate of 25 million tons a year. Pro-Western leaders found the ground removed from under them, and their ability overtly to resist combined Pan-Arab and Communist pressures was virtually destroyed. It should be pointed out in this connection that the parliament, elected in 1954, still contained a powerful group of Populists (34 deputies), who, with the Constitutional bloc, the right-wing members of the National Party, the Moslem Brotherhood, the tribal bloc, and the sympathetic independents, could easily outvote the smaller group of Baathists (18 members) and some of their independent allies. But the parliament had lost its importance during the tumultuous months of 1956 and became subject to intimidation by the pro-Egyptian and pro-Soviet army officers dominant in the military establishment, the Baath-controlled students, and street mobs.

Under these circumstances those who stood for independent Syria free of Soviet and Egyptian influence had virtually no choice but to resort to conspiracy to preserve the values and institutions they cherished. In the summer of 1956 certain leading figures of the People's Party, the Constitutional bloc, and the right wing of the National party began holding secret meetings in Beirut and elsewhere to determine the best way in which the Communist and Pan-Arab trend in Syrian politics could be arrested and the existing government changed. Impartial evidence as to whether or not their talks had reached the stage of a definite plot is not yet available. In the late fall of 1956, Colonel Sarraj's security organization disclosed that a conspiracy to overthrow the government was discovered and that the plotters were aided by Nuri's government in Iraq. On December 22 forty-seven prominent Syrian politicians were put on trial before a special military court for participation in the "Iraqi Plot." The roster of the accused read like a "Who's Who" of political conservatism in Syria, or at least of the most vigorous part of it. Among those indicted were Adnan Atassi, son of a former President of the Republic; Dr. Munir Ajlani of the Constitutional Bloc; Dr. Sami Kubbara; Mikhail Ilyan, right-wing leader of the National Party from Aleppo—all of them former ministers. On the same day Assali's cabinet tendered its resignation. The concept of "national unity" on which it was originally based no longer corresponded to the realities; conservatives and pro-Westerners were discredited and had to be removed from stewardship of the state. Ten days later, on January 2, 1957, Assali formed a new cabinet, which represented an alliance of the Baath with the left wing of the National party (Assali himself and Fakher el-Kayyali) and the ambitious pro-Soviet millionaire politician, Khalid el-Azem, who became minister of state and acting minister of defense. The remaining few posts were given to compliant neutrals anxious to dissociate themselves from those accused in the plot and their parties. Thus the once-dominant People's Party suffered its final defeat, and the last restraints on Syria's rapid sliding into the Soviet-Egyptian orbit were removed.

Act Three (1957). During this last period of separate existence before joining Egypt, Syria was controlled by a triumvirate composed of Akram Hourani, leader of the Baath (and duly elected speaker of parliament to replace the passive Populist, Nazem el-Qudsi); Khalid el-Azem; and the earlier-mentioned Colonel Sarraj, the most powerful of the three. Sarraj and Hourani represented the pro-Egyptian orientation, whereas Azem, a man with presidential aspirations, hoped to attain his objectives through an alliance with Communists and a manipulation of Soviet support. Although their final aims were different, the Sarraj-Hourani team and Azem worked well together for the time being. Unencumbered by the opposition of the conservatives—they were intimidated into silence or outward protestations of devotion to Arab unity—the leftist pro-Egyptian coalition proceeded with increased vigor to reorient Syria's position in international and inter-Arab affairs. In January 1957, on a state visit to India, President Quwatli gave emphatic publicity to "positive neutralism," and in the same month the Syrian state radio and semicontrolled press volubly attacked the newly proclaimed Eisenhower Doctrine as proof of American imperialism. Soon afterward, on February 26, the military court pronounced a number of death and long-term jail sentences on the defendants in the "Iraqi Plot" trial. Within less than two weeks the government accepted the Czech bid for the Homs refinery, thus intensifying the Soviet bloc's economic penetration of Syria. The Jordanian crisis in April acted as a further stimulant to anti-Western attitudes and policies. In the by-elections which took place in May to fill four parliamentary seats vacated by those sentenced in the "Iraqi Plot," the Baath and its allies won in three contests over a coalition of Moslem Brotherhood and the Populist-backed candidates. A highlight in this trend was the conclusion on August 6 of a Soviet-Syrian economic aid agreement. Engineered by Azem, who worked hard to bring about rapprochement with Russia, it provided for immediate credit to Syria of $140 million and Soviet assistance in nineteen development projects.

As viewed from Washington, Syria was rushing into a dangerous dependence on the Soviet Union, with its pro-Western forces intimidated, disorganized, and discouraged. This impression was confirmed when three members of the American embassy (including the military attaché) were expelled by the Syrian government on August 13. The appointment four days later of a reputed Communist, General Afif Bizri, as chief of staff of the Syrian Army was seen as conclusive proof of Syria's virtual satellization. Normal political life in Syria had come to a standstill. Even the erstwhile conservative papers were cowed into obedience, repeating in colorless and monotonous editorials the worn-out Pan-Arab slogans and applauding the anti-Western antics of the government and of its spokesman in the United Nations. An armed militia, named the Popular Resistance Force, came into being under Colonel Sarraj's supervision with the dual task of whipping up enthusiasm for the regime and intimidating any potential dissenters. Moreover, Syria's ruling group raised strong and well-publicized objections to the massing of Turkish troops on the border, accusing Turkey and the United States of planning armed intervention. Soviet assurances of assistance to Syria, coupled with threats to Turkey, were gratefully acknowledged by the Syrian propaganda agencies. The anti-Western campaign reached its climax when ten political figures were put on trial on December 11, 1957, for participation in an "American Plot" to overthrow the government. During the trial numerous witnesses testified to the deep involvement of American embassy personnel and intelligence agencies, citing names, dates, and places.[29]

Somewhat earlier, on November 18, a major move was made toward Pan-Arabism when the Syrian parliament, sitting jointly with an Egyptian parliamentary delegation, issued a declaration calling for a Syrian-Egyptian federation. Before long Baathist emissaries began pressing President Nasser of Egypt for a speedy proclamation of union between the two countries. Nasser's initial reluctance and his conditions are reviewed in Chapter XII of this study. It suffices to say here that the Baathists (and along with them the cabinet and the parliament) accepted all conditions without procrastination. Their eagerness was due to the late discovery that in the tactical alliance that linked them to the Communists the latter had made major gains in the civilian and military sectors at their expense. The classical drama of the confused "liberal" making common cause with the Communists for the attainment of some praiseworthy social and humanitarian objectives and later awakening

[29]The trial was concluded with death and prison sentences on February 16, 1958, four days after the merger with Egypt.

cheated and defeated by his ruthless and nonsentimental allies was once again enacted in the context of Syrian and Arab politics. An additional reason for the Baathists' hurry to unite with Egypt was their fear that if there was a complete Communist victory in Syria the West would intervene directly or indirectly, thus helping the conservatives to return to power. Squeezed between the dangers of Communist supremacy and conservative restoration, the Baathists saw their only salvation in union with Nasser.

When it became clear in January 1958 that the union was in the stage of earnest discussions, the Communists made a sudden turnabout, declaring their opposition on the ground that the proposed elimination of political parties (one of Nasser's conditions) was undemocratic and that the countries were not ready for complete unification. This last-minute reversal of attitudes could not arrest the inexorable march of events. Nor was General Bizri able to stem the mounting Pan-Arab tide among the army officers and outwardly conformed to their will. On February 1, 1958, union was proclaimed in Cairo by Presidents Nasser and Quwatli. When parliament ratified it on February 5, the Communist deputy, Khalid Bakdash cast the only dissenting vote and promptly left Syria to live in exile in the Soviet bloc countries. With parliament's approval the last formal step toward union was taken. Quwatli tendered his resignation from the presidency and Syria was converted into the "northern province" (or region) of the United Arab Republic.

After the Dissolution of the Union

Thanks to a successful coup carried out by the army on September 28, 1961, Syria regained her independence. The circumstances leading to this momentous event as well as the rebellion itself are described in Chapter XII. Syria and Egypt were again separate entities. The civilian cabinet installed by the army on the day of the coup had only two well-known political figures in addition to Premier Maamun Kuzbari: the minister of the interior, Dr. Adnan Quwatli, and the minister of finance, Leon Zamariya. Kuzbari had formerly been associated with Adib Shishakli. Following the latter's overthrow in 1954 he headed a political party initially formed under Shishakli's regime and called the National Liberation Movement. A lawyer of conservative tendencies, he had a keen awareness of economic matters and was anxious to restore Syria to economic normalcy. Upon assumption of the premiership, Dr. Kuzbari pledged that parliamentary elections would be held within four months. However, he maintained—with full concurrence of the Revolutionary Command (which continued to function side by side with the cabinet)— the ban on political parties. He also denied reentry into Syria to the exiled Communist leader Khalid Bakdash, although Syrian Communists abroad applauded Syria's separation from Egypt. In its first pronouncements Syria's new government stressed its attachment to the idea of Arab unity and emphasized its own Arab character. It insisted, however, that sound unity must be based on equality and not on the dominance of one party by another. It also asserted its devotion to socialism, yet with emphasis on free enterprise—in conformity with Syrian traditions—as the best means of assuring high productivity and elevated standards of living. In foreign policy it reaffirmed a course of neutralism, peaceful coexistence, and nonalignment.

Despite these neutral pronouncements, the new government was expected to be friendly to the West and to seek closer economic ties with it.

Despite its material success in overthrowing the Egyptian rule, the new regime apparently felt a compelling need to justify its separatist action to the people at home and in the Arab world as a whole. For this reason the cabinet, as well as the Revolutionary Command, issued several long statements explaining their position and describing in considerable detail all sorts of abuses perpetrated by the union regime. Their statements were followed by a lengthy memorandum from the Federation of the Syrian Chambers of Commerce and Industry, in which Cairo's economic methods—and the resulting near-ruination of the Syrian economy—were forcefully exposed. Undoubtedly aware that Pan-Arabism had taken strong hold on the emotions of the people, Kuzbari's government in mid-October 1961 issued an appeal to all Arab states proposing the early establishment of an Arab confederation, which, while achieving unity, would preserve the political systems, economies, and armies of the member states. Except for Jordan, which promptly voiced its approval, other Arab states were slow in their reactions, thus reflecting the general belief that the proposal was made hastily and primarily for propagandistic purposes.

The Twilight and End of Syria's Constitutional System

The eighteen months following the separation of Syria from Egypt were a period of transition characterized by acute ideological struggle between two rival trends, the Syrian nationalist and the Pan-Arab. From the point of view of the so-called secessionist leaders, separation of Syria from Egypt was a sound move justified by: (a) dominance of Cairo over Damascus, (b) Nasser's one-man rule contrasting with ideas of collective leadership, (c) Egypt's radical policy of nationalizations which brought Syria's economy to stagnation, and (d) the loss of autonomous power over the Syrian army. However, the Pan-Arab ideal had been propagated so long in Syria through the newspapers and broadcasts, school curricula, and speeches of politicians that whoever challenged the principle of Arab unity found himself automatically on the defensive. Thus the secessionist leaders tended to adopt apologetic attitudes when explaining their actions. This phenomenon was intensified by the fact that the separatist leadership of Syria was recruited from the upper bourgeoisie, and that, therefore, it had to combat a suspicion that secession from Egypt was not due to legitimate national causes but was undertaken merely for the purpose of satisfying its class interests.

This leadership was determined to restore a constitutional system suspended in Syria as a result of the union with Egypt. Thus on December 1, 1961, general elections were held which gave the conservatives 86 seats, the leftists 16, and the independent deputies the remaining 53 of the 155 seats in the parliament. Considering this outcome, it was not surprising that one of the most prominent leaders of the old Shaab party, Nazem el-Qudsi, was elected President of Syria by mid-December. In turn, Qudsi, with full approval of the parliament, designated another conservative leader, Maaruf Dawalibi, as prime minister. The new government's attention centered not only on the restoration of the constitutional system in Syria, including the freedom of political parties, but also on repeal or partial repeal of various revolutionary measures enacted during the period of union with Egypt. The focus was on canceling some nationalization laws and eliminating the radical aspects of the agrarian reform legislation. By the same token, estrangement from Egypt dictated to the new government a search for closer links with Iraq, even though Iraq was under the revolutionary, anti-bourgeois leadership of Abdul Karim Kassem. The common denominator between Baghdad and Damascus at that time was their distrust of Egypt and their opposition to Pan-Arab schemes based on Nasser's dominance.

Events were soon to prove, however, that the issues of Pan-Arabism versus Syrian nationalism, of democracy versus dictatorship, and of economic orientation were far from settled. Even though numerous Syrians experienced a great relief in seeing their country regain sovereignty, the restored constitutional leadership failed to entrench itself adequately either among the popular masses or in the sector where it mattered most, namely the army. And indeed on March 27, 1962, the army effected a coup d'état ousting the Qudsi government. The president, the prime minister, and such prominent leaders of the new regime as Rashad Jabri and Khalid el-Azem were placed under arrest, and on March 29, the parliament was abolished. In its first proclamation, the army leadership pledged to restore "constructive and just socialism." What followed was a period of considerable political turmoil and confusion: the pro-Nasserites fought the anti-Nasserite factions both in the military establishment and in the civilian sector. Two new prime ministers followed, Dr. Bashir Azmah and then Khalid el-Azem. Azem, with his usual political skill, succeeded not only in freeing himself from arrest but regaining a high political position. It was during this period that the Syrian Baath party formally reestablished itself at the Congress held in Damascus in May, following a period of suspension decreed as a result of the Syro-Egyptian union. To use a parallel from the Russian history, it is permissible to call this a "Kerensky period" in the political development of Syria. The situation was characterized by confusion and fluidity, and it constituted merely a prelude to further and more drastic revolutionary developments. In the name of the proclaimed socialism, the Syrian authorities decreed certain further nationalizations and reimposed the land reform law of 1958 in its full extent.

The Baath Party in Power

On March 8, 1963, the Baath party, aided by its military allies, seized power in Syria. General Louai el-Atassi emerged as the provisional Head of the State and Chairman of the Revolutionary Council with the Baath leader, Saleh el-Bitar, as prime minister. There was no need to abolish the parliament or the constitution because these were legislated out of existence already under the preceding military regime. The new dispensation differed from the previous one in that it was clearly a party-centered dictatorship. However, the Baath party, though gradually more and more entrenched, never succeeded in creating a completely monolithic party-dominated political structure in Syria. Other so-called progressive groups were not only in existence but were also, however grudgingly, recognized by the Baath leaders. Among these other "progressive" forces the Nasserite groups constituted an important segment. Considering the past record of irritations between the Baath and Nasser, the Baathists throughout their period in power had to face continuously the question of defining their relationship to the Nasserite elements in Syria. This, in turn, was inextricably linked with the broader problem of Arab unity.

It should be pointed out at this juncture that only one month earlier, on February 8, the Baath had seized power in Iraq. Thus all three leading Arab capitals, Cairo, Damascus, and Baghdad, were controlled by political groups whose twin goals were Arab unity and socialism. Regardless, therefore, of past irritations, the Baath leaderships in Syria and Iraq were obliged to legitimize their rule in the eyes of the Arab masses by promptly inaugurating unity talks with Egypt. These talks, begun in mid-March, were conducted in Cairo, the Syrian side being represented by a mixed group of Baathist and pro-Nasserite leaders with one of the Baath party's founders, Michel Aflaq, participating. As we know from the earlier account (in the chapter on Iraq), the differences between Nasser and the Baathist delegations, particularly that of Syria, centered on four points: (a) collective leadership, (b) federal or unitary state, (c) identity of the Baath party, and (d) the role of the national front, a grouping expected to embrace all "progressive" forces in the new unity scheme.[30] Despite the signing of the formal unity charter on April 24, mutual distrust between Nasser and the Syrian Baathists was so acute that by May 3 five Nasserite ministers resigned from the Syrian cabinet and the Baath resorted to a thorough purge of the Nasserites from the government machinery. This process of mutual aggravation reached its apogee on July 18, 1963, when a revolt by the pro-Nasserite elements, both military and civilian, was attempted. It was put down ruthlessly by the Baath with the inevitable bloodshed and subsequent executions. Frustrated and indignant, Nasser called Syria a "fascist" state and denounced the recently concluded unity plans as long as the Baath party stayed in power. He accompanied these remarks by calling the Baathists atheists.

The curbing of the pro-Nasserite coup triggered a change in the Baath leadership in Damascus. This time General Amin el-Hafez emerged as army commander in chief and Chairman of the National Council of the Revolution. Under the new head of state, Bitar continued as prime minister. And again, with the usual swing in Syria's political orientation, efforts were exerted to bring about a closer union with the sister Baath regime in Iraq. To this end two agreements were concluded in Baghdad on September 2 and October 8 respectively, one pertaining to an economic union and the other to a military one. Despite this, the two countries remained separate sovereign entities.

Thus, although union with Egypt was rejected as an immediate objective of the Baath, the party could not in the long run renounce the search for Arab unity as the basic tenet of its ideology. In the ensuing months and years the party politics witnessed the recurrent struggle between a pro-Egyptian and an isolationist orientation. The clash between these two orientations overlapped, moreover, another division within the party, that between the radical and the moderate groups. The radicals

---

[30]The record of these talks is in *Arab Political Documents 1963*, pp. 75–226.

were aiming at more drastic socio-economic transformations in Syria to conform to their socialist model, which was tinged with a good deal of Marxist thought. This radical trend was strongly reaffirmed at the Sixth National (Pan-Arab) Congress of the Baath party held in Damascus in October, 1963, and dominated by the extreme left-wing leader of the Iraqi Baath, Ali Saleh el-Saadi.[31] In Syria this dichotomy between the two ideological orientations found its expression in rival clusters of leadership. On the one hand, the radical group tended to rally around the person of General Saleh Jadid, who already in November, 1963, became chief of staff of the army and subsequently assumed the position of Secretary-General of the Regional (Syrian) Command of the Baath party. This group included Dr. Nureddin Atassi, Dr. Yussuf Zuayyen, and Dr. Ibrahim Makhous, physicians who had participated in the Algerian war of liberation against French colonial rule. Opposing them was the moderate group in the party, composed of the two founders, Bitar and Aflaq, Dr. Munif Razzaz, General Mohammed Omran, and Shibli el-Issami. Although there was some overlappping, basically the radicals tended to dominate the Regional Command in Syria while the moderates held the leading position in the National (Pan-Arab) Command. Insofar as the actual participation in the government of Syria was concerned, the two groups shared it, with fluctuations in favor of one or another depending on the circumstances.

While thus having to attend to its internal struggles between the competing wings, the party had also to face the challenge to its legitimacy from various other groups in Syria. The dethroned bourgeois leaders were clearly unhappy; they found natural allies in the bazaar merchants and in the religious circles in the country. The openly or implicitly expressed antireligious sentiments in the Baath Party publications as well as concrete measures aiming at the curbing of free enterprise combined to cause much resentment, which on two occasions—April 15, 1963, and January 26, 1965—gave rise to violent religious demonstrations against the Baath, the closing of the bazaar shops by the angry merchants, and repeated denunciations of the party as atheist. The April 1963 demonstrations reached the proportions of veritable local revolt in Hama, in the course of which a major mosque was bombarded by the artillery on government orders. The second demonstration centered primarily on Damascus, the government issuing a stern notice that the stores that would not reopen would be confiscated.

In the economic sector, the Baath government launched an intensive policy of nationalizations. This policy became particularly noticeable in 1965 when nationalization of 115 industrial enterprises in January was followed by another seizure, in May, of 55 ginning mills. In March, nine foreign oil companies engaged in the distribution of products in Syria were also nationalized. These measures, as could be expected, produced not only substantial flight of capital from Syria but also a considerable "brain-drain" in the form of middle and upper class, educated specialists who responded to the increasing official emphasis on class struggle, police controls, and regimentation of economy by migrating to Lebanon and the

[31] *Ibid.*, pp. 438–440; reproduced in G. Lenczowski, ed., *The Political Awakening in the Middle East* (Englewood Cliffs, N.J., 1970), pp. 134–137.

West. Gradually, sizable Syrian exile communities were making their appearance in various centers of the free world.

Supremacy of the Left-Wing Baath: Militancy and Isolation

The rivalry between the left wing and the moderates was resolved by violence. On February 23, 1966, the government of Amin Hafez and Premier Bitar was deposed by a coup accompanied by much bloodshed. General Saleh Jadid and his allies in the Regional Command of the party seized power and placed under arrest the most important members of the National Command, including the two founders of the party, Bitar and Aflaq, as well as Shibli el-Issami, Mohammed Omran, and Munif Razzaz. This move was unprecedented in the annals of the Baath party. Not only did the local, in this case the Regional, organization of the party rebel against Pan-Arab authority represented by the National Command, but it also used force and coercion. By resorting to this action, the Syrian Regional Command effectively destroyed the Pan-Arab organization of the party. The National Command which, back in the fall of 1963, was powerful enough to be able to guide and instruct the regional organizations including that of Iraq, now ceased to exist and the party lost its international character. The successful rebels promptly set up a government in which Nureddin Atassi assumed the position of head of state, Yussuf Zuayyen that of prime minister, Ibrahim Makhous that of deputy prime minister and foreign minister, and General Hafez el-Assad that of defense minister.

The advent to power of the left-wing Baath influenced Syria's position on the domestic, Arab, and international issues. In the domestic sector a militant course of repression was adopted toward the right-wing and moderate elements in the country while emphasis was put on vigorous socialist transformation of the economy. This tended further to stimulate emigration of many individuals and groups from Syria. Interestingly enough, despite its dedication to raising the level of the masses, the left-wing Baath did not succeed in stopping the phenomenon already under way before its advent to power, namely the massive migration of Syrian workers to Lebanon where they supplied much needed manpower to the booming construction industry and other economic activities. Their number by the late 1960s reached about 300,000 workers. On the Arab front, Syria's left-wing regime advocated closer links with the revolutionary-progressive camp in the Arab world while launching continuous propaganda attacks against any government with a conservative tinge, particularly Jordan and Saudi Arabia. And, in the sector of foreign policy, the regime displayed considerable hostility toward the United States, largely because of its pro-Israeli stance, and, by the same token, favored more intimate relations with the Soviet Union and the socialist bloc. This pro-Soviet attitude found its expression in four distinct ways. First, Syria's government concluded in April 1966 an agreement with the Soviet Union whereby Moscow was to extend major assistance in the construction of the projected dam on the Euphrates River. This agreement, confirmed in December, provided for a total of S.£ (Syrian pounds) 600 million of Soviet financial aid. (The dam was to be completed in 1972; actually, it was completed in 1973). Second, the Soviets extended more generously than before their economic and technical assistance to a variety of other development projects, foremost among them Syria's oil fields in Suwaidiyah, Karachuk, and Rumailan, over which appropriate agreements were signed with the Soviet Techno-Export firm in 1967. Third, the Soviet Union increased its arms supplies to the Syrian army, a process already under way but intensified since February 1966, which found its apogee after the Arab-Israeli war of June 1967. And fourth, despite its earlier record of hostility toward the Communists, the Baath party opened the door to the rehabilitation of and cooperation with the Syrian Communist Party. Thus Syria's exiled Communist leader, Khalid Bakdash, was allowed to return from exile (he spent a number of years in Russia) while at the same time two Communist leaders, Sami Attiyah and Ahmed Murad, were given ministerial posts in the cabinet in charge of communication and economics respectively.

One of the major concerns of the new regime was to gain legitimacy both inside the country and among the other branches of the Baath in the neighboring countries. The unceremonious way in which Syria's Regional Command destroyed the existing National Command while adopting coercive and vindictive measures toward the latter's members obviously placed Syria's regime in an embarrassing position. To remedy this situation, Saleh Jadid and his companions called in September 1966 the Third Regional Conference to be held simultaneously with the Ninth National Conference. The call for a national conference could have legally come only from the National Command but the latter was no more in existence. Syria's leaders contacted various branches of the Baath in other Arab countries and persuaded them to send delegates to the September meeting in Damascus. Although somewhat distrustful, some of these branches responded positively and their delegates appeared at the conference. While Syria's Regional Command was trying to form a new National (Pan-Arab) Command that would be pliable to its will and influence, a similar process was going on in Iraq. There the existing Baath Party declared itself faithful to the old National Command and invited some of its leaders, among them Michel Aflaq and Shibli el-Issami, to Iraq to continue in their old capacity. As a result of these parallel moves in Damascus and Baghdad, by 1967 two rival National Commands arose each claiming legitimacy but each, although ostensibly in charge of the entire international Baath organization, in reality was only a reflection of the regional organization in the capital in which it was based. Due to these separate proceedings the Baath party as an effective and united Pan-Arab organization ceased to exist.

In June 1967, Syria took part in the Arab-Israeli war and suffered a defeat similar to that experienced by Egypt and Jordan. Its air force was largely annihilated and part of its territory, the Golan Heights, located east of Lake Tiberias, was captured by the Israeli army. The war, which had a radicalizing effect upon Arab politics at large, intensified the radical trends already in evidence in Syria. Syria became the principal base for the Palestinian resistance movement. In contrast, however, to the experience of Jordan and Lebanon, the Syrian government never allowed the Palestinians to operate as a state within a state, and Syria's army kept close watch over and assured full subordination of the Palestinian resistance fighters to its orders. Moreover, to secure even greater influence upon the *fedayeen*, Syria sponsored the creation of a separate guerrilla organization, the Saiqa, which within the Baath party establishment became the special responsibility of General Saleh Jadid.

In a bitter mood of defeat and defiance, Syria refused to participate in the Arab summit conference held in Khartoum at the end of August 1967. The Arab leaders gathered at Khartoum, it should be pointed out, agreed on a formula advocating a "political solution" for the Arab-Israeli conflict thus rejecting the war alternative. Syria's response was to hold in Damascus the so-called Ninth Congress of the National Command of the Baath party in late August and early September. The declaration issued by the congress on September 10 covered a wide range of subjects pertaining to the Arab, foreign, and domestic policies. As a genuine and frank expression of the philosophy and behavior of the ruling group then in power in Syria, it is worth reproducing in its major points. The declaration proclaimed (a) Syria's opposition to the Arab summit meetings as likely to benefit only the reactionary regimes and dilute the revolutionary struggle for the transformation of the Arab homeland; (b) advocated an undiminished use of the oil weapon against those Western states that helped Israel; (c) castigated the United States, Britain, and West Germany for their support of Israel and Zionism, rejected any restoration of diplomatic relations with those three states, and reaffirmed that no foreign bases should be allowed to exist on any Arab territory; (d) called for closer relations with the Soviet Union and the socialist bloc countries; (e) called for union of "progressive" Arab states with specific mention of Syria, Egypt, Iraq, and Algeria to facilitate the "establishment of one single socialist base" in the Arab homeland; (f) affirmed that only armed struggle was the proper method for the liberation of the Arab homeland from the dominance of imperialism and of Palestine in particular from Israeli occupation; (g) opposed the "liquidation" of the Yemen revolution through dubious inter-Arab agreements and called for a progressive solution in South Arabia; (h) reaffirmed a radical socialist course for Syria through sacrifices and austerity; and (i) called for the establishment of "committees for the defense of the homeland" and for further development of the revolutionary paramilitary organization, the People's Army.[32]

Era of Pragmatism: The Leadership of Hafez Assad

The program outlined above clearly bore the imprint of the militant left-wing leadership of the party associated particularly with the name of Saleh Jadid. It put an emphasis on the radical internal transformation of the country, on rejection of compromise with those Arab regimes which were considered conservative or reactionary, and on anti-imperialist liberation struggle, which included rejection of a search for a peaceful solution with the state of Israel. Because the majority of the Arab states present at the conference at Khartoum definitely opted for a "political solution," such policies clearly placed Syria in a position of isolation. However, not all of the Syrian leadership shared this uncompromising and militant view. As early as the fall of 1968 cracks began to develop in the ostensibly monolithic Baath party directorate. The focus of controversy was whether the military security of the country or the revolutionary social change in a socialist spirit should have a priority. Security appeared to be the primary preoccupation of the minister of defense, General Hafez Assad, formerly commander of the air force. To promote security,

[32]Text in *The Arab World*, Weekly Report (Beirut, Lebanon), Sept. 22, 1967.

Assad believed that Syria's isolation was dangerous and that Syria should seek closer links, particularly of military nature, with Egypt and possibly with other Arab countries as well. By the same token, any militant revolutionary policy at home which was bound to produce greater divisions among the people was believed by Assad to be dangerous and harmful. General Assad rallied round himself the military wing of the party. The civilian, doctrinaire wing followed Jadid's leadership. Gradually, a serious contest for power and influence developed between these two men.

A regional Baath party conference held in Damascus in March 1969 revealed to the public the existence of this struggle while enhancing the position of General Assad. However, Saleh Jadid still retained considerable influence by securing the party's decision to have the Palestinian guerrilla organization, Saiqa, subordinated to the party's Regional Command, hence to himself, rather than to Assad's ministry of defense. The following months were a period of considerable uncertainty and confusion, during which the gap between the military and civilian wings of the party widened. In early June, the Syrian Communist party held a secret conference in Damascus, at which the longtime leader Khalid Bakdash was reelected secretary general.

It was not until September 1970, however, that the struggle between Assad and Jadid acquired such intensity that it had to be resolved by the ultimate elimination of one of the contenders. In Jordan, King Hussein despaired of reaching a compromise with the Palestinian *fedayeen* and launched a concerted military offensive against them to curb their power and compel them to subordinate themselves to the orders of the government. Responding to this drama, Saleh Jadid and his doctrinaire civilian allies in the Syrian government decided to intervene in the Jordanian civil war and to this purpose despatched a tank brigade across the border to northern Jordan. By deciding on this move Syria's government courted a possible disaster. There was a distinct possibility of escalation, with the Soviet Union, the principal arms supplier of Syria, and the United States, the protector and backer of King Hussein, likely to intervene if their respective clients were to find themselves in serious difficulties. Similarly, perceiving that Syria's intervention in Jordan might have adverse effects on Israel's security, the Israeli leadership was seriously contemplating the possibility of a countermove that might have involved the entry of Israeli troops into Jordan. King Hussein reacted to the Syrian tank invasion by ordering his air force to launch a concentrated attack on the advancing column. The Syrians suffered considerable losses and decided to withdraw. Thus an international conflagration of major proportions was narrowly avoided. But in Syria the way was opened for the elimination of Saleh Jadid and his partners from power inasmuch as they were accused by Assad and his colleagues in the military of acting without consultation, risking a major defeat, losing men and equipment, and further accentuating the division among the Arab confrontation states, which was bound to give greater advantages to Israel. Within less than a month, Assad put pressure on President Nureddin el-Atassi to resign. His resignation on October 17 was followed by the arrest of Premier Zuayyen and Foreign Minister Makhous, and the calling of the Tenth National Congress of the Baath Party. By November 21, Hafez Assad was named prime minister and the head of the Baath party both on the national and regional levels. He formed a cabinet of twenty-six members which comprised twelve Baathists and fourteen non-Baathist members including two Communists. Six days later, on November 27, under his leadership Syria declared its desire to join the newly-formed federation between Egypt, Libya, and Sudan.

Thus the left-wing Baath era came to an end and the military Baath group, more moderate in its internal policies and definitely dedicated to the promotion of closer links with other Arab states, came into power.

In the internal sector, the policies of the Assad regime were characterized by a retreat from radical socialism and by gradual moves toward a general liberalization of conditions. Syrian exiles abroad, whether businessman, technocrats, academic scientists, or political figures persecuted by the Baath leftists, were encouraged to return to Syria and work for the country. Assad made even a move to restore a measure of parliamentarism: on February 16, 1971, his government issued a decree calling into being a 173-seat People's Council to act as Syria's political representative body. Its members were to be appointed pending further constitutional development. Eighty-five seats were reserved for the representatives of the Baath party. On March 1, Assad formally assumed the presidency by being nominated by the Baath party, endorsed by the parliament, and approved by the national referendum. In May, the Fifth Baath Regional Conference legitimized formally these changes and elected Assad secretary general of the Regional Command. The process of formal transfer of power in the party was completed by the end of August when Assad was also elected secretary general of the Syrian-sponsored National Command. In contrast to the previous exclusivist policies of the Baath left wing, Assad acknowledged that Syria's political spectrum included more elements than the Baath alone. Consequently, he not only made the earlier-mentioned provision that in Syria's People's Council about half of the seats should be reserved for other progressive elements outside of the Baath party, but he also strove to create a coalition of these various progressive forces which would support him in governing the country. His efforts were crowned with success when, on March 7, 1972, the National Front was established as the highest authority in Syria. It was to be composed of the Baath party as its principal and dominant component, but it was also to include four other organizations, namely, the Arab Socialist Union (a counterpart of a similar single-party organization in Egypt), the Socialists-Unionists, the Arab Socialist Movement, and the Communist party. The governing body of the National Front was to be composed of eighteen members, as follows: the president (Assad), and nine members of the Baath, as well as two members from each of the remaining four parties. However, the National Front agreement provided that only the Baath party would take responsibility for the ideological direction of the army and student affairs. In his drive for normalization, restoration of the rule of law, and creation of greater stability and tranquillity, Assad was determined to restore to Syria a measure of constitutional parliamentarism. To this end, he not only appointed a body of experts to draft a new constitution, but, once it was drafted, he presented the product for comments and criticism to the public. Because the draft avoided any reference to Islam, considerable opposition to the proposed document developed in the more conservative circles, and religious demonstrations took place in such traditionalist strongholds as Homs and Hama, in which demands were formulated to recognize Islam as a state religion. In contrast to his predecessors who tended to respond by coercive measures to such religious manifestations, Assad accepted to some extent these demands and announced that the constitution would make it mandatory for the President of the Republic to be a Moslem. This formula, without fully conceding to the demand that Syria should be designated as an Islamic state, nevertheless constituted an important concession to popular feelings. Subsequently a referendum was held which secured an overwhelming vote in favor of the new constitution which was formally proclaimed on March 13.[33] On May 25, elections for the People's Council followed. These were the first elections held in Syria since 1961. Even though they were carried under the aegis of a military-party dictatorship, nevertheless they marked a partial return to the constitutional patterns and an end to the unchecked arbitrary rule characteristic of the previous Baath administrations. As could be expected, the Baath party secured the majority of seats in the legislature by having 111 deputies elected out of a total of 164.

An account of these internal developments would be incomplete without referring to two further points. The first was that, despite all the modern socialist slogans propagated by the Baath party, the factor of religious affiliation of its leaders did play a role in Syria's political process. In this case what really mattered was the substantial representation, particularly in the party's military wing, of the Alawite sect of Islam. This religious minority, identified geographically with the district of Lattakia, had been in the prerevolutionary era an economically depressed and socially underprivileged group in the Syrian society. The army being a great social equalizer and a channel for social advancement, many Alawis flocked into its ranks and secured commissions after graduating from the Homs military academy. Consequently, the Alawi officers emerged as a major and perhaps the single most influential group in the army. Similarly, they were inclined to embrace without too much difficulty the ideology of the Baath party as one that promised greater social equality and a more dynamic economic development with due attention to the underprivileged masses. The Alawi predominance in the army and their substantial representation in the higher party councils tended to cause some uneasiness among the Sunni Moslem majority of the population. It was one of the reasons why the Baath party could never command a real majority of popular support.

The second point pertaining to the internal developments was that, despite the turn to the right under Assad's leadership, Syria did not cease to be essentially a socialist-oriented country. By the time of his advent to power major nationalizations had been completed. Moreover, the government was committed to a centralistic planned economy closely connected with Soviet assistance. Under the circumstances, it was not surprising when on June 1, 1972, the Iraq Petroleum Company's assets in Syria, the pipelines and the terminals, were nationalized. This actually constituted Syria's immediate response to the nationalization of IPC decreed in Iraq earlier the same day. Interestingly enough, despite the parallelism of these actions

[33]Text in *ibid.*, March 18, 1972.

of the two Baath regimes, the seizure by Syria of the pipelines provoked considerable difficulty between it and Iraq over the fees to be paid for the transit of Iraqi oil to the Mediterranean terminals. In this sense, Syria's control of the pipeline proved to be more costly and troublesome for Iraq than was the case when the pipeline was controlled by private foreign interests. By the same token, a project launched back in 1966—the construction of a major dam on the Euphrates River—was completed in July 1973, and the dam was inaugurated by President Assad in the presence of a Soviet delegation without, however, much publicity being given to their visit in Syria.

Assad's Arab and foreign policies differed most conspicuously from those of his left-wing predecessors. Instead of quarreling over ideological issues and castigating other Arab regimes as reactionary traitors to the Arab cause, Assad concentrated on restoring good relations with most of the Arab states regardless of their political and ideological views. This was done in the belief that Syria could not afford to remain isolated in the face of Israeli strength. Furthermore, it is worth noting that Assad's advent to power in Syria coincided with Sadat's assumption of office in Egypt. The two leaders showed a certain similarity in that each tended to be moderate, to avoid quarrels with other Arab states, and to aim at practical Pan-Arab collaboration to assure greater coordination of Arab military efforts. Assad's main priority was placed on effective military coordination among Syria, Egypt, Iraq, and in due time, Jordan as well. Consequently, when President Sadat of Egypt began earnest preparations for an offensive against the Israeli forces occupying the Sinai Peninsula, Assad fully cooperated with him and was the only Arab leader to be let into confidence by Sadat as to the exact timing of the operations. Moreover, both leaders agreed to synchronize their operations in Sinai and the Golan Heights. As a result, the Syrian army launched an attack on Israeli positions in the Golan Heights in October of 1973 in full coordination with a simultaneous Egyptian offensive. Initially, the Syrian army made substantial advances and secured considerable territory from the Israelis. After the initial shock, however, the Israelis undertook a counteroffensive which permitted them not only to recover the areas lost through the original Syrian thrust but even to advance beyond the occupation boundary of 1967. Although the Syrian army thus ultimately suffered some reverses, its morale and spirit considerably improved because it demonstrated that the Israelis, when caught by surprise, a tactic they themselves had in the past practiced against the Arabs, were not as invincible as the growing legend tended to make them.

Although hostilities were eventually brought to a halt by a cease-fire, it was frequently violated by mutual bombings from the air and artillery exchanges. Subsequent strenuous diplomacy by the American secretary of state brought about a disengagement agreement between Egypt and Israel on the Sinai front in January 1974, but did not immediately result in a similar agreement on the Syrian front. Instead lengthy negotiations ensued which ended only on May 31 in the signing in Geneva of the "separation of forces agreement" by Syria and Israel. The agreement provided for a disengagement of forces, a UN-policed buffer zone, a gradual thinning out of troops, and a return to Syria of the town of Qunaitra.[34] The town,

---

[34]Text in *New York Times,* May 31, 1974.

incidentally, was in ruins with virtually no structure intact. It had been used as target practice by the Israeli troops when under Israeli occupation.

The signing of this disengagement agreement opened the way for a gradual restoration of relations between the United States and Syria, which had been severed after the 1967 war. In mid-June, while on a tour of the Middle East, President Nixon paid a brief visit to Damascus and, two months later, the first American ambassador appeared in Syria after an interval of seven years. Furthermore, in a move calculated to restore a modicum of normalcy between the two countries, the United States in January 1975 granted Syria $25 million for development within the so-called Middle East contingency fund. It was the first financial aid extended by Washington to Damascus since 1965. In spite of this progress in peacemaking and in restoring relations with the United States, Syria's leadership looked with considerable distrust on what became known as America's "step-by-step" diplomacy. This policy aimed at the gradual achievement of a peace settlement in the Middle East by a series of separate agreements to be concluded in succession by Egypt, Syria and Jordan with Israel under American auspices. Syria's government feared that another step giving Egypt some gains in the Sinai Peninsula might reduce Egyptian eagerness to fight for broader Arab causes and, in particular, Egyptian willingness to defend the rights of Syria thus possibly leaving it alone to face the enemy. For this reason, in a series of communications sent by personal emissaries to various Arab governments in August and September, 1975, Syria strenuously opposed the impending second disengagement agreement to be concluded between Egypt and Israel. The final signing of this agreement (Sinai II) in early September spurred the formation of the Rejectionist Front composed of Syria, Iraq, Algeria, Libya, South Yemen, and the Palestine Liberation Organization (PLO). Its members subsequently met in Tripoli, Libya, in December 1977 and—under the new name of the Arab Steadfastness and Confrontation Front—in Damascus in September 1978 to reject President Sadat's peace initiatives toward Israel as detrimental to the Arab cause. Although Syria stood to lose more than the others from a possible separate peace treaty between Egypt and Israel, it exerted a moderating influence on such resolutions as were adopted. Syria's relative restraint was attributed to its desire to avoid complete rupture with Egypt and to keep the door open to an agreement that might lead to Israel's full withdrawal from that part of the Golan Heights which still remained under its control.

In spite of this difference with Egypt, President Assad's Arab policy continued on its basic course to restore and maintain normal relations with all Arab governments regardless of the nature of their political systems. This in itself constituted a definite repudiation of a revolutionary foreign policy of his predecessors. Following this line, Assad succeeded in normalizing Syria's relations with the erstwhile target of its hostility, Saudi Arabia. There were concrete advantages to Syria, in the form of Saudi financial assistance. But such a rapprochement also paved the way for a Saudi mediation in the debate that was developing between Cairo and Damascus over the wisdom of step-by-step diplomacy. Perhaps the most spectacular act on the part of President Assad was to end the hostility prevailing between Jordan and Syria ever since the *fedayeen* uprising in September 1970. Assad believed that coordination of defense measures against Israel between Syria and Jordan should obtain absolute priority over any other consideration. Hence he initiated moves to restore normal relations and in April 1975 received King Hussein in Damascus, having assured that the king would meet with popular demonstrations of friendship. The two leaders on this occasion signed an agreement to establish joint military commands. And two months later, in June, Assad himself journeyed to Jordan on the first visit of Syria's head of state to Amman in eighteen years. He paid a second visit in December of that year.

Although thus under Assad, Syria pursued prudent and nonadventurous policies toward its Arab neighbors, in the later 1970s it became, somewhat unwillingly, involved in the Lebanese civil war. For ideological reasons Syrian sympathies were on the side of the Moslem-leftist-Palestinian coalition in Lebanon and, initially, Syria even supplied arms to this coalition. Yet, fearing further complications and a dangerous extension of the conflict, Syria also tried to bring about a reconciliation between the adversaries through unceasing mediation efforts carried out by its foreign minister, Abdul Halim Khaddam. The peacemaking venture seemed successful when in February 1976 the Lebanese government and the insurgents agreed on a program of reform. Alas, the more militant elements among the insurgents refused to abide by the agreement in the belief that the Christian side in Lebanon was so near to military collapse as to warrant a final attack leading to complete victory rather than a compromise settlement. To President Assad such a solution appeared unacceptable for three reasons: first, it would undermine his laborious efforts and moral authority as a fair mediator; second, it would result in the establishment in Lebanon of an extremist regime which might easily provoke an Israeli occupation of south-central Lebanon and further contribute to Syria's military encirclement; third, such a regime, dominated by the most militant Palestinian elements, would veer toward an alliance with Libya and Iraq, the latter known for its hostility to the Baath regime in Syria. Meeting with open defiance from Lebanon's most influential rebel leader, Kamal Jumblat, in April 1976, President Assad ordered a limited number of Syrian troops to enter Lebanese territory to pacify the war-torn country. This was followed by a full-scale invasion in June. The PLO and their Lebanese allies fought back but their resistance was overcome and within a few weeks Syrian troops established effective control of most of northern and central Lebanon down to the Litani River in the south. They did not move beyond it because Israel had made clear its objection to Syrian military presence south of the Litani. Syria's next objective was to legitimize its military presence. This end was accomplished when an Arab League meeting in Cairo resolved on June 10 to establish an Arab Deterrent Force, the bulk of which was to consist of some 30,000 Syrian troops already in Lebanon, with token contingents from Saudi Arabia, Sudan, Libya, the United Arab Emirates, and South Yemen.

Syria's military intervention thus saved the Lebanese government and its Christian allies from defeat. Before long, however, tensions began to develop between the Syrian occupation forces and the Christian militias. These groups began calling for a speedy withdrawal of Syrian troops, as they were incompatible with the Lebanese sovereignty. By 1978 an open challenge by the militias to the Syrian presence in Lebanon led to an outbreak of fighting.

While leaving further details to the chapter on Lebanon, I should mention here two more events which seriously affected Syria's position and policies. First, Syria's Lebanese adversaries began receiving arms from Israel; second, in March 1978, Israel invaded southern Lebanon, ostensibly to destroy the *fedayeen* concentrations, and remained there until June when under combined pressure from the United Nations and the United States it withdrew. Thus, though well intentioned, President Assad's decision to intervene in Lebanon brought in its wake ambivalent results: Syria's peacemaking role was frustrated, military operations proved costly, and Israel was not prevented from occupying—though temporarily—southern Lebanon. Some observers were even inclined to view Syria's involvement in Lebanon as "Assad's Vietnam" from which he would find it hard to extricate himself.

To conclude, under Assad's presidency Syria reoriented its domestic policy toward a greater liberalization of political conditions and an emphasis on the internal reconciliation of groups and classes. The new constitution and parliament, though still functioning under the aegis of military rule with a dominant party in power, represented nevertheless the first modest steps toward a revival of law and constitutionalism. In the Arab sector, Syria embarked upon a policy of moderation and cooperation with other sister nations, in contrast to the previous revolutionary policy which left Syria isolated in the midst of the Arab world. Even the intervention in Lebanon, though resulting in unforeseen complications, was basically motivated by a desire to bring peace to a neighboring country and, through this, to ensure greater security for itself.

In the foreign sector Assad's prudent course brought about the restoration of relations with the United States and at least the first step toward a possible settlement with Israel in the form of the disengagement agreement of May 1975. These definite achievements were secured by Assad with considerable risk to his own leadership in a country which for a long time had been subjected to revolutionary indoctrination. To assure full success of such policies, it was necessary that a comprehensive Arab-Israeli settlement, which would satisfy basic Syrian requirements, be achieved. Should such a settlement fail to be obtained, the new edifice of moderation and pragmatism that Assad was trying so laboriously to construct might easily be obliterated.

CHAPTER IX

Lebanon

Lebanon's postwar history can be reviewed under two headings: (1) internal politics and (2) her relations with the big powers and the states of the Middle East.

Internally the young republic continued her traditional political pattern.[1] The presidency of the republic remained in the hands of a Christian, and the position of prime minister was reserved for a Moslem. Bishara el-Khuri and Riyadh es-Sulh continued in their respective positions despite various political shifts and changes in the cabinet's membership. In the spring of 1947 the first elections since the achievement of independence took place in Lebanon in the midst of a political campaign marked by extremist tendencies and occasional violence. The return from exile of Antoun Saadeh, who established the Syrian National Social party, and of Fawzi el-Kawukji, a revolutionary of Palestinian fame who spent the war years in Germany, added to the political unrest of the country. There was a simultaneous revival of the patriotic organization Phalanges Libanaises and of the Communist party. The severance of ties with France, a quarrel over the customs administration with Syria, and unemployment resulting from the withdrawal of foreign troops, all resulted in serious economic difficulties and social unrest. The elections, which gave a substantial majority to the government's supporters (the Constitutionalist party), aroused a storm of protest from the opposition because of alleged irregularities. In September 1947 opposition groups meeting in Tripoli demanded the dissolution of the Chamber and called for new elections. No action was taken on this demand because in 1948 the attention of the people was diverted to the Palestine issue. Beginning with the fall of 1948, the government took sterner measures against those extremist groups which threatened order and security. Strict surveillance, including temporary arrests and short-term jail sentences, was applied to Mustafa el-Aris, a trade unionist chief and leader of the outlawed Communist party. On July 7, 1949, the government arrested Antoun Saadeh with a number of his associates, accusing them of a plot against the government. On the next day Saadeh was executed by order of a military court. Ten days later Lebanese police locked and sealed the headquarters of the Phalanges Libanaises, which was

---

[1]For a discussion of postwar politics, see G. E. Kirk, "Independent Syria and Lebanon," *R.C.A.J.* (July–Oct. 1948).

accused of political excesses. Furthermore, the government made a move toward stricter control of public opinion by suppressing all newspapers with a circulation of less than 1,500, as well as sixty-two political newspapers which failed to post a security bond.

Despite the outward stability of the regime (President Khuri was sworn into office in September 1949 for another term of six years, and Riyadh es-Sulh remained prime minister), there were undercurrents of unrest and violence, as exemplified by the unsuccessful attempt upon Riyadh es-Sulh's life in March 1950 by a member of the Syrian National Social party. In April 1951 the second elections in the independent republic were held under the supervision of a caretaker cabinet headed by Hussein el-Oweini. The general consensus was that this time the government had refrained from interference and the elections were termed honest by official circles and the opposition alike. The Constitutionalist party maintained its majority in the chamber, with the Progressive Socialist party of Kamal Jumblat (a Druze leader), the National Bloc party (Mediterranean Culture Group) of Raymond Eddé, the Phalanges of Pierre Gemayel, and a group of independents led by Camille Chamoun forming the opposition. No basic departure, however, could be noticed from the essentially sectarian character of Lebanese politics, and proportional representation according to religious sects was maintained in the Chamber.

Relations with the West

In international affairs, Lebanon was anxious to cultivate good relations with the powers of the West, particularly with the United States. American cultural institutions, especially the American University in Beirut, provided a significant link between the two countries, a link strengthened by increasing economic exchanges. American airlines and an oil company extended their business operations to Lebanon, the latter making Sidon (Saida) a terminal of the Trans-Arabian Pipe Line (Tapline) which carried oil from the fields of Saudi Arabia. Monetary and financial issues beclouded Lebanon's relations with France, but not to the breaking point. Lebanon's pro-Western orientation was also evidenced by the earlier-mentioned curbs on Communist activities and by her refusal to recognize some of the Soviet satellite regimes in eastern Europe. Nevertheless, Lebanon maintained diplomatic relations with the Soviet Union. The latter apparently took full advantage of this situation by converting her legation in Beirut into the reputedly greatest Soviet propaganda center in the Middle East.

Lebanon's delegate in the United Nations, Dr. Charles Malik, repeatedly went on record as favoring Western concepts of human rights and Western policies. In July 1950, Lebanon endorsed the United Nations Korean resolutions which branded the North Korean Communists as aggressors, and she seemed generally anxious to cultivate Western friendship. The Palestinian controversy revealed once again, however, the Arab character of the republic. Lebanon strongly objected to the partitioning of Palestine and subsequently sent some forces against Israel. The pro-Israel policy of the United States provoked anti-American demonstration, especially among students, but they were less violent in character than those in Syria, Iraq, or Egypt. In June 1951, Dr. Malik made a speech in Beirut foreshadowing Lebanon's practical reconciliation with the existence of Israel and even admitting that Israel, with other Arab states, would have a role to play in the defense of the Middle East against external aggression.[2]

Relations with the Middle East

Lebanon's relations with her Arab neighbors continued to be conditioned by two factors: (1) her essentially Arab character as a nation and (2) the preponderance of the Christian element in her population. While the first factor pushed Lebanon into cooperation with the Arab states through the instrumentality of the Arab League and otherwise, the second acted as a brake on the pro-Arab tendencies and dictated to the little republic a cautious course that would permit her to maintain her independence and individuality. It was this second facet of Lebanese policy which led her consistently to oppose the Greater Syria scheme advocated by King Abdullah of Transjordan, as well as to insist on the retention of full sovereignty by the members of the Arab League. This same factor made it imperative for Lebanon always to keep the door open for an understanding with the West as a time-tested guarantee against complete submergence in her Moslem environment.

The Coup of 1952 and Its Aftermath

Although Lebanon was an island of tolerance in comparison with her sister countries, her democracy suffered from two deficiencies: one was the strictly sectarian basis of her political processes; another was the narrowness of her political structure. To an impartial observer Lebanon's politics appeared like a never-ending game of musical chairs in which the principal actors were always the same, with temporary absences from the scene of this or that individual due to the normal hazards of the political profession. The people at large were expected either to mind their business in the lopsided economy of this little state or simply to conform to the wishes and ideas of their feudal lords, party chieftains, and ecclesiastical leaders (the latter abounded in this sect-ridden country). Those who found that their native land was too crowded and poor could emigrate to the more promising lands of South or North America, provided the latter were liberal enough in their immigration policies. This, in a broad generalization, was the state of affairs prevailing until the summer of 1952.

In June of that fateful year in the annals of Arab history, a new organization dedicated to radical reform came into prominence. Called the Socialist and National Front, it demanded an end of sectarian representation, a purge in the administration, and eradication of abuses in the government. Although the Front could boast of no more than eight deputies in the seventy-seven-man parliament, it had considerable appeal to the masses. Moreover, it was headed by a few reformist leaders whose reputations had not suffered in the all-pervading atmosphere of corruption. Among these leaders were Kamal Jumblat, a Druze chief and head of the Progressive Socialist party, Camille Chamoun, former minister to Britain, Emile Bustani, a self-made millionaire businessman known for his outspokenness, Ghassan Tweini,

[2]*New York Times,* June 13, 1951.

the Harvard-educated youngest member of parliament, and certain others, representing, on the whole, the antifeudal and antisectarian trends.

The Egyptian revolution of July 23 had a stimulating influence on the attitudes and activities of the Front. By the end of July three other groups raised their voices against the government. These were the Phalanges of Pierre Gemayel, the National Committee of Mohammed Khalid, and the National Congress of Mohammed Idris, who demanded the formation of an extraparliamentary cabinet, dissolution of the chamber, and speedy institution of reforms. On August 17 the Socialist and National Front held a mass rally at Deir el-Kamar, which was attended by an estimated fifty thousand people. The orators, who included Kamal Jumblat, Camille Chamoun, and Hamid Franjiyeh, called for immediate reform, threatened rebellion, and demanded the resignation of the President. In fact, it was President Bishara el-Khuri rather than the premier, Sami es-Sulh, against whom criticism was directed. On August 20, Sulh accepted the Front's demands and published a program of reforms, which embraced revision of the electoral law, dismissal of incompetent officials, sale of state lands, and creation of an economic council. His program was, however, unacceptable to certain cabinet members, who, considering Sulh as a Kerensky of Lebanese revolution, presented their resignations. On September 9 the premier appeared before the parliament, where he delivered a scathing attack on the prevailing administration of the country, choosing certain members of the president's family as his particular target. His denunciations included presidential interference with the activities of the Ministry of the Interior, prevention of the passage of measures against gambling, tolerance of and conniving with smuggling to Israel and traffic in narcotics, attempts to influence judicial processes, and usurpation of the powers of the prime minister. Having delivered this indictment, Sami es-Sulh resigned. Press censorship, dominated by the president, forbade publication of Sulh's attack.

Nevertheless, events began to move rapidly in Lebanon. On September 11 the Socialist and National Front called for a general strike to force the president to resign. Pierre Gemayel, head of the Phalanges, and his political allies seconded this appeal. Popular response was overwhelming, and on September 15 and 16 all trade and activity in Beirut, Tripoli, Saida, Zahle, and Baalbeck came to a standstill. The press declared that the strike was a virtual plebiscite in favor of the opposition. The president, in a futile gesture, appealed to General Fuad Chehab, army chief of staff, to restore order, but, meeting with a refusal, he resigned on September 18. His last constitutional act was to appoint that same general as prime minister.

Thus the opposition carried the day in a bloodless revolution which has since become known as the *Inkilab* ("overturn"). The immediate problem was to fill the vacancy created by Khuri's resignation. Had the opposition been a truly revolutionary and cohesive group, it would have suspended the constitution and established a regime of its own. But this was not the case. Although Jumblat, Chamoun, and their colleagues were united in common enmity to the Khuri regime, they lacked organization and determination to act ruthlessly if necessary. Consequently, instead of dispersing the existing Khuri-packed parliament, the Deir el-Kamar leaders chose to act through it. On September 23, in deference to the mood of the times, parliament, by a vote of 74 out of a total of 76, elected Camille Chamoun to the presidency. Thus the *Inkilab* proved to be not only a bloodless but also a "constitutional" revolution. Such an outcome had its distinct disadvantages, at least from the reformist point of view, inasmuch as it set the new president against an essentially conservative, old-regime parliament, while giving the latter a chance to recoup its strength in the days to come. This was proved soon after Chamoun's election when an attempt to form a truly reform-minded cabinet failed. Eventually a compromise formula was devised: a strictly nonpolitical cabinet headed by a diplomat, Emir Khalid Chehab, and comprising only three other members recruited from the upper bureaucracy was formed. This cabinet received from the parliament full power to legislate by decree for the succeeding six months.

Among the more notable decrees passed by the government during those months was a revision of the electoral law which reduced the number of deputies from seventy-seven to forty-four and granted the right to vote to women who held a primary education certificate. This law did not abolish the traditional sectarian representation and, at the most, gave the President of the Republic a somewhat greater chance to influence the deputies. Otherwise the "reforms" of the new cabinet revolved chiefly around the "reclassification" of civil servants and similar personnel matters. It was not a very impressive record, and soon signs of discontent and disappointment with the new regime began to appear. By the spring of 1953 relations between President Chamoun and his erstwhile associate, Jumblat, deteriorated to such a point that the Socialist and National Front was hardly a working coalition. Having risen to the highest office in the state, the president soon gave evidence of accommodating himself to the traditional pattern of Lebanese politics and in all his acts tended to tone down the original and rather radical ideals of the *Inkilab*. By contrast, the much more idealistic Jumblat insisted on the implementation of the revolutionary program, paying little heed to its practical aspects and such considerations as tactical alliances. In May most of the original members of the Front voted against the newly formed cabinet of Saeb Salam, thus returning to the opposition. The new prime minister, to be sure, spoke of the need to achieve the aims of "the September revolution," but this sounded more like lip service to virtue than sincere intention to effect radical changes in Lebanon's political and economic structure.

The basic question of whether the locus of power had shifted from the first "forty families" of Lebanon to the less-privileged strata had to await the answer of the popular ballot under the new electoral law. The electoral campaign abounded in bitterness, violence, and even assassinations. The violence of conflict was in no small measure due to the reduction of the seats in the legislature, which made the competition among the 116 candidates much more acute. In the midst of the campaign Jumblat accused the president of conspiring against his party's candidates as a result of pressure by concessionary companies, oil corporations, "Intelligence Service," and promoters of Middle East defense schemes. He also revealed a bribe offer by a representative of a foreign power if he would abstain from political activity, but he failed to substantiate his allegation.

The new parliament elected in July 1953 reflected some change in Lebanon's political scene, but the difference was not radical enough to warrant a statement that the locus of power had shifted sociologically. Of a total of forty-four deputies, twenty-three were members of the previous parliament, and the remaining twenty-one could not be regarded as representing new social strata. In a few cases traditional feudal holds on certain districts were broken, and the monopolies of certain leading families, such as the Assads in southern Lebanon, were successfully challenged by their adversaries. But there was no indication that the winners would espouse a social philosophy much different from that of their predecessors.

The political shift, if any, was indicative of the growing power of the new president, who, notwithstanding the regularity of electoral procedures, could appreciably influence the elections in keeping with the tradition of his office. The "forty families" continued to be amply represented in the new parliament, while the Progressive Socialist party managed to secure, after a fierce struggle, just one seat—for its leader. Frustrated, Jumblat expressed his disappointment in a major parliamentary speech on October 1, 1953:

> Since the events of September 1952, 3000 new officials have been appointed and an additional twelve million pounds spent. . . . The budget which one submits to us is almost entirely designed to support from nine to ten thousand officials. . . . It's not this way that one runs a State. . . . One could almost say that the State does not exist. Those in authority say that the financial situation is "healthy." The same was being said under the old regime. Well, there are many today who do not satisfy their hunger, industry is wobbly, and most of the taxpayers don't pay their taxes.
> It is absurd to continue to import to an excess and to export nothing or almost nothing, as we do now. We cannot live indefinitely on invisible receipts, on the smuggling of gold and hashish. . . . . What matters at this hour is to mete out justice to those who have betrayed the September revolution and the people.[3]

Cabinet changes were rarely due to deep policy divergencies. The trivial matter of who should represent Lebanon in Paris was sufficient to produce a crisis in the summer of 1955, resulting in the resignation of the foreign minister. On the other hand, attempts made by a few deputies to abolish the traditional system of sectarian representation made no headway whatever. The system was even vigorously defended by such prominent figures as Hamid Franjiyeh and Sami es-Sulh. The balance between numerous denominations was precariously maintained, and under the outward surface of harmony strong undercurrents of hostility between Christians and Moslems were discernible. Moslems criticized a system in which Christians, on the basis of their alleged (and slight) numerical superiority, filled not only the highest office of the state but also a disproportionately large number of civil service positions. Consequently, they insisted on a general census which, they were confident, would prove their numerical preponderance over the Christians. Christians, on their part, did not enjoy debating these matters in public but, when compelled by circumstances, argued that they contributed 80 per cent of the tax revenue and that a census would be welcome provided it included the Lebanese living overseas. The latter argument was based on the important role these predominantly Christian

[3]Quoted in *Cahiers,* 1953, 2.

emigrants continue to play in the life of the country. Whatever the faults of the religiously mixed ruling class, it seriously tried to calm and deemphasize the exaggerated sectarian zeal of the rank and file. In line with this policy, the courts sentenced to prison terms two writers found guilty of inciting religious strife.[4]

Foreign Policy Problems in the 1950s

In matters of foreign policy no appreciable change occurred after the 1952 coup. Lebanon continued her basically pro-Western orientation by accepting American technical assistance, maintaining trade and cultural relations with Western countries, and serving as a home for many Western schools and missions, including a French and an American university. But this pro-Western orientation was tempered by the realization that the rest of the Arab world was in a sulky mood toward the West and that it favored neutralism. When the Baghdad Pact began to loom as a major problem in the Middle East in 1954-1955, Lebanon was exposed to many pressures and embarrassments. She would have welcomed the military and economic assistance from the West which would follow joining the pact. And she would not have minded obtaining reassurance from Iraq and other pact powers against possible absorption by Syria. But with the Arab League on record as strongly condemning the pact, Lebanon could not afford to estrange the League without incurring grave internal and external risks. A tourist and investment boycott by Saudi Arabia and Egypt might cause her serious losses. By the same token, the traditional though unwritten entente with Egypt was too precious to be gambled away. Consequently, Lebanon tried to steer a neutral course between Cairo and Baghdad, exchanging state visits with the leaders of both blocs but refusing to join either the Baghdad Pact or the new alliance promoted by Egypt and Saudi Arabia. In keeping with this spirit of caution President Chamoun emerged as a principal advocate of reconciliation among the Arab states. His intense diplomatic activity and his calls for the preservation of Arab unity were the more remarkable in view of the fact that his country was less Arab in character than others in the League. Yet this solicitude was understandable in the light of Lebanon's smallness and vulnerability.

Relations with Israel were officially hostile (as befitted a member of the Arab League), but they lacked the bellicosity which characterized relations between Israel and Egypt or Syria. When in 1955 some Israelis were ambushed in northern Palestine by Arab assailants presumably coming from Lebanon, Lebanese authorities promptly transferred an Arab refugee camp from the frontier area to the center of the country, at the same time adopting stern measures to prevent illegal crossing of boundaries. This action conformed with the position of Lebanon, which was militarily too weak to face possible Israeli reprisals and yet too dependent on the good will of sister Arab nations to ignore their pressure for a strong stand against Israel should such a border incident develop into a major issue.

Internal and External Pressures, 1956-1958

During the period 1956-1958 Lebanon was exposed to many internal and external pressures, many of which owed their origins to the turbulence prevailing in the Arab

---

[4]Mustafa Khalidi was sentenced for writing *Moslem Lebanon Today* and Georges Shakar for his *Révolution et Contrainte*. Both judgments were delivered in 1954.

world as a whole. It was a period of growing Pan-Arabism in Syria and Egypt, of increasing cleavage between Baghdad and Cairo, of the Suez crisis and its aftermath. In Lebanon's political life domestic and foreign factors were closely interwoven and virtually inseparable. Political struggles were being carried out on two levels: (1) the level of rivalry among individual political leaders, who were linked to groups of followers in a patron-client relationship which had its roots in tradition, religious bonds, and clannish allegiance; and (2) the level of ideological struggle, in which three main trends were discernible, namely, those of Lebanese nationalism, Greater Syrianism, and Pan-Arabism. In 1956–1958, however, one could speak of increasing polarization of forces between Lebanese nationalism and Pan-Arabism. Exponents of the Greater Syria scheme (i.e., the Syrian National Social party, commonly known as P.P.S.) having suffered a defeat in Syria were ready to ally themselves with Lebanese nationalists against the common threat of Pan-Arabism.

There is no doubt that Pan-Arabism, with Nasser as its chief symbol, was having a profound impact on the thinking and emotions of Lebanon's Moslem population. The rank and file of Lebanese Moslems (especially those of the Sunni persuasion) have never developed any deep sense of loyalty to Lebanon, which they tended to regard, within its enlarged boundaries, as a somewhat artificial French-sponsored creation. It was natural for them to look toward predominantly Moslem Syria for inspiration. Syria in the meantime was steadily veering toward Pan-Arabism. Thus the initial separation of Syria and Lebanon into two sovereign states was now being widened because of the increasingly different orientations of their respective governments. While Syria definitely chose the camp of "Arab liberation," Arab unity, and neutralism, Lebanon insisted on its separateness and its right to cooperate with the West if it suited its national interest. When the P.P.S. was being crushed in Syria in 1955, Lebanon opened its doors to the refugees. Subsequently many conservative and pro-Western Syrians who opposed the Baath and army interference in their home country found refuge in Lebanon, which they sometimes used as a base of their operations. Further contrast between the two countries became evident when, at the time of the Suez crisis, Lebanon refused to break off diplomatic relations with Britain and France. Lebanon was the only Arab country which officially accepted the Eisenhower Doctrine and on March 16, 1957, signed an agreement with the United States. Lebanon's gradual pro-Western alignment was a natural reflection of the fact that about half of its population is Christian and that the latter tended to view its continuous friendly relationship with the West as the last guarantee of the country's independence. But it was also due to the will and determination of the President, Camille Chamoun, whose pro-Western sympathies and distrust of Nasser were well known.

Chamoun's refusal to follow the flock so far as Pan-Arabism was concerned contrasted with the policies of many Sunni Moslem politicians of Lebanon who catered to their constituents' sentiments by proclaiming their devotion to the ideal of Arab unity and paying homage to President Nasser whenever an opportunity arose. In reality, it was very unlikely that these Moslem leaders would have desired to exchange their position of relative power and influence (with a rotating premiership reserved for one of their group) in free Lebanon for the position of subordinate nonentities in a large authoritarian Arab state. Their tactics, however, added fuel to the already surcharged atmosphere prevailing among their followers, with the resulting tension between the latter and the Christian elements of Lebanon. The Christians considered, for example, public displays of Nasser's portraits in Moslem communities as an insult to the idea of Lebanese independence and on some occasions reacted to such provocations in a violent manner. These feuds and tensions were also reflected in the Lebanese newspapers, some of which were subsidized by foreign embassies.

The ideological cleavage had the effect of rendering the traditional struggle for power among the politicians more acute than ever before. Beginning with 1957 the central issue in this struggle was President Chamoun's ambition to be reelected for a second term in 1958. To achieve this the constitution would have had to be amended by a two-thirds vote of the parliament. Anxious to attain his goal, Chamoun did not hesitate to use his influence to secure a solid majority in the parliamentary elections of May–June 1957. As a result, certain traditional non-Christian leaders of Pan-Arab sympathies, such as Abdullah Yafi, Saeb Salam, and Kamal Jumblat were not elected. Deprived of a legal platform from which to voice their opinions, these men inevitably turned toward the street, seeking through extralegal means to reassert their role in Lebanon's political life. The conflict between Chamoun and the Pan-Arab opposition gained in intensity when Syria merged with Egypt into the United Arab Republic. Pro-Nasser manifestations in Lebanon grew in number and violence, resulting in bodily clashes between groups of different orientation as well as in intemperate editorials in the press. By the late spring the tension had reached dangerous proportions and only a spark was needed to provoke a major conflagration.

The Lebanese Civil War

Such a spark was provided when, on May 8, 1958, unknown assassins shot and killed Nassib Metni, editor of *Al-Telegraf,* a newspaper lately known for its outspoken Pan-Arabism and previously identified with Communist sympathies. Pan-Arabists immediately blamed Lebanese nationalists, while launching strong attacks on President Chamoun and Premier Sami es-Sulh for tolerating and abetting acts of terrorism against their political opponents. By May 12 antigovernment riots reached the proportions of an armed insurrection. Politically the rebels formed themselves into the so-called National Front, a loose coalition comprising those Sunni Moslem leaders who had lost parliamentary seats in 1957, the Druze faction of Kamal Jumblat, the Moslem followers of Rashid Karamah of Tripoli, the Moslem youth organization Najjada headed by the radical Pan-Arabist Adnan Hakim, the Shia Moslem faction of Ahmed Assad of Sidon (another loser in the 1957 elections), a variety of pro-Nasser elements in the Bekaa Valley and other parts of the country, and last, but not least, certain Christian elements opposing President Chamoun. The latter included the influential clan of Franjiyeh of Zgharta in northern Lebanon, represented by their kinsman René Muawad. Furthermore, in one of the ironical twists of history, the Patriarch of the Maronite Church, Paul Méouchi, gave his implicit blessing to the insurgents, largely because of a personal feud with President Chamoun. Christians participating in the National Front (though not overly active in the military sense) justified their position by the necessity of Lebanon's keeping on friendly terms with the surrounding Arab world, which, they claimed, the one-sided pro-Western and anti-Cairo policy of President Chamoun had made impossible. By the same token, the predominantly Moslem leaders of the insurrection disclaimed an exclusively Moslem character for their rebellion by pointing to their few Christian allies.

In political terms this rebel coalition was opposed, in the first place, by the government and those deputies in the recently elected parliament which supported it. These in turn were backed by the Phalanges Libanaises (Kataeb), an overwhelmingly Christian-Maronite party dedicated to the preservation of Lebanese integrity and independence, and reinforced by the militant members of the P.P.S., whose hatred of Nasserism pushed them into collaboration with Lebanese nationalists. The government, however, was gravely handicapped by its inability to count on the full support of the army. Although a majority of army officers were Christian, including its commanding general, Fuad Chehab, the rank and file were a heterogeneous group which might easily split along ideological and confessional lines if exposed to great strains. Consequently, the army played a rather passive role, contenting itself with the protection of government buildings and certain military objects, but rarely attempting an offensive.

This brings us to the military aspect of the rebellion. Insurgents had barricaded themselves in the Moslem quarter of Beirut, the Basta, under the leadership of former Premier Saeb Salam, who, strangely enough, was enjoying without hindrance the facilities of the government-controlled telephone system. The second major rebel stronghold was in Tripoli, where the scion of the local feudal family, Rashid Karamah, reigned supreme. The third was in the Shuf mountain district, where Jumblat's Druzes had taken the warpath. Furthermore, large portions of Lebanon in the south and the east, along the Syrian border, found themselves under rebel control.

The rebels were enjoying the active support of the newly formed United Arab Republic, which from its Syrian province was supplying them with arms, munitions, money, and some personnel. Furthermore, several Lebanese border ports were shelled and attacked by military raiding parties from Syria. Throughout the major part of the rebellion the government forces controlled merely 18 kilometers out of Lebanon's 324-kilometer boundary with Syria.[5] The rest was under rebel control and open to easy penetration from the Syrian side. Mule-pack trains of military equipment made regular inroads into Lebanon through these long stretches of unprotected border.

In view of the army's passive role; much of the brunt of defense against the rebels had to be borne by armed volunteer groups. Not infrequently the latter were organized and led by the members of the P.P.S., whose superior organization and experience (especially true of Syrian refugee army officers affiliated with the party) naturally placed them in a position of military leadership. It was such a heavily

[5]For a detailed account of the civil war, see Fahim I. Qubain, *Crisis in Lebanon* (Washington, D.C., 1961).

P.P.S.-staffed group which, at the "battle" of Shemlan, successfully stopped Jumblat's Druzes in their attempt to capture the Beirut airport and invade the city.

Politically, the objective of the U.A.R.'s intervention was not quite clear. To some extent it could be explained as a simple policy of revenge against President Chamoun—a man vilified in the Pan-Arab press as an agent of British intelligence—for his hands-off policy during the Suez War and for his harboring of the dissenters and plotters from Syria. Lebanon, according to this explanation, was to be punished for its treason to the Arab cause and for becoming an imperialist base directed against Arab unity and liberation. Once this punishment was inflicted, the rest remained uncertain. As a maximum target one might suspect Nasser's desire to incorporate Lebanon into the U.A.R. There is no conclusive evidence that this was Nasser's real goal. Furthermore, as mentioned earlier, it is doubtful whether Lebanon's rebel leaders (with the possible exception of Najjada's leader, Adnan Hakim) really desired it. More likely Cairo's objective was the satellization of Lebanon, leaving it an autonomous unit with its special political institutions and customs. Furthermore, it has not yet been made clear whether President Nasser initiated intervention or merely gave approval to the actions of his emotionally motivated Syrian lieutenants in Damascus.

The U.A.R.'s intervention converted the civil war from a mere domestic event into an international issue. Lebanon appealed, first, to the Arab League, where, as could be expected, it found no practical solace; then, on June 6, to the United Nations. Presenting his country's case before the Security Council, Lebanon's Foreign Minister Charles Malik accused the United Arab Republic of massive intervention. On June 10 this allegation was upheld by Secretary Dulles, who said there was "irrefutable evidence" of U.A.R. interference in Lebanon. The next day the Security Council voted to send a team of UN observers to Lebanon. The team, headed by the Swedish general Odd Bull, assembled in Lebanon a few days later. With 94 observers (166 by mid-August), the team was numerically inadequate to throw a tight cordon around Lebanon. Moreover, it did not carry out any patrols at night. Furthermore, it was denied access to certain areas controlled by the rebels. As a consequence, infiltrators could easily evade its observation posts. On July 4 the UN observer group reported to the Security Council that it found no evidence of massive Syrian infiltration. Dismayed, the government of Lebanon stated in its official commentary that the observers' findings were either inconclusive, misleading, or unwarranted. It stated that the U.A.R. had continued its massive infiltration even after the arrival of UN observers in Lebanon. Furthermore, convinced that it could not count on practical assistance from the United Nations, the government appealed to the United States for direct military aid under the provisions of the Eisenhower Doctrine.

If there was any hesitation in the State Department as to the right course to follow, it was dispelled by the revolution which occurred in Iraq on July 14. As viewed from Washington, the events in Baghdad constituted another link in a chain of dramatic developments marking the forward march of Pan-Arabism. Momentarily it looked as if the whole existing political structure of the Arab East were to crumble under the blows of militant propaganda, subversion, and aggression directed from the nerve-center in Cairo. With an eye to preventing further spread of Pan-Arab revolution (with its anti-Western implications), the United States decided to send military forces to Lebanon with the immediate task of defending the latter's sovereignty and independence. In a special statement President Eisenhower declared that this action was undertaken at the explicit request of the government of Lebanon. The first contingent of 3,600 American marines landed in Beirut on July 15, followed by further units of the army. American troops took no action in the conflict: they merely stayed, distributed on the beaches and at the airport. But their very presence constituted an important factor in the situation. Closely following them to Beirut came Robert Murphy, under secretary of state for political affairs, with the task of attempting a peaceful solution of the strife.

In the meantime President Chamoun declared that he would not seek reelection for the second term, thus depriving the opposition of their main argument for staging the revolt. This was a welcome development from the American point of view, inasmuch as it was imperative to differentiate between American defense of Lebanese independence, on the one hand, and American support of President Chamoun as a politician, on the other. After considerable negotiations, which also took Murphy to Cairo, the following solution was accepted by the interested parties: President Chamoun would stay in office until the end of his term in September 1958; then he would relinquish his position to a new, legally elected president, presumably General Fuad Chehab, commander of the army, whose compromise candidacy proved acceptable to all the warring factions (including, allegedly, President Nasser of the U.A.R.). The new regime was to follow a principle of "no victors, no vanquished" to reflect a general policy of reconciliation. The National Pact of 1943 was to be fully observed. This unwritten agreement, concluded between the principal Christian and Moslem leaders of Lebanon, Bishara el-Khuri and Riyadh es-Sulh, at the time of the struggle for independence, provided that Moslems would join Christians in a common loyalty to the sovereign state of Lebanon if the Christians (1) renounced their traditional policy of seeking Western protection and intervention and (2) shared with the Moslems in a ratio of 6 to 5 the public offices, legislative and administrative, of the republic. Implicit in these arrangements was the promise that the post-civil-war government of Lebanon would deemphasize its links with the West (such as the formal acceptance of the Eisenhower Doctrine) and would, indeed, steer a middle course between the West and its surrounding Arab environment.

It should be pointed out that in agreeing to this solution the insurgents had abandoned some of their earlier demands, such as the immediate resignation of President Chamoun and the evacuation of American troops before the election of the new president. These concessions were due partly to the removal of a valid domestic cause for continuing the insurrection and partly to the uncertainty whether President Nasser would be unwilling to continue his support of the rebels in view of the presence of American forces. On July 31, General Fuad Chehab was elected president of the Republic by the Chamber of Deputies by a 48 to 7 vote. The seven votes went to Raymond Eddé. Despite these important developments, sporadic fighting continued until early September. On September 23, Fuad Chehab assumed the duties of the presidency and on the following day he appointed as premier Rashid Karamah, former rebel leader of Tripoli. His eight-man cabinet was composed of men who had either sided with the rebellion or had been neutral in the conflict, with no representation of the former loyalist elements. This gave rise to a protest movement by the militant Lebanese nationalist party, the Phalanges, who demanded at least one seat in the cabinet for themselves and backed up this demand by proclaiming a ten-day-long general strike, since termed a counterrevolution, on September 29. Their action gained widespread support from Lebanon's Christian population, which viewed Karamah's cabinet as a victory for the rebels and a travesty of the compromise solution to which the opposing parties had pledged themselves. Finally, on October 14 Karamah formed a new cabinet, this time representing a genuine compromise. It comprised merely four members, of whom two (Premier Karamah and Foreign Minister Hussein el-Oweini) represented former insurgents, while the other two (Education Minister Pierre Gemayel, head of the Phalanges, and Raymond Eddé, minister of interior) represented the Lebanese loyalists. Peace having been restored, American troops evacuated Lebanese territory by October 24. By mid-November the UN observer group also withdrew, its task deemed accomplished. In early December the United States extended to Lebanon a $10 million grant to help it restore its economy, which had been gravely affected by the hostilities. There was a gradual return to normalcy, both in the economic and the political sectors.

The Aftermath of the Strife

Viewed in retrospect, the civil war was an unnecessary and tragic development which cost many lives, inflicted deep psychological wounds, and achieved no basic change in Lebanon's political structure or processes. The only remotely positive gain was that it reaffirmed—at a high price—certain truths about Lebanon's realities. These truths could be summed up as follows: (1) if Lebanon was to survive as a going concern, its component religious groups had to cooperate with each other on the basis of a fair compromise; an attempt by any one of them, whether Moslem or Christian, to dominate the country was bound to provoke resistance and violence; (2) while the Moslem part of Lebanon's population would always look nostalgically toward closer association with Syria and the Arab world as a whole, Lebanon's Moslem leaders had a stake in preserving Lebanon as a sovereign state, in which they were assured a position of influence and a real share in power; (3) to avoid major international frictions and enjoy prosperity, Lebanon could not afford to live in isolation either from its Arab environment or from the West; to strike the right balance between these two influences has become the principal objective of a sound foreign policy and a major test of Lebanese statesmanship; (4) inasmuch as Lebanon would always live in danger of possible intervention from its Arab neighbors, it was clear that it was bound to look toward Western counterintervention as a guarantee of its independent status.

The restoration of normalcy did not mean that Lebanon had achieved a static harmony. On the contrary, its political life continued fluctuating, with pressures and counterpressures not unlike those prior to the civil war very much in evidence. For one thing, there was the problem of interpretation of the largely verbal agreements made in midsummer 1958 between the two warring factions. For another, the political need of prominent Moslem leaders to cater to the popular Pan-Arab tastes of their constituents has not vanished as a result of the compromise formulas reached at a higher level of politics. Some former rebel leaders tended to boast of the achievements of the revolution to the annoyance of the Lebanese loyalists, who countered by emphasizing the no-victor formula. By the same token, public worship of Nasser by the former rebels continued as before. It was expressed by numerous trips to Cairo and by staging group pilgrimages of their followers to Damascus every time Nasser paid a visit to his northern province. Pan-Arab zealots would sometimes hoist the flag of the U.A.R. alongside or instead of that of Lebanon, thereby supplying provocation to the prestige-conscious Phalangists and other Lebanese nationalists. The policy of entrusting the premiership to a former rebel leader continued even after the demise of Karamah's cabinet in 1959. He was followed by Saeb Salam, who likewise continued the formula of a balanced cabinet, with this difference that, instead of four ministers, he had eighteen, thereby converting the cabinet into a little parliament in which individual ministers fought fierce personal and ideological battles among themselves. This was especially true of Pierre Gemayel, a leading loyalist holding the portfolio of public works, and Kamal Jumblat, who became minister of education. Critical of French and American influences in the Lebanese educational system, Jumblat tried to restrict them by promoting a new, Arab university, oriented toward Egypt both in ideology and in personnel, and by enlarging nonconfessional education at the expense of Western-sponsored Christian schools. To these attempts he met fierce resistance on the part of Gemayel, who strongly defended the existing private and denominational school system as productive of the highest level of literacy and education in any Arabic-speaking country. The feud between these two men and their policies was in many ways representative of Lebanon's basic dilemma: how to survive as a separate island of tolerance and freedom in the midst of the Arab-Moslem sea agitated by severe tempests of Pan-Arabism and authoritarian trends.

Persistent Issues in the 1960s and 1970s

The relative tranquillity of Lebanese politics following the 1958 crisis can be attributed partly to the exhaustion of the warring parties, partly to the felicitous choice of a president who was and appeared to many observers as a scrupulously neutral compromise figure, and partly to the fact that revolutionary forces at work in the Arab world shifted their attention and energies to other theaters than Lebanon, for Iraq emerged as the principal focus of revolutionary activity and of inter-Arab controversies. This tranquillity, however, was more apparent than real insofar as Lebanon was concerned. The crisis of 1958 did not resolve any of the basic issues that had brought it about. Lebanon's political system faced a number of problems that were bound to reemerge.

In Lebanon, it should be pointed out, the interweaving of domestic and foreign policies was always more pronounced than in any other country in the area. This tension was due to the religious heterogeneity of the Lebanese population and to the parallel and continuous searches for identity of various groups composing Lebanon. It is still useful, however, to review Lebanon's persistent problems under separate domestic and foreign headings. In the domestic sector, the central issue in Lebanon has been and continues to be that of confessionalism, that is, political representation and participation according to one's religious affiliation. When, back in 1943, the two founding fathers of the independent Lebanese Republic, Bishara el-Khuri and Riyadh es-Sulh, agreed upon a political formula since known as the National Pact, many Lebanese and foreigners believed that Lebanon's problem of sectarian rivalries and struggles was removed once and for all and that, assured of its rightful place and representation in the political process, each religious sect would play its proportional role in the system. For a number of years, the majority of the politically conscious Lebanese seemed to accept the National Pact as a reasonable and satisfactory solution. However, one should not forget that the pact was built upon the base of demographic statistics which, with the passage of time, ceased to reflect the reality. The proportion for Christian to Moslem representation was 6 to 5. But this proportion stemmed from an old population census carried out under the French mandate, whereas in the meantime Moslem population grew, and first reached parity with the Christian, and then in all likelihood exceeded it in numerical strength. Suggestions and proposals from Moslem quarters to carry out a new census in Lebanon invariably met with Christian refusals, the Christian leaders arguing that the term Lebanese should not apply merely to the inhabitants of Lebanon but also to a Lebanese "diaspora" the world over which continued to maintain strong links with the old country and to provide it with much needed financial resources. Moreover, demands for the census and the subsequent revision of the existing proportional representation usually came from younger and less established Moslem leaders. The entrenched Moslem personalities preferred to remain neutral on this issue inasmuch as they clearly saw advantages to themselves flowing from the existence of an independent Lebanon in which certain constitutionally guaranteed positions were reserved for them. A Lebanon with a clear and officially acknowledged Moslem majority might come to favor some sort of closer union or merger with the surrounding Moslem states. The consequences of union would be a radical restructuring of the society and the removal of the leading conservative Moslems from their positions of leadership.

Thus in addition to the basic problem of religious cleavage, which always loomed as a potential danger to the country, a new chasm was appearing between the old and the new leadership in the Moslem population and, to a lesser extent, among the Christians. It was characteristic of Lebanon that its political establishment experienced very little turnover during the two decades between the mid-1950s and the mid-1970s. Among the Moslem leaders (and the Druze as well) the names of such *zaims* as Rashid Karamah, Saeb Salam, Kamal el-Assad, Adel Osseiran, Sabri Hamadeh, Majid Arslan, and Kamal Jumblat seemed to be permanent fixtures of the political firmament. The premiership was frequently rotated between Karamah and Salam, with an occasional appearance of another Moslem leader such as Hussein el-Oweini, Abdullah Yafi, or Taki Eddin es-Sulh. On the Christian side, former

President Camille Chamoun, the *kataeb* leader Pierre Gemayel, the National Bloc leader Raymond Eddé, and the *zaim* of the Zgharta region in the north, Suleiman Franjiyeh, also were enjoying remarkable political longevity. These leaders drew their strength from the sectarian, feudal, and clannish nature of the Lebanese society. Breaking into this charmed circle was not easy for any newcomer. Yet with the passage of time, new forces and more ambitious younger leaders began to make their appearance.

The new forces constituted groupings based on urban, more modern, and more literate constituencies. They represented a wide spectrum of beliefs and goals and included such groups as the Communists, the Moslem Brethren, the Arab Nationalist Movement (ANM), the Lebanese branch of the Baath Party, the Syrian National Social Party (popularly known as the P.P.S. in Lebanon), various Nasserite and other radical groups. Their one common denominator was their rejection of the legitimacy of the Lebanese political system, and they were striving to transform it.

These reformist and revolutionary strivings were, of course, not divorced from the state of the Lebanese economy and its distribution of wealth. In the 1960s and 1970s Lebanon was enjoying a period of economic expansion and boom, due to such factors as the spectacular increase in the tourist traffic with corresponding influx of foreign currencies, major investments in Lebanese real estate and other ventures by the capitalists from the Arabian Peninsula, the transit of goods imported by Syria, Iraq, and Jordan, and its growing importance as the banking center of the Middle East. In fact, even though Lebanon was losing a certain part of its literate population through emigration, it was also receiving immigrants, particularly unskilled labor in the construction sectors. Thus for example, partly because of better opportunities and pay in Lebanon, partly because of the stultifying measures applied to Syria's economy under its socialist regime, close to 300,000 Syrian laborers found employment in Lebanon with little likelihood of ever returning to their home country. But this thoroughly laissez-faire economy had no substantial brake on the accumulation of excessive wealth, such as an adequate system of taxation, and it was bound to produce inequalities in the distribution of income, with certain areas of the country, particularly the southern regions inhabited by the Shia population, feeling particularly underprivileged.

Lebanon's foreign and Arab relations also caused persistent problems. The first and foremost of these was, of course, the issue of surviving as an independent entity against the propagandistic, political, and in some cases coercive policies and slogans of Pan-Arabism emanating during Nasser's time primarily from Cairo but also from other Pan-Arab centers such as Damascus. Here the essentially domestic problem of national identity was inextricably interwoven with Lebanon's foreign policy. The Lebanese were divided into the Lebanon-firsters and the Arab-firsters, and it required tremendous skill on the part of any group of leaders ruling the country to reconcile both tendencies. The issue of survival was not limited to the assertion of independence from the surrounding Arab sea. There was also the problem of security and territorial integrity vis-à-vis Israel. Ever since the establishment of the state of Israel, there was a fear in Lebanon lest Israel, following Ben

Gurion's ideas, lay claim to the southern part of the country up to the Litani River.[6] Moreover, this fear was intensified by the concern that, in case of any aggravation of relations between Israel and Syria, Israel might be tempted to enter and occupy part of the Lebanese territory in a military operation directed against Damascus.

It is not surprising, therefore, that in its position of weakness and insecurity, Lebanon looked toward some stronger foreign friends for protection. The Western nations in general and the United States in particular (especially since its military intervention in 1958) were obviously regarded by the Lebanese establishment as actual or potential guarantors of the Lebanese independence and integrity. By the same token, Lebanon's leaders were looking for a rapproachement with and assistance from conservative countries such as Saudi Arabia, Jordan, and—under propitious circumstances—even Egypt. But this search for primarily Western protection had to be done discreetly and tactfully so as not to irritate Lebanon's Pan-Arab neighbors or to stir domestic division that might lead to renewed violence. Even with their traditional friendship with the United States, the Lebanese leaders, to accentuate their ostensible freedom of action, would occasionally turn to the Soviet bloc for trade or assistance. Thus in November 1971, Lebanon and the Soviet Union concluded an agreement for the purchase of $15 million of Soviet weapons. The Lebanese government maintained that a deal of this sort did not compromise Lebanon's neutrality and was dictated merely by economic considerations.

Lebanon's relations with Syria continued to be delicate. On the one hand, Syria was the traditional heartland of Arabism. On the other, since its union with Egypt in 1958 but particularly since the rise of the Baath party in the spring of 1963, Syria was ruled by military dictatorships with socialist ideology and as such contrasted profoundly with Lebanon. Syria had many ways of exerting pressure on Lebanon: it could close its borders for transit of Lebanese goods, it could stop the flow of Iraqi or Saudi oil to the Lebanese maritime terminals, it could ban the travel of its own tourists to Lebanese resorts during the holidays and the hot seasons, it could influence the Palestinian refugees in Lebanon, and it could also use Syrian laborers working in Lebanon for political purposes. In fact, Syria resorted at one time or another to all of these measures whenever a dispute arose with the Lebanese government.

Lebanon also had to deal with the presence of many refugee Palestinians on its territory. The numerous refugee camps constituted the natural ground for recruitment of the Palestinian resistance fighters, the so-called *fedayeen*. Their growing militancy, the raids they executed from Lebanon into Israel, and their exclusion of Lebanese authorities from their camps provided a number of irritations between

---

[6]For a historical Israeli claim to southern Lebanon, see Alan R. Taylor, "Vision and Intent in Zionist Thought," in Ibrahim Abu Lughod, ed., *The Transformation of Palestine* (Evanston, Ill., 1971), pp. 20–22. Taylor gives the following quotation from *A Zionist Primer,* published in 1917 by the Zionist Organization of America: "There in our own land, we the Hebrews of long standing and you the Hebrews to come, will unitedly lay our hands on every spot which once belonged to us: from Sidon to Sukkoth, from Tadmor to Ur-Kasdim, from the Mediterranean to the Red Sea, from the mighty Euphrates to the far-stretching Desert." Moreover, Taylor's article contains a map indicating the boundaries claimed by the World Zionist Organization in 1919. For allusions to ancient Israel's access to southern Lebanon's ports, see David Ben Gurion, *Rebirth and Destiny of Israel* (New York, 1954), pp. 298–313.

them and their reluctant hosts. Moreover, their activities invariably provoked Israeli reprisals against the Lebanese territory, in the course of which civilian populations were exposed to many sufferings.

The Presidency of Fuad Chehab, 1958–1964

It is against these persistent issues and trends in Lebanese politics that one should evaluate the record of Lebanon following the 1958 crisis. The presidency of Fuad Chehab was one of relative tranquility. The president himself, who had been commander in chief of the Lebanese army, before assuming the presidential office adhered rather scrupulously to neutrality in the Lebanese political process. Having been in command of the Lebanese army during both the crisis of 1952 and that of 1958, in each case he refused to let the military forces serve the ends of one or another contender for public office even if one were actually President of the Republic. With this record he appeared a perfectly acceptable candidate for the presidency after the emotional aggravation and polarization that occurred in the course of the 1958 fighting. Actually, he was more than a mere domestic compromise candidate; he was also a compromise figure from the international point of view inasmuch as his candidacy was discussed by the special representative of the United States Robert Murphy and President Nasser prior to the presidential election in Lebanon.[7] But the very fact that he was acceptable to Nasser meant that he could not truly identify himself with the "Lebanon-first" outlook. Of course, as chief executive of an independent state, he had to guard its full independence. At the same time, however, in his public pronouncements he tried to avoid any accents that might be irritating to a Pan-Arab point of view. He appeared to have earned Nasser's trust, and therefore under his presidency Lebanon was spared the more aggressive activities of Nasser's agents, which in the past had often been geared to undermine the Lebanese system. His acceptance by Nasser and his neutrality in the 1958 civil war had earned him also popularity with Moslem masses in Lebanon. This support was an important factor in the relative stability of his presidency. Naturally, many Christian leaders were less than happy with what they believed to be Chehab's pliability vis-à-vis Cairo. On the other hand, they hesitated to launch any overt campaign against him because the country badly needed peace and time to recover after the trauma of 1958.

The Lebanese constitution had vested the President of the Republic with considerable power.[8] Chehab discernibly tended to maximize the presidential prerogatives. One of the instruments of his internal policies was the military intelligence department, popularly known in Lebanon as the Deuxième Bureau. Certain political leaders were concerned about the activities of that department and even expressed fears about an undue growth of military influence in Lebanon. By the same token, Chehab's ambivalent attitude toward Egypt and Pan-Arabism was a contributing

[7]For details on Chehab's candidacy, see Robert Murphy, *Diplomat among Warriors* (New York, 1964), p. 411.

[8]Text in Helen Miller Davis, ed., *Constitutions, Electoral Laws, Treaties of States in the Near and Middle East*, 2d ed. (Durham, N.C., 1953), pp. 291–305.

factor to a strange episode that occurred at the end of 1961. On December 31, a small military detachment led by an officer identified as a member of the Syrian Nationalist Social party (P.P.S.), using a few tanks, made an attempt to capture certain strong points in Beirut and overthrow the existing regime. The episode had certain motivational and ideological murkiness about it. Although the P.P.S. had in the past enjoyed considerable influence in Lebanon and Syria, since 1955–1956 it had lost much power and appeal. The attempt failed and the government emerged from this brief trial unscathed. The event, however, provided fresh evidence of a pervasive malaise in the Lebanese system and the possibility that some ambitious and desperate individuals would resort to violence to attain their ends.

The Presidency of Charles Helou, 1964–1970

The Lebanese constitution forbids a second term for any president. In order to be reelected, therefore, any incumbent must seek an amendment to the constitution, and in order to obtain it, he must ensure that he has an adequate qualified majority in the parliament. Almost every president in Lebanon's history has been tempted or has tried to secure such an amendment but these attempts in the past had ended in protests, disturbances, and violence. Whatever thoughts President Chehab might have had about a second term, he decided not to seek the amendment of the constitution and allowed his term to come to a peaceful end in late summer of 1964. In August of that year the parliament elected Charles Helou as president. Politically, Helou could be considered as his predecessor's protegé and nominee. Hence even despite the official abandonment of the presidential office, Chehab could still exercise influence upon the political process of Lebanon and thus ensure a certain continuity of his concepts and policies. Apart from a close relationship with President Helou, Chehab had a dedicated group of the Deuxième Bureau officers who still were inclined to follow his guidance. It should be added that the only counter-candidate was the leader of the Lebanese Phalanges, Pierre Gemayel, but in the political climate of compromise with Egypt and the Pan-Arab trends, Gemayel was strictly identified with the Lebanon-first ideology and thus was too partisan for the spirit of the times, and had no real chance of being elected.

President Helou, a former newspaper editor and writer, was a well-known figure in Lebanon's public life and somehow avoided throughout his career an identification with any strong or extreme point of view. He inherited from his predecessor the task of conciliating various centrifugal tendencies in Lebanon as well as keeping Lebanon independent and separate while maintaining good relations with revolutionary Pan-Arab centers such as Cairo or Damascus. Under normal circumstances, with tact and a modicum of diplomatic skill, this balancing act required of virtually any Lebanese president would not have been impossible. However, the regional and international situation became aggravated during Helou's presidency. Two factors in particular influenced the conditions in Lebanon: the growth of Pan-Arab militancy in Cairo and the deterioration of Arab-Israeli relations coupled with the presence of the restless Palestinians in Lebanon. This was the era of the prolonged Egyptian intervention in the civil war in Yemen, a war which lasted from 1962 to 1967 and which also involved intervention of Saudi Arabia on the side of the royalist tribes to counter the Egyptian military presence on Yemen territory. The Yemenese civil was regarded by many observers as an ideological replica of the civil war in Spain in the 1930s and as such it tended to polarize revolutionary forces against the conservatives in the entire region of the Middle East. It also had its reflection in the political processes in Lebanon.

The single event, however, that most influenced the internal and external Lebanese situation was the June 1967 war fought between Egypt, Syria, Jordan, and Iraq on the one hand and Israel on the other. This war, which ended in Arab defeat and a second Arab exodus from Palestine, intensified the feeling of hostility and desire for revenge of the Palestinian masses in exile in the states surrounding Israel. The erstwhile inactive refugee camps of Palestinian displaced persons now became recruiting ground for the *fedayeen* who began to assert themselves in Lebanon ever more aggressively. Lebanon was thus embarrassed because in contrast to Egypt, Jordan, or Syria, Lebanon was the so-called "non-confrontation state." There was, in fact, a paradox in the situation. While militant Baathist Syria served as the main shelter, recruiting and training area, and supporter of the Palestinian struggle for the recovery of their homeland, the *fedayeen* rarely if ever penetrated into the Israeli territory from Syria. Instead they chose, partly on their own and partly on Syrian instructions, to make incursions into Israel from Lebanese territory, thus provoking Israeli retaliations. This fact, plus the inability of the Lebanese authorities to gain access to the refugee camps, encouraged anti-Palestinian and anti-Pan-Arab attitudes in Lebanon. This trend found its expression in the birth of a political coalition known as the Tripartite Alliance which made its appearance in the late 1960s during Helou's presidency. It was a predominantly Christian grouping composed of Pierre Gemayel's Phalange party, Camille Chamoun's Liberal party, and Raymond Eddé's National Bloc. Their objective was to maintain full political independence of Lebanon and to assert Lebanese sovereignty both abroad and at home as against the "state-in-state" situation which the massive presence of militant Palestinians created. The Tripartite Alliance scored considerable gains in the parliamentary elections of 1968 and maintained a major influence upon both the parliament and politics in general to the end of the Helou presidency and through the first years of the next term.

That same year, 1968, was punctuated by a serious aggravation in Israeli-Lebanese relations. In retaliation for the *fedayeen* attack on an Israeli airliner in Athens, the Israelis launched a major air raid on Beirut airport in December 1968. In the course of this raid thirteen civilian airplanes were destroyed, a virtual annihilation of Lebanon's civil aviation fleet. The raid was very embarrassing, incidentally, to the United States because it came just after a sale of jet fighters by Washington to Israel.

The episode intensified the efforts of both the right-wing Christian politicians and the Lebanese authorities to curb the activity of the Palestinian *fedayeen* in and from Lebanese territory. Attempts of the Lebanese army and police to gain access to the refugee camps, by then completely under control of the armed *fedayeen* detachments, met with resistance and resulted in numerous military clashes between the two parties. At this point President Nasser offered mediation and on November 2,

1969, a Lebanese delegation headed by the commander of the army, General Emile Bustani, and the Palestinian representatives headed by Yassir Arafat concluded in Cairo an agreement which specified the mutual rights and obligations of both parties and put some restraints on the freedom of movement of the *fedayeen*. However, the *fedayeen* retained military control of the Palestinian refugee camps in Lebanon. The agreement was never formally published by the Lebanese government but its terms became known through the Lebanese newspapers.[9] General Bustani became the target of strong criticism for making concessions incompatible with the sovereignty of Lebanon, and under these pressures was obliged to resign in January 1970.

The conclusion of the Cairo Agreement was preceded by a prolonged cabinet crisis which in fact left Lebanon for seven months between April and November 1969 without a full cabinet and prime minister. These functions were performed merely on an interim basis by former Prime Minister Rashid Karamah and his former cabinet members pending the formation of a new government. For President Helou, like Chehab a compromise figure, the situation was most embarrassing. But even with his intention to cultivate the good will of the Pan-Arab circles in the Middle East region, he was compelled to declare at one point that the activities of the *fedayeen* in Lebanon constituted an infringement on Lebanese sovereignty.

For as long as he could, however, Helou tried to avoid an open showdown with the Palestinians and to reach a compromise of which the Cairo Agreement was the prime example. Similarly, he felt that it would be important to have a political leader of known Pan-Arab tendency and proven friendliness to the *fedayeen* in the key ministry of the interior. Consequently, when a new cabinet was formed in November 1969 under the premiership of Rashid Karamah, the militant Druze leader and head of the Socialist Progressive Party, Kamal Jumblat, was appointed minister of interior with the task of devising an appropriate formula for coexistence with the Palestinian *fedayeen*.

Lebanon's political life showed an increasing tendency toward polarization. Jumblat succeeded in avoiding any major crisis with the *fedayeen* but this was largely because of his willingness to ignore repeated violations of the Cairo Agreement by the militant Palestinians. Moreover, disregarding possible danger to the cohesion of the Lebanese system, Jumblat legalized in 1970 both the Communist party of Lebanon and the Arab Nationalist Movement (ANM) of George Habash. The same year witnessed the emergence of a strong leader of the Shia Moslem community, Imam Musa Sadr, under whose auspices a higher Shia council was formed. This development signaled a new political assertiveness in the Shia community in Lebanon. Hitherto the Shias constituted a rather underprivileged group which was led by major feudal families such as the Assads from their base in Sidon in southern Lebanon. In contrast, Musa Sadr was a dynamic leader whose power base rested on the peasants in the southern district as well as on the Shia migrants who, fleeing Israeli bombings of their border villages, flocked to Beirut and settled in makeshift camps around the city. A revisionist and radicalizing mood was also felt among the Sunni Moslem masses, perhaps best expressed by the demand of the

---

[9]Substance of the Cairo agreement may be found in *New York Times*, Nov. 4, 1969.

Moslem youth organization Najjada, under Adnan Hakim, that the tradition of a presidency reserved for a Christian should be abandoned in favor of an office opened to any deserving contender.

The Presidency of Suleiman Franjiyeh, 1970–1976.

The reaction of the Christian and right-wing Lebanon-first elements against Pan-Arab trends and Palestinian assertiveness found its reflection in the growing opposition to the legacy of President Chehab and his successor, President Helou. That legacy, represented by the "Nahjist" grouping in the Lebanese parliament still carried considerable weight. But by midsummer 1970 the Lebanon-first tendency appeared to be gaining in strength. The test came with the election of a new president. There were two candidates: Elias Sarkis, president of the Central Bank of Lebanon and a Nahjist (Chehabist) candidate, against Suleiman Franjiyeh, who was unaffiliated with but supported by the Tripartite Alliance. It was a close contest which resulted in Franjiyeh's election on the third ballot by a majority of one vote over his opponent. The election took place on August 17, 1970, and the new president was formally installed on September 23. This period coincided with a major showdown betwen the Palestinian *fedayeen* and King Hussein in Jordan. During this "black September," as the Palestinian militants referred to it, the *fedayeen* as an organized military force were effectively defeated by King Hussein's army and by 1971 were completely ejected from Jordanian territory. Their elimination from Jordan promptly found its sequel in the increase and intensification of their activities in Lebanon. Choosing the Arkoub region in southeastern Lebanon as a major area of concentration and freely using the so-called Arafat trail to carry supplies and personnel between Syria and Lebanon, the *fedayeen* resorted to more and more frequent incursions against Israel from Lebanese territory.

In the midst of the feverish atmosphere President Franjiyeh assumed his office. He himself was not only a typical, traditional *zaim* who based his political influence on sectarian and family-territorial factors, but also a strong Lebanon-firster determined to preserve Lebanon's sovereignty and territorial integrity and save it from the condition known (before September 1970) as "Jordanization." Although a skillful and experienced politician and parliamentarian with considerable cabinet experience, Franjiyeh had to face the almost impossible task of effecting harmony and reconciliation at a time of growing ideological and political polarization. This polarization could be observed on two levels. There was a widening chasm between the Nahjist (Chehabist) grouping credited with appeasing the Palestinians and the Pan-Arab trends in general, and the right-wing, mostly Christian elements represented by or akin to the Tripartite Alliance. On another level, an informal coalition was coming into being between the less privileged elements in the population composed of Sunni Moslem masses, militant Pan-Arab groups noted for their pro-Nasser emotionalism, a variety of socialist elements inspired or led by Kamal Jumblat, and the Shia population both in the south and in the refugee camps around the capital city. This coalition, in turn, was opposed by the more militant Christian elements particularly those grouped in or around the Phalange party of Pierre Gemayel. The elections in the spring of 1972 further accentuated this polarization.

While the Tripartite Alliance emerged largely victorious, the left-wing groups also gained ground and, in particular, Kamal Jumblat found himself in control of about fifteen votes in the parliament. This polarization led to a second showdown between the Lebanese government and the Palestinian *fedayeen*. It occurred at the end of April and the beginning of May, and this time the Lebanese army was actively involved in fighting the *fedayeen* for control of the refugee camps and authority over the movements of armed Palestinian units in Lebanese territory. The fighting was preceded by a daring Israeli raid on Beirut's residential district, in the course of which the Israeli raiders succeeded in killing three important Palestinian resistance leaders, kidnaping certain *fedayeen,* and escaping unscathed to their home bases.

The flare-up of violence had its repercussions throughout the Arab world. The leader of the revolutionary government in Libya, Colonel Muammar Qadhafi, strongly denounced Lebanon's repressive actions and pledged his support to the *fedayeen*. From then on Qadhafi, a leader known for his militant Pan-Arab views and in control of substantial financial resources, emerged as a critic and enemy of the Lebanese ruling establishment, which he repeatedly accused of subservience to the West and desire to destroy the Palestinian liberation movement. Similarly voices hostile to Lebanon were heard simultaneously, though with varying intensity, in Damascus and Baghdad. In a way typical of its behavior toward Lebanon, Syria "punished" the Lebanese government by promptly closing its border to traffic of men and goods.

It was clear that to be able to assert its full sovereignty and freedom of action, the Lebanese government would have to enlarge its military establishment both to cope more effectively with Israeli reprisal raids and to control the *fedayeen* movements. But as a parliamentary democracy Lebanon was traditionally reluctant to build up a big army. Looking at the record of many neighboring Arab states where the military had overthrown the civilian government and established dictatorships, the Lebanese leaders were afraid to create similar opportunities in their country. Added to this hesitancy was the ingrained reluctance of the oligarchical ruling group and their middle class allies to see themselves heavily taxed for the purpose of maintaining an expensive military force. True enough, in May 1974, President Franjiyeh announced that the government was determined to spend one billion dollars over the next ten years to enlarge and modernize the army. But between this declaration and the actual deeds there was a long way to go. The Lebanese army in the early 1970s numbered only 14,000 men which, added to the police forces, a miniscule navy, and a similarly small air force, gave a total maximum of 20,000 men in the armed forces of the country. At the same time, the cumulative strength of various private militias (i.e., groups controlled either by the Palestinians or by individual leaders and political parties) could easily reach 40,000 when mobilized.

The resolutions adopted by the Arab summit conference in Rabat in October of 1974, whereby the Palestine Liberation Organization (PLO) was recognized as the official spokesman for the Palestinians, and the subsequent invitation of its chairman, Yassir Arafat, to address the United Nations General Assembly had a further polarizing effect on the Lebanese political process. It was Pierre Gemayel's Phalange party that emerged as the main spokesman and actor for the Lebanon-first tendency. On April 13, 1975, a bus carrying a number of Palestinian *fedayeen* was attacked by the Phalanges and the passengers were killed. Without entering here into a discussion of the provocations that the Phalange members had experienced in the past, one may say that this single event triggered a chain reaction that developed into a full-scale civil war in Lebanon. Violence erupted between the Moslem and left-wing elements on the one hand and the Christian elements, particularly those of the Phalanges and Camille Chamoun's Liberal party, on the other. The existing cabinet of a younger but not very experienced leader, Amin Hafez, and that of his successor, Rashid es-Sulh, were unable to cope with the situation, and President Franjiyeh appointed retired General Nureddin Rifai as prime minister. Rifai formed the first military cabinet in Lebanon's history. The whole experiment, however, lasted only a few days between May 15 and 23 because of the widespread protest, particularly in the Moslem communities of Lebanon, against this type of government. Following a few weeks of a caretaker government exercised by General Rifai, on July 1, 1975, newly-appointed Premier Rashid Karamah formed a six-man cabinet from which the most militant elements of both the left and the right were excluded. Thus neither the Phalanges nor the Progressive Socialists of Kamal Jumblat had their representatives in the new government. The cabinet was composed of three Moslems: the Premier himself, Emir Majid Arslan (a Druze leader), and Adel Osseiran (a Shia leader); and of three Christians: Ghassan Tweini (Greek-Orthodox), as vice-premier, Philippe Takla (Greek-Catholic), and Camille Chamoun (Maronite). Each of the ministers was entrusted with several portfolios, that of the minister of interior being assigned to Camille Chamoun. Although the cabinet made strenuous efforts to put an end to intermittent fighting, it never gained full control over the situation. On the one side there was a Moslem-leftist coalition of various elements hostile to the existing system in Lebanon and often representing the have-not strata. On the other, there were Christian militants anxious to assert and preserve Lebanon's sovereignty and its existing socioeconomic system. Moreover, the Moslem rebel leaders, particularly Farouk Mukaddam in Tripoli and Ibrahim Quleilat in Beirut, were advancing demands for a radical overhaul of the entire political system in Lebanon. By this they meant an end to the existing confessional system, parity for Moslems and Christians as a minimum demand, an end to the Christian monopoly of the presidency, and a thorough economic and social reform for the benefit of the underprivileged masses.

Certain elements among the Palestinian *fedayeen*, particularly the Popular Front for Liberation of Palestine (PFLP) led by George Habash, participated in the struggle on the side of the Moslem-leftist coalition. But Yassir Arafat with the main body of the PLO and his own guerrilla organization, Fatah, were reluctant to commit their forces to the battle partly because of their greater moderation in the ideological sense and partly out of consideration that the Palestinian refugees as well as fighters were not entirely Moslem but included a good number of Christians. On the other hand, until midwinter 1975–1976 the government was reluctant to use the army to quell the disturbances. The responsible leaders were afraid that a multireligious army, predominantly under command of Christian officers, would disintegrate if it took part in fighting between religious factions. Despite this reluctance, the army was brought into the conflict in two stages: first, in September, it was sent to the northern area to serve as a shield separating the Moslems in Tripoli from the Christians in the president's home district of Zgharta; and then in December and January, to prevent the advancing Moslem forces from overwhelming certain districts of Beirut. Repeated cease-fires (twenty-one of them in the course of the fighting) were violated and the civil war was resumed. The situation tilted in favor of the Moslem-leftist forces in January 1976 when the PLO, reacting to the Christian Lebanese attack on the Tel-Zaatar refugee camp, entered the fight in support of the Moslem-leftist coalition.

At this stage Syria made a major mediating effort which, on January 22, resulted in an agreement between the warring parties. The truce agreement provided for immediate negotiations aiming at a reform of the Lebanese constitutional system. The negotiations had a tripartite character: the official Lebanese side, the Moslem rebel side (including the Palestinians), and the Syrians as mediators. On February 14, President Franjiyeh broadcast an announcement of a mutually agreed-upon reform program (signed in Damascus on February 7). This program to be submitted to the Parliament for approval contained the following points: (1) There would be an equality in numerical representation between Moslems and Christians in the ninety-nine-seat parliament instead of the old proportional formula of 6 to 5 in favor of the Christians. (2) The prime minister would henceforth be chosen by the parliament rather than appointed by the president. (3) The existing proportional quotas for religious communities in the civil service would be abolished except in the highest ranking posts of the government. (4) The existing constitutional custom providing for the President of the Republic to be a Maronite Christian would be maintained. (5) Likewise the constitutional custom of having a Sunni prime minister and a Shia speaker of the house would be continued.[10]

In addition to announcing these five points, President Franjiyeh reaffirmed the validity of the Cairo Agreement of November 2, 1969, regulating the relations between the Lebanese authorities and the Palestinians. The president took this opportunity to remind the Palestinians that their presence in the country should "not clash with the sovereignty of Lebanon." However, as if to reassure them he affirmed that "Lebanon is an Arab country—sovereign, free, and independent."[11]

The successful conclusion of the agreement could undoubtedly be credited to the active role of the Syrian delegation headed by Syria's foreign minister Abdul Halim Khaddam, who spent nearly a month in Beirut trying to iron out a peace formula between the warring parties. Alas, Syria was soon to experience frustration in her peacemaking role.

At the time the agreement was concluded, the military position of the Christian forces was very precarious. The extreme elements of the Moslem-leftist coalition decided to reject the agreement and press for a decisive offensive which would result in victory and in a new, dictated, settlement in Lebanon according to their

[10]Text in Kamal S. Salibi, *Crossroads to Civil War: Lebanon 1958-1976* (New York, 1976), pp. 163-164.
[11]*New York Times*, Feb. 15, 1976.

blueprints. It is in this spirit that the leftist leader Kamal Jumblat was reputed to have said to President Assad when visiting him in Damascus late in March, "Give us two more weeks and we fill finish them [the Christians]."

Angered by this defiance of his peace endeavors, in April 1976, Assad dispatched 30,000 Syrian troops into Lebanon to pacify the country and ensure the implementation of the February program. The Syrian force was accompanied by units of the Palestine Liberation Army (PLA), commanded by General Misbah el-Budeiri, and by the detachments of Saiqa, a Palestinian *fedayeen* group, both under Syria's overall control.

In deciding to intervene, Assad desired to put an end to the Lebanese civil war which caused the exodus of 300,000 Syrian workers employed in Lebanon and virtually closed Beirut as a major port of entry for imported goods destined for Syria. He also feared that the PLO and its allies, hitherto subject to Syrian influence, would form an alliance with the rival revolutionary states in Iraq and Libya. If such a militant leftist-Palestinian regime were to be established in Lebanon, it might provoke a preventive attack by Israel, with attendant deployment of Israeli forces on Syria's western border. Finally, continuation of civil war might result in the partition of Lebanon into a Christian and a Moslem state. Assad opposed such a solution as setting a dangerous precedent of political separation for territorially compact religious or ethnic groups within the existing states in the area (for example, the Alawis and Druzes in Syria) and as legitimizing Israel as a state based on religion and ethnicity.

At a meeting held in Cairo on June 10, the Arab League gave a formal seal of approval to Syria's military expedition by deciding to create a multinational Arab Deterrent Force (ADF), to be composed of Syrian, Saudi, Sudanese, Libyan, United Arab Emirates, and South Yemeni troops. The bulk of the ADF, however, was to remain Syrian.

In advancing into Lebanon, Syria encountered military and political obstacles. The leftist-Moslem-Palestinian coalition put up a stiff resistance. The paradox of the situation was that some Palestinian forces (PLA and Saiqa) as part of the Syrian command fought other Palestinians grouped in PLO and PFLP units. Eventually, the rebel forces were compelled to withdraw southward. On the other hand, Israel had publicly warned that crossing by the Syrian troops of an ill-defined "red line" (presumably the Litani River and its eastern prolongation) in the southern direction would not be tolerated. But, inasmuch as Syria decided to heed the Israeli warning, southern Lebanon became a no-man's land in which the retreating PLO troops engaged in warfare with the local Christian militias, which were increasingly supplied by Israel with arms and equipment. Thus Lebanon, for all practical purposes, became roughly divided into three zones: the northern and central-eastern part (with mixed, but predominantly Sunni Moslem population) in which Syria exercised effective authority and restored a large measure of tranquility; the central-western area with the port of Junieh as its main town, which constituted an almost purely Christian enclave likely to become a separate mini-state if Lebanon were to be partitioned; and the southern districts, with a Shia majority, which escaped Syrian pacification endeavors.

By the fall of 1976, Suleiman Franjiyeh's term came to an end and he was replaced as president by Elias Sarkis. The new president's ability to govern, however, was severely limited because the truncated Lebanese army was inferior in strength to various Christian militias and Moslem and Palestinian groups. Moreover, the Christian camp itself was divided: while Sarkis (as well as Franjiyeh before him) wanted to cooperate with Syria and preserve Lebanon as a single political entity, such leaders as Camille Chamoun and Pierre Gemayel opposed continued Syrian presence, veered toward a concept of a separate Christian state in Lebanon, and accepted arms and assistance from Israel. These differences were further accentuated by a number of political assassinations which claimed such victims as Tony Franjiyeh, the former president's son, and Kamal Jumblat.

Growing tension between Syrian troops and Christian militias led by 1978 to open warfare in the course of which the Syrians, in a protracted siege, shelled Beirut's Christian quarter of Ashrafiyeh.

In the meantime, continuous fighting in the south between the Palestinian fighters and the smaller but determined Christian militias led to an invasion of that area by Israel on March 14, 1978, and occupation of most of the Lebanese territory south of the Litani River. A Palestinian terrorist attack which claimed thirty-four victims on a bus north of Tel Aviv provided the immediate cause for Israeli invasion. More fundamental, however, was Israel's desire to "root out the terrorist bases" of the PLO in southern Lebanon.

The United States expressed support for Lebanon's territorial integrity and on its initiative the UN Security Council passed on March 19 a unanimous resolution which (a) called on Israel to withdraw from the Lebanese territory and (b) established a UN interim peace-keeping force (UNIFIL) in Lebanon. Such a force, composed of troops of neutral nations (Sweden and others), soon began its duties in southern Lebanon. After ninety-one days of occupation, in mid-June Israeli forces withdrew from the Lebanese territory.

As the year 1978 was drawing to a close, Lebanon's fundamental problems remained unresolved. Syrian occupation—legalized under the guise of the Arab Deterrent Force—failed to restore peace to the entire territory of Lebanon, partly because of militant Christian resistance and partly because of Israel's opposition to the Syrian presence in the south. In spite of the conclusion of the January 1976 agreement providing for a constitutional reform, no real progress was made on its implementation. Lebanon remained highly factionalized not only between the main Christian and Moslem parts of the population but also among the Christians themselves. If return to the concept of a unitary (though pluralistic) state proved unworkable, two other alternatives remained: partition into the Christian and Moslem entities (a solution difficult to achieve because of the pattern of demographic distribution) and cantonization. The latter involved the division of Lebanon into a number of political units based on religion or, in some cases, ethnic affiliation within a federal union. Should such a system be adopted, allocation of powers between the federal and the cantonal authorities would still require further elaboration.

Regardless of the ultimate political forms, one should bear in mind that the

Moslem-leftist rebellion had as its real cause not so much the way the highest authorities in the country were constituted as rather a series of profound socioeconomic grievances voiced by the depressed segments of the population against the dominant position of the priviledged classes. Change in the formal political system did not automatically entail the implementation of those reforms that would ensure the well-being of the masses. Any new constitutional arrangement could at the most provide only a general framework within which the wisdom and statesmanship of Lebanon's new leaders would be tested.

CHAPTER X

Israel

The hope of one day returning to the Promised Land has never died among the Jews. Religious Zionism has been cultivated in various centers of the Diaspora (Dispersion) throughout history, and in the nineteenth century a number of Jews came to Palestine to settle in Jerusalem, Safed, and Tiberias. Many of these were the so-called *Halukah* (charity) Jews, supported by funds from abroad. This yearning to return to Zion was especially strong among the Russian and east European Jews, who suffered manifold disabilities and frequent persecutions. The intensification of anti-Semitism in Russia in the last two decades of the nineteenth century gave rise to the creation, in Odessa, of the organization Hovevei Zion[1] and the establishment in 1882 of the first Zionist colonies in Palestine. These were Rishon le Zion in Judea, Zichron Jacob in Samaria, and Rosh Pina in Galilee. In the 1880s other settlements followed. They were peopled mostly by Jews from Russia, Rumania, Galicia, and Lithuania. Wealthy Jewish financiers in the West, such as Baron Edmond de Rothschild, contributed generously to aid the pioneers. A Jewish Colonization Association (ICA), founded by Baron Maurice de Hirsch, undertook the task of buying land in Palestine and provided the settlers with necessary implements and capital.

The Zionist Movement

In 1896, Dr. Theodor Herzl, a native of Budapest and Paris correspondent of the *Neue Freie Presse* of Vienna, gave Zionism a definitely political turn. At the age of thirty-six he wrote in his book *Judenstaat* ("The Jewish State") as follows: "Our national character is too historically famous and in spite of every degradation, too fine to make its annihilation desirable." "The distinctive nationality of the Jews neither can, will, nor must be destroyed." "The Jewish question . . . is a national question which can be solved only by making it a political world-question to be discussed and settled by the civilized nations of the world in council."[2]

In 1897, Herzl founded *Die Welt,* a weekly, which became an official

---

[1]With Leon Pinsker and Asher Ginsberg (Ahad Ha'am) as leaders. At the same time Eliezer Ben Yehuda preached the revival of the Hebrew tongue.
[2]Theodor Herzl, *The Jewish State* (New York, 1943), pp. 38, 24, 20.

mouthpiece for Zionism. In the same year, on his initiative, the first Zionist Congress assembled at Basle, Switzerland. The Congress adopted a resolution favoring "a home in Palestine" for the Jewish people and created the World Zionist Organization, which elected Herzl to its presidency. From that time on Herzl strove to obtain from the Ottoman government permission to create a Jewish charter company for the settlement of Palestine. Inasmuch as this was the period of German-Turkish friendship, he appealed to Kaiser William II to aid him in this quest and suggested that such a company be formed under a German protectorate.

In 1903 mass pogroms of the Jews occurred in Kishinev and Gomel in Russia; these rendered the Jewish question more acute than ever. Herzl negotiated with the British government and obtained from it the offer of Uganda as a territory for settlement. But this offer was rejected in 1904 by the Russian Zionist majority of the Seventh Congress of the World Zionist Organization. The Congress refused to consider any alternatives to Palestine.

In 1904, Herzl died, but Zionism continued to attract ever larger numbers of adherents. It soon grew into a powerful movement, ably financed by the Jewish National Fund (Keren Kayemeth), which was organized to acquire land in Palestine, and by the Palestine Foundation Fund (Keren Hayesod). It developed leftist (Poale Zion), rightist (Mizrahi), and center (General Zionists) political factions, and soon spread throughout the Western Hemisphere. In the United States the Zionist Organization recruited members largely among eastern European Jews, who at that time, because of Russian persecutions, were coming to America in large numbers. Other Jewish communities in the United States—the Sephardi (Spanish) and the German, which were more prosperous and better assimilated—were either indifferent or hostile to Zionism. Yet even among them Zionism found converts.

Zionism was and is a national movement, and as such it has encountered opposition among the Jews themselves. This opposition has been dictated by several considerations. Ultra-Orthodox Jews objected to the political aspects of the movement, believing that the return to Zion must be brought about by divine intervention and not by temporal agencies. Such views were cultivated by Agudath Israel.

The Socialists (and later the Communists) considered Zionism as a reactionary bourgeois movement. The rabbis of the reformed synagogues and their adherents opposed Zionism on the basis of its nationalist character. Believing that Judaism denotes religion and not nationality, they represented assimilationist tendencies. In Great Britain two Jewish organizations, the Board of Deputies of British Jews[3] and the Anglo-Jewish Association, opposed Zionism on this ground. Their opposition grew more vocal during World War I, when it became known that Dr. Chaim Weizmann was trying to secure an official British declaration in favor of Zionism. On May 24, 1917, Montefiore and Alexander, presidents, respectively, of the Anglo-Jewish Association and of the Board of Deputies, published an open protest against the Zionist program in *The Times*. In it they stated that political Zionism was incompatible with the religious basis of Jewry and that it introduced the concept of

---

[3]In 1917, however, a split occurred in the Board, its president being anti-Zionist while the majority were on the side of Zionism.

a secular Jewish nationality, recruited on some loose and obscure principle of race and of ethnographic peculiarity. But this would not be Jewish in any spiritual sense, and its establishment in Palestine would be a denial of all the ideals and hopes by which the survival of Jewish life in that country commends itself to the Jewish conscience and to Jewish sympathy. On these grounds the Conjoint Committee of the Board of Deputies and the Anglo-Jewish Association deprecates most earnestly the national proposals of the Zionists.[4]

Similar protests were voiced in the United States by the American Jewish Committee, headed during World War I by Jacob H. Schiff, Louis Marshall, and Mayer Sulzberger. Schiff declared on one occasion:

I believe that I am not far wrong if I say that from fifty to seventy per cent of the so-called Jewish Nationalists are either atheists or agnostics and that the great majority of the Jewish Nationalist leaders have absolutely no interest in the Jewish religion.[5]

Mayer Sulzberger, former president of the Court of Common Pleas in Pennsylvania, opposed Zionism on the ground that it constituted a denial of democracy:

Democracy, he said, means that those who live in a country shall select their rulers and shall preserve their powers. Given these principles a Convention of Zionists looking to the government of people who are in Palestine would be in contravention of the plainest principle of democracy. It can have no practical meaning unless its intent is to overslaugh the people who are in Palestine and to deprive them of the right of self-government by substituting the will of persons outside, who may or may not ever see Palestine.[6]

The Zionists insisted on the national—and to some extent racial—definition of Jewry. Dr. Weizmann in a reply to Alexander and Montefiore stated positively:

It is strictly a question of fact that the Jews are a nationality. An overwhelming majority of them has always had the conviction that they were a nationality, which has been shared by non-Jews in all countries.[7]

Following a similar line of thought, Justice Brandeis formulated a definition that contained such concepts as "blood":

The meaning of the word Jewish in the term Jewish Problem must be accepted as coextensive with the disabilities which it is our problem to remove. It is the non-Jews who create the disabilities and in so doing give definition to the term Jew. These disabilities extend substantially to all of Jewish *blood*. [They] do not end with a renunciation of faith, however sincere. They do not end with the elimination, however complete, of external Jewish mannerisms. The disabilities do not end ordinarily until

[4]Quoted by J. M. N. Jeffries, *Palestine: The Reality* (London, 1939), p. 147.
[5]*Ibid*. p. 153.
[6]*Ibid*.
[7]*Ibid.*, p. 149.

the Jewish *blood* has been so thoroughly diluted by repeated intermarriages as to result in practically obliterating the Jew.[8]

These quotations from leading Zionist and anti-Zionist authorities illustrate the profound split over the problem of Palestine among the Jewish people themselves. As H. M. Kallen has stated, it was a struggle between "assimilationist individualism and self-respecting nationalism." This struggle was difficult for the Zionists, especially for Dr. Weizmann, in England, where many prominent Jewish families, members of the British aristocracy, held influential positions in business and public life[9] and refused to compromise their British status by identifying themselves with Jewish nationalism. Yet eventually the Zionists emerged victorious. In the Balfour Declaration they obtained a formal acknowledgement of their importance as spokesmen for the Jewish world.[10] The Declaration set the stage for a new period in Jewish history—the building of a national home in Palestine. In this new period the Zionists were to transform themselves from mere missionaries into state builders. They applied themselves to the new task with zeal and vigor.

The British Mandate and the Jewish Agency

The opening of the Peace Conference brought to Paris strong Zionist delegations, both from Great Britain and from the United States. Their activities and their success have already been recounted. On April 25, 1920, the Allied Supreme Council allocated the mandate over Palestine to Great Britain, and on July 22, 1922, Great Britain was formally confirmed as mandatory power by the Council of the League of Nations. The mandate expressly provided for a Jewish national home in Palestine, incorporating into its text, almost verbatim, the Balfour Declaration. The mandatory power was to be responsible for the development of self-governing institutions. Article 4 dealt with the recognition of a Jewish Agency to co-operate with the mandatory power in establishing a Jewish national home. It added that "the Zionist organization . . . shall be recognized as such agency." Article 6 imposed upon the mandatory power the duty of facilitating Jewish immigration and land settlement "while ensuring that the rights and position of other sections of the population are not prejudiced." Article 18 contained a clause forbidding discrimination between members of the League of Nations, and Article 25 made possible the

---

[8]Italics mine. Quoted from *Brandeis on Zionism, A Collection of Addresses and Statements by Louis D. Brandeis,* with a foreword by Mr. Justice Felix Frankfurter (Washington, D.C., 1942), p. 14. H. M. Kallen, who in his *Zionism and World Politics* (New York, 1921) seems to espouse the Zionist cause, terms the Jews "members of the race" (p. 53). Dr. Weizmann similarly refers to the Jews as "an old race" in *International Affairs* (Sept.–Oct. 1936), p. 673.

[9]Such as Lord Melchett of the Imperial Chemical Industries; Sir Philip Sassoon, Lloyd George's private secretary; Sir Herbert Louis Samuel, home secretary, and other members of the Samuel family; Edwin Montagu, secretary of state for India; Marquess of Reading, lord chief justice and later viceroy of India; and the Rothschilds. Some of the above-mentioned were later converted to Zionism.

[10]See above, p. 82.

exemption of Transjordan, as part of the mandate, from the provisions of the Balfour Declaration.[11]

With the assignment of the mandate at San Remo in 1920, the British military government gave way to a civil administration. Sir Herbert Samuel, member of a prominent British-Jewish family but not a Zionist, was appointed first high commissioner of Palestine. The Jewish population of the Holy Land, at the time of the armistice, numbered 55,000 souls. (See Appendix I.) The new civil administration opened the gates for immigration into Palestine and this immediately brought Arab protests. In 1921 anti-Jewish disturbances broke out. They provoked Winston Churchill, at that time colonial secretary, into writing the so-called Churchill Memorandum (June 3, 1922), in which he reaffirmed Britain's desire to create a Jewish national home in Palestine; reassured the Arabs that the Balfour Declaration did not contemplate that Palestine as a whole was to be converted into a Jewish national state; and proclaimed that Britain would facilitate Jewish immigration to the extent dictated by the economic absorptive capacity of the country. This statement met with the formal approval of the Zionist Organization but elicited protests from Arab spokesmen. From that time on, the government of Palestine issued yearly immigration quotas, and the number of Jews in the land steadily increased.

It is proper, perhaps, at this point briefly to describe the organization of both Jewish and Arab communities. Article 4 of the mandate provided for a Jewish Agency, which would cooperate with the mandatory administration in the establishment of a national homeland. Originally the Jewish Agency was composed of Zionists only, but in 1929 it was enlarged to comprise non-Zionist Jews as well. The president of the World Zionist Organization remained, however, president of the Jewish Agency. This agency was the official spokesman of world Jewry with regard to Jewish settlement in Palestine. As such, it cooperated with the mandatory power in many fields including education, health, and agriculture. It was granted by Great Britain official right to select candidates for immigration, and as a result only those who had received the agency's "certificates" could apply for visas to Palestine at the British consulates. The agency also controlled the policies of the Jewish National Fund (Keren Kayemeth) and of the Palestine Foundation Fund (Keren Hayesod). During most of the time that the mandate was in force, Dr. Weizmann was president of the agency by virtue of his leadership in the Zionist Organization. The agency had a standing executive committee in Palestine, headed by David Ben Gurion. Its Foreign Department was administered by Moshe Shertok.

The Jewish Community

Apart from the Jewish Agency, which represented world Jewry, the Jews of Palestine had their own communal organization composed of an elected assembly and a general council (Vaad Leumi). It enjoyed certain rights of self-government. The Jewish community was composed of a number of political parties. These parties were divided into three major groups: (1) parties belonging to the Zionist Organiza-

---

[11]The full text of the mandate for Palestine may be found in Royal Institute of International Affairs, *Great Britain and Palestine* (London, 1946), p. 151.

tion, (2) the Revisionist group which did not belong to the above organization, and (3) the non-Zionist group.

The first or Zionist group was divided again into the following parties: (*a*) Mapai (Miflagath Poalei Eretz Israel), a Socialist Labor party, with the most members and the most power, headed by David Ben Gurion; (*b*) Hashomer Hatzair, a left-wing Socialist party, next largest and favoring a binational Arab-Jewish state; (*c*) Poalei Zion, a small left-wing group; (*d*) The General Zionists, representing the professional and middle class strata; divided in turn into "A" and "B" factions. The "A" faction following Dr. Weizmann's leadership was more progressive and tended to cooperate with the Socialists; and the "B" group was more conservative; (*e*) Mizrahi, an orthodox religious party within the Zionist organization; with rightist tendencies and favoring religious education; (*f*) Aliya Hadasha (New Immigrants party), formed in 1942 from the German, Austrian, and Czech immigrants; critical of the existing Zionist leadership; (*g*) Ihud (Union), an intellectual group headed by Dr. Magnes, president of the Hebrew University of Jerusalem, favoring a binational state in Palestine and largely resigned to Arab supremacy.

The second group was composed of those Zionists who had seceded from the Zionist Organization in 1935 and who had formed the New Zionist Organization, under the leadership of the extremist Vladimir Zhabotinsky. This group, also called Revisionist, violently opposed any policy of moderation and demanded the creation of a Jewish state over the whole of Palestine and Transjordan.

The third group, composed of non-Zionist Jews, organized itself into Agudath Israel, a strictly religious and nonpolitical body. In 1920, Agudath claimed to represent 20 percent of the Jewish inhabitants in Palestine. It differed profoundly from Mizrahi.

The Jewish community possessed also a number of other social and economic organizations, chief among which was Histadruth or the Jewish Federation of Labor. Histadruth was more than a mere trade union organization. It controlled many industries and agricultural cooperatives, hospitals, schools, marketing organizations, and a workers' bank. It was divided politically into the same groups as was the community as a whole. Numbering nearly 130,000 members, Histadruth was the most powerful socially minded, nongovernmental Jewish organization in Palestine.

The Jewish community displayed a marked tendency toward collectivism despite the fact that the financing of the Zionist settlement in Palestine was done mainly by contributions from wealthy Jewish capitalists abroad. One manifestation of such a tendency was the development of nearly 1,200 cooperative societies in Palestine connected with many branches of agriculture and industry. These included producers' and consumers' cooperatives; banking, credit, and insurance cooperatives; and similar societies for marketing, transport, irrigation, and land purchasing. Chief among them was Tnuva, a big organization for the distribution of the products of Jewish farms.

The early Zionists envisaged the regeneration of the Jewish nation through contact with nature and the soil. The Jew had to cast off the crippling memories of eastern European ghettos and acquire new mental and physical vigor through work on the land.[12] Palestine was also to develop specialized industries and to play the role of a small Belgium of the Middle East, supplying the surrounding Arab lands with the products of her skilled labor. Agriculture, however, was to be the main objective because of its regenerative value.

Much stress, therefore, was laid on the development of Jewish agrarian communities. These were, for the most part, collective settlements, among which three basic types predominated: the Kvutza, the Kibbutz, and the Moshav Ovdim. They differed in their degree of collectivism and of readiness to accept new members. The Kvutza was the oldest type of collective farm, it had a strictly closed membership and was communistic in its economic and social principles. The Moshav Ovdim represented the loosest form of collectivism and contained elements of individual free enterprise.[13] All these settlements bore a definite imprint of the social radicalism prevailing among most of their original founders, i.e., the Russian Jews who emigrated to Palestine in the late nineteenth and early twentieth centuries. The cooperative and semicentralized nature of Jewish agriculture permitted a lot of planning and led to monoculture trends as exemplified by the impressive development of citrus fruit. Much of the citrus produce of the Jewish agricultural settlements was earmarked for export, while other foodstuffs had to be imported. Scientific experimental stations including the famous one at Rehovoth (Dr. Weizmann's residence and laboratory), and excellent agricultural schools (such as Mikveh Israel near Tel-Aviv) contributed to the high level of Zionist agriculture.

Despite this impressive effort to return to the land, only a minority gained a livelihood from agricultural pursuits. In the interwar period only 23.8 percent of the Jewish population resided in rural areas, and, according to the Jewish Agency, only 13.2 percent of Jewish wage earners were engaged in agriculture in 1943. In fact, the trend was toward greater concentration in urban occupations.[14]

The Arab Community

The Arab community presented an altogether different picture. Politically the Arabs were far from being as efficiently organized as were the Jews. There was no Arab equivalent of the Jewish Agency, nor was there anything resembling the Jewish community organization, Vaad Leumi. The Arabs possessed their Supreme Moslem Council, whose charter was approved by the government. Originally all its members were elected, but later some were appointed by the British high commissioner. The council controlled the Moslem religious courts and charitable endowments or the *waqfs*. Its president was the grand mufti of Jerusalem, Haj Amin el-Husseini. Arab political activity was channeled through the Arab Executive, elected by the Palestine Arab Congress. This, in turn, gave way to the Arab Higher Committee, created in 1936 as a result of the union of five out of six Arab political

---

[12]He was to transform himself from a nonproductive middleman, from a *Luftmensch* (as Walter Preuss described him), into a solid farmer and producer.

[13]See H. F. Infield, *Cooperative Living in Palestine* (New York, 1944).

[14]R.I.I.A., *Great Britain and Palestine*, p. 37.

parties.[15] Considerable fluidity characterized Arab politics, but two major political groups could be discerned: the first was led by the mufti, who dominated the Arab Higher Committee; the second was led by Raghib Bey Nashashibi, who resented the mufti's influence and who leaned toward a compromise with the British. It is noteworthy that the Moslem and Christian[16] Arabs managed, to a large extent, to forget the differences handed down from the Ottoman period and to unite in the face of the Zionist challenge.

The Arab community was backward in some respects. Nearly 73 percent of the population lived in rural areas, and this number included around 65,000 nomads. Arab agricultural methods were primitive. Only 25 percent of Moslem children attended schools in contrast to 100 percent of Jewish youth. The Arabs did not get outside financial aid, as did the Zionists, and obviously could not boast of the modern schools, hospitals, and other institutions of the well-organized Jewish community.

British Attitudes

Standing between and above these two communities was the British mandatory government. Palestine was under the jurisdiction of the British Colonial Office, but service in the Holy Land was never considered very desirable in the British colonial hierarchy. Consequently the human resources of the British in Palestine were not so good as those, for example, in the Sudan, Egypt, or India. British colonial officials, who had long dealt with eastern subject races, were somewhat at a loss facing the well-educated European and often sophisticated Zionist community. In the latter, the eastern European Jew predominated—an element hitherto little known to the British. Moreover, the average Jewish intellectual, especially after the great influx of central European Jews in the middle 1930s, was more highly educated, and perhaps more intelligent, than his British counterpart in the Palestinian administration. There had been little in England's colonial experience to guide British civil servants in such situations, and inevitable tensions arose. Many a British official who initially was not prejudiced against the Jews became anti-Semitic after a tour of duty in Palestine. This was certainly true of many army officers.

Apart from these psychological difficulties, political attitudes prevented real British-Zionist friendship. It was obvious that after the Churchill Memorandum of 1922 the British government treated the Balfour Declaration as a political liability that stood in the way of a coherent policy toward the Arabs. British statesmen realized what political dynamite Zionist immigration was in the Arab world. This policy found its reflection in the mandatory administration, especially on the lower operating echelons, where pro-Arab attitudes prevailed.

In the meantime, with Jewish immigration steadily increasing, Arab opposition

---

[15]These were: (1) the Palestine Arab party (Jamal Husseini), (2) the National Defense party (Raghib Bey Nashashibi), (3) the Reform party (Dr. Khalidi), (4) the National Bloc (Abdul Latif Bey Saleh of Nablus), (5) Congress Executive of Nationalist Youth (Yakub Ghussein), and (6) the Istiqlal (Independence) party (Auni Bey Abdul Hadi).

[16]The latter were estimated at 87,000 in 1945.

was becoming more and more intense. The Arabs demanded self-determination and insisted, from the early 1920s, upon the establishment of a democratic, parliamentary form of government. Added to this were two other demands—to stop Jewish immigration and to forbid land sales by Arabs to Jews. From the beginning, the Arabs adopted a policy of noncooperation with the mandatory regime. In conformity with this policy they rejected an early British suggestion to create an Arab agency equivalent to the Jewish.

The political history of Palestine after the inception of the mandate was stormy. The Wailing Wall incidents in 1929 gave rise to violent disturbances, during which the intransigent attitude of the Arabs became manifest. Anti-Jewish riots occurred again in 1933. Hitler's rise in Germany and the resulting Jewish exodus brought a new wave of immigration into Palestine, which alone accounted for over 60,000 new arrivals in 1935. This caused renewed Arab unrest. Matters came to a head in 1937, when the Arabs began a wholesale campaign of terror, commonly referred to as the Arab Rebellion. The Rebellion lasted through 1939, nearly until the outbreak of World War II.

British official reaction to these manifestations of Arab nationalism was unvarying. After each new crisis a commission was sent to Palestine to investigate, and each time it returned with a more or less voluminous report.[17] Until 1937 these reports tended generally to be unfavorable to Zionist aspirations. They advocated restricting immigration, invoked the principle of absorptive capacity, and stressed that the Jews had no rightful claim to share in the government of the country. In 1935 the high commissioner made public a plan for a partly elected and partly nominated legislative assembly, which would give the Arabs a majority. These proposals proved unacceptable either to the Zionists or to the Arabs; moreover, they drew criticism from the Permanent Mandates Commission of the League of Nations. In 1937, the Royal Commission, having abandoned hope for a reconciliation between the Jews and Arabs, came forward with a proposal of partition. Palestine was to be divided into an Arab state, a Jewish state, and a neutral enclave around Jerusalem and Bethlehem that would remain under British administration. The Arab Higher Committee virtually rejected the scheme. The Zionist Congress which met at Zurich, August 3–17 1937, instructed the Executive to enter into negotiations with Great Britain "with a view to ascertaining the precise terms of His Majesty's Government for the proposed establishment of a Jewish State."[18]

In 1938, the British government dispatched to Palestine a technical partition commission, whose task it was to prepare a blueprint for partition, on the basis of the Royal Commission's recommendations. This new commission was at the same time authorized to make its own suggestions. Its report, in which it proposed a detailed scheme of partition, was promptly rejected by the government. Instead, Great Britain convened early in 1939 a round-table conference attended by Zionist and Arab representatives from Palestine and by delegates from the existing Arab states.

---

[17]In particular, the Shaw Commission in 1929; the Hope-Simpson Commission in 1930; the Royal (Peel) Commission in 1936; the Partition Commission in 1938.
[18]R.I.I.A., *Great Britain and Palestine*, p. 106.

The London Conference and the White Paper, 1939

The composition of the conference introduced an element of novelty into Palestinian politics. Hitherto the British had tried to settle the controversy by consultation with Arab leaders from Palestine. Now, however, yielding to the growing insistence of surrounding Arab countries, they decided to invite representatives of Iraq, Egypt, Saudi Arabia, Yemen, and Transjordan. A difficulty arose in connection with the Palestinian Arab representation. In 1937, as a result of the Arab Rebellion, the government of Palestine had arrested and deported to the Seychelles five leading members of the Arab Higher Committee.[19] Moreover, the government had deprived the mufti, Haj Amin el-Husseini, of his office as president of the Supreme Moslem Council and chairman of the General *Waqf* Committee, and issued warrants for his arrest as well as that of his relative, Jamal el-Husseini, president of the Arab party. Both the mufti and Jamal escaped, and took shelter under the protective wing of the French mandatory administration in Lebanon and Syria, respectively. The mufti continued to direct the activities of Arab guerrillas in Palestine. Led by Rahim Haj Ibrahim and Aref Abdul Razzik, the guerrillas waged a campaign of terror and intimidation, not only against the British and the Jews, but also against the moderate Arab elements headed by the Nashashibi family. It was very difficult for Great Britain to secure spokesmen for the Palestinian Arabs who could act with a degree of moderation and at the same time get support from the Arab masses. After much wrangling it was eventually decided that Palestine would be represented by six delegates, who would act on behalf of all Palestinian Arab parties. These included both moderates, such as Raghib Bey Nashashibi, and some former members of the Arab Higher Committee, released from the Seychelles. The latter were permitted to consult with the exiled mufti, who, though absent and outlawed, still wielded great influence.

The Jewish delegation comprised not only Zionists and members and nonmembers of the Jewish Agency, but also other prominent Jewish leaders from Great Britain, the United States, and the European continent. It was headed by Dr. Chaim Weizmann.

The conference met in London in February and March 1939. The Arabs and the Jews held separate meetings because of the refusal of Palestinian Arabs to sit with the Jewish delegation. The conference produced no agreement; each party adhered stubbornly to its own formula. The Arabs reiterated their demand for independence and insisted on the stoppage of Jewish immigration. The Jews made an eloquent plea for implementation of the Balfour Declaration in "this blackest hour of Jewish history" and stressed the need of continued uninterrupted immigration. British compromise proposals were rejected by both parties. The conference disbanded without producing any agreement.

On May 17, 1939, the British government issued a White Paper, which laid down new principles concerning Palestine. Reversing its former policy, the government proposed the creation, within ten years, of an independent Palestinian state to be

[19]Ahmed Hilmi Pasha; Fuad Saba; Yakub Ghussein; Dr. Hussein Fakhri el-Khalidi, Mayor of Jerusalem; and Haj Rashid Ibrahim.

linked with Britain by a special treaty. The most important provisions concerned immigration and land transfers. On both points Britain virtually gave way to Arab demands: Jewish immigration was to be limited to 75,000 for the next five years, after which it was to cease altogether; and Palestine was to be divided into three zones—the first, in which land transfers from Arabs to Jews were to be allowed; the second, in which they were to be restricted; and the third, in which they were to be forbidden.

These proposals were rejected by Arab spokesmen because they did not go far enough, but basically the Arabs had scored a considerable victory. The Zionists were profoundly shocked and promptly denounced the White Paper as a betrayal of promises and appeasement of the Arabs. The Permanent Mandates Commission of the League of Nations also voiced its criticism, declaring an incompatibility existed between the paper and the terms of the mandate.

Britain's defense was to explain that she was not bound by the principle of economic absorptive capacity but instead had to take into account the political absorptive capacity of the Arab world as a whole. The truth of the matter was that in 1938 and 1939 Nazi and Italian propaganda among the Arabs assumed alarming intensity and took full advantage of increased Jewish immigration to blame Britain and place her in a very embarrassing position. The tenseness of the international situation in the months preceding the outbreak of the war led Britain to adopt a conciliatory policy toward the Arab world, situated as it was astride the vulnerable part of the English imperial life line.

The tragedy of the Zionists stemmed from the fact that, as Jews, they had a great stake in curbing German imperialism and in desiring ultimate Nazi defeat. Any policy aimed at the strengthening of the Western camp—and such was the policy of courting Arab favor—should have been welcomed and supported by them. But this was incompatible with the basic Zionist aim of converting Palestine into a Jewish state with the immediate objective of rescuing Jewish victims of Nazi tyranny in Europe.

The Wartime Truce

The outbreak of the Second World War in September 1939 found the two protagonists unreconciled and the British more determined than ever to enforce their new policy on Palestine and to prevent the outbreak of an Arab rebellion in the Middle East.

As for the Zionists, they expressed through Dr. Weizmann their readiness to stand by Great Britain and the democracies. This was coupled with repeated demands that independent Jewish military units be created as part of the allied armies. The British responded to the latter request by allowing voluntary enlistments in the British auxiliary formations in the Middle East, by creating a Palestine Pioneer Corps, and by raising six battalions of the Palestine Companies of the Buffs. Great Britain took care, however, to open these formations to both the Jews and the Arabs, apparently unwilling to sponsor purely Jewish formations. Not until the fall of 1944 did Britain accede to Jewish demands by forming a Jewish brigade, which eventually took part in the final stages of the Allied campaign in Italy.

The war brought to Palestine an artificial truce, largely due to the presence of numerous Allied divisions, making continuance of the Arab guerrilla warfare suicidal. Arab response to the call for volunteers was not very enthusiastic. The Arabs lacked the incentive possessed by the Jews. Moreover, they could never forget the mufti, who visited Germany at the beginning of the war and joined hands with the Nazi leaders against "British imperialism."[20] Nevertheless British policy, though termed "appeasement" by the Zionists, was successful in restraining the Arab peoples from a concerted revolt against Britain in her hour of need. In Palestine it brought about a cessation of rebellion.

Need for a New Policy for Zionism

The truce lasted until 1943. In that year Palestine witnessed a new upsurge of terrorism. This time, however, the roles had changed, since it was the Jews who attacked. Their primary target was the British administration. Two factors contributed to this state of affairs. First, there was an unusual increase in illegal Jewish immigration from Nazi-occupied Europe. The unfortunate victims of Nazi persecution were arriving in Palestine on overcrowded, leaky ships, and the British authorities either forbade their entry or interned the immigrants in camps on Cyprus and in other overseas possessions. Tragic events occurred, including the sinking of an immigrant ship, the *Struma,* off the Turkish coast (the British had refused to permit it to dock in Palestine). The more extremist Jewish elements lost their patience and resorted to violence in the hope of compelling Britain to ease the immigration laws.

Second, increased pressure for a pro-Zionist solution began to be exerted by American Zionists. On May 11, 1942, the American Zionist Organization meeting in New York, adopted the so-called Biltmore Program, presented to it by David Ben Gurion, head of the Jewish Agency's executive committee. The Biltmore Program called for (1) the establishment of a Jewish state, which would embrace the whole of Palestine; (2) the creation of a Jewish army; and (3) the repudiation of the White Paper of 1939 and unlimited immigration into Palestine, which would be controlled not by the British but by the Jewish Agency.

This program went much farther than did the Balfour Declaration, and so elicited protests from more moderate Jewish groups in the West. It received endorsement, however, from the Small Committee of the General Council of the Zionist Organization in Jerusalem on November 10, 1942, and thus became official policy of world Zionism. By stepping up their demands, the Zionists gave expression to their growing conviction that a policy of moderation did not pay, that Britain could no longer be relied upon, and that it was expedient to seek the support of the United States. Allied victories at El-Alamein and in North Africa removed the danger of enemy action in the Middle East, and this encouraged the Zionists in their policy of disregarding Arab nationalism.

---

[20]For an account of the mufti's activities, see Rosalind W. Graves, "The Grand Mufti of Jerusalem," *Current History,* (Nov. 1946).

Hand in hand with the Biltmore Program went intensive Zionist activity among the leading politicians in the United States. Yielding to Zionist pleas, many state legislatures passed pro-Zionist resolutions, and in February 1944 a resolution was introduced before both Houses of Congress. The resolution called for the opening of Palestine to unrestricted Jewish immigration and for the ultimate reconstruction of Palestine "as a free and democratic Jewish commonwealth." It also requested official American intervention (good offices) to secure these goals. Had the resolution passed, it would have committed the United States to definite political action on behalf of the Zionists. At the last moment, the vote upon it was postponed because of the objections of General Marshall, then chief of staff, who, on the basis of reports from the Middle East, believed that such a resolution would harm the Allied war effort. Despite this temporary setback, it was clear that the Zionists were firmly resolved to achieve their aims in Palestine and that they found powerful allies in official Washington. In fact, after a visit of Zionist leaders a few days later, President Franklin D. Roosevelt made public a statement favoring Zionist aspirations.

Irritated by immigration restrictions and inspired by American Zionist successes, the Palestinian Zionists displayed remarkable dynamism in their struggle against Great Britain. Officially the Jewish Agency agreed to observe a truce with the Arabs for the duration of the war. But this official attitude was not shared by the extremist wing of the New Zionist Organization (Revisionists). And it was this extremist wing that set the general political tone in Palestine. The war gave the Jews a unique opportunity to equip themselves with arms, partly stolen from the Allied forces. In fact, there was considerable illegal traffic in military equipment. The Jewish community possessed three underground military forces. The first was Haganah, a large defense force, created initially to protect Jewish settlements against Arab attacks, to which belonged most of the able-bodied members of the Jewish community. Haganah was illegal, but the British tolerated it because its aims were defensive. Zhabotinsky's Revisionists had their smaller but more effective force called Irgun Zvai Leumi. Irgun used decidedly terrorist tactics, but for some time it considered itself bound by the truce. The third force was the so-called Stern Gang, a splinter group of the Irgun led by a Polish Jew, Abraham Stern. This group never accepted the truce and indulged freely in terrorism. In 1942–1943 both Irgun and the Stern Gang embarked upon a determined policy to compel the British to accede to the Biltmore Program by terrorist tactics. Terrorist activity was particularly bad in 1944. The high commissioner for Palestine, Sir Harold MacMichael, barely escaped with his life while traveling on the Jerusalem-Jaffa road. On November 2 two members of the Stern Gang assassinated Lord Moyne, British minister of state for the Middle East, in Cairo. Dozens of attacks by Irgun and the Stern groups on British police stations and on civil and military officials contributed to the steady deterioration of security in the Holy Land. These acts of terror were condemned by the official Zionist bodies and by the chief rabbis of Palestine. The New Zionist Organization even went so far as to repudiate its own offspring, the Irgun, for breaking party discipline. But it was clear that the terrorists would not have succeeded if it had not been for the support that they received in Jewish settlements or in Jewish sectors of larger towns. Their dramatic struggle eventually focused the attention of the world upon Palestine, and although it did not evoke enthusiasm in the West, it did compel Great Britain and indirectly the United States to crystallize their policies toward Zionism.

In the meantime the plight of European Jewry had become more desperate, because of the extension of Soviet dominion over eastern and central Europe. The Jews constituted a big proportion of displaced persons in the western sectors of Germany. They comprised three basic categories: (1) those victims of the Nazi persecution who had survived the ordeal and had been released from the German concentration camps by the Allies; (2) those Polish Jews who had been deported to the Soviet Union in 1939–1940 and who were after the war permitted to leave the USSR (having aquainted themselves at first hand with the realities of a Communist state, they did not want to remain in Soviet-dominated Poland, despite the policy of nondiscrimination loudly proclaimed by the new regime); (3) those Jews from eastern Europe who found that the Communist pattern of politics and economy in the Soviet satellite countries did not leave much room for the trader, middleman, or independent businessman—occupations predominantly filled by Jews in that part of the continent.

The press in Western countries either misunderstood or was unwilling to face the realities of the situation in eastern Europe in 1945 and 1946. It was thought that the Jews were emigrating because of acute anti-Semitism, which lingered even after Hitler's downfall. There was anti-Semitism in that area, but two reservations should be made. First, anti-Semitism was not a new phenomenon in eastern Europe. It had existed before the war and it had been expressed in anti-Jewish legislation. But it had never caused a mass exodus of Jews;[21] such an exodus was without doubt a result of Soviet occupation of the area in question. Second, some new acute manifestations of anti-Semitism were partly attributable to the role individual Jewish Communists played in the establishment of the puppet regimes in eastern Europe.[22] Thus, while a minority of Communist-oriented Jews benefited by the radical change in this area, the Jews as a whole were simply squeezed out of their professions and trades as a result of Sovietization in the satellite states. They lost all hope for the future.[23] The teeming camps of displaced persons in Western Germany confronted the West with a major political and humanitarian problem and added considerably to the pressure that the Zionist organization was exercising for a favorable solution in Palestine.

[21] Actually, in 1938 and 1939 there was a trend toward reemigration of Jews to their eastern European countries of origin, from both Germany and Palestine.

[22] Such as Jakub Berman, secretary general of the Council of Ministers in Poland; Rudolph Slansky, secretary general of the Communist Party of Czechoslovakia; Ana Pauker, foreign minister of Rumania; Mathias Rakosi, premier of Hungary.

[23] According to the statement made on January 2, 1946, by Lt. Gen. Sir Frederick E. Morgan, chief of the United Nations Relief and Rehabilitation Administration in Germany, thousands of Polish Jews were infiltrating into the American occupation zone in accordance with a "well-organized, positive plan to get out of Europe." This migration, he said, was sponsored by an unknown secret Jewish organization. His revelations were based on a U.S. Third Army intelligence report on the organization, by Zionist groups, of an underground route in Europe, which made it possible for the Jews to enter the American zone in Germany at the rate of 2,000 a week. These statements were partly confirmed by the U.S. commander in Europe, Gen. Joseph T. McNarney, in the latter's report to the President on January 29, 1946. Moreover,

The Anglo-American Committee of Inquiry

The stage for the next act in the Palestinian drama was set on August 31, 1945, when President Truman addressed an appeal to the British prime minister, Clement Attlee, asking for immediate admission of 100,000 Jewish refugees to Palestine. In reply the British government proposed the creation of an Anglo-American Committee of Inquiry to study the matter, thus shifting part of the burden of responsibility to the United States. The American government accepted this suggestion, and as a result both governments appointed a committee, composed of nonofficial citizens of the two countries.[24]

The joint committee held hearings in Washington and in London, visited the displaced persons camps in Germany and Austria, and made a tour of Palestine. It pursued generally an open-minded approach to the subject under its investigation, but its composition was responsible for a diversity of opinions. Three members, James G. McDonald and Bartley C. Crum of the American group and Richard Crossman, M.P., of the British group, strongly favored the Zionist cause.[25] Crum in particular resented the advice given the committee by officials of the State Department and of the Foreign Office. This advice, which was well received by many members of the British delegation, was to the effect that no political solution in the Middle East should disregard the Soviet factor[26] and that Britain and the United States should stand united in the face of the Soviet threat.[27]

Having completed its task, on April 20, 1946, the committee presented a unanimous report with three major recommendations: (1) that "the Government of Pales-

---

officials at the State Department commented that at least some of the statements made by General Morgan concerning the exodus of Jews from Poland conformed with information in the possession of the U.S. government, and added that "a number of official and semiofficial indications have been provided by the Warsaw government that it is encouraging the migration of part of its Jewish population." After issuing his statement, General Morgan was promptly suspended from his post by Herbert H. Lehman, director general of the UNRRA, on the ground of being guilty of racial bias. After an explanatory letter, however, in which he denied any anti-Semitic attitudes on his part, General Morgan was reinstated. (See *Washington Post,* Jan. 3, 4, 8, 31, 1946.)

[24]The American members of the committee were Judge Joseph C. Hutcheson, Jr., of Houston, Texas, Bartley C. Crum of San Francisco, Dr. James G. McDonald, former League of Nations commissioner for German refugees, Frank W. Buxton, editor of the *Boston Herald,* Dr. Frank Aydelotte, director, Institute for Advanced Study, Princeton, and William Phillips, former U.S. ambassador to Italy. The British group was composed of Sir John Singleton, judge, King's Bench, London, Lord Robert Morrison, a Labour peer, Richard H. S. Crossman, Labour M.P., Maj. Reginald Manningham-Buller, Conservative M.P., Wilfrid Crick, adviser to Midland Bank, and Sir Frederick Leggett, a labor conciliator.

[25]Two of them subsequently gave personal accounts of their mission: Bartley C. Crum in *Behind the Silken Curtain* (New York, 1947) and Richard Crossman in *Palestine Mission* (London, 1947).

[26]Gist of the statement made by Loy Henderson, head of the Office of Near Eastern and African Affairs, Department of State (Crum, *op. cit.,* pp. 7–8).

[27]*Ibid.,* p. 35. The author adds: "Naturally, I found my American colleagues [on the committee] much less preoccupied with anxieties over our national security," and ventures his own opinion that "there might be points at which British imperial and Russian nationalistic interests did not coincide, but surely the United States and Russia had few points at which their basic interests were in conflict." On his part, Crossman described Crum, with whom he was on excellent terms, as follows: "Indeed, he was the only American with us who had a political career in front of him, which could be made or marred by the attitude he adopted toward the Jewish question" (Crossman, *op. cit.,* p. 22).

tine be continued as at present under mandate pending the execution of a trusteeship agreement under the United Nations''; (2) "that 100,000 certificates be authorized immediately for the admission into Palestine of the Jews who have been the victims of Nazi and Fascist persecution,'' and (3) that the land transfer limitations be rescinded.[28]

The United States and Great Britain neither accepted nor rejected these recommendations. Instead the two governments appointed a new Anglo-American Commission, composed of higher officials, to devise ways to implement the committee's recommendations. As could be expected, the official approach to the Palestine problem was more conservative. The resulting Grady-Morrison plan revived the old British project of a federalized Jewish-Arab Palestine and made further Jewish immigration dependent upon common Jewish-Arab consent.

The Zionists were profoundly disappointed by these developments. They had expected that the British Labour party, which had repeatedly issued pro-Zionist statements, would favor their cause. But once in power British Labourites suddenly abandoned their old proclamations and reverted to traditional diplomacy. Ernest Bevin, Socialist foreign secretary, followed his Conservative predecessors in their policy of not antagonizing the Arab world.[29] News of the mufti's escape from Germany to the Middle East—probably with the connivance of some Western powers—added to Jewish bitterness. In October 1946, President Truman renewed his appeal for immediate admission of 100,000 Jews. Under these circumstances, the chances for a negotiated settlement of the Palestinian question became slimmer than ever.[30] Moreover, a definite swing developed in the World Zionist Organization in favor of an intransigent policy toward Great Britain. In December 1946, at a World Zionist Congress in Basle, American Zionist leaders, backed by the Revisionists, assailed Dr. Weizmann for his policy of "appeasing" Britain and asserted that British rule in Palestine was "illegal." Dr. Abba Hillel Silver, president of the Zionist Organization in America, declared that "we have the right to resist this rule and I pledge the support of American Jewry to this resistance."[31] Dr. Weizmann's retort, "I'm not impressed about speeches on resistance made in New York when resistance is supposed to take place in Palestine," elicited the cry "demagogue" from Dr. Emmanuel Neuman of the United States. American Zionist leadership carried the day, insisting on a Jewish state in all Palestine and promising more effective measures to bring this about.

Palestine before the United Nations

Britain's position was slowly becoming untenable. Subjected to official American pressure, at odds with the Zionists and with the Arabs, and facing growing disorders in its mandated territory, the British government decided to take the ques-

[28]The full text of the report is in the *New York Times,* May 1, 1946.

[29]The text of Bevin's speech at a Labour party conference at Bournemouth containing significant passages about Palestine may be found in the *New York Times,* June 13, 1946.

[30]Bevin subsequently deplored the fact that the Palestinian issue had been made "the subject of local elections" in the United States (*New York Times,* Feb. 26, 1947).

[31]*New York Times,* Dec. 11, 1946.

tion of Palestine before the United Nations. On April 2, 1947, Britain requested the calling of a special session of the General Assembly to consider the problem. The General Assembly, which met between April 28 and May 15, set up a United Nations Special Committee on Palestine (UNSCOP). The committee, composed of eleven states[32] under the presidency of a Swedish delegate, visited Palestine and presented a report to the regular fall session of the General Assembly.

The report recommended the establishment of an independent and economically unified Palestine at an early date, pending which the area would have to pass through a transitional stage under United Nations supervision. Here the unanimity ended, and the report was divided into a majority and a minority plan. The majority plan, endorsed by Canada, Czechoslovakia, Guatemala, the Netherlands, Peru, Sweden, and Uruguay, provided for the partitioning of Palestine into an Arab state, a Jewish state, and the internationalized city of Jerusalem. The minority plan, favored by India, Iran, and Yugoslavia, advocated a federated state of Palestine composed of two states, Jewish and Arab, each enjoying local autonomy. Immigration into the Jewish state would be permitted for three years up to its absorptive capacity, which would be determined by three Arab, three Jewish, and three United Nations representatives. The Arab states favored the minority plan, because it satisfied their basic desiderata, namely, a single independent state with an Arab majority and a limitation of Jewish immigration. The Zionists, somewhat reluctantly, accepted the majority plan. It did not satisfy the extremists, but at least it gave promise for a completely independent Jewish state.

Partition for Palestine

Both plans were thoroughly debated by a special Ad Hoc Committee of the General Assembly at its fall session in 1947. Arab and Jewish representatives were heard again. As the session drew to its close, it became obvious that the Zionists were determined to obtain a decision favoring the majority plan. The political atmosphere at Lake Success grew tense, and speculation was rife as to whether or not the Zionists would be able to obtain the necessary two-thirds majority, depending to a great extent on the attitude of the numerous South American and Caribbean republics.[33] On November 29, 1947—a date memorable in Jewish history—the General Assembly voted to recommend the partition of Palestine, with an economic union as proposed by the majority report.

The Arab state was to include the central and eastern part of Palestine, from the valley of Esdraelon down to Beersheba, western Galilee, and a strip of land along the Mediterranean coast from Gaza southward and along the Egyptian border to the Red Sea. Jaffa would constitute an enclave in the Jewish state, which was to extend over eastern Galilee and the valley of Esdraelon, a coastal area from Haifa to south of Jaffa, and a major part of the Negeb. Jerusalem and Bethlehem with the adjoining

[32] Australia, Canada, Czechoslovakia, Guatemala, India, Iran, the Netherlands, Peru, Sweden, Uruguay, and Yugoslavia. No major powers were included.

[33] For the political activity to secure Latin-American support, see Kermit Roosevelt, "The Partition of Palestine: A Lesson in Pressure Politics," *Middle East Journal*, 2 (Jan. 1948).

territory were to stay outside of both states and be subject to an administration responsible to the Trusteeship Council. The Assembly also took note of Britain's decision to terminate the mandate by August 1, 1948; provided for the establishment of the two states within two months after British withdrawal; established a five-nation UN Palestine Commission to implement the resolution; and called upon the Security Council to assist in its implementation of the plan, instructing it to interpret as a threat to peace any attempt to change the partition plan by force.

Thirty-three states voted for this motion, thirteen voted against, and ten abstained. Among the big powers who favored partition were the United States, the Soviet Union, and France. Great Britain and China abstained from voting, and so did Argentina, Chile, Colombia, El Salvador, Ethiopia, Honduras, Mexico, and Yugoslavia. The negative votes included the Arab states of Egypt, Iraq, Lebanon, Saudi Arabia, Syria, and Yemen and also Afghanistan, Cuba, Greece, India, Iran, Pakistan, and Turkey.

Acting in accordance with the Charter and following regular democratic procedures, the majority of civilized mankind gave its verdict on the future status of the Holy Land. Procedurally there was no flaw in the decision. Its political implications, however, were obvious. Practically the whole of ex-colonial Asia and the Near East opposed the solution, a fact which was vitally to affect Asia's affairs. To the Arabs and other Asiatics, the United Nations decision meant that once again the outside world—predominantly Western and far removed from the scene—had imposed its will upon Eastern peoples. This, in their view, was not compatible with repeated progressive-liberal protestations of respect for Asia's nationalism and self-determination.

The Arabs felt particularly resentful toward the United States, since they believed that it was this country whose presence or influence helped to rally enough votes for the partition. They also reproached Americans for "betraying" many promises made both by President Roosevelt and President Truman to the effect that no basic decision on Palestine would ever be taken without the agreement of both parties directly concerned.[34]

The Arab states challenged the resolution's binding validity from a legal point of view. They argued that, according to the UN Charter, the Assembly did not possess the right of binding decision but only of recommendation. Consequently they assumed an attitude of noncooperation. More forthrightly the Arab Higher Committee of Palestine on February 6, 1948, stated that "any attempt by the Jews or any other power or group of powers to establish a Jewish state in Arab territory is an act of oppression which will be resisted in self-defense by force."[35]

The Arab-Jewish War

Deeds were soon to confirm these words. In the neighboring Arab states volunteers were recruited for the defense of Palestine, and after January 1948 armed detachments of Arabs began entering Palestine and attacking Jewish settlements. By

[34]See below, p. 583.
[35]Larry L. Leonard, "The United Nations and Palestine," *International Conciliation* (Oct. 1949), p. 650.

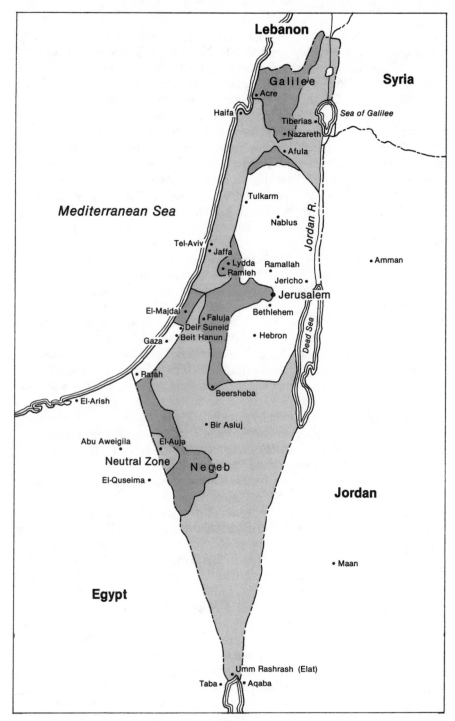

Map 5. Palestine, 1949. Light shading shows area allotted to Israel by the United Nations; dark area, that occupied by Israel.

406

February 1 these clashes had resulted in over 2,500 casualties, and the toll mounted as the days went by. Faced with this violence, Great Britain on January 1 declared that since the Jews and the Arabs could not agree on a solution, she would not aid the United Nations in the implementation of the partition plan, would terminate her mandate by May 15, 1948, and would oppose an earlier entry of the UN Palestine commission into the country.[36]

The Arab opposition also affected American policy. On March 19 the United States declared in the Security Council that, since partition proved unworkable, Palestine ought to be subjected to a temporary UN trusteeship. This change of policy met with outspoken criticism from the Zionists. Another special session of the General Assembly, which sat between April 16 and May 15, 1948, discussed this new American proposal but failed to produce majority support for it. The Soviet Union, in particular, insisted on the implementation of the November partition resolution. Eventually the Assembly recommended the appointment of a United Nations mediator and of a United Nations commissioner for Jerusalem.

On May 14, 1948, the British officially terminated their mandate over Palestine, withdrawing their last forces from the country. On the same day the National Council at a session in Tel-Aviv proclaimed the Jewish state of Israel. A few hours later President Truman extended de facto recognition to this new state on behalf of the United States.

Soon afterward Arab armies from Syria, Lebanon, Transjordan, Iraq, and Egypt entered Palestine. Arab and Jewish forces were obviously unequal. On one side were the regular armies of established Arab states, of which Egypt alone had nearly twenty million inhabitants. Among these armies, the Arab Legion of Transjordan proved to be the most effective. Commanded by Brigadier John Bagot Glubb Pasha, it employed forty British officers in key positions and played a disproportionately important role if we consider the small size and population of Transjordan. Next in effectiveness was the Iraqi force, which had to cross a long stretch of the Syrian desert to reach Palestine. The Egyptian army made a very poor showing, caused to no small degree by corruption and abuses in its rear. The regular armies of Syria and Lebanon were supplemented by a voluntary force, the Arab Liberation Army, commanded by Fawzi el-Kawukji who had been in the service of Nazi Germany during World War II. The Palestine Arabs formed the so-called Army of Judea, under the command of Abdul Kader el-Husseini, nephew of the grand mufti. Behind

---

[36]For a highly critical analysis of British policy, see *The British Record on Partition as Revealed by British Military Intelligence and Other Official Sources,* A Memorandum Submitted to the Special Session of the General Assembly of the United Nations, April, 1948, published by The Nation Associates as a supplement to *The Nation* (New York), May 8, 1948. The latter periodical as well as the group sponsoring it—The Nation Associates—have distinguished themselves by their vigorous support of the Zionist cause. Apart from the above-mentioned document, The Nation Associates in June 1948 submitted to President Truman a memorandum "pointing out—to use *The Nation's* words—how his Palestine policy has been undermined by the State Department working in close co-operation with the Middle Eastern oil companies." The basis of the memorandum was a report, allegedly written in Cairo in December 1947, by James Terry Duce, vice-president of the Arabian American Oil Company, to W. F. Moore, president of the company. A summary of this report may be found in *The Nation* of June 26, 1948, under the title "Blood and Oil, Aramco's Secret Report on Palestine," pp. 705 ff.

these Arab armies stood the Arab League, professedly united and determined to destroy Israel.

Opposing them was the army of Israel commanded by Yaakov Dori, with Colonel Yigael Yadin, a thirty-one-year-old native of Jerusalem, as its chief of operations. The backbone of the Israeli army was the old self-defense organization, Haganah. The latter was divided into the Palmah, an elite force sponsored by the leftist Mapam Socialist Labor party; Hish, a regular field force; and Mishmar, a home guard of elderly people. The Palmah insisted on retaining its special character and tended to act independently of the main force. The Israeli army numbered at its peak about 75,000 members. It had women's auxiliary services, which helped greatly by releasing men for front-line duties.

The two former terrorist organizations—Irgun[37] and the Stern Gang[38]—continued to operate apart from the army, and on a few occasions clashed with the armed forces over matters of policy. Israel's forces were handicapped somewhat by lack of over-all unity. Their morale, however, was very high and their equipment adequate. Arms and munitions, even airplanes, were purchased abroad, chiefly in Czechoslovakia, and considerable quantities were smuggled out of western Europe and the United States.[39] Jewish volunteers from the United States and from other countries, some of them with a good military education, strengthened Israeli forces.

International Repercussions

The creation of Israel and the resulting Arab-Jewish war had far-reaching international repercussions. On May 20, 1948, the Security Council appointed Count Folke Bernadotte, president of the Swedish Red Cross, as UN mediator for Palestine. Bernadotte's work and the Council's action with regard to the conflict constitute a complicated chapter in United Nations history, and it would be tedious to reproduce all the details. Suffice it to say that under UN auspices Israel and the Arabs concluded two truces, two breathing spells in the war. On September 16, Bernadotte recommended to the UN General Assembly a change in the proposed partition boundaries, which amounted to assigning the Negeb to the Arab state. The following day he was assassinated in Jerusalem by Jewish terrorists. Dr. Ralph Bunche, an American, took over his duties, and, aided by the Conciliation Commission, initiated armistice discussions between the belligerents on the island of Rhodes. Between January and July 1949 a series of armistices were concluded by Israel, on the

---

[37]Irgun was commanded by Menachem Begin. Peter H. Bergson, head of the Hebrew Committee of National Liberation in the United States, acted as Begin's chief aide for fund-collecting purposes.

[38]The Stern Gang leaders were Nathan Friedman-Yellin and Matitiahu Shmuelovitz.

[39]According to the provisions of the UN-imposed truce, an embargo was placed on all shipments of arms to the belligerent parties. Both sides adhered to this prohibition only half-heartedly and both were ready to violate it whenever they were able to do so. In this illegal contest Israel was in a stronger position than the Arab states because she had ample dollar funds to pay for the weapons supplied by the Soviet satellites. The latter were quite willing to evade the embargo, provided they were paid in dollars. This contrasted with the attitude of Britain who, by faithfully observing the embargo injunction, made it hard for the Arab states, particularly Egypt, to replenish their stocks of arms and munitions, most of which were of the British type. It may be added that treaties concluded in 1930, 1936, and 1946, respectively, between Great Britain, on the one hand, and Iraq, Egypt, and Transjordan, on the other, contained a provision that the military equipment of these Arab states should follow British patterns.

one hand, and Egypt, Lebanon, Transjordan, and Syria, on the other. Basically the armistice agreements maintained the territorial disposition resulting from the war operations. This meant that about three-quarters of Palestine came under the authority of Israel. The war extended Israel's de facto boundaries, which now included the northern, western, and southern parts of Palestine. The Arabs retained the central-eastern part adjoining Transjordan, but with a respectably wide Jewish corridor between Tel-Aviv and Jerusalem, and the so-called Gaza strip along the Mediterranean. The central-eastern part was occupied by Transjordan's Arab Legion, the Gaza strip by the Egyptians. No peace treaties were negotiated.

The Jewish-Arab war profoundly altered the strategic and political situation in the Middle East. Points of major significance are as follows:

1. Israel emerged victorious from the conflict. Except for the Arab Legion, most of the Arab forces suffered heavy defeats and proved unequal to the task.

2. Israel owed her victory to her higher morale, better equipment, and superior organization. Israel represented Western efficiency. The Arabs were defeated largely because of the poor morale of troops, bad leadership, and, above everything, political dissensions among the participating states.[40]

3. The Arab League proved to be an inadequate instrument of determined political action. Rivalry between Egypt and the Hashemite kingdoms of Transjordan and Iraq prevented cooperation. It also made impossible the creation of an Arab state in Palestine. Egypt sponsored the so-called all-Palestinian Arab government, which was proclaimed on September 20, 1948, in Gaza under the mufti's leadership. Transjordan refused to recognize its authority and eventually (December 1, 1948) annexed the east-central part of Palestine.

4. Israel owed a great deal to assistance extended from abroad and to the solidarity of Jewish people the world over. Israel's intelligence services, both in Palestine and abroad, including that in England, proved definitely superior to those of the Arabs.[41]

5. The war abounded in cruelties and violations of international law. Jewish settlements were better defended than were Arab villages. "Scores of Arab villages, deemed uninhabitable, had been razed [by the Jews] as insurance against their owner's return."[42] The Jews massacred all the Arab civilian population in the village of Deir Yasin in April 1948.

---

[40]The Arabs, not without certain justification, laid some of the blame for their poor success on the UN-sponsored truces. "Nearly every Arab, in every Arab country," observes *The Economist* (March 5, 1949), "believed and still believes that, had it not been for the first truce imposed upon them by UNO, Britain and other outsiders, they would have won the war. There is no doubt that certain Jewish areas were at this junction extremely hard pressed. Certainly, had the truce not been declared on June 11th, the Arabs would have killed more Jews than they did, which would from their point of view have been so much gain." Furthermore, as the periodical rightly points out, "Arab soldiers are not temperamentally suited to living in truce conditions. Some of them were short of pay packets, others of comforts, many found the Palestinians—particularly around Gaza—a disappointing, thieving lot. By July, therefore [at the time when the first truce came to an end], they were fighting with little heart and less skill."

[41]According to Kenneth W. Bilby, *New Star in the Near East* (New York, 1950), "Even the activities of the British Foreign Office in respect to the Arab world were reported in detail to the government at Tel-Aviv" (p. 70).

[42]*Ibid.*, p. 3.

6. The war drove nearly one million Arabs out of their homes. This flight was partly due to the fear of Jewish reprisals and partly to the urgings of Arab political leaders to evacuate probable battle areas. The refugees fled to the surrounding Arab countries or to the Arab-occupied parts of Palestine. In the spring of 1949 the number of Arab displaced persons eligible for relief was officially estimated at 940,000.[43] At the beginning of the war there were 1,320,000 Arabs and 640,000 Jews in Palestine. The establishment of Israel resulted in the displacement of nearly 70 percent of the Arab population, which the Israeli government refused to readmit.[44]

The Internal Situation in Israel

Israel is an almost unique phenomenon in the annals of history. Other nations, to be sure, have been created as a result of successive waves of immigration. But Israel did not follow the usual pattern. In the Jewish community in Palestine, emphasis was laid from the very beginning on the total social transformation of the incoming settlers, on their deurbanization and on their productivity. The immigrants, except the oriental Jews, were imbued with a pioneering spirit that made such a transformation possible. Although nothing has changed ideologically since the creation of the state, the new mass immigration has posed entirely new problems. First of all, the rate of immigration assumed tremendous proportions. In the first thirty-three months of Israel's existence 500,000 immigrants entered. In February 1951, Israel's population was officially estimated at 1,400,000 of which 170,000 were Arabs. Nearly 110,000 immigrants lived in temporary camps, i.e., 10 percent

[43]The exact number of Arab refugees is still a matter of controversy, estimates varying from well over 1,000,000 on the one hand to a little over 500,000 on the other (the latter from official Israeli sources). According to the first report of the secretary-general on United Nations Relief for Palestine Refugees, issued on November 4, 1949, the number of destitute Arabs eligible for aid was 940,000, distributed as follows: Lebanon, 127,800; Syria, 78,200; Transjordan, 94,000; Arab Palestine, 357,400; Israel, 37,600; Gaza strip, 245,000; total 940,000.

Of the above number the refugees who have actually left their homes are estimated at between 600,000 and 700,000; the remaining are those who have not moved, but who as a result of the hostilities have become destitute or homeless. (See S. G. Thicknesse, *Arab Refugees, A Survey of Resettlement Possibilities* [London, 1949]; "The Palestine Refugees," *R.C.A.J.,* Jan. 1950; and W. de St. Aubin, "Peace and Refugees in the Middle East," *Middle East Journal,* 3 [July 1949].)

[44]It may be interesting at this juncture to quote George Antonius, who in his *Arab Awakening,* written ten years before the creation of Israel, forcefully presented the Arab case in the Palestinian controversy. Said he: "The treatment meted out to Jews in Germany and other European countries is a disgrace to its authors and to modern civilization; but posterity will not exonerate any country that fails to bear its proper share of the sacrifices needed to alleviate Jewish suffering and distress. To place the brunt of the burden upon Arab Palestine is a miserable evasion of the duty that lies upon the whole of the civilized world. It is also morally outrageous. No code of morals can justify the persecution of one people in an attempt to relieve the persecution of another. The cure for the eviction of Jews from Germany is not to be sought in the eviction of the Arabs from their homeland. . . . The logic of facts is inexorable. It shows that no room can be made in Palestine for a second nation except by dislodging or exterminating the nation in possession" (pp. 411–412). Reprinted by permission of the publisher, G. P. Putnam's Sons.

In stark contrast to these words stands the following statement of the pro-Zionist writer, Dr. Joseph Dunner, in the Preface to his *The Republic of Israel:* "There is no doubt that the emergence of the first Jewish Commonwealth in nineteen hundred years has changed the course of Jewish and world history. That a people, bitterly abused, oppressed and pogromized, could rise again, must give courage and hope to all who believe in the forward march of the human race. It is proof of what the human spirit and dedication to a noble purpose can do in spite of heavily weighted odds" (p. ix).

of the total Jewish population was without permanent lodgings or work. Speedy integration of these new arrivals proved a major social and economic problem for the budding state and made orderly planning difficult. But the government adopted the policy of unrestricted immigration as one of its cardinal principles. The new immigrants did not display the same pioneering spirit as did those who had come in the early days of the mandate. Having survived Nazi persecution in Europe or escaped reprisals in the Arab countries of the East, these new settlers sought above everything security, which they conceived primarily in terms of the restoration of their old social and economic status. They tended, therefore, to settle in compact neighborhoods and to persist in their old occupations no matter how unproductive the latter might have been or proved to be in the new environment. This difference between them and the earlier settlers was deepened by their inferior economic status and accentuated by a certain bureaucratic formalism in the new state.[45]

Economic Problems

Economically Israel faced equally challenging problems. Even during the mandatory period the Jewish Yishuv had a deficit economy, but the deficit became worse after the establishment of statehood. That Israel avoided and avoids bankruptcy is due primarily to the voluntary contributions of American Jewry. The targets of the 1949 and 1950 fund drives in the United States known as the United Jewish Appeal were $250 million a year, most of which was to help Israel. These were large sums compared to the Israeli state budget, which in 1949–1950 amounted only to $285 million. In October 1949, Prime Minister Ben Gurion stated that Israel's deficit was £I (Israel pounds) 7 million ($20 million) a month.

In April 1949, Israel adopted a four-year plan—a bold program for the development of new industries and agriculture and the rehabilitation of the immigrants. But the speed of immigration continued to transcend economic absorptive capacity, and there were press reports of demonstrations by immigrants, who demanded "bread and work." Israel's economic position was not made easier by the economic boycott of the surrounding Arab states and Iraq's ban on the flow of Kirkuk oil through the pipeline to the refinery at Haifa. Some lessening of deficit spending was brought about by the conclusion of trade agreements with a number of European countries. But the main appeal had to be made to American Jews.

In October 1950, American Jewry pledged Israel one billion dollars over the next three years for the resettlement of 600,000 Jews. This was followed by flotation in the United States of an Israeli bond issue totaling $500 million. Headed by Henry Morgenthau, Jr., former American secretary of the treasury, the issue showed promise of success. In the spring of 1951, Prime Minister Ben Gurion toured Jewish centers in the United States to make a final appeal in behalf of the great fund drive.

Political Problems

Politically Israel represented, as could be expected, Western parliamentary democracy. In January 1949, elections based on universal suffrage resulted in the

---

[45]For an analysis of Israel's internal situation, see Edwin Samuel, "The Government of Israel and Its Problems," *Middle East Journal,* 3 (Jan. 1949).

establishment of a one-chamber parliament (Knesset) of 120 members. The political parties which had been in existence under the mandate continued with slight modifications in their names or composition. The moderate Socialists of David Ben Gurion (Mapai) emerged as the dominant party, with the left-wing Socialists (Mapam), Orthodox Jews, and Revisionists (Herut) as the three other most important groups. The Communist party, allowed to act freely, polled 15,287 votes and secured four seats. In February 1949 the Knesset voted by 50 to 38 to acquire a constitution "by evolution over an unspecified period of years."

From the beginning, Israel had a coalition cabinet of four parties: Mapai, holding a majority of the portfolios, Mapam, Orthodox, and General Zionist. The Revisionists were excluded from the executive branch, and at one time legal proceedings were initiated against some of their leaders. In 1948–1949 there was even some doubt, in view of their terrorist record and their independent course, whether or not they could be integrated in the new state. Experience has shown, however, that these fears were exaggerated. Nevertheless, they continued to represent the most chauvinistic and expansionist tendency in Israel. If one excepts the Communist party, which can be regarded as an instrument of an alien power, the only other group which found integration difficult was the United Religious Front. These stubborn orthodox elements, who were given three portfolios in Ben Gurion's cabinet, challenged the Socialist-espoused principle of the separation of church and state. Their refusal to acknowledge the secularization of Israel's public life brought about a serious cabinet crisis in the fall of 1950. The orthodox leaders demanded a ban on nonkosher meat imports and on transportation on Sabbath days and insisted on religious education for youth. The November 1950 municipal and rural elections brought moderate gains to parties of the right (General Zionists and the Revisionists) but the Socialist parties still commanded a strong position. Histadruth (the General Confederation of Labor) continued to occupy the key position in Israeli politics.

The second elections, held in July 1951, did not change the basic pattern of Israel's internal politics. The most significant development was perhaps the strengthening of the General Zionists (Dr. Weizmann's party), who more than doubled their representation. This could be largely ascribed to the influx of many new immigrants of a more conservative type, especially from Soviet-dominated Europe, but also from the Arab countries, who were not likely to support the traditional Socialist trends in Israel.[46]

The Arab Minority

The position and future of the Arab minority in Israel were not clear. Officially the Arabs were permitted to enjoy civic freedom and rights as citizens of the new state. Unofficially, according to some sources,[47] discrimination was practiced

---

[46]The composition of the Knesset in January 1949 and August 1951 follows (the first figure following a party is the number of seats in 1949, the second the seats in 1951): Mapai, 46, 45; Mapam, 19, 15; United Religious Front, 16, 0; Poale Mizrahi, 0, 8; Agudath Israel, 0, 2; Herut (formerly Irgun), 14, 8; General Zionists, 7, 20; Progressive, 5, 4; Sephardim, 4, 2; Communist, 4, 5; Arab parties, 2, 5; Fighter, 1, 0; WIZO, 1, 0; Yemenites, 1, 1.

[47]Norman Bentwich in his review of Dunner's *The Republic of Israel,* in *Middle Eastern Affairs* (Jan. 1951).

against them in many ways. Israel established a Ministry for Minorities, later renamed the Ministry of Police, under Sephardi Minister Behor Shitrit, and it may be assumed that internal security overrode other considerations. On May 3, 1950, Israeli forces with mortars and automatic weapons drove 12,000 Arabs from two villages near Hebron in order to clear the area for cultivation by Jewish settlers. Whether the Arabs were citizens of Israel or infiltrees from Jordan, the method employed was not consonant with Israel's professed democratic procedures. In September of the same year Egypt accused Israel of expelling 6,000 Arab nomads across the border into Egyptian territory, and the accusation was confirmed, with a slight reduction in numbers, by Major General William E. Riley, chief of staff of the Palestine Truce Commission, in his report to the United Nations Security Council.

Israel's Foreign Policy

"The Arab-Jewish struggle . . . has unsettled and poisoned the Middle East for three decades. . . . " This statement by a high Israeli official seems to penetrate to the root of the matter.[48] Israel's existence has posed one of the most baffling problems in the annals of modern diplomacy. The international relations of Israel may be divided—for the purpose of orderly presentation—into two main sectors: relations with the Middle East and with the great powers.

Middle East Relations

In her Middle Eastern diplomacy, Israel's relations with Turkey and Iran should be treated separately from her relations with the Arab world. Turkey, although she voted against partition, never manifested hostility toward Israel. In fact, she was the first in the Middle East to extend diplomatic recognition to the new Jewish state. Religious considerations could not mar this generally friendly relationship, inasmuch as Turkey had become a secularized state. Being more Westernized and prosperous than most of her oriental neighbors, Turkey even had some affinities with Israel. The main difference lay in the fact that Turkey, insisting on her European rather than her Middle Eastern orientation, definitely chose the side of the free world in the East-West struggle, while Israel was cautious not to identify herself with either political bloc.

Iran was more sensitive to the bonds of Islamic solidarity than was Turkey. For this reason her attitude toward Israel was much more reserved. During his visit in the United States in late 1949, the Shah was asked point-blank by a reporter whether or not Iran had recognized Israel and whether he "wished Israel well." In reply, he stated that Iran, as a Moslem country, could not act without due regard to the feelings of other Moslem countries and reserved her decisions until proper consultation had occurred.[49] After some lapse of time, Iran did grant Israel de facto recognition.

[48]Israel in the Pattern of Middle East Politics," by Iaacov Shimoni, director of the Asia Division of the Israel Ministry of Foreign Affairs, *Middle East Journal,* 4 (July 1950), p. 286.
[49]*New York Times,* Nov. 18, 1949.

The most vital problem for Israel centered in her relations with the Arab states. These relations, despite the armistices of 1949, have been consistently bad. The Arab countries never fully reconciled themselves to the existence of the Jewish state in their midst. They were humiliated in the war of 1948 and have not recovered from the moral and political consequences of their defeat. To preach hostility toward Israel and to promote a "second round" which would result in her complete obliteration often was the most popular line of behavior for Arab statesmen and politicians. The Arab emotional upset over Israel had become so great that it dwarfed other considerations and ideas and distorted Arab thinking on many an international and domestic problem.

This hostility to Israel was intensified by Arab fear, in part genuine and in part artificially fanned, of alleged Israeli expansionism. Although Israel's initial official policy has been one of maintaining the postwar status quo, one can point to a few facts which lend credence to Arab contentions. The first is that the extremist Revisionist bloc (Herut, former Irgun) remained very much alive in Israeli politics, and as a determined and dynamic body it was apt to wield an influence out of proportion to its real numbers. This bloc, which secured fourteen seats in Israel's first election, had a great appeal to American Jewry. Thus, for example, Menachem Begin, its leader and former head of the terrorist Irgun, visited the United States on what was believed to be a successful fund-raising trip. In New York he was received with high honors, not only by the Jewish community but also by the mayor, and he was the hero of the day in a city-sponsored motorcade through the garment district.[50]

Furthermore, even the official Israeli attitude was not entirely reassuring. During the war in 1948 Israel enlarged her territory over what was originally projected in the UN partition plan and refused to withdraw to the assigned boundaries. Israel's contention was that by invading Israel on May 15, 1948, the Arabs had invalidated the partition resolution and therefore the Arab states had no legal claims under it.[51] Israel (with the kingdom of Jordan) stubbornly rejected all proposals and official United Nations resolutions for the internationalization of Jerusalem. In fact, Prime Minister Ben Gurion challenged United Nations authority to the extent of moving Israel's capital from Tel-Aviv to the Jewish-held part of Jerusalem in late 1949.[52]

Israeli leaders had placed great stock in the authority of the United Nations at the time of the partition, but they tended to disregard the United Nations in such matters as the truces, the boundaries, and Jerusalem if UN action collided with their vital interests. This deepened Arab fears. Moreover, the Arabs showed anxiety over the prospects of Israeli economic domination of the Middle East, an anxiety nurtured by fear of the financial and banking power of world Jewry. Finally, mention should be made of Arab suspicion that the Socialist Israeli regime might set a dangerous pattern for left-wing trends in the Arab lands, upset their traditional social structures, and act as a stimulant to numerous minorities in the Arab world.

[50] See pictures of his enthusiastic reception in the *New York Times,* Nov. 27, 1948.

[51] Shimoni, *op. cit.,* p. 283 n. 5.

[52] The initial plan of the Israeli government had been to move all government offices to Jerusalem and to proclaim it the capital, in defiance of UN resolutions internationalizing the city. Because, however, of possible diplomatic objections to such a move on the part of various member states of the United Nations, the Israeli government decided to transfer only certain departments to Jerusalem, while leaving others in Tel-Aviv. The prime minister and the foreign minister continued to carry on their functions in Tel-Aviv.

The tragic problem of Arab refugees added a seemingly inexhaustible source of constant irritation. In fact, this problem hung like a sword of Damocles over the shaky Arab governments, placing them in a most embarrassing and dangerous position. On the one hand, they insisted on the right of the refugees to return to their homes. This legalistic attitude led them to refuse to study any long-range constructive resettlement projects.[53] And they were obviously unable to back up their legal claims by force, thus revealing their impotence. On the other hand, their social and economic structures were profoundly disturbed by the presence of refugee multitudes, and their public funds were strained in granting them relief. The policies of the Arab states toward the refugees were not uniform. Jordan, for example, granted all refugees citizenship. Egypt went to the other extreme of forbidding the refugees the right to work and thus condemning them to idleness, a situation full of explosive potentialities. The fact that the United Nations was not able to devote more than about $50 million a year—a pittance—to refugee relief, when at the same time the International Refugee Organization was amply provided with funds to deal with European displaced persons, added to Arab bitterness.

In the summer of 1949 the United Nations Conciliation Committee for Palestine arranged for negotiations with the Israeli and Arab delegations in Lausanne to settle all the outstanding problems including that of the refugees. But by the end of the year the conference wound up in deadlock, because of completely irreconcilable Jewish and Arab attitudes. Israel maintained that the readmission of all the refugees was utterly unrealistic and out of question and that any decision in this regard could be taken only as a part of the overall political settlement, which would transform the existing armistice agreements into formal peace treaties. The Arab delegations stood firmly on the principle that the first prerequisite of any peace settlement was the readmission of all the refugees.

Nothing was achieved, and the state of hostility between the Arabs and Israel continued. This hostility had another tragic consequence, namely, the uprooting of many old and frequently prosperous Jewish communities in Arab countries. Reprisals against the Jews of Yemen led them to emigrate en masse to Israel, causing no little trouble for the new progressive state in having to absorb a backward, oriental, and almost alien mass of refugees. No contrast could be greater than between a lice-infested, Arabic-speaking, brown-skinned, and superstitious Yemenite coolie and a London-bred and Oxford-educated English Jew, and the latter predominated in the higher echelons of the Israeli Foreign Office. The Jews of Aden, French North Africa, and Libya were also persecuted, and they flocked to Israel. The greatest tragedy was, perhaps, that of the 160,000-strong Jewish community in Iraq. Prosperous and settled in the land even before the coming of the Arabs, these Jews now found life in Iraq unbearable. By the spring of 1951 they had availed themselves of the Iraqi law which permitted them to opt for Israeli citizenship and emigrate.

The only Arab state with which Israel reached a relatively successful *modus vivendi* was Jordan. This was primarily due to the coincidence that they agreed on a

---

[53] Such as those prepared by the Clapp mission which toured the Middle East in 1949. See *Final Report of the U.N. Economic Survey Mission for the Middle East,* U.N. Conciliation Commission for Palestine, Document AAC. 25/6, Dec. 28, 1949.

few main points, while Jordan quarreled with other Arab states. Thus, for example, the disposition of the Arab-held parts of Palestine ceased to be a Jewish-Arab problem and became an inter-Arab problem, the other Arab states resenting Jordan's unilateral annexation of this area. Jerusalem was another sector where Israel's and Jordan's policies coincided. Jordan's interest in a free transit route to the Mediterranean led her to enter into negotiations with Israel for a five-year pact. In the spring of 1950, however, because of the pressure of other Arab states, Jordan decided to break off the talks. Despite all the internecine rivalries, Arab solidarity was not quite extinguished. The economic boycott of Israel, proclaimed by the Arab League and reaffirmed on many occasions, emphasized again, however imperfect it was in practice, that the Arab ocean had not reconciled itself to the volcanic eruption of the Jewish island in its midst.

Israel and the Big Powers

The friendship of Israel and the United States is an important feature of Israeli relations with the big powers. American influence was largely responsible for the UN partition resolution, and the United States was the first among the big powers to recognize the new Jewish state. Israel expected and obtained economic aid from the United States. During Dr. Weizmann's visit in Washington in May 1948 he was promised a $100 million loan. The promise was fulfilled when the Export-Import Bank announced in January 1949 that this credit had been made available to Israel. No Arab country had ever received direct financial aid from the United States of the same magnitude. In January 1949 the American government granted Israel full de jure recognition and appointed a well-known pro-Zionist, Dr. James G. McDonald, as first United States ambassador in Tel-Aviv. Israel invited American specialists such as Dr. Walter C. Lowdermilk to advise her on irrigation and other technical matters. She also concluded contracts with the Ford and Kaiser-Frazer corporations, which resulted in the establishment of motorcar assembly plants in the new state. In 1950 the two countries signed a Point Four agreement that extended to Israel further American assistance.

On the part of the United States this pro-Israeli policy was not achieved without hesitations and sudden shifts. It will be recalled that at one time the United States was prepared to abandon the partition resolution in favor of a trusteeship arrangement. Another shift occurred when Secretary of State Marshall announced official American endorsement of the Bernadotte plan in the fall of 1948. Furthermore, repeated messages were sent by Presidents Roosevelt and Truman to various Arab states and rulers, tending to reassure them that the United States would not support any solution in Palestine contrary to Arab wishes. These twists in American policy were to a large extent due to the division of responsibility between the White House and the Department of State. While the latter was concerned with the Middle East as a whole, the former tended to treat the Zionist problem in isolation from the rest of the area and as a factor of domestic politics; hence, the inconsistencies. The White House prevailed on all important occasions, and despite its tortuous ways American diplomacy could generally be described as pro-Israeli.

Israeli-British relations are in glaring contrast. Nothing could better illustrate the strange ways of human emotions than the transformation of the Jewish-British friendship of World War I into the outright hatred of Britain at the end and after World War II. Britain's policy, after as during the mandate period, continued to be pro-Arab. Even after the termination of the mandate the British, who occupied Haifa until June 30, 1948, refused to admit Jewish immigrants in that harbor. Britain endorsed the Bernadotte plan because it slightly favored the Arabs and also because by granting the Negeb to the future Arab state it promised British-protected Jordan access to the Mediterranean. Britain resumed her shipments of arms to the Arab states as soon as the conclusion of the Arab-Israeli armistice agreements eliminated United Nations rulings of this matter. And to stress her lack of enthusiasm for Israel, Great Britain abstained from voting on both occasions when Israel's application for membership in the United Nations was being decided.

Despite this political coolness, Israel was linked to Great Britain by more economic bonds than she was to any other country (if we except American charity). The British held sizable Israeli sterling balances in London; they controlled Palestine Potash Ltd., a big concern extracting salts from the Dead Sea; they owned the refinery at Haifa; and they imported considerable quantities of Israel's citrus crops. Notwithstanding the political difficulties, this great nation of traders gradually came to terms with Israel on economic lines, thus normalizing mutual relations.

Israel's relations with the Soviet Union are full of ambiguities. The original Leninist doctrine taught hostility toward Zionism as a nationalist-bourgeois movement. In the interwar period, Soviet agents in the Middle East supported Arab nationalism as opposed to Western imperialism and preached that Zionism was an instrument of British imperial policy. Soviet espousal of the partition resolution came, therefore, as a surprise to many who were acquainted with the basic Communist line. Yet it was logical as a step toward the elimination of Great Britain from this strategic area on the Mediterranean coast. Moreover, it could be explained as an expression of Russia's desire to confuse and unsettle the Middle East, so that she may eventually profit from the new ferment. Be that as it may, the fact remains that, despite her support of the partition resolution, Russia was not regarded by the Arabs as the chief villain of the drama, that role being reserved for the United States. Russia's tactics in the Middle East were tortuous, but one could discern in them a reversion to the old pro-Arab trend to the extent that it served to embarrass the West. It would not be surprising if one day the world should discover that Soviet encouragement was behind some of the popular anti-Zionist demonstrations in the Middle East. One should not forget, however, that basically Soviet policy was dedicated to the social and political revolution in the Middle East, and that all Soviet moves, either pro-Arab or pro-Jewish, had to be treated as tactics subordinated to this major objective.[54]

The Soviet Union extended full diplomatic recognition to Israel a few days after the United States and sent an envoy to Tel-Aviv. Israel sent a minister to Moscow, Golda Myerson (renamed Meir), a leader in the dominant Mapai party, who later

[54]For a typically Marxist approach to the Palestinian problem, see A. B. Magil, *Israel in Crisis* (New York, 1950). The book reveals the party line followed in 1950.

was recalled to become a member of Ben Gurion's cabinet. Relations between the two countries were highlighted by the conclusion in August 1949 of an agreement whereby all former Russian Orthodox properties (including churches, convents, and hospices) in Jerusalem and elsewhere in Israel were taken over by the Soviet government and the Soviet-controlled Orthodox Church. This arrangement placed Soviet representatives in a strategic position in the heart of Jersualem and delivered into their hands the hitherto anti-Communist Orthodox organization in Palestine. Russia promptly appointed a member of the Soviet Orthodox hierarchy archbishop of Jerusalem. Israel also concluded a number of trade treaties with the Soviet European satellites, thus linking to some extent her economy to that of the postwar Soviet empire.

Israel's policies toward Russia cannot be adequately understood unless they are related to the larger problem of the East-West conflict. In this conflict Israel has pursued a policy of neutrality, loath to commit herself to either bloc.[55] Israeli and Soviet policies were alike in that both countries extended recognition to the Communist government of China.[56] They were also alike in their opposition to the UN General Assembly's resolution in 1950 rescinding the ban on full diplomatic relations with Franco Spain. But following the Communist invasion of South Korea in June 1950, Israel declared herself opposed to any aggression and pledged her support of United Nations action. Her contribution to the allied war effort has consisted in sending some medical supplies to Korea.

A member of the United Nations since May 11, 1949, Israel has obtained diplomatic recognition from the majority of member states and has thus legally entrenched her position. The Anglo-American-French agreement of May 25, 1950, providing for the sale of arms to the Middle East for defensive purposes only added another guarantee of Israel's security. But her political future remained uncertain in view of the unabated hostility of the Arabs. It was, moreover, doubtful to what extent the strategic interest of the West could be reconciled with Israel's existence. The West, and the United States in particular, was interested in strengthening the Middle East by promoting greater technical and governmental efficiency in these underdeveloped areas, by building up their military power, and by encouraging greater political unity. But greater unity and an improved military position for the Arabs meant a greater danger to Israel, and Israeli officials did not hide their fear of Arab unification schemes. Israel argued that a transformation of the Arab states into progressive societies dedicated to the welfare of the common man would result in automatic abandonment of vindictive attitudes.[57] But this was mere speculation. It presupposed that progress would eliminate nationalism. Israel herself seemed to be a living refutation of this thesis; she was progressive but also nationalist.

---

[55]This neutrality or (later) "independence" of the Israeli foreign policy was stressed in careful statements by Israel's official spokesmen. (For an authoritative statement, see "Israel's Foreign Policy and International Relations," by Walter Eytan, director-general of the Israeli Foreign Office, *Middle Eastern Affairs,* May 1951.)

[56]It should be pointed out, in all fairness, that at that time Great Britain and a number of other non-Communist countries had also recognized Mao's government.

[57]See Shimoni, *op. cit.,* p. 285.

Internal Trends in the 1950s

Israel's cabinets in the 1950s represented coalitions of the dominant Socialist Mapai party, with the General Zionists and—to a lesser extent—religious elements. For the major part of this period the premiership remained in the hands of David Ben Gurion, who emerged not only as the practically undisputed leader of Israel but also as the living symbol of those dynamic values and the assertive spirit that characterized modern political Zionism.[58] In 1953 Ben Gurion retired from active leadership to live in a kibbutz in the Negeb, leaving the reins of government to his close lieutenant Moshe Sharett. But the darkening of the international skies in 1955 brought him back to power, first as defense minister and later, in November, as premier. Throughout these years Israel's politics were characterized by the struggle of the dominant left-of-center group to preserve the unity of the new nation on an essentially Western foundation of society. This proved to be an arduous task because of certain serious obstacles, foremost of which was the gradual orientalization of Israel's population. What originally began as a fairly homogeneous Ashkenazi community from eastern Europe had been transformed by the mid-1950s into a culturally heterogeneous group in which oriental Jews constituted over 50 percent of the population. Moreover, because of their higher birth rate, their numerical preponderance was likely to increase as time went on.

Against the background of this orientalization—with all its social and economic implications—stood the centrifugal tendency of certain elements which had never fully accepted the philosophy and program of the leading political group in the country. First among these was the orthodox religious bloc, which aimed at revival of a Jewish theocratic state. Measures advocated by this bloc included compulsory religious education, a ban on imports of nonkosher food, opposition to military service by women, compulsory jurisdiction of rabbinical courts, and general supremacy of the Torah over lay legislation. These views obviously clashed with the attitude of the dominant socialist elements who, with their Marxist antecedents,[59] had an essentially secularist and, not infrequently, atheistic approach to social problems. Another centrifugal force was represented by Herut. An heir to the Revisionist organization and to the terrorist groups of wartime, this party continued as spokesman for extreme nationalist elements that advocated expansion southward and eastward. Not only the Egyptian-held Gaza strip and Jordan's west-bank area but also the lands east of the Jordan River were objects of their territorial ambitions.[60]

[58]Dr. Chaim Weizmann, first president of Israel, had died on November 9, 1952. Soon afterward Dr. Albert Einstein, an American citizen, was offered the presidency by Premier Ben Gurion, but he refused it. On December 8, Itzhak Ben-Zvi was elected president.

[59]On May 25, 1953, four General Zionist members of the cabinet "resigned in protest against the Mapai (Socialist) party's insistence that on May Day and other labor holidays, schools in working class districts should have the right to fly the red flag, symbol of socialism, alongside the flag of Israel and to sing the Internationale in addition to the Israeli anthem" (quoted from the *Middle East Journal,* 7 [Summer 1953]).

[60]For *Herut's* program and territorial demands, see J. B. Schechtman, "Revisionism" in *Struggle for Tomorrow,* ed. by B. J. Vlavianos and F. Gross (New York, 1954), and James G. McDonald, *My Mission in Israel* (New York, 1951), p. 145.

Moreover, despite their outward adaptation to the existing parliamentary system in Israel, these extremist elements did not entirely forget their defiant attitude toward law in the mandate days, often resorting to acts and tactics hardly in keeping with the spirit of democracy. As a result there was an undercurrent of violence in Israel's politics, expressed by such manifestations as a mob attack on the Knesset during the latter's debate on German reparations; a call for a campaign of "civil disobedience" issued by the Herut leader, Menachem Begin, followed by a sabotage plot in Haifa (credited to some Herut members) in connection with the same question; and bomb explosions in the Soviet Legation and in the home of Israel Rokach, a General Zionist who was formerly minister of interior.

Communism could not be disregarded as a problem either. The knowledge now available on Communist tactics indicates that the party seldom relies on overt activities only and that it tends to employ, with increasing success, the method of infiltration into other organizations. In the Middle East in general, the line drawn between the Communists and the Socialists has never been as clear as in some more advanced countries of the West. In Israel this phenomenon found its reflection in the existence of the left-wing socialist party, the Mapam, which rather consistently showed pro-Soviet leanings. To be sure, this did not automatically mean that the party as a whole was a Communist-front organization. Yet its pronounced leftist tendency in conjunction with its pro-Soviet orientation left it open to accusations of dangerous closeness to communism. On February 21, 1952, two prominent members of the Mapam, Mrs. Hanna Landau, deputy speaker of the Knesset, and David Livshitz resigned from it on the ground that it "had become indistinguishable from the Communists."[61]

Elections to the third Knesset, which took place in July 1955, revealed that the centrifugal or even extremist trends were in the ascendant. The period of bourgeois moderation, characteristic of the 1951 elections, seemed to be over, and this time the political center lost rather heavily to the forces of the far right and the far left. The most spectacular change, perhaps, was the virtual doubling of Herut representation from 8 to 15. Otherwise leftist groups (Mapam, Achdut Avoda, Communists, and Progressives) registered gains at the expense of the center, and there was a slight increase in the strength of religious parties. Despite the orientalization of the population, political affiliations tended to follow the already existing pattern, and no successful attempt was made to build parties corresponding to the ethnic origins of the population. Such minor representation as the Yemenites and the Sephardim had had in the previous Knesset disappeared altogether in the new legislature.

The effects of this new shift in political configuration were soon felt in the composition of the cabinet. General Zionists, who were the most Western-minded members of the dominant coalition and who lost one-third of their seats in the Knesset, were removed from the government and their places were filled by the left-wing parties. The new cabinet formed on November 2, 1955, by Ben Gurion represented an alliance of Mapai (9 portfolios), Mapam (2), Hapoel Hamizrachi (2),

---

[61]*Middle East Journal,* 6 (Spring 1952).

Achdut Avoda (2), and Progressives (1). The assignment of two ministries to Hapoel Hamizrachi, an orthodox labor party, could be interpreted as a device to appease the religious groups in the country while preserving the essentially leftist character of the new coalition.[62]

Economic questions claimed, as usual, a high priority in government activities. The budget continued to show a steady deficit, which was balanced by grants from the United States, contributions from Jewish organizations abroad, and the floating of an Israeli bond issue in America. Between 1948 and 1955, Israel received $367 million from the United States government under the form of loans, grants-in-aid, and technical assistance. This compared favorably with the total of $163 million granted to all the Arab states during the same period.[63] Although the big wave of immigration had come to an end, immigrants, encouraged by the Israeli government and the World Zionist Organization, continued to flock to the country. This posed a never-ending financial problem, as it was estimated that the settling of immigrants required about $3,000 a person. Moreover, because of their oriental origin most of the new arrivals lacked the necessary skills to perform productive work in agriculture or industry, thus increasing the difficulties of absorption. The lack of adequate water resources prevented full development of contemplated irrigation schemes, while no progress was made on the utilization of the water of the Jordan River owing to the opposition of the neighboring Arab states.[64] At the same time the continuous boycott of Israel by the Arab League separated Israel's industries from their natural outlets. Stringent controls of imports and currency had to be maintained, and rationing of foodstuffs was not uncommon.

Despite all these difficulties, Israel was putting to good use the generous aid it received from abroad. Every year marked new developments in collective farming, construction, mining, and industry. Noteworthy in this connection was the agreement signed on September 10, 1952, with the Western German Republic whereby

[62]Concerning the co-operation between Socialists and "theocratic fundamentalists," see a lengthy analysis by Henry Hurwitz in "Israel, What Now?" *Menorah Journal,* 42 nos. 1 and 2 (1954).

[63]Actually, the period for the Arab states should read July 1, 1945, to June 30, 1955. Between her creation as a state and the end of 1955 Israel received an estimated total of $2 billion from external sources. This was composed of the following sums (in round figures): direct United States government aid—$367 million (grants-in-aid, $226 million; Export-Import Bank loan, $135 million; technical assistance, $6 million; Israel bonds sales in U.S., $227 million; United Jewish Appeal, $360 million; West German reparations, $160 million; other contributions (gifts, capital investments, etc.) from all external sources, $886 million.

These figures were compiled from the following sources: testimony of Arthur Z. Gardiner of the U.S. Department of State before the House Committee on Foreign Affairs on May 10, 1954 (*New York Times,* June 14, 1954); H. H. Howard, "The Development of United States Policy in the Near East, South Asia and Africa during 1954," *Department of State Bulletin,* Feb. 28, 1955; *New York Times,* Feb. 6, 1956; Eliezer Livneh, "Israel's Two Thousand Million Dollars—Where Have They Gone?" *Jewish Observer and Middle East Review,* Nov. 19, 1954; and *Operations Report, International Cooperation Administration,* Nov. 16, 1955.

[64]On October 14, 1953, Eric Johnston, prominent leader of the American film industry, left for the Middle East on behalf of President Eisenhower on a mission to secure Arab and Israeli collaboration on the development of the Jordan River with a view to benefiting all the riparian states. His proposals met with a cool reception in Arab capitals, and such negotiations as were conducted in the course of his subsequent visits to the Middle East showed little progress.

the latter agreed to pay Israel, in the course of fourteen years, $822 million in goods as reparations for the damages inflicted upon European Jewry by the Nazi regime.[65] Money thus obtained was earmarked, in large part, to finance Israel's development projects. In September 1955 an exploration party struck oil in Huleikat (Helez) in the Negeb, having completed a well abandoned years earlier by the Iraq Petroleum Company. This important discovery would open new vistas of economic self-sufficiency if the oil proved to exist in commercial quantities.

The Arab minority continued to suffer from a number of practical disabilities. It was restricted in its freedom of movement as many Arab-populated areas of Israel were subject to the authority of Israeli military commanders. Its economic opportunities were limited because such funds as Israel could obtain from abroad and such planned effort as she made to develop the country were destined to benefit Jewish and not Arab inhabitants. Except for local municipal and village offices, positions in the state administration were, to all practical purposes, denied to Arabs.

The most grievous disability resulted from an important piece of legislation known as the Land Acquisition Law of March 10, 1953. This law authorized the state to seize the property which "(1) On April 1, 1952, was not in the possession of its owners; (2) Was used or earmarked within the period from May 4, 1948, to April 1, 1952, for purposes of essential development, settlement or security; (3) Is still required for one of these purposes." Owners of such property were given the right to indemnity, which was to be based on the value of the property on January 1, 1950, with an increase of 3 percent for each year thereafter, to be paid in Israeli currency at the current rate of exchange.[66] Although primarily affecting the refugees living outside Israel's territory, the law was likely to hurt considerable numbers of Arabs in Israel because of the displacements that had occurred during or after the war of 1948. Even if some of these displacements were voluntary, in a purely technical sense, in most cases they were caused by fear such as had motivated the mass flight of refugees to the safety of the neighboring Arab states in 1948. The law did not differentiate between voluntary or involuntary absence from one's land, merely stating that it covered property "not in the possession of its owners" on a certain date. Official Israeli sources denied that the law was discriminatory, claiming instead that it applied to all absentee landowners irrespective of nationality. Such assertions, however, could not disguise the fact that Arabs were subjected to legal harassment and ill-compensated deprivation of property and that by and large they were treated as second-class citizens.[67]

---

[65]From the legal point of view this agreement was without precedent, inasmuch as it involved payments to a new state in compensation for deeds committed before the establishment of that state toward persons who might or might not have become its citizens. Politically, the agreement temporarily strained the good relations prevailing between the Bonn Republic and the Arab states. The latter accused Bonn of strengthening Israel and thus working against the Arabs. The West German government replied that shipments to Israel under the agreement would not include strategic goods. A joint Arab mission which visited West Germany failed to persuade the Bonn government to abandon the agreement. For some time Arab states contemplated an economic boycott of West Germany in reprisal, but eventually they desisted from doing so on the ground that, in their view, Germany was not a free agent in this transaction, having been prodded into it by the United States.

[66]The text is in the *Middle East Journal,* 7 (Summer 1953).

[67]For a competent treatment of the problem, see Don Peretz, "The Arab Minority in Israel," *Middle East Journal,* 7 (Spring 1953).

Israel's Foreign Relations in the 1950s

Technically at war with Israel, the Arab states not only continued their economic boycott of the new state but intensified it by drawing up additional stringent regulations and establishing regional boycott offices. Foreign commercial and industrial firms were given a choice of either continuing their business with Israel or with the Arab countries under penalty of being blacklisted. Airlines could not include Israel in routes passing through Arab territories, and merchant ships were enjoined not to call on Israeli ports during voyages that led them through Arab waters. Egypt exploited her special position in the Suez Canal and the Gulf of Aqaba to prevent Israel-bound vessels from reaching their destination. Egypt dominated the Gulf of Aqaba because the only navigable passage at the entrance of the gulf was located in her territorial waters and was effectively covered by her shore batteries. This tended to immobilize the new Israeli harbor, Elath, situated at the head of the gulf.

A peace settlement seemed far away. Israel did not cease protesting that she desired peace and that she was prepared to sign a peace treaty to replace the existing armistice agreements. The Arab states made any talk of peace conditional upon Israel's compliance with three resolutions of the United Nations, namely, those enjoining the internationalization of Jerusalem, the readmission of Arab refugees to their homes, and the rectification of boundaries so as to conform to the original partition resolution of November 1947.[68] Inasmuch as Israel steadily rejected these conditions as a prerequisite to a peace treaty, and the Arabs were adamant in insisting upon them, the likelihood of the two parties coming together was as remote as ever. In fact, one might legitimately suspect that behind this complete inflexibility on both sides was a basic reluctance to consider a peace settlement. While on many counts peace might be welcome to Israel, it also presented potential disadvantages, foremost among which was freezing of the existing modest and inconvenient boundaries—an idea repugnant to a good many Israelis long conditioned to think in terms of Palestine as a whole as their rightful possession. Also Israel could count on continued high-level generosity on the part of American Zionists so long as she was threatened with a war of revenge and so long as an aura of crisis surrounded her position in the Middle East. Any improvement in international relations might adversely affect the readiness of the American Zionist community to make heavy cash outlays for the upkeep of Israel. As for the Arabs, the bitterness engendered by their defeat in Palestine was so great and so widespread among the masses that it was unsafe for any Arab government, however strong, to go on record as favoring peace or negotiations with Israel.

[68]The Palestine partition resolution of November 29, 1947, provided for the internationalization of Jerusalem. On December 9, 1949, the General Assembly again adopted a resolution that Jerusalem should be administered under a separate international regime. The General Assembly resolution of December 11, 1948, provided "that refugees wishing to return to their homes and live at peace with their neighbors should be permitted to do so at the earliest practicable date, and that compensation should be paid for property of those choosing not to return and for loss or damage to property which under principles of international law or in equity should be made good by Governments or authorities concerned." Concerning the boundaries, the Arab states and Israel on May 12, 1949, signed agreements with the United Nations Conciliation Commission to consider the partition plan of 1947 "as a starting-point and framework for the discussion of territorial questions" (L. L. Leonard, "The United Nations and Palestine," *International Conciliation* Oct. 1949, p. 737).

Against this background of mutual inflexibility, the border situation was going from bad to worse. Violations of the armistice boundaries were frequent and were being committed by both sides. Their nature, however, differed according to who was involved. In the first place there were frequent exchanges of fire between the military outposts and clashes between border patrols, which unwittingly or knowingly crossed into alien territory. Such incidents ran into the hundreds within a single year and could be considered almost a routine matter for the Mixed Armistice Commissions which watched over the truce along the borders. Marauding Bedouin bands, traditionally accustomed to disregard boundary lines, occasionally caused minor disturbances. But so far as the Arabs were concerned, violations were usually committed by individual infiltrators, mostly refugees or farmers who crossed the boundary to rejoin their relatives or to revisit their farmlands located on the other side of the border.[69] The Israelis were determined to stop these infiltrations by a policy of retaliation, the chief advocate of which was Premier Ben Gurion himself.[70] Consequently the border violations committed by the Israelis had the character of well-organized military raids against Arab communities of the neighboring countries. Among a number of such raids, four assumed the proportions of major military operations and as a result attracted considerable attention and publicity abroad. These were the raids carried out against the Arab villages of Kibya and Nahhalin in Jordan, the Egyptian headquarters in the Gaza strip, and a Syrian village east of the Sea of Galilee. The Kibya attack was executed on October 14, 1953, by 250 to 300 "well-trained Israeli soldiers" according to the head of the Palestine Truce Supervisory Organization, Major-General Vagn Bennike. Fifty-three Arab villagers, regardless of age and sex, were killed and their houses destroyed. The pattern resembled the Deir Yasin massacre in 1948; it was an indiscriminate killing of civilians with the obvious purpose of sowing terror among the borderland Arab population. On October 15 the Mixed Armistice Commission and on November 24 the UN Security Council strongly condemned Israel for the attack. The Council actually approved by a vote of 9 to 0 a motion of censure presented jointly by the United States, Britain, and France. The Kibya raid coincided with another serious border incident, namely, an attempt by the Israelis to drain the Huleh swamps and construct a hydroelectric plant in the demilitarized zone between Israel and Syria. Inasmuch as this operation involved diversion of Jordan water to Israel, Syria lodged a protest before the United Nations. General Vagn Bennike, in his capacity as chief of the truce team in Palestine, issued an order enjoining Israel to cease work on the Huleh canal. Despite this Israel went ahead with her project, which, in turn, brought about a rather strong reaction on the part of the United States. On October 20, 1953, Secretary of State John Foster Dulles suspended aid to Israel, earmarked under the Foreign Operations Administration, until such time as Israel complied with Bennike's order.[71] This determined action seemed to be more persuasive than the rather

---

[69] In this mass of infiltrators there were some who, because of their total destitution, were intent on robbery or revenge and who, accordingly, were guilty of killings and assaults. Israel claimed an impressive number of such crimes had been perpetrated, especially in border settlements.

[70] See article by Harry Gilroy, "Policy of Retaliation Is Defended by Israel: Officials Say Reprisals Are Their Only Answer to Aggression," *New York Times*, Dec. 18, 1955.

[71] U.S. aid under the technical assistance program was not to be affected by this decision.

ineffectual United Nations resolutions, and on October 28 Israel declared that she would stop the Huleh operations. On the same day President Eisenhower declared that aid to Israel would be resumed.

The Kibya and the Huleh incidents caused considerable excitement in the Arab countries. On January 9, 1954, King Saud of Saudi Arabia declared in an interview that, if necessary, the Arabs should sacrifice up to ten million men in order to eradicate the menace of Israel, this "cancer" on their body, as he termed it. It was, no doubt, in line with this general impetuousness, that on March 17, 1954, an unknown party of assailants, presumably Arab, killed eleven Israelis riding in a bus at Scorpion Pass, near Beersheba. Israel promptly accused Jordan of the deed, but the Mixed Armistice Commission, lacking evidence, refused to condemn the Jordanian government for this action. In reply, Israel proclaimed a boycott of the Commission.

If the murder in question was an act of Arab revenge for Kibya, the subsequent Israeli retaliation again surpassed in scope the Arab action. Eleven days after the killings in Scorpion Pass two companies of the Israeli army attacked the village of Nahhalin in Jordanian territory. This time the toll was nine Jordanians killed and nineteen wounded. The village mosque was sacked. The Mixed Armistice Commission, still boycotted by Israel, condemned the latter for the attack.

Following these tragedies on the Israeli-Jordanian border, the center of difficulty shifted to the Israeli-Egyptian border area. The artificial line separating the refugee-populated Gaza strip and the El-Auja enclave from the Negeb was a constant source of irritation between the two parties, but until February 28, 1955, no major military engagements were recorded. On that day, however, an Israeli force estimated at half a battalion attacked and destroyed the Gaza garrison headquarters of the Egyptian army, killing 38 and wounding 31 Egyptians. Procedure in the United Nations was the same as before: first the Mixed Armistice Commission and then, on March 29, the Security Council censured Israel for the attack. Again the Council's resolution was based on a motion presented by the major Western powers.

The fourth major raid executed by Israel occurred on December 11, 1955, in the Syrian territory east of Lake Tiberias. A strong Israeli detachment attacked Syrian border outposts and a village, killing forty-nine persons. This time there was no pretense of spontaneity (such as was claimed in the Kibya raid), and the Israeli government openly admitted that the raid was in retaliation for sniping by Syrian border outposts against Israeli fishermen sailing close to the eastern shore of the lake. The Security Council issued the most strongly worded condemnation of Israel's action yet recorded. The British government went so far as to voice its "indignation" over the raid. American public opinion, to the extent to which it was informed of the affair, was also shocked. Even in Israel a few newspapers expressed doubts as to the wisdom of such actions.[72] There seemed to be general agreement that Israel's retaliatory deed was out of all proportion to the Syrian provocation.

These strong military measures posed the question as to whether Israel used them only as retaliation for border infiltrations or whether, perhaps, they were a device to force the Arab states to come to terms in a general peace settlement. If the latter was

[72]See Harry Gilroy, "Israelis Divided by Raid on Syria," *New York Times*, Dec. 15, 1955.

the purpose, the results did not follow expectations. Instead of becoming more pliable, Arab attitudes stiffened, and, because of the clearly demonstrated military superiority of Israel, Arab governments began to take serious steps to redress the balance of armaments. Egypt's new military rulers claimed that their original objective had been internal reform, but this had had to give place to considerations of national security after the Gaza attack. Consequently, they turned to the Soviet bloc in search of arms and before the end of 1955 consummated a deal with Czechoslovakia.[73]

Egypt's move provoked an immediate reaction in Israel, where the possibility of a preventive war was seriously discussed. The Israeli government advanced the doctrine of "balance of armaments" as a guiding principle in the maintenance of peace in the region. In the name of this doctrine Israel appealed to Washington to allow her to purchase arms in the United States. This request, strongly supported by Zionist groups in America, did not elicit an immediate reply from the Department of State, the latter having to consider many aspects of the case. Israel's raid in the Lake Tiberias area tended to slow down rather than to accelerate Washington's decision.

The bitterness of the Israeli-Egyptian conflict and the resultant race in armaments could not be divorced from the general problem of regional security in the Middle East and of the overall position of Israel vis-à-vis the major powers. Israel viewed with undisguised suspicion any attempt by the United States and Britain to forge closer links with the Arabs by drawing them into a regional defense alliance. She also expressed nervousness about any withdrawal of Western military control in the area. Thus, in 1954 when Britain and Egypt concluded their agreement concerning the Suez Canal, Israel voiced her misgivings about the removal of British troops in the Canal Zone. Also when the United States first offered arms to Iraq in order to build up a Northern Tier alliance, and later when it gave its blessing to the projected Baghdad Pact, Israel and her sympathizers launched a vigorous campaign to counter the policy of "arming the Arabs."[74] Israel had little sympathy with United States' attempts to erect a barrier against Soviet penetration in the Middle East, and, paradoxically, she shared with Egypt and Saudi Arabia a decidedly negative attitude toward the Middle East Treaty Organization.

Despite this divergence in views on regional security, Israel seemed to be veering toward the United States. This was partly due to the continuous aid Israel was receiving from the United States, coupled with the conviction that, if hostilities broke out, only the latter could be counted upon as a friend in need, and partly to the notable deterioration in Soviet-Israeli relations. This deterioration was first noted in the winter of 1952–1953 when two groups of Jews within the Soviet orbit became victims of Communist justice. The arrest and sentencing of a group of Jewish doctors in Russia for an alleged plot against the security of state resembled the familiar scapegoat techniques of Nazi Germany too much to remain unnoticed in Israel. The trials (followed by death sentences) of Rudolph Slansky, secretary-

---

[73]See below, p. 528.
[74]See *Security and the Middle East: The Problem and Its Solution,* proposals submitted to the President of the United States by a group of citizens and distributed by the Nation Associates, April 1954.

general of the Czechoslovak Communist party, and his associates, most of them Jews, had strong discriminatory undertones leading many observers to wonder whether they were not indicative of a concerted anti-Semitic drive in the Soviet bloc. These trials provoked lively comment in Israel, which reached its culmination when a bomb planted by unknown assailants exploded in the Soviet Legation in Tel-Aviv on February 9, 1953. Three days later the Soviet Union broke off diplomatic relations with Israel and did not resume them until July 15, 1953. Following this significant episode certain Soviet satellites, such as Rumania, resorted to mass persecution of Zionists, while Russia herself began to give increasing evidence of courting Arab favor, first by supporting the Arabs in Security Council debates dealing with Israel's retaliatory raids and later by offering certain Arab states arms and technical assistance at a time when Arab-Israeli relations had reached a low point. This new Soviet attitude found full expression in a speech delivered on December 29, 1955, by Communist Party Secretary Nikita S. Khrushchev, who stated that "from the first day of its existence, the State of Israel has been taking a hostile, threatening position toward its neighbors. Imperialists are behind Israel, trying to exploit it against the Arabs for their own benefit."[75]

Because of this shift in Soviet tactics, it was hard for Israel to maintain her original policy of neutrality; by the inexorable force of circumstances she was driven closer to the United States. In the meantime the latter had somewhat modified its policy toward Israel. Consequently, American response to Israeli advances was not as cordial as it had been in the first years of Israel's existence. The immediate cause of this modification was undoubtedly the victory of the Republican party at the polls in the fall of 1952. In contrast to the Democratic administration, which seemed to have leaned definitely toward Israel, President Eisenhower's administration endeavored to introduce what was officially termed "a policy of impartial friendship in the Middle East."[76] Although this new approach was far from hostile to Israel, which continued to enjoy many benefits and even priorities, it was, nevertheless, marked by a few changes. Among them could be mentioned, a visit paid by Secretary of State Dulles to the Arab capitals and Israel in the summer of 1953. Inasmuch as it was the first such visit of an American secretary of state in the area, it underlined the latter's importance and flattered the Arabs' self-esteem. Upon his return Secretary Dulles presented a realistic report in which he recommended "that the United States should seek to allay the deep resentment against it that has resulted from the creation of Israel" and recognized the existence of Arab fears "that the United States will back the new State of Israel in aggressive expansion."[77] Furthermore, all of the sensational raids executed by Israel against Jordanian, Egyptian, and Syrian territory and the Huleh dispute occurred while the Republicans were in office, and each evoked fairly strong condemnation by official Washington. While it is open to speculation whether the American reaction would have been any

[75] *New York Times*, Dec. 31, 1955.

[76] Harry N. Howard, *United States Policy in the Near East, South Asia, and Africa—1954* (Department of State Publication 5801, 1955).

[77] Harry N. Howard, *The Development of United States Policy in the Near East, South Asia, and Africa during 1953* (Department of State Publication 5432, April 1954).

different under a Democratic administration, the undeniable fact is that these raids hurt the cause of Israel in informed American opinion. When Israel, in defiance of United Nation resolutions, moved her Foreign Ministry to Jerusalem in July 1953, thus completing the process of making the latter capital of the state, the United States, along with major Western powers, refused to move its embassy from Tel-Aviv, expressing its disapproval of Israeli action. Also for the first time since the creation of Israel, the United States government voiced its doubts as to the nature of Israel as the nucleus of a worldwide community and tendered some advice to Israeli leaders. This happened on two occasions, when Assistant Secretary of State Henry A. Byroade made public statements on Arab-Israeli relations. Speaking on April 9, 1954, in Dayton, Ohio, Byroade declared:

> To the Israelis I say that you should come to truly look upon yourselves as a Middle Eastern state and see your own future in that context rather than as headquarters, or nucleus so to speak, of worldwide groupings of peoples of a particular religious faith who must have special rights within and obligations to the Israeli state. You should drop the attitude of the conqueror and the conviction that force and a policy of retaliatory killings is the only policy that your neighbors will understand. You should make your deeds correspond to your frequent utterances of the desire for peace.[78]

In another speech delivered to the American Council for Judaism on May 1, 1954, in Philadelphia, Byroade urged Israel to adopt a policy of restricted immigration inasmuch as the Arabs, fearful of Israel's possible expansion, were entitled to know "the magnitude of this new State."[79]

These statements caused considerable resentment both in Israel and among American Zionists, and Israel's government lodged a formal protest against Byroade's second speech as an unwarranted interference with Israel's sovereign

---

[78]This paragraph had its counterpart in a speech which Byroade addressed directly to the Arabs: "To the Arabs I say you should accept this state of Israel as an accomplished fact. I say further that you are deliberately attempting to maintain a state of affairs delicately suspended between peace and war, while at present desiring neither. This is a most dangerous policy and one which world opinion will increasingly condemn if you continue to resist any move to obtain at least a less dangerous *modus vivendi* with your neighbor" (*ibid.*).

[79]*Ibid.* The American Council for Judaism was formed in 1943 under the presidency of Lessing J. Rosenwald as "a group of those Jews who completely dissociate themselves and their Judaism from the national-political philosophy of Zionism; and who stand on the principle that they are individual American citizens who regard the United States of America as their single and only homeland; who have and want no other national attachments; and who believe . . . that the officers of [the United States] Government should serve the best interests of *all* Americans and America's acknowledged responsibility of leadership in the free world" (quotation from a statement by Clarence L. Coleman, president of the American Council for Judaism since 1955, *Council News,* 9, no. 11, Nov. 1955). A more complete statement of A.C.J.'s objectives can be found in "Resolutions Adopted by Eleventh Annual Conference," *Council News,* 9, no. 4 (April 1955). Commenting on Byroade's speech, Rabbi Dr. Elmer Berger, executive vice-president of the Council, declared: "Mr. Byroade's clarification is welcomed as a declaration of historic importance by American Jews who understand the history of this problem. In the face of a half-century of Zionist agitation designed to convince the governments of the world that the Jews are a nation, an American government has given a ringing, unequivocal declaration that Judaism is a religion and that Jews owe no obligations to, and possess no rights in, the political entity which Zionism calls a 'Jewish' state" (*ibid.*). The Council represents a minority of American Jews. In the words of retiring President Rosenwald, "We should, by now, realize that although our growth should be steady, it is also likely to be low" (*ibid.*).

right to formulate her immigration policies. Soon afterward the *Jerusalem Post* called for removal from the chairmanship of the Israeli-Jordanian Mixed Armistice Commission of Commander Elmo H. Hutchison, U.S.N., who was believed by Israelis to be partial to the Arab cause. Coming at a time of excitement over the contemplated American arming of the Arabs, these protests and appeals marked a low point in American-Israeli relations. In an attempt to break the deadlock created by Arab-Israeli hostility, Secretary Dulles came forward, on August 26, 1955, with a new plan to settle the Palestinian dispute. The plan proposed: (1) "resettlement and, to such an extent as may be feasible, repatriation" of the 900,000 Arab refugees whose "sufferings are drawn out almost beyond the point of endurance"; (2) "an international loan to enable Israel to pay the compensation" "due from Israel to the refugees," with "substantial participation by the United States in such a loan"; (3) "adjustments needed to convert armistice lines of danger into boundary lines of safety" inasmuch as "the existing lines separating Israel and the Arab states . . . were not designed to be permanent frontiers"; (4) "formal treaty arrangements," in which the United States would join as soon as the adjustments had been made, "to prevent or thwart any effort by either side to alter by force the boundaries."[80]

It was reported that in the winter of 1955–1956 Secretary Dulles endeavored to induce the political leaders of both major parties in the United States to keep the Arab-Israeli issue out of the forthcoming electoral campaign. Owing to the intensification of the Soviet menace to the Middle East, he wanted to promote a truly bipartisan policy which would be based on the national interest rather than on considerations of partisan advantage.

As could be expected, Arab and Israeli reactions to these American initiatives differed considerably. The Arabs viewed with suspicion any suggestion of resettlement of the refugees and definitely took exception to the granting of further loans to Israel, even if these were earmarked as compensation for the refugees. They saw no reason why, if money was to come from outside, Israel, a hostile state, should be made a dispensing agency. The American suggestion to "adjust" the frontiers was too vague and too timid to satisfy their basic quest for a substantial territorial revision. There was, incidentally, a certain change in emphasis in Arab demands. Up to this time repatriation of the refugees had always received top priority as a prerequisite to a peace settlement; in the fall of 1955 the territorial issue began to loom as perhaps the most decisive of all. As early as March 20, 1955, Major Saleh Salem, then Egyptian minister of national guidance, had stated that if the Negeb were returned to the Arabs so as to enable them to restore the land bridge between the Arab lands to the east and to the west, a major obstacle to peace might be removed. Although this was not an official policy statement either of the Egyptian government or of any other Arab state, it could, nevertheless, be taken as an indication of the new attitudes that were taking shape. As for Israel's reaction to Dulles' proposals of August 26, it was, by and large, positive, but her leaders immediately made the reservation that, so far as any change of boundaries was

---

[80]The text is in the *New York Times,* Aug. 27, 1955.

concerned, there could be only minor technical readjustments which would remove obvious inconveniences but involve no major territorial changes. With regard to Dulles' plea for keeping the Palestinian issue out of domestic politics, it would have been highly improper for Israel to take a stand on it; hence no direct comment was heard from Tel-Aviv. But Israel's sympathizers in the United States did not conceal their disapproval of this proposal.[81]

At this juncture it might be appropriate to ask what the attitude of Britain was toward these new developments in the Palestinian controversy. Beginning with the settlement of the Sudan and the Suez issues with Egypt in 1953–1954, British policy began gradually to veer toward satisfying Arab views on the matter. And inasmuch as the territorial issue began to take precedence over other points in the dispute, Britain gave her attention to the solution of that issue in the fall of 1955. Speaking at the Lord Mayor's Banquet in London on November 9, 1955, Prime Minister Sir Anthony Eden suggested that "if there could be an accepted arrangement between them about their boundaries, we—Her Majesty's Government and, I believe, the United States Government and perhaps other powers too—would be prepared to give a formal guarantee to both sides." In elucidation of the word "arrangement" he explained that he meant "some compromise" between the Arabs and the Israelis concerning the territorial settlement. He concluded his statement by offering to mediate in the conflict.[82]

Eden's statement evoked favorable response among the Arabs, some of whom hailed it as the first acceptable basis for discussion. Israel reacted negatively, suspecting British appeasement of the Arabs at the price of a major territorial concession by Israel. The State Department's reaction was cautious and noncommittal. While praising Sir Anthony's initiative for peace, American officials pointed out the difference in the British and American approaches to the problem, especially the contrast between the American formula for territorial "adjustments" and the British formula of a "compromise."

To sum up these observations about Israel's position vis-à-vis the major powers, it might be said that by the mid-1950s her relations with Russia had notably deteriorated, owing to the new Soviet tactic of wooing the Arabs, and that a definite cooling off could be noted in her relations with Britain. Under the circumstances Israel was compelled more than ever before to look to the United States for economic aid and political friendship. In the meantime the American government had had a second look at the Arab-Israeli problem, and its response to Israel had lost some of its earlier cordiality. Israel's previous appeal to the American public as a haven for Jewish refugees from Europe and as a "bastion of democracy" in the Middle East had worn off somewhat because of the new reality of nearly one million Arab refugees and because of Israel's retaliatory raids against her Arab neighbors. The traditional "biblical" appeal to Bible-conscious Americans was still powerful, and so were domestic political considerations, but both of these tended to decrease in importance as the new awareness of Soviet danger in the Middle East began to

[81] See a letter by Messrs. Moron and Pollock to the editor *New York Times,* Jan. 4, 1956.
[82] The text is in the *New York Times,* Nov. 10, 1955.

permeate the thinking of the American public. Yet it would be unrealistic to dismiss all the factors that were working for closer ties between Israel and the United States. Despite certain deviations from the previous pattern of American-Israeli relations, the United States could probably still be regarded as Israel's most reliable friend.[83]

The Suez War and Its Aftermath

As time went on, Israel's relations with her Arab neighbors not only did not show any improvement but actually suffered further deterioration. There was continuous tension on the borders, punctuated by infiltrations, raids, and counterraids, sometimes on an organized medium-sized military scale. Semivoluntary special Egyptian commando units, called *fedayeen,* were making bold incursions, some of them deep within Israeli territory, the exploits being glorified in the Arab press. The Arab economic boycott of Israel continued unabated. Arab governments refused to entertain any idea of making peace, while their spokesmen, official and semiofficial, alluded to a "second round," evoked memories of Arab victory over the Crusaders after they had dominated Palestine for more than two centuries, and threatened the Zionist "usurpers" with annihilation. They displayed a resentful negativism toward any proposal aiming at the solution of immediate practical problems such as the division and utilization of Jordan River waters—a matter repeatedly broached by Eric Johnston, President Eisenhower's special emissary. Furthermore, Egypt persisted in its refusal to open the Suez Canal to Israeli navigation and in denying Israel access to the Gulf of Aqaba from the Red Sea. It was, in fact, Egypt's policies and attitudes that perturbed Israel more than the policies of any other Arab state. Egypt's acquisition of sizable amounts of modern arms from the Soviet bloc added considerably to Israel's concern. Israel did not cease to claim that the balance of armaments, stipulated by the Tripartite Agreement among the United States, Britain, and France in May 1950, was gravely upset by the Egyptian-Soviet deals. Meeting with lukewarm response to this plea in Washington, Israel found more success in its dealings with France, which was willing to sell some new Mystère jet planes and other up-to-date equipment. Last but not least, Israel was perturbed by the growing ascendancy of Egypt's leader, Nasser, in the Arab world and his leadership in the Arab unity movement, which, if successful, threatened her with a more effective encirclement in the future.

These developments constituted the general background of the Israeli-Egyptian armed conflict which broke out at the end of October 1956. In addition, however, certain immediate causes which brought about the crisis should be mentioned. Three and possibly four of these could be pointed out. The first was the nationalization of the Suez Canal by President Nasser in late July 1956, an act which provoked a serious crisis in his relations with the major Western powers, particularly Britain and France. Thus Israel could count on at least a temporary convergence of her own and Franco-British policies. The second was the approaching national election in the United States, which, it was expected, would render the American government temporarily powerless in its ability to reach and implement any major foreign policy

---

[83]In this sense, see a significant editorial, "Israel Is Here to Stay," *Life,* March 19, 1956.

decision. The third and most immediate cause was the conclusion of a military agreement between Egypt, Syria, and Saudi Arabia, whereby a unified command of their armies under an Egyptian general was to be set up. One can only speculate as to whether or not the outbreak of the anti-Soviet revolution in Hungary was an additional factor in causing Israel's leaders to decide on an early military action against Egypt. The Hungarian drama might provide a screen behind which bold actions in the Middle East could be undertaken with greater impunity.[84]

As against this background of long-range and immediate causes, Israel's forces invaded Egypt's territory on October 30, 1956. Israel's official explanation was that this was simply a local police action aiming at the wiping out of the Egyptian *fedayeen* concentrations in the Sinai Peninsula. In reality, it was a preventive war, which Israel decided to wage with the following objectives in view: (1) to destroy the military potential of Egypt before it was too late; (2) to inflict a blow to Nasser's prestige; (3) to force Egypt to open the Suez Canal and the Tiran Strait to Israeli navigation; (4) to reopen the whole question of an Arab-Israeli peace settlement (the latter having been shelved as a result of UN intervention and the resulting armistice agreement in 1948–1949).

Israel's military operations were carried out successfully and according to plan. A group of paratroopers landed east of and not far from the Suez Canal; mechanized land forces, supported by aviation, crossed the Israeli-Egyptian border at three points in powerful thrusts into the Sinai Peninsula. Another army group swiftly occupied the Gaza strip, still another made a rapid advance along the Gulf of Aqaba coast of Sinai, capturing the Egyptian stronghold at Sharm el-Sheikh and spiking the guns which dominated the Strait of Tiran. Egyptian resistance was uneven, but never effective. To the general surprise, the Egyptian air force, with a few minor exceptions, did not engage in action, leaving Egypt's troops unprotected from the air. An attempt by the Egyptian navy to shell the Israeli port of Haifa ended in a failure when the Egyptian warship *Ibrahim el-Awal* was knocked out and captured by the Israelis.[85]

Israel's invasion was followed by military action of Britain and France against Egypt and by subsequent political intervention of the United States and Russia, each acting on its own in addition to the collective intervention under the auspices of the United Nations. A general account of these developments will be found in Chapter

---

[84]This, however, as has been pointed out, is mere speculation. In fact, one might ask whether the reverse was not true, i.e., whether the Israeli-Egyptian war did not provide Russia with an excellent opportunity to crush the Hungarian resistance, profiting from the temporary preoccupation of the West with the Middle Eastern crisis. According to one version, Lt.-Colonel Israel Beer, an Israeli engaged in espionage on behalf of Russia, secured advance information about Israel's war plans against Egypt, which he conveyed to the Soviet authorities. The latter were thus in a position to time their military action in Hungary accordingly. (*Time,* April 28, 1961). Perhaps neither Russia nor Israel had planned its military actions with reference to the other's actions; they simply reaped certain politico-psychological benefits from the fact that the world's attention was divided between the two crises.

[85]For a detailed account of the Suez War, see Robert Henriques, *One Hundred Hours to Suez: An Account of Israel's Campaign in the Sinai Peninsula* (London, 1957); Edgar O'Ballance, *The Sinai Campaign, 1956* (London, 1959); and Samuel L. A. Marshall, *Sinai Victory: Command Decisions in History's Shortest War, Israel's Hundred-Hour Conquest of Egypt East of Suez, Autumn, 1956* (New York, 1958).

XII. Here the Suez War will be investigated as a major event affecting the life and destiny of Israel.

The rather uncompromising attitude adopted by the United Nations and the United States in condemnation of aggression surprised and shocked Israel's political leaders and produced a good deal of resentment in international Zionist circles. Israel tried hard to salvage as much as possible from her military victory by, first, delaying her evacuation from Sinai and, then, by attempting to put conditions for her evacuation of the Gaza strip. These conditions revolved around Israel's insistence on free navigation in the Suez Canal and the Gulf of Aqaba and constituted the subject of intense negotiations between Tel-Aviv and Washington. Although the United States favored Israel's claim to freedom of navigation in those waters, officially the American government rejected the idea of conditional evacuation. Furthermore, Israel was penalized by the suspension of American economic aid. All in all, the Suez War produced a strain in American-Israeli relations.

Moreover, in some ways the Suez War provided a test for American policy toward Israel. This policy has often been described, by Arabs and by domestic critics, as not truly independent and as subject to the combined influence of Israel and the Zionist groups. Arab propagandists occasionally went so far as to assert that American policy in the Middle East is "directed" by Tel-Aviv. While it is undoubtedly true that, owing to the domestic political considerations—whether based on solid fact or not—both the White House and Congress often tend to lean toward the Israeli side when faced with Arab-Israeli conflict, it could be pointed out that when it came to a real crisis involving military operations in the Middle East the United States refused to align itself with Israel. This was true both in 1948, when Washington did not send any forces to defend Israel against the Arab invasion, and in 1956, when, in the name of defense of principles, President Eisenhower condemned Israel's aggression and in a televised statement insisted on unconditional evacuation of occupied territories. Yet the strain caused in American-Israeli relations by such an attitude was neither great nor of long duration. It was asserted, for example (without any formal denials from the State Department), that to pave the way for Israel's free navigation of the Gulf of Aqaba, the United States would arrange for an American vessel on its way to Port Elath to pass through the Strait of Tiran—under the protective presence of UN troops—and thus establish a precedent in favor of Israel. As soon as Israel's forces withdrew from the Gaza strip, the United States quietly but promptly unstopped the flow of its economic aid to Israel. It appeared as if both parties were anxious to erase the painful memory of the Sinai invasion and thus to restore the cordiality—genuine or simulated—of pre-Suez days.

Second in its importance to Israel was the state of Soviet-Israeli relations. These relations had been marked in the past by occasional difficulties—such as those occasioned by the Jewish doctors' trial in Moscow and the anti-Jewish purge in Prague—but it was only during the Suez War that Russia employed truly threatening terms in her notes addressed to Israel. Yet, despite the very real temporary strain, no deep and enduring hostility ensued in Soviet-Israeli relations. Ostensibly Russia had been following, especially since 1955, a very pro-Arab line. Yet Israeli leaders and the people as a whole refused to interpret this as an irrevocably anti-Israeli policy. A combination of factors might have accounted for this cautious optimism. In the first place, there was a feeling that the pro-Arab manifestations of Soviet policy were merely tactical, that in the long run genuine Arab nationalism and Soviet communism were incompatible; hence one should not attach too great an importance to loud Soviet protestations of amity toward the Arabs. Another reason for this cautious evaluation was perhaps rooted in the common Marxist background of both the Soviet and the Israeli leaders. Thus, despite the well-known differences that in the course of time divided the Communists from the Socialists, in Israel the lines tended to be blurred in some instances—such as in the case of the pro-Soviet (and yet officially non-Communist) Mapam party. Furthermore, as Menachem Begin, the Irgun leader, has pointed out in his book *The Revolt* (p. 13), "No Jew should forget two fundamental facts. Thanks to the Soviet Union hundreds of thousands of Jews were saved from Nazi hands. . . . Secondly . . . the Soviet Union . . . helped us to achieve the first stage of our independence." Moreover, Israel was not in a position to ignore that, second only to the United States, Russia and her satellites contained the greatest reservoir of potential Jewish immigrants whose fate, present and future, might to some extent depend on the state of Soviet-Israeli relations.

As for Israel's relations with Britain and France, following the Suez War they entered into a new phase marked by a great deal of cordiality in the case of France and quiet friendship in the case of Britain. Hostility toward the person of President Nasser seemed to provide a cementing material, and in the case of France friendship with Israel was enhanced by the generally anti-Arab policy France found herself following as a result of both Suez and Algeria. Consequently, in the post-Suez era France became one of the main purveyors of armaments to the Israeli military establishment.

At this juncture, it is proper perhaps to ask about the balance sheet of the Suez War from the Israeli point of view. Israel's military losses were negligible as compared to Egyptian. They amounted to 171 dead and four prisoners taken by the enemy when an Israeli plane crashed behind the Egyptian lines. These prisoners were exchanged for the 6,000 Egyptians in Israeli captivity. Although Israel's reputation as a peace-loving country suffered at the time, it does not seem that it was much affected in the long run. Israel continued to repeat emphatically time and again that she wanted peace with her Arab neighbors. It was the Arabs who steadily refused peace overtures, and this was what ultimately impressed world opinion. As to her objectives, Israel succeeded in discouraging any further *fedayeen* raids and infiltrations. The Arab-Israel borders had become much quieter since the war, and the presence of the UN Emergency Force on the Egyptian side of the border and along the Sinai coast (at least till the 1967 war) supplied an added guarantee of tranquillity. Another objective—the opening of the Gulf of Aqaba—had been fully achieved, and the gulf to all practical purposes had become an Israeli lake, at least insofar as military and naval dominance was concerned.

However, Israel had not succeeded in opening the Suez Canal to her shipping, and short of a new use of force against Egypt it was unlikely that this objective would be secured in the foreseeable future. More basic perhaps has been Israel's failure to obtain a permanent peace settlement with the Arab states. Had Israel and Egypt been left to themselves by outside powers, perhaps a peace settlement would have been achieved. But first the French and British intervention and later the United Nations' intervention made this impossible. The United Nations in particular and also the United States have insisted on the restoration of the status quo ante despite the obvious inconveniences and artificiality of the latter. The Israelis were never given the opportunity to sit down with the Egyptians to discuss peace terms. What the UN did was in effect a patch-up job of strict legalism, devoid of much vision. In fact, Israel's compliance (however reluctant) with the UN injunctions and American appeals seems somewhat puzzling in retrospect. Israel had many trump cards and could have negotiated from a position of strength: she held sizable stretches of Egyptian territory as well as 6,000 Egyptian prisoners of war. The Egyptian arsenal of Soviet arms was either destroyed or severely dislocated, and Israel's morale was understandably high. Naturally, the suspension of American aid was a weighty factor, but perhaps not as weighty as some observers were inclined to believe. Israel's decision to withdraw from these advantageous bargaining positions will undoubtedly constitute a subject of further research and study until all relevant facts are elucidated.

Israel, the Arabs, and Afro-Asia

Although the situation on Israel's borders had improved after 1956, no appreciable change could be observed in the overall relations between her and the surrounding Arab states. Israel's isolation continued; the Arab states persisted in their nonrecognition of the Jewish state as well as in their economic boycott. In due course, another complication was added to this situation—the effect that the growing movement for Arab unity might have on the relations of the two parties. Israel was concerned lest the unification of two or more of her neighbor states lead to their undue strengthening and the revival of aggressive attitudes. The union of Egypt with Syria in February 1958 was therefore received with many misgivings; yet no special action, diplomatic or military, was taken to counter it. Israel's policy appeared to differentiate between voluntary and nonvoluntary Arab unification. In practical terms, the latter type could mean only the forcible extension of Egypt's power in other Arab states, in all likelihood by subversion and revolution. It was generally believed that if the Jordanian regime was overthrown by the Pan-Arab elements friendly to Nasser, Israel would promptly react by occupying the west-Jordanian territory up to the Jordan River. In support of this belief one might quote Premier David Ben Gurion, who on October 29, 1958, warned that if a change were to occur in the status of the Jordanian Kingdom, Israel "should insist on demilitarization of Jordanian territory west of the Jordan River." Yet even voluntary inter-Arab cooperation was not accepted without reservations by Israel. Thus, two years earlier, on October 15, 1956—barely two weeks preceding the Suez War and at a time when the Hashemites still ruled in Iraq—Ben Gurion stated that Israel reserved "freedom of action" if Iraqi troops were to enter Jordan (to lend support to the latter). An additional consideration in this case was that of all the Arab states that had waged active war on Israel in 1948, Iraq was the only one which did not conclude an armistice agreement with her.

Surrounded by a hostile ring, Israel continued to stress her own military preparedness with special emphasis on quality. As early as 1956 she received her first cyclotron from Cornell University, and it was reported that by 1960 Israeli scientists were well on their way to produce nuclear fission. Despite Israeli official disclaimers that their atomic research served any but peaceful purposes, in December 1960 the State Department asked Israel for information regarding the existence and purpose of the nuclear plant in the Rehovot region. Somewhat later it was stated officially in Washington that satisfactory reassurances were obtained. Pursuing her scientific development, Israel surprised her Arab neighbors by a noteworthy achievement when on July 5, 1961, she launched her first meteorological space rocket.

With the advent of the decade of 1960s a new field of rivalry with Arab states was opened, this time in Africa. Israel made serious efforts to enter into close relations with the newly emancipated African states, while at the same time pursuing a policy of rapprochement with some underdeveloped countries of Asia. By 1961 Israel had entered into trade-and-aid as well as cultural cooperation agreements with over thirty-five states in Africa and Asia. Israel's growing industrial exports were being increasingly directed toward the Afro-Asian market, and nearly 700 Israeli experts were engaged by the Afro-Asian governments. Israeli embassies were being opened in the new African capitals, and a steady stream of official visitors from Ghana, Upper Volta, the Malagasy Republic, Burma, and a host of other countries was passing through Tel-Aviv and Jewish-held Jerusalem. Moreover, impressive numbers of African students were being attracted to Israeli schools of higher learning, and Rehovot, Jerusalem, and Tel-Aviv were the sites of special conferences of Afro-Asians with scientific, economic, and social interests.

Israel's progress in her relations with the new Africa was a source of concern to the Cairo government, whose ambitions also extended to the "African circle." Acting on the assumption that the Arabs must not lose "the African revolution," Egypt exerted major efforts to establish cordial relations with the leading African nationalists, appealing to them in the name of anticolonial solidarity, economic self-defense, geographical proximity, and sociocultural affinities. Although some Egyptian experts were sent to the new African states, emphasis was laid primarily on political solidarity. In due course the Cairo government became deeply involved in a number of controversial African questions, including that of the Congo in 1960. Cairo's activities were not without success. At the African "summit" conference held in Casablanca in early January 1961, the heads of state of Mali, Ghana, Guinea, Morocco, and the United Arab Republic as well as the premiers of Libya and the Algerian Provisional Government adopted a resolution in which they called Israel "an instrument of imperialism and neo-colonialism." It should be pointed out that Ghana and Mali had previously welcomed and received large-scale technical assistance from Israel. Although Israel's envoys to these African countries were instructed to convey their government's "disappointment and profound surprise" at this resolution, Israel was willing to continue her aid program.

Although Israel's relations with individual Afro-Asian states could be described as good, she was consistently excluded from major regional meetings which were attended by Arab states. Consequently, Israel was not invited to participate either in the Bandung conference of Afro-Asian states in 1955 or in the Belgrade conference of uncommitted states in September 1961. In both cases a line was drawn between her and the others; although geographically part of Asia, she was not a genuine member of the Afro-Asian family.

Relations with Zionism and Internal Politics

Although the independent state of Israel was the crowning achievement of Zionism, rather paradoxically certain misunderstandings and tensions arose between Israel and the world Zionist movement during Israel's first decade of statehood. The differences revolved around two major points: control of Israel's policy and immigration. While Israel's leaders welcomed the continuation of the World Zionist Organization and of the Jewish Agency, they viewed their role primarily as that of fund-collecting agencies, whose additional tasks were to provide new immigrants, assure close cultural liaison between Israel and the Diaspora, and to provide such political support outside Israel as the conditions required. Israel's leaders, however, denied these two bodies any right to interfere in the internal problems of their country and, above all, to attempt to dictate or influence its policies. Premier Ben Gurion even went so far as to say, in an address to the Hadassah organization on September 12, 1960, that the Zionist movement was like a scaffolding around the house of Israel while the latter was being erected; once the construction was finished, there would be no more need for it.[86]

Furthermore, with special reference to the Zionist movement in America, Israel's leaders were highly critical of the American Jews' unwillingness to settle in Israel in any substantial numbers. To be sure, American Zionist leaders repeatedly appealed to their co-religionists to maintain their Jewish culture and consciousness of bonds with Israel. On May 26, 1959, Dr. Nahum Goldmann, president of the World Zionist Organization, declared in Jerusalem that the emancipation of Jews from ghetto life and their integration into a free society—especially evident in the United States—represented a "new danger" to Jewish survival. "It could," he added, "easily lead to the disintegration of the Jewish communities and the loss of their consciousness of being all parts of the Jewish people."[87]

These appeals did not produce any spectacular results, at least in the form of increased immigration. Of all Israeli public figures, Ben Gurion probably felt more strongly about this matter than any other leader. On December 28, 1960, he gave vent to these feelings by declaring: "Since the day when the Jewish state was established and the gates of Israel were flung open to every Jew who wanted to come, every religious Jew has daily violated the precepts of Judaism and the Torah of Israel by remaining in the Diaspora." And he added the following Talmudic

[86]*New York Times*, Sept. 13, 1960.
[87]*Ibid.*, May 27, 1959.

citation in support of his view: "Whoever dwells outside the land of Israel is considered to have no God."[88]

The premier's statements produced something of a furore in the United States, where many members of Jewish communities resented the imputation of godlessness. Subsequently the premier's office issued reassuring explanations that his words had been addressed only to Orthodox Jews and misconstruction had resulted from an attempt at a broader application. Despite these occasional flare-ups, differences between Israel and the World Zionist were more like minor family quarrels than a serious rift beyond repair. The plain fact is that Israel and the World Zionist movement need and supplement each other.

Through the later 1950s and the early 1960s Israel's internal developments followed the course set basically during the first years of statehood. The multiparty system was maintained, though the number of parties declined somewhat. The dominant political orientation continued to be socialist, with Ben Gurion's Mapai party maintaining its position of preeminence, albeit lacking the absolute majority which would allow it to monopolize the executive branch of government. Consequently, as a rule successive Israeli cabinets represented coalitions of Mapai, the religious (Orthodox) group, and, alternating, either the center-oriented General Zionists or the left-wing socialists of the Mapam or Achdut Avoda variety.

On November 3, 1959, Israel held her fourth general election, which resulted in the strengthening of the Mapai position. Its membership in the 120-man Knesset rose from 40 to 47, still short of an absolute majority but attesting to the basic popularity of Ben Gurion's leadership. Another significant gain was that registered by Herut, which, by increasing its representation from 15 to 17, more than doubled its strength since the second election in 1951. The principal losers were the General Zionists, who nearly halved their status; lesser losses were suffered by the Achdut Avoda and the Communists.

Although the Mapai did not possess a majority in the Knesset, it generally managed to secure a majority in the cabinets. This setup began to be seriously questioned by other participating parties in 1960. Their opposition, added to certain other causes of discontent, led to a cabinet crisis in January 1961. Attempts to solve the crisis having failed in the succeeding weeks, the Knesset passed a bill calling for elections on August 15, 1961, two years earlier than provided for under normal circumstances. The new elections failed to give a decisive answer to Israel's internal political alignments. The fifth Knesset saw the Mapai representation diminished from 47 to 42, a result bemoaned by Ben Gurion as a tragic blow to his party and the state, and yet still leaving the Mapai by far the strongest party in Israel. The five seats lost by Mapai were distributed among the Communists (an increase from 3 to 5), Achdut Avoda (from 7 to 8), and the newly created Liberal party (a merger of General Zionists and Progressives), who increased their cumulative strength from 14 to 17, thus reaching parity with Herut, which until then was the second strongest party in the Knesset. All in all, however, the Knesset's basic composition was not

---

[88] *Ibid.*, Dec. 30, 1960.

altered. Israel was likely to be ruled by coalition cabinets for the foreseeable future with the attendant difficulties of apportioning portfolios to everybody's satisfaction.

Israel's politics were highlighted, at the turn of the 1950s to the 60s, by a few issues that attracted a good deal of domestic and foreign attention. One of these was the increasing orientalization of Israel's Jewish population—a result of sizable immigration from Asian and African countries since the achievement of statehood. By 1960 slightly more than a half of Jewish Israelis were of oriental origin and paradoxically Israel was confronted with her own quasi-racial problem of discrimination. In July 1959, Haifa became a scene of riots staged by North African Jews, who were protesting ill-treatment in such sectors as housing and employment.

The religious issue continued as a characteristic feature of Israel's politics. The predominance of Orthodox Judaism and its intolerance toward Reform and Conservative Judaism provoked repeated protests and complaints on the part of the latters' leaders, who, as on July 23, 1959, charged discrimination against their own types of worship. The supremacy enjoyed by Orthodox Judaism was, moreover, conducive to certain other complications, such as the impossibility of contracting mixed marriages, a ban on certain forms of entertainment including mixed swimming pools, restrictions on public transportation on Sabbath days, a ban on the importation and manufacture of non-Kosher foods, and objections to the performance of military duties by women. In 1959 and 1960 public opinion in Israel was agitated by the problem of defining a Jew, which was debated in and out of the Knesset. The problem was brought to the fore by the fact that, as a result of a new wave of immigration from Communist-held Eastern Europe in the wake of political developments in Poland and Hungary in 1956, an increased number of mixed Jewish-Christian married couples made their appearance in Israel. Inasmuch as the wives in many such cases were Christian, the rabbinical authorities of Orthodox Judaism refused to consider their offspring as Jewish, thus provoking a controversy regarding the latter's nationality and religion.

In 1960–1961 Israeli politics suffered another crisis known as the Lavon affair. Pinhas Lavon, secretary-general of the Histadruth, had been minister of defense in 1954, when an Israeli espionage ring was discovered in Egypt. The discovery resulted in a trial, at the end of which a number of Egyptian Jews were sentenced to death. Not long afterward Lavon was compelled to resign from the cabinet, and it appears that his dismissal was largely based on a document submitted by a high-ranking army officer, which blamed Lavon for the failure of a certain security operation conducted in 1954. Toward the end of 1960, however, Israel's cabinet received new evidence which seemed to indicate that the document in question was a forgery and that the security operation had been carried out without the minister's knowledge. On the basis of these data the cabinet exonerated Lavon from guilt over the protests of Premier Ben Gurion. Thus not only the cabinet but also the dominant Mapai party was rent by inner dissensions, which was largely responsible for Ben Gurion's resignation as premier in January 1961 and the resulting cabinet crisis, to which reference was made earlier. In addition, Major General Chaim Laskov tendered his resignation as chief of staff. On his part, encouraged by the cabinet's favorable report, Lavon launched a campaign aiming at the rehabilitation of his record as minister of defense. He encountered, however, a strong and unforgiving adversary in the person of Ben Gurion, who, at a subsequent meeting of the Mapai-dominated Histadruth, succeeded in deposing Lavon from the post of secretary-general. Although Ben Gurion emerged officially victorious from this test of strength, full unanimity was not restored in party ranks, and the party itself paid a penalty for these dissensions by losing five seats in the earlier-mentioned elections to the fifth Knesset in August 1961.

One further matter deserves mention in this review of Israel's politics, although it is not clear whether it should be classified as an internal or an external issue. In May 1960, Israel secret agents kidnapped in Argentina and brought to Israel Colonel Adolph Eichmann, formerly a senior officer of the Nazi SS troops. During World War II Eichmann headed the organization responsible for deportations of European Jews to extermination camps. The resulting diplomatic crisis between Israel and Argentina was brought before the UN Security Council and by midsummer 1960 was successfully patched up with the acceptance of Israeli regrets by Buenos Aires. World attention could then turn, undivided, to the fate of Eichmann himself. In due course he was indicted for crimes "against the Jewish people" (on the basis of a law passed since the attainment of statehood) and placed before a specially appointed tribunal, where he pleaded his innocence on the ground that he was responsible only for the transportation of Jewish victims and that he had acted on the orders of his superiors. His defense was conducted by a German lawyer, Dr. Robert Servatius, whose fees were paid by the Israeli government. There was general agreement that the trial (thoroughly publicized and televised; there were up-to-date facilities for 500 foreign correspondents) was staged primarily for the purpose of reminding the world of the atrocities inflicted upon the Jews by Hitler's Reich and thus shaking mankind's conscience out of lethargy and indifference. On September 11, 1961, on the occasion of the Jewish New Year, Israel's President Itzhak Ben Zvi declared:

In the year gone by, justice in Israel unfolded before the eyes of the world the magnitude of the horrifying deeds perpetrated by the Nazis and their hangers-on against the people of Israel. Here, in the independent state of Israel, it has been our prerogative to try in righteousness, in a trial recorded and public, the man indicted as one of the worst of the Nazi criminals who murdered and massacred millions of our brothers and sisters of the House of Israel.[89]

Towering above these political sensations was the truly impressive growth of Israel's economy beginning with the second decade of statehood. Between 1958 and 1961 the economy underwent a number of significant structural changes. In the field of production there was a marked shift from agriculture to industry. From 1958 to 1960 industrial production was rising at the rate of 13 to 16 percent a year (instead of the initially predicted 10 percent), a rate of increase almost unprecedented else-

---

[89] *Israel Digest,* Sept. 15, 1961. The court's hearings were concluded in August 1961, and the trial was adjourned pending the study of evidence by the judges. On Dec. 15, 1961, the court pronounced the sentence of death, from which Eichmann lodged an appeal to a higher court.

where. In Israeli pounds (£I) the relevant figures were £I 1.7 billion in 1958, £I 2 billion in 1959, and £I 2.25 billion in 1960, with an expected £I 2.5 billion in 1961. In 1960 the gross national product rose by 8 to 9 percent in real terms, following a steadily upward curve. Similarly, investment in the economy went up from £I 900 million in 1958 to £I 1 billion in 1959 to £I 1.076 billion in 1960, for the latter year rising 8 percent in industry, 12 percent in trade and services, and 28 percent in transport. Israel was rapidly developing her merchant fleet, having spent in 1960 alone £I 61 million on the purchase of ships, mostly as part of the reparations agreement with Germany. By the end of 1961 Israel's fleet was expected to amount to 700,000 tons.

Having embarked on a new policy to promote the investment of local and foreign capital—by encouraging free enterprise and deemphasizing public ownership— Israel saw foreign investments increase from $13 million in 1959 to $30 million in 1960. A number of major foreign industrial firms established local plants in Israel. The number of gainfully employed persons rose by 22,000 in 1960 to a total of 702,000, and, despite the rise of the price level by 3 to 4 percent, the real earnings of employed persons rose by 3 percent, reaching £I 265 (about $147) of average monthly income.

Especially spectacular was the increase in Israeli industrial exports, which between 1958 and 1960 rose at the rate of 35 to 40 percent a year. Israeli industrial goods effectively competed in foreign markets. This was possible partly because of the "deepening" of production—i.e., replacing the imported materials and semimanufactured components by those of domestic production—and partly because of higher productivity, which increased at the rate of 2.5 percent. "Industrial exports constituted 10 per cent of the country's direct exports. Hundreds of kinds of industrial products were being sold to over ninety countries, almost entirely for hard currency. They had almost doubled in two years, rising from $82 million in 1958 to over $150 million in 1960."[90] In 1961 they were expected to reach $180 million. Total exports, both industrial and agricultural, increased in real terms by 25 percent or $65 million from 1959 to 1960 to reach $352 million. However, imports increased by $90 million to attain $693 million. Thus, in round figures, the value of imports was twice the value of exports. This trade deficit was offset by an influx of money from four principal sources: German reparations and personal restitution payments; contributions from the United Jewish Appeal and other institutions; State of Israel Bond proceeds and other foreign loans; and private investments. The total from all these sources amounted to $350 million in 1960. This enabled Israel to increase her foreign currency reserves from $155 million in 1959 to $215 million in 1960.

Although it is true that Israel's spectacular economic development would not have been possible without the steady influx of capital from abroad, it is equally true that the Israelis, with their skill, determination, and industry, have made exemplary use of the funds thus provided. This was in contrast to much more modest achieve-

[90]From a report presented to the Knesset by Pinhas Sapir, minister of commerce and industry, on Feb. 28, 1961 (*Israel Digest,* March 17, 1961).

ments in the economies of the three principal oil-producing Arab countries, whose total income from foreign oil concessions amounted to the impressive figure of one billion dollars in 1960.

At the beginning of the 1960s Israeli leaders voiced considerable optimism as to their country's future. By the middle of 1961 Israeli bond sales had reached the $500 million mark, and further sales were anticipated. Major development of the Negeb was planned, and a long pipeline to carry water from the Jordan River to the south was being constructed.[91] An influx of 500,000 new immigrants in the 1960s was expected, and creating conditions for the absorption of two million newcomers was officially stated by Premier Ben Gurion as the goal.[92]

More broadly, the early 1960s were a transitional era in Israel's political history. These were the years of the eclipse and eventual downfall of David Ben Gurion. It is difficult to define with complete certainty what brought about the erosion of Ben Gurion's power and appeal. There is no doubt that a number of concrete and divisive political issues contributed to his repeated embarrassments and, on occasion, to the thwarting of his will. The Lavon affair profoundly shook the Mapai party while impugning Ben Gurion's probity and loyalty to his associates. His militant statements about the relationship between Israel and world Zionism exposed him to criticisms and attacks both at home and abroad. Ben Gurion was also challenged for insisting on the continuity of special military administration in the Arab-inhabited district of Israel. Lack of unanimity on this issue, despite his victory over the critics, further accentuated the fact that his moral and political authority was being increasingly questioned. Ultimately, on June 17, 1963, he resigned as premier. The Mapai party promptly designated Levi Eshkol as his successor and on June 25 Eshkol formed his first cabinet. From that time Ben Gurion's political career followed a steadily downward curve. In November 1964 he resigned and later rescinded his resignation from the Mapai central committee. This was followed in June 1965 by his formal expulsion from the central committee. Soon afterwards Ben Gurion formed the Rafi party, composed of his close followers in the Mapai. However, even his hold on the Rafi was questionable because in December 1967, over his strong protests, the Rafi voted to reunite with Mapai.

A more profound reason for Ben Gurion's eclipse was perhaps the fact that with his advancing age (he was seventy-six at the time of his resignation from premiership) he was becoming more irascible and less tolerant of opposing views. He had an authoritarian personality and, rather naturally, regarded himself as entitled to a privileged place in Israel's political establishment. He was above all a symbol of a heroic era in Israel's early history, an era of struggle and domination by the East European Ashkenazi pioneers, of power exercised by the socialist oriented elite, and of military success. In his declining years, however, all these great merits and appeals ceased to produce the same response of allegiance and trust that they had in

[91]Economic data collected from a variety of cources, including *Israel Digest, Middle East Journal,* and United Nations, *Economic Developments in the Middle East* for the years 1954–1960.

[92]"Within the next fifteen years," declared Ben Gurion in a press interview, ". . . there will be two million more Jews in Israel—about a million and half through immigration, and the rest through natural increase" (*Israel Digest,* Sept. 29, 1961).

the early years of statehood. It was indicative of his stubborn personality that he did not resign his Knesset seat until May 1970, when he was eighty-three. Ben Gurion died in 1973.

Israel's Politics after Ben Gurion

Between June 1963 and June 1977, Israel had three prime ministers: Levi Eshkol (June 1963–February 1969), Golda Meir (March 1969–April 1974), and Yitzhak Rabin (April 1974–June 1977). While all three were leaders of the Mapai party, a significant evolution was taking place in Israel's domestic politics. True enough, the basic multi-party system was maintained and in the course of those fourteen years, the Labor-affiliated coalition enjoyed a majority in the successive Knessets. However, these Labor-oriented majorities were gradually becoming weaker while, at the same time, important changes were taking place in the composition and attitudes of the Israeli electorate. The immigration and the high birth rate of the oriental Jews had placed them by the early 1960s definitely in the majority in the Israeli population while the Labor-affiliated and Ashkenazi-dominated coalitions exercised political control in the country. Similarly, a new generation of sabras—those born in Israel or pre-Israel Palestine—was coming of age and claiming its place in the political process. In spite of the Marxist background of many founding pioneers, the religious parties secured for themselves an impressively strong role in the electorate. Above all, Israel's political process was greatly affected by two wars that Israel fought with the Arab states, in 1967 and 1973. These wars, on the one hand tended to strengthen Israel's militant nationalists (especially the Herut party) and, on the other, to polarize the electorate. As a result, the 1960s and 1970s witnessed a number of realignments, mergers, splits, and regroupings in the Israeli political spectrum.

These changing attitudes and trends found their expression in the four successive elections to the Knesset. Elections to the sixth Knesset held in November 1965, in which seventeen political parties participated, gave Mapai forty-four seats, Rafi ten, a coalition of Herut and Liberal parties twenty-seven, a coalition of religious parties eighteen, and the left wing Labor Mapam party nine seats. It was clear under the circumstances that the Labor-oriented parties could continue to exercise control only if they stood united. By November–December 1967, Mapai effected a reunification with Rafi and also with Achdut Avoda. And in January 1968 the new grouping adopted formally the name of Labor Party commanding a total of fifty-nine seats in the Knesset. In the same month Golda Meir assumed the position of secretary-general of the unified party. Despite the history of early disagreements, by January 1969 the Labor and the Mapam parties formed a coalition called the "Alignment," a step that brought Israel closer to a two-party system, notwithstanding the continuous existence of smaller parties.

During the term of the sixth Knesset the Arab-Israeli war of June 1967 took place. The war is discussed in the section on foreign relations, and mentioned here for the purpose of emphasizing its impact upon the evolution of Israeli domestic politics. By March 1969, the premiership was assumed by Golda Meir, a prominent leader of the pioneering generation and an intransigent nationalist not unlike Ben Gurion. During her early months as premier elections to the seventh Knesset took place in October 1969. In these elections the Alignment (Labor party and Mapam) emerged with a plurality of fifty-six seats while the right wing opposition group Gahal (including Herut and affiliated groups) secured twenty-six seats. The religious bloc composed of the National Religious party and two other religious parties reaffirmed its strong position by capturing eighteen seats. As a result, a national unity cabinet of twenty-four—the largest in Israel's history—composed of the Labor party, Gahal, the National Religious party, and Mapam was created. In this government Herut's leader, Menachem Begin, obtained a cabinet post. Creation of a national unity cabinet reflected both the impact of the 1967 war and the fact that, henceforth, the erstwhile dominant Mapai had to share power not only with other Labor-oriented parties but also with groups that previously stood in opposition to it.

The elections to the eighth Knesset were to take place in late October 1973, but because of the fourth Arab-Israeli war, which occurred that month, they were postponed until the end of December. The results of the elections brought further erosion to the position of the Alignment by reducing its seats in the Knesset from fifty-six to fifty-three. As in earlier instances, the Labor party, still the largest but somewhat reduced in strength, was obliged to form a coalition government with the aid of the National Religious party and Independent Liberals, a combination that assured it a total of seventy-two votes in a 120-member Knesset. Despite its ability to form a parliamentary majority, the Labor-dominated Alignment and its allies suffered a further setback by the fact that the opposition right wing group, Likud (of which Herut constituted the major part) increased its position in the Knesset to thirty-nine seats (as compared to twenty-six of its predecessor Gahal in the seventh Knesset), representing 27.4 percent of the membership. Furthermore, the National Religious party (and its allies) which during the first twenty-five years of Israel's existence participated in most of the coalition governments, now began to manifest somewhat centrifugal tendencies, which made cooperation with the leading Labor groups increasingly more difficult. Consequently, it was not unlikely that sooner or later the religious parties would veer closer to the opposition grouping, Likud, and that the Labor party, in order to stay in power, would have to look for other allies in the Knesset's political spectrum. This is indeed what happened when in April 1974, General Yitzhak Rabin succeeded Golda Meir as prime minister. The coalition cabinet he created (with a bare majority of two votes in the Knesset) was formed without the National Religious party.

The erosion of Labor party's strength found its culmination in the election to the ninth Knesset in May 1977. This time the Likud grouping emerged as the single largest party in the Knesset, with its forty-three seats. The Alignment trailed behind with thirty-two seats. Its net loss of twenty-one seats represented primarily a gain for the newly formed Democratic Movement for Change (DMC) headed by a general turned archaelogist, Yigael Yadin. The DMC secured an impressive fifteen seats. The National Religious party (NRP) maintained its previous strength of twelve which, added to four of Agudath Israel and one of Poalei Agudath Israel assured the religious bloc the usual substantial representation in the Knesset. The largely Arab-dominated Communist party (Rakah) scored five. Other parties made rather symbolic appearances, as follows: General Sharon's Shlomzion party—two (he joined the Likud after the elections); Shelli (ultra-dovish toward the Arab states)—two; Flato Sharon—one; Liberal Independent—one; Civil Rights (Ratz)—one; the Arab Alignment (Arviei Maarach)—one.

The new composition of the Knesset was reflected in the cabinet which Premier Begin formed in late June. It represented a coalition of Likud with the National Religious party with an attempt to draw into it the DMC. The cabinet list as presented to the Knesset on June 20 contained nine members of Likud (representing Herut and three affiliated factions, Liberal, Laam, and Shlomzion), three members of the NRP, and one unaffiliated (Moshe Dayan, formerly of the Mapai party, as minister of foreign affairs). Three portfolios (justice, social welfare, and communications) were left vacant, reserved for the DMC once the negotiations for its affiliation were concluded. As initially constituted, Premier Begin's coalition cabinet could count on a sixty-two-vote majority in the Knesset.

The Persistent Issues

After Ben Gurion, Israel continued to face a number of political issues which had already made their appearance in the earlier period but which failed to be resolved. Indeed, some of them became intensified and played a highly divisive role in the Israeli society and political system. For the sake of clarity we will pass them in a selective review.

The Demographic Question and the Issue of the "Establishment"

The fact of the orientalization of the Jewish component of Israel's population has already been mentioned. The proportion of oriental Jews reached 55 percent in the 1970s, and these Sephardic elements continued to feel keenly the discrimination in jobs, housing, and general status and opportunities in their society. They gave expression to their feelings in angry demonstrations in May and again in August 1971. This oriental segment of the Israeli population appeared to respond positively to the appeal of the militant Likud coalition, partly as a protest against the long-entrenched Ashkenazi rule of the Labor leadership and partly as a reflection of their distrust of the Arabs and therefore their willingness to espouse more militant policies toward them.

At the same time, the native-born Israelis were also making their advance on the political ladder. A major step in this direction was taken when Yitzhak Rabin, a man born in a collective settlement in Palestine, became prime minister in 1974. Although the gradual rise of the sabras appeared inevitable, the process was slower than could be expected in the building of a new nation, because of the stubborn political longevity of the initial Israeli "establishment." Ben Gurion, Golda Meir, Levi Eshkol, Pinhas Sapir, and others enjoyed not only physical longevity but actually held on to their political offices through the first twenty-five years of Israel's existence. In certain political and government positions the turnover was minimal. Thus, for example, Golda Meir held the position of foreign minister between 1955 and 1965; and Abba Eban headed the foreign ministry between 1966 and 1974. While this undoubtedly gave Israel and especially its foreign policy a greater continuity and stability, it also acted as a deterrent to the access to power of younger elements of non-Ashkenazi origin.

The outnumbering of the immigrant Ashkenazis by both the sabras and the oriental Jews was further accentuated by the failure of Israel to attract more immigrants from Europe or the Americas. In practice, immigration from the United States and Canada could be considered nonexistent, and in fact, a resolution proposed to a conference of the World Zionist Organization that called on American and Canadian Jews to emigrate to Israel was defeated in March 1960. Similarly, western Europe provided a minimal source of immigrant manpower. The largest potential reservoir was, as usual, in the Soviet Union both because of the number of Jews living there (over three million) as well as because of the increasingly anti-Semitic policies followed by the Soviet authorities and expressed in curbs on Jewish cultural and religious life, elimination of Jews from the highest Soviet authorities, and continuous harassment of dissident Jewish intellectuals and scientists. But, both to avoid the embarrassment of a large scale emigration of a substantial segment of its citizenry and out of consideration for Arab sensibilities, the Soviet government opposed emigration as a matter of general policy. It was only in the early 1970s that, under the pressure of the United States Congress (amendments attached by Senator Henry Jackson of Washington to the United States "detente" legislation)[93] the Soviet authorities began issuing emigration visas to their Jewish citizens, with an annual quota not to exceed 35,000. In actual practice, however, this figure was reached in only one or two years; in other years the number was much smaller. Furthermore, not all Soviet Jews wanted to go to Israel and those who had an opportunity often preferred to settle in the United States or other countries of the West. While this immigration tended to be modest, an opposite phenomenon of reemigration or simply emigration was taking place. The country providing the greatest attraction was the United States, but to the shock and dismay of veteran Israeli leaders, a number of their citizens chose to emigrate to West Germany where they enjoyed a much higher standard of living under conditions of freedom and security. In the mid-1970s more Israelis emigrated than immigrated.[94]

It is a moot question whether the quality of life that Israel offered was or was not a major factor in the immigration-emigration balance. Although the Israelis enjoyed the highest standard of living among all the nations of the Middle East, an average citizen had to work hard in a hot climate and bleak environment, bear patiently all

[93]The Jackson amendment linking trade benefits with emigration of Soviet Jews was passed by the Senate by 88 to 0 votes on December 13, 1973.

[94]The relevant figures are as follows: Immigration, in 1974, 32,000; in 1975, 17,500; Emigration, in 1974, 18,000; in 1975, 18,000. Additionally, by 1976 there were 900,000 Israeli citizens living abroad, 300,000 in the U.S. alone. Emigration figures (of formally registered emigrants) do not fully reflect the actual number of Israelis leaving the country in any one given year, although many of these return eventually. For example, the total number of residents leaving Israel were: 268,834 in 1974, and 264,109 in 1975. Sources: *Statistical Abstract of Israel 1976* (Jerusalem, 1977), pp. 118 ff.; *The Middle East and North Africa 1976/77* (London, 1976), p. 412; and *New York Times*, Sept. 22, 1974; Jan. 9, 1975; July 6, 1975; Nov. 7, 1975.

sorts of austerity measures decreed by the government for economic reasons, and experience physical insecurity caused by the aggravation of relations between Israel and its Arab neighbors and the rise of the Palestinian liberation movement. Furthermore, some Israelis tended to lose faith in their political system, which initially promised equality and liberation from social fetters. In this respect, cases of corruption revealed in the highest places of the Israeli establishment in the 1970s had the effect of shattering the early dream of a Jewish utopia. In April 1973, the case of Michael Tsur, head of Israel Corporation, the Zim Shipping Lines, and Haifa Oil Refineries, gained considerable notoriety because of corrupt practices attributed to him. In December 1976, Asher Yadlin, chairman of Kupat Holim,[95] was indicted for bribery and fraud. A month later Abraham Ofer, minister of housing, committed suicide, having fallen under suspicion of bribery. And, in the spring of 1977, it was revealed that Premier Yitzhak Rabin's wife had illegally deposited $18,000 in a bank account while her husband was serving as Israeli Ambassador in Washington. Rabin, who had just won the contest for the leadership of the Labor party, had to resign as premier and party leader in favor of Defense Minister Shimon Peres. These revelations undoubtedly contributed to the demise of the existing Labor establishment in the spring of 1977.

The Religious Issue

The tension between the religious-oriented and the secular-minded Israelis was particularly aggravated in the period between 1968 and 1970. In 1968 a lieutenant commander of the Israeli Navy, Benjamin Shalit, married to a French-Scottish woman of Christian faith, tried to have his two daughters registered as Jewish by the ministry of the interior. It should be pointed out that in Israel the authorities distinguish between citizenship and nationality and that all inhabitants are required to carry identity cards indicating both. But, in the case of Jews the practice has been to equate nationality with religion. Because they were children of a non-Jewish mother, Commander Shalit's daughters could not be considered Jewish under rabbinical law. Shalit appealed to the supreme court for a ruling. In January 1970, the supreme court ruled that registration could be achieved on the basis of declared Jewish nationality rather than religion, but made it clear that its ruling referred only to the registration by the authorities and not to other more fundamental problems. The court's decree caused an uproar in orthodox religious quarters.

Bending to pressure, the Knesset on March 10 voided the ruling of the supreme court by accepting the rabbinical definition of Jewishness. According to this definition, a Jew is a person born of Jewish mother or converted to Judaism. In the same legislative act, however, the Knesset made an exception for non-Jewish spouses, children and grand-children of Jewish immigrants who were allowed to benefit from the Law of Return which had back in 1948 set the rules for immigration into the country.

As a matter of general principle, Judaism is not a proselytizing religion, in view

---

[95]Kupat Holim is the workers' sick fund of the Histadruth, the largest health organization in Israel, serving some 75 percent of the Israeli population.

of its historical concept of the chosen people. Consequently, conversions to Judaism are infrequent and when they occur, are subjected to a thorough scrutiny. Soon after the passing of the above-mentioned law by the Knesset the question arose whether conversion to Judaism under the auspices of the reform or conservative dispensation would be acceptable. On May 28, 1970, the National Religious party declared that it would accept conversions only of orthodox dispensation, under the threat of quitting the government coalition. Although the Knesset did not legislate any more on this matter, in practice the view expressed by the National Religious party was adopted because of the monopoly that orthodox Judaism enjoys in Israel. The National Religious party reconfirmed its stand in February 1974, declaring that converts are Jews only if verified by rabbinical courts.

The power of the religious establishment in Israel was attested by the presence in most of the coalition governments of three ministers representing the National Religious party, or more broadly the religious bloc, one of whom would invariably hold the portfolio of Religious Affairs.

Toward the end of the 1960s another interesting case connected with the definition of a Jew had arisen. A group of American Negroes who proclaimed themselves "Israelites" wanted to settle in Israel. Their first party, composed of about fifty persons, was admitted to Israel not under the Law of Return but on tourist visas. They were allowed to live in a not very desirable locality. When, however, some time later a group exceeding three hundred of these black Israelites arrived, they were first refused admission and were eventually compelled to leave the country under orders of deportation. This action was based on the decision that their self-proclaimed nationality had no foundation in authentic religious faith, which in the case of Jews were inseparable.

Wars with the Arab States: 1967 and 1973

While all four wars that Israel fought with the Arab states since its independence had as the common denominator Israel's quest for survival and the corresponding Arab hostility, it is possible to distinguish motivations and immediate causes in each case.

The June War of 1967

The underlying reason for the June war of 1967 was Israel's obsession with its security, which, in practical terms, could be translated—as it was in 1956—into the concept of preventive war.[96] The immediate cause, however, was supplied by an event that may have seemed accidental, but which, on closer scrutiny, was also a result of certain long-range trends. President Nasser of Egypt decided to remove from the Egyptian-Israeli borderland the United Nations' Emergency Force (UNEF)

---

[96]In the mid-1950s Menachem Begin declared in the Knesset: "I deeply believe in launching preventive war against the Arab states without further hesitation. By doing so, we will achieve two targets: firstly, the annihilation of the Arab power, and secondly, the expansion of our territory." (October 12, 1955, as quoted by S. Haddawi, *Bitter Harvest: Palestine between 1914–1967* [New York, 1967], p. 283).

that had been stationed there since the conclusion of the 1956 war. The reasons for this decision and its results are reviewed in Chapter XII. There is no hard evidence to indicate that Nasser ever had a serious intention of waging war on Israel, notwithstanding his concentration of troops in the Sinai Peninsula. In fact, despite the impressive accumulation of arms of Soviet provenance in Egypt, Nasser with his military instinct and experience would have hesitated to launch an offensive attack and thus risk his own political survival. By the same token, there always existed in Israel a school of thought, which might be called territorial-military, that viewed the existing Israeli boundaries as highly inconvenient, insecure, and inviting disaster in case of an all-out war with the Arabs. This school was in favor of an enlarged territory for Israel so as to ensure the necessary margin of strategic safety. For this school, therefore, assuming that Israel was militarily prepared, a clumsy provocation such as Nasser had conveniently provided by ordering the UNEF out supplied a welcome opportunity for waging a preventive war. That the war was indeed preventive and that the Israelis launched a well-prepared attack has long since ceased to be a matter of controversy. Although in the first days the Israeli leadership was speaking of an armed response to the Egyptian attack, this pretense was later abandoned when the Israeli military leaders willingly discussed the surprise element which so heavily weighed in their favor in the actual conduct of war.[97]

The war resulted in the virtual annihilation of the air forces of Egypt, Syria, Jordan, and Iraq, and in decisive victories against the Egyptian, Jordanian, and Syrian land forces on all three fronts. Large amounts of Soviet-supplied military equipment fell into the hands of the Israelis on the Egyptian and Syrian fronts. Many Arab prisoners of war were taken and thousands of Arab soldiers were killed or wounded. Six hundred Israels died and perhaps three times as many were wounded.

The main architects of Israeli victory were General Yitzhak Rabin, chief of staff, and General Moshe Dayan, minister of defense. The largely French-equipped Israeli air force avoided most of the Egyptian radar screens and, after an encircling move, attacked the Egyptian positions and airfields from the west, flying at low altitudes and destroying most of the Egyptian aircraft on the ground. Operations against Jordan followed soon after the attack on Egypt, partly because in fulfillment of his pledges to Nasser and misinformed about the state of affairs on the Egyptian front, King Hussein decided to enter the war, only to see his armies effectively routed. By contrast, Israel's attack on Syria was mounted subsequent to the cease-fire arranged under the UN auspices on June 9. Thus through skillful timing and apportioning of their forces the Israelis avoided simultaneous operations against Egypt and Syria.

Israel's victorious armies occupied within a few days areas about twice the size of Israel, namely the entire Sinai Peninsula up to the Suez Canal, the Gaza strip, the entire West Bank of the kingdom of Jordan, the Syrian Golan Heights northeast of the Sea of Galilee, and the Tiran and Sanafir Islands formally under Saudi sovereignty but administered by Egypt in the Strait of Tiran. On June 28, 1967, the Israeli government decreed the "administrative unification" of Jerusalem, thereby annex-

---

[97]For admission of the surprise factor, see Naphtali Lau-Lavie, *Moshe Dayan* (London, 1968), pp. 201–210; and Golda Meir, *My Life* (New York, 1975), pp. 363–366.

ing the old city and other Arab parts of Jerusalem. Israeli spokesmen repeatedly declared that the Israeli sovereignty over the unified city was not negotiable and that, as a maximum concession, in the case of a peace settlement Israel would agree to arrangements whereby the Christian and Moslem holy places would enjoy local administrative autonomy and be opened to access to members of both denominations from the Arab world and beyond.

Although on orders of its Indian commanding general, the UNEF was removed at Nasser's request from the Egyptian territory on the eve of the war, the United Nations continued to arrange for cease-fires, sent a new team of observers, passed various resolutions, and mediated for peace. The following acts of the United Nations deserve mention within the brief context of this review: (1) The General Assembly voted to censure Israel for its virtual annexation of East Jeruslaem[98] (ninety-nine votes for, none against, twenty abstentions). (2) Security Council Resolution 242 of November 22, 1967, called for the withdrawal of Israeli forces from occupied territory, the right of every state in the area to exist in peace, secure boundaries, freedom of navigation in international waters, and a solution for the Arab refugees.[99] (All four permanent members of the Council, the United States, the Soviet Union, the United Kingdom, and France, voted in favor, thereby making the resolution binding.) (3) A prominent Swedish statesman, Dr. Gunnar Jarring, at that time Sweden's ambassador to Moscow, was appointed UN representative with the task of searching for a peaceful settlement and reporting to the Council. (4) Occasional resolutions censured Israel for its massive reprisal raids directed at Jordanian or Lebanese localities or Palestinian refugee camps in those countries. (5) General Assembly resolutions censured Israel for the violation of human rights in the occupied territories (such as the Resolution of December 19, 1968).[100] (6) Israel was censured by the General Assembly for its policy of establishing Jewish settlements in the occupied territories (Resolution of December 8, 1968).

On the whole, the United Nations, particularly the General Assembly, proved to be more critical of Israel's behavior as an occupying power than of the Arab behavior. This attitude was in marked contrast to its earlier history, when, against the express will of the Arab countries and the local Arab population, the United Nations voted to partition Palestine and when, in general, the sympathies of its western majority of members appeared to be on the side of the then "underdog," meaning the dispersed Jews who survived the Nazi persecution of World War II. In the 1960s, UN membership was about four times larger than in the 1940s, and it was clearly weighted in favor of the countries of the Third World, many of which were freshly emancipated from foreign colonial rule. The sympathies of these countries were on the side of the Arabs and they tended to share the Arab view of Israel as an aggressive and expansionist state. In an era in which the issues of racial inequality and liberation from imperialism constituted major themes of international and

---

[98]Text in Ralph Magnus, ed., *Documents on the Middle East* (Washington, D.C., 1969), p. 203.
[99]*Ibid.*, pp. 205–206.
[100]Also the General Assembly resolutions of Dec. 11, 1969; Dec. 15, 1970; Dec. 20, 1971; Dec. 13 and 15, 1972; Dec. 7, 1973; Nov. 29, 1979, etc. and the resolutions of the UN Commission on Human Rights of March 4, 1969, followed by annual resolutions of similar type.

domestic politics, this attitude of the United Nations General Assembly was not surprising. In Israel, as could be expected, it provoked negative responses expressed in scorn mixed with cynicism toward the United Nations as a whole.[101]

While Egypt, Jordan, and eventually also Syria accepted UN Resolution 242, Israel was suspicious of its main provisions. Eventually, by July 31, 1970, it accepted the resolution with the major reservations that withdrawal of its forces should by no means signify evacuation of all the occupied territories, that the matter of final boundaries should be left to direct negotiation between the parties, and that there should be an agreement providing for a comprehensive peace including the establishment of diplomatic relations, trade, and tourism between itself and its Arab neighbors. Because of these major reservations it is unclear whether Israel could be regarded as really having accepted Resolution 242.

There appeared, moreover, to be a substantial difference between the Israeli views and those of the United Nations and the United States regarding the nature of the peace settlement. The formal and fairly consistent American attitude, voiced by President Lyndon Johnson, President Nixon and his Secretary of State William Rogers, and President Ford was that UN Resolution 242 should be implemented, that the Israelis should withdraw from most of the occupied territories with only insubstantial alterations of the boundaries, and that these boundaries should not "reflect the weight of conquest."[102] When, in December 1969, Secretary Rogers presented what since became known as the Rogers Plan embodying those principles,[103] the Israeli government headed by Golda Meir rather angrily rejected it. Similarly, on February 8, 1971, Ambassador Jarring presented simultaneous memoranda to the Egyptian and Israeli governments in which he asked the parties whether they were ready to abide by Resolution 242. In particular, he asked President Sadat whether he was prepared to accept the existence of Israel and agree to abandon the state of belligerency as well as to acknowledge secure boundaries, and at the same time he asked the Israeli government whether it was prepared in return for these Egytian concessions to withdraw from the occupied territories according to the terms of the resolution. He received a positive reply from President Sadat and a negative reply from Premier Golda Meir.[104] The Israelis clearly believed the *quid pro quo* contained in the Jarring memoranda was insufficient and contrary to their national interest.

The lack of progress in the search for peace found its reflection in two phenomena. On the one hand, the initial cease-fire on the Suez Canal front degenerated by 1969–1970 into what became known as the "war of attrition," with frequent exchanges of artillery fire across the canal, military aircraft duels, and an occasional Israeli raid into Egyptian territory. On one such occasion an entire

[101]In this sense, *Jerusalem Post*, Jan. 1, 1969, and *Middle East Review* (Spring-Summer 1975).

[102]See President Lyndon Johnson's speech to B'nai Brith, September 10, 1968, Magnus, *op. cit.*, pp. 208–210.

[103]Text of Secretary Rogers' speech at the Galaxy conference in Washington, D.C., December 9, 1969, in *New York Times*, Dec. 11, 1969.

[104]For details, see John Norton Moore, ed., *The Arab-Israeli Conflict: Readings and Documents* (Princeton, N.J., 1977), pp. 1148–1156.

Soviet-equipped radar installation was captured and brought back to Israel. Although numerically Egyptian losses were, as usual, much larger than those of the Israelis, the prolonged war of attrition was also painful and debilitating for Israel. By August 1970, however, a new cease-fire arranged under the auspices of Secretary Rogers put an end to continuous clashes along the Suez Canal.

Another result of the failure of the UN mediating mission was that the weight of mediation gradually passed over to the United States. This was largely because of the growing conviction of Arab leadership in Egypt, Syria, Jordan, and elsewhere that only the United States as a superpower possessed enough influence to induce Israel to accept a peace settlement according to the terms of UN Resolution 242. This conviction in the Arab capitals undoubtedly reflected a realistic appraisal of the situation. After the June war the United States gradually became the main supplier of arms and military equipment to Israel, while continuing to provide generous economic assistance. However paradoxical its role might appear, the United States, in its dual role of provider of Israeli military strength and a mediator in the search for peace, indeed had the capacity of influencing Israel's foreign policy. In contrast, however, to the policy followed by President Eisenhower in 1956 when he cut off temporarily American aid to Israel to achieve his purposes following the Suez war, this time the U.S. government used its arms grants and sales policy not as a negative weapon but as a means to generate in Israel a greater feeling of security and thus to induce it to be more receptive to the implementation of UN Resolution 242. This was definitely the line pursued by William Rogers' successor as Secretary of State, Henry Kissinger, but it was not limited to the executive branch of the government. First and foremost, Israel was enjoying strong and consistent support in Congress, particularly in the Senate. The Congress repeatedly authorized deliveries of very sophisticated American weapons systems to Israel and, with the passage of time, the combined American grants, loans, and military assistance exceeded $2 billion a year on the average.[105]

If the American arms policy toward Israel was calculated to produce a greater pliability on the part of the Israeli government it appeared to have failed in its objective in the later 1960s and the early 1970s. The Israelis were clearly in no hurry to withdraw from the occupied territories and the military school of thought, which insists on strategic-territorial safeguards rather than the uncertainties of Arab peace promises (from the Israeli viewpoint), clearly dominated Israel's political thought and behavior.

The undeniable fact was that by expanding its control over large Arab territories Israel found under its sovereign power about 1.5 million Arabs. With the exception of a small number of Egyptians in the Sinai Peninsula the overwhelming majority of these Arabs were Palestinians. About 400,000 of them constituted the Arab minority in Israel proper and the rest were inhabitants of the occupied territories. The Israeli attitude toward the Palestinians could broadly be described as negative. First,

---

[105]Figures of combined military and economic aid to Israel, in the millions of dollars, were as follows in the mid-1970s: fiscal 1974, $624.5; (Dec. 20, 1973, emergency appropriation), $2,200.0; fiscal 1975, $600.0; fiscal 1976, $2,230.0; additional appropriation, $279.0; fiscal 1977, $1,800.0. Source: *New York Times,* various issues.

ISRAEL   *453*

Israeli leaders tended to reject the notion of a distinct Palestinian nationality comparable in its identity to the Egyptians, Syrians, Iraqis, or Saudis. The tendency was to regard them as somewhat nondescript Arabs who, when displaced from their homes, could and should be assimilated by the surrounding Arab countries. Second, because a separate identity of the Palestinians was denied, the next logical step—their claim to self-determination—was also rejected by the Israelis. Perhaps the most pronounced statement in this respect was that made by Golda Meir in June 1969, the "Palestinians do not exist."[106] These attitudes of denial went hand-in-hand with Israeli territorial aspirations. Ben Gurion, for example, once deplored the fact that during the 1948 war of independence the poor judgment of some Israeli generals (including Yadin and Allon) had prevented the Israelis from seizing parts of Transjordan and the southern areas of Lebanon.[107] In fact, Ben Gurion was on record as advocating the expansion of Jewish immigration and settlement in Transjordan. Similarly ambitious was the erstwhile leader of the terrorist Irgun Zvai Leumi and eventual prime minister Menachem Begin, who, true to the tradition of the Revisionist party, advocated the inclusion not only of the West Bank but of the territory of Transjordan into the state of Israel.[108] His views were shared to a large extent by the National Religious party, which preached that the entire area of Palestine with less defined extension into Transjordan constituted the holy land and homeland of the Jews who had the duty to settle and populate it and who could not withdraw from the occupied areas without betraying their historical mission. Because the areas in question were not empty, some Israeli leaders advocated an assimilation of the Arabs into the Israeli economy. This view was opposed by one of the most important leaders of the Mapai party, Pinhas Sapir, who on several occasions (1968, 1969, and 1972) warned against the use of Arab labor by the Israeli collective settlements and business establishments on the ground that the purpose of Israel was to be a Jewish and not a binational state. He was therefore in favor of relinquishing control over the occupied territories to maintain the Jewish character of the state.[109]

Israel's victory over the Arabs in 1967 served as a powerful catalyst in the process of awakening Palestinian nationalism. Although the Palestinian Liberation Organization (PLO) and the Palestinian Liberation Army (PLA) were created as early as 1964, the June war intensified Palestinian guerrilla warfare. Palestinian terrorism brought Israeli counterterrorism expressed in regular military actions against the bases of the *fedayeen* and the localities in Jordan and Lebanon that harbored them. Furthermore, the defeat and humiliation that the Arabs suffered at the hands of the Israelis intensified radical trends in the Arab states. This radicalism was manifested both in their foreign policy—by drawing closer to the Communist bloc and rupturing diplomatic relations with the United States—and in their domestic politics by provoking the rise to power and growth in influence of militant elements bent upon

[106]Text in *Sunday Times* (London), June 15, 1969.

[107]*New York Times*, March 9, 13, and 17, 1964.

[108]For Ben Gurion's views, see Alan R. Taylor, "Vision and Intent in Zionist Thought," in Ibrahim Abu-Lughod, ed. *The Transformation of Palestine* (Evanston, Ill., 1971), p. 21. For Begin's views, see Menachem Begin, *The Revolt: Story of the Irgun* (London and New York, 1951), p. 3.

[109]*New York Times*, November 11, 1968; May 26, 1969; and November 9, 1972.

the revolutionary transformation of their societies. The Baathist revolution in Iraq of July 1968, and Colonel Muammar Qadhafi's revolution which toppled the monarchy in Libya on September 1, 1969, provided two eloquent examples of advancing radicalism.

The death of Nasser in late September 1970 was a turning point in Egypt's policies. His successor, Anwar Sadat, had initially tried to reach a peace settlement (and thereby the return of Sinai and the Gaza strip) by responding positively to the proposals submitted to him by Ambassador Jarring and Secretary Rogers. These initiatives, however, brought no tangible results. Consequently, a mood of disenchantment developed in Cairo, which, in turn, led to the search for a military solution to put an end to a likely petrification of the status quo in a hopeless "no war no peace" situation. In line with this new policy Sadat arranged intensive training of his troops while, at the same time, securing through skillful diplomacy the cooperation of other Arab states. Because of the frequency of his increasingly militant statements, which were not followed by any concrete action, and the seeming futility of Egyptian military movements on the west side of the canal zone, the Israeli army command, although well aware of these movements, did not appear to take them seriously. This attitude perhaps partly explains why in the fall of 1973 the Israeli forces were completely surprised when the Egyptians struck.

The October War of 1973

In contrast to the June war of 1967 in which four Arab countries were engaged to varying degrees, the October war was limited to Egypt and Syria, both of which launched attacks on the Israeli forces stationed in their respective occupied territories. The Egyptian attack came on October 6, the Jewish holiday of Yom Kippur during the Moslem month of fast, Ramadhan. The operations of this war are reviewed in Chapter XII. Observations here are limited to a few major points that have particular bearing on Israel's perceptions, behavior, and policies.

The October war was a traumatic experience for Israel because for the first time it suffered a surprise attack and its forces did not emerge unquestionably victorious. The myth of Israeli military invincibility was, if not shattered, at least seriously eroded. From then on Israel would have to face a front of Arab states that had regained not only self-respect after a series of humiliations but also a good deal of self-confidence, an important factor in the conduct of any war. Similarly, the traditional inability of the Arab governments and high commands to coordinate their moves gave place to a fairly well synchronized Egyptian and Syrian offensive. The initially successful crossing of the Suez Canal and the highly fortified Bar-Lev Line testified to the Arab military capacity and, to some extent, shook the "Maginot line mentality" prevailing on both sides. Furthermore, the regional conflict threatened to develop into a global confrontation between the United States and the Soviet Union, because of the massive airlift of weapons to Israel by the Americans and to Egypt by the Russians which occurred at the height of the war. This fact reconfirmed the disquieting degree of Israel's dependence on a foreign power for its security and survival; and notwithstanding the generous supply to Israel of arms (which were actually flown to the forward bases in Sinai), the United States would henceforth have to weigh the risks associated with a similar Soviet involvement on the other side. Israel could not avoid asking itself how far, after the Vietnam retreat, the Americans were prepared to go. At the same time, this very vulnerability appeared to have strengthened the military school of thought in Israel, which insisted on control of expanded territories as a proper safeguard of Israeli security. Many Israelis and their sympathizers in the United States asked what would have happened to the security of Israeli population centers and to the nation's existence had the line of defense that the Egyptians breached been located in Israel's heartland rather than in the western reaches of the Sinai Peninsula.

On the other hand, the danger of a big-power confrontation that the October war generated gave some sobering thoughts to leaders of major states the world over. It became increasingly clear to them that the neglect or failure to attend to the proper solution of the Arab-Israeli conflict could have fatal consequences for world peace. Another disturbing feature of the situation was that both the United States and Israel have found themselves somewhat isolated in the world community of nations. The NATO allies, except for Portugal (still under the fascist regime of Marcello Caetano) refused overflight permissions to the American aircraft rushing supplies to Israel. The Germans and other West European NATO powers resented the fact that certain stocks of American arms destined for the defense of their territories were rapidly depleted to accommodate Israel. The United States, designated by the Arab governments as the principal hostile power, was exposed to an oil embargo along with Portugal and Holland. The oil embargo gave Americans an occasion to consider the consequences of identification with Israel in terms of military security and economic well-being.

From the Israeli point of view there were some bright points in this generally disturbing situation. After recovering from the initial surprise, the Israeli army succeeded in stopping the Egyptian and Syrian offensives, and on the Sinai front, it recrossed the Suez Canal, establishing a bridgehead on the western bank while also surrounding the Egyptian Third Army in the southern sector of the canal zone in Sinai. Some military observers believed that if it had not been for the cease-fire that was proclaimed under UN auspices on October 22, Israel might have ended the war in a military victory by recrossing the canal and pushing back or destroying the Egyptian armies on the eastern side. Consequently, while the United States prevented the collapse of the Israeli resistance, by rushing arms to Israel, it also— through its vigorous activity in the United Nations—materially contributed to saving Egypt from a possible rout.

Operations in the Golan Heights were naturally smaller in scale but they bore some resemblance to the basic pattern in Sinai. Syrian troops launched a surprise attack on Israeli lines on October 6, breached them, and penetrated a substantial distance into the Golan area. After a few days, however, the Israelis regrouped themselves and launched a counterattack that not only restored to them the Syrian-captured territory but allowed them to advance into Syria beyond the 1967 demarcation line and to establish a foothold in a sizable stretch of land. To the Syrians the reversal was an ominous development demonstrating their vulnerability, for Damascus is located within forty miles of the original Golan front line.

Hostilities on both fronts were brought to a close by a final cease-fire on October 24. What followed was step-by-step diplomacy in which the United States played an active mediating role. As a result of these efforts three disengagement agreements were concluded. The first, known as Sinai I, signed between Israel and Egypt on January 18, 1974, left the entire Suez Canal under Egyptian control and established a new front line running parallel to the canal on its eastern side with a narrow neutral zone between the opposing forces. This arrangement meant that the Israeli force that had penetrated to the western side of the canal withdrew from its bridgehead and the Egyptian Third Army entrapped in the southeastern reaches of the canal was freed and allowed to recross to the Egyptian lines. On May 29 a similar disengagement agreement was concluded between Syria and Israel under American auspices. It provided for the retreat of Israeli forces from the additional areas captured in the course of the October war as well as from a certain stretch of the initially occupied Golan Heights and for a new demarcation line, again with a neutral zone separating the forces. The net result was that Syria regained a small part of the Golan Heights including the destroyed town of Qunaitra.[110]

In the case of Egypt, a second disengagement agreement was initialled on September 1, 1975, and formally signed on September 4. It provided for a further retreat of Israeli forces and their withdrawal from two strategic passes in Sinai, Gidi and Mitla. These passes, however, were not returned to the Egyptians; instead, they were designated along with some adjacent territory as a new neutral zone to be manned by American radar technicians. Subsequently, the United States Congress authorized the employment of Americans in that capacity. The Sinai II agreement caused considerable controversy in the Arab world. President Sadat claimed that it was another step in the Egyptian struggle to regain the areas lost in the 1967 war. He also pointed out the additional advantage of having the Abu Rudeis oil fields in western Sinai restored to Egyptian control. Critics of his policy countered by saying that not only were the territorial gains stemming from this agreement insignificant as compared with the October war effort, but that the agreement by introducing the Americans into the neutral zone had the effect of entrenching the status quo, leaving most of the Sinai and Gaza strip in the hands of the Israelis, and paralyzing Egypt in case it felt compelled to resort again to military action to regain its rights. Moreover, both President Hafez Assad of Syria and King Hussein of Jordan felt uneasy at being excluded from this second disengagement step and with varying degrees of intensity accused President Sadat of leaving them alone while attending to the interests of Egypt. Criticism in certain other Arab centers was even more intense: Iraq, Libya, South Yemen, and certain militant elements of the Palestinian Liberation Organization constituted the Rejectionist Front, attacking not only the disengagement agreements as harmful to the Arab cause but also the very concept of a peace settlement with Israel. Their view was that not only the occupied territory but the area of Israel proper should be liberated in accordance with the world-wide struggle of colonial and oppressed peoples.

---

[110]According to another version, following the May 29, 1974, disengagement agreement between Israel and Syria, Israeli combat engineers systematically demolished Qunaitra between June 7 and 26 before returning it to Syria (*New York Times,* June 8, 1974).

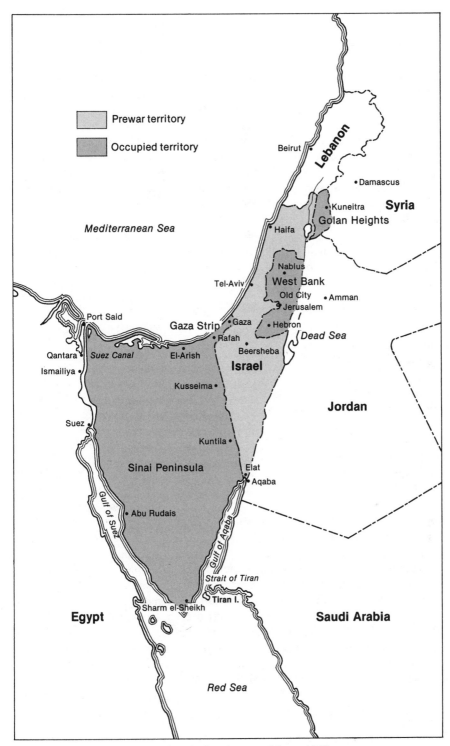

Prewar territory

Occupied territory

Map 6. Israel after the war of June, 1967.

457

The disengagement agreements were largely the result of the shuttle diplomacy carried out by Secretary Kissinger as he was flying back and forth between Jerusalem and Damascus and Jerusalem and Cairo. They undoubtedly marked an important step in the immediate tranquilization of the situation in the area but did not resolve a more fundamental question of the disposition of the bulk of the occupied territories and the ultimate peace settlement between Israel and its Arab neighbors. Officially, the principles of this settlement had been spelled out by UN Security Council Resolution 242 of 1967. These principles were further reconfirmed by UN Security Council Resolution 338 of October 22, 1973, which not only decreed cease-fire between the belligerents, but also called "upon the parties concerned to start immediately after the cease-fire the implementation of Security Council Resolution 242 (1967) in all of its parts."[111] The provisions of United States-sponsored disengagement agreements still differed substantially from the tenor of both UN resolutions. For the next two-and-half years, until the end of President Ford's term of office, no further significant progress was registered in the search for a permanent peace in the area.

The Arabs in Israel and the Occupied Territories

By the end of 1976 there were about 400,000 Arabs in Israel (mostly Israeli citizens), about 750,000 in the West Bank territory, and slightly over 400,000 in the Gaza strip. All three segments were subjected to Israel's political and military controls and they were denied the right to practice self-determination. The difference consisted in the fact that Israeli Arabs had the right to and did participate in the Israeli political process as expressed by national and municipal elections and that, with some important exceptions, they had rights and duties comparable to those of Jewish Israelis. By contrast, inhabitants of the occupied areas were subjected to the military government which was expected to follow the rules of international law pertaining to occupation of enemy territory, particularly as spelled out by the Geneva convention. Eastern Jerusalem stood somewhere between the two categories because of the Israeli act of virtual annexation. Broadly speaking, Israeli policy toward its own Arab population was more or less stabilized during the first quarter-century of Israeli statehood. Culturally, the Arab population enjoyed a degree of autonomy, with its Moslem and Christian religious courts to attend to matters of personal status according to the old Ottoman millet system, which Israel had inherited. Arabs had also newspapers and schools and elected village headmen and municipal authorities. Their participation in the national political life was in practice less effective, and there was no unified Arab representation in the Knesset. The Arabs divided their votes among a small Arab list, an Arab party cooperating with Israel's Alignment, and the communist Rakah. The government paid salaries of teachers in Arab public schools but otherwise Arab representation in the civil service was very small and on higher political levels nonexistent. This general situation was in conformity with the essentially Jewish character of the state.

The Arabs were thus a definite minority in Israel but a minority which, because of

---

[111]Text in J. N. Moore, *op. cit.*, p. 1189.

its natural birth rate, was steadily growing. From less than 200,000 in the early days of Israeli independence it doubled in size within twenty-five years. The concentration and numerical growth of the Arab population, particularly in the northern part of Israel, Galilee, caused some concern to the Israeli authorities. For example, The Koenig Report, presented to the government of Israel by one of the higher civil servants in 1976, advocated concerted measures by the government to change the predominantly Arab character of certain districts through forced displacement of the Arabs, acquisition of their landed properties, and settling of Jewish population.[112] When revealed in the latter part of 1976, the Koenig Report provoked strong protests from the Arabs both outside and inside Israel. Although it was never adopted as an official government policy, it showed a persistent concern in Israel with the so-called Arab question. In fact, in practice the government did apply measures of confiscation or forcible acquisition of land and transfers of the population in some areas. This practice was most noticeable in the annexed eastern part of Jerusalem where in one government decision over eight hundred of acres of Arab-owned land and properties were requisitioned by the state, and its inhabitants were removed to the areas outside of the city. This step was followed by an ambitious program of constructing tall apartment buildings that contrasted with the traditional architecture of the city and were designed to house Jewish inhabitants. Policies of land acquisition and population transfer were also applied in other parts of Israel, occasionally provoking Arab protest demonstrations. Some of these measures were explained by considerations of security, inasmuch as the Arab villages in question were located in militarily sensitive border zones.

Formulating policy for the occupied areas of the West Bank, Gaza, the Golan Heights, and to a lesser extent the Sinai region presented a major challenge to Israel. The Likud coalition and the National Religious party, as mentioned previously, stood for permanent incorporation of the land into Israel. Menachem Begin refused to refer to these territories as occupied and instead called them "liberated" while referring to the West Bank as Samaria and Judea. Officially the government of Israel did not commit itself to such an extreme stance, at least not until the electoral victory of Begin's coalition in late spring of 1977. In spite of this reticence the Israeli government both tolerated and encouraged Jewish settlements in the occupied territories. These took two forms. The Nahal (or semimilitary) settlements were spread along the Jordan River and in the Golan Heights close to the front line and consisted of armed populations ready to cooperate with the Israeli army in external and internal security tasks. Ordinary civilian settlements were interspersed throughout the occupied areas. By early 1977 the total number of both kinds of settlements was about seventy.[113] Although in some cases the government tried to

[112]Text in *Al-Hamishmar* (Tel-Aviv daily), Sept. 7, 1976. Reproduced in English in *Palaces of Injustice,* a pamphlet published by Americans for Middle East Understanding, Inc. (AMEU) in cooperation with American Jewish Alternatives to Zionism, Inc., as No. 7 in AMEU's Public Affairs Series. (New York, n.d., translation by Dr. Israel Shahak.)

[113]By late 1978 the number of settlements increased to 113, distributed as follows: West Bank, 62; Gaza strip and northern Sinai, 18; Golan Heights, 26; Sinai, 7. On December 6, 1978, Israel announced that soon after December 17 (i.e., three months after the Camp David agreements of September 17, 1978) seven new settlements would be established in the West Bank.

restrain the more militant groups from establishing a new settlement, especially when it was likely to produce a major outburst of Arab discontent, generally this opposition could be described as lukewarm. Sensing the official indecision in this matter, the militant elements, particularly those affiliated with the National Religious party or the Likud grouping, undertook on two occasions, in March 1975 and April 1976, major marches with the participation of twenty to thirty thousand people to certain localities in the occupied areas earmarked for potential Jewish settlements. This acquisitive policy did not limit itself to the West Bank and the Golan Heights; on a smaller scale it was practiced also in certain areas of the Gaza strip and even in Sinai where a settlement called Ophira was established by June 1975. Militant Israeli groups justified these *faits accomplis* by claiming that once the Jews were settled in the land it would be sinful and unthinkable to remove them. This policy of increasing the number of settlements caused concern not only in the United Nations but also, despite its friendship to Israel, in the United States. United States representative to the United Nations William Scranton publicly criticized Israel on March 13, 1976, for its settlement policy.

The Arabs frequently complained about harsh and arbitrary measures of the military government. The Israelis countered by saying that the economy of the occupied areas was not only restored to normalcy but even in some cases improved and that this was because of the opportunities which the adjacent Israeli economy provided as well as the "open door" policy whereby Israel permitted the West Bank inhabitants to engage in economic exchanges with Jordan east of the Jordan River.

Overshadowing these economic considerations, however, was the basic political question of Arab discontent with alien rule and the denial of national freedom. The attitudes of the Arab population could not remain unaffected by the existence of the Palestinian guerrilla movement, which found adherents among the Arabs in the occupied territories and in Israel and engaged in armed forays from bases in the adjoining Arab states. Israel's countermeasures of a purely military type against the *fedayeen* concentrations in Lebanon and Jordan have already been mentioned. The Arab population in areas under Israeli control was subjected to three types of repressive actions in retaliation for dissidence or terror. There were deportations of undesirable individuals (mostly people with leadership potential who were deported to Jordan); group expulsions, especially in the case of forced acquisition of land by Israel in certain localities; and punishments consisting of arrests and jailings, destruction or cementing in of private homes so as to prevent their further use by a given family. Characteristic of the punitive policy was the tendency to apply the principle of collective punishment in cases where the *fedayeen* were harbored or aided by a family or a village. In April 1975, Amnesty International—an organization based in London and often embroiled in controversy because of the selectivity of its targets—censured Israel for the violations of human rights in its treatment of the Arab population.[114]

Before this section is concluded, one interesting aspect of the Israeli occupation

---

[114]The report also criticized Israel and Syria for their treatment of prisoners of war during the October war of 1973. *New York Times,* April 10, 1975.

policy should perhaps be mentioned. Although Israel by virtue of the Sinai II disengagement agreement had returned the Abu Rudeis oil fields to Egypt, it continued exploration activities in the remaining parts of the Sinai Peninsula as well as offshore in the Gulf of Suez. Because these offshore areas had been granted through concession agreements to various American oil companies by the government of Egypt, a conflict over their use ensued. On September 4, 1976, an American drilling vessel operating in the Gulf of Suez was stopped by Israeli gunboats in an obvious attempt to prevent it from pursuing its task. On February 14 the State Department issued a protest over the impropriety of Israeli drilling in these offshore areas.

The Impact of War: Militarization and the Obsession with Security

The need for constant preparedness, for an efficient intelligence service to secure information about the political and military moves of foreign powers, for protection against the attacks of the *fedayeen*, and for appropriate counteractions gave the security of the state a position of primacy among all other concerns. Thus, the position of the military and of other agencies concerned with security was enhanced in Israel's political system. Moreover, the military played a major role not only as a collective, organized body but also through the influence of its leaders who frequently, upon early retirement from active service, followed political careers. Thus Israel was a democracy, in which generals in and out of military service were politically active. For instance, Moshe Dayan, at one time or another held various ministerial responsibilities in the Israeli cabinet; Yitzhak Rabin, following his service as chief of staff during the June 1967 war, served as ambassador in Washington and later became prime minister; Yigal Allon served as deputy prime minister and minister of foreign affairs; Aharon Yariv became a cabinet minister; Yigael Yadin launched the Democratic Movement for Change; Ariel Sharon founded the Shlomzion party later affiliated with Likud; and Ezer Weizmann, formerly commander of the air force, entered Prime Minister Begin's cabinet in early summer of 1977. In addition, such generals as Yehoshua Harkabi and Matityahu Peled were active as advisers, writers, and political commentators.

Security considerations led Israel not only to establish special military zones in certain Arab-inhabited areas, in which normal administrative procedures were suspended, as we know, but also to institute censorship that applied primarily to matters connected with the security of the state. Similarly, the Israeli security organization Mosad enjoyed the reputation of being effective in tracking down Arab terrorists and in mounting its own counterterror operations both at home and abroad. In fact, the deadly cloak-and-dagger game played between the Palestinian Arab guerrilla groups and the Israeli security organs expanded far beyond the boundaries of Israel and the occupied territories, with acts of assassination committed in such remote places as Rome, Paris, or Norway. Although Israel's system provided for an unquestioned supremacy of the civilian authorities over the military, doubt occasionally arose, as in the Lavon case, of the effectiveness of such controls.

Arab terrorism practiced by various *fedayeen* groups provided the main justification for Israel's countermeasures. Arab acts included many atrocities such as bombing supermarkets and theaters, hijacking planes, attacking schools and keeping the children hostage, gunning down Israeli passengers at such airports as Rome and Athens, killing the Israeli athletes at the Munich Olympic Games, and assassinating individuals. The Israelis were not reluctant to repay in kind. On April 10, 1973, the Israeli army sent a task force to Beirut which swiftly invaded the apartments of three leading PLO figures and killed them on the spot. Similarly, after proclaiming an early curfew in certain districts of Israel during the 1967 war, an Israeli army detachment gunned down all the Arab villagers, unaware of the curfew, who were returning from their fields to their homes in the village of Kfar Kassem. And in an act that caused considerable international uproar the Israeli air force shot down a Libyan airline's passenger airplane on its way from Libya to Cairo because it violated the Israeli-controlled air space beyond the Suez Canal in February 1973.

The Arab-Israeli terror and counterterror affected the behavior of certain groups outside of the Middle East. An organization called the Jewish Defense League was formed in the United States by Rabbi Meir Kahane. It assulted Arab diplomats accredited to the United Nations in New York, as well as Soviet diplomats in retaliation for the Soviet government's ill-treatment of Jews.

The primacy of security concerns had its inevitable impact on Israel's economy. While until 1967 Israel was noted for its impressive economic development, the two subsequent wars compelled the state to allocate major resources to defense. As a result, the economic pace slowed and numerous measures of austerity were introduced. This general trend was also reflected in several successive devaluations of the Israeli currency, of which the 20 percent devaluation decreed in November 9, 1974, was perhaps the most drastic. To maintain its economic viability, Israel had to rely increasingly on foreign aid provided mainly by the United States.

Foreign Relations

In the post Ben Gurion era Israel maintained strong military, economic, and cultural relations with the United States. Although no formal treaty or agreement of alliance was ever signed between the two countries, the official trend in the United States, especially in the Congress, was to consider that America had a "historical" interest in maintaining Israel's survival, security, and well-being. The rise of the United States to this position of prominence in Israeli foreign policy was related to the activities of other powers that had initially been important in the establishment and early existence of Israel. After the 1956 Suez crisis, Great Britain definitely faded away as a major factor in Israeli foreign policy. France continued to provide sophisticated arms, but under General de Gaulle the French government followed a policy of gradual reconciliation with the Arab world, especially after the recognition of independence of Algeria. After the 1967 war (in which French-supplied weapons contributed to the Israeli victory), France fairly rapidly changed her policy of closely identifying with Israel into one of forging stronger links with the Arabs. Japan experienced a real shock when it saw its oil supplies severely cut back by the Arabs in 1973-1974. Moreover, the Japanese economy was increasingly geared to supply the expanding Arab markets and to provide services to the ambitious development plans of oil-rich Arab countries.

Israel's relations with the Soviet Union and other states of the Communist bloc suffered a definite deterioration in 1967, which was reflected by the rupture of diplomatic relations between Moscow and Tel-Aviv.

Because the Arabs found many sympathizers in the Third World countries, Israel's originally promising relations with Africa also suffered. Israel was not only obliged to withdraw its technical assistance missions from a number of African countries, but also became an object of condemnation at various African conferences in which the Arab delegations caused the black African states to endorse their anti-Israeli position. An aggravating factor in this respect was a friendly relationship between Israel and South Africa, exemplified by a visit from the staunch exponent of apartheid, Prime Minister John Vorster, in April 1976. African critics of Israel were prone to draw a parallel between white supremacy in South Africa and Jewish supremacy in Israel and the occupied territories. These Third World attitudes found their dramatic expression in a resolution passed on November 10, 1975, by the UN General Assembly. The resolution defined Zionism as "a form of racism and racial discrimination."[115] It was adopted by seventy-two votes, with thirty-five opposing, and thirty-two abstentions and three absences. After the vote, the United States delegate Daniel Moynihan declared that "the United States . . . does not acknowledge, it will not abide by, it will never acquiesce in this infamous act."[116]

The American Role in the Search for Peace

Following the conclusion of the disengagement agreements between Israel on the one hand and Egypt and Syria on the other, the American role in the search for permanent peace settlement could be described as semidormant. It seemed that step-by-step diplomacy had exhausted its possibilities and that either a more decisive move would be made to resolve the fundamentals of the lingering conflict or the situation through sheer neglect would again deteriorate to the point of war.

With the new Democratic administration of President Jimmy Carter in January 1977, the United States government began to take new initiatives in the search for peace. In fact, the Carter administration gave the resolution of the Middle East problem a top priority among foreign policy concerns. President Carter received in succession Prime Minister Rabin of Israel, President Sadat of Egypt, and King Hussein of Jordan. His next move was to travel to Geneva after a conference of Western heads of state in London to see President Hafez Assad of Syria. Somewhat later, Crown Prince and First Deputy Prime Minister of Saudi Arabia Fahd ibn Abdul Aziz visited President Carter in Washington. His visit coincided with the victory of Likud in the Israeli elections and the emergence of Menachem Begin as a future prime minister of Israel. In terms of frequency and intensity of presidential contacts with Middle Eastern leaders, particularly the Arabs, this activity had no precedent. Interspersed among these meetings were various statements and press

---

[115]Text in *New York Times*, Nov. 11, 1975.
[116]*Ibid.*

conferences of the president and of Secretary of State Cyrus Vance, about the principles on which the peace settlement should be based. In the first place, the administration reiterated its support for UN Resolution 242 in firmer and clearer terms than was the case in the latter part of the Republican administration. Furthermore, the president and the secretary did not hesitate to spell out their views as to the nature of proposed settlement. These could be summed up as follows: (a) withdrawal of Israeli forces from occupied territories to the pre-June 1967 boundaries with only minor alterations; (b) the establishment of secure or defensive boundaries, with an intimation that political boundaries should be differentiated from defense lines established for the protection of Israel *within* the Arab territory and manned either by Israeli or by international forces; (c) establishment of a full-fledged peace (not merely renunciation of the state of belligerency) which would include diplomatic recognition, exchange of ambassadors, trade, tourism, and cultural relations; (d) provision for a Palestinian homeland, with a hint that preferably it should be established in conjunction with the kingdom of Jordan.[117]

Moreover, because of the well-known expansionist stance of Likud coalition and the militancy of Menachem Begin on the territorial issues, on June 27, 1977, the State Department issued a declaration on behalf of the administration directed at Israel's new government in which these principles were reiterated. Begin's visit to President Carter in July 1977 brought no further progress and it appeared that a deadlock was reached.

The stalemate, however, was broken rather unexpectedly by President Sadat's spectacular peace initiative. On November 19 Sadat flew to Jerusalem and in an address to the Knesset offered Israel recognition, full peace, and security guarantees. In return, he asked for total Israeli withdrawal from the occupied territories.

On December 25, Begin met Sadat in Ismailia and submitted to him an Israeli peace plan. On the one hand it called for a gradual withdrawal from Sinai, demilitarization of the Gidi and Mitla passes, retention of Jewish settlements in Sinai to be protected by Israeli troops, and freedom of navigation in the Strait of Tiran. On the other hand the plan offered limited administrative autonomy to "the inhabitants" (Arab and Jewish) of the West Bank and the Gaza strip. The West Bank was called Samaria and Judea in the Israeli document—to emphasize Israel's historical claim to it. According to this plan Israel was, moreover, to ensure internal and external security of the West Bank, which meant that no military withdrawal but a mere regrouping of Israeli forces was contemplated.[118] This plan followed in broad outlines the earlier unofficial plan presented by Israel's foreign minister Allon in October 1976. While conceding that the densely populated Arab areas of the West Bank should return to Arab rule, Allon had advocated creation of security zones ringing this region in which Israeli troops would be permanently deployed.[119]

Begin's proposals in essence offered Egypt a separate peace treaty with some

[117]For relevant texts, see *New York Times,* Feb. 11, 1977 (Vance), and March 10, 1977 (President Carter).

[118]Text in *New York Times,* Dec. 29, 1977.

[119]See Y. Allon, "Israel: The Case for Defensible Borders," *Foreign Affairs* (October 1976), pp. 39–53.

onerous clauses while asserting continued Israeli control over the Palestinian territories, but they fell short of Sadat's expectations and a new stalemate was developing.

To break it, President Carter resorted to a bold initiative of his own by calling for and hosting a conference at Camp David between September 5 and 17, 1978. The conference brought together Begin and Sadat, accompanied by their cabinet-rank advisers. The president played an active role, as a "full partner" in all the discussions. The Camp David meeting ended in the announcement of two "frameworks," one for the peace treaty between Israel and Egypt and the other for a multilateral treaty focusing on the West Bank and the Gaza strip. These frameworks contained the principles that were to be embodied in the subsequent final treaties.

The main principles of the first framework were as follows: (1) a peace treaty between Israel and Egypt to be concluded within three months; (2) such a treaty to be implemented between two and three years after its signing; (3) Egypt to regain sovereignty over Sinai up to the pre-1967 border; (4) Israel to withdraw its armed forces from Sinai, the first such withdrawal to take place within nine months after the conclusion of the treaty; (5) freedom of navigation for Israel to apply to passage through the Suez Canal and the Strait of Tiran; (6) a highway to be constructed between Sinai and Jordan near Eilat with guarantees of free passage to both countries; (7) limitation of Egyptian armed forces to one division within the area lying approximately thirty miles (fifty kilometers) east of the Gulf of Suez and the Suez Canal; (8) absence of Egyptian forces in the remaining part of Sinai; (9) limitation of Israeli military forces to four infantry battalions in the area within 1.8 miles (three kilometers) east of the international border; (10) United Nations forces to be stationed in specified areas to which limitations on Egyptian and Israeli military presence were to apply; (11) peace between Israel and Egypt to embody full diplomatic recognition, economic and cultural relations, termination of economic boycotts and barriers to the free movement of goods and people.[120]

"Framework of Peace in the Middle East," focusing on the West Bank and the Gaza strip, contained the following main guidelines: (1) UN Security Council resolutions 242 and 338 "in all their parts" to form the basis of the peace settlement. (2) Peace treaty to be negotiated by Egypt, Israel, Jordan, and "the representatives of the Palestinian people." (3) "Full autonomy to the inhabitants" of the West Bank and Gaza to be granted. (4) "Egypt, Israel, and Jordan will agree on the modalities for establishing the elected self-governing authority" in those areas. "The delegations of Egypt and Jordan may include Palestinians from the West Bank and Gaza or other Palestinians as mutually agreed." (5) "A withdrawal of Israeli armed forces will take place and there will be a redeployment of the remaining Israeli forces into specified security locations." (6) Once the self-governing authority ("administrative council") is established, a transitional period of five years to begin; by the end of this period the final status of the West Bank and Gaza to be determined, it being understood that "the legitimate rights of the Palestinian people

[120]Text in *Los Angeles Times*, Sept. 18, 1978.

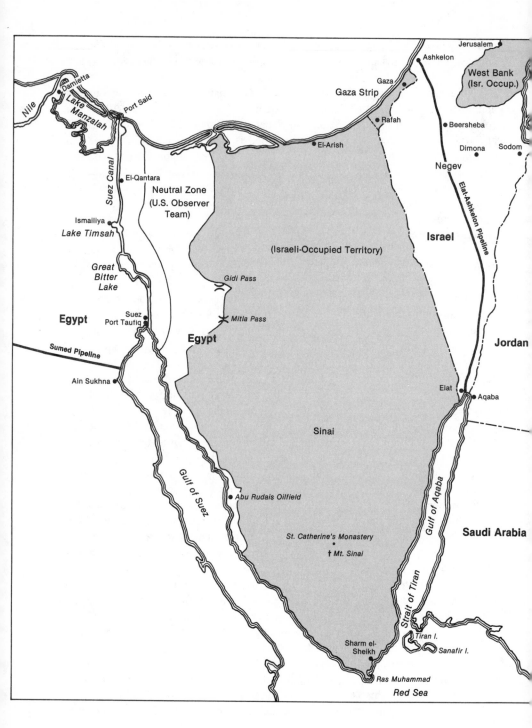

Map 7. Sinai and the surrounding area according to Egypt-Israel agreement, September, 1975.

466

and their just requirements'' be recognized. (7) "During the transitional period, the representatives of Egypt, Israel, Jordan, and the self-governing authority will constitute a continuing committee to decide by agreement on the modalities of admission of persons displaced from the West Bank and Gaza in 1967.''[121]

When, upon the conclusion of the conference, President Carter announced its results to the joint session of Congress in the presence of Begin and Sadat, the general mood was one of euphoria, and Carter's rating in opinion polls shot upwards. On closer inspection, however, one might wonder whether this uncritical enthusiasm was fully warranted. In the first place, the two framework agreements bore a striking similarity to the Allon and Begin peace plans of 1976–1977, thus creating a legitimate doubt whether the Camp David deal represented a genuine compromise or rather a capitulation to the Israeli point of view. It was hard to deny that, in a large measure, the agreements signified a reversal of President Carter's own program, announced in the spring of 1977 and providing for Israeli withdrawal from the occupied lands (with minor territorial adjustments) and a "homeland" for the Palestinians—with a connotation of political self-determination rather than a mere administrative autonomy under Israeli military control. In fact, except for Sinai, according to Camp David, Israel was not in reality committed to withdraw its forces from the areas it occupied but merely to redeploy them, very much in conformity with the Allon-Begin proposals.

In addition, the Camp David agreements failed to mention the fate of Jerusalem and the Golan Heights, the future of Jewish settlements in the occupied territories, or the Palestine Liberation Organization (PLO), and did not stipulate a linkage between the Egyptian-Israeli and the West Bank-Gaza treaties. The latter omission constituted a serious flaw because it introduced the likelihood of a separate peace treaty between Egypt and Israel which would not be followed by the other treaty and which might open the way to accusations that Sadat had, for the selfish benefit of Egypt, betrayed the Arab cause.

The United States government's policy of ignoring the PLO, which had been designated by the Arab summit meeting in 1974 as "the sole representative of the Palestinian people," was officially justified by the fact that in its charter the PLO had called for the abolition of the State of Israel and, unofficially, that it was engaging in terrorist activities. This was rather inconsistent inasmuch as the United States recognized de facto, and kept liaison with, a number of terrorist-prone guerrilla-type "liberation fronts" at one time or another, especially in Rhodesia and, in the 1950s, Algeria. Those movements, engaging in massive violence against civilian targets, each held equally uncompromising positions toward the French rule in Algeria and the white racist state in Rhodesia.

As we have seen in the earlier chapters on Syria and Iraq, the Camp David agreements provoked a strongly negative reaction in the Arab world at large. And, as pointed out in the chapter on Egypt, the threat of isolation began to have its impact on Egyptian diplomacy. It was not surprising, therefore, that when the Egyptian and Israeli delegations headed by their defense and foreign ministers

[121] *Ibid.*

subsequently (in October–November 1978) met in Washington to discuss the first of the envisaged treaties, the issue of linkage emerged as a major obstacle to the progress of negotiations.

In Israel, except for the critical attitude of fundamentalist religious and expansionist groups which valued territory more than peace, the response to the Camp David agreements was positive. This was understandable inasmuch as Camp David was viewed, rightly, as an Israeli diplomatic success. Indeed, the tenacity with which Prime Minister Begin pursued his hardline policy and his ability to win over President Carter and, under the latter's pressure, President Sadat, to what was in essence his own program, were truly impressive. Moreover, it gave Israel a psychological recompense for the partial defeat it had suffered in May 1978, when—despite its strenuous objections—the United States administration had won Senate approval for the simultaneous sale of modern jet fighter aircraft to Egypt, Saudi Arabia, and Israel.

Two major points of difference immediately arose between Prime Minister Begin and President Carter. One was the issue of Jewish settlements in the occupied lands. While Carter maintained that, according to an unwritten understanding at Camp David, Israel was to refrain from creating new or enlarging the existing settlements during the five-year transition period in the West Bank and Gaza, Begin claimed that he had given such a pledge for three months only—a rather substantial gap in interpretation. In fact, within a few weeks, Begin announced that Israel was about to "thicken" the existing settlements—a declaration that met with Washington's prompt rebuke.

The other point was that of linkage which, as we have seen, loomed large in the Egyptian-Israeli negotiations. On this issue, President Carter veered toward the Egyptian position: he maintained that the purpose of Camp David was to achieve a comprehensive settlement, that in the minds of the negotiators the two treaties were linked with each other, and that no separate peace treaty for Egypt was contemplated. By the same token, Begin steadily resisted the inclusion of the precise linkage pledge into the text of the Egyptian-Israeli treaty.

There was no doubt that by the end of 1978 the search for peace was entering a decisive phase. The American president and the Israeli premier appeared to be on a collision course. As for material strength, the United States was of course the stronger party. In terms of determination and political resources, no such clear-cut statement could be made. After the impressive victory of his coalition in the May election, Begin probably had a stronger base from which to negotiate and, if need be, to make concessions than his immediate predecessors. His country also enjoyed strong support in the United States Congress which, as an ultimate arbiter of American economic and military assistance policy, had the power to overrule the president's decisions.

In the long run, much depended on the Israelis' own vision of the nature of their state. Israel faced three alternatives: it could aim at the retention of the conquered territories while giving their Arab inhabitants full equality and thus transforming itself into a binational state; it could retain the territories and keep the Arab population in a position of inferiority legally and politically and be exposed to mounting criticisms of racialism and discrimination; or it could aim at preserving its Jewish character by returning the occupied areas in exchange for a genuine peace with all the uncertainties that reliance on written treaties and agreements would produce. Each alternative implied a risk. It was certain, however, that the choice could not be avoided.

CHAPTER XI

Jordan

In the days of the Ottoman Empire the area east of the Jordan river was a rather neglected subdivision of the vilayet of Syria. The Damascus-Medina railroad passed through it, and its only other noteworthy feature was the Greco-Roman ruins at Amman (Philadelphia), Jerash, and Petra. In its western mountainous region Transjordan supported a settled population of a quarter of a million. Its eastern parts merged into the great flat desert which divides Iraq from Syria and the Hejaz. During the First World War, Transjordan was a battleground between Faisal's Arab army and the Turks. In the course of the operations the Hejaz railway was severely damaged.

Between November 1918 and July 1920, Transjordan formed an integral part of the short-lived Arab kingdom of Syria, but its southern boundaries were ill defined. While Amman and Kerak in the north were under the Damascus government, the southern town of Maan and the port of Aqaba on the Red Sea owed allegiance to King Hussein of the Hejaz. The problem of frontiers was, however, not important at that time inasmuch as King Hussein considered himself a ruler of all Arab lands, with patriarchal authority extending over his son Faisal in Damascus. After the collapse of Faisal's government in Syria, i.e., from July 1920 to March 1921, there was no native government in Transjordan. The area was under the direct supervision of the British authorities as part of the mandate of Palestine assigned to Britain at the San Remo conference.

It will be recalled from our earlier account of the peace settlement that in February 1921, King Hussein's second son, Emir Abdullah, arrived in Transjordan from the south. His intention was to invade French-held Syria with the aim of restoring Faisal to power, but he was persuaded by the then secretary for the colonies, Winston Churchill, to accept instead the emirate of Transjordan. On April 1, 1921, Abdullah was established as emir at Amman, with a monthly subsidy of £5,000 from the British government. Born in 1882, Abdullah had always been active in politics.[1] Before the war he represented the Hejaz as a deputy in the Ottoman parliament and was one of its vice-presidents. Later he acted as his father's

---

[1] For details of his political career, see *Memoirs of King Abdullah of Transjordan* (New York, 1950) and *My Memoirs Completed* (London and New York, 1978).

foreign minister. He was always somewhat overshadowed by his warrior-brother Faisal despite the latter's younger age. His reputation suffered a severe setback as a result of the rout inflicted on him by Ibn Saud at the battle of Turaba in 1919. This did not prevent his being chosen, a year later at the Syrian Congress at Damascus, king of Iraq. Before this decision could be enforced, however, Faisal was overthrown by the French and subsequently offered the crown of Iraq by the British. Abdullah's plans were thus frustrated and he had to content himself with the rule of Transjordan. His emirate was a highly artificial unit, and its existence was threatened by Ibn Saud, who coveted large portions of Abdullah's territory. Not until the conclusion of the Treaty of Jidda in 1927 did Ibn Saud acquiesce in the retention of Maan and Aqaba by Transjordan, and even then only on a status quo basis without repudiating his legal claim.

As a part of the mandate for Palestine, Transjordan had been specifically exempted from those provisions that pertained to the establishment of a Jewish national home. Hence its interwar history lacked the controversy and sensationalism characteristic of Palestine. By the same token, no European states save Britain had any dealings with Transjordan, as a consequence of which its politics were devoid of big-power rivalry or high-level intrigue. Britain's interest in this largely barren stretch of land was dictated by three considerations: (1) it constituted a link in the British-controlled land route between the Mediterranean and the Persian Gulf; (2) its ruler was a Hashemi prince and Britain's policy was to cultivate Hashemite friendship; and (3) it was an Arab area and, no matter how unimportant, Britain did not wish to see it subjected to the influence of another power.

Government and Military Forces

The government of Transjordan was organized along the lines tested by time in similar British semicolonies. There was, in the first place, Emir Abdullah's native Arab government. Many of its civil and military servants had been formerly employed by Faisal in Damascus; they were glad, therefore, to find a new home and work when the Syrian kingdom collapsed. On April 16, 1928, an Organic Law for Transjordan was promulgated by the British authorities with Abdullah's consent. It vested "the powers of legislation and administration" in the emir, who was to be assisted by an Executive and a Legislative Council. The lawmaking authority of the emir and the Legislative Council was limited by Transjordan's treaty obligations. The Legislative Council was based on indirect suffrage and guaranteed proportional representation to the religious and national minorities as well as to the Bedouins.

Above this native structure stood the mandatory government for Palestine and Transjordan, represented in Amman by a permanent resident.[2] The resident supervised the Arab administration and assisted it through a body of British advisers and executives who were attached to various government departments. On February 20, 1928, an Anglo-Transjordanian agreement was signed in Jerusalem. It confirmed Britain's supreme authority in the area in virtue of the mandate and gave the British resident special prerogatives in regard to Transjordan's legislation, foreign rela-

---

[2]Lt.-Col. (later Sir Henry) Cox occupied this post for most of the interwar period.

tions, fiscal matters, and the protection of foreigners and minorities. By an amendment of 1934 the emir obtained the right to appoint consular representatives abroad.

From its very creation Transjordan was subsidized by the British government.
These subsidies, which on the average amounted to £100,000 per year in the 1920s,
steadily increased until in the 1940s they began to exceed the sum of £2 million.
They were dictated by economic and political considerations. Economically Trans-
jordan was poor, mostly agricultural or pastoral and with an adverse trade balance.
It was included in the Palestinian customs area and it had a reputation as a
smugglers' paradise. Its extended and ill-guarded desert borders with Syria, Saudi
Arabia, and Iraq made illicit traffic tempting and easy.

The emirate's most outstanding feature was its army, known as the Arab Legion.
Established in 1921 as a small body of 1,000 men, this picturesque desert force
gradually grew in numbers and prestige. The Legion was organized by Captain F.
G. Peake, who had commanded the Egyptian Camel Corps during the war. One of
those Englishmen who delight in making the desert their home, Peake in his seventeen years of command raised the Legion to a high level of efficiency, fought the
Bedouin raiders, repulsed the incursions of the Wahhabi *Ikhwan* and did his best to
assure order and security. For his meritorious service the emir awarded him the title
of pasha. In 1939 he was replaced by Major John Bagot Glubb, an officer with wide
experience in the Arab countries. The Legion was composed of volunteers only and
its ranks were open to any able-bodied man of Arab nationality. It had not only
Transjordanians, but also Iraqis, Hejazis, Palestinians, Syrians, and others in its
midst. It was thus the nucleus of a Pan-Arab army, should such ever be created, and
served as a valuable instrument of British policy.[3]

Apart from the Legion there existed in the emirate a formation known as the
Transjordan Frontier Force, which had been created after the Anglo-Transjordanian
treaty of 1928. Its sole function was to defend the frontiers, and because such
defense was, under the terms of the treaty, a specific British responsibility, the
Transjordan Frontier Force was a British imperial formation under the command of
the high commissioner for Palestine.

During the Second World War both formations were increased and modernized,
and both were used outside the frontiers of Transjordan. The creation, in 1940, of a
Desert Mechanized Regiment in the Arab Legion made the latter one of the most
effective Arab armies in existence. The Mechanized Regiment played an active role
in crushing the Rashid Ali rebellion in Iraq in 1941 and soon afterward took part in
the Syrian campaign. It was the increase in the size and quality of the Arab Legion
that made British subsidies to Transjordan so much higher during and after World
War II. Possession of the Legion, a force out of proportion to Transjordan's size and
poverty, enabled Abdullah to play a major role in the postwar developments in
Palestine and in the Arab world at large. In fact, during the Arab-Israeli war in 1948
the Arab Legion, commanded by Glubb[4] and employing forty British officers, was

---

[3] A first-hand account of the Legion's activities is contained in Brigadier John Bagot Glubb, *The Story
of the Arab Legion* (London, 1948). See also C. S. Jarvis, *Arab Command* (London, 1942).
[4] He held the double rank of brigadier and pasha.

the only Arab army which gave a good account of itself and which prevented Israel from overrunning the whole of Palestine.

The Interwar Period and the Second World War

The interwar history of Transjordan was relatively uneventful.[5] Internal problems consisted mainly in preserving security so as to protect trade and the settled population from the depredations of the nomads. The Transjordan sector of the Hejaz Railway was repaired and put back into operation. But owing to the controversy between the Hejaz and the mandatory powers over the legal status of the railway, its Syrian and Hejazi sectors were not restored. As a result the Transjordan sector could not play its natural role as a transit link in the pilgrim traffic and, isolated as it was within the emirate's territory, it operated at a loss.

Transjordan's minorities—about 6,000 Circassians and small groups of Shishans, Druzes, Turkomans, and Bahais, as well as 30,000 Christian Arabs—did not present any major difficulty and did not lessen its essentially homogeneous character. Its total population, estimated at 340,000 in 1944, was predominantly Arab and Sunni Moslem. Under general British supervision the emir's government, presided over by Tewfik Pasha Abul Huda for most of the interwar period, enjoyed stability and tranquillity. Amendments adopted in 1938 to the Organic Law and in 1941 to the agreement with Britain changed little of the basic political and administrative pattern of British control.

The Second World War never extended to Transjordan territory; hence it affected the emirate only indirectly. The most noteworthy event was the above-mentioned participation of the Arab Legion in the Iraqi and Syrian campaigns. For a while Amman became a place of refuge for some Iraqi statesmen who fled Baghdad during the Rashid Ali coup. Another development worth noticing was the construction, between 1938 and 1941, of the Haifa-Baghdad road, of which 340 kilometers out of a total of 1,080 passed through Transjordan. This was the long-contemplated and finally realized British imperial highway which carried great military traffic during the war, thus stressing once again Transjordan's strategic value to Great Britain.

With regard to Transjordan's international position between 1921 and 1945, little can be said because the country was weak and utterly dependent upon Britain. Ever since Ibn Saud's conquest of the Hejaz there had been, as we know, a latent hostility between him and Emir Abdullah, and while in the 1920s it was Abdullah who feared the Wahhabi expansion to the north, in the later period the roles were reversed. Abdullah's frustrated ambition led him to embrace the Greater Syria project as early as the middle twenties.[6] The plan had, however, little chance of fulfillment short of a British decision to dislodge the French from Syria, a decision unlikely to occur in the interwar period despite Anglo-French rivalry. As to British control of Transjordan, it was complete and undisturbed by manifestations of nationalism such as had

[5] A thorough analysis of the country's economic conditions may be found in A. Konikoff, *Transjordan: An Economic Survey* (Jerusalem, 1946). On the period in question, see also Baha Uddin Toukan, *A Short History of Trans-Jordan* (London, 1945).

[6] See Chapter XIX.

led to concessions to Egypt and Iraq. Politically, Transjordan and the ambitious Abdullah were Britain's reserve force with certain potentialities for the future. But bent as she was upon the preservation of the status quo, she was not anxious to make use of these potentialities in the interwar period. Britain's cultivation of Abdullah's good will was not devoid of certain aspects of *opera bouffe*. Thus the Emir was made an honorary commodore of the Royal Air Force and was consistently flattered in many small but ceremonious ways. In an exchange of notes in 1943–1944 Britain made an implicit promise to grant Transjordan independence after the war. Consequently, when the former mandates came up for discussion in the United Nations in early 1946, the British delegate declared that Transjordan would not be proposed as a trust territory because Britain intended to recognize her independence. Soon afterward, on March 22, 1946, in London, Britain and Transjordan signed a treaty of alliance largely patterned after the Anglo-Iraqi treaty of 1930. Britain recognized Transjordan as an independent state, agreed to exchange diplomatic representatives, pledged subsidies to the Arab Legion, and undertook to defend the emirate against external agression. In return she secured the right to maintain troops in its territory, to use its communication facilities, and to train Abdullah's armed forces. Both countries agreed to a "full and frank consultation . . . in all matters of foreign policy which may affect their common interests."[7]

Jordan's Postwar Position

On April 25, 1946, Emir Abdullah assumed the title of king. Politically educated circles in Transjordan were not too pleased with the terms of the treaty and demanded its revision. Inasmuch as Britain was conducting simultaneous negotiations with Egypt and Iraq for treaty revision, she agreed to review her arrangements with Transjordan as well. As a result a new Anglo-Transjordanian treaty was signed in Amman on March 15, 1948. It differed from the preceding one in that it reduced Britain's military prerogatives in the emirate. Nevertheless, Britain retained the right to possess two air bases in Transjordan (at Amman and at Mafraq). Moreover, to deal with Transjordan's external security an Anglo-Transjordanian Joint Defense Board was to be set up.

In the course of the Palestinian war of 1948, King Abdullah's Arab Legion occupied the central and eastern part of Palestine (Judea, Samaria, and the northern portion of the Negeb) but was not able to prevent the establishment of an Israeli corridor to Jerusalem. In Jerusalem itself Abdullah's forces occupied the old city. The political and military drama attending the partition of Palestine gave King Abdullah an opportunity to assert himself in the politics of the Middle East. Ambitious to extend his domains and able to do it on account of the strength of his Legion, Abdullah emerged from the obscurity of the interwar period as a new and important force in the Arab world. In 1947 he traveled to Ankara, where he called for a Turko-Arab bloc which would also include Iran, Afghanistan, North Africa, and Pakistan. This visit, as well as his trips to Baghdad and Riyadh, and a state visit (on

---

[7]Helen M. Davis, ed., *Constitutions, Electoral Laws, Treaties of States in the Near and Middle East* (Durham, N.C., 1947), p. 333.

board a British warship) in Spain in 1949 were indicative of his increasing ambition and stature. His Greater Syria scheme received more attention and publicity than ever before and, in view of the unstable character of Syrian politics, it appeared capable of realization.

Abdullah's Palestinian policy placed him at odds with the rest of the Arab League. His ambition to dominate Arab Palestine as an opening phase of the Greater Syria plan clashed, first, with the ambitions of the mufti of Jerusalem (then commuting between Cairo and the Levant), second, with Egyptian and Saudi Arabian sensibilities. Disregarding the League's wishes, he unilaterally annexed the Arab part of Palestine on December 1, 1948. By this act he almost incurred expulsion from the League and temporarily strained his good relations with the brotherly Hashemite kingdom of Iraq. To make this decision irrevocable Abdullah on April 26, 1949, adopted a new name for his country, namely, the Hashemite Kingdom of Jordan. His unification decisions were approved by Jordan's new bicameral legislature[8] on April 24, 1950. The unification of the lands west and east of the Jordan River more than doubled the kingdom's population. It resulted, moreover, in the inclusion of some Palestinian Arabs in the Jordanian cabinet. A Palestinian notable, Ruhi Bey Abdul Hadi, became Abdullah's foreign minister in May 1949. In addition, Jordan had to shelter and feed about 400,000 Arab refugees from other parts of Palestine to whom it generously offered Jordanian citizenship.

Generally speaking, Jordan's postwar position was somewhat paradoxical. On the one hand, there was Abdullah's growing stature and increased influence in the Arab world. On the other, his kingdom was more than ever dependent upon Britain's aid. An increase in the British subsidy to the Arab Legion to the sum of £3.5 million in 1949 bore eloquent testimony to this state of affairs. Because it believed that Abdullah was an outright British puppet, the Soviet Union vetoed Jordan's admission to the United Nations in August 1947 and has long continued its negative stand. In 1951 sixty-nine-year-old King Abdullah stood in the midst of the Arab world as a potential unifier of the Fertile Crescent. How realistic his dreams were it is hard to say. As a Bedouin ruler he was accustomed to changes and fluctuations in Arab politics and he knew from history that his nomad ancestors were capable of building great empires. In the person of Ibn Saud he had a living example of a chieftain who by his dogged will succeeded in unifying a major part of southern Arabia. Abdullah did not possess the martial qualities of the great Wahhabi ruler, but he possessed political skill and enjoyed the support of a great power.

His assassination on July 20, 1951, put an end to a man who, whatever his shortcomings, had bold visions of the future and consistently strove to achieve them. He was killed at the Omar Mosque in Jerusalem during the Friday prayers by a young adherent of Haj Amin el-Husseini's militant group known as the Sanctified Struggle (Jihad Muqaddas). The kingdom of Jordan, deprived of his leadership, faced a somber future. Crown Prince Talal at the time of Abdullah's death was in Switzerland undergoing treatment for a nervous breakdown, and for a few weeks it was uncertain whether he would be able to rule the country. It was reported,

[8]Established as a result of the newly won independence by the constitution of March 1, 1947.

moreover, that in contrast to his late father, Talal disliked the British and resented Jordan's dependence upon British aid. Eventually, on September 5, he was proclaimed king of Jordan, thus putting an end to the doubts concerning the succession. As to his foreign policy, Talal seemed anxious to part with certain features of his father's diplomacy. Thus he buried—at least outwardly—the Fertile Crescent scheme by allowing his premier, Tewfik Pasha Abul Huda, to deny, on September 18, 1951, any attempt on Jordan's part to effect union with Iraq. Furthermore, soon after his accession, he hastened to pay an extended visit to Riyadh (November 10–18), thus stressing, at the very outset of his reign, a desire for friendship with the rival house of Saud.

The first weeks of Talal's rule coincided with the crisis in Anglo-Egyptian relations caused by the unilateral abrogation of the 1936 treaty by Egypt (see p. 518). According to some reports Cairo made a proposal to Amman to follow the Egyptian example, denounce the Anglo-Jordanian treaty, and expel British civil and military advisers. In return Egypt was to supply her own officers for Jordan's Arab Legion and to pay the Jordanian government sums equivalent to current British subsidies. Whatever the degree of accuracy of these reports, the fact is that Talal did not avail himself of the Egyptian aid. Whether this was a reflection of his genuine loyalty to the British alliance, of disappointment in the efficacy of the Egyptian action, or of lack of trust in the alleged promises of Cairo remained a matter of speculation.

With regard to King Abdullah's tragic death, it was not clear whether the murder was the spontaneous act of a fanatic or the manifestation of some wider conspiracy among political enemies. Jordanian authorities maintained that the latter was the case. A trial before the Amman military court of a number of persons accused of complicity in the late King's assassination ended on September 3 by the sentencing to death of six men, four of whom were hanged the next day. Among the latter was Dr. Musa Abdullah el-Husseini, a cousin of Jerusalem's exiled grand mufti. Of the remaining two, who were sentenced *in absentia,* one was Colonel Abdullah el-Tell, former Jordanian governor of Jerusalem, who sometime before had deserted King Abdullah and found shelter in Egypt.

Whatever the future plans and alignments of Jordan's new ruler, it was certain that by the sudden changes in Amman British policy had suffered a serious blow. Likewise, Abdullah's death meant the removal of a stabilizing influence in the Middle East. For despite his revisionist Greater Syria policy, Abdullah was the first Arab ruler to accept the existence of American-supported Israel as a fact and to draw from it realistic conclusions.

Internal Developments after Abdullah's Death

King Talal's reign was not destined to last long. Suffering from a nervous disease, he absented himself from Jordan for lengthy periods in order to undergo treatment in European clinics. After mid-May 1952 the country was ruled by a Crown Council in the King's absence. Eventually despairing of improvement in Talal's mental capacity, the bicameral parliament on August 11, 1952, deposed him and proclaimed his son, Hussein, king of Jordan. As a minor, the new ruler was permitted to continue his studies in Sandhurst while his duties in Jordan were assumed by a Regency Council. His younger brother, Emir Mohammed (twelve years old) was proclaimed crown prince.

On coming of age (i.e., reaching his eighteenth year) Hussein was enthroned in Amman on May 2, 1953, the day on which his second cousin, Faisal II, ascended the throne of Iraq. This simultaneous accession of two young Hashemites in Amman and Baghdad meant the shelving for the foreseeable future of schemes of union of Jordan and Iraq inasmuch as it was unlikely that either of the two kings would willingly give up his throne for the sake of a merger.

Although important in an essentially authoritarian country, these matters of royal incumbency were overshadowed by more profound social and political changes that Jordan had been undergoing ever since its annexation of central Palestine. Demographic statistics bore eloquent testimony in this respect. The original population of Transjordan was estimated at 400,000. Since the creation of Jordan this number had been increased by 400,000 west-bank-of-the-Jordan residents, by 100,000 refugees from Israel who were able to support themselves, and by 472,000 Palestinians who were completely destitute and, classified as refugees, had to rely on international assistance. This total of 1,372,000 was more than three times the original population. But the resources of the country were not multiplied by three; they were not even doubled. Moreover, the Transjordan of the years before 1948 enjoyed free access to the Mediterranean through British-controlled Palestine, with attendant economic advantages. The new kingdom of Jordan was, by contrast, an almost landlocked country. Its only port on the Red Sea, Aqaba, required major investments to make it capable of handling increased transoceanic traffic; it lacked, moreover, adequate road or rail connection with the interior.

Politically, the addition of the Palestinian population had a two-fold effect on the kingdom. On the one hand, the destitute refugees provided a permanently discontented and frustrated element, which not only hated Israel, America, and Britain for having caused its misfortunes and sufferings but also envied and criticized the Jordanian government itself. On the other, the West Bank residents were, on the whole, better educated and more sophisticated than the original Transjordanians and they viewed with resentment the latter's political supremacy in the kingdom. Consequently, Jordan witnessed the rapid growth of articulate opposition to its government. This opposition was divided into a number of groups, some of which rallied around prominent personalities while others sought inspiration in ideologies. Subhi Abu Ghanima, a long-standing opponent of King Abdullah and his system, directed a clamorous group of critics from his place of exile in Damascus. The same was true of the exiled mufti of Jerusalem, Haj Amin el-Husseini, whose Jordanian followers operated openly under the leadership of Kamal Arakat, former *Futuwwah* chief, and Mustafa Bushnaq. From his place of exile in Cairo Colonel Abdullah el-Tell did his best to maintain contact with certain elements in the Arab Legion. Among those who operated in Jordan was Suleiman Pasha Nabulsi, a former cabinet minister and ambassador to London, who, having broken with the ruling group in the early 1950s, emerged as a leading personality in the so-called National Front and the National-Socialist party, both leftist organizations violently opposed to the government.

To this list of opposition leaders and groups might be added a few inter-Arab parties whose ideologies called for a revolutionary change in Jordan's system. Such were the Jordanian branch of the Moslem Brotherhood, directed by Mohammed Abdur Rahman Khalifa, and the Arab Renaissance party (Baath), whose socialism appealed to students and young people. The latter's leaders, Abdullah Rimawi and Abdullah Nawas, commanded a particularly strong following in Ramallah and Jerusalem, respectively, both West Bank centers. Nor could one ignore the existence of the outlawed Communist party, which, under the direction of Fuad Nasser, was especially active—and successful—among the numerous Palestinian refugees.

As time went on, these opposition groups gained in importance, while the Palestinian elements, whether loyal or opposed to the government, increased their influence upon politics and administration. Both phenomena were reflected in the electoral struggles and the debates of the parliaments elected after 1948. To understand the elections after that date, it may be useful to have a look at the first election, held in 1947 before the unification of the east and the west banks. At that time Transjordan had 100,000 voters, who, according to the newly adopted constitution, were to elect twenty deputies to the Lower House. The election passed without any major disturbance, the candidates campaigning either as independents or as members of the only party—El-Nahda (Revival), which was a government creation. Consequently, with the exception of Nabulsi, who was elected as an independent, all other deputies could be regarded as supporters of the government. This idyllic picture underwent a radical change soon after the merger of the territories. The West Bank was accorded twenty seats in the Chamber, whose total was increased to forty. The number of voters rose to 304,000, of whom 157,000 were Palestinians. The first postmerger election, held in April 1950, returned a parliament so strongly filled with critics of the regime as to make the government's position very embarrassing.

It was this opposition-dominated parliament which in May 1951 rejected the government-submitted budget, thus actually passing a vote of nonconfidence, a novelty in Jordan's political history. Inasmuch as the constitution did not provide for a responsible cabinet, this step was pronounced unconstitutional and, within a few days, the king dissolved the Chamber. A third election, held in August 1951, gave the government a slight majority, but the opposition counted as many as 18 members of a total of 40. It could, moreover, get the support of some progovernment members on certain issues. This new parliament at once began to press for a revision of the constitution, which would transform the hitherto nonresponsible government into a responsible one. Its efforts were successful, and on January 2, 1952, a new constitution was promulgated. Article 53 provided that a two-thirds majority against the government on a vote of confidence must result in dismissal of the cabinet. Having secured recognition of the new parliamentary principle, the opposition now began to agitate for an amendment of Article 53 so that the two-thirds vote necessary to overthrow the cabinet would be replaced by a simple majority. No decision was reached immediately.

Young King Hussein had ascended the throne, and it seemed as if the new ruler might effect a measure of political reconciliation. His first step was to remove from the premiership Tewfik Pasha Abul Huda, the "grand old man" of Jordanian politics and one of the figures most objectionable to the opposition. His position was entrusted to Fawzi el-Mulki, who chose a liberal leader, Anwar el-Khatib, as minister of economy, reconstruction, and development. In November 1953, the old opponent of the regime, Subhi Abu Ghanima, returned at the King's invitation to his homeland. In January 1954 sufficient voting strength was mustered in the parliament to amend Article 53. New vistas were opened to parliamentary democracy in Jordan.

However, this was the climax of the opposition's success. Frightened by the increasingly violent criticisms both within and without parliament, the government launched a counteroffensive aiming at the restoration of its authority and the curbing of criticism. On January 17, 1954, it dissolved all political parties and provided for the licensing of new ones. In the spring the staunchest champion of traditionalism, Abul Huda, resumed the premiership, and early in June he presented a ministerial declaration to the parliament asking for a vote of confidence. Anticipating violent opposition and an adverse vote, he had parliament dissolved on June 22. This was followed by the suspension of such political parties as were then in existence and of numerous newspapers. On August 18 defense regulations giving special powers to the cabinet were enacted. With the ground thus prepared, the government called for new elections in October, this time resolved to keep the opposition from gaining ascendancy. As might have been expected, the elections abounded in violence. Suleiman el-Hadidi, chief of the Baath party, and Suleiman Nabulsi were arrested. Abdur Rahman Shukair, leader of the National Front, and Mohammed Khalifa, head of the Brotherhood, escaped to Damascus. Opposition leaders charged intimidation and terror. But after four years of experimentation with unchecked parliamentarism, the government finally secured a friendly chamber which in its opening session gave the premier a 35-to-3 vote of confidence. Two National Front candidates campaigning as independents, were elected. Those were Abdul Qader es-Saleh and Rashad Massawadah, whom government sources promptly identified as extreme leftists.

These dramatic political changes were occurring against an extremely difficult economic background. One of the standing complaints of the opposition was the earmarking of most of the budget for internal security and nonproductive administrative purposes. The aggravating fact was that Jordan was not viable as an economic unit and for its survival as a state had to rely on continuous foreign, mostly British, aid. In 1954 its budget of over £16.5 million provided for over £8 million for military expenditures, while at the same time the British subsidy was slightly over 8.5 million. In 1954 and 1955, however, Britain made an effort to increase her economic assistance, which had been negligible up to that time. In December 1955 the British subsidy to Jordan was divided into £3 million for economic aid and £7.75 million for military aid, the latter mostly for the Arab Legion, with a small amount for the Jordanian National Guard. As for the United States, its first aid to Jordan was only through its technical assistance program, which in 1954 amounted to no more than $1 million. In June of 1954, following repeated Jordanian requests, the United States concluded with Jordan an economic aid agreement—the first negotiated with any Arab government—which provided for $8 million in aid to be taken out of a $47 million fund provided by Congress for the Arab states. The Jordanians went ahead with their economic planning. In November 1954, the Jordan Development Board announced a five-year plan of works which were to cost $200 million and embrace 274 projects.

International Position in the 1950s

These figures clearly indicate how heavily Jordan was dependent on Great Britain. If we consider the subsidies and the fairly large number of British experts employed in Jordan, we might easily conclude that Jordan was completely subject to Britain's will. Such a judgment would not be wholly warranted by the political realities in Jordan. As one author has aptly remarked, before the Palestinian war there was a king in Jordan without a people and there was a foreign power. After 1948 the missing element, the people, appeared in the form of the politically conscious mass of Palestinians.[9]

The passing of the old patriarchal king and his replacement, first by a mentally unstable individual and then by a youth just out of school, removed the traditional props and motive forces of the Jordanian state which had existed under Abdullah. Jordanian governments, especially since 1951, have been exposed to new and powerful pressures. One of these was the pressure from below of the impoverished or destitute masses. This accounted for a good deal of political radicalism and extremism. Added to it was the increasing violence on the frontier with Israel. Israeli attacks and killings at Kibya (October 1953) and Nahhalin (March 1954) so stirred emotions that no "moderate" dared advocate a compromise with the Zionist neighbor. The speeches from the throne and the ministerial declarations after Abdullah's death often reiterated the formula of "no peace, no negotiations with the Jews." In fact, at least one cabinet crisis in those years—Premier Mulki's resignation in May 1954—was generally ascribed to his objection to alleged British prodding to start negotiations with Israel. Somewhat earlier the economy minister in Mulki's cabinet, Anwar el-Khatib, contrasting the $1.4 million of Point Four aid to Jordan with the $52 million contribution by the United States to Israel, declared as follows:

> If the United States is not prepared to supplement technical assistance with cash help for economic projects, there is no necessity to keep Point Four in Jordan. . . . On the other hand, Israel is fighting with American aid. It takes dollars to buy American ammunition like that found after the Israeli raids on Nahhalin and Kibya. America is feeding her creation, Israel, and making no effort to restrain that creation from frontier attacks.[10]

The Palestine question was the source of general nationalist resentment, which intensified popular resentments caused by economic and social factors. Linked with the nationalist pressure was a third kind of pressure, one stemming from the intensified political activity of the Cairo-Riyadh axis.

[9]For the developments of this period, consult Esmond Wright, "Abdallah's Jordan," *Middle East Journal,* 5 (Autumn 1951).
[10]*New York Times,* April 2, 1954.

All these pressures came to bear upon the Jordanian government in 1955, and at one particular moment the country was very close to a revolution. The background was provided by the Turkish-Iraqi negotiations to conclude a regional defense pact, which Arab countries would be invited to join. It was generally assumed that Jordan, as a Hashemite and British-influenced country, would follow Iraq's example and become a signatory. Rather unexpectedly, however, Premier Tewfik Abul Huda and Foreign Minister Walid Salah did not take Iraq's side during the Arab League meeting in January 1955; instead they leaned toward Egypt and Saudi Arabia, both vigorous opponents of the pact.[11] Although Abul Huda's cabinet resigned shortly afterward, the new government of Said el-Mufti did nothing for over six months to revive the question.

This rather unnatural calm was disturbed in the fall by the flight of Walid Salah, who, declaring that his life was in danger because of his opposition to imperialism, sought refuge in Damascus and later in Cairo. Then early in December, Amman was subjected to new pressure as the result of a visit paid to it by General Sir Gerald Templer, chief of the British Imperial General Staff, who was reported urging Jordan's immediate adherence to the Baghdad alliance. His visit coincided with that of Egyptian Colonel Anwar el-Sadat. The latter naturally represented the opposite point of view and skillfully ingratiated himself with the people during his tour of Amman and Jerusalem. By that time it was well known that the common people in the Arab states were very hostile to the Baghdad Pact. Toward the middle of December when the Jordanian cabinet was about to reach a decision in this matter, its four West Bank ministers resigned, no doubt aware of the mood of their fellow Palestinians. This precipitated a crisis which was resolved on December 15 when thirty-six-year-old Hazzah el-Majali, former interior minister and a staunch advocate of the Iraqi alliance, formed a new cabinet. The new premier promptly declared that negotiations with Britain to bring Jordan into the Baghdad Pact would be resumed ''in proper time.'' He also revealed that the preceding government had ''approved in principle'' Jordan's adherence to the pact but that there were still differences between Britain and Jordan.[12]

His declarations touched off major riots in Amman and other towns. Angry mobs attacked many foreign and international institutions, such as the American consulate and the United Nations Relief and Works Agency headquarters. Shouting defiance of the new government, they protested against ''foreign pacts,'' imperialism, Israel, and the British hold on the Arab Legion. It appeared that the opposition parties, whether legal or outlawed, all joined in the strongest condemnation of any further link with the West. Responding to their call, government officials went on strike, thus creating a new and dangerous precedent. On December 19, Majali resigned. On the same day, yielding to public pressure, King Hussein dissolved the parliament, promising to hold new elections in April. On December 20 a sixty-seven-year-old former premier, Ibrahim Hashim, formed a caretaker cabinet which in-

---

[11]For further details on inter-Arab rivalries, see the section on the Baghdad Pact (pp. 283–286) and p. 744.

[12]*New York Times*, Dec. 18, 1955.

cluded two other former premiers, Fawzi el-Mulki and Samir er-Rifai. Following a new wave of demonstrations, he promptly pledged not to adhere to any pacts. In the meantime it was revealed that Britain had offered to increase her annual subsidy to Jordan in return for joining the pact, a revelation not likely to clear the already surcharged atmosphere. The outgoing premier, Majali, accused Saudi Arabia of a campaign of bribery, the aim of which was to weaken Jordan's government. A few days later a newly created National Committee, representing a coalition of leftist and nationalist groups and parties, met in Amman to map strategy for the forthcoming elections to the new parliament. Its agenda included a demand that Egypt, Saudi Arabia, and Syria jointly offer Jordan a subsidy to replace the British grants and thus free Jordan from Britain's dominance. Prominent among the Committee's organizers was Suleiman Nabulsi, who optimistically declared that, given free elections, the opposition would obtain 70 percent of the vote.

The ten days following Christmas witnessed a gradual return to calm and order. Misled perhaps by this recession in the clamor, the government on January 4, 1956, made public its decision to approve the finding of the Supreme Court that the dissolution of parliament decreed in December had been illegal and that the old Chamber would be reconvened. In reply, the opposition parties called a protest meeting for January 6, but the government promptly forbade it. The ban inspired new rioting, which broke out with particular intensity on January 7. This time the demonstrators not only attacked Western consulates and institutions but also marched on the royal palace in an attempt to storm it. There was widespread looting in town, a feature not conspicuous during the December riots. Moreover, excited crowds in a number of Jordanian towns, especially on the left bank, clamored for annexation of their territory by Syria, while a similar demonstration in favor of Saudi Arabia was reported in the southern town of Maan. Communist elements rather than the accepted opposition leaders were said to be in the forefront of these activities, and there were rumors about some defections from the Arab Legion, partly caused by the earlier resignation of General Ahmed Sidki el-Gindi, deputy chief of staff.

The gravity of the situation brought about the fall of Hashim's caretaker cabinet and its replacement on January 9 by one of Samir Rifai. The new premier immediately proclaimed martial law, placing a virtual blackout on the flow of news and travel from and to Jordan. At the same time, however, he bowed to public opinion by reiterating his predecessor's promise that Jordan would reject the Baghdad Pact. Soon afterward he lodged formal protests with Egypt and Saudi Arabia against their inflammatory broadcasts and incitement to disobedience in Jordan. These, in fact, were believed by many observers to be the principal cause of the upheaval, Saudi subsidies to anti-Hashemite elements being particularly potent. Jordanian protests, however, seemed to have little effect on the Cairo-Riyadh axis, which was determined to pursue its policy of opposition to the Western influence in Amman. By mid-January Egypt, Saudi Arabia, and Syria came forward with the long-expected offer to replace the British annual subsidy by one of their own. By that time, however, the government had regained its hold on the country. With self-confidence restored, it not only shelved the subsidy proposals but also, on

January 18, reconvened the dissolved parliament, thus notifying the foreign and domestic opposition that no further interference with the existing system would be tolerated.

On March 1, 1956, King Hussein in a surprise move abruptly dismissed the commander of the Arab Legion, Lieutenant-General John Bagot Glubb (with two senior British officers), and ordered his expulsion from the country forthwith. Simultaneously he appointed a senior Arab officer of the Legion, General Radi Ennab, to the position vacated by Glubb. This decision gained the king tremendous popularity, which was expressed in joyful manifestations lasting several days in Jordan, and made him overnight a hero in the Arab world at large. It did not, however, result in repudiation of the alliance with Britain, both the king and his ministers stating that they not only wanted to continue the treaty relationship but also hoped to maintain the services of a number of British officers in the Legion.

In Britain, Glubb's dismissal provoked great consternation, and *The Times,* in an editorial, called it the most "sinister" event in the Middle East since the Egyptian-Czechoslovak arms deal. Despite this the British government did not revoke its subsidies to Jordan, contenting itself with the recall of fifteen senior British officers of the Legion.[13]

In mid-March when Egypt, Saudi Arabia, and Syria met in Cairo to concert their policies and renewed their offer of a subsidy in place of the British one, they met with Jordan's refusal. In fact, within forty-eight hours of the issuance of the "Arab Big Three's" declaration (March 12, 1956) Hussein hastened to meet his cousin Faisal of Iraq in a desert border station, thus reaffirming his desire not to sever the bonds of solidarity with the other Hashemite kingdom.

Jordan's Popular Front Government

General Glubb's sudden ouster by King Hussein was calculated to gain the latter acclaim from the masses. But if this act was to have any lasting impact on the King's position, it had to be sustained by a general policy of reconciliation and understanding with the Pan-Arab-oriented nationalists, of whom the Palestinians constituted a substantial part. Such a policy was attempted by the King in the summer and the fall of 1956. It was expressed by the relaxation of political controls, thus allowing various opposition groups to hold public meetings in preparation for the parliamentary elections. Three groups in particular engaged in considerable preelectoral activity: the National-Socialists of Suleiman Nabulsi, the Arab Socialist Renaissance party (Baath), and the Communists. The latter skillfully avoided strict identification as a party, preferring to act behind the scenes in tactical alliance with the two other opposition groups. In addition, some activity was displayed by the Moslem Brotherhood, which took an independent course and was somewhat critical of leftist elements. The progovernment forces were not organized as well as the opposition. Their hard core consisted of the conservative elements, partly tribal and partly merchant, primarily from the Transjordanian part of the kingdom. Dedicated

---

[13]For General Glubb's account of his dismissal, see a series of articles by him in the *New York Times,* March 12-16, 1956; also Sir John Bagot Glubb, *A Soldier with the Arabs* (New York, 1957), pp. 419-428.

to the preservation of the status quo, i.e., the monarchy, the existing socioeconomic system, and cooperation with the West, these conservative forces stood against the general current of Pan-Arab Socialist-tinged radicalism. Their strength in Jordan, however, was not negligible, considering the support of the tribes, the army, and the state administrative machinery which they enjoyed.

Thus the elections of October 21, 1956, proved to be a close contest between the government and the opposition. Although some irregularities have crept into the electoral process (Communists and Baathists loudly complained about them), there is no doubt that these were the freest elections Jordan had had since its achievement of independence. Nabulsi's National-Socialists secured 11 seats out of a total of 40. Together with the Baathists (2 seats), Communists (3 seats), and some independent sympathizers (4 seats), they thus secured exactly half of the seats in the parliament. On October 29 Nabulsi formed a cabinet which reflected the new trend in Jordan's politics. It was a coalition, composed of eleven ministers, of whom seven were National-Socialist, one Baathist, one Communist, and two independent. Vital posts of Defense and Interior were held by a National-Socialist, Abdul Halim Nimr; Abdullah Rimawi, a Baathist, was made minister of state for foreign affairs; and Abdul Qader Saleh, a Communist (officially labeled National Front), assumed the portfolio of agriculture. Thus of all countries in the Arab East, Jordan became the first to have what it is customary to call a "popular front" government, i.e., a Liberal-Socialist-Communist coalition which, in the Middle Eastern context, was dedicated to the struggle against domestic conservatism and Western influences, while favoring closer links with the Arab countries and the Soviet bloc.

King Hussein's policy of seeking popularity by forging closer Pan-Arab links found expression, almost simultaneously, in another significant act. On October 25, Jordan, Syria, and Egypt signed an agreement placing an Egyptian in command of their armies in case of war with Israel. Egypt's minister of defense, General Abdul Hakim Amer, was appointed commander.

Thus, from the end of October onward, both through its new military alignments and through the victory of the "popular front" at the polls Jordan had embarked on a new Pan-Arab policy, which was to lead it to gradual estrangement from Britain and to violent domestic complications. The change of government coincided, furthermore, with the beginning of the Suez War, an event which caused manifold outbursts of hostility toward the West in the Arab world. Jordan, naturally, was no exception. Early in November it broke off diplomatic relations with France, and later in the month its parliament unanimously recommended abrogation of the alliance with Britain and recognition of the Soviet Union and Communist China. Furthermore, in a gesture of Arab solidarity, Saudi Arabia and Syria sent their troops to Jordan as an additional protection against possible aggression. The ensuing few months were taken up by dual negotiations. On the one hand, Premier Nabulsi negotiated with Britain with a view to abrogating the treaty of alliance. The British, seeing the futility of attempts to preserve the treaty, were amenable. However, they made it clear that such an abrogation would also put an end to the subsidies they had been paying Jordan for the upkeep of its army and for the relief of its deficit-ridden budget. While the premier was anxious to score a spectacular diplomatic victory by annulling the treaty, he was less prone to undermine the financial base of his government. His dilemma led him to the second series of negotiations, this time with Egypt, Syria, and Saudi Arabia. These three sister countries, all following at that time the so-called "policy of Arab liberation," jointly offered to replace British subsidies with their own, provided Jordan severed its treaty relations with Britain. On January 19, 1957, these negotiations led to the signing of the "Arab Solidarity" agreement, whereby the three countries undertook to pay Jordan for the next few years £E12.5 million a year in the following proportions: Egypt and Saudi Arabia £E5 million each, and Syria £E2.5 million. Soon after, on February 13, Britain and Jordan agreed to abrogate their treaty and assure a speedy evacuation of British forces from Jordan.

Thus the final act of Jordan's emancipation was consummated. But was it real emancipation? More appropriately one could call it a change of allegiance. A joint Cairo-Riyadh-Damascus "protectorate" was substituted for Jordan's former dependence on Britain. From the Arab nationalist point of view this was a desirable change, in keeping with historical process in the area. But from the point of view of the Hashemite monarchy and the native Jordanian elements allied to it the bargain had doubtful value. True enough, the king, for once, listened to the voice of the people (or at least a substantial portion of them) and thus warded off some hostility which previous Hashemite friendship with Britain had generated. But, by doing it, he threw himself on the mercy of his more powerful Arab neighbors, especially President Nasser. Furthermore, if Jordan's new Pan-Arab policy were to be carried to its logical conclusion, both Jordan as a state and the Hashemite monarchy would have to disappear. Thus Hussein's gain from following a popular policy was inherently doomed to be short-lived.

The changes effected in Jordan's political status by virtue of the above-mentioned agreements occurred in the midst of domestic effervescence. Stimulated by the Suez crisis and Nabulsi's advent to power, Pan-Arabists, Baathists, radical-minded Palestinians, and others opposed to the pre-October status quo indulged in a variety of manifestations, all designed to stress Arab unity, the need for drastic internal reform, and a revision of foreign policy toward neutralism and friendship with the Soviet bloc. Amman became a meeting ground of various Pan-Arab conferences at which flamboyant resolutions were passed. Trade-union activities came out into the open, and Jordanians played a major role in the founding of the Nasser-oriented Federation of Arab Labor Unions. The Communist press reappeared. A visiting Chinese Communist labor delegation was received by Premier Nabulsi in the midst of popular enthusiasm. Communists played an important role in most of these activities, exactly as they did during the October elections. It should be pointed out that it was still the period when Communist parties in the Arab countries consistently tried to identify themselves in the popular mind with Arab nationalism and, though preserving their own discipline and organization, increasingly infiltrated various *bona fide* Arab nationalist groups.

The Zerqa Plot and Hussein's Countercoup

Although the whole Pan-Arab trend of Jordanian politics gave King Hussein much to ponder about, it was the stimulus provided by stepped-up Communist activity which caused his special concern. As early as February 2, 1957, the king sent a letter to Premier Nabulsi, warning him of Communist infiltration and calling for effective steps against it. Nabulsi refused to heed the warning, proceeding instead to purge officials loyal to the king. Simultaneously, Baathist and pro-Egyptian officers in the army organized a plot aiming at the overthrow of the monarchy and the formation of a republic subservient to Cairo. On April 7 the plotters made their first attempt to depose the king by surrounding the royal palace with tanks, but the attempt failed. Three days later the king dismissed Premier Nabulsi. Although Nabulsi complied, the military plotters made a renewed attempt at revolt on April 13 in the army camp at Zerqa, 20 miles north of Amman. Forewarned of this action and counting on the support of loyal troops, Hussein sped to Zerqa and in a personal confrontation with his foes and friends alike he succeeded in winning the army to his side. Fourteen pro-Nasser officers, all in strategic commanding positions, were promptly arrested by loyal elements, the latter mostly recruited from Transjordanian tribes. Back in Amman the king ordered the arrest of the chief of staff, General Ali Abu Nuwar, who turned out to be a leader of the conspiracy. Instead of being tried, Abu Nuwar was permitted to escape to Syria. His successor, General Ali Hayari, remained in office for only a week and, revealing himself as another member of the plot while on a mission to Damascus, resigned on April 20. He was succeeded on an interim basis by an older officer, General Radi Ennab, whose loyalty to the throne was beyond suspicion. In due course he gave place, first to General Sadiq Sharaa and later to General Habes Majali, the latter representing a loyal bedouin tribe of Transjordan.

Having regained his control over the army, the king turned again to civilian politics and after an unsuccessful search for a conservative premier he asked a middle-of-the-road independent, Hussein Fakhri Khalidi, to form a cabinet. In the new government Suleiman Nabulsi became foreign minister. This setup was too weak and artificial to be permanent. It certainly could not please the king, who, having won a victory in the military sector, expected a more decisive solution in the political arena. On their part, despite Nabulsi's presence in the cabinet, leftists and Pan-Arabists promptly launched attacks against the new government, demanding its resignation, its replacement by a "popular front" cabinet, the repudiation of the Eisenhower Doctrine, and the expulsion of the American ambassador and his military attaché. A wave of strikes and street riots throughout Jordan was staged in support of those demands. For the second time the king found himself in grave danger, rendered even more acute by his new financial dependence on Egypt, Syria, and Saudi Arabia.

In his dire predicament the king was saved by a combination of bold military and diplomatic measures. On April 24, Hussein accepted the resignation of Premier Khalidi, appointing the octogenarian Ibrahim Hashim Pasha in his place. The new cabinet was composed entirely of ministers loyal to the king. The first moves were to proclaim martial law, abolish political parties, suspend the parliament, impose curfew, and place the security forces under army control. On the same day, Secretary Dulles announced that the United States regarded the integrity of Jordan as one of its vital interests. The following day the United States Sixth Fleet received orders to sail from its Italian bases to the eastern Mediterranean. The fleet appeared along the shores of Lebanon and Israel in a demonstration of American determination to save Jordan from collapse. On April 29 the United States extended to Jordan a grant of $10 million for budgetary support. Faced with these momentous developments and obviously displeased, Egypt and Syria stopped their payments to Jordan. Despite the reorientation of her policy toward friendship with the Hashemites, Saudi Arabia discontinued her payments as well. In due course the American government took over the task of regularly subsidizing Jordan, its subsidies reaching the level of $50 million a year by 1960.

Return of the Conservatives and the Crisis of 1958

Following the April crisis Jordan reverted to its traditional policy both in the domestic and the foreign sectors. Internally, emphasis was placed on strengthening the King's power in a system which could be described as one of royal authoritarianism. Experimentation with political liberalism ended, the regime being based on the three main props, monarchy, loyal tribes, and the army. After a transitional period of Premier Hashim's caretaker cabinet, the premiership was entrusted to Samir er-Rifai, a seasoned statesman who combined skill with force to restore stability and curb both internal opposition and outside interference. In its foreign policy the regime followed the path of virtual alliance with the West, although it did not commit itself to any formal agreements. Furthermore, profiting from the reorientation of Saudi Arabian policy, the king and Premier Rifai forged closer links with Riyadh and Baghdad in an effort to build and strengthen the "Kings' Alliance," which was designed to counteract the revolutionary Pan-Arabism emanating from Cairo and Damascus.

In the meantime a good many Jordanian leaders formerly prominent in the conspiracies against the late King Abdullah and King Hussein or in the "popular front" movement of 1956–1957 formed opposition groups in exile, notably in Cairo and Damascus, which did their utmost to keep alive the spirit of resistance to the Hashemite regime at home. Encouraged by the Egyptian and Syrian governments, these dissident groups smuggled arms and propaganda pamphlets into Jordan and resorted to all sorts of stratagems and plots to undermine the regime. They were frequently seconded by the press and the radios of Egypt and Syria, the latter branding Hussein as a "stooge of imperialism" and "traitor to the Arab cause" and occasionally calling for his assassination. As a result, almost continuous tension prevailed in the relations between the Cairo-Damascus axis and Amman.

The merger of Egypt and Syria into the United Arab Republic significantly sharpened the Pan-Arab tendencies of a substantial part of the Jordanian population. Partly to forestall any new plots against the regime and partly to strengthen the conservative-monarchial camp, Jordan and Iraq formed their own federation on February 14, 1958, scarcely two weeks after the Syrian-Egyptian merger. Barely had the foundations of the federation been laid before the Arab East experienced a new manifestation of militant Pan-Arabism in the Lebanese civil war in the summer of 1958. Jordan, a state chronically subjected to pressures of Pan-Arab activity, was again exposed to the danger of a coup. The Iraqi revolution of July 14 acted as a stimulant to anti-Hashemite forces in Amman, where the government uncovered a new plot against the regime, again involving high-ranking army officers. Faced with the problem of survival, King Hussein quelled the army plot with the customary aid of his loyal tribal units and simultaneously appealed to Britain for military help. In response, the British government promptly dispatched a paratroop force which was flown down from Cyprus over Israel despite the latter's formal protests. Simultaneous with the American landing in Lebanon, this military demonstration was instrumental in protecting the Jordanian regime from internal rebellion and possible outside aggression. British troops remained in Jordan for more than a year following this crisis.

As could be expected, Jordanian-U.A.R. relations reached a new low as a result of these events. Diplomatic relations were broken off, not to be restored until August 1959, and a fierce propaganda battle ensued. This time, however, the battle was not so uneven as in earlier periods. While Nasser's radio freely continued its old charges against the Hashemites as traitors, Hussein's government found a new and potentially promising target on which it could concentrate, namely, the asserted loss of freedom by Syria and its subjugation to the Egyptian dictatorship. From now on Cairo was obliged to weigh more carefully the gains and losses of continuing its attacks on Amman. In the ensuing years relations between the two capitals underwent a number of fluctuations, the friendly (or correct) periods alternating with the unfriendly ones. In September 1960 Jordan's new Premier, Hazza Majali, was assassinated by plotters who promptly fled to Syria. Changes in relations were due sometimes to basic policy decisions in Cairo and sometimes to mere accidents, such as a speech made on either side which contained remarks deemed offensive by the other party.

The news of the revolution in Iraq was received with shock and indignation in official Amman, where for a brief time there were hints of possible military intervention to rescue Iraq from anarchy and communism. Jordan became a place of refuge for those exiled or escaping from Iraq. By 1960, however, Jordan had accepted the new dispensation in Iraq and went so far as to restore normal diplomatic relations with General Kassem's government amid manifestations of mutual good will. The change in attitudes reflected the belief of Amman's rulers that in the long run it was not the separatist Iraq but the United Arab Republic with its militant Pan-Arab philosophy which constituted the primary challenge to Jordan's survival as an independent kingdom.

The 1960s and 1970s: Struggle for Survival

Even though the dramatic events of 1957 and 1958 ended with King Hussein's victory over his adversaries, Jordan's difficulties were by no means over. This struggle had three aspects: for survival as a political system against the attacks of both legal and illegal opposition, for independent sovereignty against various Pan-Arab schemes to incorporate Jordan into a larger Arab political entity, and for the territorial integrity of the Jordanian kingdom against the danger of division into eastern, Transjordanian, and western, Palestinian, parts.

The period between 1957 and 1967 could be described as the era of the Arab Cold

War, which was essentially political and ideological in character but occasionally erupted into physical violence. It pitted the conservative or moderate Arab regimes, mostly with monarchical structures, against the radical-revolutionary states, the latter taking their inspiration either from Nasser's Cairo or from the center of the Arab Socialist Baath movement in Damascus. Numerically, the two camps were about equally divided, with five monarchies (Saudi Arabia, Jordan, Kuwait, Libya, and Morocco) on one side and the revolutionary republics (Egypt, Syria, Iraq, Yemen, and Algeria) on the other. The revolutionaries were aggressive and militant and generally held the initiative. The monarchies were on the defensive. Jordan constituted a favorite target because of four characteristics that appeared particularly objectionable to the radical camp: Jordan was a monarchy under a dynasty with initial ties to Britain; it was pro-Western, particularly pro-American, in its foreign policy orientation; its internal system favored free enterprise while discouraging communism and various expressions of radicalism; and, finally, the regime was dominated by the conservative, partly tribal, partly military elements from Trans-jordan which, in contrast to the numerous Palestinian inhabitants of the kingdom, owed their first loyalty to the concept of independent Jordan rather than to Pan-Arab ideology.

In this struggle for survival King Hussein displayed remarkable political acumen, perseverance, and personal courage. He had to overcome many domestic obstacles inherent in the presence of large numbers of disaffected Palestinians and in the vulnerable economy of his landlocked country. Almost invariably his opponents inside Jordan, such as the Communists, the Baathists, and the Nasserites, had links with centers of power and inspiration located outside of Jordan's boundaries.[14] Virtually every step Hussein took in domestic politics was bound to affect relations with Egypt, Syria, Iraq, the organized Palestinian groups in the adjoining countries, and, after the revolution of 1969, Libya as well. Moreover, domestic stability in Jordan was also bound to be profoundly affected by the proximity of Israel, with which the Arab world at large and Jordan in particular had a number of unsettled problems.

Relations with Israel

Tension was built into Jordan's relations with Israel, for understandable reasons. First, Israel's boundary with Jordan was longer than with any other Arab state. Second, Jordan was the abode, whether permanent or temporary, of the largest number of Palestinians who had lost their homes, their farms, and their possessions as a result of the establishment of the State of Israel. It was, therefore, a natural recruiting ground for Palestinian militants who sought revenge and return to the pre-Israel status quo in the Holy Land. Third, in the 1950s and early 1960s, Israel began raising the question of the proper utilization of the Jordan waters, a matter which was bound to affect directly the people and government of the kingdom of Jordan. And fourth, the city of Jerusalem with its tremendous emotional signifi-

---

[14]For a vivid account, see King Hussein of Jordan, *Uneasy Lies the Head: An Autobiography* (London, 1962).

cance for Jews, Christians, and Moslems alike, continued to be divided between Israel and Jordan; both parties, but especially Israel, believed this division to be artificial and looked forward in the long run to a change.

Although Jordan and Israel thus had various points of potential or actual friction, King Hussein and his ministers followed a cautious policy to avoid provoking Israel into organized large-scale hostilities against the kingdom. This policy stemmed from the commonsense conviction that Jordan was militarily much weaker, that it could not count on effective help from other Arab states in case of crisis, and that any military confrontation with Israel might unleash unpredictable developments within Jordan itself, considering various centrifugal forces in which its political scene abounded. Despite this basic caution the Jordanian government could not avoid becoming embroiled in the so-called Jordan waters crisis of 1963. The crisis had arisen over Israel's publicly expressed desire to share the wate of the Jordan River with her Arab neighbors and thus be able to utilize a good portion of them for her own needs. Various attempts, including those with United States mediation in the 1950s, to reach a settlement of this issue brought no results, largely because of Arab reluctance to give an implicit political recognition to Israel by reaching any agreement with her whatsoever. Frustrated in her desire to reach an international agreement, Israel decided to proceed on her own and in 1963 publicly announced the beginning of works aiming at the diversion of a certain volume of the Jordan waters to her territory. To counter this action a meeting of the Arab heads of state (the first Arab Summit) was called on President Nasser's initiative in Cairo in January 1964. At that meeting the Arab leaders decided to prevent the use of the Jordan waters by Israel by diverting these waters at their very sources, partly in the Hasbani region of Lebanon not far from the borders of Israel and Syria, where a number of springs of the Jordan River are located, and partly by authorizing and sponsoring work on the Yarmuk River, which flows into the Jordan from the east and constitutes also the boundary between Syria and the kingdom of Jordan. The summit meeting also adopted a resolution providing for the establishment of the Palestine Liberation Organization (PLO) and the Palestinian Liberation Army (PLA), both to be financially supported by joint efforts of Arab states.

These resolutions were bound to affect Jordan materially. First, it was likely that Israel might react violently to the threat of diversion of the Jordan waters at their sources; second, the official recognition in a new organizational form of the Palestine political entity and its endowment with a regular military force was bound to have repercussions on the relations of the Jordanian government with the Palestinians both at home and outside of the kingdom's boundaries.

What was happening was a gradual escalation of tension all along the boundaries of Israel. This tension was further intensified and aggravated by the fact that various Arab states tried to outbid each other in their protestations of support for the liberation of Palestine and of hostility to Israel. This escalation eventually led to the outbreak of the Arab-Israeli war on June 6, 1967. The origins and the actual conduct of this war are discussed in greater detail in the chapters on Egypt and Israel. Jordan, in spite of her antagonistic relations with Egypt prior to that date, became involved in hostilities along with Egypt and Syria. On the very eve of the war King

Hussein signed in Cairo a mutual defense agreement with President Nasser and, when the war broke out, the Jordanian army fully participated in it. Like the armies of Egypt and Syria, it suffered a defeat as a result of Israel's superior strength and organization and the lack of adequate Arab cooperation. Actually it appears that King Hussein was misled by President Nasser in the first hours of the war when, upon inquiring on the telephone about the state of the battle, the king was assured by him that the Egyptian air force was fully engaged in effective combat against the invading Israeli forces while in reality his air force had already been destroyed by the surprise attack of the Israelis. Although by the standards of military valor, and considering that Jordan's air force had also been eliminated by the Israelis in the early hours of the war, the Jordanian army gave a good acount of itself, it was compelled to retreat beyond the Jordan River and thus not only the Arab part of Jerusalem but also the entire West Bank—the Palestinian territory incorporated into Jordan in 1950—was overrun by the Israeli forces.

The capture of the West Bank caused a new Arab exodus. Fearing Israeli presence and domination, a number of regular inhabitants of the West Bank fled to the eastern territory of Jordan. Similarly a number of Palestinian refugees who had been living in camps interspersed on the West Bank also crossed the Jordan River seeking refuge from the Israelis for the second time in their drama-filled lives. Furthermore, within a few weeks after the occupation of the territory in question, Israel proclaimed virtual annexation of eastern Jerusalem, thus drawing a clear distinction between the city itself and the rest of the occupied territory. This new exodus and the occupation of the most fertile parts of the kingdom by the enemy caused considerable economic and political dislocations in Jordan. Jordan found itself deprived of much of its agricultural produce and generally saw its economy shrink. Tourist trade suffered. At the same time the government was burdened with the task of accommodating a new wave of refugees who crowded the already strained facilities in Jordan's urban centers. With such pressures Jordan probably would have collapsed as a functioning political entity if it were not for the fact that at the Arab Summit meeting held in Khartoum in late August 1967, three oil-rich states—Saudi Arabia, Kuwait, and Libya—pledged financial assistance to those Arab states that suffered defeat at the hands of Israelis, including Jordan. Jordan was to receive about $97 million annually from these sources. In practice, this financial aid was not forthcoming regularly because it was conditioned by political considerations involving the relationship of King Hussein to the Palestinians. Of the three donor states only Saudi Arabia regularly continued its subsidy. Kuwait's subsidies were subject to suspensions, and Libya, after the overthrow of its monarchy in 1969, ceased payments altogether.

The political consequences of the war and occupation were even more momentous than the economic ones. The proportion of the homeless, destitute, and desperate Palestinians in Jordan's remaining free territory increased, with the attendant intensification of their militancy. The Jordanian refugee camps became in fact the main recruiting ground for the Palestinian guerrillas whose objective was to regain their lost homeland. This activity in the camps naturally produced new strains in the relations between Jordan and Israel.

King Hussein's policy was to avoid provoking Israel into a massive retaliatory action because of obvious inequality of military strength between the two countries. His objective was to regain control over the occupied West Bank as early as possible by diplomatic means. According to unconfirmed reports, he engaged in secret negotiations with Israeli emissaries with an eye to achieving a compromise solution.[15] Such a solution was not easy to devise, partly because there was a reluctance in Israel to return the West Bank unconditionally (certain groups in Israel opposed the return as such) and partly because of the vexing issue of Jerusalem whose annexation by Israel Hussein could not accept. At the same time, he was suspicious of the formulas proposed by the Israelis which would give the Arabs access to their holy places in Jerusalem within the framework of Israeli sovereignty. Israel's prime minister, Golda Meir, offered Jordan the guardianship of the Moslem holy places in March 1973, but this was not accepted. On the other hand, King Hussein was one of the earliest voices in the Arab world to acknowledge, in November 1967, the right of Israel to exist, thereby renouncing the ostensible all-Arab objective of abolishing or destroying the State of Israel.[16] Hussein's formal approach to his relations with Israel was perhaps best expressed in the course of various speeches and press conferences he held in the United States in 1969 when he repeatedly declared that Israel may have either peace with the Arabs or (conquered) territory, but it cannot have both.[17]

Jordanian-Israeli relations were bound, moreover, to be influenced by the state of affairs between Israel and other adjoining countries, particularly the two other Arab confrontation states, Egypt and Syria. However, it was not possible to predict exactly what effect any partial settlement between Egypt and Israel or Syria and Israel would have on the relationship between Jordan and Israel. Partial settlements (such as those achieved in the 1970s) could pave the way for a general relaxation of tension and thus facilitate some progress in Jordanian-Israeli relations or, on the contrary, they could leave Jordan isolated and facing Israel's political and military preponderance with her own meager resources. In the midst of these fluctuations a certain symbiotic relationship had developed between Israel and Jordan, expressed in the permission Israel gave to the West Bank Palestinian farmers to transport and sell their produce in the fruit-deficient areas of the free Jordanian territory east of the Jordan River.

Jordan and the Palestinians

Much in the domestic, Arab, and foreign policy of Jordan revolved around the problem of the Palestinians. Their presence in the kingdom constituted one factor, but equally important was the existence of Palestinian exiled communities in such countries as Syria, Lebanon, Kuwait, or the Gaza strip. The three million Palestinians, partly dispersed and partly under Israeli authority, began to display in the 1960s a greater group cohesion and identity, a stronger tendency to assert their

[15] *New York Times,* March 22, 1972.
[16] *New York Times,* Nov. 9, 1967.
[17] For a typical speech on April 10, 1969, see R. H. Magnus, ed., *Documents on the Middle East* (Washington, D.C., 1969), pp. 211–212.

political rights through organized action, and also to resort to military means to achieve their objectives of liberation of their homeland. Side by side with official organizations such as the PLO and PLA, groups of Palestinian militants began forming guerrilla organizations to harrass and undermine Israeli authority first in Israel proper and after 1967 in the occupied territories as well. These guerrilla organizations (*fedayeen*) embraced a great variety of groups with differing ideological orientations. The largest of them and the least ideologically oriented was the Fatah (reverse acronym for Harakat Tahrir Falastin) led by Yassir Arafat. The two best known left-wing organizations were the Popular Front for Liberation of Palestine (PFLP) under George Habash and the Democratic Popular Front (DPF) led by Nayef Hawatmeh. Both were Marxist-oriented but with a difference; the DPF was reputedly Maoist and received aid from and had its members trained in Communist China. Paradoxically, both Habash and Hawatmeh were Christians. In addition to these and other independent groups, some Palestinian guerrilla organizations were formed under the aegis of the Syrian and Iraqi governments. In Syria the group was Saiqa under the leadership of Mohsen Zuhair, and in Iraq it was the Arab Liberation Front (ALF). At one time or another the Palestinian guerrillas embraced twenty or more organizations, some of them ephemeral, some splitting into subgroups, the others merging together. Up to 1970 the PFLP, DPF, and the PFLP-General Command, a separate group under the leadership of Captain Ahmed Jebreel, represented probably the most militant expression of Palestinian nationalism. These groups engaged in hijackings of passenger airplanes and individual acts of terror. These activities were not confined to the territory of Israel or occupied areas but extended worldwide and included attacks on Israeli citizens and institutions, on airports, on Arab leaders deemed inimical to the Palestinian cause, and on selected foreigners, among whom a few high-ranking American diplomats figured prominently as victims of assassination.

While the acts of violence perpetrated by these guerrilla fighters caused much concern to the governments and security services of most civilized countries, the kingdom of Jordan was exposed on the most massive scale to the manifestations of Palestinian militancy.

By the late 1960s the *fedayeen* organizations in Jordan, with Fatah as their main component, grew into a major military force which challenged the authority of the Jordanian state. The *fedayeen* had full control over the refugee camps, they openly displayed their weapons, engaged in building of roadblocks and in search and seizure, and blithely disregarded the instructions and regulations issued by the Jordanian government, army, and police. Furthermore, they infiltrated either Israel or the Israeli-occupied territory attacking selected targets whether military or civilian. It should be pointed out, however, that they never succeeded in launching a large-scale guerrilla warfare of the Viet Cong type in the Arab areas held by Israel. Various explanations were given for this failure: on the one hand, certain observers pointed to the inhospitable, often barren, terrain of Palestine so different from the protective jungles of Indochina; on the other, especially according to the Israeli interpretation, the guerrilla movement did not evoke a profound enough response among the peaceful Arab inhabitants of the Israeli-controlled territories, thus depriving the *fedayeen* of an adequate base of support among the local population. This lack of active response did not necessarily mean lack of friendly feelings toward the *fedayeen* and their objectives. The local inhabitants might have had doubts about the ultimate effectiveness of *fedayeen* action and feared stern Israeli counteraction should large local groups of Arabs become involved in such warfare. The *fedayeen* had to rely on the territory of Jordan as a base for their operations, thereby bringing upon their host country Israeli reprisals. According to a pattern already established in the 1950s, such Israeli raids were usually large-scale, well organized, and conducted by regular armed forces which attacked selected targets, often destroying an entire village or township suspected by the Israelis of harboring the Palestinian guerrillas. Although most of such Israeli reprisal raids were successful, in some cases the Israelis encountered stiff resistance. This was particularly the case of a well-publicized attack on the *fedayeen* base at Karamah in which the Palestinian guerrillas, while losing many men, inflicted serious casualties upon the invading Israeli force.

To King Hussein this situation was deeply disturbing. The behavior of the Palestinian *fedayeen* constituted a state within a state, which if allowed to continue unchecked would ultimately result in the disintegration of the Jordanian kingdom. The king, moreover, could not help comparing the position of Jordan with that of Egypt, Syria, and Iraq, all revolutionary countries known for their militant slogans and loud support of the Palestinian cause and yet all denying freedom of action to the Palestinians and subjecting them to strong military controls through their own armies. In the early years of the PLO under the leadership of Ahmed Shukairi, relations between that body and King Hussein were full of mutual distrust. With the replacement of Shukairi by Yassir Arafat, commander of the Fatah, as chairman of the PLO, the king endeavored to establish some modus vivendi between the *fedayeen* and himself. Thus, for example, on July 10, 1970, Jordan's prime minister, Abdul Moneim Rifai, concluded an agreement with Yassir Arafat setting forth the mutual rights and obligations of the *fedayeen* and the Jordanian authorities. But the *fedayeen* were in no mood to honor such agreements, feeling confident of themselves. Ultimately, a major showdown took place in September of that year. The crisis was triggered by the hijacking of two international airliners—TWA and KLM—by the *fedayeen,* who brought them down to an airport in Jordan. The hijacking, with threats of death, some actual killings, and the eventual rescue of the passengers, brought the existing tension between the government and the guerrillas to a high pitch of intensity. Armed clashes occurred between the government forces and the *fedayeen,* quickly escalating into full-time warfare in which the Palestinians did not hide their attempt to overthrow the regime, while the king and his army were equally determined to put an end to what they regarded as the cancerous growth of a foreign body in their midst. And again, this internal upheaval in Jordan soon drew into its vortex external forces. On September 19 a Syrian tank column was despatched into Jordanian territory with the objective of assisting the fedayeen. The Syrian foray was looked upon as a matter of considerable gravity by both Israel and the United States. The Israelis were concerned lest a Palestinian-Syrian victory in Jordan complete an encircling movement from the east and therefore, create a disadvantage from the strategic point of view. The United States could not disregard a strong tie between the Soviet Union and the left-wing Baath regime then in power in Syria under the leadership of Saleh el-Jadid, and it could not view with indifference the threat posed to the survival of King Hussein's regime.[18] Accordingly, strong representations were made in both Damascus and Moscow, but the United States also warned Israel against precipitate action that might complicate and aggravate the situation. On his part, King Hussein was determined to resist, and his freshly rebuilt air force attacked the Syrian tank column, and compelled it to retreat into Syrian territory. (This reckless Syrian adventure eventually cost its initiator, Saleh Jadid, his power. He was before long replaced by a more moderate Syrian leader, General Hafez Assad, of whom an account may be found in the chapter on Syria.) The successful repulse of the Syrian attack permitted King Hussein's forces to concentrate on the *fedayeen,* whose resistance was crushed shortly afterward. The dead and wounded numbered in the thousands, there was much destruction in certain townships and villages of Jordan, and a good number of the *fedayeen* crossed the border to Syria.

The crisis in Jordan prompted President Nasser to call a meeting of Arab heads of state to Cairo to consider an appropriate solution. In the course of these meetings President Nassar died of a heart attack. Acting on the recommendations of the Arab leaders gathered in Cairo, King Hussein and Yassir Arafat concluded on October 13 an agreement to regulate the status of the *fedayeen* in Jordan. However, the situation was different from that existing before September. The king was negotiating from a position of strength and his intention was clearly never to allow the resurgence of an alien state within his kingdom. An uneasy truce that prevailed between his forces and the *fedayeen* through the rest of the year and the first half of 1971 was punctuated by an occasional minor clash. By July 1971 one could speak already of the complete elimination of the *fedayeen* as a organized force or group of forces in Jordan. Most of the *fedayeen* had by that time found their way to Syria, where they were retrained and regrouped, submitted to strict Syrian army controls, and encouraged to harrass Israel through the territory of Lebanon. This they did by establishing the so-called Arafat Trail in the Arkoub region in southeastern Lebanon from which they proceeded to make forays into Israel's northern districts.

Although the problem of the *fedayeen* presence in Jordan was resolved by the force of arms and the king's authority was entrenched, a new issue emerged in the Jordanian-Palestinian relations. This time it was the problem of who would legally represent the Palestinians in any international negotiations affecting the future of the Holy Land. As the ruler of the land in which the Palestinians constituted a majority (even in the truncated part, Transjordan), King Hussein believed that this right and responsibility was his. To renounce this claim would, furthermore, open the gate to speculation and possible controversy regarding the future of the West Bank once Israel relinquished its occupation there and, therefore, the territorial integrity and unity of the kingdom of Jordan. By contrast, the Palestinian leadership, backed often by revolutionary Arab governments, maintained that the PLO was the only

---

[18]Basic U.S. interest in Jordan's survival was expressed on April 24, 1957. See Magnus, *op.cit.,* p. 95.

legitimate representation of the Palestinian people. In an attempt to resolve the controversy, on March 15, 1972, King Hussein revealed a plan to make Jordan a federated state, with two autonomous regions, one of which would be the Israeli-cccupied West Bank. He also proposed that Jerusalem should become the capital of the Palestinian region.

Although the proposal was made in good faith and in the hope that by providing for Palestinian autonomy the plan would satisfy their yearnings for national identity and self-government, it met with an angry response from the PLO, the latter distrustful of Hussein and embittered by the defeat of September 1970. The PLO in turn was backed in its negative attitude by certain other Arab capitals including Cairo, which on April 6 went so far as to break diplomatic relations with Jordan. In turn, the king sharply criticized Egypt's leadership for what he called an appeasement of the Palestinian guerrillas.

In October 1973, Jordan witnessed the outbreak of a new war between Egypt and Syria on the one hand and Israel on the other. This time the kingdom stayed out of the conflict, its level of armaments being so inferior to that of Israel that any thought of active participation in the war would have been suicidal. Following the war, however, the problem of Palestinian representation acquired a new intensity in view of the negotiations for the cease-fires and disengagements conducted between Egypt and Syria on the one hand and Israel on the other under the United States' auspices. It should be stressed that these negotiations were taking place at a time when the United States, the Soviet Union, and other parties in the conflict were expected to meet at a conference in Geneva in a collective endeavor to seek an overall peace settlement. Under the circumstances, the question reemerged as to whether the Palestinians should have a separate representation or whether Jordan should speak in their name. Finally, on July 18, 1974, following a meeting with President Sadat in Alexandria, King Hussein recognized the PLO as the representative of the Palestinian people *outside* Jordan and agreed that the organization should be represented at the Geneva negotiations. On September 22, however, the king clarified that Jordan would continue to claim the right to speak for the Palestinians in Jordan and the occupied West Bank territory.

This formula was clearly unacceptable to the Palestinian leadership which, through intensive diplomacy, secured the backing of a number of Arab governments to its view. This backing was formalized on October 28, 1974, at a summit meeting in Rabat when the heads of twenty Arab states unanimously recognized the PLO as the sole representative of the Palestinian people on any Palestinian land that would be liberated.[19] Faced with this overwhelming decision, King Hussein accepted the verdict. Soon afterward, in November, the Jordanian parliament adopted, on the king's initiative, a constitutional amendment permitting the king to dissolve parliament and to allow a lapse of twelve months before calling for a new election. In explaining these moves, the king stated that a constitutional reform was necessary so that the kingdom could be limited to the East Bank, and the West Bank personnel could be separated from the government. Following these decisions a gradual rec-

[19]Text in *New York Times,* Oct. 30, 1974.

onciliation took place between King Hussein and the PLO, manifested by such gestures as the release of certain Palestinian prisoners held by the Jordanian authorities. The reconciliation, however, did not mean any restoration of the former military power of the *fedayeen* on Jordanian territory.

Arab and Foreign Relations

In the days of the Arab Cold War, 1957–1967, Jordan held a clearly defined place in the camp of the conservative states. After the June 1967 war and also following President Nasser's death in 1970, the Arab world witnessed a number of changes. On the one hand, the conservative camp was reduced in numbers, mostly through the advent of a revolutionary regime under Colonel Muammar Qadhafi in Libya in 1969 and partly by the ultimate assertion of authority by the republicans in Yemen following a five-year civil war. On the other hand, Nasser's death removed from Egypt a militant Pan-Arab leader whose influence was pervasive in many Arab countries and whose policies and ideological commitments generated many feuds in the Arab world. Under the leadership of President Sadat, Egypt reverted to moderate ways; however, paradoxically this new posture was not translated necessarily into better relations with Jordan, as the temporary rupture of diplomatic relations in 1972 indicated. Yet despite this lack of mutual cordiality between Amman and Cairo, under Sadat's leadership Egypt ceased to encourage active hostility against King Hussein and subversion of his regime.

Another Arab nation in which Jordan had vital interests was Syria. Relations between the two countries had reached a low level when Syria was ruled by the left wing of the Baath Party between 1966 and 1970. Jordan, along with Saudi Arabia, constituted a favorite target of Syria's propagandist attacks as a country opposed to socialism and friendly to the West. But with the arrival of President Hafez Assad in the fall of 1970, Syria's attitude toward Jordan gradually changed. Assad was giving high priority to military matters and the need for coordinated Arab action vis-à-vis Israel. As a military man he could not disregard the strategic importance of the Jordanian territory and the possible contribution of the Jordanian army to the common effort. The war of October 1973 in which Syria was engaged along with Egypt did not leave any bitter residue in the Syrian-Jordanian relations. On the contrary, Egypt's search for a partial settlement with Israel, especially expressed in the second disengagement agreement on September 1, 1975, caused marked rapprochement between Syria and Jordan, both governments feeling abandoned by Egypt and outmaneuvered by the American step-by-step diplomacy. This rapprochement took the form of an exchange of visits between King Hussein and President Assad in the midst of cordial popular manifestations—a great novelty in the relations between the two countries, considering the aggravated recent past. Their cooperation even attained certain institutional forms: on June 12, 1975, the two leaders decided to establish a joint high commission to coordinate the military, political, economic, and cultural policies. Interestingly enough, the civil war raging in Lebanon in 1975–76 provided another opportunity for a reaffirmation of the new bonds of friendship. President Assad of Syria accused President Sadat of Egypt of secretly fomenting the confict in Lebanon so that the attention of the world would be diverted from his bilateral disengagement agreement with Israel. Although King Hussein did not pronounce himself openly on this subject, nevertheless he tended to side with President Assad in this newly developing controversy between the two centers of Arab socialism, Damascus and Cairo.

In the midst of these alarms and excursions, King Hussein had to steer the ship of his state in the turbulent waters of great power politics. His basic commitment was to the West and good relations with the United States remained the foundation of his foreign policy. However, his pleas for modern arms received only a reluctant hearing in Washington, largely because of obstacles encountered in Congress. In May 1975 the United States agreed to sell Jordan a Hawk missile air defense system for $100 million. But even this transaction was subject to many embarrassing reservations. A year earlier, in June 1974, President Nixon visited Amman in the first such journey paid by an American president to Jordan. The expressions of friendship exchanged during that visit, however, did not bring about any substantial modification in the American policy, which placed the security of Israel definitely above the security of its Arab neighbors. There were indications that the Soviet Union was anxious to exploit the king's frustration over his inability to secure an adequate level of arms supplies from the United States. The king's visit to Moscow in the spring of 1976 marked an important step whereby King Hussein opened the door to a possible diversification of the sources of his arms supplies. His visit did not mean the burning of the bridges with the West. It did signal, however, to Washington that no country, no matter what its past record of reliance on American aid, could ever be taken for granted in its adherence to the pro-Western line.

PART FOUR

West and East of
the Red Sea

CHAPTER XII

Egypt

Situated at the junction of Africa and Asia, Egypt has always held a strategic position which, added to the fertility of her land, has attracted the great state builders and conquerors of the past. Egypt's strategic significance was immensely increased with the construction in 1869 of the Suez Canal. Although the canal was the property of a private, predominantly French company, strategically it fell under the control of Great Britain, who fully realized its importance to the imperial life line. Arabi Pasha's antiforeign riots gave the British an opportunity, in 1882, to occupy the delta of the Nile and to establish their rule in this still nominally Ottoman province. It was not long before Britain extended her dominion to the Sudan, although this operation encountered considerable opposition. The dervish rising of Mahdi Mohammed Ahmed in 1882, the extermination of General Gordon's British garrison in Khartoum in 1884, France's expedition to Fashoda in 1896, and Kitchener's victory at Omdurman in 1898 were steps in a process which ended January 19, 1899, in the establishment of the Anglo-Egyptian condominium over the Sudan.

Dominance of Britain

Thus in the last two decades of the nineteenth century Britain became the controlling power of the whole Nile valley. Her interests in Egypt were represented by one of the ablest empire builders of modern history, Lord Cromer. Cromer gave Egypt a sound fiscal administration and an improved irrigation system and helped her assume a leading commercial position among the countries of the Middle East. His successors, Sir Eldon Gorst (1907-1911) and Lord Kitchener (1911-1914), continued, under the nominal authority of the khedive, to exercise uncontested power in Egypt.

By the beginning of World War I Britain was so firmly entrenched that it was a mere formality for her to proclaim, on December 18, 1914, that Egypt was a British protectorate. Khedive (Viceroy) Abbas Hilmi, then on a visit in Constantinople, was deposed *in absentia* and replaced by Hussein, another member of the Mohammed Ali dynasty. With the British blessing Hussein assumed the title of sultan. Upon his death in 1917, he was succeeded by Fuad I, who, like his predecessor, enjoyed British confidence. Throughout the war Egypt was governed by Prime

Minister Rushdi Pasha, who in all important matters followed British advice. As the war progressed, Egypt became a great British military base, from which attacks were launched toward Gallipoli and Palestine. Cairo became a center of Britain's Arab diplomacy. Ever since the conclusion of the Anglo-French Entente in 1904, Britain's predominant position in Egypt had been taken for granted by the Allies, so that there was no need to include Egypt in the secret treaties of World War I. As a result, Britain's relations with Egypt during that period were devoid of the political angles of international diplomacy and were largely concerned with administrative problems.

The Rise of Nationalism

This uncomplicated relationship changed abruptly with the end of the First World War. Egypt experienced a rise of nationalism. Several factors accounted for it: the presence of large British, Australian, and New Zealand forces and the inevitable incidents deriving from it wounded Egyptian national pride; the large-scale spending of foreign armies produced inflation and profiteering from which fixed-income groups suffered severely; British recruitment of Egyptians for labor battalions depleted Egypt's labor force and resulted in a neglect of agriculture and in severe breakdowns in food production; and last, but not least, Wilson's Fourteen Points and the Anglo-French Declaration of November 8, 1918, promising independence to the Arab countries helped to arouse a keen desire for complete freedom from foreign tutelage.

In 1918–1919, Egypt witnessed intense nationalist agitation, which erupted into anti-British riots. The nationalists were led by a militant orator, Saad Zaghlul Pasha, of fellaheen origin, who had been minister of education under Cromer. In November 1918, two days after the armistice, Saad Zaghlul, accompanied by Ali Shaarawi Pasha and Abdul Aziz Fahmi Bey, called on the British high commissioner, Sir Reginald Wingate, demanding full independence for their country. This self-styled "Delegation of Egypt" (Wafd el-Masri), supported by thousands of telegrams and signatures, met with no success. Early in 1919 Saad Zaghlul founded a new party, the Wafd, which soon became the main vehicle of Egyptian nationalism.

Facing tremendous agitation in the country, the British decided to strike at the very nerve center and in March 1919 deported Zaghlul, with three other prominent Wafdists,[1] to Malta. It was of no avail. Instead of calming the atmosphere, it provoked a spontaneous uprising, commonly referred to as the Egyptian revolution, in which students, workers, and other classes acting in concert paralyzed the life of the country. On March 17, Cairo became practically isolated, and the new British high commissioner, Lord Allenby, had to rush troops from Syria to curb the insurrection.

The uprising brought home to the British the fact that Egyptian nationalism could no longer be disposed of by military measures and that some compromise was necessary to preserve their supremacy in the delta of the Nile. They released Zaghlul

[1]Hamid el-Bassel, Ismail Sidki, and Mohammed Mahmud.

from confinement and allowed him to proceed to Paris, where he laid his claims before the Peace Conference. From Paris he proceeded to London to plead Egypt's case.

In the meantime the British cabinet decided to send Lord Milner to Egypt to investigate and to advise on a proper solution. Milner's mission (December 1919 to March 1920) resulted in a report recommending the replacement of the existing protectorate by a treaty of alliance which would give Great Britain the right to defend Egypt, control the Suez Canal, and guide Egypt's foreign relations. Subsequent negotiations between London and Cairo ended in a deadlock. In 1921 there was a renewed wave of nationalist riots, whereupon Zaghlul and other leaders were again deported, this time to Aden, Gibraltar, and the Seychelles.

Unable to reach a bilateral agreement, the British government decided to proceed alone, and on February 28, 1922, in a statement issued by the high commissioner, it put an end to the protectorate and proclaimed Egypt's independence. The proclamation contained four points "absolutely reserved to the discretion of His Majesty's Government," namely, (1) the security of the communications of the British Empire in Egypt; (2) the defense of Egypt against all foreign aggression or interference, direct or indirect; (3) the protection of foreign interests in Egypt and the protection of minorities; and (4) the Sudan.[2] This declaration was satisfactory to Sultan Fuad, who on March 15 hastened to assume the title of king (*malik*), but it was rejected by the nationalists, who considered it a totally inadequate substitute for true independence.

There was no real change in the pattern of political control in Egypt, except for the abolition of martial law, which had been in force since November 2, 1914. King Fuad, by a royal rescript of April 19, 1923, promulgated a constitution which followed Western patterns but reserved considerable rights to the crown. Following an act of amnesty, Zaghlul and his associates returned from their forced exile and plunged headlong into the political campaign preliminary to the first constitutional elections. The elections, held in January 1924, gave Zaghlul's Wafd party an overwhelming victory. Commanding 188 seats as against 27 for the opposition, Zahglul was made prime minister and without delay began to press for a revision of the unilateral declaration of independence. Zaghlul's hope that Britain's Labour party cabinet headed by Ramsay MacDonald would be more responsive to Egypt's aspirations proved to be vain. Talks initiated in London between the British and the Egyptian prime ministers broke down mainly on account of the Sudan, control of which the British were unwilling to give up. As usual, the breakdown of negotiations provoked disorders in Egypt, this time resulting in frequent assaults upon British civil and military personnel.

On November 19, 1924, Sir Lee Stack, *sirdar* (commander-in-chief) of the Egyptian army and governor-general of the Sudan, was killed by a Wafdist fanatic. British reaction was unusually strong. High Commissioner Lord Allenby presented a curt ultimatum to the Egyptian government demanding punishment of the assas-

[2]See Royal Institute of International Affairs, ed., *Great Britain and Egypt, 1914–1936* (London, 1936). The full text is in Helen M. Davis, ed., *Constitutions, Electoral Laws, Treaties of States in the Near and Middle East* (Durham, N.C., 1947), p. 55.

sins, an apology, an indemnity of a half-million Egyptian pounds ($1 million), a prohibition of political demonstrations, and withdrawal of Egyptian troops from the Sudan. Moreover, he demanded the retention by Egypt of British advisers in the ministries of Finance, Justice, and the European department of the Ministry of Interior. He also informed Egypt that the area to be irrigated in the Gezira district of the Sudan would be extended. This meant that vital Nile water would be channeled to British Sudanese plantations at the expense of Egypt. To back up these demands Allenby ordered the seizure by British troops of the Alexandria customs. It was the Sudan irrigation proposal that irked Zaghlul most and rather than accept it he resigned on November 24, 1924. His successor, Ziwar Pasha, who formed a non-Wafd cabinet, accepted the ultimatum, whereupon the British evacuated the customs and, somewhat later, reversed their decision concerning Gezira irrigation. The results of these dramatic events were twofold: (1) Britain intensified her hold on Egypt by continuing to control, through her advisers, vital departments in the Egyptian government (especially internal security); (2) Egypt's influence was practically eliminated from the Sudan by the withdrawal of her troops and officials.

Egypt between 1924 and 1936

The Stack murder closed a definite chapter in Anglo-Egyptian relations. The following period (1924–1936) was characterized by two simultaneous processes: one was the prolonged and frequently interrupted negotiations with Britain for a bilateral treaty which would give ampler recognition to Egypt's national aspirations; the other was the accentuation of internal political struggle between the Palace and the Wafd.[3] Anglo-Egyptian negotiations (Chamberlain-Sarwat, 1927–1928; Henderson-Mahmud, 1929; Henderson-Nahas, 1930) were inconclusive. In May 1930 they were suspended not to be renewed until 1935. The Sudan and British troops in Egypt were the two main obstacles toward an agreement. In the meantime the unilateral declaration of February 28, 1922, remained as a basis of relations between the two countries.

Failure to satisfy nationalist demands usually produced, in the early twenties, mob demonstrations and anti-British violence. It was, therefore, noteworthy that similar failures in the decade between 1925 and 1935 did not provoke major outbursts. The explanation must be sought in Egypt's internal politics. These were characterized by two important factors. First, Saad Zaghlul Pasha passed from the political scene. Following the second elections in 1926, which again returned a strong Wafd majority, Zaghlul was a natural candidate for the premiership but he was prevented from assuming office by a British veto. The chamber then elected him to its presidency. In this somewhat obscure position Zaghlul remained for one year, but in 1927 death cut short his political career. Thus the most formidable adversary of British rule in Egypt, a man deified by the Egyptian populace, passed

---

[3]On this period, consult Anthony M. Galatoli, *Egypt in Midpassage* (Cairo, 1950); Amine Youssef Bey, *Independent Egyptian* (London, 1940); and P. A. Gargour, *Etapes de l'Indépendance Egyptienne* (Paris, 1942). For an anti-British account, see Conrad Oehlich, *Englands Hand in Ägypten* (Berlin, 1940).

away, and the Wafd lost its most inspiring leader. He was succeeded by Mustafa Nahas Pasha.

The second feature of internal politics was the determination of the king to curb the influence of the Wafd and to assert his own authority. Assisted by another center of power, the divines of the famous Moslem El-Azhar University, King Fuad succeeded in rallying around the Palace a number of aspiring politicians, who for various reasons did not accept Nahas Pasha's leadership and sought to satisfy their ambitions independently of the Wafd. Acting on their own or with the king's or Britain's blessing, these men launched a number of political parties, some quite ephemeral, some durable. In 1922, Mohammed Mahmud Pasha founded, with Adly Yeghen Pasha, the Liberal Constitutional party, which was supported by aristocratic and intellectual circles but had little popular support.[4] In 1925 Yehya Ibrahim Pasha established the Unionist (Ittihad) party, which was identified with the Palace. The party evoked very little response in the country and was notoriously unsuccessful in many subsequent elections.[5] Five years later Ismail Sidki Pasha formed the People's (Shaab) party, an organization with a rather misleading name inasmuch as it had little, if any, mass following. More significant was the split that occurred in 1932 in the ranks of the Wafd. It resulted in the establishment of a new party called Saadist (or Saadi Wafd) by two former Wafd leaders: Ahmed Maher and Mahmud Fahmi Nokrashi Pasha. This secession was the only move in party politics likely to harm the Wafd, but even this did not have much effect on the Wafd's predominance. Except for the old National (Watani) party, an insignificant and irreconcilable group of the deposed Khedive Abbas Hilmi, all these parties were more moderate than the Wafd: they were willing to support the king and ready for a realistic accommodation with Great Britain.

The pattern of Egyptian politics was roughly as follows: in a series of national elections (1923, 1925, and 1929) the Wafd emerged overwhelmingly victorious, but, except for two brief periods after Zaghlul's death (in 1928 and 1930) when Nahas Pasha headed the government, cabinets were formed by non-Wafdist premiers acceptable to the king and, indirectly, to the British. The paradox of Egyptian politics was that no Palace-supported party could ever win the elections in a free ballot because of Wafd popularity, yet the monarchy had a definite mass appeal.

The fact that hostile Wafd majorities perennially faced anti-Wafd cabinets was so frustrating to the Palace that, in 1930, King Fuad decided to curb Wafd supremacy by all the means at his disposal. To this end he appointed a "strong man," Ismail Sidki Pasha, as prime minister, dissolved the parliament, revoked the 1923 constitution, and on October 22, 1930, promulgated a new constitution and a new electoral law introducing a two-grade, indirect voting system. Thus armed with new legislative weapons and assisted by his new Shaab party, Sidki in 1931 obtained a victory in the Wafd-boycotted elections, establishing under royal authority a virtual dic-

---

[4]Other prominent members were Ahmed Gaffar Bey, Mahmud Abdul Razek Pasha, Gaffar Wali Pasha, and Heikal Pasha.

[5]Other prominent members were Hilmi Issa Pasha, Sayid Abu Ali Pasha, and Ahmed Ali Pasha.

tatorship for the next four years. This was the most peaceful period in Anglo-Egyptian relations. Sidki's government concentrated on economic issues in order to combat the depression. There was no political history to record.

The Anglo-Egyptian Treaty

The relative internal and external peace which Egypt experienced between 1930 and 1935 came to an end with the outbreak of the Italo-Ethiopian war in September 1935. A year earlier Sidki had resigned on account of ill health, and the departure of this energetic statesman from active political leadership again brought to the fore the problem of the relations between the Palace and the increasingly restive Wafd. Under strong nationalistic pressure the ailing King Fuad first suspended the authoritarian constitution of 1930 and then on December 12, 1935, notwithstanding British advice to the contrary, restored the constitution of 1923. This coincided with the creation of the so-called National Front, the result of a temporary reconciliation between the king and the Wafd. Four months later King Fuad died. He was succeeded by Farouk I, a sixteen-year-old youth who had to interrupt his secondary education in Switzerland to assume the crown.

The passing of the moderate Fuad-Sidki diumvirate and the restoration of the old constitution gave the Wafd a new opportunity to reassert itself in Egyptian politics. In May 1936 the Wafd won a resounding victory at the polls, whereupon Nahas Pasha promptly formed an all-Wafd cabinet. One of the first steps of the new government was to ask Great Britain for the renewal of negotiations to replace the status quo by a treaty. The British government responded favorably because it was anxious to reach a settlement with Egypt in view of the growing Italian menace in the eastern Mediterranean and the Red Sea basin. The realization of this menace and the object lesson Mussolini had given to underdeveloped countries by his treatment of Ethiopia also made the Egyptians more conciliatory. Repeated British offers during the preceding negotiations to defend Egypt against external aggression assumed a new significance in the light of Fascist dynamism. Egyptian moderates who privately conceded that a humanitarian British tutelage was better than outright Fascist control saw their position strenghened. After considerable interparty bickering it was decided that in the forthcoming negotiations Egypt should be represented by a thirteen-man delegation composed of seven Wafd members and six representatives of other politcal parties. Nahas Pasha headed the team. Britain was represented by the high commissioner, Sir Miles Lampson, accompanied by high-ranking diplomatic and military experts.

On August 26, 1936, the Anglo-Egyptian treaty was signed in London. It contained the following main provisions:

1. Egypt and Britain entered into an alliance, with Britain pledging to defend Egypt against aggression and Egypt placing her communication facilities at Britain's disposal in case of war;
2. Recognizing Britain's vital interest in the Suez Canal, Egypt consented to a British garrison of 10,000 men and 400 pilots in the Canal Zone, where barracks were to be constructed at Egypt's expense. British troops were to evacuate the rest of Egyptian

territory, but Britain was allowed to retain her naval base at Alexandria for eight more years;

3. British personnel in the Egyptian army and police were to be withdrawn. Instead a British military mission was to advise the Egyptian army to the exclusion of other foreigners, and Egyptian officers could not be trained abroad in other countries than Britain. Egypt regained full freedom to increase her armed forces;[6]
4. Unrestricted immigration of Egyptians into the Sudan was to be permitted and Egyptian troops were to return to the Sudan;
5. Britain was to support Egypt in her plea for the abolition of capitulations;
6. Britain promised to support Egypt's candidacy for membership in the League of Nations;
7. The British high commissioner was to be replaced by an ambassador, the latter receiving permanent diplomatic seniority rights;
8. The treaty was to be of indefinite duration, but at the end of twenty years negotiations toward its revision were allowed. It was, however, agreed that "any revision of this treaty [would] provide for the continuation of the alliance between the High Contracting Parties"[7]

If we compare these provisions with the Four Reserved Points of 1922, we see that both parties gave way in important matters. Britain retained practically undiminished her right to guard the security of imperial communications but had to compromise on the issue of defense and made a complete concession with regard to the protection of foreigners and minorities. The basic problem of the Sudan remained unsolved, Britain's consent to readmit Egyptians into the condominium being only a restoration of the situation that had existed before the ultimatum of 1924.

On December 22, 1936, the treaty was ratified by the Egyptian parliament despite some adverse criticism. To the Egyptians the treaty meant the inauguration of independence inasmuch as it replaced the unilateral British fiat of 1922. On May 8, 1937, the Montreux conference of powers who enjoyed capitulatory privileges in Egypt resulted in an agreement to abolish the capitulations but to maintain the Mixed Courts in Cairo and Alexandria for the next twelve years. On May 26 Egypt was admitted to the League of Nations.

The treaty of 1936 marked an apogee in the history of the Wafd, whose leader, Nahas Pasha, looked forward to a long period of undisputed power in Egypt. This self-assuredness brought him, however, into conflict with the young king who, like his late father, became wary of the Wafd's hold on the people. Thus the old pattern was revived, the king, backed by the rector of El-Azhar, Sheikh El-Maraghi, by the Liberal Constitutional party, and by the Saadists, opposing the Wafd. In 1937, Farouk dismissed Nahas Pasha and appointed in his place Mohammed Mahmud Pasha, a Liberal Constitutionalist. This was a repetition of the Sidki experiment of 1930–1934. Premier Mahmud Pasha again played the role of a "strong man," heading a non-Wafdist cabinet in the face of Wafdist parliamentary opposition.

As in 1931, the Palace was again determined to put an end to the abnormal situation of constant hostility between the parliment and the executive by changing

[6]Previously objected to by the British.
[7]The full text is in Davis, *op. cit.*, pp. 56 ff.

the political complexion of the parliament. Mahmud Pasha suppressed the Fascist Green Shirts (Young Egypt—Misr el-Fatat) and the Wafdist Blue Shirts, Nazi-patterned youth groups, and made preparatory moves toward national elections with the ultimate aim of ousting the Wafd from power. His task was made easier by the fact that until the conclusion of the treaty with Britain the Wafd had thrived on Anglo-Egyptian antagonism, but now this basis of popular appeal was removed. In February 1938 the king dissolved the Wafd-dominated parliament, and in the elections held in April Mahmud Pasha's progovernment coalition won a spectacular victory. The Wafd suffered an eclipse which was to keep it from power for the next four years.

Egypt During World War II[8]

Egyptian foreign and domestic politics, as we have seen, were closely interwoven. They followed, moreover, an uncomplicated pattern: on the one hand, Egypt struggled for emancipation from Britain's rule without intervention by an major outside power; on the other, Britain, with Palace connivance, strove to break the Wafd monopoly of popular appeal by encouraging splinter parties and personal rivalries in the name of the time-honored principle of "divide and rule."

With the coming of the Second World War this basic pattern continued, but it underwent some modifications—owing to the appearance of an external factor. With Britain's position in the Middle East seriously threatened by Italy and Germany, Egypt could reorient her policy of gradual emancipation and cooperation with Britain into one of open defiance and collaboration with the Axis powers. Or she could remain passive and noncommittal waiting for "the dust to settle" and then make up to the winners. Both Axis powers had been diplomatically active in Cairo a year or two preceding the outbreak of the war. A number of German staff officers, diplomats, and Nazi dignitaries (including Dr. Goebbels) paid visits to Egypt. Italy had the support of 60,000 Italian residents of Egypt, possessed influential commercial and banking establishments, and did not spare funds and efforts to create friendly feelings. German and Italian broadcasts in Arabic from Zeesen and Bari, respectively, were quite popular with Egyptian audiences. The Egyptians, to be sure, could have no particular stake in a complete victory of the Axis, but a relative weakening of Great Britain, together with self-insurance in case of her total defeat, appealed to many Egyptians as worth striving for. For many an Egyptian statesman, therefore, this was a problem of accurate appraisal, a problem not devoid of an element of gambling. The policy of obvious cooperation with the British, while commendable during the war itself in view of the presence of large British forces in the country, might boomerang in case of Axis success. On the other hand, noncooperation, depending upon its degree, might prove dangerous during the war and, in case of British victory, might ruin a political career after the war.

These considerations led to a division of opinion among the leading Egyptians when the war began. The British requested and obtained the proclamation of martial

---

[8]For a superficial, but chronologically detailed account of this period, see Jean Lugol, *Egypt and World War II* (Cairo, 1945).

law in September 1939, the institution of censorship, the rupture of diplomatic relations with Germany, the internment or expulsion of German nationals, and use of Egyptian communication facilities according to the treaty of 1936. Egypt became the principal British, and later Allied, base in the Middle East. Over half a million Allied troops, including British, Indian, Australian, New Zealand, South African, Polish, Czechoslovak, Greek, Yugoslav, and American soldiers, found themselves in the course of war on Egyptian territory. Cairo was a real hub of Allied diplomatic and economic activity. The Anglo-American Middle East Supply Center was located here, and there was hardly an Allied statesman of prominence who did not, at one time or another, visit Cairo to attend a diplomatic conference, to inspect troops, or to stop enroute to some distant place. In Cairo the British established the important wartime office of minister of state for the Middle East, occupied in succession by Captain Oliver Lyttelton, Mr. Richard Casey, and Lord Moyne. American administrators of the lend lease and other regional agencies operating in the Middle East were likewise stationed in Cairo. And last, but not least, President Franklin D. Roosevelt, Prime Minister Winston Churchill, Generalissimo Chiang Kai-shek, and Turkish President Ismet İnönü held their famous conference in the city in the late fall of 1943.[9]

At the time of the outbreak of the war the Egyptian government was headed by Ali Maher Pasha, an Independent working in close affiliation with the Saadists and Liberal Constitutionalists. He followed a policy of limited co-operation with Britain, which, as time progressed, changed into gradual hostility. The failure of the Western Allies to prevent the collapse of Poland, the defeatist period of the "phony war," 1939–1940, the German successes in the west in the spring of 1940, and the Dunkerque evacuation seemed to prove that Britain's might was on the wane. The Italian minister in Cairo, Count Mazzolini, did his best during that period to foster this impression among the Egyptians, stressing that in case of an Italo-British conflict Italy would have no iniquitous designs on Egypt. When Italy declared war on the Allies in June 1940, Britain asked Ali Maher to declare war on Italy. Ali Maher resisted and, as a result of British pressure on King Farouk, was forced to resign. From his retirement he continued to agitate against the British, which eventually led to his arrest and forcible confinement to his country residence in 1942. Ali Maher's successors did not declare war on Italy either but agreed to break off diplomatic relations. There was no question of the mass internment of Italian nationals, their large number making it impracticable, but selected individuals, usually pointed out by British security agencies, were interned. In August 1940 Italian troops in their first major offensive entered Egyptian territory. But Rome made it clear that this move was directed against Great Britain only; hence the Egyptian government did not consider it a *casus belli* and persevered in its refusal to declare war. Similarly, Egypt refused to be drawn into belligerency when General Erwin Rommel's German Afrika Korps crossed the Egyptian border in April 1941. But

[9]To this may be added a series of conferences President Roosevelt held with the following Middle Eastern and African rulers: King Farouk, King Ibn Saud, Emperor Haile Selassie, and President Shukri el-Quwatli of Syria, on board the U.S.S. *Quincy* on the Great Bitter Lake in Egypt, in mid-February 1945, following the Yalta conference.

this passive resistance was the extent of Egypt's efforts to interfere with Allied conduct of the war. There were individual attempts to cooperate actively with the Axis. Such, for example, was the unsuccessful attempt of the ex-chief of staff, General Aziz el-Masri, to join forces with the Iraqi rebel, Rashid Ali el-Gailani, in May 1941. Such also was the betrayal by some Egyptian staff officers of British defense plans concerning Siwa oasis. But generally the Egyptians were in no mood to act recklessly. The presence of large Allied contingents was, of course, a powerful deterrent against any active hostility. Moreover, the British seemed to possess effective mastery of internal security. A British subject, General Russell Pasha, was commandant of the Egyptian police, and Colonel Fitzpatrick Bey, his deputy. A Britisher was chief prosecutor in the Mixed Courts, and another Britisher headed the censorship division. British officials held strategic positions in border passport control and similar security agencies. There was little likelihood of the situation getting out of hand.

The British were anxious not to antagonize these political forces in Egypt that had influence over the masses. Any mob demonstrations or rioting, should it occur, would be a major embarrassment to Britain, whose strength had to be spared for the war effort. The British realized that the Wafd, despite its somewhat forced eclipse in 1938, still remained the most powerful single factor in Egyptian politics and that it was able to do serious harm to their position in Egypt, should it so choose. The fact that the non-Wafdist government did, after all, cooperate with Britain might have supplied the Wafd with new ammunition and might have turned it from its protreaty stand into traditional anti-British demagoguery. Moreover, the British were fully aware of Nahas Pasha's anger at being kept out of office for an unduly long period. They also knew of the thirst of Wafdist politicians for lucrative government jobs. All these considerations led the British government to decide that the safest way to keep Nahas and the Wafd out of mischief was to put them back into power. This meant, of course, a reversal of British policy. It required also persuading King Farouk, Nahas' personal enemy, to sign the act of appointment. Farouk refused and had to be coerced. On February 4, 1942, British armored units surrounded the Royal Abdin Palace in Cairo, whereupon British Ambassador Sir Miles Lampson (later Lord Killearn) accompanied by the commander-in-chief of the British forces in Egypt called on the King and gave him the choice of either signing Nahas' nomination or being deported from the country. Farouk complied, and Nahas assumed the premiership. The return to power of the Wafd necessarily resulted in increased corruption (the Wafd was known for its well-organized patronage system) and in greater governmental inefficiency. Speculation, hoarding, and similar practices showed an upward trend—the British had been fully aware that this would happen. Yet, politically, it was a shrewd move and spared them many inconveniences.

In his new role Nahas was quite cooperative, as evidenced by his willingness to confine anti-British Ali Maher Pasha to domestic arrest (the decision was not quite disinterested). He helped Britain to recruit local labor for various works in the rear bases and cooperated in tracking down spies, saboteurs, and fifth columnists. The premier's prestige suffered considerably when, some time after his appointment, he quarreled with one of his close and most able associates, a Coptic Christian, Makram Ebeid Pasha. Ebeid resigned from the cabinet and soon afterward published a documented Black Book in which he mercilessly exposed the corrupt practices of the Wafd. A number of Wafdists seceded with him, founding the new Kutla (Bloc) party. Wafd fortunes were at a low ebb, but the British continued to support Nahas to avoid ministerial crises at the time of the greatest military decisions in North Africa. By the fall of 1944 the Axis danger to the Middle East was successfully removed as a result of El-Alamein and North African victories. Consequently the British felt that they could withdraw their support from Nahas, leaving Egyptian politics to resume their natural course. As soon as this became known (October 1944), Farouk dismissed Nahas and reinstated the Saadists in power. At the elections of January 1945, which were boycotted by the Wafd, a coalition of the Saadist and Kutla parties secured a substantial majority in the parliament.

The war was drawing to an end, Britain's prestige was high, and in the person of the new premier, Dr. Ahmed Maher Pasha, the British had a friendly and realistic statesman anxious to secure a place for Egypt in the postwar community of nations. The Big Three communiqué issued at the Yalta Conference made a declaration of war on the Axis a prerequisite to attendance at the projected United Nations conference at San Francisco. The Egyptian government decided to declare war, and on February 24, 1945, Ahmed Maher appeared in parliament to make a public statement to this effect. Unfortunately he was assassinated by a fanatical student nationalist while reading the royal decree. He was succeeded by Nokrashi Pasha, another Saadist leader, who continued in office until 1946.

Nationalism and Internal Turbulence

With the end of the war a new era opened in Egyptian politics. Ahmed Maher's murder was indicative of a new trend toward extremism. The Second World War caused disturbances in the Egyptian social and economic structure similar to the First, and its effects on the political psychology of the Egyptians were analogous. It also provoked a wave of antiforeign nationalism, which tended to assume violent forms as soon as the British began to withdraw their large military contingents. Despite these general similarities between the two postwar situations, there were noteworthy differences. Whereas after World War I the Wafd became the spokesman for Egyptian nationalism, after World War II this role was taken over by other, more extreme groups. This extremism was manifested on both the left and the right wings of the political scale. On the left was the Communist party, which, as a result of Soviet world influence, gained greatly in prestige. Soviet victories during the war and the establishment of a Soviet legation in Cairo in 1942 aroused interest in communism among students and young intellectuals in particular. Financed by Henri Curiel, a bookseller and the son of a well-known Sephardi-Jewish millionaire, the Communist party, though illegal, penetrated into many editorial offices, government bureaus, organizations, and political parties including the Wafd. In the labor sector the Communists concentrated on three textile industrial centers: Mahalla el-Kubra, midway between Cairo and Alexandria; Shubra el-Khayma, on the outskirts of Cairo; and Filature Nationale in Alexandria. There they exploited legitimate labor grievances to foster their aims through strikes and disturbances. They assumed leadership in the Workers' Congress, a body created in 1946, as well as in the Egyptian representation to the leftist World Federation of Trade Unions.[10] Although the party membership probably did not exceed 5,000, the party's influence, especially on the younger intelligentsia, was out of proportion to its actual numbers.

On the right wing of the political scale stood the powerful Moslem Brotherhood (El-Ikhwan el-Muslimin).[11] Organized in 1929 in Ismailia by Sheikh Hassan el-Banna, the pro-Islamic and anti-Western Brotherhood gained a large following at the end of the Second World War, extending its influence even beyond the boundaries of Egypt. Backed by an estimated 500,000 sympathizers, Hassan el-Banna proved to be not only an inspired preacher but also an excellent organizer, who definitely aimed at the assumption of political power in Egypt. Appealing first to underprivileged lower classes, the movement eventually spread to educated classes as well, enlisting the co-operation of some influential leaders. The tactics of Hassan el-Banna were tortuous: in 1942–1944, when Nahas was prime minister, he worked in close association with the Wafd; in 1944 he gave temporary support to the Saadist party; but in 1945 he reverted to an independent course, starting a prolonged campaign of terrorism against all those whom he accused of collaboration with the British. It was rumored that part of his success has been due to subsidies received from King Farouk. The king reportedly favored the Brotherhood as a counterweight to the Wafd.

The anti-Wafd, Saadist-dominated cabinets that governed Egypt from 1944 to 1949 faced a most difficult situation. Opposed by both the Wafd and the extremist groups, they had little appeal for the masses. At the same time they had to curb repeated outbreaks of violence, strikes, and antigovernment or antiforeign demonstrations, and calm down public excitement over the Palestinian issue. The war left a sad heritage of inflation and unbalanced agricultural production, deepened the gap between the fixed-income groups and the profiteers (predominantly Levantines, who made fortunes on contracts with the Allied forces), and caused fantastic fluctuations in the cotton market and—after the withdrawal of foreign armies—large-scale unemployment among workers. Thus, although Egypt did not suffer serious war devastation[12] and even emerged as a creditor with large sterling balances, her financial status—always socially inadequate—was seriously disturbed.

Trying to maintain order, the government took measures first against the Communists. As an alien-inspired group advocating radical revolution, the Communist party became a natural target for government reprisals. In July 1946, following a wave of strikes and demonstrations, the government seized a number of leading Communists; in October and November the Egyptian police and army rounded up many Communist agitators at Fuad and El-Azhar Universities in Cairo and at Farouk University in Alexandria; and in January 1947 the government opened its

---

[10]William J. Handley, "The Labor Movement in Egypt," *Middle East Journal,* 3 (July 1949).

[11]A thorough treatment of this movement may be found in James Heyworth-Dunne, *Religious and Political Trends in Modern Egypt* (Washington, 1950).

[12]Axis bombing of Alexandria and the Suez Canal was negligible.

prosecution case against Curiel and his nineteen associates. The majority of them were given jail sentences.

Governmental action against the Moslem Brotherhood did not follow immediately. There was considerable hesitation as to what course to follow, mixed, no doubt, with thoughts that an alliance with the Brotherhood might be politically valuable. But by late 1948 it became clear that Hassan el-Banna was determined to pursue an independent policy which brooked no compromise. There were a series of terrorist acts, and on December 4, General Salim Zaki Pasha, the Cairo chief of police, was killed by a student during a Brotherhood-inspired demonstration. Four days later the government outlawed the Brotherhood. On December 28, a student member of the Brotherhood assassinated Prime Minister Nokrashi Pasha in the building of the Ministry of Interior. The murder was conceived as a punishment for Nokrashi's anti-Brotherhood reprisals and for his allegedly conciliatory policy toward Britain. The drama reached its climax when, on February 12, 1949, Hassan el-Banna was shot and killed in broad daylight by a group of young men passing in an automobile. The assassins were not discovered, and the government did not seem to show much enthusiasm in pursuing the search. The death of its leader was a severe blow to the Brotherhood, and its activities slowed down perceptibly.

At this juncture King Farouk issued an appeal for national unity and asked the Wafd to enter the government under a neutral leadership. The move was dictated partly by the deteriorating internal situation and partly by the desire to avoid another Wafdist boycott of the elections, which were due in early 1950. The Wafd replied by presenting certain conditions, and in July 1949 a coalition cabinet including several Wafdist ministers was created. The cabinet's life was short, and in November it was replaced by a caretaker preelectoral government of obscure officials.

In the January 1950 elections the Wafd obtained a resounding victory, securing 228 out of 319 seats in the chamber. The outcome was interpreted as a rebuke to the Saadists for their incompetent conduct of the Palestinian war in 1948. Seventy-one-year-old Nahas Pasha again assumed the premiership, and in June 1950 he induced the king to remove seventeen appointed senators and replace them by Wafdist nominees. By this move the Wafd secured an absolute majority in both chambers.

Problem of Treaty Revision

Against this turbulent background Egypt conducted her postwar foreign policies. As usual, Anglo-Egyptian relations dominated. Egypt emerged from the war determined to revise the treaty of 1936. The two points of special grievance were the continuing presence of British troops in Egypt and the problem of Sudan. Egyptians demanded that even the limited British forces allowed by the treaty for the defense of the Canal Zone should be withdrawn. As for the Sudan, Egypt claimed that the condominium was a screen for complete British supremacy, and insisted on the "Unity of the Nile Valley."

The Egyptian claim for reunion with the Sudan was based on historical, ethnic, cultural, economic, and strategic considerations. From the historical point of view,

Egypt had a strong case. So did she when she claimed common ethnic and cultural links with the Sudanese, although these links existed only with northern Sudan. The northern part of this huge territory is inhabited by people with a strong admixture of Arab blood who speak Arabic and are Mohammedan. The southern population is predominantly negroid and pagan and uses various non-Arabic languages. The economic argument ran as follows: The British have harnessed the economy of the Sudan to their own interests. Laying down a fine irrigation network, they have expanded Sudanese cotton plantations, especially in the Gezira province. Sudanese cotton competes with Egyptian cotton on world markets, and the Sudanese economy is competitive instead of complementary to the Egyptian. In regaining control of the Sudan Egypt would relieve her own population pressure (the Egyptian population has increased from around two million in 1800 to nearly twenty million in 1950), would help the Sudan solve her labor shortage, and would encourage the Sudanese to cultivate staple food crops which could be consumed on the spot or exported to Egypt.

The strategic argument was the most important. Egypt maintained that she could never feel completely secure so long as her water supply was controlled by a foreign nation. Egyptian publicists were not slow to quote from various British authors in support of this thesis. They also recalled the British ultimatum of 1924, which had arbitrarily announced an unlimited increase in the Gezira irrigation area as a reprisal for Sir Lee Stack's murder.

Egyptians were also irritated by the way the British handled internal Sudanese politics. There were two major political parties in the Sudan: the Umma (Nationalists) and the Ashigga (Cousins). The Umma, headed by Abdur Rahman Pasha, son of the Mahdi, stood for complete independence and separation from Egypt. Its press indulged in anti-Egyptian propaganda, and in the winter of 1946–1947, Abdur Rahman went to London to plead his party's case. The British quite obviously favored this movement.

The Ashigga party advocated a dual monarchy, which would provide for full Sudanese autonomy under the Egyptian crown. It believed in the unity of the Nile valley as necessary to both nations. Ashigga, supported by the intelligentsia of mixed Sudanese-Egyptian stock and headed by the powerful religious leader, Sheikh Ali el-Marghani Pasha, gained a considerably larger following among the Sudanese masses than did Umma. Egyptians strongly objected to the favoritism shown by the British to Umma and feared that any postponement of the solution in the Sudan would merely give the British more time to spread antiunity propaganda. The dismissal by the British governor-general of the Egyptian chief religious judge from his post in the Sudan in 1947 added considerably to Egyptians' discontent.[13]

Such, then, were the main grievances of Egypt concerning the treaty of 1936. Demands for revision had been made by Nahas Pasha as Wafd leader as early as 1942 and by the Egyptian government, then headed by Ahmed Maher Pasha, in

[13]For two views of the Sundanese problem, see Douglas D. Crary, "Geography and Politics in the Nile Valley," *Middle East Journal,* 3 (July 1949); and Mohamed Awad, "Egypt, Great Britain, and the Sudan: An Egyptian View," *Middle East Journal,* 1 (July 1947).

1945. At both times the British expressed their willingness to discuss revision after the end of the war.

Sidki Pasha, prime minister in 1946, eventually conducted the negotiations with the British government. He had decided against a large multiparty delegation and, after months of preliminary discussions, went to London alone, where, in October 1946, he concluded an agreement with Ernest Bevin, Britain's foreign secretary. The Sidki-Bevin agreement provided for the withdrawal of British forces from the Canal Zone and contained a formula concerning the Sudan. British troop protection for the Zone was to be replaced by definite Anglo-Egyptian defense arrangements which would include maintenance by Egypt of certain workshops and installations ready to be turned over to the British army in case of war. As to the Sudan, the formula adopted was as follows:

> The policy which the high contracting parties undertake to follow in the Sudan within the framework of the unity between the Sudan and Egypt under the common Crown of Egypt will have for its essential objectives to assure the well-being of the Sudanese, the development of their interests, and their active preparation for self-government and consequently the exercise of the right to choose the future status of the Sudan. Until the high contracting parties can in full common agreement realize this latter objective after consulation with the Sudanese, the agreement of 1899 will continue and Article 11 of the treaty of 1936, together with its annex and paragraphs 14 to 16 of the agreed minute annexed to the same treaty, will remain in force not withstanding the first article of the present treaty.[14]

The gist of this formula was that, for the time being, the status quo in the Sudan would continue. When the time was ripe for a change, the Sudanese would decide for themselves what form of government they desired, even if it meant complete separation from Egypt. Such at least was the British interpretation of the agreement. The Egyptians, however, interpreted it differently, believing that the words "within the framework of unity . . . under the common Crown" definitely limited Sudanese freedom of choice. This difference of interpretations led to a protracted exchange of notes, which ended in a deadlock early in 1947. It may be pointed out that the first part of the Bevin-Sidki agreement, concerning the Suez Canal Zone, was quite acceptable to the Egyptians, but they refused to ratify the agreement on account of the Sudanese question.

Egypt's Open Defiance of Britain

In December 1946, Sidki had resigned. His successor, the Saadist leader Nokrashi Pasha, decided to apply double pressure on Great Britain to obtain a solution satisfactory to the Egyptians. It is noteworthy that neither Sidki, and Independent, nor Nokrashi, a Saadist, was an extremist and that, given complete freedom of action, they probably would have agreed to a realistic compromise solution. But the pressure of inflamed public opinion and a wave of anti-British riots made it impossible for any Egyptian statesman publicly to express moderation. If the non-Wafdist coalition which was then in power had succeeded in securing a diplomatic victory

[14]The text is in *Middle East Journal,* 1 (April 1947), p. 207.

over Britain, its popularity would have been greatly increased and it might have wrested the monopoly of mass appeal from the Wafd. Added to this was the feeling that, if ever, this was the time to compel war-weary and empire-losing Britain to grant concessions.

The double pressure, previously referred to, consisted of two specific actions. One was to exploit the growing American interest in the Middle East, as evidenced by the expansion of oil business and air communications in the area, so as to supplant British supremacy by American cooperation. On June 15, 1946, the United States and Egypt had concluded a civilian air pact. In April 1947, the Egyptian chief of staff, General Ibrahim Atallah Pasha, visited the United States to sound out the American government as to its willingness to give advisory and technical assistance to the Egyptian army. At the same time it became known that Egypt was seeking an $88 million loan from the United States. On March 12, 1947, President Truman had pledged American assistance to Greece and Turkey in view of the inability of weakened Britain to continue her burdens in those countries, and in May an American fleet composed of the aircraft carrier *Leyte* and three other warships paid a courtesy call in Alexandria. Both actions were indicative of definite American interest in the security of the eastern Mediterranean. Consequently, Egyptians hoped that by skillful manipulation they might induce the United States to show more interest in Egypt and thus render the Anglo-Egyptian defense arrangements unnecessary. In September 1947, Premier Nokrashi went in person to Washington to invite the United States to send a military mission to Egypt in order to fill the gap created by the withdrawal of the British mission. He met with poor success. The American government refused to compete with Britain in what was believed to be a British preserve. It was reluctant, moreover, to create a precedent which might affect its own position in Panama.[15]

Another method of pressure was to bring the Anglo-Egyptian dispute to the attention of the United Nations. On July 8, 1947, Nokrashi Pasha accused Great Britain before the Security Council on two counts: (1) Britain was guilty of maintaining her troops in Egyptian territory against the will of the people. The presence of these troops, Nokrashi asserted, offended the dignity of Egypt, hindered her normal development, infringed upon the fundamental principle of sovereign equality, and therefore, violated the United Nations Charter. (2) Britain's occupation of the Nile valley and the pursuance of a hostile policy in the Sudan had given rise to a dispute, the continuance of which was likely to endanger international peace and the security.

For these reasons Egypt was compelled, according to Nokrashi, to request the Security Council to direct the total and immediate evacuation of British troops from Egypt, including the Sudan, and the termination of the administrative regime in the latter area. Britain's reply was that the treaty of 1936 was still valid and that there was no evidence of a threat to international peace. There the matter rested, neither country receiving definite majority support. An American motion (which failed of

---

[15] Halford L. Hoskins, "The Guardianship of the Suez Canal," *Middle East Journal,* 4 (April 1950), p. 143.

acceptance) that both parties should be directed to reopen negotiations met with resentment in Egypt. In the meantime the British, anxious to observe the treaty scrupulously, evacuated their forces from Kom el-Dik citadel in Alexandria and liquidated their naval base there. In March the last British troops left the famous Kasr el-Nil barracks in Cairo. A new headquarters was established in Fayid, in the Canal Zone.

As an eminent French writer, Paul Morand, once wrote, England and Egypt are like an old married couple: they may quarrel, but they never break their bond. This adage seemed to be proved when Egypt became involved, in 1948, in the Palestinian war. Mass feeling reached a high pitch in the delta of the Nile. Thousands of men volunteered for military service, the regular army was sent to southern Palestine, and Hassan el-Banna's desperadoes simultaneously invaded Israel in guerrilla bands. Jewish residents of Egypt, a wealthy and generally loyal community, were attacked, their property damaged, and their status endangered. What mattered, however, was the shocking exposure of the weakness of the Egyptian state. Egypt, a country of twenty million inhabitants, could send only a small and totally inadequate army to Palestine. This army, after reaching Hebron in the east and the outskirts of Jaffa in the west, suffered severe defeats and barely managed to retain a narrow Gaza strip and a small bulge around Auja on the Negeb-Egyptian border. Jewish units went so far as to make an incursion into purely Egyptian territory toward El-Arish in Sinai. At this moment the British government intervened, warning Israel that any invasion of Egypt might compel it to abide by the treaty of 1936 and take appropriate measures for the defense of Egypt. This desire to stress the validity of the treaty led Great Britain, as soon as she was free from limitations imposed by the Palestinian truce agreements, to renew shipments of arms to Egypt.

The subsiding of the Palestinian furor and the return of the Wafd to power in 1950 resulted in a reopening of the negotiations for treaty revision. Talks to this effect between the two governments began in the winter of 1950-1951, but there was little likelihood of a successful conclusion. In the first place, the Palestinian issue produced a kind of permanent tension between Britain and Egypt, which was not alleviated by Britain's desire to appear pro-Arab or at least neutral. Egypt, more humiliated than any other Arab country by the outcome of the war, was determined to prevent any oil-carrying tankers from reaching Israel, and for this reason imposed irksome restrictions upon maritime traffic in the Suez Canal.[16] In the second place, the British, who were willing to give up their installations in the canal zone in 1946 (a year of high hopes for peaceful cooperation between Russia and the West), were definitely reluctant to abandon them in 1950.

In British opinion it would have been suicidal to withdraw from Egypt when Russia threatened with invasion the whole European and Asiatic area south of her borders. It was realized, not only in London but also in Washington, that effectively to defend Greece and Turkey, Iraq and Iran, the Western democracies must possess an adequate base in the Middle Eastern hinterland, and Egypt was believed to be the

---

[16]These restrictions led Israel, in midsummer 1951, to bring the case to the United Nations. For details, see below, pp. 712-713.

only one available. Apart from her strategic position as a link between the Indian Ocean and the Mediterranean, Egypt was the only country in the Middle East possessing adequate technical facilities (stores, workshops, harbors, aerodromes, and factories) and an ample labor force and food supply so that she could be easily converted into a powerful military base. In this respect the experience of both World Wars could not be overlooked. Thus the problem of British withdrawal transcended the narrow limits of Anglo-Egyptian relations and became a truly international problem with the United States and its North Atlantic allies having a vital stake in the solution.

Under the circumstances it was, indeed, hard to see how a compromise could be reached. Egypt continued to insist on total British evacuation. This anti-British mood was a manifestation of a general anti-Western trend in Egyptian foreign and domestic policies, a trend that became obvious after the Palestinian war. Because of its pro-Israeli policy the United States became, for the first time in Egyptian history, a target of voluble criticism and denunciation.

On the outbreak of war in Korea the Egyptian government declared that it would not support the United Nations effort and would not send troops to Korea. On July 21, 1950, Egyptian Foreign Minister Saleh ed-Din Bey told a press conference that Egypt was maintaining neutrality in the conflict. His statement was corroborated on April 14, 1951, by Abdul Salam Fahmi Gamaa Pasha, president of the Chamber of Deputies and one of the leading Wafdists, who declared that in case of a general war Egypt would be neutral and at the proper time would simply abrogate her 1936 treaty with Britain.[17] These statements could not be interpreted as evidence of any agreement between Cairo and Moscow, and only a few observers were inclined to deduce from such acts as the Egyptian-Soviet trade agreements of February 1948 and July 1951 that Egypt was about to slip into the Soviet orbit. Yet there is no doubt that Egypt's neutral orientation was inconvenient to the West at a time when the West was trying hard to organize the defenses of the Free World against Soviet imperialism.

Egypt's anti-British campaign, intensified by the repercussions of the Anglo-Iranian crisis, reached its peak when, on October 8, 1951, Premier Mustafa Nahas Pasha presented to the parliament a series of decrees unilaterally abrogating the 1936 Anglo-Egyptian treaty, providing for the eviction of British troops from the Canal Zone, reuniting the Sudan with Egypt, and proclaiming Farouk "King of Egypt and the Sudan." On October 15 these decrees were unanimously approved by the parliament. A wave of anti-British riots, following these decisions, failed to induce the British to leave the Canal Zone. Britain declared Egypt's step illegal and reinforced her garrison in the Canal Zone, determined not to bend to intimidation. At the same time (October 13) in an effort to break the deadlock, the governments of the United States, Great Britain, France, and Turkey submitted to Egypt a long-

[17]See the *New York Times,* April 15, 1951. Paradoxically enough, the Egyptian navy was at the same time carrying out joint maneuvers with the British Mediterranean fleet, "to gain experience," as was explained in official Egyptian quarters.

contemplated proposal to establish an Allied Middle East Command to assure the defense of Egypt and the adjacent area. Egypt was invited to participate on a basis of equality in the proposed Command, with the understanding that the British garrison in the Canal Zone would be replaced by an allied force composed of troops of the participating nations. On October 15 the Egyptian government rejected these proposals. Two days later United States Secretary of State Dean Acheson publicly declared full American support of Britain's position and condemned Egypt's disregard of international obligations. In the ensuing few weeks it became known that proposals to join in a Middle Eastern defense pact were addressed to other Arab states and Israel as well and that the Western powers intended to go ahead with their plans even if the Arab states failed to respond favorably to these proposals.

Egypt's Middle Eastern Policy

Egypt's Middle Eastern policy revolved around the fact that she was the most advanced and richest of the Arab states. Her statesmen played a leading part in the formation of the Arab League, whose pact was signed on Egyptian soil in 1945. An Egyptian, Abdur Rahman Azzam Pasha, became secretary general of the League. Many observers felt that Egypt was trying to use the League as an instrument of her own policy and that Azzam Pasha mainly served Egyptian interests.

Owing, among other things, to the existence of El-Azhar University, the highest seat of Moslem learning, Egypt has always aspired to spiritual and political leadership in the Arab world. One of King Farouk's tutors and closest advisers had been Sheikh El-Maraghi, president of El-Azhar, and it was known that Farouk, in contrast to Mustafa Kemal of Turkey, believed in stressing Egypt's Arab and Mohammedan character as well as her links to the past. Cherishing the role of protector of the Arabs, King Farouk extended his hospitality in postwar years to such rebellious Arab leaders as Haj Amin el-Husseini, the mufti of Jerusalem; Abdul Krim, leader of the Riff tribes in Morocco; and Fawzi el-Kawukji, Syrian independence fighter.

Jealous of her leading position among the Arab states, Egypt had consistently opposed the Greater Syria scheme as likely to create a rival center of power and influence. This opposition led to political friendship with Ibn Saud of Arabia, whose fear of the Hashemi house of Iraq and Jordan made him cooperate with Egypt. In pursuance of this policy Egypt courted the short-lived dictator of Syria, Husni Zaim, in 1949.

In the spring of 1951, Egypt endeavored to bring about the conclusion of a regional Middle East defense pact that would include Turkey in addition to the Arab states. League Secretary General Azzam Pasha visited Ankara in June 1951 to sound out official Turkish opinion. Egypt's idea was to create a neutral Middle Eastern bloc, predominantly Arab, but strengthened by the inclusion of Turkey. Although no details of these talks were revealed, it was certain that such proposals could not evoke enthusiasm in Ankara because at that very time Turkey was working hard to gain admission to the North Atlantic Treaty Organization. Azzam's visit did not result in any agreements or declarations and, consequently, its results could be considered as negative. Turkey's reluctance to join the Arab bloc did not stem from the lack of interest in the regional security of the Middle East. Turkey favored regional defense arrangements and she proved it by cosponsoring, four months later, a joint Western proposal to establish a Middle East Command, to which we have referred earlier. But whe was unwilling to compromise her status as a pro-Western state by adhering to a bloc dominated by a neutralist and largely anti-Western Egypt.

Prelude to Revolution: The Cairo Riots

The excitement produced by the denunciation of the Anglo-Egyptian Treaty led to an ever-increasing number of incidents between the British forces and the Egyptians in the canal zone. British troops, collectively and individually, became a favorite target of sniping, assaults, and sometimes, attacks by guerrillas organized for that purpose by the Socialist party[18] or other extreme groups. The British countered with a policy of reprisals, which only increased the tension. On January 19, 1952, Ismailia, an important town and base on the canal, became the scene of mass fighting, which ended six days later in British occupation of the town. The Egyptian auxiliary police (Buluk Nizam) were evicted from their barracks, and sixty-four lost their lives in the course of the battle.

The Ismailia incident inspired major riots in Cairo the following day, January 26. The mobs, instigated partly by Ahmed Hussein's Socialist party and partly by the Communists, attacked and put to fire seven hundred commercial, social, and cultural establishments, mostly foreign-owned but including also a number of Egyptian-owned firms and institutions. Such well-known landmarks as the Shepheard Hotel, Barclay's Bank, the Turf Club, Groppi restaurants, and the Cicurel and Chemla departments stores were either partly or totally destroyed with attendant loss of life. The toll was 552 wounded and 26 killed after a day of rioting. The attitude of the Wafdist-controlled government during this display of violence was enigmatic. For the greater part of the day the police did not intervene to any appreciable degree, letting the rioters have their way. Only toward the close of the day did the army appear on the scene—at a time when the energy of the mobs was waning.

This was, indeed, a black day in Cairo, not only for the British and other foreigners, but for all Egyptians who had a stake in the preservation of order and authority. Foremost among the latter was none other than King Farouk himself. Traditionally hostile to the Wafd, he seized this opportunity summarily to dismiss Nahas Pasha and his cabinet on January 27 and to appoint in his place a veteran statesman, Ali Maher Pasha. The subsequent six months saw considerable turbulence, and the Palace-appointed anti-Wafdist cabinets[19] had to face either a hostile Wafd-dominated parliament or, after its dissolution on March 29, a dangerous political vacuum.

---

[18]The formerly fascist Young Egypt organization (also known as Green Shirts) founded in 1933 by Ahmed Hussein, a lawyer. In 1940, the group changed its name to the Nationalist Islamic Party, and finally after the war it adopted the name Socialist.

[19]Of Ali Maher (Jan. 27–March 1); of Naguib el-Hilali (March 1–June 28); of Hussein Sirri (July 2–20); and of Naguib el-Hilali (July 22–23).

The July Revolution

This vacuum was abruptly filled by a dynamic new force when at the dawn of July 23 a "Committee of Free Officers," a secret group formed in 1947, overthrew the government. A Revolutionary Command Council, composed of eleven young officers, assumed supreme authority in the country. The ostensible leader, Major-General Mohammed Naguib, became commander-in-chief of the armed forces, while Ali Maher Pasha was made premier. On July 26, Naguib handed to King Farouk an ultimatum to renounce the throne and leave the country forthwith. Farouk signed an act of abdication in favor of his infant son Ahmed Fuad II and on the same day left Egypt for Italy. On August 2 a Regency Council was formed. It consisted of three men: Prince Mohammed Abdul Moneim, Bahieddin Barakat, and Lieutenant-Colonel Mohammed Rashad Mehanna, the latter representing the Revolutionary Command Council (R.C.C.).

In the proclamations and statements that followed General Naguib and his fellow officers made it known that in effecting this revolution they were animated by the unselfish desire to see Egypt emancipated from imperialism and feudalism and served by an honest government that would ensure social justice, economic progress, and dignity to all citizens of the country. They emphasized the middle-class composition of their council and in their actions laid stress on rapid and radical reform. Their government, they claimed, was the first in the long history of Egypt to serve the people rather than foreign or dynastic interests.

In conformity with these utterances the military junta launched a number of reforms which, if fully implemented, were indeed likely to bring about considerable improvement in Egypt. Within a few weeks after the coup the R.C.C. abolished honorary and hereditary titles and created purge commissions in government departments. On September 8, 1952—a memorable date in the annals of the revolution—it issued a decree on agrarian reform which limited individual holdings to a maximum of 200 feddans (about 208 acres) and provided for the distribution of surplus properties to needy peasants. This was followed by the abolition of family trust estates (*ahli waqfs*), the floating of a £ E 200 million loan to finance land reform, the passing of three labor laws, and the inauguration of studies to increase the cultivable area of land in Egypt. The latter point claimed special attention by the R.C.C., which concentrated on two specific projects. The first, launched in 1953, embraced ambitious irrigation, reclamation, and development schemes in a hitherto neglected areas in the western part of the Delta, since called the Liberation (Tahrir) province. The second was the study and planning of a new high dam south of Aswan, which might add some two million feddans to the cultivable area, thus increasing it by about 30 per cent. In its solicitude for industrialization the new regime passed a notable degree on July 30, 1952, amending the company law of 1947 to permit foreigners to own 51 instead of 49 percent of the stock of corporations. This decree was followed by another, more comprehensive, on April 1, 1953, which in a number of ways encouraged the investment of foreign capital in business enterprises in Egypt.

These steps represented what one might call constructive reform. But, as with any revolution, this one had its repressive side as well. The latter was expressed by a number of measures designed to punish abuses committed by former rulers, to discredit them in the eyes of the public, and to eradicate all traces of their influence in the administration and public life of Egypt. For the purpose of accomplishing these objectives the R.C.C. instituted two special kinds of courts: the graft courts to deal with cases of corruption (December 1952) and the Treason Court (*Mahkamat el-Ghadr;* later renamed Tribunal of the Revolution) to deal with major crimes against the state (January 1953).

With regard to the legal framework of its existence the new regime was more effective in destroying the old forms than in creating new ones. On December 10, 1952, the R.C.C. abrogated the 1923 constitution, and on January 12, 1953, it appointed a fifty-man committee to redraft the constitution. Four days later, following the discovery of a plot against the regime, all political parties were dissolved and their funds confiscated. Their place was henceforth to be filled by the Liberation Movement, a body launched during the mass rallies held on January 23 in commemoration of the first six months of the revolution. At the same time the R.C.C. announced a three-year transitional period within which a "healthy democratic and constitutional regime" would be formed. February 10 saw the promulgation of a provisional constitution of eleven articles, which enunciated the principles of government to apply during the period of transition. The gist of this document was expressed in Article 8, which said: "The Leader of the Revolution, presiding over the Revolutionary Command Council, shall assume full sovereign powers, particularly in regard to measures deemed necessary to protect the Revolution, the system on which it is based to achieve its objectives, as well as the right to appoint and dismiss Ministers." Article 9 declared that "the Council of Ministers shall exercise legislative powers," and Article 11 provided for a "Congress," to be composed of the R.C.C. and the Council of Ministers, the role of which would be to "consider the general policy of the State and subjects connected with it."

In the next three years the new government made several announcements of an impending restoration of the constitutional regime, committing itself, in some cases, to a definite date. These promises were not kept, usually because of some internal emergency that made their fulfillment impracticable. Ultimately, on January 16, 1956, exactly three years after the proclamation of the transitional period, a new constitution was announced. It was subject to approval by a plebiscite scheduled to take place on June 23, 1956, on the fourth anniversary of the revolution. The new constitution provided for the election of a National Assembly, the members of which would be nominated by a single party, "the National Union." It also proclaimed Egypt to be an Islamic, Arab state under a republican and democratic form of government headed by a president whose term of office would be six years. Among the more significant provisions was the one which provided for a referendum, at the discretion of the president, on any "major issues bearing on the country's higher interests."[20]

Basically, this document, as is often the case under similar circumstances, intro-

[20]Art. 145. The text is in *Middle Eastern Affairs,* Feb. 1956.

duced little new beyond confirming the existing pattern of power in Egypt. All authority centered in the Revolutionary Command Council, which in its first three years managed to eliminate its political rivals and adversaries. The latter were numerous and rather formidable. In the first place, a "grand old party" such as the Wafd could not be expected to give up without a struggle. Fortunately for the R.C.C., the Wafd was headed by a septuagenarian, Nahas Pasha, whose vigor was declining, and its master brain, Fuad Serag ed-Din, had been subjected to violent criticism and considerably discredited before the coup of 1952, partly as a result of his responsibility for the Cairo riots of January 26. Furthermore, long years of corruption were not conducive to the breeding of heroes among the Wafdist rank and file. Consequently, when the test of strength came, especially in the first six months of the revolutionary era, the Wafd did not dare to resist the military junta openly. Other parties presented a less difficult problem. Owing their origin, for the most part, to personal rivalries or palace intrigue, they lost their ground as organized forces with the passing of the monarchy. The revolutionary government did not differentiate to any appreciable degree between them and the Wafd, considering both as representative of the old regime and applying equally stern measures to those of their leaders whom it deemed guilty of graft or treason.

No less severe was the policy of the R.C.C. toward the Communists and Ahmed Hussein's Socialists. Both movements were banned and, inasmuch as the junta operated with the double weapon of police repression and revolutionary propaganda, it succeded in dealing a powerful blow to these extremist forces.

Ultimately the Moslem Brotherhood remained as the only major organized group with which the R.C.C. had to contend. The latter was very dangerous as an adversary because it had an effective organization, possessed a persuasive ideology, and had a tradition of resistance to the old regime. In fact, in the initial period of the revolution mutual toleration if not friendship prevailed between the R.C.C. and the Brotherhood. Because it could claim that it was not a political party, the latter escaped dissolution and continued its activities long after the other parties were legislated out of existence. But in the long run the political objectives and ideology of the two movements were incompatible. Preaching the need for an Islamic state based on the Koran as the only source of law, the Brotherhood clearly aspired for power. The "Free Officers" did not intend to abdicate authority and refused to accept the idea of a theocratic state as a guiding principle. As early as November 1952, Mohammed Naguib, while visiting El-Azhar University, said that the army movement was based on "religion, union, and order" but warned that "those who speak of the religious government have but one aim—to divide the nation."[21] The proclamation of the republic at the historical meeting of June 18, 1953, which was attended by two members of the Brotherhood, was the last occasion for cooperation between the junta and the Brotherhood. From that time on the two movements diverged until in January 1954 the R.C.C. finally turned against the Brotherhood on the ground that its character was that of a political party and not a religious association. In the course of the month 450 Brethren were put under arrest, including

[21]*Cahiers*, 1952, 2.

Hassan Hodeibi, their "Supreme Guide," and six out of fourteen members of their Central Committee. Explaining this radical measure to a press correspondent, Colonel Anwar el-Sadat, a member of the R.C.C. in charge of Islamic affairs, declared:

> Immediately after the revolution, Sheikh Hassan el-Hodeibi demanded that the Koranic law be applied in all its severity, i.e., that the thief have his hand cut off, that the cinema be forbidden, that the banks be closed to prevent lending at an interest, and that foreign companies be expelled. This gives you an idea of the mentality and logic of the Supreme Guide of Moslem Brethren.... We have tried in vain to convince the Sheikh that the struggle against feudalism, injustice, misery, and British imperialism was inspired by the very essence of the *sharia* and of all the divine laws.[22]

Lieutenant-Colonel Gamal Abdul Nasser, a leading member of the Council, added in another interview:

> The Moslem Brotherhood has finished by installing a state within the state. Their chief, Hodeibi, who has not shunned collaboration with Farouk, wanted to take the Koran as the sole rule of behavior. So far as I am concerned, I have not yet understood how one can govern according to the Koran only. One may draw from it all sorts of interpretations, and mine at any rate is not that of those fanatics.[23]

The doom of the Brotherhood was not decreed, however, until the end of 1954. The immediate causes of the final stern action by the R.C.C. were the campaign of criticism that the Brotherhood had launched against the ruling group after the conclusion of a new treaty with Britain (of which more later) and the attempt on the life of Colonel Abdul Nasser, by then premier of Egypt, which had taken place on October 26. This time the Brotherhood was not only outlawed but its leaders were indicted on charges of conspiracy and treason. The sensational trial revealed the existence of the Brotherhood's military arm, whose task was to seize power in the state by terrorism and assassinations. The verdicts of the revolutionary tribunal included a number of death sentences and long prison terms. Moslem Brethren thus became the first victims of the hitherto bloodless revolution.

The R.C.C., however, stressed the fact that, far from being atheistic, it cherished and protected religion as such. Its leading members frequently displayed their piety by attending Friday prayers and performing the *hajj* to Mecca. In November 1954 the R.C.C. obtained a public condemnation of the Brotherhood's terrorism by the ulema of El-Azhar. And, finally, R.C.C.'s fast-traveling Colonel Anwar el-Sadat did major work in promoting an Islamic conference that met in Mecca in 1955 and became thereafter a permanent organization, with Sadat himself as its secretary-general.[24]

---

[22]Ibid., 1954, 1.

[23]*L'Orient* (Beirut), Jan. 31, 1954.

[24]The new regime emphasized religious tolerance and during General Naguib's leadership gave considerable publicity to the good-will visits paid by him to the religious heads of Christian and Jewish communities in Egypt. The regime's basic objective seemed to be the elimination of undue influence by Islam upon Egypt's public life. A major step in this direction was the decree of September 24, 1955, abolishing, as of January 1, 1956, the entire system of Sharia and non-Moslem religious courts.

The destruction of the Brotherhood put an end to the process of eliminating the junta's organized rivals and left it as sole arbiter of Egypt's destiny. Yet even the strongest government cannot operate in a vacuum, and it is legitimate to ask whether, apart from the army, the R.C.C. had any social support and, if so, among what groups. It is difficult to give a simple answer to this question inasmuch as the situation in Egypt, ever since July 1952, had been undergoing a rapid evolution. In the beginning the officers' movement enjoyed great popularity among both the urban and the rural masses in Egypt. The sincerity of its leaders, the charismatic qualities of a fatherly and benevolent Mohammed Naguib (son of a mixed Egyptian-Sudanese marriage), and the deep urge for change in the country as a whole combined to produce enthusiasm sometimes bordering on frenzy among the emotionally starved multitudes of Egypt. In those early days certain moderate statesmen of the prerevolutionary period (such as the generally respected Ali Maher) went along with younger intellectuals, students, and trade unionists in giving the benefit of the doubt to the R.C.C. As time went on, the enthusiasm of the masses began to abate and the inevitable restrictions on civil freedoms and economic activity gradually estranged the new rulers from the liberal-minded intelligentsia. In the beginning the R.C.C. was content to leave the cabinet posts to civilians while reserving for itself the role of a sort Politbureau, the task of which was to guide and supervise the cabinet's activity. Later civilians began to replaced by members of the R.C.C., who thus assumed the dual role of policy makers and head executives. This gradual elimination of civilians at the highest level marked a trend toward complete monopoly of power by the military.

Simultaneously, the R.C.C. underwent a number of internal readjustments, some of a very dramatic character. As was later revealed, General Naguib had not belonged to the original group of officers. He was merely "adopted" to serve as a front for the men of the R.C.C., who were both younger and more radical than he. The real leader of the movement from its very inception, Lieutenant-Colonel Gamal Abdul Nasser, resented the gradual usurpation of power by Naguib. In the ensuing contest Nasser emerged victorious, having shorn Naguib of power in three successive stages. In the first stage (February 25–March 8, 1954) the R.C.C. deprived Naguib of all his functions but, following popular demonstrations and near mutiny of the cavalry corps in his favor, reinstated him in all three of the highest positions in the state (see p. 522). In the second stage (April 18–May 31) Nasser replaced Naguib as prime minister and president of the R.C.C., leaving him in the rather nominal position of president of the Republic. In the third stage (November 14) the R.C.C. deprived Naguib of the presidency and, accusing him of complicity with certain enemies of the revolution, placed him under virtual house arrest. The presidency remained vacant, with Nasser becoming its most likely incumbent once the new constitution began to operate.

In addition to this major shift, the R.C.C. experienced a few other disaffections within its midst, most notable of which were the attempted usurpation of power by Colonel Rashad Mehanna (representing the artillery and one of the three regents for Ahmed Fuad II) in January 1953 and the above-mentioned near mutiny of the cavalry led by Major Khalid Muhi ed-Din. Both Mehanna and Muhi ed-Din were removed from the Council, the first receiving a prison term, the second being sent on a mission abroad. Similarly, after a stormy career Major Saleh Salem, minister of guidance and Sudan affairs, incurred the displeasure of the R.C.C. toward the end of 1955. He was removed from both his cabinet and his Council position.

The New Regime's Foreign Policy

In foreign policy the new government could boast of a number of achievements. Although it inherited from the previous regime two major unsettled issues—those of Suez and the Sudan—it succeeded in resolving them within two years after its advent to power. It will be recalled that Britain and Egypt had reached agreement on the canal question in 1947 but they failed to find a formula for the Sudan, as a result of which both problems were left unsolved. After the July revolution the process was reversed: the parties managed to solve the Sudan tangle considerably in advance of their final agreement on the canal. That this was so was due, in the main, to the willingness of the new Egyptian rulers to compromise. Instead of blindly insisting on the "Nile Valley Unity" formula, they agreed to a second-best solution, which consisted in giving the Sudan the right to decide whether it desired union with Egypt or independence. According to the agreement signed with Britain on February 12, 1953, the Sudan was to pass through a transitional period of three years, during which it would develop institutions of self-government preparatory to its final emancipation. At the close of this period the Anglo-Egyptian occupation would end, and the Sudanese Constituent Assembly would decide the fate of the nation. In agreeing to this formula the Egyptians believed that the Sudanese would ultimately choose union in view of the strong position of those elements in the Sudan that favored amalgamation with Egypt. Their optimism seemed to be vindicated when, in the first elections in Sudan's history, the National Unionist party (pro-Egyptian) scored a signal victory over its opponents, securing fifty out of ninety-seven seats in the Constituent Assembly.[25] Both before and after the elections Egyptian propaganda pervaded the Sudan, Egypt's position being enhanced by the popularity of General Naguib among the Sudanese. With the passage of time the Unionist-dominated government of Ismail el-Azhari began to veer from the formula of union toward that of independence. Heroic efforts on the part of Major Saleh Salem, Egypt's minister of Sudanese affairs, to instill prounion sentiment in the Sudan began to meet with increasing failure. Salem's aggressive zeal clashed with Azhari's second thoughts on the benefits of the union. By the summer of 1955 relations between Khartum and Cairo had deteriorated to the point of a personal quarrel between Azhari and Salem, and the likelihood of union appeared remote. It seemed to be buried for the forseeable future, when, in a unilateral move, the Sudanese Chamber proclaimed independence on December 19, 1955. Egypt and Britain, also the Soviet Union and the United States, promptly recognized this decision.

The Suez Canal base was the next point at issue in Anglo-Egyptian relations. Following long and frequently interrupted negotiations, the "Heads of Agreement"

[25]The elections were held on November 25, 1953. The returns were as follows: National-Unionist Party, 50; El-Umma (a party advocating separation from Egypt), 28; Independents, 11; Party of the South, 9; Republican-Socialist Party, 3; Anti-Imperialist Front, 1; total 97.

were signed on July 27, 1954, followed by the conclusion of a final Agreement on October 19. The new pact provided for the abrogation of the Anglo-Egyptian Treaty of 1936, evacuation of British troops within twenty months from the date of signiture, continuous maintenance of the Canal base by British civilian technicians under the sovereign control of Egypt, and Britain's right to reenter Egyptian territory "in the event of an armed attack by an outside power on Egypt or any country which at the date of signature of the present agreement [is] a party to the treaty of joint defense between Arab League states[26] on on Turkey." The Convention of 1888 guaranteeing freedom of navigation in the canal was reaffirmed along with recognition that the canal was "an integral part of Egypt." Valid for seven years, this agreement was accompanied by two annexes and seventeen exchanges of notes elaborating the details.[27]

By concluding this agreement Colonel Nasser's government achieved a notable diplomatic success. Yet this was not victory pure and simple inasmuch as (1) Egypt allowed the reentry of British troops within a specified period and (2) she linked her security to that of Turkey and thus, however indirectly, became involved with Western strategy. On the other hand, she made sure that any outbreak of hostilities between herself and Israel (which was not an "outside power") would not serve as a pretext for Britain's return to the base.

The Agreement had, moreover, international significance transcending the limits of Anglo-Egyptian relations. It removed an important stumbling block in the way of possible Egyptian-Western cooperation and made Egypt more eligible than before for American economic and military assistance. The optimism prevailing in Washington and London after the conclusion of the "Heads of Agreement" was strengthened when in policy statements on August 13 and September 2, Colonel Nasser declared that Egypt was basically inclined toward the West and that Russia and communism represented the only conceivable danger to Egypt's security. Both statements, however, made a serious plea that the West postpone the negotiation of any regional security pacts in the Middle East. "It is only by a period of complete independence during which mutual trust is built up between Egypt and the Western powers that Egyptians will be able to look without suspicion on any closer ties between this country and other powers," said the statement of September 2. "Cooperation based on trust and friendship, even though it is not specified by any written agreement, is better than a treaty that is regarded suspiciously by the average Egyptian." "Left alone, the Arabs will naturally turn toward the West to ask it for arms and assistance," added the statement.[28]

These friendly warnings were not, however, heeded by the West, anxious as it was to promote regional security schemes. By the end of 1954, Egypt's relations with the Western powers had suffered marked deterioration, principally on account of the impending conclusion of the Baghdad Pact. Though enjoying dictatorial powers, Gamal Abdul Nasser and his associates could not safely disregard public

---

[26]Egypt, Syria, Lebanon, Saudi Arabia, Yemen, Jordan, Iraq, Libya. The text of the Arab Defense Pact is in the *Middle East Journal,* 6 (Spring 1952).

[27]The text is in *Middle Eastern Affairs,* Nov. 1954.

[28]Compiled from the *New York Times,* Sept. 3, 1954, and *Cahiers,* 1954, 2.

opinion, which was so opposed to any "foreign pacts" as to question the wisdom of the recent Anglo-Egyptian agreement. Consequently, if only for the sake of his position at home, Nasser emerged as the principal champion of a "no pacts" policy on behalf of the Arabs, leading a frontal attack on Iraq for betraying Arab solidarity and linking her fate with that of Turkey and the West. The Egyptian premier gave forceful expression to these views at the Arab League meetings in December 1954 and January 1955, the latter actually convoked at his request to consider the Turko-Iraqi alliance. He and his delegation also stood in the forefront of the neutralist group that dominated the proceedings of the Bandung conference of Asian and African nations in April 1955. His policy of ever-increasing opposition to Western security projects led him eventually to conclude two important military agreements, one with Saudi Arabia (October 27, 1955) and another with Syria (October 20, 1955), each of which placed the signatories' armed forces under a joint command headed by Egyptian generals.[29]

Egyptian-Israeli hostility was the most important factor vitiating the chances of improving Cairo's relations with the West. After a strong and successful Israeli attack on Egyptian positions at Gaza on February 28, 1955, Egypt began paying closer attention to her military preparedness even, as Nasser admitted later, at the expense of domestic reform. The premier endeavored to purchase arms from Britain and the United States in the summer of 1955. Meeting with a virtual refusal, he turned toward the Soviet bloc and in September 1955 concluded a barter deal with Communist Czechoslovakia whereby Egyptian cotton was to be exchanged for an undisclosed quantity of heavy military equipment and munitions.

This sensational transaction, symptomatic as it was of the worsening of Arab-Western relations, led the American government to send to Cairo forthwith George V. Allen, assistant secretary of state in charge of Middle Eastern affairs, on a fact-finding and good-will mission. Whatever arguments Allen was authorized to use did not prevent the Egyptian premier from consummating his deal with the Czechs and receiving, shortly afterward, Soviet jet bombers, tanks and submarines.

The Aswan Dam and the Suez Crisis

One of the most cherished objectives of the Cairo revolutionary regime had been the construction of a new high dam above Aswan near the Sudanese border. Such a dam would harness enough Nile water to provide the delta with all the electric power it needs and increase the cultivable area of Egypt by some two million acres, representing roughly 30 percent of the existing cultivated land. Its cost had been estimated at $1350 million, a staggering sum by Egyptian standards and one that would necessitate outside assistance. Furthermore, the dam would create a 60-mile-long artificial lake, largely in Sudanese territory, resulting in the displacement of some 60,000 Sudanese farmers. Its construction would therefore call for prior agreement with Sudan, a country as dependent on the Nile as is Egypt.

Egypt's interest in the dam gained momentum in the fall of 1955, following the conclusion of the arms deal with the Soviets. In October of that year Moscow expressed a readiness seriously to consider coming to the aid of Egypt in this

---

[29]The texts are in the *Middle East Journal,* vol. 10, no. 1, Winter, 1956.

connection—a fact which undoubtedly helped precipitate the Western decision to make offers to Egypt. On December 16, 1955, the United States declared its willingness to lend Egypt $56 million for the first stage of the Aswan Dam. Britain followed suit with an offer of $14 million, to be released from the blocked sterling accounts, and the World Bank with $200 million.[30] These offers were made with an understanding that "counterpart" funds would be laid aside for construction by Egypt herself. Further conditions of Western aid included Egypt's granting priority to this project over other schemes and nonacceptance of Soviet aid.

Unhappy about these strings and in a generally sulky mood toward the West following the Cairo-Moscow arms deal, Nasser delayed his acceptance, no doubt in the expectation that a more concrete Soviet offer might come forth. In the meantime the controlled Egyptian press carried a vituperative campaign against the United States and the West for their sponsorship of the Baghdad Pact, their interference with the sovereign right of Egypt to buy arms where she pleases, their partiality to Israel, and their alleged overall hostility to Arab national aspirations. As if to accentuate its defiant attitude, the Cairo regime extended recognition to Communist China on May 16, 1956. At the same time Egyptian newspapers repeatedly hinted that a Soviet aid offer was in the making. Yet in spite of Soviet Foreign Minister Shepilov's visit to Cairo in June 1956 (to attend celebrations on the occasion of the final evacuation of British troops under the 1954 agreement), the expected Soviet offer did not materialize. Consequently, in mid-July Nasser instructed his ambassador to Washington to accept the American offer. This decision was made public by the ambassador on July 17, when he arrived in Washington from Cairo. With dismay and shock he learned from Secretary Dulles on July 19 that the American offer had been withdrawn. The official explanation of the American decision was that (1) Egypt had failed to reach a Nile water agreement with Sudan and (2) Egypt's ability to devote adequate resources to the project had become more uncertain "than at the time the offer was made." In reality Egypt was rebuffed for a number of reasons such as opposition by southern senators fearful of the competition of Egyptian cotton should the dam be constructed and by a few western senators anxious to secure funds for similar projects in their own states; the general criticism in the Senate of foreign aid programs, especially if given to neutralist countries; and, above all, Dulles' resolve to call the Soviet bluff on this particular issue and to teach Nasser, whose fresh recognition of Red China still rankled, that sustained hostility toward the West did not pay.

Nasser's reaction to the news was both sudden and violent. Angry at what he called an insult to Egypt's dignity, on July 26, 1956, he issued a decree nationalizing the Suez Canal Company. The latter's shareholders were to be compensated, the revenues from the canal were to be used for the Aswan Dam project, and navigation in the canal was to be unaffected by the new measure. We will leave a full discussion of the legal and economic aspects of the nationalization to Chapter XVIII,

---

[30]The bank's offer was hedged with reservations: one of the conditions was the availability of American and British funds. For details, see Keith Wheelock, *Nasser's New Egypt: A Critical Analysis* (New York, 1960), pp. 173-205.

restricting the present account to the political implications and consequences of this act.

The countries most directly affected by the nationalization were France and Britain, who owned the overwhelming majority of the company's stock. In their eyes, however, Egypt's rash act transcended the mere "stealing" of the company's assets: it was doubly dangerous as a threat to the Free World's unimperiled use of the canal and as a blow to Franco-British prestige. This prestige was continuously being sapped by Nasser's intrigue in the remaining British strongholds in the Arabian Peninsula, on the one hand, and by his aid to Algerian rebels, on the other. Consequently, both London and Paris condemned Nasser's action in the strongest terms possible and talked of stern measures against Egypt. Britain blocked sizable Egyptian accounts in London. Furthermore, Prime Minister Sir Anthony Eden did not conceal his strong personal animosity toward Nasser, whom he was inclined to compare to the prewar fascist dictators and therefore to regard as a menace to Britain and the world at large.

The United States' attitude was different. Neither American holdings nor American prestige was directly involved. Furthermore, despite Secretary Dulles' dislike of Nasser's neutralism and flirtation with the Soviet bloc, the State Department was not prepared to give him up as a hopeless case. With an eye to the broader issues of American-Arab relations, it believed that some *modus vivendi* could be established with Egypt's leader and that despite many irritations American policy should not acquire a punitive character. Although official Washington strongly disapproved of Nasser's seizure of a foreign corporation (and followed it up by freezing Egyptian assets in the country pending final settlement), it was just as strongly opposed to the use of force to vindicate Western rights. In the ensuing communications between Washington, London, and Paris, Dulles followed the line (the word "policy" might sound like an overstatement) of dissuading Britain and France from military action against Nasser while assuring them of his full support for the nonviolent recovery of their rights. The difficulty with this approach was that while the negative part of it (i.e., opposition to the use of force) was definite, the method of achieving the positive part (i.e., support for the Western allies) was not spelled out but was left vague and uncertain. Eventually Secretary Dulles came forth with the idea of forming a Canal Users' Association, whose function was initially conceived to be to act as a recipient of canal dues—to be apportioned later between Egypt and the expropriated company—and as a watchdog of treaty-guaranteed freedom of navigation in the canal. Such an association was indeed formed in October 1956, but it soon become clear that Dulles viewed it primarily as a dues-collecting agency on *behalf* of Egypt, thus sorely disappointing both Britain and France. The debates before the United Nations Security Council, where the matter was brought in the early fall by Britain and France, proved inconclusive and did not result in any clear censure of the Egyptian action. Instead, an agreement was reached between Egypt and France and Britain on the six principles governing the use of the canal, the most important of which was that navigation in the canal would not be subject to political discrimination. If literally applied, this formula would have opened the canal to Israel's shipping. But Egypt never meant to extend it to Israel and Israel's ships continued to be barred from passage. Although Britain and France continued to use the canal without hindrance (albeit on a reduced scale), it was clear that their disappointment at the way the matter was handled by the United States and the Security Council was great and bordered on complete frustration. Unable to obtain satisfaction under international auspices or through peaceful negotiation and convinced that their self-restraint was cynically exploited by Nasser as a sign of weakness, the two aggrieved governments in mid-October began consulting each other with a view to taking common punitive action against Egypt. According to later revelations, Israel took part in these consultations, primarily through her contacts in Paris, and a timetable for Israeli and Franco-British military intervention was adopted.[31]

Israel's exclusion from use of the canal, although not a new phenomenon, aggravated the already tense situation between Tel-Aviv and Cairo, a situation rendered more acute in the course of 1956 by the stepped-up raids into Israeli territory of the Egyptian *fedayeen,* the semivoluntary commando units. It was against a background of such international complications that in pursuance of her policy of strengthening Arab military posture vis-à-vis Israel, Egypt on October 25, 1956, concluded a tripartite agreement with Syria and Jordan, setting up a unified command for the three armies under Egyptian direction.

The Suez War

Thus toward the end of October 1956 there were in evidence at least two factors likely to contribute to an explosion: the determination of France and Britain to punish Egypt and the resolve of Israel to exploit the Suez crisis to her own advantage.

On October 29 Israel's forces invaded Egypt. Divided into four columns and executing a paratroop landing within forty miles of the Suez Canal, they occupied the Gaza strip, ejected the Egyptians from the coast of the Gulf of Aqaba, took the stronghold of Sharm el-Sheikh facing the Strait of Tiran, and penetrated deep into the Sinai Peninsula. Within six days the Israelis swiftly overcame Egyptian resistance and took about 6,000 Egyptian prisoners of war. The action of the ground troops was supported by Israel's air force, which did not encounter much opposition. Simultaneously an Egyptian warship, the *Ibrahim el-Awal,* was thwarted in its attempt to shell Haifa and after a brief engagement was crippled and captured by the Israelis. Impressive quantities of Egyptian arms and war equipment, much of it from recent Russian deliveries, fell into Israeli hands. Egyptian resistance was uneven but generally weak, despite the strategic advantage of holding key passes and road centers in the Sinai Peninsula, some of them fortified with the aid of German experts.

Israel's military action provoked multifarious reactions throughout the world. On October 30, Britain and France addressed an ultimatum to the belligerents demanding the cessation of hostilities and the withdrawal of their forces to lines ten miles

[31]For testimony and discussion of collusion, see Anthony Nutting, *No End of a Lesson: The Story of Suez* (London, 1967), pp. 90–109; and Nadav Safran, *From War to War* (New York, 1969), pp. 52–53.

from both sides of the Suez Canal within the next twelve hours. As self-appointed guardians of the peace, Britain and France claimed that their action was motivated by solicitude for the safety and availability of the Suez Canal. In reality, their ultimatum, if successful, would have rewarded the aggressor by conceding to him the still-unoccupied areas of the Sinai Peninsula up to ten miles from the canal while penalizing the victim of aggression by demanding total evacuation of Egyptian troops to the western side of the canal. On the same day the United States called for an emergency meeting of the Security Council. When the Council met the next day to consider the crisis, the United States lined up with Russia in an unusual configuration of forces against Britain and France, who promptly vetoed an American and a Soviet resolution calling for an immediate cease-fire between Israel and Egypt. The case was then transferred to an emergency session of the General Assembly, which was capable of dealing with it without the hindrance of a veto.

At the expiration of the deadline of the ultimatum Israel accepted it on the condition that Egypt accept it as well. This Egypt refused to do. On the same day, October 31, British bombers began attacking Port Said and military targets in Egypt preparatory to the landing of French and British troops in the canal zone. Egypt responded on November 1 by breaking off diplomatic relations with Britain and France, seizing their properties, and blocking the Suez Canal through sinkings and demolitions. On November 5, Franco-British paratroopers captured Port Said after a battle in which the main resistance was offered by the hastily armed civilian population. During the next two days the invading forces progressed thirty miles south of Port Said.

In the meantime the outside world was following two separate lines of action: individual and collective. The other major powers, i.e., Russia and the United States, acting individually, expressed their view on the crisis. In a series of notes and statements Russia (1) proposed that a Soviet-United States force be sent to Egypt to stop the fighting, (2) warned Britain, France, and Israel against the continuation of aggression and alluded to the possibility of using "terrible" new weapons against the aggressors (on Nov. 6), and (3) threatened to send a "volunteer" force to the Middle East to oppose the invaders (on Nov. 10). On its part the United States warned Russia that it would oppose any Soviet use of force in the Middle East. At the same time Washington pressed for a cease-fire, then followed it up with another resolution (on Nov. 7) calling for the evacuation of the Israeli and Franco-British forces from Egypt under the supervision of a special United Nations Emergency Force (UNEF), the latter to be composed of nationals of medium and small countries. In mid-November the first units of the UNEF arrived in Egypt, and the phase of gradual evacuation began. By December 22 the last British and French troops had withdrawn from Egyptian territory.

Israel was reluctant to withdraw unconditionally. Her stand can best be understood if we consider the reasons which prompted her to undertake the invasion. Officially Israel claimed that her invasion was a mere police action designed to ensure peace on her borders by eliminating heavy *fedayeen* concentrations in Sinai. This was only part of the truth. Disturbed by continuous Arab threats against her very existence, Israel was determined to arrest the process of unification of Arab forces as set forth by the earlier-mentioned Egyptian-Syrian-Jordanian agreement of October 25. Furthermore, she was anxious to secure free passage for her ships through the Suez Canal, as well as through the Gulf of Aqaba, to both of which she was denied access by Egypt. And, finally, she wished to further her basic political objective of obtaining lasting recognition from her Arab neighbors, expressed, if possible, by a formal treaty of peace, which would put an end to an abnormal state of continuous tension. Israel believed that the time was propitious to achieve these objectives in view of two favorable developments: (1) the Suez Canal nationalization crisis, which led Paris and London to consider punitive action against Egypt; (2) the approaching presidential elections in the United States, which would tend to paralyze American diplomacy in the decisive moment.

Israel's Sinai venture was a calculated risk. First of all, sacrifice of human lives was involved. This, however, proved to be not very costly, inasmuch as only 171 Israeli soldiers were killed during the whole campaign. Perhaps more important was the damage that aggressive war was likely to inflict upon Israel's much-cultivated image as a peace-loving democracy. In order to make any sense politically the war should have yielded results that would outweigh the disadvantages just mentioned. These results—i.e., the achievement of the basic objectives just mentioned—could be obtained only so long as Israeli troops held a trump card by remaining on Egyptian territory. In this connection, it should be observed that Israel was anxious to stress the difference between the territory of Egypt proper and the Gaza strip. While ready to withdraw from Sinai, Israel viewed the longer occupation of the Gaza strip as a guarantee that her war aims would not be completely frustrated. Israel's government desperately tried to reach a behind-the-scenes agreement with the United States whereby the latter would support its claim to free passage through the Suez Canal as well as facilitate, by a special arrangement, the opening of the Gulf of Aqaba to Israeli shipping. The arrangement in question was reported to be as follows: profiting by the fact that the entry to the Gulf of Aqaba, i.e., the Strait of Tiran, was momentarily out of Egyptian control (the UNEF had replaced the Egyptian artillery outpost in Sharm el-Sheikh), an American merchant vessel would sail unmolested into the Gulf with Port Elath as its destination, thereby establishing a legal precedent of free navigation without effective challenge from Egypt. By upholding the right of its own ships to navigate freely to and from the Gulf, the United States would be committed to uphold a similar right of ships under different flags.

Whether or not this rumored deal was indeed concluded has thus far not been revealed either by Tel-Aviv or the State Department. Officially, the department took an unyielding attitude, refusing to bargain with Israel. In a rather unprecedented show of determination (considering the hitherto warm relationship between the two countries) President Eisenhower took the case "to the people" by appealing to Israel in a nationwide televised speech to abide by the rules of peace and international law and to withdraw from the Gaza strip unconditionally. On March 9, 1957, Israel's forces finally evacuated the strip, thereby permitting the return of the Egyptian administration. By this act the military phase of the war came to an end.

As usual, however, military operations constituted only one aspect of the conflict. The brief Sinai war had many consequences and many ramifications. Of the reaction of the big powers we have already spoken. The salient fact in this connection was the deterioration in the relations between the United States and its two principal European allies, a development which imposed heavy strains on the North Atlantic Treaty Organization and provoked many bitter comments in London and Paris vis-à-vis America and its chief policy maker, Secretary Dulles.

The role Russia played in the Suez crisis was primarily propagandistic, inasmuch as it was unlikely that Moscow would have wanted to involve itself in a third world war on account of relatively remote Egypt, where no vital Soviet interests were at stake. In fact, President Nasser in a speech made some three years later stated that Russia had offered him aid against aggression only after the war was virtually over.[32] As a direct consequence, however, Russia's boisterous diplomacy paid good dividends in the warm and friendly reaction in the Arab East to the Soviet anti-imperialist threat and to her alleged readiness to send volunteers to Egypt. Indeed the months following the war witnessed considerable growth in Soviet and Communist influence in a number of Arab states, particularly in Syria. This was the principal factor which led President Eisenhower on January 5, 1957, to proclaim his "doctrine" of opposition to Soviet-sponsored communism in the Middle East, a policy statement which will be more fully discussed in Chapter XX.

Equally important was the general Arab reaction to the Suez War. Spiritually there was a great deal of solidarity with sister Egypt and a deep indignation against the unholy alliance of the much-hated Israel with two major "imperialist" countries. This solidarity was not, however, translated into military action. Despite the rampant Pan-Arab spirit prevailing in Syria in those days, the Syrian army did not make a move to attack or even to threaten Israel on the other front. If this was true in Syria, still less could be expected from peace-loving and commercially minded Lebanon. As for the Hashemite and Saudi monarchies in Jordan and Saudi Arabia, there was no special incentive to come to the rescue of the revolutionary regime in Cairo. These remarks do not take into account the question of the military ability of these states to engage in an offensive against Israel, an ability that was certainly debatable. Arab solidarity was expressed in other than military ways. All independent Arab states of the Middle East with the exception of Lebanon broke diplomatic relations either with Britain and France or, on the theory of French-Israeli connivance, with France alone. Saudi Arabia decreed a ban on oil exports to Britain and France. By far the most important action was the step taken by Syria, where the pumping stations of the pipeline connecting Iraq with the Mediterranean were blown up by the army. This act, together with the blocking of the Suez Canal by Egypt, stopped the flow of 70 percent of the oil toward its usual European (and partly North American) destinations. The resulting shortage of oil in Europe was remedied by a specially formed Middle East Emergency Committee composed of the major American oil corporations, which undertook to supply Europe from Western Hemisphere sources.

The Suez War generated a number of controversies regarding certain facts. The

[32] *Al-Ahram* (Cairo), March 23, 1959.

problem of asserted (and subsequently proven) connivance between Israel and France and Britain aroused much speculation, as also did the question of whether France had lent military assistance to Israel during the Israeli-Egyptian phase of the campaign. Speculation about this point was largely due to the sale by France to Israel, in the period preceding the invasion, of a number of Mystère jet planes, which, according to some reports, had come accompanied by French pilot instructors. The Egyptian thesis, which found wide currency in the Arab world, was that there were both connivance among the three aggressor states and military cooperation in the campaign. Similarly, Egyptian official quarters insisted that the "withdrawal" of their army from Sinai was due not to a defeat at the hands of Israelis but to the need to concentrate troops for the defense of the Suez Canal against the Franco-British invaders. On this point it may be remarked that the Israeli campaign in the Sinai was virtually over by the time Britain and France landed their troops in Port Said. Another puzzling point was the fact that there was very little action by the largely Soviet-equipped Egyptian air force during the Sinai phase of the campaign and that no attempt was made by the Egyptians to bomb Israel's territory. The Egyptian explanation of this paradox was that orders were issued to the air force to fly out of Egypt (to Saudi Arabia or Syria?) for the duration of the campaign so as to save this precious arm of military power for some future, presumably more important, contingency. Last, but not least, Cairo (in Nasser's speeches and other official releases) made public its own version of the military passivity of other Arab states. It was due, according to this version, to an explicit request addressed to Syria in particular not to intervene so as to deprive the "imperialists" of the excuse to invade more of the Arab homeland.

The war had many political consequences. The most important was perhaps the blow to British influence in the area. (The French had enjoyed merely a vestige of their former cultural influence since their withdrawal from the Levant in 1945.) American prestige rose for a while because of Washington's firm stand in defense of Egypt's rights, but it soon suffered a decline due to the public espousal by Dulles in 1957 of the principle of freedom of navigation in the Gulf of Aqaba. Cairo propaganda promptly said that although Washington had insisted on Israel's withdrawal from Egypt, in reality it took upon itself to secure the war aims of Israel, which included the opening of the Gulf. And, indeed, one of the important results of the war was the opening of the Gulf to Israel's shipping, which gained free passage through the Strait of Tiran. The latter was guarded by the UN Emergency Force, which, having finished its task of supervising the invaders' evacuation, was instructed to stand guard on the Egyptian-Israeli border and along the east coast of Sinai. It should be pointed out in this connection that the presence of the Emergency Force in the area of recent war operations was entirely dependent on the consent of the belligerents. Israel from the very outset rejected the stationing of the UNEF on her territory. By contrast, Egypt accepted the presence of the UNEF, not only on her side of the border with Israel but also on the coast of the Gulf of Aqaba, a decision which could be interpreted either as a sign of weakness or as a genuine expression of peaceful intentions. Although the United Nations intervened to restore peace and to maintain it, it did not secure the conclusion of a formal treaty of peace between

Israel and Egypt. In fact, the rigid insistence on the evacuation of invading armies voiced by the United Nations and the United States has delayed indefinitely the formal peace treaty by merely restoring the status quo ante of a UN-supervised armistice. Thus Israel's fundamental objective of obtaining recognition embodied in a formal instrument was not fulfilled, while Egypt achieved a signal diplomatic victory in seeing the designs of her enemies frustrated, their forces evacuated, and the canal remaining in her firm possession. Furthermore, Egypt's success was underscored by the fact that the canal was cleared at the expense of its customers under UN supervision. If we add to this that the two principal Western authors of the intervention soon retired from active political life—Eden, under a nervous strain, went to a nursing home and Mollet suffered the eclipse of his career—Nasser's triumph appeared uncontested despite the drawback of surrendering the Gulf of Aqaba to Israeli navigation. Thus, rather paradoxically, out of the military defeat in Sinai there grew around Egypt's regime and its leader an aura of victory and invincibility which greatly enhanced their prestige in the Arab world. Before long Cairo became a scene of "victory parades," the implication of which was that the victory was not only diplomatic but military as well, while the resistance of the "heroic city of Port Said" was glorified as an examplar of patriotic sacrifice.

The Pan-Arab Offensive

The Suez War irrevocably confirmed President Nasser in his role as an all-Arab leader. Actually he had begun to assume such a role in early 1955, when launching a vigorous offensive against the Baghdad Pact. His subsequent trip to Bandung, his arms deal with Russia, and the nationalization of the canal constituted further steps on the road to Arabism. By the end of 1956 his Pan-Arab and neutralist policy was fully crystallized. Consequently, it was without hesitation that he directed vigorous attacks on the freshly proclaimed Eisenhower Doctrine of January 7, 1957, claiming that it represented another imperialist attempt to meddle in Arab affiars. According to Nasser, his regime (and that of Baath-dominated Syria in 1957) represented the "Arab liberation policy," progressive, revolutionary, and committed to the eradication of Zionism, imperialism, and feudalism. He repeatedly accused the United States of a lack of sympathy with those objectives and claimed that Washington was supporting the retrograde regimes in the Arab world while denying him economic aid in an attempt to isolate him and undermine his position. The Hashemite regimes of Iraq and Jordan constituted the most natural targets of his hostility. In their zeal his propagandists did not limit their attacks to these two kingdoms but often broadened them to include monarchies in general. This led to a reappraisal of her traditional policy by Saudi Arabia and a subsequent rapprochement between Riyadh and Baghdad, both fearful of the revolutionary dynamism of the Cairo-based Pan-Arabists.

The fear was not ill-founded. Showing an amazing capacity for recuperation after the nerve-racking trials of the Suez War, the Cairo regime launched a multipronged political offensive in the Arab world. This offensive was carried out by a heterogeneous host of Egyptian teachers employed by thousands in other Arab countries, technical experts, a variety of agents, and Egyptian military attachés, some of whom were caught red-handed smuggling arms or propaganda pamphlets to neighboring states under the cloak of diplomatic immunity. Furthermore, Nasser could always count on the local fifth column of ardent sympathizers in Beirut, Baghdad, Amman, Damascus, and other Arab capitals. Especially could he rely on students and, more particularly, on the Baath Party, whose objectives of social revolution, Pan-Arabism, and anti-imperialism coincided with his own. The Baath influence grew appreciably in Jordan and Syria in 1956–1957. In both countries the Baathists entered the cabinets in the course of 1956, and for a time the foreign ministers of Syria and Jordan were members of the Baath.

In this capacity they were in a unique position to promote the idea of Arab unity, which enjoyed the highest priority in their party's program. The Baathist attempt, made in alliance with the Communists and certain other elements, to topple the Jordanian monarchy in April 1957 met with failure. By contrast, they were eminently successful in Syria, where, with the aid of the army, they began to dominate the government despite their minority status in the parliament.[33] In the latter part of 1957 leading Syrian Baathists began pressing for a speedy union with Egypt. Nasser's response to their initiative was cautious. It was one thing to propagate the idea of Arab unity in a broad sense of political solidarity, military conordination, and revolutionary progress, and another to give it a concrete political form and assume the responsibility of government. In Nasser's view the chief obstacle to Syro-Egyptian unity lay in the difference between his own military and authoritarian regime and the Syrian regime with its parliament, parties, and free press. To unite both, leaving Syrian democracy (however imperfect) in operation, would be to invite embarrassing comparisons. Nasser's formula, therefore, in his negotiations with the Syrians was as follows: the new united state should be unitary and not federal; moreover, before any two Arab countries unite, each should achieve internal union of its citizens. Consequently, before merging with Egypt, Syria must dissolve all her political parties as symbols of internal division. These conditions were accepted by the Baath leaders in the belief that, despite the formal ban, their party, as representative of Socialist and Pan-Arab ideology, would continue to wield dominant influence and would share in the new government.

Union with Syria

Following the adoption of appropriate resolutions by the Egyptian Assembly and the Syrian parliament, union between the two countries was proclaimed on February 1, 1958. On February 5, Presidents Nasser and Quwatli presented a seventeen-point program to their respective legislatures which provided for a unitary state. Executive authority was to be vested in the president, aided by executive councils in the Syrian and Egyptian regions, while legislative authority was to be exercised by an assembly appointed by the president, at least half of whose members would be

[33]See p. 342 above.

selected from the existing Egyptian and Syrian legislatures. A permanent constitution was to be adopted in due time and a plebiscite was to confirm the proposed arrangements.

On February 21 the people in both regions voted for the union and for Nasser as its first president by nearly 100 percent majorities. On March 5, 1958, the Provisional Constitution of the United Arab Republic was proclaimed by the president. It conformed in its essential features to the seventeen-point program announced a month earlier. The U.A.R. was declared to be part of the Arab nation. Society was to be organized on the basis of social solidarity and a planned economy conforming to the principles of social justice. Islam was not mentioned. Treaties concluded by Egypt and Syria were to remain valid for their respective regions. Instead of political parties the constitution called for the formation of a single organization to be called the National Union, the principles of which were to be defined by presidential decree.

On the following day President Nasser appointed the first union cabinet and the two regional executive councils. Between him and these bodies were four vice-presidents of the United Arab Republic, two Egyptian (General Abdul Hakim Amer and Abdul Latif Baghdadi) and two Syrian (Sabri el-Assali and Akram Hourani). A day later, March 8, Yemen joined in a federal union with the United Arab Republic, forming the United Arab States. In contrast to the complete merger of Egypt and Syria, the United Arab States provided for the retention by each state of its form of government and its separate diplomatic representation abroad except in the cases where by mutual consent a single mission was to be appointed. Control of common affairs was to be exercised by the Supreme Council, composed of heads of member states. It was to be assisted by the Union Council, which would include an equal number of representatives from member states, to be presided over alternately by each member state for a period of one year. In outline, this was the formal arrangement. In reality the federative link proved of the loosest kind, and Yemen stubbornly persisted in her own ways, politically and socially.

The Syro-Egyptian union had come at a time when desire for Arab unity, stimulated by Pan-Arab propaganda and external factors, had reached a high degree of intensity, especially among the nationalist intelligentsia in the Fertile Crescent. Therefore, it was not surprising that barely two weeks after the union agreement two other Arab countries, Iraq and Jordan, announced their own federation.[34] If the traditional criteria of geographic contiguity, mutual resemblance of the population, and similarity of social organization and governmental structure were to be applied, the Iraq-Jordan federation would appear more natural than the union of Egypt and Syria, where no such common features prevailed. Based on the criterion of ideological orientation, nothing was more natural than the union of Egypt and Syria, whose dominant elites were dedicated to the policy of Arab unity, social revolution, and neutralism.

If the union of Egypt and Syria was a consequence of Cairo's Pan-Arab offensive following the Baghdad Pact and the Suez crisis, it generated further intensification

[34]See p. 287 above.

of militant Pan-Arabism. Such militancy, however, was bound to provoke hostile reaction on the part of all those established governments that felt threatened by its upsurge. The inevitable estrangement between Cairo and other Arab capitals (unless they were willing to follow Syria's example) led to a series of international crises and strains of varying intensity and importance. Thus a protracted state of irritation developed between President Nasser and President Habib Bourguiba of Tunisia, who strongly resented the support given by Nasser to the Tunisian exile, Salah ben Youssef, a man condemned by Tunisian courts for a plot on Bourguiba's life. In March of 1958 a crisis broke out in Saudi-U.A.R. relations because of the alleged attempt of King Saud to bribe Syria's executive minister of interior, Colonel Sarraj, to rupture the union with Egypt and assassinate Nasser. King Saud's alleged action was viewed as a protective measure against the revolutionary intrigue carried on in Saudi Arabia by Egyptian agents, both civil and military.[35]

In late spring 1958 the United Arab Republic became strongly involved in the Lebanese civil war (see Chapter IX). Here it suffices to say that Cairo's intervention on the side of the insurgents was an important factor in intensifying the crisis as well as in bringing it from the purely domestic to the international arena. The heavy blows bestowed by pro-Nasser Pan-Arabists (Lebanese and Syrian) on President Chamoun's regime in Lebanon affected the situation in Jordan, where a renewed attempt was made by the Cairo-supported opposition to upset King Hussein's government. The resulting arrival in Jordan of British paratroops further deepened the chasm between the Pan-Arab and the pro-Western orientations in the Middle East. Furthermore, one should not underestimate the degree of which the Cairo-sponsored Pan-Arab propaganda and political activity contributed to the creation of the mental climate which led to the revolution in Iraq.

After its inception in 1955 the Pan-Arab offensive met both successes and reverses. If as a measure of success we adopt the dual test of union and radical social change, union with Syria—as long as it lasted—comes closest to this ideal model, at least outwardly. Federation with Yemen resulted in the loosest possible link between the two countries and no social change during its brief history. In fact, it might be argued that by outwardly accepting federation and thus avoiding hostile criticism and propaganda, Yemen's theocratic monarchy tried to postpone any major changes in its medieval outlook and structure. On other fronts the Pan-Arab offensive encountered resistance, in each case due to a different factor. In Lebanon the march of Pan-Arabism was checked by a combination of native Lebanese resistance and American military demonstration; in Jordan, by a combination of Hashemite determination to stay alive and British military aid; in Saudi Arabia, by the sheer weight of its medieval social structure, which made any mobilization of revolutionary forces extremely difficult; and in Tunisia and Iraq, by their own competitive revolutions which gave the masses the sense of national liberation and social change but within a strictly local rather than a Pan-Arab framework. Followers of President Nasser had frequently argued that only the governments of the artificially separated Arab states stood in the way of Arab unity. The people, they

---

[35] See note on p. 594 below.

said, are on the Pan-Arab side. This may have been true of significant segments of the populations, at least prior to an actual merger or a revolution. But it would be unrealistic to ignore the stubborn attachment to one's local self-rule and traditions which many an Arab group displays. Such an attachment might be further strengthened by the existence of natural wealth in a given territory, which the local population, regardless of the kind of government it has, is unwilling to share with or surrender to outside elements.

Internal Consolidation of Power in the U.A.R.

By the time of the merger with Syria, President Nasser's position in his native Egypt could be described as one of firmly established authority. No wonder, therefore, that any process of consolidation that took place after the merger viewed Syria as its principal objective. In Syria, Nasser's position presented a more complex picture. While initially the Baath and the elements allied with it were enthusiastic about the union and Nasser's leadership, the merchant-landowning bourgeoisie of Syria, formerly represented in conservative or Islamic political parties, had many misgivings and reservations, albeit concealed under an outward show of noisy conformity. Furthermore, the Communists, an element rapidly gaining in strength in Syria prior to the merger, in the last minute turned against the union, thus swelling the ranks of actual or potential dissenters. It is conceivable that a conservative-Communist tactical coalition might have been formed to sabotage the union. The reason this did not happen has to be sought in the fright the conservatives experienced as the result of the Communist excesses in neighboring Iraq in 1958–1959. Of the two alternatives, an independent but weak Syria subject to Iraqi influence and Communist infiltration, on the one hand, or a status of subjection to Nasser with a "respectable" socioeconomic order, on the other, the Syrian bourgeoisie preferred the latter. "Respectable," however, was in many ways a key word. To the Syrian moderates and conservatives it meant , in the first place, the preservation of their separate economy with its standard of living, which was higher than the Egyptian, and a separate currency; in the second, it meant the restraining of the revolutionary-reformist tendencies of the Baath party, whose popularity dwindled seriously once its leaders began exercising ministerial functions in the postmerger cabinets.[36] It is a testimony to Nasser's perceptiveness and political skill that he quickly sensed these realities of the Syrian situation and adapted his tactics accordingly. First, he followed a deliberately slow and cautious policy in the field of economic unification, permitting Syria to maintain her full autonomy in this sector during the first two years of the union. Second, partly in an attempt to conciliate the Syrian bourgeoisie, he began after a year of outward partnership to eliminate the Baath from power, thereby gaining much applause from Syria's conservatives. By January 1960 most Baathists, including Vice-President Hourani, were removed from the union and the provincial cabinets. It might be added here that the parting of the ways with the erstwhile Baathist allies—the group responsible for engineering

---

[36]Among the portfolios assigned to them, the Baathists held that of agriculture, which fact rankled Syria's conservatives on account of the latter's resistance to the principle and pace of the agrarian reform.

the union—lay in the very nature of the new regime. This regime, based on full authority vested in President Nasser, could not tolerate the existence of any autonomous political organization which, however informally, would preserve its machinery, cultivate its own ideology, and thus compete with the absolute center of power in Cairo. Although Nasser had consistently encouraged the exchange of civil and military personnel between the two provinces, thereby bringing Egyptians into many sensitive posts in Damascus, he still preferred to rule Syria through the Syrians themselves. From the beginning Colonel Abdul Hamid Sarraj played the role of his most trusted lieutenant. In 1960 he was elevated to the presidency of the Syrian executive council.

After the first two years of such skillful tactics, the pendulum seemed to swing again toward social radicalism. The agrarian reform, enacted for Syria on November 26, 1958, but slowed down to conciliate the landowning elements, began to be implemented with greater vigor. Furthermore, in various public utterances Nasser began equating union with revolution. Syria—this was the gist of numerous remarks—by accepting union with Egypt had opted for a far-reaching social and political revolution. Opposition to these revolutionary changes, nostalgia to restore the old party life, and desire to maintain the unjust laissez faire economy, amounted to opposition to union itself. The latter was sacred, because it embodied the ideal of Arabism, and to oppose it was sedition and treason. Step by step various revolutionary measures adopted in Egypt, such as the nationalization of banks and subordination of the press, began to be applied to Syria with increasing intensity.

To replace the old political parties, the National Union, originally formed in Egypt, was extended to Syria as well. As a single party (although the party label was strongly denied by the regime) it served primarily as a channel of communication between the government and the masses, and largely a one-way channel at that.

Dictatorial governments issuing from a revolution have a need to legitimize themselves in the eyes of the people. The method usually consists in paying lip-service to democracy by adopting formal constitutional processes while maintaining the substance of monopoly of power. Nasser's regime was no exception to this rule. In fact, it had twice conformed to it: once in 1956, when it cloaked itself with constitutional respectability in Egypt,[37] and again in 1960, when, after launching the National Union in both provinces, it produced an appointed National Assembly. The recruiting area for the candidates had been the National Union, a hierarchical organization with a congress at its uppermost level. However, the president could and did select certain members of the National Assembly outside of it. According to the earlier-mentioned provisional constitution of the U.A.R., at least half of the assembly's membership was to be recruited from among the members of the old Syrian parliament and the Egyptian National Assembly. This was the only limitation on the president's discretionary powers and the only self-imposed "constitutional" provision likely to bring into the U.A.R. legislature some element potentially criti-

[37]On Jan. 16, 1956, after the three-year transitional period, Nasser had proclaimed a constitution for Egypt, which was a prototype of the provisional constitution decreed on March 5, 1958, for the United Arab Republic. Perhaps the main difference between the two was the position of Islam, which was recognized as the state religion in the first, but not mentioned at all in the second.

cal of the regime, especially from Syria. But even here the president was not bound by any minimum figure of the old Syrian deputies to be appointed and could reduce their number to a level compatible with political safety. Ultimately, when the first U.A.R. National Assembly was appointed in July 1960, of a total of 600 members, only 37 former Syrian deputies were selected. In 1961, following the president's message, the assembly unhurriedly began to prepare the permanent constitution. Whatever the phrasing of this future document, it was certain that the regime did not intend to abdicate its political power.

While thus going through the formal procedures of legitimization, President Nasser did not neglect the ideological aspects of his exercise of power. By 1958–1959 the official philosophy was described as the building of "the socialist, democratic, and cooperative society" in the unitarian state which was part of "the Arab nation" and which was following a policy of "Arab liberation, positive neutralism, and nonalignment." Although socialism was stressed, its exact meaning was left undefined.

U.A.R.'S Foreign Relations

Nasser's neutralism was not uniformly neutral. His basic foreign commitment had always been to fight imperialism, and the latter was invariably interpreted to mean Western colonialism and political intervention. Russia's dominance over the Turkic-speaking and other Islamic groups within the Soviet Empire had been taken virtually for granted, while Soviet imperialism in Europe's satellite area, largely viewed as a settling of accounts between one and another white-European group, never evoked in Cairo any significant emotional reaction. A good example of this attitude was supplied during the Hungarian uprising of October-November 1956. Not only did the simultaneous Suez crisis completely overshadow the Hungarian tragedy in Arab emotions, but the Egyptian and the Syrian press deliberately minimized or ignored the events in Budapest.

Cairo's relations with Moscow generally tended to follow a friendly path inasmuch as (1) on the issue of Western "imperialism" their attitudes were very much alike; (2) in the Arab-Israeli conflict Moscow was inclined to side with the Arabs; and (3) in the field of economics Russia's aid to the U.A.R. embraced such sensitive areas as armaments and the Aswan Dam,[38] thereby generating in Cairo feelings of satisfaction mixed with gratitude.

Yet it should be pointed out that Nasser insisted on clearly differentiating between his commercial dealings with Russia and his attitude toward communism at home. His treatment of the Egyptian Communists had been consistently harsh and uncompromising and, with the extension of his rule to Syria in 1958, similar measures were applied to the party in the "northern region." In his policy of repression Nasser found an additional incentive in the negative stand which the Communist Party in Syria had taken toward the union and the resulting dissolution of all

---

[38] A definite Soviet offer to finance the Aswan Dam was made on Oct. 23, 1958. It resulted in an agreement providing for a loan of 400 million rubles ($100 million) for the first phase of construction.

political parties. Furthermore, following the revolution of 1958, the Communists of Iraq did their utmost to oppose any closer links with Egypt. In fact, they revealed themselves as the only effective force capable of competing with pro-Nasser elements in mobilizing street mobs and of inducing the latter to burn Nasser effigies in public.

On three occasions these tensions between Arab Communists and Nasser led to minor crises between the Soviet bloc and the U.A.R. The first crisis resulted from Nasser's charges in a major speech at Port Said on December 23, 1958, that Syrian Communists were enemies of Arab nationalism and would-be saboteurs of the Syro-Egyptian union. His speech provoked Premier Khrushchev to make critical remarks a few weeks later about Nasser's immaturity and to proclaim that the Soviet Union could not remain indifferent to the persecution of Communists in the United Arab Republic. A further exchange of angry statements followed, and for a while the Cairo government seriously considered the possibility of Russia's rupturing economic relations between the two countries.

The second crisis occurred in the relations between Communist China and the U.A.R. It was due to a speech which the Syrian Communist leader in exile, Khalid Bakdash delivered during the tenth anniversary of the Communist regime in Peking in September 1959. Both the tenor of the speech as well as the fact that its author was entertained as an honored guest in China were considered an affront by Cairo, which lodged formal protests and called its chargé d'affaires home for consultations.

The third irritation took place in May 1961, again between Cairo and Moscow and for reasons similar to those which prompted the first crisis. This time the initiator was Premier Khrushchev, who in an interview in Moscow voiced renewed criticism of the way Communists were treated both in the United Arab Republic and in Iraq. His remarks gave rise to vigorous retorts by Cairo's controlled press, in which Russia was warned not to follow the example of the West in meddling in domestic Arab affairs.

In the last analysis the status and future of Egypt's relations with Russia depend on the latter's evaluation of the situation in the Arab countries and the resultant decision either to press for a speedy Communist revolution or to assist them in their still-unfinished struggle with Western influences. Adoption of one of these alternatives does not necessarily exclude the choice of another at an appropriate time. In Moscow's eyes all methods are ultimately expected to lead to the same end. It is not certain to what degree this truth has been understood by the leaders in Cairo despite their vigilant attitude toward domestic communism.

As for relations between Cairo and Washington, they oscillated between the poles of warmth and coolness, mostly on account of American commitments to third parties who had unsettled political accounts with Nasser's regime. Yet this did not mean that they were consistently bad. Whereas the lowest point in these relations was probably reached during the Lebanese civil war in 1958, in the ensuing months and years there have been signs of improvement, translated into various agreements whereby moderate amounts of American aid have been pledged to the United Arab Republic. To be sure, Nasser and his associates could never get rid of a suspicion that despite official reassurances Washington did not genuinely desire Arab unity. But at least outwardly, Washington's correct attitude on this point contrasted with the provocative policies followed by Moscow-sponsored Communists in the Arab countries. Hence, no crisis has occured so long as proposed unity was to be voluntary. Close relations between America and Israel provided the most fertile source for irritations between Washington and Cairo. A high point in these irritations was reached in April 1960, when the International Seafarers Union in New York refused to unload the Egyptian ship *Cleopatra* in protest against the U.A.R.'s discrimination against American ships calling at Israeli ports. To Cairo this incident looked like another proof of "Washington's subservient attitude to Tel-Aviv" and in an upsurge of patriotic indignation the press and labor unions of the U.A.R. called for a complete boycott of American shipping in all Arab lands from Iraq to Morocco. In a rather impressive show of solidarity workmen in Arab ports anywhere between the Persian Gulf and the Atlantic enthusiastically accepted the call, refusing to service American shipping until the *Cleopatra*'s boycott in New York was lifted. After some hasty conferences between the Seafarers Union and the authorities in Washington, it was decided to stop the boycott. Normal relations were restored, but American prestige had been harmed and Cairo had the gleeful satisfaction of having demonstrated the strength of Arab solidarity.

Nasser's African Policy and Neutralism

If the years 1955–1958 could be viewed as those of a Pan-Arab offensive, the period following them witnessed a reorientation of Cairo's foreign policy toward the ex-colonial world as a whole, with special emphasis on Africa. Conceptually there was nothing new in this policy: as early as 1953, Nasser had proclaimed his interest in the "African circle" alongside the two other "concentric circles," the Arab and the Islamic.[39] During the first six years of the revolutionary regime in Egypt this interest was, however, more symbolic than actual. Beginning with 1959, Cairo began conducting a more vigorous African policy. Several factors contributed to this new emphasis. One was the rapid political emancipation of Black Africa, which resulted in the attainment of independence by some twenty-odd African states by 1961 and thus opened the door to direct political relations between them and Cairo. Second, apart from its positive interest in assuming the leadership of the awakening Africa, the Cairo government tried to prevent the growth of any closer links between the African states and Israel in view of the latter's attempts in that direction. Third, the African scene provided a new opportunity for the display of anti-imperialist propaganda, which had become a standard weapon in Cairo's political arsenal. Fourth, there developed in Egypt's ruling class a tendency to pose as a champion of social revolution in underdeveloped areas and to arrogate to itself the role of a militant example of success in this respect. In pursuance of this tendency President Nasser cultivated cordial relations with the revolutionary regime of Fidel Castro in Cuba and insisted on close and cordial links with the budding political

[39]In his book *Egypt's Liberation, The Philosophy of the Revolution* (Washington, D.C., 1955), pp. 109–114.

leaders of Africa. Cairo's propaganda beamed toward Africa—exemplified by ambitious radio programs and numerous broadcasts in Swahili and other native languages—was decidedly revolutionary in its character. Opposing Western imperialism, real or imaginary (without acknowledging its steady retreat from the African continent), this propaganda attacked at the same time local feudalism and tribalism in an attempt to align itself on the side of the "forces of the future." Thus its net effect was anti-Western at a time when the West, through a variety of means, was endeavoring to keep Africa from slipping into the Soviet orbit of influence. In private conversations political leaders in Cairo sometimes tried to justify their policy by asserting that by championing revolution in Africa they were competing with Russia and thus indirectly rendering a service to the Free World. While there might be some element of truth in it, there is no doubt that the close parallelism of Egyptian and Soviet policies—especially evident in the Congo crisis of 1960–1961—resulted in the strenghening of those forces in Africa which aimed a complete severance of links with the West. In pursuance of their African policy, Egyptian leaders actively participated in a number of African conferences. Such conferences were held at one time or another in Cairo, Lagos, Conakry, and Casablanca.[40]

Some critics viewed Nasser's emphasis on Africa as a compensatory mechanism for his setbacks in the Arab world since 1958. There is no doubt that his Pan-Arab drive encountered considerable opposition in several quarters and that despite his unquestionable popularity among the urban masses in the Arab world the Pan-Arab policy began to show diminishing returns.

Nasser's championship of the revolution in Africa went hand-in-hand with his role as a promoter of neutralism and nonalignment. In September 1961 the latter policy found a new expression in the sponsorship by Cairo, with India and Yugoslavia, of a twenty-two-nation conference of neutrals in Belgrade. The Belgrade meeting grouped many nations which had attended the Bandung conference in 1955. It differed from the latter in that participation was restricted to nonaligned nations, thus excluding Russia and other states of the Soviet bloc that were so conspicuously present at Bandung. Although strict neutralism was the ostensible watchword of the conference and the basis for being invited, the final resolutions still gave most prominence to the struggle against Western imperialism, Soviet imperialism being smoothly glossed over. This was all the more noteworthy in view of the fact that, on the very eve of the meeting, Russia launched a series of nuclear tests in utter disregard of the feelings and wishes of the Belgrade conferees in this respect.

Collapse of Union with Syria

While Nasser's ambition to play an increasingly active role in the world of Afro-Asia had thus involved him in a number of issues having no direct connection with the United Arab Republic, the situation in Syria was undergoing significant

---

[40]The Casablanca conference was held between January 5 and 7, 1961. For the resolutions adopted, see p. 436 above.

deterioration. Broadly speaking, Syrians began to awaken from the daze of initial enthusiasm for union and, as time went on, found multiple causes for disenchantment and discontent. The abolition of political freedoms following the union was felt as being contrary to Syrian tradition. Syria's natural political leaders, all active and vigorous before 1958, found themselves unwanted and eliminated from public affairs. Government was increasingly centralized in Cairo. For all practical purposes, Damascus became dead as a decision-making center. Syrian ministers, even those in the union cabinet in Cairo, soon discovered that they had no real authority and that important decisions, including the issuance of new laws, were being taken by Nasser without even a pretense of consultation, ostensibly in the name of the "presidential system" under which the union was expected to operate. People in Syria resented the tightening methods of a typical police state. Any dissent was quickly equated with treason, and the country swarmed with informers belonging both to the local Syrian security apparatus of Colonel Sarraj and to the Egyptian intelligence organization. There was a visible influx of Egyptian officials, experts, and officers into Syria. By 1961 their number exceeded 20,000, and as a rule, they enjoyed a privileged position, their pay often being higher than that of their Syrian colleagues. The erstwhile enthusiasts of the union—the Baathists—were in a revisionist, if not actually rebellious, mood toward their one-time hero, Nasser. The atmosphere in the schools and universities became stifling. Academic freedom was only a memory from a nostalgic past. Professors in social sciences and humanities had to outbid each other in their repetitious protestations of loyalty to Arab unity and to the principles of the revolution if they wanted to keep their positions. A standard anecdote about the secondary schools—reflecting a good deal of truth—was that if a Lebanese Moslem student failed in his examinations in Beirut, he merely had to enroll in a school in Damascus and write a zealous essay on Arab nationalism to get his diploma. The loudly advertised National Union—the regime's single party—proved to be a sham; it functioned as a haven for opportunistic careerists. The National Assembly was a paper institution. Its role was largely limited to applauding the speeches of government dignitaries. It was not consulted on any significant piece of legislation, the latter being issued by presidential decrees. The government did not even go through the motions of having such legislation formally approved by the Assembly. Syria was being ruled by proconsular methods, with Field Marshal Abdul Hakim Amer enjoying special powers delegated to him by the president.

Side by side with these curbs on political freedoms Syria's economy suffered many reverses and dislocations as a result of the union. It is important to remember that the Syrian bourgeoisie had agreed to union with Egypt in 1958 only for the sake of the principle of Arab unity. It did not visualize, or intend to give blank approval to, the extension of the Egyptian revolution into Syria. Consequently, despite the unitary rather than federal character of the United Arab Republic, Syria's landowning and business circles expected that their economy would follow its natural course and not be forcibly merged with that of Egypt. Syria's economy represented largely free enterprise, and, furthermore, Syria's standard of living was markedly higher than Egypt's. Anxious to preserve these two features, Syrian Chambers of Commerce as well as the governor of Syria's Central Bank repeatedly begged Cairo to practice restraint in its schemes of economic planning and unification. In 1958 and 1959, President Nasser was inclined to listen to this advice. His special plenipotentiary in Syria, Marshal Amer, even went so far as to order some of Syria's Baathist ministers to slow down the implementation of the agrarian reform law of 1958 in view of the complaints he had received. In 1960, however, Nasser and his associates increasingly began to equate union with revolution in their public pronouncements. Implicitly this was a message addressed to the Syrian bourgeoisie: in accepting Arab unity they had also accepted the radical refashioning of their society and economy according to the Egyptian image. Only when this refashioning was accomplished would it be possible to say that the union was based on solid foundations. One cannot deny that this reasoning contained some compelling logic. What the Syrians had in mind was a federal state, at least insofar as economy was concerned. But the dynamics of the Egyptian dictatorship, like those of any autocratic system, did not admit of a division of the united state into two parts, one controlled and the other free. Federation is possible under the conditions of democracy; otherwise the contrast in the socioeconomic systems of various component parts is bound to invite too many comparisons between the part which is free and the one which is not to be safe for the latter. Despite the inner logic of the Egyptian position, the Syrians viewed the Cairo-espoused policy of economic unification as an evil design to (1) bring down Syria's standard of living to that of Egypt and (2) subordinate entirely the Syrian to the Egyptian economy.

The tension thus produced reached a truly acute stage when President Nasser late in July 1961 issued a series of decrees introducing far-reaching socialization of the U.A.R.'s economy. The principal decrees provided for (1) nationalization of all banks and insurance companies; (2) nationalization of hundreds of industrial and commercial corporations; (3) acquisition by the government of a controlling interest (not less than 50 percent) in a long list of enterprises; (4) limitation of private stockholdings (maximum, £E10,000 or £S100,000); (5) a ban on contract works for the government unless the contracting enterprise admits the state to 50 percent ownership; (6) a new scale of income taxes, with the rates raised up to 90 percent on incomes exceeding £E5,000 a year); (8) representation of workers and employees on company boards of directors; (9) workers' sharing in profits (25 percent of the latter); (10) reduction by one-half of the maximum of landholdings allowed by the agrarian reform law of 1952; (11) acquisition by the government of a 25 percent interest in all importing agencies; (12) imposition of new real estate taxes and confirmation of the special 10 percent defense tax (meaning in practice that incomes above £E10,000 would be subject to a 100 percent tax rate); and (13) a ban on the holding of multiple jobs by one person.

Business communities both in Egypt and Syria were stunned on learning of this legislation. To the Syrian upper and middle classes this was the ultimate proof of the mistake they had made when they agreed to union in 1958. Soon afterward two new blows were delivered: in late August President Nasser abolished the existing system of three cabinets (a union and two provincial ones) and replaced it by a single cabinet for the United Arab Republic. Thus the last vestige of local autonomy, exemplified by the provincial cabinet (executive council) in Damascus, was done away with. This action was followed by the announcement that the Egyptian and Syrian currencies would be unified on the basis of the Arab dinar. This was the final blow to Syria's economic independence. Even before these summer decrees capital was being smuggled out of Syria in search of safer conditions. The process was rapidly accelerated, while new investments practically came to a standstill. Syria's bourgeoisie was in a disillusioned and rebellious mood. Yet, alone, as a civilian group, it could do little to oppose the tightening vices of Egyptian controls.

However, it was not isolated. The Syrian army was also in a state of profound fermentation, having a "second look" at its initial enthusiasm for the Pan-Arab cause. In his unceasing effort to keep the military establishment under firm control, President Nasser engaged in an ostensibly skillful personnel manipulation. Egyptian officers were being transferred to the Syrian army, and Syrian officers were being posted, sometimes with promotion, to Egypt. Yet their respective positions were not equal, Syrians being lost and isolated in the sea of the Egyptian army. By contrast, Egyptian officers in Syria frequently held important command and specialists' positions. Moreover, they often disregarded the formal hierarchical channels and communicated with the headquarters in Cairo above the heads of their nominal superiors of Syrian nationality. Some of them were equipped with short-wave transmitters for that purpose. Syrian officers resented their presence, especially in view of the fact that under the guise of artillery or tank experts, these Egyptian officers were often merely the agents of Cairo's intelligence network. Some of them lived a bit too lavishly for regular army pay, and Syrians soon learned that they possessed impressive bank accounts in Damascus. In 1960 and 1961 the U.A.R. army command issued orders that appeared to Syrians like an attempt to transfer to Egypt some high-quality weapons and deprive Syrian regiments of their munition reserves. All in all, the resentment in the Syrian army against Egyptian domination paralleled the resentment in civilian circles.

Thus the stage for some protest movement was set. A group of army officers formed a conspiracy, waiting for an opportune moment to strike. The transfer to Cairo of Colonel Sarraj (who was promoted to the rather nominal position of vice-president of the U.A.R. in the newly created single cabinet) provided such an opportunity. For a short time at least, the once-powerful Sarraj found himself cut off from his security apparatus in Syria. Although he soon resigned from his vice-presidency and returned to Damascus, his grip on Syria's coercive machine was lost. At dawn on September 28 the High Arab Revolutionary Command—as the Syrian conspiratorial junta styled itself—effected a coup and after some negotiation with Nasser's "viceroy," Marshal Amer, proclaimed the separation of Syria from Egypt. Amer and the commanding general of the First (i.e., Syrian) Army, Jamal Faisal, were arrested and deported to Egypt. A civilian cabinet headed by Dr. Maamun Kuzbari was appointed to govern Syria during the transitional period pending return to a constitutional and parliamentary system. Syria's official name was henceforth to be the Syrian Arab Republic. It would seek readmission both to the Arab League and the United Nations.

The coup was effected without much bloodshed. It was estimated that no more than fifty soldiers were killed in the few clashes that occurred between the Syrian and the Egyptian troops. The rebels assumed control of Damascus very rapidly and virtually without opposition. In Aleppo the situation was somewhat confused at first inasmuch as certain officers loyal to Sarraj tried to oppose the proindependence elements. Before the day was over, however, the latter were in full control of the city. Informed of the Syrian uprising, Nasser first gave orders to Egyptian paratroops to land in Lattakia. Within a few hours, however, he decided not to resist and ordered his troops to surrender. In subsequent broadcasts and public speeches he blamed Syria's defection on a group of "reactionaries" and "agents of imperialism."

Syria's revolution was greeted with undisguised satisfaction in all those countries of the Middle East which had some "unsettled accounts" with President Nasser. Jordan, Turkey, and Iran promptly extended their recognition to Syria's new regime, as a result of which the Cairo government broke off diplomatic relations with Amman and Ankara (relations with Iran had been severed a year earlier).

Politics and Ideology after Syria's Defection

The breakup of the union with Syria was soon followed by the termination of the federation arrangement with the kingdom of Yemen. Egyptian-Yemeni relations had been strained for some time, primarily because of the substantial differences between the respective political systems. After Egypt's socialism was ridiculed in a little poem attributed to the Imam of Yemen, it was not surprising that, in an angry reaction, Nasser put a formal end to the federation on December 26, 1961.

Syria's defection was a blow to Nasser's pride as well as the first major reverse in his triumphant progress as a Pan-Arab leader. He never fully recovered from the wound thus inflicted and, as some observers maintained, till the end of his life was obsssessed with Syria. Although officially he disclaimed any desire for forceful reunification, he neither ceased thinking of a possible reunion nor abstained from endeavors to undermine the secessionist regime in Syria. The Syrians, however, were in no mood to tolerate conspiracies and subversion by Nasser's partisans or agents, and all Nasser's attempts to bring about reunification through the overthrow of various Syrian governments proved unsuccessful.

More important perhaps, Syria's defection put into motion a soul-searching process in Egypt. Nasser and his associates were compelled to analyze the reasons why Syria defected. Before long their diagnosis could be summed up as follows: Union with Syria failed (as did the federation with Yemen) because in both cases unity lacked strong foundations, was too superficial, and thus too weak to withstand inevitable strains. Strong foundations could not be laid because of the marked differences between the political and socioeconomic systems of the component parts of the union. Both Syria and Yemen, each in its own way, were unprepared for a true symbiosis with revolutionary Egypt. To achieve a lasting union any country entering into a unity agreement with Egypt would have first to undergo profound socioeconomic and political change that would bring its system in line with that of Egypt.

If this was the diagnosis, then the next question was, what kind of system did or should Egypt have? Nasser and his colleagues experienced the need for a better elaboration of the principles of their own revolution. Consequently, during the winter and spring of 1961–62, Egypt may be said to have fallen back on its own internal problems and was less active in inter-Arab affairs.

After some preparatory work, on May 21, 1962, the National Congress of Popular Forces, composed of 1,750 participants, convened in Cairo to hear President Nasser proclaim the national charter. This lengthy document defined the ideological principles that were henceforth to guide Egypt's destiny.[41] These principles could be summed up under three main headings, socialism, nationalism, and anti-imperialism. Arab socialism admitted the existence of the private sector alongside the public sector but gave the latter primacy. The state was called upon to perform major development tasks and to control and plan the general economy. Nationalism was to be a Pan-Arab variety, therefore subordinating regional (that is, Egyptian, Syrian, and so on) interests to those of the Arab nation—from the borders of Persia to the Atlantic—as a whole. The Arab nation thus defined was to strive for unity. But unity would have to be preceded by a presumably revolutionary change in each region, which would make this unity stable and meaningful. Arabs were to struggle to emancipate themselves from any trace of imperialism and colonialism and, to ensure full success for these endeavors, they should follow a policy of neutralism, nonalignment, and close cooperation with the "socialist camp."

While this impressive document sounded radical in many respects, it did not advocate the establishment of a system identical with communism. As the well-known editor of the semiofficial *Al-Ahram*, Mohammed Hassanein Heikal, explained, there were substantial differences between Arab socialism and communism: Arab socialism was nationalist while communism was internationalist; Arab socialism rejected the concept of class warfare in favor of social harmony among all classes; its economic policy refused to sacrifice the well-being of the present generation for the sake of the future ones as was the practice of communism; and, finally, it accepted religion and rejected atheism.[42]

Socialism and Police State Methods

The next step was to put the principles of the charter into practice. Some features of it were already practiced in Egypt. Nasser's attention was focused on building up a reliable, disciplined, and ideologically motivated political organization. The old National Union was dissolved and replaced by a new entity called the Arab Socialist Union (ASU). It was to be have two types of membership: general, embracing as large a number of adherents as possible, and an active inner corps, presumably possessing a higher degree of ideological indoctrination and entrusted with more specific and demanding tasks. Special commissions were appointed to screen the candidates for membership to avoid diluting the ideological purity and organiza-

[41]The charter was approved on June 30, 1962. Text in United Arab Republic, Information Department, *The Charter* (Cairo, n.d.).

[42]Mohammed H. Heikal, "We and Communism," in *Rose el-Youssef* (weekly), Cairo, No. 1767 (April 23, 1962), quoted in full in Anouar Abdel Malek, *Egypt: Military Society* (New York, 1968), pp. 292–297.

tional cohesion of the new entity. The national assembly was continued with the provision that half of its 342 seats were to be assigned to peasants and workers. Moreover, the Arab Socialist Union would have the sole right to nominate candidates for the assembly. By 1964 a new constitution was adopted for the republic. Its ideological provisions reflected the principles already enunciated in the national charter of 1962 and it confirmed the existing political structure in the country with a strong presidency and a single licensed political organization.[43] It reaffirmed the military-ideological dictatorship in force in Egypt, and thus possessed a declaratory character. Its adoption, therefore, could not be regarded as a significant event in Egypt's political life. Furthermore, the formal structure of the state underwent a number of changes and fluctuations. At one time or another, the decrees provided for the establishment of one or more offices of the vice-president of the republic; during certain periods, the vice-presidencies were either abolished or overshadowed by the office of prime minister. And, in turn, that office would be held either by an individual appointed by President Nasser or by himself, depending on the circumstances. The office of the prime minister was held consecutively by Ali Sabri (1962-1965), Zakaria Muhieddin (1965-1966), Mohammed Sidki Suleiman (1966-67), and Nasser himself (June 19, 1967-September, 1970). These high offices were generally held by Nasser's early associates in the Revolutionary Command Council. In the later 1960s this initially very cohesive group shrank, some members disapproving of Nasser's policies and thereby making themselves politically inacceptable. Vice-President Abdul Hakim Amer's term was ended by his imprisonment and subsequent suicide in the later 1960s.

Implementation of the socialist program was signified by a wave of nationalizations decreed on August 12, 1963, when 240 private companies were taken over by the state. These measures were accompanied by arbitrary confiscations of property, including land estates, often directed against actual or suspected political enemies. These confiscations (officially referred to as sequestrations) were applied in addition to or regardless of the basic land reform program that affected many landowners. Under the Land Reform Law of 1952 the maximum allowed to a single family was two hundred *feddans* of land. This maximum was reduced first to one hundred *feddans* and later to fifty.

The attitude of the state toward foreign capital continued to be one of hostility. In the mid-1960s, however, the government, anxious to develop the country's potential oil resources, turned to certain American corporations asking them to undertake exploration for oil, primarily in the western desert but also in the Red Sea region. This way Standard Oil of Indiana and Phillips Oil Company expanded their activities to Egypt despite the basically discouraging attitude of the government toward foreign enterprise. At the same time, the state took upon itself the major task of financing the industrialization of the country. A number of projects were launched with active technical and financial assistance from the Soviet Union or East European communist-controlled states. Furthermore, the Egyptian economy was quickly

[43]Text of the U.A.R. Provisional Constitution of March 23, 1964, in Walid Khalidi and Yusuf Ibish, eds., *Arab Political Documents 1964* (Beirut, n.d.), pp. 86-99.

acquiring the directed and autarchic characteristics of the economies of socialist and communist states isolated from the world market forces. Egyptian currency was not only nonconvertible but actually suffered considerable depreciation. It was exchanged for foreign currencies at artifically pegged prices. This policy was accompanied by inevitable curbs on travel, partly for economic and partly for political reasons.

Side by side with these developments, a vast network of bureaucracy was growing. Part of it was responsible for the normal administrative functions of the state; but another, substantial, part was employed in state-owned enterprises, with inevitable inefficiency, bloated payrolls, and much political patronage. A number of army officers thus found themselves reassigned to the state-controlled economic sector as managers and executives either because they ceased to be useful in the army or to reward them for their services. Simultaneously, internal security required the development of a sizable secret police apparatus.

The gradual erosion of political freedoms found its expression in the purge and the virtual takeover of the newspapers by the government (officially by ASU) in 1966. It was at that time that Mustafa Amin, the influential editor of *Akhbar el-Yom,* was dismissed from his post.[44] These measures completed the process of extending the authorities' control over the news media, a process that had begun in 1960.

In spite of the expansion of the government's political controls over the society, cases of dissidence did occur from time to time. Although officially suppressed in the 1950s, the Moslem Brotherhood somehow managed to survive and to attract adherents. It surfaced again in February 1966, when it was accused of plotting the assassination of President Nasser, and a number its members were arrested. This wave of repression against Moslem brethren was repeated in the early fall of that same year.

The Communist party constituted a special case. Although Nasser never concealed his distrust of, and hostility to, communism, believing it to be an agency of a foreign power, he did repeatedly avail himself of the services of well-known Marxists, particularly in the press and publishing sector. On their part, the communists had to define their own attitude toward the regime. In accordance with the new tactical line adopted by Moscow in the 1960s, the Egyptian communists accepted Nasser's system as one of "revolutionary democracy," which they decided to support and in which they sought, if possible, participation. Inasmuch as Nasser was willing to accept their collaboration only on an individual basis, not as an organized political entity, the Communist party officially, on April 25, 1964, pronounced its self-dissolution. A number of its members, particularly the "intellectuals," sought admission to the ASU and offered their services, especially their literary talents, to the regime.

Nasser traditionally could count on spontaneous support from the usually radical

---

[44]He was arrested in the spring of 1965, charged with espionage for the United States, and sentenced to life imprisonment. He was released, rehabilitated, and reinstated in his editorial position in the 1970s under the presidency of Anwar el-Sadat.

and nationalist student population. Students were willing to accept restrictions on political freedom, economic inconveniences if not actual penury, and gradual isolation from the West, provided the higher values of Arab unity, nationalism, and socialism were served. Eventually, particularly after 1967, this student support began to waver, largely because of reverses in Nasser's Arab and international policies. After many years of harmony between the government and the universities, Cairo was treated to massive student demonstrations, sometimes combined with those of workers in large state-owned enterprises.

Nasser's Arab Policies in the 1960s

The principle enunciated by the National Charter of 1962, that Arab unity should be preceded by a radical change in any state wishing to enter into a union agreement with Egypt, conveyed the idea that Egypt's socialist revolution was "for export."[45] How this exportation of the revolutionary pattern was to be accomplished was not specified: A radical change might occur through native forces in a given country, or it might be instigated or supported by Egypt, depending on the circumstances. Yemen, a remote kingdom in semimedieval slumber, was to provide the first major test of Egypt's new revolutionary strategy. In September 1962, a military conspiracy overthrew the monarchy in Sana and the army proclaimed a republic. While leaving further details to the chapter on Yemen, suffice it to say here that the deposed Imam, Mohammed Badr, survived the initial attack and seizure of the royal palace, sought refuge in the mountains, and there rallied to himself faithful tribes who defied the authority of the newly proclaimed republican government. As a result, a civil war ensued. It soon appeared that the republican forces—which mostly relied on the regular army—were not in a position to impose their authority upon the entire country and that independent tribesmen of royalist sympathies not only succeeded in controlling large parts of the country, but actually threatened the survival of the new republican government. As could be expected under the circumstances, the republican leaders looked to revolutionary Egypt for support. They were not disappointed: Nasser offered help by sending substantial contingents of troops to Yemen. The Saudis, anxious to preserve the monarchical principle in Yemen, lent their support to the dethroned Imam and his loyal tribesmen, not with actual military intervention but in the form of money and supplies which began reaching northern Yemen from Saudi border localities such as Najran.

Under the circumstances, what began as a palace coup evolved first into a civil war and then into an international contest in which the prestige of the Islamic and traditionalist Saudi monarchy was pitted against Nasser's revolutionary principle. Contrary to his early expectations, Nasser soon found that the Yemen adventure necessitated a much larger military force to ensure victory for the republicans. Egyptian expeditionary forces in Yemen steadily grew in size until by the mid-1960s they reached the vicinity of 80,000 troops. Their very size, and the major economic and logistical effort that their presence in Yemen represented, testified to

[45]M. H. Heikal, "We do not want to solidarize ourselves," *Al-Ahram,* March 9, 1962. Excerpts in A. A. Malek, *op. cit.,* p. 276.

554 THE MIDDLE EAST IN WORLD AFFAIRS

the serious Pan-Arab revolutionary commitment of President Nasser. It was indeed a revolution for export. Moreover, Yemen, somewhat like Spain in the latter 1930s, became both an actual and a symbolic battlefield for competing ideologies in the Arab world.

Despite many attempts to find a compromise solution, the war with its foreign intervention dragged on until 1967. It might have lasted even longer had the Egyptian army not been defeated at the hands of the Israelis in the June war of 1967. In the aftermath of this defeat Nasser was obliged to withdraw most of his forces from Yemen and to seek peace. Finally, a settlement was achieved at a conference in Khartoum on August 30, 1967. According to its terms both Egypt and Saudi Arabia pledged to abstain from further intervention in Yemen. The existing republican government of Yemen in control of the capital city of Sana and the summer capital of Taiz remained in power. As could be expected, relations between Egypt and Saudi Arabia had deteriorated in the course of the war and, on several occasions, Egyptian military aircraft bombed Najran and other border localities in Saudi Arabia.

In the case of Yemen the Arab Cold War degenerated into a hot one. The search for all-embracing Arab unity, characteristic of the early period of Nasser's government, was replaced by attempts to effect closer unity among the revolutionary states. Two episodes deserve special attention in this connection: first, an attempt to form a union among Egypt, Syria, and Iraq in 1963; second, endeavors to establish unity between Egypt and Iraq after 1964. As for the first, the spur to the unity movement was given by the installation of the Baath in Iraq and Syria in February and March, 1963. Within a few weeks, the combined government and party delegations from Syria and Iraq converged upon Cairo to hold unity talks with President Nasser. Syria's delegation was headed by Prime Minister Salah ed-Din el-Bitar, and Iraq was represented by Premier General Ahmed Hassan Bakr. Moreover, the cofounder of the party, Michel Aflaq, was also present. Negotiations, of which published accounts subsequently became available, were difficult and sometimes acrimonious.[46] Remembering his grievious experience with the party in Syria during the union period of 1958 to 1961, Nasser distrusted the Baath leadership. On their part, Syrian Baathists wanted to avoid the mistake made in 1958 when so much power was concentrated in the hands of Nasser. Consequently, they insisted on a federal rather than unitary type of government, and on collective leadership while conceding to Nasser the presidency of the future state. Moreover, in terms of ideology, the Baath considered itself senior to Nasser's system. He clearly resented their stance in this respect and rather unmercifully tried to ridicule the modest and unassuming Michel Aflaq, whose halting speech and somewhat complicated explanations became a target of Nasser's ironical remarks and rude interruptions. Ultimately, on April 10 a federation agreement was concluded, to be implemented after its approval by referenda in the three negotiating countries.[47] The ink was barely dry on the agreement when mutual recriminations began between Syria and Egypt. The

[46]Minutes of talks in *Arab Political Documents 1963*, pp. 75–217.
[47]Text in *ibid.*, pp. 227–246.

Syrians accused Nasser of attempts to undermine and subvert their regime while Nasser was expressing his distaste for the disloyal attitudes of the Syrian Baath. On July 22 he went so far as to denounce publicly the agreement with the Syrians. Soon afterwards, an Iraqi delegation, this time headed by President Abdul Salam Aref, came to Cairo to act as a mediator in the Egyptian-Syrian conflict and to see whether anything of the proposed agreement could be salvaged. Their intervention, however, brought no results. Despite some comforting communiques at the end of their visit, the matter remained unresolved and the tripartite union never materialized.

Before long a new opportunity arose for the exploration of a possible inter-Arab unity. This time the main actor was Iraq where, in November 1963, the Baath party was overthrown by President Abdul Salem Aref who established a regime based on support of the military. Ever since 1958, when he appeared as second-in-command to General Abdul Karim Kassem at the time of the Iraqi revolution, General Aref had been an admirer of President Nasser and an advocate of Arab unity. The removal of the Baath from power was an opportunity to give practical meaning to his Pan-Arab ideas. On May 26, 1964, during Aref's visit to Cairo, the two leaders concluded an agreement establishing the joint military command in case of war and providing for the gradual implementation of federal union between the two countries.[48] A year later, in May 1965, the agreement was not only confirmed but further expanded, and a number of joint commissions and bodies, headed by the joint political leadership composed of the two presidents, was set up. In practice, however, there was no indication that either of the two countries was surrendering the essence of its sovereignty in favor of real unity. The joint commissions met and deliberated from time to time to discuss economic, cultural, and other matters, but the decision-making power was still held by the two respective leaders whose policies were dictated by concern for their own countries' interests. True enough, an attempt was made in Iraq to set up the Arab Socialist Union modeled on the organization already in existence in Egypt. This could be interpreted as Nasser's method of paving the way for a full union between the two countries, making their political systems exactly alike. However, in Iraq the formation and early activities of the local ASU provoked a good deal of resentment and suspicion. Some members of the Iraqi ruling establishment regarded the local ASU as a vehicle for the extension of Nasser's power to Baghdad. In this atmosphere of growing suspicion one could not expect much progress toward real unity. Some Iraqis actually accused Nasser of trying to overthrow Aref's government through recruited partisans in the Iraqi army while Aref was attending a Pan-Arab conference with Nasser in Casablanca in September 1965. This mutual suspicion was further accentuated during the term of office of President Abdur Rahman Aref, who succeeded his brother Abdul Salam Aref after the latter died in a helicopter accident in 1966.

Although attempts to achieve unity either with Iraq or with Syria did not produce the desired results, Nasser continued to provide broad spiritual and political leadership to a large segment of the Arab world. The displaced Palestinians invariably looked to him for guidance and inspiration, and he reciprocated by supporting the

---

[48]Text in *Arab Political Documents 1964*, pp. 217–219.

Palestine Liberation Organization (PLO), formed at a Pan-Arab meeting in Cairo in 1964, and provided it with radio facilities in his capital.

In retrospect, however, Nasser's Pan-Arab policy brought more divisiveness than unity to the Arab ranks for two reasons. First, his concept of unity ever since the breakup of the U.A.R. in 1961 was based on a revolutionary foundation; second, Egypt with himself as her leader would enjoy the position of primacy in any union. While many younger Arabs with nationalist and radical tendencies fully embraced these two propositions, Arab governments were reluctant to accept them. The conservative monarchies and other nonrevolutionary states such as Lebanon were obviously opposed to an abrupt change in their form of government and style of living. On the other hand, those states that had already undergone a revolution, for example, Syria or Iraq, were reluctant to join in a union or federation that might end in their subordination to Egypt's commands. Consequently, although the Arab cold war could be described as a political and ideological struggle punctuated by occasional violence, even the radical camp was far from reaching unity and was developing polycentric tendencies.

Foreign Policy in the 1960s

While the formally proclaimed stance was neutralism and nonalignment, in practice President Nasser drew steadily closer to the Soviet Union and the Communist bloc. The Soviets became the sole suppliers of sophisticated arms to Egypt, and the magnitude of their economic and technical assistance to the Egyptian economy exceeded that from any other country. In his public speeches Nasser frequently referred to "imperialism," but by this word he essentially meant Western policies and practices regardless of whether they were actually imperialistic. He tended to be oblivious to the fact that the great Western empires—British, French, Dutch, Portuguese—had gradually shrunk and disintegrated while the Soviet Union not only remained as the sole large empire in the world, but was also engaged in the process of expansion. Friendship with Moscow was underlined by the exhange of mutual visits. Nasser visited the Soviet capital a number of times and, in turn, received in Cairo at one time or another Chairman Khrushchev and his successors, Premier Kosygin and President Podgorny. Khrushchev attended the ceremonies of inauguration of the first stage of Aswan Dam in May 1964, while Podgorny was present at the completion of the work on the dam in January 1971, after Nasser's death.

Another major feature of Nasser's foreign policy was his insistence on the cultivation of the Third World countries, particularly those with leaders who were known as advocates of neutralism in world politics. India's Premier Jawaharlal Nehru and his daughter and successor Indira Gandhi, as well as Marshal Tito of Yugoslavia, figured prominently as Nasser's close friends with whom he held a number of bilateral or collective meetings.

Nasser's close relations with communist powers, his frequent denunciations of American imperialism, his militant posture against Israel, and his intervention in Yemen and Saudi Arabia irritated American-Egyptian relations. Nasser, however, tended to keep diplomatic communications with the United States open, allowed the continuous functioning of the American University at Cairo, and encouraged American oil investments in Egypt. The dominant factors in his relations with Washington were his stance of hostility toward Israel and his frequent criticism of America's support for that country.

The June War and Its Aftermath

The war that broke out on June 5, 1967, between Israel and Egypt, and soon drew in other Arab countries as well resulted from decisions made in various Middle Eastern capitals at the time and certain forces that had been put into motion some time earlier, which conditioned the behavior of the parties in the war. Nasser's traditional anti-Zionist and anti-imperialist attitude constituted a major force in this respect. It led him to make statements and proclaim slogans of a militant nature which were bound to intensify Israel's obsession with her own security. Nasser's militant pronouncements, however, were not invariably followed by deeds. He spoke of liberation of the Arab homeland usurped by the Israelis and gave support to the PLO but did nothing directly to implement these pronouncements. Moreover, by allowing the United Nations Emergency Force (UNEF) to be stationed on the Egyptian side of the Israeli-Egyptian border line as well as along the eastern coast of the Sinai Peninsula after 1957, Nasser appeared to accept a situation of inequality, for Israel adamantly opposed the presence of UN troops on its territory. This discrepancy between words and deeds did not escape the notice of Nasser's rivals in the Arab world. Among these could be mentioned Saudi Arabia, Jordan, and Syria. Their governments had been threatened at one time or another by Nasser's revolutionary and expansionist militancy; consequently, in the winter and spring of 1967 their media repeatedly castigated Nasser for the inconsistency of his behavior, for not matching words with deeds and, occasionally, for cowardice in hiding behind the protective shield of UNEF rather than thinking of the liberation of the Palestinian homeland.[49]

Thus, as some Arab observers would say, "Nasser became a prisoner of his own words." Irritated by these attacks and anxious to prove that he was not willing to tolerate any longer the unequal position with respect to the presence of the UN troops, Nasser demanded on May 28 that the UN force be removed from the Egyptian-Israeli border. The commander, General Rikhye of India, promptly accepted this demand and ordered his troops withdrawn not only from the Egyptian-Israeli border but from the eastern coastline of the Sinai Peninsula as well. He did it, as he later explained, in order to avoid any possible clash and bloodshed. From the legal point of view, Nasser had an uncontested right to demand the removal of this force because it was stationed on Egyptian territory by his permission. Permission could be withdrawn at any time and, in this respect, Egypt had the same right of

[49]In a speech at a mass rally at Muna as early as January 25, 1963, the crown prince and prime minister of Saudi Arabia, Prince Faisal set a pattern for such accusations: "If Egypt wants to resist aggression, there's a place nearer than the Yemen: it should start by removing the U.N. Emergency Forces from the Palestine borders. As everyone knows, the presence of these forces on the Jewish borders depends on a word from Egypt." (Full text in *Prince Faisal Speaks,* an official pamphlet published in 1963 by the Government of Saudi Arabia.)

sovereign decision as did Israel, which never permitted the force to be stationed on its side of the border.[50] Politically, however, the move was unwise unless Nasser was clearly aiming at launching a war against Israel. There is no evidence that this was his intention. Nevertheless, having removed the UNEF from the eastern marches of his country, he announced that henceforth the Strait of Tiran connecting the Gulf of Aqaba with the Red Sea would be blockaded to Israeli shipping. As for the promptness with which the commanding general of the UN troops ordered their withdrawal following the Egyptian demand, one might well debate whether he had not transcended his authority. After all, the UNEF was established as a result of a formal agreement between the United Nations (on the basis of the General Assembly's resolution) and the government of Egypt. Consequently, Nasser's demand should have been taken up by the supreme authorities of the United Nations, that is, either the General Assembly or the Security Council, and the decision should not have been left in the hands of the commanding general of the troops. Had the matter been referred to these bodies, it is quite likely that the events would have taken a different course and war might have been avoided.

With the removal of UNEF and the announcement of the blockade of the Strait of Tiran (actually the blockade was never enforced), the stage was open for a strong Israeli reaction. The Israelis considered the removal of the UNEF a hostile act, but it was Nasser's decision to blockade the Strait of Tiran that was defined by the Israeli government as a *casus belli*. Fearing the worst, the United States government engaged in intensive negotiations with both the Israelis and the Egyptians with an eye to averting war. These efforts were of no avail. On June 5 the Israelis launched a surprise attack on Egypt by air and on land and within a few days overran not only the Gaza strip but the entire Sinai Peninsula up to the Suez Canal. The Egyptian air force was virtually annihilated in the first few hours of the war. Thousands of Egyptian troops were taken prisoner and much Soviet-supplied Egyptian equipment fell into the hands of the Israelis.

By virtue of previous military agreements among Egypt, Jordan, Syria, and Iraq the other three Arab countries also became belligerents in the short-lived war, although each in a different way. In fulfillment of his pledges, King Hussein of Jordan ordered his troops into action. They experienced a strong Israeli offensive which resulted in the occupation of East Jerusalem and the entire West Bank territory of the Kingdom of Jordan. Iraq had no time to mobilize and arrange for any significant movement of troops toward the front line. A well-executed Israeli attack resulted in the destruction of the greater part of the Iraqi air force. Syria's military moves were not properly synchronized with those of Egypt, and there was no significant participation of Syrian troops in the fighting while the Israelis were advancing into Egyptian territory. The main Israeli-Syrian battle came after the proclamation of the first cease-fire, when the Israelis launched a bold attack against the Golan Heights, an area from which the Syrian army had been able to observe and

[50]Premier Ben Gurion rejected stationing of UNEF on Israeli soil after the 1956 Suez Crisis as a violation of Israeli sovereignty. See Anthony Nutting, *Nasser* (London, 1972), p. 188.

fire on the Israeli troops and civilians in the region of Lake Tiberias since 1948. After the Israeli army occupied the Golan Heights, a new cease-fire was proclaimed.

The war's operations on four separate fronts has been treated in a number of specialized works, but it is important to point out here the enormity of the Arab defeat.[51] The smaller but better organized, technologically superior, and strongly motivated Israeli armed forces scored a spectacular victory over the much larger armies of four Arab states, three of which had been generously armed and equipped by the Soviet Union. One does not need to belabor the point that to Nasser this was a traumatic experience, and it led him on June 9 to tender his resignation from the presidency. Despite the utter failure of his political and military leadership the popular masses in Cairo staged demonstrations in his favor asking that he rescind his decision. Accepting the "verdict of the people" Nasser agreed to continue as leader of Egypt.

The cease-fires as well as the establishment of an observer force were the work of the United Nations, which tried to restore peace to the area. Of these UN-sponsored activities in search of peace two deserve special mention: On July 4, 1967, the UN General Assembly condemned the Israeli decision to annex the formerly Jordanian part of the city of Jerusalem. Officially Israel called it "administrative unification," but the intent was clear, and in numerous subsequent pronouncements the Israeli leaders declared that the matter of Israeli control of the entire city of Jerusalem was not negotiable. In this vote there were nineteen abstentions, with the United States voting against the resolution. Second, by Resolution 242 on November 22, 1967, the UN Security Council adopted a plan for a peace settlement to be based on the following principles:

1. withdrawal of Israeli armed forces from territories occupied in the recent conflict;
2. termination of all claims or states of belligerency and respect for and acknowledgment of the sovereignty, territorial integrity, and political independence of every State in the area and their right to live in peace within secure and recognized boundaries free from threats or acts of force.

The Security Council also affirmed the necessity:

a. for guaranteeing freedom of navigation through international waterways in the area;
b. for achieving a just settlement of the refugee problem;
c. for guaranteeing the territorial inviolability and political independence of every State in the area, through measures including the establishment of demilitarized zones.[52]

Furthermore, the Security Council requested "the Secretary General to designate a special representative to proceed to the Middle East to establish and maintain

---

[51]Such as Edgar O'Ballance, *Third Arab-Israeli War* (London, 1972); Nadav Safran, *From War to War* (New York, 1969); Ibrahim Abu-Lughod, *The Arab-Israeli Confrontation of June 1967: An Arab Perspective* (Evanston, Ill., 1970).

[52]Text in Ralph H. Magnus, *Documents on the Middle East* (Washington, D.C., 1969), pp. 205–206.

contacts with the States concerned in order to promote agreement and assist efforts to achieve the peaceful and accepted settlement in accordance with the provisions and principles in this resolution.'"[53]

The unanimous adoption of Resolution 242 by the Security Council meant that however they might have differed in their ultimate objectives in the Middle East, both the United States and the Soviet Union reached a consensus on this issue. To be sure, the resolution did not explicitly say that Israeli withdrawal should be from *all* the territories occupied by them; it did not even use the article "the" before the word "territories," thereby leaving this sentence open to varying interpretations. However, the United States' view, both under the Johnson administration and under the Nixon administration, was that withdrawal should be substantial and that only insignificant territorial changes should be allowed in the peace settlement. This policy was expressed by President Johnson in his speech to the B'nai B'rith on September 10, 1968, when he said that "boundaries cannot and should not reflect the weight of conquest."[54] Amplifying this line of policy, Secretary of State William Rogers stated on December 9, 1969, in a speech delivered at the Galaxy Conference in Washington: "We believe that while recognized political boundaries must be established and agreed upon by the parties, any changes in the pre-existing lines should not reflect the weight of conquest and should be confined to insubstantial alterations required for mutual security. We do not support expansionism. We believe troops must be withdrawn as the resolution provides."[55]

Egypt (and subsequently Jordan and Syria) accepted UN Resolution 242 as a way of resolving the conflict.

Toward the end of August 1967 the heads of the Arab states gathered in Khartoum. The purpose of the meeting was to define a joint Arab foreign policy as well as to resolve any problems that divided the Arab states. The participants decided to seek a "political" solution for the Arab-Israeli conflict, meaning that they rejected the alternative of a renewed war. The future settlement, however, was to be based on the principle that there would be "no recognition, no negotiation, and no peace convenant with Israel." The phrasing of this declaration gave rise to subsequent Israeli criticisms that despite their talk of a "political" solution, the Arabs in reality did not want peace. These criticisms were based more on a misunderstanding or poor translation of the original Arabic text than on reality. The Arabic language has two terms referring to peace: *silm* is peace as a general condition of tranquility free of hostilities; *sulh* means a peace treaty or peace convenant. The Khartoum comunique stated that there would be no *sulh*. The Arab policy called for a condition of peace and tranquility but without formal signing of a treaty with Israel, which would involve diplomatic recognition and negotiation. While this kind of peace is obviously less perfect than one based on formally signed treaty, nevertheless history and current international relations provide many examples of such an arrangement. For example, the United States for a long time did not recognize the Soviet Union and,

[53]*Ibid.*
[54]*Ibid.*, pp. 208–210.
[55]Text in *New York Times*, Dec. 11, 1969.

after the communist revolution in China, did not recognize Mao Tse-tung's government. Yet the condition of general peace did prevail between the United States and these countries. A similar example was the United States' relations with Cuba at the time: war had been ruled out, a condition of tranquillity prevailed but there was no recognition or diplomatic connection. President Nasser was realistic enough to know that solution of the Arab-Israeli conflict by means of a renewed war was not feasible. His subsequent acceptance of UN Resolution 242 indicated that he saw advantages in conforming to it, for it promised return of the occupied territories.

Although a special envoy of the United Nations, Ambassador Gunnar Jarring of Sweden, engaged in intensive negotiations with all the parties concerned to bring about the implementation of the UN resolution, no progress was registered, largely because of Israel's reluctance to abide by its terms.

This being the case, the cease-fire along the Suez Canal suffered a gradual deterioration until it reached the proportions of continuous exchange of fire between the Egyptian and Israeli troops, a situation frequently referred to as the "war of attrition." Moreover, hostilities occasionally extended beyond the canal zone, with Israeli raids and bombings of selected targets in the interior of Egypt. At this point the United States began to exert major efforts to bring this dangerous situation to an end. Secretary Rogers came forward with a peace plan essentially based on the UN Resolution 242 and called upon both Egypt and Israel to accept a new cease-fire. The parties accepted it in August 1970.

In the meantime, the Arab-Israeli conflict acquired a new dimension that was bound to have repercussions in Egypt. The Arab defeat of 1967 spurred the rise of numerous Palestinian guerrilla organizations, the *fedayeen,* which began to engage in raids and attacks on Israeli civilian settlements and military installations. These organizations, of which the largest was Fatah, were mostly affiliated with the PLO and had their main concentrations in the kingdom of Jordan, with sizable contingents also in Syria and Lebanon. The challenge that they presented to the official authorities in Jordan led to an open armed clash between the forces of King Hussein and the *Fedayeen.*[56] While it ended in a military victory for the Jordanian forces, an attempt on a Pan-Arab scale was made to resolve the conflict, in the form of a conference in Cairo called by Nasser in September 1970. In the final stages of this conference, Nasser died of a heart attack on September 28.

The Presidency of Anwar el-Sadat

Following Nasser's death, the acting presidency was assumed by his early companion and vice-president, Colonel Anwar el-Sadat. He was elected president by the National Assembly on October 7, a decision later confirmed by a popular election. In November he was also elected chairman of the Arab Socialist Union. Upon assuming power he appointed a veteran diplomat and statesman, Mahmoud Fawzi, as prime minister. Despite the appearances of a smooth transition, Sadat was op-

[56]See above, p. 494.

posed by certain powerful factions in the ruling establishment. Their opposition stemmed partly from disappointment that it was Sadat and not themselves who were promoted to the presidency, partly from fear that their position of tremendous influence and power would be reduced or destroyed under the new dispensation, and partly from the hope of some for a more pronounced leftist orientation, a closer alliance with the Soviet Union than Sadat was prepared to espouse. The chief opponents were Ali Sabri, former vice president and former premier; Shaarawi Gomaa, minister of the interior; Sami Sharaf, minister of state; and Abdul Mohsen Abu el-Nur, secretary general of the ASU. This group conspired to remove Sadat but their plot was discovered on May 2, 1971, and all four of them, together with a number of associates, were arrested, placed on trial, and subsequently given long prison sentences. To insure the efficiency and loyalty of the security services, Sadat appointed Mamdouh Salem, a man he trusted, as minister of the interior.

Officially, the new president professed to adhere strictly to Nasser's legacy in domestic, Arab, and foreign policy. In reality, however, it soon became apparent that Sadat had launched a thorough policy of "de-Nasserization" in virtually every field of public policy. In the domestic political process Sadat inaugurated an era of liberalism that contrasted with the police methods used in the last years of Nasser's presidency. Egyptians found travel abroad easier than it had been. Citizens began to move and to express their opinions with much greater freedom. Censorship over the Egyptian press was formally removed, and editorials espousing various points of view began to appear even though the newspapers continued to be owned by the ASU. Two important newspaper editors and writers, Mustafa Amin and Ali Amin, previously victims of Nasser's hostility, were reinstated by Sadat. A writer strongly critical of past practices under Nasser's socialism, Ihsan Abdel Kuddous, was first appointed to an important job in the press establishment and eventually designated chairman of the board and editor in chief of *Al-Ahram* to replace Nasser's close associate Mohammed Hassanein Heikal. On his part, President Sadat did not cease to castigate what he called the old centers of power, composed of influential dignitaries in the intelligence and ASU organizations, who, according to him, exercized arbitrary power and were guilty of many abuses.

There was also an interesting transformation of the role of the National Assembly and the ASU under the new dispensation. While these organs could be regarded as mere appendages of the power structure under Nasser, to be freely removed or purged in case they did not follow the leader's orders and guidance, they began to acquire an autonomous position that Sadat respected. Gradually, he introduced the custom of reporting to these two bodies on his major policy decisions, encouraging free debate, and seeking their approval. It was not yet a truly democratic process according to the Western models; elements clearly hostile to Sadat, particularly those of proven or suspected association with Ali Sabri, were one way or another eliminated from meaningful participation in the political process. Furthermore, Ali Sabri's conspiracy taught Sadat that he could not dispense with the services of the secret police, the army, and other organs of security. However, on the whole the Egyptians began to enjoy a markedly greater degree of freedom than they had during the concluding period of Nasser's regime. This evolution toward liberalization reached such an advanced stage by 1976 that Sadat fully encouraged and approved the appearance within the ASU of three groupings identified with the left, center, and right of the political spectrum. In the National Assembly the left, headed by Khalid Muhi ed-Din secured 2 seats, the right under Mustafa Khalid Murad 14, and the center, headed by Mamdouh Salem (by then prime minister), 280 seats.[57] That same year, President Sadat was reelected by a popular vote to his second six-year term.

Liberalization was also proclaimed in the economic sector. First, the government announced desequestration of lands and properties arbitrarily seized from a number of citizens by Nasser's government. Second, while still officially adhering to the policy of socialism, President Sadat and his ministers repeatedly proclaimed their encouragement of the private sector, the role of which was to be enlarged. Third, the government tried to attract investments from oil-rich Arab states as well as from foreign countries. Major American oil companies such as Exxon and Mobil were granted offshore concessions in the Gulf of Suez and the Mediterranean. Moreover, the government fully cooperated with the partly foreign-sponsored project— launched during Nasser's era—the Suez-Mediterranean pipeline (SUMED), which was to carry oil from the Middle East for European destinations.

This policy of economic "opening up" (infitah) was not crowned with immediate success. After nearly two decades of socialism and arbitrary seizures and sequestrations, foreign and Arab investors required some time to become convinced that it was safe to invest in Egypt. Furthermore, the overgrown and heavily entrenched government bureaucracy, particularly in the middle and lower levels, feared a threat to its own position under a free economic system, and did its utmost to frustrate the intentions of President Sadat and members of his cabinet. Certain self-serving private entrepreneurs hastened to take advantage of the more liberal business climate to amass quick fortunes and engage in ostentatious living. This phenomenon was embarrassing to the authorities, who still adhered to Nasser's goal of greater social equality. Above all, Egypt's fundamental economic problems were not easy to solve. The population continued to grow at an explosive pace, putting great pressure on the existing scarce resources. The much advertised Aswan Dam, while advancing certain sectors of Egyptian economy such as the power network, proved to be of dubious value to agriculture because of the damming of the fertile silt which previously used to enrich the soil of Egypt's delta. The dam had also adverse effects on the fisheries in the Mediterranean. Finally, maintaining armed forces nearly half a million strong placed a heavy burden on the economy.[58] As a result, Egypt was not only continually in debt—to the Soveit Union, to oil-rich Arab states, and to certain countries in the West—but was obliged to seek new loans and grants to service old debts, to purchase wheat for its food deficit economy, and to protect itself from massive unemployment.

[57]The independents secured 48 seats.
[58]By 1978 the Egyptian military forces comprised the following: army 350,000, air force 25,000, navy 20,000; and the paramilitary: national guard 6,000, frontier corps 6,000, defense and security forces 30,000, coast guard 7,000. Source: International Institute for Strategic Studies, *The Military Balance, 1978-1979* (London, 1978), pp. 36-37.

Arab and Foreign Policy

In inter-Arab affairs, President Sadat inaugurated an altogether new policy which sharply contrasted with the revolutionary policy of President Nasser. Nasser had aimed at an ultimate Arab unity through the preparatory stage of revolution, but Sadat sought harmony among all Arab states regardless of their political structure and ideology. Thus he cultivated Saudi Arabia and other conservative oil-rich states in the Persian Gulf, hoping that by offering them immunity from revolutionary and subversive activities that had previously emanated from Cairo he could secure in turn their good will and their economic support. His calculations proved correct and the willingness of oil-rich Arab states to help Egypt in her economic difficulties became much more pronounced. Similarly, Sadat followed a policy of rapprochement and coordination with the so-called front line (or confrontation) states such as Jordan and Syria. It did not matter that the two had different political systems; their cooperation had to be secured to strengthen the common front against Israel.

There were forces in the Arab world, however, that still thought in terms of formal unity such as those advocated by Nasser. A foremost proponent of this type of Pan-Arabism was Colonel Muammar el-Qadhafi, president of the Revolutionary Command Council in Libya. Similarly, the new president of Syria, General Hafez Assad, was anxious, primarily for the sake of military cooperation, to enter into closer links with Egypt. He hoped that Syrian-Egyptian relations would improve after the change of leadership in Egypt. On his part, President Numeiri of Sudan was also eager to cooperate more closely with Egypt and was exploring the possibility of a federal agreement. The first tentative project that came out of the exchange of these ideas was the proposal to form an Egyptian-Sudanese-Libyan federation, but this plan was eventually abandoned because of domestic difficulties that President Numeiri faced. Instead, proposal for Egyptian-Syrian-Libyan federation was advanced. An agreement pledging to form such a federation and adopting its constitution was signed by the three heads of state in Damascus on August 20, 1971.[59] A more appropriate term for the new entity would be confederation inasmuch as its members retained sovereignty and no provision was made for a single federal president.

The very loose character of the new federation was disappointing to Qadhafi. Before long he began pressing for a full union between Libya and Egypt, indicating that he would be prepared to resign his presidency to achieve that objective. Although never publicly articulated, the idea frequently ascribed to him was that in return he might assume the command of the joint Egyptian-Libyan forces.

For a number of reasons President Sadat was less than enthusiastic about the idea of a full and exclusive Egyptian-Libyan union. These included the fact that the two countries were vastly different, the Egyptian urban strata being more westernized in their outlook and behavior than those of Libya. There was also a good deal of personal incompatibility between the two leaders: President Sadat was middle-aged, experienced, prudent, and practical. He knew the limitations of Egypt's economic

---

[59]Text in *The Middle East and North Africa 1975-76* (London, 1975), p. 149.

and military power. He was attuned to a pragmatic solution of his nation's problems. By contrast, Qadhafi, not then thirty years old, was idealistic, militant, and impatient, and regarded himself as the spiritual heir of Nasser. His position, for example, on Arab-Israeli relations was an uncompromising advocacy of a war of liberation against Israel and full support to the most militant elements of the Palestinian *fedayeen*. On social and cultural questions Qadhafi was dedicated to the revival of Islam. He banned alcohol in his country, closed bars and other places of entertainment and, generally, introduced a puritan style which was looked upon with concern and ridicule by the Egyptians.

Despite these misgivings, President Sadat, seeing certain economic and military advantages in closer ties with Libya, accepted Qadhafi's proposal, and on August 2, 1972, the two leaders issued in Benghazi a joint declaration agreeing to establish "unified political leadership" for Egypt and Libya in the fields of finance, education, and political and constitutional organization.[60] Furthermore, the joint declaration called for the completion of unification between the two countries by September 1, 1973, i.e. within one year. Although during that year Qadhafi's behavior (including the introduction of the "cultural revolution" in Libya) further intensified Sadat's misgivings about the wisdom of the proposed union, he again conceded to Qadhafi's pressure and on August 29, 1973, the two leaders proclaimed the "birth of a new unified Arab state." The new agreement, however, instead of stipulating the completion of unification, as originally intended, merely provided for a gradual approach to unification, by stages. Subsequently, despite the setting up of certain joint commissions, relations between the two countries gradually deteriorated and the unification agreement became a dead letter. In fact, considerable hostility developed between the two leaders. At one time—on April 17, 1974—the Egyptian authorities announced discovery of a plot aiming at the overthrow of the government and pointed to Qadhafi as the instigator. In various statements following that incident President Sadat did not hesitate to criticize Qadhafi very severely, describing his character and behavior in uncomplimentary terms.

Egyptian–Israeli Relations: The October War and Its Aftermath

From the very beginning of his presidency, Sadat was determined to seek a solution to the lingering Arab-Israeli conflict, the legacy of which was occupation by Israel of sizable parts of Egyptian territory and the need to maintain a large military force, which was a continuous burden to the Egyptian economy. Early in 1971 he made several statements promising that this would be the decisive year in resolving the conflict and restoring to Egypt its lost territory. However, as the months passed, no progress was visible despite Sadat's efforts to enlist American help in persuading Israel to accept UN Resolution 242. Moreover, the Soviet Union not only failed to deliver to Egypt certain sophisticated arms that Sadat sought to acquire but, by diverting its attention to India during the war with Pakistan in December 1971, provided a further disappointment to Sadat's expectations. At the beginning of 1972 his position in Egypt and his prestige in the Arab world were

[60]Text in *The Daily Star* (Beirut), Aug. 3, 1972.

beginning to suffer and cartoons ridiculing the discrepancy between his words and deeds began making rounds in the Arab capitals.

Sadat, however, proved to be more persistent in the pursuance of his policy than outside observers were willing to admit. He engaged in thorough preparations for a war and provided the army with intensive training for a possible offensive. In addition, he also made preparatory diplomatic moves for a possible outbreak of hostilities with Israel. His basic stance was that he was willing to recognize the existence of Israel and—as he once expressed it to the UN envoy, Gunnar Jarring—he was even ready to sign an agreement with Israel.[61] He insisted, however, on return of all the occupied territories by the Israelis. His grievance was that the no-war-no-peace situation then prevailing would prolong itself indefinitely and would eventually petrify into a de facto acceptance by the outside world of the Israeli territorial acquisitions. The only way to prevent this from happening, according to his reasoning, was to launch an attack on the Israeli forces in the Sinai Peninsula and, by provoking an international crisis, to alert the world to the inequity of the existing situation.

On October 6 Egyptian forces launched a surprise attack against the Israeli Bar-Lev line on the eastern bank of the Suez Canal. In spite of its efficient intelligence service and partly because of the Yom Kippur holiday, the Israeli army was caught off guard and the Egyptians made a breach in the Israeli defense line. After that they advanced slowly into the Sinai Peninsula. Personnel losses on both sides were substantial but even more spectacular were losses in arms and equipment, which led both sides to seek immediate relief from abroad. While the Russians rushed their arms by air to Egypt, the United States hastily organized an ambitious airlift operation to Israel. Three points deserve special mention in this connection. First, certain vital stocks of American military equipment in the NATO bases in Western Europe were depleted to meet the Israeli needs, a situation which later gave rise to complaints by American military officers.[62] Second, substantial amounts of equipment were flown from the United States by transport aircraft, which were refused landing and refueling privileges in all European NATO countries except Portugal (at that time still under the fascist leadership of President Marcello Caetano), which allowed its air base at the Azores to be used for that purpose. Third, American planes were bringing this replacement equipment not only to Israel proper but actually to advanced Israeli bases in the Sinai Peninsula itself, that is, in the theater of war. No wonder that under the circumstances the American behavior was perceived as hostile to the Arabs. On October 19 the Arab oil ministers meeting at a conference in Kuwait proclaimed an embargo on oil exports to the United States as the chief enemy of the Arab cause and coupled it with similar bans against Holland

---

[61] Text of the U.A.R. reply to Ambassador Jarring's *aide mémoire*, February 15, 1971, in John Norton Moore, ed., *The Arab-Israeli Conflict: Readings and Documents* (Princeton, N.J., 1977), pp. 1151–1153.

[62] In the spring of 1976 the Chairman of the Joint Chiefs of Staff, General George Brown, stated that "Israel was more of a burden than an asset" (*Newsweek International*, April 12, 1976) and subsequently clarified this remark by saying that Israel was a burden in the "military sense only" (see *New York Times*, Oct. 18 and 19, 1976).

and Portugal. At the same meeting, the ministers proclaimed a general cutback in Arab oil production which would affect the neutral states, but exemptions were provided for the countries that were designated as friendly.

Owing partly to the arrival of American replacement weapons for Israel and partly to the excessive prudence of the Egyptian command, which did not follow up the breach of the first defense line by rapid movement eastward, the Israelis recovered from the initial shock. They launched a counteroffensive which resulted in their recrossing of the Suez Canal and building up a substantial bridgehead on the Egyptian territory west of the canal in its middle section. At the same time, the Israelis surrounded an Egyptian army that had crossed to the east of the canal in the southern stretch of the front. From the military point of view, therefore, the initial advantage secured by the Egyptians appeared to be neutralized, and with powerful support from the United States, Israel not only stopped the Egyptian offensive but actually achieved further military successes incalculable in their consequences.

On October 16 President Sadat called for a cease-fire and Israeli withdrawal from territories seized in 1967. On October 22 a cease-fire, under the auspices of the United Nations, was declared. In spite of the cease-fires, the Israelis proceeded to seize some more territory from the Egyptians, and the war between Israel and Syria continued, the latter having synchronized its attack with the Egyptian one.

Several days after the actual cessation of hostilities on the Egyptian-Israeli front, on November 11 Major General Aharon Yariv of Israel and Lieutenant General Mohammed el-Gamazy of Egypt signed a six-point cease-fire agreement negotiated with the active participation of the United States Secretary of State Henry Kissinger. Under its terms Egypt and Israel agreed to return to positions held during the first cease-fire of October 22, to allow the supplies to reach the encircled Egyptian Third Army on the east bank of the canal, and to exchange all their prisoners of war. After substantial American mediating efforts ("shuttle diplomacy" by the secretary of state), two further "disengagement of forces" agreements were concluded between Egypt and Israel. Sinai I Agreement was signed on January 18, 1974, by the Egyptian and Israeli chiefs of staff. It called for the withdrawal of Israeli forces to a line about twenty miles away from the positions they were holding east of the Suez Canal and for a limited Egyptian force to occupy the east bank of the canal, with a UN truce force to be stationed in between.[63] It also put an end to the encirclement by the Israelis of the Egyptian Third Army which was allowed to regain the Egyptian lines. Sinai II was signed by Egypt and Israel on September 4, 1975. It provided for the Egyptian advance to the Israeli line and Israeli withdrawal to the east of the Mitla and Gidi passes, a neutral zone in which a UN force would be stationed, operation of radar warning systems in the Mitla and Gidi passes by American technicians, and Egypt's agreement to permit the passage of nonmilitary cargoes bound for Israel through the Suez Canal.[64]

Between the Sinai I and II Agreements, Secretary Kissinger mediated to produce a similar disengagement agreement between Syria and Israel. It was signed on June

[63]Text in *New York Times*, Jan. 19, 1974.
[64]Text in *Current History* (Jan. 1976), pp. 32–34 and 42.

5, 1974, and provided for the evacuation of Israeli forces from their advanced positions in the Golan Heights while leaving the bulk of the heights still under their control. Again here a neutral zone was to be established to be supervised by the United Nations Disengagement Observer Force (UNDOF).[65]

Egypt's Relations with the Superpowers

American step-by-step diplomacy thus helped to bring about concrete military disengagement agreements between the belligerents and, in the short run, helped to calm the tense political climate in the area. In the long run, however, it could not be considered as anything more than a preliminary attempt toward the solution of fundamental differences between the Arab states and Israel. Although the agreements did restore to Egypt and Syria small parts of their territory, they also provoked much criticism in broader Arab circles. The critics considered Israeli territorial concessions too small and insignificant to matter in the long run and pointed out, that, by introducing UN forces and American technicians into the neutral zones, the Israelis were being given an additional protection, thus prolonging their presence in the occupied areas and petrifying indefinitely the status quo. Furthermore, more militant Arab circles criticized Egypt for caring about her own interests exclusively while leaving Syria and Jordan, with large territories still under Israeli occupation, to their own fate. The most pronounced critics were the Palestinian *fedayeen* and their sympathizers among the dispersed Palestinians. Thus, for example, in early September 1975 a huge rally was held in Kuwait, which has a substantial Palestinian colony, to protest the signing of Sinai II Agreement by Sadat On the government level, the leaders of Libya, Iraq, and South Yemen formed what became known as the Rejectionist Front, criticizing the disengagement agreement and calling for total liberation of Palestine from Israeli control. Finally, although he had also signed a disengagement agreement, President Hafez Assad of Syria complained that he was left isolated when President Sadat concluded the Sinai II Agreement with Israel.

President Sadat angrily rejected these criticisms in a number of public statements. He pointed out that Egypt had carried the brunt of military sacrifice and that others, some of whom were far removed from the front line, had no right to teach him patriotism. Although Sadat did not say so publicly, his policy was to concentrate on the interests of Egypt first, which contrasted with Nasser's diversion of national energies to broader Pan-Arab, African, or third-world affairs. Moreover, from Sadat's point of view, the two disengagement agreements had distinct advantages for Egypt and, by strengthening Egypt, were also advantageous to the Arab camp as a whole. Among these advantages were: (1) Egypt regained control of westernmost portions of Sinai and secured the withdrawal of the Israelis from the two strategic passes which in the past served as a gateway for their invasions; (b) withdrawal of Israeli troops permitted Egypt to reactivate the Suez Canal (closed to navigation since 1967) and restore the flow of regular revenues, which in 1967 amounted to

[65]Text in *New York Times*, May 31, 1974.

$300 million and were bound to grow; (c) thanks to the Sinai II Agreement Egypt also regained access to the Abu Rudeis oil fields in western Sinai at a time when oil was becoming both a scarce and an expensive commodity.

Sadat believed that these advantages would not have been obtained without his close collaboration with the United States. Even though the United States was designated collectively by the Arabs as the principal hostile power during the actual conduct of the October war and was subjected to an oil embargo of several months' duration, nevertheless its role in producing the cease-fire and mediating in the conflict afterwards convinced Sadat that only Washington had enough influence with Israel to induce it to accept partial troop withdrawals and other compromise solutions. From that time on, Egypt's policy definitely veered toward closer economic and political relations with the United States in the belief that this was the only practical and profitable line to follow. To emphasize this friendly cooperation, President Richard Nixon paid a state visit to Egypt in mid-June, 1974; he was given a tumultuous welcome. And in turn, at the end of October 1975, President Sadat visited President Ford in Washington where he signed a number of economic cooperation agreements. These visits inaugurated a new era in which substantial American assistance to Egypt was renewed. By 1976 the amount of this aid reached the vicinity of $1 billion per year.

It is interesting to note in this connection that during the early international efforts to put an end to the hostilities of the October war the approach appeared to be multinational because it involved the machinery of the United Nations and also the participation of the Soviet Union. This was notably the case when a conference including the front-line Arab states and Israel was convened in Geneva in December 1973 under the joint chairmanship of the United States and the Soviet Union. However, with the passage of time the Soviet Union was effectively eliminated from participation in the peacemaking process and the field was preempted by the United States alone. This change was due to two factors. On the one hand, Washington wanted to avoid the complications likely to arise from too close an involvement of the Soviets in the peacemaking process. There was a strong suspicion that active Soviet participation would delay progress toward peace or disengagement because of the proven Soviet tendency to align with the militant Arab point of view. Moreover, should these joint endeavors fail, Moscow was expected to blame the United States for the failure and to make maximum use of its traditional anti-imperialist slogans to derive benefit from the breakdown in negotiations. On the other hand, President Sadat, the main Arab actor on the scene, distrusted the Soviet Union and, again in contrast to Nasser, wanted ardently to disengage himself from a client relationship with Moscow.

Sadat's reluctance to see a deeper Soviet involvement was based on the experience of the first years of his presidency. Initially, Sadat was prepared to cooperate with the Soviet Union, primarily with an eye to strengthening Egypt's position by receiving more and better arms from the Soviets. This at least could be regarded as a partial motivation for his willingness to conclude on May 27, 1971, a fifteen-year treaty of friendship and cooperation with Moscow during President Podgorny's visit in Cairo.[66] In fact, this treaty was a bold step on Sadat's part because it went counter to Nasser's official policy against the signing so-called "foreign" pacts between any Arab states and other powers. Sadat's hopes, however, of benefiting from increased Soviet arms supplies were soon disappointed. While Moscow continued arms deliveries to Egypt, it did so with great circumspection, if not actual reluctance, and definitely did not heed Sadat's requests for more sophisticated offensive weapons. The removal of Ali Sabri from office and his subsequent imprisonment and trial added another point of at least implicit irritation in Soviet-Egyptian relations, inasmuch as Sabri was generally regarded as an advocate of very close relations with the Soviet Union and a proponent of a more pronounced socialist line domestically. In addition, Sadat never made a secret of his hostility to communism and in August 1971 publicly promised to fight it anywhere in the Arab world. This declaration came soon after a serious political crisis in Sudan. A few weeks earlier, the local Communist party attempted to overthrow President Jafar Numeiri. On that occasion President Sadat threw his full support behind Numeiri and, paradoxically, provided for a substantial airlift by the Soviet Antonov transport planes of Sudanese troops from the Egyptian-Israeli front to Khartoum to help Numeiri regain his power. Following these developments, between October 1971 and April 1972 Sadat paid two visits to Moscow to press for a more definite Soviet commitment to supply him with desired weapons. His pleas were apparently to no avail. Despite their promises, Soviet leaders procrastinated and left Sadat utterly frustrated. Finally, on July 18, 1972, Sadat ordered the expulsion of all Soviet military advisers and experts from Egypt as well as the placing of Soviet bases and equipment under exclusive Egyptian control. The Soviet government complied and the world witnessed a massive exodus of fifteen to twenty thousand Soviet officers and technicians from Egyptian territory. By deciding on this radical move, Sadat undoubtedly took great risks. He not only antagonized a superpower and thereby lost some diplomatic leverage which he had had by playing one major power against another, but he also exposed himself to a possible Soviet retaliation which might take the form of refusal to provide him with much-needed spare parts for the military equipment which was almost exclusively of Soviet origin. Moscow, however, did not choose to follow the most extreme way; it continued to maintain diplomatic relations with Egypt, provide Egypt on a restricted scale with further military equipment and spare parts, and even with a modicum of economic assistance. This remarkable restraint on the Soviet part was perhaps due to its reluctance to see all the bridges burned between itself and its most important Arab partner; furthermore, it did not require much imagination for the Soviet leaders to visualize the possibility of renewed strains in Egyptian-American relations should the United States take a markedly pro-Israeli stand in any forthcoming crisis. This expectation was, indeed, fulfilled at the time of the October war the following year: Because of its determined support of Israel after the Egyptian surprise attack, the United States fell back into the role of malevolent power in the eyes of the Arab nationalists and suffered the economic consequences of its

[66]Text in G. Lenczowski, *Soviet Advances in the Middle East* (Washington, D.C., 1971), pp. 165–167.

behavior while the Soviet Union reemerged as a supplier of arms to Egypt in the hour of need. On its part, if the Soviet leadership counted on gaining Egyptian gratitude for the help extended in the October war, it clearly miscalculated. As pointed out in the preceding section, Sadat definitely preferred to rely on the United States in his search for an acceptable settlement rather than on the Soviet Union. This, of course, did not mean that the Egyptian President could be glibly taken for granted by the United States government. His policy was clearly to preserve maximum freedom of movement and, although on ideological and practical grounds friendly to the United States, it was geared to avoid pronounced dependence on any foreign power.

Sadat's and Carter's Peace Initiatives

The first half of 1977 brought forth two major developments: the inauguration of President Jimmy Carter in the United States and, following the Likud party's victory at the polls, the emergence of Menachem Begin as prime minister of Israel. As noted in our chapter on Israel, the new American president not only gave high priority to the Middle East peace settlement but also came forth with a program that called for full peace, withdrawal of Israeli forces from occupied territories, and a homeland for the Palestinians. This program, however, clashed with Premier Begin's highly nationalistic platform which reaffirmed Israel's historical rights to Samaria and Judea (the West Bank) and encouraged the demographic change in these lands through the expansion of Jewish settlements. Repeated attempts by the United States government to bring Egypt and Israel toward a compromise solution seemed to have reached a dead end by the fall of 1977.

In the midst of pervasive gloom about the prospects of a mutually acceptable solution, President Sadat announced in October that, in search of a durable peace, he was ready to go personally to Israel and speak directly to the Knesset. With impressive speed—following Israel's acceptance of this initiative—Sadat arrived in Jerusalem on November 19 for a two-day visit during which he declared in public appearances and private sessions with Israeli leaders his willingness to recognize Israel and offer it genuine peace with proper military safeguards provided Israel withdrew its forces from those Arab lands it had occupied in 1967. Sadat's initiative brought the search for peace from the multinational level of the contemplated Geneva conference (which would have included the USSR) to a bilateral level of direct Egyptian-Israeli negotiations.

Although Sadat was immediately attacked for his "go-it-alone" policy by the states of the Arab Rejectionist Front (Iraq, Syria, Libya, Algeria, South Yemen, and the PLO) which met in early December in Tripoli, Libya, he could justifiably claim that in his proposals to Israel he had not compromised any Arab rights or abandoned the Palestinian cause. His bold move produced a tremendous impact on Western, including American, public opinion: the stereotyped image of a hate-spewing Arab terrorist, a nomad camel rider, or a gold-encrusted oil sheikh (all simultaneously cultivated by the media) gave way—at least momentarily—to an image of a smiling, friendly, and civilized leader who went "into the lions' den" to seek peace.

The high hopes generated by this dramatic gesture were soon deflated. During his subsequent visit to Ismailia in late December, Begin presented his own peace plan which, in the eyes of many observers, fell short of the generous response which was expected (see the chapter on Israel). Subsequent exchanges among Israel, Egypt, and the United States brought no tangible progress and by the late summer of 1978 a deadlock seemed to have been reached.

The situation underwent another dramatic change with President Carter's initiative to convene a tripartite—American, Egyptian, Israeli—meeting at Camp David in September. The eleven-day conference ended as noted earlier in a somewhat triumphal announcement by the president of the conclusion of the "framework" agreements laying down the principles for two peace treaties, one between Egypt and Israel and the other pertaining to the West Bank and Gaza.[67]

While the Camp David agreements could be viewed as a victory for Premier Begin, they brought mixed results for President Sadat. True enough, they stipulated gradual Israeli withdrawal from Sinai and thus made it possible for Egypt to restore its sovereignty over this area (though with military limitations and with the issue of Jewish settlements in Sinai left pending). But one did not need the Camp David conference to achieve it inasmuch as already in Ismailia Begin had made an almost identical offer to Sadat. Predictably, the Arab rejectionists (now renamed the Steadfastness and Confrontation Front) held soon afterward another meeting—this time in Damascus—to denounce Egypt's betrayal of the Arab cause.

So long as Arab opposition to Sadat's peace policy was limited to a group of radical states, some of which were geopolitically peripheral, he could disregard, though without much comfort, their objections. His line of defense appeared convincing: Egypt, according to him, had done more than its duty in serving the Arab cause with the blood of its soldiers in four wars. His critics, the argument ran, were either unfair (protected by distance from Israel) or unrealistic. The door was open for them to participate in the search for peace. If they refused, Egypt had a perfect right to seek peace and security on its own.

But once the opposition to his policy enlarged to embrace the nonradical Arab states as well, his argument, though persuasive, had to be weighed not on its intrinsic merits but in terms of practical politics. Experience of inter-Arab relations has repeatedly demonstrated the danger of becoming isolated from the rest of the Arab community; Nuri es-Said's Iraq prior to 1958 provided a good example of such a risk. Consequently, when in early November 1978 the ninth Arab summit conference held in Baghdad and attended by twenty Arab states and the PLO called upon him to rescind his Camp David pledges and threatened economic sanctions if he signed a treaty according to the "framework" guidelines, Sadat was compelled to review his policy with utmost care. This explains why, in a set of instructions given in November to his main negotiators in Washington, defense minister General Hassan Ali and foreign minister Butros Butros-Ghali, Sadat put a strong emphasis on the issue of linkage between the Israeli-Egyptian treaty and the treaty pertaining to the West Bank and Gaza. If such a linkage were to be established in unequivocal and precise terms as a matter of formal obligation, he could proceed to conclude the

[67]For details, see page 465 above.

first treaty with a sense of relative security. Failing to incorporate the linkage stipulation, he ran the risk of exposing himself to a collective Arab action of punitive nature. Thus, toward the end of 1978, in spite of high hopes raised by Camp David, the fundamental question for Egyptian policy still remained wide open; which of the two values, peace with Israel or harmony with the Arab community of nations, should enjoy priority in Egypt's foreign policy and strategy?

CHAPTER XIII

Saudi Arabia

Since the eighteenth century the central province of the Arabian peninsula, the Nejd, has been the home of a militant puritanical sect, the Wahhabis. Their ruler was expelled by the rival clan of Rashids from Riyadh, the capital of the Nejd, to Kuwait in the latter part of the nineteenth century. The exile's son, Abdul Aziz ibn Saud, born in 1880, reconquered Riyadh in 1901, thereby establishing his own rule over the Nejd. During the next decade he waged constant warfare with foreign and domestic enemies. By 1913 Ibn Saud had succeeded not only in consolidating his rule in the Nejd but also in conquering El-Hasa, the easternmost province of Arabia.[1]

Power and Prestige of Ibn Saud

As a ruler whose domains extended to the Persian Gulf, Ibn Saud had attracted the attention of the government of India. The outbreak of the First World War intensified this interest, and, as we know, on December 26, 1915, Britain and Ibn Saud signed a treaty that secured the latter's benevolent neutrality. One of the consequences of this treaty was that Ibn Saud refrained from attacking his neighbor and Britain's ally, King Hussein of the Hejaz. Ibn Saud's restraint, however, was only temporary. There were enough points of friction between the Nejd and the Hejaz to produce deep hostility. A quarrel over the border oasis of Khurma led to an armed clash in the summer of 1918. The British, allied to both rulers, were at the time too hard pressed in the West to do anything about the gathering storm in Arabia.

Once started, the conflict between the Nejd and the Hejaz grew in intensity. In May 1919 the Wahhabis met the Hejazi forces commanded by Emir Abdullah at Turaba and in a fierce battle inflicted upon them a severe defeat which seriously shook the morale of King Hussein's warriors. During the next five years the adversaries lived in a state of uneasy truce while the problem of border settlements remained unsolved.

[1] For Ibn Saud's personal history see by H. C. Armstrong, *Lord of Arabia, Ibn Saud* (London, 1934), K. Williams, *Ibn Saud: The Puritan King of Arabia* (London, 1933), and H. St. John B. Philby, *Arabian Jubilee* (London, 1952).

Meanwhile King Hussein's power and prestige were following a downward curve. It will be recalled that, aided by an annual British subsidy of £2.4 million, Sherif (and after 1916 King) Hussein had raised a desert army which, under Faisal and Lawrence, fought the Turks during the First World War. Hussein's willingness to cooperate stemmed, as we know, from an exchange of letters with Britain's high commissioner in Egypt, Sir Henry McMahon. In this correspondence Britain promised to support Arab independence, presumably under Hussein's rule. As soon as the war was over, however, the British and Hussein began to differ in their interpretation of the pledge. This led to a considerable cooling off of their mutual relationship. The British subsidy to Hussein ceased in 1920, causing him immediate difficulties. Militarily Hussein's position was far from reassuring: the bulk of his army had gone with Faisal to Damascus, where in the summer of 1920 it suffered defeat at the hands of the French. With his army dispersed and no subsidy to reassemble it, Hussein had to rely on voluntary tribal cooperation. And that, as events were to prove, was too little to match the disciplined and fanatical forces of Ibn Saud.

Similarly, Hussein's diplomatic position became very precarious. This was the result of a number of political mistakes, which may be summed up as follows:

1. Hussein did not avail himself of his opportunity during the war to conclude a formal treaty with Britain which would eliminate the ambiguities contained in the McMahon correspondence. Nor did he profit from Lawrence's visit in the Hejaz in 1921 to conclude a definite alliance with Britain, which was then proffered. Lacking such an alliance he had no legal claim for British support in time of crisis.

2. He made the mistake of not ratifying the Treaty of Versailles, offended as he was by the establishment of the mandatory system in Palestine and Syria. Thus he did not become a member of the League of Nations and could not count on the collective security system when subjected to outside aggression.

3. He absented himself from the Lausanne conference in 1923 where basic questions of the Middle Eastern settlement were decided.

4. He neglected to cultivate the good opinion of the Moslem world by mismanaging the annual pilgrimages to Mecca. He allowed the essential services, including sanitary arrangements, to deteriorate to the chagrin of more liberal Moslem communities and foolishly picked a quarrel with Egypt over the memorial processions.[2]

5. He did nothing to improve relations with the large and powerful Indian Moslem community. The Indian Khilafat Committee was strongly critical of his war on Turkey as a betrayal of Islamic solidarity, and he should have tried to placate the Indian Moslems. His relations with Turkey and France were equally bad.

6. His ambition twice triumphed over sober judgment. On October 29, 1916, he had proclaimed himself "King of the Arab Countries," a title which provoked his numerous rivals in Arabia and which was much too pretentious considering the limited area under his jurisdiction. And on March 7, 1924, he made an even greater blunder by assuming the title of caliph after the expulsion of the last incumbent by the Kemalists.

This last action precipitated the crisis. Protests were heard in Moslem com-

---

[2]For similar difficulties encountered later by Ibn Saud, see next page.

munities the world over. To his neighbor Ibn Saud of the Nejd this was the last straw. On August 24, 1924, the Wahhabis attacked Taif in the Hejaz and launched an offensive against Mecca. On October 3, Hussein abdicated, and eleven days later Mecca surrendered to Ibn Saud. Hussein's oldest son, Ali, who succeeded him, withdrew to Jidda, where he remained for over a year. On December 8, 1925, however, facing a renewed attack of Saudi forces, he also abdicated and later sought refuge in Iraq. On December 23 the Wahhabis took Jidda. Ibn Saud was in effective control of the whole area. On January 8, 1926, he was proclaimed King of the Hejaz and Sultan of the Nejd and Dependencies, thus uniting into a single state the major part of the Arabian peninsula.[3] Ex-King Hussein went into exile to Cyprus. He died in 1931 when on a visit to Amman.

Ibn Saud and the Islamic World

Ibn Saud's first task was to consolidate his power. Inasmuch as the revenue and prosperity of Arabia derived largely from the pilgrim traffic, he gave high priority to the recognition of his rule by the Moslem world. On June 7, 1926, he convoked an Islamic Congress in Mecca. This was the second congress of this kind, the first having been held a few months before in Cairo to consider the perplexing question of the caliphate. In contrast to the Cairo gathering, which had been poorly attended and which had ended inconclusively, the meeting at Mecca proved a success. Ibn Saud made it clear to the sixty assembled delegates.[4] that his conquest of the Hejaz was definite and that temporal matters were to be excluded from discussion. At the same time he declared the Holy Land (meaning the Hejaz) to be the trust of Islam as a whole and asked for advice as to the best way to serve the religious needs of the faithful. The Indian Khilafat delegation, one of the most influential in the Congress, wholeheartedly supported his expulsion of the "traitor" Hussein. Nevertheless the conquest of Mecca and Medina by his "heretical" sect of Wahhabis, whose fanaticism was well known, was something of a shock to the Moslem world. It was hard to conceive of this puritanical and iconoclastic group guarding and managing the holiest places of Islam. The question of the worship of saints and of their tombs and shrines proved especially controversial, the Wahhabis opposing such worship as idolatry. This primitive strictness contrasted with Indian and Egyptian liberalism, making mutual trust difficult to achieve. To add to the difficulties a new incident connected with the Egyptian *Mahmal* occurred while the Congress was in session. The *Mahmal* is a holy litter covered by an ornate carpet, a relic of royal pilgrimages of the thirteenth century. Egypt sends it, properly escorted, to Mecca every year. To the Egyptians this is a traditional ceremony which calls for pomp, color, and music. The very idea of it, i.e., the veneration of an inanimate object, together with its colorful character, is highly offensive to the Wahhabis. Although the Egyptian government had agreed in advance to eliminate the musicians from the *Mahmal*

[3]On September 18, 1932, Ibn Saud assumed the title of king of Saudi Arabia.

[4]These delegates represented unofficial religious organizations and not the governments, and they included a delegation of Moslems from the Soviet Union. For a thorough treatment of this congress, see A. J. Toynbee, *The Islamic World since the Peace Settlement* (*Survey of International Affairs*, 1925, vol. I; London, 1927), pp. 311 ff.

procession, the escort when approaching Mecca made the mistake of playing bugle calls. This infuriated the Nejdis who, believing it a sacrilege, attacked the Egyptians. In the ensuing fight twenty-five Nejdis were killed. Only Ibn Saud's pesonal intervention restored order. But the Egyptian government ordered the *Mahmal* procession to return home without completing the pilgrimage. As a result of this incident the *Mahmal* ceremonies were suspended for the next ten years and only in 1936 did Egypt agree to their resumption.

While the *Mahmal* incident was indicative of the difficulties in the path of reconciliation between Wahhabism and the more liberal branches of Islam, these controversial issues did not prevent the Congress from achieving a good deal of harmony, especially in the practical matters of pilgrim traffic. The Congress adjourned in July after having adopted statutes that made it a permanent body to be convoked at regular intervals. Actually it never met again in Mecca, and an Islamic Congress which was called in 1931 in Jerusalem was held under different circumstances and with different terms of reference.[5] From Ibn Saud's point of view the Mecca Congress had achieved its purpose by bringing him implicit or explicit recognition from many Moslem states and by producing a friendly *modus vivendi* with the world of Islam.

Settlement with Britain

Equally important was the task of internal consolidation and of the tracing of the boundaries of his enlarged kingdom. The two problems were interrelated because internal consolidation frequently meant the elimination of some powerful tribal chieftain and the conquest of his borderland territory. We have already recounted Ibn Saud's conquest of El-Hasa in 1913. In 1920, after a brief struggle, he annexed Asir, a border principality between the Hejaz and Yemen. In 1921 he took Hail, the capital of the northern Shammar province, putting an end to the rule of his long-time rivals, the Rashids. In 1922 he extended his authority to Jauf, eliminating the Shalan dynasty. And in the same year he concluded border agreements with Iraq (at a conference at Uqair) and with Kuwait. Both agreements were negotiated with active British participation and both provided for those diamond-shaped neutral border zones which have since become a peculiarity of the maps of the area.

A major difficulty occurred in connection with the Transjordanian boundary. Transjordan was a new political entity devised, as we know, to give satisfaction to King Hussein's son, Emir Abdullah. As a geographical unit it was highly artificial, with no firm historical precedent to look to for guidance. At the time of the peace settlement Transjordan's borders had been traced in such a way as to embrace Maan and Aqaba and to secure a junction with Iraq. Ibn Saud laid claims to both these towns, asserting that they formed an integral part of the Hejaz. Moreover, he

[5]It was called under the joint sponsorship of Haj Amin el-Husseini, grand mufti of Jerusalem, and Shawkat Ali, the leader of the Indian Khilafat Committee, mainly for the purpose of cementing an alliance between the Arabs and the Indian Moslems and of securing general Moslem support for Arab claims in Palestine. A number of other politico-religious issues were also on the agenda. (For a detailed study of this congress, see H. A. R. Gibb, "The Islamic Congress at Jerusalem in December 1931," in *Survey of International Affairs,* 1934, pp. 99 ff.)

insisted on a direct boundary between his kingdom and Syria. Such a change would have meant the transfer of a sizable desert rectangle, the so-called Transjordanian Corridor, from Abdullah's to Ibn Saud's sovereignty. It could be accomplished only at the expense of Transjordan's connection with Iraq. Neither Great Britain nor Emir Abdullah liked these suggestions. Britain, exercising as she did the mandatory authority over both Transjordan and Iraq, did not want to sever her imperial land route between the Mediterranean and the Persian Gulf. Emir Abdullah was anxious to keep the permanent connection with his brother Faisal's kingdom of Iraq.

These differences were eventually composed by two instruments. The first, the so-called Hadda agreement, which was concluded on November 2, 1925, by Sir Gilbert Clayton and Ibn Saud, reaffirmed with slight modifications the postwar status quo as to the Transjordanian Corridor. But it left the question of Maan and Aqaba untouched.[6] The second was a general British-Saudi Arabian treaty signed at Jidda on May 20, 1927. Negotiated also by Clayton, the treaty reaffirmed Britain's recognition of Ibn Saud's "complete and absolute independence," provided for nonaggression and friendly relations, for Ibn Saud's acknowledgment of the special British position in Bahrein and in the Gulf sheikhdoms, and for cooperation in suppressing the slave trade. In an annexed note Ibn Saud agreed to the temporary possession of Maan and Aqaba by Transjordan but reserved his right to claim these districts at the time of the final settlement. No British subsidy was stipulated.

The treaty of Jidda made no radical change in the traditionally good British-Saudi relations but by eliminating some causes of friction it placed them on a solid footing. Britain did not ask for and did not obtain any bases or political privileges in Ibn Saud's kingdom, but her position remained preeminent. British business establishments in Jidda, such as trading, insurance, shipping, and banking, were more numerous than those of other countries. And there was a cordial personal relationship between Ibn Saud and H. St. John B. Philby, a prominent British Arabist, who had gone on his first mission to the Nejd in 1917 and who had remained ever since in close touch with the King. In 1926 Philby settled in Jidda and in 1930, having adopted Islam, accepted appointment to the King's privy council.

The first test of the treaty came in the winter of 1927–1928 when one of the warlike Nejdi tribes, the Duwaish, raided the territory of Iraq and Kuwait. The Duwaish, strict in their adherence to pure Wahhabi faith, blamed Ibn Saud for his acceptance of Western innovations, defying his orders to respect international boundaries. Their insurrection was suppressed by the combined efforts of Ibn Saud and of the British Air Force, which bombed the tribe when it crossed the Iraqi frontier. Other border incidents between the British-held territories and Arabia, which occurred as a result of tribal feuds and migrations, were subsequently settled in a spirit of friendly cooperation.

This cooperation with Britain, which was based on mutual acceptance of the territorial and political status quo in the Arab Middle East, no doubt enhanced Ibn Saud's feeling of security. But it did not completely remove his fear of the Hashemites. In fact, apprehension that one day the sons of the expelled King Hussein

<hr />

[6]For an exhaustive treatment of the boundary questions, see Toynbee, *Islamic World*, pp. 324–345.

might decide on a war of revenge always influenced Saudi foreign policy. And as the Hashemite brothers, Abdullah and Faisal, were both subject to British control, Ibn Saud was anxious to maintain friendship with Britain and to benefit from her restraining influence. In his search for stability he was glad, therefore, to conclude treaties of friendship with the Hashemite states, Iraq and Transjordan, in 1930 and 1933, respectively. The same fear of revenge caused him to pursue cautious policies toward other Arab rulers of the peninsula so as to avoid encirclement by enemies.

War with Yemen

In this respect his statesmanship was exposed to an acute test in 1934. In the spring of that year a conflict broke out between him and Imam Yehya of Yemen over the borderland of Asir. The conflict had been caused by a rebellion which had occurred in Asir a year earlier against the Saudi rule. Ibn Saud had successfully quelled it by forcing Asir's ruler, Hassan el-Idrisi, to flee to Yemen. Idrisi did not remain idle and from his safe base in Yemen, with the Imam's connivance, carried out a number of raids into his old principality. Deciding to strike at the root of the intrigue, Ibn Saud declared war on the Imam in March 1934, invaded Yemen, and inflicted severe defeats on Yehya's forces. The Imam sued for peace. In a treaty signed on June 23, Ibn Saud agreed to the restoration of the status quo ante, without insisting on territorial changes or reparations. This generous and statesmanlike behavior did not fail to impress the Imam, who ever after did his best to refrain from hostile actions. Ibn Saud's relations with the Hashemites were further improved by the conclusion, on April 2, 1936, of a treaty of nonaggression and Arab brotherhood with Iraq. Yemen, now quite friendly, adhered to it in 1937.

This sober and nonadverturous foreign policy made it possible for Ibn Saud to devote increasing attention to domestic improvements. Here his record was very commendable. At the time of his conquest of the Hejaz, banditry, assaults on pilgrims and trading caravans, and tribal raids were rife in the country. Within less than a decade the king effectively curbed lawlessness so that travel in Saudi Arabia ceased to be a hazardous venture. The king took full advantage of the Islamic institution of polygamy to marry daughters of tribal chieftains thus establishing inner political alliances. He settled considerable numbers of his own unruly Wahhabi *Ikhwan* (Brethren) in agricultural colonies. He also did much to raise economic standards and to introduce modern technical improvements. To cite an example, in 1926 there were twelve motor cars in the whole kingdom, but in 1930 there were 1,500 motor vehicles circulating between Jidda and Mecca alone.

Discovery of Oil

Of momentous significance to Saudi Arabia was the discovery of oil. On May 29, 1933, the Standard Oil Company of California obtained a sixty-year concession covering a huge area in the eastern part of the country. An operating company known as the California Arabian Standard Oil Company was established. When the Texas Company joined in the enterprise in 1934, its name was changed to the Arabian American Oil Company (Aramco). One of the first steps of the concessionaire was to give a loan of £30,000 in gold sovereigns to the Saudi Arabian government.[7] The loan came in the nick of time, when Saudi Arabia was suffering from a decrease in pilgrim traffic, caused by the world depression. The American company did it entirely at its own risk, which, considering the strangeness and remoteness of Arabia and the lack of official American interest, was considerable. Yet it paid handsome dividends in good will and soon proved economically justifiable as well. Oil wells were drilled in Dhahran, Dammam, Abqaiq, and Abu-Hadriya in the province of Hasa, and both proven and estimated reserves surpassed the boldest expectations. Oil in commercial quantities began to be extracted in the late thirties, and a new concession agreement was signed between Aramco and Saudi Arabia on May 31, 1939. It is noteworthy that in 1937, Ibn Saud had received a very advantageous offer from Japan, but believing it to be motivated by political considerations he rejected it. Germany also had designs on Saudi oil, and in the same year Dr. Fritz Grobba, German minister to Iraq and Saudi Arabia, who was stationed in Baghdad, visited Jidda. Nevertheless, Ibn Saud preferred to continue his association with the Americans: it had the advantage of assuring the economic development of the country without incurring political liabilities.

Late in 1934 another step was taken toward the development of the natural resources of the country by the creation of the Saudi Arabian Mining Syndicate. Incorporated in the Bahamas, the syndicate represented British and American capital. It undertook to exploit various minerals.

The Second World War

At the outbreak of World War II, Ibn Saud adopted a policy of neutrality. Although the majority of his advisers were inclined to believe in an Axis victory, he was convinced that the Allies would ultimately prevail. As a result his policy was markedly benevolent toward the West. Ibn Saud was highly critical of Rashid Ali's coup in Iraq and did not fail to say as much to Naji Pasha es-Suweidi whom Rashid had sent on a mission to Riyadh. The king's friendly neutrality was by no means a negligible asset to the Allies, especially to Great Britain. Had he succumbed like some Arab extremists to pro-Axis temptations, he might have preached a holy war on the West. Such a call coming from the guardian of the holy places might have caused much embarrassment to the British, both in the Middle East and in India. Actually the king not only refrained from hostility but rendered Britain a signal service by sending his son, Emir Mansur, to address Indian troops in Egypt on the eve of the decisive battle of El-Alamein in 1942.

The most significant political development affecting Saudi Arabia in wartime was, however, the growth of close cooperation with the United States. It was revolutionary in its consequences for both countries: for Saudi Arabia, because it led this medieval country into an entirely new path of progress; for the United States, because in no other area of the world had American policy undergone such a radical change as in the arid Arabian peninsula. Until 1940 the American government had

---

[7]According to K. S. Twitchell, *Saudi Arabia* (Princeton, N.J., 1947), p. 151. The amount of the loan is mentioned as £35,000 by M. Childs in "All the King's Oil," *Collier's*, Aug. 18, 1945.

practically ignored Saudi Arabia. There was no diplomatic representation in Jidda and there were no consular offices. For seven years American oil companies had carried out vast operations in eastern Arabia without the benefit of official government protection. The war changed all that.

American oil investments provided the starting point. When the war broke out, the operations of the Arabian American Oil Company were seriously curtailed owing to wartime necessities and priorities. At the same time pilgrim traffic to Mecca and Medina suffered a severe reduction. These two factors placed Ibn Saud in a very difficult position. Some way had to be found to make up for the deficit, and this could only mean foreign—Ally or Axis—assistance. In the spring of 1941 the Axis position was very strong: Germany had just completed her conquest of Yugoslavia and Greece and was about to invade Crete; the pro-Axis coup had taken place in Baghdad; Axis forces in Africa were getting ready for an onslaught on Egypt; and Japan was enviously eyeing the oil riches of the Persian Gulf. The United States still clung to its neutrality and Russia was not yet at war with Germany. Britain stood alone facing one of the gravest crises in her history, and the odds seemed overwhelmingly in favor of the Axis. Yet Ibn Saud refused to treat with Berlin or Tokyo. Instead he appealed to the Arabian American Oil Company and to the British and American governments to help him out. He pointed out that by adopting their wartime priorities Britain and the United States had deprived him of expected oil royalties and asked for a $30 million loan to be delivered in five yearly installments. His financial plight was so desperate that he threatened to cancel the concession if he failed to obtain the required funds. The company which had advanced the king £30,000 in 1933, was not in a position to satisfy his new demand. Yet the stake was too high to let the matter go by default. Consequently, the company appealed to the United States government for action. To speed up matters, Aramco's representative, James A. Moffett, saw President Roosevelt in April 1941, trying to obtain his approval for a government loan to the king. The loan would be guaranteed by the company's oil production. The President was at first hesitant, lacking the necessary legislative authority for such a transaction. Eventually, however, it was decided that the United States would request Great Britain to make funds available to Saudi Arabia out of a $425 million loan which had just been granted to her. Thus, in a somewhat roundabout fashion Saudi Arabia obtained the financial aid which made is possible for her to avoid bankruptcy. Great Britain gave the Saudi government £400,000 for one year, and these payments increased progressively until, in 1945, they reached about £2.5 million. These grants were supplemented by American lend lease, which was extended to Saudi Arabia in April 1943.

By accepting financial assistance, Ibn Saud to some extent compromised his neutrality. But this was just the beginning of a longer process which eventually brought his country into the bosom of the United Nations. This process was accelerated in 1943 when the American joint chiefs of staff reached a decision to secure a good air base in the Middle East which would link Cairo with Karachi and thus facilitate the prosecution of the war against Japan. It may be added that in the meantime Americans had constructed an impressive air base in Abadan, on the

Iranian coast. This base had been used both as a transit station to Russia and as a stopover to India. Inasmuch, however, as the Abadan airfield would have to be abandoned at the end of the war with Germany, it was deemed wise to secure another base in the Persian Gulf area. The choice fell on Dhahran in Saudi Arabia, where Aramco had its wells and installations. Negotiations to obtain Saudi Arabian permission were conducted in greatest secrecy both as a safeguard against enemy sabotage, as well as a protection for Ibn Saud, whose neutrality would be openly compromised, with the attendant risks of enemy reprisals. It is known, however, that in December 1943, Major General Ralph Royce, commanding United States forces in the Middle East, made a trip from Cairo to Riyadh where he was received by the king. He was followed the next year by a special envoy, Lieutenant Colonel Harold Hoskins, who performed numerous assignments for the United States in the Middle East. The agreement itself was concluded by an exchange of correspondence between the Saudi Arabian government and the American legation in Jidda, which, in 1943, had just been established on a permanent basis. It provided for a three-year use of the air base by American military authorities, after which period the base was to be handed over to the Saudi Arabians. The construction of the base began in 1944 (with the use of military personnel and Italian prisoners of war) and was completed in 1946.

The Dhahran air base replaced not only the Abadan base in Iran but also the Payne Field base in Cairo. It proved to be the largest and best-equipped American air base abroad outside enemy-occupied areas. And it could be easily extended over the flat desert area around Dhahran. The acquisition of the base emphasized the long way the United States had covered from its initially isolationist position. To some Americans it was a shock to realize how far-flung their country's interests had become. In November 1945, Representative Philip I. Philbin of Massachusetts and Senator Owen Brewster of Maine voiced their surprise and criticism over what they called a government investment in a "quasi private" airfield and the use of military labor in this venture.[8]

Simultaneously other important developments in Saudi-American relations were taking place. In 1942 at the request of the king an American agricultural mission headed by K. S. Twitchell arrived in Saudi Arabia to advise on irrigation and related problems with a view to improving and extending the El-Kharj oasis. In 1943, at the time of General Royce's visit, an American military mission came to Riyadh for a few months to undertake the training of the Saudi Arabian army. This mission shared the task with the British mission whom the king had also invited. In the same year two of the king's sons, Emir Faisal and Emir Khalid, paid a visit to the United States.

By 1945 relations between the two countries had reached such a level of cordiality that it was deemed appropriate to arrange a meeting between the king and the president. While on his way back from Yalta President Roosevelt received Ibn Saud in February 1945 on board the U.S. *Quincy* in the Great Bitter Lake in Egypt. The king took this opportunity to impress upon the president his concern over Palestine

[8]*New York Times*, Nov. 12, 1945, and March 29, 1946.

and—according to William E. Eddy, American minister to Saudi Arabia, (in his published account, *F.D.R. Meets Ibn Saud*)—received assurances of friendly support.[9] Two weeks later in his report to Congress the president referred to this meeting in the following words: "Of the problems of Arabia I learned more about that whole problem, the Moslem problem, the Jewish problem, by talking with Ibn Saud for five minutes than I could have learned in exchange of two or three dozen letters."[10] Afterward Ibn Saud frequently referred to Roosevelt in terms of highest praise, and the gift of a luxurious airplane no doubt deepened his friendly feelings. On March 1, 1945, Saudi Arabia declared war on Germany, and subsequently her representatives took part in the United Nations Conference at San Francisco.

Saudi-American Friendship

What followed could be described as a multiple increase of diplomatic, military, technical, and economic contacts between the United States and Saudi Arabia. It was an interesting process with no trace of compulsion on the part of the United States and with full respect for the sovereign rights and the strict Moslem character of the Arab kingdom. To Soviet critics these new methods looked like wholesale American penetration of Arabia, and they did not hesitate to use the term "dollar diplomacy." These cordial relations were marred by one problem only, the problem of Zionism. In the fall of 1946, Ibn Saud strongly objected to President Truman's appeal for the admission of 100,000 Jews to Palestine.[11] In a letter made public in the American press the king reminded the President of the statement made by the United States government on August 16, 1945 to the effect that no proposals concerning Palestine would be made by the United States without taking into account the wishes of the Arab states,[12] and he deplored the president's departure from

[9]In a subsequent letter to King Ibn Saud, dated April 5, 1945, President Roosevelt referred to "the memorable conversation which we had not so long ago" and stated as follows:

"Your Majesty will recall that on previous occasions I communicated to you the attitude of the American Government toward Palestine and made clear our desire that no decision be taken with respect to the basic situation in that country without full consultation with both Arabs and Jews. Your Majesty will also doubtless recall that during our recent conversation I assured you that I would take no action in my capacity as Chief of the Executive Branch of this Government, which might prove hostile to the Arab people.

"It gives me pleasure to renew to Your Majesty the assurances which you have previously received regarding the attitude of my Government and my own, as Chief Executive, with regard to the question of Palestine and to inform you that the policy of this Government in this respect is unchanged" (*Department of State Bulletin,* Oct. 21, 1945, p. 623).

On May 17, 1946, under the Truman administration, Acting Secretary of State Dean Acheson sent identical notes to the diplomatic representatives of five Arab states, accredited in Washington, confirming his oral assurance to them on May 10 that before the United States reached any decision concerning the report of the Anglo-American Committee of Inquiry, it would consult with Arabs and Jews (*New York Times,* May 18, 1946).

In a letter addressed to King Ibn Saud by President Truman and released to the press on October 28, 1946, the President reiterated the official American assurance that "there should be no decision with respect to the basic situation in Palestine without consultation with both Arabs and Jews" (text in *New York Times,* Oct. 29, 1946).

[10]Robert E. Sherwood, *Roosevelt and Hopkins: An Intimate History* (New York, 1948), pp. 871–872.

[11]This appeal was made on October 4, 1946.

[12]The text of Ibn Saud's letter to President Truman is in the *New York Times,* Oct. 18, 1946.

this course. The United Nations partition resolution of 1947 and the American pro-Israeli policy produced some tension, which was temporarily reflected in the negotiations concerning the extension of the Dhahran air base lease. But these matters never caused a break in relations.

In 1946, the Export-Import Bank granted Saudi Arabia at $10 million loan. A year later Crown Prince Emir Saud visited the United States, receiving from the president the order of the Legion of Merit and a citation for meritorious services to the Allies during the war. In 1948 the United States navy, entering the Persian Gulf for the first time, paid a courtesy visit in Dammam, and the next year the American legation in Jidda was raised to the status of an embassy. In the spring of 1951 by a special agreement the United States made available to Saudi Arabia technical aid under the Point Four program. Finally, the two countries moved closer to each other by signing, in Jidda on June 18, 1951, a defense agreement that extended for the next five years the lease of the Dhahran air base, enabled the Saudi Arabian government to buy military equipment in the United States, and provided for the military training of the Saudi Arabian army by American instructors. The new agreement contained a provision for renewal for the same period. It grew out of the fact that Saudi Arabia had qualified for assistance under the Mutual Defense Assistance Program as a nation "whose ability to defend itself or to participate in the defense of the area is important to the security of the United States."

There is little doubt that the growth of Saudi-American friendship hinged to a pronounced degree upon the spectacular development of the Arabian oil resources by Aramco. Commercial production began only in 1945, but by 1950 it reached the imposing figure of over 25 million tons a year. Thus Saudi Arabia emerged as the second largest producer in the Middle East—right after Iran with her 30 million-ton output. The generous royalties made it possible, consequently, to raise Saudi Arabia's revenue from a meager $300,000 to 1917 to about $90 million in 1950. At an estimated total population of six million, this meant an income of $15 per head, a rather imposing figure if we compare it with the £30 per head of social service funds in one of the most advanced countries—Great Britain.[13]

This sudden acquisition of wealth had a revolutionizing effect on the internal situation of the country. On July 17, 1947, Fuad Bey Hamza, minister of development, announced that Saudi Arabia intended to spend $270 million on the technological development of the country in the fields of transportation, electrification, agriculture and water supply, schools, and hospitals. Following this announcement the government, with American assistance, launched large-scale plans of land reclamation. An irrigation network, artificial reservoirs and catchments, water pipelines, and artesian wells were constructed. Paved roads were built between Jidda, Mecca, Medina, and other larger centers, A Saudi Arabian air service linking the Red Sea with the Persian Gulf was established under a contract with Trans World Airlines. American engineers erected a huge pier in Jidda making its hitherto dangerous harbor easily accessible to the largest ships. Furthermore, entirely new harbors were built at Dammam and at Ras Tanura. The latter had become

---

[13]For some interesting remarks on this subject, see *R.C.A.J.* (April 1950), p. 121.

a terminal point for local pipelines from Aramco's oil fields and the site of an oil refinery.

The king's cherished project was to construct a railway which would link the capital with the eastern and western coasts. With this in view he sought, in 1947, an additional $100 million loan from the United States, of which he secured $15 million from the Import-Export Bank. Between 1949 and 1951 American technicians constructed a standard-guage railroad between Dammam and Riyadh by way of the oasis of El-Kharj. Upon its completion the government announced its intention to reconstruct the old Damascus-Medina railway which was destroyed by Lawrence's irregulars during the First World War.

Anxious to promote unity in his vast country, Ibn Saud put special stress on telephone and radio communications. To this end he entrusted the American Mackay corporation with the job of erecting a powerful radio station in Jidda. To raise health standards in the country, his government after the war purchased four packaged surplus hospitals from the American army. It also invited representatives of the American University in Beirut to make a study and present recommendations concerning public education facilities.[14]

This partnership with America and the attendant growth in wealth greatly enhanced Ibn Saud's prestige among the Arab states of the Middle East. Moreover, by his championship of the Palestinian Arabs the king added new laurels to his growing popularity. Even the relatively advanced and sophisticated Egyptians began to pay attention to the deeds and words emanating from the desert capital of Riyadh. And Farouk and his ministers were glad to have Ibn Saud's support in their opposition to the Greater Syria scheme. In 1947, Cairo was pleasantly flattered when Ibn Saud came to Egypt on the first state visit he ever paid to a foreign capital. The trip of King Abdullah of Transjordan to Riyadh in 1948 in the midst of the Palestinian crisis further accentuated Ibn Saud's growing stature in Arab affairs. Saudi Arabia ceased to be an isolated island in the Arab world and began to assert her weight in the politics of the region. This was perhaps best illustrated during the Syrian crisis of 1949 when Saudi Arabia not only played an important role in bringing about Husni Zaim's reorientation, but also made full use of her new economic power by granting Syria a substantial loan for development.

With all these changes there was a paradox in Saudi Arabia's position. On the one hand, she was growing in strength and influence and she was undergoing, with American assistance, a real technological revolution. On the other hand, her government and her social system were stationary, and both the king and his associates tenaciously clung to the old traditions. Ibn Saud remained an absolute monarch subject only to the limitations of Islamic laws. His government continued along strictly patriarchal lines. The kingdom was divided into two parts: the Nejd and the Hejaz, with his sons Saud and Faisal acting as viceroys of these provinces. Emir Saud was the heir-apparent and the commander-in-chief of the army. Emir Faisal,

---

[14] An interesting firsthand account of Saudi Arabian accomplishments may be found in H. St. John B. Philby, "Golden Jubilee in Sa'udi Arabia," *R.C.A.J.* (April 1950). For a review of postwar developments, consult Richard H. Sanger, "Ibn Saud's Program for Arabia," *Middle East Journal*, 1 (April 1947).

residing in Mecca, was also foreign minister of the kingdom. Because of the ban on infidels in the holy cities, he had to transact business with foreign diplomatic representatives through Sheikh Yasin, his under-secretary. Foreign legations and embassies were not located in Riyadh, but in Jidda, which rendered all negotiations slow and cumbersome. The government continued to frown upon the entry of aliens into the land, and frequently foreigners with legitimate business in Saudi Arabia found it difficult to obtain visas.

The king seemed to be much more interested in technological improvements than, for example, in the spread of education among his subjects, of whom 95 percent remained illiterate. In fact, the shortage of properly trained talent among Saudi Arabians was such that a large number of positions in the government have had to be entrusted to citizens of more advanced Arab countries. Such were Yusuf Yasin, vice-minister of foreign affairs, a native of Lattakia; Fuad Hamza, ambassador in Paris, a Druze from Lebanon; and Hafez Wahba, minister in London, an Egyptian of Nejdi ancestry.

Despite all this, the technological progress of the country had affected social relationships. There had been a growth in urban population. The country was rapidly acquiring a class of industrial workers, skilled and unskilled, and of artisans conversant with modern mechanics. The electrification of certain towns had modified the pattern of daily life. A small "white collar" class of industrial and government employees was gradually forming. Contacts with the outside world through association with American technicians were being broadened. And the increasing prosperity of the country was not without effect on the standard of living and habits of the population.

Thus, in the mid-twentieth century change had come even to the heart of *Arabia Deserta*. It had come mainly as the result of the discovery of oil and ensuing American activity. By the old standards one might say that Saudi Arabia had become an American sphere of influence. This might be so, but there was nothing exclusive in the Saudi-American relationship to make it comparable to British treaty arrangements with Egypt, Iraq, or Jordan. Obviously it was unrealistic to underestimate the power of the American dollar and its ability to compete with other influences. But despite her dependence on the United States Saudi Arabia retained full freedom to treat with other countries and to follow policies not always compatible with American objectives in this part of the world.

Internal Developments in the 1950s

The internal changes which began in the Saudi kingdom with the discovery of oil in its subsoil became even more pronounced in the 1950s. On December 30, 1950, the Saudi government and Aramco concluded an agreement establishing a 50-50 profit formula, thus increasing substantially the government's revenue from oil operations. The amounts paid by the company to the king's treasury rose steadily from around $150 million a year—a sum obtained after the new agreement—to well over $250 million by 1956. This sudden influx of money brought a number of new problems to this underdeveloped and conservative country. Owing to the patriarchal character of its system, no division traditionally existed between the king's purse and the public treasury. But with the growing need for an orderly financial administration the Saudi government began in 1951–1952 to publish annual budgets. The next logical step was to establish a central bank of issue. The latter took the form of the Saudi Arabian Monetary Agency, which, nevertheless, was barred from engaging in normal banking activities by Koranic injunctions. Among other steps toward modernization could be listed the creation of a council of ministers in October 1953 and of a number of new ministries, such as education, agriculture, and commerce, which testified to growing governmental responsibilities in various sectors of the national life.

The basic problem, however, revolved not around changes in administrative structure but around proper utilization of revenues from oil for the public benefit. Improvements have occurred in the field of transportation (the Dammam-Riyadh Railroad was completed in 1952), in harbor development, and in an increase in hospital and school facilities. But critics insisted that an undue proportion of funds had been diverted to unproductive channels and that the high standards of probity observed in old Arabia were rapidly vanishing under the nefarious influence of easily acquired wealth. While these criticisms cannot be easily dismissed, a few points may be advanced to keep the problem of Saudi finances in proper perspective. In the first place, the kingdom faced a situation without precedent in its history. The change from a pastoral economy whose chronic deficits had to be supplemented by pilgrim fees and spending to an economy based on a steady influx of nearly astronomical revenue from one giant industry had been so abrupt that no Saudi Arab used to the old way of life could fairly be blamed for experiencing a measure of confusion and indecision. In the second place, no government operates in a political vacuum. The Saudi political system has this peculiarity that in order to keep powerful tribes out of mischief the king has to pay them steady subsidies. This item has always accounted for a considerable portion of Saudi expenditures. Even with the gradual diminution of the tribes' importance and a shift of the locus of power toward the urban centers, money still had to be spent to keep the countryside quiet, either by direct donations or by the upkeep of irregular forces which supplement—and counterbalance—the strength of the regular army. Moreover, the death on November 9, 1953, of King Ibn Saud and the ascension of his oldest surviving son, Saud ibn Abdual Aziz, introduced new factors into the power relationships in the country, and these were bound to affect the financial structure as well.

Fortunately for the stability and security of the kingdom, the succession was without incident. Upon the old king's death, Saud was promptly proclaimed king by those members of his family and notables who were around him at the time. His numerous brothers and relatives, tribal chieftains, the leading ulema, the big merchants, and the governors subsequently paid him homage assuring him of their unswerving loyalty. At the same time his younger brother, Emir Faisal, was proclaimed crown prince. This appointment gave proof of the basically unsettled question of the succession. According to accepted Western patterns in hereditary monarchies the new king's eldest son should have been appointed crown prince.

That this did not occur in Saudi Arabia was due primarily to the dispositions of Ibn Saud in this respect. But it also reflected the lack of a firm institutional framework and, by the same token, the power of a strong individual in matters of succession.

In contrast to his father, the new king from the very beginning was bound by arrangements not his own. Nor could he disregard his brothers and uncles or the early comrades-in-arms of his father, especially the leading Wahhabi ulema. He also inherited from Ibn Saud a body of royal advisers, mostly of foreign, though Arab, origin who, by virtue of their superior education and greater international experience, had assumed a position of influence in the kingdom. These were the traditionalist forces, and King Saud brought up as he was in a traditionalist environment, found it wise and proper to heed their advice.

At the same time he could not disregard the newer forces and trends, the inevitable outcome of changing economic conditions. These new forces consisted of the industrial labor (Aramco had its first major strike a month before the new king's ascension, the workers demanding the right to form trade unions); the white-collar class, substantially reinforced by Palestinian refugees; the growing merchant and entrepreneurial class, sometimes of obscure social origins, which owed its position to the opportunities presented by the expanding oil industry and the influx of wealth; the Western-trained college graduates finding employment in the Saudi government agencies; and the regular army, whose young officers were not only receiving professional military training but are also exposed to new ideas about the government and society as a result of their foreign contacts.

Most of these groups, both the old and the new, had to be catered to in some degree either by direct outlays of cash or by political behavior to obtain their approval. Inasmuch as the center of power was still located in the conservative camp, the king definitely leaned toward the latter. On numerous occasions he proclaimed his attachment to religion and to the Sharia as the only basis of legal order in the kingdom; he fully upheld the complete ban on liquor introduced shortly before the death of his father; he maintained the existing injunctions against movie theaters, music halls, and similar kinds of entertainment; he showed special interest in pilgrimage matters and in the upkeep of the holy places; and he promulgated rigorous laws forbidding Saudi youth to be educated abroad in other than academic institutions and prohibiting investment of Saudi capital in foreign countries.

The newer groups were inarticulately reformist and also nationalist. In this they conformed to the general pattern in the rest of the Middle East. However, as yet they lacked an organization or even a strong link with any specific social stratum. Western-educated Saudis often belonged to the leading families of the kingdom and consequently they did not lack opportunities for advancement in this conservative society. Hence, though fully aware of the shortcomings of the older generation, they were too well off to become iconoclastic. However, humbler elements were also getting an education, and not to be dismissed was the influence of Egyptian school teachers and military instructors and of Palestinian and Levantine clerks and officials upon the shaping of the social consciousness of the country. In the eastern part of the kingdom the proximity of Bahrain with its more sophisticated elements had added another potentially disturbing factor.

In the spring of 1955 there were rumblings in the Middle East about some disaffection in Saudi Arabia, and Levantine newspapers published accounts of repressive measures taken against the troublemakers. Saudi missions abroad staunchly denied these stories, claiming that they had originated in the minds of enemies. As a close check on the veracity of such reports was extremely difficult, one could only speculate about the significance of some personnel shifts (and disappearances), the expulsion of certain Levantine elements,[15] and concentrations of irregular forces in a number of strategic points of the kingdom. It may not be inaccurate to say that if there was any question of reformism, the latter represented a mental attitude rather than an organized movement. Under the conditions prevailing in Saudi Arabia, the challenge to stability could come not from the newer strata but from rivalries, should such occur, in the royal family itself. As will be seen in a later section, such rivalries did, indeed, begin to disturb the inner harmony of the court and government.

With regard to nationalism, to which reference has already been made, it had not only gone hand in hand with the awakening of the new social groups in the kingdom but it infected conservative circles as well. Whether these were genuinely nationalistic or whether they used nationalism as another device to strengthen their position of power was a moot question. At any rate Saudi Arabia, formerly free of other than tribal and religious loyalties, was beginning to acquire the nationalist pattern characteristic of more advanced, formerly colonial peoples.

Saudi Foreign Relations in the 1950s

Ever since the accession of King Saud, Saudi foreign policy has emphasized national sovereignty and the kingdom's role as a leading Arab and Islamic power. No doubt this conformed to the spirit of the times, but it also reflected the new king's position, which was different from that of his father. While Ibn Saud did his best to maintain friendly relations with the United States and accepted as a *fait accompli* Britain's preeminent status on the southern and eastern fringes of the Arabian Peninsula, his successor developed a new approach to these problems. Drawing ever closer to Egypt, despite a radical difference in their internal systems, King Saud soon emerged as a proponent of neutralism, a champion of Arab Palestine and North Africa, an advocate of Yemen's claims to the disputed areas in the Aden borderland, and an archenemy of the Baghdad Pact. To most of these matters, of course, his father was not indifferent, but he never allowed any of them to overshadow the vital interests of his country, as he conceived them in his untutored yet realistic way. Consequently he played down such minor difficulties as might have arisen between him and the British concerning the unsettled boundaries, and he referred to the Americans of Aramco as his "partners."

[15]In the spring of 1955 a large number of Palestinians, with a few Lebanese and Syrians, mostly employed by Aramco, were expelled from Saudi Arabia. It was understood that this measure was directed in part against the Syrian National Social Party (P.P.S.), which allegedly had found recruits among those expelled.

Shortly before his death a dispute arose between his government and Britain concerning the Buraimi oasis situated at the junction of Saudi Arabia, Muscat-Oman, and the Trucial Coast. Reportedly rich in oil, this cluster of desert villages was claimed both by the British-protected coastal rulers and by Saudi Arabia. Following Saud's advent to the throne, the matter reemerged as the cause of mutual recriminations between London and Riyadh. Here was a typical example of a dispute in which the alleged existence of oil in the oasis seemed to play a secondary role to national prestige, at least from the Saudi standpoint. In July 1954 Britain and Saudi Arabia agreed to submit the quarrel to international arbitration. Eventually, after thorough preparation of the case by the lawyers and experts of both parties, it was solved in a dramatic and unexpected way. Accusing Saudi Arabia of a campaign of bribery in the oasis to bring about a solution favorable to herself, the British member of the arbitration tribunal resigned in October 1955 shortly before the expected rendering of the verdict. Unable to reassemble the tribunal in its full strength, its president, a Belgian jurist, followed suit, thus bringing the proceedings to an end. To the accusations leveled at them the Saudis retorted that Britain had scuttled the arbitration proceedings in anticipation of an adverse decision. Shortly afterward British-officered troops of the Sultan of Muscat and the Sheikh of Abu Dhabi occupied the oasis, forcibly removing a Saudi police detachment. Saudi Arabia protested and threatened to bring a complaint to the United Nations.

The Buraimi dispute was symptomatic of the generally deteriorating relations with Britain. These relations embraced other questions too, foremost of which were Britain's support for the Hashemites in Iraq and Jordan and her sponsorship of the Baghdad alliance. King Saud's stand against the latter claimed to stem from his concern for the welfare of the Arab League and the cause of Arab unity. This provided, however, only a partial clue to behavior the motives of which were much more complex. It is highly probable that a desire to obtain prestige and to cater to popular preferences in the Arab world and also, possibly, fear of Hashemite retribution for the defeat of thirty years earlier figured prominently among the reasons that prompted him to oppose the pact so vehemently. Amply provided with funds, King Saud freely used his new economic power to back up his foreign policy. The loan of $10 million to Syria in the fall of 1955 seemed to prove this point.[16] It was publicly asserted abroad that Saudi influence was largely instrumental in bringing about the riots that shook Jordan and its monarchy in the winter of 1955–1956.[17] The upheaval followed reports that the Jordanian government planned to adhere to the Baghdad Pact.

British-Saudi relations reached their lowest level in a half-century with the rupture on Saudi initiative of diplomatic relations between the two countries as a result of British aggression in Egypt during the Suez War of 1956. However, the settlement achieved between London and Cairo in 1959 removed at least one cause for Saudi-British hostility. In 1961, Iraqi Premier Kassem's claim to Kuwait prompted both Britain and Saudi Arabia to send their troops to the threatened sheikhdom, thus

[16]By virtue of a treaty of economic cooperation, concluded on November 9, 1955. See p. 340 above.
[17]See p. 481 above.

revealing mutual interests between the two countries. At the same time efforts were being exerted by the secretary general of the United Nations to mediate in the Buraimi dispute, with both London and Riyadh anxious to cooperate. By the end of 1961 a definite improvement in the relations between the two countries could be registered.

As for Saudi-American relations, they also suffered some decline, but not as much as did Saudi relations with Britain. Thanks to the tact and foresight of Aramco's management, the company was spared the tribulations which other less fortunate corporations experienced in some neighboring countries. The one major issue that beclouded Saudi-Aramco relations was a controversy about the tankers. In February 1954, the Saudi Arabian government concluded an agreement with Aristotle Onassis, a Greek shipping magnate, concerning transport of oil in his tankers. This was contested by Aramco as violating its concession. The ensuing arbitration ended in 1958 by an award in favor of Aramco, which, however sullenly, the Saudis accepted. Regardless of how much the king may have been encouraged by his nationalist counselors to follow an anti-American line, it was certain that he did not favor an extremist policy reminiscent of Mossadegh. The basic American asset in the Arabian Peninsula was not subject to threats of expropriation during Saud's reign.

Another tangible point of interest was the Dhahran air base, leased to the United States for five years on June 18, 1951. The agreement provided for the maintenance and expansion by the United States Air Force of the existing airport facilities as well as for the training of Saudi pilots by an American mission. Although the words "military base" were carefully avoided in the text, Arab nationalists at home and abroad were prone to attack the agreement, especially in the late 1950s, as evidence of unwarranted concessions to American "imperialism." The United States, it should be pointed out, was not the only beneficiary in this deal. In addition to the training of her officers and the use of the airport by her civilian airline, Saudi Arabia was being paid a regular rent. Furthermore, the presence of the American Air Force on Saudi territory was likely to be a strong deterrent to a possible Soviet thrust toward the oil-rich Persian Gulf area. During the ensuing decade (1951–1961), the Saudi government regarded the Dhahran airport agreement as beneficial to its interests and resisted the calls for its cancellation. Eventually, as we will see in a subsequent section, it changed its attitude.

In contrast to Egypt and Syria, Saudi Arabia did not permit her neutralism to acquire a pro-Soviet hue. In 1955 the Saudi government declined a Soviet offer of arms and consistently refused to grant Russia diplomatic recognition.

Although relations with the United States have followed a not unfriendly pattern, they have not been free from occasional irritations. In 1954 the Riyadh government rather abruptly dismissed the American Point Four mission after three years of operation. In 1955 an official shipment of eighteen tanks for the use of the Saudi army was held up in American ports by the State Department as a result of Zionist picketing and protests. To the Saudis this episode appeared like another proof of America's preferential treatment of Israel, an issue which has never ceased to supply fuel to Arab grievances against the West.

Convergence of Saudi and Egyptian Policies

One of the paradoxes of inter-Arab politics in 1955–1956 was the convergence of the policies of Saudi Arabia and Egypt, two countries with diametrically opposed internal systems. This convergence had come about as a result of a few factors which have acted as common denominators. Thus, albeit for different reasons, both countries were opposed to the Baghdad Pact and both had strained relations with Great Britain, whose dominance in the Persian Gulf area and in Oman they challenged. In the case of Saudi Arabia this hostility was strengthened by a quarrel over the border oasis of Buraimi. Furthermore, Egypt and Saudi Arabia were to some extent involved in the struggle over the orientation of Syria, where there was intense rivalry between the pro-Cairo and pro-Baghdad factions. Both opposed the Iraqi influence in Damascus: Egypt by propaganda and political manipulation, Saudi Arabia by making her financial resources available to assure success. The Suez War of the fall of 1956 provided a further opportunity for Cairo and Riyadh to emphasize their solidarity.

Yet as the year 1956 drew to a close, the Saudis began having some doubts over their close association with Egypt. Egypt's policies were basically revolutionary and on two fundamental points, Arab unity and socioeconomic radicalism, potentially dangerous to the traditional status quo of the independent Saudi kingdom. The Saudis were concerned over the influx of Egyptian teachers and experts into their country. They also felt somewhat uneasy about the activities of the Egyptian military attachés and military missions in Saudi Arabia, especially in view of the fact that in 1956 such Egyptian attachés had been caught engaging in dubious activities in certain other Arab countries, such as Libya, Jordan, Lebanon, and Iraq. Other developments added to these budding misgivings. Thus many responsible Saudis were somewhat taken aback by President Nasser's hasty action in nationalizing the Suez Canal and thereby exposing the Arab world to economic inconveniences and politico-military risks resulting from the violent reaction of the west-European powers. At the time of the Suez War a Saudi contingent was sent to Jordan in a gesture of Arab solidarity. But the exposure of the hitherto isolated Saudi troops (especially their young officers) to the Pan-Arab ideas rampant among certain groups of the Jordanian population was also bound to produce doubts about the wisdom of too close an association with the more "emancipated" elements in the Arab world. Furthermore, Saudi Arabia and Egypt did not see eye to eye on their relations with Russia and on their toleration of, or cooperation with, international communism. In this respect the Saudi attitude was rigidly uncompromising in refusing Moscow any avenue of access, diplomatic or other, to their country. At the same time Cairo's policy was to distinguish between diplomatic-commercial dealings with Russia, on the one hand, and domestic Egyptian communism, on the other. The latter was discouraged; the former were promoted. Despite this distinction, the effect of Egypt's policies toward Russia in other Arab countries was to encourage cooperation, at least tactically, between Pan-Arab nationalists and Communists. This gave the Communists opportunities to grow in strength and widen their influence, particularly in Syria. These phenomena did not go unnoticed in the

Saudi ruling group, which by the end of 1956 was ready to reexamine its relationship with Cairo as well as its general posture in inter-Arab politics.

1957—Reorientation of Saudi Policy

The growth of Saudi doubts coincided with serious concern in Washington over Russia's political and psychological advances in the Arab world in the wake of the Suez War. The American concern found its expression in the proclamation on January 5, 1957, of the Eisenhower Doctrine, a policy statement conceived as a warning to the Soviets and designed to offer aid, economic and military, to any state in the Middle East which might be subject to direct or indirect aggression. Soon afterward, toward the end of January, King Saud paid a state visit to the United States. The purpose of the visit was to stress Arab-American friendship in general and to emphasize the rather special aspect of mutual trust in Saudi-American relations. By this visit, the first paid in the West after the Suez crisis, King Saud was elevated to the position of spokesman for the Arab world as a whole, and it was expected that he would help other Arabs understand United States policies better after his return. Accompanied by a large retinue and assisted by a number of counselors and cabinet ministers, the king was briefed by President Eisenhower on the significance of his new ''doctrine,'' to which he voiced no objections. At the same time his ministers negotiated with the State Department the prolongation of the Dhahran air base agreement for another five years and secured the promise of American aid in developing the port of Dammam in the Eastern Province.[18]

The king's visit in Washington provided, moreover, an opportunity for another historical meeting, that with Emir Abdul Ilah, crown prince of Iraq.[19] Abdul Ilah's overtures of peace and collaboration did not fall on deaf ears. In fact, there was a marked willingness on the Saudi side to listen and be convinced.

Thus a new phase opened in Saudi Arabia's Arab policy, a phase of rapprochement with the Hashemite monarchies of Iraq and Jordan, during which an informal bloc, called the ''Kings' Alliance'' came into being. On his way back home King Saud stopped for a brief visit in Cairo, during which he made an attempt to enlighten President Nasser on American policy. But however cordial the meeting seemed, it was an outward expression and could not disguise the reality that the two men and their respective governments were drawing further apart from each other. In fact, Nasser and his associates were annoyed by King Saud's visit to Washington. They viewed it as an attempt to draw the king into the American orbit and as another evidence of Washington's policy to isolate Cairo from its erstwhile friends and allies.

This drifting apart of the two Arab states was further accentuated through the winter of 1957–1958. While the Saudi government stopped its subsidies to the Pan-Arab and leftist Syrian press and while friendly exchanges between Riyadh,

[18]The agreement was concluded on April 2, 1957. Due to the interplay of a variety of factors, domestic and inter-Arab, the Saudi government declared on March 16, 1961, that it would not renew it after its official date of expiration on April 2, 1962.

[19]See p. 286 above.

Baghdad, Amman, and even non-Arab but monarchical Iran grew in number, Cairo-sponsored Pan-Arab tendencies made further significant advances in Syria. These tendencies found their culmination in the Syro-Egyptian union proclaimed on February 1, 1958. For official Saudi policy makers it was in many ways a shocking event which strengthened the general revolutionary Pan-Arab trend in the Middle East, an event rendered more bitter by the fact that Saudi Arabia had herself contributed to it by helping to weaken and destroy the conservative and anti-Egyptian forces in Syria in 1955–1956.

Despite outward expressions of pleasure at seeing a union between two Arab countries, in reality the Court in Riyadh was not prepared to accept the *fait accompli*. Before long, on March 5, 1958, Syria's security chief, Colonel Abdul Hamid Sarraj, made the sensational revelation that King Saud had attempted to bribe him to carry out a coup d'état which would aim at the secession of Syria from the recently formed union. According to Sarraj, he initially feigned consent but, having accepted the advance payment, he turned over the money to the treasury of the United Arab Republic. Furthermore, Sarraj stated the he was also asked to arrange the assassination of President Nasser.[20]

Assumption of Power by Prince Faisal

A strong anti-Saudi campaign in Egyptian papers and other pro-Egyptian press organs followed. As for Saudi Arabia, no formal denial was made by its government. Instead, the king appointed a commission of inquiry to make an investigation and report on its findings. Public opinion in the Arab countries and to some extent in Saudi Arabia itself tended to lend credence to the official U.A.R. allegations in this affair. As a result, the Saudi government suffered some embarrassment. Furthermore, its fiscal and economic policies brought the country to the verge of crisis. These policies, characterized by lack of regular budgeting, by overspending, and by the incurrence of substantial debts, led to marked depreciation in Saudi currency and a decrease of confidence in the solvency of the government. Politically conscious strata in the kingdom, merchants, some princes, and the budding intelligentsia, began pressing for reform and a change in government.

On March 24, 1958, the king, apparently responding to this pressure, issued a decree giving Crown Prince and Prime Minister Emir Faisal full powers to govern in the fiscal, internal, and foreign fields. Thus the rather dormant office of prime minister (virtually inactive during Faisal's prolonged absence from the kingdom due to poor health) was reactivated. Upon his assumption of power, Faisal reshuffled the cabinet, as a result of which four departments, including the ministry of finance, found themselves under his direct control. His main internal task was to bring order into the chaotic financial situation of the state. By pursuing a policy of austerity, he succeeded within a year in balancing the budget, paying off important state debts, and stabilizing the currency. In the external sector, Faisal brought about the resump-

---

[20]The total amount of the bribe was to be £S20 million, of which £S1.9 million was allegedly given in advance, the remainder to be paid after the completion of the task. In support of his statement, Colonel Sarraj produced a check drawn in his favor on the Arab Bank of Amman. Photostats of the check were published by the press in several Arab countries.

tion of correct relations with Nasser while stressing, somewhat in contrast to the king's previous policies, his country's neutralism and nonalignment in world politics. Yet in essence the Saudi foreign and Arab policies did not undergo any significant change. Faisal continued to maintain an independent policy and refused to align himself with the United Arab Republic in the summer of 1958 when, in the wake of its revolution in Iraq, a renewed quarrel broke out between Cairo and Baghdad.

Internal Rivalries, 1960–1961

The transfer of power to Emir Faisal did not freeze domestic developments in the Saudi kingdom. As usual in such circumstances, Faisal's rule had its supporters and its opponents. The policy of austerity and the attendant deflation provoked criticisms and complaints about the slowing down of the Saudi economy. The most important factor in the situation was the fact that the king did not consider the transfer of power to Faisal as final and irrevocable. Soon a group of princes and certain politically ambitious elements rallied around the king, maneuvering for the resumption of power by the latter. As time went on, tension increased until in December 1960 it culminated in a cabinet crisis. The two immediate causes of the crisis were the project of a legislative assembly and the budget. As for the first, certain "progressives" close to the king agitated for a constitution and for the establishment of a lawmaking representative assembly. These schemes were strongly opposed by Faisal, who considered them premature. As to the budget, differences arose between the royal brothers regarding the degree of detailed information about the revenues and expenditures which Faisal as prime minister was expected to convey to the king. Unwilling to agree with the king's point of view, Faisal tendered his resignation. It was accepted, and soon afterward the king appointed a new cabinet in which he personally assumed the premiership. In the new government one of the king's younger brothers, Emir Talal, a man in his early thirties, emerged as a leading figure, assuming the office of the minister of finance. In some ways this government represented a departure from the previous pattern: a majority of its members were commoners (in contrast to the predominance of princes in the preceding cabinets), and these commoners had generally had a formal university education, often secured in the West.

Talal's elevation to the position of power in the new cabinet produced jealousies and resentment in various quarters. There was some speculation regarding the young prince's ultimate aspirations. In the early fall of 1961 Talal was induced to resign after some eight months in office.

Twilight and End of King Saud's Reign

The early 1960s constituted a difficult period in the life of the kingdom. In the domestic sector there was a marked erosion of royal authority. King Saud was criticized for incompetence, mismanagement of revenues, improper toleration of extravagance of various members of the royal family, neglect of economic development, unjustified government debts, and a general antiprogressive attitude. His physical health left much to be desired and he repeatedly absented himself from the kingdom to undergo treatments or to take rest cures abroad. The king was also criticized for the handling of Saudi Arabia's foreign policy, especially in its relations with other Arab states. It will be recalled that in the early and mid-1950s the king's Arab policy ran, in a somewhat unnatural way, parallel to that of revolutionary Egypt, particularly with reference to the developments in the Fertile Crescent. At that time because of misplaced fear of a possible resurgence of the Hashemites, King Saud was opposing the policies (such as the Baghdad Pact) that were likely to strengthen the position of Iraq and, however unwittingly, was helping Nasser undermine the Syrian bourgeoisie.

When, in early 1957, the king awoke to the realities of the situation and realized that the revolutionary regime of Nasser in Egypt as well as the left-wing elements in Syria constituted a greater potential danger to Saudi Arabia than the Hashemite specter, he changed his policy, and began a line of close cooperation with the conservative Hashemite monarchies of Iraq and Jordan. This sudden turnabout came too late to save the Iraqi monarchy from a violent revolution in 1958. It also came too late to reverse the trend toward the radicalization of Syrian politics, a process which as we know ended with Syria's merger with revolutionary Egypt in 1958.

Having thus erred in his initial policy, the king now turned rather feverishly in the opposite direction, his objective being to undermine Nasser and his influence. An inevitable feud ensued between the two countries, Saudi Arabia being definitely on the defensive as an obvious and easy target for revolutionary propaganda from Cairo. The result of these sudden reversals was that Saudi Arabia, which in the early 1950s consituted a major factor in inter-Arab politics, now lost much influence and prestige. Moreover, the discovery of a plot against Nasser's life which was attributed to King Saud's instigation and which was neither repudiated nor justified in Riyadh, further contributed to the loss of prestige of the king. Gradually Saudi Arabia saw itself divorced from the main Arab currents, isolated and attacked by revolutionaries and conservatives alike for seemingly contradictory policies. The discovery that the chief of the royal garages had absconded with one of the ladies of the royal harem further added to the embarrassment of the palace.

The king's younger brother, Crown Prince Faisal ibn Abdul Aziz, who traditionally held the portfolio of the foreign minister and who in the 1950s and early 1960s was also prime minister, was known to be criticial of his royal brother's leadership. A man endowed with superior intelligence and strong character, with long experience in foreign affairs, Faisal was solicited by various quarters critical of the king and encouraged to take over the reins of power. Faisal, however, was bound by an oath given to his late father, King Abdul Aziz ibn Saud, never to use violence against his brother, and he intended to abide by it. Differences between the two brothers could not be avoided or hidden. On March 15, 1962, King Saud decided to reorganize his cabinet and assume personally the premiership. Although Faisal was appointed deputy premier and continued to direct the ministry of foreign affairs, his participation in the work of the government was reduced to a minimum and in the summer of 1962 he went for a prolonged leave of absence to the United States. The trip was effected partly to undergo medical checkups but partly also to show his disapproval of the state of affairs in the kingdom and his desire to disengage himself from responsibility for the king's actions. During his absence the signs of decay and deterioration multiplied.

By the early fall, Prince Faisal was persuaded to return to the kingdom with the understanding that he would be appointed prime minister and given free rein in choosing his own cabinet to undertake a major work of reform. The timing of these decisions was not accidental: they corresponded to the beginning of the civil war in Yemen which followed the overthrow of the monarchy in September. There was a widespread feeling both in Saudi Arabia and in Washington (where the situation in the Arabian peninsula was watched with considerable concentration) that unless a new government bent on decisive reform was installed in Riyadh, Saudi Arabia might be subjected to a revolutionary upheaval not unlike that in neighboring Yemen, with unpredictable consequences to the stability of the entire peninsula, the Persian Gulf region, and the Middle East as a whole.

What followed was a process of the phased takeover of power in the kingdom by Faisal, a process that was effected in four major acts. On October 17, 1962, Faisal returned among popular manifestations of rejoicing to Saudi Arabia and was promptly appointed prime minister. He formed a new cabinet on October 31, 1962. Between his return and the formation of the cabinet he received an encouraging letter from President John Kennedy in which the United States implicitly linked its support for Saudi Arabia's independence and integrity with the work of reform that Prince Faisal was expected to undertake.[21] In the new cabinet an important group of princes made its first official appearance: these were the Sudairi brothers (named after their mother from the great Sudairi family), two of whom were Prince Fahd ben Abdul Aziz who became minister of the interior and his brother Sultan ben Abdul Aziz who was entrusted with the ministry of defense and aviation. Faisal, moreover, retained in this cabinet a young and rising technocrat, Sheikh Ahmed Zaki Yamani, who had been appointed in March 1962 minister of petroleum and minerals in replacement of Abdullah Tariki.

Promptly upon assuming power, Faisal issued on November 6, 1972, a ten-point program of reform which covered a wide range of measures designed to improve the administration, the economy, the judicial and educational systems in the kingdom, as well as to introduce a machinery of popular representation in the form of a consultative council.[22] The ten points gained wide publicity as a serious indication of a comprehensive reform program. Prince Faisal set about energetically to implement his program, his first concentration being on finances. He cut down extravagant allowances for members of the royal family, introduced measures of austerity, and within a brief time brought the treasury of the kingdom to a position of solvency, having paid off all existing debts. These actions in turn generated increasing confidence in the stability of the kingdom and began to attract both domestic and foreign capital to invest in various development projects.

[21]Text in Magnus, *op. cit.*, p. 112.

[22]For a summary of the ten-point program, see G. Lenczowski, "Tradition and Reform in Saudi Arabia," *Current History*, February 1967, p. 101.

Through the rest of the year as well as during 1963, King Saud repeatedly absented himself from the country for lengthy periods, mostly on account of health. Despite the king's absences, Prince Faisal was not in a position to carry out his program without impediments. A state of rivalry developed between the king and the prime minister, which greatly complicated the tasks of reorganization and reform. Matters came to a head when, in a second act of the transfer of power, Prince Faisal was granted full powers on November 3, 1963. The decision was reached by a council of princes supported by an opinion of the ulema. The king was clearly unhappy with this development and in the following six months attempted to regain the lost power. He did not succeed: on March 28, 1964, the council of princes and the leading ulema had formally shorn King Saud of all power, leaving him as a mere figurehead. This purely titular position, however, was not in conformance with the tradition of the royal institution. Consequently, in the final and fourth act, on November 2 of that same year, King Saud was formally deposed and Prince Faisal was proclaimed king.[23] This time the decision was reached by three parties acting concurrently: the council of princes, the council of ulema, and the council of ministers. The dethroned King Saud went into exile, found his way first to Cairo, where he made a feeble attempt to denounce the new government and regain authority, and later settled in Athens, where he died in 1969.

The Era of King Faisal: Internal Developments

The leadership of Faisal should be viewed as a continuum in which the period of his premiership with full powers and the subsequent period as king constituted but phases of the general process of governing, the aim of which was to modernize the country in administrative and technical sectors while adhering to the traditional principles in the religious, cultural, and to some extent, social sectors. The ten-point program announced in 1962 was implemented with some unevenness. Those points that pertained to the reorganization of the executive branch of government were being carried out as efficiently as the local conditions permitted. Thus certain new ministries and government agencies were created in response to the requirements of state and society. These included the ministry of justice, the purpose of which was not only to bring greater order in the administration of justice but also gradually to enlarge the sphere of activity of civilian authorities and thus proportionately to reduce the role played by the religious courts in matters (such as traffic accidents) that had little to do with religion. In November 1962 the state Petroleum and Mineral Resources Authority (Petromin) was set up with Dr. Abdul Hadi Taher, who held his degree from the University of California at Berkeley, as its governor. The scarcity of water resources in the kingdom called for a sustained effort to assure enough fresh water for industrial and private consumption. First a department of water resources was set up within the ministry of agriculture and later a Saline

---

[23]For the text of the official proclamation, see *Arab Political Documents 1964*, p. 441. Reproduced in G. Lenczowski, ed., *The Political Awakening in the Middle East* (Englewood Cliffs, N.J., 1970), pp. 173–174.

Water Conversion Corporation, an autonomous agency, was formed under the governorship of King Faisal's second son, Prince Mohammed ben Faisal. It was responsible for the construction and supervision of a number of desalinization plants in the kingdom. In the mid-1970s a French firm was contracted to study the feasibility of bringing an iceberg from the Antarctic to the vicinity of Jidda in the Red Sea with the aim of providing both a substantial amount of fresh water and possibly also influencing to some extent the change of climate.

Oil, as usual, constituted not only the main source of revenue for the kingdom but also, through Aramco, provided the framework for the training of technical cadres as well as for the development of smaller native industries and the encouragement of private entrepreneurs.

Much attention was paid to the development of education in the kingdom. A petroleum college, later named Petroleum University, was established in 1965 in Dhahran, the existing university in Riyadh was enlarged, a private liberal arts college was founded in Jidda, and in the 1970s a new institution of higher learning, King Faisal University, was established in the eastern province. At the same time, schools for both boys and girls (coeducation was frowned upon) were founded in various centers of the kingdom. The curriculum of these schools generally followed modern patterns but laid great stress on Islamic education of the pupils. A definite sign of modernization was that a women's teachers' institute was opened in El-Hasa toward the end of 1964. Recognition that women were entitled to education and were destined to play a role in society was gradually gaining ground.

The growth of educational facilities could not be divorced from the general framework of cultural and social developments. The establishment in the 1960s of a television network was another sign of progress. Similarly, more newspapers were established, particularly in Jidda, Riyadh, and Mecca, and by the mid-1970s the first English-language dailies began to appear in the country, largely to serve the needs of the growing community of foreign technicians and experts.

Among the new government agencies was the State Planning Organization, which was responsible for drawing plans for economic development, the first during the years 1970–1975 and the second for the period 1975–1980. Although the implementation of the second plan was carried out after King Faisal's death, the foundations and preparatory work were laid during his reign. Because the second development plan came after the quadrupling of oil prices at the end of 1973, Saudi Arabia found itself receiving an unprecedented revenue from oil which, in the mid-1970s, amounted to between $25 billion and $30 billion a year. The second five-year development plan was the most ambitious in terms of expenditures of any plan ever adopted by any country thus far. It called for expenditures of close to $143 billion during five years, a staggering amount if one considers the relatively small population of the country (around five million) and the lack of many infrastructural facilities. The plan called for the building of roads and harbors, airports, hospitals, schools, and a variety of industries with an eye to the diversification of the Saudi economy. A special royal commission to supervise the development of economic infrastructure, with emphasis on two areas, Jubail in the eastern province and Yanbu on the Red Sea, was formed. An American firm, Bechtel of San Francisco, was to undertake the construction of major projects, estimated at $20 billion, with a number of other American industrial firms cooperating. The development plan required the importation of at least half a million foreign workers and specialists with varying degrees of skill because of the insufficiency of local manpower. This influx was in addition to the already considerable foreign labor force represented on the unskilled level by the Yemeni workers and on the upper technical levels by American and European specialists, with many intermediate positions held by Arab nationals from Egypt, Lebanon, Palestine, and other countries.

While definite progress could be registered in the technical and economic sectors, implementation of those points of the ten-point program which called for a gradual adaptation of political institutions to modern conditions and a greater participation of citizens in the decision-making process of the government was slow and virtually nonexistent. This slow progress was due partly to the essentially authoritarian tradition of government in Saudi Arabia and partly to the impact of the Yemen civil war. Events in Yemen filled King Faisal and his close advisors with misgivings about granting full political freedoms to a public which, in their eyes, lacked the maturity to exercise such rights with a proper sense of responsibility. Saudi Arabia therefore, as some other countries in the Middle East and more broadly in the Third World, faced the classic King's Dilemma: how to modernize the country administratively and culturally while keeping the old political order intact.[24]

Although on a comparative scale the Saudi kingdom enjoyed remarkable stability, it was not spared an occasional manifestation of political dissent. In the late 1950s and early 1960s, mostly under the impact of Nasserism, certain Saudis defected and found their way to Cairo, where they engaged in antiestablishment propaganda. One of them was Prince Talal, who freely engaged in denunciations of the Saudi political system. Later however, he recanted and returned to his country to be forgiven his trespasses.

The disastrous war which the Arab states fought with Israel in June 1967 acted as a catalyst in a number of Arab countries. Some of the results were the coup carried out by the Baath Party in Iraq in 1968 and the revolution that toppled the monarchy in Libya in 1969. Echoes of these radical movements were heard in Saudi Arabia as well: in June 1969 a plot was discovered in the Saudi air force. It resulted in the arrest of between two and three hundred officers and temporarily delayed the development of this arm of the Saudi military establishment. A few months later, in September of that year, it was reported that a plot aiming at the overthrow of the government was discovered by the security organs. It was not made clear whether this latter plot had any connection with the earlier conspiracy among the air force officers. No public trials similar to those in Iraq or Libya, however, ever took place in Saudi Arabia. It was reported that many of the arrested officers were released and possibly reinstated in the 1970s but firm figures were not forthcoming from the government.

In any authoritarian government, the loyalty of the military is crucial to its

---

[24]For an analysis of the Saudi sociopolitical system, see Manfred W. Wenner, "Saudi Arabia: Survival of Traditional Elites," in F. Tachau, ed., *Political Elites and Political Development in the Middle East* (New York, 1975), pp. 157–190.

survival and stability. In spite of the dissent among the air force officers, the overwhelming bulk of the Saudi military was loyal to the government. Following a time-honored practice, they were divided into two separate organizations, the regular army and air force under the jurisdiction of Prince Sultan ben Abdul Aziz, minister of defense and aviation, and the National Guard, a tribal force otherwise known as the White Army, subjected to another prince of the royal family (the incumbent in the mid-1970s was Prince Abdullah ben Abdul Aziz). The regular army was being energetically modernized as attested by the supply of large numbers of ever more sophisticated weapons and the construction of major military bases at Tabuk in the north and at Khamis Mushait in the south close to the Yemen border. The White Army was also being brought up to the more modern standards. In 1975 alone the spending on arms and military equipment reached $6.3 billion, tripling the figure of the previous year and making Saudi Arabia one of the biggest purchasers of modern arms, predominantly of American manufacture, anywhere in the world.

On balance, despite the occasional evidences of political dissent, the Saudi kingdom should be regarded as a very stable structure quite capable of dealing with its internal problems provided its external security was undisturbed. Culturally and politically the country remained very traditionalist insofar as the attitudes of the great majority of the people were concerned, and obedience to authority rather than challenge to it was the rule. Because of its oil revenues the country was wealthy and growing steadily more prosperous, and its development plans gave tremendous opportunities to ambitious individuals. In fact, the country had a capacity to absorb many educated people, the class that usually produces discontent and a demand for change. An educated Saudi returning from a foreign school was assured of a place in the government or the private sector with very bright prospects for promotion.

Although the kingdom had to rely on a great many foreigners, including expatriate Arabs, for its functioning and development, it followed a cautious policy toward certain groups of imported Arab nationals, particularly the Egyptians and the Palestinians, who were kept under close observation while their services were being utilized. Under King Faisal a better balance was introduced in the representation of princes and commoners in the Saudi cabinet. The princes usually retained the premiership, deputy premiership, the foreign ministry, the ministry of interior and of defense. Other more "technocratic" ministries went as a rule to the commoners, with an occasional prince assuming for some time such a civilian responsibility. Furthermore, the size of the royal family—very large owing to the practice of polygamy—provided an important guarantee of stability. It was inconceivable that the royal family would be wiped out physically in a single day as happened in Iraq, or forcibly removed from power as happened in Libya. The several thousand princes, despite a degree of rivalry among various factions, constituted a closely knit group that had excellent chances of weathering any storm. The solidarity of the royal family was, in fact, one of the most important guarantees for the stability of the Saudi kingdom.

In building this stability, modernizing the country, and launching it on the path of ambitious development and military preparedness, King Faisal played a decisive role which secured him a firm and exalted position in Saudi history. It was therefore both paradoxical and tragic that this man should be assassinated while his power was unchallenged and his position as one of the most important world leaders undisputed. He was killed by a nephew, Prince Faisal ben Musaid ben Abdul Aziz, an American-educated man in his twenties who had a personal grudge against the king, on March 25, 1975. A wide-ranging investigation made by the Saudi authorities failed to discover an organized conspiracy. The young prince was summarily tried and executed. The Crown Prince, King Faisal's brother, Prince Khalid ben Abdul Aziz, was proclaimed king. He promptly designated Prince Fahd ben Abdul Aziz, his younger half-brother, as Crown Prince and formed a cabinet under his own premiership, with Prince Fahd as the first deputy prime minister and Prince Abdullah ben Abdul Aziz, commander of the National Guard, as the second deputy prime minister. Prince Sultan retained the ministry of defense and aviation, while Prince Saud ben Faisal, son of the late king, was entrusted with the portfolio of foreign affairs. The new cabinet thus maintained substantial continuity in its composition while at the same time representing a balanced coalition of the most important groups within the royal family. As before, some two-thirds of the ministries were entrusted to commoners, among whom Ahmed Zaki Yamani, minister of petroleum, Hisham Nazer, minister of planning, Dr. Ghazi Qusaibi, minister of industry, and Mohammed Aba el-Khayl, minister of finance, were perhaps best known to the outside world, as the heads of the departments responsible for economic development and major contracts with foreign firms. On his part, King Khalid entrusted most of the executive authority to the hands of Prince Fahd, who thus, next to the king, emerged as the single most influential person in the kingdom.

Saudi Arabia's Arab Policy

Under King Faisal, Saudi Arabia's policy toward the other Arab states could be described essentially as conservative in the dual meaning of this word: first, because it was in favor of the political and territorial status quo and thus suspicious of and in practice opposed to mergers, unions, and the attendant actual or potential changes of sovereignty; second, because it opposed the revolutionary ideology with its aggressive Pan-Arab connotations as it emanated from Cairo and later from such capitals as Baghdad, Damascus, Aden, or Tripoli. In principle, Saudi Arabia sought peace and friendship with all Arab states, although being often attacked for its monarchical conservatism by revolutionary Pan-Arabists, it had no choice but to seek association with like-minded conservative countries. Inevitably, therefore, the Saudi kingdom emerged as a leader of the conservative camp during the period of the Arab Cold War, 1957–1967. Countries with which Saudi Arabia cooperated closely were royalist Yemen (until its revolution in 1962), Kuwait, Morocco, Jordan, and Libya (until its revolution of 1969). All of these, it will be noted, were monarchies that naturally drew closer to Saudi Arabia, which enjoyed a position of primacy among them. In the opposite camp were Nasser's Egypt, Syria, and Iraq under the succession of various revolutionary regimes, the People's Democratic Republic of Yemen (South Yemen, formerly Aden Crown Colony and Protectorate), Algeria, and eventually, revolutionary Libya.

Ideologically, the Saudi government tried to counter Nasser's revolutionary

Pan-Arabism by its own emphasis on Islam and Islamic solidarity. This position was natural for Saudi Arabia, the birthplace of Islam. But it encouraged cooperation with other states, provided they were Islamic. In the mid-1960s, King Faisal undertook extensive travels in a number of Islamic states in Asia and Africa. Conspicuous among them was the visit in December 1965 to the Shah of Iran, with whom, in Teheran, he proclaimed the principle of Islamic solidarity. This statement was promptly attacked by Nasser's propaganda from Cairo as reactionary and implicitly anti-Arab; moreover, the Egyptian media and spokesmen accused King Faisal and the Shah of trying to form an Islamic pact as an instrument to combat Arab unity. Actually, neither the Shah nor the king ever discussed or intended to form such a pact.

The cold war between the conservative and the revolutionary camps was considerably aggravated by the upheaval in Yemen. The overthrow of the monarchy in Yemen, which occurred in the fall of 1962, gave rise to civil war that lasted five years. After their initial shock, the royalist tribes rallied their forces and put up effective resistance to the newly proclaimed republican government. Under the circumstances, President Nasser decided to send an expeditionary force to help the republican cause, and this intervention represented Nasser's "Vietnam." From moderate beginnings the force grew to 80,000 troops. Saudi Arabia could not remain indifferent to such intervention in a neighboring country and, on its part, undertook to carry out an extensive program of supplies to the royalist party. However, it scrupulously avoided sending troops into the area. While further details of the civil war are to be found in the chapter on Yemen, suffice it to say that this war served as an arena of confrontation between the revolutionary and the status quo forces in the Arab world as a whole. Irritated by his inability to achieve a quick victory in Yemen, Nasser attempted to use violence against Saudi Arabia. Between 1962 and 1967 Egyptian aircraft bombed repeatedly the Saudi bases in Najran and other localities north of Yemen. On one occasion a major parachute drop of arms and munitions was made by the Egyptian air force in Hejaz, apparently destined to supply some ill-defined revolutionary group inside Saudi Arabia which was expected to cooperate with Egypt. As it turned out, the Saudi authorities found and impounded the supplies before any Nasserite elements could lay hands on them.

In the course of the war several attempts, some involving the mediation of other Arab countries or the Arab League, were made to effect a settlement which would restore peace to Yemen and reconciliation between Saudi Arabia and Egypt. There were Saudi-Egyptian meetings in Alexandria in September 1964 and between the warring Yemen's factions in Erkowit in Sudan that same month; there was a personal meeting between King Faisal and President Nasser in Jidda in August 1965; and a year later, the ruler of Kuwait attempted mediation. But it was not until the Arab-Israeli war of June 1967 that conditions were created for realistic attainment of a peace settlement. Egypt, as we know, suffered a humiliating defeat at the hands of the Israelis and, although many factors contributed to this defeat, there is no doubt that the diversion of Egypt's military energy to the remote theater in Yemen was one of them.

Under the circumstances, on August 31, 1967, at a conference in Khartoum attended by heads of the Arab states and convened primarily to determine Arab attitudes toward Israel after the June war, a final settlement was reached between Saudi Arabia and Egypt regarding Yemen. Nasser agreed to withdraw his forces while Saudi Arabia accepted the existence of the republican regime. This regime, interestingly enough, despite its initial close relationship with and dependence upon Egypt, was not as radical as the Saudis had originally feared. In fact, its leadership was essentially in the hands of the bourgeois elements and some of its leaders had a broadly conservative background, being by profession *qadis* (religious judges). A gradual normalization of relations between Saudi Arabia and Yemen occurred. It culminated in March 1970 in the official Saudi recognitioin of the Yemen Arab Republic and the exchange of diplomatic representations. In due time the republic, often generously assisted by Saudi financial aid, resumed its traditional position of closely cooperating with Saudi Arabia and even following its leadership.

The political security of the Arabian Peninsula was a traditional concern of Saudi Arabia. The Saudis became considerably alarmed when, under Kassem's revolutionary regime, Iraq laid sudden claim to Kuwait in 1961 as soon as Kuwait obtained its independence from Great Britain. The Iraqi claim was based on a thesis that, in the old Ottoman days, Kuwait had been a district of the province of Basra. In this attitude Iraq was isolated in the Arab community and encountered opposition to its demands from both the conservative and the revolutionary camps in the Arab world. When, therefore, the Arab League decided on a collective military intervention to assist Kuwait in preserving its independence and territorial integrity, a contingent of Saudi troops was dispatched to Kuwait.

This concern for peace and stability in the peninsula and the gulf region also led Saudi Arabia to settle a number of controversial territorial questions with its neighbors between 1964 and 1974. The boundary agreements thus concluded included the division of the neutral zone between Kuwait and Saudi Arabia, effected through two agreements of 1964 and 1966; a boundary agreement with Qatar of 1965; boundary agreements with Jordan of 1965 and 1966 which provided for the exchange of a sizable stretch of Jordanian territory in the southeast of Jordan for a smaller but important slice of Saudi territory which enlarged Jordan's access to the Red Sea southeast of Aqaba; two boundary agreements with Iran, of 1965 and 1968, pertaining to the off-shore claims and resulting in the assignment of Farsiya Island to Iran and Arabiya Island to Saudi Arabia.

That same decade saw also the settlement of a longstanding territorial dispute between Saudi Arabia and Abu Dhabi which centered on a Saudi demand for access to the Persian Gulf through a corridor separating Qatar and Abu Dhabi and the disposition of the Buraimi oasis. Because these problems were still unresolved at the end of 1971, when Abu Dhabi joined the newly created United Arab Emirates, Saudi Arabia was initially reluctant to recognize and establish diplomatic relations with the new organization. By July 31, 1974, however, both problems were resolved in such a way that Saudi Arabia obtained her access to the Gulf while relinquishing her claim on Buraimi, an oasis which thus remained under the joint jurisdiction of Abu Dhabi and the Sultanate of Oman.

In spite of the Saudi sensitivity to the territorial questions in the Gulf and the

Peninsula, its reaction to the Iranian seizure of three islands in the Persian Gulf which until then were regarded as belonging to the Trucial Coast states, in December 1971, was guarded and contrasted vividly with the flamboyant outburst of Colonel Qadhafi in Libya, who decided to punish Britain for her alleged connivance in the act by nationalizing a British oil company in his country.

The establishment of a radical, Marxist-oriented, regime in Aden following the assumption of independence by South Yemen provided a serious cause for concern to the Saudi government in view of Aden's aggressive posture. In 1969, some border clashes occurred between the South Yemeni and Saudi Arabian forces, the latter successfully repulsing the South Yemeni incursion. Another manifestation of South Yemen's revolutionary militancy was the active assistance it gave to the antigovernment guerrillas operating in the province of Dhofar within the Sultanate of Oman. The Saudis deplored this intervention and wished success to a fellow monarch in Muscat but were not in a position to assist him militarily. This role, as we know from the chapter on Iran, was assumed by the Shah, who dispatched his forces at the request of the Sultan of Oman to help him combat the rebels. From the Saudis' point of view this situation was somewhat embarrassing: on the one hand, they could not be enthusiastic about the intervention of any non-Arab country in the affairs of the Arabian Peninsula; on the other, they had to welcome the fact that a revolutionary and potentially very disturbing activity was being effectively stopped by a determined military effort in a neighboring country. Officially, therefore, the Saudis preferred to maintain a discreet silence about the Dhofar situation.

The growth and militancy of the Palestinian liberation movement in the wake of the 1967 war could not remain unnoticed in Saudi Arabia. King Faisal repeatedly voiced his support for the Palestinian cause and, by the same token, his strong opposition to Zionism, which he was prone to link with communism as a major evil. He invariably expressed full solidarity with the general Arab demands for Israeli withdrawal from the occupied territories and put special emphasis on the return of Jerusalem, as Islam's third holiest city, to Arab control. It was, therefore, natural for him to support the Palestinian Liberation Organization (PLO) and to receive from time to time its leader, Yassir Arafat, in Riyadh. Substantial funds were donated to the PLO to sustain them in their struggle for liberation. At the same time, however, the king viewed with suspicion and hostility all those groups within the Palestinian movement that were radical, that engaged in exaggerated terrorist activities (such as the hijacking of neutral nations' airliners), and that were known for their Marxist and Maoist tendencies. The strong disapproval of their actions became even more pronounced when the Saudi oil minister, Zaki Yamani, was kidnapped along with other ministers of OPEC attending a meeting in Vienna in December 1975. (Yamani was subsequently released by the kidnappers in Libya.)

The death of Nasser provided a turning point in the relations between Saudi Arabia and Egypt. These relations traditionally constituted the central issue of Saudi Arabia's Arab policy. When Egypt was trying to export its revolution, as was the case between 1962 and 1970, Saudi Arabia's security was obviously endangered. If Egypt was restrained and moderate, the Saudis invariably felt more secure. It was therefore with a great sense of relief that King Faisal and his advisors noted a substantial change in the attitudes and policies of Egypt after President Sadat's advent to power. Sadat's "de-Nasserization" policy was welcomed in Saudi Arabia and his overtures to restore friendship and coordinate policies met a positive response. King Faisal granted generous financial assistance to Egypt, recognized Egypt's military role as the main confrontation state vis-à-vis Israel, and coordinated with President Sadat his oil policy, which during the October 1973 war resulted in the proclamation of an embargo on oil exports to the United States, Portugal, and Holland and a general policy of production cutbacks adjusted in their magnitudes to the stance taken by individual consumer countries toward the Arab-Israeli conflict. Moreover, the strongly anticommunist course pursued by President Sadat and his decision to emancipate Egypt from Soviet influence in 1972 met with full approval in Riyadh. The same consideration guided Saudi policy toward Sudan, which under the leadership of General Jafar Numeiri, especially since the abortive communist coup d'etat in July 1971, was following a definite policy of disengagement from the Soviet Union.

Similarly, so long as Emperor Haile Selassie was ruling in Ethiopia, relations between that country and Saudi Arabia were friendly. After the overthrow of the monarchy in Addis Ababa by a radical military group which entered into close relations with the Soviet Union, the Saudi attitude toward Ethiopia changed profoundly. The Saudi government under both Faisal and his successors watched with some alarm the radicalization process and Soviet penetration in Somalia, where the Soviets were granted naval facilities in Berbera. These revolutionary trends and increased Soviet activity in the Horn of Africa caused Saudi Arabia to cooperate even more closely with Egypt and Sudan. Saudi Arabia also welcomed the advent of General Hafez Assad in Syria because he demonstrated moderate policies, compared with his left-wing Baath predecessors.

In the 1970s, Saudi Arabia resumed its role of leadership in the Arab world and could count on support for its policies among the smaller but oil-rich states of the Persian Gulf. A good proof of this cooperation was supplied in October 1974 when Saudi Arabia, Kuwait, and the United Arab Emirates jointly pledged $2.35 billion for economic and military purposes to Egypt, Syria, Jordan, and the PLO—the entities carrying the main burden of defense against Israel.

This resumption of an active and leading role in Arab affairs by Saudi Arabia was largely the work of King Faisal, a man of unusual intelligence, wisdom, and experience. What was remarkable about his leadership was not only that he displayed personal statesmanlike qualities but that he assured to his country an institutional foundation strong enough to survive him. Although experiencing a considerable moral shock as a result of his untimely death, the Saudi kingdom continued on its course with its political structure and its basic policies intact.

Saudi Foreign Policy under Faisal

In a broad sense, Saudi Arabia's foreign policy was dictated by its basic Islamic and conservative orientation. It had three main points of emphasis: a search for Islamic solidarity, a strong anticommunist hence also anti-Soviet stance, and a fundamentally pro-Western orientation.

The policy of Islamic solidarity has already been mentioned in the previous section on Faisal's Arab policy. The most important non-Arab but Islamic country from the Saudi point of view was their neighbor across the Persian Gulf, Iran. Conceptually, the Saudi *raison d'état* dictated a close and friendly relationship between the two monarchies. There was at the same time in certain Saudi circles a lingering suspicion of Iran's ultimate motives in the broader Persian Gulf area. Privately some Saudis were inclined to voice apprehension about what they perceived to be an expansionist trend in Iran's foreign policy. And even though Iran's military hegemony in the Persian Gulf—certainly a fact of life by the mid-1970s—had potentially beneficial effects for Saudi Arabia inasmuch as it thwarted the subversive activities of various revolutionary groups including first and foremost that of the Popular Front for the Liberation of Occupied Arabian Gulf (PFLOAG), the fact that it was Iran and not Saudi Arabia who produced this welcome result filled many Saudis with misgivings. Another point on which an occasional strain would occur between the two countries was that of the pricing of oil. When Iran and Venezuela moved for the quadrupling of oil prices at the OPEC conference in Teheran in December 1973, the Saudi oil minister tried to resist this initiative. He eventually conceded to the Iranian point of view under considerable pressure and in order not to disrupt the OPEC solidarity. Similarly, Saudi Arabia repeatedly resisted further Iranian attempts and endeavors to increase the price of exported oil. In 1976, in fact, the Saudis went so far as to break away from an additional 10 percent increase decision imposed by OPEC and proclaimed a mere 5 percent increase, thus introducing two levels of prices on the world market for oil. This steady opposition to Iranian initiatives produced considerable irritation in Teheran which, however, was careful not to attack the Saudi government or its king and crown prince directly but instead focused on personal attacks against the Saudi oil minister, Yamani.

The Saudi policy of Islamic solidarity found also practical expression in close cooperation with Pakistan, whose officers served on a contract basis in the Saudi air force, a military formation noted for its shortages of local skilled manpower.

As for the second thrust of his foreign policy, King Faisal was firmly anticommunist and refused to recognize and establish diplomatic relations with any Communist country. Even a profitable exchange of crude oil for construction of an oil refinery, concluded by the Saudi ministry of petroleum with the government of Rumania, had to be abandoned on Faisal's insistence, who was reputed to have said that he did not want "to have even a single Communist nail imported into Saudi Arabia."

Faisal's anticommunist policy was logically reflected in his tendency to seek closer relations with the West, including Western Europe. In the 1950s relations with France were clouded by the issue of the Algerian struggle against the French colonial rule. They improved notably after July 1962, when Algeria obtained independence. This friendly evolution was further accentuated as a result of General de Gaulle's policy aiming at the rebuilding of bridges with the Arab world and deemphasizing French military links with Israel.

Similarly, while in the 1950s Saudi relations with Britain had suffered as a result of the unresolved Buraimi dispute, the settlement of this question, after the with-

drawal of Great Britain from the Persian Gulf in 1971, brought about the normalization of their relations. Sales of certain types of military equipment and participation
of British firms in the Saudi industrialization process under the second development
plan marked a resumption of British presence in the kingdom.

The central issue in the foreign policies of Saudi Arabia, however, was its
relationship with the United States. The two countries had a long history of mutual
cooperation based on common concerns and complementary interests. Both were
anticommunist and opposed to radical revolutionary movements anywhere in the
world; both looked for stability and security in the Arabian Peninsula and the
Persian Gulf; and both were interested that Saudi petroleum should flow uninterrup-
tedly to the consumers in the industrialized democracies for the mutual benefit of the
buyers and the sellers. The fact that a purely American company, Aramco, was the
sole operator of oil fields on Saudi territory added to the closeness of this relationship. In fact, in the 1950s and early 1960s Saudi Arabia was often open to Nasser's
attack as a "special instrument" of United States policy in the Middle East. Because of the popularity of Nasser's nationalist slogans in the Arab world in those
days, these attacks were embarrassing enough to Saudi Arabia to warrant its decision to cancel the agreement permitting the United States to maintain an air base in
Dhahran in 1961. It was, however, indicative of the basic Saudi perception that the
United States was the ultimate guarantor of Saudi security that, when the civil war
in Yemen started and Prince Faisal returned to his country to assume the premiership in the fall of 1962, the Saudi government received with satisfaction a message
from President John Kennedy in which he stated that "Saudi Arabia can depend
upon the friendship and the cooperation of the United States in dealing with the
many tasks which lie before it in the days ahead." Moreover, in obvious reference
to the dangers stemming from the Egyptian-Saudi hostility and the Yemen civil war,
the president added: "I am fully aware that in order to accomplish your goals you
must have the requisite tranquillity—an atmosphere devoid of recrimination and
instigations from within or without. I share your concern at the tensions which
prevail in the area and which hamper your design to strengthen the fabric of government and society in Saudi Arabia. As I indicated to you in Washington, the
United States desires to be helpful in finding means of reducing these tensions."[25] It
was indeed in line with these policies that, after repeated Egyptian bombings of
Saudi borderland territory in the south, the United States air force made demonstration flights over Riyadh and other Saudi centers to reassure the government and
people of the kingdom of American power and concern for the Saudi security and
integrity.

This basically friendly relationship was emphasized by the visit that King Faisal
paid to President Johnson in June 1966 and to President Nixon in May 1971. In turn,
President Nixon visited King Faisal in Riyadh in July 1974.

The presence of Aramco undoubtedly provided the main economic link between
the two countries. On a comparative scale Aramco's concession was being carried
out in a climate of much greater harmony than was the case of Western concessions

[25] See note 21, *supra.*

in a number of other oil-producing countries. However, even Saudi Arabia could not remain unaffected by the winds of change that were characteristic of the international oil situation all over the world in the 1960s and 1970s. From 1963 on, Aramco gradually began a program of territorial relinquishment under pressure from the Saudi government. In the early 1970s, Saudi Arabia formulated a demand for participation in the ownership of Aramco. An agreement granting the Saudi government 20 percent of Aramco's stock was concluded in December 1972, followed by an agreement to increase Saudi participation to 60 percent, and the process was completed by granting Saudi Arabia total ownership of the company.[26] Basic agreements on this final transfer were negotiated in 1976. Aramco was expected to function merely as a service company under a contract to the Saudi government while its original parent companies (Standard of California, Texaco, Exxon, and Mobil) were to be given guaranteed access to specified amounts of Saudi crude oil. Because of the quadrupling of the oil prices in December 1973 and the subsequent increases in prices, the Saudi revenue from oil reached the $25 billion level in 1976 while its reserves in foreign currency, earmarked for investments, attained the figure of $45 billion in that same year. In turn, Saudi Arabia displayed considerable trust in the health of the American economy by purchasing several billion dollars worth of United States Treasury bonds in 1974 and depositing its funds mostly in American banks.

This generally friendly and harmonious relationship between the two countries suffered from one strain, namely the close realtionship between the United States and Israel. King Faisal could never overcome his puzzlement at the degree of American engagement on the Israeli side and more than once gave forceful expression to his concern about it in statements and interviews granted to foreign visitors.[27] In Faisal's perception, the United States needed to cultivate the good will of the Arab governments and peoples because of its economic, strategic, and ideological interests. Faisal believed that pronounced American partiality toward Israel is dangerous because it generates hostility toward the United States in the Arab world and thus opens the gates to Soviet, hence also communist, penetration. He believed the American policy to be illogical and hurtful to the United States' national interests; and, when reminded by his advisers of the pressure group democratic system prevailing in the United States, he invariably expressed incredulity at the ability of a small minority group to dictate the national policies of a great power.

Yet, with all these disappointments and frustrations in his relations with Washington, Faisal steadily refused to align himself with the more radical Arab countries in their minifestations of hostility toward the United States. Thus he resisted the frequent suggestions emanating from more militant Arab quarters that oil should be used as a political weapon and a means of pressure. However, with the onset of the October 1973 war, even he decided that the use of oil as a weapon could not be avoided. Consequently, on October 20, 1973, he proclaimed an em-

[26]For a fuller discussion of the changes, see G. Lenczowski, *Middle East Oil in a Revolutionary Age* (Washington, D.C., 1976).

[27]For typical interviews, see those granted to Nicholas Proffit, *Newsweek,* Sept. 10, 1973, and Wilton Wynn, *Time,* Jan. 6, 1975.

bargo on exports of oil to United States, Portugal and Holland. In reaching this decision he conformed to the resolution adopted the previous day by a meeting of the petroleum ministers representing the Arab oil-producing states. Full participation of Saudi Arabia in the Arab cutback and embargo policy was vital for its success, not only because it ensured an effective solidarity of the oil-exporting countries but also because Saudi Arabia, with its production around 8.5 millions barrels a day on the eve of the October war, constituted a major source of supply. In fact, the Saudi delegate, Yamani, played henceforth a leading and often decisive role in the subsequent meetings and decisions of the Arab oil ministers throughout the duration of the crisis in the winter of 1973–74. Furthermore, when after the conclusion of the first disengagement agreement (Sinai I), President Sadat of Egypt began advocating the lifting of the oil embargo, Saudi Arabia under Faisal's leadership was reluctant to follow this advice, insisting as it did on the fulfillment of certain conditions (such as complete evacuation of Israeli troops from occupied territories) before rescinding its decision. Ultimately, however, the Saudi government was persuaded to relent and, by July 1974, it agreed to go along with other Arab states to put an end to the embargo and cutback policy.

Positive intervention of the United States as a peacemaker materially helped to restore normal cooperative relations between Washington and Riyadh, which were eloquently expressed by the visit that the minister of the interior, Prince Fahd, paid to President Ford in Washington in June 1974. Accompanied by a group of ministers and high-ranking technocrats, the prince signed an agreement with the United States government for comprehensive cooperation between the two countries in the technical, military, energy, and other sectors. The United States was to aid Saudi Arabia in its development program on a large scale and a joint American-Saudi commission was established to supervise the implementation of this agreement. With nearly $143 billion to spend for its five-year development plan, from 1975 to 1980, Saudi Arabia became a very attractive market for American industrial, engineering, and service firms. From 1973 on, American sales of manufactured goods to Saudi Arabia began doubling and even tripling in size annually. In 1976 they reached $2.7 billion, with a promise of continued and spectacular growth. American arms sales to the Saudi kingdom also increased significantly, with multibillion-dollar contracts concluded by various American manufacturers, including the Northrop Corporation, which undertook to modernize the Saudi Arabian air force in 1976.

It was clear that despite the disturbance of the embargo in 1973–1974, Saudi Arabia had great faith in American technology and a definite preference for American goods and services, although trade with other industrial countries increased significantly.

In this promising growth of the United States-Saudi economic relationship there arose two issues likely to complicate matters. One was the reluctance of the United States Congress to approve the administration-sponsored major sales of certain types of arms to the Saudi kingdom. The main reason was the suspicion voiced by some congressmen that ultimately these weapons might find their way to the Arab confrontation states such as Egypt and therefore affect adversely Israel's security.[28] The other issue was that of the Arab boycott of Israel. By virtue of this boycott, which had been instituted as early as 1947, Arab states refused to do business with foreign firms which were substantially engaged in the development of the Israeli economy (the so-called primary boycott) and also with firms that, without doing direct business with Israel, relied on substantial supplies of goods from other firms that were in a close business relationship with Israel (the so-called secondary boycott). Interestingly enough, although these Arab boycott rules had been in force for a long time, no significant protests were raised about them in the United States until the mid-1970s. Only when the United States-Arab trade began to assume important proportions did the issue emerge to provide a source of major controversy in the United States. Pro-Israeli groups in the United States were very vocal in advocating legislation which would make it a penal offense for an American firm to conform to the Arab boycott rules. These groups found many supporters in Congress. On the other side were numerous American business firms whose success and prosperity greatly depended on a continuous and developing relationship with the Arab world, particularly with Saudi Arabia. After long debate, a law was finally passed by the Congress in 1977 which put severe restrictions on the freedom of American firms to conform to the Arab boycott rules. The way the law was phrased made the primary boycott acceptable but virtually banned the secondary boycott. While this legislation was likely to complicate, in some cases quite seriously, American business transactions with the Arab world, it did not completely close the door to such transactions. As of mid-1978 its long-range effects still had to be tested.[29]

In conclusion, by combining political authoritarianism under the aegis of the House of Saud with an emphasis on Islam and the quest for technical modernization, Saudi Arabia displayed in the 1960s and 1970s a remarkable degree of political stability and resilience. While the more liberal and progressive-minded members of its fast-growing intelligentsia might feel uncomfortable under its austere social traditionalism, the absorptive capacity of the kingdom was so pronounced as to assure any ambitious and hard-working individual a place in the society broadly commensurate with his qualifications and merits and to guarantee him fast promotion. Manifestations of discontent did occur occasionally but were weak and ineffectual and never succeeded in undermining the regime. The royal family displayed a remarkable degree of solidarity despite minor disagreements and rivalries. The rapid economic and technical development envisaged by the second plan had the potential of producing significant changes and strains in the society, not only because of the introduction of new technology but also because of the importation of much-needed

---

[28] See *U.S. Arms Policy. Hearings before the Committee on Foreign Relations and the Subcommittee on Foreign Assistance of the Committee on Foreign Relations, United States Senate, 94th Congress, Second Session on Proposed Sales of Arms to Iran and Saudi Arabia* (U.S. Government Printing Office, Washington, D.C., 1977).

[29] For a comprehensive discussion, see Nancy Turck, "The Arab Boycott of Israel," *Foreign Affairs*, 55, no. 3 (April 1977).

foreign labor on a massive scale. That same rapid development was furthermore stimulating dangerous inflationary trends which, if unchecked, might aggravate the latent social conflicts. However, the leadership provided by the House of Saud and the co-opted technocrats was intelligent, sober, and aware of the pitfalls that sudden wealth and development were bringing. Furthermore, in the foreign sector, Saudi Arabia conducted a policy characterized by prudence, lack of adventurism, a realistic appraisal of the forces at work in the world at large, and a desire to assist rather than to impede the United States and its Western allies in their opposition to communism and Soviet imperialism. In return, the Saudi government could, without signing any formal alliances, count on the support of the United States in preserving its sovereignty and the territorial integrity of its country.

CHAPTER XIV

Yemen

In contrast to Saudi Arabia, the ancient land of Yemen does not have much political history to record. Known in antiquity as *Arabia Felix,* this mountainous country is fortunate in having more rainfall and more fertile soil than the rest of Arabia and, as a consequence, is able to support a relatively dense population of about five and one-half million. Dominated by the Zaidi sect of the Shia branch of Islam, Yemen has also a considerable proportion of Sunnis, as well as—until recently—about 90,000 Jews.[1] Until 1918, Yemen formed a part of the Ottoman Empire, the ruler of its highland Zaidi region, Iman Yehya, enjoying local autonomy under Turkish sovereignty. Yehya remained faithful to Turkey during the First World War, but his anti-Ally stand had no practical influence on the conduct of the war in the Middle East. The Turkish garrison in Yemen was for the most part isolated from the rest of the Ottoman forces, and Yehya's pro-Turkish policy was to a great extent neutralized by the pro-Ally attitude of his northern neighbors, the Idrisi princes of Asir.

After World War I

After the war Imam Yehya emerged as an independent ruler, largely by default, inasmuch as there was no power ready and willing to assume imperial responsibilities in the area. No official proclamation of independence was ever issued in Sana, but Yehya quite obviously did not consider himself bound either by the Mudros armistice provisions or by the earlier British-Ottoman agreements regarding the boundaries in Arabia.

Following the armistice British troops landed on a few points of the Yemen coast and helped evacuate the wartime Turkish garrison. Having accomplished this task, they handed over the port of Loheia to their Idrisi allies while retaining temporarily the port of Hodeida. These actions greatly irked Iman Yehya, who claimed historical title to the whole of Yemen (and not to only the Zaidi-inhabited highlands).

---

[1] On September 10, 1950, Edward M. M. Warburg, chairman of the Joint Distribution Committee, announced that it was expected that by September 19 virtually all of Yemen's Jews would have emigrated to Israel. This migration was popularly known as "Operation Flying Carpet" and resulted from the growing tension that had developed between the Arab and Jewish communities of Yemen after the Palestinian war.

Consequently, at the end of 1919 he invaded Dhala and a few other frontier districts of the British Aden Protectorate hoping thereby to compel the British to evacuate Hodeida. This they did in January 1921, but instead of giving it to Yemen they turned it over to Asir. Yehya thus found himself cut off from two valuable Red Sea ports. For over five years the Idrisis were in possession of the coastal plain, known as the Tihama, but the rise of Ibn Saud seriously undermined their position. Profiting from their weakness, Yehya, in March 1925, launched an attack and, following a brief campaign, captured Hodeida and Loheia. By this act he extended his dominions to the coastal lowland, gaining secure access to the Red Sea and acquiring control of the trade routes between the above-mentioned ports and Sana, the capital. The international repercussions of this development were twofold: on the one hand, the hitherto independent Asir principality was partitioned between Yemen and the Hejaz, Asir's Idrisi rulers accepting Ibn Saud's suzerainty in October 1926; on the other, British-controlled Aden suffered economically because of the diversion of trade with the Yemen interior from Aden to Hodeida. This, in turn, suited Italian interests in the region. Italy, already in control of Eritrea on the opposite side of the Red Sea, viewed Yemen as an area for commercial and political expansion. By securing a foothold in Yemen she might find herself sitting astride the southern reaches of the Red Sea, thus threatening the British life line.

Such a development, were it to occur, was definitely not in the British interest. Moreover, Britain had come to regard the whole of the Arabian peninsula as her exclusive sphere to which something like a British Monroe doctrine should apply. Britain's attitude was not so much dictated by imperial rapaciousness (she derived no direct profit from her dealings with Arab chieftains whom she usually had to subsidize) as by the desire to keep other powers away from the approaches to India. Yet while it was relatively easy for Britain to establish her supremacy over the small sheikhdoms and sultanates of the eastern and southern coast of Arabia, it was more difficult to extend it to the inaccessible highland fastness of Yemen. Being unprepared to establish her control by outright conquest (as she had done in Aden in the nineteenth century) Britain had to rely on diplomacy.

British-Italian Rivalry

In the diplomatic duel with Italy Britain suffered defeats. Between January and February 1925 Sir Gilbert Clayton spent nearly a month in Sana trying to reach some agreement with the Imam, especially in view of the latter's continued occupation of the border areas in the Aden Protectorate. But his mission ended in failure. By contrast, on September 2, 1926, Italy succeeded in concluding with Yemen a ten-year treaty of friendship and commerce by which she recognized Yemen's "full and absolute independence," a step which Britain so far had failed to take. In June 1927, a Yemeni mission headed by Yehya's second son paid a state visit to Italy. The Yemenites were received by Victor Emmanuel and Mussolini and were shown Italian industrial establishments. As a result both parties signed an additional agreement providing for the purchase of arms by the Yemen government.

In the meantime, British-Yemeni relations had taken a turn for the worse. Imam

Yehya had not only not evacuated the Aden districts occupied in 1919 but had renewed his aggressive tactics by repeatedly raiding the Protectorate in 1927 and 1928. In the latter year he concluded a treaty with the Soviet Union, permitting the establishment of a Soviet commercial mission in Sana. Coming as it did in the year of the Sixth Congress of the Comintern and of pronounced Anglo-Soviet tension, this treaty was indicative of the Imam's growing defiance. The British retaliated by using the Royal Air Force, which drove the Yemenites back to the original boundaries and forced them to sue for a truce. Imam Yehya was still unwilling to repudiate his claims to the Aden territory, but by 1931 he decided not to press it any further and agreed to enter into negotiations with the British. His change of heart was due in part to the rise of the Wahhabi power to the north of his boundaries and in part to fear lest the British exploit his differences with the Sunni tribes of the Tihama plain and induce them to rise in open rebellion. The protracted negotiations led to the conclusion, on February 11, 1934, of the British-Yemeni Treaty of Sana which provided for friendship, mutual cooperation, and the recognition of the status quo on the Aden boundary for the next forty years. The British failed to get from the Imam a definite renunciation of his territorial claims, the explanation being that the Imam was prevented by religious restrictions from changing the God-ordained boundaries of his country. Yemen's complete independence was given express recognition.

The next month Yemen fought a war with Saudi Arabia. Defeated, Imam Yehya adopted a much more cautious policy toward his formidable northern neighbor.

Yehya's gradual reconciliation with Britain did not deflect him, however, from his policy of opposing British penetration and of favoring contacts with other powers. His was the only Arab country in which no British representative was permitted to reside. Relations with Sana were handled for Britain by the British governor of Aden, and the only Britishers living in Yemen were a medical missionary with his wife and two assistants.

Anxious to preserve complete freedom of action the Imam in 1933 concluded treaties with Holland and France, but it was Italy that remained his principal partner. In 1936 the Italo-Yemeni treaty of a decade before was renewed for one year. Next year an Italian mission visited Sana and on October 15, with impressive ceremonies, signed a new twenty-five year treaty with the Imam. A number of Italian doctors and engineers were invited to establish themselves in the country, and a quantity of arms was supplied by Italy.

The treaty of 1937 constituted the apogee of the Italian influence in Yemen. We must not forget, however, that in their essence Italo-Yemeni relations were no more than a function of Italo-British relations. Therefore any improvement in the latter was bound to be reflected in a lessening of the Italian penetration of Yemen. By an agreement signed on April 16, 1938, Britain and Italy temporarily composed their differences, regulating their respective positions in the Middle East. In the annexes to the agreement both parties undertook not to acquire "a privileged position of a political character" in Saudi Arabia or Yemen but to prevent other powers from doing so, not to intervene in the internal matters of this region, and to refrain from mutually hostile propaganda.[2] The last provision stemmed mainly from British objections to the Italian broadcasts beamed to the Arab world from Bari.

World War II and Its Effects

As for the Imam, he continued to show his preference for the Axis. In 1938 he sent one of his sons to Tokyo to attend the inauguration of a new mosque. During the Second World War he remained neutral. The full story of the pressures that the belligerents brought to hear upon him has not yet been revealed, but it is known that a few British emissaries including the well-known Arabist Miss Freya Stark visited Sana in that period.[3] The British victory at El-Alamein undoubtedly had a cooling effect on Yehya's pro-Axis proclivities, and soon afterward, on February 26, 1943, the Imam ordered the arrest of forty Italians and two Germans, thus silencing two pro-Axis radio stations operating in his territory. This action was accompanied by the severance of diplomatic relations with the Axis powers. In March 1945 Yemen joined the Arab League but, in contrast to other Arab states, she did not declare war on Germany and Japan and did not qualify for participation in the San Francisco conference. Yemen was admitted to the United Nations in 1947 as a result of a later application.

After the war Yemen gradually abandoned her traditional isolation and, like some other countries in the Middle East, sought to replace former Axis links by economic and political bonds with the United States. First contacts with Americans had been made as early as 1930 when Charles Crane and K. S. Twitchell visited Sana to help Yemen in the exploitation of natural resources. In April 1946 the first American diplomatic mission headed by Colonel William Eddy concluded a treaty of commerce and friendship with the Imam, followed by the establishment on May 11 of regular diplomatic relations. A year later, on May 24 both countries signed an agreement granting Yemen credit up to $1,000,000 for the purchase of American surplus property, and in the following July one of Yehya's sons, Prince Seif el-Islam Abdullah made a trip to the United States, where he saw President Truman and held conversations with various American industrialists.

Internal Crisis of 1948

Early in 1948 Yemen was the scene of dramatic events which focused upon her, temporarily, the attention of the outside world. On February 17 of that year Sayid Abdullah ibn Ahmed el-Wazir, former governor of Hodeida and minister of state, executed a coup d'état, in the course of which Imam Yehya, his prime minister, Qadi Abdullah Amri, Yehya's two sons, Hussein and Mohsen, and a few other persons close to the Imam were assassinated.[4] Sayid Abdullah proclaimed himself Imam and appointed Yehya's sixth son, Emir Seif el-Haqq Ibrahim, his prime minister. Ibrahim was a leader of the Free Yemeni Party, a group representing the

---

[2]Text in Cmd. 5726 of 1938.

[3]See Harold Ingrams, "A Journey to the Yemen," *R.C.A.J.* (Jan. 1946); also Freya M. Stark, *The Arab Island, The Middle East, 1939–1943* (New York, 1945), ch. on Yemen.

[4]For a detailed account of this crisis, see Eric Macro, "Yemen: A Brief Survey," *R. C. A. J.* (Jan. 1949).

commercial and landowning "bourgeoisie" of Yemen, who had grown increasingly restive under Yehya's old-fashioned and despotic rule. In 1946, Ibrahim had escaped to Aden, whence he came when the rebellion broke out. Sayid Abdullah belonged to a prominent family whose members had ruled Yemen in the past.

A few days after the coup a civil war broke out. The crown prince, Emir Seif el-Islam Ahmed, governor of Taiz, defied the new rulers, proclaimed himself Imam, and, gathering a force of loyal followers, launched an attack on Sana. In the meantime the Arab League, which met to consider the problem of recognition, decided to send a special commission to Yemen to study the situation. This commission never reached its destination, having spent considerable time in Riyadh before proceeding southward. On March 13, Crown Prince Ahmed succeeded in conquering Sana. Sayid Abdullah and his principal associates were captured and after a summary trial executed. A new government was formed. It included Mohammed Raghib Bey, Yehya's foreign minister, who resumed his old position. The Arab League was thus faced with a new situation. Opinions varied, but in the end Ibn Saud's view prevailed. The Wahhabi ruler condemned the regicide and at one moment appeared ready to intervene in Emir Ahmed's favor. Deferring to his views, the Arab League decided to uphold the principle of legitimacy and at a meeting in Beirut on March 21 granted its recognition to Seif el-Ahmed as the Imam of Yemen. Recognitions from other countries soon followed.

Yemen's International Position in the 1950s

On March 10, 1951, Yemen and Britain signed a new treaty designed to improve their mutual relations. Its principal innovation was a clause providing for the exchange of diplomatic representatives, Yemen having been reluctant to permit British diplomats to reside in the country. The treaty also provided for cooperation in the development of Yemen, should the latter so request; the creation of a mixed committee to deal with frontier problems; a mutual pledge not to change the status quo in the border regions until the committee finishes its work; and a promise to curb hostile propaganda against each other.

Despite this treaty Yemeni-British relations suffered a marked deterioration almost immediately afterward. The main cause was the unsettled territorial question and, in particular, the widely divergent attitudes of the parties toward the area situated between Yemen proper and Aden Colony, i.e., the Aden Protectorate. Composed of a number of petty principalities, this large stretch of land equivalent in size to Britain, Scotland, Wales, and Northern Ireland had at one time or another belonged to the dominion of the Zaidi imams of Sana, who were never reconciled to its subjection to British rule. Moreover, even as late as 1934—the time of the first Anglo-Yemeni treaty—British interests in this whole area were represented by no more than two officials: a political secretary and a political officer, whose main function, perforce, was to maintain liaison with Protectorate chiefs rather than to conduct a regular administration. As a result, the chiefs were largely left to their own devices, and the looseness of British control tended to emphasize their almost independent status. So long as this was the case, Yemen tolerated if she did not fully accept the status quo.

But Britain's restrained policy underwent considerable change, especially after World War II. In contrast to other areas in her empire where she gradually reduced her responsibilities, in the Aden Protectorate Britain began to assert her dominance. This came about principally in two ways. In the first place, she embarked upon a policy aiming at improvement of the social and economic conditions in the protected principalities. This led to an increase in her administrative personnel of 3,000 percent as compared to the number in 1934, naturally creating uneasiness in Yemen, which was always isolationist and suspicious of foreigners in close proximity. In the second place, in the early 1950s the British launched a project to unite the sultans, emirs, and sheikhs of the Protectorate in a federation. More precisely, the scheme was expected to comprise eighteen principalities of the West Aden Protectorate. Its principal objective, politically, would be to consolidate the British position in the area. Yemen rather naturally took a strong dislike to this plan inasmuch as she was loath to witness a gradual amalgamation of the separate petty states into a strong political unit under an aegis other than her own.

Added to this were two other considerations, both related to the internal situation in Yemen. The first and perhaps more important of the two was linked to the composition of Yemen's population. This was comprised of two principal groups: the Shafii and the Zaidi, representing two-thirds and one-third of the total, respectively. The Zaidis, inhabiting the mountainous interior, held a dominant position, the kings, nobles, and principal officeholders always being of Zaidi faith. The lowlands were peopled mostly by Shafiis as were the petty states of the Aden Protectorate. Consequently, the establishment of a predominantly Shafii federation implied the possibility that this new political center might compete with the imams of Sana for the loyalty of their Shafii subjects and thus endanger Zaidi supremacy in Yemen. The second consideration was that the markedly conservative government of Yemen could not remain oblivious to actual or contemplated changes in the economic and social life of the Aden Protectorate, inasmuch as any obvious contrast between the two areas was apt to prove disruptive to Yemen's internal stability.

For these reasons the Yemen government fought the Aden federation plan, resorting to a variety of methods to achieve its objective. For instance, it reverted to rather truculent behavior with regard to border areas. As a result, border incidents increased in number, sometimes assuming the proportions of a major Yemeni incursion into the Aden Protectorate. A Yemeni siege of Fort Mukheiras in December 1954 exemplified this tendency. The Aden authorities, on their part, reacted to these infiltrations by reinforcing the British-officered levies and policing the troubled areas with the Royal Air Force. Yemen's tactics did not stop there. The Imam's government resorted to propaganda and other inducements to win over a number of disaffected chiefs in the Aden Protectorate. In this respect Yemen profited from the general attitude of mistrust shown by the petty rulers in the Protectorate toward the British-sponsored federation plan. These rulers saw few, if any, advantages for themselves in a unification plan under British tutelage and consequently often leaned toward Yemen in this controversy.

Not content with this political action, Yemen raised certain legal points. She claimed that Britain was guilty of violating her agreements, especially the treaty of

1934, which provided for the status quo in the existing frontiers. By "frontiers" the Yemenis meant not only the rather vague demarcation line between their territory and the Aden Protectorate but also the borders between the principalities *within* the Protectorate itself. They based his claim on the plural employed in the text of the treaty when referring to the frontiers (*hudud*) and opposed the federation as likely to affect these inland border lines. In pursuance of her policy of opposition, Yemen also lodged protests against Britain's actions before the United Nations, once in July and again in October 1954. Charging Britain with "aggression," the Yemeni delegation protested against the proposed federation of what it termed Yemeni territory and in addition challenged Britain's sovereignty in the Aden Colony itself. The latter, it asserted in the Trusteeship Council, was Yemen's property which Britain had annexed by force.

While considerable doubts existed as to the legal validity of Yemen's contentions, the fact remained that it was Britain's forward policy in this hitherto fairly quiet region which lay at the root of the difficulties. Yemen's rulers could hardly be blamed for their negative reaction to moves and schemes which were apt to upset the existing political balance. By the same token, it was not illogical for Yemen in her foreign policy to line up with those states in the Arab League which, like herself, had had difficulties with Britain and leaned toward neutralism. On all major issues posed before the League, Yemen stood staunchly by the Cairo-Riyadh axis.

Internal Upheaval in 1955

Reference has already been made to Yemen's nervousness about the effect improvements in the Aden Protectorate might have on her own stability. Imam Seif el-Islam Ahmed owed his throne to the victory of conservative forces over the reformists and consequently viewed with uneasiness any movement within or without Yemen that was likely to threaten his and his allies' hold on the country. The ringleaders of the 1948 coup had all been executed, imprisoned, or exiled, but the real causes of rebellion remained, and important elements within the country had not been reconciled to Ahmed's rule. The Imam virtually acknowledged the unrest when he chose to make Taiz his "temporary" capital, ostensibly because he would not honor the people of Sana, a regicidal city, with his presence. The truth was that the people of Sana could not forget the ruthless behavior and plundering in 1948 by the tribesmen who had helped Ahmed defeat Sayid Abdullah and his reformist government. Settled, industrious, and relatively prosperous, the inhabitants of the capital resented the supremacy of the backward tribal elements to whom Ahmed owed his elevation. To be sure, the Imam took steps to develop the country, mostly by inviting a few foreign experts to carry out certain limited technical projects. But he did not adopt any comprehensive plan of development and reform, and his policy continued, by and large, to follow the traditional isolationist pattern. In the meantime, however, Yemen's participation in the United Nations and the Arab League, the growing number of Yemeni students in Cairo and other foreign centers, and increasing trade contacts with the outside world tended to counter this isolationist tendency, exposing a good many people to foreign influences and ideas. Consequently the tension already existing between the conservative and the reformist forces was increasing. In the spring of 1955 it erupted in the form of a new coup that shook the kingdom profoundly.

Toward the end of March 1955 the leaders of a new conspiracy against Imam Ahmed made common cause with disaffected army units. After having presented inacceptable demands to Ahmed, the latter struck at the royal guards in Taiz, compelling the Imam to flee the palace and seek refuge in the El-Udi fortress. Mediation attempted by religious notables brought no results. Instead, the religious and the military leaders reached agreement on March 31 to depose Ahmed and to proclaim as imam his brother and minister of foreign affairs, Seif el-Islam Abdullah. The latter was reputed to be a man of more liberal tendencies, having traveled widely and absorbed a good deal of Western culture.

Imam Ahmed's deposition was challenged, however, by his son and crown prince, Seif el-Islam Mohammed el-Badr. Badr escaped from Taiz and reached the northern stronghold of Hajja, where he appealed for aid to the Hashed and Bakil tribes whose friendship he and his father had consistently cultivated. These were, in fact, the same tribes that had restored Imam Ahmed to the throne in 1948 and subsequently sacked Sana. Badr's dramatic appeal—he reportedly threw down his turban and dagger in a gesture of humiliation—did not go unheeded. The tribesmen offered him a force of eight thousand men, who promptly set out to relieve Ahmed, the latter still besieged in El-Udi. In the fierce battle that ensued between the army and the tribesmen, the army was handicapped by a shortage of munitions and gasoline, the main depot of which was in the fortress. As a result, the tribal force emerged victorious, capturing or putting to flight the rebel leaders. On April 4, Imam Ahmed regained his throne. Fifteen leaders of the coup were promptly executed, the list including Ahmed's two brothers, Seif el-Islam Abdullah, the would-be imam, and Seif el-Islam el-Abbas, governor of the province of Sana, as well as Ahmed Yehya Salayah, instructor-general of the army. Among those arrested but later released were four sons of Yemen's prime minister, Emir Seif el-Islam el-Hassan, who at the time of the coup was on a visit to Cairo. He was subsequently removed from his position but no other steps against him were reported.

On April 17, Imam Ahmed appointed Badr head of the government and simultaneously asked him to form a study commission to modernize Yemen's administration. Soon afterward Ahmed ordered the opening of the coffers containing the treasures of the late Imam Yehya. This fortune has been variously estimated at between $56 million and $280 million. According to Yemeni declarations, the government wanted to use it for development purposes. On his part, Prince Badr declared during a visit in Cairo early in May that his father "ardently desired to establish a democratic government" which would adopt a program of reforms and that it was to be "the government of the people for the people."[5]

The subsequent granting of an oil concession to an American firm could perhaps be seen as an indication that Imam Ahmed had decided to embark upon a path of development by ending the virtual ban upon foreign penetration of the country. Signed in October 1955 between Yemen's government and Walter S. Gabler, presi-

[5] *Cahiers*, 1955, 1.

dent of the Yemen Development Corporation, the thirty-year concession provided for the exploration and development of oil and mineral resources. Simultaneously Yemen was conducting negotiations with the Soviet Union, which on October 31 resulted in the renewal of the friendship treaty originally concluded in 1928. Early in 1956 a Yemeni spokesman in Cairo declared that Russia had offered to erect factories and supply agricultural machinery and road-building equipment to his country and that this offer was linked with the recently concluded treaty. By 1957, Yemen began receiving arms from the Soviet bloc, notably from Czechoslovakia.

Yemen's New International Alignments

For about two decades, between the mid-1930s and the mid-1950s, Yemen was closely aligned with Saudi Arabia on most major international issues. Beginning in 1956, Yemen ceased to follow Saudi policies and developed an international policy of its own. Two major lines of this policy could be discerned: rapprochement with the Soviet bloc and establishment of close links with Cairo. While it is not easy to determine the exact reasons for these actions, one might venture the opinion that they were prompted partly by external and partly by domestic political considerations. On the external front, Yemen's relations with Britain suffered continuous tension due to the clash of their policies over the Aden Protectorate. Britain's determination to go ahead with the formation of a federation among the protected states was strongly resented in Taiz, whose claims to "Southern Yemen," i.e., the Aden Protectorate area, were constantly reasserted. Under the circumstances, Yemeni Crown Prince Mohammed el-Badr's mission to London in November 1957 ended in a deadlock, with neither party willing to compromise on its basic attitudes. Acting in its capacity as a suzerain power in the Protectorate, the British government continued to manipulate local dynastic politics and, reacting to hostile attitudes of the Sultan of Lahej, deposed and replaced him by another leader in the summer of 1958, thereby provoking a new outburst of Yemeni protests. The actual signing of the act of federation by the rulers of six petty states in the West Aden Protectorate on February 11, 1959, added another major obstacle to a British-Yemeni understanding, indefinitely postponing the likelihood of reconciliation.

On the domestic scene the major factor was the emergence of youthful Crown Prince Mohammed el-Badr as the leading figure, to whom his father, Imam Ahmed, entrusted an ever-widening range of responsibilities. In 1958, Badr formally assumed the duties of prime minister, but even before his formal assumption of office his influence on the country's policies had been growing steadily. Reflecting to some extent the views and attitudes of the younger Arab generation and aspiring to leave a mark of his own on the history of southern Arabia, Badr on many occasions publicly asserted his condemnation of imperialism and his sympathy for the Pan-Arab cause. In 1955-1956 the Pan-Arabists in the Middle East, following Gamal Abdul Nasser's example, were in favor of closer links with Russia, from which they expected to receive arms, economic aid, and general diplomatic support in their struggle with the remnants of Western imperialism. Badr not only followed this general line but seemed anxious to excel in it.

In June of 1956 he paid his first visit to Moscow and in August of the same year, under his prodding, the government of Yemen extended formal recognition to Communist China. Soon afterward, in the fall, Badr's new pro-Soviet orientation received another boost from the deterioration of Western-Arab relations in the wake of the Suez War. The results of the drawing closer to the Soviet bloc soon became visible in the form of arms deliveries to Yemen from Czechoslovakia and the Soviet Union. In the winter of 1957–1958, Badr made a new, extended trip to the Soviet bloc countries, visiting Rumania, Poland, Russia, and Communist China. On January 12, 1958, he signed in Peking a ten-year trade and aid agreement with the Chinese government. Before long a sizable contingent of Chinese technicians (about 500 men) was busy in Yemen constructing a road between Sana and Hodeida. Soviet experts and advisers were also much in evidence.

Officially, however, Yemen asserted that its policy was that of "positive neutralism," an expression coined in Cairo that had acquired wide currency in the Arab world. In the name of this policy Yemen's government (perhaps partly due to Imam Ahmed's more cautious approach) continued to maintain relations with the West, in particular with the United States. The latter was even permitted to establish a permanent legation administered by a chargé d'affaires in Taiz (formerly, American ambassadors to Saudi Arabia were simultaneously accredited as ministers to Yemen and limited their presence in the latter country to occasional visits.) Moreover, Yemen was willing, from time to time, to accept offers of American economic aid, such as a gift of 15,000 tons of wheat, which was sent from the United States in early 1959 to help relieve the shortages caused by drought. It should be pointed out, however, that certain factions in the Yemeni government strongly opposed the idea of accepting aid from Americans and feverishly sought to counter-balance this operation by a simultaneous deal with Russia for the delivery of a similar quantity of wheat. For a few days in the spring of 1959 Yemen's ports and its adjacent waters were the scene of a veritable race between American and Soviet ships carrying their wheat cargoes, with local port officials and operators of landing barges being involved in intrigues and counterintrigues to facilitate or delay the servicing and unloading of the ships in question.

Federation with the U.A.R. and Internal Problems

Emir Badr's public espousal of Pan-Arabism led him along the logical path of seeking closer ties with Cairo. His visits to Egypt and Syria grew in frequency, providing him with opportunities to express publicly his feelings of Arab solidarity and his devotion to the cause of Arab unity. In pursuance of such policies, his government not only warmly applauded the Syro-Egyptian union of February 1, 1958, but soon after, on March 8, 1958, joined the newly proclaimed United Arab Republic in an act of federation. The new political creation was called the United Arab States, each of the component parts, i.e., the U.A.R. and Yemen, preserving its separate identity and its form of government. In limiting their association with the revolutionary regime in Cairo to a federative link, Yemen's rulers, in contrast to Syrian, displayed a good deal of political realism, which permitted them to preserve their independence and their internal structure. In fact, in implementing even this loose federal tie, the Yemenis displayed considerable reserve and caution. Egyptians were not encouraged to travel to Yemen, and such Egyptian experts and technicians as were sent to Yemen had to secure advance permission of the Yemeni authorities to enter the latter's jealously guarded territory. Paradoxically, Yemen's government seemed to trust the Chinese and Soviet Communist technicians more than their Arab brethren from revolutionary Egypt, perhaps out of the conviction that the linguistic barrier in the case of the former groups presented a more effective guarantee against subversion than the official pledge of noninterference given by Cairo when the act of federation was signed. There were some indications that President Nasser's government viewed this Sino-Soviet-Yemeni friendship with considerable concern and tried, as discreetly as the circumstances permitted, to counteract it. In fact, a skeptic might not only question the reality of the Yemen-U.A.R. federation but also suspect that in their own Machiavellian way the Yemenis had chosen it as a method to protect themselves against the spread of the Egyptian-type revolution into their own country. By paying lip service to Arab unity and nominally recognizing Nasser's leadership in the Arab world, they tried to avoid becoming a target of Cairo's hostile propaganda and thus escape the embarrassment experienced by their neighbors when the Saudis broke openly with Nasser's Pan-Arabism in 1958.

Decline and Fall of the Imamate

The fourteen-year rule of Imam Ahmed was one of unrelieved despotism. While authoritarian rulers sometimes apply strong-arm methods to achieve certain socially desirable goals, this clearly was not the case in Yemen. Imam Ahmed was essentially reactionary, suspicious of progress, primarily concerned with his personal power, and content to see things as they were, which meant the continuous poverty and backwardness of the country. Yemen was devoid of modern roads and it was only in the later 1950s that the Soviets undertook to build a highway between Sana and Hodeida while the Americans, under the official United States aid program, launched the construction of a road linking Sana to Taiz. There was only one bank, engaging mostly in foreign exchange and short-term commerical credit, and most of the Yemeni merchants had to resort to the banking services of the British Crown Colony in Aden. The country had no other financial institutions and not even its own currency: Austrian Maria Theresa thalers were used as a means of exchange, but even these were subjected to fluctuations in value on account of their silver content. The cities were devoid of sewerage systems and only one urban center, Taiz, had a weak and continuously failing water conduit represented by a three-quarter-inch pipeline, which was frequently punctured and its water siphoned off by landowners before it reached the city. Electricity was available only to 3 percent of the population, at exorbitant rates. The educational system was rudimentary, with no university and only a few government-owned schools, a situation which compelled many young Yemenis to seek education abroad. Around 1960 there were five hundred Yemeni students in Aden, between three and four hundred in Egypt, and some seventy to eighty in the United States and Europe, mostly in the institutions of higher learning. Some also in the later 1950s went to study in the Soviet Union. At the same time certain Yemeni officers were undergoing military training in Iraq and

Egypt. Upon their return from studies these diploma-holding Yemenis—not necessarily very competent but already with aroused ambitions—constituted a chronically discontented group that was inclined to seek a radical change in the country.

The functioning of the government left much to be desired. The system of justice, based on religious law, was inadequate and clearly corrupt, as was the general state administration. Taxation was oppressive and unjust and was expressed by a maze of internal taxes including those on transport, customs duties (the main source of state revenue), pier taxes, and export taxes. Agriculture was in decline: Yemen, which traditionally—with generous rainfall as compared to the rest of Arabia—was self-sufficient in food, saw its production of cereals falling and by 1960 became a net importer. Similarly, in twenty years—between 1942 and 1962—production of Yemeni coffee fell from 12,000 tons a year to 4,000 tons. The main reason was that much of the acreage was being diverted to the production of the popularly consumed narcotic, *qat,* which gave greater cash advantages to the cultivators but deprived the country of an important export crop. Finally, such industries as existed were small and operated by manual labor. One textile factory had been built but never put into motion because the local cotton dealers persuaded the Imam that he would obtain greater revenue from taxes on exports of cotton than from a developed domestic textile industry.[6]

The following incident provides an eloquent example of the way the Imam ruled. At the time of discontent and incipient revolt in the Hashed tribal confederation, its chief and his son were invited by Imam Ahmed to Sana to negotiate a settlement and to this end were granted an official safe conduct (an institution santified by the Islamic law) by the ruler. In the course of the discussion in the royal palace the Imam flew into a rage against his visitors and ordered them to be immediately decapitated. His order was promptly carried out, turning the Hashed tribes into his sworn enemies and causing much adverse comment in the population at large, which, in spite of the widespread crudity of customs, was attached to religious principles.

Provincial rebellions on a local scale, primarily of tribal nature, were endemic. Occasionally units of the army mutinied because their pay was in arrears. The Imam was a target of repeated attempts at his life, some initiated by officers responsible for his personal safety. While subsidies to the tribes began to be used by the Imam in the late 1950s as a device of balancing the political forces in the country, they were withdrawn rather abruptly in 1962, thus provoking disappointment and widespread hostility.

Furthermore, Imam Ahmed's health began to deteriorate before and after 1960, compelling him to take long rest cures in Rome. His son and crown prince, Mohammed el-Badr, was entrusted with governing responsibilities during these absences. Badr had reformist inclinations, favored close cooperation with Nasser's Egypt and with the Soviet bloc countries, but was inexperienced and rather weak.

---

[6]For a description of the conditions under Imam Ahmed's rule, see William R. Brown, "The Yemeni Dilemma," *Middle East Journal,* 17, no. 4 (Autumn 1963).

Under the circumstances, Yemen's foreign policy tended to be erratic: formally the kingdom joined the United Arab Republic in a confederation. In December 1961, following the secession of Syria from the U.A.R., Imam Ahmed severed his relations with Egypt through the ingenious method of writing a poem which ridiculed Arab socialism and in veiled terms attacked Nasser himself.

Social Structure and Growing Dissent

During his reign, Imam Ahmed did little or nothing to bridge the gap existing between the two main parts of the Yemeni population, the Zaidi and the Shafii sects. The Zaidis, representing a little less than half of the population, were clearly a dominant class; but it was their aristocratic emanation, the *sayyids* (descendants of the Prophet), numbering about 300,000, who on account of their religious status, constituted the real ruling elite in the country. These *sayyids,* moreover, traced their origins to the legendary Arab figure, Adnan, and indirectly to Hejaz. Another important segment of the Zaidi sect was represented by those who traced their origin to Qahtan and thus considered themselves native to Yemen. The latter category was mostly represented by the tribes, especially the three big confederations of Hashed, Bakil, and Khawlan. The *sayyid* oligarchy enjoyed most of the privileges in the state, held the most important offices, including those of tax assessors and collectors, and benefited from access to state revenues, both licit and illicit. The only institution that was relatively immune to their control was the army, although its officer corps as well as most other ranks were also of Zaidi persuasion. Under the circumstances the *sayyid* ruling class favored the status quo and was opposed to any idea of progress and modernization.

As for the Shafiis, they were less tribal in their organization and the merchants among them constituted the upper leading class. The Shafiis were generally better educated than the Zaidis, individually more competitive and achievement-oriented but less organically cohesive than the Zaidis, and militarily weaker.

By 1960–1961 the position of the Imamate and the *sayyid* oligarchy was precarious; both were often hated and considered an oppressive burden by large segments of the population. Among the discontented groups those educated abroad were perhaps the most vocal. But the non-*sayyid* elements among the Zaidis (mostly of Qahtan origin) were also growing increasingly restless under the existing tyrannical rule. Among them certain tribes, particularly the Hashed (owing to their blood feud with the Imam) were very hostile. The army was also of dubious loyalty, as the seven-year imprisonment of a well-known officer, Abdullah el-Sallal, for plotting against the government indicated. It was characteristic of the erratic course of the Imam that after freeing Sallal from prison he appointed him chief of the royal guard. All these discontented elements could, as a rule, count on the support of the less privileged half of the population, the Shafiis, concentrated in the south and in the lowland plains of the Tihama. The discontent among these various groups was further fanned by the strenuous Egyptian propaganda against the Yemeni monarchy. By adopting his national charter in the spring of 1962, Nasser proclaimed a new revolutionary crusade of a Pan-Arab type and his foremost journalist spokesman,

Mohammed Hassanein Heikal, unequivocally stated that revolution should be given priority over solidarity in inter-Arab relations.[7]

Revolution, Civil War, Intervention

Imam Ahmed died, probably of natural causes, on September 18, 1962. His son, Mohammed el-Badr, was promptly proclaimed Imam. He enjoyed his new position for only eight days. On September 26 the commander of the royal guard, Brigadier General Abdullah el-Sallal, carried out a military coup d'etat and proclaimed a republic. Radio Sana announced shortly afterward that Imam Badr had been killed. This, however, proved untrue: Badr succeeded in escaping from the palace and made his way to the northern mountains where he rallied around himself loyal tribes with the aim of fighting to regain the throne.

Sallal established a revolutionary command council, composed mostly of army officers, and created the presidency council of prominent civilian and military figures, with himself as chairman and in due time as formally proclaimed president of the republic. In a swift purge he dispossessed the ruling *sayyid* oligarchy of its position of privilege and in a number of cases, again true to the Yemeni tradition, he executed his political opponents. He drew his support broadly from those discontented groups mentioned in the preceding section, with varying degrees of active engagement. Although he gained considerable applause in the discontented Shafii south, the Shafiis never played an active role in his revolution and the subsequent republican government. However, Sallal tried on the cabinet level, at least in the initial stages of his rule, to balance numerically the Zaidi and Shafii elements.

After some twenty months in power, Sallal's government adopted a constitution on April 28, 1964, which proclaimed the Yemen Republic to be ''an Islamic Arab state, independent and sovereign.'' The constitution reflected some of the ideas taken from the Egyptian patterns; a single licensed political party, the Yemeni Arab Union, was formed. There is no evidence, however, that it was ever intensively utilized by Sallal for the purpose of indoctrination or mobilization.

From the very beginning Sallal followed Egypt's example in his foreign policy: he proclaimed positive neutralism and nonalignment, and did his best to establish close relations with Moscow and other states of the Communist bloc. As early as November 1962 he sent a delegation to the Soviet Union to negotiate for economic and technical assistance and in March 1964 he concluded with the USSR a treaty of friendship. A variety of cooperative agreements were also signed with such satellite states as Czechoslovakia, Bulgaria, Rumania, and Hungary. Finally, on June 9, 1964, Sallal signed an agreement with China, a by-product of which was a Chinese undertaking to construct a highway between Sana and Sada.

Sallal's hold on power did not remain unchallenged. Despite the endemic tribal discontent with the late Imam Ahmed, there was a traditional attachment to the institution of the Imamate and distrust of the regular army. In fact, it was only the

[7]Heikal's statement in *Al-Ahram,* December 12, 1961, as quoted by A. I. Dawisha, "Intervention in the Yemen: An Analysis of Egyptian Perceptions and Policies," *Middle East Journal,* 29, no. 1 (Winter 1975), 48.

Hashed tribal confederation that openly took the side of the republicans in the early stages of the revolution. Northern tribes, acknowledging Imam Badr's authority, promptly took the warpath to restore the Imam to power. They soon made considerable progress, ejecting the government troops from various outposts, particularly in the north and the east of the country. This royalist coalition formed a government of their own under Badr's authority, with his uncle, Prince Hassan, and another relative, Prince Mohammed ben Hussein, the latter in charge of military command, and Ahmed el-Shami, foreign minister, as the most publicized figures. With the advantage of these royalist warriors, Badr turned the revolution into a full-fledged civil war.

Egyptian Intervention and Saudi Assistance

It was natural that the Saudi government became very much concerned, if not actually alarmed, by these revolutionary developments in neighboring Yemen. Inasmuch as the royalist party was not only not defeated but actually gave signs of strength and perseverance, the Saudis promptly decided to assist it by providing a variety of military, medical, and other supplies. Saudi assistance was carried out from such borderland bases as Najran, Jaizan, and Khamis Mushait. Basing their calculations on a realistic assessment of forces at play in Yemen, the Saudis hoped for a victory of the royalists who, with their loyal tribal allies, represented a military force superior to the regular army controlled by the republican government. The Saudis, however, stopped short of sending troops into Yemeni territory.

The outbreak of the revolution in Yemen was also of tremendous importance to Egypt. Within less than two weeks President Nasser sent to Yemen his two close associates, Field Marshal Abdul Hakim Amer and Colonel Anwar el-Sadat, to establish contact with the new republican authorities and report on the situation. The two envoys promptly reached the conclusion that, militarily, the republicans were too weak to cope with the tribal-royalist counterinsurgency. The military part of their assessment was correct; the political part, however, was unrealistic because they conveyed the idea that the revolution was greeted with enthusiasm by the overwhelming majority of the people—an opinion which was later reflected in Nasser's assertion that "the whole people" of Yemen supported it. In reality, distinction should have been made between the initial positive reaction of various discontented segments of the population to the fact of the revolution, including the welcome extended to it by the large masses of the somewhat underprivileged Shafiis, on the one hand, and the actual willingness to fight for the preservation of the republican government on the other. Moreover, even those who had considerable grievances against the arbitrary and unjust policies of the late Imam Ahmed did not necessarily advocate the abolition of the monarchy as an institution and would have been probably quite content to see this institution preserved provided the new incumbent were a man of humane inclinations and cared for the welfare of his people.

Basing his actions on the report of his envoys, Nasser decided to intervene on the side of the republicans and, in the second half of October, the first Egyptian troops landed in Yemen to lend a hand to the government of General Sallal. Nasser's decision did not come out of a void. There were ideological, political, and strategic reasons that provided the general background for the decision to intervene. Ever since the adoption of its national charter in the spring of 1962, Egypt was committed to spreading revolution beyond its borders, a principle which, as has been mentioned earlier, was treated as a higher value than the maintenance of inter-Arab solidarity. The revolution in Yemen provided the first opportunity to apply this principle in practice. From the political point of view Nasser had suffered a considerable blow to his prestige when, a year earlier in September 1961, Syria seceded from the United Arab Republic. Nasser's view of this act of secession was also ideologically colored: instead of analyzing carefully the Egyptians' own behavior in Syria, he developed a theory of conspiracy according to which Syria defected as a result of a sinister plot of the imperialist and reactionary forces bent upon the destruction of his Arab socialism. Consequently, the revolution in Yemen provided an opportunity to reestablish his standing as a Pan-Arab leader. Finally, from the strategic point of view, Nasser perceived an advantage in establishing a military foothold in the Arabian Peninsula, which would permit him both to threaten the Saudi monarchy and to exert influence on the developments in the Aden Crown Colony and Protectorate. This latter consideration became especially important since 1966, when the British government announced its intention of withdrawing from and granting independence to the Colony and the Protectorate as of 1968.[8]

Because of his lack of accurate knowledge about the relative strength of the various social forces in Yemen, Nasser initially sent a military contingent of a modest size, hoping that the republican side thus strengthened would deal a quick blow to the royalists and entrench itself in power. Before long he found out that his early expectation was too optimistic and that his troops needed further reinforcements. In due time more and more Egyptian troops, backed by the air force, began to arrive. The expression that they "assisted" the Yemeni republican troops should be considered a misstatement: actually, the Egyptians, throughout the entire length of the civil war, did most of the fighting. Unaccustomed to the mountainous topography of Yemen and to its harsh climate, the Egyptians suffered considerable losses. The overall Egyptian military effort was directed by Abdul Hakim Amer from Cairo. Because the Egyptian troops took the lion's share of fighting, politically the Egyptian influence became paramount in republican Yemen. The republican president, Sallal, became utterly dependent on Cairo and was obliged to consult with the Egyptians on matters both military and political.

Because of the intervention, albeit of a different nature, of both Egypt and Saudi Arabia in the Yemen civil war, that war soon assumed political proportions extending beyond Yemen's borders. It was treated by the conservative Arab camp and by their radical adversaries in the Arab world at large as a test of their respective influence and perhaps even of their ability to survive. The civil war thus became a sort of Arab "Spain" reminiscent of the struggle between the conservative and the leftist forces in the Iberian Peninsula in the 1930s.

[8]For an excellent treatment of Egypt's motivations during the intervention, see Dawisha, *op. cit.*

Alternating Warfare and Peace Negotiations

The actual and potential impact of the Yemen civil war on the regional and perhaps even global balance of forces and prospects of world peace was duly noticed abroad. The Soviet Union and the United States, the United Nations, and the Arab League expressed an active interest in the evolution of the conflict. The Soviets were clearly interested in a republican victory which would strengthen their position in the area by establishing, Moscow hoped, another client state. For this reason Russia was not interested, at least initially, in a compromise settlement of the civil war but in a decisive defeat of the royalist forces. It is interesting to note in this connection that, through its direct dealings with the Sallal regime, the Soviet Union was in a way bypassing Egypt politically. There were reasons to believe that the Egyptians were not unreservedly happy with this direct extension of Soviet influence into Yemen but, under the circumstances, they could do little about it.

The United States had an altogether different view of the situation. To President Kennedy's administration, the Yemen revolution and civil war with the attendant Saudi and Egyptian intervention constituted a complicating and embarrassing development. Because of the close identification of the preceding Eisenhower administration with the conservative governments and groups in the Middle East, President Kennedy, upon assuming his presidency, launched a policy of rebuilding the bridges with the "progressive" forces in the Arab world in the belief that these forces were destined in the long run to emerge victorious. For this reason the president embarked upon a policy of cultivating the good will of Egypt. This policy, however, could not be conducted without regard to the repercussions on the relations between the United States and Saudi Arabia. If Egypt were to threaten the Saudi sovereignty and territorial integrity, the United States could not remain indifferent and, having to choose between the two values, would have to insist on the safeguarding of the Saudi vital interests with which the interests of America were closely interwoven.[9] This being the case, the best policy was to exert efforts to bring about an early conclusion of the civil war and thus to prevent its dangerous extension on a regional scale. Accordingly, during the third week of November President Kennedy addressed a message to the Saudi and Egyptian governments in which he proposed an immediate end to their intervention, to be followed by mediation between the two parties in the Yemen civil war. His appeal was in vain: Egypt was in no mood to stop its military support for the republicans, while Saudi Arabia distrusted Egypt so profoundly that she felt most reluctant to stop her aid to the royalists even if a formal acceptance were forthcoming from Cairo. In the meantime, pressures—mostly emanating from more radical Arab quarters—were exerted on Washington to grant an early recognition to the Yemen regime and thus to prove the sincerity of its professed policy of favoring the "progressive" forces in the Arab world. After more than two months of hesitation, following a report from the American embassy in Yemen that the Sallal government held effective control over

[9] American attitudes toward the civil war are analyzed by John S. Badeau in *The American Approach to the Arab World*, esp. ch. 7, "Yemen: A Case Study" (New York, 1968).

most of the territory in Yemen, the Kennedy administration extended diplomatic recognition to the republican government in December 1962. This step was certainly welcomed in Cairo but viewed with considerable uneasiness in Riyadh. The act of recognition was followed by an intensive diplomatic activity to mediate in the conflict so that the original Kennedy message of November would be implemented. A special envoy, Ambassador Ellsworth Bunker, was dispatched to Yemen as a first step toward achievement of a settlement. One of the important points on his agenda was to persuade all parties to the dispute to accept a United Nations observer mission to be stationed in the border areas between Yemen and Saudi Arabia.

On its own part, the United Nations sent Dr. Ralph Bunche, a man known for his effort in mediating the Arab-Israeli war of 1948, on a new peace mission to Yemen. Although ostensibly playing the role of impartial mediators, both Dr. Bunche and Ambassador Bunker limited their contacts in Yemen to visits with the Sallal government, thus avoiding any contact with the royalists. Furthermore, Bunche, upon his return to UN headquarters, made public declarations praising the character of the new republican regime. This behavior caused considerable ire in Saudi Arabia, where the newly appointed prime minister, Crown Prince Faisal, felt indignant about what he believed to be the lack of fairness of both mediators. While their endeavors did not bring the parties in Yemen and their outside protectors any closer to an agreement, at least they resulted in the establishment of a UN observer force which initially was placed under the command of a Swedish general, Carl von Horn. In the later stages of the war, the UN presence in Yemen was expressed by a special civilian envoy, Pier Spinelli.

What followed was an alternating sequence of military activities and diplomatic efforts to achieve a settlement. These developments may be divided into three phases: the first phase, September 1962 to September 1964; the second phase, September 1964 to February 1966; and the third phase, February 1966 to September 1967. The nature of these phases was largely determined by the Egyptian perception of the conflict.

During the first phase Nasser's objective was to ensure the survival of the republic in Yemen by any means whatsoever, whether war or diplomacy. For this reason Nasser engaged in a policy of dissimulation: officially he asserted that he was ready to accept and consider peace initiatives but in reality he was determined to create a military situation in Yemen in which he and his republican allies would enjoy a position of strength that, in turn, would predetermine the outcome of any peace negotiations. Nasser broke off diplomatic relations with Saudi Arabia in November 1962 (they were not restored until March 1964) and followed it up with the bombing of those Saudi borderland centers which served as bases for supplies to the Yemeni royalists. It is thus that Najran, Jaizan, Khamis Mushait, and Minya, a locality south of Abha, were subjected to frequent bombings. The bombings, in turn, led the United States to issue warnings to Cairo to respect the Saudi integrity. Moreover, in July 1963, when the danger to Saudi Arabia appeared particularly severe, the United States air force made demonstrations over some Saudi urban centers to attest to the American willingness to protect their Saudi friends.

Broadly speaking, Egypt's behavior during this first phase was aggressive, both militarily and politically. In the political sector, Egypt endeavored to divide the solidarity of the conservative Arab states. It was, therefore, with satisfaction that in July 1964, Nasser received the news that the kingdom of Jordan extended recognition to the Yemeni republican government (previously, Jordan had participated with Saudi Arabia, although on a modest scale, in the assistance program to the royalists). However, despite their ambitious military program for Yemen, in the spring of 1964 Egyptian troops suffered a serious setback during a royalist offensive which resulted in the royalists regaining control over most of the northern and eastern territory of Yemen. That summer the Egyptian command undertook a major counteroffensive which, however, failed to obtain its military objectives. It was at that time, on July 13, 1964, that Egypt and Sallal's government concluded an agreement providing for close coordination with an aim of achieving ultimate unity between the two countries.[10]

This agreement constituted a sequel to Nasser's personal visit to republican Yemen in the spring. It was later learned that Nasser returned from this visit considerably disenchanted. He realized how weak and dependent on continuous Egyptian support the republican party was. He also discovered that his republican allies were not free of internecine bickering and considerable corruption, not to speak of shockingly mismanaging their administration. With the failure of his subsequent summer offensive, Nasser began to seek a way to disengage himself from his Yemeni "Vietnam" as gracefully as possible without losing face.

The second phase opened with a meeting between Nasser and Prince Faisal of Saudi Arabia at the Arab summit conference in Alexandria in September 1964. At that meeting the two leaders promised to abstain from further intervention in the Yemeni affairs and undertook to persuade their respective Yemeni protégés to seek a mutual reconciliation. This time Nasser appeared to be quite sincere in his desire to disengage because his involvement in Yemen was very costly in terms of money, equipment, and men and politically not very productive. In fact, Nasser advised a leading figure of the Yemeni government, Ahmed Numan, to seek a compromise formula with the royalists and to accept the designation of Yemen as a "state" rather than a republic. Following the Alexandria agreement the two Yemeni parties, republican and royalist, met in Erkowit in Sudan for a conference that began in November and ended in December. To the disappointment of both Nasser and Faisal, the Yemenis were much more intransigent toward each other than their respective protectors were. This was particularly true of the republican group which was afraid that, with the prospective withdrawal of all Egyptian troops from Yemen, it would be left alone to face the formidable array of tribal-royalist forces. Their interest, therefore, dictated that the Egyptian troops should stay in Yemen as long as possible and that the continuation of war was preferable to an agreement with the royalists which could be nullified as soon as the Egyptians returned home.

A period of relative calm in military operations followed, and there were partial Egyptian withdrawals from exposed northern and eastern positions, the maintenance of which required an effort incommensurate with results. It is certain that Nasser

---

[10]Text in *Arab Political Documents 1964*, pp. 271–274.

was still seeking a reconciliation and disengagement. This policy resulted in the second agreement concluded between himself and Faisal (since the late fall of 1964, king of Saudi Arabia) on August 24, 1965, in Jidda.[11] By virtue of this agreement Egypt pledged to withdraw 50,000 of its troops in the span of thirteen months, while Saudi Arabia promised to stop aid to the royalists. At the same time the two parties agreed that a plebiscite should be held in Yemen in November 1966 to decide on the form of the government for the state. As was the case of the previous Alexandria agreement, the Jidda meeting was followed by a gathering of fifty leading royalists and republicans in the northern Yemeni city of Haradh in November 1965. And again, for the second time, Nasser and to some extent Faisal miscalculated the willingness of the two Yemeni factions to come to terms with each other. The Haradh conference, like the preceding Erkowit conference, failed to bring about an agreement. To Nasser, this was very disappointing, especially in view of the fact that in anticipation of the royalist-republican conference, he called Abdullah Sallal to Cairo and arranged for a six-man presidency council (officially under Sallal's chairmanship) to run the republican government. The real power during Sallal's absence—he was a virtual prisoner of Nasser in Cairo during the several months of his stay there—rested in the hands of General Hassan Amri, the republican prime minister. But even the removal of the militant Sallal from the scene did not bring about the hoped-for agreement between the Yemeni factions. This time, however, Nasser assigned the blame for the deadlock not so much to his republican protégés in Yemen but rather to what he believed to be a reactionary conspiracy on a regional scale to prevent a settlement, to assure the victory of the royalists, and to humiliate him and his revolution. Nasser based his opinions on a number of concrete developments, two of which appeared to him as decisive. The first was a visit that King Faisal paid to the Shah of Iran in December 1965, in the course of which the two monarchs proclaimed the principle of Islamic solidarity and called for an Islamic conference. The second event was the announcement in that same month that the United States and Britain would inaugurate a major arms support program for Saudi Arabia calling for expenditures of £125 million. Moreover, by December it also became known that Iran was supplying arms to the royalists. The phase of attempted reconciliation thus came to an end.

The third phase began with a major speech Nasser delivered on February 22, 1966, in which he strongly attacked Saudi Arabia and pledged a struggle in Yemen until victory should be obtained. He followed it up the next month with an announcement of a "long breath" strategy in Yemen whereby Egyptian troops would be concentrated in the triangle of Sana-Taiz-Hodeida and would entrench themselves there to fight a protracted war. The anticipated British withdrawal from Aden added to Nasser's determination to stay in Yemen.

Paradoxically, this time the roles became reversed: it was Nasser who was belligerent, while the more moderate elements in the Yemeni republican camp under the leadership of General Amri were trying now to devise a compromise formula with the royalists. Nasser backed up his militancy by releasing Sallal from virtual deten-

[11]Text in *Middle East Journal,* 20, no. 1 (Winter 1966), 93–94.

tion in Cairo and reinstating him as head of the Yemeni government by mid-August of 1966. In fact, Amri and his friends tried to prevent the return of Sallal and put up some resistance when his airplane landed in Yemen. The Egyptian troops intervened and helped Sallal return to power. This high-handed action provoked indignation in the republican camp and a few days later a sixty-man Yemeni republican delegation (which included a number of republican sheikhs) went to Cairo to protest Egyptian interference in Yemeni internal affairs. In response, Nasser placed twenty-four members of the delegation, including General Amri, under arrest and detained the remaining members under house surveillance in Egypt. At the same time, clearly with Nasser's encouragement, Sallal announced his acceptance of Amri's resignation as prime minister. A purge in the republican army and political establishment was carried out vigorously by Sallal. A new Egyptian military offensive was launched but, like the previous ones, it was halted by fierce royalist resistance and difficult terrain. It was evident that Nasser's policy to seek a solution in Yemen by force failed.[12]

Ultimately, the denoument of the Yemen imbroglio came about as a result of the decisive defeat that Egypt suffered at the hands of Israel in the war of June 1967. This defeat demonstrated not only the bankruptcy of Nasser's policy of revolutionary intervention in the affairs of Arab states, but also made the continuation of the Egyptian presence in Yemen a physical impossibility. Consequently, when the heads of the Arab states met at the conference in Khartoum at the end of August, 1967, Nasser and Faisal reached their third and final agreement to put an end to their respective interventions in Yemen. Nasser pledged to withdraw his forces, Faisal countered with the promise of putting an end to the Saudi assistance to the royalists, and it was agreed that the Yemenis would have to resolve their differences among themselves. Soon afterward, Egyptian troops began to withdraw.

Sallal's Downfall and Iryani's Leadership

With the Egyptian withdrawal, Sallal's hold on power became very precarious. He did not survive Egyptian absence for long. On November 5, 1967, he was overthrown by a dissident republican group which established a three-man presidency council under the chairmanship of Qadi Abdur Rahman el-Iryani, with Ahmed Numan and Sheikh Mohammed Ali Othman as members. The revolt was as much against the Egyptian domination as against Sallal himself. Qadi Iryani was a conservative, Islamic-oriented individual who tried to give Yemen a civilian, constitutional rule. This policy eventually resulted in the adoption by the Yemeni government of a new constitution on January 2, 1971, a document containing strong Islamic accents.[13] Iryani also pursued a policy of reconciliation with the royalists and with Saudi Arabia. His foreign minister, Mohsen el-Ayni, went to Jidda in March 1970 to attend an Islamic conference. He received a cordial reception from the Saudis, to whom the Iryani republican regime, conservative and Islamic-oriented,

---

[12]For a thorough treatment of the civil war, see Manfred W. Wenner, *Modern Yemen, 1918–1966* (Baltimore, 1967).
[13]Text in *Middle East Journal,* 25, no. 3 (Summer 1971), 389–401.

appeared to be quite acceptable. In turn, they persuaded the royalist party in Yemen to come to terms with the republicans and, on May 19, 1970, a reconciliation agreement was concluded between the two parties. The royalists were to be represented by a member on the presidency council and to obtain four cabinet posts and twelve seats in the projected national assembly. The institution of the Imamate was quietly allowed to lapse and the Saudis as well as their royalist friends did not insist on its retention. Imam Badr remained in exile as a pensioner in Saudi Arabia. Soon afterward, in July, Saudi Arabia recognized the newly constituted republican government and this act was followed by recognitions granted by France, Britain, and Iran. The internal civil strife in Yemen thus came to end, while on the Arab front, after Nasser's death in 1970, a new era of close collaboration between King Faisal and President Sadat was launched, thus bringing to an end one of the most dangerous divisions in the Arab world.

During the constitutional rule under Iryani's leadership (1967–1974) a new challenge to Yemen developed from a rather unexpected quarter. As a result of the relinquishment of the British colonial responsibilities in Aden and the adjoining Protectorate areas toward the end of 1967, a new sovereign entity came into being. Instead of maintaining its former name of South Arabian Federation, it chose to call itself South Yemen, a name subsequently changed to People's Democratic Republic of Yemen (PDRY). Its leadership was Marxist-oriented and full of revolutionary militancy. In 1968 this new regime asserted claims to various areas on the border with Yemen. As a result, military clashes occurred repeatedly along the borderline. Furthermore, the South Yemen regime recruited certain radical followers inside Yemeni territory and these, in turn, engaged in a sporadic guerrilla warfare and acts of terrorism. Iryani's resonse to these subversive activities and border attacks was not as strong as some Yemenis would have wished it to be. He countered criticisms by invoking the Koran and saying that he wanted to avoid bloodshed between Moslems. Furthermore, he was open to suggestions for effecting a union between the two Yemens. Such a union was favored not only by the South Yemeni regime and a good number of Shafiis in the Yemen Arab Republic (YAR), as Yemen proper was officially known, but also by Libya and Algeria, whose governments were dedicated in a varying degree of intensity to the Pan-Arab ideal. As a result, in December 1972 the so-called Tripoli agreement was concluded between Qadi Iryani and the president of PDRY, Salem Rubai Ali. The agreement provided for union between the two states, to be accomplished by stages. It promptly encountered considerable opposition from the militant Zaidi elements in Yemen, who feared that the union of the two countries would give too much power to the Shafiis. Similarly, Saudi Arabia was clearly unhappy with this outcome and became critical of Iryani, a man whom the Saudis initially favored. Aware of these criticisms, Iryani went on a long vacation to a resort in Syria where, in 1973, he offered to resign but was persuaded by a delegation from his country to stay in power.[14]

---

[14]For a comprehensive analysis of the republican regime, see Robert W. Stookey, "Social Structure and Politics in the Yemen Arab Republic," Part I, *Middle East Journal,* 28, no. 3 (Summer 1974) and Part II, 28, no. 4 (Autumn 1974).

The New Military Regime

In the meantime, however, criticism of Iryani's rule became more widespread in Yemen. He was opposed not only for what his criticis believed to be an appeasing policy toward South Yemen but also for his seeming indecisiveness in reconciling the pressures emanating from Islamic-oriented Zaidi tribes with the attitudes of the Shafiis and the more progressive elements in the middle ranks of his government. Furthermore, he had to weather a plot against his regime inspired in the early 1970s by the Iraqi wing of the Baath party. While he succeeded in thwarting the plot, he took very mild measures against the conspirators, simply dismissing them from sensitive jobs and avoiding more severe penalties. This leniency was inacceptable to the Zaidi tribal chiefs who, moreover, wanted to put a stronger emphasis on Islam as the foundation of government.

This mounting opposition culminated on June 13, 1974, when a group of army officers headed by Colonel Ibrahim el-Hamdi demanded and obtained Iryani's res- ignation and promptly afterward established a new revolutionary government. There was some paradox in this situation that the army officers who took over power intended to deemphasize the religious trend in the government. It was indicative of their attitudes that they selected as their prime minister Mohsen el-Ayni, a man known for his rather anti-traditionalist views and pro-Baathist proclivities. Fur- thermore, in a seeming departure from previous patterns, the officers, whose formal organization was the Revolutionary Command Council, established a cabinet com- posed largely of civilians. This cabinet of twenty-two ministers was divided equally between the Zaidis and the Shafiis. Some ministers, such as Dr. Hassan Makki, deputy prime minister in charge of economic affairs, had held positions in the previous cabinet.

Thus, in spite of the change of government, the basic pattern of Yemeni domestic politics was maintained: a triangular relationship between the dominant Zaidi ele- ments, the army, and a third, more urban-oriented group in which the Shafii per- sonalities necessarily played an important role.

Although Hamdi was initially acceptable to the northern Zaidi leadership, with the passage of time the two became estranged. Hamdi incurred the displeasure of the Zaidis for a number of reasons. One of these was that he dissolved the tribal- dominated people's assembly, thus frustrating the Zaidi ambitions to enjoy supre- macy in Yemen's politics. Sheikh Abdullah el-Ahmar of the northern Hashed tribal confederation emerged as his strong critic. Hamdi's enemies discovered also that he was a member of a secret Nasserite movement in Yemen. The most serious, how- ever, was his tendency to cooperate with socialist South Yemen and a revelation that he was about to visit Aden to sign a mutual defense pact and an agreement for gradual unification of the two countries.

On October 10, 1977, on the very eve of his departure, he was assassinated, presumably by someone identified with forces opposed to his policies. His death brought Yemen back to the pattern of division and intermittent conflicts between the Zaidi north and the Shafii south, one conservative and pro-Saudi, the other leaning

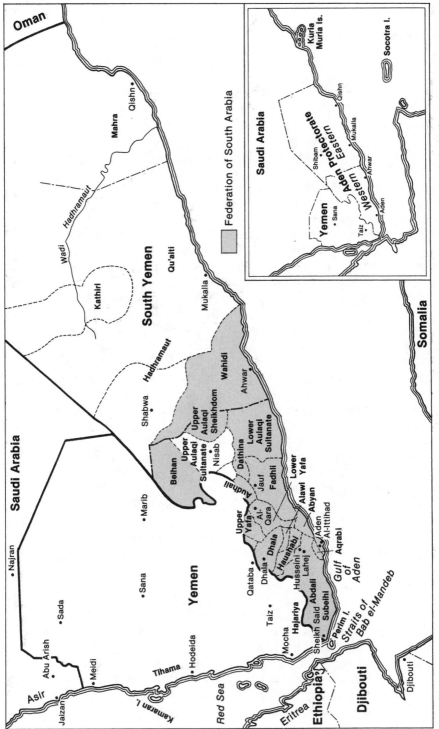

Map 8. Yemen and South Yemen, showing tribal-political divisions in South Yemen before independence.

toward closer links with Aden. This division had been at the root of the civil war of the 1960s and was marked by a subsequent series of assassinations of those leaders who—in the eyes of their adversaries—deviated too much from the even-handed position. Prominent personalities killed for pro-Saudi or pro-Aden orientation included Ahmed Numan in 1974 and Abdullah Hajri in 1977, among others.

Hamdi was replaced by Colonel Ahmed Ghashmi. One of his first acts was to call into being a largely hand-picked people's assembly which comprised primarily tribal Zaidi members and business leaders favoring closer links with Saudi Arabia and an opening to the West. Ghashmi's cabinet, headed by Abdul Aziz Abdul Ghani as prime minister, included as ministers two influential Adeni exiles, Abdullah Asnaj and Mohammed Basendwa, who had served in Hamdi's government. As refugees from Aden they opposed union with South Yemen, an attitude shared by other native Yemeni cabinet members.

The new government failed to heal the rift between the Shafii and Zaidi parts of Yemen. It experienced a notable defection when Colonel Abdullah Abdul Alem raised, in the winter of 1977–1978, a revolt in the Taiz-Turba region in the south.

With his definitely pro-Saudi orientation, President Ghashmi developed contacts with President Salem Rubai Ali of South Yemen, seemingly in an attempt to draw him away from excessive reliance on Soviet and Cuban support which was favored by the more extreme Marxist leaders in South Yemen. This policy of detaching Aden from the Soviet orbit suffered a dramatic setback when, on June 24, 1978, Ghashmi was assassinated under sensational and mysterious circumstances. He lost his life when a bomb carried in a briefcase by Rubai Ali's special emissary exploded in his office, killing the emissary as well.

Ghashmi's interim successor, Qadi Abdul Karim el-Arshi, promptly charged the Aden regime with engineering the murder. Inasmuch, however, as South Yemen's President Rubai Ali was executed by his more extreme Marxist associates two days after Ghashmi's death, the new government in Sana directed its attacks against the victors in the South Yemeni struggle for power, Abdul Fattah Ismail and Ali Nasser Mohammed. The two of them—strongly pro-Soviet—were accused of killing both presidents to prevent a reorientation of South Yemen's policies. (This critical line toward Aden was upheld when, a month later, the chief of staff, Ali Abdullah Saleh, was elected president of the people's assembly.) Saudi Arabia fully endorsed this indictment and sponsored a collective move by the Arab League to censure the South Yemeni regime.

While thus the politics of Yemen appeared to have relapsed into a pattern of instability, they became increasingly interwoven with the broader regional issues and rivalries. Foremost among these was the struggle for political influence in the Arabian Peninsula waged between Saudi Arabia and the Marxist government of South Yemen. Behind this regional struggle, however—with its extension in the Horn of Africa—loomed the rivalry on a global scale between the United States and the Soviet Union, of which the situation in the two Yemens was but a local manifestation.

CHAPTER XV

South Yemen

South Yemen, a large and arid country situated in the southwestern part of the Arabian Peninsula, was established as an independent state toward the end of 1967. It was known for a long time as Aden Crown Colony and Aden Protectorate while under British rule. In the more remote past the area in question had constituted a part of the larger Yemen and had been subjected to the rule of the Yemeni Imams at Sana. The Ottoman Turks had conquered this area, including Yemen proper in the north, in the sixteenth century. Because both Yemen and South Yemen abound in inaccessible mountains and deserts, Turkish rule never succeeded in entrenching itself in the entire territory but had to content itself with control of certain localities such as Aden which were strategicially or commercially important.

Under the leadership of Qasim the Great the Yemenis drove out the Turks in the seventeenth century and for about two hundred years (1628–1849) the Zaidi Imams of Yemen ruled not only over their own highlands but also over the lowlands stretching to the Indian Ocean. This rule, however, was also incomplete inasmuch as many local chieftains and tribes asserted their own independence or autonomy while certain governors appointed from Sana, for example a governor of Lahej, broke away from the central government and established independent fiefdoms of their own. Moreover, a vast area straddling the valley of Hadhramaut in the south central stretches of the Arabian Peninsula was so remote from Sana as to avoid subjection to its rule.

In antiquity South Yemen was primarily a transit area though which the incense routes passed, first westward and then northward along the Red Sea coast toward the major population centers in the Fertile Crescent. Certain parts of present-day South Yemen were within the confines of the ancient Minaean, Sabaean, and Himyaritic kingdoms. A number of Jews settled there after the fall of Jerusalem in A.D. 70 and, beginning with the mid-fourth century, Christianity found its way to these areas as well. Although the main Christian center in the broader area of southwest Arabia was in Najran, a church had been built in Aden by the monk Theophilus Indus. Subsequently, in the sixth century, the Ethiopians extended their rule to this area, which gave place to a short-lived Persian domination. In the seventh century Islam penetrated the area and the caliphs included it in their dominions.

British Penetration

The southern periphery of the Arabian Peninsula came to British attention toward the end of the eighteenth century when Britain, already heavily engaged as an imperial power in India, was looking for convenient transit stations which could serve as entrepôts for merchandise and provide bunkering for ships. The first move was to capture the rocky little island of Perim in the Strait of Bab el-Mandeb in 1799. The British held this strategic spot for a short time but later, in 1857, they formally acquired it by an agreement with the Sultan of Lahej. Next came the occupation of the island of Socotra in 1934. A major imperial advance was made in 1839 when, after bombardment by the British navy (due to a dispute over the ill treatment by the local ruler of the passengers from a wrecked British vessel), the British captured the port and city of Aden, which possessed a good natural harbor and was strategically located close to the entrance to the Red Sea. At that time the Ottoman Turks had made major endeavors to restore their military rule over the expanses of the Arabian Peninsula. By the mid-nineteenth century the Turks reasserted their presence in Yemen. Their southernmost outposts and the British troops operating from Aden thus began to face each other along an ill-defined line which stretched from the southwestern corner of the Arabian Peninsula eastward and northeastward toward the sandy expanse of the Rub al-Khali desert. To the Arab nationalists who interpreted these events in the mid-twentieth century, all of this appeared as a deliberate collusion of two imperialistic powers, the Ottoman and the British, with the objective of a permanent division of greater Yemen into two separate parts.[1]

Initially, Aden was administered from the Bombay Residency by a political agent whose title was later changed to Resident. After 1932 it was subjected to the direct rule of the British Government of India represented by the Chief Commissioner. Finally, in 1935, Aden was proclaimed a Crown Colony under a governor within the jurisdiction of the Department for the Colonies in London. The following year, in 1936, Aden was granted a constitution which provided for a legislative and an executive council.

After the opening of the Suez Canal in 1869, Aden gained greatly in importance as one of the major strongholds and commercial transit points along the British imperial lifeline. From a small township of barely five hundred inhabitants at the time it was conquered, it grew into a sizable city which, in addition to its major function as a coaling station, served as an important export and import harbor for its hinterland and for Yemen as well, competing with such Yemeni ports as Mocha and Hodeida. It also attracted many immigrants from Yemen, India, Somalia, Ethiopia, and other countries. In fact, by the mid-twentieth century the immigrant Yemenis became the single largest group in the city, outnumbering the native Adenis.

Covering a mere seventy-five square miles of territory, Aden developed banking, commerce, and minor industry. After nationalization of the Anglo-Iranian Oil Company with its huge refinery in Abadan, the company headquarters in London

---

[1] Such a nationalist interpretation may be found in *British Imperialism in Southern Arabia,* Information Papers no. 6 (New York: Arab Information Center, November 1958).

decided to compensate at least partly their losses in Iran by constructing in 1954 a major refinery in Aden. This was in keeping with the character of Aden which was transformed from a coaling station into a major oil-bunkering port. Another interesting development was the growth of organized labor movement. Although British rule was imperial, which means that it denied the local population the principle of full self-determination, nevertheless Britain introduced a degree of self-government through the earlier mentioned councils and allowed freedom of labor associations. By the 1950s, the Aden Trade Unions Congress (ATUC) was formed under the leadership of Abdullah el-Asnaj. It soon emerged as one of the most powerful and vocal labor organizations anywhere in the Arab world.

The Aden Protectorate

While Aden was thus transforming itself into a busy urban and maritime center which profited from its excellent location along the route linking London with its Asian and East African possessions, the sparsely populated hinterland remained in a state of backwardness and isolation. Because of its poor accessibility and lack of ascertainable mineral or agricultural resources, the British were not interested in assuming the responsibility of a direct rule over it. They tended to treat it merely as a buffer zone which would protect the Crown Colony at Aden and which would assure safe travel and communications with Yemen proper. In the 1840s, therefore, the British began a slow process of penetration aiming at the establishment of the rudiments of political control over the numerous chieftains in the area while leaving them free to govern themselves according to their laws and customs. In choosing this system, the British were following the pattern set by themselves in certain parts of India and Malaya where imperial control was exercised indirectly through the local rulers.

To formalize these relations with the local chieftains, the British concluded between 1886 and 1914 a number of protectorate treaties. These treaties followed a common pattern which contained the following main provisions: (a) Britain extended her "favour and protection" to the rulers and their tribes; (b) the ruler or chief undertook not to enter into any relations with other foreign powers; (c) the chief pledged that he would "not cede, sell, mortgage, lease, hire or give, or otherwise dispose of his territory under his jurisdiction" to any power other than the British government; (d) Britain in turn promised to pay the ruler and his successors a specified amount of Maria Theresa thalers in periodic installments.[2]

For a long time this type of agreement was deemed sufficient from the British imperial point of view. Although certain warlike tribes of the interior occasionally resorted to raids which compelled the British to intervene militarily to ensure the safety of roads and communications, by and large the last decades of the nineteenth century and the period before World War I were devoid of dramatic events. This

---

[2]For the text of a typical friendship treaty, see Charles U. Aitchison, ed., *A Collection of Treaties, Engagements, and Sanads Relating to India and Neighbouring Countries*, Vol. XI (Delhi: Foreign Office, 1933), pp. 53–179.

calm was partly due to the mutual desire of Great Britain and the Ottoman Empire to avoid unnecessary confrontations in that area. Consequently, such tribal unrest as occasionally occurred did not benefit from support of the Turkish authorities and, therefore, could be quelled by the British with relative ease. Furthermore, between 1903 and 1905 a joint British-Turkish commission drew a frontier between Yemen and the Aden hinterland. This frontier was formally confirmed in the Anglo-Turkish Convention of March 9, 1914.[3] In a Treaty of Duan of 1911 between the Ottoman Porte and Imam Yehya of Yemen, the Imam was designated as a vassal of the Ottoman Caliph and confirmed as spiritual and temporal head of the Zaidis with the right to appoint Zaidi governors and heads of courts. This emphasis on the Zaidi jurisdiction of the Imam implicitly excluded him from the rule over the Shafii-populated south under British control.

The outbreak of World War I changed the relations between the Ottomans and the British. The Turks from their base in Yemen advanced into the Aden hinterland, secured cooperation of some tribes, captured Lahej and came close to the borders of Aden. When the war ended and the Turks withdrew, the British had to begin a slow process of reasserting their authority in the hinterland area. In the meantime, Turkish defeat brought about emancipation of the Imam of Yemen who in 1919 invaded the borderland territory of Dhala and parts of the Audhali tribal country, both of which were in a treaty relationship with Britain. It was not until 1928 that the British succeeded in expelling the Yemeni forces from those districts.

The Frontier Issue: Attempts at Settlement

The 1920s and early 1930s were the years of an assertive and "forward" policy on the part of the Imam of Yemen. Claiming a historical right to rule the entire area of Yemen and South Yemen, the Imam tirelessly sponsored incursions into the British-controlled territories and encouraged tribal rebellions there (this militant policy also found its reflection in the claims that Yemen put to the border principality of Asir between itself and Saudi Arabia, a dispute that led to a brief war in the spring of 1934). To put an end to intermittent warfare and uncertainty, the British and the Yemenis concluded the Treaty of Sana on February 11, 1934. Yemen was formally recognized as an independent and sovereign state—an important advantage from the Yemeni point of view inasmuch as its formal status since the evacuation of Ottoman troops had not been clarified. As for the boundary between Yemen and the British protected areas, the treaty said that "the High Contracting Parties agree to maintain the situation existing in regard to the frontier on the date of signature of this treaty."[4] The treaty was to be valid for forty years and, in case of differences over the meaning of the text, the Arabic version was to prevail.

Before long a difference of interpretation of the text arose between the two parties. When referring to the "frontier," the British meant the existing boundary line, first established in the Anglo-Turkish Convention of 1914, and in 1934 still

---

[3]Text in Aitchison, *op. cit.*, pp. 42–43; also in G. P. Gooch and Harold Temperley, eds., *British Documents on the Origins of the War, 1898–1914*, Vol. X, Part 2 (London, 1938), pp. 340–341.
[4]Text in J. C. Hurewitz, *Diplomacy in the Near and Middle East* (Princeton, 1956), II, 196–197.

constituting the de facto border between the two countries. The Imam of Yemen, however, pointed to the Arabic text which spoke of the frontiers in plural (*hudud*), an expression which in Arabic connotes not so much a definite borderline as the idea of "border marches" somewhat reminiscent of the American notion of the "moving frontier" in the West. To him, therefore, the maintenance of the *hudud* meant the preservation of the semi-independent status of various chiefs and tribes in the British-controlled area to which he never renounced his claim.

Furthermore, within the broader area south of the British-Turkish demarcation line there were certain tribal territories which had never entered into a protection agreement with the British (for example, Radfan and the area around Shabwa, a township located to the east of the easternmost point of the line demarcated in the Anglo-Turkish Convention, hence in a territory to which both parties could lay equally valid or equally unsubstantiated claims).

Advisory Treaties and the Aden Protectorate

By the mid-1930's it was clear to the British that not only was the boundary problem not resolved by the Treaty of Sana but that, to counteract the Imam of Yemen's political activities among various chiefs of the protected tribal entities, they would have to adopt a stronger policy of political penetration and control. This policy took two forms in its implementation. First of all, by the Order-in-Council of March 18, 1937, the British government formally proclaimed a Protectorate over the whole hinterland area. In turn, it was to be divided into the Western Protectorate composed of eighteen units (sultanates, sheikhdoms, and other tribal entities) and the Eastern Protectorate composed of five major units and two smaller ones.[5]

The following is the list of the tribal units within the Western Protectorate: The title of the ruler is given in parentheses after the name of the state.

Southwestern	*Northwestern*	*Central*	*Eastern*
(west of Wadi Tiban)	(between Wadi Tiban and Wadi Bana)	(east of Wadi Bana)	(west of boundary of Eastern Protectorate)
Abdali of Lahej (Sultan)	Amiri of Dhala (Amir)	Shaibi (Sheikh)	Beihan (Sharif)
Aqrabi (Sheikh)	Radfan (Sheikh)	Upper Yafai (Sultan)	Audhali (Sultan)
	Alawi (Sheikh)	Lower Yafai (Sultan)	Upper Aulaqi (Sultan)
	Haushabi (Sultan)	Fadhli (Sultan)	Upper Aulaqi (Sheikh)
	Maflahi (Sheikh)		Lower Aulaqi (Sultan)
			Dathina Confederation (Sheikhs)

[5]For a description of British rule, see Herbert J. Liebesny, "Administration and Legal Development in Arabia: Aden Colony and Protectorate," *Middle East Journal,* 9, no. 4 (Autumn 1955).

The territory of the Eastern Protectorate (bordering on Oman and Saudi Arabia) was not contiguous with Yemen. Its real center was the Wadi Hadhramaut. It had an area about three times larger than that of the Western Protectorate and, despite its distance from the urban center of Aden, it was somewhat more advanced socially and economically. Its component units are listed below.

Western	*Central*	*Eastern*
Wahidi of Bir Ali (Sultan)	Kathiri of Saiun (Sultan)	Mahri of Qishn and Socotra (Sultan)
Wahidi of Balhaf (Sultan)	Quaiti of Shihr and Mukalla (Sultan)	
Haura (Sheikh)		
Irqa (Sheikh)		

Of these, the Kathiri Sultanate, astride the more fertile Wadi Hadhramaut, had many connections with Malaya and Singapore because many Kathiris had emigrated there and were sending remittances back home. Some of them, having made their fortunes in the Far East, have reemigrated. The Malay language was frequently used in court circles.[6]

In a parallel move, the British government began negotiating with various states of the Protectorate the so-called advisory treaties. Such treaties were concluded with many but not all states in the Protectorates between 1937 and 1952. Like the initial protection treaties, the advisory treaties also followed a common pattern. They provided for (a) a mutual reaffirmation of existing treaties; (b) a reaffirmation that the chiefs would not establish relations with any other foreign powers; and (c) a reaffirmation of the territorial nonalienation clause, with the addition that the chiefs pledged not only to desist from selling or ceding their territory to any other power but also "to a subject of any state" and that this clause would have to be carried out "in accordance with a land policy to be drawn up after consultation with the Governor of Aden;" and (d) the chiefs' agreement to accept the advice of the Governor of Aden but with the right to "address" the British Secretary for Colonial Affairs.[7] This last clause concerning advice differentiated this series of treaties from the earlier ones. Furthermore, the reference to subjects of other states in point (c) above could be interpreted as extending to the granting of concessions, particularly for oil exploration, to privately owned firms or individuals. If a British firm was not interested or available, it was conceivable that a firm of another nationality might be admitted but, clearly, only after the approval of the Governor of Aden.

The first of such advisory treaties was concluded with the Quaiti Sultan of Shihr and Mukalla (the largest state in the entire Protectorate), to be followed by other Eastern Protectorate chiefs. After 1944 similar advisory treaties were signed with Western Protectorate chiefs, beginning with the Sharif of Beihan.

---

[6]For more detail, see R. H. Smith, "Notes on the Kathiri State of Hadramaut," *Middle East Journal*, 7, no. 4 (Autumn 1953). On p. 502 there is a list—since increased—of the states of the Aden Protectorate.

[7]For typical texts, see *British Imperialism in Southern Arabia, op. cit.* For the scope and contents of some of these treaties, see Harold Ingrams, *Arabia and the Isles* (London, 1942), pp. 316–317; 338–340; 347–349.

This assertive policy of advisory treaties and the resulting intensification of British interference in the affairs of the protectorate states caused resentments and protests in Yemen. To avoid further deterioration in mutual relations, Britain and Yemen concluded on January 20, 1951, an agreement in which they pledged to form a joint commission to demarcate the borders according to the 1934 Treaty of Sana. Both parties further agreed not to alter the status quo in disputed areas. Again the British tended to interpret this as the preservation of the existing borderline, while the Imam of Yemen viewed the pledge as referring to the preservation of the independence or autonomy of various chiefs and restraining of the British from further curtailment of their rights. The forcible removal by the British of the recalcitrant Sultan of Lahej in 1952 and the subsequent installation of a relative of his who was more palatable to the British provided further fuel for the Imam's anger. (It was the newly installed sultan who agreed to sign the advisory treaty with the British.)

The South Arabian Federation

The continuous difficulties which the British experienced with neighboring Yemen in the Aden Protectorate called for a rethinking of the British political strategy in the area. According to certain British officials the loose control that Britain exercised over individual chiefs appeared insufficient and incompatible with the aim of preserving a strong buffer zone between Aden and the outside powers. With the nationalization of oil in Iran, Aden, as has been pointed out, gained in importance. Moreover, under the impact of militant Arab nationalism preached from Cairo the British were reducing their influence in Egypt—an influence that eventually came to an end with the Suez War of 1956. These officials favored the regrouping of British strength by concentrating it in southwestern Arabia and possibly the Horn of Africa. To succeed in such a scheme, it was necessary to establish a more reliable control over the Protectorate states and, paradoxical as it may sound, instead of using the method of "divide and rule" these officials proposed to unite the eighteen states of the Western Protectorate into a federation which, through union, would acquire greater strength to balance the power of Yemen. At the same time, through the proposed central organs of the federation—the cabinet, a legislative body, and a federal army—Britain would be in a position to exert a more effective influence in the region. Parallel with this went the idea that the federation would represent the almost exclusively Shafii religious orientation to counter the Zaidi Yemeni claims to supremacy.

The federative plan had been first proposed in 1954 and, as could be expected, it met with strong condemnation from Yemen. Local response in the Protectorate was hesitant but after much persuasion the British succeeded, on February 11, 1959, in establishing what was then called the Federation of Arab Emirates of the South, and concluded on that same day a treaty with the new political entity.[8] In the beginning only six states of the Western Protectorate joined. The British undertook to finance

---

[8]Text in British Parliament, *Accounts and Papers 1958/59*, vol. XXXII, cmd. 665 (London: Her Majesty's Stationery Office, 1959), pp. 701-703.

the federal army and assist materially in other sectors. The limitation of the federation to the Western Protectorate was partly dictated by the fact that it was the Western Protectorate which was mainly exposed to Yemeni propaganda and incursion and partly by the reluctance of the big states in the Eastern Protectorate to join. These states, such as Kathiri, Quaiti, and Mahri, hoped that oil would be discovered in their territories and, should this happen, were unwilling to share their expected wealth with the numerous less fortunate states in the Western Protectorate. When the Pan American Oil Company (a subsidiary of Standard of Indiana) obtained in November 1961 an oil concession from the Quaiti and Kathiri sultanates, their determination to stay away from the federation was reinforced.

Succumbing to British persuasion (and promises of more financial assistance), more states began to join the federation, the name of which was changed in 1962 to Federation of South Arabia. On January 18, 1963, membership of the federation was increased by the admission of Aden which, however, still remained a British colony under the governor.

Although the creation of the federation was conceived by the British as a defensive move against Yemen, calculated to link the "feudal" tribal chiefs of the Protectorate to the British crown, it actually provoked an even more militant policy on the part of Yemen. This time Yemen was not alone: it was assisted by strong propaganda emanating from Cairo (where many Adeni nationalists were being indoctrinated and trained). Yemen's continuous complaint was that by forming and expanding the federation the British were petrifying the division of traditional Yemen (that is, Greater Yemen), artificially fanning religious differences, violating the status quo provisions of the treaties of 1934 and 1951, and entrenching British rule in the age when imperialism was supposed to retreat. There is no doubt that, in spite of its high-sounding name, the federation was no more than an instrument of British imperial policy. The successive British governors of Aden Crown Colony served at the same time as supervisory heads of the federation. While the idea of the federation had originated under the governorship of Sir Tom Hickinbotham (1951–1956), it was being implemented by his successors, Sir William Luce (1956–1960), Sir Charles Johnston (1960–1963), Sir Kennedy Trevaskis (1963–1964), and Sir Richard Turnbull (1964–1967). After 1962 the title of Governor was changed to that of High Commissioner.

The South Arabian Independence Movement

The 1950s, partly under the impact of the Egyptian revolution, witnessed the upsurge of nationalism in the Arab world and Aden was no exception. Among various patriotic groups formed at that time, the South Arabian League, initially established in Lahej, stood out as an organization demanding independence from Britain and advocating union of Aden and the Protectorates. It was headed by Mohammed Ali Jifri and its implicit aim was to have a federated South Arabian state under the supremacy of the ruler of Lahej.

It was, however, the establishment of the British-sponsored federation in the Protectorate that gave a major spur to the intensification and radicalization of South Arabian nationalism. In addition, strong British intervention in the internal affairs of

Lahej in 1958 acted as a stimulant to this movement. In 1962 the People's Socialist Party (PSP) was formed under the presidency of Abdullah Asnaj. It could be regarded as an emanation and political arm of the Aden Trade Unions Congress, of which Asnaj had long been leader. The new party, in contrast to the SAL, asked not only for independence but also for unity with Yemen. The following year another nationalist hailing from Lahej, Qahtan el-Shaabi, self-exiled in Cairo in protest to the British-sponsored federation, organized in Sana the National Liberation Front (NLF) and soon expanded its activities into Aden. The NLF espoused not only the program of independence and unity with Yemen already advocated by PSP but insisted on a thorough social revolution to eliminate the rule of tribal chiefs and Adeni capitalists.

The outbreak of the civil war in Yemen in September 1962 and the subsequent appearance of Egyptian troops in that country acted as another powerful stimulant to the nationalist movement in Aden and the Protectorate. The new head of the republican regime in Yemen, Colonel Sallal, openly called in March 1963 for a revolution in Southern Arabia. Although having to cope with the royalist-tribal counter-rebellion in Yemen, both the Egyptians and their Republican Yemeni allies were steadily diverting a certain amount of arms to help their revolutionary friends in Aden and the Protectorate area.[9]

In October 1963, barely six months after Sallal's call for a revolution, an armed rebellion led by the NLF broke out against the British rule in the mountainous sheikhdom of Radfan, situated close to the Yemen border. From then on Southern Arabia became the scene of increasing intermittent violence expressed by tribal rebellions and terrorism directed against British troops, civilians, and those Arabs accused of collaboration with the British.

In thus intensifying their liberation struggle, the NLF and other pro-independence groups found considerable encouragement in the victory of the Labour party at the polls in Great Britain in 1964. The Labour leadership believed that it had no business supporting "feudal sultans" in Southern Arabia and elsewhere and favored curtailing British military and economic commitments east of Suez. (Britain was contributing 86 percent of the budget of the South Arabian Federation and assumed entire financial responsibility for the maintenance of the federal army.) Similarly, resolutions passed in 1963 and 1965 in the United Nations pronounced themselves in favor of an early independence for Southern Arabia. The British movement for disengagement found its culmination on February 22, 1966, with the publication of a White Paper which pledged independence to the South Arabian Federation by December 31, 1968.

The problem therefore was not when but rather how independence would be achieved and who would control the newly independent state. This concern with the ultimate assumption of power produced a number of mergers and divisions in the South Arabian nationalist movement. In 1965 the People's Socialist party joined

[9]For an account of this transitional period, see Roy E. Thoman, "Aden and South Arabia," *Current History* (Jan. 1970). For a more detailed treatment, see Tom Little, *South Arabia: Arena of Conflict* (New York, 1968).

with the committee for the Liberation of South Yemen and the South Arabian League (SAL) to form the Organization for the Liberation of Occupied South (OLOS). In the next move, in January 1966, OLOS joined with NLF to form the Federation for the Liberation of Occupied South Yemen (FLOSY) with headquarters in Taiz in neighboring Yemen, from which military and subversive action was directed in Aden and the Protectorate. This coalition, however, was too broad to satisfy the ideological preferences of some of its component parts. As a result, soon afterward the NLF and the SAL seceded from FLOSY. By 1966 three major nationalist organizations remained on the scene: FLOSY, NLF, and SAL. Of these, FLOSY was strongly allied with Egypt, while NLF was pursuing a more independent line. Both were radical, in contrast to SAL, which was bourgeois-inclined and which in time began to be regarded as an instrument of Saudi Arabian policy.

In 1966–1967 the situation in Aden and the Protectorate underwent a steady disintegration. Although committed to ultimate relinquishment of imperial rule, Britain still tried to salvage certain values in the area, hoping that a moderate nationalist government not actively hostile to Britain would take over in an orderly way. British advances and proposals to establish a provisional administration which would comprise the SAL, FLOSY and NLF elements were rejected by the latter two organizations. In June 1967 a mutiny broke out in the South Arabian Federal Army, which added to the chaos and uncertainty. A United Nations mission headed by a Venezuelan diplomat, Manuel Perez-Guerrero, paid a brief visit to Aden but accomplished nothing.

Throughout this tumultuous period the official cabinet of the South Arabian Federation proved ineffective and its administration collapsed by September 1967. It was at that time that NLF emerged as the best organized and strongest revolutionary force. Between August and October 1967 its armed detachments overthrew the rule of all the local chiefs in the Protectorate (including the seemingly well-entrenched sultans and sheikhs in the remote Eastern Protectorate) and, in most cases, compelled them to flee to Yemen and Saudi Arabia. Simultaneously, NLF staged a showdown with FLOSY. In this struggle the South Arabian Federal Army, whose loyalties tended to follow the strongest party, chose to support NLF and help the latter in routing FLOSY troops whose leaders, like the tribal chiefs, were compelled to flee for their lives abroad.

On November 27, NLF proclaimed an independent People's Republic of South Yemen and the following day NLF leader Qahtan el-Shaabi concluded in Geneva an agreement with a British delegation whereby Britain formally renounced her rule in Aden and the Protectorate. On November 29, the last British troops left Aden and the next day Qahtan el-Shaabi was proclaimed president of the newly established republic. South Yemen became thus heir to the entire Crown Colony and Protectorate area with one exception: Britain announced that the Kuria Muria islands, hitherto under the Aden administration, would be returned to the Sultanate of Muscat-Oman. However, two other island possessions, Perim in the Strait of Bab el-Mandeb and the Kamaran islands off the coast of Yemen close to the Saudi Arabian border, were retained by South Yemen.

Independent South Yemen

The new republic was born as a result of two converging processes: the struggle for independence and the social revolution. While history provides a number of examples of similar convergence, the radical transformation that the revolutionary struggle had brought about had few, if any, parallels in the past. The swiftness and thoroughness with which the NLF revolutionaries were able to remove from their traditional seats of power the ruling chiefs in the Protectorate was short of amazing. These chiefs, it should be remembered, had a deep organic relationship with their tribesmen based on natural ties of mutual need and long tradition. Nevertheless, this proved to be of no avail against the determined effort of indoctrinated, ruthless, and well-armed NLF groups which, though originally urban-based, were successful in enlisting support in remote tribal areas as well. Furthermore, the political skill of NLF was not limited to the capturing of power; it also managed to incorporate into the new system the existing military forces inherited from the old regime, the Federal Army and the Hadhrami Bedouin Legion. This move was noteworthy especially in view of the fact that most of the Federal Army soldiers and officers belonged to the Aulaqi and Audhali tribes.

What has been said about the ability of the NLF leadership to take and hold power did not necessarily apply to individual personalities in its ruling establishment. In June 1969, barely a year and a half after independence, the NLF founder and leader, Qahtan el-Shaabi, was compelled to resign from the presidency of the republic under pressure from the extreme left wing of the party. He was replaced by a presidency council initially with five members, later reduced to three, of which the chairman was a former commando officer, Salem Rubai Ali. The second most important figure of the new government was Abdul Fattah Ismail, a man of pronounced Marxist tendencies, who became minister of national guidance. This Marxist-Maoist government promptly proceeded in November 1969 to nationalize thirty-six foreign firms. It also closed the free port until then in existence in Aden for the benefit of travelers and tourists. However, the refinery owned by British Petroleum (BP, the former Anglo-Iranian Oil Company) and the cable office were allowed to continue under their old ownership and management. To stress a radical departure from the ''feudal'' past, the new regime replaced the old tribal divisions by six governorates with centrally appointed governors.

From the very beginning of its existence, South Yemen experienced considerable economic difficulties. With the departure of the British their subsidies came to an end; similarly, the country was deprived of the money spent by the British military forces and by the individual servicemen. The blocking of the Suez Canal as a result of the Arab-Israeli war of 1967 cut off the much-needed transit traffic from the port of Aden, reducing its bunkering function to a minimum and slowing down the work of its refinery. Even in normal times Aden's economy was greatly helped by the remittances of the Adenese living and working abroad, in such countries as Saudi Arabia and Ethiopia. Now, partly for political reasons, these remittances were also reduced. The country was suffering from a pronounced trade deficit: in 1970–1971 its exports amounted to £1.1 million and its imports to £14.5 million, leaving a deficit of £13.4 million. This rather desperate situation could be relieved only by massive infusions of foreign aid.

The ideological posture of the South Yemen government was definitely radical and militant. The republic and its political backbone, the NLF—later renamed the National Front—regarded themselves as a spearhead of the Arab revolution in the Peninsula as a whole. As early as December 1, 1967, Qahtan el-Shaabi defined the objectives of the new republic at a conference in the former federal capital of El-Ittihad—now renamed Madinat el-Shaab—as independence, Arab unity, socialism, nonalignment, liberation of Palestine, reunification of South Yemen with Yemen, and support for revolutionary movements. In a similar vein, the National Front at its fourth conference at Zinjibar, capital of the former Fadhli state, held in March 1968 pledged to "take up its historical responsibilities toward the Arabian Gulf and all areas of the Arabian Peninsula for the elimination of the international imperialist and reactionary forces."[10]

South Yemen's Foreign Policy

This ideological posture largely dictated the foreign policy of South Yemen. Although the regime was officially committed to nonalignment, in reality it closely aligned itself with the Communist states. Among these, Communist China and the Soviet Union became the main providers of arms and economic and technical assistance. Steadily growing involvement of South Yemen with these two countries was confirmed by an agreement of November 22, 1974, with China and a similar agreement of December 5, 1975, with the USSR. Both pledged cooperation in a number of fields, including the military. In 1972, South Yemen also inaugurated a policy of close relations with Castro's Cuba, which began sending military advisers employed not only in the training of the regular forces but also in providing support for the guerrillas who from their base in South Yemen waged a revolutionary war against the government of neighboring Oman in its westernmost Dhofar province. In connection with this export of the revolution to its eastern neighbor the regime sponsored the Popular Front for the Liberation of the Occupied Arabian Gulf (PFLOAG), whose objective was to overthrow the existing traditional and British rule in the Gulf sheikhdoms following the pattern set previously in the Aden Protectorate.

Because of its revolutionary commitment in the Peninsula as a whole, the South Yemen regime was bound to find itself on a collision course with Saudi Arabia, which was a natural target of hostility as a monarchy cooperating with the West and as a country that gave shelter to many dethroned Protectorate chiefs and dispossessed merchants from Aden. Actually, the Saudis were not passive toward South Yemen. Perceiving the Yemen regime as a threat to themselves and to the region as a whole, the Saudis were not loath to support, finance, and possibly arm as well, exiled and dissident elements from South Yemen, be they the former rulers, the FLOSY militants, the bourgeois from Aden, or even the purged individuals from the

[10]Quoted by J. Bowyer Bell in his lucid analysis "South Arabia: Violence and Revolt," *Conflict Studies,* no. 40 (November 1973).

new South Yemen regime. These dissident and exiled elements were soliciting both Saudi and Yemeni assistance and advocating joint Saudi-Yemeni intervention to overthrow the Marxist regime in Aden. Deterioration in the Saudi-South Yemeni relations inevitably resulted in border clashes between December 1969 and March 1970, which assumed considerable intensity, reflected in the use of the regular military forces and aviation by the Saudis. It was not until the spring of 1976 that Saudi relations with Aden entered a more peaceful phase of normalization. In an apparent move to outbid outside Communist influence, the Saudis extended $100 million assistance to the South Yemeni regime in a presumed belief that this gesture might dull its expansionist revolutionary policy.

In spite of its proclaimed policy to reunify the two Yemens and notwithstanding the fact that Yemen since 1962 had a republican government, the South Yemeni leadership found itself soon after its advent to power in a tense relationship with Sana. This tension was due to the fact that republican Yemen under the leadership of Qadi Abdur Rahman el-Iryani and Mohsen el-Ayni followed a moderate internal and external policy, reestablished normalcy in its relations with Saudi Arabia, and reasserted "bourgeois" Islamic values which irked the atheistic-minded leaders of the National Front in Aden. Moreover, not unlike Saudi Arabia but to a lesser extent, Yemen served as a haven to the dissident and exiled elements from South Yemen. These dispossessed leaders, while probably finding the more traditional political climate in Saudi Arabia more to their liking, often preferred to stay in Yemen, that is, closer to their own home country, in anticipation of some decisive action which might restore them to their previous positions of prominence. And it is indeed from Yemen that these exiled leaders engaged in intrigue and mounted incursions into South Yemeni territory. As a result, relations between Yemen and South Yemen deteriorated to such an extent that beginning with late September 1972 a virtual state of war prevailed between the two countries. At that time Yemen seized the Kamaran islands from South Yemen. As a by-product of this operation the Yemenis found a big depot of arms stored on the islands and supplied by the Libyan regime of Colonel Qadhafi for use by the Front of National Liberation in Eritrea which fought against the government of Ethiopia.

With Egypt and Libya acting as self-appointed conciliators, the prime ministers of both Yemens met first in Cairo on October 28 where they concluded an agreement to put an end to the hostilities. This was followed by a meeting in Tripoli on November 28 between President Salem Rubai Ali and President Iryani, who, to the considerable consternation of many foreign quarters (including Saudi Arabia), signed a pact pledging to establish a united Yemen republic, with Sana as the capital of the state.

This about-face from warfare to unity reflected both the basic instability in the region and the superficiality of the union pledges. A mere diplomatic instrument signed in a remote Libyan capital could not remove the basic incompatibility between the two regimes. And indeed, within a few months of its signing disagreements and tension reappeared in the relations between the two countries. The subsequent removal of Qadi Iryani from the presidency of Yemen and his replacement by the military government headed by Ibrahim el-Hamdi, a man favored by Saudi Arabia, made the possibility of achieving a union even less likely.

South Yemen's relations with the countries of the so-called Arab revolutionary camp oscillated between a close alignment with Iraq under Baathist rule and an ambivalent relationship with Egypt, particularly since the advent of President Sadat. Although initially Egypt had strongly supported the South Yemeni liberation movement and Cairo served as a base for indoctrination and propaganda for the Adeni nationalists, Egypt could not align itself wholeheartedly with South Yemen in view of its close relations with Yemen. Moreover, despite its reliance on Soviet arms supplies and economic aid (at least until 1972), Egypt viewed with misgivings Soviet and Chinese penetration into South Yemen, considering it in competition with its own influence and in conflict with the principles of Arab nationalism. South Yemen's relations with Qadhafi's Libya also suffered from a degree of ambivalence. On one hand, Qadhafi as an Islamic fundamentalist objected to the atheistic-Marxist proclivities of the Aden regime. On the other hand, his policies of supporting revolution in many areas of the world and his ideological crusade against the monarchies in the Arab world were bringing him closer to the South Yemeni government, thus producing a certain convergence of policies.

South Yemen strongly supported the Palestinian liberation movement and favored the most extreme elements within the Palestine Liberation Organization. A degree of cooperation between Aden and the Palestinian *fedayeen* was reached when the Israeli tanker *Coral Sea* was attacked on June 11, 1971, by a torpedo boat manned by the *fedayeen,* who launched their operation from a South Yemen base. This episode underlined the importance of the strategic island of Perim, which was a South Yemeni possession, and brought to the attention of the world maritime powers the problem of control over the Strait of Bab el-Mandeb situated between South Yemen and Djibouti, a country that was to become independent by mid-1977.[11]

Despite the poverty of its resources and its general underdevelopment, South Yemen, owing to its geographical location, enjoyed enough of a strategic advantage to be of interest to major powers. Of these, the Soviet Union and the Communist bloc seemed to pay special attention to it within the context of a broader Soviet policy in the Indian Ocean and the Horn of Africa. Symptomatic of the interest that the Communist states had in South Yemen was the fact that East German advisers were being employed to help the government organize and train its internal security force.

Thus the position of South Yemen in the Arabian Peninsula and the Arab world at large could be likened to the position of Cuba in the Western Hemisphere.

Execution of Rubai Ali and Isolation of South Yemen

In 1977–1978 South Yemen entered a new phase in its political alignments. On the one hand, Soviet and Communist satellite influence in Aden greatly increased to the detriment of Chinese influence—a trend that was connected with the growing Soviet-Chinese rivalry and reorientation of Peking's policy toward closer relations

---

[11] The legal aspect of the strait problem is reviewed in Majid Khadduri and Herbert Dixon, "Passage through International Waterways," section on Bab el-Mandeb, in M. Khadduri, ed., *Major Middle Eastern Problems in International Law* (Washington, D.C., 1972), pp. 86–88.

with the states opposed to Soviet expansionism. On the other, South Yemen's revolutionary expansionist proclivity found a new outlet in military intervention (though on a limited scale) in the Horn of Africa in favor of Ethiopia against Somalia. This, of course, was a policy fraught with danger because it put Marxist solidarity (with Ethiopia) above the Arab solidarity (with Somalia).

A rift gradually developed between Chairman Rubai Ali and two other members of the presidency council, Abdul Fattah Ismail and Ali Nasser Mohammed, both dedicated Marxists. Rubai Ali felt uneasy about excessive reliance on Russia and the growing estrangement of South Yemen from the Arab community. Without abandoning his own genuine commitment to socialism, he favored a "pragmatic" line of improvement in relations with moderate Arab states, specifically Saudi Arabia, Yemen under President Ghashmi, and Egypt. Moreover, he also differed from his two colleagues over the allocation of power between the state and the party—the National Front, which was largely controlled by Ismail.

By the early summer of 1978, Rubai Ali as chairman of the presidency council made simultaneous moves in two directions: he engaged in communications with the pro-Saudi government of Ahmed Ghashmi in Yemen and also made arrangements to receive an American diplomatic delegation which, with a degree of secrecy, left Washington for Aden in late June with a stopover in Jidda. The purpose of this visit was to resume the thus far ruptured American-South Yemeni relations and discuss possible economic cooperation. The mission, however, never reached Aden.

Both initiatives were abruptly thwarted by the assassination of President Ghashmi in Sana on June 24 and the execution of Rubai Ali in Aden two days later. The chairmanship of South Yemen's presidency council was assumed by Ali Nasser Mohammed, and Abdul Fattah Ismail emerged as the strongest figure of the reconstituted regime. According to the subsequent official announcements in Aden, Salem Rubai Ali had deviated from the strict party line and tried to prevent the "birth of the vanguard party of a new type." Moreover, in his foreign policy, he "took reactionary stands toward Arab and world revolutionary movements until the matter ended in coordination with circles of reaction and imperialism which lie in wait for the progressive regimes and national liberation movements. He also distorted our relations with the socialist community led by the Soviet Union."[12] With these motivations in mind, Rubai Ali—according to this version—attempted a coup, but failed to prevail over the National Front, its militia, and the army loyal to the regime. He and two of his principal associates from the party's central committee were pronounced guilty of sedition and executed.

The Yemeni and Saudi governments, however, in their own versions put the blame squarely on the extreme Marxist leadership (since ascended to power) in Aden. They claimed that to prevent the achievement of inter-Arab solidarity the group in question resorted to the virtually simultaneous murder of the two presidents. On Saudi initiative, a special Arab League meeting convened in Cairo to consider this matter. On July 2 it issued a strong condemnation of the terrorist

[12]Quoted in *The Middle East*, Sept. 1978, p. 50.

methods employed by the Aden government and proclaimed a "freeze" in Arab states' relations with South Yemen.

Whichever version was true, it was undeniable that South Yemen, with its Marxist leadership, had assumed a position comparable to that of Soviet satellite states. Its doctrinaire ideological commitment and its willingness to engage in revolutionary warfare against such Arab countries as Oman and Somalia effectively isolated it from the community of Arab nations and deepened its dependence on the Soviet bloc.

CHAPTER XVI

The Persian Gulf

The Persian Gulf and its extension, the Gulf of Oman, have among their riparian countries three major powers, Iran, Saudi Arabia, and Iraq, and five mini-states, Kuwait, Bahrain, Qatar, the United Arab Emirates, and the Sultanate of Oman. The major powers—major in terms of their regional importance—have been discussed in previous chapters. This chapter gives an account of the recent political development of the mini-states. The name "Persian Gulf" is a traditional one, universally accepted in the West and until recently used not only in Iran but also in the Arab world. A leading Arab nationalist, Gamal Abdul Nasser, more than once referred in his pronouncements to the Persian Gulf; the original constitution of the Baath party describes the Arab world as extending from the Persian Gulf to the Atlantic Ocean;[1] and various Arab maps of older vintage also employ this term. In the 1960s and 1970s Arab officials and propagandists began using the designation "Arab" or "Arabian" Gulf, to the considerable annoyance of the Iranians.

The mini-states of the Persian Gulf are Arab by virtue of their ruling dynasties, sometimes the majority of their population, and the language used both officially and by large segments of the population. However, some mini-states have more immigrants of non-Arab nationality than native Arabs. These immigrants are Iranians, Baluchis, Pakistanis, Pathans, Indians, and sundry others. In terms of sheer numbers of people living around the shores of the Persian Gulf and the Gulf of Oman, the Iranians with their population of 36 million constitute a group superior in number to all Arab states, both major and minor taken together. The use of the designation "Persian Gulf" has thus a historical foundation and, for a Western scholar, does not imply a political bias in favor of Iranians or against the Arabs.

Because of its strategic location as a waterway giving access to the Iranian, Turkish Ottoman, and Arab hinterland, the Persian Gulf rather early in modern history became an object of attention of major maritime powers. The Portuguese established themselves in Bahrain as early as 1507 and held that island until 1602 when they were driven out by the Iranians. Iranian rule over Bahrain lasted in turn until 1783. At the same time, the Ottoman Empire, beginning in the sixteenth century, tried to extend its dominion over virtually the entire Arab world including

[1] Article 7. Text in *Middle East Journal*, 13, no. 2 (Spring 1959), 197.

the Arabian Peninsula. However, its rule was never complete or secure over the interior of the peninsula and the eastern and southern reaches. Tribal rulers of small Arab territories or principalities along the southern shores of the Persian Gulf remained virtually independent while engaging freely in piracy.

In the early nineteenth century the British developed an interest in the Persian Gulf area. Their merchant vessels plied these waters to reach the southern ports of Iraq and Iran. But navigation was hazardous because of the unsettled political conditions in the lower gulf. To put an end to dangers and uncertainties, the East India Company entered in 1820 into a treaty of peace with the sheikhs of the lower gulf, mainly with an eye to making navigation more secure. This treaty was followed by the so-called Maritime Truce concluded with these rulers in 1835 and directed toward the suppression of piracy. The truce, of limited duration, gave place in 1853 to the Treaty of Maritime Peace in Perpetuity, this time concluded by the government of India. The main objectives of all these treaties were to put an end to piracy, to prevent traffic in slaves, to curb the widespread smuggling of arms and other goods, and to promote peaceful trade. What thus originated as a purely defensive policy to protect peaceful navigation evolved into a "forward" policy whereby Great Britain aimed at the establishment of a degree of political control over various rulers of the gulf in both its lower, or southern, and upper, or northern, reaches. In 1869 the British concluded with the rulers of what was then already known as the Trucial Coast (or Trucial Oman) a treaty in which the rulers pledged to abstain from conducting foreign relations with powers other than Britain and undertook not to cede territory or grant any concessions to powers and individuals other than Britain. Although the treaty in question did not establish in formal terms a British protectorate over these petty principalities, in fact a protectorate situation prevailed. The two main provisions of the treaty pertaining to foreign relations and territorial and other concessions were from then on referred to as the exclusivity clause and the nonalienation clause. They were to be repeated in similar treaties concluded at one time or another, renewed and revised, with other rulers of the gulf area.

Having thus secured a broad political control of these sheikhdoms, the British gradually organized their political representation in the gulf. British interests were represented by the government of India through the person of Political Resident, Persian Gulf. His early headquarters was in the coastal township of Bushire in Iran, but after World War II it was moved to Bahrain. His representatives bearing the title of Political Agents were in turn posted in Kuwait, Qatar, Bahrain, and—with the title of Political Officer—in the Trucial Coast. Muscat and Oman enjoyed more independent status and Britain was represented there by an official with the title of Consul.

At the turn of the century British hegemony over the gulf appeared to be threatened simultaneously from two quarters: by Imperial Germany with its famous Berlin-Baghdad railway project (with a possible extension to Basra) and by Czarist Russia, which at that time began sending vessels more and more frequently to the gulf waters. To counter these emerging threats, Britain's foreign secretary, Lord Lansdowne, made a major policy statement in the House of Lords in 1903 in which he declared that Britain would consider the establishment of any outpost in the Persian Gulf by other powers as a hostile act and would resist it with all the means at its disposal.[2]

In spite of these threats, Britain succeeded in maintaining its hegemony over the gulf. While the exclusivity and the nonalienation clauses in the treaties with the local chiefs resembled the pattern established by Britain in the Aden Protectorate, there was this difference: in the Persian Gulf, the British generally refrained from a specific pledge to defend the sheikhdoms, such as had been given in the Aden Protectorate area. Moreover, although British political agents and officers did interfere actively in the dynastic and territorial disputes arising among the chiefs, especially in the lower gulf area, the British basically assumed no responsibility for internal government in the sheikhdoms. The mini-states could and did follow their own traditional ways in both politics and social life.

By the time of the First World War, British presence in the gulf acquired a new dimension because the gulf provided a major strategic approach for the invasion of the Ottoman Empire mounted by British forces from India. And again, in the 1930s, a further dimension was added by the discovery of oil in some of the states of the gulf. This fact alone in many ways altered Britain's approach and intensified her interest in the gulf. It also produced international tensions as a result of the entry of American oil interests in the area. Generally, Americans, who were oblivious to British special arrangements with the local chiefs, sought concessions either directly from the chiefs or from British concession holders (sometimes adventurous individuals) who were ready to transfer the title of concession, naturally for a consideration, to an American firm. This development created in some cases a strain between the British and the local rulers who were criticized for violating the nonalienation clause. It also caused tension between the British and American governments over accessibility to natural resources anywhere in the world. The American "Open Door" policy thus clashed with the British exclusivity in the gulf. In due time, however, these differences were removed by compromise. In some cases, notably in Kuwait, an American concession holding company had to concede 50 percent of its holdings to the British; in others, notably Bahrain, the Americans were allowed to remain sole owners of the concession provided that an operating company be set up and registered in a British territory (in this case Canada) and that it would agree to employ British subjects in most of its managerial positions. Moreover, the expansion of a British-based international consortium, Iraq Petroleum Company, into certain areas of the Persian Gulf paved the way for a number of joint enterprises in which British, American, French, and Dutch interests were represented.

The spectacular growth of the oil industry and the increasing dependence on Middle Eastern oil imports of Europe, Japan, and since the early 1970s the United States as well, added a new aspect, a strategic one, to oil production in the gulf area. Control of the oil fields and of the waterways, beginning with the Strait of Hormuz,

---

[2]From Lansdowne's declaration in the House of Lords, May 5, 1903: "We should regard the establishment of a naval base or of a fortified port in the Persian Gulf by any other Power as very grave menace to British interests, and we should certainly resist it with all the means at our disposal." Quoted by Briton C. Busch, *Britain and the Persian Gulf, 1894–1914* (Berkeley, 1967), p. 256.

became a matter of vital concern to the consumer nations as well as to the producing ones. It was, therefore, something of a paradox that while from the point of view of Britain and other major Western powers the gulf was gaining in importance, the Labor government in London decided, in 1968, to relinquish British imperial responsibilities in the gulf. This decision could hardly be justified on economic grounds, inasmuch as the maintenance of modern British forces, including naval and air bases, in that region was not overly expensive and, if need be, could be accomplished by funds from either other NATO allies or even some of the local rulers of mini-states, who, after the discovery of oil in their territories, could very well provide funds for this purpose. Furthermore, this was far from a typical colonial situation: Britain protected these mini-states against external and internal enemies but refrained from imposing a British pattern of administration and life upon the native societies. In fact, the local rulers became seriously concerned about their security once the British announcement of impending withdrawal was made. They could not disregard the events of 1967 in the Aden Protectorate, where the removal of British presence resulted in the wholesale overthrow of twenty-odd sultans and sheikhs.

British withdrawal from the gulf was thus to produce a serious political vacuum, and the danger was that either the Soviet Union or China, or the local dissidents inspired by the success of the revolution in Aden, might attempt to take over. And indeed, as the date of the British withdrawal approached, the gulf area became the scene of struggle among competing forces. The revolutionaries based on Aden not only extended their struggle to the Dhofar province of Oman, but through their Popular Front for the Liberation of the Occupied Arabian Gulf (PFLOAG) attempted to influence developments in the gulf region proper. The radical regime in Iraq directed by the Baath party tried to spread its revolutionary doctrine and to enlist partisans in the gulf states. A close relationship existing between Iraq and the Soviet Union added another disquieting dimension to this southward thrust of the Baghdad government. The country that responded with greater intensity than any other to this possible disintegration in the gulf was Iran. The Shah launched a double-pronged political and military policy with the objective, first, of preventing revolutionary forces inspired by Aden or Iraq from seizing power in the gulf principalities; second, of ensuring that the Strait of Hormuz would not fall under hostile control and would be free for navigation, especially the maritime tanker traffic which carried in the mid-1970s about eighteen million barrels of oil a day to foreign destinations. With this in view, on November 30, 1971 on the eve of the formal relinquishment of British power in the gulf area—the Shah ordered his forces to seize three islands located at the western entrance of the Strait of Hormuz, Abu Musa and the Greater and Lesser Tunb. The Iranian government backed this act by invoking historical claims to these islands. On December 2, 1971, the British formally put an end to their rule in the gulf.

British withdrawal was preceded by lengthy negotiations conducted by special emmisaries, of whom Sir William Luce, previously governor of Aden, was perhaps best known. These negotiations aimed at bringing about a federation of the states of the lower gulf in the belief that, by uniting, the local chiefs would become stronger in the face of threats to their power and that such a federation would provide a better channel by which Britain could maintain friendly relations and a degree of influence in the region without the burden of a military establishment there. Although the local chiefs responded positively to the idea of federation, they were by no means unanimous. For different reasons Bahrain and Qatar decided to become independent states. The federation was ultimately limited to the seven Trucial States, but even then one of them, Ras el-Khaima, did not join for several months.

The occupation of the Hormuz Strait islands by Iran gave a new emphasis to a number of long unsettled territorial problems among the gulf states both on land and in the sea. A close look at the map of the Trucial Coast including the Musandam Peninsula reveals a crazy quilt pattern of complicated boundaries and enclaves whereby the possessions of a single minor sheikhdom may be scattered in three or four different places with territories of other sheikhdoms in between. Historically this territorial pattern has been justified by the essentially tribal and dynastic nature of politics in the area and the numerous splits and mergers that accompanied it. It was, however, the Buraimi oasis that provided the most serious bone of contention between Abu Dhabi and Oman on the one hand, and Saudi Arabia on the other. In the early 1950s the Saudis sent a mixed civilian-military group to Buraimi to assert their right to it, a right based, as they claimed, on old tribal allegiances and pattern of taxation. By 1955, however, the British-officered forces of the Sheikh of Abu Dhabi and the Sultan of Muscat-Oman ejected the Saudis and proceeded to occupy the entire oasis, actually a cluster of nine villages located at the strategic crossroads which gained importance as a result of the discovery of oil in Inner Oman.[3] This dispute, which was subjected to an abortive arbitration, did not end until May 1974, when by virtue of a final agreement Saudi Arabia renounced its claim to Buraimi in return for the cession by Abu Dhabi of a stretch of territory that gave the Saudis access to the Persian Gulf east of the base of the Qatar peninsula. By the mid-1970s most of the outstanding territorial disputes in the area were settled, with the exception of the undelimited boundary between Kuwait and Iraq, a matter which gave rise to recurrent difficulties between these two countries.

With the removal of the British military and political presence in the gulf and a token United States presence in the form of the Middle East Task Force (composed of two destroyers and a tender based on Bahrain), it was Iran's turn to assert military hegemony in the gulf area. After the occupation of the three disputed islands in 1971 Iran abstained from unilateral actions in the gulf area and, all sorts of rumors notwithstanding, it was unlikely that Iran would choose a policy of conquest and occupation that would clearly produce only resentment and alienation. However, implicitly, Iran reserved for itself the right to intervene in case any revolutionary

---

[3]For a detailed account of Buraimi within the context of eastern Arabia, see Arabian American Oil Company, *Oman and the Southern Shore of the Persian Gulf* (Cairo, 1952), pp. 141–157; and J. B. Kelly, *Eastern Arabian Frontiers* (London, 1964). The Saudi case is presented in *Memorial of the Government of Saudi Arabia,* Arbitration of the Settlement of the Territorial Dispute between Muscat and Abu Dhabi on One Side and Saudi Arabia on the Other (31 July 1955) in three volumes. Vol. 3 contains tax records. For the British case see *Memorial of the Government of the United Kingdom and Northern Ireland in Arbitration Concerning Buraimi and the Common Frontier between Abu Dhabi and Saudi Arabia,* 2 vols. (London, 1955).

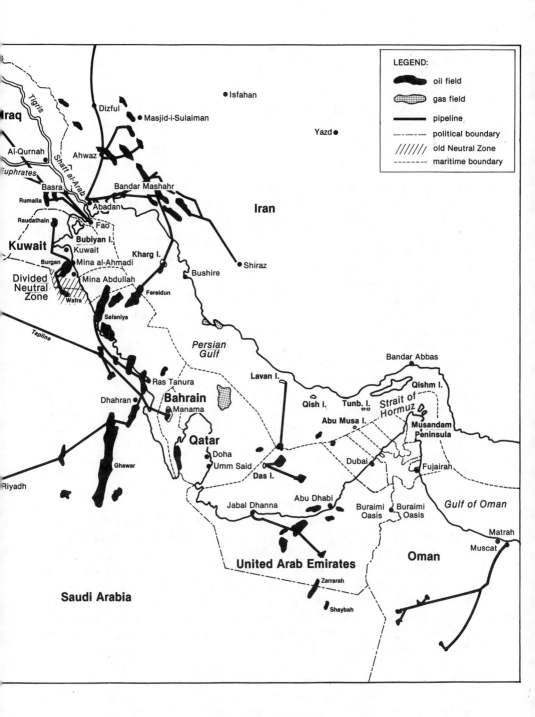

Map 9. The Persian Gulf.

group tried to upset the existing arrangements. Moreover, Iran reminded the governments of the Arabian Peninsula of its military ability by sending, at the invitation of the Sultan of Oman, forces to help him quell the Dhofar rebellion. Iran was interested primarily in the security and stability of the entire region, an objective shared by Saudi Arabia, Kuwait, the local rulers, and, ultimately, the United States and its Western allies as well.

Kuwait

Kuwait was settled in the first part of the eighteenth century by a group of tribes that, during a protracted period of drought, had left their home grounds in Nejd in search of a more hospitable environment. After a long trek that included an unsuccessful attempt to settle at the northern tip of the Qatar peninsula, these tribes found at the southern shore of Kuwait Bay relatively propitious conditions for living. Not all of them, however, decided to stay. A troupe of them headed by the Khalifa family decided to return to Qatar. Eventually, they crossed to the island of Bahrain, where they established an autonomous principality. Those who chose to remain in Kuwait were headed by the Sabah family. A leader of this family, himself named Sabah, established an autonomous sheikhdom in Kuwait about 1756. Ruling until 1762, he thus became a founder of the Sabah dynasty which has ruled Kuwait ever since. The name Kuwait derives from the Arabic word *kut,* meaning fort, and Kuwait itself means a "little fort." It was probably built by the Turks because the territory was officially within the confines of the Ottoman Empire. Its most favorable geographic feature was a bay which provided a natural shelter for ships. Kuwait Bay was a convenient harbor for ships plying trade between Iraq (Mesopotamia) and points farther south and east as far as India. The erstwhile nomadic tribesmen gradually adapted themselves to the new environment and began to excel as sailors, boat-builders, pearl fishermen, and traders.

From Dependent to Independent Status

Although officially the territory of Kuwait was part of the Ottoman Empire, as in many other areas in the Arabian Peninsula Turkish control was nominal rather than effective. For a time Kuwait was classified by the Ottoman authorities as a district of the vilayet (province) of Basra, and a descendant of the founder of the Sabah dynasty was once designated *qaimaqam* (district officer) by the Ottoman authorities. Subsequent rulers of Kuwait, however, declined to accept such a title because it implied official subjection to the Ottoman state hierarchy. In the early 1890s Kuwait suffered inner turmoil stemming from rivalries within the ruling family. A weak and ineffectual ruler, Sheikh Mohammed ben Sabah, was assassinated in 1896 by his half-brother, Mubarak, who established himself as ruler until his death in 1915. Mubarak, sometimes referred to as "The Great," was an energetic and purposeful individual whose main objective was to strengthen Kuwait against the Turks, for during his rule they made many attempts to reassert their authority over the sheikhdom.

To achieve his objective, Mubarak sought the assistance of Great Britain, which by that time had established itself as the paramount maritime power in the Persian Gulf area. British interest paralleled his own: the British feared Russian expansion in the northern gulf (as evidenced by various Russian diplomatic and commercial moves in the late 1890s) and, subsequently, German designs upon this area, symbolized by the famous Berlin-Baghdad railway plan. Actually the projected railway was not to end in Baghdad but was to proceed to Basra and, possibly, end in Kuwait.

There being thus an ascertained community of interest and objectives, Sheikh Mubarak signed, on January 23, 1899, an agreement with the British whereby Great Britain assumed responsibility for Kuwait's defense and foreign affairs. The agreement included two provisions characteristic of the agreements that Britain had at one time or another concluded with other gulf chieftains, namely the so-called exclusivity and nonalienation clauses. The first meant that the sheikh undertook not to enter into relations with any other power without British consent and the second signified his pledge that he would not grant any concessions or cede his territory to anyone without British approval. This agreement was subsequently updated in 1913 with specific reference to oil concessions.

The 1899 agreement opened the way for steady British advances in Kuwait. In 1903, Lord Curzon, viceroy of India, paid a visit to the sheikhdom. The following year a permanent British Political Agent, responsible to the British Resident in the Persian Gulf, was appointed to Kuwait. Both in turn were under the authority of the British government of India. In 1907 the British leased an anchorage in the Kuwaiti harbor of Bandar Shuwaikh and subsequently established there a naval base and a coaling station. On July 19, 1913, Great Britain and the Ottoman Empire concluded an agreement which recognized the autonomy of the Sheikh of Kuwait. Although not ratified, this agreement constituted the first official act of renunciation on the part of the Ottoman government of full sovereignty over the sheikhdoms and the official admission of the special British status there.

The period of World War I was one of considerable uncertainty and difficulty for Kuwait. In the first place, with the death of Sheikh Mubarak in 1915, Kuwait was deprived of a strong and experienced leadership. He was succeeded by his sons, Jaber (1915–1917) and Salem (1917–1921), both of whom ruled for periods that were too brief to allow them to have an impact upon the destiny of their country. Because Sheikh Salem showed an inclination toward the Ottoman side in the war, Kuwait was subjected to a British blockade that resulted in economic stagnation and considerable inconvenience to the inhabitants. Furthermore, Kuwait was subjected to the attacks of the fundamentalist Wahhabi *Ikhwan* from Nejd and barely avoided being conquered by those fanatical warriors.

The new era began with the advent of Sheikh Ahmed, son of Sheikh Jaber, who ruled between 1921 and 1950. Because of the collapse of the Ottoman Empire and the emancipation of Arab lands from Turkish rule, a necessity arose to delimit the boundaries among the various new political entities in the Arabian Peninsula. Historically, the Arabs of the peninsula were not very familiar with the concept of territorial boundaries. In contrast to Europe, there were no clear-cut ethnic divisions in the peninsula, nor were there any outstanding topographical landmarks such as major rivers or prominent mountain ranges. The authority of a given political center usually extended as far as the tribal allegiances permitted. To be sure, individual tribes had traditional claims to certain water wells or springs in the desert but they could shift allegiance from one ruler to another and, moreover, their nomadic way of life was not conducive to the development of stable territorial jurisdictions. In the period immediately following World War I the growth of the sultanate of Nejd under the leadership of Abdul Aziz ibn Saud and the gradual process of conquest and unification of large stretches of the Arabian Peninsula which he was carrying out created the need for some international agreements regarding territory to ensure stability in the area. A major diplomatic landmark in this respect was the conference in Uqair held in 1923 at which the British Resident of the Persian Gulf, Sir Percy Cox, acted as an arbiter. At that conference the boundaries of Kuwait were established, both on its northern side with Iraq and on its southern side with Nejd. The difficulty in reaching the final agreement was responsible for the decision to create the so-called Kuwait Neutral Zone, a lozenge-shaped territory in which Kuwait and Nejd (later Saudi Arabia) were to share jurisdiction and oil resources, should they be discovered.[4]

Politically, the interwar period was relatively uneventful except for renewed Wahhabi invasions from Nejd in 1927–1928. British military assistance to Kuwait proved decisive in checking these incursions and, with further consolidation of Ibn Saud's power, the militant *Ikhwan* were subjected to his stricter control and forced to abandon their warlike designs.

A major event, but one whose consequences were to be felt only a dozen years later, was the granting, in December 1934, of an oil concession to a joint Anglo-American enterprise composed of the Anglo-Iranian Oil Company and the Gulf Oil Corporation. These two firms set up as their operating affiliate the Kuwait Oil Company, which before long discovered some fifteen miles south of Kuwait town one of the largest pools of oil in the world, the Burgan oil field.

World War II found the British well entrenched in the sheikhdom, and Kuwait was an important port and naval base for the British war effort. In 1950 the throne of Kuwait was inherited by Sheikh Ahmed's first cousin, Sheikh Abdullah, who ruled until 1965. The period of his rule witnessed tremendous transformations in Kuwait's political status and economic development. In June 1961, Great Britain and Kuwait terminated their 1899 agreement. Kuwait was proclaimed an independent state and a new agreement guaranteed British military assistance in case Kuwait requested it.[5] The title of the head of state was changed from Ruler (*hakem*) to Emir (*amir*). The following month an independent Kuwait was admitted to the Arab League and in due course to the United Nations as well.

Independence was accompanied by a phenomenal economic growth under the impact of the high oil revenues. This growth in turn found its reflection in the

[4]Text in Charles U. Aitchison, ed., *A Collection of Treaties, Engagements, and Sanads Relating to India and Neighbouring Countries*, Vol. XI (Delhi: Foreign Office 1933), pp. 213–214.
[5]Text in Husain M. Albaharna, *The Arabian Gulf States: Their Legal and Political Status and Their International Problems*, 2d ed. (Beirut, 1975), p. 374.

spectacular rise in population. As late as 1949 the population of Kuwait was estimated at between 70,000 and 100,000; by 1952 the estimate rose to 160,000, and by 1958 to nearly 250,000. By 1978 Kuwait's population passed the one million mark and was expected to reach 1,250,000 by the early 1980s. Only part of this rapid growth could be attributed to the natural birth rate of the native Kuwaitis. The majority of the population was composed of immigrants, both Arabs and non-Arabs, who had flocked to this oil-rich state in search of employment and profitable business ventures. Broadly, the population was divided into Kuwaiti citizens and aliens, but beyond this formal division further differentiations had to be made. Kuwaiti citizens were ranged in two categories, native Kuwaitis and naturalized citizens whose political rights were, at least temporarily, restricted. Non-Arab aliens included a good number of Iranians, Pakistanis, Indians, Baluchis, and also quite a few Britishers, Americans, and Europeans whose technical and managerial skills were very much needed in the fast-developing Kuwaiti economy. Among the Arab immigrants, the Palestinians have emerged as a very substantial group which by the mid-1970s was estimated at some 250,000. Whether naturalized as Kuwaiti citizens or not, these Palestinians constituted a powerful pressure group in Kuwait and were subject to close surveillance by the Kuwaiti authorities.

Structure of Power

Ever since its beginning as an autonomous political entity, Kuwait has been a tribal-patriarchal society. In contrast to the urban-imperial structures of such states as the Ottoman or Persian empires, the desert-patriarchal variety of authoritarianism has been characterized by simplicity, informality, and lack of an elaborate administrative hierarchy. In the case of Kuwait, the ruling Sabah family possessed the same tribal background as other prominent families in the principality, merely differing from them in strength and prominence and maintaining this supremacy by the force of tradition.

Arab tribal societies have generally failed to develop a strict and consistent system of succession comparable to the principle of primogeniture in Europe. Succession in such tribal societies, assuming it was carried out by peaceful means, usually involved a mixture of inheritance and election, the latter often restricted to the ruling family group. Following the rule of Sheikh Mubarak, two main branches of the ruling Sabah dynasty emerged, the Al Jaber branch and the Al Salem branch. Beginning with these two rulers, it appeared that a principle of rotation between the two branches was instituted. Thus, after the death of Sheikh Salem in 1921 the man who succeeded him, Sheikh Ahmed, was not his son but the son of the preceding ruler, Sheikh Jaber. In turn, when Ahmed died in 1950, his successor was Sheikh Abdullah, his first cousin and son of the late Sheikh Salem. When Abdullah died in 1965, a perfect system of rotation would have required a member of the Al Jaber branch to succeed him. Instead the rulership was assumed by his younger brother Sabah, who ruled until his death at the end of 1977. However imperfect, the system of rotation was applied again, and Sheikh Jaber el-Ahmed el-Jaber Al Sabah, a member of the Al-Jaber branch, succeeded Sheikh Sabah el-Salem as ruler.

Actually the mechanics of succession in Kuwait usually involve two persons after the death of a ruler. The first act is to proclaim his successor, a person who had been designated a long time in advance as crown prince. Within the last few generations the person designated as crown prince has invariably been proclaimed ruler. The second act upon the succession of a new ruler is to appoint, with the concurrence of the princely family, a new crown prince, thereby introducing a greater element of certainty to the process of succession. In practice this has meant that the election of the future ruler took place a good many years before his actual accession to the throne. In the period following World War II a crown prince was generally designated within approximately six months of the accession of the new ruler.

When on the last day of December 1977 Sheikh Jaber el-Ahmed el-Jaber Al Sabah ascended the throne, the problem arose whether he would appoint as crown prince another member of the Jaber branch of the dynasty (to equalize the fact that prior to him two members of the Salem branch had ruled) or choose a descendant of the Salem branch to restore a more perfect system of rotation. This initial uncertainty was further aggravated by the fact that, under the traditional system, the crown prince has often simultaneously served as prime minister. The new ruler, Sheikh Jaber el-Ahmed, was known to favor the separation of these two functions, partly as a reflection of the concept of constitutionalism which had developed in Kuwait upon achievement of independence.

In 1961 the independent state of Kuwait elected a constituent assembly which adopted a constitution in November 1962. The constitution provided for an elective fifty-member national assembly. The first such assembly was called into being in January 1963, following which a cabinet under the premiership of the crown prince, Sheikh Sabah el-Salem Al Sabah, was constituted.

The joining of the functions of the crown prince with those of the prime minister presented some advantages and some drawbacks. The advantage was that the future ruler of the state would gain practical experience by exercising ministerial functions. The drawback was that if, according to the constitutional process, he should be removed from the premiership as the result of his inability to govern effectively, his prestige would suffer, with attendant consequences for his future performance as ruler. The matter was further complicated by the fact that the previous ruler, Sheikh Sabah el-Salem Al Sabah, in August 1976, dissolved the national assembly and suspended parts of the constitution, especially those pertaining to the freedom of the press. By doing this, Sheikh Sabah had restored the essentially traditional-patriarchal system of government under which the joining of the functions of the crown prince and prime minister was quite acceptable.

Sheikh Jaber promptly appointed a member of the Salem branch of the family, Sheikh Saad el-Abdullah Al Salem as prime minister but delayed his decision to appoint the crown prince for several months. Finally his choice fell on Sheikh Saad, thereby reflecting his decision to join the two functions and at the same time to restore the principle of rotation.

The fifteen-year experiment with constitutionalism and parliamentarism in Kuwait yielded ambivalent results. On the one hand, it demonstrated that even in a society accustomed to patriarchal rule, it was possible to establish institutions through which the voice of the people—or at least of its broader politically conscious stratum—could be heard. It also demonstrated that at the time when military dictatorships in many Arab countries were in vogue it was possible in an Arab country to tolerate opposition to the existing government. Such an opposition indeed made its appearance in the Kuwaiti national assembly, especially in 1963 when twelve members under the leadership of Ahmed el-Khatib went on record several times as critical of the government's policies. To some extent opposition in Kuwait was influenced by the nationalist trends, often those emanating from Cairo, prevalent in the Arab world in the 1960s. In Kuwait these nationalist attitudes found their reflection in two demands: (1) to lessen or sever whatever tenuous links with Great Britain still existed as a result of the 1961 treaty, and (2) to assume full control of Kuwait's oil industry. In comparison, however, with many other Arab states, social cleavages in Kuwait have never reached alarming political proportions, perhaps owing to the fact that as an oil-rich country Kuwait had sufficiently large revenues to satisfy the needs of the population and even to develop and practice the concept of a welfare state in which many services, including education and medical care, were provided free.

Kuwait's Economy

The Kuwait Oil Company (KOC) began producing and exporting oil on an increasing scale beginning in 1946. Before long Kuwait joined the ranks of the three big producing states in the Middle East (Saudi Arabia, Iran, and Iraq) and for some time during the 1950s stood second to Saudi Arabia in production volume. Kuwait's proven oil reserves have been estimated in the 1970s at around 65 billion barrels, thus making it the fourth oil-rich country in the world after Saudi Arabia, the Soviet Union, and Iran. To the original big Burgan field new discoveries were added in the north of Kuwait as well as in the Neutral Zone where since 1948 the American Independent Oil Company had operated on the basis of a concession from the Kuwait government. Actually it was a joint enterprise with the Getty Oil Company, itself holder of a concession from Saudi Arabia. Kuwait's oil production reached its peak of 3.75 million barrels a day in 1972. Kuwait's government and national assembly began to be concerned with conservation of the national resources, and eventually it was decided to reduce production to the level of 3 million barrels a day and, by 1975, further to lower it to 2 million barrels a day (composed of 1.7 million barrels a day from Kuwait proper and 0.3 million from the Neutral Zone). At this rate of production, assuming that no new discoveries were made, Kuwait could expect its oil resources to last for another seventy-seven years, the longest period of any country in the world.

The large oil revenues enabled Kuwait to engage in an impressive development of its economy. The capital city of Kuwait was developed in an imaginative way, provided with wide streets, modern public buildings, schools, hospitals, and shopping centers. The government established desalinization plants, a refinery, a fertilizer plant, and a tanker fleet. Major hotels chains such as the Hilton and the Sheraton made their appearance, catering to an increasing number of foreign visitors, businessmen, and tourists. A large new airport was constructed, and the city in general acquired a modern look, contrasting its orderliness and cleanliness with many another urban center in the Middle East.

As a result of the quadrupling of oil prices by the Organization of Petroleum

Exporting Countries (OPEC), of which Kuwait was a member, oil revenues of the state reached in 1974 the level of $9.3 billion, thus making Kuwait, along with Abu Dhabi, the country with the highest per capita income in the world. These revenues greatly exceeded the current needs of the state. Even before the rise of prices, Kuwait's oil revenue was divided into three parts: for annual current budget expenses, for development, and for long-range investments. In the mid-1970s the government adopted a $15 billion development plan. Foreign investments were mostly channeled through a special investment board operating in London, and these included important transactions such as the purchase, in December 1974, of 14 percent of the stock of the Daimler Benz Company in West Germany. Major real estate investments were also made by both the government and private citizens in the United States. In addition, the government created the Kuwait Fund for Arab Economic Development (KFAED) to assist financially the more needy Arab countries. Moreover, loans were extended to other countries of the Third World and to Ireland, Hungary, Yugoslavia, and the city of Marseilles, to mention just a few. Similarly, Kuwait has granted financial assistance to the Palestinian freedom fighting organizations and to the Eritrean Liberation Front fighting for independence from Ethiopia.

Beginning in late 1973 important changes occurred in the pattern of relations between the government and the concessionaire oil companies. In December the government proposed an acquisition of 50 percent of the Kuwait Oil Company's stock but the national assembly demanded complete nationalization. As a result, in 1974 a compromise formula resulted in an agreement with KOC's two parent companies, Gulf and BP (heir to the Anglo-Iranian Oil Company) providing for 60 percent participation of the Kuwait government. Finally, in December 1975 an agreement, retroactive to March of that year, stipulated the transfer of the remaining 40 percent of the stock to the government. By the middle of 1977 the American Independent Oil Company operating in the Neutral Zone was also fully taken over by the government. In pursuing this path Kuwait was following the patterns already under way in the neighboring oil-producing countries of the Middle East. Acquisition of 100 percent of the stock of the former concessionaire companies, however, should not be confused with outright nationalization. Nationalization is a unilateral act and has some punitive and to some extent confiscatory connotation. In contrast, the above-mentioned agreements were negotiated bilaterally between the interested parties and provided not only for compensation but also for guaranteed supplies of crude to the former concession holders. Moreover, actual exploration, production, and transportation operations were for the most part still entrusted to the old managerial and engineering teams on the basis of special service contracts. By choosing this moderate path, Kuwait avoided disruption of its production and exports.

Foreign and Arab Policy

As a small city-state located in a strategic area where the territories of its three bigger neighbors—Saudi Arabia, Iraq, and Iran—converge, Kuwait both before and after independence has been acutely conscious of its relative weakness and vulnerability. Before independence British protection assured it of survival as a separate entity. But after 1961 Kuwait was left largely to its own devices and had to adjust its policy to the new circumstances. In its relations with the neighboring Arab powers and Iran, Kuwait adopted a policy of extreme caution and official neutrality. Its tremendous wealth has added to its dangers inasmuch as it was always likely to provoke the envy of other powers. Kuwait's foreign policy could perhaps best be described as one aiming at the balancing of various influences. Moreover, its tribal and plutocratic political system automatically invited potential attacks from the centers of radical Arab nationalism and from various revolutionary movements in the Persian Gulf area.

Chronologically, the first such threat came from Iraq immediately after the achievement of Kuwait's independence in 1961. Iraq's military dictator, General Abdul Karim Kassem, laid claim to the entire territory of Kuwait on the ground that during the Ottoman regime Kuwait had been no more than a *kadha* (district) of the vilayet of Basra. Its very existence threatened, the Kuwait government turned to Britain which, by virtue of its newly concluded treaty, came to the assistance of the fledgling state by sending troops and naval units to oppose a possible Iraqi invasion. As a new member of the Arab League, Kuwait also appealed to that body, and after lengthy deliberations the League decided to send a multinational force to defend Kuwait against aggression. This force was composed of troops from Egypt (U.A.R.), Saudi Arabia, Jordan, and Sudan. But whereas the British sent their troops immediately when the Iraqi threat became known, that is, in July, the Arab League managed to mobilize its force only by September. It was therefore the decisive British intervention rather than the delayed Pan-Arab operation that saved Kuwait from being destroyed in its infancy. Furthermore, in September the United Arab Republic broke into its component parts of Egypt and Syria and this was reflected in disagreements between the Egyptian and the Syrian parts of the original U.A.R. contingent in Kuwait. These Syrian and Egyptian forces withdrew from Kuwait in December 1961 regardless of the consequences to Kuwait's security. The Jordanian, Sudanese, and Saudi Arabian forces remained until February 1963. By that time the regime of Abdul Karim Kassem in Iraq had been overthrown and the new Baath regime made certain reassuring gestures toward Kuwait, at least implicitly recognizing its legitimacy as a separate state.

The subsequent history of Kuwaiti-Iraqi relations was not, however, free from difficulties, ambiguities, and crises. In spite of many solicitations by the Kuwait government for an agreement with Baghdad on final delimitation of the boundary, the successive Iraqi governments never gave a positive response. And, after the second victory of the Baath party in Iraq in 1968, the Iraqi government repeatedly adopted a threatening attitude toward Kuwait with regard to the border areas. In March 1973 a contingent of Iraqi troops crossed the border and occupied a Kuwait military post, an act which naturally elicited Kuwait's strong protests. And between 1974 and 1976 Baghdad laid repeated claims to two Kuwait islands, Warba and Bubiyan, both strategically located along the estuary leading to the nearby Iraqi port of Umm Qasr. Umm Qasr had in the meantime increased in importance as a port of call for Soviet naval and merchant ships which, without establishing a formal Soviet base, were granted various facilities by Iraq. The conclusion in 1972 of a fifteen-year treaty of friendship between Iraq and the Soviet Union further added to Kuwait's concern over Iraqi designs in this area.

As an Arab country, Kuwait also viewed with some uneasiness Iran's forward policy in the gulf, which was expressed by an energetic program of armaments, a build-up of the Iranian navy, and the construction of various naval bases on the Iranian coast. Furthermore, toward the end of 1971, as previously mentioned, Iran occupied three strategically located islands at the western entrance to the Strait of Hormuz, the Greater and Lesser Tunbs and Abu Musa. Iranian moves in the gulf, however assertive, did not provoke in Kuwait a fear comparable to that of the threat from Iraq. In fact, privately many Kuwaitis welcomed the accretion in the strength of Iran as a counterbalancing force to Iraq.

Under the circumstances, it was natural for Kuwait to draw closer to Saudi Arabia as a country broadly similar to itself in political structure, that did not covet Kuwait's territory or riches, and was dedicated to the moderate status quo in the Arabian Peninsula and the gulf area. On their part, the Saudis tended to look upon Kuwait as a sort of "little brother" whom they should protect in case of need and to whom they might tender advice. The Saudis were concerned lest Kuwait modernize at a pace that would exceed what they considered safe and proper for the countries of the Arabian Peninsula. On two points in particular the Saudis had definite ideas about the developments in Kuwait; these were the role of the Islamic religion as a foundation of society and the maintenance of the traditional political institutions. The broad consensus in Kuwait in the 1970s was that the Saudis had not been reluctant to advise the Kuwaiti rulers on the proper system of government. When consequently, in the mid-1970s, Kuwait tightened up its regulations against the consumption of alcohol, this rather unpopular measure was generally ascribed to the influence of Saudi Arabia. Similarly, when Sheikh Sabah el-Salem Al Sabah dissolved the national assembly and suspended the constitution, the general belief was that this was done on the urging of the newly installed King Khalid of Saudi Arabia who had shortly before paid his official state visit to the Emir of Kuwait.

Although thus Kuwait kept in close touch with its powerful Saudi neighbor and was, to some extent, subject to its influence, the Kuwaitis did not always agree with Riyadh on certain policies and strategies. For example, while Saudi Arabia was generally opposed to abrupt rises in the oil prices, Kuwait was more noncommittal and on some occasions appeared to side with the "hawkish" camp within the OPEC, composed of such countries as Iraq, Iran, and Algeria in the early and middle 1970s. Similarly, when in June 1978 Saudi Arabia undertook a vigorous action within the Arab League to condemn and isolate the South Yemeni Marxist regime for its aggressive actions in North Yemen, Kuwait was openly critical of this policy as conducive to an even further aggravation and reserved for itself freedom of maintaining contact with South Yemen "for humanitarian reasons." This Kuwait policy was expressive of its general attitude in foreign and Arab affairs, namely to avoid as much as possible any rifts and conflicts likely to pit one camp of states against another. As a society with a strong merchant tradition, Kuwait was always suspicious of excessive ideological commitments and invariably sought compromise and peace. This tradition also explains a basic difference between its own and the

Saudi approach to relations with the Communist states. While Saudi Arabia never recognized the Soviet Union, Communist China, or any other Communist state, Kuwait by contrast maintained diplomatic relations with Moscow, Peking, and the countries of the Soviet bloc. The earlier mentioned loans to Hungary and Yugoslavia further underlined Kuwait's reluctance to govern its relations with foreign countries on an ideological basis. By the same token, although deeply disturbed by the unbending militancy of the Palestinians, the government of Kuwait (and even its wealthy private citizens) regularly provided financial assistance to the Palestinian liberation organizations. This, however, did not always free them from embarrassment: on September 15, 1975, following the conclusion of the Sinai II agreement between Egypt and Israel under American auspices, the city of Kuwait became the scene of a major anti-Sadat demonstration in which thousands of Palestinians and their more radical Kuwaiti allies noisily protested against what they termed a policy of appeasement.

Repeated threats from Iraq coupled with those from the radical movements in the gulf area and in Kuwait proper led the government to pay increased attention to internal security and external defense beginning with the mid-1970s. The army was increased in its numbers and a program of acquisition of arms was launched. Military equipment was primarily being purchased in the United States and the West but agreements for limited purchases of weapons were also concluded with the Soviet Union. As in the Arab affairs so in international relations, Kuwait tried to remain faithful to its nonalignment policy.

Bahrain

On August 14, 1970, Bahrain achieved independence by putting an end to the previous treaty arrangements with Great Britain. On the same day a new treaty of friendship between the two countries was concluded.[6] This date marked the end of a long era of dependent status: between 1507 and 1602 Bahrain was under Portuguese occupation. In 1602 the Portuguese were expelled and Bahrain found itself under the rule of Iran, which lasted until 1783. In that year Arab tribes from the mainland conquered the island and since 1816 it has been ruled by the Khalifa family of the Utubi tribe. Before long, however, these Arab rulers fell under the sway of Britain, which from 1820 onward established hegemony over the Persian Gulf area. The British extended their domination of Bahrain through a series of treaties. These were sometimes collective instruments such as those of 1820 or of 1853 (the Perpetual Treaty of Peace with the gulf chieftains) or, in other cases, they represented a bilateral arrangement between the British and the sheikhs of Bahrain. The latter included an agreement of 1861 directed against piracy and slavery and another, of 1880, by which the British assumed responsibility for the conduct of Bahrain's foreign relations. The treaty of 1892 further expanded Britain's dominant status by

---

[6]Texts in Great Britain, *Treaty Series,* no. 78 (1971), cmd. 4827, and no. 79 (1971), cmd. 4828. For a comprehensive treatment of Bahrain and its neighboring countries, see John Duke Anthony, *Arab States of the Lower Gulf: People, Politics, and Petroleum* (Washington, D.C., 1975).

reiterating Britain's control over Bahrain's foreign relations and the sheikh's pledge not to cede or mortgage or dispose in any way of his territory without Britain's approval, and by putting a ban on the residence of any foreign agent in the country. After that agreement the Ottoman Porte was informed that Bahrain was "now under protection of Her Majesty the Queen of England." The agreements of 1911 pertaining to the extension of British control over pearl fisheries and of 1914 by which the sheikh stipulated that he would not grant oil concessions without British approval completed the chain of legal arrangements establishing Britain's control over the archipelago.[7]

Beginning with World War I, Bahrain began to play an increasingly strategic role in the British hegemony over the Persian Gulf. It served as an assembly point for the British expeditionary force (mostly from India) which was to wage a campaign in Mesopotamia. In 1935 Bahrain became the site of the principal British naval base in the gulf after the British units evacuated their earlier bases in Henjam on the Iranian coast and in Basra. And, about thirty years later, in 1966, Britain moved to Bahrain the military base that had been headquartered in Aden.

Discovery and development of oil resources in Bahrain constituted another important element linking Britain to the island. Originally an oil concession was granted by the sheikh of Bahrain to Standard Oil Company of California in 1930. As in some other cases in the gulf—notably in Kuwait somewhat later—the grant of the concession abounded in complications arising from the fact that the ruler tended to disregard the oil nonalienation clause by which he was bound through the existing treaties. When finally the British gave their assent to the concession, it was with a provision that the operating company, although wholly owned by an American corporation, would have to register in the British territory. This demand was satisfied by registering the Bahrain Oil Company (Bapco) in Canada. In 1935 the Texas Oil Company joined as a partner on a 50-50 basis and officially the Cal-Tex Company became the owner of Bapco. Bahrain was important in the history of the oil industry in the gulf primarily in that it was the first country on the Arab side of the gulf in which oil began to be produced. Otherwise, its reserves proved to be very modest, in fact the smallest of all gulf countries. They amounted to 0.34 billion barrels as of 1974 and were steadily diminishing without new discoveries to compensate for the depletion. In fact, in 1977 it was estimated that within ten years the existing reserves would be exhausted. Bahrain, however, obtained some consolation in the fact that, by agreement with Saudi Arabia, it gained the right to half of the production of the Abu Saafah field in the offshore area, whose reserves were estimated at 6.5 billion barrels. Bahrain's own limited reserves were also reflected in the lowest production of all the gulf countries, a production which declined steadily, from an average of 70,000 barrels a day in the early 1970s to about 55,000 barrels a day toward the end of the decade. This amount, however, was supplemented by another 55,000 barrels a day which was Bahrain's share from Abu Saafah.

Additional income from the oil industry was derived from the proceeds of a

[7]See Aitchison, *op. cit.,* vol. XI, as a source for these treaties.

refinery which, linked to the Saudi Arabian mainland by a pipeline, was processing 180,000 barrels a day of the Saudi crude. Furthermore, the Organization of Arab Petroleum Exporting Countries (OAPEC) decided to establish in Bahrain an Arab shipbuilding and repair yard. The first drydock capable of servicing vessels up to 500,000 deadweight tons, designed as the first stage of the project, was completed in 1977.

Domestic Politics and Foreign Policy

Achievement of independence by Bahrain was preceded by diplomatic moves not free of international complications. The most important of these was the claim of Iran to sovereignty over the island. This matter had been lingering as an issue for many decades and occasionally assumed the proportions of a minor crisis. Iran's claim was based on a historical connection with Bahrain which dated back to Achaemenian times. Moreover, Iran maintained that in reality most of the Bahraini population was of Iranian stock, even if linguistically Arabized. In the modern period, Iran's assertion of her right to Bahrain took the form of a protest addressed to the League of Nations on November 22, 1927, as a reaction to Article VI of the British-Saudi treaty of May 20, 1927, in which reference was made to Bahrain as remaining under British protection.[8] Iranian protests were also addressed to the British and American governments between 1930 and 1933 in connection with the granting of the oil concession by the sheikh. A major move was made by Iran in 1957 when the Iranian government proclaimed Bahrain to be an integral part of Iran and assigned to it a few seats in the parliament—seats that, of course, remained vacant. The matter of Iran's claims became more pressing after Britain's announcement in 1968 of its intention to relinquish her imperial responsibilities in the gulf area. To resolve what promised to develop into a major international complication, the United Nations sent in 1970 a mission to ascertain the wishes of the Bahraini population in regard to their future. At the same time a British diplomat with long experience of service in the Persian Gulf, Sir William Luce, was engaged in protracted negotiations with the lower gulf states to explore the possibility of creating a federation. Upon completion of its work, the United Nations mission declared in the spring of 1970 that the broad consensus in Bahrain was to become independent rather than to be joined with Iran. In May 1970 the Iranian government accepted these findings and abandoned its claim to Bahrain on the condition that an independent Bahraini government would not enter into any alliances, unions, or federations. This Iranian attitude constituted an important factor in Bahrain's decision not to become a member of the federation which a few months later was formed under the name of United Arab Emirates.

Upon achievement of independence, Bahrain emerged as a patriarchal state in which the ruler (now assuming the title of Emir) still enjoyed absolute power limited merely by custom, religious law, and the principle of consultation. But Bahrain, with its population of nearly 250,000—the largest of all the lower gulf states—

---

[8]For details, see Fereydoun Adamiyat, *Bahrein Islands: A Legal and Diplomatic Study of the British-Iranian Controversy* (New York, 1955), pp. 184–203.

possessed an educated stratum more politically awakened than its counterparts in the neighboring states and more ambitious to participate in the political process. Furthermore, its largely urban working class was not only unionized but highly politicized and demanded its due share in the economy and politics of the country. In fact, Bahrain's workers, including those employed by Bapco and those in the two main urban centers of Manama and Muharraq, had a record of political militancy which, for example, during the 1956 Suez crisis resulted in riots and demonstrations. Similarly, the awakened class solidarity has led these workers on a number of occasions to go on strike as a result of economic grievances or in response to some international crisis affecting the Arab world at large. The internal political situation in Bahrain had moreover an additional complexity in the fact that more than half of its population was of Shia religious persuasion and that that part was economically underprivileged compared with the Sunni sector, from which most of the civil servants and government dignitaries were recruited.

It is no wonder that, under these circumstances, such ideologies as Nasser's Arab socialism or the socialism of the Baath Party found ready adherents in Bahrain. In the 1960s and 1970s the Arab Nationalist Movement (ANM) of George Habash (himself working from a base in Beirut but definitely displaying Pan-Arab ambitions) and the Aden-based Popular Front for the Liberation of the Occupied Arabian Gulf (PFLOAG) also found followers in Bahrain.

The existence and activity of these various dissident groups caused the successive rulers of Bahrain, Sheikh Salman Al Khalifa, and his successor, since 1971, Sheikh Isa Al Khalifa, to make certain concessions expressed by the formation of small advisory bodies. These changes however, were regarded as insufficient by the radical nationalists who demanded a full-fledged democracy. Eventually, conceding the these demands, Sheikh Isa agreed to the limitation of his powers which took the form of the constitution adopted on June 2, 1973. The constitution provided, among other things, for a free compulsory education and, characteristically, for the right to establish trade unions. On the basis of this new fundamental law the first Bahrain national assembly was elected in December 1973. It was composed of thirty members who serve a four-year term; a substantial segment among them could be regarded as standing in opposition to the government.

Adoption of the constitution and establishment of the parliament in Bahrain marked two important steps in the struggle between the democratic and the traditionalist principles of government in the Arabian Peninsula and the Persian Gulf. As the 1970s drew to a close, the outcome of this struggle was far from certain. Kuwait's experiment in constitutionalism was abruptly suspended in 1976; at the same time, Saudi Arabia, the largest and most important country in the area, clearly favored the continuation of the traditional Islamic form of government and viewed with considerable concern any deviation from this path by its smaller neighbors. On the other hand, an often Marxist-tinged militancy was characteristic of the South Yemen regime in Aden and of such offshoots as the PFLOAG. Politics in the gulf region, with Bahrain perhaps serving as a test case, were displaying a tendency toward polarization.

As a small and weak political entity, Bahrain was interested primarily in peace and survival. Its ruling Khalifa dynasty, which traced its origin to the noble Anaiza tribe (whose other offshoots were the House of Saud and the House of Sabah) made a point of maintaining close cordial relations with Saudi Arabia and Kuwait respectively. And, although officially neutral and following a policy of nonalignment, it shared with the West and the United States in particular its fear and dislike of communism and radical socialism. Consequently, it was natural that the rulers of Bahrain accepted, after World War II—with full British approval—the presence of a small United States naval force in their territorial waters and extended to it the necessary facilities. In the 1970s, however, radical pressures, both Pan-Arab and domestic, led the Bahrain government to give repeated notices of termination of these arrangements to the United States. Although the presence of this small force had no more than symbolic character for the United States, the American government was anxious to maintain this presence, particularly following Britain's withdrawal from the gulf with the attendant risk of a dangerous political vacuum. In pursuance of this policy, in September 1975 the United States raised its rent of the Bahraini naval facilities from $600,000 a year to $4 million a year. Nevertheless, the following month Bahrain declared that the facilities would be terminated as of mid-1977. Anxious to preserve its presence in the area, the United States government found itself in an extremely delicate position, particularly in view of the fact that, simultaneously, hearings were held in the United States Congress in a general political climate of opposition to the maintenance of American bases abroad. Eventually in the late 1970s the Middle East Force, as the group of three naval vessels was known, continued to ply the Persian Gulf waters and avail itself, under modified and face-saving arrangements, of certain minimal facilities in Bahrain.

Qatar

The sheikhdom of Qatar attained independence on September 1, 1971, barely two weeks after Bahrain.[9] Like other newly emancipated Arab states in the area, it promptly was admitted to membership in the Arab League and, somewhat later, to the United Nations. Its membership in other regional or functional organizations included OPEC and OAPEC but these two preceded the actual achievement of independence.

In the period following World War II, Qatar was no more than a primitive desert area inhabited by some 20,000 people. And following the general pattern, it had been under British protection and tutelage since 1916 when its Ruler concluded a treaty with Great Britain, which contained the usual nonalienation and exclusivity clauses. The treaty was supplemented in 1934 by a new agreement further extending Britain's protection obligation.

The discovery of oil brought about substantial changes in Qatar's domestic and international situation. In 1934 a concession had been granted to Petroleum Development (Qatar) Ltd., an affiliate of the Iraq Petroleum Company. Oil was discovered in the Dukhan area and production began in 1949. An oil port was con-

---

[9]For relevant texts of the changing relationship with Great Britain, see Great Britain, *Treaty Series*, no. 4 (1972), cmd. 4850.

structed in Umm Said. In the 1960s another company, Shell, was brought in to develop Qatar's gas resources. Moreover, oil was found not only inland but also in the offshore areas. Qatar's production in the 1970s was around 500,000 barrels a day. At this rate, with substantial reserves of six billion barrels, Qatar could expect its oil to last for about sixty-five years as of 1977. And, as in the case of other gulf states, oil brought with it wealth to this rather bleak country, with revenues exceeding two billion dollars a year after the OPEC-sponsored quadrupling of oil prices in 1974.

The development of oil and ancillary industries required an increase in manpower. By the mid-1970s the population rose to 125,000, of whom two-thirds to four-fifths represented immigrant labor. This work force was largely composed of Iranians, Pakistanis, Indians, Baluchis, Pathans, and other Arab nationals. At the same time there thrived in Qatar an Iranian merchant community. The Qataris themselves possessed a ruling elite composed of the princely family, high government officials, religious leaders, and wealthy merchants, among whom Abdullah Darwish established a veritable commercial empire of his own.

The ruling Thani family was very large (about 500 members); it controlled most of the important offices in the state, both during the British period and since independence. A moderate sized army, partly composed of Bedouin mercenaries from the mainland of Arabia, and a police force constituted the military props of the regime, while numerous retainers and servants together with the existing officialdom provided another group with a definite stake in the stability and preservation of the regime. The virtual lack of a native working class provided a contrast with Bahrain and was, in all likelihood, responsible for the absence of major political tensions associated with class cleavages. These cleavages existed, of course, but the labor force, being largely foreign, insecure, and liable to be deported at the slightest show of discontent, kept a low profile and concentrated on work and saving to assist their families in their respective native countries.

Under these circumstances the stability of the paternalistic regime was fairly assured and the rare strike that occurred among the oil workers was not likely to shake its foundations. The only practical possibility of political turmoil might stem from the divisions in the large princely family. In recent decades the ruling family was divided into three main branches: Bani Hamad, Bani Ali, and Bani Khalid. Between 1960 and 1972, Qatar was ruled by Sheikh Ahmed ben Ali Al Thani. Not overly interested in the practical aspects of government, Sheikh Ahmed tended to absent himself from the country on lengthy vacations in Europe or Iran. His easygoing attitude toward the affairs of state was perhaps best exemplified in that he chose to be on vacation in Switzerland when the independence of Qatar was proclaimed. This particular act of neglect might have been the decisive factor in his downfall. On February 22, 1972, he was overthrown, while vacationing in Iran, by his first cousin, Sheikh Khalifa ben Hamad, who was proclaimed Emir. Sheikh Khalifa had considerable experience in the administration, serving in a number of responsible government and cabinet positions. He soon established himself as a man of energy and practical aptitudes. Tremendous wealth accruing to the country from the oil revenue was politically most useful because it permitted the ruler and his close associates to allocate the wealth in such a way as to satisfy all potentially dissident groups in the country, including the rival branches of the princely family. Under Sheikh Khalifa's rule Qatar underwent in the 1970s a slow and prudent process of adaptation to modern times without abandoning its traditional political structure. Officially, Qatar has possessed a constitution since 1968 but it remained largely a paper document and as of the late 1970s the assembly provided by the constitution had not been elected. Being, like their Saudi neighbors, of Wahhabi fundamentalist persuasion, the ruling family favored the reaffirmation of Islamic laws and principles in public and private life, expressed for example in the ban on the importation, manufacture, and consumption of alcohol. Permission to open movie theaters (with an eye to satisfying the foreign expatriate community) was somewhat reluctantly granted only in 1970.

In its foreign relations Qatar tended to keep a low profile, anxious as it was to maintain peace with all its neighbors. Its closest relations were with Saudi Arabia, a sister Wahhabi country with whose House of Saud the Al Thanis maintained a cordial and respectful relationship. Similarly good feelings characterized Qatar's relations with Iran. For some time in the period following World War II, Qatar and Saudi Arabia disagreed on the delimitation of their mutual boundary, the Saudis laying a claim to the stretch of territory at the base of the Qatar peninsula. This matter, however, was resolved amiably by 1965, in favor of Qatar.

A more fundamental strain characterized relations between Qatar and Bahrain. The Bahraini ruling Al Kahlifa dynasty which intitially had come to Bahrain from Qatar never ceased to consider the House of Thani as usurpers. Particularly the north Qatari village of Zubarah, home of the Khalifas before their conquest of Bahrain, provided a bone of contention, the Khalifas claiming the right of jurisdiction over it. Furthermore, there was a standing disagreement about the ownership of the Hawar island close to the west coast of Qatar. Territorial disputes have also, at one time or another, clouded the relations between Qatar and its eastern neighbor, Abu Dhabi. Some of these disputes were resolved successfully, for example by recognizing Qatari sovereignty over the island of Halul and by reaching an agreement on the joint title to certain offshore oil-bearing areas.

As a cash-rich country, particularly in the 1970s, Qatar found itself catapulted into the Pan-Arab arena and began to be solicited by various Arab quarters for contributions to worthy causes. It responded positively to a number of such requests and became a member of the Gulf Organization for the Development of Egypt (GODE), which in the mid-1970s undertook to extend major financial assistance to Egypt (the other three members were Saudi Arabia, Kuwait, and the United Arab Emirates).

In the wider international arena, Qatar maintained close relations with its erstwhile patron, Great Britain, whose officers and experts continued to serve in certain executive and advisory capacities in the Qatari government while the former British Political Agency was transformed into an embassy. Similarly, a resident American ambassador was appointed to represent the United States in the capital city of Doha. Although less vocal than Saudi Arabia on ideological issues, the Qatar government followed the Saudi example in refusing to establish diplomatic relations with the Soviet Union.

The United Arab Emirates

Independence of the the United Arab Emirates was proclaimed on December 2, 1971. On the same day the newly formed federation entered into a treaty of friendship with Great Britain.[10] At the same time it adopted a provisional constitution. The federation was composed of seven states: Abu Dhabi, Dubai, Sharja, Ajman, Umm el-Qaiwain, Fujaira, and Ras el-Khaima. Initially, only the first six signed the act of federation, but by February 1972, Ras el-Khaima also adhered.

Historically known as the Pirate Coast, Trucial Coast, or Trucial Oman, this area remained through most of the nineteenth century under British tutelage. Great Britain extended control over it through the treaties of 1820, 1835, and 1953, directed at the maintenance of peace and suppression of piracy. These were further followed by the treaties of 1869 and 1892 establishing British control over foreign relations of the local chiefs and providing for the usual nonalienation and exclusivity clauses with special reference to the pearling industry and oil concessions. As in the case of other Gulf states, the area was under the supervision of the government of India which was represented by an official with the title of Political Officer, Trucial Coast, responsible to the British Resident in the Persian Gulf. An effective instrument of British control was a small military force, the Trucial Oman Scouts under the command of British officers.

The seven states comprising the U.A.E. are unequal in size, population, development, and wealth. Two of them stand out: Abu Dhabi, with a territory larger than all six others taken together, with the largest population and the greatest wealth. It is followed by Dubai, a state with a merchant tradition, a sophisticated upper stratum with a somewhat cosmopolitan outlook, and fairly close links to Iran. Oil was discovered in 1959 in Abu Dhabi and in 1966 in Dubai. The third discovery occurred in 1972 in Sharja, which joined the other two states to form an elite group within the federation. The remaining oil-less states have largely to rely on subsistence economy and in some cases are no more than small fishing villages. During the period of British control, which largely corresponded to the pre-oil era, all seven states were treated as equals. With the advent of independence and formation of the federation, as well as under the impact of the new oil-generated wealth, a substantial change occurred. The three oil-rich states, particularly Abu Dhabi and Dubai, emerged as dominant while the smaller and poorer sheikhdoms had to accept a subordinate position and to rely increasingly on the good will and generosity of the richer neighbors. As in many other areas around the gulf, discovery of oil proved to be decisive in the destinies and development of this region. Somewhat in contrast to other gulf states, however, concessions in Abu Dhabi, Dubai, and Sharja had been granted to a variety of foreign companies rather than to a few rich worldwide

[10]Text in Great Britain, *Treaty Series,* no. 34 (1972), cmd. 4941.

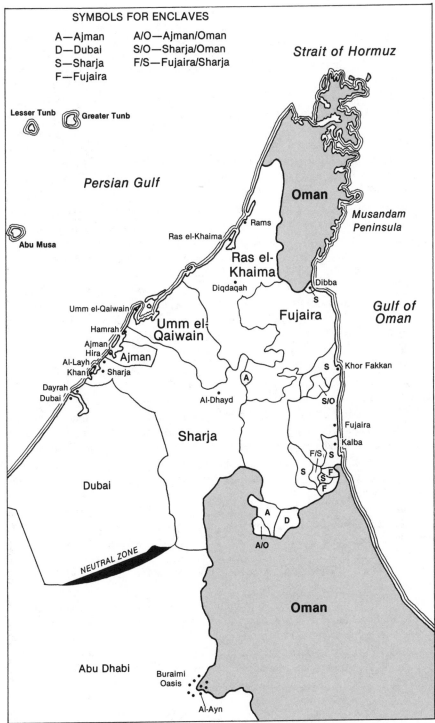

SYMBOLS FOR ENCLAVES

A—Ajman   A/O—Ajman/Oman
D—Dubai   S/O—Sharja/Oman
S—Sharja   F/S—Fujaira/Sharja
F—Fujaira

Strait of Hormuz

Lesser Tunb   Greater Tunb

Persian Gulf

Oman

Musandam Peninsula

Abu Musa

• Rams

Ras el-Khaima

Ras el-Khaima

• Diqdaqah

• Dibba
S

Fujaira

Gulf of Oman

Umm el-Qaiwain

Umm el-Qaiwain

Hamrah

Ajman
Hira
Al-Layh
Khan   • Sharja

Ajman

A

S   • Khor Fakkan

S/O

Dayrah
Dubai •

• Al-Dhayd

• Fujaira

Kalba

Sharja

F/S   S
S
S F
F

Dubai

A   D

NEUTRAL ZONE

A/O

Oman

Abu Dhabi

Buraimi
Oasis

• Al-Ayn

Map 10. United Arab Emirates: subdivisions.

established ones. The area proved very rich in oil indeed. As of 1977 its total reserves were estimated at close to 35 billion barrels, virtually equal to the reserves of Iraq. Of this figure, Abu Dhabi alone accounted for 30 billion barrels. Since the beginning of commercial production and export in the early 1960s, production volume was increasing by leaps and bounds to reach, by 1977, 2 million barrels a day. At this rate of production the reserves should last at least fifty-five-years. Correspondingly, beginning with the mid-1970s, the U.A.E. revenues reached a level of around $6 billion a year. Thus, within a decade, the hitherto primitive and neglected area had emerged as a member of the big league of oil producers and, together with Saudi Arabia, Kuwait, and Qatar, joined the GODE.

Great influx of wealth produced two inevitable results: on the one hand, the population of the sheikhdoms rose almost tenfold within less than twenty years. To illustrate this trend, suffice it to say that while in 1968 the total population of the Trucial Coast was estimated at about 179,000, by 1975 a census showed a figure exceeding 655,000 for the entire U.A.E. This total was composed of the following figures: Abu Dhabi, 236,000; Dubai, 207,000; Sharja, 90,000; Ras el-Khaima, 57,000; Fujaira, 26,000; Ajman, 22,000; Umm el-Qaiwain, 17,000. It was characteristic that not only did the population of oil-rich states leap forward in a spectacular way, but also such a miniscule entity as Ajman, whose population a decade earlier was merely 4,000, saw it increasing to 22,000.

The other result of the new oil riches was an intensification of economic activity aiming at the building of an infrastructure and general development. Ports (including the largest one in the region in Dubai), airports, roads, hotels, schools, and hospitals began to be built rapidly. They were accompanied by a moderate process of industrialization in the form of newly constructed refineries and cement and aluminum plants. The United Arab Emirates became a sort of modern El Dorado for people anxious to amass quick fortunes, and even with its prodigious spending the federation still could lay aside large surpluses. At the same time, the pattern of ownership of the existing oil enterprises underwent changes similar to those occurring in the neighboring states: the original oil concessions became modified by allowing the governments of Abu Dhabi, Dubai, and Sharja to acquire steadily increasing ownership shares and, in some cases, notably in the sector of gas, in Abu Dhabi, decrees were issued providing for national ownership of any discovered resources. The U.A.E. became a member of the OPEC and OAPEC and its oil minister, Mana el-Said Otaiba, soon established himself as an internationally known figure.

According to the provisional constitution adopted in December 1971, the U.A.E. is a federation headed by a president and endowed with three main state organs: the supreme council composed of the seven rulers of member states, the national assembly of thirty-four members representing the member states in proportion to their population, and the council of ministers or cabinet, in which rulers and members of their families serve alongside the commoners.[11]

---

[11]For details see J. D. Anthony, "Union of Arab Amirates," *Middle East Journal*, 26, no. 3 (Summer 1974). Text of the constitution, *ibid*.

The provisional constitution, the life of which was extended for another five-year period at the end of 1976, has made it possible for elected incumbents to be reelected and thus, in practice, to ensure the domination of the federation by the rulers of its three most important states. Following the proclamation of independence, the ruler of Abu Dhabi, Sheikh Zaid ben Sultan Al Nuhayyan, was elected president of the federation for a five-year term and was reelected for another term by the supreme council following a resolution of the national assembly that he should continue in power. The vice presidency was entrusted to the ruler of Dubai, Sheikh Rashed ben Said Al Maktum (also reelected in 1976). In turn, Sheikh Rashed's son, Sheikh Maktum ben Rashed Al Maktum, became prime minister while the son of the president, Sheikh Khalifa ben Zaid Al Nuhayyan, became deputy prime minister. These two leading states further reserved for themselves control, through members of their ruling families, of the ministries of finance, interior, and defense. Other cabinet posts were given to representatives of the lesser states of the federation.

Internal politics in the U.A.E. had basically a dynastic character. On the one hand a degree of rivalry existed in the relations among the rulers of the various federation states, which was in turn punctuated by occasional territorial disputes. However, common interest in mutual collaboration to safeguard the new independent status and preserve the essentially traditional and paternalistic type of government appeared to exercise a moderating influence, and the disputes were never allowed to degenerate into major confrontations or violence. On the other hand, each state had its own internal pattern of politics which, in contrast to the intrafederal relations, occasionally resulted in a violent crisis. In this respect there is no doubt that the withdrawal of British tutelage was reflected in somewhat lesser internal stability of individual states. An example of this was provided in January 1972 in Sharja. The former ruler of that state, Sheikh Saqr Al Qasimi, who had been previously deposed in 1965, decided to regain his lost position and with the aid of a group of armed retainers seized the incumbent ruler's palace while capturing him as a hostage. Saqr's triumph, however, was short-lived because the palace was promptly surrounded by forces faithful to the ruling Sheikh Khalid, and soon the rebellious group was obliged to surrender. However, Sheikh Khalid was killed in the fighting and was succeeded by his brother, Sheikh Sultan Al Qasimi, who had led a rescue force. It was worth noting that Sheikh Sultan was recognized as ruler of Sharja by Sheikh Zaid Al Nuhayyan, president of the U.A.E., even before his official proclamation as ruler in Sharja. This incident could be interpreted as indicating that the power of the federal authorities was on the increase.

The U.A.E.'s foreign policy centered primarily around its relations with Iran and Saudi Arabia. Iran's occupation of the islands of Greater and Lesser Tunb and Abu Musa on November 30, 1971, two days before the relinquishment of British rule over the Trucial Coast, introduced an understandable complication in the relations between the newly created U.A.E. and Teheran. It should be pointed out that while the Tunb islands were captured by Iran over protests and resistance of Ras el-Khaima, Abu Musa became the subject of an agreement whereby Iran would retain military control while Sharja would continue civil administration in the island;

moreover, the two countries agreed to share equally any revenues that might derive from oil on or around the island should it be discovered. Despite this crisis the newly formed U.A.E. federal authorities did not consider it opportune to intervene—which was one of the reasons why Ras el-Khaima delayed its decision to join the federation. In addition, Iran had been suspicious of the federation schemes when they were being negotiated under British auspices among the Coast rulers. Iran suspected that the creation of a federation might impede its own efforts to extend its influence in the region following British withdrawal. However, the prudent behavior of the newly formed federal government led to the establishment of normal relations between the U.A.E. and Iran.

Saudi Arabia had also had misgivings about the federation both when it was being negotiated and also in its early infancy. Over a period of time prior to U.A.E.'s independence the Saudis had established a certain pattern of relationships with individual Trucial Coast states; in many cases this relationship was of a patron-client type. A change toward political consolidation in the area might upset this pattern, although on the other hand, the Saudis were not averse to the idea that a federation might serve as a better bulwark against the inroads of radicalism in the Persian Gulf. The most immediate reason, however, for the Saudi reluctance to give early recognition to the U.A.E. was their territorial dispute with the largest of its states, Abu Dhabi, over the Buraimi oasis and the Saudi claim to a corridor linking their territory with the gulf east of the Qatar peninsula. Finally, after two and a half years, on July 30, 1974, Saudi Arabia and Abu Dhabi settled their dispute by agreeing that a part of the Buraimi oasis then under the Abu Dhabi administration (the other part being under the jurisdiction of Oman) should be recognized as an integral part of the Abu Dhabi territory, in return for which Saudi Arabia would receive access to the gulf east of Qatar in the Khor el-Udaid area. Moreover, the Zararah (Shaiba) oil field located in the Abu Dhabi-Saudi borderland should be divided. Having achieved this agreement, Saudi Arabia extended recognition to the United Arab Emirates and their mutual relations became fully normalized.

Oman

Oman is the only country among the states of the Persian Gulf with a tradition of independence dating back several centuries. It qualifies to be included within the Persian Gulf area by virtue of its possession of the Musandam peninsula, which juts northward at the eastern end of the Arab coast of the gulf, thus separating the Persian Gulf itself from the Gulf of Oman. The Musandam peninsula is separated from the main body of Omani territory by the possessions of several minor gulf states.

Long known as Muscat-Oman, the country found itself under Portuguese occupation between 1508 and 1650. In 1650 Arab tribes expelled the Portuguese. Arab rule suffered a setback in 1741 with an Iranian invasion but Iran's occupation lasted for only three years. Beginning in 1744, Muscat-Oman emerged as an independent country under the Al Bu Said dynasty. During the rule of Imam Saud ben Sultan (1804–1856), Oman extended its dominions to the east African coast, placing

Zanzibar under its rule. In fact, the capital of the country was moved to Zanzibar. After Saud's death, however, the dominions of Muscat and Zanzibar separated and two different lines of the Al Bu Said dynasty established themselves.

The ruling dynasty follows the Ibadhi sect of Islam, an offshoot of the Kharijite group of dissenters in the first century of the Islamic era. Followers of this sect deny legitimacy to the succession of caliphs except for the first two. In principle, they are in favor of an elective imamate. In practice the Al Bu Said family observed the custom of dynastic succession.

It was under the rule of Saud ben Sultan, a strong and progressive leader, that Muscat-Oman entered into relations with a number of foreign countries. In 1833 it signed a treaty of friendship with the United States, whereby the right of capitulations (that is, jurisdictional immunity) was extended to American citizens. Six years later Oman concluded a treaty with Great Britain providing for exchange of consular representatives. (This treaty followed earlier friendship agreements of 1798 and 1800.) France and the Netherlands were the two other foreign countries to enter into treaty relations with the sultan in 1844 and 1877, respectively. Upon achievement of independence in 1947, India also entered into treaty relations with Muscat.

Of all these foreign states, Britain developed a preponderant position but her relationship to Oman was never formalized in the form of a protectorate resembling her tutelage of the other gulf states.[12] To differentiate Oman's special position, the British representative in Muscat bore the title of consul general. However, British officials served in high government positions under various rulers in Muscat, including the long rule of Sultan Said ben Taimur (1932–1970). Not only did the British serve as commanders of the sultan's army and ministers of foreign affairs, but the Royal Air Force was granted the right to establish bases on the island of Masira and in other mainland localities.

A large country, Oman contains four distinct provinces, separated from each other by political boundaries or natural obstacles. In addition to the earlier mentioned Musandam peninsula, Oman includes a coastal plain facing the Gulf of Oman and the Arabian Sea, the so-called Inner Oman located to the west of the Green Mountains (Jabal el-Akhdar) merging into the sandy expanse of Rub el-Khali desert, and a separate dependency of Dhofar stretching along the southern coast of Arabia as far as South Yemen (formerly the Aden Protectorate). Similarly, Oman's population is diverse: it includes Arabs of Ibadhi and other Islamic persuasions, and a number of non-Arab nationalities, particularly in the eastern urban centers of Muscat and Matrah, where the majority of the population is Indian and Baluchi, with a small Arab ruling group above them. Muscat had always faced eastward and Indian influences on it have always been strong, as attested by the fact that Sultan Said ben Taimur was partly educated in India.

Oman's government had until recently followed a patriarchal principle. In the 1950s and 1960s, when the rest of the Arab world was being exposed to ideas of

[12]On December 20, 1951, Britain and Oman concluded a treaty of friendship with a simultaneous exchange of letters, by virtue of which British citizens and British protected persons were to enjoy immunity from local jurisdiction in criminal cases and civil matters. This agreement thus embodied the ancient principle of capitulations. Text in Great Britain, *Treaty Series*, no. 44 (1952), cmd. 8633.

progress, socialism, and Pan-Arabism, Oman remained rather effectively isolated and the not-so-benevolent rule of Said ben Taimur was characterized by backward traditionalism and a good deal of harshness. The country could not boast of any educational system except the basic religious instruction, had no hospitals except a clinic maintained by the Dutch Reformed Mission, and such elements of economic infrastructure as roads and modern communications and sanitary facilities were virtually nonexistent. There were also wide discrepancies in the economic level of its widely scattered regions. With the exception of a narrow belt of cultivable land on the Batinah coast north of Muscat and a few cultivable valleys in the mountains, the country in its eastern central and northern parts was bleak and arid and provided a bare subsistence to its inhabitants. A major exception was the Dhofar province, whose coast and the mountain ranges beyond were exposed to seasonal monsoon rains making the country green with abundant vegetation. Moreover, Dhofar was also blessed with waters rich in fish and it traditionally produced and exported seafood, including sardines, in considerable quantities. Its only drawback was that its main and attractive city of Salalah—home of a British air base until the late 1970s—did not possess a good harbor in contrast to the excellent natural harbors of Muscat and Matrah.

The Question of Inner Oman

The population of Inner Oman—the province west of the Jabal el-Akhdar—was noted for its strict adherence to the Ibadhi principles of Islam. In 1913 these interior tribes challenged the authority of the sultan in Muscat and elected their own Imam, who established himself in the mountain locality of Nizwa. Inasmuch as the then ruling Sultan Taimur ben Faisal had not enough strength to subdue the dissident tribes, an agreement called the Treaty of Sib (a coastal town north of Matrah) was concluded between him and Isa ben Saleh, leader of the dissident tribes, in 1920.[13] It provided for peace, free movement of persons between the interior and the coast, limitation of customs duties, and noninterference by the government of the sultan in the internal affairs of the signatory tribes. Subsequently, for the next thirty-five years relations between the sultan's government and the Imam of Inner Oman, Mohammed ben Abdullah el-Khalili, remained friendly and free of serious frictions. A major change occurred in 1954 when, under Imam Mohammed's successor, Ghaleb ben Ali el-Harithi, the Inner Oman tribes rose again in rebellion against the sultan of Muscat. Perhaps encouraged by the fact that since 1952 considerable tension existed between Saudi Arabia on the one hand and Abu Dhabi and Oman on the other, Imam Ghaleb established direct contact with Saudi Arabia, seeking its assistance in his struggle. By the end of 1955, however, the forces of Sultan Said ben Taimur entered Inner Oman and reestablished the sultan's authority in its main centers such as Nizwa, Adam, and Ibri. The rebellious Imam was allowed to live in retirement. However, his brother, Taleb ben Ali el-Harithi, fled to Saudi Arabia

---

[13]Text in *The Status of Oman and the British Omanite Dispute* (New York: Arab Information Center, 1957), Annex I.

and, in due course, found his way to Cairo where, under friendly Egyptian protection, he established an Oman imamate office from which he conducted an ambitious propaganda campaign. His appeals to the member states of the Arab League as well as to the United Nations were based on the assertion that by the Treaty of Sib of 1920 the sultan of Muscat had recognized Inner Oman's independence. The sultan's view, by contrast, was that the Treaty of Sib was a document pertaining to the internal affairs of his state. In the summer of 1957 Taleb returned to Oman to lead a second rebellion against the sultan's rule. He was joined by his brother, Imam Ghaleb, as well as by an important tribal leader in Jabal el-Akhdar, Suleiman ben Himyar. After desultory fighting that lasted for about twenty months, the sultan's forces finally succeeded in reestablishing his authority over Inner Oman. The rebel leaders sought refuge in Saudi Arabia, where they remained as honored guests of the king. By that time, however, the Saudi government had lost interest in actively supporting their cause. As a political issue, the matter dragged on through the mid-1960s. An attempt, in 1961, by some Arab countries to secure a United Nations resolution in favor of independence of Inner Oman failed to get the necessary majority of votes. And in 1963 a specially appointed UN commission of inquiry rejected the exiled Imam's charges of oppression practiced by the sultan's government. However, in 1965 a UN committee recommended that the British should "phase out" their domination in Oman.

A New Era under Sultan Qabus

The Inner Omanis' charge of oppression was probably not wholly without justification although it is not certain whether they in particular were the selected victims of discrimination. The entire system of government was medieval and retrograde regardless of the province to which it extended. Sultan Said ben Taimur led a secluded and virtually isolated life, oblivious to the changes taking place around him. Even the discovery of oil in 1963 (mostly in Inner Oman) and the sizable increase in the revenues of state had no effect on the sultan's reluctance to engage in the development and modernization of the country. In the meantime Oman's oil production, begun in 1967, was steadily increasing to attain, by 1977, the figure of about 350,000 barrels a day. With its oil reserves estimated at six billion barrels (equal in size to those of Qatar), Oman could look forward to long years of high revenue and development if it chose.

Sultan Said's failure to respond to these opportunities led on July 24, 1970, to a palace coup carried out by his son, Qabus ben Said, who was proclaimed sultan in his father's place. Upon his accession to the throne, Qabus, a man of about thirty, announced an ambitious program of reform and modernization. He also launched a policy of reopening broad contacts with the outside world, including the community of Arab nations. Qabus paid state visits to many foreign capitals and, in turn, received in his capital many heads of state, including those of Iran, Saudi Arabia, Egypt, Yemen, and others.

Unfortunately, his father's traditionalist attitudes and oppressive policies had caused a new wave of violent discontent, this time centered on the province of

Dhofar. Profiting from the topographical features of the area favorable to guerilla warfare, the Dhofari rebels gradually assumed control of a number of strategic points in the western parts of Dhofar. Appearing under various names, including the Dhofar Liberation Front, and merging with or cooperating with the Popular Front for the Liberation of the Occupied Arabian Gulf (PFLOAG), the rebels received encouragement and assistance from South Yemen while some members of their movement benefited from training provided by Communist China and the Soviet Union. On certain occasions Cuban fighters and advisers, dispatched from their base in Aden, joined in their activities.

The advent of Sultan Qabus caused some defection from the ranks of the rebels. The defectors were primarily those Omanis who believed that under the new government Oman could look forward to a brighter future and there was no need for violent resistance, especially one tinged with communist connections. Qabus did not hesitate to accept the services of such defectors and, in some cases, offered them high government positions.

Continuation of the rebellion, however, made it extremely difficult for the new sultan to engage in an orderly process of reform. First and foremost, order and security had to be restored to the entire area of the state. His British-officered forces, though enlarged and somewhat modernized, proved unequal to face alone a skillfully directed rebel warfare. The rebels moreover, had the advantage of being able in case of need to seek shelter by crossing the border into adjoining South Yemen. Although the sultan's forces did cross the border in the spring of 1972 in pursuit of the guerillas, Qabus was unwilling to engage in a major military confrontation with the well-armed and increasingly militant South Yemen. Under the circumstances, considering that the rebellion was not merely an internal affair of the state but had assumed international proportions, Qabus appealed to the Shah of Iran for military assistance. The Shah responded positively and in 1973 an Iranian expeditionary force was sent to Dhofar to fight the rebels. Similarly, the king of Jordan also lent military assistance, though on a lesser scale. Support, partly financial and partly diplomatic, came also from the United Arab Emirates, Saudi Arabia, Pakistan, and India, each of these countries anxious to see the independence and territorial integrity of Oman safeguarded. In the 1970s the Arab League made several attempts to bring about reconciliation between South Yemen and Oman. These endeavors generally encountered a negative attitude on the part of South Yemen. Toward the end of 1975 the competently organized counteroffensive against the rebels began to bear fruit. The rebels withdrew from their advanced positions and their pressure lessened to such an extent that in the winter of 1975–76 the Jordanian contingents helping the sultan could be withdrawn. By the end of 1976 the combined Omani and Iranian forces had succeeded in clearing Dhofar of rebel activities. Major roads were reopened and life in the main coastal and mountain centers returned to normal.

Both the Inner Oman rebellion of the 1950s and the Dhofar rebellion of the 1970s demonstrated the inadequacy of Oman's military establishment for maintaining order and defending the extensive areas of the sultanate. Under Qabus, the government made major efforts to increase and modernize its land, naval, and air forces. By 1976 the total armed forces grew to about 10,000 men, among whom there were some 600 foreigners serving on contract or on secondment. Moreover, the Dhofar warfare, involving as it did Marxist-oriented South Yemen with its close connections to the Communist bloc, contributed to the awakening of Western awareness of the strategic significance of the Indian Ocean. The leasing of naval facilities on Masirah Island by Sultan Qabus to the United States government in the 1970s provided further evidence of Washington's strategic interest in this area.

PART FIVE

Problems of
War and Peace

CHAPTER XVII

World War II and the Middle East

There was a considerable difference between the two World Wars in the Middle East. At the beginning of the first war most of the area formed part of the Ottoman Empire and the Allies had to conquer it in at least four military campaigns. When the second war broke out the Middle East was under the effective control of Great Britain and France either through mandates or through treaty arrangements with such semiemancipated countries as Egypt and Iraq. In two neutral states, Iran and Afghanistan, the Allies, using different methods in the two countries, succeeded in eliminating enemy influence. Turkey was the only truly independent major country in the Middle East, and she was the only one to preserve her neutrality.

Thus the Allies aimed at the preservation of the status quo in the Middle East and by virtue of their control of the area found their task easier than it had been during the First World War. The defense of the Middle East against the Axis received high priority in Britain, and this attitude found its reflection in the overall Allied war strategy. At one critical moment of the war, in the summer of 1942, the United States had to deplete its own reserves to rush more tanks to the Middle East.[1]

Military Operations

Because the Allies were in a relatively strong military position in the Middle East, actual fighting never occured in the heart of the area but was relegated to its fringes.[2] During World War I the Allies had fought campaigns in the Dardanelles, Mesopotamia, Palestine and Sinai, eastern Anatolia, and the Arab interior. During World War II the Axis attempted to conquer the Middle East by a pincer movement, with one arm stretching across Libya and another enveloping the area via the Caucasus. In both regions it came very close to success, but failed to reach the goal.

The Soviet campaign in the Caucasus was a separate affair, with no other Allies participating directly. Russia, of course, was receiving lend-lease aid and, more-

[1] Winston Churchill, *The Second World War* (Boston, 1950), IV, 388. This and other volumes by Britain's wartime prime minister contain many revealing chapters on the war in the Middle East.

[2] To the author's knowledge no complete history of the Middle Eastern operations during the Second World War has as yet appeared. Churchill's memoirs are probably the most authoritative source on various phases of the war in the Middle East. A number of books have been written by soldiers and newspapermen alike, but none of them is exhaustive on this subject. See the section on the Second World War in the Bibliography.

over, the British formed a rear defense line in northern Iraq with the aid of a Polish army corps in case the Caucasus was pierced by the Germans. The latter reached the farthest point of their offensive on November 19, 1942, occupying the north Caucasian oil areas up to Grozny, with only fifty miles between their front and the Caspian Sea. From that time onward they were in steady retreat.

Allied operations in the Libyan-Egyptian borderland were conducted by the British based on Egypt. It was a very mobile war, waged in three stages. In the winter of 1940–1941 (December to January) General Sir Archibald Wavell launched a rapid offensive against the Italians, who were in occupation of some border localities on the Egyptian coast, and succeeded in a brief and spectacular campaign in pushing the enemy back to El-Agheila, west of Benghazi. The British and Imperial troops captured 114,000 prisoners at a cost of 3,000 casualties. Wavell, however, overextended his lines of communication, which made it possible for combined Italo-German forces to mount a counteroffensive. Commanded by the able desert tactician General Erwin Rommel, the Axis troops drove the British all the way back to the Egyptian frontier. The British, weakened by the dispatch of 60,000 men to Greece, retreated without many casualties and managed to retain the Libyan fortress of Tobruk, which was encircled by the Axis.

Between May 29 and December 11, 1941, there was a lull in the operations, both parties preparing for a winter offensive. In December the British troops, commanded by General Sir Claude Auchinleck, launched their second offensive, during which they relieved Tobruk, captured Benghazi for the second time, but stopped short of El-Agheila (January 18, 1942). The German setbacks were largely due to a temporary depletion of their forces for the campaign in Russia. Reinforced, Rommel began a new drive into Egypt on May 27, 1942. In rather mysterious circumstances 25,000 South African troops quickly surrendered to him in Tobruk. The Germans shattered British armored formations at the battle of Knightsbridge, overcame valiant French resistance at Bir-Hakim, and drove deeply into Egyptian territory, reaching El-Alamein, only seventy miles from Alexandria.

A four months' lull followed during which Britain made her supreme effort to build up a powerful striking force between the seacoast and the Qattara depression. On October 23 the British Eighth Army under General Sir Bernard L. Montgomery began the third offensive, smashed the German line at El-Alamein, and drove Rommel back to Libya. Two weeks later, on November 8, 1942, an Anglo-American force commanded by General Dwight D. Eisenhower, made a successful landing in French North Africa. Later the Allied forces began relentlessly to pound at the Italo-German army from both east and west. On March 30, 1943, the British Eighth Army broke through the Mareth line into southern Tunisia, where it met the advanced detachments of the American Second Army Corps. By May 12 Axis resistance in North Africa had ended. Previous to that, between January and December 1941, British Imperial forces had liberated all Italian East African possessions (Ethiopia, Eritrea, and Somaliland).

Enemy air action over the British-held Middle East was not considerable, because the Axis tried not to antagonize the local population. The Axis concentrated on bombing Allied shipping and military objectives such as harbors, especially Alexandria, and the Suez Canal. Technically, the Canal was out of commission for only seventy-six days[3] during the entire war. But navigation in the Mediterranean and the Canal was very dangerous, and many convoys had to be directed by the roundabout route of the Cape. As to the other strategic waterway—the Turkish Straits—Turkey as a neutral kept them closed to Allied and Axis navies for the greater part of the war. This was one of the reasons why Russia and Britain were compelled to occupy Iran to secure a route for military supplies. But even assuming a pro-Ally stand by Turkey, the Straits would not have been too useful on account of Axis air bases in the Balkans.

Psychological Warfare

While the Allies were militarily supreme in the Middle East, their psychological position was much weaker. There was considerable anti-British feeling in a number of Arab countries, partly resulting from unfulfilled promises of independence and partly stimulated by skillful Axis propaganda.[4] This propaganda harped on the theme of liberation from British control, and it had many willing listeners. By contrast, British propaganda sounded rather unconvincing. British broadcasts depicting the horrors of the Nazi occupation in Europe with its attendant cruelties against the Jews left the Arabs skeptical and indifferent. Middle East experience with the Germans had generally been most satisfactory, and even educated Arabs or Iranians could not conceive of the Germans as anything but cultured, efficient and frequently more courteous than the colonial British. On the other hand, stories of cruelty were not likely to frighten the lower-class audience, which was apt to applaud German strength and the anti-Jewish exploits. If we add the fact that Axis propaganda was devoid of scruples and freely used the most fantastic lies as a weapon, while the Allies were restricted by certain inhibitions, we can clearly see that in this duel the Axis was able to score considerable success.

Despite all its efforts the Axis could not change the fact that British rule was not really oppressive—that, indeed, it was much more indirect and humane than any foreign rule the Arabs had known in the past. Every informed person knew that Britain did not levy tributes from the Arab states but often paid them subsidies; that she did not make requisitions but purchases for which she paid in cash; and that instead of exploiting the Middle Eastern states she enabled them to accumulate sizable sterling balances in London. Moreover, Britain and the United States assisted the Middle East to overcome wartime shortages through the Middle East Supply Center in Cairo. The Center, by its well-planned policy of allocations, averted many shortages and inconveniences.

The Arabs therefore did not have the same stake in the Second World War that they had in the First. Then they were trying to overthrow oppressive Ottoman rule, and to this end they were ready for many sacrifices. Now there was no such incentive, and all that the Arab governments really wanted was to reaffirm their independence, which they had to a considerable degree achieved prior to World War

---

[3]H. L. Hoskins, "The Guardianship of the Suez Canal," *Middle East Journal*, 4 (April 1950), p. 148.

[4]See Seth Arsenian, "Wartime Propaganda in the Middle East," *Middle East Journal*, 2 (Oct. 1948); and Nevill Barbour, "Broadcasting to the Arab World: Arabic Transmissions from the B.B.C. and Other Non-Arab Stations," *Middle East Journal*, 5 (Winter 1951).

II. Arab public opinion between 1939 and 1945 presented a combination of pro-German and neutral attitudes. There was, moreover, a widespread belief that the war was a conflict of the big powers and as such of no direct concern to the Arabs. This explains why there was relatively little anti-Ally unrest in the Middle East during the war. There were, true enough, three exceptions to this rule: the Rashid Ali rebellion in Iraq; the recalcitrant attitude of Iran prior to August 1941; and minor difficulties in Egypt resulting in the arrests of Aziz el-Masri and Ali Maher Pasha. But these manifestations could not be compared in their magnitude to the Arab Revolt of 1916. In this connection we may observe that Germany made a serious blunder by concentrating on the Arabs instead of on the Moslem peoples of the Soviet Union. There the ground was much more fertile for a popular uprising. The German Foreign Office knew it, and it tried to use the services of Haj Amin el-Husseini and of some Turkish Pan-Turanians, but its efforts were frustrated by the arrogant self-confidence of Nazi careerists from Rosenberg's *Ostministerium*.

Well-informed Arab statesmen realized the difference between British humanitarianism and Nazi brutality. But, precisely because of this, they were more anxious to ingratiate themselves with the Axis in case of an Axis victory than to prove their loyalty to the British. By the same token, Arab governments did not make their troops available to the Allies. The only exception was Emir Abdullah's Arab Legion of Transjordan. And much as the Arab leaders may have congratulated themselves on smartly staying out of the battlefields, they surely must have regretted that their armies were not stronger and more experienced when they had to face a test in Palestine in 1948.

Because the Allies had to defend the Middle East and not conquer it, they did not have the same opportunity as in World War I to incite subversion behind enemy lines. In the only area where such subversion was feasible, i.e., in Libya, the British made full use of the enmity existing between the Senussis and the Italian authorities. Exiled chiefs of the Senussis residing in Cairo were contacted, and assurances were given them that, in return for their aid to the Allies, Britain would support their independence and oppose the return of Italian rule.

The impact of the war on the Middle East was considerable. Politically the war accelerated the process of Arab emancipation which had begun a quarter of a century earlier. Syria and Lebanon gained full independence, while Iraq and Egypt secured Britain's consent to treaty revision. Indeed, one might say that as a result of the Second World War the Middle East changed position with eastern Europe. While the latter came under alien domination, the former won freedom. This is well reflected in the United Nations. Eastern European states are either not represented in the new world organization or, if represented, they act as mouthpieces of the Kremlin.[5] By contrast, all Middle Eastern and North African states have joined the organization and do not hesitate to use it as a platform for independent action, frequently in opposition to the big powers.

From the economic and social point of view the war had an unsettling effect.

---

[5]Three East European countries, Lithuania, Latvia, and Estonia, having been annexed by Russia and transformed into Soviet republics in 1940, are not represented in the United Nations.

Allied spending, war contracts, profiteering, and hoarding made some people rich, but they also caused inflation and resultant suffering on the part of the masses. Young members of the intelligentsia could not help comparing their own poverty and impotence with Western wealth and strength as exemplified by the Allied war effort. The prolonged presence of Allied armies on their soil added an element of antiforeign resentment to the already pronounced discontent and frustration. These pent-up feelings found their outlet in a powerful wave of nationalism as soon as the war was over. The intensity of these emotions made many nationalists reckless and blind to the hard strategic realities which make their part of the world vitally important to the big powers.

CHAPTER XVIII

The Middle East's
Strategic Waterways

Much of the strategic importance of the Middle East may be ascribed to its international waterways: the Turkish Straits, the Suez Canal, and the Straits of Hormuz and Bab el-Mandeb. Many political conflicts in this area have revolved around these narrow stretches of water. In fact, the Near Eastern question in the nineteenth century was essentially a rivalry on the part of the big powers for control of the Turkish Straits until the Isthmus of Suez was pierced by a canal in the latter part of the century. The canal put an end to the relative isolation of Egypt and inexorably linked that country with major world politics.

The economic significance of these waterways is obvious. Since time immemorial the Turkish Straits have been a vital trade route between the Black Sea shores and the Mediterranean. The prosperity of many a Mediterranean state, such as Genoa or Greece, has been largely dependent upon its ability to trade with the Black Sea hinterland. And, conversely, the Straits have played an increasingly important role in the foreign trade of Russia ever since the latter obtained an outlet to the Black Sea. The commercial significance of the opening of the Suez Canal, which replaced the old Cape route, is so obvious that it does not require elaboration.

The military importance of these waterways has always been considerable, and much military and naval planning of both World Wars revolved around these narrow passages. During World War II, Germany and Italy made a major effort to seize the Suez Canal, as their repeated offensives toward Egypt proved; and Britain was ready to make sacrifices in other war theaters to defend the canal. Meanwhile, the task of supplying the USSR with arms and equipment was complicated for the Allies by the closure of the Straits by Turkey and by German air bases in the Balkans. Today one may ask whether the development of aviation and modern weapons has not rendered these old plans and calculations obsolete. The ultimate answer must be reserved for the future, but the Second World War has demonstrated that nations could not be indifferent as to who was in actual control of the Turkish Straits and of the Suez Canal. And as for peacetime, it may safely be asserted that control of these waterways may prove decisive so far as the political independence of Turkey and the diplomatic alignment of Egypt are concerned.

The following sections will review and analyze pertinent facts of political interest concerning the Middle East's waterways, summing up what has been said in this volume and supplementing it with such information as may be necessary to present a unified picture of the problem.

The Turkish Straits

The Turkish Straits are composed of the Bosphorus in the northeast, the Dardanelles in the southwest, and the Sea of Marmara between them. Turkey's old capital and largest commercial center, Istanbul, is situated astride the Bosphorus. The Straits have served as the principal channel for Russia's trade with southern Europe, Asia, and Africa.

The strategic importance of the Straits to Russia matches their economic importance. Eleven hundred miles of Black Sea coast form part of Russia's southern boundary. It would be much easier for the Soviets to defend this boundary against external aggression if they were in control of the narrow bottleneck of the Turkish Straits leading into the Black Sea. And, conversely, should Russia have expansionist ambitions in the Mediterranean and the Middle East, control of the Straits would greatly enhance her chances of success.

Period of Undisputed Turkish Sovereignty

The problem of who should control the Straits has never been settled with absolute finality. The political history of the Straits abounds in "rules" and "principles" considered sacrosanct and called "universal" by those states which were able to force their acceptance under certain circumstances and which had a vested interest in maintaining the status quo. But wars and changes in power relationships often produced a change of rules and reversal of attitudes.[1] Like any other political institution, the status of the Straits has been and continues to be dependent upon the will and the ability of the states directly concerned to support it.

For three hundred years, from 1475 to 1774, the Black Sea was a Turkish lake, all its shores being under the full control of the Ottoman Empire. During that period the Ottoman government had an absolute monopoly of navigation in the Black Sea. Capitulatory rights granted to France and other countries frequently included freedom of passage through the Dardanelles so that foreign ships could reach Constantinople, but, with a brief exception in favor of Venice, none of these treaties ever extended this freedom to the Bosphorus and the Black Sea.

Russia's First Gains

The first major change in this situation occurred in 1774, when, at Kuchuk Kainardji, the Straits were opened to Russian merchant ships in time of peace. This coincided with the acquisition by Russia of a direct outlet to the Black Sea. Despite this major concession, freedom of shipping in the Straits, so far as other countries were concerned, still remained within Turkey's discretionary power. By a series of

[1] For a historical treatment of the subject, see James T. Shotwell and Francis Deák, *Turkey at the Straits: A Short History* (New York, 1941).

bilateral agreements Turkey eventually extended the freedom of passage to merchant ships of other countries, but this freedom was not yet accepted as a general principle of the public law of nations. As to foreign warships, no exception and no compromise were admitted as it was the "ancient rule of the Ottoman Empire" to exclude warships of every nation from entering the Straits. This rule, true enough, was time and again violated during the Napoleonic era, yet its validity remained unquestioned.

Russia's southward expansion throughout the nineteenth century was expressed, so far as the Straits were concerned, in attempts to obtain complete control of this waterway. To occupy and annex the region of the Straits would have been an ideal solution for Russia. Such an annexation would have meant partition and probably destruction of the Ottoman Empire, and Russia was aware that she could not obtain it short of a major war with other interested powers. The history of the Eastern question in the nineteenth century eloquently proves that, whenever Russia was on the threshold of fulfilling this ideal objective, she invariably ran into stiff opposition from Britain and other European powers, who, by concerted action, prevented her from attaining her goal.

From Unkiar Iskelessi to the First World War

Unable to solve the problem of the Straits to her best liking, Russia had to content herself with alternatives that could be achieved by diplomacy. Denied outright possession, Russia was interested in such regulation of the Straits as would most favor her needs. If the Straits were to remain outside her physical control, the second-best solution for Russia was to have a formal pledge that the guardian of the Straits (i.e., Turkey) would always keep the Straits open to Russian merchant and war vessels but that she would close them to non-Black Sea powers at Russia's will. This second-best solution Russia secured in the greatest triumph of her Near Eastern diplomacy, the Treaty of Unkiar Iskelessi in 1833. This arrangement was, needless to say, most undesirable from the British standpoint, and Britain lost no time or opportunity to effect a change in the control of the Straits. Such an opportunity came with the second act of Mohammed Ali's drama in 1839–1840. The resulting Treaty of London of 1840 and the Straits Convention of 1841 scrapped the preferential Unkiar Iskelessi arrangement and restored "the ancient rule of the Ottoman Empire" that the Straits must always be closed to foreign warships. The Straits Convention remained in force for the next eighty years as a basic law for the Straits and was raised to the dignity of the public law of Europe. It was confirmed by the Treaties of Paris in 1856, of London in 1871, and of Berlin in 1878. Its only minor modification occurred in 1871 when, by the above-mentioned Treaty of London, the sultan, hitherto obliged to keep the Straits closed to foreign warships, was given the right to open them in certain circumstances.

Thus, from 1841 until 1920, the principle of the closure of the Straits prevailed. This principle fitted well with the interests of Great Britain and certain other European powers, but not with those of Russia. It constituted an obvious obstacle to Russia's expansionist policy in the Near East, while, by the same token, it protected Britain's interests and communications in the eastern Mediterranean. There was, of course, nothing permanent in this situation. A strong Russia found the closure of the Straits a nuisance, but a weak Russia might find it beneficial. As things stood, however, in the nineteenth century Russia was or believed herself to be strong enough to prefer the open to the closed Straits. Rather naturally, her diplomacy reverted time and again to the precedent of Unkiar Iskelessi as the best solution short of actual domination of the Straits. This revisionism was particularly noticeable in the decade preceding the First World War, during which Russia made several attempts to secure a regime more to her liking. Yet, weakened as she was by the Japanese war and the revolution of 1905, she had to rely exclusively on diplomacy as she was unable in the twentieth century, in contrast to the nineteenth, to back up her demands by force. Negotiations with Britain in 1907, Austria in 1908, and Italy in 1909 aiming at the recognition of a preferential Russian position in the Straits did not bring the hoped-for results.

The Great War and the Peace Settlement

The so-called Constantinople agreement of 1915 by which the Entente powers agreed to Russian annexation of the Straits in case of victory in the war had already been discussed (Chapter II). This concession constituted a dramatic change in British and French policies, but its effects were nullified by the Bolshevik revolution and by the solemn renunciation by the Soviet government of the secret agreements.

The problem of the Straits came up at the time of the peace settlement, with a radical reversal in British (and Western) policy. Britain and her Western allies were then in a position to impose a solution independent of Russia's and Turkey's will because these two countries were kept out of the European councils in 1920. And the solution Britain chose was to declare, in the Treaty of Sèvres, the Straits open in time of peace and war to merchant and war shipping alike. This reversal stemmed from the radical change in power relationships. The new Russia was weak and, in British eyes, did not threaten the security of the eastern Mediterranean. Hence there was no point in insisting on the closure of the Straits. On the contrary, in view of increased British strength, it was advantageous to keep the Straits permanently open for the penetration of British and other Western fleets into the Black Sea, from which they could watch the movements of the new Soviet state and nip the danger in the bud should this state try to embark upon a revolutionary crusade beyond its borders.

True enough, the Treaty of Sèvres proved abortive owing to Turkey's nationalist resistance. But the new principle underlying control of the Straits remained valid in the postwar years and supplied the basis for the new regulations inscribed in the Treaty of Lausanne. Yet it was characteristic of the change in the political atmosphere between 1920 and 1923 that instead of being informed of the decisions taken in their absence, both Turkey and Soviet Russia were invited to take part in the discussions. The political configuration at the Lausanne conference was such that Britain and Russia appeared as the two main protagonists so far as the Straits were concerned. Russia desired to see the Straits closed, no doubt as a measure of protection against renewed Western intervention, and her chief delegate, Commissar Chicherin, desperately fought against the proposed international control of the Straits, defending the rights of Turkish sovereignty. Britain, by contrast, insisted on freedom of navigation and on international control (both principles incorporated in the Treaty of Sèvres), but she was willing to make concessions that would, to some extent, recognize Soviet security requirements and Turkish sensitivities.

Despite her friendship with Soviet Russia, Turkey did not entirely take the former's side. The Turks, who were very determined to have their way on many other points, were ready to accept emasculated international management of the Straits and, as to the problem whether the Straits should remain closed or open, they preferred to leave the matter to the big powers to fight over between themselves. To the Russians this Turkish halfheartedness was disappointing and, had Russia been stronger, Soviet-Turkish relations might have cooled appreciably. Because the weak Soviet state was interested in cultivating the good will of the guardian of the Straits, Turkey was spared Russian recriminations.

The Lausanne Convention

The result of these deliberations was new regulations adopted in the "Convention relating to the Straits" on July 24, 1923, the day of the signature of the principal Treaty of Lausanne. The main provisions were as follows:

Merchant ships. The principle of freedom of passage was affirmed in time of peace and war alike. The only exception applied when Turkey was at war: Turkey was then permitted to stop enemy ships but was not allowed to interfere with the free passage of neutral ships.

Warships. In peacetime, warships were allowed freedom of transit provided that the maximum force any *one* non-Black Sea power sent into the Black Sea did not exceed the most powerful Black Sea fleet. In any case, the nonriparian powers were each allowed to send into the Black Sea a force of not more than three ships, none to exceed 10,000 tons. In wartime, if Turkey remained neutral or nonbelligerent, the same principles were to apply as in time of peace. If Turkey was a belligerent, freedom of passage would apply to neutral ships only.

In addition, the region of the Straits was to be demilitarized and the Straits were to be subjected to the supervision (but not actual management) of the International Commission of the Straits composed of Turkey (president), France, Great Britain, Italy, Japan, Bulgaria, Greece, Rumania, Russia, Yugoslavia, and the United States (on adherence to the convention).[2]

The Montreux Convention

The Lausanne Straits Convention remained in force for thirteen years. On July 20, 1936, it was replaced by the Montreux Convention, which is still (1979) in force. The participants in the Montreux conference included the Soviet Union, which, as before, endeavored to reduce the freedom of the nonriparian states to enter the Black Sea. As at Lausanne, her main opponent was Britain, but the whole

[2]The Lausanne Convention, which had no termination date, was signed by the British Empire, France, Italy, Japan, Bulgaria, Greece, Rumania, Russia, Yugoslavia, and Turkey. Russia signed it on August 14, 1924, but did not ratify it. Its text may be found in *The Problem of the Turkish Straits* (Department of State, Pub. 2752, Near Eastern ser. 5, Washington, D.C., 1947).

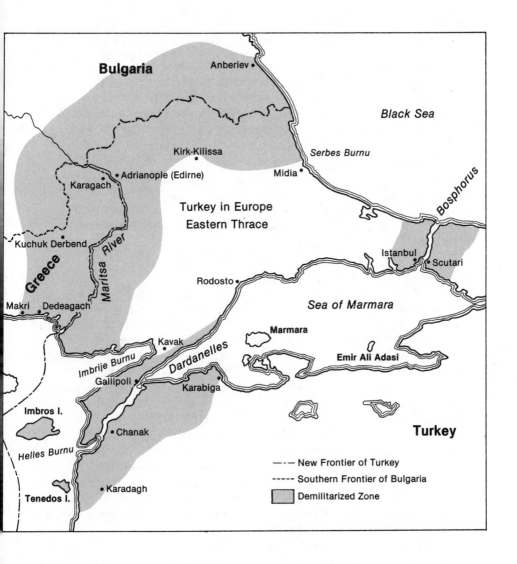

Bulgaria

Anberiev •

Black Sea

Kirk-Kilissa •

Serbes Burnu

Adrianople (Edirne) •

Midia •

Karagach •

Bosphorus

Turkey in Europe
Eastern Thrace

Kuchuk Derbend •

Istanbul

Greece

Maritsa River

Scutari •

Rodosto •

Makri • Dedeagach •

Sea of Marmara

Marmara

Kavak •

Imbrije Burnu

Dardanelles

Emir Ali Adasi

Gallipoli •

Karabiga •

Turkey

Imbros I.

• Chanak

Helles Burnu

—·— New Frontier of Turkey
----- Southern Frontier of Bulgaria
Demilitarized Zone

Tenedos I.

• Karadagh

Map 11. The Turkish Straits. The boundaries and demilitarized zones follow the provisions
of the Treaty of Lausanne, 1923.

atmosphere was perceptibly changed. Because of the rising German danger to European peace, Britain and France were willing to go rather far to accommodate Turkey and not to antagonize Russia, with whom rapprochement was being sought. As a result, both Turkey and Russia came out of the conference with tangible gains. Russia's gain consisted in a reduction in the maximum tonnage allowed in the Black Sea to nonriparian powers. This greater security was conditioned, however, on Turkey's good will inasmuch as Turkey was given much greater freedom of action in the Straits.

The Montreux Convention contained the following main provisions:

Merchant ships. In peacetime, the principle of freedom of passage was reaffirmed without a time limit. In wartime, if Turkey was neutral or nonbelligerent, complete freedom of passage was to apply. If Turkey was a belligerent, merchant vessels of countries not at war with Turkey were to enjoy freedom of passage on condition of not assisting the enemy. Should Turkey be threatened by war, freedom of passage was to apply as in peace except that ships must enter the Straits in daytime and follow the route prescribed by Turkish authorities.

Warships. In peacetime, the maximum tonnage of all foreign warships, whether riparian or nonriparian, in transit through the Straits was limited to 15,000 tons. The Black Sea powers, however, were permitted to send capital ships displacing more than 15,000 tons, provided they passed singly and were escorted by not more than two destroyers. In general, the aggregate tonnage of nonriparian powers in the Black Sea was not to exceed 30,000 tons, but this figure could be increased to 45,000 tons if the Soviet navy were to exceed by at least 10,000 tons its tonnage at the time of the signature of the convention. Warships of nonriparian powers must not stay longer than twenty-one days in the Black Sea.

In wartime, if Turkey remained neutral or nonbelligerent, freedom of passage as in peace was to apply to nonbelligerents only. Belligerents were not to pass the Straits except in cases of assistance rendered to a victim of aggression in virtue of a mutual assistance pact binding Turkey. Should Turkey become belligerent, she would acquire complete discretion as to the passage of warships through the Straits. Under a threat of war, Turkey was given the right to stop or let pass foreign warships at her discretion. Her decisions, however, were to be communicated to the signatories of the convention and to the Council of the League of Nations. A two-thirds majority of the Council, if upheld by a majority of the signatories, was permitted to reverse Turkey's decisions.

In addition to these main provisions the Montreux Convention abolished the International Straits Commission, restoring the jurisdiction to the Turkish government, and gave Turkey the right to remilitarize the Straits.[3]

The Situation during World War II

Turkey's nonbelligerency during the Second World War led her to pursue a cautious policy with regard to the Straits. Between 1939 and 1944 the Allies did not use the Straits for their supplies to Russia because unprotected merchant shipping

---

[3]For the text see *ibid*. The Montreux Convention was for twenty years. It was signed by Bulgaria, France, Great Britain, Greece, Japan, Rumania, Turkey, USSR, and Yugoslavia. Italy refused to participate in the discussions but acceded to the convention on May 2, 1938.

would have been exposed to annihilation by the enemy, and naval escorts were not practical inasmuch as Turkey would surely have prevented their passage. By the same token, the German and satellite navies were denied the use of the Straits except for a few fraudulent passages of minor importance.

All in all, Russia had no basis to complain about Turkey's attitude because Turkey proved a reliable and—as far as circumstances permitted—impartial guardian of the Straits. Earlier, in 1936—1938, Russia had used the Straits freely to send agents and supplies to Spain. During World War II, even in the darkest moments of Stalingrad, Turkey did not let Axis naval forces enter the Black Sea.[4] As soon as it was practically possible, i.e., in the fall of 1944, Turkey permitted the use of the Straits to armed or escorted ships carrying lend-lease supplies to Russia.

In the Soviet view, this dependence on Turkey did not square with the new Soviet concepts of security. These concepts, which led Russia to demand outright control of strategic approaches to her territory instead of leaving them in the hands of smaller sovereign nations, dictated a new policy toward the Straits. The first official demand for a revision of the Montreux Convention was made by the Soviet government in June 1943, and the matter was discussed at the Potsdam conference in the summer of 1945. There Russia obtained American and British consent to changing the convention, without specification, however, of the changes. It was also decided at Potsdam that the question of revision should first be explored through diplomatic channels with the Turkish government.

Postwar Attempts at Revision

The United States made the first constructive proposals concerning the contemplated revision. In a note to the Turkish government on November 2, 1945, the United States set forth the following principles for future control of the Straits: (1) the Straits were to be open to the merchant vessels of all nations at all times; (2) the Straits were to be open to the transit of the warships of Black Sea powers at all times; (3) save for an agreed tonnage in time of peace, passage through the Straits was to be denied to the warships of non-Black Sea powers at all times, except with the specific consent of the Black Sea powers or except when acting under the authority of the United Nations; and (4) certain changes were to be made to modernize the Montreux Convention, such as the substitution of the United Nations system for that of the League of Nations and the elimination of Japan as a signatory.

The contents of this note were communicated to the British and Soviet governments also. Soon afterward the British and Turkish governments expressed their agreement in principle with the American proposals. The Soviet government delayed its reply for about ten months. On August 7, 1946, it finally presented a detailed note to Ankara, transmitting copies to Washington and London. In the first part of the note Russia reminded Turkey of a number of incidents that had occurred in the Straits during the Second World War, namely, the passage through the Straits, in 1941, of the German patrol boat *Seefalke* and of the Italian auxiliary warship *Tarvisio;* the intended passage, in 1942, of 140,000 tons of auxiliary

---

[4]For an evaluation of Turkey's attitude, see Norman J. Padelford, "Solutions to the Problem of the Turkish Straits, A Brief Appraisal," *Middle East Journal,* April 1948. For a Turkish view of the problem, see Ahmed Sükrü Esmer, "The Straits: Crux of World Politics," *Foreign Affairs* (Jan. 1947).

German warships into the Black Sea; and the passage, in 1944, of eight German auxiliary warships of the *Ems* type and of five vessels of the *Kriegstransport* type. For this reason Russia believed that the Montreux Convention had not prevented the use of the Straits by hostile powers, that Turkey could not escape responsibility for these acts, and that the convention should be revised so as to "conform to present conditions." In the second part of the note the Soviet government proposed five principles to govern the Straits. Of the five, the first three were a virtual repetition of the first three principles suggested the previous year by the United States. The last two, however, were far beyond anything contemplated by the Western powers. In the fourth principle Russia proposed that "the establishment of a regime of the Straits . . . should come under the competence of Turkey and other Black Sea Powers," and in the fifth she asked that defense of the Straits should be shared jointly by Turkey and the Soviet Union.

The Soviet note set off a series of diplomatic communications among Moscow, Ankara, Washington, and London. In lengthy and detailed notes Turkey contested Soviet allegations concerning the passage of Axis war vessels through the Straits; admitted fraudulent passage of a few minor units under the guise of merchant vessels; and declared herself unable to accept Soviet proposals concerning the future administration and defense of the Straits. Russia replied in equally exhaustive statements, trying to prove Turkey's ill will or reprehensible negligence in handling these wartime incidents and insisting on her own proposals as the only solution capable of guaranteeing Soviet security. In her notes Russia more than once referred to the Black Sea as a *closed* sea. In this exchange of views Washington and London took Turkey's side, likewise refusing to accept the fourth and fifth Soviet proposals.[5]

Appraisal of the Big Powers' Proposals

In order fully to understand this Turko-Soviet duel, we must realize that, in setting forth its own suggestions in November 1945, the United States had gone far to meet the Soviet craving for increased security. A close analysis of the American proposals will show that, in their essence, they gave Russia something very similar to the conspicuously preferential treatment she received in the Treaty of Unkiar Iskelessi, back in 1833. In both cases Russia was to have complete freedom to send her warships into the Mediterranean, while this freedom was to be denied the Western powers. The Unkiar Iskelessi deal had aroused much furor and hostility in the security-conscious Britain of the 1830s. And yet, in 1945, when Russia was emerging as a military and industrial colossus dominating two-thirds of Europe and the whole of northern Asia, Washington and London, anxious for and trustful of Soviet friendship, were ready, on their own initiative, to give Moscow what a hundred years earlier had brought Russia and the West to the brink of war. Seldom, indeed, have the annals of diplomacy revealed a greater desire for peace almost at any price on the part of powerful and victorious nations. The American proposal was made essentially in the spirit of Yalta, with the obvious intention of satisfying

---

[5] For the relevant texts, see *The Problem of the Turkish Straits*.

and accommodating the Soviet Union and with little regard to strategic considerations of Western security. But, as at Yalta, this was not enough for Russia, who, rejecting compromises, renewed the ancient tsarist claim for the possession or military domination of the Straits. This was, in reality, what the Soviet demand for the "joint defense" of the Straits meant. But to the West, in the awakened political realism of 1946, this solution was inacceptable. A continuation of diplomatic exchanges among the four capitals added little to the basic positions taken in late 1946. In fact, Russia's insistence on acceptance of her demands, coupled as it was with other expansionist moves all along her periphery, produced results opposite to those expected by Moscow. By 1950 it was clear not only that the fourth and fifth of the original Soviet proposals stood no chance of acceptance by the West, but that it would be hard to expect the West to stick to its own original principles in view of the deterioration of international security. Under these circumstances no surprise was registered in the West when, on April, 27, 1950, Turkey "finally and conclusively" rejected Moscow proposals for joint Soviet-Turkish control of the Straits. With this act any further debate on revision of the Montreux Convention seemed to be closed for the foreseeable future.

Ankara's firm resistance to Soviet demands, this time clearly enjoying Western support, and the subsequent admission of Turkey to the North Atlantic Treaty Alliance apparently persuaded Moscow that it was useless to pursue the subject of revision any further. Moreover, Stalin died in March 1953 and Soviet policy, though still based on an ideological foundation and still expansionist, lost some of the direct and crude aggressiveness that was so characteristic of its daily operations during the Stalin era. On May 30, 1953, in a communication to the Turkish ambassador in Moscow, Foreign Minister Molotov declared that the Soviet Union had "no territorial claims on Turkey" and specifically mentioned the Black Sea Straits in this connection.[6] This abandonment of Soviet claims was further confirmed by Premier Malenkov on August 8, 1953, and was once again repeated by Chairman Khrushchev on June 28, 1960, soon after the Turkish military coup of May of that year.

The rise of the military to power in Turkey in 1960 did not result in any change of basic Turkish attitudes toward security and the need for continued alliance with the West. This continuity was clearly indicated by an exchange of correspondence between the Turkish president, General Gürsel, and Khrushchev in which Gürsel clearly rejected Soviet proposals that Turkey return to a position of neutrality. It was characteristic of the new, more conciliatory, Soviet tactics that Moscow did not avail itself of an opportunity to withdraw from the Montreux Convention upon the expiration of the twenty-year term for which the convention was concluded. Article 28 gave the signatories such an option provided they give notice of termination two years before the official date of expiration. The deadline for such an action was November 9, 1954, inasmuch as the convention was to expire on November 9, 1956. No signatory power having given notice of termination, it continued to be

---

[6]Text in Ferenc A. Váli, *The Turkish Straits and NATO* (Stanford, Calif., 1972), Appendix 27, pp. 298 ff. This book contains a wide range of documents pertaining to the Turkish Straits.

valid by automatic self-renewal. Although the United States was not a signatory, it observed the terms of the Montreux Convention as part of the general International Law.

Merchant and Naval Traffic in the 1960s and 1970s

There was a paradox in the position of the Turkish Straits during the three decades following the formation of NATO. In major strategic terms, with the development of air power and a variety of sophisticated missiles with nuclear warheads, the importance of any waterway was bound to decline. On the other hand, the steadily increased use that both the Soviet Union and the Western nations made of the Straits not only underlined their continuous importance to both power blocs in the world but even heightened it in economic terms and as a potentially major factor in conventional warfare.

Commercial shipping through the Straits evidenced a steady upward trend following World War I. In 1923 the total tonnage amounted to 6.5 million; by 1935 it almost doubled, to reach 12 million; and by the mid-1970s it rose to 70 million tons. The Soviet Union accounted for a major share in this growth. While in the first year after World War II, in 1946, a mere 177 Soviet ships displacing about 500,000 tons sailed to Istanbul or transited the Straits, by the mid-1970s the yearly average of Soviet ships using the Straits was in excess of 7,000, representing a tonnage of about 30 million. Thus the Soviet share in the total commercial tonnage amounted to 43 percent. A similar substantial increase could be noted in the tonnage of two other Black Sea powers linked with the Soviet Union—Rumania and Bulgaria. Between 1965 and 1975 the Rumanian transit traffic doubled in tonnage from one to two million while the Bulgarian traffic quintupled from one to five million tons. This expansion was reflected also in the numbers of their ships transiting the Straits, but not in exactly corresponding proportion inasmuch as both countries began using larger merchant ships.

The free world merchant traffic in the Straits had also followed an upward curve. The heaviest users as a group were the countries of the Mediterranean littoral, Greece, Italy, Yugoslavia, France, and Spain. Their total transiting tonnage rose from 14 million in the mid-1960s to 17.5 million in the mid-1970s, with a respective rise in the number of transiting ships from 4,500 to 5,000. The most substantial advance in the frequency of visits and transits in the Straits was made by Greece, accounting for an increase in ships from 2,500 to 3,500 and in tonnage from 6 million to 10 million in the decade under discussion. Following this group, the American maritime interests constituted the next major user, although in the mid-1970s the number of ships under United States registry hovered around a modest figure of 200 with a mere 0.9 million tonnage. To this, however, had to be added the largely American-owned ships of Panamanian and Liberian registry, representing 1.1 million and 3.5 million tons, respectively. The total of these three registries was 5.5 million tons in the mid-1970s.[7]

[7]Sources for the statistics: Harry N. Howard, *Turkey, the Straits, and U.S. Policy* (Baltimore, 1974); and République Turque, Ministères des Affaires Etrangères, *Rapport Annuel sur le Mouvement des Navires à Travers les Détroits Turcs* (Ankara, annual publication).

The Naval Traffic. With Turkey as an ally and member of the NATO and the United States maintaining its Sixth Fleet in the Mediterranean as part of its regular deployment of forces, it was natural that American naval vessels would use the Straits either for visits in Istanbul or for transit purposes. Transits through the Straits, however, were modest in frequency: the United States Navy was sending twice a year, in the spring and in the fall, two destroyers or frigates to the Black Sea "to show the flag" and to stress the principle that despite the preponderance of the Communist riparian powers it viewed this body of waters as an open sea. By contrast, United States Navy visits to Istanbul (necessitating passage through the Dardanelles Strait and the Sea of Marmara) were subject to considerable fluctuations in frequency. In the early 1950s, soon after the admission of Turkey to NATO, the frequency increased. After 1957 the visits gradually decreased (for example, fifty-four ships used the straits in 1957 and only twenty-two in 1971). This decrease in American visits could be partly attributed to the political complications that arose between Ankara and Washington in the wake of the recurrent Cyprus crises and the hostile attitudes displayed toward American naval crews by radical Turkish militants.

As for the Soviet Union, the frequency of naval passages through the Straits stood in proportion to the Soviet naval presence in the Mediterranean. Beginning with 1964, the Fifth Escadra of the Soviet navy, an offshoot of the Soviet Black Sea Command, was deployed on a regular basis in the Mediterranean. Its standard strength in the mid-1970s amounted to fifty-five ships including an average of twelve submarines. Liaison with and maintenance of this fleet required about three hundred Soviet naval passages a year through the Turkish Straits. In times of international crisis in the Middle East, the number of Soviet ships in the Mediterranean tended to increase, sometimes drastically. Thus during the October 1973 Arab-Israeli war, twelve additional ships were brought in between October 6 and 26 from the Black Sea. With other Soviet naval vessels brought in from the Baltic and the North Sea, the number of Soviet ships in the Mediterranean rose to ninety-six on that occasion. Similarly, the Cyprus crisis of 1974 and the Lebanon crisis of 1976 caused the complement of the Soviet navy in the Mediterranean to be temporarily augmented. When during the Lebanese crisis the U.S.S. *America* sailed into eastern Mediterranean waters, it was ringed by twenty Soviet ships.[8]

Political and Strategic Issues and Frictions

The increased use of the Turkish Straits by both the Soviet and the NATO navies in the post-World War II period was bound to produce tensions and disagreements. In July 1953, Moscow and Ankara exchanged communications in which the Soviet government complained about the rapidly increasing frequency of visits paid by the British and American warships to the Turkish ports in the Straits. The Soviet diplomatic notes pointed out that the number of these warships increased from thirty-three in 1950 to sixty-nine in 1952 and reached sixty during the first half of 1953.

[8]For a comprehensive account of the Soviet presence in the Mediterranean, see Jesse W. Lewis, Jr., *The Strategic Balance in the Mediterranean* (Washington, D.C., 1976).

The Soviet Union viewed these visits as "military demonstrations" and expressed its concern to the Turkish government. In response, Turkey claimed that these were merely courtesy visits not subject to any tonnage limitations under Articles 14 and 17 of the Montreux Convention.

Proper interpretation of the terms of the Montreux Convention gave rise to disagreements between the Soviet Union and the NATO powers from time to time. One problem that necessitated close watching was the transit of Soviet submarines through the Straits. In principle only surface vessels have the right to pass through the Straits. Article 12 of the Convention, however, makes an exception in favor of the Black Sea powers, as follows:

> Black Sea Powers shall have the right to send through the Straits, for the purpose of rejoining their base, submarines constructed or purchased outside the Black Sea, provided that adequate notice of the laying down or purchase of such submarines shall have been given to Turkey.
> Submarines belonging to the said powers shall also be entitled to pass through the Straits to be repaired in dockyards outside the Black Sea on condition that detailed information on the matter is given to Turkey.
> In either case, the said submarines must travel by day and on the surface, and must pass through the Straits singly.[9]

In the 1960s and 1970s two Soviet sumbarines were leaving the Black Sea and two were entering it annually on the average. In their passage they conformed to the regulations by sailing in the daylight and on the surface. It was less clear whether these passages conformed to the other specific provisions of Article 12 of the Convention. This article was included in the text because in the 1930s the Soviet Union did not possess in the Black Sea facilities to construct and repair the submarines. By the 1960s, Russia definitely had developed such facilities, although most of its effort in this respect was concentrated in its ports of Archangel and Komsomolsk.

American naval visits to the Black Sea, although limited in frequency and number of ships, were always watched with a degree of uneasiness by the Soviet authorities. Occasionally their displeasure was expressed in an unofficial medium. Thus in September 1966 *Krasnaya Zvezda* published an article deploring the visit of U.S.S. *Pratt* in the Black Sea.[10] The article claimed that the United States had violated the Montreux Convention because the vessel was armed with rockets. While the Convention makes no specific reference to rockets, it contains many specific provisions about the caliber of guns which are permissible. The question remains whether the specifications provided in 1936 encompass unforeseen technological developments that occurred several decades later.

The transit through the Straits of the Soviet aircraft carrier *Kiev* in July 1976 provided a potential for a new controversy. The Montreux Convention forbids the passage of aircraft carriers under any circumstances. To evade possible criticisms, the Soviet government labeled the *Kiev* an "antisubmarine cruiser." Although this

[9]Text in Howard, *op. cit.*, pp. 292–299.
[10]Quoted by Howard, *op. cit.*, pp. 275–276.

allegation was subject to serious reservations, neither NATO nor Turkey chose to lodge official protests with Moscow. The passage of the *Kiev* was in turn linked to another potential issue—that of the passage of Soviet helicopter carriers. The Soviet fleet in the Mediterranean has regularly included at least one such helicopter carrier of the *Moskva* type. The question remained whether these ships should be included in the category of aircraft carriers.

More broadly, the regular Soviet naval presence in the Mediterranean against the background of the spectacular expansion of the Soviet navy on a global scale in the 1970s has increased the strategic worth of the Turkish Straits to the Soviet Union. Beginning in 1964 the Soviet navy was granted a variety of facilities in the ports of Egypt, Syria, and Algeria, while visiting Libyan ports with increasing frequency in connection with military supplies to that nation. Although thus broadly successful in gaining access to various ports in the region, the Soviet Union suffered two considerable reverses when, in 1961, Albania removed a Soviet submarine base from her waters and when, on March 15, 1976, Egypt abrogated its 1971 treaty of friendship with the Soviet Union, thereby putting an end to the Soviet use of the Alexandria and Marsa Matruh harbors. The loss of Egyptian bases was particularly grievous. It caused the Soviets to rely more extensively on fourteen anchorages established in various parts of the Mediterranean, but it also enhanced the value of the Turkish Straits which Soviet warships, deprived of the Albanian and Egyptian facilities, were compelled to use more frequently.

The Suez Canal

The Suez Canal is another strategic waterway in the Middle East, which though much younger than the Turkish Straits has equaled, if not actually surpassed, them in international importance.

The Canal was opened in 1869. Its construction took a full ten years. The technical problems attending this construction were numerous and diverse though not so difficult as those attending the digging of the Panama Canal. They were definitely overshadowed by the political problems, which from the very beginning made the canal an object of intense international rivalry.[11]

The Concession

The canal owed its inception to a former French consular official in Egypt, Ferdinand de Lesseps, who turning to his advantage an old friendship with Mohammed Said Pasha, viceroy of Egypt, obtained from him on November 30, 1854, a concession to construct a canal that would link the Mediterranean with the Red Sea, and to create an international company to administer it. The concession was to be valid for ninety-nine years from the date of the opening of the canal, after which time the canal would become the property of the Egyptian government. The latter would then pay the company an indemnity for its mobile properties, to be

[11]For a thorough treatment of these rivalries, see Arnold T. Wilson, *The Suez Canal, Its Past, Present, and Future* (London, 1939); Halford L. Hoskins, *British Routes to India* (New York, 1928); André Siegfried, *Suez and Panama* (New York, 1940).

fixed by friendly negotiations or, lacking an agreement, by arbitration. The Egyptian government was to receive from the company 15 percent of the net annual profits apart from the dividends that might accrue to it as owner of a number of the company's shares. Navigation in the canal was to be based on the principle of equality of all nations. This concession was succeeded on January 5, 1856, by a new one which contained more detailed provisions concerning the rights and obligations of Egypt and the company toward each other. Thus, for example, the company was exempted from Egyptian customs duties when importing necessary materials, was authorized freely to use the mines and quarries situated along the projected canal route, and was obliged to construct a sweet-water canal from the delta of the Nile to cater to the needs of the workers. A clause in this new concession provided that four-fifths of the workers on the construction were to be Egyptian. This clause proved to be a double-edged weapon. While seemingly protecting the rights of the Egyptians, in practice it evolved into an obligation of the Egyptian government to supply the company with an adequate labor force. A viceregal decree of July 20, 1856, subsequently determined the conditions of use of Egyptian labor. When the company began its construction work, large numbers of the Egyptian workers were actually conscripted as forced labor, and it was only in 1866 that a new convention between Egypt and the company released the Egyptian government from this obligation on the payment of a considerable indemnity to the company.

Political Difficulties and British Intervention

The concessions granted to De Lesseps required ratification by the Ottoman sultan, and here the real difficulties began. Since the time of Mohammed Ali, France had enjoyed considerable influence in Egypt. England, although having important commercial interests there, could not boast of a similar position. But the situation in Constantinople was just the reverse. There British influence was paramount, especially after the beginning of the Russo-Turkish crisis of 1853, which led to the Crimean War. To obtain ratification for a firman granted by the viceroy of Egypt in favor of France or of a French citizen meant in practice to secure Britain's good will toward the project in question. As things stood then, Britain was definitely unwilling to show good will in this matter, and her government, headed by Palmerston, was opposed to the digging of the canal. This British opposition accounted for more than a decade of delay in ratification. Undaunted by these diplomatic reverses, De Lesseps went ahead with his plans. In 1858 he formed the Compagnie Universelle du Canal Maritime de Suez, the shares of which were subscribed for in a large part by the French public and by the Egyptian government, but with an understanding that an adequate part of the stock would be available to other nationalities. Then, still lacking ratification, De Lesseps launched construction work in the Isthmus in 1859. The next seven years constituted a period of nerve-racking activity for the originator of the company, who devoted his time to solving the technical, financial, and diplomatic problems, all strictly intertwined. In the meantime his good friend, Said Pasha died and was succeeded by a new viceroy, Ismail Pasha, an event which greatly complicated De Lesseps' task. Finally, having overcome most of the difficulties and, especially, having neutralized British opposition, De Lesseps secured a new convention with Ismail on January 30, 1866. This convention was ratified on March 19, 1866, by the sultan. The convention confirmed the former viceregal firman, adding some new provisions. Noteworthy among them was Article 16, which stated that the Compagnie Universelle was an Egyptian corporation and as such was to be subject to the laws and customs of the country. It provided, however, for the application of French law on corporations to the company.

The inauguration of the canal three years later, celebrated in the presence of many crowned heads of Europe and the elite of European statesmen, was a moment of great personal triumph for De Lesseps. By that time the British attitude toward the canal had radically changed. Instead of opposing it, Britain became very much interested in the canal as a commercial and strategic route. As a result of the financial difficulties of his treasury, Khedive[12] Ismail in 1875 decided to sell his stock in the company. This amounted to 172,602 shares, which were placed on the European market. Disraeli, prime minister of Britain, promptly decided to purchase them. Lacking parliamentary authorization (Parliament was then in recess), he borrowed 100 million francs from the banking house of Rothschild, instructing the latter to effect the purchase. Thus one of the boldest financial and political transactions in the world's history was made.

The purchase of Egypt's shares made Britain an important shareholder, although a majority of the shares still belonged to the French and politically the canal was under Turkish-Egyptian sovereignty. This situation underwent a radical change when Britain occupied Egypt in 1882. While Arabi Pasha's revolt supplied an excuse for this move, the occupation was largely due to Britain's desire to control the Suez Canal, this new strategic link in her imperial communications.

The Constantinople Convention

In 1888 nine major powers—France, Germany, Austria-Hungary, Spain, Britain, Italy, the Netherlands, Russia, and Turkey—concluded a convention in Constantinople defining the international status of the Suez Canal. Article 1 of the convention decreed that the Suez Canal must remain free and open to merchant and war vessels in time of war as well as in time of peace. The signatories pledged not to violate this provision and never to subject the canal to a blockade. According to further articles, hostilities in the canal were definitely forbidden, and this provision extended to the canal's entrance ports and the waters within three maritime miles around the latter. Belligerents were not forbidden to use the canal for transit purposes but were to be subject to various restrictions in order to avert hostilities in canal waters. Article 10 of the convention gave Turkey and Egypt the right to take measures as might be necessary for their defense and for the maintenance of public order. This provision was hedged with the reservation, expressly stated in Article 11, that these measures must not obstruct the free use of the canal. No fortifications

[12]A new title accorded the viceroys of Egypt by the sultan in 1867.

were allowed in the Canal Zone. Article 14 made it clear that the principle of free navigation should be permanent and not limited to the duration of the concession.[13] Thus the Constantinople Convention proclaimed the principle of free navigation in the canal for all nations, without, however, providing for the neutrality of either the Canal Zone or of Egypt as a proprietary power. This explains why there seemed to be no legal incompatibility between the British occupation of Egypt and the principle of free passage. In practice, however, it meant that henceforth Britain had become a guardian of the Suez Canal and that in case of war with other powers she would close the canal to their ships, regardless of the legal aspects of such a move.

Experience of Two World Wars

The First World War supplied evidence that such was the case, and the same can be said of the Second World War. Britain's enemies were refused access to the canal on both occasions. Whereas during the First World War Britain freely used the canal for her own purposes, during the Second enemy aviation and submarine activity in the Mediterranean and south of the Red Sea made navigation in the canal a hazardous affair for the Allied navies. This was true despite the fact that the canal was closed as a result of enemy air activity only seventy-six days throughout the whole of the Second World War. It is worth noting that during both World Wars Britain initially attempted to comply with the provisions of free passage and nonblockade of the canal by seizing enemy ships or searching neutral ships suspected of carrying contraband cargo, not in the canal proper but in the open sea just beyond the convention-provided three-mile limit. For the purpose of search these ships were usually escorted to Alexandria, whence—if neutral—they were permitted to sail freely to their destinations after having satisfied the British authorities. Eventually this practice was abandoned as inconvenient to both parties concerned. The neutral ships preferred to be subject to search at Suez or Port Said rather than to go off their course to Alexandria and thus delay their schedule.

Britain's de facto control of the Suez Canal obtained juridical confirmation by the Anglo-Egyptian Treaty of 1936. The treaty in Article 8 stated that the canal was "an integral part of Egypt," but that Britain was entrusted with the task of its defense, pending the mutually agreed upon ability of the Egyptian army to perform the task. It will be recalled from Chapter XII that Britain was authorized to keep 10,000 soldiers and 400 pilots in the Canal Zone apart from technical and administrative civilian personnel. Egypt undertook to build barracks for these troops and to supply them with water. At the time of this treaty, no one raised the problem of its compatibility with the Constantinople Convention of 1888, and it was generally assumed that the convention remained in force. It should be pointed out that at no time did the British assume direct responsibility for the administration of the canal traffic, which was left entirely to the company, and at no time did they deprive Egypt of her traditional right as the sovereign power to exercise police, customs, and sanitary controls over the canal and the adjacent area.

---

[13]This and other relevant texts concerning the Suez Canal may be found in Moustapha el-Hefnaoui, *Les Problèmes Contemporains Posés par le Canal de Suez* (Paris, 1951). This is a serious and exhaustive study, strongly tinged with Egyptian nationalism.

After the Second World War Egypt asked for a revision of the treaty of 1936 and for this purpose embarked upon negotiations with Britain, negotiations which failed and which in 1947 led to the placing of the Anglo-Egyptian dispute before the United Nations Security Council (see Chapter XII). Inasmuch as the Security Council was unable to reach any decision in the matter, the legal status of the canal remained unchanged.

Repercussions of the War in Palestine

The Palestinian war of 1948 brought the Suez Canal once again to the fore in international affairs. Egypt, as a belligerent, applied various restrictive measures against enemy ships and against neutral ships carrying contraband of war. These measures were based on Military Proclamation No. 5, issued by the Egyptian government in the early summer of 1948 and instituting a regime of inspection of ships in Alexandria, Port Said, and Suez. This proclamation, soon followed by further regulations concerning customs inspection and prize courts, did not differ from similar decrees issued, with the full approval of Egypt's British ally, between 1939–1945, which were designed to control enemy and neutral shipping during the Second World War. Although these measures interfered with normal navigation through the Suez Canal, no protests were raised by foreign maritime powers. It was silently admitted that Egypt, at war with Israel, was within her rights to adopt measures of self-defense and did not violate the Suez Canal Convention of 1888.

The Egyptian-Israeli armistice concluded at Rhodes on February 24, 1949, put an end to the hostilities and ushered in a new era of peaceful coexistence for the two states. By two regulations—of July 21 and September 14, 1949—Egypt relaxed her controls over canal shipping but did not abolish them altogether. The September regulation, confirmed by a royal decree of February 6, 1950, limited the list of merchandise destined for Israel and liable to seizure by the Egyptian authorities. This list included the following six items: (1) arms and war materials; (2) chemical and pharmaceutical materials, which might be utilized in chemical warfare; (3) fuel in all forms; (4) airplanes and their spare parts; (5) tractors and motor vehicles for military use; and (6) currencies, gold, silver, and materials necessary to manufacture money.[14]

All ships, regardless of their flags, which were found to carry the above-mentioned cargo with Israel as the direct or indirect destination, risked the danger of confiscation of the forbidden items by Egyptian prize courts. Search and inspection could be applied to all ships passing through the canal even if their destination was clearly not Israel. The Egyptian government suspected certain vessels and shipping lines of directing their cargo to Israel by a roundabout route. For this reason, Egyptian authorities drew up a list of suspect ships, shipping companies, and ports and applied to the ships in question sterner measures of search. This interference with international shipping had no parallel in peacetime. It was applied with particular thoroughness to the tankers carrying crude or refined oil from the region east of the Red Sea to Mediterranean ports and greatly affected the supply of oil to Israel.

[14]*Ibid.*, p. 203.

As a result, the predominantly British-owned Haifa refinery remained idle, and after considerable delay could be put back into partial operation only by supplies of crude oil from Venezuela. Britain protested in Cairo against this Egyptian interference, pointing out that not only Israel's but also other countries' interests were involved, and that the Egyptian action had harmful effects on the economic development of states in no way connected with the Egyptian-Israeli dispute. Britain was not the only country to voice disapproval. Nine other important maritime nations, namely, Australia, Denmark, France, Italy, the Netherlands, Norway, South Africa, Sweden, and the United States, also lodged formal protests with the Egyptian government. British annoyance over the Egyptian behavior considerably increased when on July 1, 1951, an Egyptian corvette detained and boarded a British freighter, *Empire Roach,* in the Gulf of Aqaba, not far from the Sinai coast. According to the British version the Egyptians behaved in a conspicuously unceremonious way, ordered the British crew to stay below the decks for thirteen hours, looted the ship's stores, stole £200 worth of goods, and wrecked the ship's radio. The ship was carrying supplies to the Jordanian port of Aqaba at the head of the Gulf. Egypt maintained that she was within her rights in searching the British vessel because of the suspicion that the latter was heading toward the new Israeli harbor, Port Elath, situated very near Aqaba, and because the search was made in Egyptian territorial waters.[15]

The Suez Canal Issue before the United Nations

Although not directly connected with Suez Canal traffic, this incident contributed to the deterioration of the already strained relations between Egypt and the major maritime powers and proved to be a turning point in their attitudes. Profiting from this state of mind, Israel on July 12, 1951, brought a complaint against Egypt before the United Nations Security Council. Israel's complaint included three counts. According to Israel, Egypt had violated (1) international law by exercising the rights of belligerency in time of peace; (2) the armistice of February 24, 1949; and (3) the Suez Canal Convention of 1888. The Security Council considered the matter between July 26 and September 1. The Egyptian delegate defended his country's behavior by repudiating each of the three contentions. First, he argued that the armistice was not yet a peace treaty and that Egypt was therefore still technically at war with Israel. Consequently, she was entitled to exercise the rights of a belligerent. Second, he claimed that the armistice put an end only to active military hostilities but did not forbid the parties to apply economic measures. Moreover, the Egyptian delegate asserted that Israel had violated the armistice by expelling peaceful Arab populations across the Egyptian border, by raiding certain localities in the

---

[15]In subsequent years other incidents of this sort occurred, one of them involving Egyptian firing on an American vessel carrying a cargo of grain to Jordan. The difficulty stemmed from the fact that the only navigable channel leading into the Gulf of Aqaba was located between Tiran Island and the Sinai coast, within Egyptian territorial waters. Whether or not such a channel should be considered as an international waterway, free of any restrictions that Egypt as a sovereign riparian state might want to impose, remained a moot question. There seemed to be no precedent, except for the general rules of international law, which could serve as a guide with regard to traffic in this disputed waterway.

neutral frontier zone, and by illegally attacking Egyptian territory. He also pointed to the still unresolved problem of the Arab refugees, which in his opinion could hardly permit the existing Arab-Israeli relations to be considered as a peace. Third, he asserted that the convention of 1888 specifically allowed Egypt to take self-protective measures in the Canal Zone, and that despite these measures freedom of navigation through the canal remained unimpaired, the volume of traffic actually increasing by leaps and bounds.

In the ensuing debate, representatives of Britain, France, and the United States supported Israel, at the same time attempting to reach some amicable settlement with Egypt. Owing to the latter's intransigence, however, the three above-mentioned powers felt compelled to submit a resolution condemning Egypt for her restrictions imposed on the passage of ships through the Suez Canal. During most of the debate (i.e., for six weeks) the Soviet delegate remained enigmatically silent; just before the vote was to be taken, he requested a week's delay in order to consult his government. This was accorded to him. On September 1, 1951, the resolution was submitted to a vote, which resulted in eight affirmative ballots (Brazil, Ecuador, France, the Netherlands, Turkey, the United States, the United Kingdom, and Yugoslavia) and three abstentions (China, India, and the USSR). Thus the resolution was adopted.[16] Specifically the resolution said that the armistice agreement contemplated "the return of permanent peace in Palestine," and that no party could reasonably assert that it was actively a belligerent two and one-half years after the armistice; invoked the opinions of Dr. Ralph Bunche and General Riley, chief of staff of the Truce Supervision Organization, in support of this theisis; found the Egyptian practices unjustified; and called "upon Egypt to terminate the restrictions on the passage of international commercial shipping and goods through the Suez Canal wherever bound, and to cease all interference with such shipping beyond that essential to the safety of shipping in the Canal itself and to the observance of the international conventions in force."[17]

Despite this resolution Egypt persisted in her policy of interference, as a result of which the matter was repeatedly brought to the attention of the United Nations in subsequent years. In an apparent attempt to force the issue Israel in September 1954 sent her merchant vessel *Bat Galim* through the canal via the Suez Gulf. In due course the ship was seized by the Egyptians and her crew detained. After a few months first the crew and then the ship were released, but the seizure once again underlined Egypt's contention that she was technically at war with Israel and that she would not relax her restrictive regulations with respect to maritime traffic with an enemy.

Relations between Egypt and the Suez Canal Company

The relations between the government and the company had been regulated by the original acts of concession. These acts were modified subsequently by numerous

[16]For a verbatim record of these proceedings, see *United Nations, Security Council, General,* S/PV. 549–558, July 26–Sept. 1, 1951.

[17]The full text is quoted in *Middle Eastern Affairs* (Aug.–Sept. 1951).

conventions of which there were over seventy between 1866 and 1937. Among them, three were of particular importance:

1. By a convention of March 21, 1880, the Egyptian government ceded its right to 15 percent of the company's net profits to Crédit Foncier de France, which in turn founded a special company to distribute the shares. This cession was due to the disastrous state of Egyptian finances.

2. By a convention of 1920, it was agreed to include the living quarters of personnel in the position described as material and machines in the original acts of the concession. This meant an increase in the future indemnity to be paid by the Egyptian government to the Suez Canal Company at the time of the expiration of the concession.

3. Following the Anglo-Egyptian treaty and the abolition of the capitulations, the government and the company in 1936-1937 concluded a convention regulating a number of items such as customs exemptions, the maintenance of Ismailia Municipality and the use of fresh water. This convention provided, moreover, for the annual payment of £E300,000 by the company to Egypt, thus giving the latter a financial stake in the Suez Canal for the first time since 1880.

In 1947 the Egyptian parliament passed a law on corporations operating in Egypt. The law provided that at least 40 percent of the members of the boards of directors of such corporations must be Egyptians; also the personnel of corporations must be 75 percent Egyptian and receive at least 65 percent of the total payroll. In special cases, the law gave discretionary power to the minister of commerce and industry to allow exceptions to this rule. The law was to go into force within the next three years. Inasmuch as the Suez Canal Company enjoyed a special status, the company and the government opened negotiations in order to reconcile the provisions of the law with the company's interests. After several months' negotiations the parties reached an agreement which, on March 7, 1949, was formally embodied in a convention ratified by the Egyptian parliament. This convention introduced three main modifications into the company's status:

1. The company was gradually to "Egyptianize" its personnel. The administrative employees, except pilots and the maritime personnel, were to conform to the 1947 law before the end of the concession. As regards the board of directors, its number had been thirty-two prior to 1949, and it was composed of nineteen Frenchmen, ten Britons, one Dutchman, and two Egyptians. Their terms of office extended for eight years and they were eligible for reappointment. The new convention provided for an immediate additional appointment of two Egyptians, thus raising their number to four, with the understanding that it should be raised to seven by 1964. The number of foreign members of the board was to be thirty, and was to include eighteen Frenchmen, ten Britons, one Dutchman, and—an innovation—one American.

2. The company agreed to pay the Egyptian government 7 percent of its gross annual profit, in any case not less than £E350,000. (This amounted to £E805,000 for the year 1948 alone.) By this arrangement, the Egyptian government has again become a partner, having an interest in the success of the enterprise.

3. The company also agreed to exempt from the canal toll charges small-scale

shipping (mostly low-tonnage barges and other craft flying the Egyptian flag). This concession was estimated at being worth £E50,000 per year to Egypt.

The 1949 convention laid a new basis for the relationship between the government and the company with every likelihood that it would remain in force until November 17, 1968, the date of the expiration of the concession. The convention was not greeted in Egypt with unanimous enthusiasm despite the new profits accruing to the Egyptian treasury. Fuad Serag ed-Din Pasha, secretary general of the Wafd Party, and later minister of interior in the Nahas cabinet, voiced profound criticism of the convention in the parliament. He complained that the convention practically disregarded the Egyptian law on corporations and said that the government instead of negotiating should have simply demanded that the company comply with that law. He pointed out that the number of the company's employees as of December 31, 1948, was 640, of which the foreigners constituted about 75 percent and the Egyptians barely 25 percent. Moreover, these Egyptians received only 15 percent of the total payroll. He also stressed that 25 percent were not native Egyptians but naturalized foreigners who, after the abolition of capitulations, hastily acquired Egyptian citizenship as a protective measure. Faud Serag ed-Din criticized also the government's weakness in agreeing to four instead of thirteen Egytpian members of the board, the latter number corresponding to the provisions of the law on corporations.

These criticisms elicited a reply from François Charles-Roux, chairman of the board of the company, in a statement made at a meeting of the shareholders in Paris. The chairman stated that the company had always had an exceptional character and that it had always operated under a convention. He pointed out that the preceding convention, concluded in 1936–1937, bore witness to the recognition by the Egyptian government of this special status. Hence it was logical for both parties to negotiate a new agreement in 1949. He stressed that the new convention had the virtue of slow adaptation to the new conditions, which would avert any upsets in the smooth functioning of the Suez Canal service. Provisions for the "Egyptianization" of personnel would apply only to future personnel and not to employees already on the job.

By ratifying the 1949 convention, Egypt committed herself to its terms until the end of the concession. This was the legal situation. Yet it would be unwise to underestimate such criticism as that mentioned above, which emanated from a prominent leader of the most powerful nationalist party in Egypt. It meant that Egyptian nationalists were eager to find fault with the new settlement and, granted an opportunity, might be tempted to give forceful expression to their views.

From the economic standpoint business in the canal was excellent after the Second World War. After the end of hostilities, traffic in the canal steadily increased until in 1956 it reached the high figure of 122 million tons a year, of which oil cargoes accounted for 76,860,000 tons (i.e., 63 percent). This was a considerable increase over the nearly 69,000,000 tons in 1949, which in turn represented a 25 percent increase over the preceding years.[18] The Palestinian war and the opening in

---

[18]Periodic statistics of the traffic in the canal may be found in the *Bulletin de la Compagnie Universelle du Canal Maritime de Suez*, which was published regularly in Paris.

1950 of the Trans-Arabian pipeline across the desert introduced some complicating factors into the company's business, but did not deter it from steady expansion.

The conclusion in 1954 of a new Anglo-Egyptian agreement regarding the Suez Canal base and the expected expiration of the Suez Canal Company concession in 1968 were likely to pose major problems of a political and economic nature to Egypt and other powers. By virtue of the new Suez base agreement Egypt was to regain military control of the canal by June 19, 1956, and thus become the sole guardian of the world's major strategic waterway. In view of the difference between the strength of Britain and of Egypt as well as because of the hostility prevailing in Egyptian-Israeli relations, this was bound to create an entirely new international situation. On the other hand, from 1968 on, Egypt was to become the only operator of the canal traffic and thus to assume a responsibility for rather delicate technical operations, which hitherto had been performed by a body of specially trained and competent Westerners. These new political and technical arrangements, if allowed to materialize without major complications, were expected to satisfy the deep aspirations of the Egyptian people. Whether, in the long run, they could be reconciled with the strategic interests of the American-led coalition of non-Communist nations was a moot question. Much might depend in this respect on two factors: (1) whether the transfer of the canal operations to Egyptian ownership would be effected in a peaceful and legal manner, and (2) whether, in her new role as the sole operator and guardian of the canal, Egypt would apply standards of efficiency and nondiscrimination similar to those applied before the transfer. In the following sections we will see how these plans for a peaceful transition were vitiated by the dramatic developments in the mid-1950's.

Nationalization of the Suez Canal

The story of the Suez Canal in the 1950s provides a striking illustration of the intricate relationship of events and decisions in world politics which outwardly should have had little if any connection with one another. It will be recalled from our account of Egyptian politics (see Chapter XII) that one of the cherished aims of the revolutionary regime was the erection of the High Aswan Dam. On July 19, 1956, Egypt's hopes for a monumental project which would immortalize its revolution seemed shattered. Moreover, to add to the cup of bitterness, Soviet Foreign Minister Dimitri Shepilov declared on July 21 at a press conference that Russia was not considering aid to Egypt for this particular project.

President Nasser's reaction to the withdrawal of Western offers was both swift and violent. On July 26, 1956, he nationalized the Suez Canal and declared that henceforth its revenues would go toward the financing of the High Aswan Dam project. According to the presidential decree, "The Universal Suez Maritime Canal Company S.A.E. is hereby nationalized. All its funds and rights and obligations connected therewith are transferred to the State. . . . Shareholders and holders of foundation bonds will be compensated for the shares and bonds they possess, at their value estimated at the closing rate on the Paris Bourse prior to the date on which this Law entered into effect." The decree also provided that "an independent body shall undertake the management of the traffic in the Suez Canal" and that "all funds and rights of this nationalized company in the Republic of Egypt and abroad shall be frozen." As for the personnel of the company, "They must continue to carry out their duties. No one of them is in any way, or for any reason, authorized to leave or relinquish his post except with the permission of the [governing] body." Anyone contravening the above rule "shall be punished with imprisonment in addition to his being deprived of any right to gratuity, pension, or compensation."[19]

Nasser's action was received in the Western capitals, particularly in London and Paris, with shock and indignation. Claiming that the nationalization was a violation of the international character of the canal and that it jeopardized the freedom of navigation, France and Britain threatened to use force against Egypt and began a gradual buildup of their forces in the Middle East. Although Washington joined its two allies in condemning the seizure of the canal, asserting its international character and freezing Egyptian assets in the United States, it nevertheless advised moderation. On Secretary Dulles' proposal, a conference of twenty-two interested nations convened in London on August 16 to devise means of solving the dispute. Egypt, initially invited, refused to attend. However, the Soviet Union was included and, as could be expected, took a pro-Egyptian stand in the debates. The conference ended in an agreement reached among eighteen of its participants to set up an international authority to administer the Suez Canal. A commission of five nations was appointed to negotiate international control with Egypt.[20] Its subsequent negotiations with President Nasser resulted in failure because of his absolute refusal to compromise on the principle of full Egyptian sovereignty over the canal. Faced with Cairo's adamant attitude, the Suez Canal Company ordered its pilots to leave their jobs. In reply, Egypt began recruiting pilots from outside. A number of pilots from Russia, Poland, and the satellite countries as well as some volunteers from the Free World arrived in Egypt to take over the vacated positions.

Dismayed at Nasser's intransigence, Britain and France were again inclined to use military pressure to restore their rights. But for the second time they were induced by Secretary Dulles to modify their harsh stand. On September 12, Dulles secured Franco-British approval of a new idea—the creation of a Canal Users' Association. According to Dulles,

> the users' association will not only help the vessels of members to get through the canal, but it will serve the United Nations in helping to work out a provisional solution; it will be a means of dealing with the serious economic problems that may arise for some of the member nations if the canal were blocked; and it will study alternatives which might reduce dependence on the canal.[21]

On October 1 the Suez Canal Users' Association was formally set up with fifteen member states.

Despite this joint decision, Britain and France on September 23 decided to bring

[19]Law No. 285 of 1956 Nationalizing the Universal Company of the Suez Maritime Canal, in *The Suez Canal, A Selection of Documents Relating to the International Status of the Suez Canal and the Position of the Suez Canal Company* (London, New York, 1956), pp. 41 ff.
[20]Composed of Australia, Sweden, Iran, Ethiopia, and the United States.
[21]The text is in the *New York Times,* Sept. 23, 1956.

the Suez matter to the UN Security Council. Discussions there followed a dual line of private negotiations between Egypt and the major Western powers and of open debates, which gave the Soviet delegation a renewed opportunity to assert its friendship for Egypt and its opposition to colonialism. By October 13 Egypt, France, Britain, and the United States had agreed to accept a formula elaborated by UN Secretary-General Dag Hammarskjöld, which contained the following six principles:

(1) There should be free and open transit through the canal without discrimination, overt or covert—this covers both political and technical aspects;

(2) The sovereignty of Egypt should be respected;

(3) The operation of the canal should be insulated from the politics of any country;

(4) The manner of fixing tolls and charges should be decided by agreement between Egypt and the users;

(5) A fair proportion of the dues should be allotted to development;

(6) In case of disputes, unresolved affairs between the Suez Canal Company and the Egyptian Government should be settled by arbitration with suitable terms of reference and suitable provisions for the payment of sums found to be due.[22]

These six principles were incorporated into the first part of a joint resolution presented to the Security Council by Britain and France. The second part called upon Egypt to accept the proposals formulated by the eighteen nations at their London meeting (suggesting an international board to administer the canal) and to provide suitable guarantees. Inasmuch as Russia, as well as Egypt, did not conceal her disapproval of the second part of the resolution, Britain and France agreed on a separate vote for each part. The second part was duly vetoed by the Soviet delegate. The first part was, however, unanimously adopted by the Council.

Although the six principles became officially binding, Britain and France felt disappointed inasmuch as no machinery for their implementation had been devised. The position of the Canal Users' Association, which claimed the authority to receive the tolls for the passage of the canal, remained unclear because Egypt had not officially recognized its rights and existence. The feeling of disappointment in London and Paris was mixed with resentment at Secretary Dulles for having induced them to make successive concessions to Nasser, first by proposing international control of the canal and later by abandoning this principle in favor of a formula which did not provide for a reliable method of enforcement. Under the circumstances it appeared that the Egyptian government would remain the sole arbiter of how the six principles should be carried out and interpreted, a situation which neither France nor Britain was willing to accept. This is the background for the subsequent negotiations between Paris and London, which in due course led to their intervention in the war which broke out between Israel and Egypt on October 29.

The Suez War has been treated earlier (see Chapters X and XII). Its effect on the canal was to close it for about five months because of a blockage due to Egyptian sabotage. Eventually the canal was cleared by certain Western firms (mostly German), whose fees were paid by the United Nations, the latter passing on the charges

[22]*Ibid.*, Oct. 14, 1956.

to the ships using the canal in the form of a surcharge to the existing tolls. Soviet bloc vessels refused to pay the surcharge and yet were permitted to pass. In political and legal terms the problem of the nationalization of the company was definitely closed and taken out of international diplomacy with the end of the hostilities. The only remaining issue was that of compensation of the shareholders. This was taken care of by an agreement first reached on April 29, 1958, and finally signed between Egypt and the interested parties, whereby the Egyptian government undertook to pay £E28 million to the stockholders over a five-year period in full settlement of all claims. This was accompanied by Washington's decision to unfreeze the Egyptian assets in the United States on May 1, 1958, as well as gradually to resume economic and technical assistance to Egypt and the United Arab Republic as a whole.

Legal and Technical Aspects of the Canal Operation

Franco-British opposition to the nationalization of the canal was primarily political. Both governments, however, tried hard to prove that the seizure of the canal was illegal. Their main argument was that ownership of the canal and freedom of navigation were inseparable. In this, at least initially, they succeeded in lining up the United States on their side. In a three-power statement calling for a conference of interested nations, issued on August 2, 1956, they declared:

> They do not question the right of Egypt to enjoy and exercise all the powers of a fully sovereign and independent nation, including the generally recognized right, under appropriate conditions, to nationalize assets, not impressed with an international interest, which are subject to the political authority.
>
> But the present action involves far more than a simple act of nationalization. It involves the arbitrary and unilateral seizure by one nation of *an international agency* which has the responsibility to maintain and to operate the Suez Canal so that all the signatories to, and beneficiaries of, the treaty of 1888 can effectively enjoy the use of *an international waterway* upon which the economy, commerce and security of much of the world depends.
>
> . . . . .
>
> They consider that the action taken by the Government of Egypt, having regard to all the attendant circumstances, threatens the freedom and security of the canal as guaranteed by the convention of 1888. This makes it necessary that steps be taken to assure that the parties to that convention and all other nations entitled to enjoy its benefits shall, in fact, be assured of such benefits.[23]

Egypt consistently countered these assertions by pointing out that (1) the ownership of the canal operation by the company was formally divorced from the problem of the freedom of navigation; (2) the company was Egyptian, set up under Egyptian laws, and as such was subject to the right of nationalization; (3) nationalization was not a confiscation, inasmuch as adequate provisions were made in the nationalization decree for the compensation of former owners; (4) freedom of navigation was not questioned by the government of Egypt. There is no doubt that, at least under

[23]The text is in *The Suez Canal, Facts and Documents*, published by the Selected Studies Committee (Cairo, n.d.), pp. 237 ff. Italics mine.

points 1, 3, and 4, Egypt could claim legality for its action. The Constantinople Convention of 1888 expressly provided that its principles were to apply regardless of the ownership of the operation. Article XIV of the convention stated: "The High Contracting Parties agree that the engagements resulting from the present treaty shall not be limited by the duration of the Act of Concession of the Universal Suez Canal Company."[24]

As for the argument that the company was Egyptian, it is true that the firman of the concession dated 1866 stated that "the Universal Suez Canal Company, being Egyptian, is governed by the laws and customs of the country" and that "disputes which may arise between the Egyptian Government and the Company will also be placed before local courts and decided according to the laws of the country." Yet it was also possible to argue, as the three powers did in their earlier-mentioned statement of August 2, 1956, that "the Universal Suez Canal Company has always had an international character in terms of its shareholders, directors and operating personnel and in terms of its responsibility to assure the efficient functioning as an international waterway of the Suez Canal." Moreover, once this contention was accepted, it was possible to argue that Egypt's seizure was not an ordinary act of nationalization, but a violation of a solemnly concluded contract with an alien, i.e., of the concession agreement.

Egypt's case, however, seemed rather strong when it came to the basic issue of the freedom of navigation. Not only, as we have pointed out, was the ownership question divorced from that of the principles governing the passage of vessels. In addition, one might point out that if Britain and France tried to present the company as a virtual guarantor of the freedom of navigation—which is a matter of fact rather than of law—they obviously erred in assigning to the company a task which, in material terms, could only be discharged by a power or a group of powers possessing the necessary military strength to assure respect for the convention of 1888. It was Britain herself who performed the guarantor's function between her occupation of Egypt in 1882 and her evacuation in 1954. When agreeing to leave Egypt in the latter year, the British surely knew that they were leaving physical control of the canal to the Egyptians. In terms of political decision making, that was the time to determine whether the risk was worth taking. To count on a private corporation, the Suez Canal Company, to take the place of a sovereign government in fulfilling security responsibilities appeared like a misunderstanding of the natural division of functions between private and public organisms. In fact, there was no change in the freedom of navigation through the canal before 1954—the date of the evacuation agreement—and after it, when Egypt became the sole physical guardian of the canal. There was one persistent case of discrimination, that practiced against Israel—a matter to which we shall return shortly—but it existed both during the period of British control and after its end. Consequently, the major Western powers did not have a really strong case for their claim that the continued presence of the Suez Canal Company provided the necessary guarantee for the freedom of navigation.

With regard to the technical aspects, arguments advanced against Egyptian

---

[24]The text is in *The Suez Canal, A Selection,* p. 52.

control of the operation could be narrowed down to two: (1) that efficiency and safety would suffer; (2) that with its avowed objective of channeling the canal's revenues to its domestic economic projects, Egypt would be deficient in its tasks of maintenance and development of the canal. Both allegations could not be conclusively proved or disproved at the time of nationalization because only actual practice was likely to provide convincing evidence. An attempt by the company to paralyze the operation by withdrawing its pilots failed. Egypt succeeded in finding suitable replacements, and after an initial slowdown traffic through the canal not only resumed its former pace, but with the passage of time even exceeded it, while safety standards were fully preserved. As for maintenance and development (i.e., widening and deepening the canal), every year since nationalization Egypt has made a point of earmarking a respectable portion of the revenue for these purposes. In the long run, however, some major investment, exceeding the regular annual allocations, was required and Egypt successfully solved this problem by obtaining a loan of $56 million from the World Bank in December of 1959. One further point might be mentioned. At the time of nationalization fears were expressed in Washington lest Egypt assign the newly hired Soviet pilots to American warships transiting the canal, an action unacceptable to the American government. Cairo promptly issued reassurances that nothing of the sort would be attempted, although no legal guarantees were actually given. However, it might be pointed out that the old Suez Canal Company was also free to hire any nationals it wished and that a similar problem might have arisen—at least theoretically—under the company's dispensation.

Israel and the Suez Canal

What has been said in the preceding section regarding freedom of navigation in the canal both before and after 1954, i.e., the date of the British evacuation agreement, should have one major reservation. This freedom was not complete, inasmuch as Egypt consistently denied Israel the use of the canal. Egypt's arguments on this issue have been reviewed earlier in this chapter. It suffices to say that the same arguments justifying the denial of access to the canal continued to be used after its nationalization. In actual practice, however, a certain evolution had taken place to Israel's disadvantage.

Since the establishment of the state of Israel in 1948, no Israeli ships had been allowed to pass; an attempt by the Israeli vessel *Bat Galim* to enter the canal ended in seizure of the vessel and detention of the crew. Cargoes shipped to Israel on vessels of foreign flag were refused passage if they appeared on the Egyptian "contraband list." The latter, as we know, included primarily war matériel. Furthermore, foreign vessels carrying other, noncontraband articles to Israel as well as those that had stopped at Israeli ports were black-listed by Egypt and sometimes, but not always, refused passage through the canal. According to statistics kept by the Israeli government, between May 1948 and September 1959 over 330 vessels from twenty-one countries had been placed on the black list and declared liable to Egyptian sanctions. It should be pointed out, however, that during the same years foreign vessels carrying Israeli cargoes southward to Asia and Africa were not denied passage.

This situation underwent a radical change in March 1959, when the Liberian ship

Kapetan Manolis and the West German ship *Lealott,* both proceeding from Israel, were detained and their cargoes of cement, fruit juices, and potash confiscated by the Egyptian authorities. Soon afterward, on May 21, the Danish ship *Inge Toft,* loaded with Israeli cement, potash, marble, and brass scrap was stopped and ordered to unload its cargo. Meeting with the captain's refusal to obey the order, the Egyptians detained the ship, barring it both from passage of the canal and return to its port of origin. The *Inge Toft* remained anchored at Port Said for nine months, the captain and his employers seemingly determined not to yield and hopeful that the United Nations, which in the meantime was discussing this matter on Israel's motion, would solve the dispute to their satisfaction. Their hopes, however, were disappointed, and in February 1960, faced with the restlessness of the crew, illness on board, and deterioration of the ship, the Danish owners under protest agreed to submit to the Egyptian order and unloaded the cargo. Only then was the *Inge Toft* permitted to sail away.

During the period of the *Inge Toft's* forcible detention, UN Secretary-General Dag Hammarskjöld held a number of meetings with the Cairo government, following which he informed Israel that he had informally succeeded in reaching the following agreement with the Egyptians with regard to Israeli cargoes: If Israel would agree to send her export goods through the canal in the ownership of the buyer (that is, f.o.b.) and to import merchandise under the ownership of the seller (that is, c.i.f.), the Cairo government would not deny passage through the canal to ships carrying these cargoes. Initially, Israel's reaction to this proposal was not favorable because Israel had for a long time struggled for recognition of her full right to use the canal like other nations. However, in view of her growing trade with Afro-Asia, and partly also because of strong persuasion by Hammarskjöld and certain Western governments, Israel agreed to conform to this working arrangement. It was also understood that future voyages of Israeli cargoes through the canal should be devoid of publicity so as to spare Egyptian authorities the political embarrassment likely to flow from public knowledge that Israeli goods had been allowed passage.

Acting on the basis of this understanding, Israel decided to try the new method and accordingly in December 1959 sent the Greek ship *Astypalea* loaded with 400 tons of cement purchased by an Asmara company from Haifa to Djibouti. The conditions of shipping were f.o.b. and the vessel was on "voyage charter" in the name of the purchaser. Moreover, Israel sent a prior notification to the UN Secretary-General and such "friendly" governments as had advised her to follow this method. To avoid undue publicity a complete blackout was otherwise imposed on the ship's movements. Despite all these precautions, the *Astypalea* was held up by the Egyptian authorities and her cargo confiscated. Having unloaded the cement, the ship returned to her home port in Piraeus.

Thus despite Secretary Hammarskjöld's efforts to reach a practical understanding, Cairo persisted in its adamant attitude, and Israel continued to be denied passage. Israel's leaders felt bitter about the world's indifference to their plight, and their bitterness was increased when they learned that in December 1959 the World

Bank had agreed to grant Egypt a substantial loan for the development of the canal. Israel was determined to keep the issue alive by invoking various international agreements and resolutions which, in her view, definitely upheld her right to free navigation through the canal. These were, in particular: (1) The Constantinople Convention of 1888, (2) The Security Council Resolution of October 13, 1956, by which six principles regarding Suez were unanimously adopted, (3) The Security Council Resolution of September 1, 1951, which called upon Egypt to terminate its restrictions on and to cease interference with Israeli shipping, (4) The declaration by the Egyptian government to the Secretary-General of the United Nations on April 24, 1957, in which Egypt pledged to maintain free and uninterrupted navigation for all nations in compliance with the Constantinople Convention and with the six principles adopted in 1956.

Furthermore, in support of their thesis the Israelis repeatedly quoted from a speech President Eisenhower made on February 20, 1957, in which he called upon Israel to withdraw unconditionally from Sinai territory. The President had said:

> Egypt, by accepting the six principles adopted by the Security Council last October in relation to the Suez Canal, bound itself to free and open transit through the Canal without discrimination, and to the principle that the operation of the Canal should be insulated from the politics of any country. We shall not assume that, if Israel withdraws, Egypt will prevent Israel shipping from using the Suez Canal.

The President added that if Egypt did not conform to these principles, "this should be firmly dealt with by the society of nations."[25]

In spite of the hopes thus expressed and Israel's unceasing campaign for the recognition of her demands, neither the United Nations nor the individual member states were willing to take drastic action to make Egypt admit Israel's right to free navigation. Although no state had officially accepted Egypt's contention that, being at war with Israel, it was free to deny the latter passage through the canal, in practice a line was drawn between the general community of nations and Israel, which was regarded as a "special case" not subject to the general principles regarding the navigation in the canal.

The June and October Wars

With the outbreak of the third Arab-Israeli war, Egypt (U.A.R) closed the canal to all shipping on June 6, 1967. The order of closure was accompanied by physical blockage of the waterway: mines and explosives were placed in it, some ships were deliberately sunk, and others became victims of wartime operations. The canal was clogged with remnants of airplanes, tanks, and other equipment. Some ships transiting the canal at the time were caught between these obstacles and had to remain there for several years until the canal was cleared.

Politically, the situation underwent a radical change inasmuch as Israel, as a result of military victory, established its front line on the eastern bank of the canal

---

[25]For a statement of the Israeli case by Golda Meir, minister of foreign affairs, see the *Israel Digest*, Oct. 2, 1959.

where it constructed the so-called Bar-Lev line of strong fortifications. Furthermore, to prevent a possible Egyptian recrossing of the canal, Israel planted many mines of its own in the canal waters. The war of attrition which raged along the canal in 1968 and 1969 resulted in virtual destruction of the Egyptian canal city of Ismailia, and the cities of Port Said and Suez were heavily damaged. The entire western bank of the canal became a war zone, from which the civilian population was evacuated.

On the first day of the October War in 1973, the Egyptian army crossed the canal and overcame Israeli resistance at the Bar-Lev line. For some time the entire eastern bank of the canal was under Egyptian control but in the later stage of the war, Israel's counteroffensive in the central sector of the canal resulted in the establishment of a bridgehead on its western side (the so-called Deversoir Bulge). With the conclusion of the Sinai I agreement of January 18, 1974, Israeli troops were withdrawn from the west bank and the entire canal reverted to Egypt's control. Although it had abandoned direct access, the Israeli army was separated from the canal by a narrow stretch of territory and it was easily within the reach of Israeli artillery. The Sinai II agreement, concluded on September 1, 1975, substantially increased the distance between the Israelis and the canal by providing for an advance of Egyptian troops and the creation of a UN-supervised neutral zone. Moreover, Article 7 of the Sinai II agreement provided that Egypt would permit nonmilitary cargoes on third-nation ships to and from Israel to pass through the canal.[26]

Return of control of the canal to Egypt began the process of its reopening. The physical clearing of the canal started in April 1974 and was carried out with substantial participation of the United States, Soviet, and British navies by agreement with Egypt. American minesweepers were particularly useful in retrieving American-manufactured mines which the Israelis had planted in the waters. The Soviet navy was used primarily to retrieve parts of Soviet tanks, planes, and other equipment, initially used by the Egyptians, to keep them out of American and British hands. The clearing operation was financed by a $50 million loan granted by the World Bank in December 1974, followed by $126 million from the Kuwait Fund for Arab Economic Development (KFAED) and the governments of Saudi Arabia, Qatar, and the United Arab Emirates.

Finally, after eight years of idleness, the canal was reopened on June 5, 1975. Simultaneously, the Egyptian Suez Canal Authority announced that the transit fees would be almost double those in force before June 1967. The increase was largely attributed to world inflation.

The Sinai II provision which allowed inbound and outbound cargoes for Israel to use the canal undoubtedly constituted a political gain for Tel-Aviv. But from the purely economic point of view, this newly acquired right was not very attractive because Israel in most cases could probably use more profitably its own port of Elath for trade with East Africa and the countries around the Indian Ocean. Nevertheless November 1, 1975, when a Greek freighter carrying cement to Elath passed through the Suez Canal, was an important day. And on November 18 a Liberian ship bound for Iran carried the first Israeli cargo through the canal.

[26]Text in *Current History* (Jan. 1976), pp. 32 ff.

The reopening of the canal was bound to have some strategic consequences for the major powers. For the Soviet Union, it provided a quicker access to the Indian Ocean and the Persian Gulf from the Black Sea and the Mediterranean. Moreover, virtually any Soviet naval vessel without tonnage limitations was able to pass through the canal because the Soviet Union at that time did not have aircraft carriers. While thus the potential for faster movements of the Soviet navy definitely increased, it is doubtful that the reopening of the canal made much difference in the overall strategic balance of power between the USSR and the West. Should the Soviets choose to send many ships of their Black Sea fleet and their Fifth Escadra in the Mediterranean to the Indian Ocean, they would deplete so substantially their forces closer to home as to make the gain implied by their stronger presence in the Indian Ocean somewhat illusory. As for the United States, most of its warships, including smaller aircraft carriers, could pass through the canal, but the big carriers were not able to use it. The same was true of large supertankers, of which a great number were constructed during the eight years of the canal's inactivity. These, carrying oil from the Persian Gulf to Western destinations, had to follow the route around the Cape of Good Hope; moreover, with their large capacity they became so economical that even the reopening of the canal, assuming they could use it, would not invalidate the economic advantages derived from their sheer size.

Development of the Canal and Its Economic Impact

While the removal of the war-generated physical obstacles in the canal was the first condition for its reopening, the extra silt accumulated since June 1967 also had to be removed and the eroded banks repaired. When the canal was reopened on June 5, 1975, the maximum allowable draft was thirty-three feet. The immediate objective was to attain, by dredging, the thirty-eight-foot draft of the pre-1967 period. Work was proceeding rapidly and by the end of 1975 an allowable draft of forty feet was attained.

In the long run, however, the canal had to be widened and deepened to perform well as a major world waterway. The Egyptian government and the world shipping community had not lost hope that the canal would eventually be able to allow the passage of supertankers. With this goal in view, the Egyptian government engaged the services of a British firm of engineering consultants to determine the optimum width and depth of the canal. Following these studies, it was determined that the canal should attain sixty-four feet of draft capacity (19.5 meters). To perform this work of expansion, the Suez Canal Authority signed several contracts between 1974 and 1977 with Japanese firms, and one contract with a French consortium to develop the canal in the Bitter Lakes area and to construct the Deversoir Extension canal. The target date for the completion of these development schemes was the early 1980s, depending on the sector of the canal under contract. Major financial outlays were necessary—two of the Japanese contracts were for $173 million and $112 million. The total expansion program was estimated in mid-1977 to cost $1 billion, on the assumption that the dollar would not deteriorate in value. Financing of this ambitious plan was assumed by a number of governments and institutions. The government of Japan in July 1975 pledged a $130 million loan to Egypt on very convenient terms in fulfillment of earlier promises. The governments of Saudi

Arabia and Kuwait agreed in April 1977 to lend Egypt $222 million to make the canal navigable for supertanker traffic. In addition, the Saudi Development Fund, the Islamic Bank, the government of Abu Dhabi, and the OAPEC-sponsored Arab Fund for Economic and Social Development came forth with loans in varying amounts. In the same year the World Bank loaned Egypt $100 million for twenty years. In late 1977 the Japanese government provided a second loan of $86 million. All in all, it appeared that financing was properly assured by the community of oil-producing nations and certain major consuming countries.[27]

Traffic in the canal soon resumed its prewar proportions or even exceeded them. In 1976, the first normal year of operations, the monthly general traffic was between 1,168 and 1,654 ships; 2,610 tankers used the canal, of which 1,213 were loaded and 1,397 were in ballast headed for the Persian Gulf ports. Of the latter, 150 were supertankers which could pass the canal in ballast but had to round the southern tip of Africa when loaded. The concluding weeks of 1976 saw a particular increase in the supertanker traffic under ballast to beat the deadline for loading before the scheduled OPEC increase in oil prices in January 1977. In terms of tonnage, the tanker traffic averaged 6.5 million tons a month, a total of 80 million tons a year, which was 24 million tons short of the forecast. The lower figure was attributed to the glut of oil and tankers in the world in the late 1970s.[28]

The reopening of the canal proved to be of great economic importance to Egypt. Whereas on the eve of the June war, 1967 Egypt's annual revenue from the canal amounted to about $220 million a year, beginning with 1976 it reached $450 million with a steadily upward trend. As of mid-1977 Egypt was obtaining $1.25 million a day in transit fees; her revenue from the canal in 1977 attained the $500 million level, about equal to its foreign exchange earnings from tourism and roughly 25 percent of its total foreign exchange intake.

The SUMED Pipeline

The lengthy blocking of the canal in the aftermath of the 1967 war had led Egypt to envision the construction of a pipeline between the Red Sea and the Mediterranean which would substitute for the lost revenue of the Suez Canal. Accordingly, on December 29, 1973, an agreement to establish the Gulf of Suez-Mediterranean Petroleum Company was signed by Egypt, Saudi Arabia, Kuwait, Abu Dhabi, and Qatar. The company was capitalized at $400 million with the allocation of shares being $200 million for Egypt, $60 million for Saudi Arabia, Kuwait, and Abu Dhabi respectively, and $20 million for Qatar. The Kuwait Foreign Trading, Contracting, and Investment Company undertook to arrange for a loan of $100 million with a consortium of banks. Another loan of $100 million was granted by the United States Export-Import Bank. The next step was the award of a $345 million construction contract to the Bechtel Corporation of San Francisco. The total cost was estimated to reach $400 million. A forty-two-inch pipeline was laid down between

---

[27]Data on financing are to be found in various issues of *Middle East Economic Survey (MEES)* (Beirut).

[28]Data on traffic tonnage are from *MEES, Petroleum Intelligence Weekly, Platt's Oilgram News Service,* and *Shipping Statistics and Economics.*

Ain Sukhna south of Suez and Sidi Kerir west of Alexandria. The line, with a capacity of 80 million tons a year, was opened in January 1977. The second stage of development envisaged an increase in capacity to 120 million tons a year but the decision to proceed with further work was kept in abeyance pending a review of the economic aspects of the venture.[29]

Although this chapter is devoted to the study of waterways, a brief review of the Suez-Mediterranean (SUMED) pipeline is included inasmuch as the problems of the Suez Canal and pipeline traffic are interconnected. Whereas the pipeline had been initially conceived as a substitute for the blocked canal, the decision to proceed with its construction was reached after the October War when Egypt had regained control over the canal. It was based on the assumption that the demand for oil in the consuming countries of the West would grow at a rate which would justify the existence of both transit routes. Excess of oil supply over the demand in 1975, 1976, and 1977 caused considerable underutilization of the SUMED pipeline. In fact, during the first year of its operations, 1977, the pipeline was used only up to 25 percent of its capacity. The principal users who signed contracts with Egypt for that purpose were the Exxon, Mobil, and Petrofina oil companies. Each of them undertook to transport a certain minimum tonnage through the pipeline. In that same year Egypt's revenue from SUMED amounted to about $140 million, a substantial amount in the total of Egypt's foreign exchange earnings. The forecasts for world oil consumption in the 1980s and 1990s indicated a steady increase in demand. Under the circumstances, plans for increased throughput capacity of the SUMED line as well as for further development of the Suez Canal appeared to be justified in the long run.

The Strait of Hormuz

The two main outlets from Middle Eastern waters to the Indian Ocean, the Strait of Hormuz and the Strait of Bab el-Mandeb, could never be considered negligible from the strategic point of view but in the old colonial, prepetroleum times their importance was limited and their security appeared to be adequately assured by the domination of such imperial powers as Great Britain and France. In the period following World War II the economic and strategic significance of these outlets has become dramatically evident, owing to three principal factors: first, the spectacular growth of oil traffic through these waterways; second, the political changes that have occurred in the riparian countries, notably decolonization, radicalization, and penetration by international communism; and third, a substantial expansion of the Soviet navy, expressed in the size and quality of its ships and the extension of its operations into the Indian Ocean, the Persian Gulf and the Red Sea.

Oil Traffic in the Strait of Hormuz

Although certain Middle Eastern oil fields were connected through pipelines with the eastern Mediterranean coast in the 1930s and 1940s, following World War II the

[29]Information largely based on data from *MEES* and *Quarterly Economic Review of Oil in the Middle East* (London).

bulk of oil export traffic was carried in tankers loaded in the Persian Gulf and transiting the Strait of Hormuz. The volume of this traffic was steadily increasing, corresponding to the greater production in the Middle East and growing consumption in the recipient countries. In the 1970s, with the exception of the year 1973–74 during which the Arab oil-producing countries imposed an embargo on certain consuming states, the oil traffic rose steadily until it leveled out due to the temporary world glut of oil. To take a typical set of figures for that period, we may say that in November 1977 the total oil production from the Asian part of the Middle East (excluding Egypt) amounted to 22.3 million barrels a day. To arrive at the export figures through the gulf the following calculation may be made:

Middle East production		22.3 m/b/d
Deduct:		
Iraq north	1.3 m/b/d	
Syria	0.2	
Oman	0.3	
Local consumption	1.5	
Subtotal	3.3	3.3 m/b/d
Balance		19.0 m/b/d

It should be pointed out that the figure of 19 million barrels a day included the entire production of Saudi Arabia (about 8.5 m/b/d) inasmuch as the Trans-Arabian Pipeline Company (Tapline) which had previously transported a substantial volume of Saudi crude to its terminal in Sidon in Lebanon, had ceased operations in the mid-1970s as a result of the civil war in Lebanon. Although Saudi Arabia was looking forward to replacing the Tapline outlet with a new pipeline linking Jubail in the east to Yanbu on the Red Sea, the volume transited through this new route was not expected to affect materially the amount of traffic through the Strait of Hormuz because of anticipated growth in exports in the 1980s and beyond.

The total of 19 million barrels a day thus transported through the straits was roughly equivalent to the entire daily consumption of oil in the United States and approached the amount consumed by Europe. To cater to these export demands the riparian states of the gulf developed some dozen major oil ports and a number of lesser ones. Oil was loaded on tankers in the ports of Abadan, Kharg, Bandar Mashur in Iran; Fao in Iraq; Mina Ahmadi in Kuwait; Mina Saud in the Neutral Zone; Ras Tanura, the only major Saudi port in the gulf; El-Zannah and Das in Abu Dhabi; Umm Said in Qatar; and Manama in Bahrain. The density of the traffic through the Strait of Hormuz was illustrated by the fact that approximately every fifteen minutes a tanker would sail through its waters.

The continuous presence of so many tankers in the Persian Gulf, the Strait of Hormuz, and the Gulf of Oman considerably aggravated the pollution of these waters—even without major catastrophic spills—with attendant harm to fisheries and ecology in general. Beginning in 1975, the riparian states, led by Iran and Oman, began taking steps against pollution through individual and concerted action. According to statements made in the spring of 1977 by Iskandar Firuz, head of the Iranian department of environment and assistant to the prime minister, the riparian states were undertaking collective action to implement antipollution plans that had been drawn at an earlier meeting in January 1977 in Bahrain. As early as 1975 Iran authorized its navy to search ships suspected of causing pollution within fifty miles of its coast. Similarly, the United Arab Emirates issued in 1977 instructions to its coast guard and naval units to patrol U.A.E. waters to detect cases of pollution by merchant ships and oil tankers. Generally, the riparian states showed intensified interest in the enforcement of rules against marine pollution adopted by the intergovernmental Maritime Consultative Organization.

Political Changes in the Riparian States

The most important political factor affecting the position of the Strait of Hormuz was the achievement or assertion of independence by the riparian states of the Persian Gulf, the Gulf of Oman, and the south Arabian coast. In South Yemen and in Oman's province of Dhofar militant radicalism, often taking a violent form, made its appearance, with a potential for spreading along the coast toward the north. Moreover, both the government of South Yemen and the Marxist-oriented rebels in Dhofar, as noted previously, were availing themselves of military assistance from such communist states as the Soviet Union, China, East Germany, and Cuba.

This process of radicalization was accompanied by Soviet naval expansion. The Soviet navy definitely established its presence in the Indian Ocean and acquired access to naval facilities in the ports of Aden in South Yemen and Berbera in Somalia. Similarly, the Soviet Union rendered active help to India in its war with Pakistan in 1971. The conclusion in 1972 of a friendship treaty between Moscow and the Baathist regime in Baghdad undoubtedly stimulated Soviet interest in access to the Iraqi waters. In the 1970s Soviet warships began making regular appearances in the Persian Gulf waters, nineteen visits of Soviet ships in the Iraqi port of Umm Qasr in 1974, nine such visits in 1975, fifteen in 1976, and seven during the first half of 1977. In addition, three visits of Soviet naval vessels were paid to Iranian ports ostensibly in search of water and supplies, a request which the Iranian government found difficult to refuse during the Washington-sponsored detente.[30]

Iran's Reactions to Potential Dangers

Faced with these challenges to the security of the Strait of Hormuz, Iran developed a policy of resistance to radicalism, subversion, and foreign intervention in the areas of the lower gulf and southeastern Arabia. In numerous interviews and public statements in the 1970s the Shah spoke of the need to build up a more powerful navy and advocated the expansion of Iran's "security perimeter" beyond the Persian Gulf and the Gulf of Oman into the Indian Ocean. He also expressed determination to spread "the defense umbrella of the navy and the air force to the whole of the Gulf of Oman."[31] And in a significant interview granted in May 1973,

[30]For a comprehensive analysis, see Dale R. Tahtinen, with the assistance of John Lenczowski, *Arms in the Indian Ocean: Interests and Challenges* (Washington, D.C., 1977).

[31]Rouhollah K. Ramazani, *Iran's Foreign Policy, 1941–1973* (Charlottesville, Va., 1975), p. 428. See also Alvin J. Cottrell, "Iran's Armed Forces under the Pahlavi Dynasty," in George Lenczowski, ed., *Iran under the Pahlavis* (Stanford, 1978), pp. 405–407.

the Shah linked the security of the Strait of Hormuz passage for oil with the Dhofar rebellion. Should the latter succeed, Oman, according to him, would be in hostile hands. "Just try to imagine what we would be faced with in Muscat. The capital right in front of the Strait of Hormuz. At first a few rifles and then naval guns and missiles. It's a familiar pattern. I cannot tolerate subversive activities—and by that I mean anything that is imposed from the outside." Further, to a question, "Are you saying you cannot tolerate radical regimes taking over any of the Arab sheikhdoms?" he replied, "Yes."[32]

To implement this policy of resistance to radicalism and subversion in the area, Iran engaged in three lines of action. First, on November 30, 1971, it forcibly occupied three islands in the Persian Gulf, Abu Musa and the Greater and Lesser Tunbs. Second, Iran embarked upon an intensive arms acquisition policy and in the mid-1970s became the foremost buyer of American arms anywhere in the world. And third, it embarked upon expansion of the Iranian navy and naval facilties in the gulf.

The most spectacular of these actions was undoubtedly the occupation of the three islands. Iran's policy in this respect was purposeful and calculated to reduce the adverse Arab reaction to a minimum. To achieve this objective, Iranian diplomacy displayed a good deal of skill and sophistication. In the first place, Iran engaged in negotiations with London so as to achieve control of the three islands if possible by agreement and thus to share the responsiblity for this act with Great Britain. Furthermore, although no open formal consent was obtained from the British, the Shah decided to occupy the islands two days before the termination of the British protectorate with Sharja and Ras el-Khaima. (This, incidentally, provided some justification for the claim of Colonel Muammar Qadhafi of Libya that there was British connivance in the act.) Furthermore, in an attempt to reduce friction to a minimum, Iran had negotiated an agreement with Sharja regarding control of Abu Musa. Recognition by Iran of the independence of Bahrain in advance of the move on the islands could also be regarded as a purposeful gesture to emphasize that Iran was not interested in territorial expansion but merely in the security of these waters. While all these steps were being taken, the Shah and his ministers were cultivating the good will of Saudi Arabia—a country as concerned with the threat of radicalism in the area as was Iran—to mute her expected negative reaction to the seizure of the islands. In the same category one should place the resumption, on August 29, 1970, of diplomatic relations with Egypt after ten years of rupture. It paid a dividend: when the Arab League Council was hurriedly called on December 5, 1971, to consider the occupation of the islands, Egypt was foremost in advising a moderate reaction to the Iranian move. Finally, Iran was the first nation to grant formal recognition to the newly established United Arab Emirates, within a few hours of its proclamation of independence on December 2, 1971. This act also reduced to a minimum the U.A.E.'s adverse reaction to the Iranian move on the islands.

Occupation of the islands was followed by the steady development of the Iranian navy and the expansion of its facilities. The naval headquarters were moved from Khorramshahr to Bandar Abas at the northern bend of the Strait of Hormuz and a

---

[32]Quoted by Ramazani, *op. cit.*, pp. 351–352.

new port, Chahbahar, was being developed in the 1970s on the Iranian coast of the Gulf of Oman. Its main purpose was to serve as a major base for the *Spruance* class destroyers, the purchase of which Iran was negotiating with the United States. In pursuing this forward maritime policy, Iran also expressed interest in acquiring naval facilities on the island of Mauritius—now an independent state—whose premier on a visit to Iran in December 1972 had expressed readiness to grant such an Iranian request.

In 1976 and 1977 Iran, the United States, and the gulf riparian states became alerted to the possibility of terrorist attacks against tankers transiting the Strait of Hormuz. The United States State Department issued a warning to oil shippers about the possibility of oil tankers being hijacked in the region, and a year later several riparian states took security measures to foil anticipated terrorist operations against the tankers in the Strait of Hormuz. This action was taken on the basis of some confidential reports that terrorist acts might be committed in retaliation for the West German commando raid which had released hostages of the hijacked Lufthansa aircraft at Mogadishu in Somalia. And again, in November 1977, the Iranian government put out an alert (in coordination with Saudi Arabia and the United Arab Emirates) against expected terrorist activity in the strait. Conforming to these directives, tanker captains were issued orders not to stop for any seemingly distressed vessel in those waters because of the possibility that such a ship faking distress might act as a decoy. Captains were issued instructions to stop only on orders of Iran's coast guard cutters, thus further accentuating Iran's predominant role in the Strait of Hormuz.

The Strait of Bab el-Mandeb

Located at the southern end of the Red Sea, the Bab el-Mandeb has fully earned its name (in Arabic, *the gate of lamentation*) because the unrelentingly hot and humid climate in conjunction with the bleak and uninviting coast on both sides of the strait make this region one of the least desirable in the world. The strait is divided into two channels by the small (five square miles) island, or more properly, rock, of Perim. The eastern channel closer to the coast of Arabia is two miles wide, while the western has a width of ten miles, is much deeper, and provides the main route for the transiting ships. On the Arabian side the strait is bounded by Yemen and South Yemen while on the African side it faces the republic of Djibouti. Perim Island belongs to South Yemen. Thus far there has been no legal problem arising out of the navigation through this strait. The narrower eastern channel lies definitely within the territorial waters of South Yemen while the western channel, between Perim and the African coast, constitutes also territorial waters shared by South Yemen and Djibouti. This is so because South Yemen has proclaimed a twelve-mile territorial waters limit—an act permissible by the International Law of the Sea— whereas Djibouti has not yet made any formal pronouncement on this subject and thus is entitled to at least the traditional three-mile limit. Should it also claim a twelve-mile limit as did South Yemen, the division between their respective territorial waters would run through the median line of the channel.

Although the strait is located within the territorial waters of the adjacent states, it is an international waterway allowing freedom of innocent passage. Therefore it does not require any special agreements, being generally covered by the rules of international law.[33] In 1974, however, an interesting change took place in the status of Perim Island. The island, while remaining under South Yemen's sovereignty, was placed at the disposal of Egypt in return for an annual payment of £5 million, the sum to be contributed by Saudi Arabia.

Economically, the Strait of Bab el-Mandeb has always been important because, like the Suez Canal, it has served as a passageway for the substantial shipping traffic between the Mediterranean and the Indian Ocean. In addition, it has also been a route of approach for cargo from Asia and Africa destined for the riparian states of the Red Sea, namely Yemen, Saudi Arabia, Ethiopia, Sudan, Egypt, Jordan, and Israel. Moreover, every time the Suez Canal was blocked—three times since World War II—the Bab el-Mandeb saw its Red Sea-bound traffic considerably increased. In the mid-1970s seventy ships passed through it daily on the average.

Political and Strategic Considerations

To appreciate fully the strait's importance in international affairs, it has to be treated within the broader context of political alignments of the riparian states as well as the political situation in the Indian Ocean and the Red Sea basins. Its immediate strategic value rests in the fact that, so long as the Suez Canal is also open, the Strait of Bab el-Mandeb provides the shortest access for oil tankers with European destinations. These tankers, apart from supplying the needs of European consumers, also bring oil to fuel the United States Sixth Fleet in the Mediterranean. As of the late 1970s, the Strait of Bab el-Mandeb has not generated any major political or military controversy. A single exception was the attack launched by some Palestine guerrillas—probably from a base in South Yemen—on the Iranian oil tanker *Coral Sea* sailing northward to Israel. Thus, in contrast to the perennial controversy surrounding the use of the Turkish Straits and the Suez Canal, the Bab el-Mandeb has proved to be a peaceful waterway.

In spite of this respectable record, the strait has a serious potential for causing at least four major international problems. These could be listed as follows:

1. Because both its African and its Arabian coast are controlled by Arab nations (South Yemen, Yemen, and Djibouti) with such Arabic-speaking countries as Somalia and Eritrea in close vicinity, there exists a potential for a challenge to Israel's freedom of navigation, hence to some extent to its economic well-being and security. The assumption of control by Egypt over Perim Island is indicative of Egypt's strategic interest in the strait, possibly with an eye to its relations with Israel.

2. The Strait of Bab el-Mandeb is surrounded by a number of states with radical political tendencies. These are, in particular, the Democratic People's Republic of Yemen (South Yemen), Somalia, and, since the overthrow of the monarchy in the 1970s, Ethiopia. The political behavior of such radical states has often been charac-

---

[33]For a discussion of legal aspects, see Majid Khadduri and Herbert Dixon, "Passage through International Waterways," section on Bab el-Mandeb, in M. Khadduri, ed., *Major Middle Eastern Problems in International Law* (Washington, D.C., 1972), pp. 86–88.

terized by disregard and rejection of the rules of international law, the latter treated as further evidence of the "bourgeois status quo." The leadership of South Yemen has clearly behaved in a nonconformist way in its relations with the neighboring state of Oman or with the Republic of Yemen to the north. Moreover, South Yemen's sovereignty extends not only to the island of Perim but also to the archipelago of Kamaran Islands which possess both natural harbor facilities and an airfield. These islands, located as they are 200 miles north of the Strait of Bab el-Mandeb in the Red Sea, have the potential for serving as a naval and air base to any power with ambitions in the Red Sea basin. Finally, since the overthrow of its monarchy in the mid-1970s, Ethiopia has clearly displayed a Marxist orientation. Since then Ethiopia has faced two simultaneous separatist movements, one in its southeastern province of Ogaden inhabited by the ethnic Somali population, and the other in its Red Sea province of Eritrea where an Arab-oriented nationalist movement led a rebellion with the objective of attaining full independence. These complications, as is often the case, could and did bring foreign intervention in the form of Soviet, Cuban, and Israeli assistance to the Marxist government of Ethiopia.

3. Marked Soviet penetration in the radical states in the neighborhood of the Bab el-Mandeb further added to the potential of international conflict. In fact, Soviet presence in South Yemen, Somalia (until 1977), and Ethiopia was in the long run more disturbing to the *status quo* in the area than the occasional passage of Soviet ships through the Strait of Hormuz, which borders on Iran and Oman.

Close cooperation if not an actual alliance between the Soviet Union on the one hand and South Yemen and Ethiopia on the other furthered opportunities to establish Soviet naval and air presence near the Bab el-Mandeb. The Soviet navy not only had access to the Aden port facilities but also was helping in their further development. When, on November 13, 1977, President Siad Barre cancelled the Soviet-Somali treaty of 1974 and expelled Soviet experts and military advisers and instructors, the Soviets lost the use of their naval base in Berbera and of the air base in Uanle Uen. They promptly compensated for this, however, in gaining access to the airports in Ethiopia. Their influx into that country, accompanied by an even larger influx of the Cubans (estimated at some 3,000 in 1977–1978), materially helped Ethiopia's leader, Colonel Mengistu Haile Mariam, to launch a successful counter-offensive against the Somali rebels in Ogaden and opened a possibility of the Ethiopian advance into Somalia proper with an eye to establishing a foothold on the Somali coast. From the Ethiopian point of view such an opening to the sea would be very important inasmuch as its only workable access to the sea was through the newly independent state of Djibouti, an Arab-oriented country. So long as Eritrea was in the throes of rebelliion, Ethiopia could not utilize its Red Sea ports of Assab and Massawa. Should the Eritreans succeed in their struggle for liberation and achieve independence, Ethiopia would be completely landlocked. It is no wonder, under the circumstances, that, having chosen the Ethiopian side in its struggle for the integrity of its empire, the Soviet Uniion made a major effort in assisting the Ethiopian offensive against the Eritreans as soon as Ogaden was freed from Somali danger. Should Ethiopia succeed in restoring control over Eritrea, its coastal harbor and airport facilities might become available to the Soviet Union.

In a broader sense, Russia conducted in the 1970s a forward naval policy in the Indian Ocean, where on the average ten Soviet war vessels were being kept, with the occasional presence of the 18,000-ton helicopter carrier *Leningrad*. The Soviet navy accounted for three times as many ship-days in these vast waters as the United States. It established anchorages at Socotra, a South Yemeni possession, and at Seychelles.

4. With its proclamation of independence in 1977, the Republic of Djibouti emerged as a possible trouble spot not because of any aggressive tendencies of its government but because of its weakness and vulnerability. A small area of 8,800 square miles consisting of sand and rock with virtually no vegetation and no resources, the new republic had a small population of 300,000, most concentrated in its harbor area and the rest nomadic. No sooner had it achieved independence than the heads of state of Somalia and Ethiopia began accusing one another of having plans to annex Djibouti. Djibouti's future as an independent state was indeed clouded with uncertainties. Until its emancipation, Djibouti constituted the last relic of French colonialism, in fact of Western imperialism, in that area. Save for dubious prestige, it brought no tangible benefits to France. Even after the proclamation of independence, France agreed to maintain 6,500 troops in Djibouti and help it with experts and $1.4 million annual subsidy. To safeguard its independence and integrity, Djibouti as a new member of the Arab League could count on the political and financial support of more fortunate Arab states and, possibly, on restraint of Ethiopia under the influence of the Soviet Union, which was probably unwilling to antagonize the Arab world by encouraging Ethiopian conquest of a member state of the Arab League.

There was little that the West in general or the United States in particular could do directly to strengthen freedom of international navigation in the Bab el-Mandeb. Indirectly, however, visible and close cooperation among the United States, Egypt, and Saudi Arabia in the 1970s, joined to the American naval presence in the Indian Ocean, was apt to act as a countervailing influence against the potentially disruptive trends in the Bab el-Mandeb region. As noted in an earlier chapter, in January 1975, during his visit in Washington, Sultan Qabus of Oman granted to the United States the use of facilities on Masirah Island. This was an important advantage gained by the United States inasmuch as Masirah was capable of serving as a base for two to three Polaris submarines and even of accommodating as many as 40,000 troops in case of need. The acquisition of these facilities more than compensated for the loss of full-fledged port facilities in Bahrain. Furthermore, located midway between the Bab el-Mandeb and Hormuz straits, Masirah could play a significant strategic role in the midst of the main oil tanker lanes and thus supplement the American naval presence established earlier at the Diego García Island in the Indian Ocean.

To conclude, while the issue of passage through or control of the Strait of Bab el-Mandeb has not by the late 1970s caused an international crisis or generated difficulties in a more narrow technical sense, the situation in southwest Arabia and in the Horn of Africa had the potential of materially influencing the destiny of this strategic waterway.

CHAPTER XIX

Arab Unity and Disunity

On March 22, 1945, in Cairo, seven Arab states (Egypt, Saudi Arabia, Iraq, Syria, Lebanon, Yemen, and Transjordan) signed the pact of the Arab League.[1] The League was born as the result of two influences: one was the desire for greater unity and strength, very popular among the Arabs; the other was British encouragement.

The time-tested device of all imperial governments has traditionally been to "divide and rule." How, then, could Britain reconcile her continuing supremacy over the Middle East with simultaneous support of an Arab movement for unity? This seemingly puzzling question can be answered only in the light of events that have occurred since 1914.

Background for the League

It will be recalled that with the outbreak of the First World War basic British concepts regarding the Middle East underwent a radical change. Britain abandoned her policy of maintaining the integrity of the Ottoman Empire and replaced it with a plan to build up an Arab kingdom or federation. This Arab state would then inherit the double function of the empire, namely, to serve as a friendly guardian of the British route to India and to act as a buffer against southward Russian expansion. With this end in view the British reached an agreement with Sherif Hussein that contained an explicit promise of Arab independence and an implicit recognition of the Hashemites as a ruling house. This agreement, however, was never fully implemented on account of Britain's wartime deals with the French and the Zionists. Moreover, the rise of Ibn Saud prevented its consummation in the Arabian peninsula. As a result, instead of achieving unity and independence the Arabs saw their lands divided and their freedom restricted. The Hashemites suffered grievous disappointments: King Hussein was ejected from his country by Ibn Saud; Faisal suffered

[1]On the origins and activities of the Arab League, consult Vernon McKay, "The Arab League in World Politics," *Foreign Policy Reports,* Nov. 15, 1946; C. A. Hourani, "The Arab League in Perspective," *Middle East Journal,* 1(April 1947); G. E. K., "Cross-Currents within the Arab League: The Greater Syria Plan," *World Today,* Jan. 1948; "Arab Post-Mortem," *The Economist,* March 5, 1949; Maurice Moyal, "Post-Mortem on the Arab League," *World Affairs* (April 1949); A. D., "The Arab League: Development and Difficulties," *World Today,* May 1951; G. E. Kirk, "Independent Syria and Lebanon," *R.C.A.J.* (July–Oct. 1948); also Jean Lugol, *Le Panarabisme* (Cairo, 1946).

a similar fate in Damascus at the hands of the French; and Abdullah, ready to assume the rule of Iraq, saw his hopes dashed and had to content himself with a barren tract of desert east of the Jordan River.

The peace settlement petrified the division of the Arab lands. In the interwar period Britain could implement her scheme of Arab unity only at the expense of France or the Zionists. This she was unwilling to do. Between 1939 and 1941, however, under the impact of the Nazi menace Britain regained her freedom of action. Finding it imperative to gain Arab good will Britain, early in 1939, sponsored the London conference of Arab states to consider the problem of Palestine. She thus set a pattern and a precedent for united Arab action under her protective wing. Moreover, soon after the conference and in response to Arab wishes, Britain issued the White Paper which was a blow to further Jewish immigration and expansion in Palestine. Britain took these measures with relative impunity because the Jews were unable to bargain with the two opposing camps. This time, due to Nazi policy, they had no choice but to stand by the democracies.

The second opportunity came in 1941 when the British conquered Syria and Lebanon from the Vichy French. Materially the British found themselves in a position to manipulate Arab politics throughout the Middle East because they were once again in military occupation of all Arab lands except Saudi Arabia and Yemen. Morally they felt no special inhibitions because of the French. France had not only failed them as an ally by surrendering and signing a separate peace with Germany but had gone so far as to permit Syria to be used as a base for enemy activities in the Middle East.

The conquest of Syria was the result of the dangerous situation which had developed in the Arab East in the spring of 1941. Axis influence was at its peak, and Britain felt an urgent need to make a bold bid for Arab friendship. At the end of action against pro-Nazi elements in Iraq, Foreign Secretary Eden declared, on May 29, 1941:

> The Arab World has made great strides since the settlement reached at the end of the last war, and many Arab thinkers desire for the Arab peoples a greater degree of unity than they now enjoy. In reaching out toward this unity, they hope for support. No such appeal from our friends should go unanswered. It seems to me both natural and right that the cultural and economic ties, too, should be strengthened. His Majesty's Government for their part will give their full support to any scheme that commands general approval.[2]

Barely a week later British and Free French troops invaded Syria. With Vichy capitulation a stage was set for the next move on the political chessboard. British diplomatic action centered henceforth on two strictly related tasks: (1) to free Syria and Lebanon from French control, and (2) to encourage the union of the Fertile Crescent[3] under the leadership of the Hashemites. The achievement of these aims would fulfill the original British concept of 1915—at least in major part: the Syrians

[2]*The Times* (London), May 30, 1941.
[3]Iraq, Syria, Lebanon, Palestine, and Transjordan.

and the Lebanese would be friendly to Britain for their liberation, the people of the whole area would welcome the elimination of artificial political barriers, and Britain would enhance her position by supporting the dynastic interests of the Hashemites. She would, moreover, give an opportunity to such trusted friends as Nuri es-Said of Iraq to play a major role as empire builders and unifiers of the Arab world.

From 1941 onward British action was consistent and purposeful, and it was well synchronized with the action of the Arabs themselves. In this work British interests were well served by a powerful team of experienced Arabists such as Sir Kinahan Cornwallis, ambassador to Iraq; Brigadier E. H. Clayton, brother of the late Sir Gilbert Clayton, and a man who over a quarter of a century had come to known more living Arab statesmen than any other Westerner; Brigadier Glubb Pasha, commander of the Arab Legion; Sir Walter Smart, oriental secretary (and later minister) at the British embassy in Cairo, who was married to an Egyptian lady of a prominent family; Lord Moyne, British minister of state for the Middle East who replaced Richard Casey in 1944; and General Edward Spears, chief of the British mission to the Levant. General Spears in particular did his best to remove French influence from Syria and to establish friendly relations with Shukri el-Quwatli's National Bloc party. Neither the De Gaulle-Lyttelton agreement nor official British denials could conceal the fact that, having to choose between Free French or Arab friendship, the British had chosen the latter. The situation was somewhat analogous to that prevailing in British-Zionist relations; the French, like the Zionists, could not bargain; they could only protest.

As to Arab action, the first steps were taken, as could be expected, by Nuri es-Said Pasha, prime minister of Iraq. In 1942, Nuri prepared a Blue Book in which he drew a plan of Arab union. It provided for an enlarged Syria which would include Lebanon, Palestine, and Transjordan and which would be linked with Iraq by a federative agreement. The whole would thus constitute a Fertile Crescent union. Such a union would have the merit of bringing together the countries that were near and similar to each other; it would be relatively small and therefore cohesive; and by its very modesty it would be a realistic first step in the gradual evolution toward a larger all-Arab entity. Nuri sent his plan to Richard Casey, British minister of state for the Middle East, and in 1943 circulated it privately among Arab leaders.[4] Nuri's action had Britain's full endorsement, and on February 24, 1943, Eden reiterated British support for a scheme of Arab unity. He added, however, that "the initiative in any scheme would have to come from the Arabs themselves" and that so far as he was aware "no such scheme which commands general approval has yet been worked out."[5] He thus referred to the fact that Nuri's proposals were not universally accepted. The truth was that they met considerable opposition in three distinct quarters. The first was Egypt, which feared that by the rise of a large united state in northern Arabia her own position of preeminence might be threatened. The second was Saudi Arabia, whose ruler was definitely opposed to any unification under the

[4]It was printed in Baghdad in 1943 under the title *Arab Independence and Unity* by the government press but not released to the public.

[5]Quoted in Majid Khadduri, "Towards an Arab Union," *American Political Science Review* (Feb. 1946), p. 90.

aegis of the rival Hashemite clan. And the third was Syria and Lebanon, whose "forty ruling families," prominent in the movement of the Arab awakening, preferred their republican oligarchy to a merger into a larger kingdom.

Thus Nuri's scheme suffered a setback and the initiative was taken over by Prime Minister Nahas Pasha of Egypt. Five weeks after Eden's statement Nahas presented tentative proposals for an Arab League to the Egyptian parliament. Nahas was motivated by three considerations: (1) he could not reject Nuri's plan without incurring the blame of opposing Arab unity; hence he had to come forward with some positive alternative; (2) he believed that an Egyptian-dominated Arab League might aid Egypt in achieving her national aspirations; (3) he was not devoid of personal ambition.

During the following eighteen months Nahas held conferences with the prime ministers or foreign ministers of all Arab states, who one by one visited Egypt. Nahas' concept of a loose league of sovereign Arab states gained wider acceptance than did Nuri's plan. Yet despite the nonradical character of Nahas' proposals, Saudi Arabia and Lebanon were very reluctant to commit themselves to any scheme of Arab unity. Lord Moyne's intervention finally convinced Ibn Saud that he had nothing to lose by joining the League, and Lebanon agreed to join under specific safeguards for her sovereignty.

Provisions of the Agreement

On October 7, 1944, in Alexandria, the seven Arab states of the Middle East signed a protocol in which they undertook, in the near future, to establish an Arab League according to a set of accepted principles. The protocol rejected earlier proposals for a full union, providing instead for an association of sovereign states, yet it stressed Arab unity in terms likely to evoke popular approval. Lebanon was reassured by a specific declaration guaranteeing her national sovereignty. The protocol contained, moreover, two significant provisions. One of them forbade the members to conduct policies detrimental to the league. And the other proclaimed the principle of nonintervention in the domestic affairs of the members. These two provisions were interpreted as a victory for British and Egyptian policies, respectively. The first meant that Syria and Lebanon would be prevented from concluding special treaties with France, thus confirming the gradual ouster—by British efforts—of France from the Levant. The second, by stressing the sanctity of the members' internal systems, was a rebuke to and a ban on the proroyalist unification propaganda hitherto conducted in Syria by the Hashemites. The latter was a diplomatic success for Egypt, and Azzam Pasha, future secretary of the league, hastened to remove all doubts on this point by declaring soon afterward that this provision had effectively shelved the Greater Syria plan.

When the Arab League came into being half a year later on the conclusion of the pact in Cairo, it was an even looser association than had been contemplated in Alexandria. The pact laid greater stress on the sovereignty of individual members and removed the ban on policies detrimental to the league. It provided for machinery composed of a council and six committees, and it introduced the principle of majority decisions which would be binding upon those who accepted them. The council was to convene twice a year, in March and in October, and also in extraordinary sessions upon the request of two member states. The league was to have a secretary-general, the first incumbent being named in the annex as Abdur Rahman Azzam Bey (later Pasha). Cairo was to be the seat of the league. The pact contained provisions concerning the pacific settlement of disputes but did not set up a collective security system. The main stress was laid on voluntary cooperation and consultation. Article 8 reaffirmed that "each member state shall respect the systems of government established in the other member states and regard them as exclusive concerns of those states. Each shall pledge to abstain from any action calculated to change established systems of government." But this provision was somewhat watered down in Article 9, which stated that "states of the League which desire to establish closer cooperation and stronger bonds than are provided by this Pact may conclude agreements to that end." There was no specific guarantee of Lebanon's independence inasmuch as the general principle of sovereignty covered this situation. In an annex Palestine, though not a member, was granted representation on the Council, and in another annex the League expressed its interest in the destiny and aspirations of those Arab countries that remained outside of it. Thus, the pact provided for a framework of Arab unity and cooperation. But in reality the League was created with a divided purpose. No real reconciliation was achieved between the Hashemite and Egyptian programs, and although the wording of the pact seemed to favor the Egyptian concept, neither party had renounced its ultimate ambitions.

The League at Work

A definite line can be drawn between the political and nonpolitical achievements of the league. In the nonpolitical field the league could pride itself on considerable accomplishments in the fields of cultural and technical cooperation. It sponsored exchanges of scholars and the conservation of ancient Arabic manuscripts; it called conferences of Arab engineers, doctors, archaeologists, and social scientists; it set up an Arab news agency; it prepared draft aviation agreements and other model treaties. It also reached decisions in the field of economic cooperation, especially pertaining to the boycott of Jewish goods, although in practice the latter measure fell short of expectations. But, as usual, the economic and social aspects were not decisive. It was the political action that really counted. It alone could determine whether or not the social and economic cooperation was in vain.

Politically there were two unifying factors: the problem of Palestine and the problem of the liberation of Arab peoples from foreign domination. Such points as the union of the Sudan with Egypt, the emancipation of Libya, and the freeing of Morocco could and did provide a platform for united political action and harmonious agreement.

Quarrel over Palestine

So long as the league was not expected to do more than pass resolutions and make diplomatic representations, the problem of Palestine elicited nothing but solidarity.

But as soon as the League was called upon to act, Palestine proved a stumbling block, which almost detroyed the league.

The differences over action in Palestine in 1948 stemmed from the basic conflict of ideas between the Hashemites and Egypt to which we have already referred when describing Nuri Pasha's initiative. We must remember, however, that the chief standard-bearer of the Greater Syria plan was not Nuri but Emir Abdullah, who after Faisal's death had become the recognized head of the house of Hashem. In contrast to Nuri, Abdullah was impetuous and impatient. In July 1941, right after the ouster of the Vichy French from the Levant, Abdullah declared that the union of Arab lands was the official aim of his policy. Such an open avowal of his ambitions proved somewhat embarrassing to the British, who believed it to be premature and who preferred to prepare ground by Nuri's cautious action and by slow spadework in Syria herself. Soon after this declaration Britain's minister of state for the Middle East, Oliver Lyttelton, hurried to Amman to restrain Abdullah from further hasty actions. This action was not intended to deflect Abdullah from his objective as a long-range policy. Consequently, Abdullah sent his agents to Damascus and lost no opportunity to advocate his Greater Syria plan. On two occasions, in 1943 and 1947, when the Syrians were going to the polls, Abdullah made direct appeals to them for a union under his crown. The second of these appeals provoked serious protests in Egypt and Saudi Arabia, Ibn Saud threatening to revive his claims to Maan and Aqaba. But the greatest deterrent to Abdullah's ambitions was the emergence in Syria of Quwatli's National Bloc, which was definitely resolved to preserve its monopoly of power.

Temporarily thwarted in Syria, Abdullah set his eyes on Palestine, where the impending changes seemed to offer an opportunity for aggrandizement. If he succeeded in securing control of the lands west of Jordan, he would make the first step toward the union of Arab countries and, as king of Palestine, increase his chances in Syria. Abdullah's position was strong: his Arab Legion was ready for action and a number of units were actually stationed in Palestine during the last phase of the British mandatory regime. In addition to this, Abdullah could count on the friendly cooperation of Musa Alami, representative of Palestinian Arabs in the Arab League, who during Haj Amin's absence had come to wield considerable influence in Palestine and who was known to favor the Fertile Crescent scheme.

Needless to say, such prospects were definitely distasteful to Egypt. Egypt decided that Transjordan's union with Palestine must be prevented at all costs and that the best way to achieve this was by encouraging the creation of a separate Arab state in Palestine. Saudi Arabia, Syria, and Lebanon wholeheartedly concurred. The next move was to bring the mufti of Jerusalem back from exile. Haj Amin had spent the war years in Germany and Italy. At the end of the war he was captured by the French, who placed him under house arrest in a villa near Paris. There was some talk in Allied circles of trying him as a war criminal, and Tito's Yugoslavia did list him as such for his aid in creating the Bosnian Moslem S.S. formations. But, before any such action could be taken, Haj Amin escaped from detention on board a Dutch plane and soon was welcomed by King Farouk in Egypt. His escape was engineered by the Syrian consul in Paris, Maaruf Dawalibi, who later, as a cabinet minister, went on record as favoring for Syria a policy of neutrality in the East-West conflict. The role the French authorities played in this machination was not fully clarified, but they must have had a moment of gleeful satisfaction by thus embarrassing the British. In fact, it looked like a belated revenge for their ouster from Syria. The mufti had a vested interest in keeping Palestine a separate entity. He could muster a considerable following among Palestinian Arabs. By liberally providing him with funds and arms, Egypt reintroduced him into the Palestinian scene as a counter-weight to Abdullah. The struggle for the spoils began long before Palestine was secured.

The rivalries and suspicions were reflected both during the arming of the Arab guerrilla forces and later during the war with Israel. Iraqi officers in charge of the Damascus training center did not want to issue arms to those Palestinian guerrilla leaders whom they believed to be the mufti's henchmen. On the other hand, Egypt and the mufti supplied arms to Kawukji's Liberation Army because Kawukji was anti-Hashemite, and they refused to arm those whom they suspected of connivance with Abdullah. As a result, the Arab population of Palestine was seriously short of weapons, and some of the larger centers such as Jaffa or Tiberias remained practically defenseless in the face of the total Jewish mobilization.

Likewise during the actual hostilities, cooperation between the Arab armies failed completely. Abdullah suspected that his rivals wanted his Arab Legion to take the brunt of the fighting and then, having bled it white, they would occupy Palestine with their own troops. For this reason he acted prudently, relying on his own strength and refusing to overextend his lines of communication by an advance toward the sea. By the same token Egypt instead of concentrating her troops in the coastal sector divided them into two groups, one advanced toward Tel-Aviv and the other toward Jerusalem. This division proved fatal. The Jerusalem force was badly defeated by Israel, and the Tel-Aviv force barely managed to maintain itself in a narrow strip near Gaza. Abdullah did nothing to relieve the hardpressed Egyptians.

The breakdown of inter-Arab cooperation and the resulting defeat in Palestine could also be ascribed, in some measure, to the withdrawal of British support. For at least a decade Britain had conducted a pro-Arab policy in Palestine. The White Paper of 1939 and her attitude between 1945 and 1947 proved it. But this policy did not bring the expected returns, mainly due to Egypt's policies. By assuming leadership in the Arab League, Egypt not only threw out of gear the initial British-Hashemite plan of Arab unity but actually began to use the league as an instrument of her own policy. Contributing 42 percent of the league's budget and securing a dominant voice through Azzam Pasha, Egypt exploited the league to foster her own anti-British tactics. When the matter of Palestine came before the United Nations in 1947, Britain was in a position to give substantial support to the Arab cause and, in fact, she did much to help the Arabs against the Zionists during the last phase of her administration in the Holy Land.[6] But, instead of reciprocating, Egypt chose this moment for anti-British intrigue by launching the inveterate foe of Britain, Haj Amin el-Husseini, into the Palestinian fray. The cup overflowed when Egypt, in an

[6]See footnote 36 to p. 407 above.

outburst of nationalist frenzy, brought the matter of British troops in Egypt and of the Sudanese regime to the United Nations. Premier Nokrashi's visit to Washington, in an attempt to replace Britain by the United States in Egyptian affairs, climaxed his anti-British campaign.

Under those circumstances British incentive to defend the general Arab cause in Palestine ceased to exist. Britain could help the Arabs in many ways. She could supply them with arms under the pretext that the Jews had violated the UN-proclaimed arms embargo. She could also, as a permanent member of the Security Council, prevent or delay the decision to impose the first truce on the belligerents. By halting the first bold thrust of the Arab armies the truce relieved certain hard-pressed sectors of Jewish defense and materially contributed to later Jewish victory. Moreover, her officers commanded the Arab Legion and, had they decided to rescue the Egyptian and Syro-Lebanese armies from their dire predicament, they probably could have done so. But the result would have been that large portions of Palestine would have fallen into the hands of the rabidly anti-British Egyptians, who would have hastened to install, with the Arab League's blessing, the mufti as the head of the new Arab state. Thus the anti-British camp in the league would only have been strengthened. This being so, the British thought it perferable to slow down the anti-Israel offensive and to secure some *modus vivendi* between Abdullah and the Jews. This meant that the only Arab-held part of Palestine would be the part occupied by the Arab Legion.

Such a policy, of course, hastened the defeat of the Arab armies other than the Legion, but it brought a sort of negative success to Britain. It demonstrated to the Arabs that the only Arab army capable of waging war was a British-trained force. It drove home to the Egyptians that without Britain's aid and advice their loudly advertised power was a hollow sword. It taught a stern lesson to the Quwatli bloc in Syria, who, instead of being grateful for liberation, had chosen to betray Britain and conspire with Egypt. In fact, the defeat shook the Syrian regime so profoundly as to make its continuance in power highly questionable, thus opening new vistas to British-backed Abdullah. This policy also greatly enhanced Abdullah's position: his Legion not only succeeded in the limited objectives it had proposed to attain but also proved its ability to march on Damascus and wipe out the Quwatli government should Abdullah and the British decide to do so.

The split thus produced in the ranks of the Arab League was further deepened by the formation in Gaza, on September 20, 1948, of the All-Palestine government under Egyptian auspices; by the annexation of eastern Palestine by Jordan; and by the Syrian crisis of 1949. These three events were closely interrelated, but it was the latter which particularly threatened to upset Egyptian supremacy in the League.

The Hashemite-Egyptian Feud

We dealt at some length with General Husni Zaim's coup in Chapter VIII. The downfall of the Quwatli regime, which had always stood for Syrian independence, gave Abdullah a new opportunity to press his claim for a Greater Syria. The coup, as we know, was made by the army with the connivance of some younger groups from Aleppo. It would not be surprising if future revelations proved that Abdullah's agents had a hand in engineering it. It is significant that Zaim's first moves were for a closer union with Iraq and Jordan. Unfortunately for the Hashemites Zaim soon changed his mind and turned toward Egypt and Saudi Arabia. His abrupt about-face was ascribed to clumsy handling of the affair by Nuri es-Said, who, during his visit in Damascus soon after the coup, treated Zaim too patronizingly.

With Zaim deserting Iraq and Jordan, Abdullah's star suffered an eclipse. But fate (or was it only fate?) came to his aid when, a few months later, Zaim was overthrown by Colonel Hinnawi, who, with Nazem el-Qudsi's People's Party, made the Fertile Crescent union his official plank. By the middle of December 1949, it looked as if the long-cherished plan of union were finally to be implemented, because the Syrian Constituent Assembly gave this matter high priority on its agenda. Colonel Shishakli's coup again frustrated these schemes. Shishakli's intervention did not settle Syria's destiny definitely. He was overthrown in 1954, as we know, by a coalition, which had certain Pan-Arab elements. Among them the Baath party was most conspicuous in advocating Arab unity, but in contrast to the pro-Iraqi groups came to favor close ties with Egypt.

As a result of all these events Abdullah's relations with the Egyptian-dominated majority in the league reached such a low point that he decided to boycott the spring meeting of the League Council in 1950. The absence of the Jordanian delegation was promptly exploited by Nahas Pasha, who moved that Ahmed Hilmi Pasha, prime minister of the Gaza government, be invited to attend the session. Nahas' motion was adopted, but this led Abdullah to change his mind and order his minister in Cairo, Baha ed-Din Bey Tuqan, to appear at the meeting. Baha ed-Din was instructed, however, to abstain from participation in case the Council decided to discuss territorial dispositions in Palestine.

The minister's appearance at the meeting did not heal the breach, and Egypt actually proposed that Jordan should be expelled from the League because of King Abdullah's negotiations with Israel. Such negotiations had, indeed, been conducted in 1949 and early 1950 with a view to obtaining a five-year nonaggression pact, transit facilities through Israeli territory, and a free zone in Haifa for Jordan. They had, moreover, been preceded by the so-called Shuna agreement, secretly concluded late in March 1949 (prior to the Israel-Jordan armistice), whereby the Arab Legion had conceded to the Israeli army a belt of land five miles deep along the front line. Faced with this drastic action by the league, Jordan abruptly stopped the negotiations and on April 1, 1950, joined all the other Arab states in voting to exclude from the league any member making a separate peace with Israel. Even this concession to the majority did not save Jordan from further difficulties. On May 15 she was condemned by the League's Political Committee for her unilateral annexation of eastern Palestine. A new Egyptian motion to expel her won the support of Saudi Arabia, Syria, and Lebanon. The opposition of Iraq and Yemen[7] prevented this measure from materializing.

[7]The new Imam, Seif Ahmed, was grateful to Abdullah for endorsing the principle of legitimacy at the time of the crisis in Yemen. Abdullah was the first Arab ruler to send him a telegram supporting his right of succession.

Furthermore, on Egypt's initiative the League drafted an Arab collective security pact. First adopted on April 9, 1950, by the Political Committee, the pact stated that aggression against any one of the signatories would be regarded as aggression against all. The signatories would then take all measures to repulse the aggression by armed forces, first notifying the United Nations Security Council and the Arab League Council. It also provided for a Joint Defense Council to be composed of defense and foreign ministers of member states and for a permanent committee of the chiefs of staff. On June 17, 1950, five out of seven Arab League members initialed the pact. Iraq refused to adhere because Jordan had not been present at the session. It was clear that Egypt treated the pact as an additional safeguard against possible Jordanian expansion in the direction of Syria and that, in order to preserve the status quo, she tried to transform the League from a consultative into a collective security body. This explained the reluctance of the Hashemite states to commit themselves to this new project. Eventually, on February 2, 1951, Nuri es-Said in the name of Iraq signed a revised pact after the more automatic features of collective security had been removed from the original draft. Jordan remained the only country outside the new system.

Abdullah's death at the hands of one of Haj Amin's henchmen in the summer of 1951 added a new complicating element to the already tangled picture. The removal of the main proponent of the Greater Syria plan was bound to produce far-reaching repercussions. The murder, true enough, redounded to the immediate benefit of Egypt and of other enemies of the Hashemites. But it was doubtful whether the plan of north-Arabian unity as such would be definitely buried.

In 1954–1955 Western attempts to build up a regional defense alliance led to further disagreements within the League. This time the spotlight shifted from Jordan to Iraq, whose premier, Nuri es-Said, was determined to link his country with Britain, Turkey, Iran, and Pakistan in what was to become the Baghdad Pact. Egypt, despite the change in her internal regime, strongly opposed this alliance. At an ordinary session of the Arab League Council, November 19–December 12, 1954, the general problem of Arab relations with the West came up for discussion. According to the premier of Lebanon (on whose testimony we have to rely in the absence of an official league communiqué), the following resolution was adopted: (1) The foreign policy of the Arab countries should be based on the Arab League Charter, the inter-Arab collective security and economic cooperation pact, and the United Nations Charter. This foreign policy does not admit any other pacts. (2) Cooperation between Arab states and the West should be subject to two basic conditions: (a) the West must help solve Arab problems equitably; (b) the West must help the Arab states to acquire the strength needed to defend their security and integrity against all aggression, such aid not to be prejudicial to their sovereignty. It was understood from other sources that Iraq made "clear and absolute" reservations to this resolution. In fact, her foreign minister, Musa Shahbandar, went so far as to declare in Damascus on December 22, 1954, that all the current agitation about Arab-Western collaboration did not make sense inasmuch as the Arabs had had, and continued to have, many ties with the West. In an attempt to prevent Iraq from joining the Western-sponsored alliance Egypt called an extraordinary meeting of the

Arab League Council in late January 1955. Yet despite Egypt's insistence on censuring Iraq, the conferees came to no agreement, and the session broke up with opportunities abounding for further mutual recrimination. The latter has gained in intensity, especially after an abortive visit to Baghdad following the Cairo meeting by a subcommittee of three Arab premiers. Egypt argued that, by joining the Baghdad Pact, Iraq had violated the Arab League Charter, that she had broken Arab solidarity and become the tool of imperialism, thus ultimately serving the interests of Israel. Iraq's rejoinder was that she had kept other league members informed of her intentions, that the Charter did not prohibit alliances in self-defense, that her proximity to Russia and the existence of the borderland Kurdish minority required her to seek special safeguards, and that her partnership with Turkey and eligibility for Western arms supplies made the Arab camp stronger vis-à-vis Israel. Moreover, while criticizing the Baghdad Pact, Egypt herself had entered into a Suez base agreement with Britain, permitting the latter to reenter her territory during the next seven years, without bothering to consult with sister nations. As for Saudi Arabia, argued the Iraqis, she had signed the Dhahran Air Base agreement with the United States, thus opening her territory to Western armed forces and forfeiting her moral right to criticize Iraq. The latter, stressed the spokesmen, instead of admitting foreign forces to her lands, had actually caused the evacuation of the two remaining air bases by the British.

Failing to secure a general censure of Iraq, Egypt concentrated on building a tripartite military alliance between herself, Saudi Arabia, and Syria, and by the beginning of 1956 she had succeeded in subordinating to her command the Syrian and Saudi Arabian military forces. With Saudi Arabia she countered a British attempt to bring Jordan into the Baghdad Pact by vigorous action aiming at the severance of such links as existed between Jordan and Britain in the political, military, and economic spheres. Her efforts were crowned with considerable but not full success. As a result of strong Saudi-Egyptian agitation and pressure Jordan was brought to the brink of revolution, and early in 1956 her new government promised not to join the Baghdad Pact. The abrupt dismissal and expulsion of General Glubb by King Hussein of Jordan constituted another signal victory for the Cairo-Riyadh axis. But Egypt and Saudi Arabia found it more difficult to persuade Jordan to give up British subsidies, despite formal offers of subsidies by them and Syria. By 1956 the League had experienced its second major crisis and to all practical purposes had ceased to function as an instrument of Arab solidarity. While Iraq found herself in a minority of one, Egypt had not succeeded in isolating her completely, such states as Lebanon, Jordan, and even Syria being unwilling to go on record as condemning Iraq for her action.

The history of the league demonstrated that no matter how much Britain was responsible for its birth, it soon ceased to be an instrument of British policy. In fact, by succumbing to Egyptian influence the league brought more embarrassment than benefit to Britain. It was not surprising, therefore, to hear London voices seriously questioning further continuation of the league in its present form. Suggestions were made to reform the league on purely Asiatic lines. "The withdrawal of Egypt into Africa need cause no regrets," wrote *The Economist*. "From the purely Arab standpoint, it would produce a group far more homogeneous than that formed in 1945. . . . From Britain's angle, it would remove from a group of states that is not fundamentally anti-British, a leading member that has spread much ill-will toward Britain."[8]

The Arab League and Arab Unity

In the 1950s and the early 1960s the Arab League followed a seemingly paradoxical course of Pan-Arab solidarity and deep inner conflict. The paradox, however, was more apparent than real because the policies of solidarity and internecine conflict were not mutually exclusive. Solidarity existed on most of the issues where the Arab struggle for emancipation from imperialism was involved. This solidarity was largely political and psychological. It expressed itself in resolutions, generally unanimous, and speeches, either at the league meetings or in the United Nations, on such subjects as Palestine, the Suez Canal, the Sinai war, the Oman rebellion, the British-Yemeni conflict over the Aden Protectorate, and Algeria. Some Arab states went beyond resolutions, volunteering more than words. The Cairo government followed a rather consistent policy of extending aid in the form of funds, experts, and arms to various struggling independence movements, notably to that of Algeria. Similarly, after its revolution of 1958, Iraq made a point of giving subsidies to such rebellious groups as the Algerians, the Omanis, and the Palestinians in exile. To a lesser extent this was also true of Saudi Arabia, with special emphasis on aid to inner Oman. These were, however, voluntary actions over and above the common expressions of solidarity and as such they did not produce a strain in inter-Arab relations. In one sector, however, the league as a whole went beyond a purely verbal performance: the economic boycott of Israel was carried out by all Arab states with a marked degree of efficiency, as a result of which it became increasingly difficult for major outside firms to do business simultaneously with Israel and the Arab states.

Impressive as this solidarity was in terms of its unanimity and persistence, it possessed two deflating features: it was negative, absolving from positive coordinated action; and it did not demand from member governments any significant sacrifice that would threaten their vested interests.

It was precisely their stubborn attachment to vested interests that caused the Arab League to be deeply divided despite its anti-imperialist solidarity. In an earlier section of this chapter we have reviewed the quarrel which flared up between the Hashemites and Egypt over the Palestine issue. Actually, Palestine was not the cause of this feud, but merely its forceful expression. Iraq and Egypt clashed again in 1955 over the issue of the Baghdad Pact. As viewed by Nasser (as self-appointed standard-bearer of Arab nationalism), the Hashemite kings' deviation from the common Arab front on both issues was the result of their dependence, amounting to treason, on the "imperialist" West. In reality, the feud between Cairo and Baghdad had deeper roots than that. It stemmed from a historical rivalry between the Valley

---

[8]"Arab Post-Mortem," *The Economist*, March 5, 1949, p. 422.

of the Nile and the Land of Mesopotamia, which could be traced back to ancient history and which neither the medieval caliphate nor modern Pan-Arabism was able to erase. This rivalry found many expressions, cultural and economic, throughout the ages, but the political consideration was decisive. Neither of the two centers of power and civilization was willing to become subject to the other. This was proved again in 1958. The demise of the Hashemites in Baghdad did not result in the unification of Iraq and Egypt. General Kassem's revolutionary regime was as anti-imperialist as that of Egypt. Yet it insisted on the preservation of its separate identity and sovereignty. The quarrel over Kuwait which erupted in 1961 provided further proof of this basic rivalry. When in the name of Arab unity and Iraq's historical right to its natural harbor Premier Kassem demanded the annexation of Kuwait, he encountered strong opposition from Egypt and other members of the Arab League, all of whom benefited from Britain's military action in defending Kuwait. This time it was not Iraq which was on the side of the "imperialists," but implicitly Cairo and the other Arab capitals. In fact, Cairo's insistence on separate status for Kuwait was a reversal of its policy which had hitherto repeatedly stressed that the existence of separate Persian Gulf sheikhdoms was due to the unholy alliance of local "feudalism" with British imperialism, both motivated by common greed for the gulf's oil riches. Thus it was obviously not anti-imperialism which dictated Cairo's policy on the Kuwait issue, but simply opposition to any undue accretion of wealth and power by Iraq.

What has been said of Iraq's attachment to its own independent course could be applied, in varying degrees, to all other Arab states. Thus the appeal for the unity of the Nile Valley did not cause the Sudanese to opt for union with Egypt. Despite frequent protestations of Arab solidarity, Saudi Arabia did not relinquish her sovereign status for the sake of Pan-Arab union and rather stubbornly stuck to her own political and social patterns. The same was even more true of Yemen, despite her nominal federation with the United Arab Republic. President Habib Bourguiba of Tunisia preferred a temporary severance of ties with the Arab League between 1959 and 1961 to the spread of Cairo-sponsored Pan-Arabism in his country. In Lebanon the desire for an identity of her own has persisted with great strength as against the violent attempts to submerge her in a larger Arab entity in 1958. And in Syria, despite the surrender of her independent status for the sake of Pan-Arabism in 1958, separatist forces victoriously reasserted themselves in 1961.

In calling these particularist tendencies an expression of vested interests, one should make one important qualification. A desire to preserve the separate identity and political independence of individual Arab states represented a vested interest, not only of the ruling group, but often of the people as well. This was due to a combination of social, cultural, and religious factors which tended to make a given human group reluctant to abandon its own time-tested ways in favor of some larger sociocultural model, despite the common bonds of Arabism and Islam with other Arab countries. This was one of those basic human preferences which at one time or another caused large political entities in the Western world to adopt the federative system. Furthermore, several Arab countries possessed economic resources which they were unwilling to share with others. This might be a selfish attitude, but it was nonetheless real and not limited to the ruling group alone despite the socioeconomic inequalities in many of the countries in question. In terms of actual inter-Arab politics the creation of any large political entity was bound to give Egypt, for demographic as well as political reasons, a position of preeminence, which could rapidly result in supremacy and, possibly, exploitation of others. This consideration filled some groups with fear lest they lose more than they gain from the achievement of Arab unity. Furthermore, in every country where a delicate balance existed between the ethnic-religious majorities and sizable minorities, the latter were always reluctant to agree to any change that might upset this balance in their disfavor. The Kurds and Shias in Iraq, for example, were always suspicious of anything that would adversely affect the rather important role they played in Iraq side by side with the Sunni Arab part of its population. To state this is not to deny the tremendous appeal of the slogans of Arab unity to the broad strata of the Arab populations and particularly to the poorer urban-based intelligentsia. It is merely to remind ourselves that particularism or local patriotism corresponds not only to the vested interests of the ruling groups but also to the economic, social, and political realities which make sizable groups of population unwilling to submit to a new dispensation directed from centers outside their own countries.

Viewed in this perspective, the Arab League could not be regarded as a dynamic vehicle of Arab unity. By virtue of its charter it was an association of sovereign states, and as such its role was to uphold rather than to destroy the sovereignty of its members. It could and did promote Arab solidarity on negative anti-imperialist issues and also in a broad cultural sense. But by confirming the existing division of the Arab world into a number of separate states, it was an instrument of particularism.

Thus those elements that strove for the achievement of unity were obliged to resort to other channels than the league to attain their objectives. The strongly Pan-Arab Baath Party placed main emphasis on its own organizational spread into several Arab countries. It counted more on its propaganda among youth and its infiltration of governments and armies in various countries than on the resolutions of the Arab League. Groups sponsored by, or friendly to, President Nasser sought to achieve similar ends by a variety of means, which included the calling of various Arab professional conferences. (The Association of University Graduates became particularly known for its espousal of the Pan-Arab cause). Regardless of the profession represented, these conferences invariably ended with the adoption of rather militant Pan-Arab resolutions, thus significantly cementing the bonds of Arab consciousness among their participants. Mention should also be made of the Federation of Arab Labor Unions,[9] a strongly Cairo-influenced organization, which was created in 1956 and whose Pan-Arab dynamism contrasted with the conservative ways of the Arab League.

In an earlier part of this chapter we have observed that there was a definite tendency in Egypt to use the Arab League as an instrument of her national policy.

[9] Also known as International Confederation of Arab Trade Unions. For its origins, organization, and activities, see George Lenczowski, *Oil and State in the Middle East* (Ithaca, N.Y., 1960), ch. xiv, "Pan-Arab Labor Movement."

This tendency continued throughout the years and on many issues—especially those involving the struggle against imperialism—the league voiced its support of the Egyptian stand. With the passage of time, however, it became more difficult for Cairo to line up a sufficient majority behind itself in those cases where its policies clashed with those of some other Arab states. Broadly speaking, Cairo's tactics consisted of attempts to isolate and bring about the condemnation of any Arab government that refused to follow the Egyptian-conceived policy of "Arab liberation." The early classical example of such a situation was the censure—barely missing expulsion from the league—of King Abdullah's Jordan for following policies contrary to Egypt's views on Palestine. But in later years the league could not be so easily mobilized on Egypt's side and its member states preferred to advise moderation and seek compromise in inter-Arab conflicts. In this connection the effect of the enlargement of the league upon its character might be mentioned. In the period between 1953 and 1961 five new states were admitted and one readmitted to the League, thus increasing its membership to twelve. These were Libya (1953), Sudan (1956), Tunisia (1958), Morocco (1958), Kuwait (1961), and Syria (1961). The adherence of the North African states reflected growing Arab consciousness in the hitherto remote Maghreb, thus widening, implicitly, the circle of Egyptian ideological influence. On the other hand, these new states were deeply committed to maintaining their independence and to give priority to their local interests for dynastic, economic, or social reasons. For example, when in the name of anti-imperialism and Arab-African solidarity, the Cairo government attempted to fly arms to the dissident (and friendly to Russia) government of Antoine Gizenga in the Congo in 1961, Sudan barred Egyptian airplanes from flights over its territory. Sudan's action was based on considerations of its national interest as interpreted by its own government. Thus, by enlarging its membership, the Arab League increased the number of governments which were less prone to accept uncritically Cairo's political leadership, especially in the spheres where their own local interests clashed with ideal Pan-Arab concepts.

Collective Arab Action in the 1960s and 1970s

In spite of the dissolution of the union between Syria and Egypt and the growing dichotomy between revolutionary Cairo and conservative Saudi Arabia, the community of Arab countries did not give up attempts to achieve greater coordination of their political and economic policies. These attempts were not invariably successful and sometimes gave rise to profound disagreements. Nevertheless, it is possible to identify four major issues on which endeavors to ensure collective action were intermittently undertaken by the Arab governments. The first of these issues was the *struggle against imperialism* or, more broadly, the presence or intervention of non-Arab powers in the affairs of the Arab world. Thus in the 1960s the community of Arab nations was solidly opposed to the remnants of British imperialism in Aden and southern Arabia, an area in which the local liberation movement was both militant and radical. Similarly, the independent Arab states promoted the idea of the emancipation of the Persian Gulf countries from British control, although in this case the local gulf rulers were more passive than the activists in Cairo, Damascus, and other centers of Arab nationalism. The struggle of Algeria for independence from France attracted much attention and provided the subject for many anti-imperialist resolutions in and out of the Arab League.

Although thus the chief targets of this collective action were primarily the old colonial powers, Britain and France, Arab anti-imperialism was also frequently directed against the United States. The issue was not the occupation or control of any Arab territory but rather the fact that by arming Israel and lending it continuous economic support, the United States was identifying itself with a state that the Arabs regarded as a prime example of "settler colonialism" and an aggressive and illegitimate entity bent upon expansion and the suppression of the rights of the native Palestinian population.

By the same token, Iran's action on November 30, 1971, in occupying three minor but strategically located islands in the Strait of Hormuz was regarded as a hostile and aggressive act. However, for reasons explained in another chapter of this book, Arab reaction to this move was restrained and muted.

Anti-imperialism, however, as an issue generating collective Arab action gradually lost substance in the 1970s because of the total emancipation of the Arab lands from the control of major powers. The last acts of this process were the proclamation of independence of Djibouti in 1977 in the eastern reaches of the Arab world and the relinquishment by Spain of her control over Spanish Sahara in favor of Morocco and Mauritania in 1976. Under the circumstances, the only part of the Arab world still deprived of self-determination was Arab Palestine.

Thus, despite the passage of several decades since the formation of the state of Israel in 1948 and four subsequent Arab-Israeli wars, the *issue of Israel and Palestine* became the most important (though chronologically second) focus for Arab collective attitudes and action. The Arab states manifested steady resistance to Israel's legitimacy and territorial expansion. In addition to this fundamental resentment and hostility, certain concrete issues in Arab-Israeli relations acted as a stimulant or catalyst for collective Arab action. These issues included the dispute in the 1960s over the diversion of the Jordan waters by Israel, Israel's preventive war and victory in June 1967, and Israel's occupation policy in the territories conquered during that war. This policy was punctuated by expulsions and population transfers, confiscations of land, police harrassment, blowing up of homes suspected of sheltering Palestinian guerrillas, and collective reprisals against Arab townships and villages. The establishment of increasing numbers of Jewish settlements in the West Bank, the Golan Heights, the Gaza strip, and even Sinai provided another common platform for joint Arab protest, resentment, and hostility. Arab reactions toward these measures were often expressed in terrorist acts carried out individually or by small groups. Israel's response to these acts was to engage in counterterror on various levels including massive military reprisals in the form of bombing and raids into the territory of Lebanon and organized attacks on certain border localities in Jordan. In one case, as we know, it took the form of shooting down a Libyan passenger airliner that strayed over Israeli-occupied territory in Sinai. Invariably Arab governments protested the Israeli actions in the most emphatic terms. Last but not least, Arab defeat in the 1967 war acted as a catalyst for the development of a joint political and military strategy against Israel.

The third area in which a good deal of Arab cooperation and coordination took place was that of *oil affairs*. Oil matters were linked with the issue of Arab-Israeli relations when the Arab states developed a policy of using oil as a political weapon. This policy passed through especially intensive stages in connection with the October war of 1973, during which Arab oil production was reduced and an embargo imstituted against certain countries, including the United States, for their support of Israel or as a punitive measure against their racist and colonial policies in Africa.

But concern with oil had also its more positive aspects: the oil-producing Arab states engaged through the 1960s and 1970s in many joint efforts to assert national control over their resources, to develop independent technical facilities (joint tanker and repair yard ventures), and to establish training and educational facilities for their own technical oil cadres while stimulating a greater "oil awareness" in the Arab world at large.

The fourth area of Arab collective action was in *the resolution of inter-Arab conflicts and disputes,* which claimed as much if not more attention from the Arab governments as the problem of Israel and Palestine. After the collapse of the Syro-Egyptian union in 1961, the Arab world experienced at least eight major conflicts among its member states. These were: the Kuwait-Iraqi dispute over Iraq's claim to sovereignty to Kuwait, 1961; the Yemen civil war which, in addition to the two Yemeni factions, also involved Egypt and Saudi Arabia, 1962–1967; intermittent disputes involving border warfare and assassinations which pitted in the 1970s South Yemen against Yemen and Saudi Arabia; the confrontation between Jordan and the Palestinian guerrillas, a brief but fierce conflict which was further complicated by Syrian intervention, 1970; a protracted conflict between South Yemen and Oman linked to the Dhofar rebellion, 1972–1976; intermittent hostility and actual border fighting between Egypt and Libya in 1977; a tripartite conflict between Algeria on the one hand and Morocco and Mauritania on the other over the control of the former Spanish Sahara, 1976; and finally, the Lebanese civil war that involved two outside parties, the PLO and Syria, which began in 1975 and continued with interruptions and renewals into the late 1970s. Except for the first case, that of the Kuwait-Iraq dispute in 1961, where the timely arrival first of the British and then of Arab League troops prevented the conflict from reaching a violent stage, every other of these disputes assumed a violent character involving regular and irregular military forces and in some cases reaching proportions of full warfare.

Vehicles and Instruments of Collective Action

To attend to the four types of issues mentioned in the preceding section, the Arab states resorted to the Arab League as the first and most suitable body whose task was to represent collectively Arab interests toward the outside world and act as an arbiter of inter-Arab disputes.[10] Thus the records of various organs of the Arab League are

[10]With the passage of time, membership of the Arab League increased from the original seven to twenty as more Arab countries achieved independence. By the end of 1978, the member states were: Algeria, Bahrain, Egypt, Iraq, Jordan, Kuwait, Lebanon, Libya, Mauritania, Morocco, Oman, Qatar, Saudi Arabia, Somalia, South Yemen, Sudan, Syria, Tunisia, United Arab Emirates, and Yemen. In addition, the Palestine Liberation Organization enjoyed the status of associate member. Djibouti, having become independent in 1978, was expected to apply for membership.

full of resolutions pertaining to the struggle against imperialism, opposition to and condemnation of Israel, the use of oil as a weapon, and arbitration in inter-Arab quarrels. The effectiveness of these resolutions differed from case to case and frequently they were no more than verbal protests that were not backed up by truly concerted action. Perhaps the greatest influence exerted by the Arab League was on the pacification of inter-Arab disputes, but it was not due so much to any compulsory judicial function of the league, as to the league's mediating role in convincing the parties to a dispute to desist from further hostile action against each other. In other words, the final decision to stop fighting and practice restraint was invariably within the realm of sovereign actions of the governments directly involved in the conflict.

The meetings of Arab oil ministers constitute a special subcategory, especially in 1973-1974 in the wake of the October war. At these meetings important decisions regarding production cutbacks, differentiation between friendly, hostile, and neutral states, and the imposition as well as the termination of embargoes were made.[11] It should be pointed out that these oil ministers' meetings were held outside of the framework of the Organization of Arab Petroleum Exporting Countries (OAPEC) formed in 1968, whose nonpolitical objective was to promote technical and economic cooperation among the Arab states. Similarly, the Arabs neither wanted to nor actually did use the Organization of Petroleum Exporting Countries (OPEC) to achieve their political purposes. That body, composed of Arab and non-Arab states in about equal numbers, served as a platform for joint action of oil producers to achieve their economic objectives. In the 1950s and 1960s a number of Arab oil congresses had taken place. These were generally sponsored by the Arab League and provided a forum in which both the economic and the political demands of the Arab states were often voiced. It was at these oil congresses, particularly during the Nasser era, that Arab spokesmen, foremost among whom was perhaps the minister of oil of Saudi Arabia, Sheikh Abdullah Tariki, presented increasingly radical demands to put an end to foreign concessions and to ensure full control of their oil resources by the producing states.

Arab governments used a variety of other conferences, especially those of the Third World nations, to propagate their ideas and promote their causes. These were the conferences of nonaligned countries, for example, a conference in Algiers in September 1973 during which the Arab point of view regarding Israel was forcefully presented. Similarly, international Islamic conferences provided a forum for the discussion of the Arab-Israeli conflict. Such was, for example, the Islamic conference held in Rabat in September 1969 at which a resolution condemning Israel for the burning, during the preceding month, of the Al-Aqsa mosque in Jerusalem was unanimously adopted. And in the same vein, at the Islamic conference held in Lahore in February 1974 strong resolutions critical of the United States' support for Israel were passed. The periodic meetings of the Organization of African Unity (OAU) gave its Arab member states a repeated opportunity to engineer resolutions

---

[11]For a survey and analysis of these decisions, see George Lenczowski, *Middle East Oil in a Revolutionary Age*, National Energy Study no. 10 (Washington, D.C., 1976).

with a distinctly anti-Israeli character. At the OAU conference in Algiers in 1968, a resolution enjoining member states to break off diplomatic relations with Israel was adopted.[12]

The United Nations, gathering in the 1970s over 140 states of which the overwhelming majority were underdeveloped with a colonial past, provided a forum in which Arab grievances, particularly those pertaining to Israel, had probably the greatest multiplier effect. The annals of the meetings of the UN General Assembly, and occasionally also of the Security Council, are replete with Arab-sponsored resolutions in which Israeli actions, such as massive reprisal raids on the neighboring states, its occupation policies, or the establishment of Jewish settlements in occupied territories, are the subject of repeated official condemnation.[13] On a somewhat smaller scale but no less effectively, the Arabs used certain affiliated agencies to press their point of view, for example when, in November 1974, the United Nations Economic, Social and Cultural Organization (UNESCO) adopted a resolution excluding Israel from its European regional group.

The most important vehicle of collective Arab action, however, was the summit meeting, conferences of the Arab heads of state. They were held irregularly and always on the occasion of some major event in the Arab world. Because of the predominantly authoritarian nature of the Arab political structures, the summit meetings had a greater inherent capacity for producing decisions and ensuring their implementation than any other instrument of Arab collective action.

The Summit Meetings

The Arab summit meetings were usually convened when the matters to be decided upon were deemed important enough to warrant the presence of the heads of Arab states. A monograph of substantial length would be necessary to do full justice to the causes, motivations, bargaining processes, and decision-making of such meetings. For the purposes of this study we will have to limit ourselves to the briefest possible description and analysis.

The first summit meeting took place in January 1964 in Cairo at the invitation of President Nasser. The main item on the agenda was the problem of Israel's declared intention to divert the Jordan waters for its own use. (Israel had tried a number of times in the past to reach an agreement with other riparian states regarding the sharing of the waters, but being unsuccessful in these endeavors it decided to act unilaterally.) The summit meeting reached the decision not to go to war with Israel over this issue but to counteract the Israeli move by arranging for the diversion of the Jordan at its headwaters, specifically by diverting the waters of the Hasbani River (or springs) in Lebanon and the Banias River in Syria. An important by-

---

[12]Similarly, the OAU conference in Kampala (July 28–August 1, 1975) likened Israel to white African states practicing discrimination by stating "that the racist regime in occupied Palestine and racist regimes in Zimbabwe and South Africa have a common imperialist origin forming a whole and having the same racist structure and being organically linked in their policy aimed at repression of the dignity and integrity of the human being." *New York Times*, Nov. 11, 1975.

[13]The strongest of these was probably the UN General Assembly resolution determining "that Zionism is a form of racism and racial discrimination." Text in *ibid*.

product of this conference was the decision to establish the Palestine Liberation Organization (PLO) and the Palestine Liberation Army (PLA), a regular uniformed force which was to be stationed in Syria, Jordan, and Egypt.

The second summit meeting took place in Alexandria in September 1964. It was called in fulfillment of the resolution taken at the first meeting that the summit conferences should convene regularly at stated intervals—a decision which with the passage of time ceased to be strictly observed. The meeting reaffirmed support for the PLO and PLA, pledged a common struggle against British imperialism in the Arabian Peninsula and the "Arabian Gulf," and ended in the signing of the Joint Arab Defense Pact by all those in attendance.

The third summit meeting was held in Casablanca in September 1965, a period of considerable intensity in the so-called Arab Cold War, which was reaching a "hot" stage in the hostilities in Yemen. The purpose of the meeting was to put an end to inter-Arab conflicts. With this in view, the meeting registered two ostensible achievements: a Saudi-Egyptian agreement on the termination of hostilities in Yemen and a general Arab "solidarity pact," by which the signatories pledged to desist from further hostile propaganda against each other. Neither decision was subsequently implemented. The Yemen civil war and the Saudi and Egyptian interventions dragged on for another two years. As for the solidarity pact, the radical political centers in the Arab world considered it to be advantageous only to the conservative regimes inasmuch as it was supposed to put a halt to continuous attacks by the radicals on the existing monarchies. Before long, the mutual hostile media campaigns resumed. Moreover, despite all the talk about Arab harmony, two dissonant notes could already be heard during the conference itself: on behalf of Tunisia, its president, Habib Bourguiba, declared that his government refused to attend and would boycott all Arab League meetings so long as Nasser continued to attempt to dominate the Arab states. On the other hand, Jordan rejected the proposed presence of the Iraqi and Saudi troops in its territory to assist in protecting the diversion works on the Jordan River headwaters.

The fourth summit meeting was held in Khartoum at the end of August 1967 to agree on a united policy in the wake of the crushing Arab defeat sustained in the war with Israel during the preceding June. On September 1, the participating heads of state issued a lengthy declaration in which they proclaimed their intention to seek a "political solution" (rather than a military one) to their conflict with Israel. The declaration included the formula that there should be "no recognition, no negotiation, no peace covenant with Israel." Three oil-rich states, Saudi Arabia, Kuwait, and Libya, pledged financial assistance to the "confrontation states," the U.A.R., Syria, and Jordan. As a by-product of the conference a final reconciliation was effected between the U.A.R. and Saudi Arabia regarding their intervention and civil war in Yemen. The conference was considerably influenced by the conservative states, particularly Saudi Arabia. To the more militant Arab states it appeared as a betrayal of the Arab cause of liberation of the whole land of Palestine. The conference was boycotted by the chairman of the PLO, Ahmed Shukairy, and denounced by Syria. Another by-product of the conference was the decision to end the embargo on exports of oil to the United States, Great Britain, and West Germany which had been imposed when the June war broke out.

The fifth summit meeting took place in Cairo between September 22 and 27, 1970, on the initiative of President Nasser. Its main purpose was to resolve the civil war raging in Jordan between the government of King Hussein and the PLO. It was attended by the heads of nine states who, on September 27, signed a fourteen-point pact which called for the immediate cessation of hostilities in Jordan. The pact was signed by, among others, King Hussein of Jordan and Yassir Arafat, who had succeeded Ahemd Shukairy as chairman of the PLO. The conference created a committee to be headed by Premier Ladgham of Tunisia to supervise the implementation of the agreement. The tension that President Nasser experienced as host and mediator of the meeting precipitated his death of a heart attack on September 28 when the heads of Arab states were leaving Cairo.

The sixth summit meeting gathered in Algiers in November 1973, this time in the aftermath of the October war between Israel and the Arabs. Like the Khartoum meeting of 1967, this summit was called to map a common Arab strategy following the war. The pros and cons of the oil weapon were discussed and the conference adopted a resolution calling for the continuation of restrictions and embargoes on the export of oil until Israel's withdrawal from occupied territories, notably Jerusalem, and until the realization of the national rights of the Palestinians. The conference approved Egypt's decision to enter into peace negotiations with Israel at the forthcoming Geneva conference slated to meet in December. Libya and Iraq boycotted the conference.

The seventh summit meeting, which met in Rabat in October 1974, debated the financial aid to be extended to the confrontation states. Such aid was pledged by Saudi Arabia, Kuwait, and the oil-rich states of the lower Persian Gulf, but not by Iraq and Libya. The most important decision was to grant recognition to the PLO as the "sole legitimate representative of the Palestinian people." At the same meeting it was decided that the Arab League would lease from South Yemen for ninety-nine years the strategic Perim Island, a concession for which South Yemen was to receive $150 million. (The island was subsequently placed at the disposal of Egypt.) It is worth noting that the four most militant Palestinian groups, namely the Popular Front for the Liberation of Palestine, the Arab Liberation Front, the Popular Struggle Front and the Popular Front for the Liberation of Palestine—General Command, rejected the Rabat decisions as unsatisfactory in terms of their ultimate objectives.

Arab Groupings and Divisions

Even a cursory review of the inter-Arab disputes and the Arab summit meetings reveals two simultaneous trends at work in the Arab world: one toward unity and coordination and the other toward disunity. The divisions within the Arab world could be traced to a number of causes. Some were due to deep ideological differences, some to dynastic quarrels (although with the demise of the Hashemite dynasty in Iraq these gradually faded away). Some were based on personal rivalries among leaders of individual states, and others on discrepancies in social, economic, and cultural levels.

The ideological differences between the revolutionary and the conservative regimes were primarily responsible for the phenomenon of the Arab Cold War between

1957 and 1967.[14] In those years Cairo acted as the mainspring of Pan-Arab and revolutionary ideology, with the socialist regimes of Syria, Iraq, Algeria, Yemen, and eventually South Yemen as its allies. This revolutionary-radical group was in turn opposed by a virtual coalition of monarchies, namely Saudi Arabia, Jordan, Libya, Kuwait and other gulf states, and Morocco. Somewhere in between, following a cautious neutral path, stood Lebanon, Sudan, and Tunisia. This division in the Arab community of nations was, however, not permanent. In the later 1960s and 1970s important changes occurred: with the overthrow of its monarchy, Libya joined the revolutionary camp. On the other hand, following the Khartoum settlement of the Yemen civil war, the republican regime that emerged followed a prudent and moderate policy that brought it into a close and friendly relationship with the Saudi monarchy. The most important change, however, has undoubtedly occurred in Egypt since the advent of President Sadat. In the 1970s Egypt rapidly abandoned its Pan-Arab militancy, ceased interference and subversion in other Arab states, and with its policy of close cooperation with Saudi Arabia and the United States it emerged as a powerful force for moderation in the entire region. Moreover, President Sadat's initiative toward the end of 1977 to seek a genuine peace settlement with Israel on the basis of the recognition of its right to existence not only accentuated Egypt's moderate stance in international politics but also generated fierce opposition to its policies. This opposition took the form of the so-called Rejectionist Front which first made its stand known during the negotiations preceding the Sinai II agreement of 1974. It comprised Iraq, Libya, Syria, Algeria, and South Yemen. The front's objections to the Egyptian policies probably reached an apogee after Sadat's visit to Jerusalem in November 1977. Within two weeks, the rejectionist leaders met in Tripoli (December 2–5) where, hosted by Colonel Muammar Qadhafi of Libya, they condemned Egypt's "high treason" and called for a "freeze" in relations with her, but under the moderating influence of Syria stopped short of a complete rupture of relations and boycott of Egypt.[15]

While no similar organized grouping to oppose the Rejectionist Front was formed around Egypt, nevertheless a number of Arab governments headed by Saudi Arabia and Sudan continued to support Egypt both diplomatically and financially.

As a result of the repeated Arab-Israeli wars, particularly those of 1967 and 1973, a new informal grouping arose within the Arab community: these were the so-called confrontation states of Egypt, Syria, Jordan, and Iraq. Cooperation between Iraq and the other three members of this group followed a tortuous path, passing through stages of friendliness and mutual recrimination. However, between 1970 and 1974, Syria and Egypt tended to coordinate closely their military policies. This harmony was in no small part due to the vision and mutual good will of presidents Hafez Assad and Anwar Sadat, who had come to power at approximately the same time in 1970. Similarly, an increased degree of military coordination was characteristic of the relations between Syria and Jordan in the 1970s in spite of the differences

[14]For a comprehensive account, see Malcolm H. Kerr, *The Arab Cold War: Gamal 'Abd al-Nasir and His Rivals, 1958–1970,* 3d ed. (London, 1971); also George Lenczowski, "The Arab Cold War," in Willard A. Beling, ed., *The Middle East: Quest for an American Policy* (Albany, N.Y., 1973).

[15]For subsequent collective Arab protests against Egyptian-Israeli negotiations, see p. 571 ff. above.

between their political systems. With the exception of Iraq, whose "confrontation" status was somewhat in doubt owing to its geographical distance from Israel, the confrontation states did not belong to the rich league of oil producers. As countries having to carry the heaviest military burden of defense preparations against Israel, they needed economic support, and this was generally available from the wealthier states of the Arabian Peninsula.

A discussion of the divisions and groupings within the Arab world should also take into account the effect that partial unions or federations, which group only a few states, might have on the existing divisions. In terms of public ethos the politically conscious Arab strata are in principle dedicated to the proposition of institutionalized Arab unity. As the achievement of total unity is out of reach in the foreseeable future, some Arab governments at various times have attempted to conclude unions or federations of a more limited scope. While aiming at the promotion of harmony and unity among the signatories of such partial pacts, these unions at the same time often accentuated the existing cleavages in the Arab community of nations.

Arab Unity Schemes in the 1960s and 1970s

Much of what follows in this section has already been mentioned in chapters dealing with individual countries. The purpose of reviewing Arab unity schemes here is to consolidate the available material while comparing and contrasting the policies that led to union attempts, their successes, and their failures.

As a rule it was the radical regimes with a Pan-Arab orientation that advocated the idea of Arab unity and time and again made attempts to achieve it. There occurred two exceptions in this trend: between March and July 1958 there was a short-lived federation of two monarchies, Iraq and Jordan. This federation was more a response to the just-concluded (February 1958) Syrian-Egyptian union than a result of a genuine desire of the two monarchies to unite. The revolution that took place on July 14, 1958, in Iraq put an end to this experiment. The second exception occurred in late 1971 when seven small Trucial Coast states decided, with the encouragement of the retreating British, to form the United Arab Emirates. Their purpose was to strengthen the capacity of survival of the lower gulf sheikhdoms whose miniscule populations and general underdevelopment made them individually more vulnerable to foreign conquest and influence or revolution.

As for the revolutionary regimes, the 1960s and 1970s witnessed a number of attempts at unity. The break-up of the Syro-Egyptian union in September 1961 constituted a traumatic experience for the revolutionary Pan-Arabists. In Cairo, as noted earlier, it gave rise to a thorough rethinking of the Pan-Arab strategy. Analyzing the reasons for the collapse of the union (and the subsequent withdrawal of royalist Yemen from a federative agreement with Cairo), the Egyptian leadership under Nasser came to the conclusion that the union had broken up because of the substantial ideological, political, and economic differences that existed between revolutionary Egypt and the still bourgeois Syria. Henceforth, it was decided in Cairo, one must not rush blindly into unions without first paying proper attention to the sociopolitical structure of each candidate country. Union, according to this reasoning, could not succeed unless the contracting countries underwent a thorough revolutionary preparation internally. This new philosophy or strategy had dual consequences. On the one hand, whenever a revolution occurred or was about to occur in any Arab country the Egyptian leadership felt duty bound to assist such revolutionaries, morally, politically, and even militarily, as the massive Egyptian intervention in Yemen beginning in 1962 proved. On the other hand, no sooner had a given country established a revolutionary regime than both it and the government in Egypt began to explore the possibility of some form of union.

The first major test of this policy came in the spring of 1963 following the victory the Baath party, first in Iraq (in February) and then in Syria (in March). Within a few weeks after these two revolutions, delegations from Iraq and Syria arrived in Cairo to conduct tripartite unity negotiations. The result was the conclusion in April of a unity agreement providing for a federated state to be composed of three regions.[16] The ink was barely dry on the document when profound disagreements between Egypt and Syria put an end to this unity scheme for all practical purposes. The reason for the failure of this new creation had to be sought primarily in the profound distrust that existed between Nasser and the Baathist rulers of Syria. Bearing in mind the recent experience of the abortive United Arab Republic in which Egypt had assumed a dominant rule in Syria, the Damascus leaders were obsessed with their survival as a group and as a political movement and tried to hedge the union agreement and its implementation with many safeguards against the recurrence of a situation such as existed between 1958 and 1961. On his part, Nasser could not easily forget what he believed to be the disloyal behavior of the Baathists at the time of the Syrian-Egyptian union and was clearly opposed to the continued separate existence of the Baath party. In fact, within a few weeks after the signing of the agreement his agents in Damascus made an abortive attempt to overthrow the Baathist regime. In this drama the Baathist leadership of Iraq tried to mediate between Cairo and Damascus but its efforts came to naught. The failure to achieve unity among three countries ostensibly professing the same ideology of Pan-Arabism and socialism demonstrated the appearance of a new phenomenon in Arab politics: revolutionary multicentrism. So long as Cairo was the only Arab capital where the revolution had seized power and established itself as a regular government, it served as a "Mecca" for revolutionaries from Syria, Iraq, Yemen, Algeria, and other countries. Once, however, these revolutionaries attained power in their respective countries, their taste for exercising that power and not surrendering it to Egypt in the name of unity exceeded their zeal for mergers regardless of the form they were to take.

Nevertheless, ideologically all such leaders were committed to seeking unity. The incessant propaganda both before and after the revolutions in their respective countries stressed Arab unity as the highest ideal. Under the circumstances, it was not surprising that when, in the fall of 1963, Colonel Abdul Salam Aref, a man known for his admiration of Nasser, seized power in Iraq, he promptly began exploring the possibility of union between his country and Egypt. And indeed, in May 1964,

---

[16]Text in *Arab Political Documents 1963, op. cit.,* pp. 227–246.

barely half a year later, Aref and Nasser concluded an agreement pledging the establishment of an Iraqi-Egyptian union by stages, the first being the creation of a joint presidential council and certain ancillary bodies.[17] This agreement, however, like the preceding attempts, did not bear the expected fruit. For one thing, Nasser was too prone to interpret any unity pact as legitimizing the extension of his political influence into another country. Thus a new political organization set up in Iraq under the name of the Arab Socialist Union (a namesake of the only licensed political party in Egypt) was soon suspected of being an instrument of Egyptian policy in Iraq. For another, President Aref might have been speaking genuinely of union when he was an aspiring revolutionary. Once in power, he simply liked his job and was not about to deliver it, as the Syrians might say, "on a silver platter to Nasser." As a result, some meetings of the newly constituted joint bodies not-withstanding, Egypt and Iraq remained separate entities and each conducted its policies according to its national interests. Furthermore, when both Nasser and Aref attended, in the fall of 1965, the Casablanca summit meeting (the one that produced the solidarity pact), Nasser's agents attempted a coup d'état against Aref in Baghdad. The attempt failed and, naturally, it further cooled Aref's ardor for unity schemes with Cairo.

After this unsuccessful experiment there was a six-to-seven year pause in the search for new unions. This period further emphasized the trend toward revolutionary polycentrism in the Arab world. Thus, for example, the Baath party regained power in Iraq in July 1968. But instead of rushing into union with a sister Baath regime in Syria, it developed an active dislike and hostility toward it. The Syrian Baathists reciprocated in word and in deed. They raised the tariff for the Iraqi oil transiting Syria through a pipeline to a rate so high as to cause Iraq to seek alternate routes for export by concluding a pipeline agreement with Turkey. And each regime, while officially adhering to the Baathist ideology, repeatedly accused the other of betraying the Baathist principles and ideals. Even the fact that the two countries became client states of the Soviet Union, at least in terms of dependence on Soviet arms supplies, did not reduce the mutual hostility between them. Syria's behavior during the Lebanese civil war in the mid-1970s and her subsequent dispatch of a peace-keeping force to that country brought a further avalanche of accusations from Baghdad.

The number of Arab radical centers increased with the installation of a military regime in Libya in September 1969. While this book does not include Libya or other countries of the Arab West (Maghreb), the role of Libya must be mentioned here within the context of the Arab unity schemes. The twenty-eight-year-old new ruler of Libya, Colonel Muammar Qadhafi, combined a great admiration for Nasser with his own beliefs in Arab unity, socialism, and Islam. Consequently, he projected himself onto the general Arab scene as a strong advocate of Arab unity and an uncompromising promoter of the Arab liberation movement directed both at Israel and at the remnants of Western imperialism. It was on his initiative that on December 27, 1969, President Nasser of Egypt and President Jafar Numeiri of Sudan

---

[17]Text in *Arab Political Documents 1964, op. cit.*, pp. 217–219.

signed with him the Tripoli Declaration establishing a triple alliance and a revolutionary Arab front. The realization of the principles contained in this declaration had to be postponed when Nasser died in September 1970. However, soon after the installation of Anwar Sadat in Cairo, Egypt, Libya, and Sudan signed in Cairo on November 8, 1970, an agreement pledging to establish a federation. It was widely commented at the time that such a federation would create a strong base of Arab power: Egypt would provide manpower and technical and managerial skills, Libya would supply oil money to fuel economic development and increase military strength, and Sudan with its great agricultural riches would be the granary of the federation. Moreover, the advantage of this tripartite union would be that all three Arab countries with their vast territories were adjacent to each other, in contrast to the Syrian-Egyptian and Iraqi-Egyptian union schemes in the past. The element of geographic contiguity was not, however, decisive. Anxious not to remain isolated and to benefit from military and financial advantages that such a union might bestow, President Hafez Assad of Syria adhered to the Cairo agreement less than three weeks later, on November 27. The road appeared open for the implementation of a really grandiose union scheme.

On April 17, 1971, the heads of state of Egypt, Syria, and Libya gathered in Benghazi where they signed an act establishing the Federation of Arab Republics (FAR). This time President Numeiri of Sudan was absent and eventually abstained from signing the act of the federation, largely because substantial segments of the Sudanese population opposed the idea of such a union. Subsequently, various joint councils and commissions were formed for the federation.[18]

The establishment of the federation did not change the political realities of the participating member states. Each had its own particular concerns and each followed its own path. There occurred a considerable influx of Egyptians into Libya, which was chronically short of skilled manpower. The number of Egyptians in the early 1970s finding employment in oil-rich Libya was estimated at nearly 200,000. Their presence did not appear to endear them to the Libyans, who, ever since the Italian control of their country, were prone to display somewhat xenophobic tendencies even toward fellow Arabs. In a way, too much familiarity brought contempt in its wake. The Egyptians tended to look upon their Libyan hosts as uncouth and lacking in intellectual and social refinements. On the other hand, the Libyans viewed the Egyptians as greedy and grasping, merely interested in the high salaries that Libya could pay them and often grossly overstating their specialized skills. A good example of these mutually less than cordial attitudes was supplied when a Libyan airliner with many Libyans aboard was shot down by the Israelis over the Sinai peninsula where it strayed. The Libyan populace for some unexplained reason blamed the Egyptian authorities for permitting it to happen and in a rush of anger attacked Egyptian-staffed hospitals and other institutions in Benghazi and other cities.

Mutual disenchantment did not deter Qadhafi from pursuing a more perfect

---

[18]For the text of the consititution of FAR, see *Middle East Journal,* 25, no. 4 (Autumn 1971), 523–529.

union. Deeming the structure of the tripartite FAR too loose, he conceived the idea of a full merger of Egypt and Libya and declared himself prepared to step down as head of the Libyan state in favor of Sadat. He succeeded in persuading Sadat to sign, on August 2, 1972, an agreement pledging complete union between the two countries within a year. Some observers of the Arab scene believed that Qadhafi's militant advocacy of full merger stemmed from the fact that as a leader with Pan-Arab ambitions (and one who considered himself a spiritual heir to Nasser), Qadhafi felt stultified in Libya, which he considered insufficient as a solid base for truly Pan-Arab action. Such action, went this reasoning, could be provided only by a large and centrally located country such as Egypt. Should Qadhafi, under Sadat's presidency, assume the supreme command of the armed forces of the merged state, he would acquire the coveted platform for action. This explanation, naturally, represents mere speculation for which documentation is lacking. However, it is hard to deny that the suggested scenario appears to have strong elements of probability.

Anxious to pursue his scheme of full unity with Egypt, Qadhafi paid an extended visit to Cairo in late June 1973. In addition to his official conversations with Sadat, he made himself available to various social and professional groups in the Egyptian capital to which he spoke freely of his ideas regarding the future union. It should be pointed out that only a few months earlier, in the spring of that year, Qadhafi had launched in Libya what became known as the popular or the cultural revolution. It followed certain patterns of the earlier cultural revolution in Communist China and consisted largely of the formation of worker and student committees to govern the state and private enterprises as well as the schools and universities. For example, students were given the right to dismiss professors, to elect deans, and to be promoted to a higher class without examinations. At the same time, Qadhafi announced and enforced strict Islamic regulations such as the ban on alcohol, closure of cabarets, and so on. Flying squads of students and minor employees began raiding the better furnished offices of their managers and executives, rifling through their desks in search of suspicious material, and generally terrorizing the population. Simultaneously, young people, regardless of the level of education and physical adaptability, were being sent to work camps in the countryside. In the midst of all this Qadhafi proclaimed that there is a "third way" between communism and capitalism which is the Islamic way and which he hoped would in due time be embraced by the whole world. He also strongly opposed the movement for the emancipation of women.[19]

Qadhafi revealed those ideas in many interviews and discussions with various groups in Cairo. They produced a real shock among the intelligentsia of Egypt, which is largely westernized, enjoys Western patterns of entertainment and leisure, admits women to full participation in social and intellectual activities, and is generally opposed to any fundamentalist fanaticism. Their fears and misgivings were not assuaged when Qadhafi declared that in adhering to the union Libya was "prepared to sacrifice" its wealth but not its "cultural revolution." He also warned, rather

[19]For further details, see George Lenczowski, "Popular Revolution in Libya," *Current History* (Feb. 1974).

puzzlingly, that if complete union was not reached by September first, that is, within the next nine weeks, he would resign his post in Libya. His subsequent appearance before the Egyptian national assembly brought about a heated discussion between him and the inquisitive members.

The next step had the flavor of a comic opera. On Qadhafi's orders a caravan of about 20,000 Libyans set out in trucks and cars for Egypt to pressure Cairo into agreeing to a full merger. Sadat reacted to this uninvited expedition with anger. He issued orders to his forces to intercept and stop the marching multitude before it reached the densely populated areas of the delta. The Libyans withdrew. Soon afterward, Sadat declared that union with Libya should be carried out in stages and that emotion was not a firm foundation for unity. Undaunted by these difficulties, Qadhafi persisted in his schemes and on September 1, 1973, issued with Sadat a joint statement pledging that the two countries would (a) establish a constituent assembly to draft a joint constitution; (b) adopt a new monetary unit, the dinar; (c) exchange resident ministers to replace the existing diplomatic representations; and (d) set up a joint secretariat to assist the constituent assembly and resident ministers.

Like many previous endeavors at Arab unity, this ambitious scheme did not materialize either. Soon afterward, in October, Sadat launched an attack on the Israeli forces on the east bank of the Suez Canal. While he coordinated his moves with Syria's Assad, he did not consult Qadhafi, who was left completely out of the planning and execution of the war. Frustrated, he closed down the Libyan embassy in Cairo in December and soon afterward issued orders to the Egyptians working in Libya to prepare to leave his country. From then on relations between the two countries steadily deteriorated, to the point that in July 1977 an armed clash occurred between the Libyan and Egyptian forces in the border area.

Thwarted in his initiatives in Egypt, Qadhafi now turned to his western neighbor, Tunisia. In January 1974 he succeeded in persuading President Habib Bourguiba that their two countries should merge into a single Arab Islamic republic. Considering Bourguiba's political past, his fierce attachment to independence, and his frequent denunciations of Nasser's meddling in the affairs of other Arab countries, Bourguiba's agreement to effect union with Libya has not yet been satisfactorily explained. This scheme, however, also misfired. Within a year, in January 1975, Tunisian foreign minister Habis Chatti declared that relations with Libya were "frozen" due to differences over the merger agreement of January 1974.

To complete this review of ambitious schemes and broken hopes, mention should be made of an agreement signed between the governments of Yemen and South Yemen on November 28, 1972, to establish a union. Considering that the government of Yemen, while republican, was nevertheless moderate and inclined toward collaboration with Saudi Arabia and the government of South Yemen was radical and pro-Marxist, the agreement appears as puzzling as the one between Libya and Tunisia. And, like so many Arab pacts before, it just faded away. While there is evidence that the Saudis were seriously perturbed by the proposed union, the very incompatibility of the philosophies of both Yemen governments made it highly unlikely that it would succeed. Before long relations between Yemen and South

Yemen reverted to the previous state of tension punctuated by occasional border clashes.

Conclusion

As is clear from the foregoing review, the record of the Arab movement for unification is replete with many grandiose schemes and solemn agreements but it is also punctuated with almost as many failures. We have noted earlier that profound differences between the cultural and social levels, discrepancies in economic wealth, and contrasts in ideologies and political structures among Arab states largely accounted for the failure to achieve the desired unity. Moreover, it is a fact of life that those who actually hold power, whether they are conservatives or radicals, never cherish the idea of parting with it. Arab striving for unity often stemmed from emotion and exaggerated idealism and lacked a solid social and cultural foundation. While there were areas in which Arab leaderships and masses alike seemed able to reach consensus, notably in their oppositon to imperialism— now largely a thing of the past—and in their resistance to Israel and particularly to its territorial expansion, they were divided on many fundamental issues. Thus for example, Iraq and South Yemen, with their close ties to the Communist bloc, considered themselves part of the "socialist camp," whereas countries such as Saudi Arabia and, under Sadat's leadership, Egypt, definitely arranged themselves among the nations of the free world. It was also questionable to what extent the established Arab governments shared the maximalist platform of the Palestine Liberation Organization which, in its original charter, had asked for the abolition of the state of Israel and an uncompromising struggle for liberation. While some Arab governments, such as Libya and Iraq, supported PLO's maximalist objective, this was clearly not the case with Egypt and certain other Arab states that either explicitly or implicitly were willing to accept the existence of Israel provided it be contained within the pre-June 1967 boundaries.

As a matter of more fundamental political thinking, it seems that the Arabs, perhaps as a result of the psychological complex as former victims of colonialism, had not yet recognized the historical fact that the linguistic unity which they possess on the literate level is not in itself a sufficient foundation for political unity. The example of the English-speaking British Empire and later Commonwealth appears to point to centrifugal rather than centripetal tendencies. While there is a considerable degree of cultural community prevailing among the white nations of the Commonwealth, countries such as Canada, Australia, New Zealand, or Rhodesia have all asserted their complete sovereignty and are in no way subject to directives from London. A similar observation may be applied to Latin America. There, in the Spanish- and Portuguese-speaking world, the nations are fiercely independent and fully sovereign. They cooperate with each other within the framework of the Organization of American States but without losing the ultimate freedom of sovereign decisions.

It seems that with the advent of Sadat to power in Egypt a greater dose of realism was injected into Arab political thought. In contrast to Nasser, Sadat ceased to conduct Egypt's policy on an ideological basis. By demonstrating some restraint, he significantly contributed to the restoration of harmony among the Arab states, and if his relations with any Arab country showed strain, it usually was not due to his aggressive postures. Sadat emerged as a leader who instead of advocating unattainable unity schemes preferred to promote cooperation among the sovereign Arab states on the basis of their common interests, regardless of their ideological orientation. In the long run, this approach might prove more practical and beneficial to the Arab world as a whole.

CHAPTER XX

Foreign Powers and the Middle East

Great Britain

In the nineteenth century Britain's basic objectives in the Middle East could be described as follows: (1) to protect India; (2) to safeguard the lines of communication between the metropolis and the empire; (3) to promote British trade; and (4) to assure respect for a minimum of humanitarian standards. To attain these objectives Britain developed a policy which was rather remarkable for its consistency and which was based on the observance of a set of principles. The first of these was to defend the independence and integrity of both the Ottoman and the Persian Empires as against the threats and encroachments of Russia and, later, Wilhelmian Germany. Although Britain could have absorbed Persia and at least some portions of the Ottoman Empire and have converted them into a colony like India, she preferred to uphold them as living political organisms over which she would seek to exert influence but not domination. Her interest in seeing both the Ottoman Empire and Persia as viable political entities capable of withstanding Russian pressures led her to support reform movements aiming at the strengthening of their governments and societies: the *Tanzimat* in Turkey and the constitutional movement in Persia. In some cases her own strategic needs were given precedence over the maintenance of Ottoman integrity. Thus in her persistent policy of building a chain of naval strongholds between the metropolis and the East, Britain acquired Gibralter (1704), Malta (1800), Aden (1839), Cyprus (1878), and control of the Suez Canal (1882). The last two acquisitions were achieved at the expense of the Ottoman Empire. The purpose, however, was to establish outposts of strategic strength rather than to absorb and colonize major land areas. As such, these acquisitions were not wholly inconsistent with the basic principle of preserving the independence of the Ottoman Empire as a protective bulwark against Russian imperialism.

Britain's interest in safeguarding her life line to the East led her, inevitably, to concentrate on major routes to India. This explains the purchase of the Suez Canal stock by Disraeli in 1875 as well as the occupation of Egypt in 1882. By the same token, Britain was determined to assume uncontested supremacy in the Persian Gulf. In pursuance of this objective, she concluded a series of exclusive agreements with virtually all petty Arab principalities on the western and southern shores of the

765

gulf as well as with the sultan of Muscat in the course of the nineteenth century. Furthermore, in an attempt to frustrate German and Russian designs aiming at penetration of the Persian Gulf from the north, Britain opposed the Berlin-Baghdad Railway plan and in 1903—through Lord Lansdowne—gave formal warning to her would-be rivals that she would resist, with force if necessary, the establishment of any naval or commercial stronghold in the Persian Gulf by other powers.

Side by side with these political moves, Britain sought commercial opportunities in the area. In the Ottoman Empire her interests in this respect were looked after by the dedicated corps of the Levant Consular Service. In Persia her subjects sought and obtained important concessions to develop banking and the natural resources of the country. The most significant result of these endeavors was the establishment in 1909 of the Anglo-Persian Oil Company, in which, in due time, the Admiralty acquired a majority of the shares.

Britain's defense of humanitarian principles was expressed in her attempts to suppress the slave trade in the Persian Gulf and Sudan, as well as in her solicitude for the welfare of certain minorities, such as the Jews and Druzes, who were likely to suffer under the discriminatory policies of the Moslem states in which they lived.

The advent of World War I brought about a reorientation of British policy. Committed to fight and destroy the Ottoman Empire, Britain adopted a new "grand design," namely, the erection of an Arab political structure which would fill the void caused by the collapse of the Ottomans. This design, however, could be carried out only in part. Its implementation was vitiated by the concessions Britain made to France and Zionism under wartime duress. As a result, a hybrid system combining liberalism and imperialism was developed in the form of mandates. At the same time, encouraged by wartime promises of independence, the Arab peoples clamored for full self-determination. Faced with this pressure, Britain tried to devise a compromise solution which would give basic satisfaction to the Arabs while preserving British influence in the area. This solution consisted, in the interwar period, in freeing Iraq and Egypt from direct imperial control while linking them both to Britain through treaties of alliance, which treaties were to preserve her military and political preponderance. A similar pattern was applied to Jordan somewhat later. To strengthen these links with her erstwhile wards, Britain supported the Hashemite and the Egyptian monarchies, as well as the tribal and conservative elements in general. Furthermore, realizing the vigor of the anti-Zionist upsurge in the Arab East, in 1939 Britain stopped implementing the Balfour pledge and issued the White Paper on Palestine. Designed to court Arab favor at the time of the growing Axis threat to the Middle East, the White Paper virtually banned Jewish immigration and put an end to further land acquisitions in Palestine by the Zionists.

World War II found Britain—a status quo power—defending the Middle East against the onslaughts of Germany and Italy. The defense was a success and the military danger was eliminated. Politically, however, the process of withdrawal initiated in the interwar period was both resumed and accelerated. Arab nationalism, restive under enforced wartime suspension and stimulated by the presence of foreign armies, now reemerged in a modified form, the form of Pan-Arabism. Although any encouragement of Arab unity was contrary to the time-tested principle of *divide et impera,* Britain formally endorsed the plan for an Arab League. The elimination of France from the Levant and the reneging on the pledges to Zionists were viewed in London as the removal of two major obstacles to British-Arab friendship. Rather than oppose the current for Arab unity, Britain chose to identify herself with it, while continuing to support the conservative elements in the Arab world.

Although not perfect, this arrangement was defensible on grounds of political realism. Yet it was not allowed to come to full fruition. It was again vitiated by the upsurge of Zionism, which, far from meekly accepting the "frozen" situation in Palestine, set its sights on an early achievement of statehood for the Jews. Harassed and embarrassed by the violent terrorist attacks against her military and civilian administration in the Holy Land, Britain did not succeed in finding a positive solution to her difficulties. Instead she chose to escape the need for decision by dumping the Palestine problem onto the United Nations. Two conceivable advantages were to be derived from this course of action: one was the absolution of Britain from direct responsibility for the events in Palestine; the other was the possible transfer of the onus to the United States, whose two successive presidents, Roosevelt and Truman, had been inclined to advise pro-Zionist solutions without pledging American power for their implementation. This second advantage was undoubtedly achieved: through its role in securing the UN partition resolution as well as through its subsequent policies toward Israel, the United States became the prime target of Arab hostility for events in the Holy Land. Nevertheless, Britain did not obtain the first of the two advantages. She still continued to be blamed for her role in the Palestinian imbroglio, particularly for the cession of sizable stretches of territory to Israel by the British-commanded Arab Legion of King Abdullah of Transjordan.

To the failure to salvage her reputation on the issue of Palestine should be added another aggravating feature of Britain's position in the Middle East, namely, her control of the Persian Gulf and the south of the Arabian Peninsula. Whereas her supremacy in the Persian Gulf was intially based on her interest in the routes to India, Britain now viewed this area as the main supplier of oil to her industrial economy and her military establishment. This being the case, she was determined to maintain her control over the Persian Gulf and the southern coastlines of the Arabian Peninsula despite her concessions to the principle of self-determination in other, more advanced centers. But because Arab nationalism of the mid-twentieth century displayed unitary tendencies, it was no longer appeased by victories achieved in local national centers, such as Egypt or Syria. It tended to embrace in a broad sweep the whole of the Arab world, from Iraq to Morocco, demanding self-determination even for the most backward and remote areas.

Thus despite her attempt to espouse the cause of Arab unity through the medium of the Arab League and to shake off the burden of Palestine onto the shoulders of the United Nations, Britain was still blamed for Zionism, colonialism, economic imperialism, and alliance with reactionary traditionalism—the four devils of modern Arab nationalism. Under the circumstances it was almost inevitable that a strong tension should develop between her and the most vocal exponent of this nationalism, Colonel Nasser of Egypt. This tension, notwithstanding the attempt to reach a final settlement in 1954, culminated in a major clash over the issue of the Suez Canal in 1956. Although Nasser's nationalization of the canal was a reaction to certain American rather than British policy moves, it was ultimately British decisions which determined the course of events in the Middle East. Convinced that Nasser's nationalism had exceeded the bounds of decency and that it had acquired aggressive features reminiscent of the fascist totalitarianisms of the 1930s, Prime Minister Eden decided to put an end to further "appeasement" by striking, in conjunction with France, a military blow against Egypt. Although debatable on moral and other grounds, this policy could have been justified if it had been carried out consistently and to its logical conclusion. Eden's (and Britain's) tragedy was that it was conceived hastily, without proper weighing of various international factors, and executed poorly. The first major error was to equate ownership of the canal operation with a safeguard to free navigation. Such a safeguard was voluntarily removed by Britain in 1954, when she agreed to evacuate her troops from Egyptian territory. The second error consisted in lack of a clear decision whether to use force against Egypt regardless of the American attitude. Apparently Eden hoped that Washington would not object to the use of force or that its objections would be purely nominal. This proved to be a miscalculation. Eventually force was used, but the military operation was stopped halfway because of the combined pressures of the United States, the United Nations, and, possibly, of the Soviet Union. Finally, the third major error was that force was used under the worst possible circumstances from the political point of view. Instead of acting only in cooperation with France, Britain chose to exploit the Israeli advance into the Sinai Peninsula to foster her objectives. Thus, with a single stroke she erased whatever gains she had made in the past by trying to dissociate herself from Zionism. From now on Arab belief in the existence of British-Zionist connivance and conspiracy seemed to receive confirmation. Moreover, Britain's official explanation of her military intervention reached a high level of hypocrisy when she stated that her only objective was to separate the Israeli and Egyptian armies from each other and to protect the canal from the ill effects of hostilities. In reality, the aim was to defeat Nasser militarily and politically and to safeguard freedom of navigation in the canal by reimposing imperial control (or threat of it). Rebuffed by Washington and the United Nations, Britain achieved neither of these objectives. On the contrary, the canal was closed to navigation through the invasion-triggered act of Egyptian sabotage, and Nasser emerged triumphant, pointing to another signal victory over imperialism. Britain's prestige suffered grievous damage, thereby contributing to the creation of a political vacuum which various forces hostile to the West were eager to fill as rapidly as possible. Once dominant in the Arab world, Britain now saw her diplomatic relations broken with Egypt, Syria, and Saudi Arabia, her assets sequestrated in Egypt, and her supplies of oil interrupted both through the Suez and the Syrian routes. Her only links with the independent Arab states were maintained through the Hashemite monarchies in Iraq and Jordan and pro-British President Chamoun of Lebanon. But even there powerful forces were at work to upset the existing regimes and whatever remained of British influence. The civil war in Lebanon in 1958 put an end to the government which openly defied Nasser and replaced it with a compromise regime which carefully avoided identification with Britain. In the same year the Hashemite dynasty of Iraq was physically destroyed in a violent revolution, thus removing one of the traditional pillars of British policy in the area. And Jordan, though protected by British troops from internal subversion and Pan-Arab aggression, was henceforth to be a common ward of Britain and the United States.

By the end of the 1950s British influence in the major centers of the Arab world—Cairo, Baghdad, Damascus, and Riyadh—had diminished, faded away, or collapsed altogether. British presence, still of a colonial or semicolonial nature, continued through the 1960s only in the peripheral areas: Aden and the Aden Protectorate, the Persian Gulf, and, as an extension of wartime military campaigns, the eastern portion of Libya.

In the 1960s Britain resumed diplomatic relations with some of the states of the area that had broken them as a result of the Suez crisis. But this process was uneven: in 1965 President Nasser broke off relations with Britain in protest against colonial policies in Aden and Rhodesia. During the June 1967 Arab-Israeli war, Britain's popularity was still so low in the Arab world that, along with the United States and West Germany, she was subjected to a short-lived oil embargo.

Despite these reverses, Britain's fortunes took an upward path in the later 1960s, partly due to Britain's role in the United Nations in the aftermath of the June war. Great Britain figured as the main author of the United Nations Security Council Resolution 242 calling for the withdrawal of Israeli forces from occupied Arab territories (Lord Caradon initially drafted the resolution). Furthermore, by the end of 1967 Britain relinquished imperial control over Aden and the South Arabian Federation. The announcement the following year of British intention to withdraw from the Persian Gulf further helped restore Britain to a position of esteem in Arab nationalist circles. In 1970, the British withdrew their last forces from the El-Adem military base near Tobruk in Libya and the formal ending of their rule in the Persian Gulf came December 2, 1971. This last act of withdrawal, however, caused another complication when, incensed at Britain for allowing the Iranian seizure of three strategic islands in the Strait of Hormuz, Libya's revolutionary ruler, Colonel Muammar Qadhafi, nationalized the concession held in his country by the British Petroleum Company. He also publicly admitted providing arms and financial support for the Irish nationalists struggling against British rule in Northern Ireland.

All in all, however, the decade of the 1960s witnessed the gradual rebuilding of Britain's relations with the Arab countries. In Saudi Arabia, for example, Britain undertook first to establish and later to maintain a complex air defense system. In the 1970s this process of normalization quickened its pace in both the political and economic realms. Britain became a supplier of substantial quantities of arms and military equipment to various Arab states. Arms sales were an important compensation for the huge amounts of money that Britain had to spend on imported oil, the price of which was quadrupled in 1974. As traders and arms suppliers, the British had to compete with the United States, France, and other industrial powers for their share in the steadily growing Middle East market. They had to do it without the privilege of monopoly that their former imperial position in the area had afforded, but also without the encumbrance of resentments and hostility that imperial ventures had generated.

France

Historically, the role of France in the Middle East had been that of a protector of Latin Christianity and a carrier of culture. The imprint that France's *mission civilisatrice* had made in the area could perhaps best be measured by the fact that the upper classes of Egypt and the countries of the Levant adopted French as their second language, which in some cases they knew better than their native Arabic. Numerous French schools, lay and religious, the University of St. Joseph in Beirut, and numerous research institutes and archeological missions further emphasized the intellectual influence of France. Politically, France had supported the Ottoman Empire against the aggressive designs of Russia, playing in this respect a role similar to that of Britain but somewhat less emphatic. Although we have grown accustomed to speaking of a British lifeline linking England with her Indian and Far Eastern possessions via the Mediterranean and the Red Sea, we must not underestimate the usefulness of the Suez Canal, constructed by the French and then largely owned by them, in reducing the distance between France and her colonial possessions in Indochina.

Following World War I, France appeared in the Middle East in a new, colonial aspect: she became a mandatory power over Syria and Lebanon. Thus her interests for the first time clashed seriously with Arab nationalism, a fact which was accentuated by the forcible ejection from Damascus of the newly elected king of Syria, Faisal of the Hashemite dynasty. But from a perspective of several decades, the colonial presence of France in the Levant was no more than an interlude which came to an end with the achievement of sovereign statehood by Syria and Lebanon at the end of World War II. After 1945, France was thus prepared to resume her traditional position as friendly power and provider of culture. French hopes, however, that relations with the Arab world would regain the earlier level of friendship and normalcy were frustrated by the struggle for the emancipation of Algeria. It should be pointed out that in the 1950's the French relinquished without too much friction their imperial dominion over Morocco and Tunisia. Because of the presence of many French *colons,* Algeria was regarded as an integral part of France (*France d'outre-mer*), with deputies sitting in the French parliament. To agree to Algerian independence thus meant not only parting with territory but also changing the basic political concept underlying French presence there and abandoning the million Europeans who had greatly contributed to the economic development of Algeria. As a consequence, the Algerian struggle for liberation was violent and protracted. In fact, indirectly it contributed to the collapse of the Fourth Republic in France and the return of General Charles de Gaulle to power in 1958. Furthermore, because Arab nationalism, stimulated as it was by Nasser's Pan-Arab ideas, knew no geographical boundaries, the cause of Algeria became the cause of the nationalists in the Arab East as well.

A further complication in Franco-Arab relations occurred as a result of the nationalization of the Suez Canal by Egypt. By invading the Suez Canal Zone jointly with Britain in 1956, France not only resumed an imperial-aggressive character in Arab eyes but also became guilty of collusion with the Arabs' worst enemy, Israel. France's relations with the regime of President Nasser in Egypt were particularly strained: while he supported with arms and money the Algerian revolution, France became the biggest single provider of arms to Israel.

Between General de Gaulle's return in 1958 and the achievement of Algerian independence in 1962, relations between France and the Arab world were in a period of transition. Although some French arms were still flowing to Israel, firms such as Renault, decided to abide by the rules of the Arab boycott of Israel and withdrew their facilities from that country. Similarly, Air France refused to enter into an agreement with the Israeli authorities.

The liberation of Algeria opened a new chapter in the relations between France and the Arab world, highlighted by a visit of Egypt's vice president, Marshal Abdul Hakim Amer, to General de Gaulle in 1965, which was marked by great mutual cordiality. General de Gaulle publicly praised Nasser for his statesmanship, and the two governments reached an agreement providing for the desequestration of French property seized during the Suez crisis.

The growing friendliness toward the Arabs had its counterpart in the steadily worsening relations between France and Israel. General de Gaulle was highly displeased by the Israeli attack on Egypt in June 1967 inasmuch as he did not consider that the removal of the UN Emergency Force and Egypt's announced intention to block the Gulf of Aqaba provided sufficient reasons for war. He was also disturbed by and critical of the Israeli occupation of extensive Arab territories. He opposed Israeli annexation of eastern Jerusalem, proclaiming his preference for internationalization of the city. He gave the initiative for the Big Four series of meetings in the late 1960's with the aim of not only achieving but perhaps also imposing a settlement on Israel. That settlement, in his view, would require virtually total Israeli withdrawal from the occupied territories.

Under de Gaulle—and also under his successors Georges Pompidou and Valery Giscard d'Estaing—France also radically reversed its arms policy toward the Middle East. In 1968 the French government cancelled the promised sale of fifty Mirage jets for Israel and in early 1969, after the Israeli raid on Beirut which was executed in French helicopters, it proclaimed a complete ban on arms sales to Israel. That same year, to maintain a modicum of a balanced policy, France proclaimed an embargo on offensive arms to the so-called confrontation states. This permitted France to effect in 1970 the sale of 110 Mirage jets to Libya on the ground that Libya was not a combatant country. When Israel protested this transaction, pointing to the possibility or vitual certainty of the transfer of some of these aircraft to Egypt, the French disregarded Israeli complaints. A further irritation in the Franco-Israeli relations occurred that same year when the Israelis engineered the capture of five gunboats earlier ordered by them but sequestered by the French authorities, from the port of Cherbourg. In 1973 a new tension arose when President Pompidou criticized the planned visit of the Israeli premier, Golda Meir, to Paris to attend a meeting of the Socialist International on the grounds that it would constitute Israeli interference in French domestic affairs. Nevertheless, Meir made a hurried trip to the conference. To accentuate its pro-Arab stance, the French government agreed in 1975 to the opening of a PLO office in Paris and in the same year lifted its earlier ban on arms for the confrontation states. Finally, a bitter moment was reached in 1977 when the French authorities permitted the escape from France of the freshly arrested Abu Daoud, sought by European police agencies for his role as mastermind of the massacre of the Israeli athletes at the Munich Olympic games a few years earlier.

It was clear that in the 1970s France was determined to follow a path of reconciliation and friendship with the Arab world. Paying a visit to two Arab capitals, Beirut and Damascus, in the summer of 1971, French minister of state for foreign affairs Jean de Lipkowski declared, ''The purpose of our presence here is to guarantee Lebanon's independence,'' thereby indicating a resumption by France of an active political role in the region.[1]

This new policy brought its rewards to France, especially in the economic sector. In 1968 a French government-owned enterprise, ERAP, entered a joint venture in Libyan oil. The following year construction of the Sumed was launched by a French-led consortium in Egypt. When on June 1, 1972, the Iraq Petroleum Company was nationalized by the Baathist givernment in Baghdad, its French shareholder, Compagnie Française des Pétroles (CFP), was offered an option to negotiate a separate favorable agreement with Iraq in appreciation of her support of the Arab cause. And indeed, eighteen days later, Iraq's vice president, Siddam Hussein, concluded such a preferential agreement with the French during his visit in Paris.

It was no surprise, therefore, that during the October war of 1973 France was placed by the oil-producing Arab states on a list of friendly nations immune to embargo and entitled to the prewar level of deliveries. Nevertheless, disturbed by the turmoil the war had produced in international oil economics, France sought to safeguard her position in case of future emergencies and disruptions. To this end she concluded early in 1974 a bilateral oil agreement with Saudi Arabia providing for delivery of 800 million tons over a period of twenty years in return for arms supplies to the Saudi kingdom. This move was accompanied by further expansion of French-Saudi relations, as exemplified by agreements to provide all sorts of technological services to Saudi Arabia, including an ambitious project of mineral exploration. From the mid-1970s France engaged also in wide-ranging activity aiming at the export and construction of nuclear plants in various Arab countries and Iran. She also concluded nuclear cooperation agreements with Iraq and Libya while exploring with Egypt the possibility of joint ventures for the production of military aircraft and other weapons.

In pursuing this dynamic policy of rapprochment with the Islamic countries of the Middle East, France did not appear to be disturbed by ideological preferences. Her internal political process, though frequently punctuated by crises, was free from the ethnic group pressure syndrome which, in the case of the United States, made the

---

[1]Quoted by *Middle East Journal,* 25, no. 4 (Autumn 1971), 513.

formulation of a coherent foreign policy so difficult. Within two decades following de Gaulle's presidency France could be said to have regained her position of influence in the Middle East.

Germany

German involvement in the Middle East began in the late nineteenth century during the reign of Wilhelm II. The ambitious and militaristic German emperor courted the favor of Sultan Abdul Hamid II and, on a visit to the Holy Land at the turn of the century, proclaimed himself friend and protector of Islam.

Substantial differences could be observed between Germany, on the one hand, and Britain and France, on the other, in their relationship to the Middle East. Even before they became entrusted with mandatory responsibilities over the Fertile Crescent, Britain and France were deeply involved in the politics and economics of the area. Britain was in possession of Aden and its hinterland, exercised a tutelage based on special treaties over the Persian Gulf, controlled Cyprus, and had occupied Egypt since 1882. At the same time, the French entrenchment in the economy of Egypt and in the cultural institutions of the Levant was substantial. By contrast, Germany was a newcomer trying to force an entry into the area through promotion of various economic and technical schemes, foremost of which was the Berlin-Baghdad railway in 1902. But this project, with its contemplated Kuwait terminal, posed a threat to the British position of dominance in the Persian Gulf and, naturally, Britain reacted strongly against it. Basically, therefore, Germany strove to effect a change in a situation that favored Britain and, to a lesser extent, France.

This revisionist tendency in the German policy displayed a sharp edge during World War I when, on the one hand, German agents and emissaries stirred up revolts in southern Iran and infiltrated Afghanistan and, on the other, Imperial Germany made a substantial manpower investment in the Ottoman war effort. Moreover, the establishment of a pro-German dissident Iranian government in Kermanshah during the war further accentuated the German objective of upsetting the status quo.

In the interwar period, particularly after the rise of Hitler, Germany resumed the economic and technical penetration of Iran and, to a lesser extent, of certain Arab countries. World War II provided new opportunities for German intervention in the area. German agents, particularly Schulze-Holthus, again became active among the tribes of southern Iran while infiltrating certain segments of the Iranian army. In Iraq, Germany supported the anti-British rebellion of Rashid Ali el-Gailani in 1941. A German armistice mission was busy establishing closer links with the anti-Western nationalists in Syria and to some extent in Lebanon. And, last but not least, a powerful German expeditionary force under General Erwin Rommel spearheaded a combined German-Italian offensive from Libya into Egypt.

Thus there is no doubt that in the first half of the twentieth century Germany accumulated a record of multifarious attempts, economic, technical, and military, to penetrate the Middle East. In pursuing these policies, however, Germany suffered from certain disadvantages. First of all, it lost both world wars, hence its prestige suffered. Secondly, its policies experienced interruptions and discontinuities as a result of abrupt changes from the Imperial regime to the Weimar Republic, the rise of Hitler, and then the collapse of the Nazi Reich at the end of World War II. Potentially, however, Germany enjoyed an advantage over its British and French rivals in that it had no tradition of imperial domination of the Middle East, never gave reason to excite the hostility of local nationalists, and invariably appeared as a friendly power anxious to promote trade, assist in development, and share its superior technology with the nations of the area.

The years immediately following World War II were not noted for much German activity in the Middle East. Truncated in its territory, with its industries severely damaged as a result of the war, Germany had first to concentrate on its own recuperation from defeat and on reestablishing itself as a respected state in the Western community of nations. But by the 1960s the German Federal Republic (West Germany) had made an impressive comeback as an exporter of industrial commodities, a major consumer of Middle Eastern oil, and provider of technology both in the Northern Tier and in the Arab world. Germany's economic advances often met with a positive response from the freshly emancipated Arab states. In the Arab part of the Middle East, West Germany seemed to be pursuing two objectives: one was to effect reconciliation with Israel and thus to erase the bitter memories of the Nazi persecution of Jews; the other was to establish close economic and technical links with the Arab world within the framework of regular diplomatic relations. Reconciliation with Israel (treated as an heir to the once thriving Jewish community in Germany) took the form of one billion dollars' worth of reparations paid between 1952 and 1966; it was also expressed through consistent effort to normalize relations with Israel, with which no diplomatic relations were maintained for two decades after World War II. The absence of mutual diplomatic representation was largely due to the reluctance of Israel to commit itself to a full-fledged diplomatic recognition. This reluctance was expressed in a resolution passed by the Israeli Knesset in 1962, by virtue of which strict limits were imposed on student and scientific exchanges, mutual visits of sports teams and entertainers, and so forth, between Israel and West Germany.

These two objectives were not easy to reconcile because any German move toward a closer relationship with Israel was bound to produce adverse Arab reactions, and by the same token, any significant warming up of relations with the Arab countries was certain to generate criticism in Israel. And indeed, a number of complications arose in the relations between West Germany and both Israel and the Arab countries. Thus, in the 1950s, Israel repeatedly complained that West German arms experts were employed by Egypt and rejected as invalid the formal German arguments that these experts were in Egypt in a private capacity. On their side, the Arab countries were increasingly critical of expanding German arms sales to Israel, especially between 1960 and 1965. Arab anger reached a high pitch in 1965 when it was learned that, by virtue of a secret agreement, a substantial number of American-made M-48 tanks were transferred, at the request of the United States, by West Germany to Israel. Furthermore, during the period following the June 1967

Arab-Israeli war, West Germany was the site of terrorist activity, a situation which produced considerable strains in its relations with Israel and the Arab countries as well. The relatively free use that the Palestinian *fedayeen* organizations were making of the West German territory and the links that were revealed between them and the native German terrorist gangs of the Baader-Meinhof type caused the federal German government to effect a crackdown on Arab organizations in its territory, an act that evoked protests in the Arab Middle East. On the other hand, Germany became the target of Israeli attacks for mishandling the situation arising from the massacre by Arab terrorists of the Israeli athletic team in Munich in 1972.

The year 1965 proved to be one of crisis in Germany's relations with the Arabs. Angered by mounting evidence of German arms supplies to Israel, Nasser, in March of that year, granted recognition to the German Democratic Republic (Communist-dominated East Germany) in spite of repeated warnings from Bonn that such a recognition might result in the suspension of German economic assistance to Egypt and expose political relations between the two countries to a great strain. That same month, in pursuance of a policy inaugurated some time earlier, West Germany reached an agreement with Israel to establish diplomatic relations. (This decision was the result of a mission undertaken on orders of Chancellor Ludwig Erhard by Dr. Kurt Birrenbach, chairman of the board of the Thyssen Steel Corporation and member of the Bundestag.) As a result, the first West German ambassador arrived in Tel-Aviv in May 1965, meeting with some hostile demonstrations but received courteously by the Israeli government.

Promptly reacting to this new development, the Arab League had met in March 1965 to map out joint action against West Germany. A resolution to sever diplomatic relations was adopted and implemented by Iraq, the U.A.R., Sudan, Saudi Arabia, Algeria, and eventually the majority of the League member states. The breach between the Arab world and West Germany was bound to be costly to both sides. Shortly before the rupture in diplomatic relations, Cairo and Bonn had agreed on nearly $80 million of German assistance to Egypt. This amount brought total postwar aid from West Germany to about $400 million, as against a mere $30 million that Egypt had received by then from East Germany. Moreover, just prior to the crisis Nasser had warned Bonn of possible retaliatory suspension of $200 million in Egyptian debts to West Germany. Under the circumstances it was not surprising that when an oil embargo was proclaimed by the Arab states in the wake of the June 1967 Arab-Israeli war West Germany was subjected to its provisions.

In spite of these political difficulties, German economic involvement in the Arab world continued through the 1960s. It included oil concessions in Libya and Oman; irrigation projects in Saudi Arabia; industrial projects in Iraq, Jordan, and Yemen; fairly comprehensive economic relations with the countries of the Maghreb (Tunisia, Libya, and Morocco chose not to sever relations with West Germany); and even participation in the research and development of the Qattara Depression in Egypt.

With the advent of the 1970s, West Germany began gradually normalizing relations with the Arab countries, as evidenced by the resumption of diplomatic relations and expansion of economic cooperation. At the same time, Bonn took care not to antagonize Israel. In fact, during his visit in that country in 1971, Foreign Minister Scheel declared that the Federal Republic's "special relationship" with Israel would continue. On the other hand, resumption of friendly relations with the Arab states made West Germany immune to the oil embargo declared in the wake of the October war of 1973. It was listed among the "friendly" states.

West German relations were not limited, of course, to the Arab countries and Israel alone; they also extended to the Northern Tier, with Iran as a major partner largely owing to its increasing oil wealth. German exports to Iran increased considerably to provide technology for the development plan and consumer goods for the population. On its part, Iran showed interest in investing its financial reserves in German industry, with the purchase of 25 percent of the stock of the Krupp Company by the Iranian government providing a major highlight of this trend.

By carefully refraining from interference or mediation in the Arab-Israeli conflict and by concentrating on economics, technology, and to some extent cultural exchanges, West Germany successfully reestablished itself as a partner of Middle Eastern states by the mid-1970s.

The Soviet Union

During the past century and a half Russia had been the most persistent of Britain's rivals in Asia. The Soviet revolution did not change this basic pattern of rivalry; it only added a new ideological flavor to it. This Russian position differed from the British in this important respect: that while Britain was *in* the Middle East, especially after 1918, Russia remained *outside* it. What Russia strove for was to exchange these roles; hence her policy was a policy of change.

Trying to penetrate the Middle East and to dislodge Britain (as well as France), Russia used diplomatic, military, economic, and ideological weapons according to the need of the moment. Her first attempts after the revolution were both diplomatic and ideological. At the Congress of the Peoples of the East, held in Baku in September 1920 under the auspices of the Communist International, Russia put forward the slogan of liberation of the colonial and semicolonial peoples from the imperialist yoke.[2] The Comintern continuously harped on this theme, and at its Sixth Congress of 1928 prepared blueprints dealing with the doctrinal and tactical aspects of the revolution in the East. Their sharp edge was directed against the colony-owning Western powers, and no line of these "Theses" was repudiated even at the time of the Popular Front policy in the middle 1930s or during the actual alliance with the West in World War II.

The diplomatic action of the Soviet Union was synchronized with this ideological offensive and was designed to capture public opinion in the Middle Eastern countries and to secure the cooperation of their governments. The first round came in 1921 when Russia concluded treaties with Turkey, Iran, and Afghanistan. These

[2] An account of the Baku Congress may be found in George Lenczowski, *Russia and the West in Iran, 1918-1948* (Ithaca, N.Y., 1949), pp. 6ff.

treaties were well timed because their conclusion corresponded to the postwar deterioration in relations between Britain and the three countries in question. Turkey was then fighting her War of Liberation against British-supported Greeks, Iran was experiencing one of those paroxysms of xenophobia so characteristic of her emotional instability, and Afghanistan was frantically seeking to assert her newly won independence after the Third Afghan War. These treaties were all alike in that they used anti-imperialist phraseology calculated to impress the awakening masses of the East.

When it came, however, to their actual implementation, Russia's southern neighbors soon discovered that while the Kremlin was anxious to stir anti-Western moods, it was definitely reluctant to abandon the traditional objectives of tsarist imperialism. From the economic standpoint the new Russia was as eager to dominate the northern provinces of Iran and Afghanistan as was the old one. From the territorial angle the Soviets did not hesitate to use force to dislodge the Kemalists from Batum, to occupy Gilan in 1920, and to indulge in petty but aggressive bickering about the Atrek and Oxus boundaries with Iran and Afghanistan, respectively. Moreover, their much-vaunted support of self-determination proved to be no more than an anti-Western propaganda device that did not stand the test of reality when the Soviets brutally crushed national independence movements in the Caucasus and Central Asia. Finally, Soviet support of separatist tendencies among the Turkic-speaking groups across their southern border and the subversive activities of local Communist parties were not conducive to mutual cordiality. As time went on, relations between the Soviets and their southern neighbors cooled. This trend is perhaps best symbolized by the fact that, whereas between 1926 and 1928 Iran, Turkey, and Afghanistan had concluded a series of mutual friendship treaties under Soviet auspices and prodding, ten years later, in 1937, these same countries plus Iraq, signed the Saadabad Entente, implicitly directed against Soviet infiltration of the area. And this process of estrangement was far advanced in 1939 when Iran and Afghanistan entered into cordial relationships with Nazi Germany while Turkey veered toward an alliance with Britain and France.

There was practically no direct relationship between the Soviets and the Arab countries in the interwar period. The Arab East at that time was under the direct or indirect control of Britain and France, and there was no reason why these two powers should facilitate any contacts between revolutionary Russia and their colonial wards. Only with Saudi Arabia and Yemen, two states really independent after the First World War, did the Soviets establish diplomatic relations (in 1926 and 1928, respectively), and a Soviet commercial mission operated for a brief period in Sana. But to foment proletarian revolution in these isolated and remote regions where there was no proletariat and no strong anti-Western feeling was a losing proposition, and after some time Russia gave up her attempt to establish a foothold there.

Thus deprived of direct diplomatic relations, the Soviets acted through the Comintern and through the small and rather inefficient Communist parties in Arab lands and in Palestine. The official party line was to favor Arab nationalism and to side with it against Zionism. The latter, officially described as a petty-bourgeois capitalist ideology,[3] was considered an instrument of British imperialism and as such it was vigorously opposed both in Palestine and in Russia herself. This, however, did not prevent the Russians from sponsoring a Communist party among the Jews of Palestine.[4] But care was taken to keep it separate from the Arab Communists in the same country.

Generally speaking, Communist influence in the Middle East in the interwar period was not great. Turkey, homogeneous, reformed, and nationalist, had her own ideals and definitely rejected the ideology so alien to her spirit. Iran and Afghanistan, with their conservative societies and their knowledge of Soviet intrigue among borderland groups, could not be expected to fall an easy prey to foreign ideological innovations. And the Arab peoples, physically isolated from Russia, conscious of the naval power which Russia did not possess, largely uninformed and devotedly Islamic, were not likely to become excited by the new Communist gospel.

Russian Activities during and after World War II

This situation underwent a radical change as the result of the Second World War. Britain's wartime pro-Soviet policy resulted in the lifting of the ban on Soviet diplomatic missions in Arab capitals, and from 1942–1943, Cairo, Baghdad, Beirut, and Damascus witnessed a real invasion of Soviet diplomats as well as commercial and cultural representatives. Once established behind the cloak of diplomatic immunity, these Soviet agents diplayed considerable energy and versatility in their multifarious activities. They established contact with existing trade unions and helped to organize new ones. The Soviet-dominated World Federation of Trade Unions took an active interest in the Arab and Iranian labor movement and lost no opportunity to send visiting missions and to enhance the prestige of such Communist labor leaders as Reza Rusta in Iran or Mustafa el-Aris in Lebanon. A number of pro-Soviet dailies and periodicals sprang into existence in Teheran and the Arab capitals. The Middle East experienced a sudden growth of Soviet friendship societies and other front organizations ostensibly dedicated to the cause of culture, peace, or female emancipation. "Houses of culture," bookstores carrying Communist literature, exhibits of Soviet art, concerts and shows of Soviet artists, lectures of Soviet scholars, and Soviet motion pictures constituted just so many examples of Soviet infiltration. Iranian and Arab intellectuals and artists were conducted on free tours of Asiatic centers in the Soviet Union and lavishly entertained. And the cooperation of some "unemployed millionaires"—usually idle and frustrated heirs of large fortunes in Teheran or Cairo—was skillfully secured.

Soviet propaganda was like a good taxation system: it assumed various forms, sometimes open and sometimes well concealed but always pursuing its main objective. Of special interest was the encouragement given to national minorities and compact borderland groups. The Turkish-speaking population of Iranian Azerbaijan

---

[3]J. Stalin, *Marxism and the National and Colonial Question* (Marxist Library, n.d.), p. 289.
[4]See Martin Ebon, "Communist Tactics in Palestine," *Middle East Journal*, 2 (July 1948).

was an object of special solicitude, but other groups in a similar geographical position were equally subjected to Soviet blandishments. The Turkomans of the Iranian and Afghan northern plains, the Afghan Uzbeks and Tajiks, and above all the Kurds were consistently encouraged in their national aspirations. The creation in 1945 of a Soviet-sponsored Kurdish republic at Mahabad bore eloquent testimony to Soviet ambitions and tactics.

Courting as they did national minorities, the Soviets scored considerable success with the Armenians. This unfortunate nation, scattered all over the Middle East and unpopular with Arabs, Iranians and Turks alike, successfully preserved its identity and culture on the basis of its loyalty to the Armenian Orthodox Church. The fact that the headquarters of its leader, the *catholicos,* was situated in Echmiadzin in Soviet Armenia gave Russia a chance to influence Armenian public opinion abroad. Moreover, the structure of Armenian society, which contains large numbers of skilled workers, mechanics, and intellectuals, all somewhat frustrated by discrimination and lack of opportunity in their foster countries, facilitated the spread of Communist ideology among their rank and file. Soviet propaganda among them was so ingenious that it even succeeded in causing the Dashnak party to falter in its anti-Soviet stand.

In 1946 the Soviet Union loudly advertised and carried out the "repatriation" to Soviet Armenia of many thousands of Armenians living in the Middle East and elsewhere.[5] In performing this feat the Soviets turned to their benefit the peculiar psychological complexes of a race both persecuted and scattered. Hope for greater social justice under the Communist system (enhanced by a somewhat naive conviction that in the Armenian SSR things might look much brighter than in other parts of the Soviet Union), inner rebellion against the hostility of their adopted countries, belief in the myth of Russian invincibility, and a mystical longing to die in the shadow of Ararat—all combined to give this exodus the semblance of a mass pilgrimage. As to Russia, she scored a diplomatic success by proving that there were people willing to accept the Soviet system with enthusiasm; she enlarged her contacts with the Armenian community as a whole, using them when necessary for anti-Turkish propaganda; and through the new settlers she gained a lever of pressure on their relatives who remained abroad.

The many-faced character of Soviet political activity was well illustrated by the frequent recourse to religious propaganda. Ever since 1941 Soviet publications and broadcasts had laid great stress on the alleged freedom of religion in the Soviet Union and on the good will of the government toward Islam. In the later stages of the war and in the postwar period delegations of Soviet Moslems made pilgrimages to Mecca and paid visits to Iran. Care was taken to staff Soviet legations and embassies in the Middle East with a certain number of Soviet Moslems, sometimes of high diplomatic rank. These officials skillfully displayed their piety by making their Friday prayers in the most-frequented mosques. The degree of Soviet support to fanatical religious societies, such as the Moslem Brotherhood in Egypt or

[5]For an account of this exodus, see Bertold Spuler, "Moskaus kirchenpolitische Offensive im Vorderen Orient," *Ost-Probleme,* June 2, 1951.

Fadayan Islam in Iran, remains a matter of speculation, but in view of their inherently anti-Western character, it would not be surprising if we should learn some day that Soviet money was at least partly responsible for some of their actions.[6] In Britain, at any rate, opinions were voiced that the trouble-making Fakir of Ipi on the Afghan-Pakistan frontier had been a steady recipient of Soviet subsidies.

The Soviets did not hesitate also to use the Russian Orthodox Church as an instrument of their policy.[7] Special efforts were made to bring to Moscow Orthodox bishops from the Middle East to attend the Holy Synods, whose business it was to elect the patriarchs. The aim of these tactics was to subordinate the Orthodox hierarchies in Turkey, Greece, Syria, Palestine, and other parts of the Middle East to the supremacy of the Russian Church. In some cases these tactics failed, but in some—notably in Jewish-held Jerusalem—they succeeded.

The action of Soviet diplomatic missions was obviously well coordinated with that of local Communist parties. For some time, especially during the Western-Soviet alliance during the war, these parties enjoyed immunity from official molestation. In Iran the Tudeh party grew in numbers and influence and so did the Communist parties in Iraq and Egypt. This artificial truce did not, however, last long, and in 1947–1949 stern measures were taken against the Communists in Iran, Iraq, Egypt, and Syria. As a result, in some countries the parties went underground, but as events in Iran proved in 1951, they did not cease to be active.

Over and above these indirect activities were various manifestations of direct Soviet pressure. Apparently encouraged by the easy manner in which the West had surrendered eastern Europe to her mercy, Russia, right after the war, made a bold bid for the control of Iran and Turkey and for an opening in the Mediterranean. The chapters on Iran and Turkey have described in some detail how Russia engineered a rebellion in Azerbaijan and how she intimidated the Iranian premier to grant her an oil concession, and what demands she presented with regard to the Turkish Straits and the east-Anatolian border areas. We may add that at the inter-Allied Potsdam conference of 1945 the Russians requested a trusteeship over Tripolitania or Eritrea. Early in 1947 Soviet pressure, through Communist guerrillas, had become so dangerous in Greece that the President of the United States found it necessary to proclaim what amounted to a new doctrine in American foreign policy.

Soviet Tactics: Aid and Trade

The year 1955 constituted an important landmark in Soviet relations with the Middle East. It closed the period during which foundations were laid for the defense of the Northern Tier against Soviet encroachments and aggression. By concluding the Baghdad Pact, Turkey, Iran, Iraq, and Pakistan clearly defined their attitude toward the West and communism, in return for which they received guarantees from, and were assured cooperation by, Great Britain and the United States.

But if the Baghdad Pact was meant to be a barrier to Soviet expansionism, its

---

[6] Philip W. Ireland, "Islam, Democracy, and Communism," in *Islam in the Modern World,* a symposium edited by D. S. Franck (Washington, 1951), p. 65.

[7] Albion Ross, "Soviet Revives Tie to Levant Church," *New York Times,* July 17, 1950; see also Spuler, *op. cit.*

usefulness soon proved limited to the Northern Tier alone. Rather than try to force it down, the Soviet Union chose to bypass it by concentrating on the Arab Core of the Middle East. Here the method adopted was not to threaten but to woo. The aggression and intimidation practiced vis-à-vis the Northern Tier gave way in the Arab East to gradual infiltration and friendly dealings with the existing governments regardless of their character. Slogans of peaceful coexistence, mutual respect for independence and sovereignty, and noninterference in internal affairs were proclaimed and skillfully repeated by a variety of media. In actual practice Russia (with the aid of the satellites) began to conduct a vigorous aid-and-trade policy extending low-interest loans and technical assistance to Egypt, Syria, Yemen, and, since the revolution of 1958, Iraq.[8] The Soviet-Egyptian arms deal of September 1955 was a major opening move in this new policy, symbolizing Russian determination to skip the Northern Tier defenses in her new concentration on the Arabs. In this policy Russia consistently endeavored to turn to her advantage any differences which had arisen between the Arab world and the West. Such controversial issues as Palestine, the Baghdad Pact, the purchase of arms, the Suez Canal, and Algeria were methodically exploited by Soviet propaganda to blacken the reputation of the West while presenting Russia as a disinterested friend of the Arabs and their ally in the struggle for "liberation." Russia's advances in the Arab world were greatly aided by the fact that historically the Arabs have never been exposed to continuous Russian imperialism. The subjection of millions of Turkic- and Persian-speaking Moslems to tsarist and Soviet imperial rule left the Arabs cold and indifferent. They reacted much more intensely to any manifestation of Western imperialism, despite the latter's steady retreat from Asia and Africa. Russia's brutality toward her own and conquered peoples alike might be occasionally (and privately) deplored, but it was also regarded as proof of her strength and her capacity to checkmate the West— hence not an unwelcome phenomenon from the Arab point of view. In this respect the psychological reactions of the Arabs were not entirely unlike those toward Nazi Germany two decades earlier.

Did the results of this policy warrant the heavy investment of time, funds, and energy from the Soviet point of view? If promotion of an immediate Communist-inspired revolutionary movement is used as a yardstick, the answer would have to be negative. If, however, one were to look at the long-range trends and at the opportunities which such a policy afforded for establishing various advance positions for further penetration of the Middle East and Africa, then the answer might be cautiously affirmative. Russia's gains could be observed in two broad sectors: economic and psychological. In the economic sector certain countries, particularly Egypt, had become heavily dependent on Russia in three ways: (1) by redirecting toward the Soviet bloc most of their trade hitherto transacted with the West; (2) by making the success of their development plans conditional on the steady stream of

[8]For further details, see Robert Loring Allen, *Middle Eastern Economic Relations with the Soviet Union, Eastern Europe, and Mainland China* (Charlottesville, Va., 1958); Joseph S. Berliner, *Soviet Economic Aid: The New Aid and Trade Policy in Underdeveloped Countries* (New York, 1958); and U.S. Congress, Senate, *Soviet Economic Penetration in the Middle East* (Sen. Doc. 58; Washington, D.C., 1959).

Communist economic and technical assistance; and (3) by supplying their armies with Soviet bloc weapons and equipment, the latter in constant need of spare parts which only the original suppliers could provide.

As for the psychological gains, they were less tangible, but by no means negligible. By engaging in diplomatic and commercial deals with the Arab governments Russia was acquiring a reputation of almost bourgeois respectability, a quality which, for a variety of reasons, the Arabs were not too prone to bestow upon her before 1955. She was thus becoming, in Arab eyes, a state like any other great power, intent upon promoting her national interests, which luckily did not seem to conflict in any major way with Arab national interests. It was significant in this connection that, side by side with her aid-and-trade deals with the Arab states, Russia insisted on and obtained the conclusion of cultural pacts. The world ''cultural'' has a specific meaning in the Communist vocabulary. This gives the so called cultural pursuits in any Soviet-controlled area a character altogether different from that of those in the West. Briefly, in the Soviet world music, dance, painting, literature, and the like are merely vehicles by which the official ideology and party line are expected to be propagated. As in Iran during the war and Afghanistan in the 1950s, the Arab countries now experienced an invasion of Soviet and satellite cultural missions. Considerable emphasis was placed on the exchange of students and, to a lesser degree, of mature scholars. The student exchange was largely of a one-way type, i.e., providing for numerous scholarships for Arab students in Russia and the satellites. Even Bulgaria figured prominently as a center of learning for Arab youth! Nationalist Arab leaders tended to look with optimism at these cultural relations, claiming that the intense nationalism of their students made them immune to the inroads of Communist ideology and that by acquiring special skills (technological, medical, scientific, and the like) in the Soviet bloc these students were the real beneficiaries. This allegation probably held true in a great many cases—but not in all. By converting even a selected few to their own creed and preparing them to serve as well-trained instruments of their policy, the Russians were gaining a valuable foothold which had previously been denied them in the Middle East.

Russia had to contend with the intentions of Communist China in the Middle East. In the 1950s the Chinese were active at the Bandung Conference, extended their influence to the Afro-Asian People's Solidarity Organization headquartered in Cairo, formed links with the Pan-Arab labor movement, and multiplied their contacts with revolutionary Iraq. Their actions ran parallel to those of Russia in an ostensible harmony between the two. But in the 1960s, especially since the Twenty-second Congress of the Communist Party of the Soviet Union in 1961, a definite rift occurred between Moscow and Peking. In some cases that rift was to lead to reversals in Chinese policy, such as a switch from a negative to a positive attitude toward Iran as a country withstanding Soviet attempts at penetration.

Soviet Policy under Brezhnev and Kosygin

The removal of Khrushchev in 1964 brought no major changes in Soviet policies pursued during his rule. The collective leadership that followed him, headed by

Leonid Brezhnev, Aleksandr Kosygin, and Nicolai Podgorny—and later Brezhnev alone—broadly continued his policy of restraining from threats and normalizing relations with both the Northern Tier and the Arab countries of the Middle East. These policies were characterized by increasing aid and trade, support for various nationalist causes so long as they were directed against the West, and increasing supplies of arms. In the Northern Tier where alliance ties existed with the United States and its Western partners, neutralism was encouraged. In Turkey and Iran, the Soviet Union made consistent efforts to lull these countries into a false sense of security. It was helped in the pursuit of this objective by the fact that the generation that grew to political awareness and maturity in the 1960s and 1970s was ignorant of or at the most had an imperfect recollection of the Soviet record of aggressive behavior toward these countries in the 1940s. Concern over domestic political, social, and economic issues often overshadowed in the minds of this younger generation their consciousness of external dangers. The inauguration of the American policy of detente with Russia, strongly promoted by Henry Kissinger and endorsed by President Nixon and Ford, further contributed to this false sense of security among the masses if not among the ruling elites of Iran and Turkey. In both countries whatever political dicontent there was often tended to take the violent form of urban terrorism, a phenomenon which was upsetting to both countries and from which the Soviet Union could not but benefit indirectly.

The long-range Soviet objective of detaching Turkey from close ties with the West and gaining influence came closer to realization as a result of the repeated Cyprus crises. In handling the Cyprus situation, the Soviets showed a remarkable degree of flexibility and opportunism. During the first Cyprus crisis, in 1964, the Soviets were on the side of Greece and of the Cypriot Greek president, Archbishop Makarios, while warning Turkey against the contemplated military action in Cyprus. But the subsequent bitter exchange of letters between Turkish Premier Inönü and President Lyndon Johnson brought such a substantial deterioration in American-Turkish relations that Russia was quick to exploit it to her own benefit. All sorts of political and economic overtures were made to Turkey, and by the time of the second Cyprus crisis, in 1974, when Turkey finally did invade that island, the Soviets ranged themselves squarely behind Turkey. Soviet-Turkish relations were further strengthened by the American embargo on the export of arms to Turkey. The Soviet fleet in the Mediterranean was simultaneosly being strengthened and the Turkish Straits, as noted in the chapter on the strategic waterways, became a veritable highway for Soviet merchant and naval vessels moving in both directions.

The decade of the 1960s was also marked by an increase of Soviet exchanges with Iran. On Soviet initiative, the Shah made a state visit to Moscow in 1965, where he negotiated wide-ranging economic collaboration agreements. The Soviets pledged to construct a steel mill and metallurgical complex in Isfahan and a gas pipeline linking Iran's southern oilfields with the Soviet territory, and to help Iran with a number of development projects. And, paradoxically, the Soviet Union undertook to supply for the first time Iran—an ally of the West—with $110 million worth of military equipment (to be sure, of a simple, unsophisticated type). By the late 1970s the number of development projects in which the Soviet Union was engaged in Iran

THE MIDDLE EAST IN WORLD AFFAIRS

amounted to 134. Although Iran was clearly unhappy with the lack of American support to Pakistan in its repeated conflicts with India and had a skeptical view of the military effectiveness of CENTO, no emotional issue comparable to that of Cyprus stood in the way of an essentially close Iranian-American relationship. In spite of all the economic collaboration projects, Iran's leadership continued to display distrust of the Soviet Union, based on a feeling of gradual Soviet encircle-ment of Iran by proxy, that is, through the extension of Soviet influence in countries such as Iraq, Afghanistan, and the more distant but geopolitically important coun-tries such as South Yemen, Somalia, and Ethiopia, all located in the proximity of vital oil tanker lanes. Furthermore, support the Soviets granted to the South Yemen-based rebels in Dhofar further strengthened the Shah's suspicions and fears of a concerted Soviet strategy of encirclement.

In the third country of the Northern Tier, Afghanistan, the military coup that toppled Premier Daoud from power in April 1978 resulted in a further increase of Soviet influence in that country. The new premier, Nur Mohammed Taraki, was an avowed Marxist, while the officers who constituted a virtual military junta behind him were mostly Soviet-trained and possibly impressed with the appeal of Soviet ideology.

The Soviet Union and the Arab World in the 1960s and 1970s

While the Soviet Union was anxious to open up and maintain relations with any Arab country regardless of ideology and system of government, it concentrated on those that were most receptive to its advances, the "revolutionary democracies" of Egypt, Syria, Iraq, Yemen, and Algeria. In due course, with the achievement of statehood by South Yemen and the revolution in Libya, these two countries with their own versions of radicalism became objects of Soviet interest and solicitude. The Soviet policy of identifying itself with the strivings of Arab nationalism, in both its anti-Western and anti-Israeli aspects, not only continued but received a consider-able boost as a result of the Arab-Israeli wars of 1967 and 1973 and the attendant deterioration of Arab-American relations. Soviet policy, particularly toward the revolutionary Arab states, was one of multipronged penetration in the economic sphere, as well as the supply of arms, and the acquisition of naval facilities. The construction of the Aswan Dam (completed in 1971) in Egypt, the launching of work on the Euphrates Dam in 1968 in Syria, and the agreement to exploit the rich oil resources of the North Rumaila Field in Iraq in 1970 were outstanding examples of Soviet economic and technical involvement. Similarly, in the sector of arms supplies, Soviet activity reached remarkable levels. Prior to the 1967 Arab-Israeli war Soviet deliveries of arms to Egypt alone were estimated at $1.5 billion worth. Inasmuch as most of this equipment was destroyed during the June war, Russia proceeded to rearm Egypt in excess of the previous levels. Finally, during the October 1973 war the Soviets undertook a massive airlift of arms to sustain their Egyptian partner. Estimates of the total worth of these supplies to Egypt have varied considerably, but a figure between $5 and $6 billion would not appear exaggerated. Supplying arms to Egypt, a country notoriously short of cash, was not beneficial from a financial point of view to Moscow. But then the motivation in arming Egypt was not economic. By contrast, when in 1975 Libya and in 1976 Iraq concluded with Russia agreements providing for $1 billion worth of arms supplies each, Russia expected and received payment in hard currencies from these two oil-rich revolutionary states.

While Soviet interest in the strategic waterways in the Middle East is discussed in another chapter, it is worth recording here that close political relations with a number of revolutionary states resulted in Soviet access to several naval facilities along the eastern and southern shores of the Mediterranean as well as in the northwestern reaches of the Indian Ocean.

Despite its concentration on Arab revolutionary states, the Soviet Union did not neglect the conservative camp. It maintained diplomatic relations, engaged in aid and trade, and in some cases even supplied arms to such states as Kuwait, Jordan, and Morocco. Among the major Arab countries only Saudi Arabia stubbornly resisted recognizing the Soviet Union or any Communist government. Under Saudi influence, the United Arab Emirates also refrained from exchanging diplomatic representations with Russia.

If we assume that the broad Soviet objective in the Arab world was not to convert it in the near future into a congeries of Communist states but rather to acquire strategic strongholds and to gain political ascendancy through the instrumentality of client states while reducing Western presence and influence, there is no doubt that, particularly in the late 1960s and early 1970s, the Soviet Union could boast of considerable success. Some of this was due to its own astuteness, flexibility, and tactical cleverness; some to the weaknesses and failures in American policy. Soviet tactics varied according to the occasion and were noted for a high degree of opportunism. If circumstances warranted, Russia would cement a close relationship with a given country through a formal treaty. This was notably the case of Egypt in 1971, Iraq in 1972, and—in a more peripheral but increasingly important region—Somalia in 1974. These treaties followed a similar pattern of pledging mutual political cooperation and consultation, Soviet military assistance, struggle against imperialism and colonialism, and Soviet aid in economic development, the latter explicitly or implicitly along "noncapitalist lines." Mention of any military bases or facilities for the Soviet Union in the countries in question was carefully avoided. The Soviet-Iraqi treaty expressed Iraq's concern about Israel in the following words: "The High Contracting Parties . . . will continue to wage a steadfast struggle against imperialism and Zionism and for the complete and unconditional elimination of colonialism, neocolonialism, racism and apartheid and to advocate the complete and earliest possible implementation of the U.N. Declaration on the Granting of Independence to Colonial Countries and Peoples."[9]

By articulating the common objectives of the signatory parties, the treaties to some extent supported Soviet propaganda goals in the Arab countries and the Third World at large. But not every revolutionary regime was willing to enter into a treaty relationship with the Soviet Union. Syria, for example, declined to sign such a treaty, clearly preferring an informal though close relationship. Libya, under Col-

[9]Text in *The Current Digest of the Soviet Press*, 24, no. 14 (May 3, 1972), 12.

onel Qadhafi, went even farther: not only did it oppose the idea of a treaty but, upon learning of the conclusion of the Soviet-Iraqi treaty, Colonel Qadhafi expressed his loud displeasure and recalled his ambassador from Baghdad. His argument was that by concluding a separate treaty with the Soviets Iraq was breaking the ranks of Arab solidarity. Aware of this reluctance on the part of certain revolutionary regimes to enter into a formal treaty relationship, Moscow was content to conduct her business with such governments on a nontreaty basis. And, in fact, Libya was a case in point: in spite of Qadhafi's critical attitude toward communism (as a fundamentalist Islamic leader), Soviet arms supplies and participation in development projects in Libya markedly increased in the 1970s. Moreover, Soviet influence in those countries displayed varying degrees of entrenchment. Perhaps three basic arrangements could be distinguished in this respect. One involved a considerable amount of Soviet aid and trade plus arms supplies but no clear commitment on behalf of the recipient state to cooperate with the Soviet Union in the political sector. The second could be described as a client-patron relationship in which the economic and military dependence of the Arab partner on the Soviet Union was pronounced and strengthened by a certain parallelism of political interest. In the third situation the Marxist orientation of the Arab partner provided a common ideological platform for close political cooperation and its far-reaching dependence on Soviet support. The last of these three alternatives could be found in the 1970s in the People's Democratic Republic of Yemen (South Yemen), whose radical Marxist government not only relied heavily on Soviet aid but, in spite of its inherent weakness, displayed adventurous and aggressive tendencies in its relations with Yemen and Oman.

It was characteristic of Soviet tactical flexibility that Moscow could and easily did change sides in a given conflict when it suited its purposes. Perhaps the first notable example of this flexibility was given in 1947 when, after voting for the partition of Palestine in the United Nations—an act clearly favorable to the Zionist program— Russia rapidly reversed her policy in favor of the Arabs. But the 1970s provided further examples of such behavior. Thus after the initial heavy investment in favor of the Republican regime in Yemen, the Soviets gradually lessened their interest in that country and transferred it to South Yemen despite its intermittent outbursts of hostility toward its northern neighbor. A similar *volte-face* took place when, during the deterioration of relations between Egypt and Libya in the mid-1970s, the Soviets began to support Colonel Qadhafi against President Sadat. A Soviet switch of support in the latter 1970s from Somalia to the newly established Marxist regime in Ethiopia further accentuated this trend. In the 1970s, the Soviets abandoned without much compunction their erstwhile support for the Kurdish cause of emancipation and threw their weight behind the Baath government in Iraq in its policy of suppressing the Kurdish rebellion.

Another characteristic tactic of the Soviets was the use of proxies. This tactic could be understood in a broader and a narrower sense. For example, from the Iranian point of view both Baathist Iraq and Marxist-oriented Afghanistan (after its revolution of April 1978) could be viewed as bases for the spread of Soviet influence in the area. The use of the Czechoslovaks in concluding the original arms deal with Egypt and the presence of Cubans and East Germans in South Yemen and Ethiopia were typical proxy situations, in the narrower sense.

Soviet Setbacks

While the advances of the Soviet Union in various parts of the Arab world were undeniable, it also experienced some serious setbacks. Thus in the summer of 1971 a Communist-inspired coup in Sudan misfired and in consequence brought about a marked cooling off of relations between the government of General Jafar Numeiri and the Soviet Union. That same year marked the beginning of the steady, and occasionally dramatic, deterioration of relations between Egypt under the new leadership of President Sadat and Moscow. In the spring an attempted coup by the pro-Soviet group headed by Ali Sabri failed, resulting in a growing distrust toward the Soviets on the part of Sadat. In July 1972 he ordered the expulsion of thousands of Soviet military experts. His intermittent negotiations with Moscow for more and better arms caused much frustration, and in April 1974, Sadat proclaimed an end to Egypt's sole reliance on Soviet armaments. Even the massive airlift of Soviet arms during the October war of 1973 did not dispel the basic lack of confidence between the two governments. In March 1976, Sadat announced the abrogation of the Soviet-Egyptian treaty of 1971, and some eighteen months later, dismayed at the Soviet refusal to ease the schedule of Egyptian debt payments, Sadat proclaimed the suspension of debt servicing and stoppage of cotton exports to Russia and certain East European countries. It was during this period of rapid deterioaration in relations that he also cancelled the privileges hitherto granted to the Soviets to use naval facilities in certain Egyptian ports.

The diminution of Soviet influence in Yemen was less drastic. It corresponded, true enough, to the simultaneous transfer of Soviet interest to South Yemen, as previously mentioned; but it was not entirely of the Soviets' own making: much of Yemen's reorientation could be ascribed to the emergence in that country of a more moderate leadership and to the growth of Saudi Arabian influence, backed by considerable transfusions of funds.

Issues and Dilemmas for Soviet Policy

Even when the Soviet Union was scoring successes, its policy in the Middle East was not free from dilemmas. Although support for the national liberation movements in the Third World has been a time-honored principle of Soviet strategy ever since the 1920s, even the most patient and farsighted Communist theorists could legitimately experience some doubts as to the final outcome of helping men like Nasser or Sadat, whose firm opposition to communism at home was a matter of public record. For Moscow was faced with the choice between support for their persecuted comrades in the Egyptian or Iraqi Communist parties and aid to the governments guilty of persecution. In the name of long-term strategy, Soviet rulers were usually willing to sacrifice their comrades for the sake of higher goals. But the decision was painful and fraught with dangers, especially since the appearance in the 1960s of Communist China as a serious rival for the allegiance of the Marxist-oriented radical elements in those societies. Sometimes Soviet patience seemed to have neared a limit. This was the case in late 1958 and the spring of 1959 when Khurshchev publicly admonished Nasser for his rough treatment of Communists in the United Arab Republic. The emergence of socialist-oriented Arab regimes in the 1960s posed the need to determine the role of the Communists in such systems. Should they continue to stay in opposition to these governments, in the name of the purity of Leninist principles and with the ultimate hope of seizing power, or should they cooperate? By the early 1970s, a new line of behavior was devised for them by Moscow: henceforth they should participate in their countries' efforts at socialist construction, and the instrument of such participation was to be a National Front in which the ruling exponents of Arab socialism (Nasserites, Baathists, or others) would participate along with the Communists. In terms of the traditional Communist concept of the National Front, a concept initially geared to the formation of an effective anti-imperialist coalition in the colonial and semicolonial countries, this line represented a new departure. The National Front was to serve not as an instrument of opposition but as a vehicle which would permit the Communists to share, directly or indirectly, in the government of the country. Following this new principle, National Front coalitions came into being in the early 1970s in Syria and Iraq, and in both cases Communists were rewarded by the ruling Baath parties with some cabinet posts, albeit remaining in a subordinate position.[10] Even this stratagem, however, did not completely resolve the problem of ultimate loyalties and the tension between the Communists and their fellow Arab socialists. Achievement of some influence by the Communists invariably led to the temptation to increase it, the highest stake being the establishment of a reliable foothold in the armed services through the creation of Communist cells. This pattern fits events in Iraq in the spring of 1978: the Iraqi Baathist authorities discovered a disturbing network of Communist penetration in the military and, claiming that the Communists were preparing a coup d'état, arrested and executed twenty-one culprits. As in similar situations in the past, Moscow's displeasure with these events did not lead to a rupture of relations with Iraq, for too much was invested politically, economically, and militarily to be cast lightheartedly aside.

Another major dilemma was the degree of Soviet support against Israel. In numerous declarations both before and after the creation of Israel, Russia had a record of opposing Zionism. Occasionally this critical attitude took a more severe form, as when in 1964 the Soviet government lodged a protest in Israel against Zionist propaganda carried out inside the Soviet Union by Israeli diplomats. In the 1960s and 1970s the problem of Jewish emigration from the Soviet Union to Israel assumed the proportion of an international crisis which also involved the United States. In contrast to the earlier periods of Communist rule in Russia when Jews frequently held high positions in the Soviet civil and military hierarchies and when Jewish memories of persecutions under the tsars seemed to sway many of them toward support of the Soviet system, the 1960s and 1970s witnessed a substantial

---

[10]For a fuller discussion of the National Front concept, see George Lenczowski, *Soviet Advances in the Middle East* (Washington, D.C., 1971), p. 16; and A. Benningsen, "The National Front in Communist Strategy in the Middle East," in W. Z. Laqueur, ed., *The Middle East in Transition* (London, 1958).

change in the orientation of many Jews in Russia. Apparently disillusioned not only with the totalitarian nature of the system but also with the growing discrimination against them, many expressed a desire to emigrate, Israel and the United States being the countries of their preference. The Soviet authorities opposed this emigration for two reasons: first, they never cherished the idea that a substantial number of disgruntled citizens would find their way abroad and there, profiting from the freedom of expression in the capitalistic countries, reveal the truth about the Soviet government and society, particularly in the liberal circles of the West; second, any substantial Jewish migration to Israel was bound to provoke Arab protests. On the other hand, the detente policies launched by Washington and Moscow created an opportunity to benefit from the flow of American goods and technology and to make the United States accept the reality of Soviet conquests in eastern Europe at the end of World War II. But, largely as a result of Senator Henry Jackson's initiative, American trade agreements concluded at that time with the Soviet Union were hedged with reservations enjoining the Soviets to ease restrictions on Jewish emigration. Thus Moscow was caught in the dilemma of having to choose the least harmful line of conduct from the point of view of its interests abroad. The result was a compromise whereby certain quotas of Jews, numbering in the thousands, were given permission to emigrate, usually through a relay point in Vienna, from which they could proceed to Israel or to any other destination. Although this Soviet behavior constituted an obvious irritant to the radical nationalist regimes in Iraq, Syria, Libya, and other countries, they chose not to make it a major political issue in their relations with Moscow in order not to jeopardize interests with higher priorities.

Another question is whether heavy arms supplies by the Soviet Union to the Arab revolutionary states should be interpreted as an encouragement to aggressive military action against Israel. While no documented answer can be provided, it appears that Moscow was more interested in controlled tension than in actual warfare. War, after all, presented a risk, and should its client states be defeated—as they were time and again—the Soviet Union would have to make an additional effort to save them from collapse and to resupply them with new and costly weapons. Soviet gains or losses from the June war of 1967 generated much debate among Western political analysts. Some of them have maintained that the defeat of Soviet client states—Egypt, Syria, and Iraq—constituted a blow to Soviet prestige and weakened the Soviet position in the area. This conclusion, however, appears to be somewhat hasty because it equates the military defeat and loss of Soviet-supplied arms by her protégés with the loss of political influence. Actually, a strong case could be made that, ultimately, Russia emerged as a beneficiary of this defeat, first because it deepened Arab frustration and anger against the United States, and second because it generated a wave of Arab radicalism more militant than ever before, as expressed by the revolution in Iraq in 1968, the revolution in Libya in 1969, and the intensification of the Palestinian guerrilla movement. The war, moreover, caused Moscow to break diplomatic relations with Israel and provided a renewed opportunity for Russia to reassert its identification with the Arab nationalist movement.

Under the circumstances, it was natural for the Soviet Union to back UN Security

Council Resolution 242, the main provision of which called for the withdrawal of Israeli forces from occupied territories. Subsequently the Soviet Union repeatedly called not only for the total withdrawal of the Israelis but also for the recognition of the right to self-determination of the Palestinian people. At the same time, however, the Soviets refused to embrace entirely the extreme Palestinian position, which called for the abolition of the State of Israel. On April 14, 1969, the magazine *Soviet Russia* expressed the opinion that "the liquidation of the State of Israel is not realistic." This statement reflected a more fundamental policy which was voiced by Soviet spokesmen on other occasions as well.

Crystallization of appropriate policy toward the PLO and other *fedayeen* groups constituted another dilemma for the Soviets. Initially, Russia's attitude toward these Palestinian groups was negative. First, the Soviets had no control over their behavior, and second, there was a possibility that the excessive militancy of the guerrillas might provoke a retaliatory war by Israel which could end in a new Arab defeat and produce a collapse of such "progressive" regimes as those of Egypt, Syria, and Iraq. With the passage of time, however, Soviet attitudes underwent a transformation: not only did they welcome the formation of a small and rather unimportant separate Communist group among the *fedayeen,* but they embarked upon a policy of close contacts with the leadership of the PLO and, by 1974, permitted it to establish an office in Moscow. Assistance in the form of arms supplies accompanied these diplomatic moves. The Soviets undoubtedly based their policy on a view that sooner or later a separate Palestinian state would emerge and that it was useful to establish a friendly relationship with its future leaders.

Arab revolutionary polycentrism posed another dilemma for Soviet policy. While from the Soviet point of view the proliferation of Arab radical regimes was looked upon with favor, these regimes, as noted in the earlier part of this book, did not necessarily unite or even live in harmony with each other. For the Soviet Union this presented the problem of having to choose sides in case of any conflicts among these governments. Rather remarkably, in spite of the mutual hostility bordering on hatred that separated the Baathist regimes in Damascus and Baghdad, the Soviets managed to maintain good relations with both. However, when in the spring of 1976, President Hafez Assad of Syria decided to intervene in the Lebanese civil war by throwing his 30,000-strong expeditionary force against the PLO and the Lebanese leftist coalition, he incurred Soviet displeasure, and admonitions were voiced by various Soviet media. But again, with a remarkable show of self-restraint, the Soviet Union did not allow this quarrel to overshadow its more basic interest in cultivating Syria, especially when Syria joined the "rejectionist front" against the American-Egyptian peace initiatives in the Middle East.

This brings us to the last element in the complex picture of the Big Powers' attitude toward the Arab-Israeli conflict. Officially, the Soviet Union repeatedly favored a peace settlement provided it conformed to UN Resolution 242, preferably according to the Arab interpretation of this document. Unofficially, having in mind broader benefits deriving to it from the implementation of the detente with the United States, Russia was not likely to jeopardize them by encouraging the renewal of armed conflict in the Middle East. However, Russia's dedication to peace had an important reservation, that it should be a cosponsor of a peace settlement. For this reason it not only participated in the Big Four negotiations that took place in the late 1960s but also accepted participation in the subsequent Geneva Conference in which the Soviet and American governments were to serve as cochairmen. When, however, American policy, especially after the October war of 1973, followed the line of excluding the Soviet Union from the peacemaking process, Moscow consistently opposed American and later Egyptian peace initiatives and supported the Arab rejectionist front.

Despite adherence to the never-repudiated ideal of the Communist world revolution, the Soviet Union in its relations with the Middle East displayed considerable flexibility. Occasionally its behavior was heavy-handed, as when it allowed relations with Egypt to deteriorate to the breaking point in the 1970s. But considerations of saving face never prevented the Soviet Union from reaching an accommodation with a party with which it might have quarreled provided that long-range interests in the area were furthered. Russia undoubtedly experienced a major setback with the defection of Sadat from the Soviet camp. How permanent this Egyptian policy was to be depended on a number of factors, of which an appropriate American policy toward the Arab-Israeli conflict was perhaps the most important. Russia, a proverbial "scavenger of the revolution," was also a scavenger of other states' mistakes. Should American policy become definitely tied to the Israeli concept of territorial expansionism and denial of self-determination to the Palestinians, the defection of Egypt from the American camp and return to the Soviet one was not inconceivable. In the meantime, the Soviet Union had lost an impressive stronghold in the very heart of the Arab world. It continued to maintain a rather strong position in Iraq and Syria despite some humiliations experienced in both countries. Its endeavors appeared to be directed particularly toward certain peripheral but strategically vital regions such as southern Arabia, the Horn of Africa, the approaches to the strategic waterways, and revolutionary Libya in the mid-Mediterranean area. Its political, economic, and military, particularly naval, policies seemed to be well synchronized to ensure the maximum extension of Soviet influence and the replacement, wherever possible, of Western presence. Above all, the Soviet Union had a definite stake in the radicalization of the Arab world, a phenomenon closely linked to any aggravation in American-Arab relations, with Israel as a focal point in regional politics.

The United States

Relations between the United States and the Middle East may be divided into three distinct periods: the first, ending with the year 1941; the second, embracing the war period, 1941–1945; and the third, after 1945.

In the first period, the United States displayed no steady political interest in the area. For a long time Protestant missionaries and educators were the only Americans to pay serious attention to the Middle East. Such institutions as the American University of Beirut (founded as Syrian Protestant College in 1866), the American University at Cairo, and Robert College and the American Women's College in Istanbul, as well as the secondary schools known as "colleges" in Teheran and

Baghdad, bore testimony to the cultural links established between the New World and the ancient Bible lands. There were, in addition, American Presbyterian missions in a number of Middle Eastern countries which combined religious with charitable and medical work. All these institutions made America popular in the eyes of the peoples who had come into contact with them, and the fact that the American government had no political axe to grind in connection with their activities only strengthened the general good will toward American democracy.

The first instance of American political intervention occurred in 1918–1919 at the time of the Peace Settlement. Point Twelve of Wilson's Fourteen Points specifically dealt with the disposition of the Ottoman Empire, and the general principle of national self-determination enunciated therein made a profound impression on the literate public of the Middle East. Judging by their reaction to these statements, one might assert that the American crusade for a just and honorable world order evoked more hopeful expectations than the simultaneous social radicalism beamed from revolutionary Russia. Anxious to implement his principles, President Wilson sent two missions to the Middle East to ascertain the will of the people directly concerned: the King-Crane mission to Syria and Palestine and the Harbord mission to Armenia. But the play of power politics in Paris largely frustrated Wilson's designs and resulted in the compromises which only thinly disguised traditional European imperialism. Following Wilson's death and the repudiation of the Versailles Treaty, the United States withdrew altogether from world politics, thereby leaving the Middle East to its own devices.

Subsequent American interest in the area was of sporadic nature. The United States, in its concentration on economic issues as the only ones which seemed to matter, insisted on and defended the principle of the Open Door, especially with regard to the areas mandated by Britain. In 1924 this solicitude led to an Anglo-American agreement concerning equality of opportunity in Palestine. The discovery of oil in Iraq, on the other hand, led to a temporary controversy between the interested American companies and Britain over the spoils of prewar Turkish Petroleum Company. This controversy was complicated by the fact that at the same time another American group, known as the Ottoman-American Development Company, headed by Admiral Chester, sought to ratify in Turkey its old (1909) concession which had failed in 1913 because of British and German opposition. On April 9, 1923, Turkey awarded Chester an exclusive mineral, railway, and oil concession which covered "twenty kilometers on either side of a 2,400 mile right-of-way, beginning at Ankara and going, by way of Sivas, Kharput, and Diarbekir, on straight through Mosul to the border of Persia."[11] The inclusion, shortly before the Lausanne Treaty, of the controversial Mosul territory in this concession meant that the interests of the Chester group were bound to clash with Britain's claim to Mosul in her capacity of a mandatory power for Iraq. Somewhat earlier, in 1922, the Standard Oil Company of New Jersey had reached an agreement with Britain whereby it secured a 25 percent share in Iraq's oil resources, thus acquiring a vested interest in Britain's control of Mosul. Both industrial groups looked, of course,

[11] Benjamin Gerig, *The Open Door and the Mandates System* (London, 1930), p. 146.

toward their government for support, and for a moment it appeared that the United States might be drawn into an unpleasant political controversy. The whole affair remained in abeyance for two more years inasmuch as the Lausanne Treaty did not definitely dispose of the Mosul question. But with the award, in 1925, of the contested area of Iraq by the Council of the League of Nations, Chester's rights were automatically repudiated. This opened the way for a definite agreement between the American oil group and the British government, an agreement which had the blessing of the Department of State because it implemented the Open Door principle.

Apart from these economic issues the attention of the United States government was drawn to the Middle East in connection with the Palestinian problem.[12] The Balfour Declaration of 1917, as we know, owed its birth to the influence of American Jews, supported by the friendly attitude of their government. But with the establishment of the mandate, which explicitly provided for the fulfillment of the Declaration, official American interest in Palestine somewhat slackened, it being taken for granted that the mandate had basically satisfied Zionist aspirations. Two other factors accounted for diminished American interest: one was the fact that the leadership of World Zionism rested in the hands of Britain; and the other was the fact that, until 1939, Britain had not drastically limited Jewish immigration into Palestine, thus allowing the Jewish national home to grow.

All in all, the political approach of the United States toward the Middle East up to 1941 could be described as one of indifference, good will, and a conviction that the area was a British preserve where no major American interests were involved. Even the entry of the American oil business into the scene, with its concessions in Iraq, Bahrain, and Saudi Arabia, did not materially change this aloof attitude.

World War II

During the second period (1941–1945) the United States suddenly developed multiple contacts with the Middle East as a result of the war emergency. The conduct of the war in this area ceased to be a purely British affair. American troops appeared in Iran to handle the supplies to Russia; they also came to Egypt and Palestine, mainly to accomplish various technical tasks connected with the American armor with which the British army was being equipped. The American navy and merchant marine played a vital role in conveying supplies to the Middle East theater. And the United States air force established a chain of bases linking North Africa with the India-Burma-China theater. This military tie with the area was strengthened by several economic measures: the United States extended lend lease to most of the Middle Eastern countries, gave active support and guidance to the Middle East Supply Center, and took an active interest in the interim arrangements concerning oil production. Mainly to serve American strategic needs in the Far East, the Anglo-Iranian Oil Company adjusted its facilities to produce high-octane avia-

[12]See Carl J. Friedrich, *American Policy toward Palestine* (Washington, 1944); for a general American policy toward the area, see Walter Batsell, *United States and the System of Mandates* (New York, 1925), and Harvey P. Hall, *American Interests in the Middle East* (Headline Series, No. 72, Nov.-Dec. 1948).

tion gasoline. And in 1943 Harold Ickes, administrator of the American petroleum authority, suggested active government participation in the projected pipeline through the Arabian desert. American responsibilities in this respect grew to such an extent that in 1944 the government found it necessary to appoint a high-ranking official, James Landis, as United States economic minister to the Middle East. It was significant that at the same time the government created the post of petroleum attaché for the whole region, attached to the American embassy in Cairo.

The government also grew more alert to the political problems of the Middle East. Colonel Donovan, director of the Office of Strategic Services; Wendell Willkie, acting as the President's personal representative; Ambassador Harriman; and a number of other highly placed persons visited the area during the war. Even President Roosevelt, although mortally tired after the Yalta conference, found time to devote a few days to a conference with Arab rulers in the Suez Canal Zone. The United States had shown friendly helpfulness to Saudi Arabia at the time of her economic crisis, and to Syria and Lebanon in their struggle for emancipation.

After the War

In the postwar period this increased interest in the Middle East expanded. Oil, Palestine, and the Soviet menace provided three avenues of approach. The spectacular development of oil production in Saudi Arabia and Kuwait, with American holdings in Bahrain, Iraq, and Egypt, brought home to American leaders the strategic importance of the region. The virtual repudiation by Britain of the Balfour Declaration, through the White Paper of 1939, and the attendant renewal of strife in Palestine placed before the United States the necessity of defining its position, the necessity being made more urgent by the fate of Jews in Europe and by the transfer of Zionist leadership to American Jewry. And last, but not least, growing Soviet expansionism has compelled Washington to formulate policies and take steps to protect the Middle East and safeguard the vital interests of the West therein. The first test case came in Iran in 1945–1946, when Russia made a bold bid for the subjugation of that country through her support of the Azerbaijan rebellion and her acquisition of an oil concession by coercive measures. The United States' response was to encourage Iran to resist Soviet pressures and, as was later revealed by President Truman, to warn Russia against further aggressive actions.[13]

The Iranian crisis was not yet over when Washington was presented with a new Communist threat, this time toward Greece and Turkey. Exhausted and impoverished by World War II, Great Britain had to withdraw her support from these two countries, thus producing a dangerous power vacuum. Convinced that lack of

[13]In 1957 former President Truman described his part in this episode as follows: "After the end of World War II, Stalin and Molotov brazenly refused to keep their agreement to withdraw from Iran. They persisted in keeping their troops... in northern Iran. Formal steps were taken through diplomatic channels and the United Nations to get the Russians to withdraw. The Soviet Union persisted in its occupation until I personally saw to it that Stalin was informed that I had given orders to our military chiefs to prepare for the movement of our ground, sea, and air forces. Stalin then did what I knew he would do. He moved his troops out" (quoted from "Truman Charges Inaction on Syria: Asks Vigorous Steps to Halt 'Communist Subversion' in Strategic Region," NANA dispatch, *New York Times*, Aug. 25, 1957).

action would result in a dangerous extension of Soviet power southward, President Truman on March 12, 1947, proclaimed American readiness to come to the rescue of the two menaced countries by pledging financial aid for economic and military purposes. The official policy statement (to be known as the Truman Doctrine) clearly recognized the threat: "The very existence of the Greek State is today threatened by the terrorist activities of several thousand armed men, led by Communists, who defy the Government's authority at a number of points, particularly along the northern boundaries." As for Turkey, its "integrity is essential to the preservation of order in the Middle East." American policy was defined in the statement as the "creation of conditions in which we and other nations will be able to work out a way of life free from coercion. . . . We shall not realize our objectives, however, unless we are willing to help free peoples to maintain their free institutions and their national integrity against aggressive movements that seek to impose upon them totalitarian regimes." Having thus defined American objectives, the President asked Congress for authority to provide assistance to Greece and Turkey in the amount of $400 million and to detail civilian and military personnel to both countries to assist and supervise the implementation of the aid program.[14]

This was the first major step in recognizing the Soviet threat and responding to it. Subsequent inclusion of Greece and Turkey in the Marshall Plan benefits and their admission as members of the North Atlantic Treaty Organization in 1950 were a logical outcome of this first basic policy statement. The Truman Doctrine proved to be a success: aided and financed by the Americans, the Greek government wiped out the Communist guerrillas and thus saved itself from sharing the fate of its less fortunate Balkan neighbors; similarly, strengthened in her economy and her military posture, Turkey successfully resisted Soviet pressures for the control of the Straits and the annexation of her eastern provinces. The Northern Tier was saved.

Encouraged by this success and anxious to promote regional defensive cooperation patterned on the NATO alliance, Washington now endeavored to draw the Arab countries into a broader military scheme which would encompass the Middle East as a whole. Here, however, American policy met with a negative response. The leading Arab country, Egypt, refused to accept the proposals for a Western-sponsored Middle East Command and instead proclaimed a policy of positive neutralism. Other nationalist Arab centers followed Egypt's example. By 1953 it was clear that further attempts to create a regional alliance with massive Arab participation would be useless. Secretary of State John Foster Dulles realistically acknowledged this upon his return from a Middle Eastern tour in the spring of that year.[15] The reasons for Arab reluctance could be summed up as follows: (1) the Arab world was still unreconciled to the existence of Israel, which it regarded as a creation and an outpost of Western imperialism; (2) the surviving remnants of west-European colonialism in the Arab world were regarded as a greater threat to Arab independence and well-being than seemingly remote Soviet imperialism; (3) Arab

[14]The text is in 81st Congress, Senate, *A Decade of American Foreign Policy, Basic Documents, 1941–49* (Sen. Doc. 123; Washington, D.C., 1950), pp. 1253–1257.

[15]The text of Secretary Dulles' report is in J. C. Hurewitz, ed., *Diplomacy in the Near and Middle East: A Documentary Record* (Princeton, 1957), II, 337–342.

nationalists resented the prospect of a patron-client relationship which military cooperation with the West would entail and suspected the latter to be a device of neocolonialism; (4) they wanted to save their countries from becoming battlefields as a result of the possible extension of future wars into their territories.

Rebuked in the Arab Core of the Middle East, Washington turned back to the area where the consciousness of the Soviet menace was ever present, i.e., the Northern Tier. The Baghdad Pact of 1955 was the outcome. It united in a military alliance three non-Arab countries (Turkey, Iran, and Pakistan), one Arab country (Iraq), and one Western country (Britain). Paradoxically, the United States did not formally adhere, partly out of fear lest it irrevocably alienate the revolutionary regime in Egypt and all those elements in the Arab world which followed its lead. Before long American civil and military representatives were active on various committees of the Baghdad Pact organization, thus making the United States a member in fact if not in name of this defense alliance.

But if defense of the whole of the Middle East (including the Arab part of it) was the objective, then the Baghdad Pact was only a partial and even a dubious success. This was so because, from a military angle, the Western commitment to defend the Northern Tier states was more important than cooperation among the latter. In fact, virtually the same objective of arming these states, training their personnel in new military techniques, building bases on their territory, and generally coordinating defense activities could be achieved without the mechanism and overhead of the Baghdad Pact organization. Although the pact provided also for significant technical and economic cooperation among its members, such cooperation could have been secured by specific agreements divorced from the military aspects and as such not subject to the violent objections which the pact generated in the neutralist centers of Arab nationalism.

Thus the conclusion of the Baghdad Pact could be regarded as superfluous for the purpose of defending the Northern Tier, while at the same time presenting no serious obstacle to Soviet advances in the Arab world. These advances were different from the tactics pursued by Russia vis-á-vis the Northern Tier. In the north, as we have seen in the preceding section, she threatened and intimidated. In the Arab world, she courted. The Baghdad Pact providing for military defense of the Northern Tier proved no obstacle to Soviet blandishments in the countries of the Arab Core. It certainly did not prevent Russia from arming Egypt and Syria and identifying herself with the aspirations of Arab nationalism.

Beginning with the Baghdad Pact (with the Palestine issue providing a general background), the United States was exposed to a chain reaction in the course of which a succession of political moves deepened the cleavage between itself and the Arab nationalists. The Moscow-Cairo arms deal was the second major event in this sad story, to be followed by the withdrawal of the Aswan Dam offer, the nationalization of the Suez Canal, and the Suez War. The war provided an opportunity to repair much of the damage of the past few years inasmuch as the United States clearly and strongly came forth in defense of the victim of aggression, Egypt. In fact, there was a brief period during which recognition of the American stand and gratitude for it were voiced by Nasser and other Arab nationalists. These gains were soon to be dissipated by two American acts of policy. One was the endorsement by Secretary Dulles of the principle of freedom of navigation in the Gulf of Aqaba. The second, and more fundamental, was the President's policy statement of January 5, 1957, known as the Eisenhower Doctrine.

The origin of the doctrine may be found in Washington's concern over the penetration of the Arab world by international communism in the wake of the Suez War and the attendant collapse of British influence in the area as well as the resurgence of nationalist hostility toward the West. It was believed that Russia should be warned to keep her hands off (to prevent Korea-like miscalculations) and that the nations exposed to Soviet-sponsored Communist aggression or infiltration should be assured of American help to defend their integrity. Although formally addressed to the whole of the Middle East (including even such far-flung extensions as Pakistan and Morocco), this declaration was aimed primarily at the Arab world, where Soviet advances and local Communist activity were most conspicuous. In this sense the Eisenhower Doctrine complemented the Truman Doctrine of ten years earlier, the latter having focused on the Soviet threat to the non-Arab Northern Tier. While complementing the old doctrine, the new one differed from it in one important respect: it committed American forces to defend the threatened countries. Actually, the President proposed, and sought the authorization of Congress for, three types of action: (1) to assist the Middle East to develop its economic strength; (2) to undertake programs of military assistance; and (3) "to include the employment of the armed forces of the United States to secure and protect the territorial integrity and political independence of such nations requesting such aid against overt armed aggression from any nation controlled by international communism." "The proposed legislation," said the declaration in a later paragraph, "is primarily designed to deal with the possibility of Communist aggression, direct and indirect."[16]

Although as a policy statement clarifying the American attitude toward the security of the Middle East, the Eisenhower Doctrine appeared to be a logical corollary to earlier statements and instruments of policy, it was not tailored to fit the situation in the Arab world. The doctrine made two assumptions: that there was danger of overt Soviet aggression and that there was a likelihood of indirect aggression, i.e., presumably Communist subversion, the latter varying from simple infiltration of governmental apparatus to guerrilla warfare. The first assumption could be eliminated as not corresponding to the realities of Soviet-Arab relations during that period. As for the second, it implied a degree of interference in the internal affairs of the countries in question even if the formality of asking for United States aid was duly observed. It is no wonder, therefore, that the doctrine met with immediate violent denunciation in Cairo, Damascus, and other militant Pan-Arab circles in the Middle East. Their argument was that the United States was attempting to defend them against the imaginary danger of Soviet aggression, whereas the real danger stemmed from the presence of Israel and the frustrated ambitions of France and Britain, who only a few months earlier had given tangible evidence of their aggres-

---

[16]The text is in the *New York Times,* Jan 6, 1957.

sive policies by invading Egypt. Thus, they argued, the doctrine was highly suspect and betrayed America's intention of introducing her armed forces into the Arab East and possibly helping some unpopular regimes to hold on to power against the progressive movements of national liberation. These views were by no means unanimously held in the Arab world: Iraq welcomed the doctrine (rather naturally as a member of the Baghdad Pact), Saudi Arabia did not object to it, and Lebanon even formally accepted it in a joint declaration of March 16, 1957. Despite these exceptions, the critical view was predominant.

The bad reception accorded the doctrine by Arab nationalists should not, of course, serve as the only criterion of its wisdom and utility. As pointed out earlier, the doctrine also served as a warning to Russia and as such might have had some educational impact on the Soviet rulers. Furthermore, like any important policy statement, it was also addressed to the public at home. By dramatizing the situation in the Middle East, it was likely to contribute to the awakening of the American people to the dangers inherent in the unsettled conditions in that area and to induce them to think more seriously about them in terms of the national interest.

Both in 1957 and in 1958 the doctrine was tested in practice. In April 1957 the Jordanian monarchy was gravely shaken by an attempt at a coup staged by the pro-Nasser faction in the army and supported by a civilian coalition which included the Baathists and the Communists. Washington's reaction to those events was to send the United States Sixth Fleet to eastern Mediterranean waters in a demonstration of its active interest in developments in that area. Simultaneously Secretary Dulles made a statement that the United States regarded "the independence and integrity of Jordan as vital" to its national interests.[17] In the summer of 1958 the United States intervened in the civil war in Lebanon by sending its troops there at the request of President Chamoun. In both cases the doctrine was stretched somewhat to suit the circumstances. While it was true that the independence and integrity of Jordan and Lebanon were gravely threatened, the assaults had come not from Russia but primarily from Nasser's Egypt and her fifth column in both countries. Communists played a merely ancillary role in both upheavals. This did not prevent official Washington from claiming that its rescue actions were directed against the aggressions of "international communism." Thus, in practical application the Eisenhower Doctrine became an instrument of a status quo policy which was aimed as much at stopping militant Pan-Arabism as preventing Russia and her agents from upsetting the friendly and legally established regimes in the Arab East.

Although understandable and, in its external aspects, justified, the status quo policy carried with it one important drawback. It could be both abused and misconstrued by being applied in an oversimplified manner to the internal situations of Middle Eastern countries, thus identifying the United States with social and economic conservatism in the area. An unfortunate feature of the economy in a number of Middle Eastern countries is that it tends to follow the extremes of either an antiquated mixed feudal and lassez-faire system or an exaggerated statism, with not enough scope for a progressive and responsible capitalism of the Western type. Of these two extremes, the statist proves less tolerant and less friendly to foreign

[17]The text is in the *New York Times,* April 25, 1957.

private investments, applying to them various curbs and restrictions, which occasionally end in expropriation. Under the circumstances, Western free enterprise—and its home governments—frequently prefer the other extreme as a lesser evil. This choice should not, however, be interpreted as approval by the West in general, and the United States in particular, of the old socioeconomic patterns. On the contrary, the extension of technical and economic aid to underdeveloped areas has been an integral and important part of American foreign policy ever since the end of World War II. Such aid has been geared to the objective of developing abundant economies and progressive societies, free from the tensions and instabilty which general poverty and great contrasts in wealth between various strata tend to induce. Thus, on closer scrutiny, the unqualified equation of American policies with support of conservatism is a distortion of the truth. This distortion, however, has been widely propagated by elements hostile to the United States in the Middle East.

This inimical propaganda has been further strengthened by the continuous allegation that, in contrast to Soviet, American aid has had "strings attached to it." There is no doubt that the United States, like any major power aiding less fortunate countries, has often faced the dilemma to whom and on what conditions, if any, aid should be given. The natural tendency has been to help one's friends, i.e., allies, in the first place, and this view has been reflected in legislation authorizing loans and grants, especially those made under the general heading of mutual security. However, in a number of cases the United States has been extending substantial amounts of aid to many neutralist countries, such as India, Afghanistan, and even Egypt, although strictly military assistance was understandably channeled to countries linked to Washington by instruments of mutual defense. Thus the "political strings" were often more a myth than a reality.

Of course, American loans and grants were often given to finance a specific project or development scheme under the condition that the ventures should be properly supervised by mixed local-American teams to prevent waste, embezzlement, and inefficiency. Although such supervision could be and sometimes was resented as an interference in the domestic processes of the recipient country, it really served the latter's true interests. The progressives in the country should have welcomed such safeguards against the squandering of the much-needed capital by corrupt or inefficient elements. If they have not, it has often been due to some more basic cause of an essentially political nature. Thus, for example, both Egypt and Syria have often voiced criticisms of American aid programs (Syria refusing to accept any prior to 1958), largely because of the resentments caused by American policies toward Palestine. It would appear, therefore, that if good use was to be made of the American assistance both in terms of economic benefits for the recipient nations and psychological advantages for the giver, such assistance should have been carefully coordinated with an overall political policy and serve as an instrument of the latter rather than as its substitute.

The Northern Tier: Strains and Stresses in the Alliances

The American policy toward the Northern Tier, with special focus on Turkey and Iran, could be considered a success during the first two decades following World War II inasmuch as it achieved its goal of containing Soviet expansionism and preserving the independence and territorial integrity of these countries. The United States used the unilateral, multilateral, and bilateral instruments in its relations with the Northern Tier in pursuance of this policy. The Truman Doctrine, the inclusion of Turkey (and Greece) into NATO, the formation of CENTO, and the signing of the mutual security agreements with Turkey, Iran, and Pakistan in 1959 testified to the variety of these approaches, all focusing on the survival of the countries in question and the creation of an interlocking system of mutual guarantees. But ultimately what counts beyond any written document is the will and determination to implement it. In those years the United States did possess such a will and determination to help its allies if necessary through military intervention and this, in turn, was bolstered by American credibility which was established by American actions in Korea, in Lebanon, when Israel was compelled to withdraw from Sinai and Gaza in 1956, when Russia was forcefully persuaded to withdraw its missiles from Cuba in 1962, and, closer to home, by decisive American interventions in Guatemala and Santo Domingo. Under those circumstances, the Northern Tier countries developed respect and trust in America and, to the extent to which their own capacities permitted, reciprocated in loyal cooperation as attested by the participation of the Turkish troops in the Korean war.

After the mid-1960s, American credibility suffered considerable erosion. Among the causes of this change could be mentioned the following (not necessarily in chronological order): (a) the retreat from Vietnam; (b) the Watergate scandal and the attendant weakening of the office of the presidency in favor of the less informed and less stable Congress; (c) the inner tumoil of the United States in the 1960s, especially on the campuses, which showed a disturbing rejection by the younger elements in American society of the leadership of the free world; (d) a greater ability of ethnic pressure groups to influence and often distort the national foreign policy for their own reasons; (e) a campaign of denigration aimed at crippling, through legislative and other means, the ability of certain vital defense organs, such as the Central Intelligence Agency, to work effectively for the security of the nation; (f) the emergence of a special brand of neoisolationism in which the extreme right and the extreme left in American politics combined to prevent the government from intervening effectively in certain international situations, such as Angola; and, finally, (g) a spirit of appeasement toward the Soviet Union, espoused by various segments of the society, including certain business groups, and generated by the official policy of detente.

It is no wonder, then, that the confidence of both the Northern Tier states and the world at large in America's strength and firmness slackened and that reverses in the United States initial containment policy, imaginatively inaugurated under bipartisan leadership during the Truman and Eisenhower administrations, were experienced.

Correspondingly, disturbing trends appeared in the Northern Tier itself. Three of these deserve particular attention:

1. A new generation in Turkey and Iran (composed of young people who were children at the time of the traumatic Soviet threats of the 1945–46 period or who were born afterward) developed a different perception of their country's relations with the United States: America was no longer hailed as a shield and savior of their

independence and integrity but often presented in a sinister light as a country dominated by the industrial-military complex, to be distrusted and blamed for real or imaginary ills in the world at large.

2. Deterioration in the internal stability of the Northern Tier countries was the second major factor. This was often based on discontent of various social groups in Turkey and Iran, born of greater expectations—often unrealistic considering the economic and cultural lag between them and the advanced industrial societies—and often due to the shortsightedness of their ruling groups and the greed and corruption of their elites and administrative structures. Thus the thousands of Turkish migrant workers who found temporary jobs in western Europe became impressed with the better life, greater honesty, greater productivity, greater efficiency they saw there. By the same token, tens of thousands of Iranian students pursuing their studies abroad were in their daily lives exposed to democratic systems and permissive attitudes of Western societies and hoped, somewhat unrealistically, to transpose such patterns to their home ground. In Iran in particular, the sudden accretion of wealth as a result of the quadrupling of the oil revenues in 1974 did not prove an unmixed blessing: while it provided the financial base for rapid development and modernization, it also produced rampant inflation which severely hurt certain classes of people and accentuated the social cleavages already in existence. Growing impatience with the *status quo* in both countries was the result and this, in turn, gave rise to urban guerrilla groups and endemic acts of terror in both countries, especially in the 1970s.

3. Local and regional conflicts tended to overshadow more fundamental security priorities. In the case of Turkey, the Cyprus crisis in its two stages of 1964 and 1974 created an issue of such emotional intensity as to defeat, at least partly, the more rational considerations based on proper regard for the position of Turkey as the main eastern anchor of NATO. In the case of Iran, considerable disillusionment developed in its ruling circles in connection with the American hands-off policy in the Pakistan-India conflicts, particularly the war of 1971 which resulted in the loss of Pakistan's eastern region and the creation of Bangladesh. In those regional conflicts the United States was either unwilling to help or, as in the case of Cyprus, tried to act as a mediator but earned only reproaches, whatever it did. A marked disagreement developed between Turkey and Iran on the one hand and the United States on the other over the interpretation of their mutual alliance or security agreements: while the United States conceived them as defensive mechanisms against possible Soviet aggression and not as guarantees of support in other local conflicts, both Teheran and Ankara held the opposite view. This dissonance, in the case of Turkey, was further aggravated by the widespread conviction that the pressures of the Greek lobby in the United States Congress were the main reason that the American government did not respond positively to Turkish pleas. A degree of cynicism crept into the attitudes of political leaderships in both Turkey and Iran. It was translated into the belief that it did not quite pay to be a United States ally; it was perhaps more profitable to sit on the fence and practice neutralism while engaging in political blackmail to get the maximum economic aid from both of the superpowers.

The result of these changes of attitude was that following the rather precipitous congressional decision to embargo arms to Turkey, the use of American bases in that country was drastically curtailed in retaliation. Pakistan virtually inactivated its CENTO membership. Iran was still anxious to preserve a special relationship with the United States, but developed nagging doubts about the seriousness of the American intention to honor its obligations toward Iran and about the military effectiveness and usefulness of CENTO as well.

Paradoxically, while these strains and stresses were eroding the close links forged between the Northern Tier and the United States in the early postwar era, the dangers to the Northern Tier and, indirectly, to the United States and its Western allies, were clearly increasing. The Soviet Union did reach (or exceeded) nuclear parity with the United States while promoting rapid growth in its conventional arms strength, especially through a spectacular development of its navy, now deployed in all the oceans of the world. Russia's political influence in Iraq—through its friendship treaty with the Baghdad government—and Afghanistan, particularly after the Marxist coup of the spring of 1978, was definitely on the rise. And in Marxist-oriented South Yemen the Soviets established a political base of operations from which they could render effective assistance to the revolutionary forces in southern and eastern Arabia.

Yet, with all these negative signs, the essentials of the American-Northern Tier relationship could still be preserved and even strengthened if accurate perception of the dangers, followed by an imaginative and purposeful action, were displayed in Washington. There were indeed signs during the first two years of the Carter administration, 1977-1978, that after some confusing statements in which the electoral campaign had abounded (for example on arms sales abroad and on the need to keep a weapons embargo on Turkey) the United States launched a policy designed to heal the wounds and restore its relations with Turkey and Iran to the previous levels of mutual trust. In midwinter 1977–1978 President Carter and Shah Mohammed Reza Pahlavi exchanged visits in their respective capitals, during which the president stressed his dedication to the security of Iran and repeatedly used the word "alliance" to describe their mutual relationship. The American side tactfully refrained from questioning the Shah's judgment about appropriate armaments levels for Iran, while the Iranian side expressed willingness to cooperate fully with Washington and Riyadh in preventing escalation in oil prices. Even more notable perhaps was a breakthrough effected in the strained American-Turkish relations when, following a persistent advocacy by the administration, the Congress by a narrow vote canceled in midsummer 1978 its earlier ban on arms sales to Turkey.

The United States and the Arab World since the Kennedy Administration

For analytical purposes it is possible to divide American-Arab relations into three sectors: (a) direct, bilateral relations between the United States and various Arab countries pertaining to concrete matters of mutual interest such as aid and trade, arms sales, maintenance or liquidation of military bases, and so on; (b) issues arising from inter-Arab relations, particularly those focusing on problems of Arab unity and disunity; and (c) problems related to the triangular relationship between the Arab world, Israel, and the United States. Although having some merits in terms of classification, this division should be subject to this reservation, that no event or policy can be fully isolated in Arab affairs; all of them are to some extent interrelated, even those that at first glance appear to be a purely bilateral matter between the United States and a given Arab country. The totality of these relationships has invariably been affected by the protracted Arab-Israeli conflict.

Each president of the United States since World War II has left the imprint of his personality and policy on Arab-American relations. While President Truman will be mostly remembered within this context for his early recognition of Israel and his friendly but not excessive support for that state, President Eisenhower's administration will go into history for the strong diplomatic intervention to resolve the Suez crisis of 1956 and the American military intervention in Lebanon in 1958. Moreover, under Eisenhower the United States became largely identified with the conservative forces in the Arab world, in opposition to Nasser's expansionist Pan-Arab policies so as to prevent, as Ambassador John Badeau expressed it, his "meddling" in the affairs of other Arab states. Interestingly, after heavy involvement in the Arab-Israeli issue due to the Suez crisis, the United States experienced some respite from that conflict in the period of 1957 to 1967, spanning the presidencies of Eisenhower, Kennedy, and Johnson. This relief was largely due to the relative tranquility that prevailed in the Arab-Israeli relations after the Israeli withdrawal from Sinai and Gaza in 1956–57 and to the primacy that the Arab Cold War assumed in Arab politics during that decade.

President John F. Kennedy's inauguration brought a degree of reorientation of American policy toward the Arabs. The new thesis prevailing in Washington was that the United States should be on the side of those forces in the Third World that would have a decisive voice in politics in the future. With reference to the Arab world it meant that the United States should range itself on the side of "progressive" forces such as Egypt's Nasser and his followers throughout the Arab world. Consequently, a new policy was launched aiming at the rebuilding of those bridges to the centers of revolutionary Arab nationalism that had been badly damaged during the last years of the Eisenhower era. Symbolic of this policy was the appointment of a noncareer man, John Badeau, former president of the American University at Cairo, as ambassador to Egypt. While this vision of a new American-Arab relationship might have had some appeal because of its conceptual neatness, in practice it soon encountered difficulties. Inauguration of this policy coincided with the beginning of the civil war in Yemen and the resulting massive intervention of the Egyptian forces. Clearly if there was a question of Egyptian "meddling" in other countries' affairs, this was it. Furthermore, even with the best intention of cultivating good relations with Cairo, the United States could not ignore Nasser's aggressive behavior toward Saudi Arabia, Egyptian bombing of Saudi cities, and the threat presented to an oil-rich monarchy maintaining close and friendly relations with America.[18] Thus during Kennedy's brief presidency this new concept of American policy was already undergoing a severe strain. Kennedy's untimely death prevented the policy from being fully tested.

Under President Johnson the initial tendency for the United States was to keep

---

[18]For a fuller discussion, see John S. Badeau, *The American Approach to the Arab World* (New York, 1968), esp. ch. 6, "Dilemmas."

matters in the Middle East as undisturbed as was feasible. To this end American policy strove to keep a working relationship with such revolutionary states as Egypt, Syria, and Iraq, to continue its friendly cooperation with Saudi Arabia and Jordan, and to extend regular assistance to Israel. However, in 1967 the outbreak of the June war between Israel and its Arab neighbors (partly generated by inter-Arab rivalries) put a spoke into the wheel of American policy. Esteem for America reached a new low in the Arab world, diplomatic relations with Washington were broken by a number of Arab governments, and a three-month oil embargo against the United States was decreed by the Arab producing states. What began as a hopeful development of American-Arab relations in the early part of the Johnson administration ended in considerable aggravation. Moreover, the year 1967 opened an era of marked Israeli ascendancy in Washington. This was primarily expressed by the increasing amount of financial assistance and steadily growing supplies of sophisticated American weapons to Israel. By the same token, the defeat-generated radicalization in various Arab countries, for example, the revolutions in Iraq and Libya, enlarged the group of Arab governments highly critical of or actually hostile to the United States.

Following his election to the presidency but even before he was inaugurated, President Nixon sent his personal friend, former governor of Pennsylvania William Scranton, on a goodwill and fact-finding trip to the Middle East. On his way home Scranton expressed the view that American policy toward the area should be more "even-handed." This statement met with such a critical response in Israel and among its friends in the United States that in subsequent statements Nixon carefully avoided using this expression. In fact, during his presidency Israel was accorded preferential treatment, especially in terms of arms supplies. Part of this was due to the weakening of the domestic position of the president himself, as a result of which he could ill afford to alienate powerful segments of opinion in the American political spectrum. But a substantial part could also be ascribed to the Democratic-dominated Congress which was prone to nullify any presidential attempt to improve materially Arab-American relations. The outbreak of the October war in 1973 further complicated Nixon's task. The United States was made the target of an Arab oil embargo as a "hostile" country. Yet, because the October war ended with a modicum of Arab success, in contrast to the 1956 and 1967 Arab-Israeli wars, Egypt was less frustrated than before and willing to accept, albeit with reservations, the new American "step-by-step policy," personified by Kissinger's shuttle diplomacy between Cairo, Damascus, and Jerusalem. In contrast to the ban on oil sales to certain countries instituted by the Arab states in the summer of 1967, the embargo of 1973-74 affected much more seriously the economies of the industrialized countries, including the United States, and gave some sobering thoughts to the policymakers regarding their approach to the Arabs and their grievances. The lifting of the embargo some time after the conclusion of the Sinai I agreement was therefore greeted with relief in Washington and other Western capitals. Although the embargo was abolished without achieving the initial Arab condition of Israeli withdrawal from the occupied territories, enough goodwill was displayed by the Nixon administration through its mediation in the Sinai I agreement to create a climate of greater mutual confidence between Washington and the Arab capitals. A visit in the United States by Crown Prince and Deputy Minister Fahd of Saudi Arabia in June 1974 resulted in the conclusion of a comprehensive and ambitious cooperation agreement by which the United States committed its powerful technological resources to aid Saudi Arabia in her well-financed development program.

Under President Gerald Ford the step-by-step diplomacy continued. In November 1974, Ford met Brezhnev in Vladivostok where, in an official communique, they spoke of "the legitimate interests of the Palestinian people." The United States government aimed at further partial withdrawal of the Israeli forces away from the Suez Canal and the creation of a more secure neutral zone in Sinai. It encountered strong opposition to any further concessions on the part of Israel, which led President Ford in late March 1975 to announce a "reassessment" of the American policy toward the Middle East conflict. This was a diplomatic way of saying that the United States would now have to have a hard look at the policy of unconditionally delivering to Israel massive amounts of the most sophisticated weapons and attending to its economic needs. Israel's reaction was to mobilize its supporters in the media and on Capitol Hill. On May 21 of that year seventy-five senators addressed a collective letter to President Ford in which they called for a presidential aid request to Congress that would be "responsive to Israel's urgent military and economic needs."[19] The letter, however, in spite of its bipartisan backing, did not deter Ford from meeting President Sadat in Salzburg early in June and pursuing his reassessment policy. The Sinai II agreement signed on September 4, 1975, was an outcome of these endeavors. The novelty of this document in terms of American involvement consisted in the introduction of a team of American observers, radar technicians, into the neutral zone between Israeli and Egyptian forces.

But once this new important stage in the search for a settlement was attained, the step-by-step diplomacy seemed to have lost is usefulness. What was needed was a formula for a comprehensive settlement, in the spirit of UN Security Council Resolution 242, to which all the administrations beginning with that of Lyndon Johnson have adhered. The task of devising such a comprehensive settlement fell on the shoulders of President Carter, who immediately after his inauguration in January 1977 opened a series of meetings with the Arab and Israeli leaders. Before long the president announced in two statements on March 9 and 16 the principles that an Arab-Israeli peace settlement should incorporate. These were (a) a "substantial withdrawal" of Israeli troops with only "minor adjustments" in boundaries; (b) the right of Israel to exist within the framework of full peace with its neighbors; and (c) the need to create a "homeland" for the Palestinian people.[20] Although broadly consonant with the provisions of UN Resolution 242, these principles were actually beyond its provisions in two important respects: instead of calling for mere nonbelligerency they envisaged a full-fledged peace with diplomatic relations and trade and cultural exchanges between Israel and the surrounding Arab states—a proposal designed to evoke a positive response among the Israelis. Secondly, the concept of a

[19]Quoted in *New York Times*, May 22, 1975.
[20]See *New York Times*, March 10 and May 27, 1977, and *Washington Post*, March 17, 1977.

homeland for the Palestinians also went beyond Resolution 242's mere mention of justice for the Palestinian refugees. It signified recognition by the president that a claim for national self-determination of a sizable ethnic group in the latter part of the twentieth century could not be safely ignored.

In comparing the attitude of four presidents, from Johnson to Carter, to the Arab-Israeli conflict it is possible to detect, despite individual differences of approach, considerable continuity and consistency in their policies. All four supported UN Resolution 242, as previously noted. On June 5, 1967, President Johnson proclaimed five principles of peace which broadly coincided with the subsequent UN resolution. Similarly, in a speech delivered before a B'nai B'rith audience on September 10, 1968, Johnson insisted that there must be no territorial aggrandizement "by weight of conquest." Under President Nixon, a more detailed articulation of American policy was undertaken by Secretary of State Rogers, who on December 9, 1969, in his well-publicized Galaxy Educational Conference speech, pronounced himself against territorial expansionism, called for Israeli withdrawal, and for only minor territorial boundary adjustments. Nixon himself spoke in February 1971 of the "legitimate aspirations of the Palestinian people," and Ford's joint communique with Brezhnev referring to the Palestinian rights, previously noted, provided a further link in this chain of continuity. As for President Carter, he not only pursued this consistent line but gave a new dimension to some of the principles enunciated earlier.

Taken as a whole, these high-level American pronouncements clashed with the Israeli views on territory and the fate of the Palestinians. Israel's political strategy was to convince the United States that its very survival was threatened by any substantial territorial withdrawal and by conceding to the Palestinians the right of self-determination. The view of the successive American administrations was that one had to differentiate between Israel's survival and expansion. The message of all four presidents was that the United States was committed to the survival of Israel but opposed its expansion.

In addition to these fundamental differences there were subsidiary points on which Washington and Tel Aviv disagreed. Thus when during the June war of 1967 an American research and intelligence-gathering ship, U.S.S. *Liberty* was attacked in successive waves by Israeli aircraft and lost thirty-four members of its crew, killed in the process, the United States lodged a protest, although Israel denied that the action was deliberate. The United States did eventually accept the Israeli regrets and reparations payments to the families of victims, but lingering doubts remained as to the true motivation of this attack. Following the 1967 war, the United States repeatedly raised objections against Israel's actions in the occupied Arab territories. The unilateral annexation of Arab East Jerusalem in the summer of 1967 was opposed and, as late as March 1976, United States delegate to the United Nations Scranton reiterated that the future of Jerusalem must be determined not through unilateral action but only through negotiation. Israel's practices in occupied territories, such as land expropriation and expulsion of populations from certain areas were also criticized by the United States government. The United States objected forcefully against the establishment and proliferation of Jewish settlements on the West Bank, Golan Heights, Gaza strip, and Sinai. Ambassador Scranton in the earlier mentioned statement called these settlements "an obstacle to peace"; State Department spokesmen referred to them as "illegal"; and the United States delegation supported the UN Security Council statement on November 11, 1976, which deplored the establishment of Israeli settlements in occupied Arab territories and declared "invalid" the absorption of East Jerusalem into Israel. By the same token, the United States Department of State termed "illegal" the oil drilling by Israeli crews in the Gulf of Suez in February 1977. Intimidation by Israeli armed forces of the American drilling crews exploring for oil in the Suez waters on the basis of concessions granted by Egypt added another irritant to American-Israeli relations. More broadly, the United States was critical of the excessive retaliations practiced by Israel against the neighboring states, particularly in 1976, 1977, and 1978 against Lebanon as a country from which the Palestinian *fedayeen* organized raids against Israeli territory. The use by Israel of American-supplied cluster bombs in some of these massive strikes against specific prohibitions gave cause to another American protest.

Generally, the question of arms supplies and transfers provided another area of disagreement. The United States was delivering weapons to Israel on the condition that they should not be resold. In spite of this clause Israel tried to negotiate a sale to Ecuador of 24 Kfir jet fighters equipped with American-made engines. Learning of the proposed transaction, the United States blocked the sale on February 7, 1977. That same month, the United States government stopped the sale to Israel of concussion bombs. More broadly, American arms deliveries to Israel were often affected at the cost of depleting NATO-related arsenals on both sides of the Atlantic. This was one of the reasons why the chairman of the Joint Chiefs of Staff, General George Brown, declared in October 1977 that Israel was a "burden" on the United States. In 1977–1978, by virtue of previous pledges, the United States government tried to obtain congressional authorization for substantial arms deliveries to Saudi Arabia and Egypt, a measure vigorously opposed by Israel and its backers in the Congress. To avoid accusations of one-sidedness, the Carter administration proposed an arms package deal which would provide for simultaneous authorization of arms sales to Saudi Arabia, Egypt, and Israel, with Israel receiving the most advanced type of military aircraft. The struggle between the administration and the pro-Israeli forces in the House and the Senate was intense. Rather untypically, it ended on May 15, 1978, in the administration victory when the Senate approved the proposed measure by a 54 to 44 vote.

But if the above listing of points of difference and irritations between the United States and Israel conveys the idea of some basic divergence of policies between the two countries, an even longer list of clearly pro-Israeli and implicitly anti-Arab actions by the United States can be supplied. Thus, to begin with, the Israeli attack on the American research ship in 1967 did not receive the searching scrutiny of a widely publicized investigation that it perhaps warranted. Six years later, during the October war of 1973, the United States engaged in a massive air lift of arms to Israel to halt the Egyptian offensive; moreover, weapons and equipment were delivered to forward Israeli bases in Sinai, thus making the United States an indirect participant in the war operations themselves. The United States was prepared to do this in response to a simultaneous massive Soviet airlift to Egypt but the question which of the two superpowers was the first to begin may be open to further research and investigation. It is certain that the United States was willing to undertake such an action despite the obvious strain it produced within the NATO alliance, whose members, except for Portugal, refused to grant permission for American overflights through their airspaces.

President Nixon's decision on October 19, 1973, to request immediate appropriations of $2.2 billion of arms to Israel was the act that triggered the decision of Saudi Arabia, followed by other Arab states, to impose an oil embargo on the United States. In turn, the embargo generated certain warnings mixed with implicit threats from the United States to the Arabs. In November 1973, Kissinger declared that the United States would consider countermeasures if the embargo continued "unreasonably and indefinitely." Defense Secretary James Schlesinger followed with a statement in January 1974 that the Arab states would run the risk of violence if they used oil "to cripple the larger mass of the industrialized world," and a year later, January 1975, spoke of the possibility of the use of force against the oil-producing countries: "I am saying that there [are] no circumstances where we would not use force . . . but it is one thing to use it in the case of dispute over price; it's another where there is some actual strangulation of the industrialized world."[21]

Consistently high appropriations for arms deliveries and economic assistance to Israel provided another example of Washington's friendly attitude. These appropriations averaged about $2 billion a year since 1973. The Sinai II agreement of September 4, 1975, provided a good illustration of this trend. According to one observer, "Israel had exacted a high price. Washington was to supply $2.2 billion in aid and replace all oil lost from Sinai production. American and Israeli positions would be 'coordinated' in the future. The United States agreed to look favorably on a request for a new range of sophisticated weapons including the Lance surface-to-surface missile."[22]

Although the United States delegation at the United Nations occasionally expressed its disapproval of certain Israeli actions, by and large the delegation opposed various resolutions critical of Israel if they appeared too one-sided or too strong. While in the first two decades of the United Nations' existence the Soviet Union frequently used the instrument of veto inasmuch as it so often found itself outvoted by the majority in the Security Council, in the 1970s it was the turn of the United States to find itself in a minority of one on several occasions even if its West European allies favored some measure. Five American actions in the United Nations may serve as an illustration of these attitudes: (1) Because some Third World countries were exploring the possiblity of eliminating Israel from the United Nations in a way reminiscent of the ban applied to South Africa and Rhodesia, Secretary Kissinger warned in July 1975 that the United States would take a "definite and clear action" if the United Nations suspended Israel "in violation of the charter."

[21] *Business Week,* Jan. 2, 1975.
[22] Georgiana Stevens, "1967–1977: America's Moment in the Middle East," *Middle East Journal,* 31, no. 1 (Winter 1977), 14.

(2) On November 10, 1975, the UN General Assembly passed a resolution condemning Israel for its racism. In response, United States delegate Daniel Patrick Moynihan (later senator from New York) strongly deplored the resolution as an "infamous act." (3) On December 8, 1975, the United States vetoed the Security Council resolution that would have condemned Israel for the air attack on Lebanon without also condemning violence used against Israel. (4) Similarly on January 23, 1976, the American delegation vetoed a draft resolution submitted by six members of the Security Council which affirmed the Palestinians' right to self-determination and statehood and the right of Palestinian refugees to return home or receive compensation, required Israel to withdraw from all Arab lands occupied in 1967, and required guarantees of territorial integrity of all states in the area. (5) On May 26, 1976, the United States dissociated itself from a majority statement of the Security Council which deplored Israeli measures altering the demographic character of the occupied territories.

The Arab boycott of Israel provided another area where the Israeli and American policies converged. Although the boycott was practiced for a long time—ever since the establishment of the State of Israel in 1948—the matter did not receive much attention or publicity until the mid-1970s when, owing to the rise in the oil prices, the wealthy Arab markets began to present tremendous opportunities for American export trade. A strong campaign was launched in the United States Congress to pass legislation which would not only prevent American firms from complying with the Arab League's boycott regulations but also make such a compliance a punishable crime. It generated a lively national debate in which semantics—with the use of the words "participation" and "cooperation" with the Arab boycott—added to the emotionally charged atmosphere. In this case, the administration, although basically opposed to the boycott, counseled moderation so as not to close the doors to the American economic transactions with the Arab world. It should be pointed out, furthermore, that the United States itself had a record of applying boycotts through unilateral or collective decisions to such countries as Cuba, Communist China, South Africa, Rhodesia and on a selective basis to a number of Communist bloc countries. Ultimately, on May 5, 1977, the Senate passed the antiboycott law which represented a compromise between the proponents and opponents of the earlier more drastic proposals.

The Camp David agreements of 1978 fall into the category of ambiguous acts of the administration. They represent substantial retreat from the earlier position of President Carter regarding Israel's withdrawal, a homeland for the Palestinians, and the need to take the PLO into account in the peacemaking process. In fact, the intransigence of Israel's Premier Begin on these issues apparently paid handsome dividends to Israel: both the basic Israeli proposals, the Allon plan of 1972 envisaging Israel's military presence in the West Bank and the Begin plan of December 1977 calling for internal autonomy for the Palestinians in the West Bank and Gaza, were incorporated, with minor changes in verbiage, in the Camp David "framework for peace" agreements. Moreover, President Carter did not obtain from Begin any formal commitment to desist from further expansion of Jewish settlements in the West Bank and the Gaza Strip and did not insist on return of Arab sovereignty over these areas. On the credit side for the president one could mention Israel's agreement to withdraw from Sinai and to ensure continuous American involvement in the peacemaking process. But even these gains may appear illusory if one takes into account that the Begin plan of December 1977, without any special American pressure, did also offer Israeli withdrawal from Sinai. Finally, the American pledge to replace the Israeli airfields in Sinai by constructing at America's expense two powerful air bases in the Negeb, both to be equipped with costly and sophisticated instruments, added another significant dimension to Israel's diplomatic victory at Camp David.

Conclusion

We began this section by mentioning three main reasons for the United States' concern with the Middle East: the Soviet menace, oil, and Palestine. Within the thirty-five years since the concluding stages of World War II, these three reasons still provided the essence of America's interest in this strategic region. But the experience of this postwar era showed that a piecemeal handling of each of the three problems, that is, the absence of a coordinated and integrated approach, was clearly insufficient and abounded in contradictions which ultimately might defeat the main American purpose of keeping this area free from Soviet domination, guaranteeing access to its oil resources, and ensuring political stability. Stability, in turn, could be achieved through orderly economic development that would satisfy legitimate aspirations of the masses and through peace based on justice. International justice, in terms of twentieth-century political standards, was inconceivable without due regard being paid to the national self-determination of once dependent peoples.

Because the principle of self-determination and the desire to ward off Soviet menace supplemented each other in the Northern Tier, America's main goal of preserving the freedom and independence of Turkey and Iran could be and was pursued without major contradiction. Even the complications in American-Turkish relations arising from the Cyprus affair and the dubious effect of the American human rights crusade of 1977–1978 on Iran's stability did not erase the basic community of interests between the United States and the Northern Tier.

But in the Arab area of the Middle East the situation grew more complex because first the establishment of Israel, and later its territorial expansion, could not be easily reconciled with the principle of national self-determination and was bound to subject American-Arab relations to considerable strain. Growing alienation of the Arabs from America not only dangerously eroded their earlier friendship but also brought in its wake three undesirable consequences: (a) left-oriented radicalization of a number of Arab political systems, (b) opening the gates to Soviet penetration, (c) threats and interruptions in the supply of Arab oil to the United States and some of its Western allies.

This dichotomy became especially aggravated after 1967 when Israel occupied extensive Arab areas about twice the size of its original territory. Annexation of Arab Jerusalem, confiscation of private Arab lands, expulsions and forcible deportations of Arab inhabitants, and the planned proliferation of Jewish settlements in the occupied territories added new obstacles to the achievement of peace as envisaged by the Four Power-supported UN Security Council Resolution 242.

Israel's concept that its security and survival depended on its continued control of all or at least substantial parts of the occupied territories clashed with the American concept—as voiced by consecutive presidents from Johnson to Carter—that one must distinguish between Israel's right to secure existence within its essentially pre-1967 boundaries and its expansion. The first, from the American point of view, was to be supported by political, economic, and military means; the second was to be opposed in the name of justice and out of consideration for Arab sensibilities.

The years following the 1967 June war thus witnessed the continuous struggle between these two concepts. Periods of aggravation alternated with periods of relaxation. Lyndon Johnson's formula of no territorial acquisitions reflecting the weight of conquest, Scranton's "even-handed policy," and Secretary Rogers' pronouncement against expansionism alternated with a certain reticence on the part of Nixon—himself embattled in the wake of Vietnam and Watergate—to press for Israeli concessions and, again, the subsequent "reassessment" of American policy ordered in 1975 by Ford. In this struggle between the consecutive American presidents and Israeli premiers—Golda Meir, Itzhak Rabin, and Menachem Begin—the United States Congress acted as an arbiter and, at least until the spring of 1978, the Israeli premiers as a rule emerged victorious over the American presidents. This outcome was reflected in generous allocations (totaling some $10 billion between 1967 and 1977) of economic and military assistance to Israel, repeated investigations, spurred by congressional committee staffs, regarding the supplies of oil and generally characterized by hostility to the Arabs, and stringent anti-boycott proposals followed by restrictive legislation aimed at hindering American-Arab economic exchanges. Broadly, these congressional endeavors could be viewed as an attempt to demonstrate that the Arab countries were not too important to the strategic and economic interests of the United States, that only certain industrial groups in America stood to gain by the close American-Arab relationship, that Israel was America's most dependable ally (despite the lack of a formal pact) in the Middle East, and that the distinction which American presidents tried to establish between Israel's territorial integrity and its expansionism was uncalled for.

The thwarting of presidential policies by Congress appeared more feasible and, therefore, more successful, when the president and the congressional majority represented different political parties (that is, under Nixon and Ford). When both the president and the majority in Congress belonged to the same party, there were some signs that the president was able—though not invariably—to have his view prevail. It was under Johnson that the United States delegation cast its vote for the UN Resolution 242 calling for Israeli withdrawal and it was President Carter who in the spring of 1978 persuaded the Senate to adopt the arms package bill for Israel, Egypt, and Saudi Arabia in spite of strong opposition mounted by Israel and its backers in Congress. But these presidential victories were often followed by defeats or at least by retreats from original positions, as noted in our remarks on the broad thrust of Camp David agreements.

The general lesson from the study of American policies toward the Middle East—especially in the Arab-Israeli area, is that it has been very difficult to formulate and implement a consistent policy truly reflecting America's long-range national interest. The American democracy, based as it is on the aggregation and articulation of pressure group demands, is always prone to advance competing definitions of national interest. Adoption by a congressional majority at a given moment of one of such definitions does not guarantee its accuracy. The right and safe policy may sometimes emerge only after a protracted struggle between the executive and the legislative branches of the government and within the legislative branch itself, and the struggle is apt to be replete with sudden shifts in moods, alignments, and concepts. Moreover, as the Korean bribery case in 1977–1978 vividly demonstrated, the people's representatives are not immune to temptations of foreign pecuniary inducements, not to speak of their interest in being reelected, and thus they cater to pressure groups that are likely to influence their victory at the polls.

To achieve satisfactory results in a foreign policy which would correspond to long-range national interest, conceived in the most rational terms possible, is in a democracy a painful and often slow process. In spite of the obstacles the United States has faced in developing its national policy toward the Middle East, some guarded optimism might be justified: the basic objective of keeping that area free from dominance by a hostile power and the traditional moral guideline of American policy—respect for self-determination of nations—did not contradict each other. Moreover, rational considerations were likely to have greater effect on shaping a policy as a result of demonstrated danger stemming from neglect—with the October crisis of 1973 serving as a warning—and there was a greater awareness of the area's strategic importance, an awareness that was bound to grow with the spread of unbiased information and accurate knowledge among the politically conscious American public.

Appendix Tables,
Bibliography, and Index

Appendix Tables

I. Area and population of the countries of the Middle East, 1978

	Area				Population of the capital city	
	sq. km.	sq. mi.	Population			
Afghanistan	850,000	250,000	20,400,000	Kabul	750,000
Bahrain	369	231	345,000	Manama	85,000
Egypt	1,000,000	384,000	40,000,000	Cairo	7,000,000
Iran	1,648,000	636,000	36,300,000	Teheran	4,000,000
Iraq	440,000	168,000	12,500,000	Baghdad	1,500,000
Israel	20,300	7,800	3,700,000	Jerusalem	366,000
Jordan	97,700	37,700	3,000,000	Amman	700,000
Kuwait	17,600	6,800	1,100,000	Kuwait City	120,000
Lebanon	10,400	4,000	3,100,000	Beirut	800,000
Oman	330,000	120,000	835,000	Muscat	50,000
Qatar	11,000	4,250	205,000	Doha	140,000
Saudi Arabia	2,150,000	830,000	5,000,000	Riyadh	670,000
Syria	185,000	71,500	8,000,000	Damascus	850,000
Turkey	780,000	301,000	42,000,000	Ankara	1,700,000
United Arab Emirates	83,000	32,000	875,000	Abu Dhabi	250,000
Yemen (North)	195,000	75,000	7,200,000	Sana	450,000
Yemen (South)	338,000	130,000	1,800,000	Aden	270,000

Statistics are based on composite sources: UN annual demographic yearbooks, the International Institute of Strategic Studies, the Europa Yearbooks, and the *National Geographic Atlas of the World*. In a number of cases figures are estimates or represent projections from censuses taken several years earlier. All figures, except those for the area of Bahrain, are rounded.

II. Crude oil production in the Middle East and certain other countries (thousands of barrels per day)

	1972	1973	1974	1978
Abu Dhabi[a]	1,055	1,305	1,410	1,447
Bahrain	70	68	67	53
Dubai[a]	153	220	242	362
Iran[a]	5,050	5,861	5,024	5,159
Iraq[a]	1,454	1,969	1,945	2,622
Kuwait[a]	2,999	2,753	2,276	1,866
Neutral Zone[a]	559	509	542	458
Oman	282	293	291	315
Qatar[a]	482	570	519	482
Saudi Arabia[a]	5,733	7,342	8,211	8,070
Other Mid-East	240	182	254	202
Total Middle East (in Asia)	18,077	21,072	21,781	21,035
Algeria[a]	1,022	1,055	943	1,225
Egypt	217	168	145	482
Gabon[a,b]	n.a.	n.a.	177	225
Libya[a]	2,227	2,187	1,491	1,990
Nigeria[a]	1,818	2,051	2,251	1,898
Other Africa	345	429	291	293
Venezuela[a]	3,220	3,366	3,976	2,163
Mexico	444	470	565	1,190
Ecuador[a,c]	n.a.	199	165	202
Other Latin America	1,152	1,100	1,096	1,184
Canada	1,532	1,793	1,715	1,317
Indonesia[a]	1,076	1,294	1,401	1,639
Western Europe	439	448	449	1,779
Other Eastern Hemisphere[d]	779	940	968	1,162
Sino-Soviet Area	8,921	9,568	10,505	13,589
United States	9,451	9,188	8,786	8,685
Total Free World	40,055	44,009	43,511	46,470
Total World	48,976	53,577	54,016	60,059
Total OPEC	26,848	30,681	30,416	29,829
Total Arab Countries	n.a.	18,535	18,226	19,564

Source: Statistical bulletins of the Standard Oil Company of California.

[a]Members of Organization of Petroleum Exporting Countries. Abu Dhabi, Dubai, and Sharja (which is not listed separately) are constituent units of the United Arab Emirates, a member of OPEC.

[b]Not member of OPEC in 1972, 1973, 1974.

[c]Not member of OPEC in 1972.

[d]Except Sino-Soviet area.

III. Approximate proven reserves of oil in the Middle East and North Africa, end of 1978 (in thousands of barrels)

Middle East	
Abu Dhabi	30,000,000
Bahrain	250,000
Dubai	1,300,000
Iran	59,000,000
Iraq	32,100,000
Israel	10,000
Kuwait	66,200,000
Neutral Zone	6,480,000
Oman	2,500,000
Qatar	4,000,000
Saudi Arabia	165,700,000
Sharja	16,000
Syria	2,080,000
Turkey	360,000
Total Middle East	369,996,000
North Africa	
Algeria	6,300,000
Egypt	3,200,000
Libya	24,300,000
Morocco	125
Tunisia	2,300,000
Total North Africa	36,100,125
Grand total	406,096,125

Source: *Oil and Gas Journal,* Dec. 25, 1978.

IV. Oil revenue of major producing countries in the Middle East and North Africa (millions of dollars)

	1965	1975	1978
Bahrain	17	280	400
Iran	522	19,900	20,700
Iraq	375	7,600	10,400
Kuwait[a]	671	7,900	9,000
Oman	—	900	1,700
Qatar	69	1,800	2,200
Saudi Arabia[a]	655	26,700	36,000
United Arab Emirates	33	6,500	8,200
Total Gulf Area	2,342	71,580	88,600
Algeria	n.a.	n.a.	5,100
Libya	371	5,200	9,200
Total North Africa	n.a.	n.a.	14,300
Grand total	n.a.	n.a.	102,900

Sources: For the years 1965 and 1975, Exxon Background Series, *Middle East Oil,* 1976; for 1978 the revenue figures are calculated on the basis of oil export values contained in International Monetary Fund, *International Financial Statistics,* 32, no. 3, March 1979 (Washington, D.C.).

[a]Includes one-half Neutral Zone.

V. Military and development budgets of selected countries in the Middle East (thousands of dollars)

Country	Year	Ordinary budget expenditure		Development budget expenditure
		Military	Total	
Egypt	1977–78	4,370,000	13,770,000[a]	4,125,000
Iran	1977–78	8,000,000	33,000,000[b]	
Iraq	1976–77	1,190,000	17,000,000	n.a.
Israel	1977–78	2,770,000	6,300,000	1,830,000
Jordan	1976–77	186,000	420,000	396,000
Kuwait	1977–78	320,000	7,100,000[b]	
Saudi Arabia	1977–78	950,000	10,400,000	21,200,000[c]
Turkey	1976–77	1,750,000	8,000,000	n.a.

Sources: Courtesy information services of the respective governments.

[a]At official exchange rate of *LE* 1 = $2.55; tourist rates are *LE* 1 = $1.42 and represent a more accurate value of the Egyptian pound.

[b]Includes development budget.

[c]Includes $8 billion in military expenditures.

VI. Development plans of selected countries in the Middle East (thousands of dollars)

Country	Period	Total Planned Expenditure
Iran	1973–1978	62,340,000
Iraq	1976–1980	33,800,000
Jordan	1976–1980	2,300,000
Kuwait	1976–1981	17,400,000
Saudi Arabia	1975–1980	142,500,000

Sources: Courtesy information services of the respective governments.

VII. Military forces of selected countries in the Middle East, 1978

Country	Army		Navy		Air Force		Total personnel
	Troops	Tanks	Troops	Combat ships	Troops	Combat aircraft	
Egypt	350,000	1,680	20,000	73	25,000	612	395,000
Iran	285,000	1,870	28,000	23	100,000	459	413,000
Iraq	180,000	2,020	4,000	19	28,000	339	212,000
Israel	138,000[b]	4,525	5,000	21	21,000	543	164,000
Jordan	61,000	500	200	—[a]	6,650	76	67,850
Saudi Arabia	45,000[c]	325	1,500	—[a]	12,000	171	58,500
Syria	200,000	2,600	2,500	14	25,000	392	227,500
Turkey	390,000	2,800	45,000	90	50,000	339	485,000

Source: International Institute for Strategic Studies, *The Military Balance 1978–1979*.
[a]Only small coastal patrol craft.
[b]Includes women.
[c]In addition, the National Guard has 35,000 troops.

Selected Bibliography

The Area in General

Abboushi, W. F. *Political Systems of the Middle East in the 20th Century*. New York: Dodd, Mead, 1970.

Allen, Robert Loring. *Middle Eastern Economic Relations with the Soviet Union, Eastern Europe, and Mainland China*. Charlottesville: University of Virginia Press, 1958.

Anshen, R. N., ed. *Mid-East: World Center*. New York: Harper, 1956.

Badeau, John. *The American Approach to the Arab World*. New York: Harper & Row, 1968.

Belgrave, Sir Charles. *Personal Column*. London: Hutchinson, 1960.

Beling, Willard A. *Pan-Arabism and Labor*. Cambridge, Mass.: Harvard University Press, 1960.

Belot, Raymond de. *The Struggle for the Mediterranean, 1939–1945*. Princeton: Princeton University Press, 1951.

Bentwich, Norman. *The Mandates System*. London, New York: Longmans, 1930.

Bill, James, A., and Leiden, Carl. *The Middle East: Politics and Power*. Boston: Allyn & Bacon, 1974.

Bonné, Alfred. *State and Economics in the Middle East: A Society in Transition*. Rev. ed. London: Routledge & Kegan Paul, 1955.

Boutros-Ghali, B. Y. *The Arab League, 1945–1955*. (International Conciliation, no. 498.) New York: Carnegie Endowment for International Peace, 1955.

Brockelmann, Carl. *History of the Islamic Peoples*. New York: Putnam, 1947.

Bullard, Sir Reader. *Britain and the Middle East*. New York: Longmans, 1951.

———. *The Camels Must Go: An Autobiography*. London: Faber & Faber, 1961.

Campbell, John C. *Defense of the Middle East*. 2d ed. New York: Praeger, 1960.

Caroe, Sir Olaf K. *Wells of Power, the Oilfields of South-West Asia: A Regional and Global Study*. New York: Macmillan, 1951.

Cumming, Henry H. *Franco-British Rivalry in the Post-War Near East*. New York: Oxford University Press, 1938.

Davis, Helen Miller, comp. *Constitutions, Electoral Laws, Treaties of States in the Near and Middle East*. 2d ed. Durham, N.C.: Duke University Press, 1953.

Ellis, Harry B. *Challenge in the Middle East*. New York: Ronald Press, 1960.

———. *Heritage of the Desert: The Arabs and the Middle East*. New York: Ronald Press, 1956.

Eudin, Xenia Joukoff, and North, Robert C. *Soviet Russia and the East, 1920–1927: A Documentary Survey*. Stanford, Calif.: Stanford University Press, 1957.

Evron, Yair. *The Middle East: Nations, Superpowers and Wars*. New York: Praeger, 1973.

Faris, N. A., and Husayn, M. T. *The Crescent in Crisis: An Interpretive Study of the Modern Arab World*. Lawrence: University of Kansas Press, 1955.

Fernau, F. W. *Moslems on the March*. Trans. E. W. Dickes. New York: Knopf, 1954.

Finnie, David H. *Desert Enterprise: The Middle East Oil Industry in Its Local Environment*. Cambridge, Mass.: Harvard University Press, 1958.

Fisher, Sydney N. *The Middle East: A History*. New York: Knopf, 1959.

_____. *The Military in the Middle East*. Columbus: Ohio State University Press, 1963.

_____, ed. *Social Forces in the Middle East*. Ithaca, N.Y.: Cornell University Press, 1955.

Fisher, W. B. *The Middle East: A Physical, Social and Regional Geography*. London: Methuen; New York: Dutton, 1950.

Gerig, Benjamin. *The Open Door and the Mandates System*. London: Allen & Unwin, 1930.

Golan, Galia. *Yom Kippur and After: The Soviet Union and the Middle East Crisis*. Cambridge: Cambridge University Press, 1977.

Hall, H. Duncan. *Mandates, Dependencies and Trusteeship. Washington, D.C.: Carnegie Endowment for International Peace, 1948*.

Harari, Maurice. *Government and Politics of the Middle East*. Englewood Cliffs, N.J.: Prentice-Hall, 1962.

Hitti, Philip K. *The Arabs: A Short History*. Princeton: Princeton University Press, 1943.

Hoskins, Halford L. *The Middle East: Problem Area in World Politics*. New York: Macmillan, 1954.

_____. *Middle East Oil and United States Foreign Policy*. Washington, D.C.: Library of Congress, 1950.

Hurewitz, J. C. *Middle East Politics: The Military Dimension*. New York: Praeger, 1969.

_____, ed. *Diplomacy in the Near and Middle East: A Documentary Record*. 2 vols. Princeton: Van Nostrand, 1956.

_____, ed. *Soviet-American Rivalry in the Middle East*. New York: Praeger, 1969.

Ismael, Tareq Y., et al. *Governments and Politics of the Contemporary Middle East*. Homewood, Ill.: The Dorsey Press, 1970.

Izzeddin, Nejla. *The Arab World: Past, Present, and Future*. Chicago: Regnery, 1953.

Kazemzadeh, Firuz. *The Struggle for Trancaucasia (1917–1921)*. New York: Philosophical Library, 1952.

Kedourie, Elie. *England and the Middle East*. London: Bowes and Bowes, 1956.

Kerr, Malcolm H. *The Arab Cold War: Gamal 'Ab'd al-Nasir and His Rivals, 1958–1970*. London: Oxford University Press, 1970.

Kimche, Jon. *Seven Fallen Pillars*. Rev. ed. New York: Praeger, 1953.

Kirk, George E. *The Middle East, 1945–1950*. New York: Oxford University Press, 1954.

_____. *The Middle East in the War*. London: Royal Institute of International Affairs, 1953.

_____. *A Short History of the Middle East: From the Rise of Islam to Modern Times*. Rev. ed. New York: Praeger, 1955.

Knatchbull-Hugessen, Sir Hughe. *Diplomat in Peace and War*. London: J. Murray, 1949.

Lacoste, Raymond. *La Russie Soviétique et la Question d'Orient*. Paris: Editions Internationales, 1946.

Laissy, Michel. *Du Panarabisme à la Ligue Arabe*. Paris: Maisonneuve, 1949.

Laqueur, Walter Z. *Communism and Nationalism in the Middle East*. New York: Praeger, 1956.

_____. *The Soviet Union and the Middle East*. London: Routledge & Kegan Paul, 1959.

_____, ed. *The Middle East in Transition*. London: Routledge & Kegan Paul, 1958.

Lawrence, Thomas E. *Seven Pillars of Wisdom*. London: J. Cape, 1935.

Lenczowski, George. *Middle East Oil in a Revolutionary Age*. National Energy Study No. 10. Washington, D.C.: American Enterprise Institute, 1976.

_____. *Oil and State in the Middle East*. Ithaca, N.Y.: Cornell University Press, 1960.

_____, ed. *The Political Awakening in the Middle East*. Englewood Cliffs, N.J.: Prentice-Hall, 1970.

_____, ed. *Political Elites in the Middle East*. Washington, D.C.: American Enterprise Institute, 1975.

_____. *Soviet Advances in the Middle East*. Washington, D.C.: American Enterprise Institute, 1971.

————, ed. *United States Interests in the Middle East*. Washington, D.C.: American Enterprise Institute, 1968.

Lerner, Daniel, and Pevsner, Lucille W. *The Passing of Traditional Society: Modernizing the Middle East*. Glencoe, Ill.: Free Press, 1958.

Longrigg, Stephen H. *Oil in the Middle East*. 2d ed. New York: Oxford University Press, 1961.

McFadden, Tom J. *Daily Journalism in the Arab States*. Columbus: Ohio State University Press, 1953.

Magnus, Ralph, ed. *Documents on the Middle East*. Washington, D.C.: American Enterprise Institute, 1969.

McLaurin, R. D. *The Middle East in Soviet Policy*. Lexington, Mass.: D. C. Heath, 1975.

Malone, Joseph J. *The Arab Lands of Western Asia*. Englewood Cliffs, N.J.: Prentice-Hall, 1973.

Mandelstam, André N. *Politique Russe d' Accès à la Mediterranée au XXe Siècle*. In Hague, Academy of International Law. Recueil des Cours, 1934, I.). Paris: Hachette, 1935.

Al-Marayati, Abid A., and others. *The Middle East: Its Governments and Politics*. Belmont, Calif.: Duxbury Press, 1972.

Marlowe, John. *Arab Nationalism and British Imperialism*. New York: Praeger, 1961.

Marriott, J. A. R. *The Eastern Question*. Oxford: Clarendon Press, 1917.

The Middle East. London: Europa Publications, 1948–.

Mikesell, Raymond F., and Chenery, Hollis B. *Arabian Oil, America's Stake in the Middle East*. Chapel Hill, N.C.: University of North Carolina Press, 1949.

Monroe, Elizabeth. *Britain's Moment in the Middle East, 1914–1956*. London: Chatto & Windus, 1963.

Monteil, Vincent. *Les Musulmans Soviétiques*. Paris: Editions du Seuil, 1957.

Nuseibeh, Hazem Zaki. *The Ideas of Arab Nationalism*. Ithaca, N.Y.: Cornell University Press, 1956.

Peretz, Don. *The Middle East Today*. New York: Holt, Rinehart & Winston, 1963.

Polk, William R. *The United States and the Arab World*. Cambridge, Mass.: Harvard University Press, 1965.

Romainville, François de. *L'Islam et l'U.R.S.S.* Paris: Hermès, 1947.

Roosevelt, Kermit. *Arabs, Oil and History: The Story of the Middle East*. New York: Harper, 1949.

Royal Institute of International Affairs. *British Interests in the Mediterranean and Middle East*. London: Oxford University Press, 1958.

Rubinstein, Alvin. *Red Star on the Nile: The Soviet-Egyptian Influence Relationship since the June War*. Princeton: Princeton University Press, 1977.

Sayegh, Fayez A. *Arab Unity: Hope and Fulfillment*. New York: Devin-Adair, 1958.

The Security of the Middle East: A Problem Paper. Washington: The Brookings Institution, 1950.

Seton-Williams, M. N. *Britain and the Arab States: A Survey of Anglo-Arab Relations, 1920–1948*. London: Luzac, 1948.

Sharabi, Hisham B. *Governments and Politics of the Middle East in the Twentieth Century*. Princeton: Van Nostrand, 1962.

Shwadran, Benjamin. *The Middle East, Oil and the Great Powers*. New York: Praeger, 1955.

Smith, Wilfred C. *Islam in Modern History*. Princeton: Princeton University Press, 1957.

Spector, Ivar. *The Soviet Union and the Muslim World, 1917–1958*. Seattle: University of Washington Press, 1959.

Stevens, Georgiana, ed. *The United States and the Middle East*. Englewood Cliffs, N.J.: Prentice-Hall, 1964.

Storrs, Sir Ronald. *Memoirs*. New York: Putnam, 1937.

Thicknesse, S. G. *Arab Refugees: A Survey of Resettlement Possibilities*. London: Royal Institute of International Affairs, 1949.

Warriner, Doreen. *Land Reform and Development in the Middle East*. New York: Oxford University Press, 1957.

Wright, Quincy. *Mandates under the League of Nations*. Chicago: University of Chicago Press, 1930.

Zeine, Zeine N. *Arab-Turkish Relations and the Emergence of Arab Nationalism*. Beirut: Khayat, 1958.

_____. *The Struggle for Arab Independence: Western Diplomacy and the Rise and Fall of Faisal's Kingdom in Syria*. Beirut: Khayat, 1960.

The First World War and the Peace Settlement

Adamov, Evgenii A. *Die Europäischen Mächte und die Türkei während des Weltkrieges*. Dresden: C. Reissner, 1932.

Antonius, George. *The Arab Awakening*. New York, London: H. Hamilton, 1938.

Bowman-Manifold, Sir Michael G. E. *An Outline of the Egyptian and Palestine Campaigns, 1914 to 1918*. Chatham: Mackay, 1922.

Dane, Edmund. *British Campaigns in the Nearer East, 1914–1918*. 2 vols. London: Hodder and Stoughton, 1917–19.

Emin, Ahmed. *Turkey in the World War*. New Haven: Yale University Press, 1930.

Howard, Harry N. *The Partition of Turkey*. Norman: University of Oklahoma Press, 1931.

Larcher, Maurice. *La Guerre Turque dans la Guerre Mondiale*. Paris: Berger-Levrault, 1926.

Lawrence, Thomas E. *Revolt in the Desert*. New York: Doran, 1927.

Storrs, Sir Ronald. *Orientations*. London: Nicholson and Watson, 1937.

Survey of International Affairs, 1925. London: Oxford University Press, 1927.

Temperley, H. W. V., ed. *A History of the Peace Conference of Paris*. Vol. VI. London: Henry Frowde and Hodder and Stoughton, 1924.

Townshend, Charles V. *My Campaign in Mesopotamia*. London: T. Butterworth, 1920.

The Second World War

Australia. *Active Service: With Australia in the Middle East*. Canberra: Australian War Memorial, 1941.

Beaton, Cecil. *Near East*. London: Batsford, 1943.

Churchill, Winston S. *The Second World War*. Vol. III: *The Grand Alliance;* Vol. IV: *The Hinge of Fate*. Boston: Houghton Mifflin, 1949–1950.

Cowie, Donald. *The Campaigns of Wavell: The Inner Story of the Empire in Action*. London: Chapman, 1942.

De Guingand, Maj.-Gen. Sir Francis. *Operation Victory*. London: Hodder and Stoughton, 1947.

Hill, Russell. *Desert Conquest*. New York: Knopf, 1943.

Moorehead, Alan. *Don't Blame the Generals*. New York: Harper, 1943.

_____. *Mediterranean Front*. New York: Whittlesey, 1942.

Paiforce: The Official Story of the Persia and Iraq Command, 1941–1946. London: H. M. Stationery Office, 1948.

Talbot, Godfrey. *Speaking from the Desert*. London: Hutchinson, 1944.

Young, Desmond. *Rommel, the Desert Fox*. New York: Harper, 1950.

Minorities

Adamson, David C. *The Kurdish War*. New York: Praeger, 1964.

Arfa, Hassan. *The Kurds: A Historical and Political Study*. London: Oxford University Press, 1966.

Cohen, Hayyim S. *The Jews of the Middle East, 1860–1972*. New York: John Wiley, 1973.

Eagleton, William, Jr. *The Kurdish Republic of 1946*. London: Oxford University Press, 1963.
Edmonds, C. J. *Kurds, Turks, and Arabs*. London: Oxford University Press, 1957.
Fany, Messoud. *La Nation Kurde et Son Evolution Sociale*. Paris: Rodstein, 1933.
Hamilton, A. M. *Road through Kurdistan*. London: Faber & Faber, 1958.
Hourani, Albert H. *Minorities in the Arab World*. New York: Oxford University Press, 1947.
Joseph, John. *The Nestorians and Their Muslim Neighbors: A Study of Western Influence on Their Relations*. Princeton: Princeton University Press, 1961.
Landshut, S. *Jewish Communities in the Muslim Countries of the Middle East*. London: Jewish Chronicle, 1950.
Luke, Harry C. *Mosul and Its Minorities*. London: Hopkinson, 1925.
Makarem, Sami N. *The Druze Faith*. New York: Caravan Books, 1974.
Malek, Yusuf. *The British Betrayal of the Assyrians*. Chicago: Assyrian National Federation and the Assyrian National League of America, 1935.
Meinardus, Otto F. A. *Christian Egypt: Faith and Life*. Cairo: American University Press, 1970.
Rambout, Lucien. *Les Kurdes et le Droit*. Paris: Editions du Cerf, 1947.
Rondot, Pierre. *Les Chrétiens d'Orient*. Paris: Peyronnet, 1955.
Safrastian, Arshak. *Kurds and Kurdistan*. London: Harvill Press, 1948.
Schmidt, Jane Adams. *Journey among Brave Men*. Boston: Little, Brown, 1964.
Soane, E. B. *To Mesopotamia and Kurdistan in Disguise*. London: J. Murray, 1926.
Stafford, Ronald S. *The Tragedy of the Assyrians*. London: Allen & Unwin, 1935.
Vratzian, Simon. *Armenia and the Armenian Question*. Boston: Hairenik Publishing Co., 1943.
Wakin, Edward. *A Lonely Minority: The Modern Story of Egypt's Copts*. New York: William Morrow, 1963.

Strategic Waterways

Avram, Benno. *The Evolution of the Suez Canal Status from 1869 up to 1956: A Historico-juridical Study*. Paris: Librairie Minard, 1958.
Bloomfield, L. M. *Egypt, Israel, and the Gulf of Aqaba in International Law*. Toronto: Carswell, 1957.
Boutros-Ghali, B., and Chlala, Youssef. *Le Canal de Suez*. Alexandria: Société Egyptienne de Droit International, 1958.
Connell, John. *The Most Important Country: The True Story of the Suez Crisis and the Events Leading to It*. London: Cassell, 1957.
Foot, Michael, and Jones, Mervyn. *Guilty Men, 1957: Suez and Cyprus*. New York: Rinehart, 1957.
Hallberg, Charles W. *The Suez Canal*. New York: Columbia University Press, 1931.
Hefnaoui, Moustapha el-. *Les Problèmes Contemporains Posés par le Canal de Suez*. Paris: Guillemot et de Lamothe, 1951.
Hoskins, Halford L. *British Routes to India*. New York: Longmans, 1928.
Howard, Harry N. *Turkey, the Straits, and U.S. Policy*. Baltimore: Johns Hopkins University Press, 1974.
Khadduri, Majid, ed. *Major Middle Eastern Problems in International Law*. Washington, D.C.: American Enterprise Institute, 1972.
Lauterpacht, E., ed. *The Suez Canal Settlement*. New York: Praeger, 1960.
Lewis, Jesse, W., Jr. *The Strategic Balance in the Mediterranean*. Washington, D.C.: American Enterprise Institute, 1976.
Longgood, William F. *The Suez Story: Key to the Middle East*. New York: Greenberg, 1957.
Reinhard, Ernst. *Kampf um Suez*. Dresden: Kaden, 1930.
Schonfield, Hugh J. *The Suez Canal*. New York: Penguin, 1939.
_____. *The Suez Canal in World Affairs*. London: Constellation Books, 1952; New York: Philosophical Library, 1953.

Shotwell, James T., and Deák, Francis. *Turkey at the Straits: A Short History.* New York: Macmillan, 1940.

Siegfried, André. *Suez and Panama.* New York: Harcourt, Brace, 1940.

Váli, Ferenc A. *The Turkish Straits and NATO.* Stanford, Calif.: Hoover Institution Press, 1972.

Wilson, Sir Arnold T. *The Suez Canal, Its Past, Present, and Future.* London: Oxford University Press, 1939.

Afghanistan

Adamec, Ludwig W. *Afghanistan, 1900–1923: A Diplomatic History.* Berkeley and Los Angeles: University of California Press, 1967.

————. *Afghanistan's Foreign Affairs to the Mid-Twentieth Century.* Tucson: University of Arizona Press, 1974.

Dupree, Louis. *Afghanistan.* Princeton: Princeton University Press, 1973.

Dupree, Louis, and Albert, Linette, eds. *Afghanistan in the 1970s.* New York: Praeger, 1974.

Franck, Peter G. *Afghanistan between East and West.* Washington, D.C.: National Planning Association, 1960.

Fraser-Tytler, Sir Kerr. *Afghanistan: A Study of Political Developments in Central Asia.* London: Oxford University Press, 1950.

Grassmuck, George, Adamec, Ludwig, and Irwin, Frances, eds. *Afghanistan: Some New Approaches.* Ann Arbor: University of Michigan, Middle East Studies Center, 1969.

Gregorian, Vartan. *The Emergence of Modern Afghanistan: Politics of Reform and Modernization, 1880–1946.* Stanford, Calif.: Stanford University Press, 1969.

Griffiths, John C. *Afghanistan.* New York: Praeger, 1967.

Kamrany, Nake. *Peaceful Competition in Afghanistan: American and Soviet Models for Economic Aid.* Washington, D.C.: Communication Service Corporation, 1969.

Newell, Richard S. *The Politics of Afghanistan.* Ithaca, N.Y.: Cornell University Press, 1971.

Nollau, Günter, and Wiehe, Hans J. *Russia's South Flank: Soviet Operations in Iran, Turkey, and Afghanistan.* New York: Praeger, 1963.

Poullada, Leon B. *Reform and Rebellion in Afghanistan, 1919–1929.* Ithaca, N.Y.: Cornell University Press, 1973.

Wilber, Donald N., ed. *Afghanistan.* New Haven, Conn.: Human Relations Area Files, 1956.

Egypt

Abdel Malek, Anouar. *Egypt: Military Society: The Army Regime, the Left, and Social Change under Nasser.* Trans. C. L. Markmann. New York: Random House, 1968.

Abdel Nasser, Gamal. *The Philosophy of the Revolution.* Buffalo, N.Y.: Smith, Keynes & Marshall, 1959.

Ahmed, Jamal Mohammad. *The Intellectual Origins of Egyptian Nationalism.* London, New York: Oxford University Press, 1960.

Area Handbook for the United Arab Republic (Egypt). By Harvey H. Smith and others. Washington, D.C.: U.S. Government Printing Office, 1970.

Baer, Gabriel. *Studies in the Social History of Modern Egypt.* Chicago: University of Chicago Press, 1969.

al-Barawy, Rashed. *The Military Coup in Egypt: An Analytic Study.* Cairo: Renaissance Bookshop, 1957.

Berger, Morroe. *Bureaucracy and Society in Modern Egypt: A Study of the Higher Civil Service.* Princeton: Princeton University Press, 1957.

————. *Islam in Egypt Today: Social and Political Aspects of Popular Religion.* Cambridge: University Press, 1970.

Bowie, Robert R. *Suez 1956.* New York and London: Oxford University Press, 1974.

Published under the auspices of the American Society of International Law in the series entitled International Crises and the Role of Law.

Chedid, Henry. *Political Organizations in the United Arab Republic since 1952: The Arab Socialist Union.* Beirut, 1969.

Cromer, Evelyn Baring. *Modern Egypt.* 2 vols. New York: Macmillan, 1908.

Dawisha, A. I. *Egypt in the Arab World.* New York: John Wiley, 1976.

Dekmejian, R. Hrair. *Egypt under Nasir: A Study in Political Dynamics.* Albany: State University of New York Press, 1971.

Haddad, George M. *Revolutions and Military Rule in the Middle East: The Arab States.* Part *II: Egypt, the Sudan, Yemen and Libya.* Vol. 3. New York: Robert Speller, 1973.

Haykal, Muhammed Hasanayn. *The Cairo Documents: The Inside Story of Nasser and His Relationship with World Leaders, Rebels, and Statesmen.* Garden City, N.Y.: Doubleday, 1973.

Heikal, Mohammad. *The Road to Ramadan.* New York: Quadrangle, The New York Times Book Co., 1975.

Hofstadter, Dan, ed. *Egypt and Nasser.* 3 vols. New York: Facts on File, 1973.

Holt, Peter M., ed. *Political and Social Change in Modern Egypt: Historical Studies from the Ottoman Conquest to the United Arab Republic.* London: Oxford University Press, 1968.

Hussein, Mahmoud. *Class Conflict in Egypt: 1945–1970.* Trans. Michel Chirman, Susan Chirman, et al. New York: Monthly Review Press, 1973.

Issawi, Charles. *Egypt in Revolution: An Economic Analysis.* London: Oxford University Press, 1963.

Lacouture, Jean. *Nasser.* Trans. Daniel Hofstadter. New York: Knopf, 1973.

Landau, Jacob M. *Parliaments and Parties in Egypt.* Tel-Aviv: Israel Publishing House, 1953.

Landes, David S. *Bankers and Pashas: International Finance and Economic Imperialism in Egypt.* Cambridge, Mass.: Harvard University Press, 1958.

Mansfield, Peter. *Nasser's Egypt.* Rev. ed. Baltimore: Penguin, 1969.

———. *The British in Egypt.* New York: Holt, Rinehart & Winston, 1972.

Marlowe, John. *Four Aspects of Egypt.* London: Allen & Unwin, 1966.

Mayfield, James B. *Rural Politics in Nasser's Egypt: A Quest for Legitimacy.* Austin: University of Texas Press, 1971.

Neguib, Mohammed. *Egypt's Destiny: A Personal Statement.* Garden City, N.Y.: Doubleday, 1955.

O'Brien, Patrick K. *The Revolution in Egypt's Economic System: From Private Enterprise to Socialism, 1952–1965.* London: Oxford University Press, 1966.

President Gamal Abdel Nasser's Speeches and Press Interviews. Cairo: U.A.R. Information Dept. 6 vols.

Rejwan, Nissim. *Nasserist Ideology: Its Exponents and Critics.* Jerusalem: Israel University Press; New York: John Wiley, 1973.

Royal Institute of International Affairs. *Great Britain and Egypt, 1914–1951.* Rev. ed. London: Royal Institute of International Affairs, 1952.

Rubinsten, Alvin Z. *Red Star on the Nile: The Soviet-Egyptian Relationship since the June War.* Princeton: Princeton University Press, 1977.

El Sadat, Anwar. *Revolt on the Nile.* London: Allan Wingate, 1957.

Sadat, Anwar el-. *In Search of Identity: An Autobiography.* New York: Harper & Row, 1978.

Safran, Nadav. *Egypt in Search of Political Community: An Analysis of the Intellectual and Political Evolution of Egypt, 1804–1952.* Cambridge: Harvard University Press, 1961.

Stevens, Georgiana G. *Egypt: Yesterday and Today.* New York: Holt, Rinehart & Winston, 1963.

United Arab Republic. *The Charter.* Cairo: U.A.R. Information Department, 1962.

Vatikiotis, P. J., ed. *Egypt since the Revolution*. New York: Praeger, 1968.

———. *The Egyptian Army in Politics: Pattern for New Nations?* Bloomington: Indiana University Press, 1961.

Wynn, Wilton. *Nasser of Egypt: The Search for Dignity*. Cambridge, Mass.: Arlington Books, 1959.

Iran

Algar, Hamid. *Religion and State in Iran, 1785 to 1906*. Berkeley: University of California Press, 1970.

Amirie, Abbas, and Twitchell, Hamilton A. *Iran in the 1980s*. Teheran: Institute for International Political and Economic Studies, 1978.

Amirsadegh, Hossein, ed. *Twentieth-Century Iran*. Assisted by R. W. Ferrier. London: Heinemann, 1977.

Amuzegar, Jahangir. *Iran: An Economic Profile*. Washington, D.C.: The Middle East Institute, 1977.

Amuzegar, Jahangir, and Fekrat, Ali. *Iran: Economic Development under Dualistic Conditions*. Chicago and London: University of Chicago Press, 1971.

Arfa, Gen. Hassan. *Under Five Shahs*. London: John Murray, 1964.

Avery, Peter. *Modern Iran*. New York: Praeger; London: Benn, 1965.

Baldwin, George B. *Planning and Development in Iran*. Baltimore: The Johns Hopkins Press, 1967.

Banani, Amin. *The Modernization of Iran, 1921–1941*. Stanford, Calif.: Stanford University Press, 1961.

Bayne, E. A. *Persian Kingship in Transition: Conversations with a Monarch Whose Office Is Traditional and Whose Goal Is Modernization*. New York: American Universities Field Staff, 1968.

Bill, James A. *The Politics of Iran: Groups, Classes, and Modernization*. Columbus, O.: Charles E. Merrill, 1972.

Binder, Leonard. *Iran: Political Development in a Changing Society*. Berkeley: University of California Press, 1962.

Blücher, Wipert von. *Zeitenwende in Iran. Erlebnisse und Beobachtungen*. Biberach an der Riss: Koehler & Voigtländer, 1949.

Browne, Edward G. *The Persian Revolution of 1905–1909*. Cambridge: The University Press, 1910.

Chelkowski, Peter J., ed. *Iran: Continuity and Variety*. New York: New York University Press, 1971.

Chubin, Shahram, and Zabih, Sepehr. *The Foreign Relations of Iran: A Developing State in a Zone of Great-Power Conflict*. Berkeley and Los Angeles: University of California Press, 1974.

Cottam, Richard W. *Nationalism in Iran*. Pittsburgh: University of Pittsburgh Press, 1964.

Denman, D. R. *The King's Vista*. Berkhamsted, Herts.: Geographical Publications Ltd., 1973.

Elwell-Sutton, L. P. *Modern Iran*. London: Routledge, 1941.

———. *Persian Oil: A Study in Power Politics*. London: Lawrence & Wishart, 1955.

English, Paul Ward. *City and Village in Iran: Settlement and Economy in the Kirman Basin*. Madison: University of Wisconsin Press, 1966.

Fatemi, Nasrollah S. *Diplomatic History of Persia, 1917–1923: Anglo-Russian Power Politics in Iran*. New York: R. F. Moore, 1952.

Frye, Richard N. *Iran*. New York: Henry Holt, 1953.

Hamzavi, Abdol Hossein. *Persia and the Powers: An Account of Diplomatic Relations, 1941–1946*. London and New York: Hutchison, 1946.

Issawi, Charles, comp. *The Economic History of Iran: 1800–1914*. Chicago: University of Chicago Press, 1971.

Kazemzadeh, Firuz. *Russia and Britain in Persia, 1864-1914: A Study in Imperialism*. New Haven: Yale University Press, 1968.

Keddie, Nikki R. *Religion and Rebellion in Iran: The Iranian Tobacco Protest of 1891-1892*. New York: Humanities Press, 1966.

Lambton, Ann K. S. *Landlord and Peasant in Persia: A Study of Land Tenure and Land Revenue Administration*. New York: Oxford University Press, 1953.

_____. *The Persian Land Reform, 1962-1966*. Oxford: Clarendon Press, 1969.

Lenczowski, George, ed. *Iran under the Pahlavis*. Stanford, Calif.: Hoover Institution Press, 1978.

_____. *Russia and the West in Iran, 1918-1948: A Study in Big-Power Rivalry*. With a *Supplement*, 1954. Ithaca, N.Y.: Cornell University Press, 1949. Reprinted, New York: Greenwood Press, 1968.

Looney, Robert E. *The Economic Development of Iran, 1959-1981*. New York: Praeger, 1973.

Mohammad Reza Pahlavi Aryamehr, Shahanshah of Iran. *The White Revolution*. Tehran: The Imperial Pahlavi Library, 1967.

Mohammed Reza Shah Pahlavi. *Mission for My Country*. New York: McGraw-Hill, 1961.

Millspaugh, Arthur C. *Americans in Persia*. Washington, D.C.: The Brookings Institution, 1946.

Niedermayer, Oskar von. *Under der Glutsonne Iran's*. Munich: Einhorn, 1925.

Nirumand, Bahman. *Iran: The New Imperialism in Action*. Trans. from the German by Leonard Mins. New York: Monthly Review Press, 1969.

Ramazani, Rouhollah K. *The Foreign Policy of Iran: A Developing Nation in World Affairs, 1500-1941*. Charlottesville: The University Press of Virginia, 1966.

_____. *Iran's Foreign Policy, 1941-1973: A Study of Foreign Policy in Modernizing Nations*. Charlottesville: The University Press of Virginia, 1975.

Sadeeg, Javad. *Nationalities and Revolution in Iran*. New York: Distributed by Pathfinder Press, 1974.

Schulze-Holthus, Bernhardt. *Daybreak in Iran: A Story of the German Intelligence Service*. Trans. M. Savill. London: Staples Press, 1954.

Shuster, William M. *The Strangling of Persia*. New York: Century, 1912.

Sykes, Christopher. *Wassmuss, "The German Lawrence."* London: Longmans, 1936.

Sykes, Sir Percy M. *A History of Persia*. London: Macmillan, 1930. 3d ed. Reprinted, London: Routledge & Kegan Paul, 1969.

Upton, Joseph M. *The History of Modern Iran: An Interpretation*. Cambridge: Harvard University Press, 1960.

Warne, William E. *Mission for Peace: Point Four in Iran*. Indianapolis: Bobbs-Merrill, 1956.

Wilber, Donald N. *Iran: Past and Present*. 7th ed. Princeton: Princeton University Press, 1975.

_____. *Riza Shah Pahlavi: The Resurrection and Reconstruction of Iran, 1878-1944*. Hicksville, N.Y.: Exposition Press, 1975.

Yar-Shater, Ehsan, ed. *Iran Faces the Seventies*. New York: Praeger, 1971.

Zabih, Sepehr. *The Communist Movement in Iran*. Berkeley: University of California Press, 1966.

Zonis, Marvin. *The Political Elite of Iran*. Princeton: Princeton University Press, 1971.

Iraq

Bell, Lady Florence, ed. *The Letters of Gertrude Bell*. 2 vols. London: Benn, 1927.

Birdwood, Baron Christopher B. B. *Nuri as-Said: A Study in Arab Leadership*. London: Cassell, 1969.

Caractacus (pseud.). *Revolution in Iraq: An Essay in Comparative Public Opinion*. London: Gollancz, 1959.

Dann, Uriel. *Iraq under Qassem: A Political History, 1958–1963*. New York: Praeger, 1969.

Gabbay, Rony. *Communism and Agrarian Reform in Iraq*. London: Croom Helm, 1978.

De Gaury, Gerald. *Three Kings in Baghdad, 1921–1958*. London: Hutchinson, 1961.

Foster, Henry A. *The Making of Modern Iraq: A Product of World Forces*. Norman: University of Oklahoma Press, 1935.

Gallman, Waldemar J. *Iraq under General Nuri: My Recollection of Nuri al-Said, 1954–1958*. Baltimore: The Johns Hopkins Press, 1964.

Harris, George L. *Iraq: Its People, Its Society, Its Culture*. New Haven: Human Relations Area Files Press, 1958.

Khadduri, Majid. *Independent Iraq, 1932–58: A Study in Iraqi Politics*. 2d ed. London and New York: Oxford University Press, 1960.

_____. *Republican Iraq: A Study in Iraqi Politics since the Revolution of 1958*. London and New York: Oxford University Press, 1969.

_____. *Socialist Iraq: A Study in Iraqi Politics since 1968*. Washington, D.C.: The Middle East Institute, 1978.

Kimball, Lorenzo K. *The Changing Pattern of Political Power in Iraq, 1958–1971*. New York: Speller & Sons, 1972.

Longrigg, Stephen H. *Iraq, 1900 to 1950: A Political, Social, and Economic History*. London and New York: Oxford University Press, 1953.

Longrigg, Stephen H., and Stoakes, Frank. *Iraq*. New York: Praeger, 1959.

Sluglett, Peter. *Britain in Iraq, 1914–1932*. London: Ithaca Press, 1976. Published for the Middle East Centre, St. Antony's College, Oxford.

Israel

Allon, Yigal. *Shield of David*. London: Weidenfeld & Nicolson, 1970.

Begin, Menachem. *The Revolt: Story of the Irgun*. London: W. H. Allen, 1951.

Ben Gurion, David. *Rebirth and Destiny of Israel*. New York: Philosophical Library, 1954.

Berger, Elmer. *Judaism or Jewish Nationalism: An Alternative to Zionism*. New York: Bookman, 1957.

Bernstein, Marver H. *The Politics of Israel: The First Decade of Statehood*. Princeton: Princeton University Press, 1957.

Bober, Arie, comp. *The Other Israel: The Radical Case Against Zionism*. Garden City, N.Y.: Anchor Books, 1972.

Brecher, Michael. *Decisions in Israel's Foreign Policy*. London: Oxford University Press, 1974.

Bull, General Odd. *War and Peace in the Middle East: The Experiences and Views of a U.N. Observer*. Boulder, Colo.: Westview Press, 1977.

Bulloch, John. *The Making of a War: The Middle East from 1967–1973*. London: Longman Group, 1974.

Burns, Lt. Gen. Eedson L. M. *Between Arab and Israeli*. London: George G. Harrap, 1962; New York: Ivan Obolensky, 1963.

Cattan, Henry. *Palestine, the Arabs and Israel: The Search for Justice*. London: Longmans, Green, 1969.

Chaliand, Gérard. *The Palestinian Resistance*. Trans. Michael Perl. Harmondsworth: Penguin, 1972.

Cooley, John K. *Green March, Black September: The Story of the Palestinian Arabs*. London: Frank Cass, 1973.

Crosbie, Sylvia Kowitt. *A Tacit Alliance: France and Israel from Suez to the Six-Day War*. Princeton: Princeton University Press, 1974.

Davis, John H. *The Evasive Peace: A Study of the Zionist-Arab Problem*. New York: New World Press, 1970.

Dayan, Moshe. *Diary of the Sinai Campaign*. New York: Harper & Row, 1966.

Eden, Sir Anthony. *Full Circle: The Memoirs of the Rt. Hon. Sir Anthony Eden*. Boston: Houghton Mifflin, 1960; London: Cassell, 1960.

Elizur, Yuval, and Salpeter, Eliahu. *Who Rules Israel?* New York: Harper & Row, 1973.

Ellis, Harry B. *The Dilemma of Israel.* Washington, D.C.: American Enterprise Institute, 1970.

Fein, Leonard J. *Politics in Israel.* Boston: Little, Brown, 1967.

Golan, Matti. *The Secret Conversations of Henry Kissinger: Step-By-Step Diplomacy in the Middle East.* New York: Quadrangle, 1976.

Halpern, Ben. *The Idea of a Jewish State.* 2d ed. Cambridge, Mass.: Harvard University Press, 1969.

Handel, Michael I. *Israel's Political-Military Doctrine.* Occasional Papers in International Affairs no. 30. Cambridge, Mass.: Harvard University, Center for International Affairs, 1973.

Harkabi, Yehoshafat. *Arab Attitudes to Israel.* New York: Hart, 1972.

――――. *Palestinians and Israel.* New York and Toronto: John Wiley, Halstead Press, 1974; Jerusalem: Israel Universities Press, 1974.

Heradstveit, Daniel. *Arab and Israeli Elite Perceptions.* New York: Humanities Press, 1974.

Hertzberg, Arthur, ed. *The Zionist Idea: A Historical Analysis and Reader.* New York: Doubleday, 1959.

Herzl, Theodor. *The Jewish State: An Attempt at a Modern Solution of the Jewish Question.* New York: Scopus, 1943.

Herzog, Chaim. *The War of Atonement: October 1973.* Boston: Little, Brown, 1975.

Hurewitz, J. C. *The Struggle for Palestine.* New York: Norton, 1950.

Hutchinson, Elmo H. *Violent Truce: A Military Observer Looks at the Arab-Israeli Conflict, 1951–1955.* New York: Devin-Adair, 1956.

Isaac, Rael Jean. *Israel Divided: Ideological Politics in the Jewish State.* Baltimore: Johns Hopkins University Press, 1976.

Jabber, Fuad. *Israel and Nuclear Weapons: Present Options and future Strategies.* London: Chatto & Windus for the International Institute for Strategic Studies, 1971.

Kadi, Leila S. *Arab Summit Conferences and the Palestine Problem (1936–1950), (1964–66).* Beirut: Research Centre, Palestine Liberation Organization, 1966.

Kerr, Malcolm H., ed. *The Elusive Peace in the Middle East:* Papers by Fred Khouri, Aharon Cohen, George Haddad, John Campbell, and E. L. M. Burns. Albany: State University of New York Press, 1975.

Khalidi, Walid, ed. *From Haven to Conquest: Readings in Zionism and the Palestine Problem until 1948.* Beirut: Institute for Palestine Studies, 1971.

Khouri, Fred J. *The Arab-Israeli Dilemma.* New York: Syracuse University Press, 1968.

Kraines, Oscar. *Government and Politics in Israel.* Boston: Houghton Mifflin, 1961.

Landau, Jacob M. *The Arabs in Israel: A Political Study.* London: Oxford University Press, 1969.

Laqueur, Walter. *Confrontation: The Middle East and World Politics.* New York: Bantam Books, 1974.

――――, ed. *The Israeli-Arab Reader: A Documentary History of the Middle East Conflict.* New York: Citadel Press, 1969.

Lilienthal, Alfred. *What Price Israel?* Chicago: Regnery, 1953.

Lorch, Netanel. *Israel's War of Independence, 1947–1949.* 2d rev. ed. Hartford, Conn.: Hartmore House, 1968.

Lucas, Noah. *The Modern History of Israel.* New York: Praeger, 1975.

Magnes, Judah Leon. *Palestine—Divided or United? The Case for a Bi-National Palestine before the United Nations.* Jerusalem: Ihud (Union) Association, 1947.

Moore, John Norton, ed. *The Arab-Israel Conflict: Readings and Documents,* 3 vols. Princeton: Princeton University Press, 1974. Sponsored by the American Society of International Law.

Naamani, Israel, Rudavsky, David, and Katsh, Abraham, eds. *Israel: Its Politics and Philosophy; An Annotated Reader.* New York: Behrman House, 1974.

Nutting, Anthony. *No End of a Lesson: The Story of Suez.* New York: C. N. Potter, 1967.

O'Ballance, Edgar. *Arab Guerilla Power: 1967–1972*. Hamden, Conn.: The Shoe String Press, 1973.

———. *The Sinai Campaign of 1956*. New York: Praeger, 1960.

———. *The Third Arab-Israeli War*. Hamden, Conn.: Archon Books, 1972.

Patai, Raphael, ed. *Encyclopedia of Zionism and Israel*. 2 vols. New York: Herzl Press, 1971.

Peretz, Don. *Israel and the Palestine Arabs*. Washington, D.C.: The Middle East Institute, 1958.

Pfaff, Richard H. *Jerusalem: Keystone of an Arab-Israeli Settlement*. Washington, D.C.: American Enterprise Institute, 1969.

Pranger, Robert J. *American Policy for Peace in the Middle East, 1969–1971: Problems of Principle, Maneuver and Time*. Washington, D.C.: American Enterprise Institute, 1971.

Quandt, William B. *Decade of Decisions: American Policy Toward the Arab-Israeli Conflict, 1967–1976*. Berkeley: University of California Press, 1977.

Quandt, William B., Jabber, Fuad, and Lesch, Ann Mosely. *The Politics of Palestinian Nationalism*. Berkeley: University of California Press, 1973.

Reich, Bernard. *Quest for Peace: United States-Israel Relations and the Arab-Israeli Conflict*. New Brunswick, N.J.: Transaction Books, 1977.

Roberts, Samuel J. *Survival or Hegemony? The Foundations of Israeli Foreign Policy*. Baltimore and London: The Johns Hopkins Press, 1973.

Rodinson, Maxime. *Israel: A Colonial Settler State?* New York: Monad Press, 1973.

Royal Institute of International Affairs. *Great Britain and Palestine, 1915–1945*. 2d ed. London: Oxford University Press, 1946.

Safran, Nadav. *From War to War: The Arab-Israeli Confrontation, 1948–67*. New York: Pegasus, 1969.

Safran, Nadav. *Israel: The Embattled Ally*. Cambridge, Mass.: Harvard University Press, 1978.

Schechtman, Joseph B. *On Wings of Eagles: The Plight, Exodus, and Homecoming of Oriental Jewry*. New York: T. Yoseloff, 1961.

Schmidt, Dana Adams. *Armageddon in the Middle East*. New York: John Day, for *The New York Times*, 1974.

Sharabi, Hisham. *Palestine and Israel: The Lethal Dilemma*. New York: Pegasus, 1969.

Sheehan, Edward R. F. *The Arabs, Israelis, and Kissinger: A Secret History of American Diplomacy in the Middle East*. New York: Reader's Digest Press, 1976.

Smetsinger, John. *Truman, the Jewish Vote and the Creation of Israel*. Stanford, Calif.: Hoover Institution Press, 1974.

Syrkin, Marie. *Golda Meir, Israel's Leader*. Rev. ed. New York: Putnam, 1969.

Taylor, Alan R., and Tetlie, Richard N., comps. *Palestine, A Search for Truth: Approaches to the Arab-Israeli Conflict*. Washington, D.C.: Public Affairs Press, 1970.

Teveth, Shabtai. *Moshe Dayan: The Soldier, the Man, the Legend*. Boston: Houghton Mifflin, 1973.

Tahtinen, Dale R. *The Arab-Israeli Military Balance Today*. Foreign Affairs Studies no. 9. Washington, D.C.: American Enterprise Institute, 1973.

———. *The Arab-Israeli Military Balance since October 1973*. Foreign Affairs Studies no. 11. Washington, D.C.: American Enterprise Institute, 1974.

Weizmann, Chaim. *Trial and Error: The Autobiography of Chaim Weizmann*. New York: Harper & Row, 1949.

Jordan

Abdallah, King of Jordan. *My Memoirs Completed (Al Takmilah)*. Trans. Harold W. Glidden. London and New York: Longman, 1978.

Abdullah, King of Transjordan. *Memoirs of King Abdullah of Transjordan*. Ed. Philip R. Graves. London: Jonathan Cape, 1950.

Abidi, Aqil Hyder H. *Jordan: A Political Study, 1948–1957*. New York: Asia Publishing House, 1965.

Area Handbook for the Hashemite Kingdom of Jordan. By Howard C. Reese et al. Washington, D.C.: U.S. Government Printing Office, 1959.

Aruri, Naseer Hasan. *Jordan: A Study in Political Development (1921–1965).* The Hague: Nijhoff, 1972.

Benvenisti, Meron. *Jerusalem: The Torn City.* Minneapolis: University of Minnesota Press, 1976; Jerusalem: Isratypeset, 1976.

Cohen, Saul B. *Jerusalem—Bridging the Four Walls.* New York: Herzl Press, 1977.

Copeland, Paul W. *The Land and People of Jordan.* 2d ed. Philadelphia: Lippincott, 1972.

Dearden, Anne. *Jordan.* London: Robert Hale, 1958.

Glubb, John Bagot. *A Soldier with the Arabs.* New York: Harper, 1957.

———. *The Story of the Arab Legion.* London: Hodder and Stoughton, 1948.

Goichon, A. -M. *Jordanie Réelle.* Paris: G. -P. Maisonneuve and Larose. Vol. I: 1967; Vol. II: 1972.

Harris, George L., et al. *Jordan: Its Peoples, Its Society, Its Culture.* New Haven, Conn.: Human Relations Area Files, 1958; New York: Grove Press, 1958.

Hussein, King of Jordan. *Uneasy Lies the Head: An Autobiography.* London: Heinemann, 1962.

Ingram, O'Kelly, ed. *Jerusalem: Key to Peace in the Middle East,* including papers presented in the conference on Jerusalem in Jewish, Islamic, and Christian Perspectives at Duke University, November 11 and 12, 1977. Durham, N.C.: Triangle Friends of the Middle East, 1978.

Johnston, Sir Charles Hepburn. *The Brink of Jordan.* London: Hamilton, 1972.

Morris, James. *The Hashemite Kings.* New York: Pantheon, 1959.

Patai, Raphael. *The Kingdom of Jordan.* Princeton: Princeton University Press, 1958.

Sanger, Richard H. *Where the Jordan Flows.* Washington, D.C.: The Middle East Institute, 1963.

Schleifer, Abdullah. *The Fall of Jerusalem.* New York and London: Monthly Reivew Press, 1972.

Shwadran, Benjamin. *Jordan: A State of Tension.* New York: Council for Middle Eastern Press, 1959.

Vatikiotis, P. J. *Politics and the Military in Jordan: A Study of the Arab Legion, 1921–1957.* New York: Praeger, 1967.

Lebanon

Area Handbook for Lebanon. By Harvey H. Smith and others. Washington, D.C.: U.S. Government Printing Office, 1969.

Baaklini, Abdo I. *Legislative and Political Development: Lebanon, 1842–1972.* Durham, N.C.: Duke University Press, 1976.

Binder, Leonard, ed. *Politics in Lebanon.* New York: John Wiley, 1966.

Chamoun, Camille. *Crise au Moyen-Orient.* Paris: Gallimard, 1963.

Christopher, John B. *Lebanon: Yesterday and Today.* New York: Holt, Rinehart & Winston, 1966.

Entelis, John P. *Pluralism and Party Transformation in Lebanon: Al-Katā'ib, 1936–1970.* Leiden: E. J. Brill, 1974.

Hitti, Philip K. *Lebanon in History: From the Earliest Times to the Present.* 3d ed. London: Macmillan, 1967; New York: St. Martin's Press, 1967.

Hudson, Michael C. *The Precarious Republic: Political Modernization in Lebanon.* New York: Random House, 1968.

Koury, Enver M. *The Operational Capability of the Lebanese Political System.* Beirut: Catholic Press, 1972.

Meo, Leila M. T. *Lebanon, Improbable Nation: A Study in Political Development.* Bloomington: Indiana University Press, 1965.

Qubain, Fahim I. *Crisis in Lebanon.* Washington, D.C.: The Middle East Institute, 1961.

Rondot, Pierre. *Les Institutions Politiques du Liban: Des Communautés Traditionelles à l'Etat Moderne.* Paris: Institut d'Etudes de l'Orient Contemporain, 1947.

Salem, Elie A. *Modernization without Revolution: Lebanon's Experience*. Bloomington: Indiana University Press, 1973.
Salibi, Kamal S. *The Modern History of Lebanon*. New York: Praeger, 1965.
Suleiman, Michael W. *Political Parties in Lebanon: The Challenge of a Fragmented Political Culture*. Ithaca, N.Y.: Cornell University Press, 1967.
Winder, Viola (Hitti). *The Land and People of Lebanon*. Philadelphia: Lippincott, 1965.

Persian Gulf

Adamiyat, Fereydoun. *Bahrein Islands: A Legal and Diplomatic Study of the British-Iranian Controversy* New York: Praeger, 1955.
Allfree, P. S. *Warlords of Oman*. London: Hale, 1967.
Amirie, Abbas. *The Persian Gulf and Indian Ocean in International Politics*. Teheran: Institute for International Political and Economic Studies, 1975.
Anthony, John Duke. *Arab States of the Lower Gulf: People, Politics, Petroleum*. Washington, D.C.: the Middle East Institute, 1975.
Baharna, Husain M. al-. *The Arabian Gulf States: Their Legal and Political Status and Their International Problems*. 2d ed. Beirut: Librairie du Liban, 1973.
Barger, Thomas C. *Energy Policies of the World: Arab States of the Persian Gulf*. Newark, Del.: University of Delaware, Center for the Study of Marine Policy, 1975.
Burrell, R. M. *The Persian Gulf*. Washington, D.C.: Georgetown University, 1973.
Busch, Briton C. *Britain and the Persian Gu'f, 1894-1914*. Berkeley: University of California Press, 1967.
Cottrell, Alvin J., and Burrell, R. M., eds. *The Indian Ocean: Its Political, Economic, and Military Importance*. New York: Praeger, 1972.
Dickson, Harold R. P. *Kuwait and Her Neighbours*. London: Allen & Unwin, 1956.
Fenelon, Kevin G. *The United Arab Emirates: An Economic and Social Survey*. London: Longmans, 1973.
Freeth, Zahra (Dickson). *Kuwait Was My Home*. London: Allen & Unwin, 1956.
The Gulf: Implications of British Withdrawal. Washington, D.C.: Georgetown University, Center for Strategic and International Studies, 1969.
Hay, Sir Rupert. *The Persian Gulf States*. Washington, D.C.: The Middle East Institute, 1959.
Ibrāhīm, Hasan A. al-. *Kuwayt: A Political Study*. Kuwayt: Kuwayt University, 1975.
Long, David E. *The Persian Gulf: An Introduction to Its Peoples, Politics, and Economics*. Boulder, Colo.: Westview Press, 1976.
Kelly, J. B. *Eastern Arabian Frontiers*. London: Faber & Faber, 1964.
Mallakh, Ragaei el-. *Economic Development and Regional Cooperation: Kuwait*. Chicago: University of Chicago Press, 1968.
Marlowe, John. *The Persian Gulf in the Twentieth Century*. New York: Praeger, 1962.
Morris, James. *Sultan in Oman: Venture into the Middle East*. New York: Pantheon, 1957.
Nakhleh, Emile A. *Arab-American Relations in the Persian Gulf*. Washington, D.C.: American Enterprise Institute for Public Policy Research, 1975.
_____. *Bahrain: Political Development in a Modernizing Society*. Lexington, Mass.: D. C. Heath, 1976.
Phillips, Wendell. *Unknown Oman*. New York: McKay, 1966.
Ramazani, Rouhollah. *The Persian Gulf: Iran's Role*. Charlottesville: The University Press of Virginia, 1972.
Skeet, Ian. *Muscat and Oman: End of an Era*. London: Faber & Faber, 1974.
Tahtinen, Dale R., with the assistance of John Lenczowski. *Arms in the Indian Ocean*. Washington D.C.: American Enterprise Institute for Public Policy Research, 1977.
_____. *Arms in the Persian Gulf*. Washington, D.C.: American Enterprise Institute for Public Policy Research, 1974.
Townsend, John. *Oman: The Making of a Modern State*. London: Croom Helm, 1977.
Vicker, Ray. *The Kingdom of Oil*. New York: Scribner, 1974.

Wilson, Sir Arnold T. *The Persian Gulf: A Historical Sketch from the Earliest Times to the Beginning of the Twentieth Century.* London: Allen & Unwin, 1954.

Yodfat, A., and Abir, Mordecai. *In the Direction of the Gulf: The Soviet Union and the Persian Gulf.* Frank Cass, 1977.

Saudi Arabia

Arabian American Oil Company. *Aramco Handbook: Oil and the Middle East.* Rev. ed. Dhahran, Saudi Arabia, 1968.

Area Handbook for Saudi Arabia. By Norman C. Walpole and others. Washington, D.C.: U.S. Government Printing Office, 1971.

Armstrong, Harold C. *Lord of Arabia, Ibn Saud: An Intimate Study of a King.* London: A. Baker, 1934.

Benoist-Méchin, Jacques G. *Le Roi Séoud ou l'Orient à l'Heure des Relèves.* Paris: A. Michel, 1960.

Cleron, Jean Paul. *Saudi Arabia 2000: A Strategy for Growth.* New York: St. Martin's Press, 1978.

De Gaury, Gerald. *Faisal, King of Saudi Arabia.* New York: Praeger, 1967.

Eddy, William A. *F. D. R. Meets Ibn Saud.* New York: American Friends of the Middle East, 1954.

Halliday, Fred. *Arabia without Sultans.* New York: Random House, Vintage Books, 1975.

Hassouna, Hussein A. *The League of Arab States and Regional Disputes: A Study of Middle East Conflicts.* Dobbs Ferry, N.Y.: Oceana Publications, 1975; Leiden: A. Sijthoff, 1975.

Howarth, David A. *The Desert King.* New York: McGraw-Hill, 1964.

Long, David E. *Saudi Arabia.* Washington, D.C.: Center for Strategic and International Studies, Georgetown University, 1976.

Meulen, Daniel van der. *The Wells of Ibn Saud.* New York: Praeger, 1957.

Nakhleh, Emile A. *The United States and Saudi Arabia: A Policy Analysis.* Washington, D.C.: American Enterprise Institute for Public Policy Research, 1975.

Philby, H. St. John B. *Arabian Jubilee.* London: Hale, 1952. New York: Day, 1953.

————. *Saudi Arabia.* New York: Praeger, 1955.

Sanger, Richard H. *The Arabian Peninsula.* Ithaca, N.Y.: Cornell University Press, 1954.

Tahtinen, Dale R. *National Security Challenges to Saudi Arabia.* Washington, D.C.: American Enterprise Institute for Public Policy Research, 1978.

Troeller, Gary. *The Birth of Saudi Arabia: Britain and the Rise of the House of Sa'ud.* London: Frank Cass, 1976.

Wells, Donald A. *Saudi Arabian Development Strategy.* Washington, D.C.: American Enterprise Institute for Public Policy Research, 1976.

Winder, Richard Bayly. *Saudi Arabia in the Nineteenth Century.* New York: St. Martin's Press, 1965.

South Yemen

Belhaven, Lord. *The Uneven Road.* London: John Murray, 1955.

Brinton, Jasper Y. *Aden and the Federation of South Arabia.* Washington, D.C.: American Society of International Law, 1964.

Foster, Donald S. *Landscape with Arabs: Travels in Aden and South Arabia.* Brighton: Clifton Books, 1969.

Hickinbotham, Sir Tom. *Aden.* London: Constable, 1958.

Ingrams, William H. *Arabia and the Isles.* 3d ed. New Yrok: Praeger, 1966.

Little, Tom. *South Arabia: Arena of Conflict.* New York: Praeger, 1968.

Trevaskis, Sir Gerold K. N. *Shades of Amber: A South Arabian Episode.* London: Hutchinson, 1968.

Syria

Abouchdid, Eugenie Elie. *Thirty Years of Lebanon and Syria (1917-1947).* Beirut: Sader Rihani, 1948.

Area Handbook for Syria. By Richard F. Nyrop and others. Washington, D.C.: U.S. Government Printing Office, 1971.

Catroux, Gen. Georges. *Dans la Bataille de Méditerranée*. Paris: Julliard, 1949.

Haddad, George. *Fifty Years of Modern Syria and Lebanon*. Beirut: Dar al-Hayat, 1950.

Hitti, Philip K. *History of Syria*. New York: Macmillan, 1951.

Hourani, Albert H. *Syria and Lebanon: A Political Essay*. London: Oxford University Press, 1946.

Longrigg, Stephen H. *Syria and Lebanon under French Mandate*. London: Oxford University Press, 1958.

Petran, Tabitha. *Syria*. New York: Praeger, 1972.

Rabinovich, Itamar. *Syria under the Ba'th, 1963–1966: The Army-Party Symbiosis*. Jerusalem: Israel Universities Press, 1972; New York: Halsted Press, 1972.

Seale, Patrick. *The Struggle for Syria: A Study in Post-war Arab Politics, 1945–1958*. London: Oxford University Press, 1965.

Torrey, Gordon H. *Syrian Politics and the Military, 1945–1958*. Columbus: Ohio State University Press, 1964.

Weygand, Maxime. *Recalled to Service: The Memoirs of General Maxime Weygand of the Académie Française*. Trans. E. W. Dickes. Garden City, N.Y.: Doubleday, 1952.

Ziadeh, Nicola A. *Syria and Lebanon*. London: Benn, 1957.

Turkey

Armstrong, Harold Courtney. *Grey Wolf, Mustafa Kemal: An Intimate Study of a Dictator*. London: A. Barker, 1932; New York: Minton, Balch, 1933.

Ataöv, Türkkaya. *Turkish Foreign Policy, 1939–1945*. Ankara: Ankara Universitesi Basimevi, 1965.

Berkes, Niyazi, ed. *Turkish Nationalism and Western Civilization: Selected Essays of Ziya Gökalp*. New York: Columbia University Press, 1959.

Caroe, Olaf. *Soviet Empire: The Turks of Central Asia and Stalinism*. London: Macmillan, 1953.

Czaplicka, Marie A. *The Turks of Central Asia in History and at the Present Day*. Oxford: Clarendon Press, 1918.

Davison, Roderic H. *Turkey*. Englewood Cliffs, N.J.: Prentice-Hall, 1968.

Dodd, Clement H. *Politics and Government in Turkey*. Berkeley: University of California Press, 1969.

Eren, Nuri. *Turkey Today and Tomorrow: An Experiment in Westernization*. New York: Praeger, 1963.

Frey, Frederick W. *The Turkish Political Elite*. Cambridge, Mass.: M.I.T. Press, 1965.

Giritli, Ismet. *Fifty Years of Turkish Political Development, 1919–1969*. Istanbul: Istanbul University Publications, 1969.

Graves, Philip P. *Briton and Turk*. London: Hutchinson, 1941.

Haddad, William W., and Ochsenwald, William, eds. *Nationalism in a Non-National State: The Dissolution of the Ottoman Empire*. Columbus: Ohio State University Press, 1977.

Harris, George S. *The Origins of Communism in Turkey*. Stanford, Calif.: Hoover Institution Press, 1967.

———. *Troubled Alliance: Turkish-American Problems in Historical Perspective, 1945–1971*. Washington, D.C.: American Enterprise Institute, 1972; Stanford, Calif.: Hoover Institution Press, 1972.

Heyd, Uriel. *Foundations of Turkish Nationalism: The Life and Teachings of Ziya Gökalp*. London: Luzac, 1950.

Hostler, Charles W. *Turkism and the Soviets: The Turks of the World and their Political Objectives*. New York: Praeger, 1957.

Howard, Harry N. *The Partition of Turkey: A Diplomatic History, 1913–1923*. Norman: Oklahoma University Press, 1931. Reprinted, New York: H. Fertig, 1966.

———. *Turkey, The Straits and U.S. Policy*. Baltimore and London: The Johns Hopkins University Press in cooperation with The Middle East Institute, 1975.

Karpat, Kemal H. *Turkey's Politics: The Transition to a Multi-party System*. Princeton: Princeton University Press, 1959.

————, ed. *Social Change and Politics in Turkey: A Structural-Historical Analysis*. Leiden: E. J. Brill, 1973.

Kili, Suna. *Kemalism*. Istanbul: Robert College, School of Business Administration and Economics, 1969.

Kinross, John Patrick D. B. *Atatürk: The Rebirth of a Nation*. New York: William Morrow, 1965.

Kushner, David. *The Rise of Turkish Nationalism: 1876–1908*. London: Frank Cass, 1977.

Lewis, Bernard. *The Emergence of Modern Turkey*. 2d ed. London and New York: Oxford University Press, 1969.

Lewis, Geoffrey. *Turkey*. 3d ed. London: Benn, 1966.

Luke, Sir Harry C. J. *The Making of Modern Turkey*. London: Macmillan, 1936.

Mango, Andrew. *Turkey*. Walker, 1968.

Moyzisch, L. C. *Operation Cicero*. New York: Coward-McCann, 1950.

Özbudun, Ergun. *Social Change and Political Participation in Turkey*. Princeton: Princeton University Press, 1976.

Ramsaur, Ernest E. *The Young Turks: Prelude to the Revolution of 1908*. Princeton: Princeton University Press, 1957.

Robinson, Richard D. *The First Turkish Republic: A Case in National Development*. Cambridge, Mass.: Harvard University Press, 1963.

Shaw, Stanford H., and Shaw, Ezel Kural. *History of the Ottoman Empire and Modern Turkey. Volume II: Reform, Revolution, and Republic: The Rise of Modern Turkey, 1808–1975*. New York and London: Cambridge University Press, 1977.

Sousa, Nasim. *The Capitulatory Regime of Turkey: Its History, Origin, and Nature*. Baltimore: The Johns Hopkins Press, 1933.

Váli, Ferenc A. *Bridge across the Bosphorus: The Foreign Policy of Turkey*. Baltimore: The Johns Hopkins Press, 1970.

Vere-Hodge, Edward R. *Turkish Foreign Policy, 1918–1948*. Ambilly-Annemasse: Imprimerie Franco-Suisse, 1950.

Webster, Donald E. *The Turkey of Atatürk: Social Process in the Turkish Reformation*. Philadelphia: The American Academy of Political and Social Science, 1939. Reprinted, New York: AMS Press, 1973.

Weiker, Walter F. *Political Tutelage and Democracy in Turkey: The Free Party and Its Aftermath*. Leiden: Brill, 1973.

————. *The Turkish Revolution, 1960–61: Aspects of Military Politics*. Washington, D.C.: The Brookings Institution, 1963.

Yalman, Ahmet Emin. *Turkey in the World War*. New Haven: Yale University Press, 1930.

Yemen

Ingrams, William H. *The Yemen: Imams, Rulers and Revolutions*. London: John Murray, 1963.

Macro, Eric. *Yemen and the Western World since 1571*. New York: Praeger, 1968.

O'Ballance, Edgar. *The War in Yemen*. Hamden, Conn.: Archon Books, 1971.

Phillips, Wendell. *Qataban and Sheba*. New York: Harcourt, Brace, 1955.

Schmidt, Dana A. *Yemen: The Unknown War*. New York: Holt, Rinehart & Winston, 1968.

Somerville, Peter. *Tribes and Tribulations: A Journey in Republican Yemen*. London: Hale, 1967.

Stookey, Robert W. *Yemen: The Politics of the Yemen Arab Republic*. Boulder, Colo.: Westview Press, 1978.

Wenner, Manfred W. *Modern Yemen, 1918–1966*. Baltimore: The Johns Hopkins Press, 1967.

Index

Library of Congress Cataloging in Publication Data

Lenczowski, George.
  The Middle East in world affairs.

  Bibliography: p.
  Includes index.
  1. Near East—History—20th century. 2. Near East—Politics and government. I. Title.
DS62.8.L46   1980   956   79-17059
ISBN 0-8014-1273-0